Revel enables students to read and interact with course material on the devices they use, **anywhere** and **anytime**. Responsive design allows students to access Revel on their tablet devices, with content displayed clearly in both portrait and landscape view.

Highlighting, **note taking**, and a **glossary** personalize the learning experience. Educators can add **notes** for students, too, including reminders or study tips

Revel's variety of **writing** activities and assignments develop and assess concept **mastery** and **critical thinking**.

Superior assignability and tracking

Revel's assignability and tracking tools help educators make sure students are completing their reading and understanding core concepts.

Revel allows educators to indicate precisely which readings must be completed on which dates. This clear, detailed schedule helps students stay on task and keeps them motivated throughout the course.

Revel lets educators monitor class assignment completion and individual student achievement. It offers actionable information that helps educators intersect with their students in meaningful ways, such as points earned on quizzes and time on task.

LIVING DEMOCRACY

2016 Presidential Election

Fifth Edition

Daniel M. Shea
Colby College

Joanne Connor Green
Texas Christian University

Christopher E. Smith
Michigan State University

330 Hudson Street, New York, NY 10013

Portfolio Manager: Jeff Marshall
Content Producer: Kimberly Dunworth
Content Developer: Rebecca Green, Ohlinger
  Publishing Services
Field Marketer: Brittany Pongue-Mohammed
Content Production Manager: Melissa Feimer
Content Development Manager: Beth Jacobson,
  Ohlinger Publishing Services
Content Developer, Learning Tools: Claudine Bellanton
Art/Designer: Kathryn Foot

Digital Studio Course Producer: Tina Gagliostro
Full Service Project Management: Valerie Iglar-
  Mobley, Integra Software Services, Inc.
Compositor: Integra Software Services, Inc.
Printer/Binder: LSC Kendallville
Cover Printer: Phoenix Color
Cover Design: Lumina Datamatics, Inc.
Cover Credit: igorstevanovic/Shutterstock
Text Font: Adobe Caslon Pro 10/13.5

Acknowledgments of third party content appear on the appropriate page within text or on page 631, which constitutes an extension of this copyright page.

Library of Congress Cataloging-in-Publication Data
Names: Shea, Daniel M., author. | Green, Joanne Connor, author. | Smith,
  Christopher E, author.
Title: Living democracy /Daniel M. Shea, Joanne Connor Green, Christopher
  E. Smith.
Description: 5th edition. | Hoboken, N.J.: Pearson Higher Education, 2018. |
  Includes bibliographical references and index.
Identifiers: LCCN 2016028498 | ISBN 9780134625782
Subjects: LCSH: United States–Politics and government–Textbooks.
Classification: LCC JK276 .S34 2018 | DDC 320.473–dc23
LC record available at https://lccn.loc.gov/2016028498

1   16

Instructor's Review Copy:
ISBN 10:   0-134-62738-5
ISBN 13: 978-0-134-62738-0

Brief Contents

Contents

To The Student

I t's probably natural that each generation feels as though they are at the cusp of great political transformation. Certainly those coming of age in the 1950s and 1960s could make that claim. Television burst onto the scene, quickly transforming how Americans would spend their leisure, how products were sold, and how candidates would run for office, among much else. New modes of political activism, like mass protests, rallies, sit-ins, marches, and boycotts were used with great effect to advance feminism, civil rights, anti-Vietnam war and environmental movements. Money became a key factor in electoral campaigns, campaign consultants replaced local party activists, and the explosion of interest groups stunned even the most seasoned observers.

Many feel the same way about our current political scene. In the past few years, we have witnessed incredible changes in the way average Americans experience government and politics. Only a few decades ago the election of an African American to the presidency seemed impossible, and just as remote were the prospects of electing a woman to lead the nation. That changed in 2008, of course. The Internet, with social networks, online fundraising, video sharing sites, blogs, and Twitter, is transforming the way Americans interact. The exact depth and breadth of recent partisan polarization has been a source of scholarly dispute, but at the minimum we have not seen this intensity in generations. The mushrooming weight of social media, the continued strength of the partisan press, and the breadth of demographic changes are remarkable. The number of twists and turns witnessed during the 2016 presidential election was incredible.

Yet the heart of the American political experience remains constant: Change happens when citizens become involved. When concerned citizens—young and old—roll up their sleeves and enter the political trenches, the system responds. Unfortunately, too many young Americans doubt their ability to bring about change by utilizing the political process. They fret about problems and injustices but believe their efforts to change the system would be meaningless. Part of this despondency likely springs from bewilderment over how our political system works. It is true that quite often these changes come slowly, and it can take a concerted effort by many, but individual political action matters.

Living Democracy, the book in your hands, was conceived after the 2000 election, when youth electoral turnout was at historic lows. There have been signs of improvement in some areas, but on the whole, we are confronted with a generation divorced from politics. So one goal is to help readers learn about our political system, but we also want the reader—you—to come away with a greater appreciation of how to use our political system to bring about a better nation. We look forward to being on that journey with you.

Meet Your Authors

DANIEL M. SHEA is a Professor of Government and Director of the Goldfarb Center for Public Affairs and Civic Engagement at Colby College in Waterville, Maine. He has received numerous awards for his teaching and scholarship and has authored or co-authored numerous books and articles on the American political process.

JOANNE CONNOR GREEN is a Professor of Political Science and former Director of Women and Gender Studies at Texas Christian University. She has won numerous teaching awards and her research and teaching interests include the role of gender in congressional elections and issues of substantive representation in state legislatures.

CHRISTOPHER E. SMITH is a Professor of Criminal Justice at Michigan State University. He previously taught at the University of Akron and the University of Connecticut at Hartford. As a specialist on courts and constitutional law, he has written more than 20 books and more than 100 scholarly articles on law and politics.

To The Instructor

Those who have been fretting about levels of youth political engagement breathed a sigh of relief after the 2008 election. Turnout for voters younger than 30 grew from 35 percent in 2000 to 51 percent in that election. Other indicators of political behavior—such as participating in campaign events, talking about politics with friends and family, and attention to the news—seemed to suggest greater interest. Yet we now know that this was probably a temporary surge rather than a sea change. Youth turnout in the 2010 midterm election reached just 22.8 percent—less than four years earlier. Turnout for those under 30 once again dropped in 2014—with 37 percent overall and 21 percent under 30 voting. In the 2016 presidential contest, it was once again lackluster: just 49 percent of those under 30 came to the polls. This was rather surprising given that the race was so long and hotly contested and, of course, the importance of the outcome. Stated simply too many young people shun politics and are indifferent to the duties and responsibilities of democratic citizenship.

So if we can agree that young citizens are generally indifferent to politics, and that things may have gotten worse in recent decades, what are we to do about it? Should instructors of American Government care about this trend? If so, is this really an issue we might confront in meaningful ways?

Instructors of American Government especially understand the fragility of democracy and the importance of participation from a broad spectrum of citizens. A generation turned off from politics is a problem. Many have come to understand that introductory courses in American Government offer a unique opportunity to make a difference, as we have a captive audience for at least 45 hours per semester! And a stunning number of Americans take this course each year—upward of nearly one million. What a unique opportunity. There are numerous objectives in the introductory course, but surely one should be the cultivation of civic skills and an understanding of how average citizens can bring about change.

Our goal in writing and organizing this book has been to provide a tool to engage students—not only in the democratic process, but in the course itself. This course is fascinating, important, and fun—and we bring that feeling into the pages of this book.

We want the reader to understand that government and politics are not distant, abstract concepts but rather forces that shape their lives now and will greatly shape their lives in the future. Students should understand the workings of their government and the value of their engagement. We pull the reader into the subject matter by offering anecdotes and illustrations that "connect," by localizing politics whenever possible and by using a writing style that is clear and accessible.

Can a single course or the right textbook turn students into activists or politicians? Perhaps not. But we do believe that the material reviewed in this course is important and that offering content in novel and lively ways can help young readers appreciate their potential in a democracy. It is their system, too, and students should understand the workings of their government and the value of their engagement. This persistent indifference to politics compelled our work when we began this project a decade ago, and inspired our efforts and innovations with this new edition.

New to This Edition

American politics has undergone dramatic changes in the past few years, and this edition attempts to capture many of these adjustments—from the ramifications of **stunningly important elections**, a policy process framed within record level of individual and institutional partisan polarization, **landmark court cases**, immense cultural changes (including the growing acceptance of LGBT rights), the mushrooming importance of social media, and the continued rise of the partisan press. Simply stated, the pace of change in American politics in the last few years has set aback even the most seasoned observers. So much is different, yet so much of our politics is new.

As for key changes in the larger political universe, this new edition picks up after the 2016 elections—as Donald Trump takes over the White House. Not only will this be a change of administrations and a shift in public policy, but the former reality star will likely usher in a very different approach to governance. The pages to follow explore many of the forces that led to his assent, the numerous twists and turns in the electoral process that contributed to his victory over Hillary Clinton, and how Trump's brand of leadership will impact the presidency—perhaps for generations. We are at a unique, perhaps critical juncture in our politics. We have done our best to incorporate these big changes within the framework of historical and contextual forces. Our goal is to help students better comprehend what a Trump presidency might imply—the good and the bad—for our experiment in democratic governance.

A central aspect of this book has always been to offer stories of how average citizens—both in the United States and abroad—confront politics, respond, and make a difference. In this edition, we have updated these anecdotes to keep them as current as possible.

Chapter 1: This introductory chapter sets the stage for our understanding of how average citizens can play a meaningful role in our government by incorporating the latest data on political engagement. In light of so many significant recent developments in our politics, can citizens still make a difference?

Chapter 2: Our system has always wrestled with a desire to bring new, bold leaders into government, with the need for stabile governance through seasoned, experienced officials. The struggle between "new" and "establishment" has been recurrent, and this knowledge certainly helps us make better sense of the 2016 presidential election. New material in this chapter puts the rise of candidates like Donald Trump and Bernie Sanders in historic context.

Chapter 3: The latest trends in federalism, including the controversies surrounding Medicaid expansion, Supreme Court decisions regarding same-sex marriage, contraception, health care exchanges and other issues relating to the Affordable Care Act, are highlighted.

Chapter 4: Civil liberties issues are illuminated by the most important recent court decisions including: the Supreme Court declining to examine municipal restrictions on ownership of assault weapons (Friedman v. Highland Park, 2015); use of evidence against a driver who had broken no laws but was wrongly stopped by a police officer who misunderstood state traffic laws (Heien v. North Carolina, 2014); and limits on police authority to search the contents of drivers' cell phones during traffic stops (Riley v. California, 2014).

Chapter 5: This chapter now highlights the most controversial civil rights issues in the past year, the policing issues highlighted by the Black Lives Matter movement and the Supreme Court's approval of same-sex marriage in Obergefell v. Hodges (2015).

Chapter 6: New material in this chapter allows readers to better appreciate the breadth and consequence of polarization in Congress and how the prospects of continued gridlock will be shaped by the results of the 2016 election. It also dives into the make-up of the 115th Congress and how the changes ushered in by the 2016 election will continue to redefine the "People's Branch."

Chapter 7: New material in this chapter will help readers understand the forces that will shape Donald Trump's Administration. It provides the most up-to-date look at the development of his cabinet, the role of different advisors, how the new president will work with Congress—particularly Speaker Paul Ryan in the House of Representative, and how Trump may harness social media to put a unique spin on the "powers to persuade." New to this edition is also a more robust discussion on presidential unilateral actions.

Chapter 8: Problems involving the federal bureaucracy are illustrated by contemporary controversies about care at Veterans Administration hospitals and efforts to push the Department of Education to protect student loan borrowers against unfair practices.

Chapter 9: The political deadlock over the 2016 nomination of Judge Merrick Garland for a seat on the Supreme Court to replace the late Justice Antonin Scalia illustrates the efforts of presidents, senators, and political parties to shape the composition of the judiciary because of its importance in creating law and policy.

Chapter 10: A new section on the impact of social media on public opinion and political action is included as well as an expanded section on religion and party identification and public opinion, noting changes over time as well as contemporary dynamics.

Chapter 11: This chapter is significantly updated to include far more information about the lack of diversity in the news media and the concern over media bias. A good deal of attention is placed on the growing role of technology in the delivery of news, the use of social media and "citizen journalists," the controversies around viral videos and police violence, and divergent consumption patterns and access to technology based upon demographics and ideology. A new section on digital first news media is included as well as data comparing public support for a vigorous and free press in the United States and other counties around the world.

Chapter 12: A new section on online activism is included, with special attention paid to examining whether or not online activism helps engagement or provides the illusion of being involved without the necessary commitment of time and energy. All data in the chapter is updated, with new information about Super PACs and nonprofit election spending.

Chapter 13: New to this chapter is a discussion of the legitimacy of the presidential nomination process, a topic brought to light by the candidacies of Donald Trump and Bernie Sanders. It also provides turnout data from the 2016 election, as well as the most recent campaign finance reports and polling data on voters' attitudes and behaviors. What factors explain Donald Trump's surprise victory? How did the Republicans maintain control of both the House and Senate? What will happen to the Democratic Party in the years to come? Many believe the presidential election process has been forever changed by what happened in this election, and this chapter confronts many of these issues.

Chapter 14: The opening vignette and conclusion now focus on the 2013 government shutdown and debate over the Affordable Care Act. The discussion about the Obamacare court cases has been updated to include *King* v. *Burwell* (2015). The chapter now mentions the Flint water crisis as an addition to the issue-attention cycle and discusses the international Paris Agreement on climate change. All budget numbers in the chapter, including defense spending numbers, are updated. Some discussion of how economic policy was debated during the 2016 presidential primaries is also included.

Chapter 15: The opening vignette and conclusion discuss new, hot global issues, including the Syrian Civil War, ISIS, a more aggressive Russia, and a more assertive China. American involvement in Afghanistan and Iraq has been updated for recent developments as well. The chapter now mentions NATO and Operation Inherent Resolve against ISIS. The discussion of CAFTA has been replaced with a discussion of Trade Promotion Authority. The chapter also looks at President Obama's Iran deal (the Joint Comprehensive Plan of Action, or JCPOA).

The number of special features in this edition has been streamlined, tightening the focus on the central theme of the book and making the most of students' allotted reading time. We have also added **polling questions** throughout each chapter to help students connect the material to their daily lives and explore their opinions on a variety of current issues. Revel takes these polling questions one step further, allowing students to compare their positions with those of their classmates, all *Living Democracy* readers, and national polling data.

The photos in this edition serve important purposes. They capture major events from the last few years, of course, but to illustrate politics' relevancy, they show political actors and processes as well as people affected by politics, creating a visual narrative that enhances rather than repeats the text. Also, all of the **figures and tables** reflect the latest available data.

Features

Informed by cognitive psychology and proven learning concepts, the 2016 Presidential Election Edition of *Living Democracy* structures the material in ways that are consistent with effective, research-based pedagogy. We use a scaffolding process, for example, where new information builds on an established foundation.

One of the key pedagogical features of this book is the pathway of politics concept. We posit that democratic politics filters down into five "pathways" of change: the court process, elections, lobbying, grassroots activism, and cultural change. Many instructors have told us that this approach simplifies the process for students, and it helps them understand that voting is not the only route to change. American government can seem overwhelmingly complex and intricate—because it is! So we introduce this model early and use it throughout every chapter to untangle key concepts and thus aid student learning.

Living Democracy opens with an examination of the historical context and structure of our government, paying close attention to our constitutional system and our civil liberties and rights. Next, we move into a comprehensive examination of our political institutions and introduce students to the complex organization of our federal government. We are careful to place contemporary issues in historical and comparative context so that students understand the political intricacy of contemporary issues. Political linkage mechanisms are presented next, exposing students to various entities that tie us to our government and promote (and complicate) democracy. The last two chapters introduce students to the policymaking process by using economic and foreign policies as case studies. The text will help you teach students how to be active participants in the political process by giving them the knowledge and skills they will need to be interested and informed consumers throughout their lives.

- **Pathways of Action** sections illustrate how citizens—often average citizens—have made key changes in the system. At times these changes have been very broad, but in other instances, they have been much more localized.
- **Policy Timelines** explore the "when, where, and why" of significant changes in our political history in every chapter.
- **Confronting Politics and Policy** features close every chapter by laying out an important, on-going issue—a topic that could affect the readers' lives—and suggesting a series of steps they can take to become more informed and involved, and to make a difference. The goal is to explore a real issue and to suggest concrete steps for the reader's engagement.
- Every chapter includes **learning objectives** and a **marginal glossary** to support students' understanding of new and important concepts at first encounter. For easy reference, learning objectives and section summaries and key terms are repeated at the end of each chapter. There is also an end-of-book glossary.

Participation is surely at the center of this book. But so is pedagogy. We have worked diligently to incorporate research-based learning strategies. Our "pathways" approach is part of that, but so are all of the features described above. Our goal is to offer core information and proven learning tools to help the student feel better about the class and about future involvement in politics. If we have done our job, this text will encourage a deeper level of connection to the system, and afford the reader a foundation of understanding—a framework for a lifetime of democratic engagement.

Revel™

Educational technology designed for the way today's students read, think, and learn

When students are engaged deeply, they learn more effectively and perform better in their courses. This simple fact inspired the creation of Revel: an immersive learning experience designed for the way today's students read, think, and learn. Built in collaboration with educators and students nationwide, Revel is the newest, fully digital way to deliver respected Pearson content.

Revel enlivens course content with media interactives and assessments—integrated directly within the authors' narrative—that provide opportunities for students to read about and practice course material in tandem. This immersive educational technology boosts student engagement, which leads to better understanding of concepts and improved performance throughout the course.

- Chapter-opening and closing **Current Events Bulletins** feature author-written articles, refreshed twice a year, that put breaking news and current events into the context of American government. The end-of-chapter bulletins, new to the 2016 Election Edition, lay out two sides of a hot-topic debate and encourage students to develop their own informed opinions.

Chapter 10
Political Socialization and Public Opinion

- **Videos** vividly illustrate key moments in American government. **News footage** provides examples from both historical and current events, from pinnacle civil rights demonstrations and hallmark presidential speeches to extensive coverage of the 2016 election and the issues that resonate with students today like climate change and new media. In addition, popular **Sketchnote videos** illustrate the material's "pathways" framework, showing individuals how they can make a difference, and walking students through difficult-to-understand concepts such as how a bill becomes a law and the policymaking process. Through the visual storytelling approach, Sketchnote videos cater to visual and audio learners and hit a high level of engagement in students who can see the concept come to life.

Watch   MARCH ON SELMA REMEMBERED 50 YEARS LATER

Watch   JOHN OLIVER ON MAKING CURRENT EVENTS FUNNY

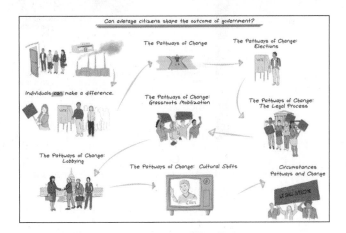

- **Interactive maps and figures** featuring Social Explorer technology allow updates
  with the latest data, toggles to illustrate movement over time, and clickable hot
  spots with pop-ups of images, detailed data, and captions.

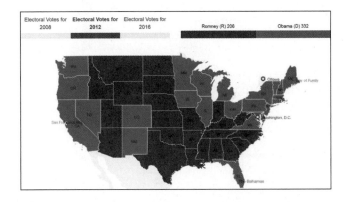

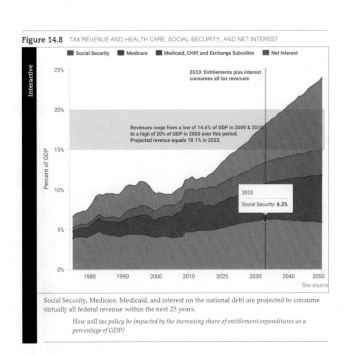

Figure 14.8   TAX REVENUE AND HEALTH CARE, SOCIAL SECURITY, AND NET INTEREST

Social Security, Medicare, Medicaid, and interest on the national debt are projected to consume
virtually all federal revenue within the next 25 years.

*How will tax policy be impacted by the increasing share of entitlement expenditures as a
percentage of GDP?*

- **Interactive simulations** allow students to apply each chapter's concepts in real-world scenarios and explore critical issues and challenges that the country's Founders faced and that elected officials, bureaucrats, political activists, and average citizens still face today.

- Primary source **documents**, such as Thomas Paine's *Common Sense*, the Emancipation Proclamation, and various Supreme Court cases and *Federalist Papers*, open alongside the material's narrative so that they can be read in context.

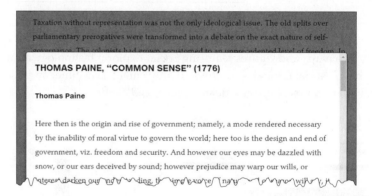

- **Interactive timelines** in each chapter allow students to explore important events and the development and different sides of key issues in American political history.

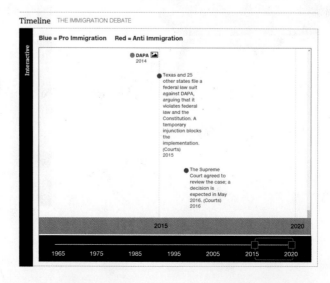

- **Polls** encourage students to explore their own views on important political issues and often compare their opinions to similar national polling results.

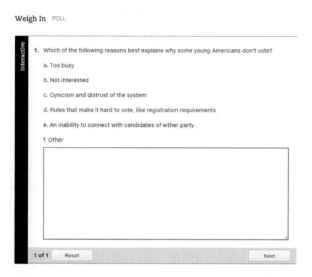

- Interactive **Review the Chapter** summaries that utilize learning objectives and flashcards featuring key terms and definitions allow students to review the chapters and reinforce the content.

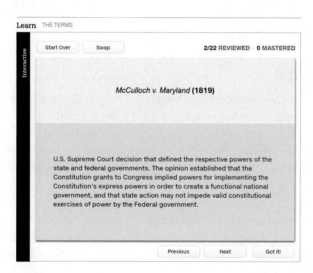

- **Assessments** tied to primary chapter sections, as well as full chapter exams, allow instructors and students to track progress and get immediate feedback.

- **Integrated Writing Opportunities** To help students reason and write more clearly, each chapter offers two varieties of writing prompts:

  - **Journal prompts** ask students to think critically and apply what they have learned.
  - **Shared writing prompts** encourage students to consider how to address challenges described in the chapter. Through these prompts, instructors and students can address multiple sides of an issue by sharing their own views and responding to each other's viewpoints.

Learn more about Revel:
www.pearsonhighered.com/revel/

Supplements

Make more time for your students with instructor resources that offer effective learning assessments and classroom engagement. Pearson's partnership with educators does not end with the delivery of course materials; Pearson is there with you on the first day of class and beyond. A dedicated team of local Pearson representatives will work with you to not only choose course materials but also integrate them into your class and assess their effectiveness. Our goal is your goal—to improve instruction with each semester.

Pearson is pleased to offer the following resources to qualified adopters of *Living Democracy*. Several of these supplements are available to instantly download on the Instructor Resource Center (IRC); please visit the IRC at **www.pearsonhighered.com/ irc** to register for access.

TEST BANK Evaluate learning at every level. Reviewed for clarity and accuracy, the Test Bank measures this book's learning objectives with multiple- choice, true/ false, fill-in-the-blank, short answer, and essay questions. You can easily customize the assessment to work in any major learning management system and to match what is covered in your course. Word, BlackBoard, and WebCT versions available on the IRC and Respondus versions available upon request from **www.respondus.com**.

PEARSON MYTEST This powerful assessment generation program includes all of the questions in the Test Bank. Quizzes and exams can be easily authored and saved online and then printed for classroom use, giving you ultimate flexibility to manage assessments anytime and anywhere. To learn more, visit **www.pearsonhighered.com/ mytest**.

INSTRUCTOR'S RESOURCE MANUAL Create a comprehensive roadmap for teaching classroom, online, or hybrid courses. Designed for new and experienced instructors, the Instructor's Resource Manual includes learning objectives, lecture and discussion suggestions, activities for in or out of class, research activities, participation activities, and suggested readings, series, and films as well as a Revel features section. Available within Revel and on the IRC.

POWERPOINT PRESENTATION WITH LEARNING CATALYTICS™ Make lectures more enriching for students. The PowerPoint Presentation includes a full lecture outline and photos and figures from the textbook and Revel edition. With integrated Learning Catalytics™ questions, get immediate feedback on what your students are learning during a lecture. Available within Revel and on the IRC.

Acknowledgments

Although it required the work of numerous people to make this revision possible, several deserve special recognition. Our editor, Jeff Marshall, offered important insights and guidance, particularly regarding the integration of hard copy and electronic elements. Development Editor Rebecca Green helped guide the revision process along, and we benefited from the skills and knowledge of several others at Pearson, including Kimberly Dunworth and Tina Gagliostro. Valerie Iglar-Mobley provided excellent project management. Tara Cook at Metrodigi was instrumental in helping us develop and fine-tune the electronic components.

The author team would especially like to thank Grant Ferguson of Texas Christian University for his keen insights and work on the two policy chapters. Joanne would like to thank her students in her American Politics classes, who have solidified her love of the subject. They are a continuing source of inspiration and motivation. A special thanks goes to her family, Craig, Emma, and Connor—to whom her efforts are devoted—for their continued patience. Chris thanks his wife, Charlotte, and children, Alicia and Eric, for their support and encouragement. Dan would like to thank his colleagues in the Department of Government and the Goldfarb Center for Public Affairs and Civic Engagement at Colby College for their assistance and encouragement. And, as always, he offers a special thanks to his wonderful family—Christine, Abby, Daniel, and Brian—for their love, guidance, and unwavering support.

We are grateful to the Test Bank Advisory Board members who provided feedback used to improve our assessment questions: Willie Hamilton, Mt. San Jacinto College; Will Miller, Flagler College; James Starkey, Pasadena City College and Long Beach City College; V. James Strickler, Valdosta State University; Ronald Velten, Grayson College; Ryan Voris, University of Kentucky.

Finally, the authors wish to thank the many professors and researchers who provided detailed feedback on how to improve content and who gave their invaluable input during professional conferences and Pearson-sponsored events. They gave generously of their time and expertise and we are, as always, in their debt.

APSA 2015: Brian Califano, Missouri State University; David A. Caputo, Pace University; Lori Cox Han, Chapman University; Joshua Dyck, University of Massachusetts, Lowell; Maurice Eisenstein, Purdue University Calumet; Bryan Gervais, UTSA; Ben Gonzalez, Highline College; Mel Hailey, Abilene Christian University; Kerstin Hamann, University of Central Florida; Meredith Heiser, Foothill College; Erika Herrera, Lone Star College; Judith Hurtado Ortiz, Peralta; Gabe Jolivet, Ashford University; Ryan Krog, George Washington University; Jessica Lavariega Monforti, Pace University; Liz Lebron, LSU; Andrew Levin, Harper College; Stephen Meinhold, UNC-W; Keesha Middlemass, Trinity University; Samantha Mosier, Missouri State University; Jason Myers, CSU Stanislaus; Todd Myers, Grossmont Community College; Sharon Navarro, Univeristy of Texas at San Antonio; John Payne, Ivy Tech Community College; Anne C. Pluta, Rowan; Dan Ponder, Drury University; David Ramsey, UWF; Jason Robles, Colorado State University; John David Rausch, Jr., West Texas A&M University; Jon Ross, Aurora College; Erich Saphir, Pima College; Justin Vaughn, Boise

State University; Peter Wielhouwer, Western Michigan University; Patrick Wohlfarth, University of Maryland, College Park; Chris Wolfe, Dallas County Community College; Youngtae Shin, University of Central Oklahoma.

APSA 2016: Cathy Andrews, Austin Community College; Sara Angevine, Whittier College; Benjamin Arah, Bowie State University; Yan Bai, Grand Rapids Community College; Michael Bailey, Georgetown University; Karen L. Baird, Purchase College, SUNY; Richard Bilsker, College of Southern Maryland; Russell Brooker, Alverno College; Christopher M. Brown, Georgia Southern University; Jonathan Buckstead, Austin Community College; Camille Burge, Villanova University; Isaac M. Castellano, Boise State University; Stefanie Chambers, Trinity College; Anne Marie Choup, University of Alabama, Huntsville; Nick Clark, Susquehanna University; Mary Anne Clarke, RI College; Carlos Cunha, Dowling College; John Diehl, Bucks County Community College; Joseph DiSarro, Washington and Jefferson University; Margaret Dwyer, Milwaukee School of Engineering; Laurel Elder, Hardwick College; Melinda Frederick, Prince George's Community College; Amanda Friesen, IUPUI; Jason Giersch, UNC, Charlotte; Mauro Gilli, ETH; Margaret Gray, Adelphi University; Mark Grzegorzewski, Joint Special Operations University; John Hanley, Duquesne University; Jacqueline Holland, Lorain County Community College; Jack Hunt, University of Southern Maine; Clinton Jenkins, George Washington University; Nadia Jilani-Hyler, Augusta University; Christopher N. Lawrence, Middle Georgia State University; Daniel Lewis, Siena College; Joel Lieske, Cleveland State; Nancy Lind, Illinois State University; Matt Lindstrom, College of St. Benedict /St. John's University; Eric D. Loepp, UW-Whitewater; Kevin Lorentz, Wayne State University; Gregory Love, University of Mississippi; Abbie Luoma, Saint Leo University; Linda K. Mancillas, Georgia Gwinnett College; Buba Misawa, Washington and Jefferson College; Martha Musgrove, Tarrant County College – South Campus; Steven Nawara, Lewis University; Tatishe Nteta, University of Massachusetts, Amherst; Dr. Mjahid Nyahuma, Community College of Philadelphia; Matthew Platt, Morehouse College; Marcus Pohlmann, Rhodes College; Adriane M. Raff Corwin, Bergen & Brookdale Community Colleges; Lauren Ratliff, The Ohio State University; Dr. Keith Reeves, Swarthmore College; Ted Ritter, Virginia Union University; Joseph W. Roberts, Roger Williams University; Amanda Rosen, Webster University; Scot Schraufnagel, Northern Illinois University; John Seymour, El Paso Community College; Ginger Silvera, Cal State, Dominguez Hills; Kyla Stepp, Central Michigan University; Ryane Straus, College of Saint Rose; Maryam Stevenson, Troy University; Tressa Tabares, American River College; Bernard Tamas, Valdosta State University; Lee Trepanier, Saginaw Valley State University; Kevin Wallsten, California State University, Long Beach; Richard Waterman, University of Kentucky; Joe Weinberg, University of Southern Mississippi; Jonathan Whatron, Southern Connecticut State University; Elizabeth G. Williams, PhD, Santa Fe College.

2016 WebEx meetings for Revel: Maria Albo, University of North Georgia; Hendel Cerphy, Palm Beach State College; Karl Clark, Coastal Bend College; Amy Colon, SUNY Sullivan; Lishan Desta, Collin College; Agber Dimah, Chicago State University; Dr. Barbara, Arkansas State University; Kathleen Ferraiolo, James Madison University; Terri Susan Fine, University of Central Florida; Maria Gonzalez, Miami Dade College; Joe Gaziano, Lewis University; Dion George, Atlanta Metropolitan State College; Colin Glennon, East Tennessee State University; Mike Green, Southern New Hampshire University; Jan Hardt, University of Central Oklahoma; Kathryn Hendricks, MCC – Longview; Julie Hershenberg, Collin College; Jeneen Hobby, Cleveland State University; Andy Howard, Rio Hondo College; Nikki Isemann, Southeast Community College; Nicole Kalaf-Hughes, Bowling Green State University; Frederick M. Kalisz, Bridgewater State University; Lance Kelley, NWTC; Eric Loepp, University of Wisconsin, Whitewater; Benjamin Melusky, Franklin and Marshall College; David Monda, Mt. San Jacinto College; Laura Pellegrini, LBCC; Dave Price, Santa Fe College; Jennifer

Sacco, Quinnipiac University; Larry W. Smith, Amarillo College; J. Joel Tovanche, Tarrant County College.

Spring 2016 WebEx Meetings: Cathy Andrews, Austin Community College; Yan Bai, Grand Rapids Community College; Richard Bilsker, College of Southern Maryland; Jonathan Buckstead, Austin Community College; Adriane M. Raff Corwin, Bergen & Brookdale Community Colleges; Carlos Cunha, Dowling College; Margaret Dwyer, Milwaukee School of Engineering; Jacqueline Holland, Lorain County Community College; Nadia Jilani-Hyler, Augusta University; Nancy Lind, Illinois State University; Eric D. Loepp, UW-Whitewater; Abbie Luoma, Saint Leo University; Martha Musgrove, Tarrant County College–South College; Steven Nawara, Lewis University; Maryam Stevenson, Troy University; Lee Trepanier, Saginaw Valley State University; Elizabeth G. Williams, PhD., Santa Fe College.

2016 Texas WebEx Meetings: Ralph Angeles, Lone Star College; Delina Barrera, University of Texas Pan American; Jennifer Boggs, Angelo State University; Bryan Calvin, Tarrant County College Northwest; William Carroll, Sam Houston State University; Anita Chadha, University of Houston-Downtown; Jennifer Danley-Scott, Texas Woman's University; Bianca Easterly, Lamar University; Reynaldo Flores, Richland College; Katie Fogle Deering, North Central Texas University; Sylvia Gonzalez-Gorman, Texas Tech; Peyton Gooch, Stephen F. Austin; Donald Gooch, Stephen F. Austin; Cheri Hobbs, Blinn College; Cynthia Hunter-Summerlin, Tarrant County College Trinity River; Joe Ialenti, North Central Texas College; Dominique Lewis, Blinn College; Eric Lundin, Lonestar College; Sharon Manna, North Lake College; Holly Mulholland, San Jacinto College Central; Hillel Ofek, University of Texas at Austin; Lisa Palton, San Jacinto Community College; William Parent, San Jacinto College Central; Cecil Pool, El Centro College; Jennifer Ross, Brookhaven College DCCCD; Lane Seever, Austin Community College; Max Seymour, West Texas A&M University; Les Stanaland, North Central Texas College; Dustin Tarver, Blinn College; James Tate, Richland College; Blake Tritico, Sam Houston State University; Karen Webb, Texas Woman's University.

May 2016 Hoboken /Boston Focus Groups: Flannery Amdahl, Hunter College; Thomas Arndt, Rowan University; Ben Christ, Harrisburg Area Community College; Mary Anne Clarke, RI College; Ken Cosgrove, Suffolk University; Melissa Gaeke, Marist College; Todd M. Galante, Rutgers University-Newark; Jack Hunt, University of Southern Maine; Ed Johnson, Brookdale Community College; Frederick M. Kalisz, Jr., Bridgewater State University; M. Victoria Perez-Rios, John Jay College of Criminal Justice, CUNY; Francois Pierre-Louis, Queens College, CUNY; John Seymour, El Paso Community College; Ursula C. Tafe, University of Massachusetts Boston; Anh Tran, Baruch College; John Trujillo, Borough of Manhattan Community College; Aaron Zack, John Jay College.

AMERICAN GOVERNMENT

DEMOCRACY IN ACTION

Efforts to expand the legal protections for LGBT Americans have produced significant changes in recent years due to the will and dedication of average Americans. In a very real way, our democracy has been created and redefined through the centuries by citizens demanding change.

Do you think most Americans, particularly younger citizens, today believe they can make a difference in the conduct of government?

→ LEARNING OBJECTIVES

1.1 Illustrate how citizens participate in a democracy and why this is important.

1.2 Relate the themes of this book to American politics today.

1.3 Outline the various "pathways" of involvement in our political system.

1.4 Analyze the forces of stability in American politics.

uring the 1950s, lesbian, gay, bisexual and transgender (LGBT) Americans were subjected to widespread discrimination. Early in the decade, a Senate report said "homosexuality" was mental illness, and that this group constituted a security risk because "those who engage in overt acts of perversion lack the emotional stability of normal persons."[1] Two years later, the American Psychiatric Association listed homosexuality as a sociopathic personality disturbance and in 1953 President Eisenhower signed an executive order banning gay and lesbian citizens from working for the federal government. These citizens were subjected to an array of treatments to find a "cure," including electroshock therapy. By the 1960s, 82 percent of American men and 58 percent of American women believed that only Communists and atheists were more dangerous than "homosexuals."

Things began to change. In the 1960s, a number of local organizations began to emerge—likely drawing energy from other civil and human rights movements. Sit-ins and other small-scale protests started to take place. In June of 1969, the patrons of the Stonewall Inn in Greenwich Village (a neighborhood in Manhattan) rioted when police officers raided the popular gay bar. Over the course of three days, thousands of protestors stood their ground against the police. Many believe the Stonewall Riots ignited the modern LGBT rights movement.

The pace of change accelerated in the 1980s and 1990s, but there were also setbacks. The AIDs crisis, which affected a disproportionate number of gay men, rekindled fears of the LGBT lifestyle. In 1996, President Bill Clinton signed the Defense of Marriage Act—a law that defined marriage as a legal union between one man and one woman, and stipulated that states were not required to recognize same-sex marriages performed in other states. A rash of state ballot initiatives and constitutional amendments were passed to prohibit gay marriage. Many candidates were sent to office on an anti-gay marriage platform.

And yet, the LBGT movement continued. The tide of public opinion turned, pushed along by shifts in popular culture. State after state began passing laws to protect LGBT citizens. The military changed course on "don't ask, don't tell" and several states allowed gay marriage. In June of 2015, precisely 46 years to the day after the Stonewall Riots, the U.S. Supreme Court ruled that gays and lesbians have a constitutional right to marry in *any* state.

Amy Snow and Christelle show their wedding rings as they celebrate the Supreme Court ruling on same-sex marriage on June 26, 2015. The Supreme Court has said that same-sex couples have a constitutional right to marry nationwide without regard to their states' laws.

■ *Do you think the decision will settle the gay marriage issue once and for all?*

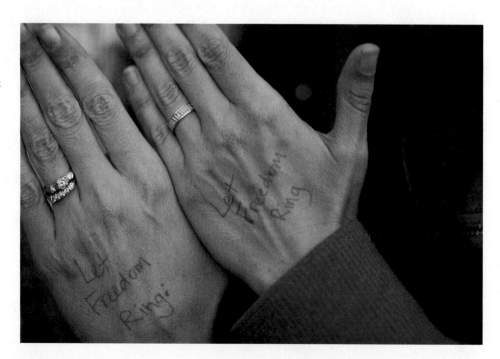

CAN AVERAGE CITIZENS PLAY A MEANINGFUL ROLE IN AMERICAN POLITICS?

For those who suffered discrimination and hatred because of their sexual orientation, the pace of change was surely not swift enough. And of course the issue of gay marriage remains controversial in many states and communities; some believe the issue has not been settled. But in historic terms, the pace of the gay rights movement has been rapid.

How did this happen? As with all significant political movements in our nation's history, a host of forces came together. At the very heart of this transformation, however, were countless acts by ordinary citizens. Struggles took place in large and small protests, voting booths, courtrooms, and legislatures. Political action took place in classrooms, in bars, and at kitchen tables across the nation. The acts of public officials were instrumental, but these moves were made possible because average citizens refused to sit on the sidelines.

As you will see throughout the pages of this book, there are forces that suggest ordinary citizens cannot make much of a difference in our political system. The United States is not a perfect democracy, as we all know. But political engagement matters—and it always has. Time and again, ordinary men and women have shifted the course of government. The story of the LGBT rights movement underscores a fundamental and enduring truth that our government can be responsive, so long as citizens demand to be heard.

It's Your Government

1.1   Illustrate how citizens participate in a democracy and why this is important.

On some level, everyone knows that government affects our lives. We must obey laws created by government. We pay taxes to support the government. We make use of government services, ranging from police protection to student loans. It is easy, however, to see government as a distant entity that imposes its will on us. It provides benefits and protections, such as schools, roads, and fire departments. But it also limits our choices by telling us how fast we can drive and how old we must be to get married, purchase alcoholic beverages, and vote.

Would your view of government change if a new law dramatically affected your choices, plans, or expectations? Imagine that you and your four best friends decide to rent a house together for the next academic year. You find a five-bedroom, furnished house near campus that is owned by a friendly landlord. Then, you sign a lease and put down your deposit. During the summer, however, the landlord sends you a letter informing you that two of your friends will need to find someplace else to live. The city council has passed a new ordinance—the kind of law produced by local governments—declaring that not more than three unrelated people may live in a house together.

Now what would you think about government? After your initial feelings of anger, you might resign yourself to the disappointment of moving back into a dormitory or finding a different apartment. You might also ask yourself an important question: Is there anything that I can do about this new ordinance?

A distinguishing feature of democracy—the form of government in the United States—is that people have opportunities to influence the decisions of government. One individual cannot realistically expect to control the government's choice of priorities or the laws that are produced. However, in some circumstances, individuals can participate in activities that ultimately change government and lead to the creation of new laws and regulations—as was suggested in the opening section on the LBGT rights movement. Let us take the example of the housing ordinance and consider what you might do to attempt to change that law:

- You could encourage students to register to vote and help with political campaigns for city council candidates who promise to listen to students' concerns and get rid of the housing ordinance. In some college towns, individual students have become so energized by specific political issues that some have actually run for and been elected to city councils. These activities, *voting* and *elections*, are the most familiar forms of citizen participation in a democracy.

- You could organize your friends to contact members of the city council asking them to change the restrictive new law. You could also go to city council meetings and voice your opposition to the law. We often characterize these activities as *lobbying* lawmakers in order to pressure or persuade them to make specific decisions.

- You could talk to the local landlords' association about whether it might file a lawsuit challenging the ordinance on the grounds that it improperly interferes with the landlords' right to decide how to use their private property. You might talk to an attorney yourself about whether, under the laws of your state, a new ordinance can override the rental lease agreement that you and your friends had already signed. If the new ordinance violates other existing laws, then taking the issue to court by filing lawsuits—a process known as *litigation*—may provide the means for a lawyer to persuade a judge to invalidate the city council's action.

- You could write articles in the college newspaper or blog about the new ordinance to inform other students about the effect of the law on their off-campus housing choices. You could publicize and sponsor meetings in order to organize *grassroots activities*, such as marches, sit-ins, or other forms of nonviolent protests. These actions would draw news media attention and put pressure on city officials to reconsider their decision.

There is no guarantee that any of these approaches would produce the change you desire. But each of these courses of action, depending on the circumstances in the community and the number of people who provide support, presents the possibility of changing the government's decision.

Each one of these approaches is part of **politics**. You should understand that politics concerns the activities that seek to affect the composition, power, and actions of government.

American government should *not* be viewed as "distant," "all-powerful," or "unchangeable." Although government buildings are often designed to instill feelings of respect and admiration and to convey permanence, stability, and power, they are much more than awe-inspiring works of architecture. They are *arenas of activity* that determine **public policy**—what government does and does not do. The

politics

The process by which the actions of government are determined. For example, by appealing to members of the city council to change the new housing ordinance, several students decided to roll up their sleeves and become engaged in local politics.

public policy

What government decides to do or not do; government laws, rules, or expenditures. For instance, it is state public policy that you must be 21 years old to purchase alcohol.

Pictured here are demonstrators, marking the one-year anniversary of the shooting of Michael Brown, in Ferguson, Missouri. Black Lives Matter, a grassroots protest organization, has drawn a lot of media attention.

■ *Do you think the group's efforts have been effective in helping to bring change?*

TABLE 1.1   Government Is All Around Us

Many doubt that government plays a role in your daily life. If you agree, consider the following timeline of a typical day in the life of an average college student and the number of times governmental control comes into play. Keep in mind that this is only the tip of the iceberg.

Time	Event	Government Agency
6:22 A.M.	You awaken to the sounds of a garbage truck outside. Annoyed, you realize that you forgot to bring the recyclables to the street last night.	Local department of sanitation; local recycling program
6:49 A.M.	Unable to get back to sleep, you take a shower, thinking about the cost of rent for your apartment and wondering if your next place will have a decent shower.	Local water filtration plant; federal Department of Housing and Urban Development
7:22 A.M.	You read the news, noting that interest rates are going up and that troop levels in Afghanistan are on the rise.	Federal Reserve Board; Selective Service; Department of Defense
8:34 A.M.	Driving to class, you notice the airbag, but you don't notice dirty car exhaust. You also note that your inspection sticker is about to expire.	Federal Environmental Protection Agency, state and local environmental agencies; state Motor Vehicle Bureau
8:43 A.M.	You stop at a gas station and are so pleased that prices seem to be going down.	Federal government investments in oil exploration and alternative fuels; presidential oversight of the Strategic Oil Reserves; federal trade agreements
9:05 A.M.	You arrive on campus, find a parking space, and walk to class.	State and federal support for higher education; state and federal tuition support and student loan programs
11:00 A.M.	In accounting class, you discuss the CPA exam.	State professional licensing program
12:09 P.M.	At lunch, you discuss the upcoming elections. Your best friend realizes that she won't be able to vote because she missed the registration deadline.	State election commission; Secretary of State Office
3:00 P.M.	You receive a paycheck for your part-time restaurant job. In spite of the low hourly wage you receive, a bunch of money has been deducted for taxes.	Federal and state minimum wage laws; local, state, and federal income tax regulations; federal unemployment program; federal Social Security program
4:15 P.M.	You figure out a customer's bill, carefully adding the sales tax to the total.	Local and state sales taxes
9:47 P.M.	You settle in for some television after studying and wonder why profanity is allowed on some cable shows, but not on network television.	Federal Communications Commission
11:49 P.M.	You collapse into bed and slip into a peaceful sleep, taking for granted that you are safe.	Local police department; state militia; U.S. military

laws and policies produced by government in these arenas affect the lives of everyone in the United States—including students like you, as suggested in Table 1.1. It is essential for you to understand that laws and policies are influenced by the actions of groups and individuals and that *you* can play an important role in the policy process.

Our Unique Political System

The United States is different from other countries in the world. Our government and laws reflect our unique history as a group of former British colonies that fought a war for independence, expanded westward across a wilderness through the efforts of pioneers, experienced waves of immigration, and survived a bloody civil war that occurred, in large part, over the issue of race-based slavery. While many aspects of American government, such as elections and the right to a fair trial before being convicted of a crime, can be found in other countries, the organization of American elections and the rights possessed by criminal defendants in American courts differ from those found elsewhere in the world. For example, in the United States, defendants are presumed innocent until proven guilty, which forces the government to prove someone's guilt, rather than compelling individuals to prove their own innocence. In addition, judges at the federal level are appointed for life, a scheme designed to remove them from the pressures of public opinion. Compared to judges in other democracies, American judges also possess significant power to invalidate laws and policies created by other government decision makers. Thus, Americans have unique opportunities to use litigation as a means to influence government. Yet another example of our uniqueness is the fragmented nature of our system—the check and balances, sharing of powers, bicameral legislature, federated system, and much else. Likely, this scheme has led to stability, but also a slow-moving, incremental policy process.

If we look at countries around the world, we can discover a variety of forms of government. By classifying forms of government according to two factors, citizen participation in governmental decisions and freedom for individuals, a number of different types of governments emerge. Freedom House, a nonprofit, nonpartisan organization, makes just such an assessment. Every year, it issues a rating of countries according to the extent of political rights (for example, voting) and individual liberties (for example, freedom of speech) that their citizens have. Countries are rated on a scale from 1 to 7, with 1 meaning the highest level of political rights. Political rights are evaluated based on a number of factors, including whether the process of candidate selection is free from government approval, whether voters are presented with genuine choices at the ballot box, and whether the elections and governments are free from military involvement. Representative findings are shown in Figure 1.1.

At the top end of the scale are **democracies**, including the United States, in which citizens enjoy a large measure of personal freedom and have meaningful opportunities to participate in government through voting, organizing protests against government policies, and other forms of free speech and political action. At the other end of the scale are countries with **totalitarian regimes**, in which the leaders of the government hold all of the power and control all aspects of society.

Unlike residents living in countries with totalitarian regimes, you can actually use your knowledge, critical analysis skills, time, and energy to improve America's

democracy

A political system in which all citizens have a chance to play a role in shaping government action and are afforded basic rights and liberties.

totalitarian regime

A system of government in which the ruling elite holds all power and controls all aspects of society. Nazi Germany was a totalitarian government in the 1930s and early 1940s.

FIGURE 1.1   Global Ratings on Political Rights, 2016

■ *Do you find anything in this figure surprising, or are the ratings as you expected?*

SOURCE: Freedom House, Inc., http://www.freedomhouse.org.

Free   Party Free   Not Free

laws and policies. Your efforts might be aimed at decisions by local government, as in the example of the controversial housing ordinance, or you might roll up your sleeves to help an underdog candidate win an election. There are numerous pathways for your involvement, and you can seek to affect government at the local, state, and national levels. The chapters of this book will help you to see how you can actively participate in processes that influence the decisions and actions of your government.

Themes of This Book

1.2   Relate the themes of this book to American politics today.

A merican government is complex. The functions of government are divided among different institutions and people. While in some countries, a national government creates law and public policy to handle all issues and priorities for its people, in the United States, by contrast, there are multiple governments. In addition to the familiar institutions of the national government—including the president, Congress, and the U.S. Supreme Court—there are parallel institutions and actors in all 50 states, plus additional agencies and actors in cities, counties, and townships within each state.

To illustrate how government works and how you can affect the way it works, this book first shows the opportunities for *citizen participation in democratic government*. Second, the text identifies and analyzes the *pathways of action* through which individuals and groups can seek to influence law and public policy in American government. Third, the text emphasizes the importance of American society's *diversity and the effect that has on government and our participation in it*. Let's take a moment to consider these three themes in greater detail.

Citizen Participation in Democratic Government

As we noted earlier, a distinguishing feature of democracy is that it provides opportunities for citizens to participate in their government. In nondemocratic governing systems, people have few lawful ways, if any, to shape law and policy. For example, *totalitarian governments* swiftly arrest and even kill people who express opposition to the central authority. When 50,000 people stormed into the streets of Moscow in December 2011 to protest what they believe to be rigged parliamentary elections, the leader of the protest was promptly arrested. After what many believed would be an opening of the system by the so-called "Arab Spring," leaders in Egypt moved aggressively to detain and sentence some 41,000 people between July 2013 and May 2014 for speaking out against the government. Thousands were held without a trial and human rights groups reported hundreds of deaths due to medical negligence, illtreatment, and torture.[2] In some of the oppressive countries, the only option available to citizens who want to affect change is an armed revolt—using violence to change the system of government.

In contrast, people in the United States have opportunities to express their viewpoints and take actions to influence the government without resorting to violence. These opportunities to participate help create and maintain a stable society. You will find many examples throughout this book of such opportunities.

> POLL   Generally speaking, would you say students at your college or university are very interested in public affairs, somewhat interested in public affairs, or not at all interested in public affairs?

These options for engagement will not be fully effective, however, unless people actually become engaged in public affairs. If large numbers neglect to vote, fail to keep themselves informed about the government's actions, or passively accept all decisions by lawmakers, governing power may come to rest in the hands of a small number of individuals and groups. The quality and effectiveness of laws and policies suffer if there is inadequate input from the full range of people who will be affected by them. Without knowledge about carbon dioxide emissions, for example, well-intentioned decisions to address climate change by Congress and the president may be misdirected and fail to get at the actual source of the problem. In the same way, lawmakers might make more effective laws concerning financial aid programs for college students, if students provide information and express their viewpoints about the best courses of action. In other words, the laws and policies of a democracy will reflect the preferences and viewpoints of a diverse country only if citizens from all segments of society make their voices heard.

Now look at the comparison of voting rates in Figure 1.2. Does this raise any concerns about whether Americans are active enough in shaping their government's decisions? Note that some of the countries with the highest voting rates impose fines on citizens who fail to register to vote and cast their ballots. Would such a law violate Americans' notions of freedom?

To many, it seems ironic that the legal opportunities to participate in the electoral process have expanded greatly during the past 50 years, but a bare majority of Americans seem willing to do so. Numerous measures of political engagement suggest a somewhat disengaged citizenry in the United States. In the past few years, the Pew Research Center has been tracking levels of engagement in the United States. Figure 1.3 includes some of their findings. It should also be noted that election turnout continues to shrink. In fact, turnout for the 2014 midterm elections was the lowest recorded since World War II. In the 2016 election that swept Donald Trump into the

FIGURE 1.2 A Comparative Look at Voting Rates Since 1992

Historically, Americans have voted less often than citizens in other countries. However, in the last two elections, the percentage of voters in the United States participating in the election increased.

■ *Why do you suppose this is true?*

SOURCE: International Institute for Democracy and Electoral Assistance, "Voter Turnout," accessed July 30, 2014, at http://www.idea.int/vt/viewdata.cfm#.

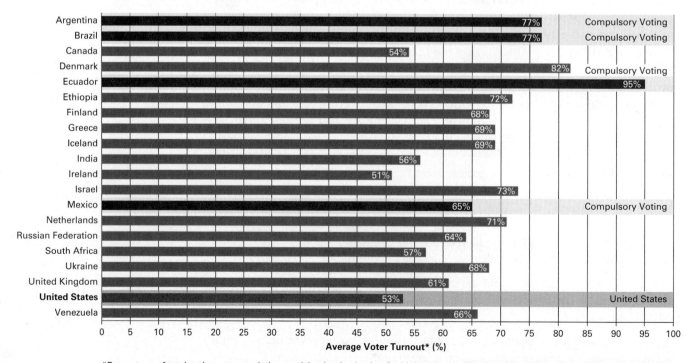

*Percentage of total voting-age population participating in election for highest-level office (president of the United States, for example).

FIGURE 1.3   Levels of Political Engagement

America has always been a "beacon of democracy," but levels of political engagement have been quite modest in recent years.

■ *Are there problems when elections choose most of our public leaders and most citizens sit on the sidelines during these contests?*

SOURCE: Pew Research Center, "Political Engagement and Activism," June 12, 2014, accessed at: http://www.people-press.org/2014/06/12/section-5-political-engagement-and-activism/; Pew Research Center, "Civic Engagement in the Digital Age," April 25, 2013, http://www.pewinternet.org/2013/04/25/civic-engagement-in-the-digital-age/.

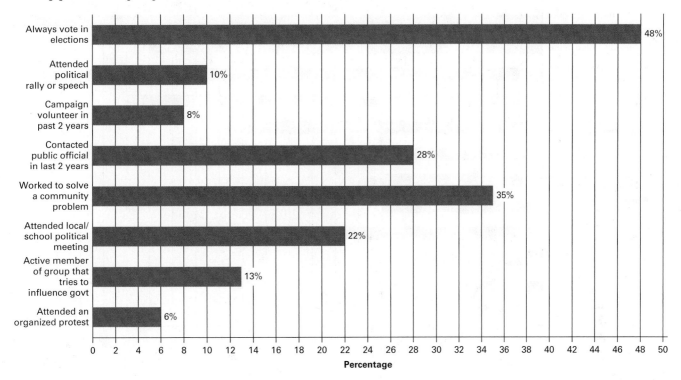

presidency, the story of election turnout was a bit mixed. Overall, roughly 55 percent of Americans came to the polls—roughly the same as in previous elections. There was a bit of a decline for some groups, such as younger citizens and African Americans, but a surge in white, working-class voters. In fact, it is likely that surge was the key to Trump's victory. As you can see in Figure 1.4, levels of engagement seem rather modest, given the openness of our system and the opportunities for involvement. These figures are also a bit low given advancements in our ability to organize and to receive information (social networks and Internet sources), and given what many suggest is a politically active period in our history.

As noted, active participation by citizens is necessary in order for a democracy's laws and policies to reflect what people want. Yet, there will always be disagreements and conflicts among an active citizenry, which can prolong decision making and make democracy seem inefficient. Laws and policies in a democracy often represent compromises between the viewpoints and interests of different individuals and groups. On top of this, the framers, the individuals who drafted the U.S. Constitution, worried a great deal about sudden shifts in public policy, and so they sought to create a system that would produce slow, moderate change. What does all of this mean? It means that active citizen participation does not produce smooth, dramatic policy making. Instead, it ensures that a range of viewpoints and interests are presented before compromises are reached.

Pathways of Action

Pathways of action are the activities, institutions, and decision points in American politics and government that affect the creation, alteration, and preservation of laws and public policies. In other words, they are the methods to bring about change in our system of government. Certain pathways are open to citizens, who can cast their

pathways of action

The activities of citizens in American politics that affect the creation, alteration, and preservation of laws and policies. For instance, average citizens can change the course of public policy by bringing new officials into government through elections and by lobbying existing legislators.

FIGURE 1.4 An Index of Political Engagement

The National Conference on Citizenship measures and promotes civic participation and engagement. Since 2006, they have published yearly reports called America's Civic Health Index. This data is based on the results of several surveys of thousands of Americans in 2010.

■ *Overall, do you think this graph depicts an engaged public?*

SOURCE: National Conference on Citizenship, "Some Political Engagement Continued after the Election," Accessed at: http://www.ncoc.net/2gp65.

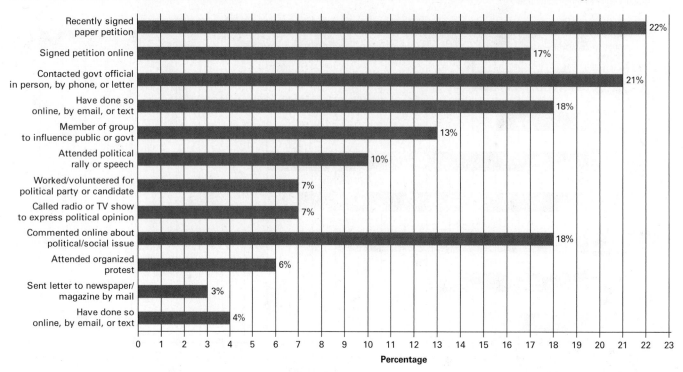

votes, initiate lawsuits, and organize public demonstrations as a means to influence government. The effectiveness of activities within these pathways may depend on the resources, organizational skills, and knowledge possessed by the people making use of them. For example, people who have a lot of money may be able to use litigation more effectively, because they can hire experienced lawyers and carry their lawsuits through all levels of the court system. Resources and organizational skills can also affect people's efforts to conduct petition drives, advertise community meetings, and stage public rallies. Because resources, knowledge, and skill can enhance the effectiveness of citizen participation, powerful organized groups—such as the National Rifle Association, the Chamber of Commerce, and the AARP—are often better positioned than single individuals to achieve their public policy goals through specific pathways.

As you will see, not all pathways of action are equally open to all people. For example, effective lobbying and the use of personal contacts to influence decisions by Congress may require resources and skills possessed only by organized groups and experienced, well-connected individuals. However, because personal freedom in the United States includes opportunities to publicize ideas and form political organizations, highly motivated individuals may be able to gain the resources and contacts necessary for active participation in these less accessible pathways of action. For example, Mothers Against Drunk Driving (MADD) was started in 1980 by a small group of ordinary people with friends or family members who had been killed by drunk drivers. Nearly four decades later, MADD has over 3 million members and continues to exert substantial influence over national, state, and local policies concerning alcohol consumption and traffic enforcement. The organization also claims that because of

their efforts and the passage of new drunk driving laws, some 27,000 young lives have been saved.[3]

The existence of several pathways of action to influence American government does not mean that people in the United States always resolve conflicts peaceably. The bloody Civil War of 1861–1865, which resulted in over 600,000 American deaths (more American deaths than in any other war), reflected the nation's inability to use democratic processes to resolve the controversial issues of race-based slavery and federal versus state control of public policy. In addition, if individuals fundamentally object to the nature and existence of the democratic governing system of the United States, they may resort to terrorism. Timothy McVeigh's politically motivated bombing of a federal office building in Oklahoma City in 1995, killed 168 people, and showed that some individuals and groups reject nonviolent pathways of action in a democratic society.

Brief episodes of public disorder and violence also erupt periodically in urban neighborhoods, sometimes fueled by individuals or groups who perceive their opportunities for effective political participation and economic success to be blocked by racial, ethnic, or social-class discrimination. Some may participate, in part, because they do not believe that pathways of action, such as voting, lobbying, and organized protests, provide realistic opportunities to make their viewpoints heard and understood by decision makers in government. Throughout American history, we can identify instances in which people, seeking to express themselves and influence government, used violence instead of the pathways of peaceful action presented in this book. However, the relative stability of American society and the longevity of its governing system are attributable to the existence of nonviolent pathways that provide opportunities for meaningful participation in democratic government.

The chapters are organized to highlight important pathways of action that provide opportunities for participation in and influence over American government. As you consider these opportunities for action, think about how you might contribute to or participate in activities within each pathway. Figure 1.5 shows the 10 steps for choosing a pathway of action. As an example, we review the creation of tough drunk driver laws in the past three decades.

ELECTIONS PATHWAY American government is based on representative democracy, in which voters elect leaders and then hold those leaders accountable for the decisions they make about law and public policy. If the voters disagree with the decisions that leaders make, the voters can elect different leaders in the next election. Because government leaders in a democracy are usually concerned about maintaining public support in order to gain reelection, they feel pressured

FIGURE 1.5 The Ten Steps in Choosing a Pathway of Action *An Illustration: Toughening Drunk Driving Regulations*

In this case, the pathway selected was grassroots mobilization. MADD began with a massive letter-writing campaign, attracted media attention, and changed public opinion. In the end, decision makers had little choice but to respond.

STEP 1 HISTORICAL CONTEXT
It is essential that the activist understand the legal context, the history surrounding the issue, past governmental and political developments, and previous actors. It is especially important to understand the successes and failures of similar movements and the pathways that were used. → Drunk driving and related injuries and deaths are rampant in the United States. In 1980, some 25,000 are killed by drunk drivers.

STEP 2 THE TRIGGER
Why did you become involved in an issue? What fueled your motivation? Was it a steady development or a sudden event that motivated you to act? → 13-year-old Cari Lightner is killed by a drunk driver as she walks down a quiet street. Her grieving mother, Candy, sets her sights on tougher drunk driving laws and in 1980 forms Mothers Against Drunk Driving (MADD).

STEP 3 ACTORS THAT WILL HELP
Who might you expect to help your efforts and what are their motivations? Who are your potential supporters and what would trigger their action? → Other grieving parents, those in communities that have seen horrific drunk driving accidents, youth advocacy groups such as Students Against Destructive Decisions (SADD).

STEP 4 ACTORS WITH THE OPPOSITION
Who is likely to oppose your efforts and why? How motivated will they be? → Tavern and restaurant owners, liquor industry, civil libertarian groups such as the Center for Consumer Freedom.

STEP 5 TIMING
When might you best proceed with your efforts? Will there be particular stages or a singular bold stroke? How long will things take? → As new data are revealed on drunk driving accidents, after a high-profile event stirs public emotions.

STEP 6 YOUR RESOURCES
What resources will you bring to the cause? A partial list includes your time, intelligence, passion, financial resources, networks of like-minded activists, ability to garner sympathetic media attention, expertise and experience in similar endeavors, and much else. → Passion, time, media attention, public sympathy.

STEP 7 YOUR OPPOSITION'S RESOURCES
What will your opposition bring to the table? Will its resources be similar or different? If they are similar, how can you take best advantage of your resources and minimize the effectiveness of your opponents' resources? → Lobbyists, money, long-standing access to decision makers, campaign resources.

STEP 8 PATHWAY ACCESS
Even though your resources might suggest a particular course of action, not all issues fit each of the pathways. For example, there might be no way to pursue a legal course of action. Along similar lines, decision makers might be more receptive to efforts directed down certain pathways. For instance, judges often express indifference to rallies and protests surrounding an issue. → No clear court pathway point of access, yet the cause is ideal for attracting public attention. Graphic stories and visuals are available.

STEP 9 PATHWAY SELECTED BY THE OPPOSITION
What pathway has your opposition used, and has it proved successful? If your efforts are successful, which pathway will the opposition likely take? → Lobbying decision makers; elections.

STEP 10 HOW TO MEASURE SUCCESS
How will you measure success? How will you sustain your efforts until success is reached? Establishing incremental goals can allow for celebration as they are achieved to create and sustain momentum. → New laws passed, data shows a shrinking number drive while intoxicated, fewer are injured and killed by drunk drivers.

*Note: It is critical that the activist understand that the selection of a pathway is not fixed, but rather is dependent upon new developments, successes and failures, and the adjustments of the opposition. Yet, all political action begins with a step down a pathway of action. Also, remember that several pathways often exist to pursue your objectives—if you are not successful using one pathway, look to another. History has proved that diligence is often the key to success.

to listen to the public and to please a majority of the voters with their actions. Even officials who do not plan to run for reelection or who have served the maximum number of terms the law permits—such as a president who has been elected to a second, four-year term—demonstrate their concern for voters' preferences because they want to help the election chances of other members of their political party.

A variety of activities, actors, and institutions are involved in the elections pathway. For example, political parties organize like-minded individuals into groups that can plan strategies for winning elections, raise money, and provide public information to help elect leaders who share the party's specific values and policy preferences. Activities in the elections pathway include voter registration drives, fundraising, political campaigning, and each individual voter's action in casting a ballot.

LOBBYING PATHWAY Legislatures are the central lawmaking bodies at the national, state, and local levels of government. At the national level, the federal legislature is Congress. States also have their own legislatures, and local legislatures include city councils, county commissions, and village boards. Legislatures are made up of elected representatives who must regularly face the voters in elections. Unlike the elections pathway (the mechanisms by which candidates are chosen to fill offices), the lobbying pathway involves attempting to influence the activities, actors, and institutions of government by supplying information, persuasion, or political pressure. Lobbying activities target legislatures and executive officials, such as presidents and governors, as well as the bureaucrats who staff government agencies.

In the lobbying pathway, individuals and organized groups present information and persuasive arguments to government officials. The aim is to convince these decision makers either to support specific proposed laws or to oppose proposed changes in existing laws and policies. Lobbying occurs in the context of the decision-making processes used by each institution. In the legislature, individuals and organized groups can testify before committee hearings attended by legislators. With the president or a governor, the individual or group representative seeks a direct appointment with the decision maker or presents information and arguments to the executive's top aides. Lobbyists also seek meetings with legislators, often buying them meals or taking them on trips that will supposedly educate them about issues. Information and persuasion may well be accompanied by financial contributions to the reelection campaigns of legislators or elected executives.

Lobbying, in the form of information and persuasion, can also be directed at permanent employees in government agencies who have the authority to create government regulations, such as rules concerning the environment, business practices, and consumer products. Effective lobbying typically requires money, time, and other resources, such as a large organizational membership to flood officials' offices with letters and e-mails, or personal relationships between lobbyists and government officials, as when interest groups hire former members of Congress to represent them in presenting information and arguments. Under the right circumstances, people who lack resources may effectively influence government by getting the attention of key officials. For example, research has shown that letters, e-mails, and phone calls from ordinary citizens are an important source of ideas for new laws and policies.[4]

COURT PATHWAY In the United States, judges have broader authority than in other countries to order the government to take specific actions. Because people in

TIMELINE

The Immigration Debate

Many controversial issues in American politics could be used to help illustrate how different pathways are used by different political actors. This timeline offers a glimpse into the ongoing struggle over immigration reform.

Before 1882, anyone who wished to live in the United States could. Things have changed dramatically since that time. Some of the more controversial issues facing our government today include who should be allowed to immigrate to our country, what we should do to secure our borders, and what should be done with immigrants illegally residing in the country.

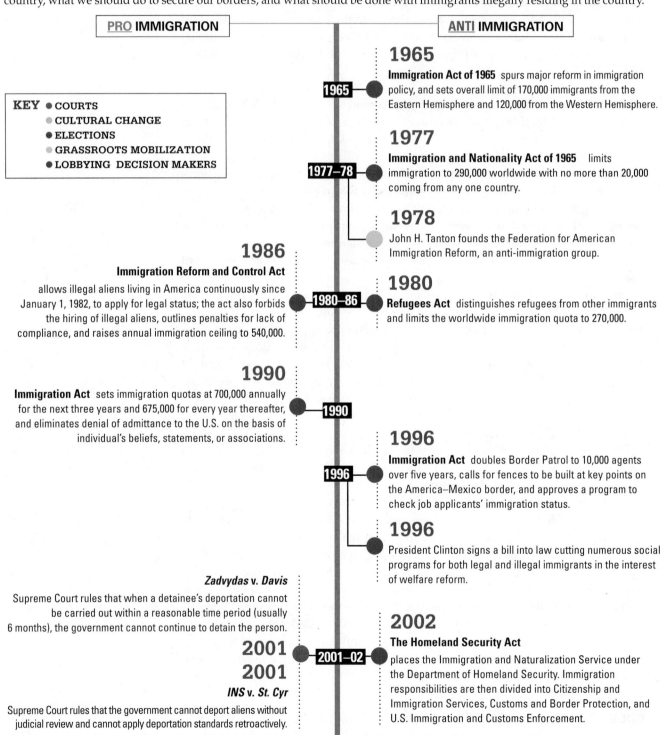

PRO IMMIGRATION | ANTI IMMIGRATION

KEY ● COURTS
● CULTURAL CHANGE
● ELECTIONS
● GRASSROOTS MOBILIZATION
● LOBBYING DECISION MAKERS

1965
1965
Immigration Act of 1965 spurs major reform in immigration policy, and sets overall limit of 170,000 immigrants from the Eastern Hemisphere and 120,000 from the Western Hemisphere.

1977
1977–78
Immigration and Nationality Act of 1965 limits immigration to 290,000 worldwide with no more than 20,000 coming from any one country.

1978
John H. Tanton founds the Federation for American Immigration Reform, an anti-immigration group.

1986
Immigration Reform and Control Act
allows illegal aliens living in America continuously since January 1, 1982, to apply for legal status; the act also forbids the hiring of illegal aliens, outlines penalties for lack of compliance, and raises annual immigration ceiling to 540,000.

1980–86
1980
Refugees Act distinguishes refugees from other immigrants and limits the worldwide immigration quota to 270,000.

1990
Immigration Act sets immigration quotas at 700,000 annually for the next three years and 675,000 for every year thereafter, and eliminates denial of admittance to the U.S. on the basis of individual's beliefs, statements, or associations.

1990

1996
Immigration Act doubles Border Patrol to 10,000 agents over five years, calls for fences to be built at key points on the America–Mexico border, and approves a program to check job applicants' immigration status.

1996

1996
President Clinton signs a bill into law cutting numerous social programs for both legal and illegal immigrants in the interest of welfare reform.

Zadvydas* v. *Davis
Supreme Court rules that when a detainee's deportation cannot be carried out within a reasonable time period (usually 6 months), the government cannot continue to detain the person.

2001
2001

2001–02

2002
The Homeland Security Act
places the Immigration and Naturalization Service under the Department of Homeland Security. Immigration responsibilities are then divided into Citizenship and Immigration Services, Customs and Border Protection, and U.S. Immigration and Customs Enforcement.

INS* v. *St. Cyr
Supreme Court rules that the government cannot deport aliens without judicial review and cannot apply deportation standards retroactively.

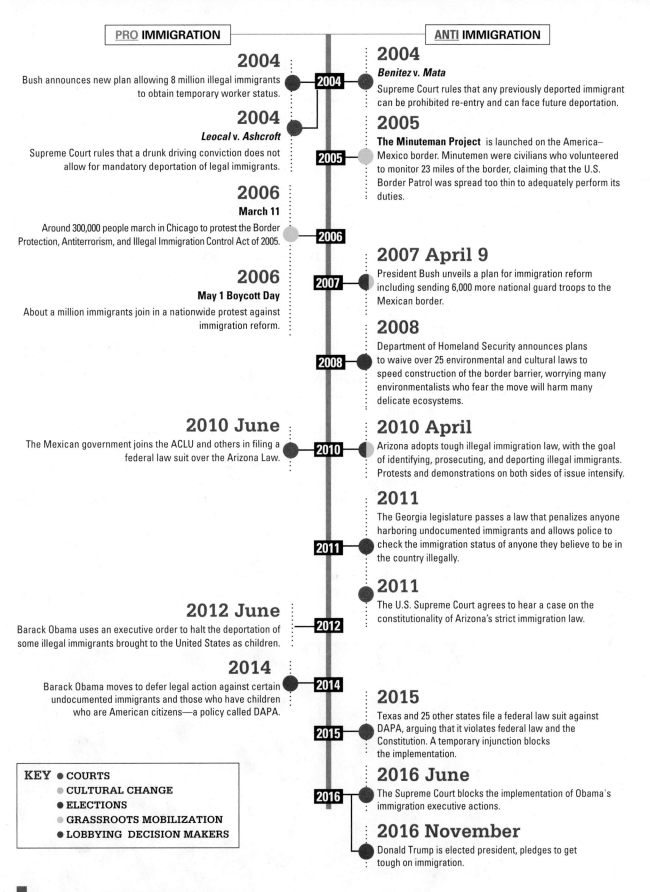

PRO IMMIGRATION

2004
Bush announces new plan allowing 8 million illegal immigrants to obtain temporary worker status.

2004
Leocal v. Ashcroft

Supreme Court rules that a drunk driving conviction does not allow for mandatory deportation of legal immigrants.

2006
March 11

Around 300,000 people march in Chicago to protest the Border Protection, Antiterrorism, and Illegal Immigration Control Act of 2005.

2006
May 1 Boycott Day

About a million immigrants join in a nationwide protest against immigration reform.

2010 June
The Mexican government joins the ACLU and others in filing a federal law suit over the Arizona Law.

2012 June
Barack Obama uses an executive order to halt the deportation of some illegal immigrants brought to the United States as children.

2014
Barack Obama moves to defer legal action against certain undocumented immigrants and those who have children who are American citizens—a policy called DAPA.

ANTI IMMIGRATION

2004
Benitez v. Mata

Supreme Court rules that any previously deported immigrant can be prohibited re-entry and can face future deportation.

2005
The Minuteman Project is launched on the America–Mexico border. Minutemen were civilians who volunteered to monitor 23 miles of the border, claiming that the U.S. Border Patrol was spread too thin to adequately perform its duties.

2007 April 9
President Bush unveils a plan for immigration reform including sending 6,000 more national guard troops to the Mexican border.

2008
Department of Homeland Security announces plans to waive over 25 environmental and cultural laws to speed construction of the border barrier, worrying many environmentalists who fear the move will harm many delicate ecosystems.

2010 April
Arizona adopts tough illegal immigration law, with the goal of identifying, prosecuting, and deporting illegal immigrants. Protests and demonstrations on both sides of issue intensify.

2011
The Georgia legislature passes a law that penalizes anyone harboring undocumented immigrants and allows police to check the immigration status of anyone they believe to be in the country illegally.

2011
The U.S. Supreme Court agrees to hear a case on the constitutionality of Arizona's strict immigration law.

2015
Texas and 25 other states file a federal law suit against DAPA, arguing that it violates federal law and the Constitution. A temporary injunction blocks the implementation.

2016 June
The Supreme Court blocks the implementation of Obama's immigration executive actions.

2016 November
Donald Trump is elected president, pledges to get tough on immigration.

KEY
- COURTS
- CULTURAL CHANGE
- ELECTIONS
- GRASSROOTS MOBILIZATION
- LOBBYING DECISION MAKERS

CRITICAL THINKING QUESTIONS

1. Write an essay in which you critically examine the various proposals presented, being certain to indicate which proposal(s) you think would be most effective in addressing illegal immigration.

2. Should states have the right to adopt their own immigration laws when they believe the federal government is not acting accordingly?

the United States are granted specific legal rights, they can use those rights as a basis for filing lawsuits against the government. For example, if a man was charged under an old state law for the crime of shouting profanity in front of women and children, his lawyer could challenge the validity of the law by asking a judge to declare that it violated the man's legal right to freedom of speech. Such a case actually occurred in Michigan in 1998, where judges eventually ruled that the law violated the man's free speech rights because it was too vague to give him guidance about what words were illegal.[5] Individuals can also file lawsuits asking judges to order the government to follow its own laws. This often happens in cases concerning environmental issues or consumer products when people believe that government officials are failing to enforce the law properly.

Litigation is expensive. People who use this pathway must hire an attorney and pay for gathering and presenting evidence to a court. Organized groups interested in the issue may use their resources to help people carry their cases through the courts. For example, the National Rifle Association (NRA) may provide assistance to individuals who sue to invalidate firearms regulations, or the American Civil Liberties Union (ACLU) may supply attorneys to represent people who believe that their rights to freedom of speech have been violated by the government. Many important policies have been shaped by the actions of individuals and groups who successfully used the court-centered pathway. The U.S. Supreme Court's decision in *Brown* v. *Board of Education of Topeka* (1954), which prohibited state and local governments from engaging in racial discrimination in public schools, is one of the most famous examples of this pathway in action. The origins of the case can be traced to a lawsuit filed by the father of Linda Brown, an African American girl in Topeka, Kansas, who was not permitted to attend an all-white public school near her home. Lawyers from an interest group, the National Association for the Advancement of Colored People (NAACP), represented the Brown family.

GRASSROOTS MOBILIZATION PATHWAY Highly motivated individuals can seek to attract the attention of government officials and influence the direction of law and policy by mobilizing others to join them in taking strategic actions.

Immigration reform has been a hot button issue for some time. Some believe it has become more contentious as the nation's economy has changed.

■ *Why might that be the case?*

Historically, when members of certain groups in society feel that the government is unresponsive to their concerns (as expressed through lobbying and elections activity), they seek other means to educate the public and pressure those officials. Martin Luther King Jr. became a nationally known civil rights figure in the 1950s as a result of his role in organizing and leading a boycott of the public transit system in Montgomery, Alabama, to protest racial segregation on buses. A boycott is a coordinated action by many people who agree not to buy a specific product, use a specific service, or shop at a specific store until a policy is changed. Boycotts can place financial pressure on businesses and governments that rely on daily revenue, such as bus fares or the sale of products, in order to stay in business. Advocates of racial equality and gender equity, opponents of the Vietnam War, individuals concerned about restrictive immigration policies, gay rights groups, those speaking out against police brutality, and others have organized protest marches as a means to attract public attention and pressure the government to change laws and policies. These actions are seldom instantly successful, but over time, they may draw more and more supporters until elected officials begin to reconsider past decisions. Successful grassroots mobilization requires organizational skill, publicity, careful planning, and a solid core of committed activists who are willing to take public actions in support of their cause.

CULTURAL CHANGE PATHWAY   The cultural change pathway is an indirect approach to influencing government. It is a long-term strategy that requires persistence and patience. Through this approach, individuals and organized groups attempt to change the hearts and minds of their fellow citizens. By educating the public about issues and publicizing important events, the dominant values of society may change over time. This can lead to changes in law and policy as newly elected officials bring the new values into government with them.

Until the twentieth century, for example, many Americans—both men and women alike—believed that women should devote themselves to the roles of wife and mother. Federal, state, and local laws reflected this belief, generally preventing women from voting in elections and working in certain occupations. Over a period of several decades, beginning before the Civil War, activist women and their male supporters used newspaper articles, speeches, and demonstrations to educate the public about women's capabilities and about the need to grant women opportunities to live and work as citizens equal to men.

In the late nineteenth and early twentieth centuries, women finally gained the right to vote, first on a state-by-state basis but eventually through passage of the Nineteenth Amendment (1920), which guaranteed the vote to women nationwide. But discriminatory attitudes toward women remained prevalent through the 1960s, requiring decades of continued educational work. Gradually, laws and policies changed to protect women against gender discrimination. Eventually, most Americans accepted the idea of women becoming doctors, lawyers, police officers, and elected officials at all levels of government—even president and vice president. Law and policy changed through the long-term effort to change the culture and values of American society.

Individuals and groups can use the cultural change pathway to try to affect changes in laws and policies related to a variety of issues, including abortion, the death penalty, environmental protection, and the rights and opportunities of lesbian, gay, bisexual, and transgender (LGBT) citizens, as noted at the start of this chapter. For people who seek to change society's values, the ultimate outcome of the cultural change pathway can be quite uncertain. Indeed, for some issues, change may occur long after the passing of the people who initiated the efforts to alter public opinion and social values. And sometimes change never comes.

FIGURE 1.6 Can Average Citizens Play a Meaningful Role in American Politics?

Many Americans believe they can't play a meaningful role in politics. While it is true that change can sometimes come slowly, and that certain citizens have more resources than others, our history also suggests that steadfast, determined individuals and groups can make a big difference by using the five pathways of change: elections, courts, lobbying, grassroots mobilization, and cultural change.

■ *Will any of these pathways become more or less influential in the digital age? Why or why not?*

	👍 STRENGTHS	👎 WEAKNESSES	❓ CRITICAL THINKING QUESTIONS
Elections	Elections are generally egalitarian; everyone's vote is counted equally, so the "majority will" can be harnessed to create change.	Hefty resources shape the outcome; the "majority will" can sometimes stifle democratic change.	Given the "checks and balances" inherent in the structure of government, how can we expect the election of a particular leader, such as a new president or governor, to shape the outcome of public policy?
Courts	Elections are generally egalitarian; everyone's vote is counted equally, so the "majority will" can be harnessed to create change.	Change can come about slowly; litigation can be expensive.	How democratic can the court pathway be when federal judges (and many state judges) are appointed and serve for life?
Lobbying	Big change can occur quickly behind the scenes.	Effective lobbying often entails "connections," which requires big resources.	Many are critical of "special interest lobbying," but what's wrong with citizens promoting their own interests?
Grassroots Mobilization	Grassroots efforts can be effective at getting decision makers to pay attention to an issue.	Changes are seldom effective immediately; organizational skill, careful planning, and truly committed activists are necessary.	Can you think of a time in American history when policymakers turned a deaf ear to massive public demonstrations?
Cultural Change	Cultural change can involve a variety of issues, particularly those that are at first opposed by the majority.	Change takes a long time to be effective and is by no means certain.	How does popular culture, such as music, television, and sports, ultimately shape public policy?

PATHWAYS OF ACTION

NEW STUDENT ACTIVISM...OR THE CODDLING OF YOUNG MINDS?

Every year, the Higher Education Research Institute at UCLA conducts a survey of first year students. The report offers a snapshot of a broad range of topics for each college class, as well as a historical context. Their 2015 study received a good deal of attention because it suggested today's college freshman are more likely to participate in a campus protest than any class of students in the last 50 years. This includes students of the late 1960s and early 1970s, when campuses seemed to erupt with disputes.

What is driving today's campus activism? There are likely a host of hot button issues like the growing cost of higher education, campus diversity (including challenges to affirmative action plans), awareness of the challenges confronted by LGBT students, broader political forces like the 2016 presidential election, the ability to use on-line organizational tools, and an increased willingness to speak out on a range of issues. For those concerned about the long-term stability of our political process with a turned-off generation, this finding led to a collective sigh of relief. Young Americans—or at least college students—seem to have rediscovered the power of activism.

And yet, some commentators have started to worry that the growing number of campus protests may stifle freedom of thought and speech. There have been many news stories about fervent protests over the expressions of unpopular ideas. In a powerful, widely-circulated 2015 article in the *Atlantic*, dubbed "The Coddling of the American Mind," Greg Lukianoff and Jonathan Haidt chart how college students, with an eye to their own emotional well-being, increasingly demand protection from words and ideas they do not like.[6] College campuses, the theoretical bastions of free thought and intellectual discovery, have become intolerant and close-minded, they argue. At the very least, they raise an interesting question: Has the campus protests culture gone too far?

Diversity in American Society

This book's third theme is the impact of diversity on American government and on the laws and policies that government produces. Many of the issues facing American government are products of the country's history, and many policy issues have their roots in America's history of race-based slavery. Slavery and its consequences, including blatant discrimination against African Americans, which persisted until the 1970s, are at the heart of such difficult contemporary problems as chronic poverty, decaying urban neighborhoods, disproportionate minority unemployment rates, and lingering racial and ethnic hostility and mistrust.

Cultural change eventually created a widespread consensus in American society about the need to eliminate overt racial discrimination. Laws and policies, such as the Civil Rights Act of 1964 and the Voting Rights Act of 1965, were enacted in the second half of the twentieth century to prohibit many forms of discrimination that had been endorsed and enforced by various levels of government. However, there is no consensus on how to address other problems arising out of the legacy of slavery and racial discrimination. Attempts to apply specific remedies, such as court-ordered busing to achieve public school desegregation, affirmative action programs to increase minority enrollment in colleges and universities, and programs to diversify government employment and contract opportunities have all caused bitter debate and political conflict.

> **POLL** In your view, should immigration be kept at its present level, increased, or decreased?

Immigration is another challenging policy controversy related to the nation's diversity. Contemporary debates about immigration often focus on undocumented workers arriving from Mexico and other countries in violation of American law. Some Americans want stronger measures to prevent illegal immigration, but many businesses hire undocumented workers because they often work for less money than U.S. citizens. At the same time, Latinos in the United States have grown in numbers. In 2004, Latinos became the nation's largest minority group. As shown in Figure 1.7, the Hispanic population in the United States is expected to double in the next few decades. Hispanics have also expanded their political power by becoming a significant voting presence in many cities and winning an increasing number of important offices. Many native-born and naturalized Latino citizens are wary of certain anti-immigration proposals, fearing that they may contribute to ethnic discrimination against U.S. citizens while treating noncitizens unduly harshly. Immigration reform was clearly a hot topic in the 2016 presidential election.

The policy debates over immigration show how America's diversity contributes to political controversies at the same time that it adds complexity to the mix of actors seeking to use various pathways of change. Indeed, the timeline dealing with the immigration debate (see Timeline, pp. 14–15) highlights the history and the complexity of the issue, as well as the various approaches used by concerned individuals to shape the outcome of the debate. All these pathways—elections, lobbying, courts, grassroots mobilization, and cultural change—have been used by a diverse array of Americans, including women, people with disabilities, gay and lesbian individuals, and people of color, who have felt excluded from meaningful participation in American government.

Now that we have highlighted the book's important themes, in the next section we'll consider an example that illustrates how citizen participation and pathways for action affect the operations of American government.

FIGURE 1.7 The Face of a Changing Nation

SOURCE: U.S. Census Bureau, "International Database, Table 094," http://www.census.gov.

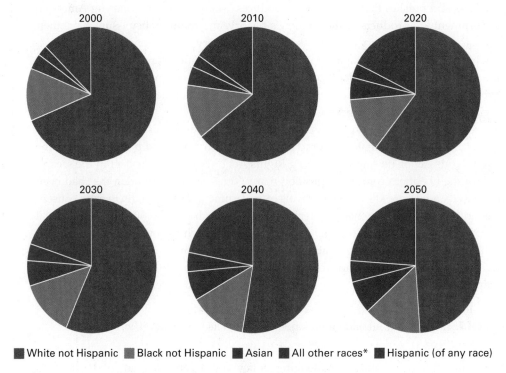

■ White not Hispanic ■ Black not Hispanic ■ Asian ■ All other races* ■ Hispanic (of any race)

*Includes American Indians and Alaska Natives, Native Hawaiians, other Pacific Islanders, and people who belong to two or more racial designations.

Citizen Participation and Pathways: The Example of Abortion

1.3 Outline the various "pathways" of involvement in our political system.

Abortion is a divisive, wrenching issue that continues to generate controversy among Americans nationwide. Several major institutional components of American government, including Congress, the president, the U.S. Supreme Court, and state governments, have been involved in defining and changing abortion laws and policies. Thus, the abortion issue helps show how American government operates and how citizens can use pathways of action to influence the results of those operations.

Although women gained the right to vote nationwide in the early twentieth century, advocates using the *lobbying pathway* failed to persuade state legislatures to enact abortion choice laws until the 1960s, and then only in a few states. In the early 1970s, however, two young lawyers in Texas volunteered to help a woman who unsuccessfully sought an abortion after she claimed that she had been raped. The lawyers began a legal case to challenge the Texas law that made it a crime to obtain or perform an abortion. The case worked its way through the levels of the court system until it reached the U.S. Supreme Court. In a landmark decision in *Roe v. Wade* (1973), the justices of the Supreme Court voted 7-2 to strike down the Texas law as a violation of women's right to privacy in making personal choices about reproduction. Much more will be said about this case in subsequent chapters. For now, you should understand that the *court pathway* was used to change the law for the entire nation.

Of course, opponents of abortion were anxious to move government in a different direction. In the aftermath of *Roe* v. *Wade*, opponents of abortion mobilized supporters and organized political action groups. They used several pathways in their efforts to reimpose legal prohibitions on abortion. In the *elections pathway*, they sought to recruit and elect candidates who pledged to fight abortion. They used the *lobbying pathway* to pressure and persuade elected officials to pass new laws that would place restrictions on abortion that would be acceptable to the courts. They also used the *grassroots mobilization pathway* to organize protest marches and, especially, demonstrations at abortion clinics intended to discourage women from entering to seek abortions. A few opponents of abortion even rejected democratic processes as a means to seek change, instead engaging in such violent acts as firebombing abortion clinics and assaulting or even killing doctors who performed abortions.

Abortion opponents who worked within the governing system achieved partial success in many state legislatures and in Congress. New laws were adopted imposing restrictions that could discourage or hinder women's efforts to obtain abortions—for example, blocking the use of government funds to pay for poor women's abortions. During the heated negotiations over health care reform in 2009, the issue of whether government-assisted insurance plans should include any reimbursement for abortions became a central and hotly debated issue. Laws also limited the ability of teenagers to obtain abortions without informing their parents or obtaining the permission of a judge. States imposed new requirements for counseling women about abortion procedures and, after the counseling session, making them wait 24 hours before making a second trip to the clinic to have the abortion procedure performed by a doctor.

Throughout the three decades in which abortion opponents used these pathways to seek restrictions on abortion, they also focused on the *elections pathway* in an effort to elect Republican presidents who might appoint new Supreme Court justices willing to overturn *Roe* v. *Wade* and to elect senators who would confirm these justices. As a result, the process of obtaining the U.S. Senate's approval of the president's nominees for the Supreme Court became part of the political battles over abortion. Both opponents and supporters of women's abortion rights used the *lobbying pathway* to pressure senators to either endorse or oppose judicial nominees on the basis of their perceived stance on abortion.

The struggle between opponents and defenders of abortion choice moved between *different* pathways. With each legislative success that abortion foes won, advocates of choice returned to the *court pathway* to challenge the laws on the grounds that they improperly clashed with the Supreme Court's declaration in *Roe* v. *Wade* that women had a constitutionally protected right to choose to have an abortion. Although the Supreme Court and lower federal courts struck down some state laws as conflicting with *Roe* v. *Wade*, the courts also upheld many laws that imposed regulations.

In March 2006, shortly after Justices John Roberts and Samuel Alito, both nominated by President George W. Bush, were confirmed by the Senate, state legislators in South Dakota acted quickly to enact a statute that would virtually abolish abortion in their state. Under the law, abortion would be permitted only to save the life of a pregnant woman. Doctors faced criminal prosecution and prison sentences for performing other abortions, including those performed in the aftermath of rape or incest. The purpose of the statute, in large part, was to generate a legal challenge that might ultimately lead the newly constituted Supreme Court to overturn *Roe* v. *Wade*.

A protester holds a sign in favor of Mississippi's Personhood Amendment in November of 2011. The ballot initiative, which was ultimately defeated by voters, would have established "personhood" at the moment of conception.

■ *Can you imagine abortion continuing to be a controversial issue for years to come?*

A countermove by pro-choice forces might have been a lawsuit, but opponents of the law chose a different strategy instead. They gathered petition signatures to place the measure on the general election ballot for a statewide vote—a process called a *ballot initiative*, which is possible in 23 states. Their strategy worked: The abortion ban was rejected by 55 percent of South Dakota voters in 2008.

The same sort of process was played out in Mississippi in the fall of 2011. This time conservative activists moved to place a measure before voters that would outlaw all abortions and most contraceptives. Broadly known as the "personhood" amendment, Initiative 26 would have changed the state Constitution to define life "to include every human being from the moment of fertilization, cloning or the functional equivalent thereof." Mississippi is a conservative state, but the measure failed, netting just 43 percent of the vote. Voters in Colorado and North Dakota rejected similar moves in 2014.

In recent years, many of the state legislatures dominated by Republicans have continued to pass laws aimed at eliminating abortions. For example, a 2014 North Carolina law required women to receive an ultrasound and listen to the doctor describe the fetus before getting an abortion, and a 2015 Mississippi measure requiring abortion doctors to obtain admitting privileges from local hospitals, a complicated bureaucratic arrangement. Both measures were struck down in lower courts, but were then appealed. Federal Circuit Court judges upheld a similar law in Texas that requires abortion facilities to comply with costly hospital-like standards and doctors at these facilities to have admitting privileges at area hospitals. Because few of the current abortion centers could comply with these standards, this measure effectively shut down most facilities. The constitutionality of this law was taken up by the Supreme Court and in the spring of 2016 it ruled the measure was indeed unconstitutional. These standards created, wrote the Court, an undue burden on the reproductive rights of women.

Both sides in the abortion debate have attempted to shape public opinion through the *cultural change pathway*. Supporters of choice seek to persuade the public that control over "reproductive freedom" is a key component of women's equality in American society. They also raise warnings about the risks to women's health if abortion is banned, referring to the time when abortion was illegal and women turned to abortionists who were not doctors, causing many desperate women to die from bleeding and infections. Opponents of abortion insist that abortion is murder and use graphic pictures of both developing and aborted fetuses in their publicity campaigns.

This brief snapshot of the abortion issue illustrates how law and policy develop and change through the complex interaction of the pathways of action and the American government's various institutions. Throughout this continuing battle over abortion, both sides rely on the participation of individual citizens for lobbying, contributing money, campaigning, voting, engaging in public protests, and carrying out the specific activities of each pathway of action.

Change and Stability in American Government

1.4 Analyze the forces of stability in American politics.

As we have seen, the pathways of action provide opportunities for citizens to take nonviolent actions to make their voices heard by decision makers in American government. The existence of these pathways is also important for the preservation of the American governing system. No form of government is automatically stable. No form of government automatically functions smoothly. If disagreements within the population are great enough, or if a segment of the population does not accept the design and operation of the governing system, then even democracies will experience violence, disorder, instability, and collapse. The American Civil War vividly reminds us of what can happen when pathways fail to resolve controversies. In that example, the divisive issues of slavery and state government authority were inflamed rather than resolved through actions in the elections pathway (the election of Lincoln as the antislavery president) and the court-centered pathway (a Supreme Court decision that helped the spread of slavery to western territories— *Dred Scott* v. *Sandford*, 1857).

To understand American government and its ability to endure, we must examine the factors that contribute to stability as well as those that help Americans change what their government does. This book focuses on pathways of action as a key element for understanding how American government operates. These pathways help explain why the American system of government continues to exist, even after two centuries that included significant social changes and a bloody civil war.

Every nation experiences periods of transformation. These are eras in which new issues, fundamental changes in social and economic conditions, or major events spur adjustments in society and in the priorities and actions of government decision makers. These transformations can also produce changes in a country's system of government. In the 1990s, the world witnessed the emergence of new governing systems in places such as South Africa and the formerly communist countries of Eastern Europe and Russia, and in the last few years a number of North African and Middle Eastern nations have witnessed a spat of democratic changes. In the United States, we have maintained the same Constitution and general blueprint for government through more than 220 years of significant changes in society, politics, and the economy—topics taken up throughout the book.

Sources of Stability

Stability in American government and in the governing systems of other countries cannot be taken for granted. We cannot automatically assume that governing systems will be stable or remain stable for any predictable period. Stability in any political system is the result of three closely related elements:

- A broadly accepted political and economic framework
- A stable, powerful political culture
- A variety of ways for citizens to seek and achieve policy changes

We will discuss each of these elements in turn.

BROADLY ACCEPTED FRAMEWORK: REVERENCE FOR THE CONSTITUTION AND CAPITALISM Early in his political career, Abraham Lincoln delivered a speech in which he urged that our Constitution be the "political religion of the nation."[7] We have taken his advice to heart. Indeed, one of the interesting and somewhat unique aspects of American politics is our reverence for the structure of our governing system. Some would say that we treat the Constitution as our non-religious "bible"—the written document that Americans deeply respect and obey.

The authors of the Constitution, the framers, would likely have found this surprising. The Constitution they developed was a collection of compromises, ambiguities, and generalized grants of authority to the national government. It divided powers between the national government and the states, and it tried to compel the sharing of powers among three branches of government, with an elaborate system of

checks and balances

A system in our government where each branch (legislative, executive, judicial) has the power to limit the actions of others. For example, even though President Obama announced a decision to send 30,000 additional troops to Afghanistan in December 2009, it did not automatically mean that Congress would appropriate the funds necessary to carry out the plan.

capitalism

An economic system where business and industry are privately owned and there is little governmental interference.

socialism

An economic system in which the government owns and controls most factories and much or all of the nation's land.

checks and balances to limit the actions of each branch. However, the Constitution replaced an earlier governmental blueprint, the Articles of Confederation. If the Constitution had been rejected by the American public or had failed to work well, they might have been forced to go back to the drawing board to write a third version. In other words, to the framers, the Constitution was a practical plan for creating a government. It was not a set of sacred principles. Yet today, Americans express a shared belief in the special wisdom of the Constitution's authors for creating a system of government that would both endure and embody important principles of democracy. Citizens may strongly oppose particular policies or desperately hope to change the personnel of government, but rarely do they challenge the governing framework.

Americans' reverence for the institutional framework of our political system extends to our economic system as well. Indeed, the "American dream" rests mostly on the notion that intelligence, ingenuity, and hard work will lead to economic success. Faith in **capitalism** is deeply ingrained in Americans' values and beliefs. Capitalism is the economic system based on free enterprise in which individuals compete with each other for jobs, operate privately owned businesses that may succeed or fail, and focus their efforts on accumulating wealth for themselves and their families. In an alternative economic system, **socialism**, the government owns and controls key factories and sometimes also the land. It may even use that control to assign individuals to specific jobs. Socialist systems may focus on the ideal of individuals working for the good of society rather than pursuing self-interest. In the United States, by contrast, most people have always believed that society as a whole benefits through the continuous creation of new businesses, new jobs, and increased wealth when all individuals pursue their own interests and have opportunities to use their own private property and businesses to create jobs and generate income.

The American idea that we have ample opportunities to become economically successful through our own hard work is not always fulfilled in practice. Historically, racial and gender discrimination have limited opportunities for many Americans to find good jobs or start their own businesses. The ability of rich people to provide superior education for their children and pass on their wealth to family members provides and perpetuates advantages that most Americans do not

One of the best illustrations of our nation's reverence for the Constitution and capitalism is our currency. On one side of the dollar bill we pay tribute to the hero of the Revolution and the first president, and on the other side we find the Great Seal of the United States (front and back). The pyramid symbolizes strength, and its 13 steps represent the original 13 colonies. The unfinished summit on the pyramid implies a "work in progress."

■ *Do you think the larger message is that our government's fate is linked to the future of free enterprise in America? Or, as capitalism goes, so goes our system of government?*

share. The significant power wielded by corporations in the United States and vast disparities of individual wealth have led to occasional calls for a change in the American economic system. Various plans for a redistribution of wealth to assist poor people have been proposed—for example, through higher taxes on the rich to fund antipoverty programs. In the spring of 2016, Democratic presidential candidate Senator Bernie Sanders of Vermont, who calls himself a Democratic-Socialist, drew attention to what he dubbed the "greed and corruption of corporations." He also advanced the idea of government taking over key parts of the economy, mainly the creation of a "single payer" (meaning government-run) health care system. Sanders was defeated by Hillary Clinton, of course, but many were a bit surprised by the traction of his message. Indeed, many would also suggest that Donald Trump's surprising assent to presidency was built on many of the same issues. Support for free enterprise and capitalism remains strong even when critics point out that the United States falls short of its ideals of equal economic opportunities for all Americans. Particular policies might be changed, but there is little support for broad adjustments to our economic system.

Americans believe strongly in the core elements of our political and economic system. Lincoln's hope that Americans would protect their system through an almost religious reverence has come to pass. James Madison and the other framers of the United States would presumably be pleased—and perhaps surprised—to know that the experimental governing system they designed has survived for more than two centuries. They would be doubly surprised to see how Americans cherish the Constitution—the experimental document full of compromises—as the crown jewel of democracy.

POLITICAL CULTURE: THE "AMERICAN CREED"   Scholars have long recognized the powerful influence of a nation's *political culture*. Much more will be said about this concept in Chapter 10, but for now, simply note that this term refers to the fundamental values and dominant beliefs that are shared throughout society and that shape political behavior and government policies. It is the umbrella under which political activities take place, and it defines the arena where political questions are resolved. Political culture incorporates both citizens' personal values—that is, their ideas about what is right and wrong—and their shared ideas about how they should be governed.[8]

A nation's political culture springs from a number of sources, including the origins of the nation (sometimes called the nation's "creation myth"), historical struggles in the nation's history, the deeds and thoughts of past leaders, important documents and texts, economic conditions, and distinct subcultures. Religion may also play a role, depending on a nation's history and culture. To some extent, a nation's popular culture, including its entertainment, fashions, and media, also contribute to its political culture. For instance, the counterculture movement in the 1960s (hippie culture) had a direct impact on the political process—especially on policies related to gender equity, civil rights, and the war in Vietnam. And many observers suggest that the portrayal of gay men and women in film and on television in recent years has raised levels of tolerance toward LGBT citizens throughout society. Indeed, when Vice President Joe Biden announced his support of gay marriage in the spring of 2012 he suggested the sitcom *Will & Grace* had done more to advance the cause of gay rights than any act by a public official. When some or all of these pieces are missing or are not clearly defined, the nation's political identity becomes less clear. Nations with a strong, clearly defined political culture are generally more stable.[9]

Alexis de Tocqueville (uh-lek-see de TOKE-vil), a French scholar who traveled throughout the United States in the early 1830s, found our nation's emerging political culture to be distinctive and powerful. The essence of American politics, Tocqueville wrote in *Democracy in America*, lies not in the complex maze of political institutions but rather in the shared values of American citizens. In fact, he suggested, along with this powerful political identity comes a downside: "I know of no country in which there is such little independence of mind and real freedom of discussion as in America."[10] The widespread nature of shared values and beliefs among Americans, which was observed by Tocqueville and continues today, has tended to limit the range of discussions about government and public policy. As with the economic system, people tend to focus on fixing specific problems within the current system rather than suggesting that the system itself should be changed.

American political culture, as noted by the Swedish social scientist Gunnar Myrdal (GUN-er MEER-dahl) in 1944, is "the most explicitly expressed system of general ideals" of any country in the West[11]—so much so that he saw fit to call our belief system the "American Creed." At least in the abstract, Americans embrace the concepts of "freedom," "equality," "liberty," "majority will," "religious freedom," and "due process under the law." According to Myrdal, "Schools teach the principles of the Creed; the churches preach them; the courts hand down judgment in their terms."[12] According to historian Arthur Schlesinger Jr., "Myrdal saw the Creed as the bond that links all Americans, including nonwhite minorities, and as the spur forever goading Americans to live up to their principles."[13] Yale University political scientist Robert Dahl echoed this idea a few decades later when he called our set of beliefs the "democratic creed." He wrote that this view suggests that not only is our system democratic, but is indeed the most perfect expression of democracy in the world, and that for a citizen to reject this way of thinking is to renounce their own Americanism.[14]

America has always had a deep sense of patriotism, especially when it comes to honoring those who have defended our country during times of war.

■ *Is it possible to be truly patriotic while at the same time speaking out against our involvement in war?*

There are many things that define the American Creed, many of which will be discussed in later chapters. The important point here is to understand that the United States possesses a powerful political culture that is clearly defined and long-lasting. The historical national consensus on political values and democratic institutions helped create stability during times of profound social change. As waves of change transformed the workplace, home life, leisure patterns, and intellectual fabric of the nation, Americans found strength in the stability of their political system.

NUMEROUS AVENUES OF CHANGE Two necessary conditions for any country's political stability are broad popular acceptance of its government and economic system and a clearly defined political culture. But they do not guarantee stability. For a democratic system to remain stable, its citizens must believe that they can influence the outcome of government activity. The design and operation of government must permit popular participation. In addition, the political culture and laws must encourage civic involvement and protect activists from being silenced either by the government or by majority opinion. There must also be a variety of ways to achieve desired ends. Severe limitations on citizen participation and influence can lead to frustration, cynicism, and in the end, conflict and potential upheaval. Stated a bit differently, stability in a democratic regime springs from a system that allows participation, a culture that promotes involvement, and a set of options (or, shall we say, "pathways") to help redirect public policy.

Many Americans assume that all young activists are liberal, but this is certainly not the case.

■ *Are young voters attracted to particular issues pushed by conservatives like Ted Cruz?*

Conclusion

A key feature of all democracies is the opportunity for citizens to participate in public affairs in order to influence the decisions of government. The design and operation of American government provide a variety of opportunities for citizens to make their voices heard at the national, state, and local levels. In the United States, individuals can use the different pathways for action to influence government and public policies, and occasionally even the moves by large multinational corporations. These pathways include opportunities to participate in campaigns and elections, to file lawsuits in the courts, to lobby government officials, and to mobilize large groups of people to pressure officials or seek to change the culture and values of society.

The issue of youth engagement is featured prominently in this chapter. The story of significant policy changes on LGBT rights underscores the reality that average citizens can make a difference. Young people were key players in this movement, and this generation played a key role in several recent elections—particularly 2008. But levels of engagement in other forms of political action and in other, non-presidential elections, is spotty. Youth-centered groups are again forming, but the overall level of commitment to changing the course of public policy in America is quite modest among this generation—particularly compared to previous generations. At the very least, young Americans now seem rather certain that their involvement in community civic engagement matters. But they are less confident that their efforts can impact other important aspects of government and politics. Their turnout in the 2016 presidential election—a very important, dramatic contest—was lackluster.

In the next chapter, we examine the design of American government, beginning with the blueprint developed in the Constitution. Subsequent chapters will discuss key elements in government and politics, such as the news media and public opinion, as well as the specific institutions of government, such as Congress and the U.S. Supreme Court. As you learn about these key elements and institutions, think about which pathways of action are most important for each aspect of American government. You should also consider how you can participate as an engaged citizen when you want to assert influence over the decisions and priorities of your government.

CONFRONTING POLITICS AND POLICY

As you think about your daily life, are there laws or government policies that you regard as unfair or misguided? Listen to the people around you. Are they debating issues that affect their lives? Many people disagree about whether motorcyclists should be required to wear helmets. Some think it unjust that one can vote at age 18 but can't drink alcohol until age 21. Other people feel deeply about issues such as abortion, American military actions overseas, or growing economic disparities between the rich and the poor. Some of your classmates may believe that public universities have raised their tuition and fees to a level that is too high for the average individual to afford. Yet others may feel most strongly about the availability of health insurance for students and other individuals with limited incomes. Throughout the country, Americans debate such issues as gay marriage, gun control, and affirmative action. Do you worry about whether Social Security funds will be available when you retire? Or what should be done about immigration? Should dramatic steps be taken to reduce climate change? Unfortunately, many people, including students, appear to feel helpless, and they act as if there is no point in getting involved in contemporary issues. This may explain, in part, why voter participation rates in the United States are low compared to those in many other democracies.

ACTION STEP

1. As you evaluate your views about government and society, ask yourself the following question: As a college-educated person, do you really want all laws and policies that affect your life and determine what happens in your country to be decided by other people? If not, consider the steps that an engaged citizen should take to be effective in politics. In short, get informed, get organized with others, and get active.

⟩ REVIEW THE CHAPTER

It's Your Government

1.1 Illustrate how citizens participate in a democracy and why this is important. (p. 3)

Many Americans, especially young Americans, believe "government" and "politics" are distant, beyond their immediate world. In reality, government is around us; it shapes our lives in important ways every hour of every day. That is why it is particularly important for citizens in a democracy to become involved. Government matters, and you can make a difference.

Themes of This Book

1.2 Relate the themes of this book to American politics today. (p. 7)

There are numerous ways to investigate and explore our political system. This book focuses on three essential themes. First, in a democracy, it's essential that citizens become participants and not merely spectators of the political process. Second, while many in the United States believe their options for effective involvement are limited, there are numerous pathways for change. Indeed, throughout American history, different political actors have used different pathways to achieve their goals. Finally, issues of diversity have and will continue to shape the process and outcome of our political system. America's diversity contributes to most political controversies, while at the same time adding complexity to the mix of actors seeking to affect change.

Citizen Participation and Pathways: The Example of Abortion

1.3 Outline the various "pathways" of involvement in our political system. (p. 20)

Abortion is one of the most controversial issues of our day, and this long, heated debate has been played out though the five pathways of change: lobbying, courts, elections, grassroots mobilization, and cultural change. As one side has begun to achieve its goals via one pathway, the other side has responded by heading down a different pathway. The story of abortion says a lot about various routes of change in all of American politics.

Change and Stability in American Government

1.4 Analyze the forces of stability in American politics. (p. 22)

There is no doubt that our nation has undergone significant change in the last three centuries. At the same time, however, core elements of our political system have remained remarkably stable. This is due to reverence for democracy and free market capitalism, to a well-crafted Constitution, and to numerous pathways for average citizens to voice their concerns and redirect the course of public policy.

⟩ LEARN THE TERMS

politics, p. 4
public policy, p. 4
democracy, p. 6

totalitarian regime, p. 6
pathways of action, p. 9
checks and balances, p. 24

capitalism, p. 24
socialism, p. 24

⟩ EXPLORE FURTHER

In the Library

Ainsworth, Scott, and Thad Hall. *Abortion Politics in Congress: Strategic Instrumentalism and Policy Change.* New York: Cambridge University Press, 2011.

Almond, Gabriel A., and Sidney Verba. *Civic Culture: Political Attitudes and Democracy in Five Nations.* Princeton, NJ: Princeton University Press, 1963.

Baumgartner, Frank, and Jeffrey Berry. *Lobbying and Policy Change: Who Wins, Who Loses, and Why.* Chicago: University of Chicago Press, 2009.

Frantzich, Stephen F. *Citizen Democracy: Political Activism in a Cynical Age,* 3rd ed. Boulder, CO: Rowman and Littlefield, 2008.

Halperin, Morton, Joseph T. Siegle, and Michael M. Weinstein. *The Democracy Advantage: How Democracies*

Promote Prosperity and Peace, Revised Edition. New York: Routledge, 2009.

Hendershott, Anne. *The Politics of Abortion*. New York: Encounter Books, 2006.

Sanger, Alexander. *Beyond Choice: Reproductive Freedom in the 21st Century*. New York: Public Affairs, 2004.

Tocqueville, Alexis de. *Democracy in America*. New York: Signet Books, 2001. (Originally published 1835–1840.)

On the Web

To see comparisons of the United States and other countries in terms of political rights and individual freedom, visit the Freedom House Web site at *http://www.freedomhouse.org*.

To see comparisons of the United States and other countries in terms of voter turnout, see the Web site of International IDEA at *http://www.idea.int*.

To read about one organization's strategies for using various pathways to affect government policy concerning firearms, see the Web site of the National Rifle Association at *http://www.nra.org*.

Another good example of a powerful political action organization is the AARP, a massive, nationwide unit that works to protect the interests of older Americans: *http://www.aarp.org/*.

There are numerous youth and student political action organizations. To read about the Student Environmental Action Coalition, see http://www.seac.org/.

One of the most prominent, well-organized groups to defend abortion rights is Planned Parenthood: *http://www.plannedparenthood.org/*.

There are many organizations dedicated to ending abortions. One such group is the National Right to Life: *http://www.nrlc.org/*.

There are numerous sites to explore events in American history, including this one: *http://www.americanheritage.com/*.

EARLY GOVERNANCE AND THE CONSTITUTIONAL FRAMEWORK

The 2016 race for the White House was nothing if not spirited. There were a host of issues that separated Hillary Clinton and Donald Trump. Underneath it all were two very different types of candidates. Clinton represented experience, stability. Trump offered a radical change—a bold experiment.

■ *Under what conditions are voters more likely to back change over the status quo?*

→ LEARNING OBJECTIVES

2.1 Identify the difference between government and politics.

2.2 Differentiate between different types of governments.

2.3 Describe how forces in Colonial America helped set the stage for the American Revolution.

2.4 Identify the core principles of the American Revolution.

2.5 Determine the reasons for the failure of the Articles of Confederation.

2.6 Assess how compromises at the Constitutional Convention shaped our political system.

2.7 Identify the core principles of the Constitution.

2.8 Analyze how the ratification debate structured the nature of our democracy.

During the 2016 presidential election, there was a good deal of discussion about "establishment" versus "outsider" candidates. Is it better to have leaders well-versed in governance, with long resumes of public service, or political novices who can bring bold ideas to office? Clearly, candidates like former Florida governor Jeb Bush and Hillary Clinton reflected the establishment perspective, due to their lengthy experience in government and their relationship to former presidents. Jeb Bush's father and brother were both presidents; and, of course, Clinton lived in the White House with her husband Bill for eight years. Senator Bernie Sanders of Vermont and especially Donald Trump of New York were considered outsider candidates.

It might come as a surprise that the debates between the so-called establishment and outsiders is not new; and, in fact, extends back to when the nation was created. The framers of our system understood they were creating a democracy and the system had to be open to new ideas, perspectives, and people. There would be no right to office through heredity, social standing or even prior experience in government. The length of term for each office was a very important topic of discussion at the Constitutional Convention. Other than federal judges, public officials should have a "dependence on the people;" meaning they would be selected by citizens in periodic elections. There would be no oligarchy, a term introduced below meaning a preferred class of ruling elites.

At the same time, many worried about structuring public policy based on the whims of the citizenry. Even James Madison, who was always concerned about the democratic character of the new system, suggested that members of Congress should "enlarge and refine the public will." They should do what is right for the country regardless of what is popular with citizens. The constitutional framers believed the government would function best if well-educated, virtuous citizens were called to lead. In today's terms, most of the framers would probably fall in the establishment camp.

What about the role of heredity? Would the new system favor certain families—bloodlines of leaders—as was common throughout Europe at that time? They were adamant that it should not. Madison writes in *The Federalist*, No. 39, "It is essential [that the government be] derived from the great body of the society, not from an inconsiderable proportion, or a favored class." The republic would fail, the framers believed, if certain members of society were given preference over others. Power must flow through the ballot, not the blood line. They went on record as objecting to power through heredity, declaring in the U.S. Constitution that "no title of nobility shall be granted by the United States."

HOW DOES OUR NATION'S FORMATIVE PERIOD CONTINUE TO SHAPE CONTEMPORARY POLITICS?

And yet, we know that a handful of families have played a disproportionate influence in public affairs. John Adams and his son, John Quincy Adams, both served as president, as did William Henry Harrison and his grandson, Benjamin Harrison. There was Theodore Roosevelt and three decades later his cousin Franklin D. Roosevelt. George H.W. Bush was followed by his son, George W. Bush, just eight years later. And of course Bill and Hillary Clinton have been key members of the Washington establishment for nearly 30 years. At the state level, powerful political families have been common—including the Kennedys of Massachusetts, the Longs of Louisiana, the Cuomos of New York, and many others. A recent study found that members of Congress have a 40 percent chance of someone in their family also later serving in Congress.[1]

So which model is better—bringing to office experienced leaders, perhaps from a prominent family, or outsiders with fresh ideas? It seems that the willingness of voters to cast aside experience and familiarity for something new is a function of broader forces, like the nation's economic well-being. As we witnessed in the 2016 election, the desire for something new—perhaps even something bold—can be powerful. Exit polls from the 2016 election suggest much of Donald Trump's support came from voters worried about their futures. During times like that, establishment candidates face an uphill battle, to say the least.

> **POLL** Generally speaking, is it better to bring someone into office who has a good deal of experience in government, or someone from the outside who can offer fresh perspectives?

The Nature of Government and Politics

2.1 Identify the difference between government and politics.

In real ways, *government* is all around us. Government is the formal structures and institutions through which binding decisions are made for citizens of a particular area. We might also say that it is the organization that has formal jurisdiction over a group of people who live in a certain place. Government is *not* the process by which things take place in a political system; rather, it is the "rules of the game" and the structures (the institutions) that make and enforce these rules. However, the rules of the game can, and do, shape the political process. For example, due in large part to the Supreme Court's view that giving and spending money during elections is akin to speech, and thus protected by the First Amendment of the Constitution (government), money has become a fundamental aspect of the elections process (politics).

In the United States, institutions include legislatures like city councils, state legislatures, and Congress; executives like mayors, governors, and the president; the courts; the bureaucracy; and a few independent agencies, such as the Federal Reserve System. However, political parties, interest groups, and public opinion are key elements of our political system but not formal parts of the governmental structure.

This definition of government helps clarify the different types and layers of government. The rules and formal structures of a city government apply to the people living in that city. The rules of a school or club government apply only to the students in that school or the members of that club.

What does it mean to be "under the rule of the government?" At the most basic level, this suggests that government has the power to enforce its regulations and collect the resources it needs to operate. Rules can be enforced in many ways. One way, called *civil law*, is for citizens to be required to pay money as a penalty for breaking a rule. *Criminal law*, by contrast, prescribes that citizens who do not follow regulations pay a monetary penalty (a fine), be removed from society for a period of time or even permanently through a sentence of death or of life imprisonment without parole, or both. Taxation is the most common way to collect revenue to make the government run.

The words *power* and *authority* are related to government's ability to enforce its rules and collect resources. **Power**, in the political context, is the ability to get individuals, groups, or institutions to do something. Power determines the outcome of conflicts over governmental decisions; it charts the course of public policy. When the ranks of an interest group grow to the point that governmental decision makers are forced to listen, that group is said to have power. If a handful of corporate elites can persuade public officials to steer public policy their way, they have power.

Authority is defined as the *recognized* right of a particular individual, group, or institution to make binding decisions. Most Americans believe that Congress has the authority to make laws, impose taxes, or draft people into military service. We may not like the decisions made in Washington, in our state capital, or at city hall, but we recognize that in our system of government, elected officials have the authority to make those decisions. However, many people balk at the idea of *appointed* bureaucrats making regulations, given that they are not elected, which means that they don't have to answer to the people, only to those who appointed them. Thus bureaucrats have *power* but lack *authority*.

Some individuals, groups, and institutions have both power and authority. Congress has the authority to make laws, and federal law enforcement units have the power to enforce those laws. Perhaps the best contemporary example of when power

power

The ability to exercise control over others and get them to comply. For instance, the National Rifle Association wields power because many legislators fear upsetting their large, active membership.

authority

The recognized right of an individual, group, or institution to make binding decisions for society. While some might disagree with certain Supreme Court decisions, for instance, most recognize the Court's authority in our system of government.

and authority collide would be the individual health insurance mandate. Barack Obama signed into law the Patient Protection and Affordable Care Act in the spring of 2010 after a very contentious, drawn-out process. The controversy has not abated, as repealing "Obamacare" has become a rallying cry of the Republican Party. One of the most contentious aspects of the law is a fine for those who do not have health insurance by 2014. Supporters of the law argue that to keep health care costs down, everyone must have insurance. Setting aside the validity of this argument, others contend that the federal government does not have the authority make individuals buy insurance. It might have the power to prohibit certain acts, but it does not have the authority to punish someone for inaction. Needless to say, the federal courts were asked to resolve this issue. In 2012, the Supreme Court ruled on a 5–4 vote that the individual mandate is constitutional under Congress's taxation powers.

A final term to consider is *politics.* Politics is the *process* by which the character, membership, and actions of a government are determined. It is also the struggle to move government to a preferred course of action. All citizens might agree that a change is needed, but how to reach the desired goal can be hotly disputed. Given that governmental decisions create winners and losers—that is, acts by the government rarely please everyone—politics is a process that causes many to be left frustrated and at times angry. Moreover, politics can prove to be a slow process. The famous German sociologist Max Weber once suggested that politics is the "strong and slow boring of hard boards," and this makes good sense.[2]

The key difference you should keep in mind is that politics is the *process,* whereas government involves the *rules* of the game. An analogy that might be helpful is as follows: The baseball rulebook is long and complex. It states how runners can arrive at first base safely, how outs are made, and how a team wins. Most rules are clear and have remained the same for generations. But the actual *conduct* of the game is another matter. The rulebook says nothing about split-finger fastballs, change-ups, bunts, intentional walks, double steals, pitching rotations, closers, stoppers, line-up strategy, and other aspects of how the game is played. The rulebook represents government; the way the game is played is politics (see Figure 2.1).

FIGURE 2.1 Government and Politics: What's the Difference?

It is important that you understand the difference between government and politics. We suggest government is analogous to the official rules of baseball, and politics is similar to how the game is actually played.

■ *What is another analogy that might help you and your classmates better understand the difference between governmental institutions and the political process?*

SOURCE: Steve Mount, *U.S. Constitution Online,* http://www.usconstitution.net.

Baseball		American Government	
Official Rules (Government)	**How the Game Is Played (Politics)**	**Official Rules (Government)**	**How the Game Is Played (Politics)**
1. Pitchers can start from either the windup or the stretch position.	Pitchers grip the ball in different ways to throw fastballs, curveballs, or knuckleballs. Also, pitchers release the ball at different points to change the batter's view of the ball.	Article I, Section 2 The House of Representatives shall choose their speaker and other officers	The majority party uses their power to elect a speaker and other officers from their party, thus enabling them to push their legislative agenda.
2. Batters must keep both feet in the batter's box while hitting.	Batters can "crowd the plate" by standing close to the inside edge of the box.	First Amendment Freedom of the Press	Corporate conglomerates own media outlets.
3. A batter will run to first base after hitting a ball in fair territory.	Batters do not always make a full swing with the bat (for example, bunting).	Article I, Section 7 Presidential Veto	Presidents can threaten to veto a bill before it passes through Congress in order to influence the legislation.
4. All fielders must be in fair territory when that team's pitcher delivers the ball.	Defense can shift to accommodate for a batter who tends to hit in a certain direction.	Article I, Section 3 Each Senator shall have one vote	Lobbyists can provide information on issues and influence the way a Senator or Representative votes.
		Article I, Section 2 The House of Representatives shall be composed of members chosen every second year by the people of the several States	Candidates raise money and campaign before election day to influence the opinions of the voters.

Types of Governments

2.2 Differentiate between different types of governments.

Governments come in many forms and modes of operation. Perhaps the best way to think about these differences is to focus on two critical questions: Who is allowed to govern? And how are governmental decisions reached?[3] In terms of *who* is allowed to set the rules and regulations and to enforce them, there are several broad possibilities. **Monarchy** is a system of rule in which one person, such as a king or queen, possesses absolute authority over the government by virtue of being born into a royal family and inheriting the position. Monarchies have been the most common form of rule in world history, and they are still in place in some nations around the globe. For example, Saudi Arabia still relies on a royal family for ultimate authority. In history, few monarchies were truly "absolute;" kings were normally limited by custom and by the need to consult powerful groups. But in theory, the monarch's authority was unlimited. Almost all kings and queens today head **constitutional monarchies** in which they perform ceremonial duties but play little or no role in actually governing their country. Examples include the United Kingdom, Spain, Belgium, the Netherlands, and Japan.

A **dictator** is also a sole ruler, but often this person arrives at the position of power through a violent overthrow of the previous government, such as Sudan's Omar Al-Bashir. Sometimes contemporary dictators, such as North Korea's Kim Jong-un, succeed to power like a king or queen on the death of a parent. Like an absolute king, a dictator theoretically has unlimited control of the government, but again this power is often limited by the bureaucracy, the military, the ruling party, or even members of the dictator's family.

In some forms of government, a small group, such as military leaders or the economic elite, holds the reins of power. This is known as elitism or **oligarchy** (rule by a few). Decisions in such systems are often made through a council. Some have suggested that Russia has become an oligarchy in recent years due to the growing power of a small group of leaders. **Pluralism** occurs when a number of groups in a system struggle for power. In a pluralist system there are multiple centers of power.

monarchy

A system of government in which the ruler is established through heredity. This person (sometimes an entire family) holds absolute governmental power.

constitutional monarchy

A system of government in which a royal family, and often a king or queen, serves as a symbolic figurehead. Real government authority rests with another body, usually a parliament.

dictator

A ruler who holds absolute governmental authority and usually arrives at the post through a violent uprising.

oligarchy

A system of government in which a small group of elites, sometimes the very wealthy or an assembly of religious leaders, control most of the governing decisions.

pluralism

A system of government in which there are multiple groups vying for power.

Pictured here is Kim Jong Un, leader of the Democratic People's Republic of Korea (DPRK), during a military parade celebrating the 70th anniversary of the ruling Workers' Party of Korea in 2015. Kim is one of the world's most strident dictators.

■ *Are systems able to change when leaders control freedom of speech and expression?*

democracy

A political system in which all citizens have a chance to play a role in shaping government action and are afforded basic rights and liberties.

republic

A system of government in which members of the general public select agents to represent them in political decision-making. For example, most campus student governments can be considered republics because elections are held to choose student representatives.

representative democracy

A system in which citizens select, through an open and fair process, a smaller group to carry out the business of government on their behalf.

totalitarian regime

A system of government in which there are no limits on the power and authority of the rulers.

authoritarian regime

A system in which leaders have no formal or legal restraints, but are constrained by informal structures like religious groups or military leaders.

constitutional government

A system where there are both formal and informal constraints on the exercise of power.

Consider the arduous battle over health care reform in the United States. Just a sampling of the concerned groups included the insurance industry lobby, hospitals, health care professionals, labor unions, health reform advocates, conservative groups, liberal organizations, and so forth. On nearly every contentious issue there are multiple groups struggling to shape the outcome.

A **democracy** is a political system in which all citizens have a right to play a role in shaping government action—a mechanism often referred to as *popular sovereignty*. Citizens in a democracy are afforded basic rights and liberties, as well as freedom from government interference with private actions (that is, *liberty*). In a *direct or pure democracy*, all citizens make all decisions. Some tiny Swiss cantons (states) operate in this way, and a small number of communities in the United States are governed through town hall meetings, where everyone in the community has a say in making town policy.

Finally, a **republic** is a system of government in which a small group of elected representatives acts on behalf of the many. If these representatives closely follow the wishes of their constituents (the people they are sent to represent), and if they are elected through a fair and open process in which everyone has the same opportunity to participate, the system is considered a **representative democracy**. The United States is a republic—as are most of the industrialized nations of the world (though some are constitutional monarchies). Whether or not we are a true representative democracy, however, is a point of dispute.

The second important question to consider is *how* decisions are reached in a government. In a **totalitarian regime**, leaders have no real limits on how they proceed or what they do. Formal constitutions might exist in such regimes, seemingly full of limits on power, but in practice, such limits are meaningless. Totalitarian governments control—or at least try to control—almost every aspect of society.[4] The term *totalitarian* was invented in the 1920s by Benito Mussolini in Italy, although in practice, his government exercised less than total control. Nazi Germany, the Soviet Union under Joseph Stalin, China under Mao Zedong, and present-day North Korea are the clearest examples of truly totalitarian dictatorships. Under a dictatorship, there may be an individual ruler, a small group, or even a number of groups, but none of these acknowledges any formal limitations.

In an **authoritarian regime**, government policies are kept in check by informal limits, such as other political forces (maybe political parties), the military, and social institutions (for example, religious groups). Leaders face real limits, but there are no formal or legal restrictions. A good example would be the African nation of Chad, and its leader, General Idriss Déby Itno. The nation's constitution stipulates that the President be elected, but once in office he is given exceptional powers—including the ability to appoint a prime minister and a cabinet, and to remove judges and other public officials at his will. Thus, Déby has ruled Chad with an iron fist since the early 1990s, leading this nation to be ranked at the top of corrupt governments across the globe. But his powers are not absolute, however. In recent years opposition political parties have gained some strength, likely fueled by recent democratic movements throughout Africa and the Middle East. And of course there are the politics of oil. A few years ago the World Bank lent Chad money to construct a 1,000 mile oil pipeline under the conditions that much of the revenues help alleviate the widespread poverty. When Déby moved to divert proceeds from food aid to purchase arms, the World Bank quickly cut off funding, leading to a backlash among many of his constituencies. When there are both informal and legal limits, the system is a **constitutional government**. In the United States, for example, government action is controlled by strong social and political forces (including religions, interest groups, political parties, and the media) and by what the laws, the courts, and the Constitution allow (see Table 2.1).

TABLE 2.1 Types of Government Systems

Government Systems	Definition	Examples
Who is Allowed to Participate?		
Monarchy	Individual ruler with hereditary authority holds absolute governmental power	Bhutan, Saudi Arabia, Swaziland
Constitutional Monarchy	Monarch figurehead with limited power, actual governing authority belongs to another body	Denmark, Japan, United Kingdom
Dictatorship	Individual ruler with absolute authority, often comes to power through violent uprising	Hussein's Iraq, North Korea
Oligarchy	A small group of the rich or powerful controls most of the governing decisions	Tunisia, 20th-century South Africa, Pakistan
Pluralism	Multiple centers of power vying for authority	Canada, Great Britain, United States
How are Decisions Reached?		
Pure Democracy	Citizens make all governmental decisions	Some Swiss states, some towns in New England
Representative Democracy	Citizens elect representatives to carry out government functions	United States, Germany, France
Totalitarian Regime	Leaders have no limits on authority	Nazi Germany, 1920s Italy
Authoritarian System	Leaders have no formal legal restraints on authority but are limited by informal forces (for example, the military, religious forces)	South Korea, Singapore, Taiwan, Chad
Constitutional System	Government has both informal and legal restraints on the exercise of power	United States, Germany, France, Mexico

Early Governance in America

2.3 Describe how forces in Colonial America helped set the stage for the American Revolution.

In 1620, a tiny group of English people consisting of 41 men and an unknown number of women and children sailed across the Atlantic to what was called at the time the *New World*. They were crammed into a leaky old ship called the *Mayflower*. Some members of this band would later be dubbed the **Pilgrims**, because they were coming to America in hopes of finding religious freedom. But other passengers were not part of this religiously motivated group. All of the *Mayflower* passengers were bound for Virginia, where they expected to join an English colony that had been founded a few years earlier, in 1607. Unfortunately, the place where they landed—New England—was outside the recognized boundaries of Virginia, and the captain of the ship refused to go any farther because winter was coming. When spring arrived, the captain took his ship back to England, leaving the passengers on the coast of New England.

Recognizing that they were stuck in this bleak place, the Pilgrim leaders insisted that everyone, Pilgrim and non-Pilgrim alike, sign the **Mayflower Compact**, a document legalizing their position as a "civil body politic" under the sovereignty of King James I. Most important for our concerns is that these people, finding themselves in a place outside the jurisdiction of English rule, sought a system where laws, not a small group or a single person, would rule their society.

From the Mayflower Compact until the American Revolution, a mixed system characterized colonial governance. On the one hand, most of the colonies were established through charters from England. There was no question that these settlements would be governed under English rule. Governors were appointed by the Crown to oversee different colonies and were responsible only to the king. On the other hand, the New World was an ocean away. Settling an untamed wilderness created its own set of problems, and ideas favoring self-governance grew in intellectual circles both in America and in England. The compromise came in the form of colonial assemblies. Here, colonists elected representatives to speak on their behalf and to counsel the governors on the best courses of action. Every colony had an assembly, usually located in the largest city. These bodies had little legal authority. But while the governors did not have to listen to the

Pilgrims

Puritans who sailed from Europe in the early 1600s to North America with the aim of settling the land and starting a new life. More generally, this term can mean a person who journeys to a holy land.

Mayflower Compact

A document setting-up a set of laws for the Pilgrims who landed at Plymouth, Massachusetts, in 1620. It was truly significant because they did not simply pick a leader to make decisions, but instead established rules that all would follow.

This painting depicts a critical moment in the history of world governance: when the pilgrims to America signed the Mayflower Compact.

■ *Imagine you have arrived with your family, friends, and a group of strangers in a land without any formal rules or regulations. What type of government would you seek to establish? Would it make more sense to rely upon a few smart or powerful leaders to get things started, or would you try to establish a system of laws from the very beginning?*

French and Indian War

Also called the Seven Year's War, this was a series of military battles between Britain and France in North America between 1754 and 1763. The French received support from a number of Indian tribes. Britain won the war, but it proved quite costly—leading to novel ways of raising money from the colonists.

Great Squeeze

A period prior to the American Revolution when the British Parliament sought to recoup some of the costs associated with the French and Indian War by levying new taxes and fees on colonists. Two examples of these measures would be the Sugar Act and the Stamp Act.

advice of the assemblies, they often did so in order to win the esteem of citizens. This mix of appointed rule and self-governance seemed to work, at least at first.

Two developments upset this balance. First, many colonists brought with them the political customs and traditions from their homeland, meaning that the debate over the extent of royal authority in the conduct of government came along as well. As in England, those supporting the Crown were often the wealthiest, having received immense land grants and special privileges from the king. Those who were not part of the political in-group were deeply suspicious of the favored elite, and their numbers swelled as the years passed. On top of this, if a local governing authority proved oppressive, colonists had the option of simply packing up and moving. This made opposition to royal and elite control easier.

Second, and more significantly, new financial pressures were thrust on the colonists in the mid-1760s. The **French and Indian War** in North America, which began in 1754 and ended nine years later, pitted Great Britain against France. The war, part of a larger Anglo-French struggle for global power, began over control of the upper Ohio River valley. However, the larger issue was which nation would eventually control the continent. Most of the settlers in this area were British, but the French had entered into trade agreements (and later a military alliance) with many Indian tribes. Through a series of spectacular military engagements over the course of several years, the British defeated the French and took control of North America, with relatively little colonial assistance.

All wars are expensive, but given that this one had been waged an ocean away, the price of protecting Britain's New World empire proved very high. Facing massive debt and grumbling taxpayers, Parliament, with the king's blessing, looked for new ways of raising revenue. Because the war had been fought to protect the colonists, it seemed logical that they should bear much of the responsibility for paying the bill. Thus began a period known as the **Great Squeeze**, in which Parliament passed one measure after another—including the Sugar Act (1764), the Stamp Act (1765), the Townshend Acts (1767), and the Tea Tax (1773)—all designed to wring as much revenue from the colonists as possible. To make matters worse, the Great Squeeze came after more than a generation of what was called "salutary neglect," a policy of casual, loose enforcement of trade laws in the colonies. Parliament had hoped that this freedom would stimulate greater commercial growth, leading to greater profits for British investors. Parliament's decision to raise revenue through a number of taxes after a century of trade freedom proved a bitter pill for the Americans.

PATHWAYS OF ACTION

THE TRIAL OF PETER ZENGER

One of the themes of this book is that political change can come through different pathways. The trial of publisher Peter Zenger is a vivid illustration of how the court system can be used not only to protect individual liberties, but to draw attention to emerging issues, thus changing political culture.

During much of the pre-Revolution period, relations between the royal governors and the colonists were generally congenial. But in the 1730s, the New York Province was ruled by Governor William Cosby, a notorious scoundrel. By all accounts, Cosby was a greedy, unsavory character and after he replaced the popular Chief Justice Lewis Morris with one of his friends, criticism grew intense. Soon a group was formed and an opposition newspaper founded. After a series of critical articles, the publisher of that paper, Peter Zenger, was thrown in jail for libel. He stayed there for eight months.

The story of the corrupt governor and the group that dared challenge his rule spread throughout the colonies. The best lawyer in land, Andrew Hamilton of Philadelphia (no relation to Alexander Hamilton), was hired to defend Zenger. Rather than suggest Zenger was innocent of the charges, Hamilton spoke passionately at the trial about the right of citizens to air grievances and the necessity of a free press: "It is a right, which all free men claim, that they are entitled to complain when they are hurt. They have a right publicly to remonstrate against the abuses of power in the strongest terms...." The jury freed Zenger and Hamilton's defense of rights and liberties planted the idea in the American psyche that no public officials, no matter how powerful, should be above criticism.

In truth, the new taxes were not severe, and colonial Americans were probably among the least taxed people in the Euro-American world at the time. But the colonists were in constant fear of the corruption that, in their eyes, a faraway and arbitrary government could impose on them. ("Corruption" to eighteenth-century Americans included the distribution of government favors to what we would today call "special interests.") It seems, then, that the colonists' obsession about corruption and tyranny and their insistence on guaranteeing limited, accountable government became fundamental to Americans' ideas of just governance—surely an explicit theme in the Constitution. The relationship between the royal governors and the colonial assemblies soured. Because it was the duty of the governors to enforce these unpopular revenue-raising acts, they became the targets of colonial outrage.

The American Revolution

2.4   Identify the core principles of the American Revolution.

The causes and meanings of the American Revolution are best broken into two broad categories: financial (pragmatic) and ideological. With regard to the financial concerns, the Great Squeeze made life in the colonies harder and the prospects for a profitable future seem dimmer for all colonists. The Stamp and Sugar acts were viewed as tyrannical, and the backlash against them was fierce. Parliament also passed many measures that placed lands in the western regions under British control. Because land represented profits—from sales of acreage, lumber, or farm products—many colonists saw this move as unbearable. The Acts for Trade were an additional series of moves by Parliament to channel money back to the commercial class in Great Britain. King George III (along with Parliament) sought to save money by demanding that each colony pay for the upkeep of the British soldiers occupying its territory. On a practical level, the Revolution was about the money.

At a deeper level was a growing desire among Americans to create a system in which all citizens (at least all white, male, propertied citizens) would have a say in the conduct of government and in which basic freedoms of life and liberty would be protected. Echoing this idea, one of the rallying cries during this period was "No taxation without representation." The essence of self-governance, Americans argued, was the ability to control taxes. After Parliament imposed yet another revenue-raising measure, this time giving the bankrupt but politically powerful East India Company a monopoly

This painting depicts a political protest by the 'Sons of Liberty' known as the Boston Tea Party on December 16, 1773, in Boston, Massachusetts.

■ *Is the destruction of property and violence justified when a group seeks freedom and equality?*

on importing tea into the colonies, a band of enraged colonists, disguised as Indians, stormed a merchant ship in Boston Harbor in the dark of night and threw the company's tea overboard. For many colonists, the so-called Boston Tea Party was a galvanizing event that rallied patriotic sentiment. For Parliament and George III, the event reflected growing unrest in the colonies—it was an act of insolence that had to be punished and suppressed. Parliament quickly passed five new measures, which the British called the Coercive Acts and the colonists referred to as the Intolerable Acts. In short, these were punitive measures, designed to punish the rebellious colonists: One act closed the Port of Boston; another altered the Massachusetts government to bring it under British control; anther made the quartering of soldiers in colonial homes easier; and so forth. Of course, these new measures only stoked the flames of rebellion.

Taxation without representation was not the only ideological issue. The old splits over parliamentary prerogatives were transformed into a debate on the exact nature of self-governance. The colonists had grown accustomed to an unprecedented level of freedom. In Great Britain and throughout Europe, laws and customs limited access to trades and professions, controlled land usage, and compelled people to belong to established churches. The Pilgrims had come to the New World in search of religious freedom, and in large measure, they had found it. The generations that followed began to consider and demand what they saw as their "rights."

During this period, a good deal of attention was paid to the writings of great philosophers on the rights of citizens and the proper conduct of government. The English political theorist John Locke (1632–1704), in particular, had written a number of widely read essays on the subject, most notably *Two Treatises of Government,* which first appeared in 1690. Locke argued that all legitimate governing authority is based on the consent of the governed and that all individuals have "natural rights." Later, in the eighteenth century, the Scottish economist Adam Smith (1723–1790) wrote about the importance of limiting government in order to protect the economic rights of citizens.

In the colonies, a number of people started to write on liberty, including a young Massachusetts lawyer named John Adams (1735–1826), who would later become president of the new nation. In 1765, he began publishing a series of essays in which he offered a fervent defense of patriotism. "Liberty must at all hazards be supported," he argued.[5] The writings struck an immediate chord, noted one historian.[6] That same year, a group of delegates from the colonies gathered to discuss the new Stamp Act and to consider responses to it. The Stamp Act Congress produced the Declaration of Rights and Grievances, a powerful statement on the rights of citizens that was widely circulated.

A decade later, when Americans found themselves debating the fateful step of seeking independence, Thomas Paine (1737–1809) wrote a highly influential and persuasive tract, *Common Sense,* promising freedom, equality, and the prospect of democracy.

The Declaration of Independence

By September 1774, in the aftermath of the Coercive Acts and the Boston Tea Party, events seemed to be spinning out of control. Every colony except Georgia sent delegates to the First Continental Congress in Philadelphia. At this point, few openly spoke of breaking ties with Great Britain; most still hoped to find a compromise that would protect the rights of Americans and pull back the harshest tax measures. Still, in the absence of dramatic changes by George III and Parliament, the delegates called on the colonists to boycott all British goods.

Matters did not improve. Within a year, the royal governor of Massachusetts, Thomas Gage, ordered his troops to seize what was believed to be a growing supply of arms from the colonists at Concord. Before the 700 red-coated British troops sent from Boston reached Concord, however, 77 "Minutemen" (militia) met them at the small town of Lexington. Shots were fired, and the Minutemen retreated. The Redcoats pressed forward, but by the time they arrived at Concord, the Patriot forces had swelled to more than 300. After another battle, the royal troops had to retreat and were attacked repeatedly as they marched back to Boston. In the end, some 270 British soldiers and 95 colonists were killed. The event sent shockwaves throughout the colonies and across the Atlantic Ocean. The wheels of war had been set in motion.

Although there was still strong sentiment in America for reconciliation with Great Britain, many of the delegates who attended the Second Continental Congress in 1775 considered compromise impossible. They understood that war had, in fact, begun. But they still had to convince others throughout the colonies that armed rebellion was their only remaining chance. Not all Americans were convinced. British oppression had been real, but a war for independence was an altogether different matter. Many of those who had protested British abuses still remained loyal to England. At the very same time that delegates were arriving at Philadelphia, petitions were circulating in towns and villages throughout the colonies calling for reconciliation with Great Britain. Something needed to be done to convince more colonists to rebel, to move with force toward a system of self-governance. A committee of five was formed, and the task of writing a clearly written rationale for rebellion was given to a young, rather shy delegate from Virginia by the name of Thomas Jefferson.

Jefferson's Declaration of Independence is today regarded as one of the most lucid statements ever written on the rights of citizens and the proper role of government in a free society. It is one of the world's great democratic documents and has been an inspiration to people yearning for freedom around the globe. While the message is certainly a poignant one, it is the strength of the language and rhetorical skill that gives it power. The core of the statement can be found in just 83 words:

> We hold these truths to be self-evident, that all men are created equal, that they are endowed by their Creator with certain unalienable Rights, that among these are Life, Liberty and the pursuit of Happiness. That to secure these rights Governments are instituted among Men, deriving their just power from the consent of the governed, That whenever any Form of Government becomes destructive of these ends, it is the Right of the People to alter or abolish it, and to institute new Government....

Rarely has more been said in so few words. Let us examine this passage in detail. First, Jefferson presents a notion of **natural rights**. That is, individuals possess certain privileges—certain guarantees by virtue of being human. Second, these rights are *not* granted by government but instead by God, whom Jefferson calls the Creator. They cannot be given, nor can they be taken away. Third, Jefferson introduces the **social contract theory**, drawn in large measure from the writings of John Locke. Humans have the option of living alone in

natural rights
Basic rights that no government can deny. For example, the right to a fair, impartial trial would be considered a natural right, as would the right to speak out against government corruption.

social contract theory
A political theory that holds individuals give up certain rights in return for securing certain freedoms. If the government breaks the social contract, grounds for revolution exist. This notion was at the core of the Declaration of Independence.

TIMELINE

Thinking About a "Government by the People"

In the 1830s, French writer and philosopher Alexis de Tocqueville traveled around the United States taking notes. His subsequent book, *Democracy in America*, suggested our system was a "grand experiment," a bold effort to create a popular government. He was right. But the idea of a democracy, a limited form of government, did not emerge quickly or with any particular event. Rather, it was an idea that emerged over decades; a broad notion that was eventually blended with the unique circumstances of colonial life, British politics, dynamic personalities, and world affairs. This timeline charts some of the more important philosophical foundations of our system of government. It ends with the ratification of the Bill of Rights but you should realize that this list of ideas, documents, and events has grown, and will continue to grow, for generations. Ours' is a democracy in motion, a system ever-moving toward a "more perfect union."

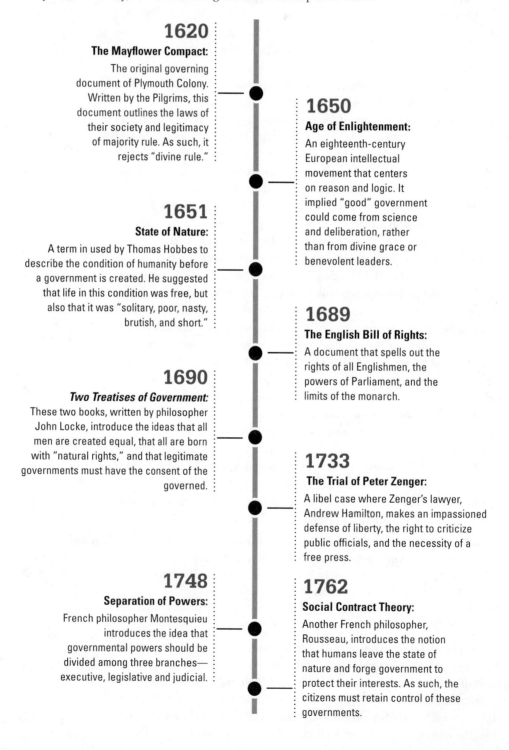

1620

The Mayflower Compact:
The original governing document of Plymouth Colony. Written by the Pilgrims, this document outlines the laws of their society and legitimacy of majority rule. As such, it rejects "divine rule."

1650

Age of Enlightenment:
An eighteenth-century European intellectual movement that centers on reason and logic. It implied "good" government could come from science and deliberation, rather than from divine grace or benevolent leaders.

1651

State of Nature:
A term in used by Thomas Hobbes to describe the condition of humanity before a government is created. He suggested that life in this condition was free, but also that it was "solitary, poor, nasty, brutish, and short."

1689

The English Bill of Rights:
A document that spells out the rights of all Englishmen, the powers of Parliament, and the limits of the monarch.

1690

Two Treatises of Government:
These two books, written by philosopher John Locke, introduce the ideas that all men are created equal, that all are born with "natural rights," and that legitimate governments must have the consent of the governed.

1733

The Trial of Peter Zenger:
A libel case where Zenger's lawyer, Andrew Hamilton, makes an impassioned defense of liberty, the right to criticize public officials, and the necessity of a free press.

1748

Separation of Powers:
French philosopher Montesquieu introduces the idea that governmental powers should be divided among three branches—executive, legislative and judicial.

1762

Social Contract Theory:
Another French philosopher, Rousseau, introduces the notion that humans leave the state of nature and forge government to protect their interests. As such, the citizens must retain control of these governments.

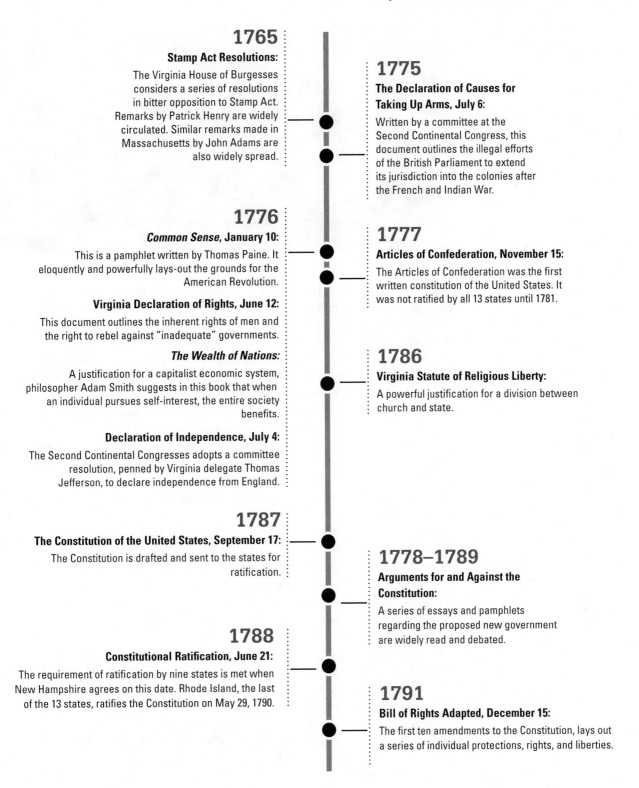

1765

Stamp Act Resolutions:

The Virginia House of Burgesses considers a series of resolutions in bitter opposition to Stamp Act. Remarks by Patrick Henry are widely circulated. Similar remarks made in Massachusetts by John Adams are also widely spread.

1775

The Declaration of Causes for Taking Up Arms, July 6:

Written by a committee at the Second Continental Congress, this document outlines the illegal efforts of the British Parliament to extend its jurisdiction into the colonies after the French and Indian War.

1776

***Common Sense*, January 10:**

This is a pamphlet written by Thomas Paine. It eloquently and powerfully lays-out the grounds for the American Revolution.

1777

Articles of Confederation, November 15:

The Articles of Confederation was the first written constitution of the United States. It was not ratified by all 13 states until 1781.

Virginia Declaration of Rights, June 12:

This document outlines the inherent rights of men and the right to rebel against "inadequate" governments.

The Wealth of Nations:

A justification for a capitalist economic system, philosopher Adam Smith suggests in this book that when an individual pursues self-interest, the entire society benefits.

1786

Virginia Statute of Religious Liberty:

A powerful justification for a division between church and state.

Declaration of Independence, July 4:

The Second Continental Congresses adopts a committee resolution, penned by Virginia delegate Thomas Jefferson, to declare independence from England.

1787

The Constitution of the United States, September 17:

The Constitution is drafted and sent to the states for ratification.

1778–1789

Arguments for and Against the Constitution:

A series of essays and pamphlets regarding the proposed new government are widely read and debated.

1788

Constitutional Ratification, June 21:

The requirement of ratification by nine states is met when New Hampshire agrees on this date. Rhode Island, the last of the 13 states, ratifies the Constitution on May 29, 1790.

1791

Bill of Rights Adapted, December 15:

The first ten amendments to the Constitution, lays out a series of individual protections, rights, and liberties.

CRITICAL THINKING QUESTIONS

1. Given this list of impressive, important documents, which do you believe has the greatest impact on your day-to-day life? Put a bit differently, which of these documents shape the way average Americans conduct their lives?

2. What's next? That is, if you were responsible for composing a document that would add to this list, what issues would you confront? Are there topics that the authors of these documents—all white men, by the way—could not have imagined, but are fundamental in any modern democracy?

This famous picture depicts one of the greatest moments in the history of democratic governance—the signing of the Declaration of Independence.

■ *Did you know that these men all feared they were signing their own death warrants? Indeed, if the British had won the war, it is highly likely that these men would have been hanged as traitors. Would you have put your life on the line for the "cause of liberty"?*

what Locke called "the state of nature." According to this theory, humans originally lived without government or laws, enjoying complete personal freedom. Yet the state of nature meant "a war of all against all," in which—in the words of another philosopher, Thomas Hobbes—life was "solitary, poor, nasty, brutish, and short." To end this perpetual conflict and insecurity, people created governments, thereby giving up some of their freedoms in order to protect their lives and their property. Fourth, Jefferson agreed with Locke that governments, having been created by the people to protect their rights, are limited; they get their powers from the will of the people and no one else. (In arguing this, Locke was attacking the traditional claim that kings ruled by the will of God.) Finally, said Jefferson (again following Locke), when a government fails to respect the will of the people—that is, when it appears no longer to be limited—it becomes the right, indeed the obligation, of citizens to change the government. This passage is Jefferson's call for revolution.

How effective was the Declaration of Independence in rallying support behind the Revolutionary cause? This is a difficult question to answer because there were no accurate ways to measure public opinion in those days. While we know that many New Yorkers were so inspired on hearing these words that they toppled a statute of King George and had it melted down to make 42,000 bullets for war,[7] many balked at joining the Revolution and even enlisted in the British Army. We also know that public support for the Continental Army, headed by George Washington, lagged considerably throughout the Revolution. Most Americans were deeply suspicious of professional armies, fearing them as a threat to liberty. There were no mechanisms to collect funds to support the Continental Army; state contributions were very stingy, which helps explain the terrible conditions that the troops suffered at Valley Forge in the winter of 1777–1778. "The supply problem," writes historian Joseph Ellis, "while catastrophic in its immediate consequences, was eminently solvable....A veritable caravan of grain and livestock flowed from the countryside into the city to feed British troops...." We often point to the valor of soldiers at Valley Forge, but fail to recognize that the very reason for the widespread starvation was because area farmers chose to sell their produce to the British Army—who were willing to pay a higher price.

Either way, war had begun between the most powerful nation in the world—Great Britain—and the American colonies. At first, things looked grim for the Patriot cause, and many Americans feared that all would be lost within a matter of weeks. By December 1776, the end seemed near. But three startling developments seemed to turn the tide.

First, with bold leadership from George Washington, the Continental Army was able to gain a few high-profile victories, which served to assure patriots and foreign governments that the war could, in fact, be won and that financial contributions to the war effort would not be wasted.

Second, from 1776 to 1783, Thomas Paine espoused the virtues of democracy in his sixteen famous "Crisis" papers. Their tone is apparent in the famous opening of "The

American Crisis, Number 1," published on December 19, 1776, when Washington's army was on the verge of disintegration:

> These are the times that try men's souls. The summer soldier and the sunshine patriot will, in this crisis, shrink from the service of their country; but he that stands it now, deserves the love and thanks of man and woman. Tyranny, like hell, is not easily conquered; yet we have this consolation with us, that the harder the conflict, the more glorious the triumph.

This was powerful writing, and Washington ordered the pamphlet read to all of his troops.[8]

Third, the French government decided to support the Revolutionary forces. This decision came, after a prolonged diplomatic effort spearheaded in Paris by Benjamin Franklin, upon news that the Americans had inflicted a serious defeat on the British Army at Saratoga in October 1777. Financial support, arms and ammunition, and military assistance from the French government proved immensely helpful—particularly on occasions when the prospects for victory still seemed bleak.

The Colonial Experience and the Pathways of Change

Having some gripes with your government is one thing; deciding to break away and form a new government is quite another. A move of this sort would seem especially momentous given that in 1776 Britain had the world's most powerful army and navy. It has been said that the signers of the Declaration of Independence assumed they were signing their own death warrants.

How did things come to this? Ideas of liberty, equality, and self-governance—captured so well by Jefferson's pen—had simmered throughout the colonies for decades. Jefferson's prose captured a sentiment, but he did not bring the idea of democracy to life. Like flowers bursting from the ground after a long winter, liberty and equality were destined to blossom in the American soil. Also, as we noted in Chapter 1, governments whose citizens yearn for liberty are stable only if those citizens have avenues of change—that is, the means to move public policy in new directions as times and circumstances change. What pathways of change had been available to the colonists? Could they have elected a new government or petitioned the courts for redress? Might average citizens have effectively lobbied members of Parliament, an ocean away? Their protests, such as the Boston Tea Party, were met with additional acts of repression. There seemed no option for change. Their only recourse was to declare independence and prepare for war. In a very real way, the American Revolution underscores the importance of our pathways concept.

This is, of course, the famous picture of George Washington crossing the Delaware on Christmas Eve, 1776.

■ *How important was it to have a strong, high-profile leader to rally the patriot cause?*

The Articles of Confederation

2.5 Determine the reasons for the failure of the Articles of Confederation.

Less than a week after the signing of the Declaration of Independence, the Continental Congress set to work drawing up a system of government for the self-declared independent American states. After a year's effort, the model that emerged was called the *Articles of Confederation*. The idea was to draw the 13 states together but, at the same time, to allow each state to remain independent. In this system, the central government could coordinate and recommend policies, but it had no ability to enforce these policies if the states refused. An analogy would be today's United Nations, where each nation has one delegate and one vote and the representative serves at the discretion of the home government. On paper, at least, this Congress had power to conduct foreign affairs, wage war, create a postal service, appoint military officers, control Indian affairs, borrow money, and determine the value of the coinage.[9] But the Articles did not give the national government the power to force its policies on the states, nor did it allow the levying of taxes to support the federal government (see Table 2.2). It was up to the states to contribute to the federal government's support as they saw fit, just as each member nation of the United Nations contributes what it wishes to the UN budget. And the Articles said nothing about judicial matters.

The fact that the Articles guarded state sovereignty is really not surprising. In a very real way, our first system of national government was designed to be the opposite of what colonists had experienced under authoritarian, centralized British rule. It was also widely believed at the time that democracy was possible only when government was local.

Limitations of the Articles of Confederation

The Articles of Confederation failed for several reasons. First, the national government had no way to collect revenue from the states or from the states' citizens. No government can survive without some means of obtaining the resources it needs to operate. Second, the national government had no way of regulating commerce. Third, the national government was unable to conduct foreign affairs—that is, to speak to other nations with a unified voice. Fourth, the mechanism to alter the Articles proved too difficult, as any change required the unanimous consent of all 13 states. So even if adjustments, such as giving the national government the power to collect taxes, could have improved matters, the chances of achieving unanimous agreement to do so were slim.

Yet another shortcoming of the Articles was the lack of leadership and accountability within the national government. There was no one in charge. This issue of accountability came to a head in 1786 with an event that rocked western Massachusetts.

During the mid-1780s, the nation had experienced an economic depression. Particularly hard-hit were farmers, who received much less for their crops than in previous years due to a flood of imports. Desperate for relief, a group of farmers led

TABLE 2.2 Powers of Congress Under the Articles of Confederation

What Congress Could Do	What Congress Could Not Do
Borrow money	Regulate commerce
Request money from states	Collect taxes from citizens
Conduct foreign affairs	Prohibit states from conducting foreign affairs
Maintain army and navy	Establish a national commercial system
Appoint military officers	Force states to comply with laws
Establish courts	Establish a draft
Establish a postal system	Collect money from states for services
Control Indian affairs	

by Daniel Shays, a veteran Patriot militia captain who had fought against the British at Bunker Hill in 1775, gathered to demand changes. Frustrated that their calls for help seemed to fall on deaf ears at the state legislature, Shays's forces grew to nearly 1,200. Soon violence broke out as the group clashed with state militia forces. The governor and state legislature appealed for assistance in putting down the protest, which they argued had deteriorated into a full-blown riot. But there was no person or group outside Massachusetts to take the call for assistance, and no help was available.

Many of the rebels were captured and sentenced to death for treason, but all were later pardoned. Yet **Shays's Rebellion** had a profound impact on the future of our nation, because it suggested that liberty and freedom—that is, an open democratic society—carried risks. A few months after the uprising in Massachusetts, a meeting was organized to revise the Articles. This was the **Constitutional Convention**.

Shays's Rebellion: An Alternative Look

Why would Shays and his followers turn to violent protest? Were there no other pathways for change?

Money, especially specie or "hard money" (silver and gold coin), became very scarce throughout the United States in the 1780s, resulting in a severe depression that lasted nearly a decade. But not everyone was affected the same way. Hardest hit were working-class citizens and small farmers. Because these people had little or no hard money with which to pay their debts, bank foreclosures skyrocketed. By the mid-1780s, demands for action grew louder. Very much in keeping with the structure of government during this period, people's cries for assistance were directed to the state legislatures. "Stay laws" were passed by state legislatures to postpone foreclosures, and "tender laws" allowed farmers to use agricultural products (rather than hard money) to help pay loans. Partly as a result, inflation surged, and as paper money became more widespread, it became easier to use this inflated currency to pay off debts, such as the mortgage on a farm.[10]

However, in Massachusetts, the legislature dragged its feet. What made this state different? For one thing, business interests dominated the state legislature. Instead of helping small farmers, the legislature saw fit to levy heavy taxes in an attempt to pay off the state's wartime debts, with most of the money going to wealthy business owners in Boston. From this vantage point, Shays's Rebellion broke out because the channels of the democratic process were *not* working in Massachusetts. There seemed to be no other viable pathway for change, and violence erupted.

This perspective also allows us to reconsider the motivations of the delegates to the Constitutional Convention. Today, many believe that the aim of that meeting was to fine-tune the democratic process and create a stronger national government. In some ways, this is true. But the policies of the state governments designed to protect farmers and laborers during the depression of the 1780s created hardship for a different group—the economic elite. As noted earlier, there are always winners and losers in politics, and during this period, much that was given to the farmers was taken from business owners and bankers. Perhaps, then, some of the rationale for calling delegates to Philadelphia was to revise the Articles in order to make sure that state governments could not limit the "liberty" of the economic elite.

Shays's Rebellion
An armed uprising in western Massachusetts in 1786 and 1787 by small farmers angered over high debt and tax burdens. This event helped bring about the Constitutional Convention, as many worried that similar events would happen unless there were changes.

Constitutional Convention
A meeting in Philadelphia in 1787 at which delegates from the colonies drew up a new system of government. The finished product was the Constitution of the United States.

The Constitutional Convention

2.6 Assess how compromises at the Constitutional Convention shaped our political system.

In late May 1787, some 55 delegates from every state except Rhode Island came together at the Pennsylvania State House in Philadelphia for the purpose of proposing changes to the Articles of Confederation. Congress itself had authorized the

TABLE 2.3 The Virginia Plan

- Have three branches of government—a national legislature, an executive, and a judiciary.
- Force each of the branches to rely on the others.
- Grant each branch the ability to keep an eye on the other two so that no one segment of the government becomes too powerful.
- Have a legislature with an upper and lower house, with members of the lower house chosen by the people in the various states and the upper chamber made up of legislators chosen by the lower house from a list of nominees put forward by the state legislatures.
- Allow each state a number of seats in the national legislature based on its population (thus the larger states would have more delegates and the smaller states fewer).
- Have an executive, selected by the legislature and serving a single term.
- Have judges who would be appointed to the bench by the legislature for life terms.
- Establish a "council of revision," with members from both the executive branch and the judiciary, which would review all national and state laws; this body would have some control over national legislation and an absolute veto over state legislation.
- Be supreme over the state governments—that is, acts of the new national government would override state law.

Virginia Plan

A plan made by delegates to the Constitutional Convention from several of the larger states calling for a strong national government with a bicameral legislature, a national executive, a national judiciary, and legislative representation based on population. Much of this plan found its way into the Constitution, shaping the system we live under today.

New Jersey Plan

A scheme for government advanced at the Constitutional Convention that was supported by delegates from smaller states. It called for equal representation of states in a unicameral legislature. Under this approach, each state would have the same say in the national legislature, and the executive branch would have modest powers.

meeting, but it did not expect that the Articles would be completely replaced by a new system of government. The delegates were not "average" men but rather included many of America's leading political, economic, and social figures of the time. (Thomas Jefferson, then serving as U.S. minister to France, was not present.) In a move designed to lend legitimacy to the event, George Washington was selected as the convention's presiding officer and on May 29, the delegates set to work. Interestingly, and perhaps contrary to what you might think, the convention deliberated in total secrecy—even to the extent of nailing the windows shut!

Opening the convention, Governor Edmund Randolph of Virginia offered a series of resolutions that amounted to an assault on the Articles. Rather than attempting to modify them, Randolph argued, the Articles should be dumped altogether. The delegates agreed; something new and vastly different was needed. Small groups were formed, charged with drawing up plans for a new government. In the end, five plans were submitted for consideration, but the delegates quickly narrowed their consideration to two.

The first was the **Virginia Plan**, named for the home state of its principal author, James Madison. The delegates from the more populous states favored it. Table 2.3 provides an overview of what the new government would look like under this plan.

Most delegates agreed with the core idea of the Virginia Plan—that the central government should be strengthened. Yet big differences in population between the states seemed a problem. The most populous states were Virginia, Pennsylvania, North Carolina, Massachusetts, and New York; the smallest states included (besides absent Rhode Island) Georgia, Delaware, Connecticut, and New Jersey. Delegates from the smaller states realized that this scheme would put them at a real disadvantage in the national government—a smaller state's interests would be overwhelmed by those of the larger states. Opposition to the Virginia Plan grew. William Paterson of New Jersey offered an alternative approach. His **New Jersey Plan** was designed to stick closer to the Articles of Confederation and create a system of equal representation among the states: Each state would have the same number of national legislators. Table 2.4 is an overview of this plan.

Although it might seem that both models were similar in terms of the supremacy of the national government, this was not the case. A national legislature was at the core of both plans, but under the New Jersey Plan, each state would have equal say in the making of public policy. Since a majority of state governors could change the makeup of the executive council, this plan was more state-centered and in keeping with the confederation model that underlay the Articles. In contrast, the Virginia Plan clearly laid out what was called at the time a "consolidated government"—one that all but absorbed the states.

TABLE 2.4 The New Jersey Plan

- Have three parts of government—a national legislature, an executive council, and a judiciary.
- Have a legislature consisting of one body, in which each state would have one vote.
- Have a multiperson executive council, chosen by the legislature, with the responsibility of executing national laws; its members could be removed by a vote of a majority of state governors.
- Have a judiciary appointed by the executive council.
- Have a national legislature with the ability to tax the states, proportional to their population.
- Be supreme over the state governments, with the national legislature having the right to override state law.

The Great Compromise

All the delegates at the convention knew that the legislative branch was critical, but the argument over the allocation of seats in the legislature nearly ended the proceedings. The dispute was serious, because the delegates believed that if the new national government had real powers (as they all hoped), control of the legislative branch would be critical.

The issue also boiled down to different views of representation: a *state-based approach* versus an *individual-based approach.* It should be remembered that at this time most Americans felt loyalty to their state over any sort of national allegiance. At the time, even Thomas Jefferson considered Virginia, not the United States, "my country." A widespread sense of national citizenship did not emerge until after the Civil War, some 80 years later. So the argument over representation came down to which states would have more sway in the new system, and delegates of the smaller states were not about to join a union that would put their own people at a disadvantage. *States* were the units to be represented, not the citizens. But the large states relied on an individual-based notion of representation. The new national government should speak on behalf of *citizens,* not states. If one state had significantly more citizens than another, it was self-evident that the bigger state would have more national representatives.

On June 30, 1787, Roger Sherman of Connecticut presented a compromise plan: The national legislature would have a House of Representatives, based on proportional representation (as under the Virginia Plan), but a second branch, the Senate, would contain an equal number of representatives from each state (as under the New Jersey Plan). This **Great Compromise**, sometimes called the **Connecticut Compromise**, settled the matter (see Table 2.5). Few of the delegates were completely satisfied. Indeed, some walked out of the proceedings, but most agreed that it was the best possible solution. Several of the states had tried this in their own legislatures, with much success. The plan was accepted, and the convention continued.

Great Compromise/Connecticut Compromise

An agreement at the Constitutional Convention that the new national government would have a House of Representatives—in which the number of members would be based on each state's population—and a Senate—in which each state would have the same number of representatives.

TABLE 2.5 Differences Between the Virginia Plan, the New Jersey Plan, and the Great Compromise

Issue	Virginia Plan	New Jersey Plan	The Great Compromise
Source of Legislative Power	Derived from the people and based on popular representation	Derived from the states and based on equal votes for each state	A mix; from the people for one house, from the states for the other
Legislative Structure	Bicameral	Unicameral	Bicameral; one house of equal representation, and another based on population
Executive	Size undetermined; elected and removable by Congress	More than one person; removable by state majority	Single executive; removed by impeachment
Judiciary	Life tenure, able to veto legislation in council of revision	No power over states	Life tenure, judicial review ambiguous
State Laws	Legislature can override	Government can compel obedience to national laws	National supremacy
Ratification	By the people	By the states	Ratification conventions in each state, thus allowing both the people and the states to be involved

This compromise—the creation of a Senate with an equal number of representatives from each state—has proved incredibly significant through our history. Time and again, a handful of Senators from sparsely populated states, representing a mere fraction of the overall public, has stopped a piece of legislation in its tracks. Coupled with procedural rules that give small groups of senators exceptional powers (namely the filibuster), the Senate has become the epicenter of the policy process. (This topic is discussed in greater detail in Chapter 6). Some would argue that the Senate is one of the *least* democratic institutions in our government. Others would argue that it is an institution that reflects state interests and also leads to careful, incremental policy change. As we have tried to highlight throughout this chapter, developments during the formation period continue to shape contemporary politics.

The Three-Fifths Compromise

If one of the chambers of the national legislature was to be based on population (the House of Representatives), and if taxation was to be fixed around each state's population, how would the inhabitants of each state be counted? The delegates quickly agreed that a census (a complete count) would be conducted every 10 years, and this was written into the Constitution. But *who* might be counted as an inhabitant was a vastly more difficult matter. Here we find one of the most distressing parts of the Constitutional Convention. The issue boiled down to slavery. A vast majority of slaves in North America were located in a handful of southern states, namely Georgia, Maryland, North Carolina, South Carolina, and Virginia. The delegates from these states argued that for the purposes of allocating House seats, slaves should be counted. This was quite a twist, given that slaves were considered property and were not given any rights of citizenship in these states—and the delegates from the northern states retorted as much. Yet given the huge slave populations in the southern states (40 percent or more in some states), not counting them would prove significant. If slaves were not counted, the southern states would have just 41 percent of the seats in the House; if slaves were counted, the South would have 50 percent.

One of the tragic ironies of our nation's formative years is that while notions of freedom and liberty warmed the hearts of patriots, slavery was sanctioned in the Constitution. It took two centuries and the courageous acts of men and women, like these civil rights demonstrators in Birmingham, AL, to advance the cause of liberty.

■ *Why do you suppose there was such a gap between what was preached and what was practiced?*

Once again, the convention came to a standstill, delegates threatened to bolt, and a compromise was reached. Population would be used to determine each state's delegation to the House of Representatives, and slaves would be counted as three-fifths of a white person. Put a bit differently, five slaves would equal three white persons in the census. Slaves would not be allowed to vote or to have any of the rights that Jefferson had written about in his Declaration, but they would be counted as inhabitants—or rather as three-fifths of an inhabitant—in order to get both sides to agree to the Constitution. Our history is filled with such tragic ironies.

The Sectional Compromise

Still another deal reached at the Constitutional Convention—what James Madison and some historians have called the most important compromise—related to slavery and commerce.[11] Many Northerners hated slavery and pointed out the irony of celebrating the American Revolution and creating a free nation while preserving the institution of slavery. However, southern delegates were not about to join a government that stripped them of their slaves, and even Northerners realized that abolishing slavery would shatter the South's economic base. According to one observer, "The subject haunted the closed-door debates."[12]

Most delegates agreed that the new Congress would have the power to regulate commerce, but many also worried about the potential for abuse. This was a very important power. Southern delegates in particular worried that because the House of Representatives would be based on proportional representation and the power to regulate commerce would reside in the new national government, their states' economic future was at risk. They argued that Congress should require a supermajority (a two-thirds vote, rather than a simple majority) whenever it attempted to regulate commerce. The northern delegates said no, once again worried about giving too much power to less populous states.

This led to another compromise: The Atlantic slave trade would be protected for at least 20 years. Article 1, Section 9, Clause 1 of the Constitution prohibited Congress from stopping the importation of slaves from overseas until 1808. (Slave trading within and among states was not mentioned.) In exchange, it was agreed that a simple majority of both houses of Congress would be needed to regulate commerce. Sometimes it is difficult to see how the acts of the framers have a direct bearing on our lives. Rest assured, congressional regulation of commerce has, and continues, to shape the world in which we live—from the products we buy at the store, to the roads we drive on, to what we watch on television. In short, this is one compromise that has proved extraordinarily important throughout the centuries.

The U.S. Constitution

2.7 Identify the core principles of the Constitution.

On September 17, 1787, following five hot, argumentative months, the delegates to the Constitutional Convention finished their work. After hearing the clerk read the entire document, Ben Franklin rose to the floor to remark that although the form of government they had drafted was not perfect, it was the best that could have been achieved under the circumstances. He then made a motion that each delegate sign the final version. Thirty-nine of the original fifty-five who had begun the convention did so.

Most Americans believe that our Constitution is one of the greatest schemes of government ever devised—due in no small measure to the overarching structural framework that created a vibrant yet controlled government, a system that is both rigid and flexible. Much more will be said of the provisions in the Constitution in subsequent chapters, but some key points are outlined here.

The Constitution breaks down into seven articles:

Article I: The Legislative Branch (Congress)

Article II: The Executive Branch (President)

Article III: The Judicial Branch (Courts)

Article IV: Guidelines for Relations Between States

Article V: The Amendment Process

Article VI: Federal–State Relations (Supremacy Clause); Oath for Officers

Article VII: How the Constitution Will Be Ratified

Let us consider several core principles embodied in the Constitution:

- **Three Branches of Government.** Understanding both the complexity of governance and the potential for corruption, the framers saw fit to create a system with different branches of government—legislative, executive, and judicial. The legislature would *make* the laws, the president would *enforce* the legislature's will, and the judicial branch would *interpret* the laws and *resolve* disputes according to the law.

- **Separate Institutions Sharing Powers.** One of the greatest challenges the framers faced was creating a system that was neither too weak nor too strong. A weak government would suffer the fate of the Articles of Confederation, but too strong a government might lead to corruption and an excessive concentration of power, minimize the role of the states, infringe on individual rights, and perhaps collapse in civil war. The framers believed that they had found a middle ground through the granting of specific powers for each branch while at the same time making each branch partly dependent on the others for carrying out its powers. This is called the **sharing of powers**.

    We will say a lot more about the powers and duties of each branch and the connections between the branches in the chapters that follow, but a few examples might be helpful here. Although Congress passes laws and appropriates funds, the executive branch enforces these laws and spends the money. The judicial branch can pass judgment on disputes that arise, but it must rely on the executive branch to enforce its rulings. The president can negotiate treaties with other nations, but the Senate must ratify these agreements before they take effect.

- **Checks and Balances.** Just as each branch shares powers with the others, each branch is limited ("checked") by the other two. That is to say, each branch can review, and in some ways restrict, the acts of the other branches. For instance, Congress passes laws, but the president can veto proposed legislation—and if both houses of Congress can put together a two-thirds vote, they can override a presidential veto. The president can be impeached by the House and, if convicted by a two-thirds vote in the Senate, can be removed from office. Federal judges can likewise be removed by impeachment and conviction. The judiciary can invalidate acts of Congress or the president when they are considered unconstitutional, but Congress and the states can enact amendments to the Constitution that get around judicial decisions (see Figure 2.2).

- **Representative Republicanism.** The framers wanted to create a limited government, a government "by the people," but they worried that the whims of public opinion would lead to an unstable government and perhaps even mob rule or "anarchy." As noted in the introduction to this chapter, Madison suggested the government "enlarge and refine" the public's will. Representative republicanism proved to be the solution. The system would not be a direct democracy—where each person has a say on all public matters—but rather a representative republic—in which a small group of elected leaders speak and act on behalf of the many. Members of

sharing of powers

The U.S. Constitution's granting of specific powers to each branch of government while making each branch also partly dependent on the others for carrying out its duties. For example, the Supreme Court ruled that "separate but equal" educational systems were unconstitutional in 1954, but the task of actually desegregating schools was left to President Eisenhower.

FIGURE 2.2 Shared Powers, Checks, and Balances

Many applaud this unique system of government in which each branch is somewhat dependent on the others, and each branch is in some ways checked by the others. Our system's longevity would suggest this model works, but others argue that this model makes change difficult—especially when different political parties control other branches of the government.

■ *What do you think? Does this system favor pathways for change, or does it stifle the will of the people?*

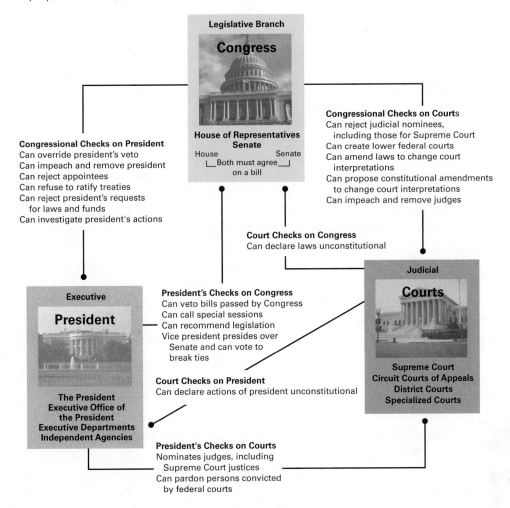

Legislative Branch

Congress

House of Representatives Senate

House   Senate
└─ Both must agree ─┘
on a bill

Congressional Checks on President
Can override president's veto
Can impeach and remove president
Can reject appointees
Can refuse to ratify treaties
Can reject president's requests
  for laws and funds
Can investigate president's actions

Congressional Checks on Courts
Can reject judicial nominees,
  including those for Supreme Court
Can create lower federal courts
Can amend laws to change court
  interpretations
Can propose constitutional amendments
  to change court interpretations
Can impeach and remove judges

Court Checks on Congress
Can declare laws unconstitutional

Executive

President

President's Checks on Congress
Can veto bills passed by Congress
Can call special sessions
Can recommend legislation
Vice president presides over
  Senate and can vote to
  break ties

Court Checks on President
Can declare actions of president unconstitutional

**The President
Executive Office of
the President
Executive Departments
Independent Agencies**

President's Checks on Courts
Nominates judges, including
  Supreme Court justices
Can pardon persons convicted
  by federal courts

Judicial

Courts

**Supreme Court
Circuit Courts of Appeals
District Courts
Specialized Courts**

the House are elected directly by the voters; under the original Constitution, senators were to be selected by the state legislatures (a provision that changed to direct popular election when the Seventeenth Amendment was adopted in 1913); and the president would be chosen by an electoral college—envisioned in 1787 as a gathering of a small group of notable leaders in each state to select the federal chief executive. The Constitution rests firmly on the representative Republican principle.

• **Federalism.** None of the framers intended to create a centralized government; instead, they envisioned a system in which a viable national government would undertake certain responsibilities and state governments would handle others. This is known as *federalism*—a system of government in which powers and functions are divided among different layers of the system. The Constitution clearly defines many of the powers of the national government, which are referred to as the **expressed powers**. State governments were considered closest to the people and thus best able to look after their health, safety, and well-being. These powers were called **police powers**. The national government, for its part, would focus on commercial matters, foreign affairs, and national security. The precise division of powers between the federal government and the states has been an ongoing, often heated issue for two

expressed powers

The powers explicitly granted to the national government in the U.S. Constitution. For instance, Article I, Section 8 grants Congress the power to regulate commerce, and Article II, Section 2 stipulates that presidents will be commander in chief of the Army and Navy.

police powers

The powers reserved to state governments related to the health, safety, and well-being of citizens. For example, many consider the job of educating children to be the concern of local governments—a police power.

centuries. Much of the energy behind the recent Tea Party movement, for example, centers on what they believe to be usurpations by the federal government.

> **POLL** Do you think the federal government has too much power, has about the right amount of power, or has too little power?

- **Reciprocity Among the States.** Although the Constitution permitted each state a degree of independence, delegates to the convention were concerned that citizens should be treated equally in every state. The framers had in mind, for example, that a marriage in one state would be recognized in other states. Two "comity" clauses accomplished this goal. The full faith and credit clause (Article IV, Section 1) said that each state must accept the legal proceedings of the other states, and the privileges and immunities clause (Article IV, Section 2) mandated that out-of-state citizens have the same legal rights as citizens of that state. While on vacation in New York, for instance, you have the same rights as people living there.

- **A Fixed System Open to Change.** The framers had in mind a rather fixed scheme of government, something that would not change with the winds of public opinion or the shifting personnel of government. What good would a constitution be if it could be changed each time new issues emerged or new people took office? At the same time, they recognized that their document was not perfect and that new pressures would arise as the nation grew and society changed. The outcome was to create a difficult but navigable route for change. The Constitution can be amended by a total of four procedures, as noted in Figure 2.3. The amendment process entails two steps: proposal and ratification, and there are two approaches for each step.

FIGURE 2.3 How the Constitution Can Be Amended

The framers wanted to create a fixed system, but at the same time allow for some modifications under certain circumstances.

■ *With just 27 amendments since 1789, would you say they got things right?*

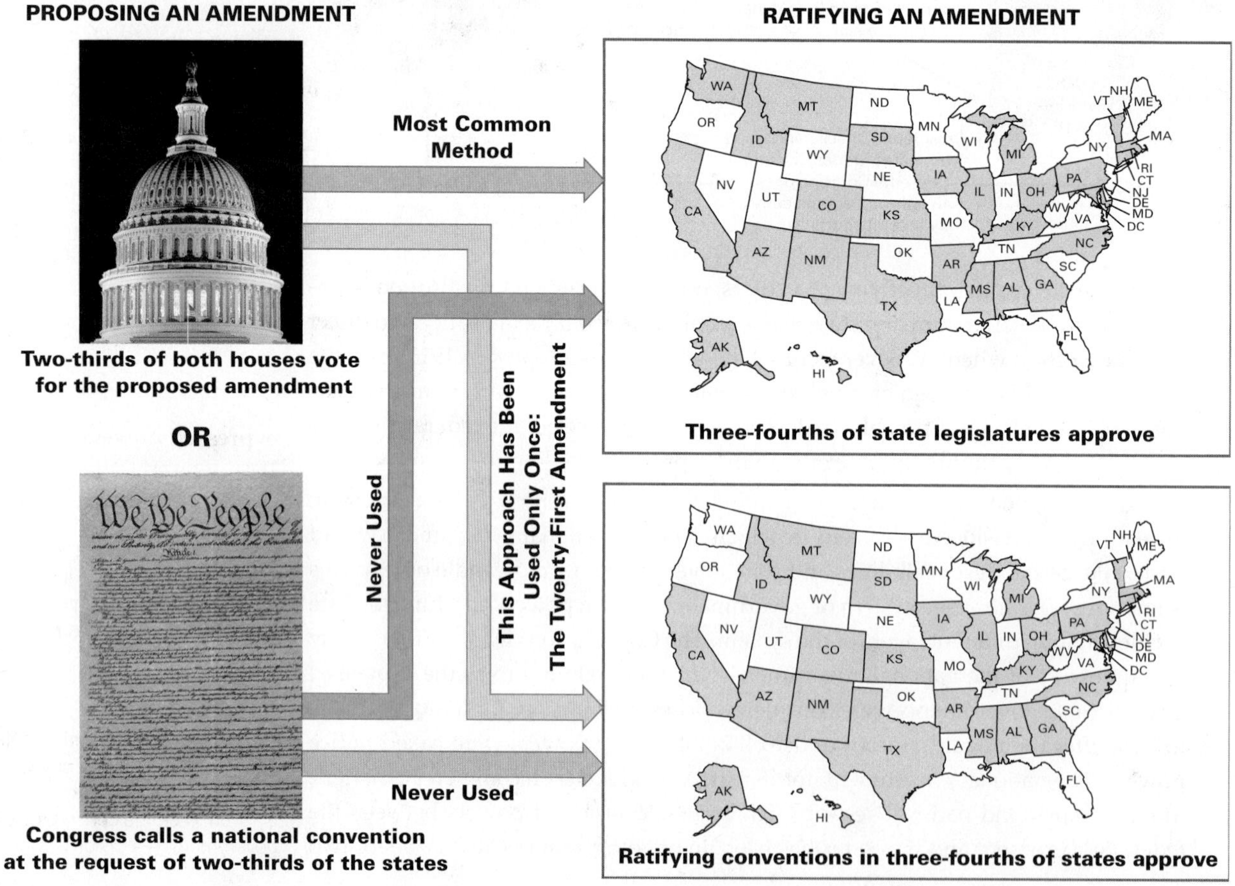

PROPOSING AN AMENDMENT

Two-thirds of both houses vote for the proposed amendment

OR

Congress calls a national convention at the request of two-thirds of the states

Never Used

This Approach Has Been Used Only Once: The Twenty-First Amendment

Most Common Method

Never Used

RATIFYING AN AMENDMENT

Three-fourths of state legislatures approve

Ratifying conventions in three-fourths of states approve

TABLE 2.6 The First 10 Amendments to the Constitution (the Bill of Rights)

Safeguards of Personal and Political Freedoms

1. Freedom of speech, press, and religion, and right to assemble peaceably and to petition government to redress grievances
2. Right to keep and bear arms

Outmoded Protection Against British Occupation

3. Protection against quartering troops in private homes

Safeguards in the Judicial Process and Against Arbitrary Government Action

4. Protection against "unreasonable" searches and seizures by the government
5. Guarantees of a grand jury for capital crimes, against double jeopardy, against being forced to testify against oneself, against being deprived of life or property without "due process of law," and against the taking of property without just compensation
6. Guarantees of rights in criminal trials, including right to speedy and public trial, to be informed of the nature of the charges, to confront witnesses, to compel witnesses to appear in one's defense, and to the assistance of counsel
7. Guarantee of right of trial by a jury of one's peers
8. Guarantees against excessive bail and the imposition of cruel and unusual punishment

Description of Unenumerated Rights and Reserved Powers

9. Assurance that rights not listed for protection against the power of the central government in the Constitution are still retained by the people
10. Assurance that the powers not delegated to the central government are reserved by the states, or to the people

- **Stability.** While the delegates at the Constitutional Convention were anxious to establish a limited government—a government that responded to the wishes and concerns of citizens—their foremost goals were to create a stable system and to provide the national government with real powers. In actuality, many of the provisions in the Constitution limit the direct role of citizens, including the Electoral College, the indirect election of Senators (changed by the Seventeenth Amendment), the lengthy terms for members of the Senate, and the lifetime appointment of federal judges. The idea was to slow the democratic process and to create a powerful and stable new government.

Since the Constitution's ratification, there have been thousands of proposals for constitutional amendments, but only 27 have made it through the journey to formal amendment. The first 10 amendments, which make up the **Bill of Rights** (see Table 2.6), were enacted during the very first session of Congress, in large part as a response to criticisms of the original Constitution by its opponents during the ratification process. It would seem that the framers accomplished their goal of creating a fixed structure that could also be changed at critical times. The Bill of Rights and several of the other amendments are discussed in greater detail in subsequent chapters.

Bill of Rights
The first 10 amendments to the U.S. Constitution, ratified in 1791, protecting civil liberties. Freedom of speech, for instance, is one of our core civil liberties, protected in the First Amendment.

The Struggle Over Ratification

2.8 Analyze how the ratification debate structured the nature of our democracy.

Reaching agreement at the Constitutional Convention on the framework of government was the first step. But for the Constitution to become the law of the land (replacing the Articles of Confederation), it would have to be ratified by 9 of the 13 states. Most contemporaries also understood that if larger states, such as Virginia, Pennsylvania, and Massachusetts, failed to ratify the document, the chances for the long-term success of the new government were slim. The framers said that nine states were needed, but most hoped that ratification would be unanimous. The document was sent to the states, where special *ratification conventions* would be held. The use of conventions was significant because it signaled the issue should be decided by a group of citizens, not simply by state legislatures.

As soon as the ratification process began, two sides emerged. The Constitution's supporters became known as **Federalists**, and its opponents were called **Anti-Federalists**. Both sides took their dispute to state capitals, to city halls, to taverns, and to kitchen tables across the nation. In the end, the matter was settled peacefully, through logic, persuasion, eloquence, and deliberation. It was the first test of our new take on democracy—and we passed.

The Federalists believed that a representative republic was possible and desirable—especially if populated by citizens "who possess [the] most wisdom to discern, and [the] most virtue to pursue, the common good of society."[13] The Anti-Federalists countered with the argument that representatives in any government must truly reflect the people, possessing an intimate knowledge of their circumstances and their needs. This could be achieved, they argued, only through small, relatively homogeneous republics, such as the existing states. A prominent Anti-Federalist put it this way: "Is it practicable for a country so large and so numerous [as the whole United States] … to elect a representative that will speak their sentiments? … It certainly is not."[14]

The Federalist Papers

Persuading citizens that the Constitution should be approved was no simple matter. Today the battle for public opinion would be fought on cable news programs, through television and radio advertisements, in direct mail, and over the Internet. In the late 1780s, the battle raged in interpersonal settings, such as formal meetings or casual tavern conversations, and in newspapers and pamphlets, which were often read aloud in group settings or passed from hand to hand. Three leading Federalists—James Madison, Alexander Hamilton, and John Jay—teamed up to write a series of essays, known collectively as ***The Federalist Papers***, on the virtues of the Constitution. These 85 essays were published in a New York City newspaper, because New York State, where Anti-Federalist sentiment ran high, was a key battleground in the campaign for ratification. The three authors adopted the *nom de plume* Publius (Latin for "public man").

Step by step, *The Federalist Papers* worked their way through the most fought-over provisions in the Constitution, laying out in clear logic and powerful prose why each element was necessary. The essays also explained what the framers had been thinking in Philadelphia while hammering out the document. Indeed, in many places, the Constitution is vague, and if you are interested in understanding what the framers had in mind, *The Federalist Papers* are the best place to look. Constitutional lawyers and Supreme Court justices still cite them.

The Federalist, No. 10, written by James Madison was particularly important. Madison begins with a detailed discussion of the dangers of "factions," groups that form to pursue the interests of their members at the expense of the national interest. "Measures," Madison notes, "are too often decided, not according to the rules of justice and the rights of the minor party, but by the superior force of an interested and overbearing majority." What can be done about factions? Madison takes the reader through different alternatives, suggesting that suppressing them would be a huge mistake: "Liberty is to faction what air is to fire." Instead, he presents a two-part solution. First, if the faction is less than a majority, then the "Republican principle" will solve things, meaning that elected officials, representing the wishes of a majority of constituents, will do the right thing. But if the faction constitutes a majority, which often happens in a community or a state, Madison writes,

> Extend the sphere, and you take in a greater variety of parties and interests; you make it less probable that a majority of the whole will have a common motive to invade the rights of other citizens; or if such a common motive exists, it will be more difficult for all who feel it to discover their own strength, and to act in unison with each other.

Using powerful, direct reasoning, Madison explains why one large nation is preferable to many smaller ones—thus challenging the logic of many political theorists who argued that only small democracies could survive. *The Federalist*, No. 10, is a lucid justification for forming the United States of America, and Madison's insistence on this seeming paradox makes him one of the greatest political philosophers of all time.

Another important essay is *The Federalist*, No. 51, also written by Madison. Here he explains the logic behind the sharing of powers and the essence of checks and balances. It is an awkward scheme of government, he admits, but also the best way to give the new government power but not *too much* power. "If men were angels, no government would be necessary," he writes. And "if angels were to govern men, neither external nor internal controls on government would be necessary." Since neither condition prevails, other precautions are needed. Madison proposes that "ambition must be made to counteract ambition"—a truly innovative idea, since all Republican thought for 2,000 years had focused on schemes to make citizens more virtuous. In brief, a system of shared powers and of checks and balances would secure the democratic character of the government. Madison also introduces a "double security": Not only will each branch of the national government be dependent on the others, the federal system itself—in which powers are divided between national and state governments—will help secure the rights of the people. Madison's argument is incredibly innovative when viewed from the standpoint of classical political theory. It had always been assumed that virtue (truly good citizens) could ensure the survival of a republic—a view that stretched back to Plato in ancient Greece. Madison, by arguing that ambition can be harnessed and checked by other ambitions through a layered system of governments, was turning political theory on its head.

The Anti-Federalists' Response

The Anti-Federalists offered clear and thought-provoking counterarguments, many of which also appeared in newspapers. Some of these essays, published under the byline Brutus (the name of the ancient Roman Republican leader who had assassinated Julius Caesar to stop him from establishing a monarchy), called attention to the very nature of democracy. Echoing traditional Republican ideology, one of the important Brutus essays insists that large governments could not heed the wishes of average citizens: "If respect is to be paid to the opinion of the greatest and wisest men who have ever thought or wrote on the science of government, we shall be constrained to conclude, that a free republic cannot succeed over a country of such immense extent...." What is more, if we want legislators to speak on behalf of citizens, as democracy demands, these leaders must know the interests of their constituents. When districts are large, as they would have to be in the proposed government, the number of constituents per legislator would be excessive. How could a legislature actually know the wishes of 30,000 residents, the number proposed for House districts? (Today there are more than 660,000 residents per House district!) The Anti-Federalists further argued that the president would inevitably build up too much power and dominate the other branches. Indeed, much of their concern centered on Article II of the Constitution, the office of president. Their worries were only slightly eased by the realization that if the Constitution were ratified, George Washington, with his spotless reputation for honesty and patriotism, would be chosen as the first president. One of the arguments against ratification of the Constitution that continues to be used today against the current political system is what appears to be the expanding scope of presidential powers.

Finally, the Anti-Federalists argued that the Constitution did not contain provisions to protect individuals. There were checks on each branch of government but none against the government's infringement on individual rights and liberties. This omission would seem glaring, yet Madison took exception to the criticism, arguing that the national government would be limited exclusively to the powers outlined in the document. It could not infringe on the rights of citizens, because it did not have the power to do so. The absence of such provisions, argued Madison, would be a clear check. But many people found this "protection by omission" worrisome.

In response to these objections, the Federalists gave in: If the states would ratify the Constitution, they agreed that the first matter of business for the new government would be to amend the Constitution to include a list of individual safeguards—a list of individual protections, which became known as the *Bill of Rights*. With this guarantee, the tide of public opinion shifted, and by June of 1788, the necessary nine states had ratified the Constitution (see Figure 2.4). In the end, all the states did so. (North Carolina at first rejected the Constitution but then hastily reconvened a ratification convention after the other states had accepted the document. Rhode Island also at first rejected the Constitution and then waited until 1790, when its convention finally voted to join the Union.) The vote in many of the state conventions was quite close. In New York, the margin was 30 to 27; in Massachusetts, 187 to 168; in New Hampshire, 57 to 47; in Virginia, 89 to 79; and (eventually) in Rhode Island, 34 to 32.

FIGURE 2.4 The Ratification of the Constitution, 1787–1790

Clearly, support for ratification of the Constitution was more robust in some parts of the country than others.

■ *Why was this true? Do you think commercial interests might have been an important factor?*

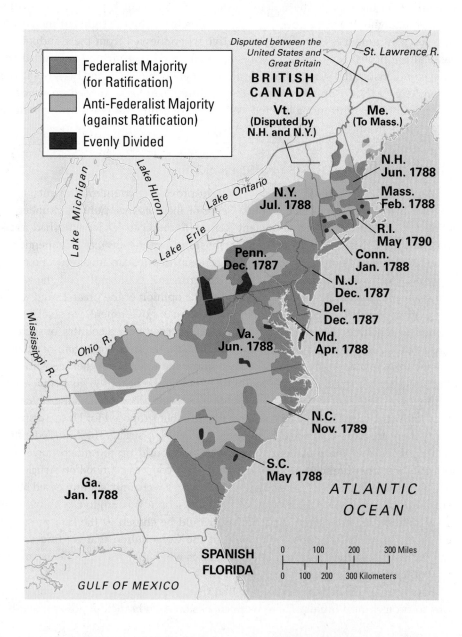

The Federalists kept their word and moved to amend the Constitution with the goals of protecting individuals from government infringements. Numerous changes were offered, and eventually 12 amendments were voted on. Ten of these amendments were successful—all passed in 1791. One additional draft amendment did not receive ratification by three-fourths of all the states until 1992, whereupon it finally became the Twenty-Seventh Amendment. This amendment delays any increase in compensation for members of Congress by at least one election cycle.

It is important to understand that the arguments advanced by the Anti-Federalists have not faded into the history books. The essence of many policy disputes center on the proper role of government and the powers of particular branches of the government. For instance, in response to the tragic events on 9/11, George W. Bush and the Congress moved quickly with a package of measures to protect citizens—dubbed the Patriot Act. But does the government, even under extreme circumstances, have the right to tap telephones without warrants? Can the federal government shape local school policies, as it did through No Child Left Behind, or tell citizens where they can and cannot build their homes, as directed by the Environmental Protection Agency? Should all business matters fall under the purview of Congress's commerce powers? Does the power to tax extend into health care policy and the ability of Congress to require citizens to have insurance? Again, many of the concerns voiced in recent years by both conservative and liberal activists center on the proper role of the federal government. Thus many of the worries of the Anti-Federalists have been given new life in recent years.

A Second Revolution?

We often assume that the war against the British had a singular focus, even though two names for the conflict are often used interchangeably: the War for Independence, and the Revolutionary War. These names suggest different ways of interpreting the same event. To some observers, the war was about breaking away from British control. A distant government had imposed laws and taxes on Americans without the input of Americans. British citizens had rights and liberties that were for some reason not extended to those citizens living in the new lands. After repeated appeals, it seemed only proper that a new nation be established—the better to protect these liberties. After victory had been won, there would be a return to the established order, much as before. Liberty and equality were wonderful theoretical constructs, but day-to-day rule should be entrusted to enlightened gentlemen, to whom ordinary people should accord great deference. Those holding this perspective argued that once rulers were elected based on the agreed upon constitutions, it was up to the people to trust and obey these rulers, not question them.

To others, the war was not only about independence but also about a dramatic change in the nature of governance. It was about shifting control from a small group of elites to *all* citizens. It was a revolution in governance and in thinking about the proper nature of government and politics. The "Spirit of '76" was about liberty, equality, and the creation of a limited government. The Revolution was a social upheaval in which common men seized equal rights, liberties, and opportunities from the wealthy landowners in America as well as the British rulers abroad.

The distinction between these perspectives—a war for independence or a revolution—was very important during the early years, as we began the difficult process of taking our first steps as a sovereign nation. The matter came to a head in the late 1790s as big issues—namely, a series of economic and foreign policy questions—pulled Americans into a debate about the role of average citizens in governance. Alexander Hamilton, Washington's secretary of the treasury, proposed a series of measures that he believed would secure the nation's long-term economic future. But many believed these policies would help the business class at the expense of the poor. As for foreign policy, our allegiance in the war between England and France was fiercely debated. Should we help England, our principal trading partner, or France, our ally in the Revolution? The group in power during this period, led by the second president, John Adams, had adopted the name Federalists (inspired by the leaders who had worked to get the Constitution ratified a few years earlier). The other group, led by Thomas Jefferson and James Madison, had begun referring to itself as the Republicans or the Democratic-Republicans, the distant precursor of today's Democratic Party.

The ferocity of the debate and the depth of feelings on each side seemed to threaten the nation in its infancy. Republicans believed that the economic policies of the Federalists and their moves to stifle criticism were an assault on free government. For many people, the issue boiled down to the role of average citizens in society and in the conduct of government. Things came to a head during the election of 1800, which pitted John Adams against Thomas Jefferson. Jefferson narrowly defeated his former friend. Republicans swept into the Congress and state legislatures across the nation.

Beyond policy changes, the election of 1800 marked three critically important events. First, one administration (led by the Federalists) was removed from power peacefully, being replaced by its political rival. A "Second Revolution" had occurred without violence—a rarity in history. This in itself was a stunning success for the new government. Americans rejected violence as an acceptable means of bringing about change. Second, efforts to stifle criticism of government leaders, through the Alien and Sedition Acts (measures passed by Adams and the Federalists), backfired. The notion of "legitimate opposition" took hold, meaning that it would be healthy for our system to have an out-of-power group keeping an eye on the in-power group. Third, the election of 1800 seemed to signify that there should be no privileged class in American politics. The process set in motion by the Declaration of Independence was indeed a revolution, not simply a war for independence.

Conclusion

One of the virtues of our political culture has been the widespread celebration of our formative period. However, a vibrant democracy did not arrive with the Boston Tea Party, the signing of the Declaration of Independence, the victory of the Continental Army, the ratification of the Constitution, or any other event. Rather, the American story has been one of triumphs and tragedies, great achievements and monumental setbacks, fits and starts. The early period began the journey of liberty and equality in our country, but most observers would agree that we have not yet arrived at a final destination.

We might also underscore the interplay of political power, authority, and legitimacy. As noted, even though a government might have the power to compel action by citizens, it may not have the authority; the cry of "no taxation without representation" by the Sons of Liberty clearly echoed this notion. But after independence was secured, the tables were turned. On paper, the Articles of Confederation seemed to give Congress an avenue for collecting funds, but the scheme contained few provisions to impose the will of the national government on the states. The central government simply lacked power. And of course, the true challenge of the framers was to find a balance between power and legitimacy.

Another theme springing from these pages is the importance of political participation. Citizens stood up, demanded liberty and freedom, and forged their own system of government. We often hear that the framers were an atypical lot—much wealthier and better educated than average citizens. Although this may be true, we still need to remember the role played by average men and women during this period, not the least of which were the patriots who helped fill the ranks of the Continental Army and local militias. Our democracy would have stumbled— indeed, it would not have taken its first step—were it not for the hard work of citizens fighting for a better life and a better system of government. Widespread political and civic engagement has been one of the many things that has distinguished the American system of government.

The American Revolution was about creating a limited government—a government that would reflect the concerns of the people. Yet the framers had to fashion a system that was both responsive and stable. In some very real ways, the Constitution limits the democratic process and harnesses the will of the people, with the goal of creating a powerful, secure system of government. On its face, you might be hard-pressed to label the original Constitution (before the amendments) a plan to enhance democratic principles. But thanks to changes to the original framework (the Bill of Rights, in particular) and the toil and sacrifice of countless citizens, numerous pathways have emerged to make the system more democratic.

Finally, we opened this chapter with a story about the perceived importance of bringing experienced leaders to power, juxtaposed with the value of fresh faces and ideas. The American Revolution was a bold move—a dramatic assault against the establishment (Parliament and King George III). In fact, one can certainly interpret Jefferson's Declaration of Independence as a call for new ideas and fresh faces. Revolutions are not "revolutionary" unless new people are brought to power. However, not long after the war ended, efforts were made to create a more powerful, stable national government. There was a hunger for well-known and trusted officials. One of the critically important selling points for the ratification of the Constitution was that George Washington, the tried-and-true leader of the Revolution, would be at the helm. After more than a decade of turbulence, there was a craving for familiarity.

During his term, Washington made a series of moves that signaled the rejection of titles of nobility and any sense of a preferred class of leaders. After a prolonged struggle to figure out what citizens might call the new leader, for example, Washington settled the matter by insisting that it be simply "Mr. President" or "Mr. Washington." He also rejected the wearing of his military uniform or other ceremonial garb, and most importantly stepped down after two terms—setting a precedent that would last for the next 150 years.

As was witnessed in the 2016 election, the struggle between the two models of leadership can be spirited. Vermont Senator Bernie Sanders called his vigorous struggle for the Democratic presidential nomination a "revolution," and many in Donald Trump's camp labeled their efforts similarly. Indeed, the battle between experience and new leadership, between well-known political families and true newcomers, has been on-going since the formation of our nation. A cyclical process is probably at work, where citizens yearn for change and fresh ideas, but after a period of time seek constancy and stability. In other words, if you favored experience in the 2016 election, rest assured there will be other opportunities in the years ahead.

CONFRONTING POLITICS AND POLICY

Throughout the course of our nation's history, a number of constitutional provisions have proved to be controversial. One of those areas of recurrent dispute has been the precise reach of the federal government. As noted in this chapter, one of the key differences between the Articles of Confederation and the Constitution is that the latter boasts explicit powers (detailed mostly in Article I). Yet, the Tenth Amendment—the last of the Bill of Rights—provides states with certain powers. It states, "The powers not delegated to the United States by the Constitution, nor prohibited by it to the States, are reserved to the States respectively, or to the people." The idea behind the amendment was simple: Lay a foundation for state prerogative, and assuage fears of a large, tyrannical federal government. But as the federal government moved into more and more aspects of American life, and as judicial decisions buttressed broad federal powers, the Tenth Amendment seemed to lose relevance. In the past few years, however, there has been a growing movement, mostly among conservative activists, to rein in the federal government by adding new life to the Tenth Amendment. One proposal that has proven particularly controversial is for certain state governments to take control of federal lands. In Utah, for instance, the state legislature and the governor passed a resolution calling on the federal government to "return" millions of acres of federal lands to the state. Most notably, the state would lay claim to the Grand Staircase-Escalante National Monument in southern Utah, some of the 1.9 million-acres set aside by President Bill Clinton in 1996. This measure, and many others like it, is strongly backed by state's rights advocates. But, as you might imagine, many are opposed to such measures, particularly as they relate to national lands and forests.

ACTION STEPS

1. Do you agree that the federal government has been given too much power in recent decades, and that steps should be taken to return some of these powers to the states?

2. Where do other Americans stand on these types of issues? For example, do a majority of citizens believe that the federal government has become too powerful?

3. If you do believe in "reinvigorating the Tenth Amendment," would you go so far as to shift control of lands from federal to state control? If so, would that include national parks?

4. What other issues of this sort will emerge in the coming years?

› REVIEW THE CHAPTER

The Nature of Government and Politics

2.1 Identify the difference between government and politics. (p. 33)

Before beginning our exploration of American government, it is important to understand the difference between government and politics, power and authority, and legitimacy. Government refers to the official rules and institutions that structure the development and implementation of public policy (what government does). Politics, on the other hand, refers to the various ways individuals and groups seek to influence the final outcome of policy disputes. A governmental entity is said to have authority if there is a legal foundation for a particular action. Legitimacy means that most citizens believe an action taken is proper. Thus, authority is based on institutional elements, but legitimacy is based on perceptions. For example, while the federal government might have the authority to regulate elementary school curricula, many think this should be done at the local level.

Types of Governments

2.2 Differentiate between different types of governments. (p. 35)

There are many types of governments, the foremost distinguishing characteristics being who is allowed to participate and how decisions are made. Using these two dimensions, systems such as monarchies, oligarchies, and totalitarian regimes are more easily understood. In brief, as the number of participants in a system expands, the system moves more toward a democracy. This section also explores the differences between a democracy and a republic. In a direct democracy, all citizens participate in all policy questions, but in a republic, citizens ask others—usually elected officials—to make policy decisions.

Early Governance in America

2.3 Describe how forces in Colonial America helped set the stage for the American Revolution. (p. 37)

During the pre-Revolution period, governance was not exactly democratic. Royally appointed governors ruled most colonies with few checks by citizens. Yet, the seeds of a democratic movement were planted. For example, most colonies had assemblies, where delegates came to discuss issues of concern, and to provide reports and suggestions to the governors. We might say that these were budding legislative institutions. Moreover, notions of liberty and equality were increasingly discussed during this time.

The American Revolution

2.4 Identify the core principles of the American Revolution. (p. 39)

When Abraham Lincoln spoke of our nation's birth as "Four score and seven years ago," he was referring to the Revolution and to the signing of the Declaration of Independence, not to the ratification of the Constitution in 1789. This is because the core of the "American experiment" in self-governance springs from this revolutionary period. Ideas of liberty, equality, self-governance, and economic advancement set in motion a revolution, and later a new, democratic system of government.

The Articles of Confederation

2.5 Determine the reasons for the failure of the Articles of Confederation. (p. 46)

Our first stab at self-governance was a flop, because there was no way for the new national government to regulate commerce, raise needed funds, or conduct foreign policy. Most significantly, the system was unstable, ready to collapse at any moment. However, the experience under the Articles of Confederation shaped the motivations of the framers, thus shaping the Constitution and our system of government.

The Constitutional Convention

2.6 Assess how compromises at the Constitutional Convention shaped our political system. (p. 47)

We often hear that the framers came to the Constitutional Convention eager to create a stronger national government. But the truth is more complex. Numerous, often conflicting motivations drove this historic event, and from these concerns our Constitution was born. The many compromises, such as dividing power between states and the federal government, and between branches of government, also speak to the interests of the framers and to the nature of our political system. We have a democracy, but also a system of government that seeks to "enlarge and refine" the public will.

The U.S. Constitution

2.7 Identify the core principles of the Constitution. (p. 51)

The Constitution is made up of both broad principles, such as the sharing of powers and the checks and balances, and specifics, such as the enumeration of congressional powers. In order to understand how our government operates, both elements must be acknowledged. For example, while the Constitution affords Congress the duty to create public policy, the bicameral legislature may lead the Senate to have a very different take on policy questions. Added on top of this, the president can veto legislation and is also responsible for implementation of legislation. And, finally, the courts may declare all or parts of legislation unconstitutional.

The Struggle over Ratification

2.8 Analyze how the ratification debate structured the nature of our democracy. (p. 55)

While Lincoln might have been right to assert that our nation began in 1776, this does not mean that who we are as a people was defined at that point. There have been numerous transformative events in our history, and this short section takes a look at the election of 1800. Here, political parties—each representing different versions of what they believed was "just" public policy—fought to win the presidency. In the end, the Jeffersonian Republicans won the contest, and John Adams was sent into private life. More importantly, the election of 1800 showed that the new system of government could change leaders and policies peacefully—a rarity in world history at that time. Perhaps political parties were not so bad; they could even play an important role in the new system of government.

❭ LEARN THE TERMS

power, p. 33
authority, p. 33
monarchy, p. 35
constitutional monarchy, p. 35
dictator, p. 35
oligarchy, p. 35
pluralism, p. 35
democracy, p. 36
republic, p. 36
representative democracy, p. 36
totalitarian regime, p. 36

authoritarian regime, p. 36
constitutional government, p. 36
Pilgrims, p. 37
Mayflower Compact, p. 37
French and Indian War, p. 38
Great Squeeze, p. 38
natural rights, p. 41
social contract theory, p. 41
Shays's Rebellion, p. 47
Constitutional Convention, p. 47
Virginia Plan, p. 48

New Jersey Plan, p. 48
Great Compromise, p. 49
Connecticut Compromise, p. 49
sharing of powers, p. 52
expressed powers, p. 53
police powers, p. 53
Bill of Rights, p. 55
Federalists, p. 56
Anti-Federalists, p. 56
The Federalist Papers, p. 56

❭ EXPLORE FURTHER

In the Library

Bailyn, Bernard. *The Ideological Origins of the American Revolution.* Cambridge, MA: Harvard University Press, 1967.

Bowen, Catherine Drinker. *Miracle at Philadelphia: The Story of the Constitutional Convention May–September 1787.* Boston: Back Bay Books, 1986.

Burns, James MacGregor. *The Vineyard of Liberty.* New York: Knopf, 1982.

Butler, Jon. *Becoming America: The Revolution Before 1776.* Cambridge, MA: Harvard University Press, 2000.

Collier, Christopher. *Decision in Philadelphia: The Constitutional Convention of 1787.* New York: Ballantine Books, 2007.

Ellis, Joseph J. *Founding Brothers: The Revolutionary Generation.* New York: Vintage Books, 2002.

Ellis, Joseph J. *American Creation.* New York: Vintage, 2007.

Jensen, Merrill. *The Articles of Confederation: An Interpretation of the Social-Constitutional History of the Revolution, 1774–1781.* Madison, WI: University of Wisconsin Press, 1959.

Ketcham, Ralph. *The Anti-Federalist Papers and the Constitutional Convention Delegates.* New York: Signet, 2003.

Morgan, Edmund S. *The Meaning of Independence: John Adams, Thomas Jefferson, George Washington.* New York: Norton, 1978.

Parenti, Michael. *Democracy for the Few.* 9th ed. New York: Wadsworth, 2010.

Sharp, Gene. *From Dictatorship to Democracy.* New York: Serpents Tail, 2012.

Smith, Page. *The Shaping of America: A People's History of the Young Republic.* New York: McGraw-Hill, 1979.

Wills, Garry. *Inventing America: Jefferson's Declaration of Independence.* New York: Random House, 1978.

Wood, Gordon S. *The Radicalism of the American Revolution.* New York: Vintage Books, 1993.

On the Web

Many theorists have written about the relationship between power and authority. This Web site offers some thoughts from Montesquieu, an eighteenth-century French philosopher whose writings had a great impact on the framers of our political system: *http://www.lonang.com/exlibris/montesquieu/sol-02.htm.*

Numerous Web sites chart differences between types of governments around the world. Two of interest include *http://home.earthlink.net/~kingsidebishop/id2.html* and *http://www.stutzfamily.com/mrstutz/WorldAffairs/typesofgovt.html.*

To better understand some of the developments from the first 100 years of our nation's history, visit From Revolution to Reconstruction: *http://odur.let.rug.nl/~usa.*

For general information on numerous early American documents, try the Avalon Project at Yale University at *http://avalon.law.yale.edu.*

Visit the Annenberg Learning Center: A Biography of America at *http://www.learner.org/biographyofamerica.*

Learn about the periods before, during, and after the Constitutional Convention at the History Place Web site at *http://www.historyplace.com.*

To access the Declaration of Independence, the Constitution, and other key documents in our nation's history, see the Library of Congress, Primary Documents in American History at *http://memory.loc.gov/ammem/help/constRedir.html.*

For an online, searchable copy of *The Federalist Papers,* see *http://www.law.ou.edu/hist/federalist.*

For an online look at the Anti-Federalist Papers, see *http://thefederalistpapers.org/anti-federalist-papers.*

FEDERALISM

Michelle Obama has made nutrition and fitness a hallmark of her time as First Lady. The less controversial element of her initiative to fight childhood obesity and promote healthy living is the "Let's Move" campaign. Less popular is the push to have more nutritionally balanced lunches provided in public schools. Many argue that local school districts should have flexibility in determining options for students; others are concerned about the costs associated with the nutritional guidelines.

■ *Do you think the federal government should be involved in promoting healthy eating in schools, or should local school districts be free to feed students whatever they feel appropriate even if it isn't nutritious?*

→ LEARNING OBJECTIVES

3.1 Explain how and why the framers divided authority between layers of government.

3.2 Characterize dual federalism both before and after the Civil War.

3.3 Compare and contrast cooperative and creative federalism.

3.4 Trace the evolution of federalism in recent decades.

Promoting healthy nutrition for school-aged children seems like a high consensus and low conflict issue. Childhood obesity has risen at alarming rates. Today, more than one-third of children and adolescents are overweight or obese with the percent of adolescents being obese quadrupling between 1980 and 2012.[1] We know that obesity is linked to diet and exercise so promoting both seems logical.

Michelle Obama has made fighting childhood obesity her hallmark issue with her Let's Move Campaign. The campaign is designed to raise a healthier generation of children and end childhood obesity within one generation. The program promotes healthy nutrition and physical action. The National Football League (NFL®) has even gotten on board with the NFL Play 60 campaign designed to encourage children to play 60 minutes a day to reverse the trend of childhood obesity.

Given these initiatives and research linking childhood obesity to long-term adult health issues, it should be of little surprise that the federal government has moved to update nutritional standards in school lunches. The United States Department of Agriculture (USDA) sets the rules for nutritional standards and has recently moved to require schools to increase the availability of fruits, vegetables, whole grains, and low-fat milk as well as to reduce the amount of sodium and saturated fats in school lunches. Sounds reasonable, right?

Not so fast. States are very concerned as these new standards are likely to cost state and local schools $479 million each year. These federal guidelines are not associated with extra funding and are only one of many new mandates that will be imposed on the states. Another example of a new unfunded mandate comes from the Environmental Protection Agency (EPA). The EPA issued a new rule on emission standards [rule 111(d)] which will reduce hazardous air pollutants (including mercury). Once again, sounds positive, right? The rule will be positive to promote clean air, but the Office of Management and Budget (OMB) estimates that this rule will cost state, local, and tribal governments approximately $294 million in 2015 alone. Concerns about unfunded mandates prompted Congress to pass the Unfunded Mandates Reform Act of 1995, however federal agencies often issue new rules without looking at the economic impact as required by the law.

Examples like these of rules designed to promote healthy nutrition for children and clean air for us all seem positive until we begin to examine the costs associated with the programs. Many states, while they support the goals of the programs, argue that they cannot afford to comply with these new federal rules and continue to urge Congress to examine and limit the use of unfunded mandates by executive agencies.[2]

HOW HAS FEDERALISM IN THE UNITED STATES EVOLVED?

Increasingly we turn to our federal government to address what were traditionally seen as local issues—from environmental cleanups to the treatment of the flu. Many are concerned that we rely too heavily upon Washington and that we need to decrease the authority and budget of the federal government. Others are comfortable with an active federal government, arguing that an energetic and vigorous national government is necessary to respond quickly to health and national security threats and to promote equality. At what point do we hold states and localities liable, and conversely, what responsibility does the federal government have to ensure the health and welfare of its citizens?

Dividing Governmental Authority

3.1 Explain how and why the framers divided authority between layers of government.

Governmental authority in the United States has been a source of conflict for more than two centuries. Unlike countries such as the United Kingdom and France, which are governed under a **unitary system** (that is, a system in

unitary system
A system of government in which political power and authority are located in one central government that runs the country and that may or may not share power with regional subunits.

federal system

A system of government in which power and authority are divided between a central government and regional subunits.

which all ruling authority rests in a single national government), the United States divides powers and responsibilities among layers of governments, in a **federal system**.

The framers included in the Constitution a division of power and responsibility between the national and state governments to create yet another check against potential abuses. Yet, our unique system has created much uncertainty and many practical management problems. At times in our history, it has even led to violence. Indeed, the greatest crisis in our history, the Civil War, was very much about "states' rights" versus the authority of the national government. We can imagine why foreign policy would fall under the scope of the national government, but what about the general welfare of American citizens? Is crime a problem for a local government, a state government, or the national government? Should the national government be able to control the conduct of doctors and regulate what services they can or cannot provide? How about lawyers, electricians, or hairdressers? If a state considers the medical use of marijuana permissible, should the federal government be able to step in and ban it? Should the federal government be allowed to dictate to states who should be eligible to marry whom?

Then there is the issue of transportation. Just because the Constitution says that Congress shall regulate commerce, does that mean the federal government is responsible for fixing all roads and bridges? Would we want the federal government telling us how many stop signs to put up on a stretch of road? That may seem an extreme example, yet the issue of speed limits has been controversial for decades. In the mid-1970s, when the nation faced a fuel shortage, one of the measures used to save energy was fixing the national speed limit at 55 mph. Many states, especially those in the West, refused to abide by the federal law. In response, Congress threatened to cut off federal highway aid to any state that did not enforce this law. Some states rejected the money and set the speed limits they wanted. Others simply lowered the fines for speeding tickets. The federally mandated 55 mph limit has since been dropped, but some states still abide by it while others allow up to 80 mph (a few roads in Texas allow speeds up to 85 mph). If you exceed the 80 mph limit in Montana, you might get a $40 fine. In many other states, it could cost you more than $300.

In education, law, medicine, transportation, environmental protection, crime, and many other areas of American life, the line between federal and state control has been controversial and fluid. For example, until more recently, education had been largely the domain of state and local governments. However, No Child Left Behind, which George W. Bush helped enact in 2001 with high levels of bipartisan support, instituted standards-based education reform that required states to develop assessments of basic skills as a condition for receiving additional federal funding for education. A more recent example of the federal government getting involved in education is the Common Core State Standards (which aims to raise student achievement in math and language arts/literacy). The Department of Education has also gotten more involved in higher education with more aggressive investigations in sexual assaults on college campuses (under the authority of Title IX). Another example of the increased interaction between the state and federal levels comes in the area of cleanup after natural disasters. It used to be that cleanup after a flood or hurricane was entirely the responsibility of state and local governments. Today, everyone expects the federal government to take the lead. Indeed, one of the low points in President George W. Bush's administration was the federal government's inept response following Hurricane Katrina in the summer of 2005. Ironically, many of these critics are the same people who argue that the federal government is getting too big and should stay out of the affairs of local governments.

You might be tempted to draw a conclusion that things have moved toward more federal control, but even if this is true in some policy areas, in other spheres the states have been given more control and greater responsibility. Politicians eager to promote local control often suggest that state governments are the "laboratories of democracy,"

The Common Core has generated much criticism across the country. Many are concerned over the federally mandated tests as well as the proposal of tying teachers' performance to the test results. Pictured here are children at a rally in New York City urging local officials to opt out of Common Core testing.

■ *Do you think tying teacher performance to test results promotes accountability or places too much emphasis on testing?*

a concept first enunciated by Supreme Court Justice Louis Brandeis in 1932, meaning that difficult challenges are more likely to be resolved when 50 entities are working to find innovative solutions rather than just the federal government.

This chapter explores the complex issues surrounding federalism in the United States. As with other elements in our political system, many changes have occurred over the years. Today, the relationship between the states and the federal government is vastly different from what it was at the dawn of our nation's history. Rather than being simply a unique, interesting aspect of our government, the debate over governmental authority has been at the center of most of the trying events in our history, and it is likely to influence future directions in American government.

The goal of this chapter is to help you understand that public policy does not spring simply from "government" but rather from different *layers* of government. It would make little sense, for example, to lobby members of Congress to change the zoning laws in a particular town or to ask a city council to help lower the cost of prescription drugs. Different governments are responsible for different policies in the United States. This chapter explains why we have such a unique system, examines its advantages and disadvantages, and explores changes over the past 225 years. Politics is not simply about pushing government in a given direction; instead, it is about knowing *which* government to push and how.

National Government: Reasons for Federalism

The federal structure of the United States is not unique. But most countries, whether or not they are democratic, have unitary systems (see Table 3.1). In those countries, viable and active local authorities may exist, but the national government has **sovereignty**. This means that the national government has the ultimate governing authority and the final say. In the United Kingdom, for example, Parliament can change city and town government boundaries at any time. It may allow certain regions to create their own government, as has been the case with Scotland and Northern Ireland, but at any point, Parliament can abolish these structures and override any of their policies.

Why, then, would the United States choose to create a federal system in which sovereignty is divided among different levels of government? The history of government in North America provides one explanation. During the period of exploration and discovery, set into motion by Christopher Columbus's voyage in 1492, a number of nations—including England, France, Spain, Portugal, and the Netherlands—sought

sovereignty

The exclusive right of an independent state to reign supreme and base absolute power over a geographic region and its people.

TABLE 3.1 Federal, Confederate, and Unitary Systems of Government

Each type of governmental system uses a different means to enact policies.

■ *Look at this table carefully; which system do you think works best? Why?*

Federal	Confederation	Unitary
Governmental authority is divided between a national government and state governments.	Ultimate authority comes from the states.	Ultimate governmental authority comes from the national government.
United States under the Constitution (1789–present), Australia, Brazil, Germany, Mexico, Nigeria	United States under the Articles of Confederation (1781–1789), Confederate States of America (1861–1865), Confederation of Independent States (states of the former Soviet Union)	France, Spain, Tanzania
Let's Consider How Each System of Government Would Work to Promote Clean Water Restoration Plans.		
The federal government would pass broad guidelines and provide some financial incentives, but the implementation of the clean water plans would be left to state and local governments.	The central government would pass broad guidelines with the hope that state governments agree to comply.	The central government would pass specific guidelines and ensure that local governments comply with national decrees.

to establish colonies in the New World. England eventually planted more than 13 colonies on the North American mainland. As settlers eventually moved to these colonies, they set up their own governments.

Before setting foot on American soil in 1620, the Pilgrims drew up the Mayflower Compact, which was essentially an agreement to form a government. In the Virginia colony, a legislative body called the House of Burgesses was established. Eventually, each colony established its own governing structure. These governments were not sovereign, of course, given that the English Parliament and king could dissolve them at any time (and did so on various occasions), but as our nation began to take shape, many distinct governing entities existed. Moreover, there existed a great deal of suspicion and rivalry among the colonies and among the early states. One of the greatest hurdles confronted by those anxious to break ties with Great Britain on the eve of the American Revolution was to get people to consider themselves as citizens of an American nation rather than just citizens of their individual colonies.

After independence had been won, the central point of dispute over the ratification of the Constitution in 1787 and 1788 was the extent to which the new national government might, at some future time, take over the role of state governments. Many Americans agreed that a stronger national government was needed to regulate commerce and deal with foreign nations, but few envisioned that the national government would be fully sovereign.

One explanation for our federal system lies, then, in the historical roots of the United States. Our nation was born through the fusing of independent states—states that would never have agreed to a merger if giving up their independence had been part of the deal. Federalism was a compromise. We might also point to the writings of philosophers John Locke, Adam Smith, and Thomas Hobbes who guided the thinking of the framers of our system. Another influential philosopher was the Frenchman Baron de Montesquieu, who in the early eighteenth century wrote about the virtues of dividing power and authority between different parts of the government. This might be done, he argued, by having different branches of government *and* by creating layers of governmental authority. James Madison echoes Montesquieu's idea in *The Federalist*, No. 51:

> In the compound republic of America, the power surrendered by the people is first divided between two distinct governments, and then the portion allotted to each subdivided among distinct and separate departments. Hence a double security arises to the right of the people.

In other words, federalism, coupled with the checks and balances and the sharing of powers at the national level, would help guarantee a republican government.

Montesquieu also argued that republican institutions were more likely to flourish in smaller political systems, yet such small states were incapable of defending themselves against attack. The problem could be solved by the creation of a system that would permit a consensus for domestic affairs among the separate governing units but provide unified action for the common defense.[3]

Still another significant factor behind federalism is the geographic, cultural, and economic diversity of the United States. The distinctiveness of different American regions has eroded dramatically in recent decades, due in large measure to changes in transportation, entertainment, and the economy. A Wal-Mart in Boise, Idaho, looks exactly the same as a Wal-Mart in Bath, Maine. Kids in Albany, Georgia, watch the same Saturday morning cartoons as kids in Albany, New York. However, throughout most of our history, culture, language, demographics, economic conditions, and other aspects of life varied in different regions, states, and even communities. And the United States remains one of the most diverse nations in the world, which has contributed to a sense of a localized citizenship.

Finally, federalism made sense in the American setting for practical reasons. Historians agree that if in 1787 the separate states had not been permitted to have significant powers, the Constitution would never have been ratified.

State and Local Governments

Our local and state governments control nearly all aspects of our daily lives, many of which go unrealized. State and local governments are responsible for police and fire departments, utilities, sewage systems, schools, libraries, and zoning laws. Most of our interactions—from parking and speeding tickets to building permits and issuing marriage licenses—are with local and state governmental officials. State and local governments make many of the decisions that impact our families and our occupations. For example, states determine how easy or difficult it is to end a marriage and divorce. They also intervene when families are in trouble from domestic violence, oversee custody battles, and manage child protective services. State and localities make many decisions about how local schools function, what they teach, and who they hire. They regulate our professions and our transportation. States and localities administer many of the social programs—like Medicaid, unemployment benefits, and public housing—that are funded by the federal government. Interestingly, though state governments make many decisions that contribute directly to the quality of our lives, we tend to be less interested in, participate less in, and are less informed about state and local governments than our national government.

In *The Federalist*, No. 10, James Madison stated "the federal Constitution forms a happy combination in this respect; the great and aggregate interests being referred to the national, the local and particular to the State legislatures." Consequently, aggregate issues like printing money, declaring war, protecting the national defense (through the maintenance of the army and navy and negotiating treaties with foreign governments), regulating interstate and foreign commerce, and establishing a post office are tasks assigned by the Constitution to the federal government. Other issues that impact localities such as issuing licenses for driving, hunting, and marriage; regulating intrastate commerce; conducting elections; and caring for public health and safety are left to the state and local governments. This sharing of power, while not perfect and often controversial, is one of the key features of our governmental structure.

The Tenth Amendment to the United States Constitution states, "The powers not delegated to the United States by the Constitution, nor prohibited by it to the States, are reserved to the States respectively, or to the people." Consequently, state governments have a constitutional right to exist and a long tradition of significance in American politics. To ensure proper functioning, all states have constitutions that are often far more elaborate and complicated than the federal Constitution.

All state constitutions are legally inferior to the federal Constitution (as the federal Constitution is the supreme law of the land) but in many aspects some are more progressive than the federal Constitution. For example, the Vermont Constitution, adopted in 1777, abolished slavery long before the federal Constitution did with the Thirteen Amendment in 1865. State constitutions tend to be much longer than the U.S. Constitution. Alabama currently has the longest state constitution, with over 770 amendments, many of which only apply to particular localities within the state. State constitutions average about four times longer than the federal Constitution and tend to be much easier to amend. Most state constitutions are modeled after the federal Constitution and typically include a bill of rights and outline the structure of the state government. While the federal Constitution mandates that all states uphold a "republican form" of government, the three-branch structure is not a requirement though all states do divide authority similarly among the legislative, executive, and judicial branches.

Structure of State Governments

Many states allow for more direct representation in government than does the federal Constitution (which relies more heavily upon representative democracy). In many states, multiple offices within the executive branch are directly elected. In all but eleven states, members of the judicial branch are subjected to election at some point during their judicial tenure. Many states allow citizens to vote directly on public policy provisions through initiatives and/or referendums and nineteen states have provisions that allow voters to remove elected officials from office. These provisions are based upon the premise that state and local governments ought to be directly and closely linked to the people.

STATE LEGISLATURES All state legislatures are bicameral except Nebraska's, which is unicameral and nonpartisan. The larger chamber is typically called the house of representatives but can sometimes be called the assembly or house of delegates. They vary in size from 40 members in Alaska to 400 in New Hampshire although the average is 108 members. In nearly all states, members of the lower house serve two-year terms but in a handful of states they serve four-year terms. The other chamber, the senate, is on average composed of approximately 40 individuals typically serving 4-year terms, although 11 states have senators with two-year terms.[4]

State legislatures can be differentiated by the level of institutionalism present. Some state legislatures are highly institutionalized—which political scientists characterize as having high levels of membership continuity, long sessions, autonomous and specialized committee structures, large professional staffs and resources, and an emphasis on seniority in according leadership positions. Legislatures, which are considered institutionalized, are also called "professional," while those that are not structurally institutionalized are considered "amateur." Amateur legislatures are characterized by shorter sessions, high turnover rates, small professional staffs, and low wages. The amateur model is supported by those who prefer a limited state government constituted by representatives with ties to their communities who will serve for a short period of time then return to their permanent careers. Service is seen as a public good that is to be shared. States that have more professional legislatures see service as a profession that values experience addressing complex issues. About one half of state legislatures are seen as professional and one half are seen as amateur. Currently 22 states pay their legislators $20,000 or less per year, with 7 states paying nominal per day or monthly wages to legislators while in session. The rest of the states opt for a more substantial salary as service is seen as a full-time job. California currently has the highest pay scale, with legislators making an average of $100,113 per year. In contrast, Texas, a diverse state with many divergent needs and a large population, only pays its legislators $7,200 a year.[5] New Hampshire only pays its state legislators $200 per two year term, with no per diem to offset travel and other expenses. The idea of a part-time citizen-legislator (which characterizes those serving in amateur legislatures) is attractive to many, but having experience dealing with the complicated problems facing states can be of great value. Additionally, amateur legislatures may attract more elite individuals as many cannot afford to give up their full-time paychecks to travel to the state capital for minimal compensation while the legislature is in session. The attraction with citizen-legislators is one of the factors justifying term limits (which are in place in 15 states). Term limits were instituted in most states in the early 1990s to reform state legislatures. Most were instituted to promote turnover with the ideal of electing citizen-legislators who would serve for a few years then return to their communities and prior occupations.

State legislators today are more likely to be older, white, Christian, affluent, and well-educated, but the ranks of legislators are becoming more diverse. For example, the occupational backgrounds of legislators are becoming more varied. In 1976, 22 percent of state legislators were attorneys—since 2007, that number has remained around 15 percent. More legislators today, than ever before, consider themselves full-time legislators. Eight percent of current legislators consider themselves retired (down from 12 percent in 2007) and 13 percent are business owners (down from 16 percent in 1976). The average age of legislators is 56 (three years younger than the average age of Congress but nine years older than the national average). Male legislators are on average two years younger than women legislators and members of state senates are older than members of state houses. The National Conference of State Legislatures notes that the youngest state legislator in 2016 was 20-year-old Saira Blair (Republican from West Virginia, first elected in 2014 when she was 18 years old) and the oldest legislator was 95-year-old John Yates (Republican from Georgia). State legislators are better educated than the public with 40 percent having advanced degrees (compared with only 11 percent of the general population).[6] The percent of women elected to the state legislature has increased steadily since the 1970s, but has seen little increase in the last 10 years (see Figure 3.1). As seen in Figure 3.2, the percent of African Americans and Latinos elected to state legislatures nationally has increased slightly in the last 20 years, but both groups, like women, remain underrepresented. In 2017, Republicans control 25 state governments, Democrats control 5, and 19 are split between the parties (Nebraska has a non-partisan, unicameral legislature).

FIGURE 3.1 Women in State Legislatures

SOURCE: Center for American Women and Politics, Fact Sheet Archive on Women in State Legislatures, accessed on February 3, 2016 at http://www.cawp.rutgers.edu/fact-sheet-archive-women-state-legislatures-1975-2016 (the most current data available at the time of publication).

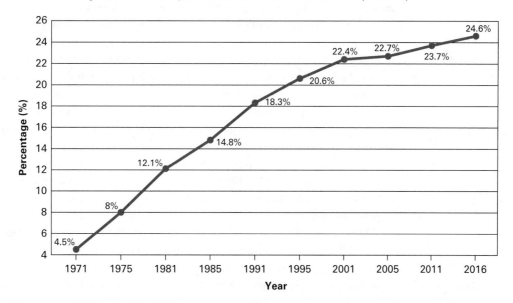

FIGURE 3.2 Percentage of National Legislators Who are African American and Latino

SOURCE: Data compiled from legislator data published by the National Conference of State Legislatures, National Black Caucus of State Legislators, and NALEO Educational Fund, accessed on February 3, 2016, http://www.ncsl.org/portals/1/documents/about_state_legislatures/raceethnicity.pdf.

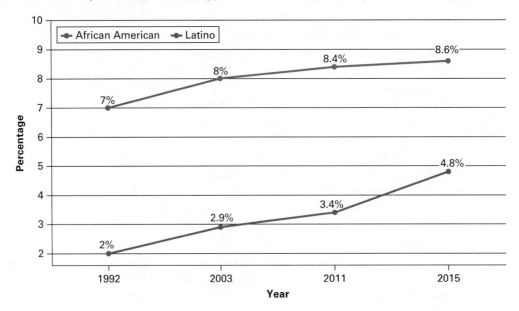

EXECUTIVE Governors serve four-year terms in all states, except in New Hampshire and Vermont, where they have two-year terms. All states, except Virginia, allow governors to serve consecutive terms and all states have a direct election of governors. Currently, 36 states have some form of term limit for governors, the most common allows for two consecutive terms, re-eligible for election after 4 years. Throughout the country, there exists a great variety of power accorded to governors. In some states, the governor is a very powerful office. In other states, like Texas, other officials (like the lieutenant governor) can exert more influence and have more power in state politics than the governor. Gubernatorial salaries range from a high in Pennsylvania of $190,823 in 2016 to a low in Maine of $70,000 with the average being $134,160.[7]

The formal and informal powers of the governor have grown throughout time. Most states reluctantly created an executive. Initially, the power of the executive was very limited and shared. In most state constitutions executive authority is divided among a governor, lieutenant governor, secretary of state, treasurer, and attorney general. Currently, many governors have the power of appointment. Many have formal influence over policy decisions and exert considerable power in the legislature. Most governors prepare the state budget, are given the power to serve as commander-in-chief of the state's National Guard, and can pardon or commute criminal sentences. Most states give the governor a veto power, which the state legislature can override. In most states, governors have a line-item veto that allows them to accept part of an appropriations bill while rejecting other components of the same law. The line-item veto is a power not given to the president and is thought to encourage fiscal responsibility. Political scientist Margaret Ferguson has measured and characterized the formal and informal powers for governors across the country as their powers vary considerably (see Figure 3.3). Strong governors typically have significant appointment powers, can serve for multiple terms, can veto legislation, and have significant budgetary powers.

Throughout the history of the United States, the vast majority of governors have been white, Christian, older males. Thirty-seven women have served as governor in 27 states (and one woman has served as the governor of Puerto Rico). All states except Maine have elected a female to state-wide elective office. In 2017 five women

FIGURE 3.3 Ranking of Formal Powers of Governors—From Strong to Weak

SOURCE: Margaret Ferguson, "Governors and the Executive Branch" in *Politics in the American States: A Comparative Analysis*, 10ᵗʰ ed., eds. Virginia Gray, Russell L. Hanson and Thad Kousser (Washington D.C.: CQ Press, 2013).

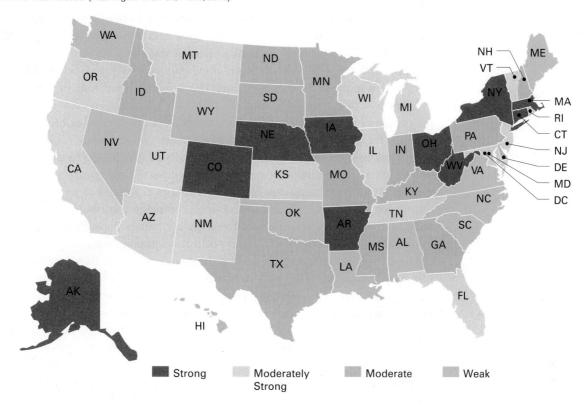

■ Strong   ■ Moderately Strong   ■ Moderate   ■ Weak

serve as governors (two Democrats and three Republicans). In 2017, two governors are Hispanic, one is Indian-American, one is of Japanese descent, and 46 are white. Forty-six are publicly declared Christians, with the largest single denomination being Roman Catholic. No openly homosexual person has served as governor, though Jim McGreevey announced he was gay when he resigned as governor of New Jersey in 2004 (after which the press revealed that he had an extramarital affair with a man). Most states hold elections in nonpresidential-election years to help insulate state politics from national trends. One consequence of off-presidential-year elections is lower turnout rates in gubernatorial elections. In 2017, 33 governors were Republican, 17 were Democratic (at the time of publication, the gubernatorial election in NC was remarkably close, but the Democratic candidate Roy Cooper was ahead pending calls for a recount). All but 5 states have lieutenant governors, although in only 25 do they get elected together like the president and vice president. The rest of the states select the governor and lieutenant governor separately.

STATE COURT SYSTEMS Each state has its own court system, so it's difficult to generalize across the nation. However, most states have three general categories of courts: minor courts (largely dealing with misdemeanors), trial courts of general jurisdiction, and appellate courts. Minor courts handle the largest volume of cases stemming from violations of minor laws as well as traffic cases and civil cases entailing small sums of money. Most states refer to these courts as municipal courts and are divided by function: family, juvenile, small claims, and traffic courts. State trial courts are referred to by a variety of names—including circuit courts, superior courts, courts of common pleas, and in New York state supreme courts. These courts are the main trial courts in the state system. Above these courts are the appellate courts. Most states have two levels of appellate courts: intermediate and highest state appeals courts (typically called supreme courts, but also referred to simply as courts of appeal). These courts typically sit in panels of three, five, seven, or even nine judges or justices depending on the system.

State courts hear most criminal cases, probate cases (involving wills and estates), most contract cases, tort (personal injury) cases, and family law (marriages, divorces, adoptions). State courts are the final arbiters of state laws and constitutions. Federal questions involving the interpretation of federal law, treaty, or U.S. Constitution may be appealed to the U.S. Supreme Court. The Supreme Court may or may not choose to hear these cases. State court judges are tenured in a variety of ways—election by the people or by the legislature, appointment for a given number of years, appointment for life, or some combination (most commonly appointment for a specified time period followed by an election). The vast majority of state judges face election at some point in their careers, most of which are nonpartisan. Concerns have risen in recent years about the increasing cost of judicial elections and the sources of funds. Judicial candidates are increasingly dependent upon campaign contributions from attorneys, law firms, businesses, and special interest groups, raising significant concern over the impartiality and objectivity that are implicitly important in our system of justice. Most political scientists and lawyers favor a merit-screening plan (typically known as the Missouri Plan), which allows a professional commission to screen nominees for competency. Most states that use this plan allow the commission to nominate three candidates from whom the governor will select his/her appointment. After a year or so, the judges face election in which voters have to decide if they should retain their positions, called retention elections. The salaries for state judges vary considerably across the nation and even within a state depending upon the type of court. The range for the chief justice of a state supreme court is from $126,000 (in Montana and Mississippi) to $232,060 (in California).[8]

LOCAL GOVERNMENTS   There are two tiers—counties, boroughs, or parishes and municipalities (towns and cities)—below the state governmental level. The structure of each varies partly depending on size and local tradition. Nearly all states have county governments, which are the largest local governmental unit. Below counties are municipalities (usually organized around population centers) and townships (primarily used in the northeast). Large cities that are usually economic and cultural centers for the region are called metropolises. Communities with developed areas adjoining a metropolis are called metropolitan areas. One example of a metropolitan area is the Dallas-Fort Worth Metroplex which has approximately 7.1 million residents from 12 counties (Collin, Dallas, Delta, Denton, Ellis, Hunt, Johnson, Kaufman, Parker, Rockwall, Tarrant, and Wise) and 13 cities with more than 100,000 inhabitants each (Dallas, Fort Worth, Arlington, Garland, Irving, Plano, Carrollton, Denton, Frisco, Grand Prairie, McKinney, Mesquite, and Richardson). A large number of rural communities have no local government below the county level; consequently the size, budget, and responsibilities of local governments vary considerably across the country.

When most people think about "the government," they think about the government in Washington, D.C., but there is a long-standing tradition in the United States of active and powerful local governments. In the earliest days of colonial America, many colonies were actually federations of local governments. In fact, newly independent states often included stipulations in their first constitutions to guarantee that local governments would retain influence over their own affairs. Some states held on to the English tradition of weak local governments. A ruling in 1868 by Judge John Dillon of the Iowa Supreme Court held that local governments could rule only in areas explicitly permitted by the state government, providing a legal framework for this view of state–local relationships. His decision became known as **Dillon's rule**. Legally, state governments create and control local governments. Because of this, state governments have great influence on the nature and character of local municipalities. States that

Dillon's rule

Iowa state court decision in 1868 that narrowly defined the power of local governments and established the supremacy of state governments when conflict exists with localities. Subsequently upheld by the Supreme Court.

FIGURE 3.4 Forms of Local and Special Governments

There are more than 180,000 types of governments in the United States, and the branches of government stretch far and wide, giving residents many points of access to governmental officials and leaders. Thus there are numerous pathways that can be used to initiate change or promote the status quo.

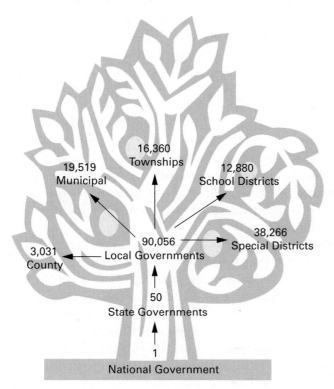

16,360 Townships

19,519 Municipal

12,880 School Districts

90,056 Local Governments

38,266 Special Districts

3,031 County

50 State Governments

1 National Government

follow Dillon's rule give local governments very narrow and explicit power to fulfill their responsibilities. Consequently, these state governments are very powerful and have a great deal of influence over municipalities within the state. Currently, 39 states follow Dillon's rule, though some more stridently than others.[9]

In contrast are states that follow the theory of **home rule**, which holds that city governments can do anything to serve the needs of their residents that is not prohibited by state law. Although city ordinances must comply with state laws and state legislatures can preempt local laws, home rule states give far more authority to the local governments, which are very important for the administration of many governmental services. There were 90,056 local governments at the time of the last census, the largest of which were special governments.[10] Some states rely very heavily upon local governmental units while others rely less heavily. For example, Hawaii only has 21 local governmental units, Massachusetts has 857, and Illinois has 6,963 local governments. While local governments are multipurpose, **special governments** exist to fulfill one or a few special needs, the most numerous of which are natural resource, fire, housing, and community development districts. It is difficult to imagine life without our local governments.

home rule

The right of a city with a population of more than 5,000 to adopt any form of government residents choose, provided that it does not conflict with the state constitution or statutes.

special governments

Local governmental units established for very specific purposes, such as the regulation of water and school districts, airports, and transportation services. Decisions made by special governments tend to have a very large impact on the daily lives of individuals but typically garner less media attention.

Dual Federalism

3.2 Characterize dual federalism both before and after the Civil War.

The people who wrote and ratified the Constitution did not share a consistent, clear vision of the meaning of American federalism. Fairly broad agreement about the need for a stronger national government had led to the end of the Articles of Confederation and the drafting of the Constitution, but there remained strong disagreements about exactly how much power the states kept under the new governing document. As a result, arguments about federalism played a central role in shaping the country's political system.

During the 1800s, both before and after the Civil War, the theory of federal–state relations that prevailed was one known as **dual federalism**. Under this system, state governments and the national government are equally authoritative; the national government is not superior. The national government possesses authority over its powers listed in the Constitution, such as coining money and establishing post offices and military forces, while the Tenth Amendment specifically reserves to the states all other governmental powers not discussed in the Constitution.

Before the Civil War

In the United States, disputes are often resolved through lawsuits that call on federal judges to interpret constitutional provisions defining the extent of federal authority. The judiciary's role in shaping American federalism is not a modern development. Judges have issued rulings on federalism since the first decades after the Constitution's ratification.

In 1816, Congress enacted legislation to charter the Second Bank of the United States. Two years later, the Maryland legislature imposed a tax on all banks within the state that were not chartered by the state legislature. James McCulloch, an official at the Baltimore branch of the federally chartered Bank of the United States, refused to pay the tax. The dispute arrived before the U.S. Supreme Court as the case of *McCulloch* v. *Maryland* **(1819)**, and it presented Chief Justice John Marshall with the opportunity to define the respective powers of the state and federal governments.

Marshall's opinion in the case first examined whether the U.S. Constitution granted to Congress the power to charter a bank. Such a power is not explicitly stated anywhere in Article I of the Constitution, which defines the authority of the national legislature. But Marshall focused on the constitutional provision that grants Congress the power to make "all laws which shall be necessary and proper, for carrying into execution the foregoing powers, and all other powers vested by this constitution, in the government of the United States, or in any department thereof." This phrase in the Constitution, known as the **Necessary and Proper Clause**, does not specify what powers, if any, flow from its words. Nevertheless, Marshall relied on the Necessary and Proper Clause to conclude that Congress possessed the power to charter a national bank. The Chief Justice concluded that the creation of the Bank of the United States was "necessary and proper" as a means to carry out other powers that Article I explicitly granted to Congress, such as the powers to collect taxes, coin money, and regulate commerce. Marshall's opinion rejected Maryland's claim that the word *necessary* granted only powers that were absolutely essential. In this case, Marshall interpreted the Constitution in a way that enhanced the powers of the federal government and empowered Congress to make choices about how it would develop public policy.

After establishing that Congress had properly chartered the bank, Marshall's opinion went on to invalidate Maryland's efforts to impose taxes on the federal government's agencies. "The power to tax," wrote Marshall in a memorable phrase, "is the power to destroy." Realizing that states could use taxation to weaken or destroy federal institutions, the chief justice asserted that the federal government necessarily retained the power to preserve its creations. According to Marshall, the people of the United States grant powers "to a government whose laws, made in pursuance of the Constitution, are declared to be supreme. Consequently, the people of a single state cannot confer a sovereignty" on their own government that would extend beyond the borders of the state. By invalidating Maryland's tax on the bank chartered by Congress, Marshall made a strong initial statement about the superior position of the national government in the evolving system of federalism.

---

dual federalism

A theory stating that the powers of the federal and state governments are strictly separate, with interaction often marked by tension rather than cooperation. Under a system of dual federalism, governments have separate spheres of responsibilities and influence and do not cooperate among themselves.

McCulloch v. *Maryland* **(1819)**

U.S. Supreme Court decision that defined the respective powers of the state and federal governments. The opinion established that the Constitution grants to Congress implied powers for implementing the Constitution's express powers in order to create a functional national government, and that state action may not impede valid constitutional exercises of power by the Federal government.

Necessary and Proper Clause

A statement in Article I, Section 8, of the U.S. Constitution that grants Congress the power to pass all laws "necessary and proper" for carrying out the list of expressed powers providing basis for implied Congressional power. Also known as the Elastic Clause as it stretches Congressional power and authority.

Chief Justice Marshall also led the Supreme Court in making other decisions that shaped the law affecting federalism. In *Cohens* v. *Virginia* (1821), for example, brothers who had been convicted under a Virginia law for selling tickets in a lottery approved by Congress appealed to the U.S. Supreme Court. Virginia claimed that the Court had no authority to review decisions by its state courts. Marshall wrote an opinion rejecting that argument and asserting that the U.S. Supreme Court had ultimate authority over judicial matters concerning federal law, whether or not earlier decisions on the matter had been issued by state courts or by lower federal courts.

In *Gibbons* v. *Ogden* (1824), Marshall's Court considered a challenge to a New York law that granted specific steamboat operators the exclusive privilege of providing service between New York and New Jersey. The Chief Justice announced a broad definition of the power granted to Congress by the Constitution to regulate commerce "among the several states." His opinion concluded that Congress possessed exclusive authority over the regulation of interstate commerce, including navigation, and therefore New York and other states had no power to grant such exclusive licenses to steamboat operators. In short, by these and other key decisions, the early U.S. Supreme Court, under Marshall's leadership, shaped federalism by interpreting the Constitution to give the federal government superior powers in certain matters of public policy, thereby imposing limits on the powers of the states.

Despite these decisions, however, the wording of the Constitution raised many questions about the powers of states and the national government. The most prominent source for debate regarding the distribution of power rests with the Tenth Amendment. Many Americans viewed this amendment as embodying a fundamental premise of the Constitution: Governmental powers not explicitly granted to the federal government continue to reside with the states. This viewpoint supported the theory of dual federalism, which says that governments and the national government are equally authoritative; the national government is not superior.

In practice, in early nineteenth-century America, dual federalism faced criticism from two directions. Advocates of a strong national government believed that where their spheres of activity overlapped, the powers of the federal government must be superior to those of the states. For example, both the states and the federal government sought to regulate certain aspects of business and commerce, and the Marshall Court had ruled in *Gibbons* v. *Ogden* (1824) that Congress has exclusive authority over "interstate commerce." Others saw the states as the central, sovereign governmental entities in the American governing system. These advocates of "states' rights" asserted that the states possessed specific powers superior to those of the national government.

Before the Civil War, many southern leaders and advocates of states' rights relied on a **doctrine of nullification**, which declared that each state had retained its sovereignty upon joining the United States. The doctrine asserted that the government established by the Constitution, represented a voluntary pact between states and that the federal government had limited powers. If the federal government exceeded the power that had been delegated to it by the Constitution, then a state could declare any laws or actions of the national government "null and void" if they clashed with that state's interests and goals. In the 1830s, the South Carolina legislature voted to nullify federal tariffs that were believed to help northern manufacturing businesses while hurting southern planters and slave owners. The state later cancelled its action after Congress passed a compromise tariff bill, and no other states acted on the nullification doctrine. Many who wanted to protect southern agricultural interests and to prevent Congress from interfering with slavery, however, advocated the idea.

doctrine of nullification

Theory that state governments had a right to rule any federal law unconstitutional and therefore null and void. The doctrine was ruled unconstitutional but contributed to the secession of southern states from the Union and ultimately the Civil War.

The bloody Civil War reflected the failure of the pathways of political action to solve disagreements about slavery and federalism. The usual democratic mechanisms of lobbying, elections, and litigation could not forge a compromise resolution.

■ *Are there reasons that make another civil war highly improbable in today's United States? What are they?*

doctrine of secession

The theory that state governments had a right to declare their independence and create their own form of government. Eleven southern states seceded from the Union in 1860–1861, created their own government (the Confederate States of America), and thereby precipitated the Civil War. The Civil War demonstrated that the doctrine was invalid, but the idea that state governments ought to be very powerful and act in their own self-interest has resurfaced from time to time.

The most extreme expression of dual federalism before the Civil War was the **doctrine of secession**. By asserting that states retained sovereignty and were not subordinate to the national government, advocates of secession claimed that states could choose to withdraw from the United States if they had profound disagreements with laws and policies produced by the national government. In 1861, when 11 states acted on this theory by leaving the United States and forming the Confederate States of America, a bloody, four-year civil war erupted. The Confederacy's defeat in 1865 ended—presumably forever—the idea that dual sovereignty could be carried to the point of justifying secession. Many Americans believe that competing conceptions of federalism were the root cause of the Civil War; however, historians have convincingly demonstrated that slavery and regional economic differences—not federalism—were the key causes of the war. Until the second half of the twentieth century, students in many southern states were taught to call the conflict of 1861–1865 the "War Between the States." This label was based on an understanding of the war as reflecting profound disagreements about the rights of states to manage their own affairs without interference from the federal government, and it coincided with efforts by southern whites to defend state-mandated racial segregation. By contrast, elsewhere in the United States, students learned to call the bloody event the "Civil War" and to interpret it as having been fought over North–South disagreements about the institution of slavery and the southern states' unlawful assertion of a right to secede. The policy issue of slavery was intertwined with disputes about federalism, because the slave states resisted any move by the federal government to outlaw slavery in new territories and states.

The doctrines of nullification and secession were put to rest with the Union victory in the Civil War. The war's outcome did not, however, end all attempts to preserve a "states' rights" conception of federalism. Such arguments remained common, for example, by those southerners who during the 1950s and 1960s resisted passing and enforcing federal voting rights legislation and other antidiscrimination laws seeking to prevent the victimization of African Americans. The term *states' rights* is seldom used today because of its discredited association with efforts to preserve slavery and, later, to deny civil rights to African Americans.

THE CIVIL WAR AND THE FAILURE OF AMERICAN POLITICS

Throughout, we describe the pathways of American politics that produce public policies and shift the balance of power between different political actors and governing institutions. However, the Civil War represents the best example of a policy dispute that was not controlled by one of the pathways of American politics.

The operation of the pathways depends on the American people's shared democratic values, commitment to the preservation of the constitutional governing system, and willingness to accept individual policy outcomes that are contrary to their personal preferences. In the case of slavery, however, no workable compromise balanced the interests of those who sought to abolish or at least prevent the territorial expansion of slavery and those who wanted to preserve the institution. As a result, people turned to violence to advance their interests.

Many battles and more than a half-million deaths occurred before American policy regarding slavery and secession could stabilize. The bloodshed of the Civil War stands as a reminder about what can happen when Americans fail to use the pathways of action to settle policy disputes.

After the Civil War

In the aftermath of the Civil War, the Constitution was amended to prevent specific assertions of state authority, particularly with respect to the treatment of newly freed African Americans. The Thirteenth Amendment (1865) banned slavery, thereby eliminating that issue as a source of conflict between states and the national government. The Fourteenth Amendment (1868) sought directly to limit states' authority to interfere with certain rights of individuals. "No State," the Fourteenth Amendment declares, shall deny "due process of law" or "the equal protection of the laws." According to the Fifteenth Amendment (1870), the right to vote shall not be denied "by the United States or by any State on account of race, color, or previous condition of servitude" (that is, slavery). In addition, each of the three post–Civil War amendments contained a statement empowering Congress to enact legislation to enforce them. These amendments specifically limited state authority and enlarged that of the federal government.

For nearly a century after the passage of these amendments, federal institutions—courts, Congress, and presidents alike—failed to vigorously apply the powers granted by these amendments to protect African Americans from discrimination at the hands of state and local authorities. However, in what was called "nationalizing the Bill of Rights," federal courts in the 1920s and 1930s slowly began using the Fourteenth Amendment to strike down state laws and state-sanctioned policies that violated the Bill of Rights in such areas as criminal justice, freedom of speech, and the separation of church and state. And as early as the 1940s, presidents began issuing executive orders designed to ensure the equal treatment of racial minorities and enforce antidiscriminatory court decisions and congressional legislation. In the 1960s, the Supreme Court revived nineteenth-century federal antidiscrimination statutes affecting contracts, housing, and other matters by declaring that they were appropriate exercises of congressional power under the Thirteenth Amendment. Congress meanwhile relied on the Fifteenth Amendment to enact important voting rights legislation aimed at preventing discrimination in state elections.

In the decades following the Civil War, American society transformed enormously. Many new technologies developed that helped reshape the economy. The expanded use of railroads, telegraph, and industrial machinery shifted the country away from an agriculture-based economy to one deriving most of its wealth from urban industry. Cities grew with the spread of factories. Industrial demands for energy expanded employment opportunities in coal mines, in shipyards, and on railroads. People left farms and small towns to seek jobs in factories, urban offices, and retail businesses. Increasing numbers of job-seeking immigrants arrived from

The Civil War Amendments promised that slaves would be freed and politically equal, being afforded the equal protection of the laws and the right to vote. However, these promises of political equality were not truly granted until over one hundred years later with additional constitutional amendments and federal civil rights laws.

■ *Do you think that these promises have been fully achieved or is there more work to be done until all Americans have true political equality?*

Europe and East Asia in search of new lives in American cities. In addition, large corporations grew, attempting to consolidate control over entire industries. The changes brought by urbanization and industrialization presented the country with new kinds of economic and social problems. Many government officials believed that new policies were needed to foster economic growth, prevent predatory business practices, protect the interests of workers, and address the growing problems of urban poverty.

In the late nineteenth century, Americans looked first to their states to deal with the effects of industrialization and urbanization. But in most states, corporate interests had significant influence on the state legislatures, which therefore did relatively little to address these issues. Because industries, like the mining companies in West Virginia, could use their substantial resources to influence politics and policy, only a few state legislatures enacted economic regulation and social welfare legislation.

At the federal level, Congress enacted statutes intended to address specific concerns that affected the entire nation. For example, the Interstate Commerce Act of 1887 established the Interstate Commerce Commission, a regulatory agency responsible for implementing rules for transporting goods by rail and ship. The Sherman Antitrust Act of 1890 sought to prevent individual companies from controlling entire industries

Although the Civil War put to rest the most extreme arguments advocating states' rights, such claims lingered for decades afterward, often as a means to justify discrimination against African Americans. In the 1950s, for example, President Dwight Eisenhower sent federal troops to Little Rock, Arkansas, to protect nine brave African-American students who were attempting to desegregate Central High School. State and local officials in Arkansas were opposed to desegregation.

■ *What circumstances today might require the president to use the military in order to force state and local officials to comply with the law?*

and to stop companies from working together to rig prices at artificially high levels. The government thought that **monopolies**, companies that gained control over most or all of a particular industry, could harm the national economy and consumers by raising prices in unjustified ways—there would be no competition to which consumers could turn. Congress wanted to encourage the existence of a variety of companies in each industry so that market forces, in the form of competition between companies, would keep prices at economically justifiable levels. But such federal legislation did relatively little to curb the excesses of big business.

Many laws passed in response to changing social conditions and problems were tested in the court. But unlike Marshall's Supreme Court a century earlier, which had consistently sought to strengthen and expand the powers of the federal government, the justices of the Supreme Court of the late nineteenth and early twentieth centuries handed down decisions that generally limited governmental authority to regulate commerce and address issues of social welfare. For example, in 1895 the Supreme Court rejected the government's charge that the American Sugar Refining Company had become an illegal monopoly in violation of the Sherman Antitrust Act, even though the company, by buying up competing sugar businesses, had gained control of over 98 percent of the country's sugar-refining capacity (*United States* v. *E. C. Knight Company*). The Court concluded that although the Constitution empowered Congress to regulate interstate commerce, "manufacturing," such as sugar refining, was a separate activity from "commerce." Therefore, the federal government could not regulate the company and other manufacturing enterprises.

In *Hammer* v. *Dagenhart* (1918), the Supreme Court struck down the 1916 federal statute barring the interstate transport of goods produced by child labor. The Court said that because the goods themselves were not harmful, the statute had improperly sought to regulate child labor. It ruled that Congress, in exercising its power over "interstate commerce," possessed only the authority to regulate the *transportation* of goods. Decisions like these temporarily limited the expansion of federal governmental authority during decades when Congress sought to become more active in regulating the economy and advancing social welfare goals.

monopolies
Exclusive control by companies over most or all of a particular industry.

Through the first decades of the twentieth century, it was common for American children to work long hours under harsh and dangerous conditions in textile mills (like that pictured here), mines and in other industrial settings. Until the late 1930s, the U.S. Supreme Court blocked legislative efforts to enact laws that would protect workers, including children, from danger and exploitation in the workplace.

■ *What would labor laws be like today if all regulation was controlled by state governments?*

The Supreme Court's actions in limiting federal power did not necessarily mean that the justices intended to shift federalism's balance of power in favor of the states. The Court also struck down similar laws enacted by state legislatures. In 1905, for example, in *Lochner* v. *New York,* the Supreme Court invalidated a New York State statute that sought to limit the working hours of bakery employees to not more than 10 hours per day or 60 hours per week. Although the New York legislature intended to protect the health and well-being of bakers, the Court found that the statute interfered with the workers' liberty to work as many hours as they wished to work. (Of course, workers typically toiled such long hours because hourly wages were so low that they had no choice.) In effect, the Supreme Court's decisions reflected the justices' views on the limits of legislative power generally, both state and federal.[11] Still, the judicial decisions of this era had the primary effect of preventing the federal government from expanding its authority.

Cooperative and Creative Federalism

3.3 Compare and contrast cooperative and creative federalism.

With the advent of the twentieth century and the heightened complexity brought by industrialization and urbanization, the rigid separation mandated by dual federalism no longer allowed the government to address the pressing social, political, and economic problems facing the nation. Responding to increased expectations from citizens, our leaders began to see the need for a more dynamic view of federalism.

The New Deal: Cooperative Federalism

The stock market crash of 1929 signaled the beginning of the Great Depression, which would last through the 1930s. Manufacturing dropped, banks failed, and by early 1933, nearly one-quarter of the American workforce was unemployed. Elected president in 1932, Franklin D. Roosevelt (FDR) was inaugurated in early 1933 at the depth of the economic crisis, and he immediately sought to use the federal government's power to spur economic recovery and revive employment. FDR's domestic policy, known as the **New Deal**, included programs to regulate farm and industrial production; to provide government jobs in construction, environmental conservation, and other public sector projects; and to give relief to people suffering from economic hardships. It also established the Social Security system.

President Roosevelt used the power of the presidency and his remarkable personal skills to sell his New Deal programs and new vision of federalism to the American people. Under his leadership, the power and influence of the federal government changed dramatically, as did the relationship between the national and state governments. Many of FDR's programs involved unprecedented interactions and cooperation between the states and the national government to deal with complexities of the economic crisis. Political scientists refer to this relationship as **cooperative federalism**—the belief that state and national governments should work together to solve problems.

Programs that involved joint involvement were far-ranging, including public works projects, welfare programs, and unemployment assistance. Morton Grozdins, a historian of federalism, aptly contrasted a layer cake and a marble cake in describing the shift from the older, dual federalism to the new, cooperative federalism with its high levels of national–state interaction.[12] In a marble cake, the two types of cake are separate, like state and federal governments, but they exist next to each other rather than resting exclusively in separate layers. The marble cake analogy symbolically portrays state and federal government as coexisting and cooperating in a variety of policy areas.

Many of the New Deal programs that Congress enacted collided with the conservative views of the Supreme Court justices on the limits of government authority, and the Court initially struck down several important laws that Roosevelt had sponsored. In 1936, for example, the Court decided that Congress lacked the power to impose minimum wage and maximum work hour regulations on coal mines (*Carter* v. *Carter Coal Co.*). President Roosevelt criticized the Supreme Court for blocking New Deal economic and social welfare laws.

In 1937, after he had been elected to a second term, Roosevelt proposed changing the Supreme Court so that the president could appoint a new justice whenever a sitting justice reached the age of 70. At the time, six justices were older than 70. This proposal became known as Roosevelt's **court-packing plan**. Even though Roosevelt had won reelection by an overwhelming popular margin, the public responded negatively to this proposed change, and Congress rejected the proposal. In the late 1930s, after several elderly conservative justices left the bench, Roosevelt was finally able to reshape the Supreme Court by appointing new justices, whom the Senate confirmed. Their views on congressional commerce power and federalism led them to uphold the constitutionality of the New Deal's expansion of federal power.

For decades thereafter, the Court permitted Congress to justify nearly any kind of social, economic, and civil rights legislation as an exercise of power under its constitutional authority to regulate interstate commerce. Congress used this power to enact a variety of laws, some of which clearly had primary goals other than the regulation of commerce. For example, in 1964 Congress enacted Title II of the Civil Rights Act of 1964, barring racial discrimination in restaurants, hotels, movie theaters, and other "public accommodations" provided by private businesses. Although the public widely recognized that the statute was created to advance civil rights and combat discrimination, the Supreme Court rejected challenges to the law and accepted the federal government's argument that Title II regulated commerce by attacking a major barrier to interstate travel by African Americans. The Court's decisions in this and other cases seemed to indicate that Congress had nearly unlimited authority to make laws under the premise of regulating interstate commerce. The expansion of federal lawmaking affected federalism by simultaneously limiting the scope of the states' authority to control their own affairs in certain areas (see Figure 3.5).

New Deal
Programs designed by President Franklin D. Roosevelt to bring economic recovery from the Great Depression by expanding the role of the federal government in providing employment opportunities and social services, advanced social reforms to serve the needs of the people, greatly expanding the budget and activity of the federal government. Its ultimate success helped redefine the very nature of federalism and how Americans viewed their national government.

cooperative federalism
A system in which the powers of the federal and state government are intertwined and shared. Each level of government shares overlapping power, authority, and responsibility.

court-packing plan
President Franklin D. Roosevelt's unsuccessful proposal in 1937 to permit the appointment of additional justices to the U.S. Supreme Court to enhance the support for New Deal initiatives.

FIGURE 3.5 Distribution of Powers between National and State Governments

The Founders of our government created a system that divided power, authority, and responsibility between the federal and state governments. Some powers are exclusive to one entity (delegated powers represent powers that are given—delegated—to the federal government, while reserved powers remain with the states), but many are shared (concurrent powers). Throughout our history, the power of the federal government has grown, but states remain important actors in our political system. Unfortunately, many in our country are overwhelmed with the size of the government and do not correctly understand which level of government is responsible for different issues.

■ *How do you think we can better explain to individuals how power is divided and shared?*

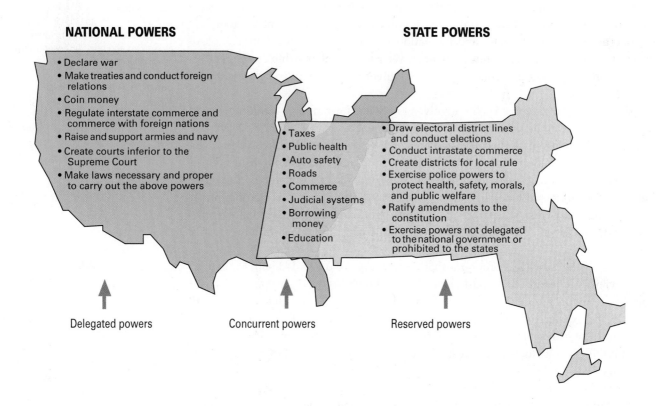

NATIONAL POWERS

- Declare war
- Make treaties and conduct foreign relations
- Coin money
- Regulate interstate commerce and commerce with foreign nations
- Raise and support armies and navy
- Create courts inferior to the Supreme Court
- Make laws necessary and proper to carry out the above powers

- Taxes
- Public health
- Auto safety
- Roads
- Commerce
- Judicial systems
- Borrowing money
- Education

STATE POWERS

- Draw electoral district lines and conduct elections
- Conduct intrastate commerce
- Create districts for local rule
- Exercise police powers to protect health, safety, morals, and public welfare
- Ratify amendments to the constitution
- Exercise powers not delegated to the national government or prohibited to the states

Delegated powers   Concurrent powers   Reserved powers

The Great Society: Creative Federalism and Federal Grants

The nature and role of the federal government and of federalism itself changed throughout the twentieth century. The presidency of Lyndon B. Johnson (1963–1969) marked a critical point in the evolution of federalism. Johnson proposed many new social programs to achieve what he called the *Great Society*. Of crucial importance in his vision was the *War on Poverty*, which channeled federal money to states, local governments, and even citizen groups to combat poverty and racial discrimination. Funds were allocated to a variety of social programs for urban renewal, education, and improving the lives of underprivileged children. The money was used to advance the agenda of President Johnson and liberal Democrats in Congress, the direct result of which was to bypass governors, state legislatures, and local officials. This new view of federalism, coined **creative federalism**—articulated by Johnson as an expanded partnership between the federal and state governments—began to infiltrate policymaking in the 1960s and early 1970s.

As we see in Figure 3.6, federal departments such as agriculture and commerce, which Democratic leaders did not target, saw only limited growth in the 1960s, while agencies with responsibility for health care, education, and community

creative federalism

A system in which the role of the federal government is expanded by providing financial incentives for states to follow congressional initiatives. Creative federalism establishes programs that are funded and regulated by Congress centralizing congressional authority over the states to provide social services. Many oppose this system because they believe that it usurps the authority of states and makes the national government too powerful.

FIGURE 3.6   Grants-In-Aid from the Federal Government to States (1965–1972)

The pattern of distributions of federal grants-in-aid is a good indicator of the priorities of our government and its leaders. During the 1960s, we saw enormous growth in grants for health care, education, income security, and community development and housing. While there was an increase in grants for agriculture/rural development and commerce/transportation, the rate of growth was substantially less than the other categories, reflecting the policy priorities of Lyndon Johnson and the Democratic leadership in Congress.

SOURCE: "Federal Aid to State and Local Governments: 1965 to 1972," *Statistical Abstract of the United States: 1972*, No. 655, 413.

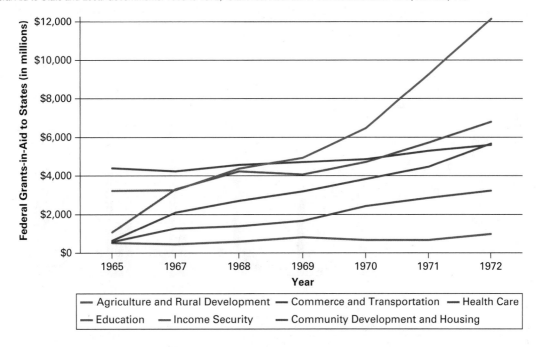

development saw dramatic growth during Johnson's presidency. These patterns reflected the domestic priorities of Johnson and the liberal wing of the Democratic Party, especially concerning urban development. Figures 3.6 and 3.7 show the remarkable increases in federal grants for subsidized housing and in urban renewal grants.

Under President Johnson, the federal government funneled record amounts of money to states to combat discrimination and fight poverty. Many states (especially in the South) were blamed for dragging their feet in carrying out social reforms to promote equal rights. If the federal authorities decided that states and local communities were not cooperating, they withheld funds. By using a reward-and-punishment system to allocate resources, the federal government was successful in getting the states and localities to comply. This use of financial incentives was the key device Johnson and the Democrats in Congress employed to fulfill their vision for a just society.

Grants-in-aid—federal funds given to state and local governments on the condition that the money is spent for specified purposes defined by officials in Washington—are a key tool of creative federalism, and they became a crucial means for redistributing income. Under this system, money collected from all citizens by the national government in the form of taxes is then allocated by the federal government for the benefit of certain citizens in specific cities and states. These grants often work to reduce notable inequalities among states, as many are based on economic need. However, grant money always comes with stipulations to ensure that the money is used for the purpose for which it was given; other conditions are designed to evaluate how well the grant is working. Both give rise to complex reporting and accounting requirements.

Grants-in-aid go back to our earliest days. The national government gave money to the states to help them pay debts from the Revolutionary War. One of the most important early examples of grants-in-aid was the decision of the national government

grants-in-aid

Funds given from one governmental unit to another governmental unit for specific purposes. Such grants cover a wide array of programs, helping to equalize services among states and allow the federal government to influence policy-making at state and local levels.

FIGURE 3.7   Grants-In-Aid Selected Programs 1965–1972

Federal grants for food stamps increased from around $32 million in 1965 to $2.02 billion in 1972 while grants for medical assistance increased from $272 million to $4.4 billion during the same time period. Spending for work training and urban renewal also increased dramatically over the same time period. During that decade, we saw greater demands for minority voting rights and protection from racial and ethnic discrimination. As a larger number of less affluent people got involved in politics, using the grassroots mobilization and elections pathways, the manner in which we allocated federal grants changed.

SOURCE: "Federal Aid to State and Local Governments: 1965 to 1972," *Statistical Abstract of the United States: 1972*, No. 655, 413.

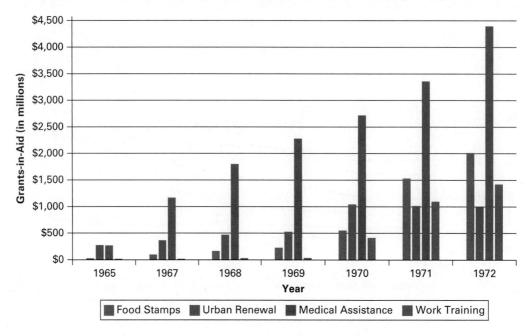

in the mid-nineteenth century to give the states land grants for educational institutions and to build railroads that promoted westward expansion. In fact, many of today's leading public universities were founded with the proceeds of these grants. Cash grants-in-aid did not become common until the twentieth century. Today, they are enormously important. It is estimated that in 2013, the federal government spent more than $546.2 billion in grants-in-aid to state and local governments (up from $461 billion in 2008 but down from $601 billion in 2011), benefiting millions of Americans.[13]

Categorical grants are federal funds targeted for specific purposes. Typically, they have many restrictions, often leaving little room for discretionary spending. Two types of categorical grants exist: formula grants and project grants.

Formula grants are funds distributed according to a particular formula, which specifies who is eligible and for how much. For example, the number of school-age children living in families below the poverty line is used to allocate federal funds to each state to subsidize school breakfasts and lunches. The states must spend this money on school meals, according to a very specific formula allowing no flexibility. The money at stake under grants of this type is one reason why the state population figures and other demographic data revealed each decade by the national census are so important—and so controversial. Consider what happens when Congress proposes to allocate money to states for homeless shelters based on the number of homeless people in each state. States that are better at finding and counting the homeless would receive more money than states that are less successful or less diligent in accounting for their homeless population—a problem compounded by the irregular lives of many homeless people, who often migrate for a variety of reasons (including the weather).

Project grants, the second type of categorical grants, are awarded on the basis of competitive applications rather than a specified formula. Consider homeless shelters: A community could apply for a project grant to develop a new model of a shelter, one that not only houses the homeless but also involves the efforts of other community

categorical grants

Grants of money from the federal government to state or local governments for very specific purposes. These grants often require that funds be matched by the receiving entity.

formula grants

Specific type of categorical grant in which money is allocated and distributed based upon a prescribed formula.

project grants

A type of categorical grant in which a competitive application process is required for a specific project (often scientific or technical research or social services).

organizations to provide education, job training, and substance abuse counseling. The community could receive federal grant money based on the strength of its application and its prospect for innovation.

Typically, state governments must contribute some money of their own, but many times the federal funds support the primary cost of the program. State and local officials have often found these grants frustrating, because they are defined so narrowly and may not fit the needs of the locality. For example, money might be available to hire more public school teachers, but a local school district may actually need money to purchase new textbooks and build new schools. Under most categorical grants, school districts lack discretion: They must either follow Washington's requirements (hire new teachers, for example) or forgo the funds. The lack of flexibility has often meant that local needs are not well served and that money is wasted.

Congress created **block grants** in 1966 as a response to these problems. Block grants are still earmarked for specific programs, but they are far more flexible. To continue our earlier example, a categorical grant for education might specify that the money be used for teacher salaries, even if that is not the greatest need in the school district. A block grant, by contrast, would still be available to improve education, but the school district could decide (within specified parameters) how to spend the money—it might choose to buy textbooks rather than hire more teachers. Because block grants allow greater spending flexibility, many observers feel they are a more efficient and more effective form of federal grants.

block grants

Funds given to states that allow substantial discretion to spend the money with minimal federal restrictions. State and local governments tend to prefer block grants to other forms of grants-in-aid, as there is more flexibility in how the money is spent.

Recent Trends in Federalism

3.4 Trace the evolution of federalism in recent decades.

The power and influence of the federal government expanded dramatically in the twentieth century. Every president since Richard Nixon (1969–1974) has voiced concern over the size and influence of the federal government. In 1976, Georgia Governor Jimmy Carter successfully ran for the White House as an outsider who opposed federal mandates (requirements imposed by the government without funding), which as governor he had disagreed with for a variety of reasons. Although as president Carter did cut back federal grant expenditures, his cuts paled in comparison to those of his successor, Ronald Reagan.

Winning the election over Carter in 1980, Reagan pledged to promote a new form of federalism that returned more power and responsibility, including financial responsibility, to the state. Reagan strongly disagreed with the diminishing role of state governments that had developed over the previous decades. He saw states as vital instruments in our governmental apparatus and vowed to increase their presence. His goals were reflected not only in his rhetoric but also in his budgetary policies. In addition to large income tax cuts, Reagan proposed massive cuts in domestic spending that would roll back and even eliminate many programs created by the Democratic administrations from the New Deal to the Great Society. Reagan successfully pressed Congress not only to reduce the amount of federal grant money that it disbursed but also to shift more money into flexible block grants, which fell into four broad categories—income guarantees, education, transportation, and health. He argued that the states knew best how to serve their citizens and that mandates from Washington were wasteful, failing to meet the needs of the people and also taking away legitimate authority from state and local governments.

This idea of state authority is not new; it goes back to a view of states as laboratories for public policy experiments. However, this view of states' independence and control over their own affairs had diminished over the course of the twentieth century. By the 1980s, with the power and the budget of the federal government reaching record levels, the idea of strengthening states and curbing the federal government

FIGURE 3.8 Total Outlays for Grants to State and Local Governments: 1940–2019 (In Billions of Constant (FY 2009) Dollars)

Beginning in the 1960s, the federal government has played an increasingly important role in providing funds for states and localities. In the 1980s, under the Reagan administration, we saw the grant expenditures decline. This trend changed beginning in 1987 with a steep and clear upward trajectory in place ever since. The large increase in 2010 was in reaction to the Great Recession, with grant levels returning to more normal levels in 2012. As you will see in Figure 3.9, much of this growth is due to the aging population and health care costs.

■ *What problems do you see with having the federal government providing so many grants to states and localities to subsidize programs?*

SOURCE: Office of Management and Budget, "Table 12.1 – Summary Comparison of Total Outlays for Grants to State and Local Governments: 1940–2019," *Fiscal Year 2015, Historical Tables: Budget of the U.S. Government*, https://www.whitehouse.gov/sites/default/files/omb/budget/fy2015/assets/hist.pdf.

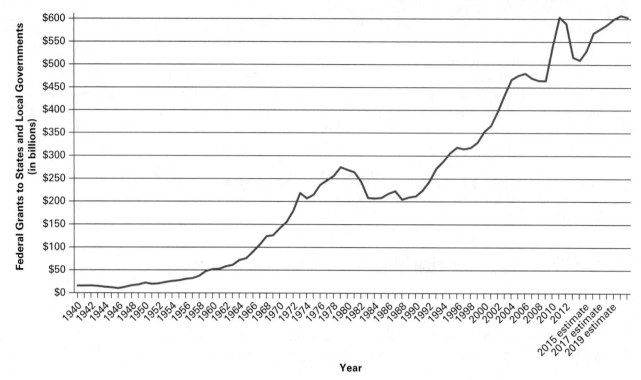

struck a chord with the American public. As is evident in Figure 3.8, Reagan was successful in fulfilling his pledge to reduce the role of the federal government in funding state and local government budgets. During the "Great Recession," states have been increasingly dependent upon federal funding. In 2008, 27.4 percent of state and local governments' budgets came from federal grants-in-aid. Only two short years later, that percentage increased over 10 points to 37.5 percent. Since 2010 state reliance on the federal government has steadily decreased, from 34.7 percent in 2011 to 31.6 percent in 2012 to around 30 percent in 2013 and 2014. However these averages mask significant variation, ranging from 19 percent in North Dakota to 43 percent in Mississippi.[14] Even with these reductions, substantial portions of state budgets come from Washington, leaving one to wonder if this trend will continue in the future.

devolution

The transfer of jurisdiction and fiscal responsibility for particular programs from the federal government to state or local governments. State governments generally like certain components of devolution, most notably responsibility over decision making that impacts their residents; however, the fiscal responsibility that often comes with devolution is often difficult for states and localities to bear.

Devolution

Americans and elected leaders of both the Republican and Democratic parties continued to voice concerns about the power and influence of the national government after President Reagan left the White House. Republicans objected to the national government asserting such a large role in the federal system. In 1994, the Republican congressional leadership announced its "Contract with America," which called for reducing the size of the federal government and for returning money, responsibility, and power to the states—what has come to be known as **devolution**, or the transfer of power to political subunits. With Republican majorities elected in the House and Senate in 1994,

FIGURE 3.9 Grants over Time by Type

In 1992 Bill Clinton's campaign strongly emphasized the need for health care reform (correctly anticipating the heightened financial needs for an aging population). As you can see, health care costs have escalated steeply since the early 1990s, with states increasingly dependent upon the federal government to subsidize the health care of their residents. The government has also provided much larger amounts of money for income assistance, training and employment assistance (which peaked during the Great Recession) and transportation (if you excluded health care costs from the graphic, you can better see these trends). In contrast, funding for veterans benefits has remained relatively low.

▪ *Are you surprised by these spending trends? Do you agree with the distribution of resources?*

SOURCE: Office of Management and Budget, "Table 12.3 – Total Outlays for Grants to State and Local Governments by Function, Agency and Program: 1940-2016," *Fiscal Year 2015, Historical Tables: Budget of the U.S. Government,* https://www.whitehouse.gov/sites/default/files/omb/budget/fy2015/assets/hist.pdf.

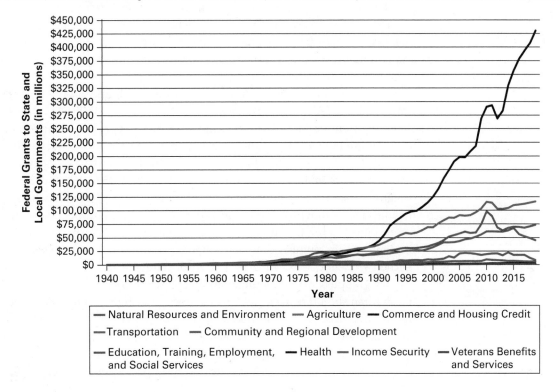

interest in minimizing the role of the federal government increased. The Republican initiative focused, in part, on returning power to the states and having states complete what had once been federal tasks. One prominent example of this is welfare. Congress passed reforms (which the Democratic President Bill Clinton signed) that returned management of welfare programs to the states. With the aim of moving welfare mothers into the workplace, Congress enacted new rules to limit the number of years women with dependent children could continue receiving public assistance. Another way that Republicans tried to limit the scope of the federal government was to pass the Unfunded Mandates Reform Act of 1995 (signed into law by President Clinton). The law was an effort to reduce the number of mandates (requirements) imposed on the states, localities, and tribal governments without adequate funding and to increase communication between the layers of government. However, as we saw in the example of new nutritional rules for school lunches, the federal government often bypasses this law and passes regulations which can cost state and local governments significant amounts of money.

Devolution has been motivated by a number of factors, including an ideological belief that the federal government is less effective than the states and localities in delivering services and solving problems. Many supporters of devolution believe that the state governments are best equipped to solve their own problems and that they only need the power and flexibility to do so. Worry over increasing federal deficits also fuels devolution, with the aim of transferring not only power but also fiscal responsibility to the states. However, many policy advocates are opposed to devolution, fearing a return to the days of great inequality among states and among citizens within states. The weak economies of some states prevent them from keeping pace with other states in education funding, highway construction, and other vital services unless they have financial support from the federal government.

In economic hard times, the number of people in need grows dramatically, while the tax revenues required to satisfy these needs shrink. Thus, at a time of great hardship, states often have little ability to meet their citizens' needs adequately (trends evident in Figure 3.8). Moreover, most state and local governments are legally prohibited by their own state constitutions from incurring budget deficits, whereas the federal government can freely cover whatever deficits it incurs by selling bonds. So when their tax revenues fall, states have to make the difficult choice between raising taxes and cutting services. Devolution has complicated state and local politics by forcing states to compete for fewer and fewer federal grants.

Many state governments (especially in the South and on the border) are frustrated with the federal government's unwillingness or inability to address concerns stemming from immigration. Consequently, in recent years, a number of states and localities are taking it upon themselves to pass stricter laws to tackle the problems associated with undocumented immigrants. In the first half of 2015, for example, state legislators in 46 states and Puerto Rico enacted 153 laws and 238 resolutions designed to address various elements of immigration.[15] Issues such as these raise the question as to which level of government, the states or the federal government, are responsible for the immigration question and how to handle undocumented residents. As the number of unaccompanied children crossing the southern boarder reached epidemic levels in 2014 and 2015, state and local governments across the country grappled with the humanitarian crisis. Some states and localities argue that the children should be welcomed as refugees, offering to shelter them. Others assert the children need to be deported as quickly as possible so as not to encourage others to migrate. The courts have been and will continue to be called upon to strike a balance in this controversial issue that goes to the heart of our federal system of government and which has the potential to impact large numbers of families and can threaten civil liberties and rights.

A Return to Creative Federalism?

When Barack Obama was elected president, the country was in the middle of the worst economic crisis since the Great Depression. Hoping to stem the downturn, Obama ushered into effect dramatic changes involving the federal government in businesses and localities in extraordinary ways. Facing a battered stock market, a precarious banking system, decreased exports, a desperate car industry, and a housing crisis, the president made a number of unprecedented proposals. He advocated for direct and immediate aid to individuals around the country in the form of extended unemployment benefits and homeowner relief. He proposed providing automobile and home-buying incentives to jump-start consumer spending. He urged Congress to authorize funds to rescue banking institutions and domestic car companies on the brink of collapse, because their failure would have had a long-term and far-reaching impact on our economy. And on February 17, 2009, President Obama signed the American Recovery and Reinvestment Act, a $787 billion economic stimulus bill dramatically expanding the scope of the federal government for the foreseeable future. Some believe that these changes have overextended the role and responsibilities of the federal government in a dangerous way. Others believe that more needed to be done. Time will tell whether or not this shift marks a dramatic turn in the nature of our federal system.

One of the most significant changes in the relationship between the federal and state governments in recent years involves health care. Under the Patient

Protection and Affordable Care Act (Obamacare or ACA) millions of previously uninsured Americans became eligible for affordable health care through the expansion of Medicaid. Medicaid is a program to provide health care to the nation's poor. States were allowed to decide if they would expand Medicaid by changing eligibility requirements above the federal minimum requirements (eligibility is largely determined by income and family size relative to the federal poverty level). By late-2016, 31 states and the District of Columbia expanded eligibility thereby allowing millions of additional Americans to get health insurance. Nineteen states opted out of the expansion (the remaining were in the process of deciding what was best for their citizens). The decision to expand eligibility was controversial in many states as the federal government would only pay 100 percent of the cost of the program in 2014, 2015, and 2016. After this time, the percentage would decrease to 95 percent in 2017, 94 percent in 2018, 93 percent in 2019, and 90 percent in 2020 and all subsequent years. The law initially required states to participate in the expansion or opt out of the Medicaid program entirely, however the Supreme Court (in *NFIB* v. *Sebelius,* 2012) ruled that this provision was coercive and declared that states must be allowed to maintain levels of coverage pre-ACA. While the vast majority of states have expanded eligibility, a very large proportion of the nation's poor live in the states opting out resulting in a large number of poor remaining uninsured.

Although the idea of having more powerful and more independent state governments has been popular under a theory of "new" federalism, we have yet to see it reach fruition, and many observers doubt that this vision will ever become a reality. The very issues that brought about a more active federal government—poverty, economic instability, complex relationships at home and with other global powers—still exist. It is therefore difficult to imagine that the federal government might become substantially less active and less involved in the wide array of policy issues. Consider what would happen if one state did not maintain high educational standards. The economy of the entire region could be harmed as the quality of the workforce deteriorated, encouraging employers to relocate their businesses. If the health care system of one state became significantly substandard, neighboring states would experience a crisis as people flocked to them seeking better services. Population shifts can create new burdens for states. With increased globalization and the resultant international competition for scarce resources, the days of big national government are not likely to end.

The Supreme Court's Shift in Perspective

Since 1968, Republican presidents have selected 12 of the 16 new justices who have served on the Court (President Obama's nomination of Mr. Merrick Garland to the Supreme Court to replace Justice Antonin Scalia was not acted upon). Through their judicial opinions, several of these justices have expressed concern about a steady lessening of states' authority to manage their own affairs. By the mid-1990s, justices who were concerned about striking a new balance of power in American federalism gained a slim 5-4 majority. And beginning in 1995, the Supreme Court issued decisions limiting the power of the federal government and consequently opening the way for states to control a greater number of policy issues. In *United States* v. *Lopez* (1995), the Supreme Court struck down the Gun-Free School Zones Act of 1990, which made it a crime to possess a firearm near a school. The Court's majority concluded that congressional power to regulate interstate commerce did not include the authority to create this particular law. The Court made a similar decision in striking down portions of the Violence Against Women Act of 1994, in which Congress had permitted victims of sexual violence and gender-based attacks to file federal lawsuits against their attackers (*United States* v. *Morrison,* 2000).

TIMELINE

Legalizing Marijuana

Concern over drug use in the United States is not new; however, more controversy over drugs exists today than ever before. Should the government work to legalize marijuana, treating it similarly to alcohol, or should the government continue to minimize its use by keeping it criminal? The issues surrounding the legalization debate are more far-reaching than simply drug policy—they strike at the very heart of our federal system of government. Under federal law, marijuana is considered a Schedule I drug (meaning that it is considered as having a high potential for abuse and has no proven or acceptable medical use). Other Schedule I drugs include heroin, LSD, and ecstasy. However, marijuana is currently legal (with varying restrictions) in 25 states and the District of Columbia. The Obama administration has decided not to prosecute those complying with state law—even though they are violating federal law.

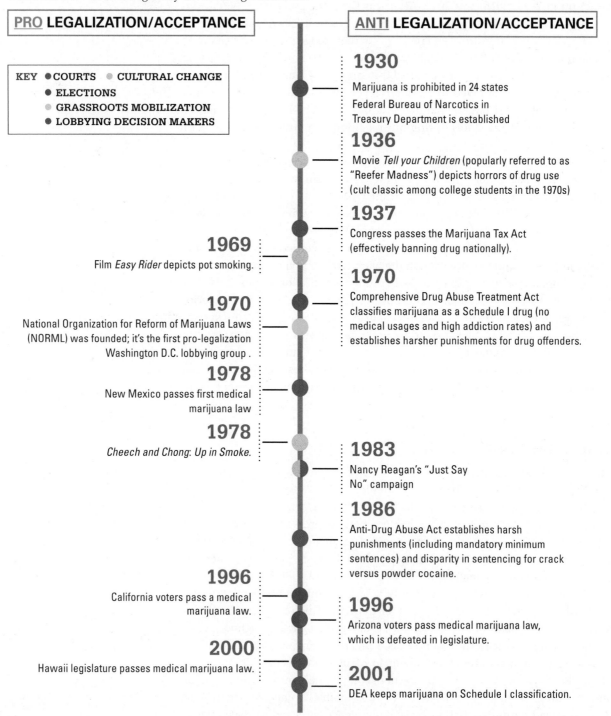

PRO LEGALIZATION/ACCEPTANCE

ANTI LEGALIZATION/ACCEPTANCE

KEY ● COURTS ● CULTURAL CHANGE
● ELECTIONS
● GRASSROOTS MOBILIZATION
● LOBBYING DECISION MAKERS

1930
Marijuana is prohibited in 24 states
Federal Bureau of Narcotics in Treasury Department is established

1936
Movie *Tell your Children* (popularly referred to as "Reefer Madness") depicts horrors of drug use (cult classic among college students in the 1970s)

1969
Film *Easy Rider* depicts pot smoking.

1937
Congress passes the Marijuana Tax Act (effectively banning drug nationally).

1970
National Organization for Reform of Marijuana Laws (NORML) was founded; it's the first pro-legalization Washington D.C. lobbying group .

1970
Comprehensive Drug Abuse Treatment Act classifies marijuana as a Schedule I drug (no medical usages and high addiction rates) and establishes harsher punishments for drug offenders.

1978
New Mexico passes first medical marijuana law

1978
Cheech and Chong: Up in Smoke.

1983
Nancy Reagan's "Just Say No" campaign

1986
Anti-Drug Abuse Act establishes harsh punishments (including mandatory minimum sentences) and disparity in sentencing for crack versus powder cocaine.

1996
California voters pass a medical marijuana law.

1996
Arizona voters pass medical marijuana law, which is defeated in legislature.

2000
Hawaii legislature passes medical marijuana law.

2001
DEA keeps marijuana on Schedule I classification.

PRO LEGALIZATION/ACCEPTANCE	ANTI LEGALIZATION/ACCEPTANCE

2001
Supreme Court (*U.S.* v. *Oakland Cannabis Buyers' Cooperative*) re-affirms federal drug law.

2001
Portugal decriminalizes drugs.

2005
Supreme Court (*Gonzales* v. *Raich*) – Congress may criminalize production and use of medical marijuana (under the commerce clause) despite state law allowing it.

2009
Attorney General Eric Holder Jr. says that Obama administration will defer to state medical marijuana laws and not prosecute those complying with state law Medical marijuana legal in Washington D.C. when Congress allows a D.C. council bill to become law.

2006
FDA says marijuana has no medical value and can be harmful.

2011
Sixteen states have legalized medical marijuana.

KEY ● COURTS ● CULTURAL CHANGE
● ELECTIONS
● GRASSROOTS MOBILIZATION
● LOBBYING DECISION MAKERS

October 2011
Gallup reports 50 percent of Americans (highest ever) favor legalizing marijuana.

November 6, 2012
Colorado and Washington voters legalized recreational use of marijuana.

2015
23 states and DC have laws allowing legalized use of marijuana in some form, 4 states and DC allow for recreational use—rest have either decriminalized small amounts and/or allow use for medical purposes, 57% of men and 49% of women favor legalizing marijuana.

2016
9 states had ballot initiatives to either legalize recreational or medical use of marijuana. All but one passed.

❯ **POLL** Given that the majority of Americans favor legalizing marijuana, do you think the federal government should reclassify it so that it is considered legal in the United States?

SOURCE: October Gallup poll found 58% of country favored legalization – 71% of 18-34-year-olds (up from 44% fifteen years earlier) – compared to 58% of 50-64-year-olds and 35% of those over 65, http://www.gallup.com/poll/186260/back-legal-marijuana.aspx.

CRITICAL THINKING QUESTIONS

1. Should marijuana be reclassified as Schedule II Controlled Substance (substances considered Level II have a high potential for abuse which may lead to dependency but do have a recognized medical use, like morphine, opium, OxyContin, and Ritalin)? Many see marijuana as a gateway drug often leading to more dangerous drugs that are more addictive and heighten criminal behavior in addicts. What do you think? Should all states legalize marijuana?

2. Do you think the Obama administration is correct to order the agencies of the federal government (such as the Drug Enforcement Administration) to ignore sales of medical marijuana? Are such inconsistencies between federal and state law acceptable? What about neighboring states who want to keep drugs out of their borders—does legalization in one state impact the ability of others to keep their citizens drug free?

SOURCE: Michael Cooper, "2 Governors Asking US to Ease Rules on Marijuana to Allow for Its Medical Use," *New York Times,* November 30, 2011, accessed on December 1, 2011, http://www.nytimes.com/2011/12/01/us/federal-marijuana-classification-should-change-gregoire-and-chafee-say.html; Peter Katel, "Legalizing Marijuana," *CQ Researcher* 19 (June 2009) update July 21, 2010: 525–548; Frank Newport, "Record-High 50% of Americans Favor Legalizing Marijuana Use," October 17, 2011, accessed on December 1, 2011, http://www.gallup.com/poll/150149/Record-High-Americans-Favor-Legalizin g-Marijuana.aspx.

The Violence Against Women Act of 1994 was passed to enhance the investigation and prosecution of violent crimes perpetrated against women. The law provided federal funds to local law enforcement agencies and allowed victims of gender-based violence the right to sue for compensation in federal court. The Supreme Court ruled that the component of the law guaranteeing victims greater power to seek redress in federal court was unconstitutional (*United States v. Morrison*, 2000). After a controversial process, the law was reauthorized in 2013 and now includes protections for Native Americans living on reservations, undocumented immigrants, and gays, lesbians, and transgender individuals.

■ *Do you think that Congress should address domestic violence? Or, should this be left to the states? Do you think enough is being done to end partner violence in the United States?*

The Court also revived the Tenth Amendment, a provision of the Constitution that was generally treated as a powerless slogan by justices from the late 1930s through the mid-1990s. In *Printz* v. *United States* (1997), the Court declared that Congress cannot require state and local officials to conduct background checks on people who seek to buy firearms. In *Gonzales* v. *Raich* (2005), the Court rules that Congress can criminalize the production of cannabis under the Constitution's Commerce Clause, even if states have approved the drug for medical uses. The Court's decisions on the Tenth Amendment's protection of state authority and the limits of congressional power to regulate interstate commerce indicated that the Supreme Court would no longer automatically endorse assertions of federal power at the expense of state authority. The Supreme Court was called upon to examine the constitutionality of several components of the Affordable Care Act. In 2012, the Supreme Court upheld the law but declared that states must be allowed to opt out of Medicaid expansion (*NFIB* v. *Sebelius*). The Court ruled that the ACA was not a mandate but was rather a tax (uninsured Americans may now have to pay a tax and those who opt in may receive a reduction in taxes). In a second case (*King* v. *Burwell*, 2015), the Supreme Court upheld tax credits for state-run health exchanges (a key component of the law). However, the Supreme Court issued a blow to the Obama administration in *Burwell* v. *Hobby Lobby Stores* (2015). The Court ruled that "closely held corporations" (generally thought to be one in which the majority of the stock is held by no more than five people) cannot be required to provide health insurance which covers certain forms of contraception that violate deeply held religious convictions (the ACA required such coverage for private businesses).

〉 POLL Do you agree with the Supreme Court's decision in *Burwell* v. *Hobby Lobby* (that companies should be able to decide which types of contraceptives the health insurance for their employees should cover)?

While the federal government remains actively involved in a wide array of public policies, recent decisions indicate that the Supreme Court stands ready to selectively reject specific assertions of federal power that it considers excessive under its new vision of the Constitution's framework for federalism.

Current Challenges Facing State and Local Governments

As we grapple with the balance of authority and responsibility that should be accorded to each level of government, we realize that answers are difficult to come by and that the problems facing our country are very complex. In many cases, states and localities are presented with the real need to balance services against tax rates. Local communities and states tend to desire lower tax rates so that they can attract and retain businesses. They like to promote their communities as attractive places to live and do business, so they have to make tough fiscal choices. As such, localities rarely introduce redistributive policies, which promote equality by redistributing resources from the more affluent to those in need. State governments are also often reluctant as they want their states to be seen as favorable to business investments; consequently, the promotion of equality and providing public services are often not top priorities for state governments either. Thus, economic disparity across the nation is increasing. The poverty rate in urban areas is extremely high. The United States stands out among advanced industrial societies as having among the worst income inequality in the world. America ranks in the bottom half of nearly 90 countries studied by the Center for Global Development, behind most of Western Europe, Eastern Europe, India, Niger, and Ethiopia.[16] Income differentials based upon educational attainment are the highest in our history. Consequently, the economic gap is likely to continue to widen rather than decrease. Poverty often hits localities hard and many are unable to address the needs of their residents. Not only do states have to worry about increased demand for services in times of economic hardship, they also have to contend with lower revenue. For example, in 2008, states collected $358.8 billion in sales taxes, but that figure declined to $322.4 billion in 2010 (the worst year in sales tax during the recession). By 2011 the figures rose to $369.6 billion and have increased every year since. In 2013, sales taxes increased to $393.8 billion, accounting for 46.5 percent of total revenue.[17] During economically difficult times, states become more dependent upon other forms of revenue as sales taxes decline. Many states become increasingly reliant upon property taxes. For example, in 2008, states collected $12.7 billion in property taxes, but that figure rose to $14.5 billion in only two years. Consequently, during the recession, when the worst of the housing crisis was hitting localities across the country, states were increasingly relying upon property taxes as an important source of revenue.[18] In many instances, individual homeowners are finding it increasingly difficult to pay their tax bills and renters are seeing their rents increase. Another challenge facing states are the costs associated with crime. Prison costs have skyrocketed to the point that correction costs consume one in every 15 state discretionary dollars.[19] The United States is the world's incarceration leader. We have only around five percent of world's population but confine 25 percent of the world's prisoners.[20] Moreover, state spending on corrections increased by 700 percent since the late 1970s, and currently is the fourth largest expenditure category in state budgets.[21] Several states are considering significant reforms to their criminal justice systems, many of which include reexamining punitive policies toward drug offenders put into place in the 1980s and early 1990s.

Throughout the history of our country the Supreme Court has been called upon to decide some very controversial decisions. Pictured here are protesters outside the court building the morning the justices were hearing oral arguments in *Obergefell* v. *Hodges*. Many heralded the decision as a triumph for equality while others saw it as violating the rights of states to regulate marriage.

■ *Do you think the Supreme Court overstepped its boundaries or was their action dictated to enforce the Equal Protection Clause of the Fourteenth Amendment?*

States are also reconsidering mandatory minimum sentences and first offender programs to reduce the size of the prison population and ideally to minimize recidivism rates. However, not all states are reducing drug sentences. Maine reduced sentences for some drug possessions but increased the penalty for cocaine and fentanyl powder (an opioid similar to heroin).

The changing demographics in our country are also creating a number of problems for state and local governments. Health care systems in many communities are overwhelmed, as are local school districts that may be ill prepared for the needs of immigrant communities. Demographic changes impact states differentially. For example, some states have little or no need for bilingual education while others are overwhelmed. Intense conflict exists in many states over immigrant communities. Anti-immigrant sentiment is not new. For example, the Know Nothing Party (later renamed the American Party) was a nativist party, which was organized to oppose changes brought about by German and Irish immigrants (largely Catholic) who threatened the dominant Anglo-Saxon Protestants in the late 1840s and 1850s. However, the level of anti-immigrant sentiment today seems higher than in previous times (we have no reliable social scientific data regarding public opinion during these earlier time periods) and made more salient by technology, which allows nativist groups to solidify their support and network.

Conclusion

We have outlined some practical and theoretical reasons for a federal system—why a democracy such as ours might have layers of governmental authority. The foremost original explanation for federalism in the American setting was the need for compromise. Most Americans understood the necessity of a stronger national government given the failures of the Articles of Confederation, but many also worried about a distant, unresponsive, and potentially tyrannical national government. Why not look to one level of government to regulate commerce, conduct foreign policy, and safeguard national security while another level provided basic services and looked after law and order? Dual federalism seemed natural, even logical, during the early years of our republic. Yet, determining precisely which layer of government is responsible for certain functions—and, when push comes to shove, which layer is superior—has never been simple. The struggle over appropriate governmental authority has been at the heart of nearly all critical periods in American history.

Given that there is no clear or universally agreed upon way to allocate responsibilities among layers of our government, the nature of federalism has been shaped by the individuals who happened to be in charge of government, either as elected officials or as judges, during crucial periods. In effect, the course of federalism is like a pendulum that swings between different approaches to allocating national and state authority, depending on the problems faced by the nation and the viewpoints of the individuals in positions of political and judicial power. From the New Deal until the 1980s, for example, the Democrats controlled the federal government most of the time, and argued that a strong national government offered the best means of helping citizens reach their potential and ridding society of its ills. Their approach called for merging each layer of government into unified action to attack these problems. The use of categorical grants under Lyndon Johnson's Great Society program is a clear example of how officials in Washington have used federal monies to advance their priorities at the state and local levels.

The election of Ronald Reagan in 1980 and of a Republican Congress in 1994 produced a shift to less federal intervention—and less federal money—at the state level. George W. Bush's 2001–2008 budget proposals reflected an even more constrained view of the federal government's role in many domestic policy areas. In direct contrast to this, in February 2009, with the nation facing a severe economic crisis, President Obama signed into law a massive federal economic stimulus package. The package rekindled the debate about the proper role of the federal government and federalism itself. With the passage of Obamacare, the federal government's role in state health care systems increased dramatically. The current dilemma over drug policy and illegal immigration demonstrates the difficult challenges facing our country. When federal and state law conflict, like it currently does with regard to marijuana, or when states become frustrated by the lack of action in addressing problems stemming from illegal immigration, we once again are forced to examine the proper balance of power between the federal and state governments. These problems with drug policy and illegal immigration renew the debate about our federal system and the vitality of state governments.

Make no mistake, state and local governments will remain vital in the United States no matter which party controls Congress, the White House, or the federal judiciary. But exactly how much federal help (or interference) states and communities will receive is an open question. One thing is certain: Anyone who is interested in playing a role in politics should pay close attention to the federalism debate. The pathways of change are not simply about pushing government in a certain direction but rather about pushing the *correct level* of government in a new direction.

CONFRONTING POLITICS AND POLICY

During Thanksgiving time, most Americans think about turkey, family, and football. But this perspective is not the case for law enforcement officers in Southern California. Each November, drug agents seize incredible quantities of drugs crossing the boarder from Mexican marijuana crops harvested in October in underground tunnels. On November 29, 2011, drug agents discovered a 600-yard sophisticated tunnel with electric carts, hydraulic lifts, ventilation, and more than 32 tons of marijuana. More than 80 similar tunnels have been found since 2006. In November 2010, authorities found two tunnels between San Diego and Tijuana with over 52 tons of marijuana on both sides of the boarder.[22] In April 2014, two drug-smuggling tunnels were found between San Diego and Tijuana, with a 73-year-old California woman allegedly running one tunnel. Despite a nearly 50-year-long war on drugs, the demand for illegal drugs in the United States is high. In October 2015, a "super tunnel" with a railway, electricity and reinforced metal beams stretching the length of eight football fields was found between warehouses in Tijuana and San Diego. Authorities confiscated over twelve tons of marijuana worth over $6 million. Law enforcement agents seem to be fighting a losing battle. Consequently many feel that we need to reexamine our national drug policy. What do you think? Can we stop the supply without adequately addressing the demand?

ACTION STEPS

1. Imagine the National Organization for Reform of Marijuana Laws (NORML) hired you to develop a new public relations campaign to encourage Congress to reexamine our national drug policy. What do you think are the two most compelling arguments you could offer to legalize marijuana? What are the two largest obstacles that you'd anticipate facing? How would you run an ad campaign to mobilize support for your organization?

2. Why do you think most Americans see the drug violence in our southern neighbor to be a Mexican problem? How can we convince people that the demand in the United States for illegal drugs is largely to blame for the violence? What, if any, responsibility does the United States have for the problems in Mexico resulting from drug trafficking?

❯ REVIEW THE CHAPTER

Dividing Governmental Authority

3.1 Explain how and why the framers divided authority between layers of government. (p. 67)

Unlike most democracies in the world, which have unitary systems of governance, the United States has a federal system. In this country, power and authority are divided between layers of government. There are many explanations—historical, theoretical, cultural, and pragmatic—for why the United States relies on a federal system. Probably the best explanation is that dividing power between the national government and the state governments was a compromise that kept the Constitutional Convention on track.

Dual Federalism

3.2 Characterize dual federalism both before and after the Civil War. (p. 77)

During the early years of our republic, there was much confusion over the division of authority, and this controversy produced crucial Supreme Court cases such as *McCulloch* v. *Maryland* (1819). Until the Civil War, dual federalism existed, meaning that neither the state nor the federal government was superior, and each had specific duties and obligations. To a large extent, the Civil War was fought over the issue of supremacy—determining which level of government, state or national, should be supreme. In the years after the Civil War, as a consequence of Supreme Court decisions, the power of the federal government was limited until the Great Depression.

Cooperative and Creative Federalism

3.3 Compare and contrast cooperative and creative federalism. (p. 84)

The nature of federalism in the United States changed irrevocably during the Great Depression as Franklin Roosevelt's New Deal thrust the federal government into nearly every realm of domestic governance and ushered in an era of cooperative federalism. For the next several decades, the power of the federal government continued to grow. Beginning with Johnson's administration and the Great Society programs, federalism became more creative with the use of federal grants to promote national goals; these grants continue to be controversial today.

Recent Trends in Federalism

3.4 Trace the evolution of federalism in recent decades. (p. 89)

As our society continues to change, so too does federalism. Federalism is best viewed as a "pendulum model," whereby power and authority continually shift, reflecting the perspective of the people in power, the social and economic conditions, and the outlook of the courts. Although fewer and fewer policy areas exist where the reach of the national government does not extend, a growing concern, especially among conservative politicians, has been to revive local governing authority. Devolution is the term used to describe the return of authority from the federal to the state level, and this occurred in some policy areas during the Bush administration. However since Obama's first year in office in 2009, the trend toward devolution evident under the Bush administration began to end. With the passage of the federal bailout and Obamacare, the size and scope of the federal government grew considerably.

❯ LEARN THE TERMS

〉 EXPLORE FURTHER

In the Library

Barber, Benjamin R. *If Mayors Ruled the World: Dysfunctional Nations, Rising Cities.* New Haven, CT: Yale University Press, 2013.

Burgess, Michael. *In Search of the Federal Spirit: New Theoretical and Empirical Perspectives in Comparative Federalism.* New York: Oxford University Press, 2012.

Gagnon, Alain-G., Soeren Keil and Sean Mueller, eds. *Understanding Federalism and Federation.* New York: Routledge, 2016.

Gulasekaram, Pratheepan and S. Karthick Ramakrishnan. *The New Immigration Federalism.* New York: Cambridge University Press, 2015.

Hudak, John. *Presidential Pork: White House Influence over the Distribution of Federal Grants.* Washington, D.C.: The Brookings Institution, 2014.

Keech, William R. *Economic Politics in the United States: The Costs and Risks of Democracy,* 2nd ed. New York: Cambridge University Press, 2013.

Nolette, Paul. *Federalism on Trial: State Attorneys General and National Policymaking in Contemporary America.* Lawrence, Kansas: University Press of Kansas, 2015.

Reed, Douglas S. *Building the Federal Schoolhouse: Localism and the American Education State.* New York: Oxford University Press, 2014.

Thomson, Vivian. *Sophisticated Interdependence in Climate Policy: Federalism in the United States, Brazil, and Germany.* New York: Anthem Press, 2014.

On the Web

The Federalist Society: *http://www.fed-soc.org/.*

The Council of State Governments: *http://www.csg.org/.*

The History of U.S. Federalism: *http://www.cas.sc.edu/poli/courses/scgov/History_of_Federalism.htm.*

National Governors Association: *http://www.nga.org.*

United States Conference of Mayors: *http://www.usmayors.org.*

Real Food Challenge: Uniting students for just and sustainable food: *http://realfoodchallenge.org/.*

The Office of Management and Budget: *http://www.whitehouse.gov/omb/.*

CIVIL LIBERTIES

Police officers possess the authority to stop drivers for traffic violations or ask questions of passing pedestrians. Police can also use their discretion to place people under arrest and take them to jail when there is evidence of criminal activity. Yet, under the U.S. Constitution, police are not supposed to have unlimited authority because Americans possess constitutional rights to protect aspects of their liberty and privacy.

■ *Under what circumstances, if any, do you believe that police officers should be able to examine someone's cell phone to look for evidence of a crime?*

→ LEARNING OBJECTIVES

4.1 Explain how the Bill of Rights came to protect individuals against actions by state governments.

4.2 Distinguish between the two dimensions of freedom of religion in the First Amendment.

4.3 Specify the limits on free speech in the United States.

4.4 Assess the test for justifying governmental limitations on written words and images.

4.5 Specify the protections afforded to criminal suspects in the Bill of Rights.

4.6 Evaluate the legal protections that seek to ensure only guilty people receive criminal punishment.

4.7 Explain why the right to privacy is controversial.

In January 2016, Martin LaLonde, a member of Vermont's state legislature, proposed a law that would authorize that state's police officers to examine "portable electronic devices" inside vehicles when they make traffic stops. The intent of the law was to enable officers to catch people who violated the "distracted driving" law by texting on their cellphones while behind the wheel of a car. The law would operate on the same basis as "implied consent" laws throughout the country in which licensed drivers are presumed to have agreed to submit to breathalyzer tests. Refusal to submit to such tests can be used as evidence in drunk driving cases and can be the basis for suspension of drivers' licenses. Thus a driver's refusal to hand over a cellphone to police during a traffic stop could have similar consequences under Vermont's proposed law.[1] Would any constitutional rights be violated by mandating that police officers gain access to drivers' cellphones during traffic stops? What if officers scrolled through text messages, email, and photos on a driver's cellphone? If you were a driver stopped by police, would you feel that your rights had been violated if officers examined the contents of your phone?

The proposed Vermont law could collide with citizens' rights under the Fourth Amendment to the U.S. Constitution. In particular, if the law was challenged in court, judges would need to decide whether such examinations of drivers' cellphones violate the protection against "unreasonable searches." In 2014, the U.S. Supreme Court declared that just such a Fourth Amendment violation had occurred when police officers looked through photos on a cellphone after arresting a driver. Photos discovered on the phone provided evidence of the driver's possible involvement in a gang-related shooting. In its decision in *Riley* v. *California* (2014), the Supreme Court said that officers must seek a search warrant from a judge before examining the contents of an arrested driver's cellphone. The officers in the *Riley* case acted on their own in examining the cellphone. By contrast, if the Vermont law was enacted, officers in that state would enjoy specific authorization under state law to examine drivers' cellphones. The phrase "unreasonable searches" in the Fourth Amendment is vague, much like many other constitutional phrases that announce the civil liberties and rights possessed by Americans. Thus the determination of whether a constitutional right is affected by the proposed Vermont law would rest on the interpretive decisions of the judges called upon to clarify the meaning of the Fourth Amendment. Do you believe such warrantless examinations of drivers' cellphones should be prohibited as "unreasonable searches"?

DO AMERICANS HAVE TOO MANY OR TOO FEW CIVIL LIBERTIES PROTECTIONS?

The Supreme Court's decision in *Riley* v. *California* (2014) limited the ability of police officers to find evidence of crimes that might be easily discovered through a quick look at a driver's cellphone. Yet the Supreme Court's justices felt obligated to protect people from such searches, even in a situation in which evidence from an attempted murder would be excluded from use in court because they deemed the cellphone examination to be an improper search. Judges make decisions that define the civil liberties—individuals' freedoms and legal protections that cannot be denied by actions of government—guaranteed by the Bill of Rights and the Fourteenth Amendment. When judges conclude that a legal protection exists, it is available even for individuals whose ideas and actions anger most Americans, including those involved in serious, violent crimes. Definitions of civil liberties change over time as new judges assume office and interpret the Constitution in different ways or as sitting judges change their views.

The Bill of Rights in History

4.1 Explain how the Bill of Rights came to protect individuals against actions by state governments.

civil liberties

Individual freedoms and legal protections guaranteed by the Bill of Rights that cannot be denied or hindered by government. For example, burning an American flag during a protest, as was done at the Republican convention in 2016, is protected as a form of symbolic speech under the First Amendment.

As you've seen in earlier chapters, the 10 constitutional amendments that make up the Bill of Rights were added to the U.S. Constitution in 1791 to provide **civil liberties** for individuals. These amendments were enacted in response to fears that the Constitution had failed to provide enough legal protections for individuals. The experiences of eighteenth-century Americans with British rule gave the Founders reason to be concerned that a government might become too powerful and thereby fail to respect individuals' liberty and property. The Bill of Rights spelled out the legal protections that individuals could expect from the federal government. Later, the Fourteenth Amendment added words to declare the existence of legal protections against state governments, such as the right to "due process." Mere words on paper, however, do not, by themselves, provide protection against actions by government officials. Those words must be respected by officials, and there must be judges willing to interpret and enforce the underlying meanings.

Early Interpretation of the Bill of Rights

During the first years after ratification of the U.S. Constitution and the Bill of Rights, the tiny federal court system handled relatively few cases. The U.S. Supreme Court was seen as a weak institution that did not have much influence over major issues of public affairs. The U.S. Supreme Court's most important cases from this era involved decisions that defined the authority of the various institutions of American government and clarified the respective powers of state and federal governments. The Supreme Court played an important role in interpreting constitutional provisions in ways that created a workable distribution of power among branches of government and defined the relationships between state and federal governments.

The Supreme Court's role as a guardian of civil liberties did not emerge until the 1950s, when the Bill of Rights became a central focus of decisions by federal judges. One reason that the federal courts did not focus much attention on the Bill of Rights was because of the way the Supreme Court first interpreted the legal protections for individuals contained in the Constitution. In an early case, a man named Barron sued the city of Baltimore over road construction work that damaged his wharf at the harbor. He claimed the city violated his Fifth Amendment right against the government taking private property "without just compensation." The Supreme Court's decision in *Barron* v. *Baltimore* (1833) was written by Chief Justice John Marshall, a crucial figure who shaped the Supreme Court's role in the nation during the federal judiciary's formative decades (1801–1835). After examining the arguments in the case, Marshall concluded the following:

> We are of the opinion that the provision in the Fifth Amendment to the Constitution … is intended solely as a limitation on the exercise of power by the Government of the United States, and is not applicable to the legislation of the States.

Marshall's decision reflected the original intent of the Bill of Rights as well as the literal words at the start of the First Amendment, which refer to the federal government: "Congress shall make no law…." The effect of Marshall's decision went beyond merely limiting the Fifth Amendment's protections; it also established the fact that all the provisions of the Bill of Rights protected *only* against actions by the *federal* government, not against actions by state and local government.

Think about the implications of the Court's decision. Although Americans take justifiable pride in the Bill of Rights as an important statement about civil liberties, during most of American history those protections have applied only against actions by the federal government. State constitutions provided protections for individuals within the boundaries of individual states, but the rights listed in these documents varied from state to state and were defined and implemented in varying ways. Many state courts did not rigorously interpret and enforce individual rights. The actual civil liberties enjoyed by citizens could differ dramatically, depending on which state a person happened to live in or be visiting. As a result, many states had laws restricting speech, press, assembly, and other aspects of civil liberties, and these laws were unaffected by the existence of the idealistic language of the Bill of Rights.

The Incorporation Process and the Nationalization of Constitutional Rights

Three amendments were added to the Constitution after the Civil War (1861–1865). Members of Congress proposed the amendments primarily to provide protections for African Americans who were newly freed from slavery. However, one of the amendments, the Fourteenth (ratified in 1868), gave the Constitution language granting legal protections for all individuals against actions by state and local officials. The key language in the first section of the Fourteenth Amendment says,

> No State shall make or enforce any law which shall abridge the privileges or immunities of citizens of the United States; nor shall any State deprive any person of life, liberty, or property, without due process of law; nor deny to any person within its jurisdiction the equal protection of the laws.

The words of the Fourteenth Amendment specified that these constitutional protections were aimed against actions by states, but the precise protections were not clear. It would require interpretations by judges to determine what specific protections, if any, would be provided by the phrases "privileges or immunities of citizens," "due process of law," and "equal protection of the laws." One scholar has called the Fourteenth Amendment "probably the most controversial and certainly the most litigated of all amendments adopted since the birth of the Republic."[2]

Lawyers used the court pathway to present arguments to the U.S. Supreme Court and other courts about specific legal protections that they believed the Fourteenth Amendment should provide for their clients. In particular, they asked the Court to interpret the **Due Process Clause** of the amendment as providing specific civil liberties to protect individuals against actions by state and local officials.

For several decades, the Supreme Court generally refused to specify the protections provided by the phrase "due process." In 1925, however, the Court began to move in a new direction by declaring that the First Amendment right to free speech is included in the protections of the Fourteenth Amendment's Due Process Clause. According to the Court's decision that year in *Gitlow* v. *New York*, individuals enjoy the right to freedom of speech against actions and laws by state and local governments. (The state of New York had prosecuted Benjamin Gitlow, a member of the Socialist Party, for distributing publications that advocated overthrowing the U.S. government.) Although the Supreme Court said that individuals enjoy the protections of free speech against actions by state governments, Gitlow's conviction was upheld because the Court did not regard his advocacy of socialism as protected by the First Amendment. Today the Supreme Court takes a broader view of free speech, and Gitlow could not be imprisoned for criticizing the government or advocating change.

In subsequent years, the Court began to bring other specific civil liberties under the protection of the Fourteenth Amendment's Due Process Clause. For example, in *Near* v. *Minnesota* (1931), the Court included freedom of the press under the Fourteenth

Due Process Clause

A statement of rights in the Fifth Amendment (aimed at the federal government) and the Fourteenth Amendment (aimed at state and local governments) that protects against arbitrary deprivations of life, liberty, or property. The Fourteenth Amendment phrase is also interpreted by the Supreme Court to expand a variety of rights, such as identifying a right to privacy in the concept of personal "liberty" that the clause protects against arbitrary government interference.

Amendment. The Court added the First Amendment's right to free exercise of religion under the Due Process Clause in 1934 (*Hamilton* v. *Regents of the University of California*) and firmly repeated that conclusion in 1940 (*Cantwell* v. *Connecticut*).

The process through which the Supreme Court examined individual provisions of the Bill of Rights and applied them against state and local officials is called **incorporation**. Over the course of a half-century, the Court *incorporated* specific civil liberties from the Bill of Rights into the meaning of the Due Process Clause of the Fourteenth Amendment. The Court used a process of selective incorporation as lawyers sought the incorporation of a specific right, such as free speech or free exercise of religion, in a particular case. As discussed in Pathways of Action, in its most recent incorporation case in 2010 (*McDonald* v. *Chicago*), Supreme Court justices voted 5-4 to incorporate the Second Amendment's right for law-abiding adults to keep a handgun in their homes for self-protection. Incorporation gave individuals throughout the nation the same civil liberties protections against actions by state and local governments.

The Supreme Court's narrow definition of the Second Amendment right has had little impact on the most law-abiding Americans' ability to obtain a variety of firearms and to obtain permits to carry concealed weapons. The Court left open the opportunity for governments to regulate firearms, but few places have acted in the manner of Highland Park, Illinois, by banning specific weapons. Instead, opportunities for gun ownership seem well-protected, not by the courts pathway, but by the elections pathway. Actual opportunities to own and carry guns are most affected by the success

incorporation

The process used by the Supreme Court to protect individuals from actions by state and local governments by interpreting the Due Process Clause of the Fourteenth Amendment as containing selected provisions of the Bill of Rights. For example, in *Klopfer* v. *North Carolina* (1967), the U.S. Supreme Court held that the Sixth Amendment right to a speedy trial is fundamental to the criminal justice process and therefore applies to state criminal trials through the Fourteenth Amendment's Due Process Clause.

PATHWAYS OF ACTION

THE RIGHT TO OWN GUNS

The Second Amendment says "A well-regulated Militia, being necessary for the security of a free State, the right of the people to keep and bear Arms, shall not be infringed." Americans have long debated the meaning of this amendment. Does it give people a right to own or carry firearms? Do the words "well-regulated Militia" mean that only members of a state's National Guard are entitled to possess guns? Is the phrase about "Militia" separate from the final phrase about "the right of the people"? The answers to these questions are in the hands of the justices of the U.S. Supreme Court as well as other federal judges, all of whom possess the authority to interpret the words of the Constitution.

For most of American history, the U.S. Supreme Court avoided cases that sought interpretation of the Second Amendment. In 2008, however, a five-member majority on the Supreme Court declared that Washington, D.C., and other federal jurisdictions cannot prohibit law-abiding citizens from keeping handguns in their homes for the purpose of self-defense. These five justices declared that the Second Amendment provided a limited right to handgun ownership (*District of Columbia* v. *Heller*, 2008). The four dissenting justices argued that the Second Amendment's opening words about a "well-regulated Militia" merely meant that states are entitled to arm their state militia, now known as the National Guard.

The decision in the *Heller* case, a long-sought victory for gun-rights advocates, encouraged like-minded individuals to file parallel lawsuits against various cities and states in order to seek incorporation of the Second Amendment. In 2010, one such lawsuit led the Supreme Court to incorporate the Second Amendment and apply it against a City of Chicago ordinance that sought to ban the possession of handguns within city limits (*McDonald* v. *City of Chicago*). The words of the Second Amendment have not changed, but the words gained new meaning through the Court's decisions in 2008 and 2010.

Although the Second Amendment is now recognized as applying against prohibitions imposed by federal, state, or local governments that would prevent people from keeping handguns at home, some people believe that the Second Amendment has broader meaning. Many Americans argue that they have a Second Amendment right to carry concealed firearms, carry firearms in public, and own semi-automatic assault rifles. Yet, the Supreme Court has limited the definition of the Second Amendment right to handguns kept at home. Moreover, the Court's decisions have specifically left open opportunities for governments to regulate who can own firearms (such as possible exclusions for ex-felons and people with certain diagnosed mental illnesses), which firearms can be owned, and how firearms can be sold. Indeed, in December 2015, the Supreme Court declined to consider a challenge to a municipal ordinance in Highland Park, Illinois, that banned ownership of semi-automatic assault rifles and firearms with a capacity to hold more than ten bullets (*Friedman* v. *Highland Park*). By declining to accept the case, the Court seemed to reinforce its decision that the Amendment only protects ownership of handguns kept at home.

The Supreme Court has ruled that the Second Amendment guarantees law-abiding adults the right to keep a handgun in the home for self-protection. Many Americans believe the Second Amendment should be interpreted to protect gun rights more broadly, including a right to carry firearms—either concealed or openly—throughout society. Other Americans would like to see strict limits on selling and carrying firearms.

■ *Because the Supreme Court has only protected the right to keep handguns in the home, why are people in many states able to own a variety of other weapons and carry those weapons in public?*

of gun rights interest groups in lobbying legislators to enact laws that permit buying and carrying guns in ways that exceed the Supreme Court's definition of the Second Amendment right.

> POLL Would you prioritize the protection of Second Amendment rights ("the right to bear arms") or gun control legislation?

However, total incorporation of the Bill of Rights did not occur. A few provisions of the Bill of Rights have never been incorporated and thus still provide protections solely against actions by the federal government. Several provisions have yet to be incorporated:

- Third Amendment's provision against housing troops in private homes
- Fifth Amendment's right to a grand jury
- Seventh Amendment's requirement of jury trials in civil cases contesting any amount over $20
- Eighth Amendment's prohibition of excessive bail

The incorporation process served to apply most of the provisions in the Bill of Rights everywhere within the United States in order to protect individuals against actions by all levels of government. Thus, the process of incorporation is also referred to as the "nationalization" of the Bill of Rights. Figure 4.1 illustrates key Supreme Court decisions that established important civil liberties.

First Amendment Rights: Freedom of Religion

4.2 Distinguish between the two dimensions of freedom of religion in the First Amendment.

Many political scientists believe that the drafters of the Bill of Rights placed special importance on the rights listed first. Indeed, several Supreme Court justices have argued that First Amendment rights should be regarded as "preferred freedoms" that receive extra attention from judges.[3]

FIGURE 4.1 Key Decisions on Civil Liberties

The Bill of Rights initially protected individuals' civil liberties only against actions by the federal government. The Fourteenth Amendment (1868) added language to the Constitution to prohibit state and local officials from violating the right to "due process." Over the course of several decades, the U.S. Supreme Court interpreted the phrase "due process" in ways that required state and local officials to respect specific civil liberties protections in the Bill of Rights. The Supreme Court also interpreted specific provisions in the Bill of Rights to expand the legal protections enjoyed by individuals.

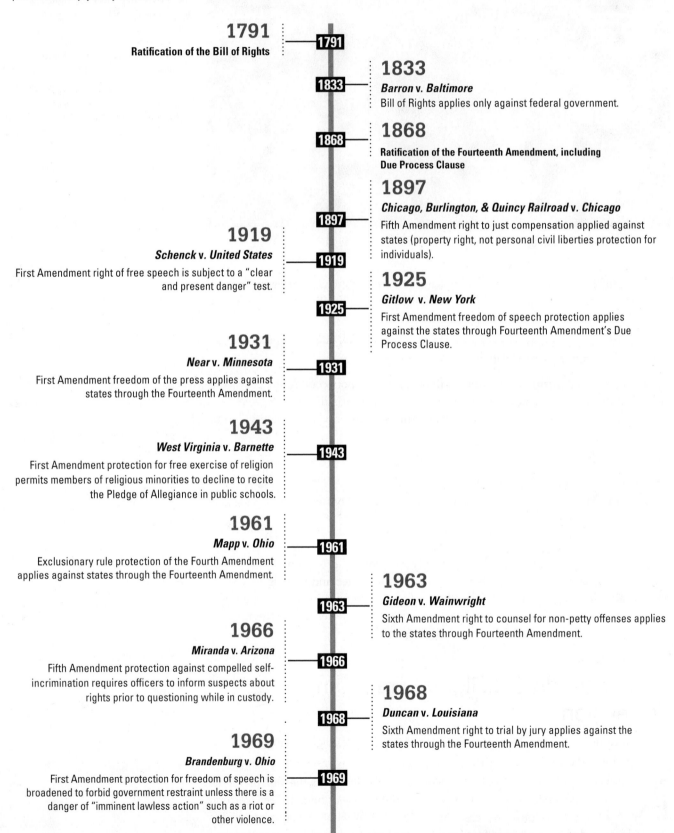

1791
Ratification of the Bill of Rights

1833
Barron* v. *Baltimore
Bill of Rights applies only against federal government.

1868
Ratification of the Fourteenth Amendment, including Due Process Clause

1897
Chicago, Burlington, & Quincy Railroad* v. *Chicago
Fifth Amendment right to just compensation applied against states (property right, not personal civil liberties protection for individuals).

1919
Schenck* v. *United States
First Amendment right of free speech is subject to a "clear and present danger" test.

1925
Gitlow* v. *New York
First Amendment freedom of speech protection applies against the states through Fourteenth Amendment's Due Process Clause.

1931
Near* v. *Minnesota
First Amendment freedom of the press applies against states through the Fourteenth Amendment.

1943
West Virginia* v. *Barnette
First Amendment protection for free exercise of religion permits members of religious minorities to decline to recite the Pledge of Allegiance in public schools.

1961
Mapp* v. *Ohio
Exclusionary rule protection of the Fourth Amendment applies against states through the Fourteenth Amendment.

1963
Gideon* v. *Wainwright
Sixth Amendment right to counsel for non-petty offenses applies to the states through Fourteenth Amendment.

1966
Miranda* v. *Arizona
Fifth Amendment protection against compelled self-incrimination requires officers to inform suspects about rights prior to questioning while in custody.

1968
Duncan* v. *Louisiana
Sixth Amendment right to trial by jury applies against the states through the Fourteenth Amendment.

1969
Brandenburg* v. *Ohio
First Amendment protection for freedom of speech is broadened to forbid government restraint unless there is a danger of "imminent lawless action" such as a riot or other violence.

FIGURE 4.1 Continued

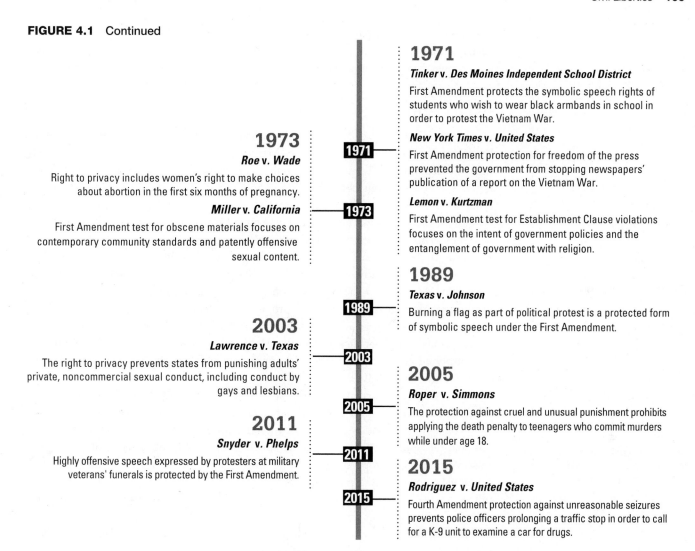

1971

Tinker* v. *Des Moines Independent School District

First Amendment protects the symbolic speech rights of students who wish to wear black armbands in school in order to protest the Vietnam War.

New York Times* v. *United States

First Amendment protection for freedom of the press prevented the government from stopping newspapers' publication of a report on the Vietnam War.

Lemon* v. *Kurtzman

First Amendment test for Establishment Clause violations focuses on the intent of government policies and the entanglement of government with religion.

1989

Texas* v. *Johnson

Burning a flag as part of political protest is a protected form of symbolic speech under the First Amendment.

2005

Roper* v. *Simmons

The protection against cruel and unusual punishment prohibits applying the death penalty to teenagers who commit murders while under age 18.

2015

Rodriguez* v. *United States

Fourth Amendment protection against unreasonable seizures prevents police officers prolonging a traffic stop in order to call for a K-9 unit to examine a car for drugs.

1973

Roe* v. *Wade

Right to privacy includes women's right to make choices about abortion in the first six months of pregnancy.

Miller* v. *California

First Amendment test for obscene materials focuses on contemporary community standards and patently offensive sexual content.

2003

Lawrence* v. *Texas

The right to privacy prevents states from punishing adults' private, noncommercial sexual conduct, including conduct by gays and lesbians.

2011

Snyder* v. *Phelps

Highly offensive speech expressed by protesters at military veterans' funerals is protected by the First Amendment.

The very first rights listed in the First Amendment concern freedom of religion, speech, and press:

> Congress shall make no law respecting an establishment of religion, or prohibiting the free exercise thereof; or abridging the freedom of speech, or of the press; or the right of the people peaceably to assemble, and to petition the Government for redress of grievances.

The importance of these rights to the Founders of the United States is quite understandable. Many colonists came to North America from Europe because their membership in minority religious groups led them to seek a land where they could worship as they pleased without interference by the government. Similarly, the authors of the Bill of Rights were angry that people in the American colonies had been punished for criticizing the British government. Many scholars of government regard freedom of expression as an essential element for any democratic system. If people cannot freely criticize government officials, there is little opportunity to share information and opinions that will keep government officials accountable to voters.

Religious liberty is the very first right protected by the Constitution's First Amendment: "Congress shall make no law respecting an establishment of religion, or prohibiting the free exercise thereof." The amendment's first section, called the **Establishment Clause**, concerns the connections between government and religion. The Establishment Clause can be characterized as providing "freedom *from* religion"— namely, limiting government's ability to favor specific religions or impose religion on the people. The second section, the **Free Exercise Clause**, focuses on people's ability to

Establishment Clause

A clause in the First Amendment guaranteeing freedom from religion by providing a basis for Supreme Court decisions limiting government support for and endorsement of particular religions.

Free Exercise Clause

A clause in the First Amendment guaranteeing freedom to practice one's religion without government interference as long as those practices do not harm other individuals or society.

practice their religion without governmental interference. This clause provides "freedom *of* religion." Individuals and interest groups have used the court pathway to challenge governmental actions related to both of these aspects of the First Amendment.

Establishment of Religion

Agreement is widespread that the Establishment Clause forbids the designation by government of a national religion. Many people describe this clause as mandating "the separation of church and state." However, significant disagreements exist about what connections between religion and government are permitted by the First Amendment. Under a strict **separationist** view, government must avoid contacts with religion, especially those that lead to government support or endorsement of religious activities. This perspective argues not only for preventing government-sponsored religious practices, such as teachers leading prayers in public school classrooms, but also strict limits on government financial support for religion-connected practices. Separationists advocate prohibitions on government financial support for religious schools, religion-based rehabilitation programs in prisons, and the display of religious items in public buildings and parks, such as posters showing the Ten Commandments or Christmas nativity scenes. Advocates of this viewpoint see such actions as improperly implying governmental favoritism or endorsement of one religion over others—or even of religion itself.

> **separationist**
>
> An interpretive approach to the Establishment Clause of the First Amendment, which requires a "wall of separation" between church and state, including prohibitions on using government money for religious programs.

By contrast, the **accommodationist** view would permit the government to provide support for religion and associated activities. For strong accommodationists, the Establishment Clause is primarily intended to prevent the creation of an official, national religion. Advocates of this perspective argue that religious displays are permissible on public property and that government can even give financial support to religious schools for the nonreligious aspects of education, such as having teachers who are paid from taxpayers' money provide instruction in math, science, and other nonreligious subjects at Catholic schools.

> **accommodationist**
>
> An interpretive approach to the Establishment Clause of the First Amendment that would permit government financial support for certain religious programs, or would permit government sponsorship of religious practices, such as prayer in public schools.

During the 1960s, the Supreme Court issued two controversial decisions that tilted toward the strict separationist perspective. In *Engel* v. *Vitale* (1962), the Court found a violation of the Establishment Clause in the common public school practice of beginning each day with a teacher-led prayer. Parents in New York filed lawsuits to challenge the practice. According to Justice Hugo Black's majority opinion, "When the power, prestige, and financial support of government is placed behind a particular religious belief, the indirect coercive pressure upon religious minorities to conform to the prevailing officially approved religion is plain."[4] A second decision barred public schools from reading the Lord's Prayer and Bible verses over their public address systems (*School District of Abington Township, Pennsylvania* v. *Schempp*, 1963). By declaring that long-standing practices provided improper government endorsement and pressure on behalf of religious beliefs, the Supreme Court generated a storm of controversy that continues today. Although many Americans wonder whether such governmental practices actually cause any harm, the Court has been sensitive to the concern that nonbelievers or members of minority religions, especially children, will feel pressured to participate or will be ostracized by others if they decline to participate.

In the years following these decisions, critics complained that the Supreme Court had "improperly removed God from the schools" and thereby reduced morality and social order in society. Some state legislatures and local officials challenged the Court's decision through various means, such as mandating public display of the Ten Commandments in schools, teaching Bible-based creationism in public school science classes, and conducting student-led school prayers or moments of silence. Such practices were challenged in the court pathway by parents who viewed government-sponsored religious activities as inconsistent with civil liberties under the Establishment Clause.

TABLE 4.1 Two Pillars of Religious Freedom in the First Amendment

"Congress shall make no law respecting an establishment of religion, or prohibiting the free exercise thereof."

Establishment Clause	Free Exercise Clause
Prohibits:	Protects:
1. The establishment of a national religion by Congress	1. The freedom to believe
2. Government support for or preference of one religion over another or of religion over nonreligious philosophies in general	2. The freedom to worship and otherwise act in accordance with religious beliefs

In deciding cases concerning Establishment Clause issues, the Supreme Court has usually instructed judges to follow the so-called **Lemon test** (*Lemon* v. *Kurtzman*, 1971). Under this test, a court is to ask three questions about any governmental practice challenged as a violation of the Establishment Clause (see Table 4.1):

1. Does the law or practice have a secular (nonreligious) purpose?
2. Does the primary intent or effect of the law either advance or inhibit religion?
3. Does the law or practice create an excessive entanglement of government and religion?

If a law or government practice flunks any of the three questions, the law or practice violates the Establishment Clause and is unconstitutional. The Supreme Court has used the test to invalidate programs that provided public support for religious schools (*Grand Rapids* v. *Ball*, 1985), school-sponsored benediction prayers at public school graduation ceremonies (*Lee* v. *Weisman*, 1992), and mandatory instruction in "creation science" as an alternative to evolutionary theory in high school science classes (*Edwards* v. *Aguillard*, 1987).

In the past two decades, several justices on the Supreme Court have harshly criticized the *Lemon* test and sought to replace it with an accommodationist perspective. In a case concerning public school graduation prayers (*Lee* v. *Weisman*, 1992), the test may have come close to being eliminated. The justices originally voted 5-4 to permit such prayers, but during the process of drafting opinions, Justice Anthony Kennedy changed his mind. He provided the decisive fifth vote to declare such prayers unconstitutional, because a high school student could have, in his words, "a reasonable perception that she is being forced by the State to pray in a manner her conscience will not allow."[5]

In recent years, the Court issued two Establishment Clause decisions that highlighted the difficulties experienced by the justices in attempting to interpret the First Amendment in a clear, consistent manner. In *McCreary County* v. *ACLU* (2005), a majority of justices applied the *Lemon* test to rule that copies of the Ten Commandments could not be posted in Kentucky courthouses. A different combination of justices declared that the *Lemon* test need not apply, however, when those justices formed a majority in *Town of Greece* v. *Galloway* (2014) to permit a town in New York to open its town council meetings with Christian prayers led by local ministers. The justices regarded the two situations as distinctively different, because the Kentucky courthouses displayed documents with a specific religious purpose whereas the town's prayers followed a long tradition of legislative prayers opening sessions in Congress and state capitols. Justice Anthony Kennedy said adults expect to encounter speech with which they disagree, thus making these ceremonial prayers different than prayers imposed on children in public schools. In light of the divergent viewpoints within the Supreme Court, future directions in Establishment Clause decisions are difficult to predict and may change as new justices are appointed.

Lemon **test**

A three-part test for Establishment Clause violations announced by the U.S. Supreme Court in *Lemon* v. *Kurtzman* (1971) that examines whether government policies support religious programs or cause excessive entanglement between government and religion.

Free Exercise of Religion

The Free Exercise Clause concerns the right of individuals to engage in religious practices and to follow their beliefs without governmental interference. Several of the important cases that expanded civil liberties in this area were pursued by Jehovah's Witnesses. Just prior to World War II, the Supreme Court ruled that public schools could punish Jehovah's Witness students for refusing to salute the flag and recite the Pledge of Allegiance, even though the students claimed that being required to salute anything other than God violated their religious beliefs (*Minersville School District* v. *Gobitis,* 1940). Shortly afterward, several justices had second thoughts about the issue, and the Court reversed itself in *West Virginia* v. *Barnette* (1943). Justice Robert Jackson's opinion contained a lofty statement about the importance of freedom of thought and religious belief:

> If there is any fixed star in our constitutional constellation, it is that no official, high or petty, can prescribe what shall be orthodox in politics, nationalism, religion, or other matters of opinion or force citizens to confess by word or act their faith therein.

This does not mean, however, that the free exercise clause provides an absolute right to do anything in the name of religion. For example, if a person believed that his religion demanded that he engage in human sacrifice or cannibalism, the Supreme Court would permit legislation to outlaw such practices. In 1990, an opinion written by Justice Antonin Scalia declared that the "right to free exercise of religion does not relieve an individual of the obligation to comply with a 'valid and neutral law of general applicability'" (*Employment Division of Oregon* v. *Smith*).

Many members of Congress want judges to look carefully at laws that would override religious practices. In effect, these legislators want judges to apply an analysis called **strict scrutiny** (or the compelling government interest test), which places the burden on the government to demonstrate the necessity of a specific law in order to outweigh an individual's desire to engage in a religious practice. The Supreme Court already applies the compelling government interest test to analyze whether other fundamental rights have been violated. In 1993, Congress enacted the Religious Freedom Restoration Act, which protects individuals' free exercise of religion against actions by the federal government. This act was used by the Supreme Court in 2014 when it found that the government did not have a compelling justification to force a family-owned company to include coverage for contraceptives in employee health insurance. The owners claimed that such coverage required them to violate their religious objections to certain contraceptives (*Burwell* v. *Hobby Lobby Stores*). The government believed that for-profit corporations cannot claim religious rights and that the compelling justification of advancing public health supported the health insurance law. Yet, a five-member majority of the Court narrowly rejected those arguments.

There are often apparent conflicts between civil liberties protected under the Establishment Clause and those protected under the Free Exercise Clause. For example, some critics argue that the Court's Establishment Clause decisions barring sponsored prayers in public schools effectively violate the free exercise rights of students who wish to pray. The apparent clash with free exercise of religion, however, is less substantial than it may first appear. Students can pray on their own in school as long as school officials do not organize or lead the prayers. In addition, the Supreme Court has not ruled against student-organized and student-led prayers in public schools except when those prayers are conducted in a manner that implies sponsorship by school officials, such as a student reading a prayer over the stadium public address system before high school football games (*Santa Fe Independent School District* v. *Doe,* 2000).

strict scrutiny

An exacting test for violations of fundamental rights by requiring the government to demonstrate a compelling interest when policies and practices clash with certain constitutional rights. The government may persuade judges, for example, that national security interests or health and safety interests outweigh the exercise of free speech or religion in specific situations.

Although the First Amendment guarantees the free exercise of religion, controversies arise when government officials conclude that they must prohibit dangerous activities that are components of religious practices. For example, in some rural areas of the United States, ministers have used poisonous snakes during religious services to show their belief that God will protect them. People sometimes are bitten and die when snakes are handled during religious services.

■ *Should the government outlaw handling poisonous snakes and other dangerous practices or should these practices be considered part of free exercise of religion?*

First Amendment Rights: Freedom of Speech

4.3 Specify the limits on free speech in the United States.

The First Amendment protections for speech and press are expressed in absolute terms: "Congress shall make no law … abridging the freedom of speech, or of the press; or the right of the people peaceably to assemble, and to petition the Government for redress of grievances." Although the words of the amendment seem to say that the government cannot impose *any* limitations on your ability to speak, write, or participate in peaceful public demonstrations, you can probably think of several kinds of expressions that are limited under American law—for example consider the following:

- If you claimed you were exercising your right to freedom of speech when you telephoned the leaders of Iran and told them how to build nuclear weapons
- If you claimed you were using freedom of speech and freedom of the press when you filled bottles with tap water and sold them through advertisements falsely calling them "The Amazing Liquid Cure for Cancer"
- If you wrote a novel about the life of a college student by copying sections, word for word, from other novels about college life

These examples raise questions about whether freedom of speech is absolute or whether the government can impose limitations. Judges interpret the First Amendment in ways that seek to strike a balance between individual liberty and important societal interests. In the first example, national security interests may outweigh an individual's desire to transmit a specific communication. In the second example, the government can regulate product advertisements and medicines in ways that protect society from harm, even when they limit an individual's speech and written expression. And the third example concerns the protection of intellectual property—such as books, songs, and poems—which is an individual's or a group's creative expressions, protected through copyright laws. Freedom of expression is important for democracy and liberty in the United States, but these and other limitations are regarded as essential for protecting individuals and society against specific harms. Judges typically demand that governmental regulations concerning speech and the press be supported by strong, persuasive justifications before they can be applied to limit individuals' opportunities to express themselves.

During American involvement in World War I (1917–1918) and the years immediately after, the federal government prosecuted people for publishing pamphlets that were critical of the war or that called for a socialist form of government. The Supreme Court took a narrow view of the right to free speech and upheld these criminal convictions. In a famous majority opinion, however, Justice Oliver Wendell Holmes argued for a **clear and present danger test** that would permit prosecution only for speeches and publications that actually posed a tangible, immediate threat to American society (*Schenck* v. *United States*, 1919). Holmes illustrated his point with an especially famous descriptive example: "The most stringent protection of free speech would not protect a man in falsely shouting fire in a theater, and causing a panic."

Throughout the twentieth century, advocates of free speech pursued cases in the court pathway to challenge laws that limited people's ability to express their beliefs and viewpoints. By the 1960s, the Supreme Court had adopted, expanded, and refined Holmes's suggested test so that political protests, whether by civil rights advocates, antiwar activists, or communists, could express critical viewpoints as long as the nature and context of those expressions did not pose an immediate threat. As expressed by the Supreme Court's decision in *Brandenburg* v. *Ohio* (1969),

> The constitutional guarantees of free speech and free press do not permit a State to forbid or proscribe advocacy of the use of force or of law violation except where such advocacy is directed to inciting or producing imminent lawless action and is likely to incite or produce such action.

Nowadays, commercial speech can be regulated to protect people against misleading advertising. However, it is difficult for people to be prosecuted for political speech that expresses their viewpoints about government and public affairs. In a controversial decision in 2010, the Supreme Court strengthened the free speech rights of corporations in the political arena by striking down campaign finance laws aimed at limiting expenditures by corporations seeking to influence elections (*Citizens United* v. *Federal Election Commission*). Critics contend that political speech and campaign expenditures as an expression of free speech should be protected only for people, not for corporations.

How far has the Supreme Court moved in broadening the concept of freedom of speech? In 1989, the Court considered the case of Gregory Johnson, a protester at the 1984 Republican National Convention who burned an American flag during a political demonstration. He was convicted under a Texas law prohibiting flag desecration. However, a five-justice majority on the U.S. Supreme Court overturned his conviction by declaring that burning the flag is **symbolic speech**, a protected form of political expression that falls within the coverage of the First Amendment (*Texas* v. *Johnson*, 1989). In the words of Justice William Brennan, who wrote the majority opinion, "If there is a bedrock principle underlying the First Amendment, it is that the Government may not prohibit the expression of an idea simply because society finds the idea itself offensive or disagreeable." There are several contexts in which the Supreme Court is more willing to permit government-imposed limitations on First Amendment rights. The Court accepts **reasonable time, place, and manner restrictions** on political assemblies—government regulations on the way in which speech is expressed, to prevent threats to public safety. Judges recognize that chaos and disruption might harm society if protesters can freely block roadways, jail entrances, hospital parking lots, and other locations in a community. However, this recognition does not give government officials the power to prohibit protests because they do not support the ideas being expressed. Any regulation of speech must strike an appropriate balance between protecting important societal interests and permitting people to express their view. In 2011, for example, eleven college students received probation sentences after being convicted of violating a state law against disrupting public speeches. They temporarily delayed a speech by a diplomat at the University of California-Irvine by shouting.[6]

clear and present danger test

A test for permissible speech articulated by Justice Oliver Wendell Holmes in *Schenck* v. *United States* (1919) that allows government regulation of some expressions, such as prohibiting people from creating danger by falsely shouting "fire" in a crowded theater, words that are likely to cause people to be needlessly injured when they rush to flee the building.

symbolic speech

The expression of an idea or viewpoint through an action, such as wearing an armband or burning an object. Symbolic speech can enjoy First Amendment protections.

reasonable time, place, and manner restrictions

Permissible government regulations on freedom of speech that seek to prevent disruptions or threats to public safety in the manner in which expressions are presented, such as blocking a street to stage a protest march. Such regulations cannot be used to control the content of political speech.

The students' right to free speech did not permit them to disrupt the event by shouting in the auditorium. By contrast, in 2014, the Court rejected a state law seeking to keep abortion protesters away from clinics (*McCullen* v. *Coakley*).

A contemporary controversy concerns *hate speech,* the expression of ideas that cause hostility toward people because of their skin color, ethnicity, gender, religion, or other characteristics. Advocates of restrictions on hate speech argue that certain words and phrases serve to degrade, insult, and injure people in especially harmful ways, because they perpetuate historic prejudices, harassment, and discrimination. These advocates have characterized hate speech as falling under the Supreme Court's *fighting words doctrine*. According to this doctrine, government can prohibit and prosecute expressions that constitute insults likely to provoke a fistfight or some other immediate breach of the peace. Courts have examined hate speech laws as well as related forms of regulations, such as public universities' conduct codes (which may include restrictions on students' expressions of hatred or prejudice). Although judges' decisions often support free speech, even when it is offensive, people may be convicted of violating such laws, especially if they do not possess sufficient resources to hire an attorney who will challenge the government through the entire course of the court pathway.

A U.S. Supreme Court decision on the issue concerned Virginia's law against the symbolic hate speech underlying cross burning, a traditional form of intimidation used by the Ku Klux Klan and other groups advocating racial hatred (*Virginia* v. *Black,* 2003). The Court concluded that "the First Amendment permits Virginia to outlaw cross burnings done with the intent to intimidate." Thus, certain forms and contexts of hate speech may be limited by government regulation when there is proof about the underlying intent.

The Ku Klux Klan is an organization founded after the Civil War to terrorize African Americans. As shown in this photo of a Klan demonstration in Texas, when the Klan holds protests today, the police must often protect their right to free speech by guarding them against attacks by counterprotesters who object to their philosophy of racial hatred.

■ *Do Klan members have a right to express their ideas, or should they be prohibited from using hate speech? What reasons might you give for prohibiting the use of hate speech?*

First Amendment Rights: Freedom of the Press and Obscenity

4.4 Assess the test for justifying governmental limitations on written words and images.

Throughout the world, it is common in many countries for governments to prevent journalists from reporting information that illuminates problems for which officials may be blamed. In the United States, by contrast, freedom of the press is specifically mentioned as a protected value in the First Amendment. Questions arise, however, about whether certain information should be kept from the public in order to protect national security or safeguard other interests, such as insuring that criminal defendants have fair trials. In addition, open access to published information, opinions, and photographs can raise issues about perceived harms to society, such as harms that some people believe come from profanity and pornography. Thus, judges must decide cases that determine whether and how publications can be limited by government.

Freedom of the Press

Like free speech, freedom of the press is guaranteed by the First Amendment's absolutist language, and Americans regard this freedom as an essential element of democracy. Voters need free-flowing, accurate information in order to evaluate their elected leaders. They have little hope of using democratic processes to hold their leaders accountable or to elect new legislators and executive officials unless they have access to information. Limitations on freedom of the press, like limitations on speech, are based on important government interests such as national security (see Figure 4.2).

prior restraint

Effort by government to prohibit or prevent the publication of information or viewpoints. Since its decision in *Near* v. *Minnesota* (1931), the U.S. Supreme Court has generally forbidden prior restraint as a violation of the First Amendment protection for freedom of the press.

The Supreme Court issued a strong statement against **prior restraint** of publications that criticize public officials in *Near* v. *Minnesota* (1931). Prior restraint is the government's attempt to prevent certain information or viewpoints from being published. In the *Near* case, the Supreme Court struck down a state law intended to prevent the publication of articles or editorials that used inflammatory language to criticize government officials. As a result, the government generally cannot prevent articles from being published. However, the principle of no prior restraint does *not* prevent authors and publishers from later being sued for the publication of false or misleading information that harms people's reputations. Such civil lawsuits are for defamation—false, harmful statements either through spoken words (*slander*) or through written words (*libel*). The Court's decision established the basic presumption that the government will not censor the news media, except perhaps in the most extreme circumstances.

In 1971, the Supreme Court faced a case that raised the issue of prior restraint when the federal government claimed that publication by newspapers of a top-secret internal Defense Department study concerning the Vietnam War would seriously damage national security. When the *New York Times* and *Washington Post* began to publish this book-length document, under the title *History of the U.S. Decision-Making Process on Vietnam Policy,* the government sought a court order to stop the newspapers. The two newspapers in question, arguably the nation's most prominent at that time, had the money and legal expertise to battle the government on equal terms in the court pathway. The Supreme Court majority declared that the newspapers could continue to publish the report (*New York Times Company* v. *United States*, 1971). The decision demonstrated that many judges would require exceptionally compelling proof of harm to society before permitting government censorship of publications about public affairs.

Such compelling government interests can exist, especially with respect to national security interests. For example, in recent years WikiLeaks established itself as

FIGURE 4.2   Freedom of Speech and Press

Civil liberties protections enjoyed by Americans are defined by judges' interpretations of the words in the Bill of Rights. For the First Amendment and several other provisions of the Bill of Rights, judges often seek to strike a balance between protecting the liberty of individuals and acknowledging the need to protect important interests of society. Thus there are limitations on many civil liberties.

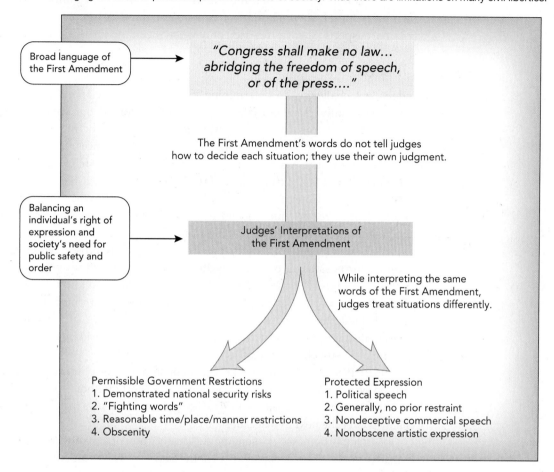

Broad language of the First Amendment

"Congress shall make no law... abridging the freedom of speech, or of the press...."

The First Amendment's words do not tell judges how to decide each situation; they use their own judgment.

Balancing an individual's right of expression and society's need for public safety and order

Judges' Interpretations of the First Amendment

While interpreting the same words of the First Amendment, judges treat situations differently.

Permissible Government Restrictions
1. Demonstrated national security risks
2. "Fighting words"
3. Reasonable time/place/manner restrictions
4. Obscenity

Protected Expression
1. Political speech
2. Generally, no prior restraint
3. Nondeceptive commercial speech
4. Nonobscene artistic expression

an international organization that sought to publish online secret information about governments and corporations that it believed the public was entitled to know. It obtained and published secret information about American diplomatic and military affairs. An investigation by U.S. officials led to the arrest of a U.S. Army private who was eventually sentenced in 2013 to 35 years in prison (with parole eligibility after 7 years) upon being convicted for supplying secret military information to WikiLeaks.[7] In such cases, it is likely that judges would have agreed to prevent such publications based on national security interests if WikiLeaks had been based in the United States and therefore was susceptible to orders from American courts.

The interests of the press can clash with governmental priorities when reporters have information sought by the government and refuse to share it with prosecutors and other officials. Reporters claim that a free press can survive only if they can protect the identities of their sources of inside information. Otherwise, people would not be willing to provide reporters with controversial and even potentially incriminating information about governmental activities and issues of public interest. Government officials argue in response that reporters, like other citizens, should be required to cooperate with criminal investigations to ensure that criminal enterprises are thwarted and that guilty people receive appropriate punishment.

Advocates for the news media feel that the First Amendment should be interpreted to recognize a **reporter's privilege**, the right of news agencies to decline to provide information requested by the government. Although some states have enacted **press shield laws** to protect reporters in state justice processes, the federal courts have

reporter's privilege

The asserted right of news reporters to promise confidentiality to their sources and to keep information obtained from sources, including evidence of criminal activity, secret. The U.S. Supreme Court has held that reporter's privilege is not a component of the First Amendment's protection for freedom of the press.

press shield law

A statute enacted by a legislature establishing a reporter's privilege to protect the confidentiality of sources.

refused to recognize a constitutional privilege to protect reporters nationwide. Thus reporters are occasionally jailed for contempt of court if they refuse to cooperate with criminal investigations. For example, Vanessa Leggett, a freelance writer in Houston who was conducting research for a book on a controversial murder case, spent 168 days in jail for refusing to testify before a federal grand jury about her interviews with criminal suspects. She was released only when the grand jury ended its investigation.[8]

Obscenity

Judges face challenges in determining if expressions that offend the sensibilities of some community members fall under the protection of the First Amendment. In particular, legislators have regularly sought to prohibit or regulate material with sexual content, such as books, magazines, live performances, films, and Web sites. The Supreme Court has said anything that is "obscene" falls outside of the First Amendment and is not considered part of free expression. It has been very difficult, however, for the Court to provide a clear definition of *obscene*. This issue can cause major conflicts because images and performances that some people consider artistic expression can be regarded by others as harmful to the morals of society.

In the early twentieth century, people were regularly prosecuted in various communities for possessing or selling written materials or pictures with sexual content. James Joyce's novel *Ulysses,* published in France in 1922 and today regarded as one of the great works of modern literature, could not legally be printed, imported, or sold in the United States because it contained four-letter words and certain sexual allusions. Only in 1933 did a federal judge lift the ban after a leading American publisher brought a lawsuit challenging it.

In the 1950s, the Supreme Court developed a test for obscenity. Its initial efforts focused on whether the work in question was "utterly without redeeming social importance" (*Roth* v. *United States,* 1957). This test was refined as the Court's composition changed over the next two decades.

In an important case challenging the prosecution of a man who mailed brochures that advertised sexually explicit books, the Supreme Court articulated a new test for obscenity. According to Chief Justice Warren Burger's opinion, materials that met a three-part test for obscenity could be prohibited by legislation and lead to prosecutions. The Court's test was stated as follows in *Miller* v. *California* (1973):

> The basic guidelines for the trier of fact must be: (a) whether the "average person, applying contemporary community standards" would find that the work, taken as a whole, appeals to the prurient interest; (b) whether the work depicts or describes, in a patently offensive way, sexual conduct specifically defined by the applicable state law; and (c) whether the work, taken as whole, lacks serious literary, artistic, political, or scientific value.

The test for obscenity is thus based on "community standards," and those standards change over time. For example, in the 1960s, actors portraying married couples in movies and on television were often shown sleeping in separate single beds so as not to convey any sexual implications by having a double bed on the set. Today, by contrast, scantily clad performers in sexy embraces and dance routines are everyday fare for music videos shown around the clock on cable. It seems clear that "community standards" regarding acceptable entertainment have changed over the years. Does this mean that "anything goes" in American entertainment media? No. The Federal Communications Commission (FCC) continues to regulate television and radio broadcasts, and it imposes fines for profanity and sexual content that it believes has gone too far. Broadcasting is subject to stricter government control than newspapers, because the government has the power to regulate use of the public airwaves. The uproar over the momentary exposure of singer Janet Jackson's bare breast on television during the halftime show for the 2004 Super Bowl served as a reminder that there are still limits to expression, especially when that expression is broadcast to the televisions and radios of unwitting consumers who assume that certain standards are in place.

Obviously, a different situation exists for consumers who intentionally seek sexually explicit material in specific magazines or specialty stores or online. Generally, pornographic films and magazines that once would have led to prosecution in most communities are now widely available in the United States and without legal repercussions, as long as the sellers and distributors of such materials take steps to keep such items away from children.

Indeed, except for content standards for broadcasts regulated by the FCC, most regulation of obscenity today focuses on the exposure of children to obscene material or their exploitation in its production. Laws impose prison sentences for the creation, dissemination, and possession of child pornography.

Civil Liberties and Criminal Justice

4.5 Specify the protections afforded to criminal suspects in the Bill of Rights.

Several amendments in the Bill of Rights describe protections afforded people who are subject to police investigations, prosecutions, sentencing, and criminal punishment. The protections described in these amendments do not merely safeguard civil liberties for people who have committed crimes. These amendments are designed to protect everyone in the United States, including innocent people, from excessive actions by overzealous law enforcement officials who are seeking to prevent and solve crimes.

Search and Seizure

The Fourth Amendment is focused on protecting people against improper searches and seizures. In the words of the amendment,

> The right of the people to be secure in their persons, houses, papers, and effects, against unreasonable searches and seizures, shall not be violated, and no Warrants shall issue, but upon probable cause, supported by Oath or affirmation, and particularly describing the place to be searched, and the persons or things to be seized.

The two key parts of the amendment are the prohibition on "unreasonable searches and seizures" and the requirements for obtaining search and arrest warrants. Like other provisions of the Constitution, the Fourth Amendment contains inherently ambiguous language that must be interpreted by judges. The word *seizure*, for example, includes arrests when people are taken into police custody (that is, seizures of people) as well as situations in which officers seize property that may be evidence of criminal wrongdoing. But how do you know whether a search or seizure is "unreasonable"? Clearly, such a determination is a matter of judgment, and all people will not agree about whether specific actions are "searches" or whether they are "unreasonable."

The U.S. Supreme Court endorsed application of the **exclusionary rule** in *Weeks* v. *United States* (1914). Under this rule, evidence obtained improperly by the police cannot be used to prosecute someone accused of a crime. The intent of the rule is to stop police from undertaking illegal searches or improperly questioning suspects and to remedy the violation of suspects' civil liberties. At first, the rule applied only against federal law enforcement officials, such as FBI agents, but the Supreme Court—in the famous case of *Mapp* v. *Ohio* (1961)—subsequently applied it to all police officers throughout the country. The *Mapp* decision provoked a storm of controversy and has led to decades of debate about whether the exclusionary rule

exclusionary rule

A general principle stating that evidence obtained illegally cannot be used against a defendant in a criminal prosecution. The Supreme Court has allowed certain exceptions to the rule in particular circumstances, such as when evidence obtained through an improper search would have eventually been discovered by the police later through actions permitted by law.

reflects an appropriate interpretation of the Constitution. Critics claim that the rule improperly "ties the hands of the police" and lets guilty people go free due to honest errors by law enforcement officials. Social science research shows that the rule does benefit some guilty people but affects the outcomes of only a small percentage of cases.[9] These cases usually are based on the possession of an illegal item, such as drugs or weapons.

As Republican presidents appointed new justices in the 1970s and 1980s who interpreted civil liberties under the Bill of Rights in a narrower manner, Chief Justice Warren Burger (1969–1986) was able to lead the changing Court toward creating limitations on and exceptions to the exclusionary rule. The narrowing of the exclusionary rule continued during the eras of Chief Justice William Rehnquist (1986–2005) and Chief Justice John Roberts (2005–current). The rule went from being a broad, clear restriction on police after *Mapp* v. *Ohio* (1961) to one with many situational exceptions. The limitations on the exclusionary rule now in effect include the following:

- The prosecution may use evidence obtained through certain kinds of improper questioning, if the questioning was conducted in the midst of a situation that threatened "public safety" (*New York* v. *Quarles*, 1984).

- The prosecution may use improperly obtained evidence, if it would have been "inevitably discovered" by the police later through the use of a legal search (*Nix* v. *Williams*, 1984).

- The prosecution may use evidence obtained through the use of an improper search warrant, if a judge made an error in issuing the warrant and the police honestly, albeit mistakenly, believed they had sufficient evidence to justify a warrant (*United States* v. *Leon*, 1984).

- The prosecution may use evidence based on a search that was conducted based on inaccurate records in a law enforcement or court database that erroneously indicate the existence of an arrest warrant for a specific person (*Herring* v. *United States*, 2009).

- The prosecution may use evidence based on a traffic stop of a driver who had broken no laws but was wrongly stopped by a police officer who misunderstood state traffic laws (*Heien* v. *North Carolina*, 2014).

The rule still applies in many situations, but law enforcement officers now have greater leeway to make errors in conducting searches and questioning suspects without automatically facing the exclusion of evidence.

warrant

A judicial order authorizing a search or an arrest. Under the Fourth Amendment, police and prosecutors must present sufficient evidence to constitute "probable cause" in order to obtain a warrant from a judge.

With respect to a **warrant**—an order from a judge authorizing a search or an arrest—the Fourth Amendment specifically requires the police and prosecutor to show the judge sufficient reliable information to establish "probable cause" about the location of evidence or a person's criminal behavior. Probable cause is generally understood to mean that reliable information shows it is more likely than not that specific items that provide evidence of criminal activity will be found in a certain location (*search warrant*) or that a specific individual committed a crime (*arrest warrant*). As indicated by the two kinds of warrants, search and arrest, the concept of "seizures" governed by the Fourth Amendment can refer to the government taking possession of either property items (for example, a gun, car, or jewelry) or a person who is a criminal suspect.

Other searches conducted without warrants are governed only by the prohibition on "unreasonable searches and seizures." The Supreme Court has identified specific situations in which warrants are not required, because these searches are considered reasonable. For example, officers can conduct a warrantless search when the owner of a home or the driver of a car gives permission. Thus police officers are often trained to automatically ask drivers during traffic stops, "Do you mind if I look around inside your car?" If drivers consent to a search, then there is no need for a warrant. Other permissible warrantless searches include the following:

- "Stop and frisk" searches of a suspect's outer clothing on the streets when officers have a reasonable basis to suspect that person is involved in criminal behavior and potentially poses a danger to the public (*Terry* v. *Ohio*, 1968)
- Searches of a suspect at the scene of the suspect's arrest in order to make sure that the suspect does not have a weapon and that no evidence will be lost (*Chimel* v. *California*, 1969)
- Automobile searches done without warrants so that the vehicles do not drive away with the evidence, although the officer must have a justification for searching each portion of the automobile and its contents (for example, *California* v. *Acevedo*, 1991)
- Searches based on "special needs" beyond the normal purposes of law enforcement, such as luggage searches at airports, searches at national border-crossing points, drug tests of high school student athletes and certain government employees, and police roadblocks serving as sobriety checkpoints to identify drunk drivers (for example, *Michigan Department of State Police* v. *Sitz*, 1990)

The creation of these categories of warrantless searches demonstrates how judges' decisions in the court pathway define rights and clarify the authority of law enforcement officials. As the United States continues to develop homeland security policies in response to the terrorist attacks of September 11, 2001, new cases will arise that test the government's authority to conduct searches and surveillance. Congressional enactment of the controversial USA Patriot Act, for example, expanded government authority to investigate suspected terrorists through wiretaps, searches of business records, and surveillance without a warrant. Many critics argue that the use of these powers under the administrations of both President George W. Bush and President Barack Obama undercuts the protections that Americans are supposed to receive under the Fourth Amendment. Controversies continue to arise as news reporters discover and reveal to the public the broad scope of the federal government's monitoring of Americans' phone calls and the use of new technology by federal, state, and local officials to intercept communications without a search warrant.[10]

Self-Incrimination

The Fifth Amendment describes several rights related to criminal justice, including the concept of **double jeopardy**, which refers to the protection against being tried twice for the same crime. Many controversial cases arise concerning another protection: the privilege against **compelled self-incrimination**. In the words of the amendment, no person may be "compelled in any criminal case to be a witness against himself." This does not mean that people cannot provide evidence against themselves. During questioning, criminal suspects can fully confess or provide police with partial details about their involvement in crimes. However, they cannot be *compelled* to provide statements that will be used against them. In order for their incriminating statements to be used by the prosecution, the statements must be made *voluntarily*. The police cannot use threats of violence—or actual violence—to obtain confessions.

If an individual is not free to walk away from police questioning, the police must make it clear that the person has a right to remain silent and to have an attorney present during questioning. The latter requirement emerged from the Supreme Court's famous and controversial decision in *Miranda* **v.** *Arizona* **(1966)**. Television programs with crime themes regularly show police officers reading people their "*Miranda* rights:"

> You have the right to remain silent. Anything that you say can and will be used against you in a court of law. You have the right to have an attorney present during questioning. If you cannot afford an attorney, one will be appointed to represent you.

double jeopardy
Being tried twice for the same crime, a practice prohibited by the Fifth Amendment.

compelled self-incrimination
Being forced through physical abuse or other coercion to provide testimony against oneself in a criminal case, a practice that is prohibited by the Fifth Amendment.

Miranda **v.** *Arizona* **(1966)**
A U.S. Supreme Court decision that requires police officers, before questioning a suspect in custody, to inform that suspect about the right to remain silent and to have a lawyer present during custodial questioning. These warnings are intended to protect people from feeling pressured to incriminate themselves without being aware of their rights.

After criminal suspects have been arrested, police officers are required to inform them of their *Miranda* rights before questioning them. These rights are intended to limit the risk that suspects will feel pressured into providing incriminating information about themselves.

■ *Because the arrest process, including being handcuffed, fingerprinted, and jailed, can be upsetting and stressful, are there risks that suspects will not listen closely to and fully understand their* Miranda *rights when they are scared and upset?*

Police are required to inform people of their *Miranda* rights only if individuals are in police custody and are not free to walk away, as would be the case if they have been arrested. When police question people on the street, or when people come to the police station voluntarily, the police do not have to inform them of their rights. The primary exception to this rule concerns motorists stopped for traffic violations who are not free to drive away; the police can ask them questions without informing them about their *Miranda* rights. When the Supreme Court announced its decision in the *Miranda* case, critics complained that the Court had extended Fifth Amendment rights too far. Over the years, however, the Court has given police more flexibility about when and how to give *Miranda* warnings. For example, in *Florida* v. *Powell* (2010), the Court approved a version of *Miranda* warnings that did not clearly inform the suspect that he could request an attorney even after police began to question him.

Trial Rights and Capital Punishment

4.6 Evaluate the legal protections that seek to ensure only guilty people receive criminal punishment.

The nation's founding documents focused on individual liberty as a premier value. The determination of criminal guilt and the imposition of punishment pose particular threats to the ideal of liberty if they are not carried out in ways that are accurate and fair. Thus, the Bill of Rights contains many legal protections that guide the processing of criminal cases.

Trial Rights

The Sixth Amendment contains a variety of legal protections for people who face criminal trials:

> In all criminal prosecutions, the accused shall enjoy the right to a speedy and public trial, by an impartial jury of the State and district wherein the crime shall have been committed, which district shall have been previously ascertained by law, and to be informed of the nature and cause of the accusation; to be confronted with the witnesses against him; to have compulsory process for obtaining witnesses in his favor; and to have the Assistance of Counsel for his defense.

The rights to **confrontation** and **compulsory process** are considered essential to providing fair trials for criminal defendants. The right to confrontation permits the defendant to be present in the courtroom when the victim and other witnesses provide testimony about the defendant's alleged guilt. The entitlement to compulsory process permits the defendant to use the power of the court to require witnesses to appear at court and to obtain needed documents that might be relevant to the case. If defendants had no ability to compel others to appear and present testimony, they might have little hope of counteracting the evidence being presented against them by the prosecution.

The right to a speedy and public trial provides important protections for criminal defendants. For instance, it ensures that the government cannot hold secret proceedings that prevent citizens from knowing whether evidence exists to prove a defendant's guilt. Under a system that permits secret trials, individuals can be convicted of crimes and sentenced without the government demonstrating that it properly exercised its powers to deprive people of their liberty through incarceration.

The right to a speedy trial prevents the government from ruining a person's life by holding charges over his or her head for an indefinite period of time. When individuals have been charged with a crime, they may lose their jobs or see their families disintegrate if they sit in jail awaiting trial. Even if they gain release on bail, they may be ostracized by the community and find it difficult to obtain employment. Thus, the Sixth Amendment obligates the government to move forward in presenting its evidence of criminal activity. However, the Supreme Court has not provided a clear time limit for prosecutions; instead, judges must examine each case to make an individual determination about whether the right to a speedy trial has been violated.

The right to **trial by jury** evolved in England more than seven centuries ago. Before this, it was presumed that God would indicate an accused person's innocence by allowing him to win in hand-to-hand combat with his accuser. Today, jury trials can be seen as the democratic component of the judicial process by permitting citizens to be involved in important decisions. Initially, the Sixth Amendment right to trial by jury applied only to federal cases, but the Supreme Court incorporated the right in 1968 and applied it to state proceedings (*Duncan* v. *Louisiana*).

Although dramatic scenes from jury trials are a central feature of television shows such as *Law and Order*, in reality only about 10 percent of criminal convictions result from trials, and only half of those are the result of jury trials.[11] The other trials are **bench trials**, in which the verdict is determined by a judge without a jury. Defendants may request bench trials because they are afraid that jurors may be biased and emotional, especially if there are controversial charges involving sex offenses, guns, or drugs. The other 90 percent of criminal convictions are obtained through **plea bargaining**, a process approved by the Supreme Court in which prosecutors and defense attorneys negotiate a guilty plea in exchange for a less-than-maximum number of charges or a less severe sentence. Plea bargaining has become an essential way to dispose of the vast number of cases that otherwise would overwhelm the resources of the criminal justice system if they all proceeded to trial. Figure 4.3 illustrates the path of criminal cases and how specific civil liberties protections from the Bill of Rights apply at each stage of the criminal justice process.

The Sixth Amendment's exact words—"In all criminal prosecutions, the accused shall enjoy the right to … an impartial jury"—have not been enforced by the Supreme Court. According to the Court, the right to a trial by jury applies only in cases concerning "serious offenses" that are punishable by six months or more in jail or prison (*Lewis* v. *United States*, 1996). For lesser crimes, the accused can be forced to accept a bench trial. Because jury trials are expensive and time consuming, it appears that the Court's interpretation is designed to reduce the costs and administrative burdens that courts otherwise would face.

confrontation

A right contained in the Sixth Amendment for criminal defendants to see their accusers in court and hear at first hand the accusations and evidence being presented against them.

compulsory process

A right contained in the Sixth Amendment to enable criminal defendants to use court orders to require witnesses to appear and to require the production of documents and other evidence.

trial by jury

A right contained in the Sixth Amendment to have criminal guilt decided by a body of citizens drawn from the community.

bench trials

Trials in which a judge presides without a jury. The judge makes determinations of fact and law.

plea bargaining

Negotiation process in which prosecutors seek a quick, certain conviction without a trial by agreeing to reduce charges or recommend a less-than-maximum sentence in exchange for the defendant's voluntary plea of guilty.

FIGURE 4.3 Civil Liberties and the Criminal Justice Process

Specific civil liberties from the Bill of Rights apply at each stage of the criminal justice process. These are legal protections for individuals that help to reduce the risk that innocent people may be convicted of crimes or that unfair processes will be used to decide which people will be punished.

▪ *Are there too many rights for people accused of crimes? If so, which rights do you believe provide "too much" protection or otherwise improperly prevent police and prosecutors from doing their jobs?*

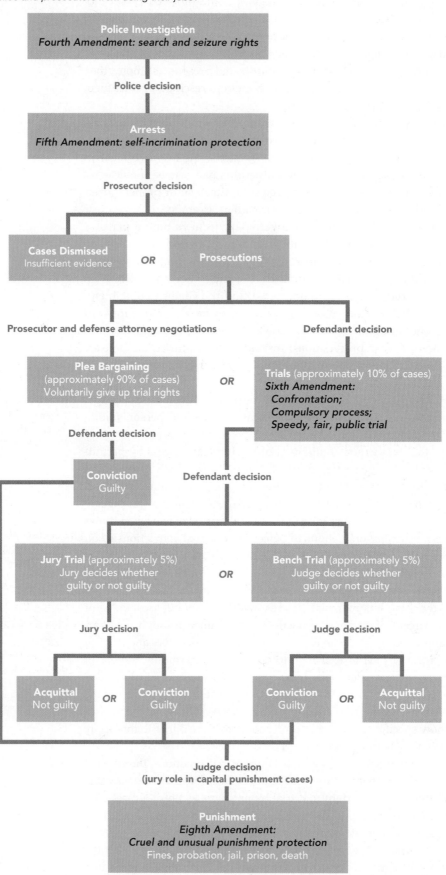

The right to counsel is an especially important part of the Sixth Amendment. As early as 1932, the Supreme Court, in *Powell* v. *Alabama,* recognized the value of this legal protection by requiring Alabama to provide attorneys for nine African American youths who had previously been convicted and sentenced to death. Their brief, attorneyless proceeding was based on rape accusations from two white women, one of whom later admitted that her charges were false. Many people in the North had viewed these death sentences as a reflection of extensive racial discrimination in the courts of southern states. Interest group lawyers volunteered to assist the youths, and large protest marches occurred in Washington, D.C., and elsewhere. Many observers see the Supreme Court's decision in this case as having been influenced by pressure from both the court pathway and the grassroots mobilization pathway.

Later, the Supreme Court required that the government provide attorneys for all indigent defendants facing serious criminal charges in federal court (*Johnson* v. *Zerbst,* 1938) and state courts (*Gideon* v. *Wainwright,* 1963). Indigent defendants are people who do not have enough money to hire their own attorneys. If people have sufficient funds, they are expected to hire an attorney, and the Sixth Amendment right merely means that the government cannot prevent them from seeking legal advice.

The right to counsel for indigents was expanded to all cases in which the potential punishment involves incarceration, even if only a short stay in jail (*Argersinger* v. *Hamlin,* 1972), as well as initial appeals (*Douglas* v. *California,* 1963). There are many kinds of cases, however, for which indigent people are not automatically entitled to have an attorney provided by the government: appeals to state supreme courts, petitions to the U.S. Supreme Court, civil lawsuits between private individuals, and civil rights lawsuits by people against the government.

Capital Punishment

The Constitution also provides rights for people who have been convicted of even the very worst crimes. The Constitution does not require people to forfeit all of their rights if they violate society's rules. The words of the Eighth Amendment include a prohibition of "cruel and unusual punishments." This clearly implies some limitation on the government's ability to punish. Criminal sanctions must not violate this provision, either by being similar to torture or by being disproportionate to the underlying crime. The Supreme Court has said that the phrase "cruel and unusual punishments" must be defined according to society's contemporary standards, so the meaning of the phrase changes as society's values change (*Trop* v. *Dulles,* 1958).

An important battleground for the meaning of the Eighth Amendment has been cases concerning **capital punishment** that are appealed through the court pathway.[12] As you can see in the Timeline Capital Punishment and the Courts, although the courts have produced many major decisions on the issue over the past four decades, supporters and opponents of capital punishment have also used elections and lobbying to influence state laws on the subject. In 1972, the Supreme Court ruled that the death penalty was unconstitutional, as it was then being administered (*Furman* v. *Georgia*). Some justices thought that the death penalty was unconstitutional, because it was "cruel and unusual" according to the values of contemporary civilization. Other justices believed that the punishment was applied too inconsistently and unfairly and thus violated the Fourteenth Amendment right to due process.

The death penalty was reinstated in 1976 after the latter group of justices became persuaded that states had adopted fairer procedures for administering capital punishment cases (*Gregg* v. *Georgia*; see Figure 4.4). The special procedures for death penalty cases include *bifurcated proceedings* (separate trials to determine guilt and to decide on the appropriate sentence). In addition, judges and juries look specifically for *aggravating factors* that make a particular crime or offender worse than others, such as a murder by a repeat offender or a killing in the course of committing another felony. They

capital punishment

A criminal punishment, otherwise known as the death penalty, in which a person is subject to execution after conviction. Reserved for the most serious offenses of murder and treason.

FIGURE 4.4 Executions by State 1976–February 2016

The number of executions carried out in a state does not depend on the number of people murdered or the murder rate in the state. The frequency of executions is determined by the political culture in that state and the values and beliefs of politicians and the public. Thus the cultural change pathway may ultimately play an important role in determining whether the use of capital punishment expands or shrinks.

■ *How might political values explain the relatively large number of executions in certain southern states and the small number of executions in California, a large state with many murders?*

SOURCE: Data from Death Penalty Information Center, http://www.deathpenaltyinfo.org/documents/FactSheet.pdf.

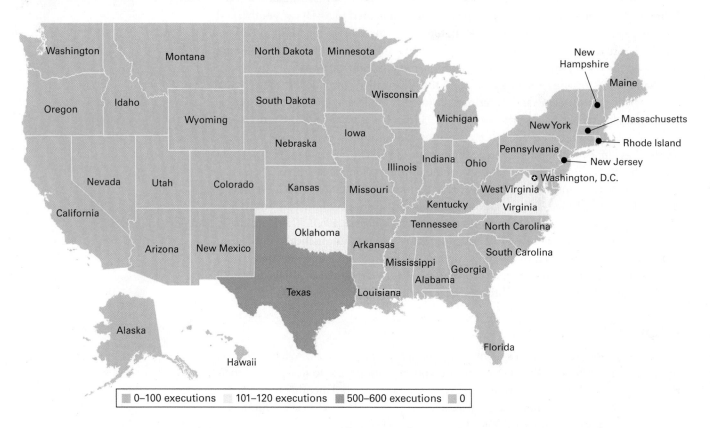

also weigh *mitigating factors,* such as the offender's age or mental problems, which might make an offender less deserving of the death penalty.

The weight of scholarly evidence suggests that the death penalty does not deter crime.[13] Advocates of the death penalty argue that only the ultimate punishment can satisfy victims and survivors and show how strongly society disapproves of the worst crimes. Yet, many states have discovered significant problems with the accuracy of their legal proceedings. Between 1973 and 2016, a total of 156 people condemned to death in the United States were later released from prison when it was discovered they were actually innocent.[14] Debates therefore continue about whether the American legal system is capable of imposing capital punishment accurately and fairly.

> POLL Do you think the death penalty is an appropriate punishment for homicide?

Because the Supreme Court has addressed so many issues concerning capital punishment, the court pathway has significantly shaped public policy. For example, the justices have forbidden the execution of developmentally disabled killers (*Atkins* v. *Virginia,* 2002) as well as individuals who committed murders before having reached the age of 18 (*Roper* v. *Simmons,* 2005). The Court has also banned the use of capital punishment for the crime of rape, including rape of a child (*Kennedy* v. *Louisiana,* 2008). A majority of justices on the Court view such executions as violating the prohibition on cruel and unusual punishments by being out of step with contemporary values.

The Court refused, however, to recognize statistical evidence showing that racial discrimination affects decisions about which offenders will be sentenced to death,

For nearly all executions in the United States, the condemned prisoner is strapped down and a series of lethal drugs are injected into the offender's veins as news reporters and family members watch through a glass window. The U.S. Supreme Court rejected a challenge to Oklahoma's choice of lethal injection drugs in 2015, but the 5-to-4 decision in the case raised questions about whether changes in the Court's composition could lead to abolition of the punishment.

■ *Are there any other legal arguments that opponents of the death penalty might use to seek an end to capital punishment?*

even when scholars produced studies that show death sentences are disproportionately imposed on African-American defendants convicted of killing white victims (*McCleskey* v. *Kemp,* 1987). In addition, in *Glossip* v. *Gross* (2015), by a 5-to-4 vote the justices narrowly rejected a claim that the drugs used in Oklahoma's lethal injections violate the Eighth Amendment's prohibition on "cruel and unusual punishments."

Other more recent policy changes have come through lobbying and electoral politics. New Jersey's legislature voted to abolish that state's death penalty in December 2007, and New Mexico's legislature did the same in 2009, as did the Illinois legislature in 2011 followed by Connecticut in 2012, Maryland in 2013, and Nebraska in 2015. By contrast, change came through the courts pathway in 2016 when the Delaware Supreme Court ruled its state's death penalty to be unconstitutional.

Privacy

4.7 Explain why the right to privacy is controversial.

The word *privacy* does not appear in the Constitution. The Supreme Court has nevertheless used its interpretive powers to recognize a **right to privacy** that protects people from government interference in a number of contexts. The justices first explicitly recognized a right to privacy in 1965. In this case, Connecticut had a statute that made it a crime to sell, possess, use, or counsel the use of contraceptives. After the law was challenged in the court pathway, the Supreme Court struck it down (*Griswold* v. *Connecticut*, 1965). The majority opinion by Justice William O. Douglas concluded that a right to privacy exists as an unstated element of several rights in the Bill of Rights: the First Amendment right to freedom of association, the Third Amendment protection against the government housing troops in private homes, the Fourth Amendment protection against unreasonable searches, and the Fifth Amendment privilege against compelled self-incrimination. Douglas wrote,

> The present case ... concerns a relationship lying within the zone of privacy created by several fundamental constitutional guarantees.... Would we allow the police to search the sacred precincts of marital bedrooms for telltale signs of the use of contraceptives? The very idea is repulsive to the notions of privacy surrounding the marriage relationship.

right to privacy

A constitutional right created and expanded in U.S. Supreme Court decisions concerning access to contraceptives, abortion, private sexual behavior, and other matters, even though the word privacy does not appear in the Constitution. A majority of Supreme Court justices since the 1960s have identified privacy protections as among the rights within the concept of protected liberty in the Due Process Clause of the Fourteenth Amendment.

TIMELINE

Capital Punishment and the Courts

Debates about capital punishment continue to rage, just as they have since the 1960s. Opponents of capital punishment have had limited success using the election pathway. Instead, they have focused their efforts on the court pathway. Supporters of the death penalty, on the other hand, have used the elections and lobbying pathways to push revisions of state capital punishment laws that would satisfy the Supreme Court. Highly publicized cases of innocent people being convicted and later released from death row have helped spur grassroots mobilization and pardons and moratoriums by governors. However, the fear of crime and terrorism attacks may have solidified public support for the death penalty in specific cases, such as convicted terrorists and serial killers.

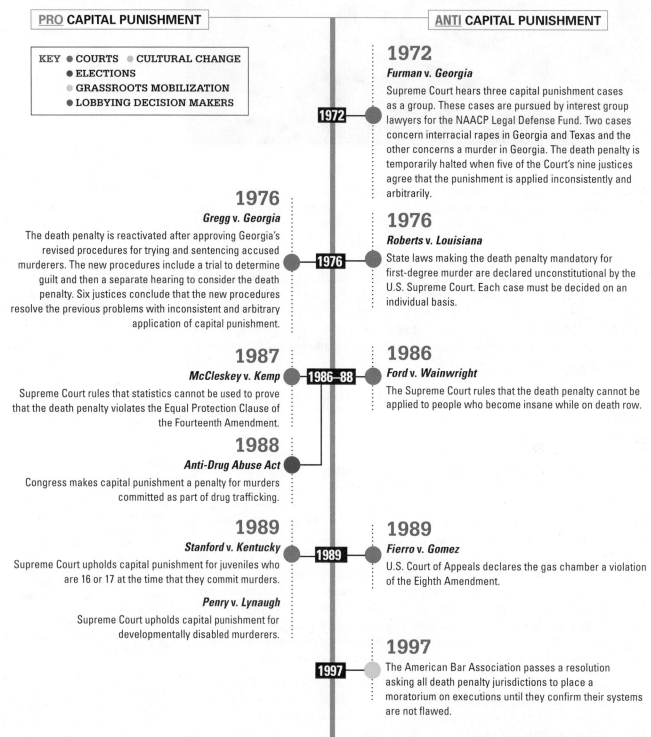

PRO CAPITAL PUNISHMENT

ANTI CAPITAL PUNISHMENT

KEY ● COURTS ● CULTURAL CHANGE
● ELECTIONS
● GRASSROOTS MOBILIZATION
● LOBBYING DECISION MAKERS

1972

1972
Furman v. *Georgia*
Supreme Court hears three capital punishment cases as a group. These cases are pursued by interest group lawyers for the NAACP Legal Defense Fund. Two cases concern interracial rapes in Georgia and Texas and the other concerns a murder in Georgia. The death penalty is temporarily halted when five of the Court's nine justices agree that the punishment is applied inconsistently and arbitrarily.

1976
Gregg v. *Georgia*
The death penalty is reactivated after approving Georgia's revised procedures for trying and sentencing accused murderers. The new procedures include a trial to determine guilt and then a separate hearing to consider the death penalty. Six justices conclude that the new procedures resolve the previous problems with inconsistent and arbitrary application of capital punishment.

1976

1976
Roberts v. *Louisiana*
State laws making the death penalty mandatory for first-degree murder are declared unconstitutional by the U.S. Supreme Court. Each case must be decided on an individual basis.

1987
McCleskey v. *Kemp*
Supreme Court rules that statistics cannot be used to prove that the death penalty violates the Equal Protection Clause of the Fourteenth Amendment.

1986–88

1986
Ford v. *Wainwright*
The Supreme Court rules that the death penalty cannot be applied to people who become insane while on death row.

1988
Anti-Drug Abuse Act
Congress makes capital punishment a penalty for murders committed as part of drug trafficking.

1989
Stanford v. *Kentucky*
Supreme Court upholds capital punishment for juveniles who are 16 or 17 at the time that they commit murders.

Penry v. *Lynaugh*
Supreme Court upholds capital punishment for developmentally disabled murderers.

1989

1989
Fierro v. *Gomez*
U.S. Court of Appeals declares the gas chamber a violation of the Eighth Amendment.

1997

1997
The American Bar Association passes a resolution asking all death penalty jurisdictions to place a moratorium on executions until they confirm their systems are not flawed.

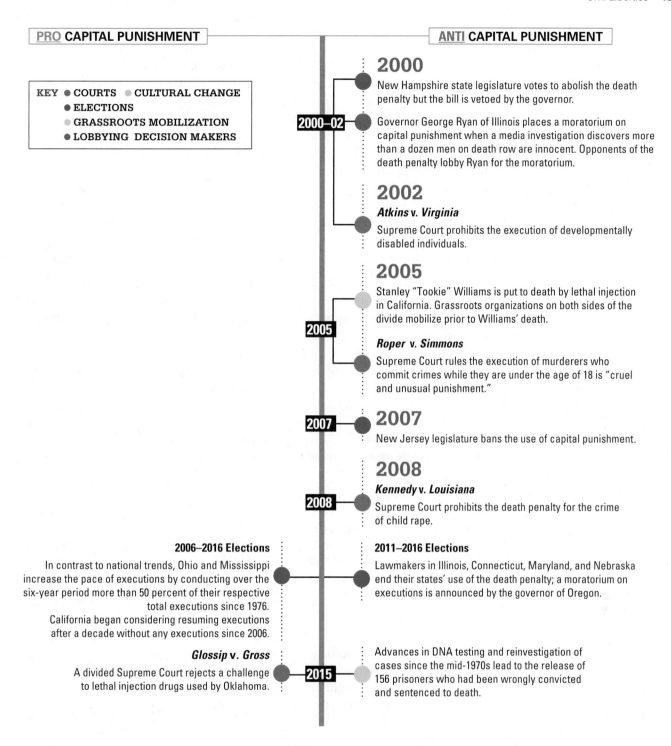

PRO CAPITAL PUNISHMENT ──────────────── **ANTI CAPITAL PUNISHMENT**

KEY ● COURTS ● CULTURAL CHANGE
● ELECTIONS
● GRASSROOTS MOBILIZATION
● LOBBYING DECISION MAKERS

2000

New Hampshire state legislature votes to abolish the death penalty but the bill is vetoed by the governor.

2000–02
Governor George Ryan of Illinois places a moratorium on capital punishment when a media investigation discovers more than a dozen men on death row are innocent. Opponents of the death penalty lobby Ryan for the moratorium.

2002

Atkins v. *Virginia*

Supreme Court prohibits the execution of developmentally disabled individuals.

2005

Stanley "Tookie" Williams is put to death by lethal injection in California. Grassroots organizations on both sides of the divide mobilize prior to Williams' death.

Roper v. *Simmons*

Supreme Court rules the execution of murderers who commit crimes while they are under the age of 18 is "cruel and unusual punishment."

2007

New Jersey legislature bans the use of capital punishment.

2008

Kennedy v. *Louisiana*

Supreme Court prohibits the death penalty for the crime of child rape.

2006–2016 Elections

In contrast to national trends, Ohio and Mississippi increase the pace of executions by conducting over the six-year period more than 50 percent of their respective total executions since 1976.
California began considering resuming executions after a decade without any executions since 2006.

2011–2016 Elections

Lawmakers in Illinois, Connecticut, Maryland, and Nebraska end their states' use of the death penalty; a moratorium on executions is announced by the governor of Oregon.

Glossip v. *Gross*

A divided Supreme Court rejects a challenge to lethal injection drugs used by Oklahoma.

2015

Advances in DNA testing and reinvestigation of cases since the mid-1970s lead to the release of 156 prisoners who had been wrongly convicted and sentenced to death.

CRITICAL THINKING QUESTIONS

1. Many observers expect the Supreme Court to turn its attention to the question of whether it is "cruel and unusual" to execute murderers suffering from mental illnesses. Imagine that you are a lawyer. Choose a side—for or against—and create arguments concerning this issue.

2. Several states are attempting to create more careful processes that will guard against the risk that innocent people will be convicted of murders and sentenced to death. Create three suggestions for ways to reduce the risk of mistakes in murder trials. Explain how your suggestions will improve the process.

Critics complained that the Court's decision created a new constitutional right that was not grounded in the Bill of Rights. In the words of Justice Hugo Black's dissenting opinion, "I like my privacy as well as the next [person], but I am nevertheless compelled to admit that government has a right to invade it unless prohibited by some specific constitutional provision." Critics feared from this that a five-member majority on the Supreme Court could invent any new rights that the justices wanted to impose on society. By contrast, defenders of the flexible approach to constitutional interpretation claimed that the Court is obligated to adjust the Constitution's meaning to make sure that it remains consistent with the changing values and needs of American society. In subsequent cases, the Court's flexible approach to constitutional interpretation led to the application of a right to privacy to new situations.

Abortion

Roe v. Wade (1973)
Controversial U.S. Supreme Court decision that declared women have a constitutional right to choose to terminate a pregnancy in the first six months following conception.

In 1969, two young lawyers in Texas, Linda Coffee and Sarah Weddington, met a woman who claimed that she had become pregnant as the result of being raped. Because Texas, like other states, made abortion a crime, the woman could not legally terminate the pregnancy. Although the woman gave birth to the baby, she wanted to use her case to challenge the Texas statute through the court pathway. The lawyers took the case, *Roe v. Wade*, all the way to the U.S. Supreme Court. ("Jane Roe" was not the woman's real name; it was used in the case to protect her privacy.) Her lawyers argued that the Texas statute violated the woman's right to make choices about abortion. In 1973, after the Supreme Court heard arguments from lawyers on both sides of the issue, the justices voted 7-2 that the Texas statute violated the Constitution. Justice Harry Blackmun wrote the majority opinion:

> The Court has recognized that a right of personal privacy, or a guarantee of certain areas or zones of privacy, does exist under the Constitution.... This right of privacy, whether it be founded in the Fourteenth Amendment's concept of personal liberty and restrictions upon state action, as we feel it is, or as the District Court determined, in the Ninth Amendment's reservation of rights to the people, is broad enough to encompass a woman's decision whether or not to terminate her pregnancy.

Several state legislatures and city councils sought to counteract the Court's decision by enacting statutes and ordinances to make obtaining abortions more difficult by specifying expensive medical procedures and other matters during the second trimester. In addition, abortion opponents in Congress fought against the Court's decision by using their authority to limit public funding for abortion. Initially, the Court struck down several of these restrictive state laws. Later, however, as new justices were appointed, the Court became more flexible about accepting regulations. In *Webster v. Reproductive Health Services* (1989), for example, a majority of justices upheld Missouri's new abortion regulations.

Abortion became a central consideration in the appointment of newcomers to the Supreme Court. Interest groups on both sides of the abortion issue sought to influence the composition of the Supreme Court by lobbying presidents and senators to either favor or oppose specific judicial nominees. Presidents Ronald Reagan (1981–1989) and George H. W. Bush (1989–1993) vowed to use their appointment powers to put new justices on the Court who would work to overturn the right of choice established in *Roe v. Wade*. Thus the stage seemed set for a reconsideration of *Roe v. Wade* when the case known as *Planned Parenthood v. Casey* (1992) reached the Court.

Pennsylvania had enacted statutes requiring that doctors provide women seeking abortions with detailed information about fetal development, mandating a 24-hour waiting period before a woman could proceed with an abortion, and specifying that minors obtain parental consent and that married women notify their spouses before obtaining an abortion. These regulations were challenged as interfering with women's rights to make choices about their own health care. In 1992, only one member of *Roe*'s seven-member majority, Justice Blackmun, remained on the Court to defend that decision. In a ruling that surprised observers, however, three appointees of Presidents Reagan and Bush joined in writing an opinion that preserved the right of choice originally created by *Roe*.

Justices Sandra Day O'Connor, Anthony Kennedy, and David Souter applied an "undue burden test" that accepts government regulations, as long as they do not pose an undue burden on women's choices about abortion during the first six months of pregnancy. This test, developed by Justice O'Connor in several of her opinions in abortion cases, became influential in determining how the Court examined abortion issues. However, Justices O'Connor, Kennedy, and Souter believed that a decision to overturn *Roe* after nearly 20 years would cause "profound and unnecessary damage to the Court's legitimacy, and to the Nation's commitment to the rule of law" by making it appear as if the right of choice disappeared merely because the Court's composition changed. Justice Blackmun, an appointee of President Nixon, and Justice John Paul Stevens, an appointee of President Ford, also voted to keep the *Roe* precedent. Thus, by a 5-4 vote, the Court approved most of Pennsylvania's regulations but preserved the essence of the right of choice by declining to overturn *Roe*.

Subsequent decades saw new cases challenging the actions of various states that sought to limit access to abortion. In 2016, the Court issued a decision rejecting Texas's imposition of new requirements for equipment and personnel at medical facilities that would have effectively reduced the number of abortion clinics in the state.[15] The Court has generally approved increasingly restrictive regulations, yet appointments to the Supreme Court during the administrations of Presidents Bill Clinton, George W. Bush, and Barack Obama effectively preserved the Court's narrow five-member majority supporting the underlying right of choice. The unexpected death of 79-year-old Justice Antonin Scalia in February 2016 during the middle of the Supreme Court's term added drama and uncertainty to the Court's future. When Scalia, an opponent of *Roe*, is replaced by the appointee of new Republican president-elect Donald Trump, the Supreme Court's set of justices who are critics of *Roe* v. *Wade* is expected to grow in strength. The U.S. Senate remained narrowly under Republican control after the November 2016 election, so new President Trump should be able to gain confirmation for his appointee to the Supreme Court. In addition, as of 2016, three justices (Ruth Bader Ginsburg, Anthony Kennedy, and Stephen Breyer) are age 78 or older and, as with anyone their age, face risks of a sudden health crisis that could also force them from Court. Because a Republican was elected as the new president, if Ginsburg, Breyer, or Kennedy leaves the Court during Trump's first term, the possibility exists that the *Roe* precedent will be overturned by new appointees to the Court.

Although some people hope—or fear—that legal abortion will disappear if *Roe* is eliminated, in reality the Court's decision merely tells states what laws they *cannot* create. Although overturning *Roe* would permit states to prohibit or severely restrict abortion, it is likely that abortion would remain legal in certain states, even if it were no longer recognized by the Supreme Court as a constitutional right. Therefore, debates and political battles about abortion may ultimately have direct effects on only two groups of women: those who are too poor or too young to travel to a state where abortion is legal and available.[16]

Private Sexual Conduct

Griswold v. *Connecticut* (1965), the case that produced the Supreme Court's first explicit recognition of a constitutional right to privacy, concerned married couples' personal lives. The public did not generally object to recognizing a right to privacy in this context. By contrast, the private sexual conduct of nonmarried adults can produce controversy.

Both opponents and supporters of abortion rights use the grassroots mobilization, elections, and lobbying decision makers pathways as well as the court pathway.

■ *If you chose to become involved in actions to influence the abortion issue, which pathway would you recommend for your allies to use? Why?*

In *Bowers* v. *Hardwick* (1986), a young gay man in Georgia was charged with violating the state's sodomy law—which mandated sentences of up to 20 years in prison for sexual conduct other than intercourse between a man and a woman—when a police officer entered his home and found him in a bedroom having sex with another man. The Supreme Court was deeply divided on the question of whether the right to privacy should protect the private sexual behavior of gays and lesbians. The five-member majority of the Court treated the case as if it only concerned, in Justice Byron White's words, "whether the Federal Constitution confers a fundamental right upon homosexuals to engage in sodomy." To that question, the majority answered no. By contrast, the four dissenters, who argued that the law was unconstitutional, viewed the Georgia law as making a general attack on privacy. According to Justice Harry Blackmun's dissenting opinion,

> This case is about "the most comprehensive of rights and the right most valued by civilized men," namely "the right to be let alone." The statute at issue denies individuals the right to decide for themselves whether to engage in particular forms of private, consensual sexual activity.

Seventeen years later, the Supreme Court revisited the issue in *Lawrence* v. *Texas* (2003), a case challenging the constitutionality of a Texas statute that criminalized sexual conduct between persons of the same gender. This time, however, the majority on the Supreme Court overruled *Bowers* v. *Hardwick* and declared that the right to privacy protects the private, noncommercial sexual conduct of adults, including gays and lesbians. In the words of Justice Anthony Kennedy's majority opinion,

The petitioners are entitled to respect for their private lives. The State cannot demean their existence or control their destiny by making their private sexual conduct a crime. Their right to liberty under the Due Process Clause gives them the full right to engage in their conduct without intervention by the government.

Do you believe that the Supreme Court has gone too far in identifying and defining the right to privacy? Some people are concerned that judges will do whatever they want to do in creating new rights and affecting public policy. Because of new technology as well as increased governmental surveillance efforts related to computer crime, Internet child pornography, and antiterrorism efforts, additional privacy issues are likely to emerge concerning government intrusion into e-mail, computer systems, and wireless communications. For example, in 2012 the Supreme Court rejected the government's claim of legal authority to secretly—and without a warrant—attach a GPS (Global Positioning Satellite) device to the car of a suspected drug dealer in order to continuously monitor his movements and pinpoint locations (*United States* v. *Jones*). It remains to be seen whether or how the Court will define privacy protections in other contexts.

Conclusion

Civil liberties are an especially important part of the governing system in the United States. They reflect the high value that the U.S. Constitution accords to personal liberty, individualism, and limited government. The Bill of Rights, as well as other provisions in the Constitution and in the state constitutions, describes legal protections for individuals and at the same time imposes limitations on what government can do to individuals. The specific civil liberties enjoyed by individuals are defined and changed through decisions by judges who interpret constitutional provisions.

As you saw with respect to incorporation and the death penalty, judges may use flexible approaches to interpretation that enable them to recognize new rights and expand or shrink existing rights. The vagueness of the words *due process of law* enabled the U.S. Supreme Court to interpret them to mean that many provisions of the Bill of Rights should protect people against actions by states and cities as well as actions by the federal government. Debates about the meaning of such constitutional phrases continue to this day, as we saw in the chapter opening example concerning the meaning of "unreasonable searches." The justices applied those words to cover police officers' examinations of photos contained in cellphones of drivers who have just been arrested. Similarly, the words *cruel and unusual punishments* in the Eighth Amendment are vague; judges must give them specific meaning in evaluating which murderers are eligible for the death penalty and which methods of execution are permissible.

The Supreme Court and other courts will face new issues that arise from changing developments in society, such as post-9/11 questions concerning whether suspected terrorists in government custody are entitled to the protections of the Bill of Rights and how far the government can go in conducting warrantless wiretaps of people suspected of being in contact with terrorist organizations. The ever-changing world in which we live continually produces conflicts between individuals and government that lead to intense battles in the court pathway. Judges are therefore likely to remain highly influential in determining aspects of public policy related to issues of civil liberties.

Many civil liberties issues, such as school prayer, abortion, capital punishment, and government's use of technology to intercept citizens' communications, are extremely controversial. Thus individuals and groups who are disappointed by judges' decisions often raise questions about the extent of proper judicial authority and whether judges' decisions have "gone too far." These controversies have also made the process of nominating and confirming appointments to federal court positions, especially to the Supreme Court, a matter of high-stakes politics. Americans' lack of agreement about the meaning of the Bill of Rights guarantees that these debates will continue and that presidents will use their appointment powers to try to influence civil liberties cases through the selection of federal judges who share their values and beliefs.

CONFRONTING POLITICS AND POLICY

In September 2015, news reports described a dispute at Hinds Community College, a large public college in Mississippi. Two students said that they were arrested for allegedly violating the college's rule against having "sagging pants," even though they both claimed that they were wearing belts and complying with the policy. One student claimed that he was pushed into a wall by the officer who handcuffed him. Fellow students were upset by what happened and protested against the arrests of their two classmates. The news reports about this situation raise possible civil liberties issues.

ACTION STEPS

1. Should the manner in which one wears clothing be regarded as protected "symbolic speech" under the First Amendment? As long as students do not violate state laws against public nudity, should officials at a state college have rules that regulate how fully-clothed students wear their clothing? List two reasons for your answers to each of these questions.

2. An arrest is a form of "seizure" under the Fourth Amendment and all such seizures must be reasonable. Does it violate the Fourth Amendment prohibition on "unreasonable seizures" to arrest a student and take that student to jail for wearing sagging pants? Give two reasons for your answer.

3. If students wanted to push the college to change its dress code rules, what would be the best pathway of action? Have the arrested students file lawsuits for asserted constitutional rights violations? Lobby the state legislature to reduce the power of college officials? Protest marches? Explain your choices.

〉 REVIEW THE CHAPTER

The Bill of Rights in History

4.1 Explain how the Bill of Rights came to protect individuals against actions by state governments. (p. 104)

Civil liberties, drawn from the Bill of Rights and judicial decisions, provide legal protections for individuals and limit the authority of government. The Supreme Court originally applied the Bill of Rights only to protect individuals against the federal government, but by the end of the 1960s, through its incorporation of decisions interpreting the Fourteenth Amendment's Due Process Clause, it was applying most of those protections to the actions of state and local officials as well.

First Amendment Rights: Freedom of Religion

4.2 Distinguish between the two dimensions of freedom of religion in the First Amendment. (p. 107)

Americans consider the civil liberties contained in the First Amendment—which cover freedom of speech, press, assembly, and religion—essential to the maintenance of a democracy and a free society. Freedom of religion in the First Amendment consists of two components: the Establishment Clause and the Free Exercise Clause. Judicial decisions concerning the Establishment Clause have forbidden sponsored prayers in public schools and other activities that are judged to provide excessive government support for or entanglement with religion. Congress has sought to protect the free exercise of religion by requiring courts to apply a strict scrutiny or compelling government interest test to such cases. This test forces the government to show a compelling reason for laws and policies that clash with the free exercise of religion.

First Amendment Rights: Freedom of Speech

4.3 Specify the limits on free speech in the United States. (p. 113)

The actual protections for freedom of speech are less absolute than implied by the words of the First Amendment, because the Supreme Court has accepted time, place, and manner restrictions as well as other limitations that serve society's interests regarding safety, order, and the protection of national security, intellectual property, and personal reputations.

First Amendment Rights: Freedom of the Press and Obscenity

4.4 Assess the test for justifying governmental limitations on written words and images. (p. 116)

Courts generally rule against government efforts to impose prior restraints on the press, although the possibility for prior restraint exists if military plans or national security interests are at stake. If individuals' reputations are harmed by inaccurate news articles or other untrue communications, they can seek compensation afterward by suing for defamation based on false written statements (libel) or false spoken statements (slander). However, freedom of the press claims by reporters can clash with other priorities, such as the government's need to gather evidence about witnesses and suspects in criminal cases. The government can also regulate commercial speech in order to protect the public from false or deceptive advertising. The First Amendment does not protect obscenity, but the Supreme Court has struggled to develop a workable definition of what materials are "obscene." As a result, governmental prosecution of obscene material focuses primarily on child pornography, a subject for which a broader consensus about the harm from published materials exists.

Civil Liberties and Criminal Justice

4.5 Specify the protections afforded to criminal suspects in the Bill of Rights. (p. 119)

The Fourth Amendment protection against unreasonable searches and seizures requires significant interpretation by courts, especially because so many different situations arise in which the government examines people and their property for evidence of crimes. The Supreme Court has approved a list of situations in which no warrant is required for searches because those searches are regarded as "reasonable." Individuals subjected to unreasonable searches may gain protection from prosecution through the exclusionary rule, but the Supreme Court has created exceptions to this rule that permit the use of improperly obtained evidence in some situations. The Supreme Court's requirement of *Miranda* warnings prior to the questioning of suspects in custody serves as a central component of the Fifth Amendment privilege against compelled self-incrimination.

Trial Rights and Capital Punishment

4.6 Evaluate the legal protections that seek to ensure only guilty people receive criminal punishment. (p. 127)

The Sixth Amendment contains trial rights, including the right to confrontation, the right to compulsory process, and the right to trial by jury. Without these rights, there would be greater risks of innocent people being convicted of crimes. The right to trial by jury applies only for "serious" charges, and the right to counsel applies only for specific stages of the criminal process.

Capital punishment is a controversial issue that has divided the Supreme Court's justices over questions about whether it is "cruel and unusual" and therefore in violation of the Eighth Amendment. The Supreme Court's decisions create rules and restrictions that seek to make death penalty trials produce careful decisions. The Supreme Court's rulings also limit the categories of offenders eligible for the death penalty.

Privacy

4.7 Explain why the right to privacy is controversial. (p. 129)

The Supreme Court used its interpretive powers to identify and develop a right to privacy that has been applied to give individuals rights related to choices about abortion, contraceptives, and private, noncommercial sexual conduct by adults. These are issues about which many Americans vigorously disagree. The identification and expansion of the right to privacy has been especially controversial because the word privacy does not appear in the Constitution; the right was produced through interpretive decisions by the Supreme Court.

〉 LEARN THE TERMS

civil liberties, p. 104
Due Process Clause, p. 105
incorporation, p. 106
Establishment Clause, p. 109
Free Exercise Clause, p. 109
separationist, p. 110
accommodationist, p. 110
Lemon test, p. 111
strict scrutiny, p. 112
clear and present danger test, p. 114

symbolic speech, p. 114
reasonable time, place, and manner restrictions, p. 114
prior restraint, p. 116
reporter's privilege, p. 117
press shield law, p. 117
exclusionary rule, p. 119
warrant, p. 120
double jeopardy, p. 121
compelled self-incrimination, p. 121

Miranda v. *Arizona* (1966), p. 121
confrontation, p. 123
compulsory process, p. 123
trial by jury, p. 123
bench trials, p. 123
plea bargaining, p. 123
capital punishment, p. 125
right to privacy, p. 127
Roe v. *Wade* (1973), p. 130

〉 EXPLORE FURTHER

In the Library

Abraham, Henry J., and Barbara Perry. *Freedom and the Court: Civil Rights and Liberties in the United States*, 8th ed. Lawrence, KS: University Press of Kansas, 2003.

Amar, Akhil Reed. *The Bill of Rights*. New Haven, CT: Yale University Press, 1998.

Bollinger, Lee, and Geoffrey Stone, eds. *Eternally Vigilant: Free Speech in the Modern Era*. Chicago: University of Chicago Press, 2003.

Costanzo, Mark. *Just Revenge: Costs and Consequences of the Death Penalty*. New York: St. Martin's Press, 1997.

Coyle, Marcia. *The Roberts Court: The Struggle for the Constitution*. New York: Simon & Schuster, 2013.

Epps, Garrett, ed. *Freedom of the Press*. New York: Prometheus Books, 2008.

Friendly, Fred W. *Minnesota Rag: Corruption, Yellow Journalism, and the Case that Saved Freedom of the Press*. Minneapolis, MN: University of Minnesota Press, 2003.

Hull, N.E.H., and Peter Charles Hoffer. *Roe v. Wade: The Abortion Rights Controversy in American History*. Lawrence, KS: University Press of Kansas, 2001.

Levy, Leonard W. *The Establishment Clause: Religion and the First Amendment*. Chapel Hill, NC: University of North Carolina Press, 1994.

Lewis, Anthony. *Freedom for the Thought that We Hate: A Biography of the First Amendment*. New York: Basic Books, 2008.

Maclin, Tracey. *The Supreme Court and the Fourth Amendment's Exclusionary Rule*. New York: Oxford University Press, 2013.

Smith, Christopher E. *Constitutional Rights: Myths and Realities*. Belmont, CA: Thomson-Wadsworth, 2004.

Smith, Christopher E. *John Paul Stevens: Defender of Rights in Criminal Justice*. Lanham, MD: Lexington, 2015.

Stevens, John Paul. *Six Amendments: How and Why We Should Change the Constitution*. Boston: Little, Brown and Co., 2014.

Thomas, George C., III, and Richard A. Leo. *Confessions of Guilt: From Torture to* Miranda *and Beyond*. New York: Oxford University Press, 2012.

On the Web

Compare competing perspectives on defining civil liberties and deciding which freedoms are most important for Americans by examining the Web sites of interest groups: *http://www.acslaw.org* (American Constitution Society) and *http://www.fed-soc.org* (Federalist Society).

Examine Web sites of organizations focused on issues of religious liberty: *http://www.becketfund.org* (Becket Fund for Religious Liberty), *http://www.rluipa.com* (issues focused on the Religious Land Use and Institutionalized Persons Act), and *http://www.aclu.org* (American Civil Liberties Union).

Many contemporary free speech issues are discussed at the Web site of the First Amendment Center: *http://www.firstamendmentcenter.org/*.

Examine the Federal Communications Commission's presentation on its duty to prevent obscene and indecent materials over the regulated airwaves on television and radio: *http://www.fcc.gov/eb/oip/Welcome.html*.

Examine the U.S. Supreme Court's decisions on the exclusionary rule and *Miranda* warnings at *http://supreme.justia.com*.

Compare the competing perspectives on capital punishment presented by the Criminal Justice Legal Foundation at *http://www.cjlf.org* and the Death Penalty Information Center at *http://www.deathpenaltyinfo.org*.

Compare the competing perspectives on abortion presented by the National Right to Life Committee at *http://www.nrlc.org* and NARAL Pro-Choice America at *http://www.prochoiceamerica.org*.

CIVIL RIGHTS

Since 2014, controversial shootings of unarmed men by police officers have called attention to evidence of racial disparities in stops, searches, arrests, and sentences for criminal offenses. Public protests in response to the shootings have also raised concerns about the relationship between police departments and the minority communities that they are supposed to serve.
▪ *Do the public protests against police actions show that the United States has moved backward in its aspiration for equal rights and equal justice or are they a reminder that the United States has never progressed as far as many had hoped toward the goal of equality?*

→ LEARNING OBJECTIVES

5.1 Describe the idea of equality that underlies the governing system of the United States.

5.2 Trace the historical development of civil rights in the United States.

5.3 Analyze how litigation strategies contributed to the dismantling of official racial segregation.

5.4 Differentiate between the various tests used by the Supreme Court when deciding discrimination claims under the Equal Protection Clause.

5.5 Identify the events and factors that influenced the development of the grassroots civil rights movement.

5.6 Compare and contrast the civil rights struggles of women, Latinos, Native Americans, and African Americans.

5.7 Evaluate the continuing debates, lawsuits, and protests over civil rights in the twenty-first century.

The images from Ferguson, Missouri, in late 2014 captured national attention: unarmed African American protesters, hands held high as a symbol of nonviolence, face-to-face with heavily armed police officers, including officers pointing guns directly at them. Related protests were repeated in cities across the country with only a few places experiencing property damage and arson, primarily by a subset of angry community members in Ferguson and Baltimore. Typically, the marches were peaceful expressions of the communities' anger and frustration. The deaths of unarmed African American men at the hands of police officers generated the protest marches. In Ferguson, unarmed teenager Michael Brown was shot and killed by a police officer who claimed that he feared Brown would attack him after they had an altercation over the officer's order for the teen to stop walking in the street. In New York City in December 2014, protest marches were organized after Eric Garner died from a chokehold applied by an officer who sought to stop Garner from illegally selling cigarettes on the sidewalk. Neither officer was charged with a crime. People in other cities organized protest marches in support of protesters in Ferguson and New York City. Subsequently, parallel protests emerged in such places as Baltimore in April 2015 and Minneapolis and Chicago in November 2015 in reaction to similar deaths caused by police officers' actions.[1]

The continuing race-based differential treatment that is perceived by activists from their own observations and experiences is well-documented in studies showing significantly greater application of stops, searches, arrests, use of force, and enhanced punishments for African Americans.[2] In 2013, activists concerned about racial discrimination, excessive use of force by police, and the killing of African Americans by whites who were never punished began using the Twitter hashtag "#BlackLivesMatter." They initiated social media-messaging protests around these issues. The death of Michael Brown and the subsequent protests in Ferguson mobilized the Black Lives Matter movement as larger numbers of people affiliated themselves with the organization. People from across the country came to join the organization's protests in Ferguson. Others used the Black Lives Matter slogan in organizing protests in their own cities.[3]

For many participants and observers, the Black Lives Matter movement represented a rejuvenation of the civil rights protests of the 1960s as activists called attention to continuing issues of racial discrimination, especially unfair treatment by police and justice system officials. The persistent existence of such discrimination in the twenty-first century was made crystal clear when the U.S. Department of Justice issued a scathing report in 2015 about the police and court system in Ferguson. City officials in Ferguson encouraged police officers to write many unjustified citations targeting poor African Americans in the community. When they could not pay their fines, the fine amounts were doubled, they were jailed, and the city gained increased revenue as a single traffic ticket could end up costing an individual hundreds and hundreds of dollars over time. Officials funded city government through discriminatory and oppressive treatment of African American citizens. The city retained the services of a particular part-time judge specifically because he generated so much revenue for them by compounding punitive fines on poor people. Officials also used their connections to help whites with traffic and other citations avoid facing the same fines and punitive actions that were imposed on African Americans. The revelations about Ferguson's discriminatory justice system generated media attention about parallel problems elsewhere in the country.[4] For example, judges illegally jailed people who were too poor to pay fines, and cities permitted private companies to administer probation services in profit-maximizing, predatory ways that treated poor African Americans especially unfairly.[5]

By 2016, the Black Lives Matter organization and movement had such visibility that presidential candidates were asked questions about problems underlying the resurgence of civil rights activism. Moreover, the movement began to translate its protests into other forms of political action. The Black Lives Matter organization put forth specific policy proposals for improving the fairness of policing and the justice system.[6] In addition, leaders of the organization began to run for elective offices, including Congress, the Minnesota state legislature, and the mayor's office in Baltimore.[7] In this way, the Black Lives Matter movement followed in the footsteps of earlier civil rights activists who used a variety of pathways of action in seeking to end discrimination and achieve political equality.

› **POLL** Do you think law enforcement in your community treats minorities fairly?

WHICH PATHWAYS OF ACTION SHAPED CIVIL RIGHTS TO ADVANCE THE IDEAL OF EQUALITY?

The United States has a long history of discrimination, most famously based on race but also on national origin, gender, sexual orientation, and other characteristics. This history clashes with the nation's ideals about equality. Various pathways of policy change—including litigation in courts, mass protests on the streets, and lobbying in legislatures—have been used by people seeking their civil rights—namely, equal political participation, such as the right to vote, and equal opportunities to seek education and employment. In this chapter, we examine the American ideal of equality and political action undertaken to advance the fulfillment of this ideal.

The Ideal of Equality

5.1 Describe the idea of equality that underlies the governing system of the United States.

civil rights
Public policies and legal protections concerning equal status and treatment in American society to advance the goals of equal opportunity, fair and open political participation, and equal treatment under the law without regard to race, gender, disability status, and other demographic characteristics.

political equality
Fundamental value underlying the governing system of the United States that emphasizes all citizens' opportunities to vote, run for office, own property, and enjoy civil liberties protections under the Constitution.

The concept of **civil rights** concerns legal protection for equality and participation in the country's governing processes. As we've discussed in earlier chapters, the founders of the United States wanted to enjoy **political equality**, which would allow them to express their views, own property, and participate in what they called a "republican" governing system. The most famous expression of the founders' emphasis on equality is in the words of the Declaration of Independence: "All men are created equal." The founders believed that political equality was an essential element of the natural world and a fundamental principle of human life, and they considered that principle to be violated when a social system or government granted extra status and power to favored individuals.

The Declaration of Independence focused on equality for *men.* The nation's founders simply took it for granted that women need not participate as important decision makers in political affairs. Women were viewed as being destined for such roles in society as cooks, maids, wives, and mothers. In addition, the founders intended equality to apply in practice only to certain men of European ancestry. Many of the founders of the United States were slave owners, and even some who did not own slaves viewed African Americans as less-than-equal beings. Nor did the founders view Native Americans as equal to whites. From the mid-seventeenth century through the late nineteenth century, Native Americans were pushed from their lands, often through military force and other violence.

In practice, the founders did not even view all white men as completely equal for purposes of political participation and influence over public policy. Thus, many laws at first restricted voting rights to white men who owned land. Men without property, it was feared, would be too easily controlled by their employers or creditors to act independently.

Despite this, the statement that "all men are created equal" has served as a beacon of inspiration for Americans. Instead of accepting the founders' original limited idea of equality, people have focused on the underlying ideal and asked themselves and their fellow Americans, "Shouldn't I be included in that statement?" Women, African Americans, Latinos, the disabled, and gays and lesbians, among others, have worked through various pathways to broaden the Declaration's original ideal of equality.

Civil rights protesters use graphic examples to remind the American public of our country's history of violence and unequal treatment aimed at members of racial minority groups.

■ *Are such reminders just an attempt to generate guilt, or does this history still have relevance for the problems that we face today?*

Over the course of American history, several factors have contributed to widespread acceptance of a redefinition of political equality that extends beyond white males. These factors include grassroots mobilization, legislative action, legal cases, and even the bloody Civil War of the 1860s. Political activity and social changes over many decades produced new—and now widely accepted—ideas about equality that embrace women and members of racial and other minority groups (see Table 5.1). Public acceptance of other aspects of change, concerning the disabled, gays and lesbians, and others—who see themselves as treated unfairly—is still developing. Many people think it is appropriate, for example, that the disabled or gays and lesbians be barred from certain occupations, including military service. Such groups that are not universally regarded as victims of unjustified discrimination may find their civil rights claims to be viewed by critics as improper attempts to gain special treatment.

The founders' ideal of equality focused on political participation and civil liberties. By contrast, it is possible to have a governing system that emphasizes equal economic status or **equality of condition**. Some governing systems use policy decisions rather than constitutional rights as the means to ensure that everyone has access to important goods and services, such as education, medical care, housing, and at least a modest income. For example, the system of taxation and government benefits in Sweden, the Netherlands, and several other European countries seeks to lift low-income people into the middle class.

The American system seeks to advance **equality of opportunity** or equal opportunities for participation in the economic system and in public life. This goal has expanded beyond the founders' original concept of political equality to also include the elimination of *some* discriminatory barriers to education, employment, and public accommodation. Some forms of discrimination are perfectly legal in the United States, while the law bans others. For example, universities are not obligated to admit students who failed all of their courses during high school. They can legally discriminate in admissions based on high school grades. Universities can also discriminate in hiring professors by requiring successful applicants to have specific graduate degrees and rejecting those applicants who do not possess those degrees. Universities cannot, however, discriminate by race or gender in hiring because employment discrimination laws prohibit those forms of discrimination, as they interfere with the goal of providing equal employment opportunity for similarly qualified applicants. The system does not claim to seek the *elimination* of all differences and disparities or to provide goods and services to everyone. The American

equality of condition

A conception of equality that exists in some countries that value equal economic status as well as equal access to housing, health care, education, and government services. For example, governing systems that emphasize equality of condition provide health care, generous unemployment benefits, and government-financed opportunities to attend universities.

equality of opportunity

A conception of equality that seeks to provide all citizens with opportunities for participation in the economic system and public life but accepts unequal results in income, political power, and property ownership.

TABLE 5.1 Rights, Pathways, and Results in Advancing Equality of Opportunity

Various groups used specific pathways in order to seek the promise of equality outlined in the Declaration of Independence and the Equal Protection Clause of the Fourteenth Amendment. Multiple pathways were employed, and each group used different strategies.

Group	Minority Right	Pathway	Outcome
African Americans	Basic civil rights, prohibit discrimination, voting rights	**Equal access to education:** court pathway **Prohibit discrimination:** grassroots mobilization, elections, and court pathways **Voting rights:** grassroots mobilization pathway	*Brown* v. *Board of Education* (1954) [school desegregation]; Civil Rights Act of 1964 [no discrimination in employment and public accommodations]; Voting Rights Act of 1965
Women	Voting rights, prohibit discrimination	**Voting rights:** grassroots mobilization and elections pathways **Prohibit discrimination:** elections, court, and cultural change pathways	Nineteenth Amendment (1920) [women's right to vote]; Equal Pay Act of 1963; *Reed* v. *Reed* (1971) [no discrimination in inheritance laws]
Japanese Americans	Compensation for deprivation of rights during World War II	**Compensation for rights' deprivation:** elections pathways	American Japanese Claims Act of 1948; Civil Liberties Act of 1988
Disabled	Prohibit discrimination	**Prohibit discrimination:** elections and grassroots mobilization pathways	Section 504 of the Rehabilitation Act of 1973 [no discrimination in federally funded programs]; Americans with Disabilities Act of 1990 [no discrimination in employment and public accommodations]
Older Workers	Prohibit discrimination in employment	**Prohibit discrimination, employment:** elections pathway	Age Discrimination in Employment Act of 1967 [no discrimination against workers age 40 and over]
Latinos	Basic civil rights, prohibit discrimination	**Basic civil rights and prohibit discrimination:** Grassroots mobilization and elections pathways	Agricultural Labor Relations Act of 1975 (California state law) [right of farm workers to unionize]; Voting Rights Act of 1975 [no discrimination against language minority groups]
Gays and Lesbians	Basic civil rights, prohibit discrimination	**Basic civil rights and prohibit discrimination:** court and elections pathways	*Obergefell* v. *Hodges* (2015) [right of gays and lesbians to marry]; *Romer* v. *Evans* (1996) [protection against laws targeted at gays and lesbians]; state and local antidiscrimination laws
Native Americans	Basic civil rights, prohibit discrimination, economic development	**Basic civil rights, prohibit discrimination, economic development:** elections pathway	Covered by federal antidiscrimination laws concerning race and ethnicity that were primarily spurred by African Americans; economic development, including gambling enterprises, through state laws

political ideology and our free-enterprise economic system emphasize individual achievement and the acquisition of wealth through hard work. People are expected to be self-reliant and to earn enough money to buy their own goods and services. If the government chooses to provide a service, such as public schools or health care for the elderly, it cannot discriminate by race, gender, or ethnicity in serving members of the public. However, the U.S. Constitution does not require the government to provide those services.

The drive for civil rights in the twentieth century focused on two areas: equal access to voting and the prohibition of certain forms of "categorical discrimination," which meant exclusion—by reason of race, gender, or disability—from public education, employment, housing, and public accommodations (restaurants, hotels, and stores). The advancement of these opportunities does not, however, mean that the American governing system is committed to complete equality of opportunity. Belief in the values of individualism and self-reliance in American ideology leads people to benefit from social networks, contacts, and the achievements of their friends and relatives.

Many people, for example, get jobs through referrals from family members and friends. (As a college student, you may very well have seen such preferences in action.) Some people inherit money from wealthy relatives and use that money to start businesses. People with wealth and social contacts typically have many more educational and employment opportunities than poor people. This disparity is an

The United States has a diverse society. Discrimination may be directed at groups along a number of dimensions, including race, religion, or disability status. During the 2016 presidential election, critics raised concerns that some candidates appeared to express hostility toward adherents of the Muslim faith. Here, Muslim women protest against a retail store's refusal to hire a woman because she wore a head scarf in compliance with her religious beliefs.

■ *Which pathway of action is most promising for Muslims seeking to counteract religious or national-origin discrimination?*

accepted aspect of the American free-enterprise system and its emphasis on individualism. As a result, the equality of opportunity advanced by civil rights is limited to specific contexts and does not reflect a comprehensive goal that is vigorously pursued by the American governing system.

Equal Protection of the Law

5.2 Trace the historical development of civil rights in the United States.

From the 1600s, people who were abducted and brought by force from Africa, and their descendants, worked as slaves in North America. Slavery existed in all 13 American colonies, although in the North, it was less extensive and abolished years earlier (within several decades of the American Revolution) than in the South. State laws mandating the gradual emancipation of slaves in New York and Connecticut, for example, meant that there were still small numbers of slaves in those states as late as 1827. Slavery was a brutal life, with dehumanizing effects for the African Americans subjected to violence and oppressive controls. It also fostered an ideology of racial superiority and animosity in white slave owners to justify their mistreatment of dark-skinned people.

Slaves worked from sunup to sundown under harsh conditions. They were forced to live in circumstances of limited nutrition, housing, medical care, and clothing, and they had few opportunities to use their creativity, intelligence, and effort to improve the quality of their lives. Slaves were beaten and whipped. Families were forcibly divided, as husbands, wives, and children were separated from their loved ones to be sold at auction and never seen again.[8] Race-based slavery and the subsequent decades of racial discrimination laid the foundation for today's racial gaps in wealth, education, housing patterns, and employment opportunities.[9] These enduring disadvantages for Americans of African ancestry have often proved extremely difficult to undo or overcome (see Figure 5.1).

The descendants of whites could enjoy the benefits of education, business contacts, and employment opportunities through social networks. Throughout the United States, freed slaves and their descendants faced the problem of starting from scratch without accumulated or inherited assets. To succeed in the economic system, they needed to seek access to education, employment, political participation, bank loans, land leases, and business contracts—all sectors of society dominated by whites until the late twentieth century. Yet the visibility of their skin color made African Americans easy to exclude by whites who wished to use discrimination to preserve their superior

FIGURE 5.1 Educational Attainment and Income by Race (Percentage of Adults) Over Time

Differences in educational attainment and poverty rates are evident among major ethnic groups in the United States. Over time, some of these disparities have become less stark than in the past. However, these issues that affect millions of Americans have not changed easily or swiftly.

NOTE: Hispanic data is not available prior to 1974 for educational attainment and 1972 for income and poverty rate.

SOURCE: U.S. Census data.

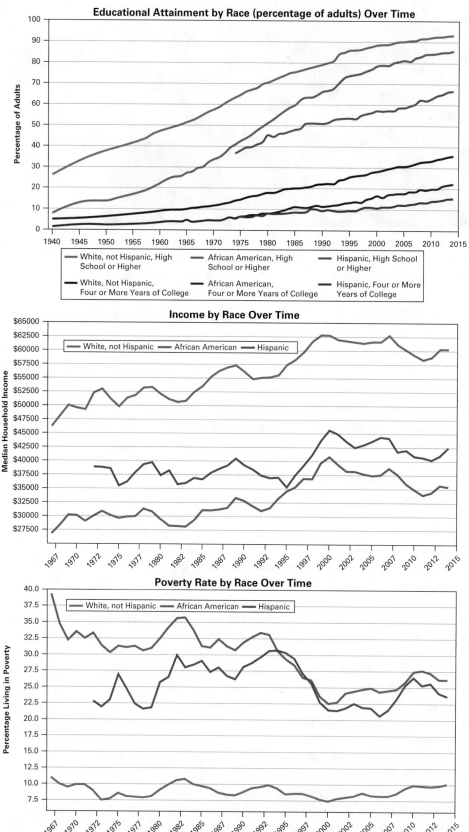

status and to monopolize educational, political, and business opportunities. To varying degrees, women, Latinos, and members of other minority groups have faced parallel problems of exclusion and discrimination.

One central question continues to be debated by individuals and groups who seek to shape American civil rights law and policy: How much should government do to make up for the nation's history of discrimination and its continuing effects? There are significant disagreements about which governmental actions appropriately advance Americans' limited concept of equality of opportunity.

The Fourteenth Amendment and Reconstruction

Immediately after the Civil War, between 1865 and early 1867, President Andrew Johnson—who had succeeded Abraham Lincoln after his assassination—permitted southern whites to determine how the South would reconstruct itself. Not surprisingly, they created laws that sought to maintain white superiority and power. As described by the historian Eric Foner,

> Southern state governments enforced [their] view of black freedom by enacting the notorious Black Codes, which denied blacks equality before the law and political rights, and imposed on them mandatory year-long labor contracts, coercive apprenticeship regulations, and criminal penalties for breach of contract. Through these laws, the South's white leadership sought to ensure that plantation agriculture survived emancipation.[10]

Members of Congress from the North also led the effort to create three constitutional amendments after the Civil War to provide important protections for African Americans. However, they could not transform society and create equality merely by adding new words to the Constitution. According to the historian David Kyvig,

> Each of the three Civil War amendments represented an effort to define the rights of free slaves and to give those rights constitutional protection. Each provided less protection than intended, whether as a result of sloppy draftsmanship, deliberate compromises that produced ambiguous perceptions, or determined resistance.[11]

The Thirteenth Amendment (1865) abolished slavery. The Fourteenth Amendment (1868) extended to former slaves the rights of full citizenship, including the equal protection of the laws and the right to due process under the law. The Fifteenth Amendment (1870) sought to guarantee that men would not be denied the right to vote because of their race. Women had not yet gained the right to vote and were deliberately excluded from the purview of the Fifteenth Amendment—over the bitter opposition of women's rights crusaders, who had also been abolitionists.

The language and intended meaning of the Thirteenth and Fifteenth Amendments were relatively straightforward, although as we will discuss later in this chapter, it took additional legislation and court decisions to fulfill the Fifteenth Amendment's goal of ensuring voting rights without racial discrimination. In contrast, the words of the Fourteenth Amendment were ambiguous and required extensive judicial interpretation over many decades. The Fourteenth Amendment has had a great impact on the definition of civil rights for all Americans, because it contains the Equal Protection Clause that victims of discrimination rely on when they go to court to seek judicial protection against unequal treatment by state and local government. Unlike the Bill of Rights, which was originally intended to protect individuals against actions by the federal government and only during the twentieth century came to be applied against state and local governments, the Fourteenth Amendment was aimed directly at actions by state governments. The amendment says that "no State shall" deprive people of specific rights. The ratification of this amendment two years after it was approved by Congress marked the first time that the ideas of birthright citizenship and equal rights for all Americans were articulated in the Constitution.

Today, we view the Fourteenth Amendment as protecting against various forms of discrimination. However, the Amendment's creation was motivated by northern congressmen's concerns about the treatment of newly-freed African Americans in the South. Despite efforts during that era by activists, such as Susan B. Anthony and Elizabeth Cady Stanton, who had worked since the 1840s to press for voting rights and equal treatment for women, the Amendment's Equal Protection Clause was not regarded as providing protection against gender discrimination. The U.S. Supreme Court, with its exclusively male membership until more than a century later when Justice Sandra Day O'Connor was appointed in 1981, endorsed discrimination against women shortly after the ratification of the Fourteenth Amendment through its decision *Bradwell v. Illinois* (1873). In *Bradwell,* the Court upheld an Illinois statute that prohibited women from becoming licensed attorneys in that state. Justice Joseph P. Bradley's now-discredited opinion relied on prevailing social values and nineteenth-century assumptions about women's "natural destiny" to work solely in the roles of wives and mothers:

> The natural and proper timidity and delicacy which belongs to the female sex evidently unfits it for many of the occupations of civil life. The constitution of the family organization, which is founded in the divine ordinance, as well as in the nature of things, indicates the domestic sphere as that which properly belongs to the domain and functions of womanhood.

The attitudes evident in the *Bradwell* opinion continued for many decades and help to explain why women did not obtain the right to vote nationally until ratification of the Nineteenth Amendment in 1920. In the 1970s, the Fourteenth Amendment's Equal Protection Clause was finally applied to protect civil rights and equal treatment for women.

The Rise and Persistence of Racial Oppression

The disputed outcome of the presidential election of 1876 between Republican Rutherford B. Hayes and Democrat Samuel Tilden affected the fates of African Americans. Election returns from several southern states were in dispute, preventing either Hayes or Tilden from claiming an Electoral College victory. After a special commission (consisting of members of Congress and the Supreme Court) awarded Hayes all the disputed electoral votes, Hayes became president and promptly withdrew the federal occupation troops from the South. Ending federal occupation permitted southern states greater freedom in developing laws and policies.[12]

The absence of federal troops unleashed the Ku Klux Klan and other violent, secret societies that terrorized African Americans—by beatings, house burnings, and murders—to prevent them from voting or otherwise asserting political and social equality. After 1876, in one southern state after another, self-styled "conservative," white-dominated governments came to power and did everything possible to raise legal barriers to black political participation. These laws could not simply say "black people cannot vote," because such wording would clash with the Fifteenth Amendment's prohibition on racial discrimination in voting. Instead, the new laws did such things as impose literacy tests and "government knowledge" tests as a condition of voter registration. These could also be used to exclude poor whites from voting. In some places, white county clerks administered the tests in a discriminatory fashion to fail all African American applicants while permitting whites to pass. Intimidation and violence were also used by police to prevent African Americans from voting. As a result, between the 1870s and the 1890s, the number of African American men who were registered to vote in southern states dropped from tens of thousands to only a handful.

The white-dominated, conservative state governments also began enacting **Jim Crow laws**, labeled after a minstrel song that ridiculed African Americans. These laws mandated rigid racial segregation throughout southern society. State and local governments required that African Americans attend separate schools and use separate public facilities. By the early twentieth century, this policy had evolved into designating separate and inferior

Jim Crow laws

Laws enacted by southern state legislatures after the Civil War that mandated rigid racial segregation. For example, such laws not only required separate bank teller windows and elevators but also separate Bibles for swearing in African American witnesses in court.

waiting areas in bus stations, public restrooms, and even public drinking fountains. Often, no attempt was ever made to provide separate public facilities; public swimming pools and parks, for example, were set aside for the use of whites only.

With the rise of state-enforced racial discrimination, life for many African Americans was little better than slavery. They were generally stuck in slavelike positions as poorly paid agricultural workers and other laborers. They were virtually unprotected by the law. If whites committed crimes against African Americans, including such horrific acts as rape and murder, there was little likelihood that any arrest would be made.

In the 1890s, a light-skinned African American man named Homer Plessy, described in court papers as "7/8ths white," worked with lawyers from the North in planning a legal challenge to the rigid segregation of Jim Crow laws. Plessy illegally sat in a "whites only" railroad car and refused to move when asked. As he and his lawyers had planned, Plessy was arrested for violating the law when he disobeyed the racial separation mandated by Louisiana's state law. When the case reached the Supreme Court (*Plessy v. Ferguson* (1896)), Plessy's lawyers argued that racial segregation laws violated the Equal Protection Clause of the Fourteenth Amendment. In a 7-1 decision, however, the Supreme Court decided that there was no violation of the constitutional right to equal protection when states had "separate but equal" facilities and services for people of different races. The Court's decision effectively endorsed racial discrimination by government, because the separate facilities provided for African Americans, including railroad cars, public restrooms, and schools, were always inferior to those provided for whites. The majority of the justices did not examine whether the separate facilities were equal. It was merely assumed that they were, and the Court turned aside African Americans' hopes for civil rights protection under the Fourteenth Amendment.

Justice John Marshall Harlan, who grew up in a Kentucky family that had previously owned slaves, was the lone dissenter in the *Plessy* case. He wrote one of the Court's most famous opinions. "Our Constitution is color-blind," he said. As if looking in a crystal ball, he accurately predicted that "the destinies of the two races in this country [whites and African Americans] are indissolubly linked together." The Court's decision endorsing the infliction of harm on one race would, he foresaw, lead to long-term consequences that would adversely affect the entire nation. In Harlan's words, "The common government of all [should] not permit the seeds of race hate to be planted under the sanction of law."

From the introduction of slavery through the first five decades of the twentieth century, African Americans were victimized by horrific violence and enjoyed little protection from the legal system. White mobs lynched African Americans—hanged and often mutilated innocent people—based on rumors of criminal acts or even for violating white people's expectations that they show deference and obedience.

■ *Which pathway had the greatest impact in moving the United States from these gut-wrenching scenes to where we are today—the court pathway, elections pathway, grassroots mobilization pathway, lobbying decision makers pathway, or cultural change pathway?*

Plessy v. Ferguson (1896)

A U.S. Supreme Court decision that endorsed the legality of racial segregation laws by permitting "separate but equal" services and facilities for African Americans, even though the services and facilities were actually inferior, such as markedly inferior schools for African American children.

The "separate but equal" doctrine led to strict racial separation in many aspects of American life, especially in southern states. Although some whites argued that separation affected both races equally, the inferiority of services and facilities provided for African Americans made it very clear that the policy targeted one particular group for victimization.

■ *Did your parents or other relatives observe or experience aspects of racial segregation? If so, what effect did those experiences have on them?*

de jure segregation

Racial segregation mandated by laws and policies created by government officials.

de facto segregation

Racial segregation in housing and schools that was presumed to occur through people's voluntary choices about where they wanted to live but was actually facilitated by the discriminatory actions of landlords, real estate agents, and banks.

In the southern states, rigid segregation and exclusion of African Americans from political participation continued through the 1960s. Black people continued to be intimidated by violence, including lynching, and remained unprotected by the law. Southern whites maintained their superior status and economic benefits. After 1900, many African Americans began leaving the South and seeking employment in the industrial centers of the North, where they also faced racial discrimination. The South practiced **de jure segregation**, in which state and local laws mandated discrimination and separation.

Northern cities used less formal means, often labeled **de facto segregation**. Patterns of segregated housing in the North were usually justified by a presumption that African Americans preferred to live together in the poorest section of each city. Many private decision makers, especially real estate agents and mortgage bankers, steered African Americans into ghettos by refusing to show them houses or to finance their attempts to purchase homes in white neighborhoods. In turn, northern school boards used these discriminatory housing patterns as a way to keep African Americans segregated into the worst, most crowded schools in each district. Other school boards redrew school boundaries and transported students to new locations in order to keep African Americans from attending schools with white students. African Americans were also victimized by employers' hiring decisions and police officers' discretionary decisions about whom to stop, search, and arrest.

Other groups also faced discrimination. For example, immigrants from China began to come to the United States before the Civil War, but they were invariably forced into difficult, low-paying jobs with little opportunity for advancement. At various times, Congress actually banned further immigration from China, and Chinese who lived in the United States always faced severe prejudice and discrimination.[13] In 1927, the U.S. Supreme Court upheld a Mississippi law that barred Chinese-American children from white schools and required them to attend inferior, segregated schools for African Americans (*Gong Lum* v. *Rice*). People of Japanese heritage were victimized by similar treatment in California and other West Coast states where most of them settled. They were also forced from their homes and placed in isolated internment camps during World War II—unjust treatment experienced by very few German Americans or Italian Americans, even though their ancestral homelands also fought against the United States during the war. In short, unequal treatment and racial discrimination were pervasive aspects of American life throughout the United States for a full century following the Civil War, in spite of the amendments that prohibited slavery and promised "equal protection of the laws."

Litigation Strategies

5.3 Analyze how litigation strategies contributed to the dismantling of official racial segregation.

The **National Association for the Advancement of Colored People (NAACP)**, a civil rights advocacy group founded by African Americans and their white supporters in 1909, sought to use the court pathway to attack the forms of segregation and discrimination endorsed by the Supreme Court's decision in *Plessy v. Ferguson* (1896). The group originated during a period that historians regard as one of the worst for African Americans. In the first three decades of the twentieth century, racial attacks on African Americans, often called "race riots," broke out in dozens of northern and southern cities, sometimes over nothing more than an African American crossing an invisible dividing line at a segregated beach. In these riots, whites typically roamed the streets assaulting and murdering African Americans and destroying homes and businesses. Lynchings of African Americans by white mobs continued in the South as well as the North.[14] Thus, the NAACP began its strategic actions at a moment when African Americans faced their greatest hostility from American society.

Instead of directly attacking the "separate but equal" *Plessy* rule, the NAACP's lawyers initiated a series of cases that helped to demonstrate how, in practice, the rule had plenty of "separate" but virtually no "equal." In the 1930s, the organization represented an African American resident of Maryland who was denied admission to the law school at the University of Maryland despite being an outstanding graduate of prestigious Amherst College. Although Maryland sought to defend against the lawsuit by offering to pay for the man to attend an out-of-state school, the state's supreme court recognized in *Murray* v. *Maryland* (1936) that the alternatives offered by Maryland would not be equal for the purposes of someone who planned to practice law in Maryland. Over the years, the NAACP pursued similar lawsuits and eventually won cases in the U.S. Supreme Court that banned specific discriminatory graduate school admissions practices at universities in Missouri, Texas, and Oklahoma.

Having won a series of court victories in cases demonstrating the lack of equality caused by racial segregation in law and graduate schools, the NAACP took the next step: pursuing a similar claim with respect to the public education provided for school-age children. This step was very risky. It was widely—and correctly—assumed that whites would have an easier time accepting the presence of small numbers of college-educated African Americans in graduate schools than they would the prospect of their children attending grade school and high school with students of a race that many of them feared and despised.

In 1953, the Supreme Court heard the case ***Brown* v. *Board of Education of Topeka***, concerning racial segregation in the public schools of Topeka, Kansas. NAACP attorney Thurgood Marshall, who in 1967 became the first African American appointed to serve as a Supreme Court justice, presented the case and argued that the *Plessy* rule of "separate but equal" was inherently unequal. The Court's new chief justice, former California governor Earl Warren, felt strongly that racial segregation violated the Equal Protection Clause. Using his leadership skills and effective persuasion, he convinced his reluctant colleagues to join a strong opinion condemning racial segregation and overturning the "separate but equal" doctrine of *Plessy* v. *Ferguson*.[15] When the Court announced its highly controversial *Brown* decision in 1954, it became clear that an important branch of government, the federal judiciary, endorsed a new concept of equality that forbade racial segregation by state and local governments, including public school districts.

The *Brown* decision did not immediately end racial segregation. A second Supreme Court decision concerning the *Brown* case (*Brown* v. *Board of Education*, 1955—known as "*Brown* II") left it to individual lower court judges and school districts to design and implement desegregation plans "with all deliberate speed." Ultimately, it took two decades of lawsuits against individual school systems throughout the country, both in the South and in the North, to produce the hundreds of court orders that chipped away at racial segregation. Some observers contend that the Supreme Court has been given too much credit for advancing civil rights, because it was actually the long, slow process of many lawsuits and court decisions after *Brown* II that finally ended official segregation. Still, there is broad agreement that the Supreme Court's first *Brown* ruling was a bold and necessary step in the process of increasing civil rights protections for African Americans by withdrawing the judiciary's earlier endorsement of racial segregation.

National Association for the Advancement of Colored People (NAACP)

Civil rights advocacy group founded by African Americans and their white supporters in 1909 that used the court pathway to fight racial discrimination in the 1930s through the 1950s and later emphasized elections and lobbying pathways.

***Brown* v. *Board of Education of Topeka* (1954)**

A U.S. Supreme Court decision that overturned *Plessy* v. *Ferguson* (1896) and declared that government-mandated racial segregation in schools and other facilities and programs violates the Equal Protection Clause of the Fourteenth Amendment.

President Dwight D. Eisenhower sent U.S. Army troops to protect nine African American students who faced violence and harassment when they enrolled at the previously all-white Little Rock Central High School in Arkansas. The effectiveness of pathways of change also depends on the actions of individuals who carry out new laws and policies. This may include physical courage, as illustrated by the Little Rock Nine, and the political courage of leaders such as Eisenhower.

■ *Can citizens create societal change through nonviolent protests if no government institutions or officials ever support their efforts?*

Additional lawsuits also challenged racial restrictions imposed by government in other aspects of American life. One of the final breakthroughs occurred in 1967, when the Supreme Court struck down state laws that prohibited people from marrying individuals of a different race (*Loving* v. *Virginia*). Today, many people are surprised to realize that little more than five decades ago, it was a crime in several American states for people of different races to marry.

The courts barred laws and governmental actions that enforced segregation, but they did not ensure that schools were integrated or equal in quality. Eventually, the Supreme Court even limited desegregation by requiring all court orders to only affect students within the boundaries of a single school system (*Milliken* v. *Bradley*, 1974). Today, racial separation results from housing patterns reflecting boundaries of cities and suburbs and the inability of poorer people to afford housing in affluent school districts. Judicial decisions prevent racial segregation created by law, but they do not prevent the sort of racial separation that exists in many metropolitan areas.

Clarifying the Coverage of the Equal Protection Clause

5.4 Differentiate between the various tests used by the Supreme Court when deciding discrimination claims under the Equal Protection Clause.

On several occasions, advocates of gender equality pursued cases with the hope that the Supreme Court would interpret the Equal Protection Clause to prohibit discrimination against women. However, the Supreme Court's 1873 decision in *Bradwell* v. *Illinois* had established a long-standing precedent that provided judicial endorsement of laws that discriminated against women because of their gender—much as the 1896 *Plessy* case did with respect to African Americans. In later decades, additional cases tested whether the Court would alter its interpretation of the Equal Protection Clause to advance civil rights for women. In *Goesaert* v. *Cleary* (1948), for example, the Court upheld a Michigan statute that prohibited women from working in establishments that served alcoholic beverages unless they were the wives or daughters of the owner. Like many other statutes that mandated unequal treatment by gender, this law was justified by the state's purported desire to protect women. Such attitudes still dominated the thinking of legislatures and courts in the 1960s, as shown by the Supreme Court's endorsement of a Florida law that automatically excluded women from jury duty unless they asked to serve (*Hoyt* v. *Florida*, 1961). This law led to an overrepresentation of men on juries—and even to many all-male juries—yet the justices endorsed the law by noting that a "woman is still considered as the center of home and family life." The Court concluded that states could enact protective laws that sought to avoid interfering with women's "special responsibilities" as wives and mothers. In light of the continuing disparities in employment opportunities and compensation between men and women, questions remain whether there is a continuing legacy from this history of discrimination (see Figure 5.2).

During the 1970s, the Women's Rights Project of the American Civil Liberties Union (ACLU) tried to copy the approach of the NAACP by using the court pathway to argue for application of the Equal Protection Clause to gender discrimination. The Supreme Court first struck down a gender-based law as discriminatory in *Reed* v. *Reed* (1971), a case concerning Idaho's inheritance statute that mandated preferences for men. Led by law professor Ruth Bader Ginsburg, who in 1993 would be appointed the second woman justice on the U.S. Supreme Court, the ACLU hoped to persuade the justices in other cases that the Equal Protection Clause should protect against gender discrimination in the same manner that the courts used the clause to prohibit racial discrimination by government.

As part of the ACLU's litigation strategy, Ginsburg sought to illuminate the issue of gender discrimination for the then all-male Supreme Court by demonstrating that many discriminatory laws treated men in an unequal fashion. Ginsburg wanted to show that gender discrimination was not merely a "women's rights" issue. In *Craig* v. *Boren* (1976), a key case in which Ginsburg submitted written arguments as an amicus brief, a majority of justices struck down an Oklahoma law that mandated a higher drinking age for men than for women. In making this decision, the Court clarified how lower court judges should apply the Equal Protection Clause to claims of gender discrimination.

The Supreme Court analyzes equal protection cases through three different tests, depending on the nature of the discrimination alleged in the case (see Table 5.2). The three tests are strict scrutiny, intermediate scrutiny, and the rational basis test. In cases alleging discrimination by race or national origin, the Court directs judges to provide the greatest level of protection for individuals. In such cases, the courts apply *strict scrutiny*, a concept mentioned in Chapter 4, with respect to alleged violations of fundamental rights. For these cases, the courts require the government to show a compelling justification for any laws, policies, or practices that result in racial discrimination (or the denial of fundamental rights).

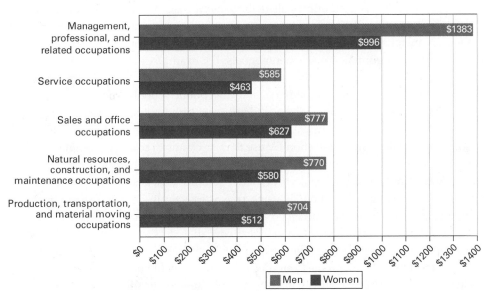

FIGURE 5.2 Median Usual Weekly Earnings of Workers in Selected Occupational Groups by Sex

Median earnings are the wages earned by workers at the midpoint of the salary scale for this occupation group. Disparities could result from discrimination in educational opportunities or job promotions as well as from different pay rates for men and women.

SOURCE: Bureau of Labor Statistics, *Economic News Release: Usual Weekly Earnings Summary*, January 22, 2016, available at http://www.bls.gov.

TABLE 5.2 Three Tests for the Equal Protection Clause

Types of Rights and Discrimination Claims	Types of Tests	Continuing Controversies
Strict Scrutiny Test		
Fundamental freedoms: religion, assembly, press, privacy. Discrimination based on race, alienage (foreign citizenship), ethnicity: called "suspect classifications" (i.e., such bases for discrimination are especially suspicious in the eyes of judges)	Does the government have a compelling reason for the law, policy, or program that clashes with a fundamental freedom or treats people differently by "suspect" demographic characteristics (i.e., race, alienage, ethnicity)? If there is a compelling justification for the government's objective, is this the least restrictive way to attain that objective? **Example:** *Loving* v. *Virginia* (1967) Virginia has no compelling justification for prohibiting marriages between whites and people from other races.	*Grutter* v. *Bollinger* (2003). A slim, five-member majority of the Supreme Court approved race-conscious affirmative action programs in admissions decisions at public universities by concluding that the advancement of diversity is a compelling government interest.
Intermediate Scrutiny Test		
Gender discrimination	Is gender discrimination from a law, policy, or government practice substantially related to the advancement of an important government interest? **Example:** *Mississippi University for Women* v. *Hogan* (1982). The preservation of a public university as a single-sex institution is not an important government interest that can justify excluding men from a graduate nursing program.	*Rostker* v. *Goldberg* (1981). Despite the service of and casualties suffered by female military personnel in the war zone of Iraq, the Supreme Court has said that the government is advancing an important interest in military preparedness by limiting mandatory Selective Service registration to males, because women were ineligible for combat roles prior to 2016.
Rational Basis Test		
Other bases of discrimination, including age, wealth, and other classifications not covered by strict scrutiny or heightened scrutiny	Is the government's law, policy, or practice a rational way to advance a legitimate government interest? **Example:** *San Antonio Independent School District* v. *Rodriguez* (1973). Despite the extra money generated for children in wealthy school districts and the reduced funding for children in poor districts, the use of a property tax system for financing public schools was rational and acceptable.	In *Bush* v. *Gore* (2000), the Supreme Court terminated the Florida vote recount that might have affected the outcome of the contested presidential election by asserting that the recount procedures would violate the equal protection rights of individual voters. The Court decision did not directly answer whether this case signaled the Court's willingness to thereafter look at voters as claimants deserving of higher levels of scrutiny for equal protection claims.

affirmative action

Measures taken in hiring, recruitment, employment, and education to remedy past and present discrimination against members of specific groups. For example, affirmative action efforts can range from advertising employment and educational opportunities in publications with primarily minority or female readers to giving extra credit in university admissions processes to underrepresented groups, including racial minorities, poor people, women, and the disabled.

By contrast, the Supreme Court applies *intermediate scrutiny* to claims of gender discrimination. In such cases, the government need only show a substantial justification, rather than a compelling reason, to explain the different treatment of men and women. This lower level of protection against gender discrimination explains, for example, why the courts accept differential treatment of men and women in military matters, such as the requirement that only men must register with Selective Service (for draft eligibility) when they reach the age of 18.

The third level of scrutiny, called the *rational basis test,* applies for other kinds of equal protection claims. In these cases, the government can justify different treatment by merely providing a rational reason for using a particular policy or practice that advances legitimate governmental goals. For example, the government can have policies and programs that adversely affect the poor. The Supreme Court made this point clear in approving methods of financing public schools, such as property tax systems, which give advantages to residents in wealthy school districts (*San Antonio Independent School District* v. *Rodriguez,* 1973). Similar issues would arise if people sought to use the Equal Protection Clause to raise claims in court concerning discrimination based on age, disability, sexual orientation, and other characteristics.

Although it is very difficult under strict scrutiny analysis for the government to show a compelling justification for using race as a factor in how people are treated, a slim majority of justices has accepted as compelling the limited use of race as one factor in certain admissions decisions in higher education, a practice commonly known as **affirmative action**. In *Bakke* v. *University of California Board of Regents* (1978) and *Grutter* v. *Bollinger* (2003), the Supreme Court declared "that student body diversity is a compelling state interest that can justify the use of race in university admissions."[16] According to the Court, all students benefit from learning in the environment of a diverse student body. Elite universities had long given preferences in admissions to the children of alumni and to recruited athletes, including numerous white athletes with test scores below the average of other admitted students. However, these forms of preferences would fall under the rational basis test in any litigation and therefore survive. By contrast, because the use of race in admissions triggers equal protection principles under the strict scrutiny test, such preferences in admissions, unlike those given to alumni children and athletes, continue to be the focus of controversy, debate, and lawsuits.

The Supreme Court's decisions have made it clear that the Equal Protection Clause is available only to prohibit specific kinds of discrimination by government, especially race and gender discrimination. It does *not* require the government to treat all people in an equal fashion. As a result, the court pathway does not provide all groups with an equally promising means of advancing civil rights issues by relying on the Equal Protection Clause. The disabled, the elderly, and other groups can use the court pathway to enforce legislatively-created *statutes,* such as the Age Discrimination in Employment Act, which protect them from specific kinds of discrimination. It is much more difficult for them to use the Equal Protection Clause, because nearly all government policies and

Obergefell **v.** *Hodges* **(2015)**
The U.S. Supreme Court's momentous decision that declared same-sex marriage is a protected right under the Fourteenth Amendment's Due Process and Equal Protection Clauses.

PATHWAYS OF ACTION

EMERGING CLAIMS FOR EQUAL TREATMENT UNDER THE LAW

In 2015, the U.S. Supreme Court issued a highly-anticipated blockbuster decision in **Obergefell v. Hodges** declaring that the Due Process and Equal Protection Clauses of the Fourteenth Amendment forbid states from depriving same-sex couples of their fundamental right to marry. In the preceding years, many individuals presented claims concerning a right to same-sex marriage in the court pathway when they believed that their treatment by the government violated their civil rights. During the twenty-first century, several court cases struck down laws prohibiting same-sex marriage, but there were also lower court decisions upholding other states' laws. As illustrated by the Timeline later in this chapter, the political movement toward recognition of same-sex marriage as a protected right included action in various pathways, including grassroots action and successful efforts to legalize same-sex marriage through the actions of a few state legislatures. When the Supreme Court settled the issue in 2015, however, its discussion of marriage as a fundamental right as a component of constitutionally-protected liberty interests did not clearly establish that discrimination against gays and lesbians would be subject to protective strict scrutiny analysis under the Equal Protection Clause. The Court said that equal protection principles prohibited states from denying fundamental rights to gays and lesbians, but that conclusion did not establish that sexual orientation discrimination would be given the close legal attention given to discrimination by race and sex. Thus courts regularly receive claims concerning unequal treatment, including discrimination against gays and lesbians, that seek to clarify, expand, and strengthen the protections of the Equal Protection Clause.

For example, Shari Hutchinson, an employee of the Cuyahoga County child support enforcement agency in Ohio, filed a lawsuit alleging that her supervisors passed her over for several promotions because of her sexual orientation. The county's

attorneys argued that the Equal Protection Clause does not protect at all against discrimination based on sexual orientation, but a federal judge ruled that such protection exists under the rational basis test.[17] Federal appellate courts did not have the opportunity in this case to clarify whether discrimination based on sexual orientation deserves a more protective level of analysis under the Equal Protection Clause. After the district court decision, Hutchinson accepted a $100,000 payment from the county government to settle the case and terminate her claim. Undoubtedly, future discrimination cases will seek to clarify this issue.

In yet another example of a lawsuit seeking to expand equal protection principles under state law, seven people were killed and dozens were injured at the Indiana State Fair in August 2011 when an outdoor stage collapsed into the audience under heavy winds as fans gathered for a concert by the musical group Sugarland. Under Indiana law, the state's liability for deaths and personal injuries is capped at a total of $5 million for such an event. That amount of money had to be divided among all victims and no victim's family could receive more than a $700,000 portion. The victims' families believed that it was unfair that they would receive much less compensation for these tragic deaths than would have been available in a lawsuit against a private entity. They filed a lawsuit claiming that they were being treated unequally under the law as compared to victims' families from other events caused by private businesses or government agencies outside of Indiana. The claim was eventually rejected in a split decision by the Indiana Supreme Court in 2015.[18] However, the victims received larger amounts of money from settlements with private companies involved in setting up the concert stage.

The variety of claims illustrated by these lawsuits demonstrates that the court pathway remains an important avenue of action for people who believe that their civil rights have been violated through unfair treatment by government.

practices can be justified under the rational basis test, even if they adversely affect the disabled, the elderly, children, or members of other groups not protected by the strict scrutiny (race and national origin) or intermediate scrutiny (gender) test. In spite of these challenges, as described in Pathways of Action, individuals and groups use the court pathway to file lawsuits that ask judges to expand the coverage of the Equal Protection Clause and protect civil rights in a wider variety of circumstances.

Grassroots Mobilization and Civil Rights

5.5 Identify the events and factors that influenced the development of the grassroots civil rights movements.

Judicial interpretations of the U.S. Constitution had important but limited effects on the advancement of equality and civil rights. Judicial decisions, as we've seen, primarily limit what governments can do to impose certain kinds of discrimination based on race and gender. However, the Constitution did not cover forms of discrimination practiced by private individuals in making decisions about hiring people for jobs, selling or renting houses, and providing goods and services. Thus, judicial decisions based on the Constitution could not, by themselves, transform the daily lives of discrimination victims. Changes in these other aspects of discrimination developed as a result of grassroots mobilization and evolving social values that eventually produced both new legislation and new attitudes about equality.

African Americans and Civil Rights

Protest marches and other forms of grassroots mobilization were used by various groups before the civil rights movement of the 1950s. American labor unions, veterans' groups, and other organizations had long attempted to mobilize support for their goals. Later, African Americans and their supporters became famous for their courage, their visibility, and their success in changing both laws and societal attitudes.

Several events in the mid-1950s drew the American public's attention to civil rights. In 1954, the Supreme Court's monumental *Brown* decision got significant attention—including outrage and vows of resistance by southern whites. One year later, a 14-year-old African American youth from Chicago named Emmett Till, who was visiting relatives in Mississippi and probably unaware of local ways, was brutally murdered and mutilated after he allegedly whistled at a passing white woman. Charles Diggs, an African American congressman from Michigan at the time of the murder, observed that a photograph in *Jet* magazine, an African American publication, showing Emmett Till's mutilation "was probably the greatest media product in the last forty or fifty years, because that picture stimulated a lot of interest and anger on the part of blacks all over the country."[19] Despite being identified by eyewitnesses, the defendants were quickly found "not guilty" by the all-white jury. Reaction was swift. African Americans held protest rallies in major cities throughout the country, and editorials in major newspapers condemned the verdict. As one commentator noted, the Till case had a powerful mobilizing effect on Americans, both African Americans and whites:

> Through the extensive press coverage, all America saw the injustice that had taken place. But black Americans, particularly in the South, saw something else as well.... They saw black people stand in a court of law and testify against white people.[20]

A major problem for the mobilization of African Americans, especially in the South, was the fact that whites controlled the region's entire criminal justice system, including the police and the prosecutors.[21] Any African American who challenged the status quo by complaining about discrimination and inequality ran the risk of being arrested on phony charges, beaten by the police, or even killed by whites who knew that they would not be convicted for their crimes. Thus, the grassroots mobilization of African Americans required great courage in the face of violence by many whites dedicated to preserving the privileges that a segregated society gave them.

One instance of grassroots mobilization was especially important for drawing national attention to racial discrimination and for helping to develop southern organizations for civil rights activism. In December of 1955, African Americans in Montgomery, Alabama, began a boycott of the city bus system in protest against a Jim Crow ordinance that forced them either to sit in the back of the bus or to stand whenever a white person needed a seat. The local chapter of the NAACP had been thinking about initiating a boycott like the ones that had been attempted in other cities. Around that time, one of the organization's active members, a 43-year-old seamstress named Rosa Parks, refused to surrender her seat to a white man who boarded the bus after she did. The bus driver had her arrested, and she was convicted of violating segregation laws.

In response, the NAACP and ministers of local African American churches organized a boycott.[22] In selecting a leader for the boycott organization, the Montgomery Improvement Association (MIA), the civil rights advocates turned to Martin Luther King Jr., a 26-year-old minister who had only recently arrived in town to lead a local Baptist church. King proved to be a thoughtful and charismatic leader whose powerful speeches and advocacy for nonviolent methods of protest carried him to the forefront of the national civil rights movement.

The Montgomery bus boycott lasted 13 months. The MIA purchased station wagons to carry African Americans to work, and blacks who owned cars, as well as sympathetic whites, volunteered to drive the boycotters to work as well. Many people walked rather than ride the bus. White leaders fought back against the boycott by prosecuting African Americans for congregating on corners while waiting for rides. Other whites firebombed the homes of King and other boycott leaders, and snipers fired at African Americans.

Eventually, the prosecutor in Montgomery charged King and dozens of other leaders with violating a state law against boycotts. King's trial and conviction brought national news media attention to the boycott, and he was invited to give speeches throughout the country about racial discrimination and civil rights.[23] King's prominence as a civil rights leader enabled him to advocate the benefits of nonviolent, mass mobilization as a means for policy change.

Because African Americans had long faced violent treatment at the hands of both white citizens and the police without being protected by law and courts, some activists argued that achieving equal rights would require meeting force with force. There was little reason for civil rights activists to feel confident that governing institutions, such as legislatures and courts, would be responsive and address the unfair discrimination and inequality that motivated the grassroots mobilization. Dr. King also had cautious critics who believed that it was morally wrong to break the law, even if the law was unjust. Yet King was a firm believer in the necessity of a commitment to nonviolence in protest actions, including protests that broke laws against "unlawful" assemblies. To those arguing for forceful confrontations, King said that nonviolent action can better attract attention and create pressure for change without giving police a justification to use violence against activists. To those who worried about breaking the law, King argued that morality is separate from law and therefore people must follow a higher moral code that included disobedience to unjust laws.

The boycott ended after the MIA used the court pathway to file a successful lawsuit asserting that, in accordance with the recently developed principles of *Brown*, enforced racial segregation on the buses was illegal. The actions in Montgomery inspired African Americans in other southern cities to launch their own bus boycotts against segregation. The boycott also inspired the formation of new grassroots organizations, such as the Southern Christian Leadership Conference.

As grassroots protests against racial discrimination continued in many cities, other events contributed to move public opinion as well as the federal government's political power away from acceptance of segregation. For example, the national news media gave great attention to the Little Rock Nine, a group of African American students who attempted to enroll at all-white Little Rock Central High School in Arkansas after a successful court case in 1957. President Dwight D. Eisenhower sent hundreds of troops from the U.S. Army's 101st Airborne Division to escort the students into the school and provide protection for them after they were barred from the school and subjected to harassment, threats, and violence.

Acts of violence against African Americans and white civil rights activists continued to capture headlines and produced gripping television footage. In 1962, whites rioted at the University of Mississippi, leading to two deaths and hundreds of injuries, as they attempted to prevent one man, Air Force veteran James Meredith, from enrolling as the university's first African American student. After dozens of federal marshals were injured, President John F. Kennedy sent soldiers to restore order.[24] In 1963, television showed the vicious use by city police of fire hoses, tear gas, and attack dogs to subdue peaceful protesters in Birmingham, Alabama.[25] The bombing of a Birmingham church that year, which took the lives of four young African American girls attending a Bible study class, shocked the nation. "Revulsion at the church bombing," wrote one historian, "spread swiftly around the world."

In 1964, two young white men from the North, Michael Schwerner and Andrew Goodman, and an African American civil rights worker from Mississippi, James Chaney, were abducted and murdered in Philadelphia, Mississippi, as they sought to register African American voters. The vehemence and violence of white resistance to desegregation helped move national public opinion in favor of the African Americans' cause, and it pushed the federal government to take long-overdue action in support of civil rights.

People came from around the country to participate in the 1963 March on Washington to express support for legislation to combat discrimination and enforce civil rights. The quarter of a million participants included tens of thousands of whites.[26] Among the many leaders who spoke to the crowd from the steps of the Lincoln Memorial was the keynote speaker, Martin Luther King Jr., who delivered what later came to be known as his "I Have a Dream" speech, one of the most famous public addresses in American history. News coverage showed a nationwide television audience the huge throng of people, both African American and white, who peacefully rallied for the cause of civil rights. A few months after President Kennedy was assassinated, the new president, Lyndon Johnson, was able to use public sentiment aroused by the martyred president's death as well as growing concerns about racial discrimination to push the **Civil Rights Act of 1964** through Congress. The Act sought to stop discrimination in various aspects of American life, yet significant inequality continues to exist (see Figure 5.3).

In 1965, national attention was drawn to Selma, Alabama, where protests focused on registering African American voters. Many locales across the South used rigged literacy tests in which African Americans were flunked by officials no matter how accurate their responses and thus denied the opportunity to vote. A protest march, planned to proceed from Selma to the state capital, Montgomery, was stopped by dozens of Alabama state police, who attacked the peaceful marchers and beat them with clubs. The brutality of the police attack received significant coverage in newspapers and on television.[27] Public reactions to the violence directed at civil rights protesters helped push Congress into enacting the **Voting Rights Act of 1965**, the long-sought federal legislation that finally facilitated the participation of African Americans through voting and campaigning for elective office.[28]

Civil Rights Legislation

As attitudes about racial equality changed, people pressured legislators to create new civil rights laws. Many of these new laws were directed at discrimination practiced by private individuals and businesses—discrimination that was beyond the reach of the

---

Civil Rights Act of 1964

A federal statute that prohibited racial discrimination in public accommodations (hotels, restaurants, theaters), employment, and programs receiving federal funding.

Voting Rights Act of 1965

A federal statute that effectively attacked literacy tests and other techniques used to prevent African Americans from voting.

FIGURE 5.3 Equal Opportunity?

The civil rights efforts in the grassroots, judicial, and legislative pathways of action have sought since the 1950s to achieve the goal of racial equality. Although these efforts have eliminated formal racial discrimination that was previously enshrined in American law, significant inequality remains in American society, as indicated by statistics concerning education, employment, and income.

■ *What barriers remain to the attainment of equal opportunity? What actions, if any, should the government take to facilitate greater equality in American society?*

SOURCE: Carmen DeNavas-Walt, Benadette D. Proctor, and Jessica C. Smith, *Income, Poverty, and Health Insurance Coverage in the United States: 2012*, Current Population Reports: Consumer Income, U.S. Census Bureau, September 2012; U.S. Census Bureau, "Educational Attainment" online tables, 2013; U.S. Bureau of Labor Statistics, "Labor Force Statistics from the Current Population Survey" online tables, 2013.

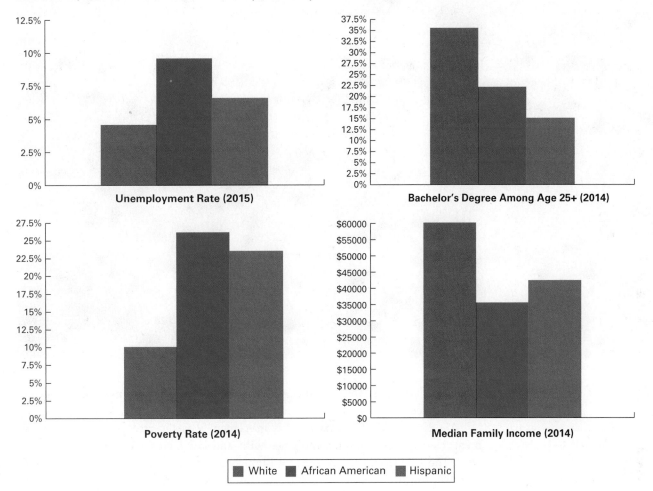

Equal Protection Clause. Title II of the Civil Rights Act of 1964, for example, forbids discrimination by race, color, religion, or national origin in "public accommodations," which include hotels, restaurants, gas stations, movie theaters, and sports stadiums.

The Voting Rights Act of 1965 was not the first congressional legislation that sought to prevent the racial discrimination that limited African Americans' access to the ballot—discrimination that the Fifteenth Amendment had sought to outlaw back in 1870. The Civil Rights Acts of 1957, 1960, and 1964 all contained provisions aimed at barriers to voting. However, because they relied on litigation for enforcement, they all proved ineffective, as states frequently found new ways to discriminate. The Voting Rights Act of 1965 (and its subsequent extensions in 1970 and later years) barred the literacy tests that had been used to keep African Americans away from the polls. Figure 5.4 shows the impact of the Voting Rights Act in increasing the registration of African American voters. The act was also more powerful and effective because of its "preclearance" provision, which required officials in designated districts, primarily in southern states, to obtain the permission of the attorney general before making any changes in elections and voting procedures. However, a five-member majority on the Supreme Court invalidated parts of the Voting Rights Act in 2013 (*Shelby County* v. *Holder*). The controversial decision created

The 1963 March on Washington showed a national television audience that tens of thousands of African Americans and whites were working together to advance the cause of civil rights. The "I Have a Dream" speech given by Dr. Martin Luther King Jr. on the steps of the Lincoln Memorial is considered by many observers to be one of the most inspirational moments in American political history.

▪ *How might such memorable events contribute to cultural change?*

uncertainty about the Voting Rights Act's continued effects at the same moment several states enacted new laws that could limit voting in poor and minority communities.

Another result of the civil rights movement was the creation of new government agencies to monitor compliance with and enforcement of antidiscrimination laws. The U.S. Commission on Civil Rights, created in 1957, was given the task of investigating and reporting to Congress about discrimination and the deprivation of civil rights. The U.S. Equal Employment Opportunity Commission, created in 1964, was charged with investigating complaints about illegal employment discrimination.

FIGURE 5.4 Percentage of Eligible Citizens Registered to Vote

Voter registration rates for African Americans in southern states increased dramatically after the Voting Rights Act of 1965 helped to eliminate discriminatory barriers.

SOURCE: Data from Bernard Grofman, Lisa Handley, and Richard G. Niemi, *Minority Representation and the Quest for Voting Equality*, (New York, NY: Cambridge University Press, 1992), pp. 23–24; U.S. Census Bureau, "Voting and Registration in the Election of November 2014," (2015).

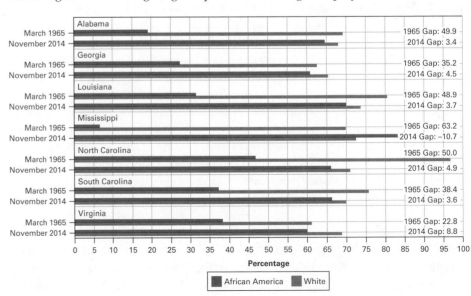

Subsequently, states and cities created their own agencies to investigate and enforce their own civil rights laws. These agencies are typically called "civil rights commissions" (for example, the Iowa Civil Rights Commission), "human rights commissions" (for example, the San Francisco Human Rights Commission), or "equal opportunity commissions" (for example, the Nebraska Equal Opportunity Commission).

Other Historic Struggles for Civil Rights

5.6 Compare and contrast the civil rights struggles of women, Latinos, Native Americans, and African Americans.

While the African American struggle for civil rights frames much of our discussion, many other groups have had a long path to equality as well. One should bear in mind that while slavery cast a dark cloud over the formation of the American system and racial discrimination has been a defining characteristic of our politics, many other groups have struggled to achieve basic rights of citizenship and dignity in an open and free society. Unfortunately, the list of these groups is rather long.

Women and Civil Rights

Beginning with public meetings and speeches in the first half of the nineteenth century, grassroots mobilization played a crucial role in obtaining the right to vote for women. After the Civil War, the Fifteenth Amendment sought to give African American men the right to vote. Because advocates for women's civil rights were disappointed that the amendment did not help women get the vote, they took action to mobilize supporters in favor of **universal suffrage**—the right to vote for all adult citizens. One of the most prominent organizations, the National Woman Suffrage Association, was founded in 1869 and led by Susan B. Anthony and Elizabeth Cady Stanton.[29]

universal suffrage
The right to vote for all adult citizens.

The first American jurisdiction to grant women the permanent right to vote was the Territory of Wyoming in 1869, followed by the Territory of Utah in 1870. When Wyoming became a state in 1890, its admission effectively permitted its female residents to be the first women in the country to vote in presidential and congressional elections. Colorado and Idaho followed later in the decade. Activists continued to press for suffrage throughout the rest of the country. Over the years, in addition to lobbying legislators and educating the public through publications and speeches, advocates of suffrage organized protest marches and other public demonstrations. Anthony and other activists intentionally faced arrest and prosecution by attempting to vote on Election Day. Women went to jail for picketing at the White House, and while incarcerated, they went on hunger strikes to draw public attention to their harsh treatment and their cause.[30]

Another important strategy involved trying to place the question of women's suffrage on statewide ballots as often as possible. As described by one historian, "From 1870 to 1910, there were 480 campaigns in thirty-three states, just to get the issue submitted to the voters, of which only seventeen resulted in actual referendum votes."[31] In the early twentieth century, the suffrage movement gained momentum after winning successful ballot-issue campaigns in Washington (1910), California (1911), Arizona (1912), Kansas (1912), and Oregon (1912). In 1917, several state legislatures gave women the right to vote for specific elections, such as the presidential election or primary elections.[32] Finally, in 1918, the women's suffrage amendment received sufficient support to pass through Congress and be sent to the states for approval. It was ratified as the Nineteenth Amendment and added to the Constitution in 1920.

The right to vote came through organized political action over the course of eight decades. Figure 5.5 illustrates the universal struggle for women's suffrage in the United States and other countries. The mobilization of supporters alone did not lead to women's suffrage. American society gradually changed as women gained

FIGURE 5.5 Women and the Right to Vote

At the time that several territories and states in the American West granted women the right to vote in the late nineteenth century, women were not yet permitted to vote in other countries. The women's suffrage effort in the United States coincided with efforts elsewhere in the world to authorize women to vote, although the American national right to vote was not approved until after women began to vote in several other countries. Even when white women gained the right to vote in the United States in 1920, barriers still remained for many years for African Americans and Native Americans. Similar racial barriers took years to dismantle in other countries, such as Australia, Canada, and South Africa. Women's suffrage efforts have continued for decades as women in Saudi Arabia finally gained permission to vote in municipal elections in 2011 and voted for the first time in that country in 2015.

SOURCE: "Timeline of Women's Suffrage Granted, by Country," Infoplease.com, Pearson Education, 2012.

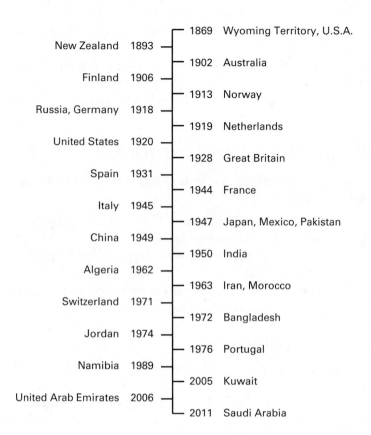

	1869 Wyoming Territory, U.S.A.
New Zealand 1893	
	1902 Australia
Finland 1906	
	1913 Norway
Russia, Germany 1918	
	1919 Netherlands
United States 1920	
	1928 Great Britain
Spain 1931	
	1944 France
Italy 1945	
	1947 Japan, Mexico, Pakistan
China 1949	
	1950 India
Algeria 1962	
	1963 Iran, Morocco
Switzerland 1971	
	1972 Bangladesh
Jordan 1974	
	1976 Portugal
Namibia 1989	
	2005 Kuwait
United Arab Emirates 2006	
	2011 Saudi Arabia

opportunities to enter the workforce, obtain education, and enter professions that had previously excluded them. All of this contributed to the societal changes necessary for women to be viewed as legitimate participants in political processes.

Ratification of the Nineteenth Amendment did not ensure that women would enjoy equal rights. Large segments of the public continued to see women as properly destined for subservient roles as wives and housekeepers or in a few "helping professions," such as nursing, teaching, and secretarial services. Women frequently could not gain consideration for other jobs. After graduating near the top of her class at Stanford Law School in the 1950s, even Sandra Day O'Connor—who eventually became the first woman appointed to the U.S. Supreme Court—received offers to work only as a legal secretary, not as a lawyer. It took decades for women to be elected to public office in appreciable numbers. Even in the twenty-first century, despite the increasing frequency with which women win elections for Congress, governorships, and state judgeships, they remain underrepresented.

Legislatures took little action to initiate laws that would protect women from discrimination until a new grassroots women's movement emerged in the 1960s and 1970s. By then, larger numbers of women were attending college, entering the workforce, participating in campaigns and elections, and challenging traditional expectations about women's subordinate status in society.

Latinos and Civil Rights

Latinos share a Spanish-speaking heritage, but ethnically and racially, they are highly diverse. Also referred to as Hispanics, Latinos' ancestors came from Mexico, Puerto Rico, Cuba, or other places in Latin America. They have long faced discrimination in the United States. Some Americans perceive Latinos to be recent arrivals who may have entered the country without proper permission from immigration authorities. In reality, many Latinos are descended from people who lived in the territory that became the United States even before whites became the numerically dominant group.

Women in New York City march for suffrage in 1913. Advocates of voting rights for women went to great lengths over the course of many decades to educate the public about the need for universal suffrage. The ratification of the Nineteenth Amendment, which established women's right to vote, represented a major change in the American political system.

■ *Are there still assumptions about politics, government, and women that hinder women candidates in their efforts to gain election to top leadership positions in government?*

For centuries, Latino people lived in parts of what are today California, Texas, New Mexico, and Arizona—all states whose territory originally belonged to Mexico, which the United States annexed in the 1840s after the Mexican War. Latinos from Puerto Rico and Cuba began moving to New York and Florida in the late 1800s. The United States gained control of both islands after the Spanish-American War (1898). Cuba later became an independent country, but Puerto Rico remains under American sovereignty as an "associated commonwealth." Its people can travel freely to the mainland to live and work.

When the Mexican Revolution broke out in the early twentieth century, thousands of Mexicans came north in search of safety and employment. Many American businesses actively recruited workers from Mexico and elsewhere in Latin America.[33] The recruitment and hiring of these workers, including undocumented workers who entered the United States in violation of immigration laws, continued throughout the twentieth century.

Prior to the enactment of federal civil rights laws in the 1960s, Latinos in the United States often received less pay than white workers, while being assigned the most difficult and burdensome tasks. Migrant farm workers, who were typically of Mexican or Central American origin, traveled throughout the country harvesting crops, receiving very low pay, and facing difficult living conditions. Latinos suffered discrimination and segregation in housing, employment, public accommodations, and education—and often harsh treatment from police officers and other government officials.[34]

Latinos formed labor unions and civil rights organizations in the early twentieth century at the same time that others in the United States were forming such groups. Other civil rights organizations emerged when Latinos mobilized in conjunction with the highly publicized civil rights movement of African Americans.

The best-known grassroots movement was led by César Chávez, who founded the National Farm Workers Association, later renamed the United Farm Workers (UFW). As you will see in Chapter 12, in the discussion of effective, charismatic interest group leaders, Chávez led protest marches and organized a national boycott of grapes harvested by nonunion workers during the 1960s. He also went on hunger strikes to protest poor pay and working conditions for farm workers as well as other issues, such as their exposure to dangerous pesticides.[35] He worked on voter registration drives to encourage more Latinos to vote (see Figure 5.6). His efforts brought public attention to the issues of poor working conditions for agricultural workers as well as

FIGURE 5.6 Hispanic Voting Power, 2014

Because of trends in population growth, Hispanics will become an increasingly important segment of the American electorate. Political strategists from both the Republican and Democratic parties are already hard at work on plans for persuading Hispanic voters to favor their political party.

SOURCE: U.S. Census Bureau.

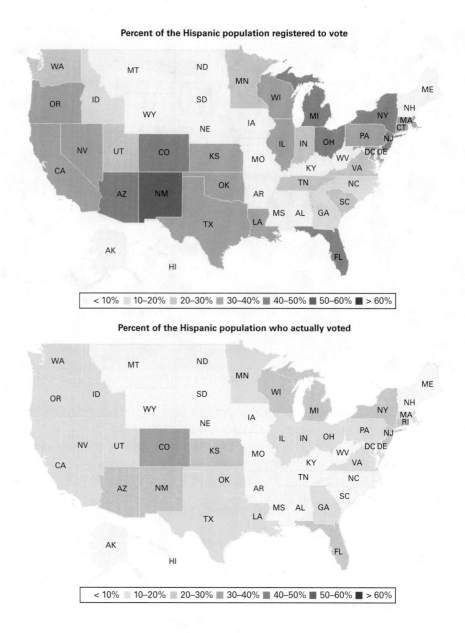

Percent of the Hispanic population registered to vote

< 10%   10–20%   20–30%   30–40%   40–50%   50–60%   > 60%

Percent of the Hispanic population who actually voted

< 10%   10–20%   20–30%   30–40%   40–50%   50–60%   > 60%

discrimination against Latinos. As a result, his struggle contributed to the enactment of new statutes to provide protection for farm workers.

The issue of civil rights and equal treatment for Latinos continues in the twenty-first century, especially because Latinos are now the largest minority group in the United States, surpassing the number of African Americans in 2003 and continuing to grow at a faster rate than most other demographic groups. Latino activists continue to be concerned about such issues as unequal treatment in employment, housing, and the criminal justice system. For example, in 2015 the federal government's Consumer Financial Protection Bureau and the U.S. Department of Justice took action against a mortgage company for charging higher fees to Latino and African American borrowers.[36] Individual state legislatures, most notably in Arizona and Alabama, enacted laws ostensibly aimed at combatting illegal immigration but that generate criticisms about the impact on Latino citizens who may be treated with suspicion. The Arizona law required people to carry immigration papers and authorized police officers to detain people in order to verify their citizenship or immigration status. These provisions initially triggered fears that police officers would stop and detain Latinos based on their perceived ethnicity and subject Latino citizens to police surveillance, stops, and searches that were not directed at other

Americans. The U.S. Supreme Court later struck down portions of the law in its decision in *Arizona* v. *United States* (2012). The Court left intact the provision for state and local police to check the immigration status of people lawfully stopped and arrested. However, the Court prohibited the state from detaining people solely on the grounds of being undocumented immigrants. The federal government possesses the exclusive authority over such detention decisions.

The Alabama law was similar but with even more requirements and sanctions, such as requiring schools to collect immigration status data on students, imposing stricter requirements on everyone in the state seeking drivers' licenses and other documents, and affecting the validity of contracts by those who do not prove their immigration status. Backlash against both laws took the form of lawsuits and organized protests by civil rights groups.[37] Some observers believe that the nation's treatment of undocumented workers who entered the country in violation of immigration laws—many of whom have lived, worked, and raised families in the United States for years—is an important contemporary civil rights issue. Indeed, President Obama helped to place the issue into the policy debates surrounding the 2012 presidential election by issuing an executive order to suspend deportations of law-abiding undocumented immigrants who were brought into the United States illegally by their parents. He also endorsed the DREAM ACT, a legislative proposal that provides a path to citizenship for law-abiding undocumented immigrants. Subsequently, these immigration issues became central campaign positions for the 2016 Republican presidential candidates who opposed President Obama's viewpoints and actions. In addition, several states used the courts pathway to successfully challenge President Obama's actions when a divided Supreme Court ruled against the suspension of deportations (*United States* v. *Texas*, 2016). Thus the status and treatment of undocumented immigrants will remain a controversial issue with implications for the nation's policies on the treatment of people living within its borders.

Native Americans and Civil Rights

Issues of equal treatment under the law have long been a matter of concern for Native Americans as well. They have suffered from overt discrimination, nonexistent economic opportunities, government-facilitated loss of their property, and widespread poverty. They faced many challenges through the twentieth century to secure voting rights, the right to practice their religions, and, especially, historic land rights. Because

Protesters raised public awareness about immigration policies that led to the deportation of foreign-born parents of American-born children. The treatment of undocumented workers and their children presented a key point of disagreement for Republican and Democratic presidential candidates in 2016.

■ *Are there risks that Latinos who are U.S. citizens will face hostility and discrimination because some people may assume that they are undocumented workers?*

of their relatively small numbers and isolated locations, Native Americans have not enjoyed success through the grassroots mobilization strategies. In recent years, however, they have advanced their cause through the court pathway, especially the case of *Cobell* v. *Kempthorne,* originally filed in 1996 and finally decided in favor of the Native Americans in January 2008. In this case, the federal judge found that over the years, the U.S. Department of Interior's Bureau of Indian Affairs had mismanaged and lost billions of dollars owed to Native Americans for oil and gas revenues and other leases on their lands administered by the federal government. In December 2009, the federal government agreed to settle the claims for $3.4 billion. The slow-moving court process did not instantly solve the problem, but it did set into motion the events that enabled Native Americans to receive compensation. It also put political pressure on members of Congress to provide greater oversight for the Bureau of Indian Affairs.

Contemporary Civil Rights Issues

5.7 Evaluate the continuing debates, lawsuits, and protests over civil rights in the twenty-first century.

Much of the twentieth-century American civil rights movement centered on efforts to prohibit overt discrimination mandated by government laws and practiced by private businesses. As we have now seen, women, African Americans, and Latinos used both grassroots mobilization and court processes to gain the right to vote and to produce laws against discrimination in employment, education, and other contexts. After laws were changed in the 1960s to forbid rather than mandate open discrimination, however, unequal treatment and inequality still remained. Some forms of discrimination became more subtle, such as racial profiling, when police officers use their discretion to stop African American and Latino drivers by alleging minor traffic violations when they really want to search a vehicle for drugs. Studies of police actions on some highways have shown that members of minority groups are significantly overrepresented among those who are stopped and searched by the police, despite evidence that their rate of violating traffic laws does not exceed that of more numerous white drivers.[38]

The discretionary decisions of police officers, especially with respect to the use of lethal force against unarmed young men, triggered the protests, civil unrest, and civil rights activism of the Black Lives Matter movement described in the opening of the chapter. This activism to advance equality generated specific beneficial impacts. In particular, these impacts included President Obama's appointment of a task force on policing that made recommendations for policy changes in 2015. Moreover, the Police Executive Research Forum produced a report in 2016 on thirty principles for police use of force that emphasize communication, de-escalation of conflict, retreating for the purpose of reassessing a situation, and other strategies to reduce the use of lethal force.[39] The publicity surrounding the Black Lives Matter protests heightened the sensitivity of police officials and politicians to both the deterioration of police-community relations and the need for new policies and training for officers.

Laws that seek to prevent discrimination typically require strong, clear proof of improper treatment to justify judges' orders for remedies. However, many kinds of discrimination, especially those based on discretionary decisions, are very difficult to prove. Discretionary decisions are those guided by a decision maker's values and judgments and they are not dictated by a precise set of rules. Why, for example, are women and members of minority groups seldom chosen by boards of directors to lead large corporations? Why are women's salaries, on average, lower than men's for the same occupations? Why are murderers who kill white people often given more severe sentences than those who kill African Americans?[40] These and other outcomes are the products of discretionary choices by decision makers. How can one know—let alone prove—whether any intent to discriminate underlies the decisions that produce these results? Unequal outcomes continue to exist that are not remedied by laws, which typically prohibit only open forms of discrimination.

Inequality can be perpetuated by social conditions that are a legacy of past discrimination, such as disadvantages endured by poor minority group members whose parents, because of past discrimination, could not afford to accumulate sufficient assets to move within the boundaries of the top public school systems or save enough money to send their children to college. Discrimination also continues to result from less visible decisions by employers, police officers, and others whose discretionary authority affects their fellow citizens.

Further efforts to address continuing issues of inequality and discrimination may depend on the evolution of societal values and politics through the cultural change pathway rather than through judicial decisions in the court pathway. In the future, the elections pathway may also be a source of policy change regarding civil rights, as immigration and differential birthrates among ethnic groups make whites less numerically dominant among the voting-age population.

Complexity of Issues

The role of discretionary decisions in the continuation of discrimination and unequal outcomes for members of different demographic groups has made contemporary civil rights issues more complex. Although society's values and laws have changed to reflect general agreement that people should not be excluded from government programs and jobs because of their race or gender, deep disagreements remain about what, if any, additional policies are necessary to provide full civil rights and full equality for all Americans. Some people believe that equality of opportunity has been created through the enactment of laws that forbid discrimination by race and gender. Others believe that more policy actions are necessary to achieve equality for members of groups that have been held back by discrimination.

〉 POLL Do you think new civil rights legislation is necessary to protect African Americans?

For example, some people regard the preferential university admissions policies of affirmative action as an essential tool to counteract the country's history of discrimination, open opportunities for members of groups that are underrepresented in business and professions, and enable all students to study and interact within an environment that reflects an increasingly diverse country. By contrast, critics argue that such preferences are really a form of reverse discrimination rather than an effective means to remedy social problems. This debate demonstrates that there are disagreements about whether preferences based on race, gender, or other categories are a necessary element of equal opportunity in a society in which discretionary decisions and other factors continue to provide evidence of unequal treatment and outcomes. The Supreme Court revisited the issue in 2016 after an appeals court upheld the University of Texas's admissions program in 2014 (*Fisher* v. *University of Texas*). In the case, a white applicant denied admission claimed less qualified minority students were admitted. Observers predicted that the remaining eight justices would be equally divided on the issue after the death of Justice Antonin Scalia in 2016. However, Justice Anthony Kennedy reversed his previous opposition to affirmative action and wrote the 4-to-3 majority opinion providing the Supreme Court's renewed endorsement of universities' use of race in admissions decisions. Justice Elena Kagan did not participate in the case.

Legal disputes persist over the creation of legislative districts at both the federal and the state level. As you will see in Chapter 6, legislative districts are drawn in varying geographic sizes and shapes. They are required to have equivalent populations, but they do not have to be drawn as rectangular entities with straight boundary lines. Usually, districts are designed to advance the prospects of either Republican or Democratic candidates, depending on which party controls the state's legislature. Issues

Disabled protesters crawled up the steps of the U.S. Supreme Court in 2004 as the Court prepared to hear a case about the accessibility of courthouses for people who must use wheelchairs.

■ *Which pathways of action seem most likely to advance disabled people's goals for new laws and policies to advance their interests?*

of race and ethnicity can arise when districts are redrawn, which occurs after every 10-year census and sometimes more frequently. Should lines be drawn to facilitate the election of African American and Latino legislators by concentrating voters from those groups in specific districts? The creation of these so-called *majority-minority districts* has generated much controversy. White voters in some states have challenged the creation of such districts, while some civil rights advocates see the existence of such districts as important for increasing the likelihood of minority representation in legislatures. Other critics contend that creating a few majority-minority districts actually helps white conservatives, who thereby gain a larger number of "safe" seats in areas where fewer liberal-leaning minority voters live.

Emerging Groups

The visibility and success of litigation strategies by African Americans and women and of grassroots mobilization strategies of those groups and Latinos provided examples for plans and action by other individuals who saw themselves as victims of discrimination. For example, beginning in the 1970s, people with disabilities lobbied legislators and held public demonstrations protesting discrimination in employment and public accommodations. People who use wheelchairs, for example, often found themselves rejected for jobs merely because an employer assumed that they were incapable of working. Similarly, they often could not be served as customers at restaurants, entertainment facilities, and other public accommodations that lacked wheelchair access. In the Rehabilitation Act of 1973, Congress prohibited discrimination against people with disabilities who work in government or who seek services from federally funded programs. The Americans with Disabilities Act, passed in 1990, provided protection against discrimination in employment and public accommodations.

Advocates of civil rights protections for gays and lesbians have used legislative lobbying, litigation, and grassroots mobilization to seek legal protections comparable to those provided for African Americans and women. Prior to the Supreme Court's decision legalizing same-sex marriage in *Obergefell* v. *Hodges* (2015), lobbying pushed legislatures in several states to enact laws permitting such marriages. Although no federal law prevents employment discrimination based on a worker's sexual orientation, some states and cities have enacted statutes and ordinances to prohibit such discrimination in housing and public accommodations. In 2009, however, Congress enacted a new law making it a federal offense to commit a violent hate crime against someone because of the victim's sexual orientation or gender identity. Another important development occurred in 2010, when President Obama's Department of Defense asked Congress to change the rules for military service so that gays and lesbians would no longer be required to keep their sexual orientation secret in order to have military careers.

Americans are divided over whether new civil rights laws should address discrimination against gays and lesbians. The U.S. Supreme Court's first two cases concerning this issue did not command state and local governments to take particular actions to advance equality. In *Romer* v. *Evans* (1996), the Court declared that cities such as Aspen, Boulder, and Denver could pass antidiscrimination laws to protect gays and lesbians if they chose to do so. The Court relied on the Equal Protection Clause in striking down a statewide referendum approved by Colorado voters that had banned the passage of such local antidiscrimination laws. However, in *Boy Scouts of America* v. *Dale* (2000), the Court found that New Jersey's law against sexual orientation discrimination in public accommodations could not be used to require the Boy Scouts to accept a gay man as a troop leader. According to the Court, such an application of the state law would violate the Boy Scouts' First Amendment right of expressive association, which means that a private group cannot be forced to accept a member it does not want. By 2015, cultural changes in American society and public pressure on the group led the Boy Scouts to reverse the organization's position and announce that gays and lesbians would be welcomed as leaders.[41]

> POLL What racial, religious, and/or sexual-orientation groups of people do you think face the most discrimination in America?

Early successes for equality advocates came on a state-by-state basis. Wider success for these goals is occurring as Americans show increasing public support for the need to protect the civil rights of gays and lesbians. In 2015, by a narrow 5-to-4 vote, the U.S. Supreme Court made a momentous decision that declared same-sex marriage is a protected right under the Fourteenth Amendment's Due Process and Equal Protection Clauses (*Obergefell* v. *Hodges*). For a detailed examination of political and legal battles over same-sex marriage, see The Struggle over Same-Sex Marriage Policy Timeline.

Changes in laws and governmental rules opened the way for gays and lesbians to serve openly in the military and also legalized same-sex marriage. Here, a same-sex couple prepares to say their wedding vows. These changes reflect actions over the course of several decades through court decisions, state statutes, and cultural change affecting viewpoints in American society.

■ *Does the attainment of legal equality for military service and marriage indicate that gays and lesbians are certain to gain legal protection against other forms of unequal treatment?*

Conclusion

Political equality is an important component of democracy. If voting rights are restricted and certain groups are excluded from full participation in society, the governing system will represent only the interests of those who have status and wield power. The efforts to obtain civil rights for excluded groups in the United States constitute an important chapter in this country's history. Without these efforts, the American governing system would fall well short of its professed aspiration to be a democracy that sets an example for other countries around the world. The court and grassroots mobilization pathways have been especially important for the advancement of civil rights. In the twentieth century, the NAACP's litigation strategy helped make the Fourteenth Amendment's Equal Protection Clause a viable tool for challenging governmental laws and policies that foster discrimination. Advocates of civil rights for members of other victimized groups could copy the NAACP's strategies in using the court pathway to advance their own causes. Beginning in the 1960s, when Congress and state legislatures began enacting additional civil rights laws, opportunities arose to use the court pathway as a means to gain judicial enforcement of statutes intended to prevent discrimination.

TIMELINE

The Struggle Over Same-Sex Marriage

Same-sex marriage is one of the most controversial issues of the twenty-first century. Law and policy have developed through actions and reactions in multiple pathways of change. When same-sex couples first claimed an equal legal right to marry in the 1970s, their claims were quickly rejected. In the 1990s, however, some legislative proposals and court decisions supported the concept, reflecting the first stirrings of cultural change within specific states. Legislatures and voters reacted against these initial events by enacting new legal measures to ban same-sex marriage. In a counter-reaction, supporters of same-sex marriage challenged these legal measures in the courts. By 2015, action in the courts pathways led to the legalization of same-sex marriage nationwide.

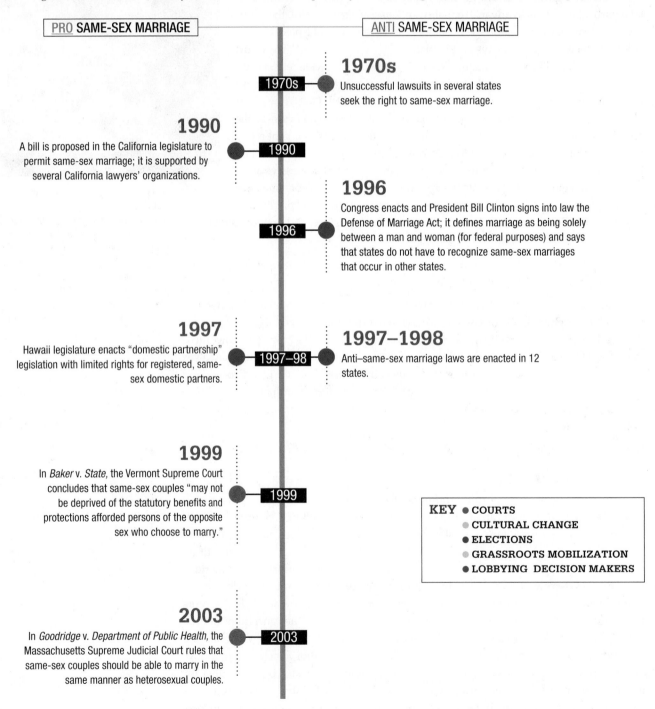

| PRO SAME-SEX MARRIAGE | | ANTI SAME-SEX MARRIAGE |

1970s

1970s — Unsuccessful lawsuits in several states seek the right to same-sex marriage.

1990

A bill is proposed in the California legislature to permit same-sex marriage; it is supported by several California lawyers' organizations. — *1990*

1996

1996 — Congress enacts and President Bill Clinton signs into law the Defense of Marriage Act; it defines marriage as being solely between a man and woman (for federal purposes) and says that states do not have to recognize same-sex marriages that occur in other states.

1997

Hawaii legislature enacts "domestic partnership" legislation with limited rights for registered, same-sex domestic partners. — *1997–98*

1997–1998

Anti–same-sex marriage laws are enacted in 12 states.

1999

In *Baker* v. *State*, the Vermont Supreme Court concludes that same-sex couples "may not be deprived of the statutory benefits and protections afforded persons of the opposite sex who choose to marry." — *1999*

KEY
- COURTS
- CULTURAL CHANGE
- ELECTIONS
- GRASSROOTS MOBILIZATION
- LOBBYING DECISION MAKERS

2003

In *Goodridge* v. *Department of Public Health*, the Massachusetts Supreme Judicial Court rules that same-sex couples should be able to marry in the same manner as heterosexual couples. — *2003*

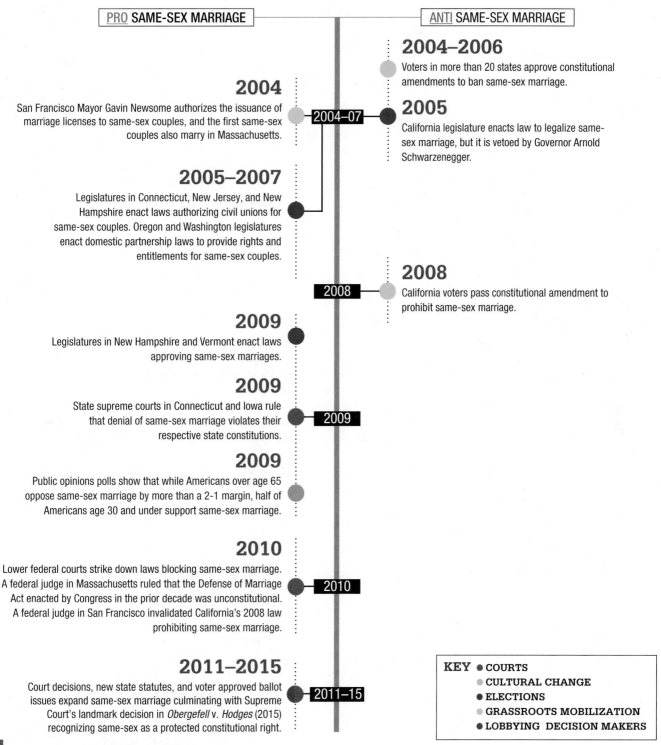

PRO SAME-SEX MARRIAGE

ANTI SAME-SEX MARRIAGE

2004–2006
Voters in more than 20 states approve constitutional amendments to ban same-sex marriage.

2004
San Francisco Mayor Gavin Newsome authorizes the issuance of marriage licenses to same-sex couples, and the first same-sex couples also marry in Massachusetts.

`2004–07`

2005
California legislature enacts law to legalize same-sex marriage, but it is vetoed by Governor Arnold Schwarzenegger.

2005–2007
Legislatures in Connecticut, New Jersey, and New Hampshire enact laws authorizing civil unions for same-sex couples. Oregon and Washington legislatures enact domestic partnership laws to provide rights and entitlements for same-sex couples.

2008
California voters pass constitutional amendment to prohibit same-sex marriage.

`2008`

2009
Legislatures in New Hampshire and Vermont enact laws approving same-sex marriages.

2009
State supreme courts in Connecticut and Iowa rule that denial of same-sex marriage violates their respective state constitutions.

`2009`

2009
Public opinions polls show that while Americans over age 65 oppose same-sex marriage by more than a 2-1 margin, half of Americans age 30 and under support same-sex marriage.

2010
Lower federal courts strike down laws blocking same-sex marriage. A federal judge in Massachusetts ruled that the Defense of Marriage Act enacted by Congress in the prior decade was unconstitutional. A federal judge in San Francisco invalidated California's 2008 law prohibiting same-sex marriage.

`2010`

2011–2015
Court decisions, new state statutes, and voter approved ballot issues expand same-sex marriage culminating with Supreme Court's landmark decision in *Obergefell* v. *Hodges* (2015) recognizing same-sex as a protected constitutional right.

`2011–15`

KEY
- COURTS
- CULTURAL CHANGE
- ELECTIONS
- GRASSROOTS MOBILIZATION
- LOBBYING DECISION MAKERS

CRITICAL THINKING QUESTIONS

1. We often think of policy changes as driven by new laws and court decisions. However, would those laws and court decisions be produced if the dominant social values in society did not change in a way that supports these developments? Does the legalization of same-sex marriage reflect activists' effects on legislatures and courts or the product of social change based on positive images and acceptance of gays and lesbians on television and elsewhere in society?

2. Do you foresee any other changes affecting law and policy either advancing or reducing equality in the future based on either activists' efforts or cultural change? What about the status of undocumented immigrants? The treatment of Muslims in immigration and national security policy based on Americans' terrorism fears? The treatment of children? How about the treatment of animals from the "animal rights" movement that advocates legal rights for animals? Why or why not?

Grassroots mobilization is a long-standing method of seeking changes in public policy, going all the way back to the origins of the United States. Over the years, various groups in our society, including labor union organizers and veterans seeking government benefits, have used this pathway. The African American civil rights movement of the 1950s and 1960s had an exceptionally powerful impact on the attitudes of ordinary citizens and eventually convinced the government to create and enforce antidiscrimination laws. Seeing the effectiveness of African Americans' protests, other groups emulated these tactics. Years earlier, women's rights advocates used meetings and protests to educate the public about their struggle to gain the right to vote. Civil rights advocates did not invent grassroots action, but they have employed it in an especially successful manner. As illustrated by the chapter opening, many observers believe the Black Lives Matter movement is effectively using grassroots mobilization and other pathways to call attention to continuing issues of racial discrimination in the justice system.

CONFRONTING POLITICS AND POLICY

In January 2016, several dozen students at the University of California at Santa Barbara (UCSB) held signs and chanted slogans outside an on-campus job fair to protest the presence of recruiters from the U.S. Customs and Border Security agency. The protesters objected to federal government policies and practices of deporting undocumented immigrants and, prior to deportation hearings, holding detainees in overcrowded and otherwise inadequate conditions in jail-type facilities. The students were objecting to policies and practices of the Obama administration but their statements also effectively expressed objections to the campaign statements of Republican presidential candidates who promised their supporters that their administrations would be even tougher in finding and deporting people who entered the United States without proper approval from immigration officials.

Can such a small, local protest have any impact on debates about national immigration policies? A student commentator who wrote an opinion column in the UCSB student newspaper said: "[N]ot all protests have to produce concrete results in order to be successful.... It doesn't have to be about accomplishing something, or creating a dialogue. Sometimes, it can simply be about the pure emotion of the matter."[42]

ACTION STEPS

1. The UCSB protest concerned the treatment of certain people living in the United States amid great political debate about whether these people should be permitted to stay because of their immigration status. Is this a contemporary civil rights issue? Why or why not? Give two reasons for your answer.

2. Do you agree with the student commentator's statement that a protest about a policy matter can be "successful" just by embodying the expression of the protesters' emotions? Why or why not? Are there other actions that these student protesters could take if they actually wanted to push for policy impact? List three suggested actions for these student activists.

› REVIEW THE CHAPTER

The Ideal of Equality

5.1 Describe the idea of equality that underlies the governing system of the United States. (p. 140)

"Civil rights" concern issues of equality and involve the development of laws and policies that prevent discrimination, especially forms of discrimination that exclude members of selected groups from full participation in the economic and governing systems. The founders of the United States advocated an ideal of equality for white men that was to become a source of inspiration for women, African Americans, Latinos, and others who sought full inclusion in society. Equality in the United States and laws that advance the American vision of equality focus on equality of opportunity, not on equality of condition.

Equal Protection of the Law

5.2 Trace the historical development of civil rights in the United States. (p. 143)

In the United States, a long history of discrimination inspired the development of civil rights action. After the Civil War, three amendments (the Thirteenth, Fourteenth, and Fifteenth Amendments) were added to the Constitution to prohibit slavery and provide legal rights for African Americans.

The racial segregation that existed in the states was produced by formal laws as well as by less formal means. The Supreme Court endorsed formal discrimination in 1896 and thereby helped to facilitate the spread of separate public schools and other public facilities, especially in southern states.

The history of slavery and violent racial oppression in the United States as well as the pervasive discrimination that existed for a century after the abolition of slavery produced lingering inequalities that continue to affect American society today.

Litigation Strategies

5.3 Analyze how litigation strategies contributed to the dismantling of official racial segregation. (p. 148)

The U.S. Supreme Court originally endorsed racial segregation in *Plessy* v. *Ferguson* (1896), but Thurgood Marshall and the NAACP initiated a litigation strategy in the 1930s to attack the "separate but equal" principle from *Plessy*. They filed lawsuits narrowly focused at unequal, and often nonexistent, facilities for African American college graduates seeking education in state university law schools and graduate programs. After winning several cases over the course of two decades, they filed a similar case against a public school system. As a result, the U.S. Supreme Court became the first major governing institution to firmly reject all segregation laws as violating the Equal Protection Clause (*Brown* v. *Board of Education of Topeka*, 1954).

Clarifying the Coverage of the Equal Protection Clause

5.4 Differentiate between the various tests used by the Supreme Court when deciding discrimination claims under the Equal Protection Clause. (p. 150)

The Court uses three tests to address equal protection claims. Claims of racial discrimination are analyzed by judges under the strict scrutiny test, which examines whether the government can present a "compelling" justification for treating racial group members differently. Claims of gender discrimination are analyzed through the moderate or intermediate scrutiny test, which asks whether the government has "important" reasons for treating men and women differently. Nearly all other kinds of discrimination claims filed under the Equal Protection Clause are examined through the rational basis test, which merely asks whether the government has reason to distinguish between people in order to pursue a legitimate government objective. The government almost never wins when there is proof of racial discrimination and the strict scrutiny test is applied. However, the government usually wins when the rational basis test is applied.

Grassroots Mobilization and Civil Rights

5.5 Identify the events and factors that influenced the development of the grassroots civil rights movement. (p. 154)

A number of significant events in the 1950s and 1960s mobilized African Americans to mount organized, nonviolent protests despite death threats, sniper bullets, and police brutality directed at them. These events included the murder of teenager Emmett Till, the Montgomery bus boycott in response to the arrest of Rosa Parks, and the murders of civil rights workers. The violent response of southern whites to African Americans' nonviolent demonstrations helped dramatize the need for civil rights protections by changing public opinion and spurring the federal government to take action.

The civil rights movement pushed Congress and state legislatures to enact a variety of statutes including the Civil Rights Act of 1964 and the Voting Rights Act of 1965.

Other Historic Struggles for Civil Rights

5.6 Compare and contrast the civil rights struggles of women, Latinos, Native Americans, and African Americans. (p. 159)

Women, Latinos, and Native Americans suffered from many decades of discrimination in employment and other aspects of American life. Although they had not experienced the centuries of enslavement directed at African Americans, they still found themselves denied full and equal participation in American government and society. While African Americans relied on a litigation strategy to produce their major civil rights breakthrough in the twentieth century through the Supreme Court decision in *Brown v. Board of Education* (1954), women and Latinos focused on grassroots mobilization in order to gain political rights and economic opportunity. Native Americans gained a relatively recent litigation victory over the federal government yet many still suffer from severe problems due to lack of economic opportunities and poverty as a historic legacy of being forced from their lands as well as a long history of harsh discrimination.

Contemporary Civil Rights Issues

5.7 Evaluate the continuing debates, lawsuits, and protests over civil rights in the twenty-first century. (p. 164)

Twenty-first century civil rights issues are increasingly complex. As statutes and judicial decisions have barred formal discrimination by race and gender, new questions emerge about how to remedy existing inequality, how to prevent discrimination in government officials' discretionary decisions, and what standards of proof should be required to win discrimination cases in court. The Black Lives Matter movement that gained national momentum beginning in 2014 called attention to issues of differential treatment based on discretionary decisions of justice system officials. Some efforts to address these issues, such as the use of affirmative action to address continuing racial inequality, are very controversial.

Additional groups have emerged to seek civil rights protection through the court and grassroots mobilization pathways. These groups include the disabled as well as gays and lesbians. While disabled people have been successful in pushing for laws to guard against discrimination in employment and public accommodations, gays and lesbians are still working toward similar coverage in state and local laws. Yet, there is evidence of significant change in the status of gays and lesbians as evidenced by the legalization of same-sex marriage and the elimination of barriers to their service in the U.S. military.

⟩ LEARN THE TERMS

civil rights, p. 140
political equality, p. 140
equality of condition, p. 141
equality of opportunity, p. 141
Jim Crow laws, p. 146
Plessy v. *Ferguson* (1896),
    p. 147

de jure segregation, p. 148
de facto segregation, p. 148
National Association for the
    Advancement of Colored People
    (NAACP), p. 149
Brown v. *Board of Education of Topeka*
    (1954), p. 149

affirmative action, p. 152
Obergefell v. *Hodges* (2015),
    p. 153
Civil Rights Act of 1964, p. 156
Voting Rights Act of 1965,
    p. 156
universal suffrage, p. 159

⟩ EXPLORE FURTHER

In the Library

Ackerman, Bruce. *We the People: Foundations.* Cambridge, MA: Belknap/Harvard, 1991.

Alexander, Michelle. *The New Jim Crow: Mass Incarceration in the Age of Colorblindness.* New York: The New Press, 2010.

Baer, Judith, and Leslie Friedman Goldstein. *The Constitutional and Legal Rights of Women.* New York: Oxford University Press, 2006.

Blackmon, Douglas A. *Slavery by Another Name: The Re-Enslavement of Black Americans from the Civil War to World War II.* New York: Anchor Books, 2008.

Branch, Taylor. *Parting the Waters: America in the King Years, 1954–1963.* New York: Simon and Schuster, 1988.

____. *Pillar of Fire: America in the King Years, 1963–1965.* New York: Simon and Schuster, 1998.

Epp, Charles R., Steven Maynard-Moody, and Donald Haider-Markel. *Pulled Over: How Police Stops Define Race and Citizenship.* Chicago: University of Chicago Press, 2014.

Flexner, Eleanor, and Ellen Fitzpatrick. *Century of Struggle: The Women's Rights Movement in the United States.* Cambridge, MA: Belknap/Harvard, 1996.

Foner, Eric. *The Story of American Freedom*. New York: W.W. Norton, 1998.

Gerstmann, Evan. *Same-Sex Marriage and the Constitution*, 2nd ed. New York: Cambridge University Press, 2008.

Gutierrez, David G. *The Columbia History of Latinos in the United States Since 1960*. New York: Columbia University Press, 2006.

Kluger, Richard. *Simple Justice: The History of Brown* v. *Board of Education*. New York: Random House, 1977.

Litwack, Leon F. *Trouble in Mind: Black Southerners in the Age of Jim Crow*. New York: Knopf, 1998.

McDonald, Laughlin. *American Indians and the Fight for Equal Voting Rights*. Norman, OK: University of Oklahoma Press, 2011.

Sterba, James. *Affirmative Action for the Future*. Ithaca, NY: Cornell University Press, 2009.

Takaki, Ronald. *A Different Mirror: A History of Multicultural America*. Boston: Little, Brown, 1993.

Tushnet, Mark V. *Making Civil Rights Law: Thurgood Marshall and the Supreme Court, 1936–1961*. New York: Oxford University Press, 1994.

On the Web

Read about the idea of equality in Sweden, which emphasizes equality of condition, rather than just equality of opportunity, in many aspects of society: *https://sweden.se/society/*.

The Web site of the Public Broadcasting System (PBS) presents maps, photos, and other materials about the post–Civil War Reconstruction period: *http://www.pbs.org/wgbh/amex/reconstruction/*.

Examine the Web sites of the NAACP and the NAACP Legal Defense and Educational Fund to see the goals and current activities of these organizations: http://www.naacp.org and *http://www.naacpldf.org*.

Examine the Web sites of two organizations focused on women's issues to see how they define and pursue their markedly different goals: National Organization for Women (*http://www.now.org*) and Eagle Forum (*http://www.eagleforum.org*).

Read about the Civil Rights Memorial in Montgomery, Alabama, at *https://www.splcenter.org/news/2014/11/05/civil-rights-memorial-celebrates-25th-anniversary*. A monument and a visitor center honor the people who lost their lives during the civil rights movement, either as a result of their political activism or because of the color of their skin. The Web site of the U.S. Commission on Civil Rights describes its work: *http://www.usccr.gov/*.

The Web site of the Susan B. Anthony Center for Women's Leadership at the University of Rochester provides historical information about women's efforts to obtain the right to vote: *http://www.rochester.edu/SBA/suffragehistory.html*.

Learn about contemporary issues affecting farm workers, especially Latino farm workers, at the Web site of the United Farm Workers union, which was founded by César Chávez: *http://www.ufw.org/*.

Read about litigation and advocacy efforts by the attorneys at the Native American Rights Fund, a nonprofit law firm that litigates concerning such issues as religious practices and land rights for Native Americans: *http://www.narf.org/*.

Read about competing perspectives on affirmative action at the Web sites of the National Leadership Network of Black Conservatives (*http://www.nationalcenter.org/AA.html*), and the American Association for Affirmative Action (*http://www.affirmativeaction.org/*). You can also learn about disability rights organizations (*http://www.ndrn.org/*) and gay rights organizations (*http://www.glaad.org/mission*) as you try to understand their role in emerging civil rights issues.

CONGRESS

Throughout much of the 2016 presidential campaign, media pundits speculated that Donald Trump would lose, perhaps badly, and by doing so would drag down the entire Republican ticket. Paul Ryan, the Speaker of the House, might lose his job as Speaker. To make matters worse, Ryan refused to campaign for Trump. But, of course, neither of those outcomes happened.
■ *How do you think Trump and Ryan will get along in the coming years?*

→ LEARNING OBJECTIVES

6.1 Differentiate between the various ways legislators represent the interests of their constituents.

6.2 Identify the key constitutional provisions that shape the way Congress functions.

6.3 Establish the importance of committees in organizing the legislative process.

6.4 Assess how political parties and leaders manage the legislative process while advancing their own initiatives.

6.5 Show how the rules and norms of behavior help ensure a more orderly, efficient legislative process.

6.6 Outline the process by which a bill becomes a law.

6.7 Determine whether members of Congress mirror America's demographic diversity and why this matters.

6.8 Compare the state of congressional ethics with Americans' perception of the legislative branch.

In the spring of 2016, as Donald Trump's nomination grew more likely, operatives in both political parties scrambled to understand the potential implications for House and Senate candidates. Most speculated that Trump's high negatives would create an uphill slog for marginal Republican senatorial candidates. Control of that chamber might flip to the Democrats if Republican voters stayed home on Election Day. Historically, when the head of the ticket (the presidential candidate) is weak, "down ballot" repercussions can be significant.

That's not what happened. Donald Trump stunned many pundits, scholars, and average Americans by decisively beating Hillary Clinton. Many of the House and Senate seats that Republicans feared they would lose were held by what appears to be a late surge of support. The Republicans did drop a few seats—two in the Senate and six in the House—but they maintained control of both chambers. The margin is slim in both houses, but Donald Trump will come to power with a unified government.

This does, however, bring up a broader question. All told, some 97 percent of House and a large majority of Senate incumbents (those candidates running for reelection) were sent back to office. This was true for both Republicans and Democrats. Why was there so little turnover in Congress when it seems the voters were desperate for change? Why didn't Trump's antiestablishment message spread to House and Senate races?

The answer is simple: there were very few competitive House elections. The most frequently cited explanation as to why so many House seats are safe or noncompetitive, is so-called gerrymandering—a term discussed later in this chapter. After the historic, inclusive ballot sweep by Republicans in 2010, congressional district lines were carefully assembled by Republican state legislatures to insulate their colleagues. Political scientists have been reluctant to put too much stock in artfully-drawn district lines, however, because the empirical evidence seems thin. There is another explanation—one with potentially greater implications. Many scholars now believe that Americans are starting to choose where to live based on politics, a process called geo-political sorting. We may be clustering in ideological uniform communities. Whether it is based on life-style preferences (which of course are linked to political preferences), on ideology, or some mix of factors, the homogenization of American communities is shifting electoral dynamics as well as how the House of Representatives operates.

When it comes to the work of Congress—the focus of this chapter—sorting could create any number of big problems. When members of Congress come from competitive districts, finding compromise solutions seems tolerable. When most voters in the district are moderate, middle-ground solutions make sense. But when legislators come from rabidly Democratic or Republican communities, compromise is viewed as treason. Legislators from sorted districts are more worried about their next primary election than they are about the next general election. As will be seen in the pages to follow, gridlock and stalemate seems all-too-common in Congress, with citizens frustrated by the process. How could compromises be so elusive? Deepening partisanship in the chamber could be part of the answer, but so too might be our growing fondness for living with like-minded neighbors. One of the jobs of the Speaker of the House is to move the process forward; to produce necessary changes in public policy. Ironically, the very forces that have allowed Paul Ryan to remain Speaker may also make his job exceptionally difficult.

The Nature and Style of Representation

6.1 Differentiate between the various ways legislators represent the interests of their constituents.

There are a number of important questions that we can ask about the precise job of members of Congress. Whom do they represent? What do they seek to accomplish? At the core, the job of any representative is to speak and act on behalf of others.

FIGURE 6.1   Representing the Will of the People

There are different approaches to representation, as this figure suggests.

■ *Should legislators act as their constituents would if they were present, or should they work to "enlarge and refine" the public will? Does it depend on the issue at hand? Are there contemporary forces pushing legislators toward one perspective?*

Delegate Model	Politico Model	Conscience Model	Trustee Model
The job of a legislator is to stick to the will of the people	A legislator might follow his or her own sense of what is right until the public becomes involved in the issue, at which point he or she should heed their wishes	A legislator follows the will of the people in most instances until conscience pulls him or her in a different direction	The job of a legislator is to use information and the powers of deliberation to arrive at his or her own assessment; to "enlarge and refine the public's will"
"To say the sovereignty rests in the people, and that they have not a right to instruct and control their representatives, is absurd to the last degree." —**Representative Elbridge Gerry** (1744–1814) of Massachusetts during a debate over the ratification of the First Amendment	"The average legislator early in his career discovers that there are certain interests or prejudices of his constituents which are dangerous to trifle with." —**Senator J. William Fulbright** (1905–1995) of Arkansas	Former House member **Sherwood Boehlert** (1936–) of New York called this the "pillow test." He argued that the job of a legislator is to follow the will of constituents until doing so keeps the legislator awake at night.	"Have the people of this country snatched the power of deliberation from this body? Are we a body of agents and not a deliberate one?" —**John C. Calhoun** (1782–1850) of South Carolina, vice president and member of the House and Senate during a debate over a bill fixing compensation for members of Congress

delegate model of representation

The philosophy that legislators should adhere to the will of their constituents. If most constituents want a particular measure, a legislator with this view would feel compelled to support it, regardless of his or her personal feelings.

trustee model of representation

The philosophy that legislators should consider the will of the people but act in ways they believe best for the long-term interests of the nation, at which time, the precise "will of the people" is set aside.

politico model of representation

Legislators follow their own judgment until the public becomes vocal about a particular matter, at which point they should follow the dictates of constituents.

conscience model of representation

The philosophy that legislators should follow the will of the people until they truly believe it is in the best interests of the nation to act differently.

Thomas Paine, the revolutionary propagandist and political thinker, suggested in his famous 1776 pamphlet *Common Sense* that legislators must "act in the same manner as the whole body would act, were they present." This perspective has been called the **delegate model of representation** (see Figure 6.1). Here, the legislator does his or her best to discern the will of the people and then acts accordingly.

A very different approach is called the **trustee model of representation**. This was the outlook favored by most of the delegates at the Constitutional Convention. It holds that the legislator should consider the will of the people but then do what he or she thinks is best for the nation as a whole and in the long term. Advocates of this approach would suggest that a legislator should use his or her experiences, knowledge, and judgments to make decisions, and not simply follow the whims of public opinion.

There is no right or wrong model; each has held more sway at different points in our history. Although the trustee perspective was dominant in the early years of the Republic, several changes have made the delegate model more popular today. For example, the number of career legislators has shot up in recent decades. To retain their seats, legislators are often eager to appease the public. "Public opinion" is also much easier to discern, given the accuracy and frequency of polls. Two contemporary American political scientists conclude, "The core dictate of this new breed of politician, as we might expect, is to win reelection each year. This means keeping your votes in line with the wishes of those in the district."[1,2] Moreover, many legislators are now finding that wandering from the wishes of *primary* elections voters can prove perilous—as noted above.

Of course, there are middle-ground perspectives, too. The **politico model of representation** holds that legislators should feel free to follow their own judgment on matters where the public remains silent. Another perspective is called the **conscience model of representation**, or what we might call the "pillow test." On most matters, representatives are delegates and heed the wishes of constituents, but if a particular position really disturbs representatives to the point that they can't sleep at night, they turn into trustees and vote the other way.

Mitch McConnell of Kentucky is the Senate Majority Leader. Until Donald Trump's victory, McConnell had only served in this post with a Democrat, Barack Obama, in the White House.

■ *Do you think his job will be different, perhaps even harder, now that his party is in charge of the presidency?*

There is also the issue of whether legislators should spend their time working on broad-based policy initiatives or on direct constituency needs. We might call this a question of *representational style*. Some legislators focus on major policy matters, such as health care reform, foreign policy, national defense, international trade, and immigration; others concentrate on helping constituents get their share from the federal government. Constituent service (also called *casework*) makes up a great deal of what legislators and their staff do on a daily basis.

Finally, there is the issue of symbolic representation. Many analysts have argued that an important facet of the legislators' job is to speak on behalf of the groups they belong to—especially their demographic group. Members of ethnic or racial groups feel great pride and validation when another member of their group is elected to the Congress. This also gives them confidence that they will have better representation as a result. On top of this is partisan loyalty. A growing number of legislators believe it is their job to support the policy agenda of the party or group that aided them in the last election. Many Republicans in the 114th Congress, for example, seemed unwilling to veer from the wishes of the conservative groups in their districts.

Congress and the Constitution

6.2 Identify the key constitutional provisions that shape the way Congress functions.

A Bicameral Legislature

Article I, Section 1, of the Constitution established a two-chamber or **bicameral legislature** (see Table 6.1). The House of Representatives, with its legislators directly elected by the people to relatively short terms of office, seemed to stick closely to the spirit of 1776. That is to say, the House reflected the idea that average citizens should select leaders who would follow their wishes rather closely. Yet the other chamber of the legislature, the Senate, allowed state legislatures to pick senators. By granting senators 6-year terms, the Constitution seemed to check the democratic impulses of the day. We might say, then, that the battle of the Virginia Plan against the New Jersey Plan in the Philadelphia Convention had involved two conflicting Revolutionary Era visions of representation: sovereign people versus sovereign states.

bicameral legislature

A legislature composed of two houses. Not only is Congress bicameral, consisting of the House and the Senate, but 49 of the 50 states also have a two-house legislature. Since 1934, Nebraska has had a unicameral (one house) legislature.

TABLE 6.1 Key Differences Between the House and the Senate

How do these differences shape the way members of each chamber approach their job of representing the "will of the people"?

House of Representatives	Senate
435 members (apportionment based on state population)	100 members (2 from each state)
2-year terms	6-year terms
Less flexible rules	More flexible rules
Limited debate	Virtually unlimited debate
Policy specialists with an emphasis on taxes and revenues	Policy generalists with an emphasis on foreign policy
Less media coverage	More media coverage
Centralized power (with committee leaders)	Equal distribution of power
More partisan	Somewhat less partisan
High turnover rate	Moderate turnover rate

This balancing act would be revisited throughout much of our history. Before the Civil War, for example, John C. Calhoun, a representative and, later, a senator from South Carolina, as well as vice president under Andrew Jackson, advocated a theory of "nullification." Calhoun's idea was that within their own borders, states had the right to nullify—to declare null and void—acts of Congress. Roughly 100 years later, southern lawmakers again argued that "states' rights" and "state sovereignty" granted them the right to ignore desegregation mandates from the federal courts. More recently, battles over controversial issues such as health care mandates, education policy, medical marijuana, immigration, and same-sex marriage have elicited similar arguments.

Who Can Serve in Congress?

Article I, Section 2, of the Constitution sets the length of terms for House members (2 years) and specifies the basic qualifications for service. House members must be 25 years of age, a citizen of the United States for at least 7 years, and a resident of the state where they are elected. Notice, however, that the Constitution does *not* say that House members must reside in the district they represent. Throughout our history, on a number of occasions, politicians have been elected to represent districts in which they did not live. Nor does the Constitution put any limit on the number of terms a representative may serve. In the early 1990s, a number of states tried to limit the terms of members of Congress—both in the House and in the Senate. The Supreme Court, however, in *Term Limits, Inc.* v. *Thornton* (1995), found such restrictions unconstitutional. It seems, then, that the only way to limit the number of terms for members of Congress would be a constitutional amendment.

Article I, Section 3, begins with the method of selecting a senator. Originally, the Constitution stated that each state legislature would select its two U.S. senators. This changed with ratification of the **Seventeenth Amendment** in 1913, and senators are now elected directly by the voters of their state. The next clause deals with the length of senatorial terms (6 years) and makes a special provision called **rotation**. Rather than have all senators come up for election every 6 years, the Constitution divides the Senate into three "classes," each of which must stand for election every 2 years. Rotation ensures that the Senate's membership can never be changed all at once just because the public has become outraged over some issue. This gives the Senate greater stability than the House—exactly what the framers intended.

Seventeenth Amendment

Change to the U.S. Constitution, ratified in 1913, which provides for the direct election of senators. Without this change, we would not vote for our senators, but instead they would be chosen by the state legislature.

rotation

The staggering of senatorial terms such that one-third of the Senate comes up for election every 2 years. Even if voters are ripping mad throughout the nation, only one-third of the Senate can be removed in a particular election.

A senator must be 30 years old, a citizen of the United States for at least 9 years, and a resident of the state he or she represents. The Constitution, however, does not stipulate *how long* the person has to be a resident of that state before serving in the Senate. Occasionally, politicians are elected to represent a state where they had not previously lived. A good example was the election to the Senate in 2000 of Hillary Rodham Clinton, a native of Illinois and a resident of Arkansas (where her husband had been governor before becoming president), to represent the state of New York.

Congressional Elections

Article I, Section 4, of the Constitution outlines the congressional election process. Each state can decide the time, place, and manner of elections to the national legislature—so long as Congress remains silent on the matter. For the most part, Congress has left the regulation of congressional elections to the states, but it has stepped in at important and controversial times. Poll taxes, literacy tests, and excessive residency requirements were used, particularly in many southern states, to keep African Americans from voting (in defiance of the Fifteenth Amendment). Congress responded with the Voting Rights Act of 1965. Later, in 1993, hoping to get more Americans to the polls, Congress passed the National Voter Registration Act (also known as the "Motor Voter Law"), which mandates that all states allow citizens to register to vote at certain frequently used public facilities, including motor vehicle offices. More recently, Congress moved to standardize the manner of voting after the recount fiasco in Florida during the 2000 presidential election (the Help America Vote Act of 2002).

Lawmaking

Article I, Section 7, of the Constitution addresses how a bill becomes law and also specifies the checks and balances between the two houses of the legislature and between the other branches of the government. The same piece of legislation must be approved by a majority of each house of the legislature before it goes to the president for signature into law. If the president signs the bill, it becomes law. Should the president fail to act on the bill for 10 days (not counting Sundays), it becomes law anyway—unless Congress has adjourned in the meantime, in which case it is known as a **pocket veto**. If the president vetoes the bill, however, a two-thirds vote in both houses is necessary to override the veto.

pocket veto
The president's killing of a bill that has been passed by both houses of Congress, simply by not signing it within 10 days of the bill's passage when Congress has adjourned.

Article I, Section 8, lists the powers of the legislative branch (see Table 6.2). This list of enumerated powers is one of the most important sections of the Constitution, but it was controversial for two reasons: First, although the framers thought it important to define the powers of Congress, there was still widespread public resistance to giving excessive power to the national government. Second, even though the framers were willing to give the national government broad powers, listing them carried a risk of leaving something out—something that might later prove significant. Inclusion of the last clause of Section 8 seemed to provide a solution. This provision, often called the **Elastic Clause** or the **Necessary and Proper Clause**, states that Congress has the power to make all laws "necessary and proper" to implement any of the other powers mentioned in the section. This clause suggested that many congressional powers were *implied* rather than spelled out in detail.

Elastic Clause/Necessary and Proper Clause
Constitution grants Congress the power to pass all laws "necessary and proper" for carrying out the list of expressed powers. This allows Congress to move on a broad host of matters so long as they can be linked to one of the enumerated (specifically stated) powers. It greatly enhances the power of the national government.

By 1819, the Supreme Court had put the argument for implied powers on a stronger foundation. In his majority opinion in the case of *McCulloch* v. *Maryland*, Chief Justice John Marshall made it clear that Congress did, indeed, have "implied powers." The case concerned a branch of the federally chartered Bank of the United States located in the state of Maryland. The Maryland legislature had levied a tax on the Bank of the United States. But could a state government tax an institution created by the

TABLE 6.2 Powers of Congress Under the U.S. Constitution

One of the dangers of listing an organization's powers is that all circumstances may not be covered. The framers of the Constitution understood this and added the final element to deal with unforeseen circumstances. Yet, the "Elastic Clause" has proved controversial because the Supreme Court has interpreted it in broad terms, thus granting Congress sweeping powers.

■ *Do you think the national legislature should have these expansive powers?*

Clause	Power Granted in Article I, Section 8
1	Levy and collect taxes and duties and provide for the common defense
2	Borrow money on credit
3	Regulate commerce with foreign nations and between the states
4	Establish rules on naturalization and bankruptcy
5	Coin money
6	Create punishments for counterfeiting
7	Establish post offices
8	Promote the progress of science and the arts
9	Constitute tribunals below the Supreme Court
10	Punish crimes on the high seas
11	Declare war
12	Raise and support the army
13	Provide and maintain a navy
14	Make rules for the use of armed forces
15	Call out the militia
16	Organize, arm, and discipline the militia
17	Exercise exclusive legislation over the district of the seat of the federal government
18	Make all laws deemed "necessary and proper" for implementing these powers

national government? And—resurrecting the question that Jefferson and Madison had asked back in 1790—where does the Constitution give Congress the power to create a national bank?

As to the first question, Marshall wrote, "The power to tax involves the power to destroy." That would suggest some sort of supremacy. Yet the Constitution is clear that the national government is supreme, so the tax (which could, if heavy enough, put the national bank out of business) was unconstitutional. As to the broader question—the power to charter a bank—Marshall wrote the following:

> Let the end be legitimate, let it be within the scope of the constitution, and all means which are appropriate, which are plainly adapted to that end, which are not prohibited, but consistent with the letter and spirit of the constitution, are constitutional.

In one clean sweep, Marshall's ruling greatly expanded the scope of the national government's power. This issue has been contentious at different points of American history, and in recent years the debate has intensified. Some suggest that the Elastic Clause, particularly when coupled with the powers to regulate commerce, seems stacked against the Tenth Amendment. This amendment reserves to states powers not granted to the federal government. If Congress can regulate nearly any issue because it can somehow be linked to commerce, what then is left to the states?

Redistricting

The Great Compromise had stipulated that Congress be divided into two chambers, one with an identical number of legislators from each state (the Senate) and the other based on population (the House of Representatives). But how would we know the number of citizens in each state? The Constitution also stipulates that a census be conducted every 10 years and that seats be allocated to each state based on this count. However, if a state gets more than one seat (and most states do), who then is responsible for drawing the boundaries of legislative districts—or should there even *be* legislative districts? The Constitution left these questions to the states to decide, and they have caused considerable controversy ever since.

In the earliest days of the Republic, some states did use **at-large districts**. If they were granted three seats in the House, they would simply elect three members from the entire state. Those states had no districts. Most states, however, chose to divide their territory into a number of congressional districts equal to the number of seats they were allocated in the House of Representatives. The idea of changing legislative districts in response to population shifts stems from the American idea of geographic representation. That is, our representatives should be directly responsible to a group of people living in a specific geographic location. Today, drawing the boundaries for congressional districts has become a tricky and controversial process. In all states except very small ones that have only a single representative (there are seven), the process must be undertaken every 10 years to reflect changes in the state's overall population relative to the rest of the country, as well as to respond to population shifts within the state. This process of redrawing the boundaries of legislative districts is called **redistricting**. The Constitution gives state legislatures the redistricting power. Because these bodies have nearly always been partisan (controlled by a majority of members from one party), the process causes a lot of partisan wrangling.

Gerrymandering is the drawing of legislative districts for partisan advantage. The word immortalizes one Elbridge Gerry, who as governor of Massachusetts around 1810 persuaded his followers in the state legislature to draw an odd-shaped district, wiggling across the state, designed to elect a political ally. Looking at the map, someone said that the new district looked like a salamander, to which someone else replied that it wasn't a salamander but a "Gerrymander" (see Figure 6.2).[3] The name stuck. Gerrymandering means the creation of oddly shaped districts as a means of controlling the results of future elections in those districts. This has been done in a number of ways, but mostly through either *packing* or *cracking*. Packing is lumping as many opposition voters as possible into one district. For instance, if the state has five districts, the idea is to fill one of these districts overwhelmingly with supporters of the other party. The party in power—the politicians drawing the lines—would give up that one seat, but the other four districts would have boundaries that nearly guarantee that candidates of their party would win. Cracking involves splitting up groups of voters thought to favor the opposition so that they do not make up a majority in any district and thus cannot win in any district.

An example may be helpful. After the 2010 Census, the Democratic majority in the Maryland State Legislature drew eight congressional district boundaries to make seven of them safe for Democrats. A federal judge, called upon to look into the matter, suggested one of the districts looked like a "broken-winged pterodactyl, lying prostrate across the center of the state."[4]

The redistricting process has also been used to minimize the representation of minority groups. Thirty percent of a state's population, for example, might be black, but through cracking, it could be fixed so that these voters would never be able to elect an African-American legislator without the help of white voters. Or, through packing, most of the black population might be concentrated in one virtually all-black district, enabling whites to elect representatives from the other districts. This issue came to the fore in 2011 when Texas was given four additional House seats because of the state's rapid population growth. While most of the increase was due to Hispanic citizens, only one of the new districts had a sizable Hispanic population. The legislature was

at-large districts

Districts encompassing an entire state, or large parts of a state, in which House members are elected to represent the entire area. Small states, like Wyoming and Vermont, have at-large legislators because they have just one legislative district (the entire state).

redistricting

The process of redrawing legislative district boundaries within a state to reflect population changes. The shifting of district boundaries can have massive political implications. At times, two sitting legislators are placed in the same district, for example. They are forced to run against each other.

gerrymandering

Drawing legislative district boundaries in such a way as to gain political advantage. With the rise of partisanship in most state legislatures, many assume that party-based gerrymandering will be more common in the years to come.

FIGURE 6.2 That's Not a Salamander; It's a Gerrymander!

As Governor of Massachusetts in 1812, Elbridge Gerry prompted his fellow Republicans in the state legislature to draw congressional district lines that favored their party. As the story goes, a reporter looked at one of these new districts and commented that it looked like a salamander. Another noted, "That's not a salamander, that's a Gerrymander!" Partisan-based redistricting is an age-old problem.

■ *Should legislatures allow nonpartisan groups to draw new district lines?*

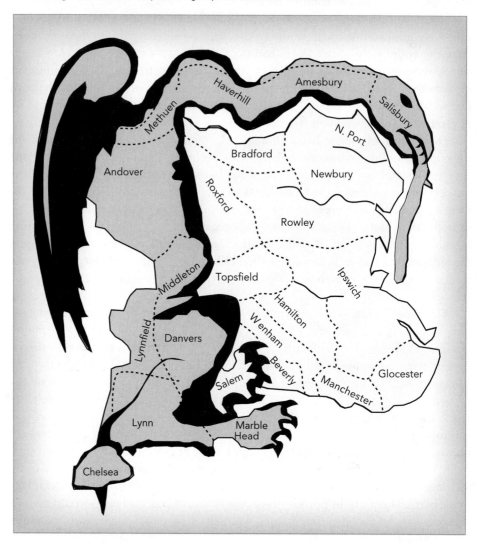

controlled by Republicans. The issue swirled in the federal courts and eventually the state redrew the lines, creating two Latino-dominated districts.

Some states have moved toward using nonpartisan organizations to draw district lines. Iowa has taken this trend furthest, using a complex computer program administered by a nonpartisan commission to draw geographically compact and equal districts. The state legislature then votes these districts up or down, but it cannot amend them. This process has spared Iowa from court challenges and has generally produced competitive congressional races. For example, in the 2006 election, 3 out of 5 of Iowa's U.S. House races were considered competitive, compared to only 1 out of 10 in the rest of the nation.[5] The voters of California passed a ballot measure in 2010 for the creation of a nonpartisan Citizens Redistricting Commission, and several other states—including Arizona, Hawaii, Idaho, New Jersey, Washington, and Montana—have made similar moves. In several other states, "back up commissions" have been established in the event that the state legislature is unable to agree on a redistricting plan. Likely, these changes are being considered in light of new research that suggests that districts drawn by courts or commissions are typically much more competitive than legislatively drawn districts. So by that measure, they are successful.

For the most part, redistricting has been a tricky issue for the courts. On a number of occasions, the courts refused to get involved in the controversy.[6] However, in more recent decades, the courts have signaled a greater willingness to hear such cases. The complexity of the reapportionment process continues to makes judicial intervention difficult, however. In those occasions where courts are called upon to assess draw lines, they must contend with the thorns in the "political thicket." They confront entrenched partisan interests, the interests of incumbent legislators, pressure groups' preferences, democratic principles of representation, and struggle to align those interests with standards articulated in *Baker* and other voting rights cases. Are civil rights violated, for instance, when districts are drawn for partisan political purposes? What constitutes an "irregular" shaped district?

POSITIVE GERRYMANDERING Amendments to the Voting Rights Act of 1965, which were passed in 1982, approached the racial gerrymandering issue from an entirely different direction. If the redistricting process has been used in the past to limit minority representation, could it not be used to *increase* minority representation? Perhaps census data could be used to construct districts that would better ensure the election of minority legislators. After the 1990 census, 24 majority-minority districts—districts in which a minority group made up a majority of the population—were created in different states. Fifteen of these districts had majorities of African-American voters, and nine had a majority of Hispanic voters.

The scheme seemed to work: In each of these districts, the voters chose a minority legislator. Nevertheless, two issues came up. First, the resulting districts were often oddly shaped. In North Carolina's 12th Congressional District, for example, a roughly 100-mile strip of Interstate 85, on which almost no one lived, connected black communities in Durham and Charlotte. Second, the overt consideration of race in drawing highly irregular districts was challenged in the courts as an affront to the Equal Protection Clause of the Fourteenth Amendment. In a series of decisions in the 1990s, the Court generally supported plans that improved the likelihood of minority representation but seemed reluctant to allow highly irregularly shaped districts (*Shaw v. Reno*, 1993) or to approve schemes that use race as the primary criterion for drawing district lines (*Miller v. Johnson*, 1995). In the *Miller* case, the court ruled that race could not be the "predominant" factor in drawing district lines. In recent years, many states have moved to create minority-majority districts as a means of heading-off litigation. Conversely, plans that dilute minority voting strength are quickly challenged in the courts. The issue became even more complicated in 2013 when the Supreme Court, in the case of *Shelby County v. Holder*, invalidated sections of the Voting Rights Act that required states with a history of discrimination to have their redistricting plans approved by the Justice Department.

NUMBER OF RESIDENTS PER DISTRICT Related to the difficult issue of drawing district lines is the question of the number of residents per district. Oddly enough, the Constitution is silent on this matter, and for most of our history, many states did not ensure that every district had the same number of constituents.

The issue of malapportionment came to a head in the mid-twentieth century when a group of Tennessee residents claimed that the state legislature had denied them equal protection under the law by refusing to draw districts with the same population. In 1961, the Supreme Court decided that the Tennessee districts were so out of proportion that they violated the plaintiffs' constitutional rights. This case, **Baker v. Carr**, wrote the "one person, one vote" principle into federal law.[7] It also sparked a revolution in the way legislative districts were drawn.

In the post-*Baker* era, geographic concerns took a backseat to ensuring equal population in all districts. These later cases also mandated that redistricting happen every

Baker v. Carr (1961)
Supreme Court case that set the standard that House districts must contain equal numbers of constituents, thus establishing the principle of "one person, one vote."

10 years, even if the size of the state's congressional delegation remained unchanged. This was mandated because population shifts over a decade would mean that old districts would be unlikely to have equal populations. Perhaps most important, *Baker* v. *Carr* inserted the federal courts into the redistricting process, thereby leaving any plan open to a court challenge. Along with the mandate under the Voting Rights Act of 1965 to prevent racial discrimination in voting, *Baker* v. *Carr* has made redistricting a tedious process of moving district lines block by block until the population balance is correct, while constantly facing the threat that a federal court will find the entire scheme unconstitutional.[8]

The most recent spin on this issue came in 2016 when the Supreme Court heard *Evenwel* v. *Abbott*. In this case the court wrestled with whether the doctrine of "one-person-one-vote" should be based on the state's general population or its voting population. Historically, it has been general population—that is, residents. Urban areas, which lean toward Democrats, have a higher percentage of residents who are not eligible to vote, mostly immigrants and other minority groups, so a change to this precedent would have significant electoral implications. In a unanimous decision the court ruled that states will have to continue to use all residents in determining congressional district size. As noted by Justice Ruth Bader Ginsburg, "Nonvoters have an important stake in many policy debates."

reapportionment

The process by which seats in the House of Representatives are reassigned among the states to reflect population changes following the Census (every 10 years). In recent decades Sun Belt states have netted more seats, and Rust Belt states have lost seats.

REAPPORTIONMENT Finally, the redistricting process is controversial because the allotment of seats per state shifts with each new census (see Figure 6.3). The process of shifting the number of seats allotted to each state is called **reapportionment**. Originally, the Constitution set the ratio of residents per House member at 1 to 30,000, meaning there were 65 House members in the first Congress. As the nation's population grew, so did the number of representatives in the House. The membership of the House jumped from 141 in 1800 to 240 in 1830. By 1910, the House had grown to 435 members. That seemed large enough, so its membership was capped by Congress. Today, there are roughly 710,000 residents for each House district.

Reapportionment implies that the fastest-growing states gain seats after each census and that seats are taken from the slower-growing states. For instance five states have lost at least five congressional seats over the last 40 years, and all of them come from the Upper Midwest, also called the Rust Belt.[9] The "winning" states over the same period have been in the South, and especially the West and Southwest. As a result of the 2010 Census, for example, 8 of 12 new congressional seats are west of the Mississippi River, while the other 4 are in the Southeast. This is the first time that the population in the West exceeds the population in the Midwest. Florida gained two more seats and Texas netted an additional four. These trends reflect the shift of the U.S. population toward the Sun Belt and away from the old industrial and farming states.

Losing seats in the national legislature can be devastating for a state because much of the federal government's domestic spending is proportionate to a state's population. Having fewer residents means getting fewer federal dollars.

An interesting argument has also emerged over the actual population of each state, similar to the dispute noted above. Democrats often charge that many citizens are missed in the counting process of the census. They argue that statistical models for estimating populations would actually yield more accurate results than trying to physically count everyone. Republicans, on the other hand, often point out that the Constitution stipulates a full *person-by-person* count; until the Constitution is changed, they say, there is no alternative. The battle over the census counts is partisan, because most analysts agree that the chance of citizens being missed is greatest in the northeastern urban states, which lean Democratic. Arguments made by both sides get louder every 10 years when a new census is conducted, but for now, the Republicans seem to have the courts on their side.

FIGURE 6.3 Distribution of Congressional Power

The framers mandated that a census be taken every 10 years and that the allocation of House seats to each state be reapportioned accordingly. This map shows the changes after the 2010 Census.

■ *What are some of the patterns that emerge? What will be some of the political implications of population changes in the decades to come?*

SOURCE: U.S. Census Bureau and http://www.electiondataservices.com/NR-Appor2010ESRI-finalwTableMap.pdfs.

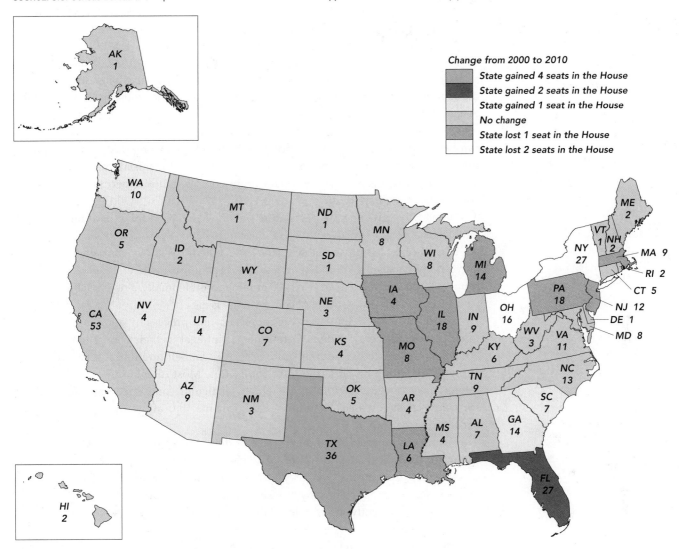

Change from 2000 to 2010
- State gained 4 seats in the House
- State gained 2 seats in the House
- State gained 1 seat in the House
- No change
- State lost 1 seat in the House
- State lost 2 seats in the House

Organizing Congress: Committees

6.3 Establish the importance of committees in organizing the legislative process.

The national legislature is called upon to undertake numerous important functions, which include creating legislation, overseeing federal agencies and departments, creating policies for the collection and appropriation of federal monies, serving constituents (often referred to as *case work*), investigating public issues and matters of growing concern, and providing the president with advice and consent on treaties and appointments to federal offices. Much of this work is defined in the Constitution, but the Constitution says very little about *how* the two legislative chambers should be structured and organized to fulfill these critical governmental functions.

The issues of structure and organization are also important when considering how policy change might be accomplished through the legislative process and how individual citizens might make a difference. Each of the organizing elements discussed in the next three sections gives citizens points of access into the policy development process. We look at the key organizing forces within the legislative process, the nonconstitutional components that help hundreds of individual legislators merge into a lawmaking, appropriating, and oversight body. We begin with the workhorses of the legislature: committees.

Standing Committees

Standing committees are the permanent structures that perform the detailed work of a legislature, such as drafting bills for consideration. There are many advantages to the standing committee system, which was first set up in the House in 1810 and in the Senate shortly thereafter.

First, members of each committee become experts in that policy area so that they can better determine the importance and implications of proposals. To accomplish this, each committee acquires a staff of experts who help legislators make informed decisions. As issues become more and more complex, the "expertise function" becomes even more important.

Second, by dividing the legislature's work between dozens of committees, or "minilegislatures," a vast number of measures can be considered simultaneously. As two leading congressional scholars have noted, "Without committees, a legislative body consisting of 100 senators and 441 House members could not handle roughly 10,000 bills and nearly 100,000 nominations biennially, a national budget over $3 trillion, and a limitless array of controversial issues."[10]

Third, this system enhances the representation process by allowing legislators to sit on committees that deal with issues of interest to their constituents. For example, many legislators from the midwestern Farm Belt might best serve their constituents by sitting on an agriculture committee. Most often, however, constituent interests are varied, making the fit with a particular committee impossible. Even so, many legislators seek committee assignments that allow them to serve their constituents better.

Fourth, committees have taken on a "safety valve" function by becoming the forum for public debate and controversy. They give average citizens a place to vent concerns and frustrations, and they can absorb conflict and resolve the strains of a democratic system. Of course, by blocking action on measures that some citizens and interest groups ardently support, legislative committees can also promote conflict and increase tensions.

Finally, and much related to the pathways of change, committees offer citizens many points of access into the legislative process. It might be too much to expect a citizen or a small group of like-minded citizens to persuade an entire chamber, but shifting the course of committee decisions may be more manageable. Given that very few measures are considered by the full legislature without first being passed at the committee level, and given that committee votes are often won or lost by a few votes, swinging a couple of legislators to your point of view can sometimes change the fate of a piece of legislation. This heightens the power of citizens in the policy process.

The number of standing committees has varied over the years. Different subject areas have been more important in some periods than in others. Today, there are 20 standing committees in the House and 16 in the Senate (see Table 6.3). The size of each committee varies as well, but generally speaking, House committees consist of about 50 members, and Senate standing committees have roughly 20 members. The balance of power between the parties in each chamber is reflected in each committee.

Although standing committees are clearly the most important, there are four other types of legislative committees. Nearly all standing committees have one

TABLE 6.3   Standing Committees of the 115th Congress

Imagine for a minute that you have been elected to Congress.

■ *Given your interest, and the concerns of people in your community, which of these committees would you request to serve on? Which committee would make the least sense?*

Committees of the Senate		Committees of the House	
Agriculture, Nutrition, and Forestry (21 members)	**Homeland Security and Governmental Affairs** (17 members)	**Agriculture** (46 members)	**Judiciary** (40 members)
Appropriations (30 members)	**Judiciary** (19 members)	**Appropriations** (60 members)	**Natural Resources** (49 members)
Armed Services (26 members)	**Rules and Administration** (19 members)	**Armed Services** (62 members)	**Oversight and Government Reform** (41 members)
Banking, Housing, and Urban Affairs (20 members)	**Small Business and Entrepreneurship** (19 members)	**Budget** (39 members)	**Rules** (13 members)
Budget (23 members)	**Veterans' Affairs** (15 members)	**Education and Labor** (49 members)	**Science and Technology** (44 members)
Commerce, Science, and Transportation (25 members)	**Senate Special or Select Committees**	**Energy and Commerce** (59 members)	**Small Business** (29 members)
Energy and Natural Resources (23 members)	**Aging** (21 members)	**Financial Services** (71 members)	**Standards of Official Conduct** (10 members)
Environment and Public Works (19 members)	**Ethics** (6 members)	**Foreign Affairs** (47 members)	**Transportation and Infrastructure** (75 members)
Finance (23 members)	**Intelligence** (19 members)	**Homeland Security** (34 members)	**Veterans' Affairs** (29 members)
Foreign Relations (19 members)	**Indian Affairs** (15 members)	**House Administration** (9 members)	**Ways and Means** (41 members)
Ethics (10 members)	**Health, Education, Labor, and Pensions** (23 members)		

or more **subcommittees** under their jurisdiction. Much the same rationale for apportioning legislative work to committees also applies to subcommittees, whose members and staffers specialize, thus breaking down a broad policy area into more manageable parts. Any piece of legislation that comes before a committee usually is quickly referred to the appropriate subcommittee. Most of the day-to-day lawmaking and oversight of Congress occur at the subcommittee level.[11]

Today, both chambers also establish select committees to deal with a particular issue or problem. They are temporary, so they disappear either when the problem is resolved or, more likely, when the congressional session ends. They serve primarily in an investigative role and cannot approve legislation or move it forward. Of much more significance is the **conference committee**. For legislation to become law, both branches of the legislature must first pass exactly the same bill. When each chamber passes similar but not identical legislation, a conference committee is assembled to work out the differences and reach a compromise. Some conference committees are small, consisting of the chairs of corresponding House and Senate committees and a few members; others, dealing with higher-profile matters, can have hundreds of members. In some ways, these conference committees actually write legislation—the version that emerges from conference often contains vital details that differ from what either house originally passed and may deal with entirely unrelated matters. So important are conference committees that some have dubbed them the "third house of Congress." Finally, joint committees are composed of members selected from each chamber. The work of these committees generally involves investigation, research, and oversight of agencies closely related to Congress. Permanent joint committees, created by statute, are sometimes called standing joint committees.

subcommittees

Specialized groups within standing committees. For example, a subcommittee of the House Education and Labor Committee is Early Childhood, Elementary, and Secondary Education.

conference committee

A committee of members of the House and Senate that irons out differences in similar measures that have passed both houses to create a single bill. The goal of the committee is to find common ground and emerge with a single bill. This process has become more difficult in recent years.

What Committees Do

Committees are critical to the lawmaking process, and it's impossible to imagine a modern legislature functioning without them. But what, exactly, do committees do? Let's take a closer look.

REFERRAL AND JURISDICTION   The Legislative Reorganization Act of 1946 stated that every piece of legislation introduced for consideration must first be referred to a committee. This may sound rather mechanical, simply matching the topic of the bill with an appropriate committee. However, the process is much more complex, and at times it can be quite contentious. The job of referral is given to the Speaker of the House or, in the Senate, to the majority leader.

During most of our nation's history, bills were referred to just one committee. Sometimes which committee a bill got referred to depended less on jurisdictional fit than on the impact, positive or negative, that the chair of that committee might have on its fate. Referral to one particular committee would often either seal a proposed measure's doom or give it a good chance of enactment. This helped ensure that the committee process was closed and undemocratic. By the early 1970s, the House adopted a process of multiple referrals. Now, instead of assigning a new bill to just one committee, it is possible to send the measure to several committees at the same time. It has become customary to designate a "primary committee" that considers a bill but also to assign the bill to other committees as well.

HEARINGS AND INVESTIGATIONS   The vast majority of bills that are introduced in the House or Senate, assigned to a committee, and then assigned to a subcommittee wind up being killed (deemed unworthy of consideration). If a measure is not moved out of the committee considering it, that measure dies at the end of the legislative term. Roughly 90 percent of all measures stall in committee.

For measures that have a modest chance of committee approval, **hearings** are often the first step. These are fact-finding, informational events that usually take place in a subcommittee. Experts are asked to testify at hearings. These experts can include the sponsor of the bill, state and federal officials, interest group leaders, private officials, and (if arranged for by the bill's sponsor, by its opponents, or by advocacy groups) even ordinary citizens making highly emotional pleas, largely for

hearings

Committee sessions for taking testimony from witnesses and for collecting information on legislation under consideration or for the development of new legislation.

On occasion, congressional hearing can be high-profile events. Pictured here is Hillary Clinton in 2015, as she testified before a congressional panel on the U.S. Embassy attack in Benghazi.

■ *Do you think hearings of this sort will be used more often in the future as a partisan weapon to attack and embarrass members of the other party?*

the benefit of the media. Occasionally, on high-visibility issues, celebrities also get to testify. "Quite candidly, when Hollywood speaks, the world listens," a former senator once commented.[12]

MARKUP   If the measure is still considered important after hearings and investigations have been held, the next step in the process is called markup. Here, the actual language of the bill is hammered out. The member responsible for crafting the language is called the *prime sponsor*. Often, but not always, the prime sponsor is the subcommittee chair. The language of the bill must address the concerns of the sponsor, but it also must win the approval of the committee and then the full chamber.

REPORTS   For the fraction of measures that win committee approval, the next step is to send the bill to the floor for consideration. At this point, the staff of the committee prepares a report on the legislation. This report summarizes the bill's provisions and the rationale behind them.

THE RULES REPORT   There is another step—and a critically important one—before a bill is sent to the floor. Every bill in the House must pass through a Rules Committee. This committee establishes rules regarding the consideration of the legislation, which helps streamline the process and make things fair.

BUREAUCRATIC OVERSIGHT   Another critical committee function is **oversight**, the responsibility of Congress to keep a close eye on the federal bureaucracy's implementation of federal law. The Constitution neither spells out a congressional oversight role, nor prohibits such work. By keeping an eye on the bureaucracy (see Chapter 8) Congress helps create greater accountability in an otherwise "distant" part of the federal government. Congress can investigate issues; call agency heads to testify; compel

oversight
The responsibility of Congress to keep an eye on agencies in the federal bureaucracy to ensure that their behavior conforms to its wishes. Perhaps not surprisingly, many see this function as taking a more partisan flavor in recent years—particularly when one party controls Congress and the other the White House.

PATHWAY OF ACTION

FIXING OUR ROADS AND BRIDGES

With upwards of 4 million miles of roads and nearly 600,000 bridges, no other nation boasts a ground transportation infrastructure like the United States. It's not even close. The highway system has been a key ingredient in economic growth; it has made the U.S. strong and vibrant. The problem is that many of the nation's highways and bridges were built decades ago – many after World War II – and today are in disrepair. A quick fix is out of the question and with Congress seemingly unable to come together, the problem has gotten worse.

The snag, of course, is how to pay for it. Historically, a tax on gas at the pump helped fund the highway bill. The more you drove – and the more you used the roads and bridges – the more you pay. But with cars getting more miles per gallon and with a growing list of needed repairs, the gas tax does not provide enough. Conservatives in Congress have argued that the gas tax should not be increased, but instead new funds should come from cuts in other areas of government. Liberals balk at domestic cuts and also argue that hiking the gas tax would be wrong, as it is regressive (meaning that everyone, regardless of their income, pay the same tax). A better approach, they argue, would be to take money from the general fund (based mostly on income taxes). The outcome of this philosophical difference has been stalemate. At most, Congress passed a short-term, stopgap fix, leading to uncertainly and little real progress on the issue.

To the surprise of many, real change came in the spring of 2015 when Congress passed a $305 billion highway bill. It was less than the Obama Administration had in mind, but it was a five-year agreement, thus ending the process of "kicking the can down the road," as Obama referred to it. It was a rare example of compromise, too. Republicans were able to hold the line on any additional tax at the pump, and some of the money would come from cuts in domestic programs. But Democrats were able to keep those cuts at a modest level and to pull some of the money from the general fund. And of course there were sweeteners for both sides. One provision allowed states to repeal what some thought to be onerous burdens on farmers; another to improve child support enforcement for the benefit of struggling parents and their children; and several others to enhance small banks' ability to lend to businesses and families. Obama was able to secure the reauthorization of the Export-Import Bank, which he argued helps companies compete around the world.

This begs the question of why members of Congress seem unable to find compromise solutions on so many other issues. Perhaps this issue is unique because all voters, regardless of their partisanship, grimace at potholes, congestion and crumbling bridges. It is also likely that the old adage by the former Speaker of the House, Thomas "Tip" O'Neill that "all politics is local" echoed through the halls of Congress in the spring of 2015.

changes in regulations, programs, and activities; modify levels of funding (including cut funding altogether); and pass legislation to redirect the agency. Oversight is especially time-consuming and contentious in times of divided government (when the president is of one party and the opposition party controls at least one house of Congress).

THE IMPORTANCE OF COMMITTEE STAFF   Given the hectic schedules of members of Congress and the ever-growing complexity of policy alternatives, it should come as no surprise to learn that staffers do most of the committees' work. "Committee staff spend a lot of their time on policymaking activities," the political scientist David Vogler has noted. "They research issues and generate information relevant to administrative oversight; draft bills; prepare speeches, statements, and reports; organize and help run committee hearings; and sometimes engage directly in legislative bargaining."[13] Furthermore, the size of the committee staff—what some observers have termed the "unelected representatives"[14]—grew tremendously in the late twentieth century. In 1967, there were roughly 600 committee staffers at work on Capitol Hill, but in recent years their number had jumped to more than 3,000.[15] As for personal staff, each House member has about 15 employees, and each senator boasts about 34.

Organizing Congress: Political Parties and Leadership

6.4   Assess how political parties and leaders manage the legislative process while advancing their own initiatives.

One of the great ironies of our system of government is that the very organizations that the framers of our system feared the most – political parties – are today instrumental in helping the legislature work. James Madison wrote about the dangers of "factions" and George Washington used most of his farewell address to warn the nation about the emergence of political parties. And yet, within a few decades most understood that something was needed to organize the electoral and legislative processes – to help create unified action. Political parties served that role. Indeed, it is hard to imagine Congress or any legislature functioning without political parties.

Parties in the Legislatures

Parties in the legislature serve an orientation function—the job of familiarizing new members of Congress with the procedures, norms, and customs of the chamber. The job of legislating has always been difficult, but during the past few decades, it has become exceedingly complex. Being a good legislator requires a great deal of time and effort, and few prior positions can prepare anyone for a job as a member of Congress. Both parties conduct extensive orientation sessions for incoming members of Congress. These events often last several days and cover a range of topics. "Beyond the briefings on everything from setting up the office, ethics, legislative customs, and rules," note two scholars of the legislative process, "these orientations help break new representatives into the social fabric of the capital. Scores of receptions and dinners help newcomers feel welcome and at the same time socialize the new representative to the ways of the legislative world."[16]

Second, parties in the legislature set the agenda for the coming session and establish priorities. Each legislator comes to Washington with an agenda, a list of issues that he or she would like to address and in some way resolve. These issues originate with constituents, interest groups, and other elected officials, and they also reflect the convictions of the legislators themselves. Combined, this would make a long, dizzying array of topics. Parties allow rank-and-file members to express their concerns to the leadership, where they are prioritized into an agenda for the session. This process not only narrows the list but also focuses members' efforts on priority items. No longer, for example, are there 200 different members of the same party independently fighting for some type of prescription drug program but rather (or so the party leaders hope) 200 legislators working in a unified, synchronized effort toward a common goal.

Third, parties give their members an important time-saving tool when it comes to committee service and floor voting. Thousands of complex measures are introduced and considered each term. Expecting legislators to be fully informed on all, or even most, of these measures is simply impossible. Parties help legislators cut though the complex maze of initiatives by providing briefs and, more important, **voting cues**. Party leaders will often take positions on issues, thereby "suggesting" to other members of their party that they do the same. Members of Congress do not have to follow this cue from leadership, and occasionally, they do not—but quite often they do.

voting cues
Summaries encapsulating the informed judgment of others in the legislature; members of Congress rely on these to streamline the decision-making process.

Finally, parties organize the committee appointment process. We noted earlier that legislators try to sit on committees that cover topics of most importance to their constituents. This does not mean, however, that every committee assignment is equally desirable. Some committees, such as those dealing with the raising and distribution of money (Budget, Appropriations, Finance, and Ways and Means), are in more demand than others. There is an important pecking order. Party leaders handle the difficult and sometimes contentious chore of committee appointments—and being a "regular" who goes along with the leadership certainly helps a member get a choice assignment.

THE IMPORTANCE OF MAJORITY STATUS Beyond these organizing functions, another issue to consider is the majority or minority status of political parties. In each branch, there is a majority party and a minority party, determined by the number of legislators in each party. The majority party has many significant advantages. For one, the majority of members on all committees belong to the majority party. The majority party sets the ratio of party representation on each committee, which reflects the size of the majority it enjoys in that chamber, and it names the chair of each committee and subcommittee. And as we have discussed, the majority also manages the critically important Rules Committee in the House, thus controlling the flow of legislation to the floor.

The majority party selects the leaders in each chamber. The House elects a **Speaker**, who has a number of advantages, including the power of referral. These votes to "organize" the House, which are conducted as soon as each session of Congress convenes, are always along party lines, inevitably leading to the victory of someone from the majority party. Similarly, the Senate chooses a **majority leader**, who has many of the same advantages, although Senate tradition dictates that individual members have more leeway than House members to do what they please. Finally, given the advantages of majority status, external players—interest groups and the media, for example—are much more interested in their interactions with the majority party's members.

Speaker
The presiding officer of the House of Representatives, who is also the leader of the majority party in the House.

majority leader
The head of the majority party in the Senate; the second-highest-ranking member of the majority party in the House.

LEGISLATIVE PARTIES AND CHANGE There are numerous partisan-based groups in Congress, allowing members in each chamber to come together to promote issues of mutual concern. The term "caucus" can be a verb (working together to accomplish a common goal), and it is also a noun. Congressional caucuses are also sometimes called coalitions, study groups, and task forces. In brief, they are informal, voluntary groups of legislators who have enough in common to meet regularly. The goal is to share information and strategize on policy matters. For example, the Blue Dog Coalition, formed in 1994, is comprised of roughly 25 Democratic House members who are more conservative than average Democrats. This group played a critically important role in shaping health care reform legislation in 2009. By 2015, their numbers had shrunk to 14, however. On the other side, the Republican Study Committee is comprised of about 170 truly conservative House members. There are racial- and ethnic-based caucuses as well, most notably the Congressional Black Caucus and the Congressional Hispanic Conference. The number varies from session to session, but generally speaking there are at least a dozen such caucuses. There are no formal requirements that a member join a caucus; one might be a conservative Democrat but not belong to the Blue Dogs, for instance. But legislators have realized that there is power in numbers, and these sorts of groups are increasingly popular.

The largest caucus is the *party conference,* which is comprised of all members of a political party in each chamber. If a legislator ran for Congress under one of the two major parties, then he or she is automatically a member of that party's conference. At times, minor party legislators are allowed to join one of the conferences as well. For example, Democratic senators voted to allow Independent senator Joseph Lieberman of Connecticut and Democratic-Socialist Bernard Sanders of Vermont to join the Senate Democratic Conference in 2007, and they did the same for Angus King, an independent from Maine, in 2013. Members of the conference may disagree with their colleagues or the party leadership on any range of topics, but there is one vote deemed critical: Each member of the conference must support a fellow partisan for all leadership positions. For example, a member of the House Republican Conference would find himself in hot water (likely kicked out of the Conference) if he voted for a Democrat for the position of Speaker.

Legislators vote with their party on most matters. Party leaders *hope* that all in the conference will "stay the line," but traditionally, elected officials have been able to stray without serious repercussions. Still, the single best predictor of how legislators will vote on any given bill is their party affiliation. One way to assess the extent to which legislators vote with their fellow partisans is through **party unity scores**— measures of party unity based on a gauge of how often members of the same party stick together. Since 1954, there has been a clear pattern of greater unity, echoing what many see as an increasingly polarized Congress.

In fact, many are concerned that record levels of party polarization have made compromise—a mainstay of the legislative process—even more difficult. A series of high-profile retirements from the House and Senate underscored the problem. Two-term Democratic Senator Evan Bayh of Indiana, known for being a moderate, was direct in his rationale for stepping aside in 2010: "For some time, I have had a growing conviction that Congress is not operating as it should. There is too much partisanship and not enough progress—too much narrow ideology and not enough practical problem-solving. Even at a time of enormous challenge, the people's business is not being done."[17] (Surprising many, Bayh attempted to return to the Senate in the 2016 election but was defeated the by the Republican Todd Young.) New York City Congressman Gary Ackerman, who served in the House for 30 years, left for similar reasons in 2012: "It's a different era. People more than ever since I can remember are concerned about being out of step and out of line with their political party and won't cross over. There is nobody, man or woman, who wants to be left out, and people are fearful of that. People are fearful of their leadership as well."[18]

What does this brief discussion of the weight of partisanship say about the pathways of change? On the one hand, all other things being equal, an activist would surely find it more profitable to lobby and work with members of the majority party than with members of the minority party. In fact, most seasoned political activists consider it so important that the first step of their lobbying strategy is to focus on elections. But on the other hand, steadfast partisan allegiances in Congress—likely propelled by hardcore partisan activists, the reemergence of a partisan press, and maybe even geo-political sorting—seem to have created unprecedented levels of gridlock. Without a willingness to find common ground, little gets done in the legislature— even on matters of national concern. Speaking of the emerging crisis of huge federal deficits, former GOP Senate leader Alan K. Simpson of Wyoming noted, "There isn't a single sitting member of Congress—not one—that doesn't know exactly where we're headed. And to use the politics of fear and division and hate on each other—we are

party unity scores
Various measures of how often legislators of the same party stick together. When these measures are high, the level of bipartisanship is low. In recent years, party unity scores have been at record high levels.

Historically, both parties boasted members that were considered "centrists." Often legislation hinged on the willingness of these lawmakers to back a measure; they carried a great deal of sway. In recent years, however, there are fewer and fewer moderates. Pictured here are a few of the Blue Dog Democrats.

■ *Why are there a shrinking number of middle-of-the-road legislators when most Americans are still centrists?*

at a point right now where it doesn't make a damn whether you're a Democrat or a Republican if you've forgotten you're an American."[19]

> POLL Which do you think is more important in a politician: the ability to compromise to get things done, or a willingness to stand firm in support of principles?

Legislative Leadership

The framers of the Constitution believed that giving one legislator, or a group of legislators, more power in the system would upset what should be an enlightened, deliberative process. The Constitution states that each chamber will have "leaders": in the House, a Speaker (the title *speaker* was used in the British House of Commons and in the colonial assemblies), and in the Senate, a president. The framers assumed these posts were meant to aid organization; each was to be a mere parliamentarian who structured debate, made sure that rules of order were followed, guaranteed equal access, and so forth. Leaders were to be impartial. And this is precisely what occurred for the first few decades; legislative leaders simply helped create an orderly process. It was rare, in fact, for leaders of either chamber to even cast a vote.

All that changed in the 1820s. First, the election of 1824, leading to the so-called Corrupt Bargain, reinvigorated party spirit in the United States, and partisanship soon intensified in both houses of Congress. Second, Henry Clay of Kentucky had been elected Speaker in 1823. An affable, whiskey-drinking, card-playing master of politicking in the Washington boardinghouses where members lived during sessions of Congress, Clay was also aggressive, outspoken, ambitious, and highly partisan. Speaker of the House Clay, in fact, contributed enormously to building what eventually became the Whig Party, and the role of Speaker as moderator faded into the history books.[20] In the Senate, the move to aggressive leadership happened more slowly, given the smaller size of the chamber and most senators' insistence on their greater political independence. However, within two decades, the Senate also developed aggressive, partisan leadership.

At the beginning of each legislative term—that is, at each two-year interval—every member of the House casts a vote for a Speaker. Since the 1820s, the winner of these internal elections has always been a member of the majority party. It has become customary for the members of each party to decide on their choice for Speaker in advance and to expect every member to vote for that person. Because deviations from this party line vote never occur, the majority party's candidate always prevails.

Rather than having one leader, a hierarchy of leadership now exists for both parties in both chambers. In the House, the most powerful person after the Speaker is the majority leader, followed by the majority **whip**—an assistant to the majority leader responsible for garnering support for the party's agenda and for making sure that the party leadership has an accurate count of the votes both for and against different pieces of legislation. In brief, majority leaders and whips work with the Speaker to coordinate strategy and to advance the party's policy goals. If members of the party are inclined to vote against a measure deemed important to the leadership, it is the whip's job to help those legislators think otherwise—that is, to "whip" them into line. They also have the added responsibility of passing information along to other members and of working to ensure that members of their party show up for important floor votes.

The Constitution stipulates that the vice president of the United States shall be president of the Senate. Under the Constitution, however, the vice president can vote only to break a tie. The first vice president, John Adams, came into office expecting that even if he did not vote, he would also be able to take a leading role in Senate deliberations—and he was bitterly disappointed and offended when the senators told him that all he could do was preside, in silence. "The most insignificant office that the mind of man ever devised" was Adams's sour verdict on the vice presidency.

When the vice president is not present—which is usually the case except on solemn occasions or when a tie vote is expected—the Senate is formally led by its elected president pro tempore (*pro tempore* is a Latin phrase meaning "for the time being" and is usually abbreviated to *pro tem*). Through tradition, this position has become purely ceremonial and is always bestowed on the most senior member of the majority party. The real job of moderating debate in the Senate usually falls to a junior member of the majority party, chosen for that assignment on a rotating basis. The job confers little real power. Much more power in the Senate rests with the majority leader. In some ways similar to the Speaker in the House, the majority leader of the Senate is elected and is the head of his or her party. Correspondingly, the Senate **minority leader** is the top dog of the minority party. Each has an assistant leader and a whip, charged with much the same responsibilities as those in the House. There are also conference chairs for both parties in the Senate.

LEADERSHIP POWERS   What makes legislative leaders powerful? The answer is a mix of formal and informal powers. Speakers of the House refer legislation to committee, preside over floor proceedings, appoint members to conference and other joint committees, and set the rules of how legislation will be debated and how long such debates might last. They establish the floor agenda, meaning that they decide which bills will—and will not—be scheduled for consideration on the floor. These are weighty formal advantages, but they are just the beginning. The Speaker can also use the force of personality and prestige to persuade other members of the legislature to go along with his or her wishes. Great Speakers have been able to merge their formal and informal powers. The ability of the Speaker to attract national press attention has become another powerful tool. Few Speakers were more adept at seizing national press coverage, and thus enhancing their power base, than Georgia Republican Newt Gingrich in his first term (1995–1997) and Nancy Pelosi (2007–2011).

Great as the powers of the Speaker may be, however, they are not absolute. On a number of occasions, Speakers have been humbled by their fellow legislators. Although Newt Gingrich was a powerful Speaker at first, many members of his own party conference soon thought him too heavy-handed. He also lost favor with the public because of his confrontational ways and his advocacy of heavy cuts in popular government programs. When challenged for the post after the 1998 midterm election, in which the Republicans lost seats, Gingrich resigned from the House. John Boehner, who served as Speaker from 2010 to 2015, faced the daunting challenge of pulling

whips

Assistants to House and Senate leaders, responsible for drumming up support for legislation and for keeping count of how members plan to vote on different pieces of legislation. Given the rise of partisanship in Congress, the job of the whips has become much more intense.

minority leader

The leading spokesperson and legislative strategist for the minority party in the House or the Senate.

together hard-core-conservative and moderate Republicans to both oppose Barack Obama's agenda and also move the government forward. A fair assessment would be that he had mixed success.

In the Senate, the majority leader's powers are broad but not as extensive as the Speaker's. Majority leaders have great influence on committee assignments, on the scheduling of floor debate, on the selection of conference committee members, and in picking their own conference's leaders. Yet majority leaders have less sway in the Senate for several reasons: first, because of the institution's somewhat different internal rules; second, because of the long-standing notion that the Senate is the "upper chamber," filled with more experienced and higher-status politicians; and third, because Senate norms dictate a more egalitarian process. In other words, Senate rules protect each member's right to participate far more than House rules do.

Organizing Congress: Rules and Norms

6.5 Show how the rules and norms of behavior help ensure a more orderly, efficient legislative process.

The final organizing elements in any legislative body are its formal and informal rules of behavior. Let's begin with the formal regulations. The Constitution states that each house establishes its own rules. Not surprisingly, given the different sizes of the two chambers, the House has a longer set of rules than the Senate. It is difficult to list all the regulations that structure proceedings in the House, but a few of the most significant deal with how measures proceed from committee to floor consideration and with the actions that might be taken to modify a measure once it reaches the floor. Scheduling refers to floor (full-house) consideration of committee-approved measures. All bills approved at the committee level must be scheduled for consideration on the floor. This might seem a straightforward matter, but many issues come into play with this process, including when—if ever—the bill will be considered. If a measure finds itself on a floor calendar, the rules regarding amendments become important, as noted earlier.

The Filibuster

The Senate is somewhat less bound by formal rules than the House, but this does not mean that anything goes. Three formal rules stand out as most significant. First, leaders of both parties in the Senate quite often will informally negotiate the terms for debate and amendment of a bill scheduled to be sent to the floor. This is called unanimous consent, because all senators must be in agreement. The idea is to try to establish some limits and control in order to expedite floor actions and to impose some predictability. To block legislation or confirmation votes, Senate minorities may resort to use of the **filibuster**—an unlimited debate in which one senator or a group of senators keeps talking without interruption unless three-fifths of the chamber (60 senators) votes to end the discussion.

Conservative southern Democrats were particularly known for filibustering civil rights bills in the second half of the twentieth century. The longest filibustering speech in American history occurred in 1957, when Senator Strom Thurmond of South Carolina (a Democrat who later became a Republican) held the floor for more than 24 hours in an effort to block a vote on what became the Civil Rights Act of 1957. More recently, members of both parties have threatened to use this maneuver to stall the approval of controversial legislation and judicial nominations.

To some observers, use of the filibuster is a clear violation of majority rule. However, where you stand on the strategic use of the filibuster is most likely a function of the issue under consideration. When the filibuster was used to block civil rights legislation in the 1950s and 1960s, Democrats argued that it thwarted the majority will. Republicans

filibuster

A process in the U.S. Senate used to block or delay voting on proposed legislation or on an appointment of a judge or other official by talking continuously. Sixty senators must vote to end a filibuster. With a hyper-partisan legislature, the requirement to get 60 votes to move things along has created a very slow process. Some would suggest this rule worsens legislative gridlock.

The longest speech in the history of the U.S. Senate was made by Strom Thurmond of South Carolina. Thurmond, a Democrat who later became a Republican, spoke for 24 hours and 18 minutes during a filibuster against passage of the Civil Rights Act of 1957.

■ *Are filibusters undemocratic, or are they an important procedural tool?*

cloture

A rule declaring the end of a debate in the Senate. In most instances it takes 60 votes for cloture, meaning that even a minority of senators can hold up legislation.

were outraged by the widespread use of the filibuster during much of George W. Bush's administration, but when Barack Obama took over as president, they seemed quite comfortable with it on a wide range of policy matters and appointments. Since then, the Democrats have voiced outrage over the widespread use of this rule, and others, to slow the pace of legislation and the confirmation of judicial appointments.

Without a unanimous-consent agreement, extended debates can become a problem. A filibuster can be used, but another delay variant is to switch control of floor discussion from one member to another, thereby postponing a vote. The goal is to tie things up until the other side backs down or decides to compromise. The tool used to cut off these debates is called **cloture**. Here, three-fifths of the senators (60) must vote to end the discussion of a bill—that is, "to invoke cloture." This rule can be used for general floor debate or to end a filibuster. Still another variation is called a hold: A senator signals to the rest of the chamber that it would be pointless to bring a piece of legislation to the floor, because he or she intends to use delaying tactics to stave off a final vote. A hold can be trumped, of course, with 60 votes for cloture.

In 2005, frustrated by what they perceived to be unreasonable delaying tactics by the Democrats in the Senate with respect to the confirmation of court nominees, Republicans responded by threatening the "nuclear option." The plan was for the Senate president to rule that the U.S. Constitution prohibited filibusters against judicial nominations, and then a vote would be held on an appeal. If that happened, only 51 votes would be needed to uphold the ruling. A few years later, as the Democratic Conference hovered around the 60-member mark (the so-called magic number), the validity of procedural rules to delay legislation were again called into question. In 2010, as the fate of health care reform and numerous appointments remained uncertain, Vice President Joe Biden suggested a drastic change is needed: "As long as I have served, I've never seen, as my uncle once said, the Constitution stood on its head as they've done. This is the first time every single solitary decision has required 60 senators. No democracy has survived needing a supermajority."[21]

Change to the filibuster came in fall of 2013. Some 52 Democratic and independent senators voted to alter the chamber's rules regarding the approval of executive and judicial nominations. The threshold for cloture would drop from 60 to 51 votes. The move did not include approval for Supreme Court nominees, but it was widely viewed as controversial and certainly a sign of the times. As the Republicans took control of the Senate in 2015, they kept the 2013 rules in place.

UNWRITTEN RULES You might think that informal rules or legislative norms and customs are less significant than the formal regulations. In fact, informal rules likely do *more* to structure the day-to-day legislative process than any other organizing mechanism. More than 40 years ago, a distinguished political scientist, Donald Matthews, noted the power and importance of "folkways" in the legislature.[22] While the times have changed, much of what Matthews suggested still applies today.

Seniority stipulates that the longer a member of either chamber has served, the greater deference and the more power he or she should have. Such senior members usually deserve respect because of their long service and accumulated wisdom, but Senate traditions normally also grant them more power in the chamber. It is no longer a hard-and-fast rule that the longest-serving member of a committee becomes its chair (or, if in the minority party, its ranking minority member), but it still occurs. Senior members are often given a greater share of their appropriation requests than a novice, and they are more likely to have their bills at least considered by a committee. In recent years, junior members perceived to be vulnerable to an election defeat are helped by the party leadership, but generally speaking, seniority still matters.

Along with seniority, there is a powerful apprenticeship norm. In the past, novice legislators were expected to work hard, get along, be deferential and polite, keep their mouths shut most of the time, and study the legislative process. They were to be "workhorses" instead of "show horses." This was true even when House members moved to the Senate; junior senators were expected to be seen and not heard. In recent years, this norm, like that of seniority, has been observed less and less. Democratic Senator Al Franken of Minnesota was a particularly outspoken critic of several GOP senators in his very first year in the chamber, and the same might be said of Republican Senator Rand Paul of Kentucky. In fact, in some instances, party leaders have advised first-term senators to speak up and make a name for themselves. Texas GOP Senator Ted Cruz received a great deal of attention during his first session in Congress for his outspoken behavior and occasionally bombastic rhetoric. At times, Cruz's verbal assaults were aimed at his Republican colleagues!

Civility is another powerful norm in both chambers. Regardless of party, ideology, or position on issues, it is expected that members accord each other respect and a high, even exaggerated level of courtesy. Even when tempers rise, politeness is to remain. "Political disagreements should not influence personal feelings,"[23] suggests Matthews. By tradition, a senator or a representative refers even to his or her bitter political rivals and personal enemies as "the distinguished gentleman [or lady] from" whatever the state might be. When members publicly lapse from this norm of civility, they are expected to apologize, which they very often do. The norm of civility extends to presidents when they formally address Congress. It is taken for granted, for example, that when a president enters the House of Representatives, all members stand and applaud. That is why so many people were shocked on the evening of September 9, 2009, when South Carolina Congressman Joe Wilson shouted "You lie!" at Barack Obama. The president had been giving an address to a joint session of Congress on the subject of health care reform. Later that evening, Wilson issued a formal apology, which President Obama accepted. However, that did not stop Wilson's House colleagues from issuing a formal reprimand. As perhaps a sign of changing times, within a matter of days Wilson had raised over $2 million dollars for his reelection.

seniority

Length of time served in a chamber of the legislature. Members with greater seniority have traditionally been granted greater power.

specialization

A norm suggesting that members of both chambers have extensive knowledge in a particular policy area. One member might specialize in military matters, while another might focus on agricultural issues. This norm serves the needs of the full chamber.

reciprocity/logrolling

Supporting a legislator's bill in exchange for support of one's own bill.

earmarks/pork-barrel legislation

Legislation that benefits one state or district; also called *particularized legislation*. For example, a legislator might work diligently to get federal monies for the construction of a new stretch of an interstate highway.

Specialization is a norm that suggests members of both chambers are expected to become well versed in a small number of policy areas. Specialization allows members to defer to their colleagues on some policy matters rather than try to bone up on every issue that might come before the legislature. In this, there is an expectation of **reciprocity**. That is, members are expected to support each other's initiatives on a "you scratch my back, and I'll scratch yours" basis. According to Matthews, "Every senator, at one time or another, is in the position to help out a colleague. The folkways of the Senate hold that a senator should provide this assistance and that he [or she] be repaid in kind."[24] This is often called **logrolling**, which means that members reciprocally exchange support, often on **earmarks**, or what is sometimes termed **pork-barrel legislation**. *Pork* is slang for particularized assistance: federal money and programs that largely or wholly benefit just one state or congressional district. Every member wants to "bring home the bacon" to his or her district, and the constituents expect it. One way to get it is through logrolling. For instance, a House member from Tennessee might agree to support a New York City member's appropriation to build a commuter rail station in her district in return for her support for a new stretch of interstate through his part of Tennessee.

How a Bill Becomes a Law

6.6 Outline the process by which a bill becomes a law.

Bills must cross many hurdles in order to become law. Here, we'll walk through this process in greater detail. Please keep in mind that this outline is a theoretical model and that in practice, things are rarely this neat. Also, the process is similar in both chambers, but it is not exactly the same. What follows is a general pattern (see Figure 6.4).

General Steps

Step 1. Introduction of a Bill. The idea (and frequently the language) of a bill can originate from many sources. Often, an administrative agency will draw up a bill. Interest groups also often have a hand, both in the broad outlines of a measure and in its exact wording. Yet to begin the actual process of legislating, a member of Congress must always introduce a bill in one chamber of that body. This person becomes the **bill sponsor**, the official "parent" of the legislation. With the exception of tax bills, which under the Constitution can only be introduced in the House of Representatives, any member of the national legislature can introduce any measure he or she sees fit.

Step 2. Referral. Soon after a bill is introduced, it is referred to a committee (occasionally, to two or more committees), and from there, it is usually sent to the appropriate subcommittee.

Step 3. Committee Consideration. Most measures go no further than the subcommittee level. As we've seen, hearings are held, the language is sometimes modified (in the markup process), and if a bill is approved at this level, it is reported back to the full committee. Additional changes are sometimes made at the full-committee level, but the committee often will simply accept or reject the measure offered by the subcommittee.

Step 4. Rules for Floor Action. Any bill approved by a full committee is sent to the floor for full-chamber consideration. In the House of Representatives, however, a required stop is the Rules Committee. Here, many procedural issues are set, such as the length of time the bill will be debated and the types of amendments, if any, that can be accepted. Once again, the majority party controls the Rules Committee. There is no similar procedure in the Senate.

bill sponsor

The member of Congress who introduces a bill.

FIGURE 6.4 How a Bill Becomes a Law

Some would say that the system of checks and balances weeds out unnecessary measures, but others argue that the system is too cumbersome and that it makes change too difficult.

■ *Does this complex process serve the nation well, or does it inhibit needed change?*

How a Bill Becomes a Law: Every Student Succeeds Act of 2015

This bill amends the Elementary and Secondary Education Act of 1965 (ESEA), by addressing issues such as accountability and testing requirements, distribution requirements for grants, fiscal accountability requirements, and the evaluation of teachers.

Trigger

No Child Left Behind was a federal education reform bill that was signed into law by President George W. Bush in 2001. The bill had wide bipartisan support and was actually sponsored in the Senate by Democrat Edward Kennedy. But over the last several years many on both sides of the political isle have argued that the law shifted too much control and responsibility to the federal level. Many believed that states and local communities should have greater control of education issues, particular how to evaluate teachers and improve schools.

Step 1. Introduction

House: On May 7, 2015, Minnesota Republican John Kline, chairman of the House Committee on Education and the Workforce, pushes his own bill in the House of Representatives.

Step 1. Introduction

Senate: On April 30, 2015, Tennessee Republican Senator Lamar Alexander introduces Every Student Succeeds Act.

Step 2. Referral and Committee Action

House: House Committee on Education and the Workforce considers the bill in the spring of 2015.

Senate: The Senate Committee on Health, Education, Labor, and Pensions considers the bill in the spring of 2015.

Step 3. Floor Action

House: After a series of debates and minor amendments, the bill passes in the House, 243-to-18, on November 17, 2015.

Step 3. Floor Action

Senate: After some floor debate and a minor amendment, the bill passes in the Senate, 81-to-17, on November 16, 2015.

Step 4. Resolving Difference Between Bills

Members of both chambers are appointed to a conference committee. Their chore is to hammer out differences and emerge with one bill. They do so and on November 30, 2015, a conference report is filed, and the measure is sent to both chambers for consideration. The House approves the measure on December 2, 2015, in a 359-to-64 vote. The Senate approves the bill on December 9, 2015, on a 85-to-12 vote.

Step 5. Presidential Signature

President Barack Obama signs the Every Student Succeeds Act of 2015 into law on December 10, 2015. At the signing ceremony the president comments, "There is nothing more essential to living up to the ideals of this nation than to make sure every child is able to live up to their God given potential." At the ceremony he is surrounded by many Democrats and Republicans, as well as educators, parents, and students.

Step 5. **Floor Consideration.** This is where every member of the chamber has an opportunity to express his or her support (or lack of support) for the bill. Most measures do not entail a lengthy floor debate. The reason for this is that most measures are low-profile, highly technical matters (such as adjustments to complex statutes) that draw little public interest. When the public becomes involved, however, floor debate can be intense.

Step 6. **Conference Committee.** For a bill to become a law, an identical version must be approved in both houses. Measures passed in one house but not the other house are called one-house bills. If the other chamber has also passed an identical version of the bill, it goes to the president to be signed—or to face a veto (see Step 7). Sometimes a similar (but not identical) bill is passed in the other chamber. To reconcile differences, a conference is created. Three outcomes from conference deliberations are possible. First, one of the versions of the bills might be accepted as the final agreement. When this occurs, the chamber accepting changes has to vote on the measure again (as each chamber must approve exactly the same wording). Second, some sort of compromise position might be crafted, making it necessary for both houses to vote again on the compromise version. Finally, compromise might not be possible (this often happens when Congress is about to adjourn), and each measure remains a one-house bill.

Step 7. **Presidential Action.** When the president is of the same party as the majority in both houses, it is rare that important measures are approved without the president's blessing. (If they are, it is a sure sign that the president is in deep political trouble.) Even when there is a divided government, most bills approved by Congress do wind up winning presidential support. A bill becomes a law when the president signs it. If 10 days pass without the president having signed the bill—a rare occurrence that generally indicates the president does not like the bill but does not want to cause an uproar by vetoing it—the bill becomes law. Or the president can veto the bill, sending it back to the Congress. When the president does not sign a bill within 10 days and Congress goes on recess during this time, the bill does not go into effect. This is called a pocket veto. Vetoes have recently become quite rare, especially compared to the number of measures that win presidential approval. Given a president's grave concern about having his or her veto overridden, when the president does reject an important bill, it certainly makes news.

Step 8. **Overriding a Presidential Veto.** Presidential vetoes are always accompanied by a written message—a statement to Congress that says why the measure was rejected. The measure can still become a law if two-thirds of each house of Congress votes to override the veto.

Unorthodox Lawmaking

The steps outlined previously explain the process used throughout most of our nation's history for a bill to become law. However, a number of adjustments in recent decades continue to transform the lawmaking process. Many have documented these changes, but at the forefront of this research has been UCLA scholar Barbara Sinclair. In a series of important books and articles, Sinclair documented the routes of "unorthodox lawmaking."[25] She notes, for example, that multiple referrals are increasingly common, and there are occasions when bills will bypass committees altogether. For instance, at the start of the 111th Congress, Democratic House leaders pushed for fast action on several high-profile measures, including the Lilly Ledbetter Fair Pay Act, a bill that made it easier for plaintiffs to sue employers over pay discrimination, and thus bypassed the committee stage.

It is also increasingly common for each chamber to pass generic bills, knowing that the true details of the legislation will be ironed-out in conference committee. In a very real sense, these bills are written and deliberated on in the conference committee, not in the standing committees in both houses. Another approach to reconcile differences, dubbed "ping-ponging," is for each chamber to make amendments back and forth until disagreements are resolved. On occasion, particularly at the end of the legislative session when there is a push to tie up loose ends, bills can "ping-pong" back and forth between the House and Senate on an hourly basis. Omnibus measures, where one bill contains numerous issues and topics, are also no longer rare. Nor are congressional-executive summits, where congressional leadership works with the president and his staff to forge acceptable language—even before any sort of committee deliberations or markup occur.

The traditional route also implies that bills that do not receive approval from a committee are doomed. While this is generally the case, there are a few options available to dislodge a bill, if the committee refuses to report it to the full chamber. One of these methods is a dislodge petition, which is designed to overrule the committee leadership (and often the majority party leadership). Here, a House member must gather 218 signatures from other members (a majority of the members) and then the bill will eventually be sent to the floor for consideration. A second, more controversial method of dislodging a bill is for the Rules Committee to simply discharge a bill without committee approval, to bypass reluctant committee chairs.

Why have these changes to the traditional lawmaking process occurred? Sinclair and others argue that the increased partisan polarization of Congress has made the traditional legislative process more difficult. There seems to be less and less common ground. Majority party leaders have been granted greater leeway from their members to insert themselves more directly into key stages of the process with the goal of producing results, and there is no question that *both* parties are using unorthodox approaches to advance their initiatives in the contemporary Congress.

Emergency Legislation

The process of passing legislation can be lengthy. Occasionally, however, emergencies arise during which the legislature is called upon to act quickly and to condense the process into a few days.

Such was the case with the Emergency Economic Stabilization Act of 2008, the so-called Wall Street Bailout Bill. By mid-September of that year, the subprime mortgage crisis had reached a critical stage, with then Secretary of the Treasury Henry Paulson openly concerned about an imminent crisis and the necessity for immediate action. Americans were told this was the most serious economic crisis since the Great Depression.

Paulson, in close consultation with Federal Reserve Chairman Ben Bernanke, proposed a plan under which the U.S. Treasury would acquire up to $700 billion worth of mortgage-backed securities. By doing so, they argued, banks would again start lending money. The plan was backed by President George W. Bush, and negotiations began with leaders in Congress to draft the appropriate legislation. President Bush and Secretary Paulson told the public and members of Congress that a quick agreement was vital; it had to happen within just a few days.

Congress acted quickly, but not as fast as the Bush administration had hoped. On the one hand, many legislators understood that a massive governmental intervention was the only hope to stave off a financial collapse. On the other hand, many also knew that average citizens saw the proposed measure as helping the business elite. In short, the scheme was very unpopular back home.

Early measures passed in the Senate, but the House balked. The election was only weeks away: Every House member would be up for reelection, but only one-third of the Senate would face the voters. The process unfolded precisely as the framers of our system envisioned, with the Senate better able to rise above public opinion and the House seemingly beholden to it. Through a great deal of persuasion, negotiation, compromise, and added "sweeteners" (elements that aided particular districts), the measure passed on October 3, 2008.

A few lessons can be drawn from this issue. First, when emergencies arise, Congress can move quickly, but not nearly as rapidly as the executive branch can. This, too, is what the framers envisioned—immediate action from the executive branch, but greater deliberation in the legislature. Second, members of Congress face particularized constituencies. What is good for the nation might be unpopular in specific districts or states. The president, on the other hand, faces a national constituency. Third, the Senate, with 6-year terms and rotation, seems better able than the House to confront important but unpopular measures. Finally, there is no easy answer to the age-old question of whether legislators should be delegates, trustees, or something in between.

Making Laws: A Summary

While the number varies somewhat from year to year, roughly speaking, in the 2 years that any Congress sits, more than 10,000 measures are introduced. Of these, roughly 400 become law.[26] Sometimes the percentage is even lower. In the 113th Congress, for example, some 10,637 bills were introduced but only 296 became law. That is under 3 percent![27] Most of these are low-profile, technical adjustments to existing laws; only a handful of truly significant measures gets passed each session.

The road from introduction to presidential signature is long and difficult—deliberately so. On the one hand, we might suggest that the difficulty of the process implies a shortcoming in the legislative process: The will of the people should be more easily and more quickly expressed through the national legislature. Partisan polarization surely makes things even more difficult, as has been suggested throughout this chapter. On the other hand, many people would agree that the process *should* be difficult, and that there *should* be many potholes, roadblocks, and detours along the pathway. They would argue that the federal government must act cautiously when deciding the laws citizens must obey. That, after all, was the intent of the framers of our Constitution.

Who Sits in Congress?

6.7 Determine whether members of Congress mirror America's demographic diversity and why this matters.

As we have emphasized in discussing representative democracy, *representation* means that someone speaks and works on behalf of others. Perhaps this process can be enhanced when the representative understands the issues and concerns that confront a district, and perhaps this is more likely to happen when he or she reflects the demographic makeup of the constituency of the district. Many people feel that, at the very least, a legislative body should look like the nation as a whole. According to this viewpoint, race, ethnicity, gender, sexual orientation, occupation, age, and other demographics matter. This preference for *symbolic* or *descriptive representation* is the logic behind the drive, discussed earlier in this chapter, to create majority-minority districts. In this section, we examine some demographic characteristics of the Americans who have been members of Congress.

Gender

The first woman elected to the House of Representatives was Jeannette Rankin of Montana in 1916. She was elected even before women nationally got the right to vote under the Nineteenth Amendment. A peace activist, Rankin voted against declaring World War I. She was also in the House in 1941, where she cast the only vote against a declaration of war after Pearl Harbor. The first woman to serve in the Senate was Rebecca Felton from Georgia in 1922, who was appointed to fill a vacant seat. There were very few female members of either chamber during the following

Even though the number of women in Congress has grown in recent years, their numbers lag far behind men. Pictured here is the House Woman's Soft Ball Team and their captain, Minority Leader Nancy Pelosi (D-California), in 2015. They are celebrating a victory over a team comprised of female journalists—and of course any time politicians can beat the media, it's time to rejoice!

■ *Do you think more women will be sent to public office in the coming years?*

decades—about a dozen in the House and just two in the Senate. By the 1950s, there were 17 female national legislators in House and Senate combined, and that number actually dipped during the 1960s and 1970s.

Prior to the 2010 midterm election, there had been a steady increase in the number of women serving in Congress since the 1980s, with a big jump that came after the 1992 election (called by journalists the "Year of the Woman" because of the large number of women who ran for office that year). In the 114th Congress, there was a record number of women, including 20 in the U.S. Senate (equal to the total number of women who had served in all the years before 1978) and 85 in the House of Representatives. After the 2016 elections, 104 women (78 Democrats, 26 Republicans) will serve in the 115th Congress. Some 21 of these women will serve in the Senate (16 Democrats, 5 Republicans). There will also be 37 women of color in Congress, a record number. Women fill 24.4 percent of the 7,383 available seats nationwide for state legislatures and 22.5 percent of the seats nationwide for state senates (see Figure 6.5). Although this is slightly higher than the national figures of 19.4 percent and 20 percent for the House and the Senate respectively, it still appears that parity is impeded on both a local and national level.[28]

Race and Ethnicity

The picture for African Americans in Congress in some ways resembles that for women, and in other ways it is even more vexing. The first black elected to the House of Representatives was Joseph Hayne Rainey of South Carolina in 1870.

FIGURE 6.5 Percentages Of Women In State Legislatures

▣ *Why do you suppose these figures are generally higher than in Congress, and what would explain regional difference? Why are the percentages so much higher in the West?*

SOURCE: http://www.ncsl.org/legislators-staff/legislators/womens-legislative-network/women-in-state-legislatures-for-2015.aspx.

| 5–14.9% | 15–24.9% | 25–34.9% | 35–44.9% |

Rainey was a slave as a child and was requisitioned for labor by the Confederacy during the Civil War. He escaped on a blockade-runner ship and made his way to Bermuda, a British colony where slavery had been abolished. After the Civil War, he returned to South Carolina and began working with the Republican Party. He was sent to the House after a special election in 1870, where he served for 8 years.[29] The first African American was also elected to the Senate in 1870: Hiram Rhodes Revels, representing Mississippi. Interestingly, he was elected by the "reconstructed" state legislature to complete Jefferson Davis's unfinished term. (Davis had left his place in the U.S. Senate to become president of the Confederacy.) After serving only 1 year, Revels left the Senate to become president of Alcorn State College.[30]

In all, only nine African Americans have ever served in the Senate. In the House, just over 120 African Americans have served. These are discouraging statistics, but as with women, the numbers have improved since the 1980s. In recent years, about 40 members of the House have been black—roughly 9 percent of the chamber. Given that African Americans make up about 13 percent of the national population, we might say that the situation is improving.

Hispanic Americans (Latinos) are the fastest-growing demographic group in America and have recently succeeded African Americans as the nation's largest minority group. It is estimated that by 2028, there will be roughly 60 million Hispanic Americans, making up some 18 percent of the population. The U.S. Census Bureau estimates that Hispanics have accounted for 40 percent of the nation's population growth since 1990. Their representation in Congress, however, has lagged far behind. Today, about 30 members of the national legislature, or about 7 percent, are of Hispanic descent.

Why are so few women and minority citizens elected to Congress? One reason is that historically, fewer women and minorities have sought office, likely because of a wide range of factors, including biases in the campaign process, discriminatory voter attitudes, and lags in the number of these groups who entered professions—especially the law—that have typically led to a political career. For whatever reason, some Americans still find it difficult to vote for minority and female candidates. One prominent elections scholar has observed that one way "to achieve fairer and more equal representation for minorities is to eliminate the allegiances and attitudes (some consider them biases and prejudices) that favor the majority."[31]

A related explanation lies in the nature of our electoral system and specifically in our reliance on single-member districts. There is no requirement in the Constitution that specific districts be drawn within each state, only (as noted earlier) that states receive an overall number of representatives relative to that state's population. We might consider an at-large system, under which states that have two or more representatives would have no distinct districts: Voters would vote for at-large candidates, and these candidates would get into the House in descending order according to the number of votes they won. Alternatively, large states like California and New York could be divided into a number of large districts, each of which would elect a group of at-large representatives. Under such a system, if a minority group makes up one-fifth of a state's population, which is often the case, and that state has been allotted 10 seats in the House of Representatives chosen at large, we might expect that more minority candidates—perhaps two—would be elected. When one candidate is selected from a single district, however, that same 20 percent minority group is simply drowned out by the majority. And if attitudes about supporting minority candidates do not change, the prospects for that group gaining a voice in the legislature will be small.

Income and Occupation

When it comes to income and occupation, we find that, once again, the national legislature does not reflect America very well. Members of Congress are far better educated and far wealthier than the average American (Table 6.4). (And that is what the framers of the Constitution—themselves drawn from the elite—expected.) The Senate is often called the "millionaires' club." By 2014, it was reported that a majority of members of Congress were millionaires. Some 268 had a net worth of over $1 million. Perhaps surprisingly for some readers, the same report found that there was not much difference between the two parties—congressional Democrats had a median net worth of $1.04 million, as compared to about $1 million for Republicans.[32] There are, however, significant differences between the Senate and the House. In the former, the average net worth is nearly $3 million, and

TABLE 6.4   10 Richest Members of Congress, 2014

Darrell Issa (R-Calif)	$436,500,015
Jared Polis (D-Colo)	$387,864,231
Mark Warner (D-Va)	$242,889,630
John K Delaney (D-Md)	$214,902,588
Michael McCaul (R-Texas)	$160,340,931
Dave Trott (R-Mich)	$113,844,576
Vernon Buchanan (R-Fla)	$106,912,071
Nancy Pelosi (D-Calif)	$101,273,023
Dianne Feinstein (D-Calif)	$94,202,571
Richard Blumenthal (D-Conn)	$81,745,158

SOURCE: Open Secrets: http://www.opensecrets.org/pfds/.

TIMELINE

Voting Rights Act of 1965

During any Congress, thousands of bills are introduced, but only a handful of these measures are passed and sent to the president for signature. Of those bills, most are non-controversial, often technical adjustments to existing legislation. In other words, major pieces of legislation—measures that dramatically impact public policy and the world we live in—are very rare. In fact, some would suggest that there have only been a few dozen major acts by Congress, and most of these occurred in the 19th century. All would agree, however, that at the top of any list of major legislation would be the efforts by Congress in the 1960s to ease the legacy of discrimination: the Civil Rights Act of 1964 and the Voting Rights Act of 1965. This timeline charts the latter—the move by Congress to ensure that all Americans would have equal access to the voting booth. What made the Voting Rights Act so momentous, and also so difficult to pass, was not only the opposition of many legislators from the South. Rather, throughout most of our nation's history, issues of voting rights and regulations were left to the states. This bill helped ease discrimination, but it also dramatically changed the nature of federalism. As you will see below, the driving force behind this change was the groundswell of grassroots activism. It is often said that members of Congress ignore the public, but of course that is not true. They listen, often very closely. The call for change became deafening by the mid-1960s.

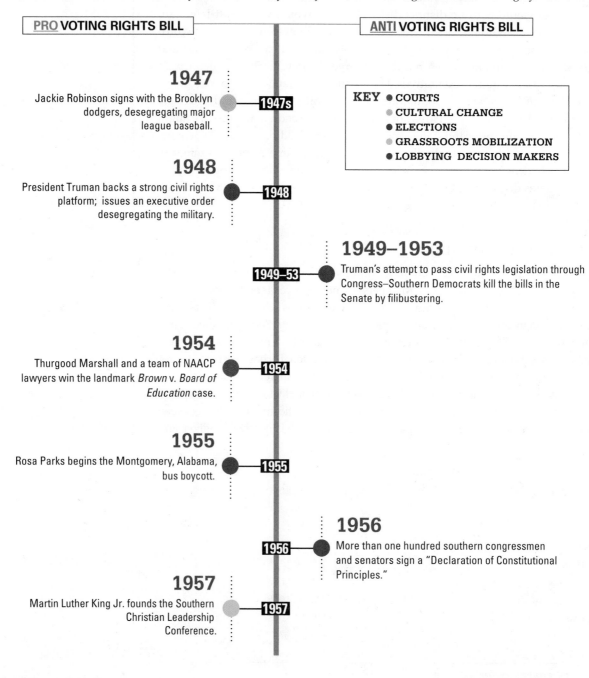

PRO VOTING RIGHTS BILL

ANTI VOTING RIGHTS BILL

KEY
- COURTS
- CULTURAL CHANGE
- ELECTIONS
- GRASSROOTS MOBILIZATION
- LOBBYING DECISION MAKERS

1947 — 1947s
Jackie Robinson signs with the Brooklyn dodgers, desegregating major league baseball.

1948 — 1948
President Truman backs a strong civil rights platform; issues an executive order desegregating the military.

1949–53 — **1949–1953**
Truman's attempt to pass civil rights legislation through Congress—Southern Democrats kill the bills in the Senate by filibustering.

1954 — 1954
Thurgood Marshall and a team of NAACP lawyers win the landmark *Brown* v. *Board of Education* case.

1955 — 1955
Rosa Parks begins the Montgomery, Alabama, bus boycott.

1956 — **1956**
More than one hundred southern congressmen and senators sign a "Declaration of Constitutional Principles."

1957 — 1957
Martin Luther King Jr. founds the Southern Christian Leadership Conference.

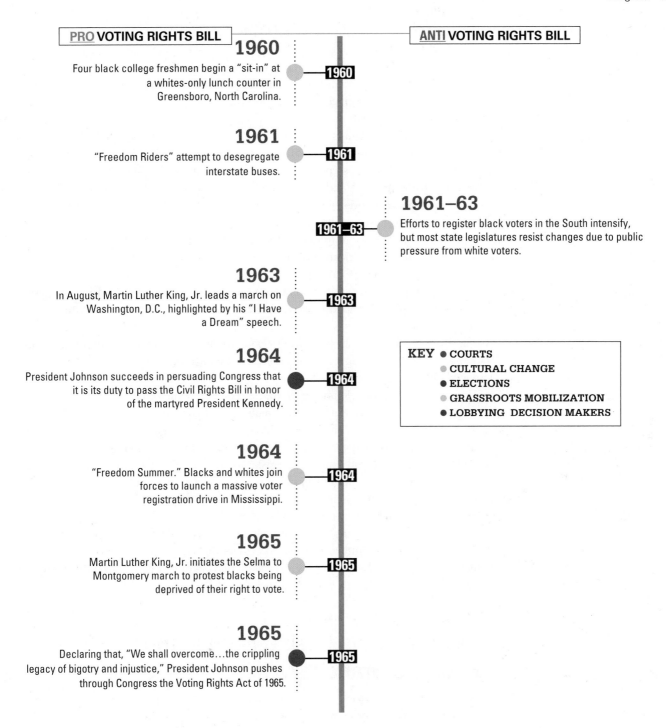

PRO VOTING RIGHTS BILL

ANTI VOTING RIGHTS BILL

1960
1960

Four black college freshmen begin a "sit-in" at a whites-only lunch counter in Greensboro, North Carolina.

1961
1961

"Freedom Riders" attempt to desegregate interstate buses.

1961–63
1961–63

Efforts to register black voters in the South intensify, but most state legislatures resist changes due to public pressure from white voters.

1963
1963

In August, Martin Luther King, Jr. leads a march on Washington, D.C., highlighted by his "I Have a Dream" speech.

1964
1964

President Johnson succeeds in persuading Congress that it is its duty to pass the Civil Rights Bill in honor of the martyred President Kennedy.

KEY
- COURTS
- CULTURAL CHANGE
- ELECTIONS
- GRASSROOTS MOBILIZATION
- LOBBYING DECISION MAKERS

1964
1964

"Freedom Summer." Blacks and whites join forces to launch a massive voter registration drive in Mississippi.

1965
1965

Martin Luther King, Jr. initiates the Selma to Montgomery march to protest blacks being deprived of their right to vote.

1965
1965

Declaring that, "We shall overcome…the crippling legacy of bigotry and injustice," President Johnson pushes through Congress the Voting Rights Act of 1965.

CRITICAL THINKING QUESTIONS

1. Clearly, passage of the Voting Rights Act came about by numerous pressures, particularly grassroots mobilization efforts. Can you imagine similar waves of protest these days? That is, has the Information Age changed the way citizens push for policy change? If so, are there any drawbacks to this shift?

2. Again and again, the filibuster was used by southern senators to halt the passage of civil rights legislation. President Lyndon Johnson, a former majority leader in the Senate, was forced to use every scheme and trick in the book to overcome these efforts. Perhaps that begs an important question: is the filibuster an anti-democratic rule? Why is it being used so often these days? What would happen if it were abandoned?

in the later just over $1 million. During roughly the same time, the average American household brought in $45,000, and only about 5 percent of Americans earned more than $200,000 per year. Less than 1 percent of Americans are worth a million dollars or more.[33] Of course, a dramatic income disparity between elected officials and their constituents has always been true, but given growing concerns about the income inequities more generally, this issue has drawn increased attention.

And there have always been lawyers in Congress—lots and lots of lawyers. Roughly 40 percent of members of Congress serving at any given time are attorneys. Bankers and business professionals make up about the same percentage, and educators (schoolteachers and professors) account for roughly 15 percent.[34] All other occupational backgrounds—including clergy, farmers, and retired military personnel—have been represented by only 5 percent of the members. Laborers, small farmers, homemakers, service employees, and other blue-collar workers, who make up a vast majority of the American workforce, have never accounted for more than a tiny fraction of the members of Congress (see Figure 6.6).

Perhaps it makes sense that some occupations are overrepresented in Congress. Lawyers, after all, are trained to understand the nuances of the law; it is natural that they would take the lead in writing laws. We might hope that the best and the brightest would serve in the national legislature—perhaps the same kinds of individuals who have earned advanced degrees and succeeded at their profession (that is, made lots of money). Of course, it is possible that such representatives can understand the concerns of diverse groups of people and work on their behalf. Some of the greatest legislative champions of women's rights have been male legislators, and some of the most aggressive advocates for the poor in Congress have been rich. Many white legislators fought valiant battles against slavery and segregation. Moreover, given that all Americans have the right to vote and that most legislators do everything they can to stay in office, we can imagine that members of Congress would be very attentive to *all* of their constituents—especially to large blocs of voters, many of whom are far from affluent. Yet many of those who are underrepresented in the halls of Congress—women, African Americans, Asian Americans, Hispanics, blue-collar workers, farmers, gays and lesbians, persons with disabilities, and the poor—feel that their concerns would get more attention if more members of their group were players on the field rather than simply spectators from the sidelines or the bleachers.

Are Americans Losing Faith in the "People's Branch"?

6.8 Compare the state of congressional ethics with Americans' perception of the legislative branch.

When the Republicans captured control of the House in 1994, Tom DeLay, a Republican from Texas who was first elected in 1984, quickly emerged as a powerful player. By the spring of 2005, however, DeLay's fortunes had taken a dramatic downward turn: A grand jury in Austin, Texas, indicted him on criminal charges of conspiracy to violate election laws. In the spring of 2006, he was forced to relinquish his post as majority leader and by summer, DeLay had withdrawn his name from the November ballot; he had decided to leave the House altogether.

About the same time that DeLay was stepping down from his leadership position, an influential lobbyist named Jack Abramoff, who had been under investigation by federal law enforcement officials for some time, was hit with a string of indictments. Abramoff quickly agreed to cooperate with the prosecutors in exchange for a lighter sentence. A year later, Idaho Senator Larry Craig was arrested for lewd behavior in a men's bathroom at the Minneapolis–St. Paul Airport, and Alaska Senator Ted Stevens

FIGURE 6.6 Occupations, Education, Party Profile, and Gender Composition of the 115th Congress

■ *What conclusions can you draw about the occupations, education, and gender of Congress? How can it become more diversified and representative of the average citizen?*

Note: As of November 15, 2016.

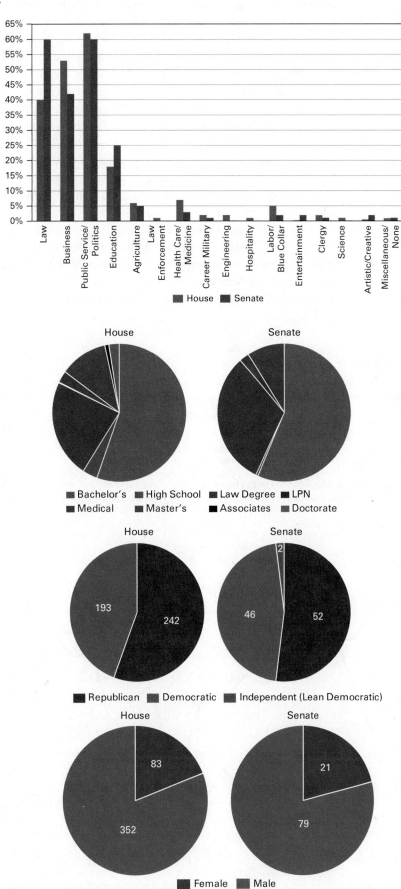

came under investigation by the FBI and the IRS for possible corruption (Stevens was later acquitted of the charges). New York House Representative Anthony Weiner was forced to resign in the summer of 2011 due to a "sexting" scandal, and a year later the chairman of the House Financial Services Committee, Spencer Bachus of Alabama, was placed under investigation for insider trading. In an earlier edition of this book we profiled Aaron Schock of Illinois, who was elected to the House in 2007 at the age of 27. He was thought to be a rising star in the Republican Party—that is, until the spring of 2015 when he was forced to resign. He had allegedly used piles of government funds for lavish, personal use. Among other things, he had spent more than $100,000 to redecorate his congressional office in the aristocratic style of the television series *Downton Abbey.*

Mark Twain's oft-cited line that Congress is the only "distinctly native American criminal class" still seems accurate to many Americans. In one national survey, only 20 percent of Americans rate the ethics of members of Congress as "high" or "very high"[35] (see Figure 6.7).

However, close observers of the legislative branch argue that in the past few decades, members of Congress have actually become more ethical and more upstanding than at any point in our nation's history. According to Fred Harris, a political scientist and former Democratic senator from Oklahoma, members of the national legislature are a good deal cleaner than the average American.[36]

FIGURE 6.7   Public Opinion Poll on Congressional Ethics

This figure suggests that over the last three decades, Americans have been skeptical about the ethical standards of members of Congress—even though most scholars believe the actual level of corruption has grown.

▪ *Do you think the president has anything to do with the perceptions Americans have of honesty and integrity in Congress? What role might divided government play in public perceptions?*

SOURCE: Lydia Saad, "Honesty and Ethics Poll Finds Congress Image Tarnished" Gallup, December 9, 2009. Reprinted by permission of Gallup, Inc. Updated for 2015 from: http://www.gallup.com/poll/1654/honesty-ethics-professions.aspx.

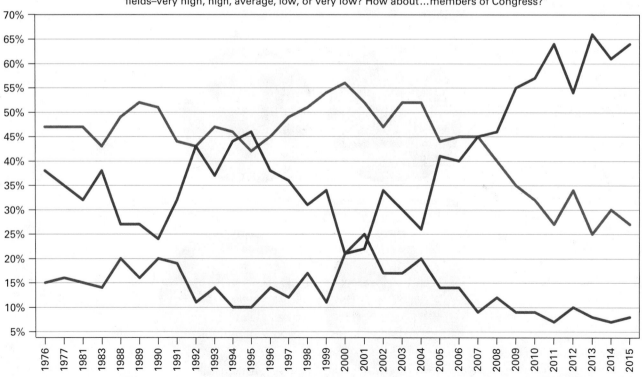

What, then, might explain the gap between perceptions and reality? There are a number of plausible explanations. For one, there is simply much more reporting of ethical transgressions than in the past. Particularly after the Watergate scandal in the early 1970s, when President Richard Nixon resigned from office on the eve of an impeachment trial over his activities in covering up a criminal investigation, aggressive investigative journalism became an omnipresent force in American politics. Members of Congress are also subject to tougher rules and procedures and to far more public scrutiny than in the past.

> **POLL** Do you think members of Congress are generally ethical and honest?

In very important ways, however, it is the perception of the public that really matters. Beyond overt corruption, there are strong signs that the general public may be losing faith in Congress. In a series of surveys conducted by the Gallup organization, the job approval of Congress has dropped from roughly 50 percent in 2004, to 13 percent in 2016.[37] The source of this outrage is likely multifaceted, but surely a large part stems from concerns over partisan-based gridlock—the very change that has pushed many moderates from the legislature and propels sitting members to reject compromise solutions

Conclusion

Representation is the linchpin of our democracy. It is true that in some tiny communities, all citizens can participate directly in governmental decisions, but direct democracy is rare, is impracticable in all but the smallest settings, and presumes that all citizens *should* be involved in every decision. Our system relies on a small group to speak and act on behalf of the many. Ours is a representative republic, and few Americans would have it any other way.

Congress was established as the "first branch," because the framers believed it would be the part of our government closest to the people. Today, the real issues surrounding Congress have little to do with the value or legitimacy of legislative bodies or whether they should be seen as first among equals. Rather, what we worry about is how to make the system more efficient or more egalitarian. No one could realistically imagine getting rid of standing committees, leadership roles, or party structures, for instance; but at the same time, most people agree that these components do modify the character of the institution. Not every initiative that comes before Congress gets treated the same way, and not every legislator has the same input in the process. In many ways, an open, egalitarian system is sacrificed in the name of efficiency. Also, for many Americans who are critical of Congress, the *kind* of person who gets to serve in our legislature raises deep questions about the breadth and quality of representation.

What does all this mean for individuals who want to change public policy by lobbying their representative or senator? For one thing, it means that many of Congress' organizational components create points of access for effective citizen action, but it also implies that the actors must be well versed in the nuances of legislative procedure—the precise route that measures travel from introduction to law, as well as the numerous pitfalls along the way. Insiders familiar with the complexity of the legislative process and with access to decision makers are in high demand. It is little wonder that former members of Congress are sought—and are very well paid—as lobbyists.

Beyond the complexity of the legislative process, this chapter also underscored a rather dramatic change. Since the earliest years, members of Congress have been partisans—advocates of a party platform. They were endorsed by a party committee in their home state, ran for office under a party label, and once elected caucused with fellow partisans. Parties have always been an important factor in the legislative process. But partisan allegiances were tempered by pragmatism—a desire to find common ground to get things accomplished. Believe it or not, at some points in our history, such as in the 1960s and 1970s, political scientists fretted that levels of party cohesion in Congress were actually too low! Stanford University scholar Morris Fiorina has written of that period, "National politics had degenerated into a free-for-all of unprincipled bargaining...."[38]

Those days are a distant memory. Today party-line unity is at historic highs, and it seems that hyper-partisanship may be distorting the very nature of representation. But if anything is true about the American national legislature it's that the legislative process evolves and changes. Just as we look at Professor Fiorina's comments about "unprincipled" legislators as odd given what seems to be such high levels of partisanship, it is entirely possible that a few years from now we will marvel at why coming together seemed so difficult. Let's hope.

CONFRONTING POLITICS AND POLICY

One of the fastest moving public policy issues in recent years has been the legalization of medical marijuana. In 1970, the Justice Department defined marijuana as a "Schedule I" narcotic—meaning that it was considered one of the most serious drugs. Ironically, it was about the same time that medical researchers began to find cannabis helpful for a range of illnesses. In 1986, several federal measures were passed to toughen marijuana-related prison sentences, but within a decade several states had moved to decriminalize marijuana use for medical purposes and by 2016, it was legal in 22 states. That same year, 70 percent of Americans agreed that marijuana should be legal for medical use and over 60 percent for recreational use.

But what if you live in a state where both uses—medical and recreational—are illegal? Additionally, marijuana continues to be a federally prohibited drug. Under the Obama administration the Department of Justice issued a memorandum saying that it would rely on state laws and essentially not enforce federal laws, but that could change with the new administration. Someone could be charged with a felony for using marijuana in one state, but in the neighboring state you might be able to pick some up on the way home from work for the evening barbeque. What if you were interested in creating one national policy on marijuana usage?

ACTION STEPS

1. The first step would be to take a look at marijuana policies in your state. Have there been efforts to change that policy? Does your state allow ballot initiatives? If so, have the voters of the state weighed in on the issue?

2. Have your federal representatives—members of the House and Senate—taken a position on this issue? One quick way of finding this out is to call one of the district offices and request information. Most members of Congress are very attentive to inquiries (they want to be responsive) and you would likely get their position on the issue quickly—along with other information.

3. The next step would be to consider joining a group interested in reforming marijuana policy. There are several national organizations and likely several in your state. These units will also have information on where your federal delegation stands and, importantly, how you might get involved.

4. Finally, after becoming familiar with the issue and joining a pro-marijuana group, you might start sending letters to your representatives and to local newspapers. You might pull together an event—maybe a rally on campus—and start reaching out to groups on neighboring campuses. Keep in mind that the federal policy process can move slowly, but with sustained efforts individuals, like you, can make a difference.

〉 REVIEW THE CHAPTER

The Nature and Style of Representation

6.1 Differentiate between the various ways legislators represent the interests of their constituents. (p. 175)

There are many approaches to "representation" and many ways a member of Congress might spend his or her time. The trustee approach suggests legislators should consider the wishes of constituents but in the end do what they feel is best for the long-term good of the nation. The delegate model implies legislators should simply reflect the will of the people. There are also middle ground perspectives, including the politico model and the conscience model, but it seems clear that numerous forces are pushing legislators toward the delegate model.

Congress and the Constitution

6.2 Identify the key constitutional provisions that shape the way Congress functions. (p. 177)

The framers of our system of government placed a great deal of faith in the legislative branch and provided it with clear, extensive powers. Article I, Section 8, details the numerous powers of the legislative branch, and it also includes a key provision for expanding powers: the Elastic Clause. Combined, the list of powers and the opportunity to broaden the scope of powers when "necessary and proper," have greatly expanded the reach of congressional action in American society.

Organizing Congress: Committees

6.3 Establish the importance of committees in organizing the legislative process. (p. 185)

Congress is comprised of 535 members, each with their own concerns and unique constituency. The forces promoting self-interest and individual action are great, but collective outcomes happen. One of the main ways collective outcomes happen is through committees, which are the workhorses of the legislature.

Organizing Congress: Political Parties and Leadership

6.4 Assess how political parties and leaders manage the legislative process while advancing their own initiatives. (p. 190)

Americans often bemoan "partisanship" in Congress, but political parties and their leaders have served key organ-izing functions for over 200 years. Parties orient new members, set policy agendas, denote leaders, and afford rank-and-file members time-saving voting cues. And for all the talk of "nonpartisan" solutions and "independent-minded" legislators, the role of parties in Congress has actually increased in recent years. Whether or not things have gone too far toward partisan polarization is an open question.

Organizing Congress: Rules and Norms

6.5 Show how the rules and norms of behavior help ensure a more orderly, efficient legislative process. (p. 195)

While there are important differences between the House and Senate, formal rules and informal norms of behavior help structure the legislative process in both chambers. For example, as a bill moves from a committee to the floor in the House, a set of rules defines how long the bill can be debated, and how many and what type of amendments might be made. A powerful but informal rule in both chambers is specialization, whereby members are expected to become experts in certain policy areas. A norm of civility helps make compromise more likely. Adherence to these modes of behavior streamlines, but limits, the democratic character of the process.

How a Bill Becomes a Law

6.6 Outline the process by which a bill becomes a law. (p. 198)

The process by which a bill becomes a law is complex, with numerous hurdles and pitfalls along the way. In brief, the process moves from specialized subcommittees, where hearings are generally held, to larger standing committees, and then to the full chamber. The Senate version of a bill must be merged with the House version of the same bill through a conference committee. If this challenge is met, the bill is sent to the president for his signature. Some believe the process may be too difficult, but others argue that the bar should be set high and that the framers envisioned a slow, deliberate process, with numerous checks along the way.

Who Sits in Congress?

6.7 Determine whether members of Congress mirror America's demographic diversity and why this matters. (p. 202)

It is likely no surprise that the "people's branch" does not exactly look like the rest of America. Congress is comprised of a vastly greater share of men than the rest of society, and a disproportionate number of wealthy whites, Protestants, and lawyers. Some believe this is a problem and that true representation implies not only the reflection of policy preferences, but also the gender, racial, ethnic, and occupational backgrounds of constituents. The trend in both chambers seems to be improving, but there is a long way to go before Congress mirrors the diversity of American society.

Are Americans Losing Faith in the "People's Branch"?

6.8 Compare the state of congressional ethics with Americans' perception of the legislative branch. (p. 208)

Long ago, a comedian once joked that our nation has "the best Congress money can buy." Today, many Americans share that sentiment, believing that most legislators are unethical and self-interested; a number of high-profile events have reinforced the perception that the "people's branch" is filled with crooks. However, many scholars suggest that there have been real improvements in the area of ethics due in part to tougher and more robust ethics rules and greater surveillance.

〉 LEARN THE TERMS

delegate model of representation, p. 176
trustee model of representation, p. 176
politico model of representation, p. 176
conscience model of representation, p. 176
bicameral legislature, p. 177
Seventeenth Amendment, p. 178
rotation, p. 178
pocket veto, p. 179

Elastic Clause/Necessary and Proper Clause, p. 179
at-large districts, p. 181
redistricting, p. 181
gerrymandering, p. 181
Baker v. *Carr* (1961), p. 183
reapportionment, p. 184
subcommittees, p. 187
conference committee, p. 187
hearings, p. 188
oversight, p. 189
voting cues, p. 191
Speaker, p. 191

majority leader, p. 191
party unity scores, p. 192
whip, p. 194
minority leader, p. 194
filibuster, p. 195
cloture, p. 196
seniority, p. 197
specialization, p. 198
reciprocity/logrolling, p. 198
earmarks/pork-barrel legislation, p. 198
bill sponsor, p. 198

〉 EXPLORE FURTHER

In the Library

Abramowitz, Alan I. *The Disappearing Center*. New Haven, CT: Yale University Press, 2010.

Bzdek, Vincent. *Woman of the House: The Rise of Nancy Pelosi*. New York: Palgrave Macmillan, 2008.

Davidson, Roger H., Walter J. Oleszek, and Frances E. Lee. *Congress and Its Members*, 12th ed. Washington, D.C.: CQ Press, 2009.

Davidson, Roger H., Susan Webb Hammond, and Raymond W. Smock, eds. *Masters of the House*. Boulder, CO: Westview Press, 1998.

Deering, Christopher J., and Steven S. Smith. *Committees in Congress*, 3rd ed. Washington, D.C.: CQ Press, 1997.

Devins, Neal, and Keith E. Whittington, eds. *Congress and the Constitution*. Durham, NC: Duke University Press, 2005.

Fenno, Richard. *Homestyle: House Members in Their Districts*. Glenview, IL: Scott Foresman, 1978.

Fiorina, Morris. *Disconnect: The Breakdown of Representation in American Politics*. Norman, OK: University of Oklahoma Press, 2009.

Hamilton, Lee. *How Congress Works and Why You Should Care*. Bloomington, IN: Indiana University Press, 2004.

Hilton, Stanley G., and Ann-Renee Testa. *Glass Houses: Shocking Profiles of Congressional Sex Scandals and Other Unofficial Misconduct*. New York: St. Martin's Press, 1998.

Lee, Francis. *Beyond Ideology: Politics, Principles and Partisanship in the U.S. Senate*. Chicago: University of Chicago Press, 2009.

Matthews, Donald R. *U.S. Senators and Their World*. New York: Vintage Books, 1960.

Mayhew, David R. *Congress: The Electoral Connection.* New Haven, CT: Yale University Press, 1974.

Oleszek, Walter J. *Congressional Procedures and the Policy Process.* Washington, D.C.: Congressional Quarterly, 2010.

Schroeder, Pat. *24 Years of House Work ... and the Place Is Still a Mess: My Life in Politics.* Kansas City, MO: McMeel, 1998.

Shea, Daniel M., and Morris Fiorina. *Can We Talk? The Rise of Rude, Nasty, Stubborn Politics.* Upper Saddle River, NJ: Pearson Longman, 2012.

Sinclair, Barbara. *Unorthodox Lawmaking: New Legislative Processes in the U.S. Congress*, 3rd ed. Washington, D.C.: CQ Press, 2007.

Stone, Peter. *Heist: Superlobbyist Jack Abramoff, His Republican Allies, and the Buying of Washington.* New York: Farrar, Straus and Giroux, 2006.

Theriault, Sean, M. *Party Polarization in Congress.* New York: Cambridge University Press, 2008.

Thurber, James, ed. *Rivals for Power: Presidential-Congressional Relations.* Lanham, MD: Rowman and Littlefield, 2009.

On the Web

To learn more about the history of the U.S. Congress, see *http://clerk.house.gov/art_history/house_history/index.html.*

To read the specifics of Article I and to search for related court cases, see *http://caselaw.lp.findlaw.com/data/constitution/article01.*

To explore the Census Bureau's redistricting data, see *http://www.census.gov/rdo.*

Learn more about committees, specific pieces of legislation, roll call votes, and much more at *http://thomas.loc.gov.*

Learn more about leadership in both chambers as well as party unity scores over time at *http://clerk.house.gov/* and *http://www.senate.gov/pagelayout/senators/a_three_sections_with_teasers/leadership.htm.*

For an online directory of members on Congress and details on how to contact them, see *http://www.contactingthecongress.org/.*

For an up-to-date look at what is happening on Capitol Hill, go to *http://www.rollcall.com.*

Believe it or not, many students enjoy seeing "Schoolhouse Rock" from their childhood, an animated cartoon that explains how a bill becomes a law. To see this, visit YouTube at *https://www.youtube.com/watch?v=FFroMQlKiag.*

For an extensive look at the history of women in Congress, see *http://womenincongress.house.gov/.*

For a biographical database of all members of Congress, including your congressperson, go to *http://bioguide.congress.gov/.*

For a detailed timeline of congressional scandals, go to *http://www.foxnews.com/story/0,2933,181733,00.html.*

THE PRESIDENCY

One of the most important norms of American governance is the peaceful transition of power. Here President Barack Obama and President-Elect Donald Trump meet in the White House following the 2016 election. They met behind closed doors for 90 minutes.

What do you think they spent most of their time talking about?

→ LEARNING OBJECTIVES

7.1 Explain the framers' decision to bestow the president with real powers despite their concerns about potential abuses.

7.2 Outline the changes that have led to the expansion of presidential powers.

7.3 Establish how the "power to persuade" expands presidential power beyond the Constitution.

7.4 Identify the duties and functions of modern presidents.

7.5 Evaluate the qualities that contribute to presidential success or failure.

One of the better films about U.S. elections is *The Candidate* (1972). The protagonist, Bill McKay, is played by Robert Redford. Reluctant at first, McKay slowly grows into the part. He develops an affinity for the campaign trail, and the crowds swell. He's charismatic and, well, looks like Robert Redford. McKay remains convinced, however, that the outcome is a foregone conclusion—that he will lose to the incumbent senator. At the end of the film, when McKay is declared the winner, a telling scene takes place. Retreating from the horde of well-wishers at the victory party, McKay and his campaign manager find themselves in an elevator. "The candidate" stares into his manager's face and asks, "What do we do now?" Both appear gaunt, stunned. Silence follows. Running for office is one thing, serving the public is all-together different.

Few, including perhaps the candidate himself, thought Donald Trump would win such a decisive victory against Hillary Clinton in 2016. Within several hours of the polls closing, as one blue state dropped after another, it became clear that one of the greatest upsets in American electoral history had occurred. The pundits, scholars, and practitioners got it wrong. Donald J. Trump would be our next president. What do we do now?

There would be much to do in the days and weeks following the election, as a new administration would have to be created from scratch. But the first and perhaps most important step would be a meeting between the president-elect and the president. On the Thursday following the election, Barack and Michelle Obama hosted Donald and Melania Trump at the White House. The importance of this "chat" was not lost; the world was watching. They had been steadfast political adversaries. Trump has risen in conservative, far right ranks by challenging the president's legitimacy to the office by suggesting he was not born in the country, and thus not a real citizen. To many, this was a humiliating, racist charge. Throughout the campaign, Obama leveled an array of attacks against Trump, not the least of which was that he was temperamentally unfit for the office. They couldn't be more opposite on any number of political and personal characteristics. And yet, Obama extended this invitation, and Trump graciously accepted. In the United States, elections are sovereign, and the transition from one administration to the next is done respectfully, peacefully. Ever since John Adams lost in the ugly, mean-spirited election of 1800 to Thomas Jefferson, presidents relinquish the reins of power without fuss, without disgruntlement. As Obama noted after the 90-minute meeting, Americans should pray for Donald Trump's success. If he succeeds, America succeeds.

A turbulent, unprecedented campaign had come to an end. There is a winner. One presidential administration readied to leave, another to take the reins of power. And so it goes in the American system.

The President and the Constitution

7.1 Explain the framers' decision to bestow the president with real powers despite their concerns about potential abuses.

The framers of our system of government were ambivalent about the role of the executive branch under the Constitution. On the one hand, the history of strong executives with whom the framers were familiar was unsettling. From the beginning of history, whenever human beings came together to form governments, the result was either autocracy (rule by one) or oligarchy (rule by a few).[1] Yet governing systems *without* executive power seemed ripe for discord and anarchy. In the end, there were several reasons why the framers were inclined to bestow the president with real powers despite concerns about potential abuses.

A Powerful Executive

The framers were well versed in the philosophies of Hobbes, Montesquieu, and other theorists of the seventeenth and eighteenth centuries who agreed that although we might wish for a political system without a powerful executive, governments that had none had proved ineffectual and short lived. The English political philosopher

prerogative power
Extraordinary powers that the president may use under certain conditions, such as during times of war.

John Locke, who was greatly admired by the framers of our Constitution, argued that legislative politics should be at the heart of a limited government—but also that it was necessary to give executives the powers to do "several things of their own free choice, where the law is silent, and sometimes, too, against the direct letter of the law, for the public good."[2] Locke called such action **prerogative power**.

Also, the experience under the Articles of Confederation suggested the need for a strong executive; for, under the Articles, the national government lacked the power and the ability to respond quickly to emergencies. Advocates of an effective executive had an ideal republican leader readily at hand: George Washington, the hero of the Revolution.[3]

Debate at the Convention

At the Philadelphia Constitutional Convention in 1787, the first scheme for a new government that the delegates discussed, the Virginia Plan (authored principally by James Madison), was vague on the basic questions, including whether one person or a group of people would hold executive power, how long the term of office would be, whether the president could be reelected, and even what the precise powers of the presidency should be. The second scheme to emerge at the convention and gain early support, the New Jersey Plan, was more state centered, and although many of its provisions were also vague, it envisioned a relatively weak executive office.

However, concerns that the executive branch would be overwhelmed by the power of the legislature led some of the most prominent and most talented delegates, including James Wilson and Gouverneur Morris of Pennsylvania, to push for a stronger model.[4] Ultimately, on the question of whether the president would have real powers—that is, be an authentic player in the system instead of merely an administrator of what Congress decides—the answer was yes.

There would be no blank checks, wrote one scholar, and nearly all the presidential powers would be shared with Congress, but presidents were meant to be significant players in the system.[5] The principal powers granted by the Constitution to presidents allowed them to influence the judiciary by appointing judges to the bench, to have a modest say in making legislation, to conduct foreign policy, and to be the commander of the nation's armed forces during times of war. As we'll see in this chapter, these formal powers have proved to be merely the foundation of presidential authority.

Article II and Ratification

Previous chapters have noted that many of the fears about the new system of government were calmed by the central role the legislature would play. But if Article I (the legislative branch) calmed citizens' fears, Article II raised an alarm. What was this "presidency," and what sorts of power would its occupants have? How long would this person serve? What would stop this person from gaining too much power and becoming another tyrant? Moreover, the scheme laid out in Article II was unfamiliar. As noted by a leading presidential scholar, "Not only was the presidency the most obvious innovation in the proposed plan of government, but its unitary nature and strong powers roused fears of the most horrifying political specter that most Americans could imagine: a powerful monarchy."[6]

Both proponents and opponents of the Constitution presented their arguments in the form of essays published in newspapers. Several essays in opposition were published under the pseudonym Cato in the *New York Journal*. (Cato, who lived from 95 B.C. to 45 B.C., was a defender of republican virtues—such as freedoms and liberty—and he was an outspoken opponent of Julius Caesar.) One piece, appearing on September 27, 1787, only 10 days after conclusion of the Constitutional Convention, was a powerful assault on the executive branch:

> The deposit of vast trusts in the hands of a single magistrate, enables him in their exercise, to create a numerous train of dependents—this tempts his *ambition*, which in a republican magistrate is also remarked, *to be pernicious* and the

duration of his office for any considerable time favors his views, gives him the means and time to perfect and execute his designs—*he therefore fancies that he may be great and glorious by oppressing his fellow citizens, and raising himself to permanent grandeur on the ruins of his country.* [Emphasis in original.]

Cato worried that the scheme outlined by the framers would allow the president to use his long term of office to take such a firm hold of the reins of power that it would ruin the democratic experiment.

Alexander Hamilton had the difficult chore of countering Cato's argument. He undertook the task of easing fears about the presidency in *The Federalist,* No. 69. There, Hamilton sought to "place in a strong light the unfairness of such representations" of the proposed executive branch. Repeatedly, Hamilton worked to underscore the differences between a president and a king. He notes that while the president is elected for only 4 years, a king gains his post through heredity and holds it throughout his life. The president can be impeached for treason, bribery, and other high crimes or misdemeanors, but the king can be subjected to no punishment—he is "sacred and inviolable." A president may be able to veto legislation, but this decision can be overridden by the legislature. In contrast, a king's judgment is absolute.

In the end, however, it was not persuasive arguments that carried the day; rather, it was public sentiment toward one political leader. Everyone knew that George Washington would be the first president. He had not abused his authority as the commanding officer of the Continental Army, and many simply could not imagine such a great man amassing power and making himself a king. Faith in Washington allowed citizens to overcome their fears (for the moment) about a powerful executive.

The Evolution of the Presidency

7.2 Outline the changes that have led to the expansion of presidential powers.

The fact that the Constitution *allows* for a powerful president does not mean that it *mandates* one. The scope of presidential powers has been a function of the men who have served in the position and used those powers. In addition, the overall evolution of the presidency has been toward ever-greater powers, so much so that today few of us can imagine a time when the president was not at the center of the federal government. But indeed, there have been such times in our history.

Models of Presidential Power

As we saw in Chapter 6, the framers of our system believed that Congress would be the primary branch of government. And that was precisely what occurred during the first century of our nation's history. Presidents seemed quite willing to follow Congress. There were, of course, strong presidents, such as George Washington, Thomas Jefferson, Andrew Jackson, and Abraham Lincoln. They were exceptions to the rule, however, and their powers sprang from extraordinary circumstances.

There were a number of reasons why it made sense that the presidency was not at the center of nineteenth-century American government: the national economy still centered on agriculture, and the supervision and guidance of economic matters was not as important during this time as it would be after industrialization and urbanization; the United States was not a central player in world affairs; and nineteenth-century political campaigning was party centered, with less emphasis on presidential candidates and more attention on party platforms and the entire "ticket." On top of this was the general belief among presidents themselves that they should not be at the center of government. Most nineteenth-century presidents—and a few in the twentieth-century—held closely to the idea that presidents are limited to the powers *explicitly* stated in the Constitution or explicitly granted to the executive branch by Congress in the years since the Constitution was written. This has been dubbed the **Whig model** of presidential powers.

Whig model

A theory of restrained presidential powers; the idea that presidents should use only the powers explicitly granted in the Constitution. Under this approach Congress, not the president, would lead the policy process.

This view of executive power, however, had begun to erode by the end of the nineteenth century, in part due to changing economic and geopolitical conditions. The nation's economy shifted from farming to industry, and its position in global affairs expanded. Moreover—and perhaps most significantly—some of the men who occupied the White House after 1901 transformed the job of the president.

Most historians agree that the first truly assertive president who did not confront extraordinary circumstances was Theodore Roosevelt (1901–1909). Before becoming president, Roosevelt, or "TR" as the press called him, had been a vigorous, reform-minded governor of New York. There he learned the power of shaping public opinion and using public support to push his reform agenda through the state legislature. As president, he took the same route, transforming the office into a unique opportunity to preach to and inspire a "national congregation." One historian offered this description: "As a master of political theater with an instinctive understanding of how to dramatize himself and the policies he favored, TR was our first modern media president, and a brilliant huckster."[7]

stewardship model

A theory of robust, broad presidential powers; the idea that the president is only limited by explicit restrictions in the Constitution. This model, now completely accepted, set the stage for a broad expansion of presidential powers.

Theodore Roosevelt held firmly to a new view of presidential powers, one with no restrictions on presidential authority except what was strictly *forbidden* in the Constitution. This perspective, often referred to as the **stewardship model**, reversed the earlier approach. Instead of using only the powers expressly granted, Roosevelt believed that *all* was possible *except* what was prohibited. This was especially true, he argued, when the good of the nation was at stake. Looking back on his presidency, TR boasted, "I did not usurp power, but I did greatly broaden the use of executive power....I acted for the common well-being of our people...in whatever manner was necessary, unless prevented by direct constitutional or legislative prohibition."[8]

Woodrow Wilson, the twenty-eighth president (1913–1921), also subscribed to the stewardship model. He believed that the president should lead not only in national politics but also in international relations. Following World War I, Wilson set his sights on creating an international body to settle disputes between nations, which he called the League of Nations and which he tried, unsuccessfully, to have the United States join. (The League was the predecessor of the United Nations, which the United States would help form at the end of World War II.) Wilson's efforts have not been lost on historians such as Robert Dallek, who wrote, "No vision in twentieth-century presidential politics has inspired greater hope of human advance or has done more to secure a president's reputation as a great leader than Wilson's peace program of 1918–1919."[9]

Theodore Roosevelt believed that presidents should use their position to articulate values, offer policy alternatives, and challenge accepted wisdom. That is to say, presidents should lead public opinion rather than simply follow it.

■ *But what if this "bullish" advocacy leads to a divided public? Should presidents be responsible for finding compromises and common ground?*

Not all of the presidents who came after Wilson shared his activist views of presidential power. For example, his successors Warren G. Harding (1921–1923), Calvin Coolidge (1923–1929), and, to a lesser extent, Herbert Hoover (1929–1933), followed the Whig model by deferring to congressional leadership.

However, the election to the presidency in 1932 of Franklin Delano Roosevelt (FDR) ushered in what many historians would describe as the **modern presidency**. Roosevelt—a distant cousin of TR and, like him, a former governor of New York—ran for the White House at the depths of the Great Depression. He swept into the presidency on a wave of public anger, frustration, and fear. Within a day of being sworn in, FDR took charge of the federal government.

With panicked depositors withdrawing their savings from bank accounts (which at the time were not insured) and thus threatening the country's banking system with collapse, his first move was to declare a national bank holiday—something that most people doubted he had the legal authority to do. Legally or not, Roosevelt ordered every bank in the country temporarily closed until federal inspectors could go through its books and declare it sound, thus reassuring depositors. Then, with equally dubious legality, he banned the buying and selling of gold and halted the practice of linking the value of the dollar to the price of gold. Next, he sent Congress an emergency banking reform bill, which the House passed in 38 minutes and the Senate accepted with very little debate that same night. This was just the beginning of a comprehensive package of measures designed to pull the nation out of the economic crisis. During the Hundred Days, as it was called, Roosevelt submitted to Congress a stream of proposed reform measures, all of which were quickly enacted into law. Roosevelt demanded "action—and action now." The **New Deal**, the name he gave to his series of programs and initiatives that transformed the national government, gave birth to the welfare state and shaped the modern presidency.[10]

Today, there no longer seems to be any question about the proactive role of the executive branch. Presidents are expected to lead the nation. They must come up with innovative solutions to our problems, give aid and comfort to American citizens in times of need, maintain a healthy and growing economy, and protect our nation from foreign and domestic threats. In times of peace and prosperity, we congratulate the president (who expects to be rewarded in the polls and at the ballot box), and in bad times, we place the blame squarely on the White House. This transformation has thus presented presidents with a double-edged sword, but there is little question that the stewardship model, first articulated by Theodore Roosevelt, guides the contemporary presidency. Presidents have no choice but to lead—or else stand condemned as failures.

Institutional Changes

Along with the shifting role of the chief executive in the federal government have come changes within the institution of the presidency. We refer here to the cabinet, support staff, and the various offices and agencies designed to help the president succeed, as well as to the changing role of the vice president.

THE CABINET Since the very beginning, presidents have relied on their staff. The framers of the Constitution rejected the idea of creating any type of council of presidential advisers, but once in office, Washington immediately realized that specific executive departments should handle the responsibilities of the federal government. The people who took charge of these departments became the president's **cabinet** (see Table 7.1). The cabinet consists of the secretaries of the major departments of the bureaucracy on whom the president relies heavily to carry out public policy. These officials are appointed by the president and are confirmed by the Senate. They can be removed at the president's will without the consent of the Senate. Unlike the rules in parliamentary systems, members of the cabinet cannot also be members of Congress: The Constitution dictates that no one can hold more than one post in the federal government at the same time.

modern presidency
A political system in which the president is the central figure and participates actively in both foreign and domestic policy.

New Deal
A set of policies and programs advanced by Franklin D. Roosevelt in the 1930s with the aim of pulling the nation out of the Depression.

cabinet
A group of presidential advisers, primarily the secretaries of federal departments. The size of the cabinet has varied through the years, but lately it has been composed of roughly 20 members.

President George W. Bush meets with his cabinet, including U.S. Secretary of State Colin Powell, left, and Secretary of Defense Donald Rumsfeld, in the Cabinet Room of the White House after the September 11 terrorist attacks.

■ *How do you think Donald Trump will use his cabinet?*

TABLE 7.1 Departments of the President's Cabinet

Presidents have always surrounded themselves with policy advisers, especially as the powers and duties of the executive branch broadened with FDR's administration. One source of support comes from the cabinet.

■ *Why have the number of cabinet positions increased over time?*

Department	Created	Responsibilities
State	1789	Create foreign policies and treaties
Treasury	1789	Coin money, regulate national banks, and collect income taxes
War, Defense	1789, 1947	Security and defense
Interior	1849	Maintain national parks and natural resources
Agriculture	1862	Protect farmland, nature, and wildlife; provide resources to rural and low-income families; ensure agricultural products are safe for consumers
Justice	1789	Ensure justice and public safety by enforcing the law
Commerce	1903	Promote economic stability, growth, and international trade
Labor	1913	Protect the rights of working citizens and retirees; monitor changes in employment and economic settings
Health and Human Services	1953	Promote research; provide immunizations and health care to low-income families; ensure safety of food and drugs
Housing and Urban Development	1965	Guarantee everyone a right to affordable housing; enhance communities and increase the number of homeowners
Transportation	1966	Provide an efficient and safe transportation system that meets the needs of the American people
Energy	1977	Provide reliable energy and promote science while protecting the environment and national and economic securities
Education	1979	Ensure that all citizens can obtain a quality education
Veterans Affairs	1989	Provide support for the nation's veterans
Homeland Security	2002	Protect the United States from threats

SOURCES: Accessed at http://www.whitehouse.gov; Cabinet Web sites.

In Washington's administration, there were four cabinet members: secretary of state (Thomas Jefferson), to handle foreign affairs; secretary of the treasury (Alexander Hamilton); attorney general (Edmund Randolph); and secretary of war (Henry Knox), in charge of the U.S. Army. In later administrations, a secretary of the navy was added, and after that, secretaries of the interior, commerce, agriculture, labor, and other departments were also added. Some more recent presidents expanded their cabinets by creating new departments. Jimmy Carter pushed Congress to create the Department of Education. Following the terrorist attacks of September 11, 2001, George W. Bush and Congress created the Department of Homeland Security.

Different presidents have used the cabinet in different ways. Some, such as Andrew Jackson, Dwight D. Eisenhower, Gerald Ford, and Jimmy Carter, staffed their cabinets with their closest advisers and allies. Other presidents have kept their cabinets at arm's length, consulting with members only for routine matters or for policy concerns within their particular area. President John F. Kennedy once commented, "Cabinet meetings are simply useless.... Why should the Postmaster General sit there and listen to a discussion of the problems of Laos?"[11] Bill Clinton rarely spoke directly with many of his cabinet officers, and Ronald Reagan once mistook his secretary of urban affairs for another official when they were later introduced. Furthermore, most presidents informally establish an "inner" and an "outer" cabinet, with the former being the most important secretaries, usually those representing the departments of state, defense, treasury, and justice. Denis McDonough, Barack Obama's chief of staff, was a very close confidant, and in the **inner cabinet**, several other members, such as John Kerry, Jack Lew, Loretta Lynch, and Ashton Carter, also regularly offered the president advice. President Obama relied on a broad range of advisors, and these groups shifted with different policy questions.

inner cabinet
The advisers considered most important to the president—usually the secretaries of the departments of state, defense, treasury, and justice.

EXECUTIVE OFFICE OF THE PRESIDENT   Before Franklin D. Roosevelt, all presidents had a handful of clerks and personal assistants. A few nineteenth-century presidents also relied on informal input from a trusted circle of advisers—for example, the political cronies whom Andrew Jackson named his "kitchen cabinet," who were not part of his official cabinet. As the role of the president in developing and carrying out federal programs expanded, however, so did the number of his personal advisers. FDR needed lots of experts, a great deal of information, and more staff, and he pushed hard for institutional changes. The greatest single leap in this direction was the creation of the **Executive Office of the President (EOP)** in 1939.

An act of Congress established a number of groups of advisers under the broad heading of the EOP, including the White House staff, the Bureau of the Budget, and the Office of Personnel Management. Through the years, new divisions have been created, including the National Security Council, the Council of Economic Advisers, and the Office of Management and Budget. In Barack Obama's administration, the EOP consists of many offices, each with a group of members and a large support staff (see Table 7.2).

Executive Office of the President (EOP)
A group of presidential staff agencies created in 1939 that provides the president with help and advice. Many suggest the growing powers of the presidency spring in large measure from the expansion of the EOP.

TABLE 7.2   Executive Office of the President in 2016

- Council of Economic Advisers
- Domestic Policy Council
- National Economic Council
- National Security Council
- Office of Administration
- Office of Management and Budget
- Office of National Drug Control Policy
- Office of Science and Technology Policy
- Office of the United States Trade Representative
- President's Intelligence Advisory Board and Intelligence Oversight Board
- White House Military Office
- White House Office

Each component of the EOP is important, but some have proved more significant than others. The National Security Council (NSC) was established in 1947, and although its membership varies from administration to administration, it always includes the vice president and the secretaries of defense and state. The job of the NSC is to provide the president with information and advice on all matters concerning national security, including foreign and domestic threats. One of the key players of this group is the national security adviser, who is appointed by the president without confirmation and is not officially connected with the Department of State or the Department of Defense. As such, he or she is expected to give the president independent, unbiased advice on important national security matters.

Office of Management and Budget (OMB)

A cabinet-level office that monitors federal agencies and provides the president with expert advice on fiscal policy-related topics.

The **Office of Management and Budget (OMB)** has a number of sweeping responsibilities that include preparing the president's annual national budget proposal, monitoring the performance of federal agencies, and overseeing regulatory proposals. The Council of Economic Advisers (CEA), established in 1946, is led by three members—usually eminent economists—who are appointed by the president and confirmed by the Senate. Their duties include assisting the president in preparation of an annual economic report to Congress, gathering timely information concerning economic developments and trends, evaluating the economic impact of various federal programs and activities, developing and recommending policies that boost the nation's economy, and making recommendations on economy-related policies and legislation.

Along with the expansion of presidential responsibilities has come a rapid growth in the president's personal staff. Today, the White House Office is a critical part of the Executive Office of the President. FDR expanded his personal staff significantly, to an average of 47. This number grew to 200 under Harry Truman and to 555 under Nixon. When Ronald Reagan left office, some 600 full-time employees had been working for him. These days, the number of White House staffers hovers around 450, scattered through numerous offices. The most important of the president's personal staff assistants is the *chief of staff*. Presidents have used their chiefs of staff differently; some have been granted more control and autonomy than others. Generally speaking, the chief of staff is especially close to the president and oversees all that the president might do on a typical workday, including who is allowed to meet the chief executive, what documents the president reads, and even what issues take up the president's time. Needless to say, this gatekeeping role makes the chief of staff one of the most important figures not only in the executive branch but also in the entire federal government.

Social Security

A federal program started in 1935 that taxes wages and salaries to pay for retirement benefits, disability insurance, and hospital insurance.

PATHWAYS OF ACTION

FDR TAKES CHARGE!

When Franklin D. Roosevelt began his presidency in 1933, voters were looking for bold leadership and dramatic changes. Understanding his mandate, Roosevelt took the lead in redirecting the federal government. In doing so, he forever transformed the nature of the presidency. Many of the ideas for his New Deal programs came from a group of advisers, some of them college professors or other intellectuals, whom he called his "Brain Trust." Roosevelt's advisers and cabinet members did not always agree with one another—sometimes, in fact, their ideas were flatly contradictory—but in a crisis, FDR was willing to try anything that seemed as if it might work. In fact, his leadership style included always listening to advice from different viewpoints, always making the final decision himself, and always keeping his options open to try something else.

A partial list of Roosevelt's policy achievements included the Federal Deposit Insurance Corporation (FDIC), which insured savings deposits to prevent future banking crises; the Securities and Exchange Commission (SEC), which protects investors from fraudulent stock market practices; the Wagner Act of 1935, which strengthened the organizing power of labor unions; and several measures designed to help homeowners finance mortgages and keep their homes. Maximum work hours and minimum wages were also set for certain industries in 1938. The most far-reaching of all the New Deal programs, however, was **Social Security**, enacted in 1935 and expanded in 1939, which provided benefits for the elderly and widows, unemployment compensation, disability insurance, and welfare programs for mothers with dependent children. (Medicare and Medicaid were added to Social Security in 1964.)

Riding a wave of popular support, Franklin D. Roosevelt transformed the nature of the presidency and the federal government. His New Deal program ushered in a series of programs and policies designed to pull the nation out of the Great Depression. In doing so, he forever placed the executive branch squarely at the center of American politics.

◾ *What would the framers think about the burgeoning powers of the executive?*

RAMIFICATIONS OF STAFFING CHANGES Many observers of the American presidency have noted that the nature of the office has been transformed by the dramatic expansion of the presidential staff. The modern presidency is a massive network of offices, staff, and advisers, requiring a complex organizational chart to keep track of duties and responsibilities. The result is that presidents have become central to the policy process. Scholars now use the term **institutional presidency** to describe the burgeoning responsibilities and scope of presidential powers. Some suggest that the massive expansion of support staff has tipped the balance of power between the branches such that the president is now at the center of the federal government and Congress has, in some respects, taken a back seat. While it is true that over the years congressional staffs have also increased, they have not increased at nearly the pace of those in the executive branch. Others point out that the duties and responsibilities of modern presidents (discussed later in this chapter) have greatly expanded, making all this support necessary.

A second ramification of staffing changes has been growing internal conflict—that is, the balance of power *within* the executive branch seems to be shifting. In the past, cabinet secretaries and other policy experts played a key role in the executive branch. The president could always reject their advice, but it was taken for granted that they would have the president's ear—that they would provide counsel on important issues. However, in recent decades, presidents have surrounded themselves with White House staff members, who are essentially *political* experts—with the goal of helping their boss win reelection, boost his poll ratings, and build his historical legacy—and policy advisers have often been pushed to the side. That is to say, the battle for the president's ear has become intense, and most analysts agree that the political experts are winning over the "policy wonks."

Finally, when it comes to shaping the outcome of government, the explosion of executive branch staff has made citizen action a bit more complex. On the one hand, we might say that the number of people to talk to has increased, quite similar to what we saw in Chapter 6 in the case of Congress. Persuading a staffer close to the president can often be an effective means of shaping public policy. On the other hand, direct access to the president has become difficult. In an effort to protect their boss, White House aides may well be transforming the connection between the president and the people.

institutional presidency

The concept of the presidency as a working collectivity—a massive network of staff, analysts, and advisers with the president as its head.

Ronald Reagan, the so-called Great Communicator, gives the State of the Union Address in the House Chamber in January, 1988. This event, held each year, can be a powerful tool for building public support for the president's policy agenda. Historically, many Americans have watched this speech.

■ *What sort of "communicator" do you think Donald Trump will be?*

The Transformation of the Vice Presidency

Throughout most of American history, the vice presidency was considered an insignificant office. Benjamin Franklin once quipped that the vice president should be addressed as "your Superfluous Excellency."[12] Thomas Marshall, the vice president under Woodrow Wilson, once told a story of two brothers: "One ran away to sea; the other was elected vice president. And nothing was heard of either of them again."[13] In 1848, Senator Daniel Webster—who as one of his party's most influential figures had long hoped to gain the presidency—declined the vice presidential place on the Whig Party ticket. "I do not propose to be buried until I am dead," he snorted.[14] John Nance Garner, FDR's first vice president and a former speaker of the House, is quoted as saying that the vice presidency is "not worth a pitcher of warm spit."[15]

When Lyndon B. Johnson was asked by John Kennedy to be his running mate, the powerful Texas senator was reluctant to accept. Like Webster, LBJ worried about his political future. The job of vice president was mostly ceremonial—attending the funerals of dignitaries, dedicating bridges and parks, and sitting in the Senate on special occasions—and as majority leader of the Senate, Johnson stood at the hub of the federal government. But he was convinced by friends and colleagues to take the place on the ticket, because he would be a "heartbeat away from the presidency." And as fate would have it, Johnson did become president on November 22, 1963, upon the assassination of JFK. Indeed, the job of vice president has always been, first and foremost, to stand ready. Nine times in American history, a vice president has assumed the presidency: John Tyler, Millard Fillmore, Andrew Johnson, Chester Arthur, Theodore Roosevelt, Calvin Coolidge, Harry Truman, Lyndon Johnson, and Gerald Ford.

With the advent of the Cold War after 1945 and the proliferation of nuclear weapons, concerns grew about the vice president's readiness to take the helm at a moment's notice, fully abreast of world and military developments.[16] Truman, who became president on FDR's sudden death in April 1945, had been kept in the dark about the American project to build an atomic bomb. He was also not fully apprised of the rapidly mounting tension between the United States and its ally, the Soviet Union, as World War II drew to its close. Truman had to learn everything "on the job"; fortunately for him and for the nation, he was a man of intelligence and strong character.

By the 1950s, in an age of nuclear missiles, many Americans believed that there should be no learning curve for new presidents. Dwight Eisenhower remarked, "Even

It is likely that Delaware Senator Joe Biden, shown here speaking with reporters at the Capitol, would not have agreed to run as Barack Obama's vice presidential candidate if he had not believed that he would be a "player" in the White House.

■ *What are some of the changes in our world that compel an expanded role by vice presidents?*

if Mr. Nixon (his vice president) and I were not good friends, I would still have him in every important conference of government, so that if the Grim Reaper [death] would find it time to remove me from the scene, he is ready to slip in without any interruption."[17] Thus began a move toward bringing vice presidents into the inner circle, and as a result, the job of the vice president changed.

Walter Mondale had full access to President Carter and became a trusted adviser on all important matters. Al Gore, Bill Clinton's vice president for 8 years, was given numerous important responsibilities and also had full access to the president, including weekly one-on-one lunch meetings. Gore was very much in the inner circle: "one of three or four people whose advice Clinton sought on virtually every important matter."[18] And Dick Cheney played a very powerful role; some have suggested that he was the most powerful vice president in American history. Joe Biden continued the trend toward more powerful vice presidents. For example, Biden attended most strategy sessions in the Oval Office, and he was a key player in Obama's push for health care reform. In addition, Biden participated significantly in the discussions about whether or not to expand U.S. forces in Afghanistan. Ultimately, of course, the vice president has only as much power as the president allows him.

As to what powers Mike Pence, Donald Trump's vice president, will have, only time will tell. By all accounts, Pence is a smart, serious public official, and one can certainly imagine the president leaning on him for much advice. As noted above, however, the extent to which the vice president is consulted by his boss varies from one administration to the next. We will have to see.

The Informal Powers of the President

7.3 Establish how the "power to persuade" expands presidential power beyond the Constitution.

In 1960, political scientist Richard Neustadt published an important book called *Presidential Power.* It suggested that the formal powers of the presidency, as outlined in the Constitution, were rather minor: They amounted to little more than a clerkship, by which the occupant of the White House is in the position to provide services to others in the federal government.[19] Instead, Neustadt argued, presidential power is the power to persuade.

FIGURE 7.1 The Evolution of Presidential Powers

The framers were unsure about executive powers, which helps explain the vagueness of Article II. While they knew that future presidents and events would help fill in the blanks, they likely could not have imagined the steady expansion of executive powers. The irony, of course, is that while presidential powers have greatly expanded, there are growing forces that extend beyond a president's control.

■ *Would the framers have accepted the expansion of presidential power as necessary, given the nature of our world? Or would they have balked at the pivotal role that presidents play in nearly every aspect of modern American governance?*

How have presidential powers evolved since the adoption of the Constitution?

CRITICAL THINKING QUESTIONS

1789–1797 **George Washington** sets the precedent of a powerful but constrained executive.	Other presidents follow Washington's lead, and Congress becomes the focal point of American government.	What if Washington had decided to stay in office for life? Why was it so important for him to have stepped down after serving for only two terms?
1861–1865 **Abraham Lincoln** takes charge during the Civil War.	Lincoln establishes "presidential prerogative." Future presidents recognize that the executive branch should have weighty powers during times of crisis.	While most agree that presidents should have broad powers during times of crisis, what sort of dangers does this type of leeway create for a democracy?
1901–1908 **Theodore Roosevelt** uses the "bully pulpit" to shape public opinion and push his Progressive Movement reforms through Congress.	Teddy Roosevelt introduces the stewardship model, where presidential powers extend to everything except that which is prohibited by the Constitution.	What if Teddy Roosevelt had not used the bully pulpit to generate public support for his progressive reforms? Would he have been as successful in getting Congress to act?
1933–1945 **Franklin D. Roosevelt** takes office in the midst of the Great Depression, and his New Deal programs create new federal agencies and institutions, which transform the national government.	FDR forever shatters the constrained presidential model, changing the nature of federalism. The new Executive Office of the President places the president at the center of American governance.	What if a different president had been elected instead? Were FDR's personality and leadership skills central to the institutional changes that occurred? Or would the changes have occurred regardless of who was in the White House?
1945–1953 **Harry S. Truman** presides over America's rise as a military superpower, in an era of increased global economic interdependence.	The role of presidents in both domestic and foreign affairs is heightened.	What if Truman had not made the decision to use the atomic bomb on Japan to end World War II? What is it about modern warfare that heightens the powers of American presidents?
1981–1989 **Ronald Reagan,** the "Great Communicator," takes office and makes use of new modes of communication to sell the public on his agenda.	Presidents are able to speak directly to the American public with the aid of television (and later the Internet). By persuading the public, presidents can help shape congressional activities.	Can modern presidents be successful today if they are not great communicators? Has the Internet made this "qualification" more or less important?
1993–2001 **Bill Clinton** appoints his wife, Hillary Clinton, to lead a task force on health care reform, ushering in an era of expanded influence for running "mates": first ladies and vice presidents.	Vice presidents and first ladies have become important elements of increased presidential powers, especially with the advent of television and the Internet.	Is it also possible for missteps by running "mates" to decrease presidential powers?

The Power to Persuade

The real powers of any president are to use a combination of personality and political skills to lobby members of Congress. A president who feels strongly about a program or a policy initiative can tap into the many informal tools that the office makes possible, including the office's prestige, charm, the fear that others have of retribution, the need for special favors, and bargaining skills. Neustadt's book was very much a prescription—a guide for presidents to understand the true breadth of their powers. Both John F. Kennedy and Bill Clinton, for example, were said to have kept *Presidential Power* next to their beds.

Barack Obama employed a battalion of informal tools, such as invitations to the White House, trips on Air Force One, and telephone calls, to persuade wavering members of Congress to back health care reform in the spring of 2010. Indeed, many attribute the success of the final push for reform to Obama's ability to persuade members of his own party to stay on the ship. The same sort of pressure was used to help secure the extension of the payroll tax credit in December of 2011. Republicans are quick to point out, however, that while Obama may have been persuasive with members of his own party, his ability to bridge the partisan gap—to reach out to members in the other party—was lackluster, at best.

The ability (and necessity) to persuade has more or less always been central to a successful president. As president, Thomas Jefferson was a master of this tactic, holding dinner parties at which matters of state were informally discussed and decided by his cabinet and key members of Congress. New routes to persuasion opened up in the twentieth century, much to the benefit of presidential power. With the successive developments of radio, television, and the Internet, presidents have had widening opportunities to speak directly to the public—a process known as **going public**. Winning the public's hearts and minds was found to be even more potent than persuading a few members of Congress.

Franklin D. Roosevelt, who broadcast "fireside chats" on the radio, first showed how a president could establish a deep personal bond with the American people. John F. Kennedy used television to build an image that was both glamorous and admired. Ronald Reagan, dubbed "The Great Communicator" by the press, was especially skillful at connecting with the public on television, due in no small measure to his years of training as an actor. As suggested by Figure 7.2, some presidents have been more successful at gathering support than others.

Barack Obama was the first president to make extensive use of on-line communication tools. Building on his successful "net-root" presidential campaigns in 2008 and 2012, the White House launched a robust Web site (Whitehouse.gov) where citizens could keep abreast of policy developments, news stories, novel pictures, and the president's daily schedule, and click on a dizzying array of links to information on federal programs and events. Nearly all of the president's activities were documented on this site, and of course they had a very active Facebook page. By putting all press conferences and other official notices and speeches on YouTube, the White House was able to bypass traditional media outlets and connect with the public directly. Given Donald Trump's propensity for using Twitter and other social media outlets, one can certainly imagine he would continue these sorts of outreach techniques.

going public
Appealing directly to the people to garner support for presidential initiatives. For instance, presidents will often hold a press conference or an address in the White House Rose Garden when they are looking to build public support for a proposal that is languishing in Congress.

The Political Context

Stephen Skowronek, a Yale University scholar, advances another explanation for the evolution of informal presidential powers.[20] He argues that a president's power is largely determined by broader political forces, what scholars call the *political order* or context. An approach that works in one era might fall flat in another.

Skowronek identifies four distinct periods. In the first period, stretching from the early years of the nation to the reelection of Andrew Jackson in 1832, presidents garnered power through close, personal interactions with political elites. If the president was able to forge close, personal relations with a small group of decision makers, he was more likely to prevail. Presidential powers during the second period, from 1832 until the end

FIGURE 7.2 The Ups and Downs of Presidential Approval Ratings

Presidents may benefit or suffer from the winds of public opinion. But on closer inspection, we see a pattern where most presidents begin their term of office with high approval ratings and end their stay with lagging support.

■ *Are presidents bound to fail in the eyes of the public? What made Gerald Ford, Ronald Reagan, and Bill Clinton the exceptions?*

SOURCE: Gallup Poll, 1960–2016 Gallup, Inc. From http://www.gallup.com/poll/124922/presidential-approval-center.aspx.

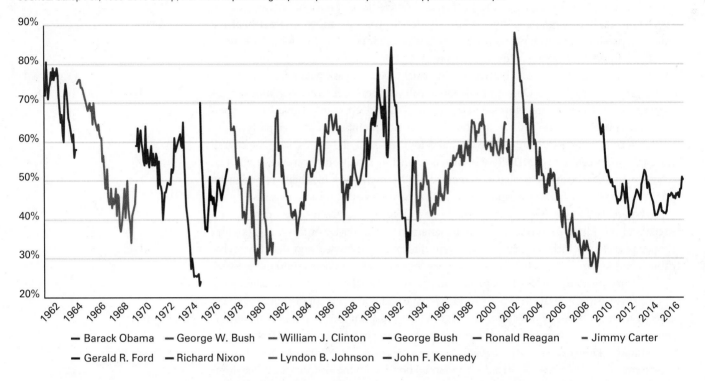

- Barack Obama - George W. Bush - William J. Clinton - George Bush - Ronald Reagan - Jimmy Carter
- Gerald R. Ford - Richard Nixon - Lyndon B. Johnson - John F. Kennedy

of the nineteenth century, hinged on the ability of presidents to forge agreements with local party bosses. The period from the turn of the nineteenth century until the departure of Richard Nixon in 1973 exemplified pluralist politics. Here, presidential power sprung from the ability to bargain and negotiate agreements among competing interests. Finally, the most recent era has featured plebiscitary politics, in which forging a personal connection with the public is imperative. Central to Skowronek's approach is the suggestion that informal presidential powers are dependent on the political order of the day.

First Ladies

Finally, another critically important source of presidential power has always been first ladies. From Martha Washington to Michelle Obama, these women have provided informal advice, advocated significant policy reform, undertaken a host of symbolic functions, and lobbied lawmakers and foreign dignitaries.

During most of our nation's history, first ladies limited their political work to informal, behind-the-scenes activities. For instance, the profound role played by Abigail Adams in helping her husband John maintain a cool head during his entire political career—and especially his presidency—is well documented. Another critically important first lady was Edith Bolling Galt Wilson. Her husband, Woodrow, suffered a stroke and was left partly paralyzed in 1919. He was incapacitated for several months, during which time Edith spoke and acted on his behalf. Her critics called her the "first lady president."

The activities of first ladies became much more public with Eleanor Roosevelt, the wife of Franklin D. Roosevelt. She traveled extensively and spoke on behalf of her husband's New Deal policies as well as her own concerns (centering mostly on the condition of poor children in America). She also wrote a newspaper column and worked tirelessly for Democratic candidates across the country. After her husband's death, Eleanor Roosevelt became a U.S. delegate to the United Nations, taking a lead on issues related to human rights and world poverty.

Perhaps the most dramatic change to the role of first ladies came about with Hillary Rodham Clinton. As a Yale-trained lawyer, Clinton had spearheaded a successful education reform task force while her husband was governor of Arkansas, in the process drawing national media attention. As she and her husband took up residence in the White House, her role as a powerful and public aide to her husband, President Bill Clinton, continued. Upon leaving the White House in 2000, Hillary Clinton was elected U.S. senator of New York and later was named Secretary of State in the Obama administration in 2009. She served in that office until 2013.

Michelle Obama undertook the more traditional approach of being a close confidant to her husband but not a key participant in most policy debates. She took the lead on issues that were important to her, including support for military families, helping women balance careers and family, and the promotion of national service. She also brought attention to the problems of obesity and poor eating habits among children in America. As her husband's reelection approached, however, Michelle Obama spent much more time at campaign rallies and fundraising events.

As for what role Melania Trump will play as first lady, it is difficult to say. We do know that she played a very modest role during the campaign, but it is certainly possible that her real influence will be behind closed doors. Many of the most important first ladies wielded great influence, while maintaining a low public profile. Also of note, she will become the first foreign-born first lady since John Quincy Adam's wife, Louisa, in 1825.

The Roles of Modern Presidents

7.4 Identify the duties and functions of modern presidents.

Contemporary presidents are called on to perform a staggering number of duties and to play a dizzying variety of roles. It has been said that no job can prepare you for the presidency, and no job is similar. Still, we can break down a modern president's tasks into several categories or functional roles.

The President as Chief of State

When George Washington took the helm of the federal government in April 1789, his role in ceremonial events was unclear. On the one hand, everyone understood the importance of ritual and formal events. There would be occasions when the nation would need a leader to perform such functions—addressing Congress, greeting

There are times when we look to presidents to help heal the nation, to help us with our sorrow and grief.
The casket of Rev. Clementa Pinckney sits beneath the podium as President Barack Obama delivers the eulogy during his funeral service, Friday, June 26, 2015, in Charleston, S.C. Pinckney, a well-known civil rights leader, was assassinated in his church during a Bible study session.

foreign dignitaries, speaking on the nation's behalf during times of celebration and grief, or even meeting ordinary citizens. If the president would not perform these functions, who would? In most political systems throughout the world, both then and now, a monarch or dictator undertakes chief-of-state functions.

Washington rejected all titles. Vice President John Adams proposed to the Senate that the president be addressed with a dignified title, such as "His High Mightiness," but neither the senators nor Washington himself accepted such an idea, which would have been hated by most Americans of the time. Nor did Washington wear any sort of robe, crown, or military uniform. It was Washington who established two acceptable titles for all future chief executives: "Mr. President" or "Mr. [last name]." In many ways, presidents would be regular citizens.

Still, all presidents perform ceremonial functions. Washington held formal gatherings, called *levees,* at which citizens would line up and be greeted one by one with a grave presidential bow. That, in the late eighteenth century, was expected, as a way of investing the presidency with dignity. But even that seemed too kingly to many Americans, and beginning with President Jefferson, a more informal tone permeated the presidency. Today, we expect presidents to make a telephone call to the winning Super Bowl team, to throw out a baseball at the start of the World Series, and to pardon the White House turkey on Thanksgiving. We also look to presidents for stability, wisdom, and composure during times of crisis. When the nation was shattered and shaken to its core by the terrorist attacks on September 11, 2001, we all turned to George W. Bush to steady the ship, to bring us together, and to help us move on. And when 29 miners died in West Virginia in the spring of 2010, the worst mining accident in 40 years, it was Barack Obama who gave the eulogy at the memorial service. He did the same in June 2015 after nine people were shot at the Emanuel African Methodist Episcopal Church in Charlestown, South Carolina. Some critics look down on the chief-of-state role, suggesting that these sorts of activities are all fluff. But whether we live on a dairy farm in Vermont, in the suburbs of Los Angeles, or on a beach in North Carolina, we are all Americans. Ceremonial dinners and occasions to toss a baseball out at a special game might seem extraneous, but through these and many other events, our diverse nation becomes more unified.

The President as Chief Legislator

Article I of the Constitution states that Congress will undertake legislative functions—the passing of laws and the collection and distribution of funds. Article II makes the executive branch responsible for implementing the will of the legislative branch. At the same time, in keeping with the design of shared power, presidents are given some legislative authority: the power to veto bills, the ability to recommend measures for consideration, and the duty from time to time to inform Congress as to the "state of the union."

Consistent with the restrained view of presidential powers, occupants of the White House were reluctant to dig deeply into legislative matters during the first 140 years of our nation's history. Presidents believed it their role to wait for Congress to act. In the eight years of his presidency, George Washington expressed an opinion on only five pieces of legislation.[21] Some presidents during this period—especially Andrew Jackson, Abraham Lincoln, Theodore Roosevelt, and Woodrow Wilson— were deeply immersed in legislative matters, but they were exceptions to the rule. A good estimate is that during this period, only about one-quarter of all significant policy initiatives originated with the executive branch.

This changed in 1933 with the inauguration of Franklin D. Roosevelt. Amid the crisis of the Great Depression, not only did FDR send a stream of measures to Congress for consideration, he and his aides also plunged into the legislative process with gusto, writing bills and twisting congressional arms to make sure that they passed. No one doubted that FDR was in charge of making policy during his first two terms, that he was very much the chief legislator.

All presidents since FDR have sought to lead the policymaking process, but some of them have been better at legislative matters than others. Lyndon Johnson was particularly good at "working the legislature." As a former member of the House, and especially as the Senate's majority leader, Johnson understood how the system worked, including the incentives that might be most effective with a legislative leader or a rank-and-file member. He was aggressive about getting his way, routinely giving reluctant members of Congress the "Johnson treatment." Jimmy Carter's story was altogether different. Having never worked in Washington before moving into the White House, Carter was simply unfamiliar with how things worked in the national legislature. In the end, Carter got only modest support from Congress, even though his own party (the Democrats) controlled both chambers (see Figure 7.3). President Barack Obama's decision to hire former legislative leader Rahm Emanuel as his chief of staff and his early legislative successes indicate that he truly understands the process and appreciates the importance of legislative dynamics.

LEGISLATIVE TOOLS: THE VETO   Presidents have at their disposal a number of tools and resources to aid their efforts with the legislature. The **veto** is critical. Presidents can shape legislation by rejecting measures passed by Congress. Sometimes presidents veto measures on principle, because they strongly disagree with the proposal (for example, when George W. Bush vetoed a measure to increase funding for stem cell research) or think it unconstitutional; at other times, they may consider the goals laudable but the

veto

The disapproval of a bill or resolution by the president. A veto can be overturned by two-thirds vote in both houses of Congress.

FIGURE 7.3 Congressional Support for Presidential Initiatives

This figure charts the percentage of presidential initiatives that are approved by Congress. Clearly, some presidents are more successful with the legislature than others. What makes this figure especially interesting is that presidents can be successful even when the other party controls Congress.

■ *What force do you suppose leads to greater success with Congress, even when the president faces a "hostile" legislature?*

SOURCE: Harold Stanley and Richard Niemi, *Vital Statistics on American Politics, 2016.*

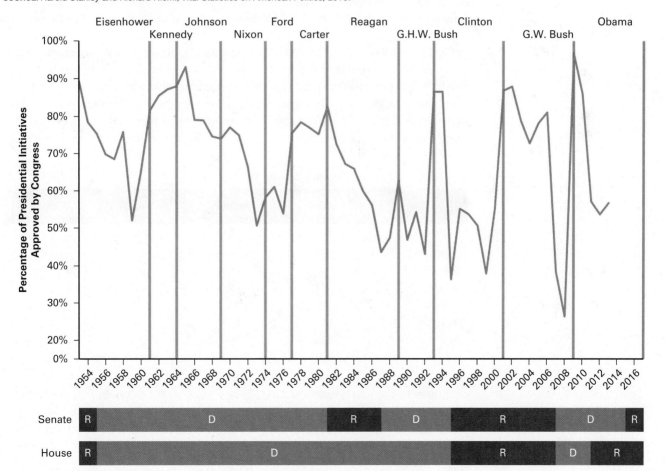

details wrong. There are two types of vetoes. One approach is to simply send the legislation back to Congress with a message as to why the president disapproves—this is called a *veto message*. The legislation can still become law if two-thirds of both houses of Congress vote to override it. Overrides are very rare; only about 3 percent of all vetoes have been overridden because presidents are reluctant to lose face by vetoing bills that are likely to be overridden. If a president fails to act on a piece of legislation within 10 days, it becomes law. If Congress adjourns within those 10 days, however, the president can let the measure die through a *pocket veto*. Here, there is neither a signature nor a veto message. Pocket vetoes are quite rare, especially on major legislation.

Some modern presidents have been more willing than others to veto bills, as Table 7.3 suggests, even when Congress has been controlled by the same party. However, this table is also misleading. Actual vetoes are less significant in the legislative process than the *threat* of their use. Not wanting to be embarrassed by the president or to waste everybody's time, the legislature often responds to the threat of a veto by either not moving on the measure or by crafting a version of the bill that is acceptable to the president. Sometimes the threat is quite public. When Bill Clinton sought to reform the nation's health care system, he picked up a pen during a State of the Union address, waved it back and forth, and declared that if Congress did not send him a bill that covered all children, he would gladly use the pen to veto the bill. In the spring of 2012, the House approved a measure keeping student loan interest rates at 3.4 percent. Barack Obama supported this measure, but he threatened to veto the bill because the Republicans, who controlled the chamber, sought to finance the measure by removing funding for the Prevention and Public Health Fund in the Affordable Care Act of 2010—Obama's first term signature achievement. His threat essentially killed the bill, as the Senate did not even bring it up for a vote. Many veto threats are delivered in private, either directly by the president or by presidential aides. It is difficult to know how often the threat of a veto is used, but observers of congressional and presidential dynamics agree on its significance. For more information on the push for health care reform in the Unites States, see the Timeline.

LEGISLATIVE TOOLS: THE STATE OF THE UNION The presidential duty to inform Congress about the state of the union each year has become another powerful legislative tool. Rather than seeing this as a chore, presidents now understand it as a rare opportunity to set the legislative agenda for the coming year. For about the first 100 years of the nation's history, these messages were written. Since then (with a few exceptions), they have been formal speeches delivered in the House Chambers. It is an opportunity

TABLE 7.3 Presidential Vetoes, 1933–2016

	Regular Vetoes	Pocket Vetoes	Total Vetoes	Vetoes Overridden
F. Roosevelt	372	263	635	9
Truman	180	70	250	12
Eisenhower	73	108	181	2
Kennedy	12	9	21	—
L. Johnson	16	14	30	—
Nixon	26	17	43	7
Ford	48	18	66	12
Carter	13	18	31	2
Reagan	39	39	78	9
G. H. W. Bush	29	17	46	1
Clinton	36	1	37	2
G. W. Bush	11	1	12	4
Obama	12	0	12	1

SOURCES: John Woolley and Gerhard Peters, "The American Presidency Project," http://www.presidency.ucsb.edu/data/vetoes.php.

to lay out broad principles and to offer concrete measures. Even more important, it is an opportunity to speak directly to the American people. Many Americans watch the State of the Union address, and presidents use this rare occasion to try to shape public opinion, which of course goes a long way in persuading legislators.

The President as Chief Diplomat

Presidents are in charge of foreign affairs. This is what the framers had in mind, it is strengthened by over 200 years of precedent, and it has been confirmed by several Supreme Court decisions. As stated by the Supreme Court in *United States* v. *Curtiss-Wright* (1936), the president is the "sole organ" in conducting foreign affairs, and his powers are "exclusive." Indeed, the president enjoys a freedom from congressional restrictions that "would not be admissible where domestic affairs alone are involved."[22]

There are a number of ways in which presidents can conduct foreign policy. Obviously, they can travel around the world, meeting with the leaders of other nations, forging ties and formal alliances. The Constitution states that they can appoint and receive ambassadors. In appointing ambassadors, which the Constitution requires them to do with the advice and consent of the Senate, presidents can choose officials who share their outlook toward a given nation or foreign affairs more generally. Accepting ambassadors might seem a less significant act, but it can be used as a powerful tool. When presidents "accept" the emissary of another nation, it signifies that the United States recognizes that nation's existence and that its leaders hold power legitimately.

Another critically important foreign policy tool is the **treaty**, a formal agreement between the United States and one or more other sovereign nations. The intent of the framers was that the Senate would work closely with the executive branch to negotiate and ratify treaties. This approach did not last long, as George Washington became frustrated with both the slow pace of the Senate and the difficulties of arriving at a consensus. From that point onward, presidents have negotiated treaties independently and then asked the Senate to ratify them by the two-thirds margin that the Constitution requires. For example, in April 2010, Barack Obama negotiated a treaty with Russian President Dmitry A. Medvedev to reduce each nation's nuclear warheads and launchers. The Strategic Arms Reduction Treaty—known by its acronym, START—was signed into effect on April 7, 2010. Given that presidents have usually been of the same party as the majority in the Senate, it should come as no surprise that the Senate has rejected very few treaties. Of the approximately 1,500 that have been sent to the Senate, only 15 have been voted down. However, a good many, roughly 150, have been withdrawn because they appeared to lack support.

In some ways more important than treaties are less formal **executive agreements**—also known as "arrangements"—between the United States and other nations. Whereas treaties are generally high-profile matters, attracting a great deal of media attention, executive agreements are often arranged in secret. They do not require Senate approval, which makes them especially appealing to presidents—particularly if they confront a hostile Congress—but the Case Act of 1972 requires the president to inform Congress of executive agreements within 60 days.

Presidents may make executive agreements only in areas where they have the power to act, and they often deal with relatively minor concerns, such as tariffs, customs regulations, or postal matters. Yet some presidents have used executive agreements in very important ways. In 1973, President Nixon used an executive agreement to end the American conflict (never a declared war) with North Vietnam and to exchange prisoners of war. Such an agreement was also used by President Reagan in 1981 to form a strategic alliance with Israel. Perhaps not surprisingly, given the growing importance and complexity of world affairs as well as the potential roadblocks to winning Senate approval of treaties, the number of executive agreements made by presidents has increased greatly in the past few decades.

treaty
A formal agreement between governments. For example, in the 1970s the United States joined many other nations in agreeing to limit the testing and development of nuclear weapons.

executive agreements
Binding commitments between the United States and other countries agreed to by the president but, unlike treaties, not requiring approval by the Senate.

With the hopes of delaying their development of an atomic weapon for a decade or longer, Barak Obama forged an agreement with Iran in June 2015. Crippling sanctions against Iran would be eased and the United States and other allies would release $150 billion in frozen assets, if Iran agreed to drastically reduce its stockpile of uranium and reduce by about two-thirds the number of its gas centrifuges (used to make atomic bombs) for 13 years. The deal had all the markings of a treaty, but because Obama knew that he would not get it ratified by the Republican-controlled Senate, he used an executive agreement-like maneuver. It was agreed that the deal could be scuttled if Congress could pass a resolution of disapproval. Such a move would have to survive a presidential veto, however. The deal took effect on October 18, 2015.

The President as Commander in Chief

Article II, Section 2, of the Constitution appoints the president commander in chief of all American military forces. When they take the oath of office, presidents swear that they will "preserve, protect, and defend" our nation. The framers of our system believed it essential that one person be responsible for decisive action during times of crisis—in the event of an invasion, for example, which was a real threat in the late eighteenth century. As for the oversight of an ongoing conflict or the direction of prolonged military engagements, however, presidents share power with Congress. That is, the president is commander in chief of the armed forces, but Congress is charged with declaring wars (in Article I, Section 8). Also, Congress has the responsibility to raise and support armies (i.e., to raise and allocate funds for military matters).

During the first few decades of our nation, the president's decision to go to war was clearly shared with Congress. In 1803, for example, Thomas Jefferson sent the U.S. Navy to fight the Barbary pirates—North African rulers who were seizing American merchant vessels in the Mediterranean Sea and enslaving their crews unless the United States paid them tribute. But Congress had authorized this attack in advance.[23] Presidential war powers took a leap forward during the Civil War. Congress was in recess when the southern states seceded at the end of 1860 and in early 1861, as well as when fighting began at Fort Sumter in April 1861, only a few weeks after Lincoln's inauguration. Without congressional authorization, Lincoln called up the state militias, suspended the writ of habeas corpus, and slapped a naval blockade on the rebellious southern states. Critics claimed that Lincoln's acts were dictatorial, but he argued that they were necessary to preserve the Union. His defense of his "doctrine of necessity" is rather compelling:

> [My] oath to preserve the Constitution to the best of my ability imposed upon me the duty of preserving, by every indispensable means, that government....Was it possible to lose the nation and yet preserve the Constitution? By general law, the limb must be protected, yet often a limb must be amputated to save a life; but a life is never wisely given to save a limb. I felt the measures otherwise unconstitutional might become lawful by becoming indispensable to the preservation of the Constitution through the preservation of the nation.[24]

Essentially, Lincoln acted and left it to Congress either to accept or cancel his action later. Presidents since Lincoln have taken this "presidential prerogative" to heart, arguing that they are uniquely situated to protect the nation and should be given a free hand in all military emergencies.

In 1950, Harry Truman ordered troops to defend South Korea against a North Korean attack without requesting congressional authority (he said that the United States was engaging in a "police action" in support of a United Nations act). In the 1960s and early 1970s, both Lyndon Johnson and Richard Nixon waged the Vietnam War without a formal congressional declaration. Indeed, many observers think that the days of Congress actually declaring war—which last happened right after Japan's 1941 attack on Pearl Harbor—may now be over.

In 1973, after the United States and North Vietnam signed a peace agreement, Congress attempted to rein in presidential war making by passing the **War Powers Resolution**—and then overriding President Nixon's veto of it. This act requires that the president consult with Congress in "every possible instance" before sending troops to combat, that the president report to Congress in writing within 48 hours after ordering troops into harm's way, and that any military engagement must end within 60 days unless Congress either declares war or otherwise authorizes the use of force (provisions allowed for 90 days under certain circumstances).

Since 1973, every president has claimed that the War Powers Resolution is unconstitutional. Nevertheless, rather than defy the act and test its constitutionality in the federal courts, and also in an effort to build broad public support (a critically important factor in waging successful long-term wars), all presidents who have sent American forces into battle have first sought congressional support for their action in the form of resolutions. For example, President George W. Bush sought and received a broad congressional authorization before invading Afghanistan in 2001 and Iraq in 2003. Barack Obama consulted with Congress before air strikes against ISIS in Syria and Iraq in 2014. It should also be noted that many believe the War Powers Resolution may actually expand presidential war-making powers given that their moves are virtually unchecked for the first 90 days. These days a great deal of war making can take place in three months.

Nearly 7,000 American lives have been lost in the wars in Iraq and Afghanistan. Here coffins of U.S. military personnel are prepared to be offloaded at Dover Air Force Base. While public support for our military efforts there was high in the early years, as the massive costs of both wars and the number of casualties grew, Americans seemed to lose faith in the effort.

■ *How does Congress have the right (and obligation) to step in and change the course of military engagements after a period of time? At what point should it take such action?*

> **POLL** Which of the following best reflects your view regarding the war powers in the United States?

1. The president should be left unchecked when it comes to war making.
2. The president should be the leader during times of war, but he or she should consult with members of Congress when possible.
3. War making powers should be evenly divided between the president and Congress.
4. Congress should be at the helm when it comes to war making. Presidents should simply implement Congress's will.

Contrary to popular belief, modern presidents do not have unlimited foreign policy powers; Congress has the power to allocate or deny funds for military engagements. For example, in 1974, Congress cut off further funding for the war in Vietnam. But what if a situation arises in which the president sees military action as being in our nation's interest but Congress disagrees and fails to appropriate the necessary resources? This issue came to a head in the 1980s in the **Iran-Contra affair**, when aides to Ronald Reagan channeled U.S. funds to rebels fighting the leftist government in Nicaragua—even though Congress had passed a measure forbidding it. To many people, this was a clear violation of the law: Congress had spoken, and President Reagan, the executive, had thwarted its will. The Justice Department moved forward and eventually secured a number of felony convictions. The lesson from the Iran-Contra affair is that while presidents see their commander-in-chief authority as sweeping, Congress still has one crucial power—the power of the purse.

War Powers Resolution

A measure passed by Congress in 1973 designed to limit presidential deployment of troops unless Congress grants approval for a longer period. Every president since the passage of this measure has argued that it is unconstitutional, and has not agreed to abide by its provisions.

Iran-Contra affair

The Reagan administration's unauthorized diversion of funds from the sale of arms to Iran to support the Contras, rebels fighting to overthrow the leftist government of Nicaragua.

The President as Chief Executive

We have discussed several important elements of the president's chief executive function, including the assembling of staff and the cabinet, enforcing laws, and spending the funds that are allocated and appropriated by Congress. The president is in many ways the nation's chief administrator and head bureaucrat. This role might suggest that the president's hands are tied by the will of Congress—that this function affords little leeway to shape policy—but this is only partially correct. At times, Congress makes its will clear with exact instructions to the executive branch. At other times, only vague outlines are provided, thereby leaving a great deal of ambiguity and leeway. This gives presidents and the federal bureaucracy a chance to shape public policy.

Second, many authorities believe the very size of the federal bureaucracy has shifted the balance of power toward the executive branch. During the first few decades, our government had only about 1,000 federal employees (most of whom staffed local post offices). Even so, President Jefferson thought that there were too many officials and carried out a severe staff reduction! In recent years, the number of federal employees has climbed to roughly 2.6 million (excluding active-duty members of the military). Although the vast majority of federal employees are civil service workers, the power to appoint certain high officials who lead the massive agencies and set their policies is an important executive function.

executive order

A regulation made by the president that has the effect of law. In the summer of 2012, for example, President Obama issued an executive order limiting the deportation of some illegal immigrant children brought to the United States by their parents.

On top of this, presidents can issue **executive orders**, which are essentially rules or regulations that have the effect of law—as noted above. At times, executive orders are used to clarify existing legislation, but at other times, they have the effect of making new policy. There are three types of executive orders: *proclamations*, which serve the ceremonial purpose of declaring holidays and celebrations, and *national security directives* and *presidential decision directives*, both of which deal with national security and defense matters. Three of the most famous executive orders were used to ease some of the barriers to black men and women caused by generations of racial discrimination. Abraham Lincoln issued the Emancipation Proclamation, freeing the slaves of the South in 1863. Harry Truman issued an executive order in 1948 ending segregation in the armed forces, and Lyndon Johnson issued an executive order in 1966 making affirmative action a federal policy. George W. Bush used an executive order to create the White House Office of Faith-Based and Community Initiatives in 2001, and in 2010, to persuade certain House Democrats to back the health care initiative, Barack Obama issued an executive order affirming that no federal monies would be used for abortions. In the spring of 2012 Obama issued an executive order limiting the deportation of certain illegal immigrant children who came to the United States with their parents—a move that was later checked by the Supreme Court. By the end of this first term, Barack Obama had issued roughly 170 executive orders.

signing statement

A written proclamation issued by the president regarding how the executive branch intends to interpret a new law. Occasionally these statements seem to contradict what Congress had in mind, making them quite controversial.

Another tool that presidents have at their disposal to shape public policy is what is known as a **signing statement**—a written proclamation issued when a president signs a bill into law that states how the executive branch will interpret the measure, which is often different from what Congress intended. Controversy has arisen over the constitutionality of signing statements—especially the large number of statements issued by George W. Bush. During his tenure in office, Bush issued nearly 200 signing statements, challenging over 1,200 provisions in various laws. By contrast, at the end of Barack Obama's first term he had issued only about two dozen signing statements.

Regulatory review can be used as a unilateral executive action. When Congress passes legislation, the details of how these acts are to be implemented is usually left vague. The federal bureaucracy is charged with policy implementation, and of course, the president controls this part of the government. The vagueness of the laws therefore allows presidents to tweak and sometimes dramatically alter the execution of the law through rules created by the agencies involved. Presidents can sometime fail to enforce a statue they disagree with, also. This is controversial, but again more common than you might think. Barack Obama, for instance, refused to defend the federal Defense of Marriage Act, a number of immigration laws, and to aggressively prosecute marijuana-related crimes.

Finally, presidents can shape public policy by working to secure funding for new or existing programs. While Congress has the ultimate authority to set federal budget policies, each year presidents offer their own budget plans. Developed by an extensive staff of experts with the Office of Management and Budget (OMB), the president's budget is generally considered the starting point for congressional negotiations.

Because the president is "first off the mark" with a budget outline, and because of the expertise of the OMB, savvy presidents often get a great deal of what they want, especially when Congress is controlled by the same party.

Congress will often agree with a president's unilateral action and there will be no response. This is more common when the government is unified (meaning that one party controls both the Congress and the presidency). When Congress disagrees with a president's action, they can pass laws to restrict the move or to clarify a statute's implementation. The president has the upper hand, however, as he or she can veto the new legislation. One final retort would be to sue the president in the federal courts. For example, Senator Rand Paul (R-Ky.) filed a federal suit against Barack Obama's decision to allow the National Security Agency to collect telephone data without a warrant. Suits of this sort are rarely successful, but they do draw attention to the issue.

The President's Other Roles

While the list of duties and responsibilities outlined previously is long, there are many additional roles. For instance, some have suggested that modern presidents must be economists in chief. That is, they are expected to keep a close eye on the nation's economy and to take immediate and effective actions when conditions dictate. Presidents are also expected to be moral leaders and to set an ethical tone in both politics and society. Many supported George W. Bush in the 2000 election because they believed he would set a higher moral standard than his predecessor, Bill Clinton. Many also expect presidents to be the heads of their political party, pushing the party's policy agenda and helping other party members raise money during elections.

The Two Presidencies

Scholars have tried to merge these various roles of the president into a neat model. The most successful attempt has been an approach advanced by political scientist Aaron Wildavsky in 1966. He introduced the "two presidency" thesis (sometimes called the dual presidency model).[25] Wildavsky suggested that the numerous roles of the presidency could be broken down into two categories: domestic affairs and defense/foreign policy. Wildavsky argued that presidents are often frustrated when it comes to domestic affairs, given the numerous actors and Congress's ability to check presidential initiatives. Instead, presidents are significantly better equipped to lead in foreign policy and defense matters. Not surprisingly, presidents will often turn to foreign policy matters later on in their tenure, likely due to frustration over the difficulties in advancing domestic policies. Many scholars have offered critiques of the two presidency model, including the idea that the lines between the two areas have blurred in recent years. Yet, the core logic—that presidents confront unique challenges and opportunities in both domestic and foreign policy—is important to bear in mind when considering all that presidents are asked to do.

Presidential Greatness

7.5 Evaluate the qualities that contribute to presidential success or failure.

The term **personal presidency** describes the mounting expectations that the public places on the president—"expectations that have grown faster than the capacity of presidential government to meet them."[26] In short, Americans have developed a personal connection, an emotional bond, with their presidents. A number of changes have led to this development, including the growing size and importance of the federal bureaucracy, the expansion of presidential powers, and the heavy use of television advertising during campaigns, which forces candidates to promise things they cannot deliver once in office.

personal presidency
The notion that there are greater and greater expectations placed on presidents, due in large measure to the way they run for office. At the same time, presidents are often unable to deliver on the promises they made during campaigns.

TIMELINE

The Battle Over Health Care Reform

Are democratic governments responsible for the well-being of their citizens? Most would agree that governments should provide military, police, and fire protection, as well as a safety net for those citizens unable to care for themselves. But when it comes to basic medical care for all citizens, not everyone agrees. President Barack Obama's drive for health care reform brought change to our system. While some believe that the reforms are modest compared to what is found in other systems, others suggest that with passage of the Health Care and Education Reconciliation Act of 2010, the nation took a dangerous step toward socialism.

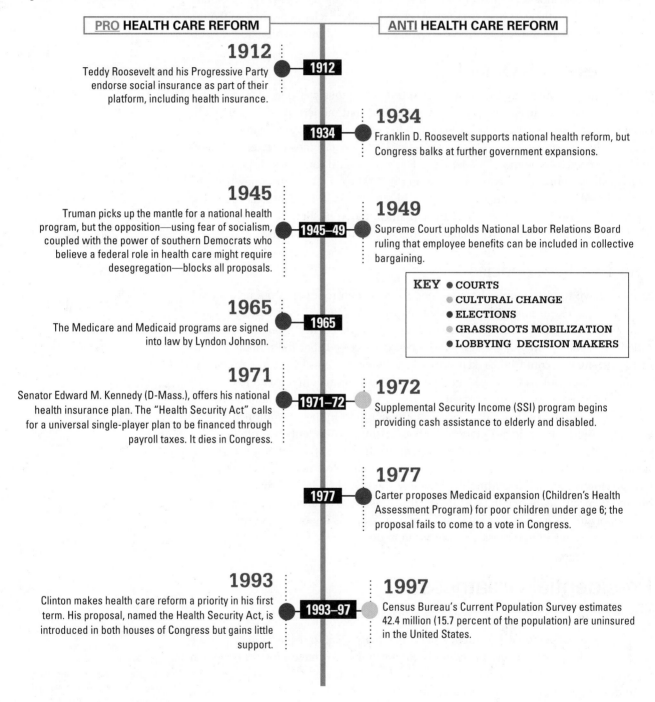

PRO HEALTH CARE REFORM **ANTI HEALTH CARE REFORM**

1912
Teddy Roosevelt and his Progressive Party endorse social insurance as part of their platform, including health insurance.

1934
Franklin D. Roosevelt supports national health reform, but Congress balks at further government expansions.

1945
Truman picks up the mantle for a national health program, but the opposition—using fear of socialism, coupled with the power of southern Democrats who believe a federal role in health care might require desegregation—blocks all proposals.

1949
Supreme Court upholds National Labor Relations Board ruling that employee benefits can be included in collective bargaining.

KEY ● COURTS ● CULTURAL CHANGE ● ELECTIONS ● GRASSROOTS MOBILIZATION ● LOBBYING DECISION MAKERS

1965
The Medicare and Medicaid programs are signed into law by Lyndon Johnson.

1971
Senator Edward M. Kennedy (D-Mass.), offers his national health insurance plan. The "Health Security Act" calls for a universal single-player plan to be financed through payroll taxes. It dies in Congress.

1972
Supplemental Security Income (SSI) program begins providing cash assistance to elderly and disabled.

1977
Carter proposes Medicaid expansion (Children's Health Assessment Program) for poor children under age 6; the proposal fails to come to a vote in Congress.

1993
Clinton makes health care reform a priority in his first term. His proposal, named the Health Security Act, is introduced in both houses of Congress but gains little support.

1997
Census Bureau's Current Population Survey estimates 42.4 million (15.7 percent of the population) are uninsured in the United States.

PRO HEALTH CARE REFORM | ANTI HEALTH CARE REFORM

2002

Bush launches Health Center Growth Initiative, expanding the number of community health centers.

2006

Massachusetts implements measure to provide health care coverage to all state residents. Legislation requires residents to obtain health insurance coverage. Vermont makes a similar move.

KEY
● COURTS
◐ CULTURAL CHANGE
● ELECTIONS
◐ GRASSROOTS MOBILIZATION
● LOBBYING DECISION MAKERS

2008

Presidential campaign focuses early on national health reform, but it is overshadowed later by the housing crisis and economic downturn.

2008

Senator Baucus, Chairman of the Senate Finance Committee, releases White Paper on health reform outlining a plan based on the Massachusetts model.

2010

Obama signs the Health Care and Education Reconciliation Act of 2010.

July, 2012

In a 5–4 decision, the Supreme Court upholds a key provision of the Affordable Health Care Act—the individual mandate.

November 6, 2012

Obama wins reelection; even hard-core Republicans accept the Affordable Health Care Act as the law of the land.

August 30, 2012

Romney is given Republican presidential nomination; pledges to overturn "Obamacare" as one of his first acts.

CRITICAL THINKING QUESTIONS

1. If we have a limited government that is by and for the people, should we expect help with health care costs? If we presume government will provide an education for all citizens, how is health care any different?

2. Why do you suppose so many presidents proposed health care reform, only to see their initiatives stopped in Congress? Is there a difference between the president's constituency and the constituencies of members of Congress? Are members of Congress more responsive to the influence of lobbyists than presidents?

SOURCE: Recreated by authors based on information from "Timeline: History of Health Reform Efforts in the U.S.," The Henry J. Kaiser Family Foundation, 2010, http://healthreform.kff.org/flash/health-reform-new.html. This information was reprinted with permission from the Henry J. Kaiser Family Foundation. The Kaiser Family Foundation is a non-profit private operating foundation, based in Menlo Park, California, dedicated to producing and communicating the best possible analysis and information on health issues.

Americans put more and more faith in their presidents to solve their problems and meet all challenges, both foreign and domestic. The problem, however, is that the executive branch is only one piece of the federal government and only one element of the world's economy. The majority of Americans believe that the president is the powerful center of life in America—this is comforting because the president appears to be in charge. But the truth is that the president must convince many other people to get on board with his policies in order for them to take effect. The outcome is dissatisfaction. Presidents often fail to meet our expectations, and we are left feeling disappointed and cynical. Some people would argue that this explains a string of "failed" presidencies.

Harry Truman and Lyndon Johnson—both of them vice presidents who entered the White House upon their predecessors' deaths—were rejected by their own party after leading the nation into controversial military entanglements. Having won reelection in a landslide in 1972, Richard Nixon just 2 years later resigned in disgrace, facing impeachment and likely conviction, after his criminal misconduct in the Watergate Affair was exposed. Jimmy Carter was perceived as bungling the nation's economy and being indecisive during the Iranian hostage crisis (which lasted for more than 12 months between 1979 and 1981), and the voters ejected him from office after just 4 years. Ronald Reagan faced a congressional inquiry into the Iran-Contra affair and may have escaped impeachment only because he was on the verge of retirement. George H. W. Bush was riding high early in his presidency and drew record high approval ratings after victory was won in the first Gulf War—but one year later, Bill Clinton defeated him, largely because of a downturn in the economy. Clinton served for two full terms but was impeached by the House—on grounds stemming from personal misconduct. George W. Bush left office with very low approval ratings, and Barack Obama saw his number drop by over 20 points during his first term in office. Half way through his second term Obama's ratings have dropped even lower, to roughly the 40 percent mark. One might conclude that modern executives are destined to fail, that "presidential greatness" is a thing of the past.

But what is presidential greatness? What is it that makes one chief executive better than another? Are there ingredients that can be combined to create a successful, distinguished presidency? Perhaps it is only when our nation confronts adversity that greatness can emerge. The three presidents who top nearly all scholarly lists of great chief executives—Washington, Lincoln, and Franklin D. Roosevelt—each confronted a major national crisis. Washington led the nation in its founding years, when the very success of the federal experiment hung in the balance; Lincoln had to preserve the Union and chose to abolish slavery during a civil war that cost 600,000 lives; and Roosevelt faced the gravest economic crisis in the nation's history and then fought World War II. No other presidents, even those who rank relatively high, had to surmount crises as dangerous as these.

George W. Bush has said that his presidency was shaped by the events of September 11, 2001. Some might conclude that he was a good president because he met the challenge of our new realities. Others will see his tenure in the White House as a failure because of the war in Iraq; they will argue he took the United States into the wrong war at the wrong time and against the wrong enemy.

Perhaps simple luck has much to do with successful or failed presidencies. But bad luck can only explain so much. Herbert Hoover—a man superbly qualified by education and early experience for the presidency—claimed to be the

Lyndon Johnson was masterful at engineering compromises and pushing through important domestic policies. The war in Vietnam spun out of control during his administration, however, and his popularity plummeted. Modern presidents are powerful, but they are far from omnipotent.

■ *How much leeway should presidents have in conducting military engagements? They are the commander in chief, but only Congress can declare a war. What's the proper balance?*

unluckiest president in history, given the stock market's collapse on his watch in 1929. Yet Hoover was crippled by his rigid attempts to apply orthodox economic theories to a situation that required innovative thinking. Lyndon Johnson inherited the unwinnable conflict in Vietnam from his White House predecessors, and despite his noble championing of the civil rights movement and his policies aimed at eradicating poverty, his presidency was plagued by riots and massive antiwar demonstrations on college campuses. In addition, after the glamorous and eloquent Kennedy, LBJ seemed an uncouth, untrustworthy, and ruthless wheeler-dealer who spoke with a widely mocked Texas drawl. Jimmy Carter's hands were tied when the Iranian militants who had seized the U.S. embassy in Tehran threatened to kill the American diplomats whom they had taken hostage. He also faced skyrocketing oil prices and a stagnating economy.

It is worth remembering the words of the man always ranked as one of the greatest presidents, Abraham Lincoln, responding in 1864 to a reporter's question: "I claim not to have controlled events, but confess plainly that events have controlled me." How Lincoln *did* act when confronted with those events, however, is the measure of his greatness.

Abraham Lincoln once noted, "I claim not to have controlled events, but confess plainly that events have controlled me."

■ *Do you think this is true, or simply modesty on Lincoln's part? Put a bit differently, can presidents be great without confronting exceptional circumstances?*

Circumstances matter. Yet even unlucky events can turn into triumphs of leadership if the president has the necessary character. And what defines great character in a political leader? Scholars and biographers have wrestled with this question for thousands of years, and there is no shortage of lists. The historian and presidential scholar Robert Dallek suggests that five qualities have been constants in the men who have most effectively fulfilled the presidential oath of office:[27]

1. *Vision:* All great presidents have had a clear understanding of where they wanted to lead the nation in its quest for a better future.

2. *Pragmatism:* All great presidents have been realists—leaders who understood that politics is the art of the possible and that flexible responses to changing conditions at home and abroad are essential.

3. *Consensus building:* All great presidents understood that their success depended on the consent of the governed. Moving government in a new direction, often down a difficult path, requires building a national consensus first.

4. *Charisma:* All great presidents have been able to capture and retain the affection and admiration of average citizens.

5. *Trustworthiness:* All truly successful presidents have had credibility and have earned the faith of their fellow citizens.

Many groups have attempted to measure presidential greatness. The conservative Federalist Society, joining forces with the *Wall Street Journal* in November 2005, undertook one such effort. The study involved 78 randomly selected presidency scholars: historians, political scientists, and law professors. Another, conducted by C-SPAN in 2009, also surveyed scholars, whose responses seem to have been slightly weighted in favor of the more liberal or "progressive" presidents. Table 7.4 shows the results from both polls. Still another ranking was pulled together by the American Political Science Association (APSA) in 2015. The results of their findings are found in Figure 7.4.

Although we might argue over the precise order of these rankings—whether one president should be ranked higher than another, whether Washington was better than Lincoln, or whether Harding, Buchanan, or Andrew Johnson was the worst of all—nearly all assessments of past presidents suggest similar groupings. Lincoln, Washington, both Roosevelts, and Jefferson were great leaders, and those at the bottom of this list, the presidents whose names seem the most obscure to us, are generally considered failures. The interesting part of this exercise is not the precise order but rather a consideration of the personal qualities and historical events that contributed

TABLE 7.4   Rankings of American Presidents

Wall Street Journal Ranking		C-SPAN Ranking	
Rank	Name	Rank	Name
1	George Washington	1	Abraham Lincoln
2	Abraham Lincoln	2	George Washington
3	Franklin D. Roosevelt	3	Franklin D. Roosevelt
4	Thomas Jefferson	4	Theodore Roosevelt
5	Theodore Roosevelt	5	Harry S. Truman
6	Andrew Jackson	6	John F. Kennedy
7	Harry S. Truman	7	Thomas Jefferson
8	Ronald Reagan	8	Dwight D. Eisenhower
9	Dwight D. Eisenhower	9	Woodrow Wilson
10	James K. Polk	10	Ronald Reagan
11	Woodrow Wilson	11	Lyndon B. Johnson
12	Grover Cleveland	12	James K. Polk
13	John Adams	13	Andrew Jackson
14	William McKinley	14	James Monroe
15	James Madison	15	Bill Clinton
16	James Monroe	16	William McKinley
17	Lyndon B. Johnson	17	John Adams
18	John F. Kennedy	18	George H. W. Bush
19	William Howard Taft	19	John Quincy Adams
20	John Quincy Adams	20	James Madison
21	George H. W. Bush	21	Grover Cleveland
22	Rutherford B. Hayes	22	Gerald R. Ford
23	Martin Van Buren	23	Ulysses S. Grant
24	Bill Clinton	24	William Howard Taft
25	Calvin Coolidge	25	Jimmy Carter
26	Chester A. Arthur	26	Calvin Coolidge
27	Benjamin Harrison	27	Richard M. Nixon
28	Gerald R. Ford	28	James A. Garfield
29	Herbert Hoover	29	Zachary Taylor
30	Jimmy Carter	30	Benjamin Harrison
31	Zachary Taylor	31	Martin Van Buren
32	Ulysses S. Grant	32	Chester A. Arthur
33	Richard M. Nixon	33	Rutherford B. Hayes
34	John Tyler	34	Herbert Hoover
35	Millard Fillmore	35	John Tyler
36	Andrew Johnson	36	George W. Bush
37	Franklin Pierce	37	Millard Fillmore
38	Warren G. Harding	38	Warren G. Harding
39	James Buchanan	39	William Henry Harrison
		40	Franklin Pierce
		41	Andrew Johnson
		42	James Buchanan

NOTE: William Henry Harrison, who died after just 30 days in office, and Garfield, who was mortally wounded 4 months after his inauguration and died 2 months later, are omitted from the *Wall Street Journal* ranking.

SOURCE: For the 2005 *WSJ* rankings: James Taranto, "How's He Doing?" *Wall Street Journal,* September 12, 2005, http://www .jamestaranto.com/average.htm; C-SPAN Rankings, 2009: "C-SPAN Ranks Presidents: Abe Still on Top, Shocker at the Bottom," *Los Angeles Times,* February 16, 2009, http://latimesblogs.latimes.com/washington/2009/02/presidents-cspa.html.

FIGURE 7.4   Presidential Scholars' Ranking of Top President

SOURCE: Rendered based on data from Brandon Rottinghaus and Justin S. Vaughn, "Measuring Obama Against the Great Presidents," *Brookings*, February 13, 2015, https://www.brookings.edu/blog/fixgov/2015/02/13/measuring-obama-against-the-great-presidents/.

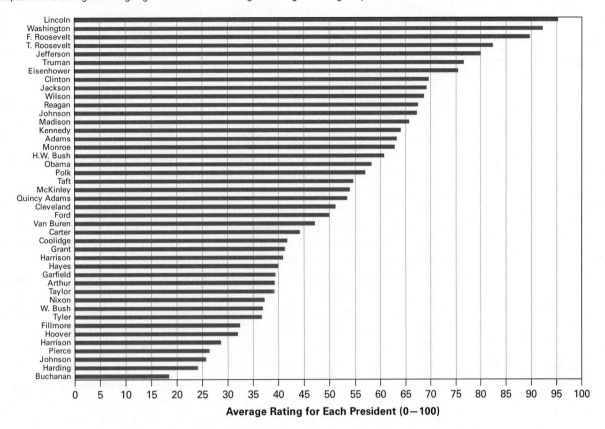

to the success or failure of a given president. Why are James Madison and John Quincy Adams, who made enormous contributions to this country, not ranked among the greatest presidents? Why was Ulysses S. Grant at best only mediocre, and why did Gerald Ford fail as a president? Why is James K. Polk listed in the top tier in some rankings? And who *was* James K. Polk, anyway?

As for George W. Bush's place in the rankings, the C-SPAN survey places him in 36th position. After his first 4 years in office, some began to speculate he would fall in the "average" range, but during his second term, the economy weakened, budget deficits grew, there were few legislative accomplishments, and the war in Iraq continued. His approval ratings languished in the 30 percent range for the last three years of his presidency. It seems likely that most historians will assess his tenure in office in an unfavorable light. By 2006, one commentator noted, "George W. Bush's presidency appears headed for colossal historical disgrace. Barring a cataclysmic event on the order of the terrorist attacks of September 11th, after which the public might rally around the White House once again, there seems to be little the administration can do to avoid being ranked on the lowest tier of U.S. presidents."[28]

Most seem to agree that Barack Obama had a solid presidency. The APSA ranking puts him at the 18th spot—slightly above average. To his credit, the economy rebounded after the Great Recession of 2008, and his signature achievement, the Affordable Care Act, ushered in monumental changes. Nearly all would agree that he conducted himself with integrity, and of course his election as the first African American president was very important. And yet, others argue that he was not able to bridge the partisan divide in Congress or across the nation. To many, he was a polarizing president. A number of simmering issues, like stagnant wages for the middle class and immigration reform, remained unchecked by the end of his administration. Some have also suggested that Donald Trump's success, and the defeat of Hillary Clinton (who seemed to want to continue many of Obama's policies) is an indication of a modestly successful presidency. Others are quick to point out that Obama left office with a rather high approval rating.

> POLL   How would you rate Barack Obama's overall performance as president? Would you say he did an excellent, good, fair, poor, or very poor job?

Conclusion

The framers of our system could not have imagined many of the things that we take for granted. How would we even explain the Internet, YouTube, Twitter, and selfies? Could they even conceive of nuclear bombs, satellite surveillance, and drones? Could they even fathom that one of the most grievous attacks on American soil came from jet planes flying into skyscrapers, killing thousands of civilians?

And yet, these men were visionaries and right about the presidency. They anticipated grievous attacks against the United States and the necessity for an immediate response. They understood that after tragic events, citizens would look to a leader to calm, resolve, and console. They held that the heart of their new republic would be found in the legislature, but they also understood that a strong executive would keep the nation together during times of crisis. It is hard to imagine how our nation would have responded to any of the great challenges without the leadership of the president.

Our first years under the Constitution were uncertain and turbulent, but to some extent, the steady hand and vision of George Washington helped keep the peace and ensure that the Union survived. Congress or state governments did not save the Union in 1861–1865, but the will, intellect, and political skill of Abraham Lincoln helped it to survive and be reborn. Congress and the Hoover White House were paralyzed by the strife and anguish of the Great Depression, so not until Franklin D. Roosevelt took the helm did the federal government respond. From his first inaugural address, FDR calmed the waters by reminding us that "the only thing we have to fear is fear itself," and he rallied a nation horrified by the Japanese attack on December 7, 1941—"a date," he said, "which will live in infamy." After the humiliations of the 1970s, Ronald Reagan made Americans once again feel proud of their nation, and it was through his unwavering mixture of determination and moderation that the Cold War was brought to a peaceful end. The will of the American people is best expressed through representatives, but our resolve, our spirit, and our sense of united purpose rests in the hands of the president. This is especially true during times of crisis.

Much as we may praise the advantages of a single leader, however, endowing this person with too much prerogative distorts the balance of power that the framers so carefully built into the constitutional system. Our nation has grown from fewer than 4 million people in 1790 to more than 300 million today, requiring the federal government to step into all aspects of American life—and the power of the chief executive has mushroomed along with that explosive growth. Facing dramatically different realities from what was envisioned by Madison and his colleagues in Philadelphia in 1787, modern presidents have three main tasks: (1) to develop a legislative program and work to persuade Congress to enact it; (2) to engage in direct policymaking through bureaucratic actions that do not require congressional approval; and (3) to lead a massive network of staff with the singular goal of helping the occupant of the White House succeed in achieving these first two goals.[29]

As touched upon at the start of this chapter, running for the office and serving as president are two very different things. One can certainly imagine elements of one helping the other. For example, Donald Trump was able to arouse the passions of the public. His followers were engaged, filling one large campaign venue after another. Public support is a president's best friend—particularly when there is pushback from Congress. Trump was astute at using the media to persuade the public, and that too could come in handy when his administration bores down on difficult policy questions.

But it is also fair to say that his aggressive, often bombastic rhetoric may cause difficulties when trying to forge compromise solutions with members of his own party and the Democrats. Successful presidents are often pragmatic, meaning willing to work behind the scenes to forge compromises. At least during the campaign, the ability to find common ground did not seem to be one of Donald Trump's overt character traits.

Donald Trump will be called upon to heal the nation and to follow through with his promises—hefty challenges, to be sure. Americans put a great deal of stock in their presidents—and it is exceedingly difficult to deliver on campaign promises. It may come to pass that Trump, like many of his predecessors, will be reminded of that adage that you should be careful of what you ask for because you might just get it.

CONFRONTING POLITICS AND POLICY

Many Americans are frustrated at the pace of government. Gridlock and stalemate seem to be the order of the day and many worry about the democratic character of the government. Does the system still respond to the will of the people? Consider two important policy issues—gun control and immigration reform. A large majority of Americans would like greater restrictions on the sale of guns, especially on automatic weapons and magazine clips that hold a large number of bullets. Most would like background checks on all gun sales. And yet, Congress seems unwilling to make even the smallest change. The National Rifle Association and other pro-gun groups are very active and flex their muscles at election time, and few legislators seem willing to take them on. The same can be said about immigration reform. Most Americans want a change, but deep partisan differences in Congress have led to stalemate. The legislature seems unable to respond to important policy questions.

Under these circumstances, should the president act unilaterally? There is, after all, only one elected official with a national constituency; meaning that the president alone represents all Americans. Perhaps the president is uniquely situated to act on behalf of the nation, not being beholden to a narrow geographic or ideological constituency. Shortly after the horrific shooting of 20 children and six adults at Sandy Hook Elementary School in December 2012, for example, Barack Obama signed 23 executive agreements on gun control. The changes were minor, but many thought they were a step in the right direction. After immigration reform negotiations stalled in Congress, he signed the so-called Dreamer Act in November 2014, protecting millions of children of undocumented immigrants from deportation. Both of these moves and many other unilateral acts were controversial. But they demonstrated that at least parts of the government can address a problem.

One of the fundamental principles of governance is that democracy and deliberation are juxtaposed with efficiency. Deliberative bodies move slowly. The framers of our system wanted public policy to spring from the legislature, the most democratic and, admittedly, the least efficient branch of government. But things seem very different these days and that deliberation has led to deadlock. Presidents, especially modern presidents, can act decisively, without delays. Should we welcome a president's unilateral action?

Let's switch to another issue. Many Americans are concerned about sensitive areas of land in their state and are anxious to have it preserved for future generations. Young Americans, in particular, seem quite concerned about large landscape conservation. They worry about beautiful, unique tracts of land that seem to be threatened by development, and the state seems unwilling to move. Is this true in your state? Are there sensitive areas under the threat of development? If so, one route would be to push Congress to designate it as protected federal properties or even a national park. Another option would be to persuade the president to act unilaterally: to designate it a national monument. It can be done with a stroke of a pen. One move is more democratic, the other more efficient.

ACTION STEPS

1. Find out the various issues surrounding the designation of lands as federal property.

2. Understand who and what groups are on each side of the issue and why. Do your best to sit down with representatives of these groups and understand their points of view.

3. Get the position of the members of Congress from not only the area in question, but the entire state. Do they support or oppose the federal land control and why?

4. Explore when and under what conditions presidents have designated lands as national monuments. You will find that it is done quite often, usually at the end of the president's term of office.

5. Organize groups to make contact with officials in the Department of Interior to make your case. Work to get favorable news coverage of your position, with the hope of swaying public opinion.

❭ REVIEW THE CHAPTER

The President and the Constitution

7.1 Explain the framers' decision to bestow the president with real powers despite their concerns about potential abuses. (p. 217)

Unlike other branches of the new government, the framers of the U.S. Constitution were a bit unsure about the presidency. On the one hand, they wanted to vest the office with real powers—to afford "energy in the executive," as one noted. On the other hand, many worried that giving a president too much power would lead to corruption and perhaps even a new monarchy. In the end, they set aside most of their reservations because they had afforded Congress with an extensive list of powers, and they wanted the presidency to serve as a check on that power. In addition, they knew that George Washington would be the first president and would set the tone of a powerful yet constrained leader.

The Evolution of the Presidency

7.2 Outline the changes that have led to the expansion of presidential powers. (p. 219)

During much of the nineteenth century, most presidents held to the Whig model of presidential power, meaning that they were limited to the powers expressly granted in the Constitution. Beginning with Teddy Roosevelt, and continuing with his cousin Franklin D. Roosevelt, the more activist stewardship model of presidential powers took hold. In addition, a host of intuitional changes broadened presidential powers, including the Executive Office of the President, a swathe of additional advisors, the growing opportunities to use unilateral actions, and an expanded role for the vice president. Today, there is little question that the presidency is at the very center of our political system.

The Informal Powers of the President

7.3 Establish how the "power to persuade" expands presidential power beyond the Constitution. (p. 227)

Astute presidents have learned that much of their power comes from their own skills, the trappings of the office, and a steadfast spouse. That is, the powers outlined in the Constitution are just the beginning. Successful presidents have harnessed an array of tools to push their agenda forward and have understood that the most effective tools are those that best match the larger political context of the day.

The Roles of Modern Presidents

7.4 Identify the duties and functions of modern presidents. (p. 231)

No job prepares a person for the presidency. Along with expanding powers comes a dizzying array of jobs and responsibilities in both domestic and foreign affairs. The president is a chief of state and must lead the nation in ceremonial events. The president is a chief legislator and must recommend measures to Congress and report to Congress on the "state of the union." The president is a chief diplomat and must appoint and receive ambassadors and represent the United States abroad. The president is commander in chief and must make decisions about when to deploy the armed forces. Finally, the president is chief executive and must carry out the will of Congress: enforcing laws and spending the funds that are allocated and appropriated.

Presidential Greatness

7.5 Evaluate the qualities that contribute to presidential success or failure. (p. 239)

While there is no formula for success, there are shared characteristics of great presidents. Truly successful presidents have vision, but they are also pragmatic. They understand the importance of public conscience, and they are trustworthy and charismatic. Perhaps because of growing demands and forces beyond their control, however, it seems that successful presidents are increasingly rare.

⟩ LEARN THE TERMS

prerogative power,
  p. 218
Whig model, p. 219
stewardship model, p. 220
modern presidency, p. 221
New Deal, p. 221
cabinet, p. 221
inner cabinet, p. 223

Executive Office of the President
  (EOP), p. 223
Office of Management and Budget
  (OMB), p. 224
Social Security, p. 224
institutional presidency, p. 225
going public, p. 229
veto, p. 233

treaty, p. 235
executive agreement, p. 235
War Powers Resolution,
  p. 237
Iran-Contra affair, p. 237
executive order, p. 238
signing statement, p. 238
personal presidency, p. 239

⟩ EXPLORE FURTHER

In the Library

Ellis, Joseph J. *His Excellency: George Washington.*
  New York: Knopf, 2004.

Greenstein, Fred I. *The Presidential Difference: Leadership
  Style from FDR to George W. Bush.* Princeton, NJ: Princeton University Press, 2004.

Milkis, Sidney, and Marc Landy. *Presidential Greatness.*
  Lawrence, KS: University of Kansas Press, 2001.

Neustadt, Richard E. *Presidential Power: The Politics of
  Leadership.* New York: Free Press, 1991.

Schlesinger, Arthur M., Jr. *The Imperial Presidency.* Buena
  Vista, VA: Mariner Books, 2004 (repr.).

Stephen Skowronek, *The Politics Presidents Make: From
  John Adams to George Bush.* Cambridge, MA: Harvard
  University Press, 2008.

Weisberg, Jacob. *The Bush Tragedy.* New York: Random
  House, 2008.

On the Web

To explore a range of topics on the presidency, go to the
  American President: An Online Reference Resource at
  http://millercenter.org/academic/americanpresident.

You can view some 52,000 documents at the American
  Presidency Project at *http://www.presidency.ucsb.edu/
  index.php.*

Doing a research project on a president or a related topic?
  Check out the National Archives Web site at *http://
  www.archives.gov/presidential-libraries/research/guide.html*
  and the National First Ladies' Library at *http://www
  .firstladies.org/.*

The American Presidents Web site at *http://www.ameri-
  canpresidents.org* contains a complete video archive of
  the C-SPAN television series *American Presidents: Life
  Portraits,* plus biographical facts, key events of each
  presidency, presidential places, and reference materials. You might also take a look at one of the presidential libraries. For links to them, try *http://www.archives
  .gov/presidential-libraries/.*

For a wealth of scholarly information on each of the
  presidents, visit the Miller Center of Public Affairs
  Web site at *http://millercenter.org/academic/
  americanpresident.*

The White House Web site at *http://www.whitehouse.gov*
  provides a wealth of information about the current
  presidency.

BUREAUCRACY

Military veterans, politicians, and members of the public reacted with outrage to news reports about long delays in obtaining medical appointments at Veterans Administration hospitals as well as examples of veterans who died while waiting for care. *Is a large bureaucracy in the national government capable of providing timely, essential services, such as medical care for veterans, or are government bureaucracies inevitably underfunded and inefficient?*

→ LEARNING OBJECTIVES

8.1 Trace the development of specific federal departments and agencies.

8.2 Analyze the debate over whether the heads of federal agencies should be policy experts or loyal political appointees.

8.3 Describe the image people have of the federal bureaucracy, and evaluate the bureaucracy's advantages and disadvantages.

8.4 Assess the mechanisms and processes that influence and oversee the federal bureaucracy.

IS THE BUREAUCRACY AN ESSENTIAL CONTRIBUTOR TO THE SUCCESS OF GOVERNMENT OR A BARRIER TO EFFECTIVE GOVERNMENT?

What does this case show us about government agencies? Americans expect government agencies to provide services and respond to crises, including tasks ranging from delivering mail to cleaning up major environmental disasters. Yet, the connections between government officials, interest groups, and politics—as well as other issues, such as limited funding and overwhelming tasks—create risks that agencies will be hampered by controversy. There are also debates about whether these agencies operate effectively.

Shocking news reports emerged in 2014 about military veterans who died while waiting for weeks to get appointments to see doctors at Veterans Health Administration hospitals. These hospitals are commonly referred to as VA Hospitals and are under the management of a federal government department, the U.S. Department of Veterans Affairs. Other reports revealed that administrators at these hospitals manipulated reports in order to hide the fact that many veterans were not receiving the medical and mental health care that they needed in a timely manner.

In other countries, medical care for military veterans is handled under the same medical systems that provide care for all other citizens. In Great Britain, veterans receive care from the National Health Service, a government agency that provides medical services for everyone. In Canada, veterans receive government-supported health insurance and, like other Canadians, they use this government health insurance to pay for services from private doctors and hospitals. In the United States, by contrast, it was not until the twenty-first century that Congress and the Obama administration put into place a national program, the Affordable Care Act, intended to make medical insurance and treatment available to all Americans. Thus a special government agency was founded in 1930 to make sure that American military veterans had access to medical treatment. As a result, the federal government has spent decades running a system of hospitals and medical clinics specifically for veterans.

News about the VA hospital system scandal led opposing political parties in Congress to blame each other for the problems. Republicans claimed the issues stemmed from mismanagement of the hospitals under the Democratic administration of President Obama. Democrats, by contrast, pointed to underfunding of the VA hospital system. Despite the increase in the number of veterans needing care from the wars in Iraq and Afghanistan that began during the administration of Republican President George W. Bush, Republicans in Congress were accused of failing to support adequate budget increases for the Department of Veterans Affairs. Eventually, Congress approved budget increases for VA hospitals, but by late 2015, the system still struggled to hire enough doctors and nurses willing to work for a government agency. Wait times also continued to be too long at some VA hospitals. Is the hospital system too big to be properly managed by government officials? Is the system underfunded because, unlike other hospital systems, it must depend entirely on money allocated by Congress and cannot freely impose increased charges on its patients to cover rising costs?[1]

The Federal Bureaucracy

8.1 Trace the development of specific federal departments and agencies.

In this chapter, we'll examine the agencies of the executive branch of the federal government that are collectively known as "the bureaucracy." The word **bureaucracy** refers to an organization with a hierarchical structure and specific responsibilities, which operates on management principles intended to enhance

bureaucracy

An organization with a hierarchical structure and specific responsibilities intended to enhance efficiency and effectiveness. In government, it refers to departments and agencies in the executive branch. For example, the Internal Revenue Service (IRS) is an agency in the federal bureaucracy that carries out national tax laws through collection of income taxes and investigation of individuals and businesses that fail to pay the taxes required by the laws created by Congress.

efficiency and effectiveness. Bureaucracies exist in businesses, universities, and other organizational contexts; however, the general term *bureaucracy* is most frequently used to refer to government agencies. Action or inaction by these agencies determines whether and how policies are implemented and how these policies will affect the lives of Americans.

The departments that comprise the executive branch of the federal government work under the direction of the president to carry out the nation's laws. Some of them, such as VA hospitals, provide specific services. Others regulate specific activities and enterprises, such as the Environmental Protection Agency (EPA) ensuring that businesses and local governments do not violate air and water pollution standards. Other agencies, such as the Federal Bureau of Investigation (FBI), enforce laws after conducting investigations. Departments and agencies do not simply decide for themselves what entities, activities, and services should be subject to their regulation and supervision. They must act within the guidelines set by Congress and the president. These guidelines typically leave room for agency officials to make specific decisions, but these officials cannot act beyond the scope of their authority as defined by law. In essence, Congress and the president write laws to define public policy; the officials who work in federal agencies then act to carry out those laws and policies.

Agency officials can shape public policy through their authority to create rules for administering programs and for enforcing laws enacted by Congress and the president. They are also the source of information and ideas for members of Congress who wish to propose new statutes about various policy issues. The policy preferences of individual agency officials affect the day-to-day actions that these bureaucracies undertake, as do those officials' interactions with representatives from outside interest groups.

Ideally, the officials who work in federal agencies possess knowledge and experience concerning the policy matters that they handle. We want them to be expert professionals who are dedicated to public service for all Americans. We do not want them to be politicians who serve the interests of a particular political party. Despite this idealistic vision of government workers, these officials are not necessarily removed from the world of politics. Because the bureaucracy is part of the executive branch (and, thus, under the president's authority) policymaking decisions within government agencies can be affected by partisan political considerations. Moreover, the president's political appointees assume the top positions in each agency. In making their decisions, agency officials may be influenced by lobbying from legislators, state and local officials, and interest groups. Thus, the bureaucracy becomes another arena of action for the policy-shaping pathway that relies on the lobbying of decision makers.

Development of the Federal Bureaucracy

The roots of the federal bureaucracy go back to the original U.S. Constitution of 1787. Article I, Section 8, gives Congress the power to enact laws for specified purposes. These include matters such as "lay and collect taxes," "coin Money," "establish Post Offices," and "provide and maintain a Navy." The president, as the head of the executive branch, is responsible for carrying out the nation's laws.

It soon became apparent that agencies must be created to administer specific policies and programs. Post offices, tax agencies, and mints (where money is coined) handle tasks that require specialized personnel and facilities. Indeed, Article I makes reference to congressional authority to "make all laws necessary and proper for carrying into Execution... all other Powers vested by this Constitution in the Government of the United States, or in any Department or Officer thereof." Thus, the founding document explicitly acknowledged that

government agencies, called "departments," would be established to carry out laws and programs.

Article II of the Constitution, which discusses the president and executive power, provides further acknowledgment of the need to create governmental departments that will execute the laws under the president's supervision and control. For example, Article II says that the president "may require the Opinion, in writing, of the principal Officer in each of the executive Departments, upon any subject relating to the Duties of their respective Offices."

Although the Constitution clearly anticipated the existence of executive departments, the actual development and organization of those departments over the course of American history were shaped by social developments and the country's response to emerging policy issues and priorities.

THE FIRST DEPARTMENTS During the nation's first century, the federal government was involved in only a limited range of policy areas. The original departments of the federal government focused on policy matters related to specific powers granted by the Constitution to Congress and the president. Most policy issues came under the authority of state governments. This explains why the federal government after 1789 had only four departments:

Department of State—responsible for diplomacy and foreign affairs

Department of War (in 1947 consolidated, along with the Department of the Navy, a later creation, into the *Department of Defense*)—responsible for military matters and national defense

Department of Justice—responsible for legal matters under federal law

Department of the Treasury—responsible for tax revenues and government expenditures

Note how many of these agencies focused on matters that had motivated the Constitutional Convention to replace the Articles of Confederation with the new U.S.

PATHWAYS OF ACTION

STANDARDS FOR AIR POLLUTION

The Clean Air Act was enacted by Congress in 1970 to protect air quality. Scientific studies estimate that hundreds of thousands of Americans have been spared from lung problems and deaths through limits on air pollution. In addition, cleaner air reduces economic costs from medical treatment and lost days of work for the people who would otherwise suffer severe health problems from breathing polluted air.[2] The Environmental Protection Agency (EPA) is the unit in the federal government responsible for creating and enforcing air pollution regulations under authority delegated by Congress.

Many scientific studies point to carbon dioxide emissions into the air as a primary cause of global warming. Continued emissions into the atmosphere are projected to lead to life-altering climate change, including: melting polar ice; rising ocean levels; flooding of coastal cities; changing weather patterns; spreading of tropical insects and diseases; and turning sections of current farmland into deserts. Those who accept the results of these scientific studies advocate policy actions to reduce emissions from coal-burning power plants and other sources of carbon dioxide. By contrast, those who reject the notion that man-made activities are affecting the earth's climate complain about the expense of proposals to limit airborne emissions.

The Obama administration made the issue of global warming one of its priorities. As a result, the EPA developed a rule that requires power plants to reduce their carbon emissions by 32 percent prior to 2030. Compliance with the rule would require expensive changes for power plants in many states, especially those that rely heavily on burning coal in order to produce electricity. The Obama administration was seeking to push states to develop alternative energy sources, such as wind and solar power, as well as alter coal-based facilities to produce fewer emissions. Local governments argued that they could not afford to make such upgrades, particularly during a period of economic problems in which their budgets were shrinking from declines in tax revenues. Businesses argued that the increased expenses would lead to a loss of jobs as some power plants and factories would be forced to close when they could not afford the required upgrades. Thus more than half the states as well as several energy companies filed a lawsuit alleging that the EPA exceeded its authority in issuing the new rule about carbon emissions. In addition, these states and their business allies lobbied Congress to pass a resolution to forbid the EPA's rule.

In late 2015, the Republican-controlled Congress acted to block the EPA rule. However, in December 2015, President Obama used his veto power to nullify the congressional action and keep the rule in place.[3] Subsequently, in a surprise move, the Supreme Court announced in February 2016 that the EPA must put the rule on hold until after the lower federal courts had the opportunity to hear arguments and evidence on the issue. Four of the nine justices objected to the order issued by the high court. Normally, the Supreme Court would decline to issue any decision until after the lower courts had heard the case.[4]

The Supreme Court's decision led many observers to predict that five justices were prepared to strike down the EPA rule when it reached the high court. However, just a few days after the order to put the rule on hold, Justice Antonin Scalia—one of the five justices presumed to be skeptical about the rule—died in his sleep. Thus the future of any final ruling on the EPA's authority under the Clean Air Act and the specific rule intended to slow global warming suddenly became uncertain as the nation waited to see if the Republican-controlled Senate would approve President Obama's next appointee to the Supreme Court—the justice who would presumably cast the deciding vote on the issue.

This story reflects the types of actions that occur in regulatory politics. The rules produced by the bureaucracy can be shaped or blocked by interactions with and responses to other actors involved in a specific policy issue. Scientific experts provide influential information and interest groups and other affected entities apply political pressure through lobbying and litigation.

Constitution. Under the Articles, the national government had lacked authority to handle taxation and the military. As Congress and the president expanded the scope of federal activities in law and policy, departments were created to operate in new areas. First came the Department of the Navy. Then, in the mid-nineteenth century, Congress created the Department of the Interior to manage federal lands and the Department of Agriculture to assist the nation's most important industry.

During the last decades of the nineteenth century, the United States began to undergo significant changes. Industrialization, urbanization, and immigration shaped a new economy in which people moved to cities to work in factories and service occupations. Congress became increasingly assertive in using its constitutional authority to enact laws regulating interstate commerce to prevent business monopolies, control the exploitation of child labor, improve dangerous working conditions, and deal with other problems created by the new industrial economy. In the first decade of the twentieth century, Congress created the Department of Commerce and the Department of Labor to address these emerging issues.

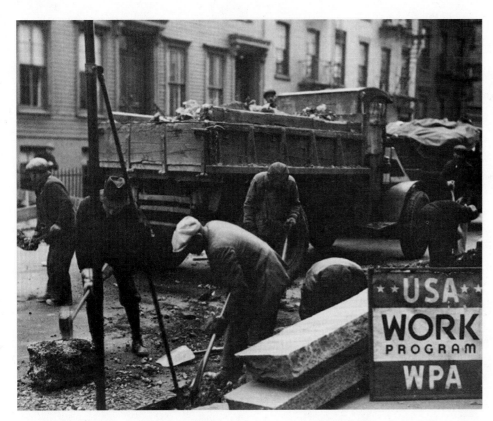

During the Depression, the Roosevelt administration expanded the size of government by creating programs to permit unemployed workers to earn money while repairing roads and undertaking other public service projects.

■ *In light of recent economic difficulties, should the federal government maintain permanent programs to employ people who cannot find jobs? Why or why not?*

THE NEW DEAL AND ITS AFTERMATH   The Great Depression, which began with the stock market crash of 1929, brought years of record-high unemployment and economic problems. At the depth of the Depression in 1932, Franklin D. Roosevelt (FDR) was elected to the presidency. He believed that the federal government had to take an active role in the economy in order to overcome the economic stagnation and correct the underlying causes of the Depression. He called his program the New Deal. The Roosevelt administration (1933–1945) contributed enormously to the growth in the federal bureaucracy by initiating various governmental programs, first in response to the Great Depression and later to wage World War II.

For example, in 1935, Congress created Social Security to provide income for senior citizens and dependents of deceased workers. It later added coverage for disabled workers and their dependents. Other New Deal programs created jobs for the unemployed and regulated economic activity. The size and complexity of the federal government increased tremendously during the Roosevelt administration (see Figure 8.1). By the end of FDR's presidency in 1945, not only had the public accepted the federal government's involvement in a variety of policy issues, many Americans had come to *expect* federal action on important matters, eventually including such areas as education and criminal justice, which had traditionally been the exclusive preserve of state and local governments. Moreover, World War II had demonstrated the necessity of combining the War and Navy departments (as well as the newly created Air Force department) within a single structure, the Department of Defense.

In the 1950s, expanded public expectations of the federal government and the consequently broader range of legislative activity undertaken by Congress led to the creation of the Department of Health, Education, and Welfare (HEW). (In the 1970s, HEW was split into two agencies, the Department of Education and the Department of Health and Human Services.) The framers of the Constitution never expected the federal government to become increasingly involved in policy areas that were traditionally under the control of states.

Heightened public awareness of urban decay, racial conflict, and poverty during the 1960s produced a new social welfare federal bureaucracy, the Department of

FIGURE 8.1 Growth in the Size of the Federal Bureaucracy

The Roosevelt administration's programs to address the Depression and World War II dramatically increased the size of the federal bureaucracy.

◼ *After these crises had passed, why didn't the government shrink back to its size in the early years of the twentieth century?*

SOURCE: Author created with data from Office of Personnel Management.

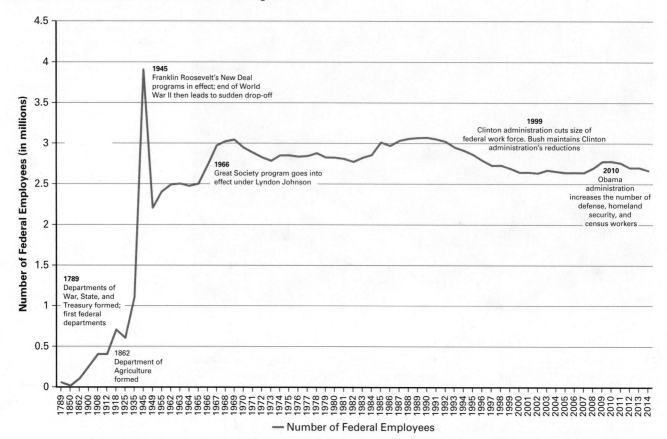

Housing and Urban Development (HUD). Similarly, the Department of Transportation, created during the same decade, reflected concerns about urban mass transit as well as a recognition that air travel was expanding.

Organization of the Federal Bureaucracy

Today, the federal bureaucracy consists of four types of organizational entities: departments, independent agencies, independent regulatory commissions, and government corporations (see Table 8.1). **Departments** typically are large organizations responsible for a broad policy realm, such as education, national defense, or transportation. Independent agencies have narrow responsibilities for a specific policy issue, such as the environment. They are independent in the sense that they are not subunits of a larger department, but like departments, their leaders are appointed by and under the control of the president.

By contrast, independent regulatory commissions are not under the control of the president or a department. They have a focused policy mission governing a specific issue area, but they are run by a body of officials drawn from both political parties and appointed in staggered terms over the course of more than one presidential administration. Government corporations have independent boards and are intended to run like private corporations. They handle a specific function, such as the postal system or the passenger railroad, which Congress believes would not be handled effectively by private businesses, either because of the huge scope of the operation or because of issues of profitability.

department

Any of the 15 major government agencies responsible for specific policy areas whose heads are usually called secretaries and serve in the president's cabinet. For example, the U.S. Department of State, led during the Obama administration by Secretary John Kerry, the former U.S. senator from Massachusetts, is responsible for managing relationships with foreign governments and issuing passports to U.S. citizens.

TABLE 8.1 Cabinet Departments and Examples of Other Agencies

Departments	Independent Agencies
Agriculture	Environmental Protection Agency
Commerce	Peace Corps
Defense	Social Security Administration
Education	**Independent Regulatory Commissions**
Energy	Federal Communications Commission
Health and Human Services	Federal Trade Commission
Homeland Security	Federal Reserve System and Board of Governors
Housing and Urban Development	Nuclear Regulatory Commission
Interior	**Government Corporations**
Justice	National Railroad Passenger Corporation (Amtrak)
Labor	Overseas Private Investment Corporation
State	United States Postal Service
Transportation	
Treasury	
Veterans Affairs	

SOURCE: https://www.usa.gov/branches-of-government.

As you consider the role and operation of each of these components of the federal bureaucracy, ask yourself whether there might be a better way to organize the government. Alternatively, consider whether some of the bureaucracy's functions could be handled effectively and appropriately by private businesses without the expenditure of taxpayers' money.

Changes Since the 1960s

As the nation faced changing political and economic circumstances, Congress reacted to specific issues that it perceived to be the most difficult, immediate challenges by creating new departments to address those matters. The creation of a new department

During the 1960s, President Lyndon B. Johnson tried to expand the activity and influence of federal government agencies in order to address poverty and racial discrimination. The Department of Housing and Urban Development (HUD) was created during his presidency.

■ *Has expanded action by the federal government actually helped to solve social problems?*

represents an opportunity to reorganize the use of governmental resources and apply expertise to address pressing concerns. It also represents a method of showing constituents that Congress is taking action even if members of Congress are unsure about whether the new department will be effective.

DEPARTMENT OF ENERGY   In 1973, the energy crisis struck. That year, the nation's ever-growing thirst for oil, natural gas, and other fossil fuels collided with the determination of the oil-producing countries to increase their profits. Many Americans found themselves waiting in long lines at gas stations and paying skyrocketing prices to fill up their gas-guzzling cars. Responding to the crisis atmosphere, Congress created the Department of Energy to implement new laws and develop policies designed to encourage fuel efficiency, develop new sources of energy, and relieve the nation's dependence on foreign oil producers.

DEPARTMENT OF VETERANS AFFAIRS   At the end of the 1980s, the Veterans Administration (created in 1930) was elevated to the status of a separate department called the Department of Veterans Affairs. By the 1980s, a huge group of World War II veterans had become senior citizens, and they looked to the federal government for health care and other benefits. Korean War veterans and middle-aged Vietnam War veterans followed closely behind, increasingly in need of benefits and services. The long-lasting military actions in Afghanistan and Iraq produced an additional surge in veterans needing medical care in the twenty-first century.

When an agency gets the status of an executive department, its head becomes a member of the president's cabinet and is literally "at the table" when the president's top executive appointees discuss policies and budgets. The cabinet plays an especially important and influential role in advising the president. Creation of the Department of Veterans Affairs implied a promise that veterans' interests would be taken into account in those discussions. Congress symbolically demonstrated its concern about veterans and simultaneously sought the political benefits of granting increased attention and stature to an important constituency.

DEPARTMENT OF HOMELAND SECURITY   After terrorists attacked the World Trade Center and the Pentagon on September 11, 2001, public shock and congressional demands for action resulted in the creation of the federal government's newest department: the Department of Homeland Security (DHS). Like other departments, the DHS represented a response to a policy issue that had moved to the top of the nation's priorities.

The creation of the DHS involved the development of new agencies, such as the Transportation Security Administration (TSA), and the consolidation of existing agencies from other departments, to better coordinate government actions related to domestic security issues. Many observers recognized that creating a new department that included agencies from elsewhere in government would inevitably pose a variety of problems. Would agencies engage in "turf wars" over who should be in charge of specific tasks? Would employees resist a move to an unfamiliar department with unproven leadership and a still-developing mission?

To give you an idea of the scope of the reorganization, this short list identifies a few of the agencies absorbed into the new department as well as their previous homes within the bureaucracy.

> **Federal Emergency Management Agency (FEMA)**—previously an independent agency
>
> **Immigration and Naturalization Service (INS)**—previously in the Department of Justice
>
> **Coast Guard**—previously in the Department of Transportation
>
> **Secret Service**—previously in the Department of the Treasury

The slow response and general ineffectiveness of FEMA during and after Hurricane Katrina in 2005 led many critics to complain that the DHS was too big. They claimed that individual agencies within the department had lost resources and suffered from diminished focus on their domestic mission in light of the department's broader concerns about preventing attacks by international terrorists.

Departments and Independent Agencies

8.2 Analyze the debate over whether the heads of federal agencies should be policy experts or loyal political appointees.

In order to understand how the bureaucracy operates, you must recognize the policy areas that fall under the authority of the *departments* (governmental units) run by the president's cabinet. By contrast, other kinds of agencies exert more independent influence over certain policy issues, because they are not directly under the supervision of the president and the cabinet.

Departments

During every presidential administration, the president's cabinet consists of the heads of the executive departments. These department heads typically have the title of secretary, such as Secretary of Defense for the head of the Department of Defense. The head of the Department of Justice, however, is known as the Attorney General of the United States. Because new departments have been created over time, the cabinet has grown to include 15 departments as well as the administrators of three agencies within the Executive Office of the President: the Office of Management and Budget (OMB), the Office of National Drug Control Policy, and the Office of the U.S. Trade Representative. The head of one independent agency, the EPA, also has cabinet rank.

At earlier points in American history, the members of the cabinet would advise the president, debate policy options, and develop ideas to determine the president's agenda. In recent administrations, presidents have relied most heavily on their staffs and key cabinet members for advice. Cabinet meetings now serve the function of reporting to the president on the activities of each department. Cabinet members are expected to be loyal to the president to avoid any public indication that they question the president's agenda or actions. Presidents need agency leaders who are willing to support and implement the president's policies. Thus, top department and agency leaders are political appointees who serve during one president's administration rather than as permanent employees. However, political appointees sometimes do not have sufficient expertise about the policy issues addressed by their agencies, and their relatively short terms in office can inhibit the effective development and implementation of programs.

The various departments are divided according to areas of policy responsibility. Within each department, various agencies are assigned to implement laws, keep detailed records, and make consistent decisions in accordance with established rules. Table 8.2 lists the 15 cabinet-level departments and some of the agencies housed in each. You'll notice many familiar agency names on the list, but you may be surprised about which department houses each agency. For example, many people don't realize that the National Weather Service is in the Department of Commerce and that the Financial Crimes Enforcement Network belongs to the Department of the Treasury rather than to the primary law enforcement department, the Department of Justice. The location of some agencies is a product of history and politics as much as of topical focus.

Table 8.2 also indicates the number of people employed in each executive department. The Office of Personnel Management reported in 2014 that 2,663,000 civilians

TABLE 8.2 Departments in the Executive Branch of the Federal Government with Selected Subunits and Total Number of Employees, 2012

Department of Agriculture (99,503 employees)	Department of Homeland Security (191,326 employees)
Agricultural Research Service	Coast Guard
Animal and Plant Health Inspection Service	Customs and Border Protection
Cooperative State Research, Education, and Extension Service	Federal Emergency Management Agency
Economic Research Service	Secret Service
Farm Service Agency	**Department of Housing and Urban Development (8,655 employees)**
Forest Service	Government National Mortgage Association (Ginnie Mae)
Natural Resources Conservation Service	Office of Healthy Homes and Lead Hazard Control
Department of Commerce (44,317 employees)	Public and Indian Housing Agencies
Bureau of the Census	**Department of the Interior (76,827 employees)**
Bureau of Export Administration	Bureau of Indian Affairs
International Trade Administration	Bureau of Land Management
National Institute of Standards and Technology	Fish and Wildlife Service
National Oceanic and Atmospheric Administration	Geological Survey
National Weather Service	National Parks Service
Patent and Trademark Office Database	Office of Surface Mining
Department of Defense (729,559 civilian employees)	**Department of Justice (117,016 employees)**
Air Force	Bureau of Alcohol, Tobacco, Firearms, and Explosives
Army	Drug Enforcement Administration
Defense Contract and Audit Agency	Federal Bureau of Investigation
Defense Intelligence Agency	Federal Bureau of Prisons
Marine Corps	United States Marshals Service
National Guard	**Department of Labor (17,752 employees)**
National Security Agency	Mine Safety and Health Administration
Navy	Occupational Safety and Health Administration
Department of Education (4,250 employees)	**Department of State (41,438 employees)**
Educational Resources and Information Center	**Department of Transportation (57,972 employees)**
National Library of Education	Federal Aviation Administration
Department of Energy (15,632 employees)	**Department of the Treasury (112,461 employees)**
Federal Energy Regulatory Commission	Bureau of Engraving and Printing
Los Alamos Laboratory	Bureau of Public Debt
Southwestern Power Administration	Internal Revenue Service
Department of Health and Human Services (74,017 employees)	Office of the Comptroller of the Currency
Centers for Disease Control and Prevention	United States Mint
Food and Drug Administration	**Department of Veterans Affairs (323,208 employees)**
National Institutes of Health	

SOURCE: ProQuest, *Statistical Abstract of the United States, 2014*, Lanham, MD: Bernan, 2014, 346.

were employed in the executive branch of government. More than two-thirds of these worked in the executive departments and the rest were employed in independent agencies that we'll discuss later in this chapter. Although people's perceptions of impersonal, impenetrable bureaucracies often lead them to believe that all federal government agencies are huge, the departments actually vary significantly in size. They range from the Department of Education, which has fewer than 4,300 employees, to the Department of Defense, which has more than 700,000 civilian employees in addition to 1.4 million uniformed military personnel.

There are also approximately 2,000 people who work directly for the president in the Executive Office of the President and its constituent agencies. Because they come under the direct control of the White House, these employees and agencies are typically considered an arm of the presidency rather than agencies within the federal bureaucracy.

Not all government employees are hidden away in office buildings or criticized by the public for inefficiency. The U.S. Coast Guard, for example, an agency within the Department of Homeland Security, is widely recognized for providing valuable services that rescue people at sea and keep ports running smoothly and safely.

■ *Which agencies do you respect and admire for their effectiveness in providing essential services?*

The organizational chart for the U.S. Department of Homeland Security in Figure 8.2 illustrates the complexity of departments in the federal government. Within each department, there are various offices responsible for specific aspects of the department's administration and mission. Bear in mind that all of the agencies within the Department of Homeland Security, especially those listed along the bottom row of the organizational chart, each have their own organizational structure with various internal offices that would look similar to that of the overall chart for the department.

Political Appointees in the Bureaucracy

Presidential appointees who run federal executive departments are expected to be loyal members of the president's team. This means that they will defend the administration's policies and avoid public disagreements with the president. After being appointed by the president, they must be confirmed by the U.S. Senate. These appointees work directly for the president and try to guide and push the bureaucracy to act in accordance with the president's policy preferences.

Secretaries and assistant secretaries who are appointed by the president do not necessarily possess expertise on the policy issues and laws administered by their departments. For example, a former member of Congress or former governor from the president's political party may be chosen to run an agency, in part as a reward for political loyalty. However, they may also be chosen because the president thinks the person will be an effective spokesperson or good administrator.

Other high-level appointments in the departments, such as assistant secretaries and inspectors general, may go to people with policy experience, but they may also go to party loyalists or to the children of prominent political figures. Critics have cited President George W. Bush's appointment of Michael Brown as the director of the Federal Emergency Management Agency (FEMA) as an example of an appointment based on political connections and loyalty rather than on qualifications and experience. Brown's lack of experience in emergency management received widespread news attention amid the federal government's slow and ineffective response to the destruction, death, and human suffering in New Orleans when Hurricane Katrina struck the city in August 2005. Before gaining a political appointment to a senior leadership position at

FIGURE 8.2 Organization of the Department of Homeland Security

The Department of Homeland Security contains a variety of governmental agencies that are not necessarily closely connected with each other.

■ *How would you decide if a department of the federal government was too large and therefore needed to be divided into two or more smaller departments?*

SOURCE: "Organizational Chart," U.S. Department of Homeland Security, accessed March 3, 2012, http://www.dhs.gov/xabout/structure/editorial_0644.shtm.

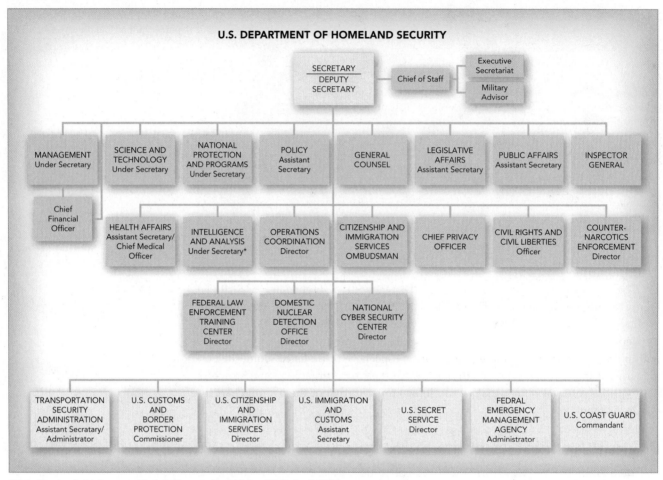

* Under Secretary for Intelligence and Analysis title created by Public Law 110-53, Aug 3, 2007.

FEMA in 2001, Brown had previously been a lawyer for the International Arabian Horse Association and had little, if any, training or experience in emergency management.[5]

In the confirmation process, senators may expect that the secretaries and other appointed officials in specific departments possess relevant experience and expertise. This is most likely to be true for the departments of State, Defense, and the Treasury, owing to the overriding importance of foreign affairs, national security, and the economy. For other positions, senators look less closely at the nominees' qualifications because they believe that presidents should generally be permitted to choose their own representatives to lead government agencies. Even the president's political opponents in the Senate may vote to confirm nominees simply because they would like other senators to show the same deference for appointments by future presidents from a different political party.

Presidents do not merely reward loyalists in their appointments. They also use the upper-level appointed positions to place above the bureaucracy knowledgeable political figures who will vigorously enforce the laws and regulations with which the president agrees—or alternatively, will fail to enforce, enforce weakly, or attempt to change the laws and regulations with which the president disagrees. These elite actors influence the use of the bureaucracy's power and resources in shaping public policy.

Since the final decades of the twentieth century, presidents have also used their appointment power to demonstrate a commitment to diversity as a means of pleasing their constituencies and attracting more voters. Women and members of minority groups increasingly receive appointments to highly visible positions at the top of executive departments. Presidents also seek geographic diversity so that the cabinet can be regarded as representing the nation. The composition of President Barack Obama's cabinet in 2016 illustrates this aspiration for diversity. Among the heads of the 15 major executive departments were a former U.S. senator and a one former governor. There were four women who headed the departments of Justice, Interior, Commerce, and Health and Human Services. African American men served as the Secretary of Transportation and Secretary of Homeland Security, and an African American woman was Attorney General of the United States. Hispanic men headed the Department of Labor and the Department of Housing and Urban Development. As previous presidents have done during their time in office, in his initial term after the 2008 election, President Obama sought to demonstrate bipartisanship by appointing two Republicans to his cabinet: Defense Secretary Robert Gates, a holdover from the Bush administration, and former congressman Ray LaHood as Secretary of Transportation. Both of them served for several years before resigning to return to private life.

Independent Agencies, Independent Regulatory Commissions, and Government Corporations

The executive branch includes nearly 100 **independent agencies**, **independent regulatory commissions**, and **government corporations** that operate outside the 15 executive departments. Table 8.3 provides examples of some of the independent organizational entities in the federal government.

independent agencies
Federal agencies with narrow responsibilities for a specific policy issue, such as the environment, not covered by one of the fifteen federal departments.

independent regulatory commissions
Organizational entities in the federal government that are not under the control of the president or a department.

government corporations
Agencies with independent boards and the means to generate revenue through sales of products and services, fees, or insurance premiums that are intended to run like private corporations.

TABLE 8.3 Examples of Independent Agencies, Independent Regulatory Commissions, and Government Corporations, by Type

Independent Agencies: Facility or Program Administration
General Services Administration
National Archives and Records Administration
National Aeronautics and Space Administration (NASA)
Peace Corps
Selective Service System
Smithsonian Institution
Social Security Administration
Independent Agencies: Grants of Funds
Harry S. Truman Scholarship Foundation
National Endowment for the Arts
National Endowment for the Humanities
National Science Foundation
Independent Regulatory Commissions
Consumer Product Safety Commission (toys, appliances, other products)
Federal Communications Commission (radio, television, cell phones)
Federal Elections Commission (campaign contributions, campaign advertising)
Federal Trade Commission (consumer credit, deceptive advertising)
National Labor Relations Board (labor unions, union voting, unfair practices)
National Transportation Safety Board (collisions involving aircraft, trains, trucks, other vehicles)
Nuclear Regulatory Commission (nuclear materials)
Securities and Exchange Commission (stock market, financial investments)
Government Corporations
Federal Deposit Insurance Corporation
National Railroad Passenger Corporation (Amtrak)
Overseas Private Investment Corporation
Pension Benefit Guaranty Corporation
United States Postal Service

SOURCE: http://www.usa.gov/Agencies/Federal/Independent.shtml.

These agencies do not have identical functions. Some provide government grants or administer a specific government facility, such as a museum. Others are regulatory agencies that exert significant influence over public policy, because Congress has delegated to them broad authority to interpret statutes, create regulations, investigate violations of law, and impose sanctions on violators. The regulatory agencies are typically called *commissions* or *boards,* and as such names imply, they are led by a group of officials. The heads of these agencies often serve staggered terms so that no new president can replace the entire commission or board upon taking office. For example, the members of the Board of Governors of the Federal Reserve Board serve 14-year terms, with one new member appointed to the seven-member board every 2 years. The Federal Reserve Board acts independently to shape monetary policy by, for example, setting certain interest rates that affect the cost of borrowing money.

For some other commissions, the authorizing legislation requires that the appointees contain a mix of Republicans and Democrats. For example, the Federal Communications Commission (FCC) and the Federal Trade Commission (FTC) each have five members, but the law requires that no more than three members can be from one political party. The FCC regulates television, radio, cell phones, and other aspects of communications. It also investigates and imposes sanctions for violations of law and policy. The FTC enforces consumer protection laws, such as fining companies that do not comply with rules concerning the fair treatment of applicants for credit or loans.

Some independent agencies are government corporations with their own boards of directors. For example, the National Railroad Passenger Corporation manages Amtrak, the nation's national system of passenger trains. These agencies generate their own revenue through the sale of products or services, fees, or insurance premiums. They must convince Congress to provide them with whatever operating funds they need beyond what they can raise from customers. Some members of Congress see Amtrak, the U.S. Postal Service, and similar agencies as providing services that could be handled more efficiently by private businesses. This explains why arguments are sometimes made for cutting off government funding for such enterprises. Defenders of these agencies argue that these essential services must be maintained and that private businesses may cut back or eliminate unprofitable enterprises.

Independent agencies are responsible for government facilities—such as the national museums in Washington, D.C., administered by the Smithsonian Institution—or specific programs—such as the Peace Corps, which sends American volunteers to teach and provide community service around the world. Such facilities and programs are likely to be considered too unique and important to ever be subjected to privatization. Similarly, special agencies, such as the National Aeronautics and Space Administration (NASA), the space exploration agency, may do things that are so expensive and important that private organizations cannot match the federal government's ability to pursue the agency's goals.

The Nature of Bureaucracy

8.3 Describe the image people have of the federal bureaucracy, and evaluate the bureaucracy's advantages and disadvantages.

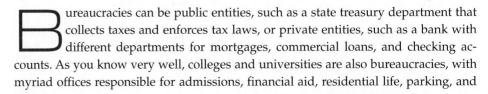Bureaucracies can be public entities, such as a state treasury department that collects taxes and enforces tax laws, or private entities, such as a bank with different departments for mortgages, commercial loans, and checking accounts. As you know very well, colleges and universities are also bureaucracies, with myriad offices responsible for admissions, financial aid, residential life, parking, and

People may wait in long lines while seeking to use government services. In federal offices, this may occur in such places as the post office or Social Security offices. At other levels of government, public-contact offices may be similarly slow or understaffed when people seek unemployment benefits, job placement services, or subsistence benefits. Students at colleges and universities may be accustomed to similar encounters with bureaucracies at a registrar's office or financial aid office.

■ *What are your negative—or positive —experiences in dealing with bureaucracies?*

security. In a bureaucracy, workers typically have specific tasks and responsibilities, and there are clear lines of authority in the organization's pyramid of supervision and leadership. One person is responsible for leading and supervising the organization, and beneath the leader lie different levels of responsibility and supervisory authority. In a private organization, such as a business corporation, the leader might be called the president or the chief executive officer. In a government agency, the title of the head person may depend on the nature of the agency and the definition of the positions under relevant constitutional provisions or statutes. Departments are generally headed by a secretary, while independent regulatory commissions typically have a chairman.

The Image of Bureaucracy

In the minds of most Americans, the word *bureaucracy* does not conjure up idealistic notions of efficient organizations that carry out specialized responsibilities for the public's benefit. Instead, *bureaucracy* can convey an image of gargantuan organizations filled with employees who push paper around on their desks all day and worry only about collecting their paychecks and earning their pensions. In government service, because these employees have secure jobs, they may be perceived to feel no pressure to work industriously or efficiently.

A poll concerning the performance of five federal agencies conducted by the Pew Research Center for the People and the Press found that the agencies get low ratings for administrative ineffectiveness, being slow in carrying out tasks, and making rules, regulations, and forms that are too complicated.[6] The negative image of the bureaucracy may be enhanced by Americans' expectations that the government ought to operate for the benefit of the people in accordance with Abraham Lincoln's familiar words describing a "government of the people, by the people, and for the people." When people's anticipated Social Security checks are late or Medicare benefits are denied, citizens often feel frustrated and resentful about their treatment at the hands of bureaucrats who are paid by taxpayers, yet do not seem responsive and obedient to the public. Frustration can be compounded by the fact that many government employees enjoy job protections that make them very difficult to fire, even if they are rude or incompetent and have been the subject of many complaints by people who come into contact with a particular office or agency. Perhaps you have felt such frustration in dealing with student loan applications, waiting for a tax refund, or otherwise seeking responsiveness from a government agency. This negative image of bureaucracies obviously includes generalizations about large organizations and the frustrations that individuals may face in dealing with the officials who work there. On the other hand, specific government agencies, such as the Postal Service and National Park Service, are viewed favorably by most Americans, as indicated by a poll in 2015.

> **POLL** Do you approve of the way the following are doing their jobs?

- U.S. Postal Service?
- Homeland Security?
- Social Security Administration?
- IRS?
- Veterans Affairs?
- Congress?
- Supreme Court?

What is your image of a bureaucracy? When we talk about the bureaucracy in terms of government agencies rather than banks, corporations, and universities, does your image of bureaucracy depend on which government officials come to mind? When a firefighter rushes into a blazing house and saves a child's life, few of us would associate this hero with the negative image of a bureaucracy. Yet the firefighter belongs to a bureaucracy: The fire department is a government agency, hierarchically organized and with specialized responsibilities for each rank, from the chief down through the captain and the individual firefighters.

As this example shows, our perceptions of government agencies may depend on actual experiences. When government officials respond quickly and provide expected services directly to us, there's no reason to associate these officials and their agency with the negative image of a bureaucracy. On the other hand, when responses to our requests are slow and we can't understand why we must fill out complicated forms or meet detailed requirements, the negative images come galloping back.

Because of their size and distance from many citizens, federal agencies may be especially susceptible to generating negative images. When citizens go to their local Social Security Administration office to apply for retirement or disability benefits, the office staff may need to seek approval from other officials back at Social Security headquarters. Meanwhile, citizens must fill out many forms and provide copies of various documents—and then wait weeks for an answer. "Red tape!" they mutter. Direct services from a local firefighter or police officer put a human face on much-appreciated and immediate government services. But federal officials are often distant, faceless decision makers whose contacts with citizens are based on slow and frequently disappointing correspondence in response to questions and requests about important matters such as taxes, Social Security benefits, and medical assistance for veterans.

Unlike the equally faceless customer service representatives for online merchants and credit card companies, who nevertheless seem eager to respond to our phone calls and questions, the government officials with whom we communicate may appear detached and unresponsive—and (it seems) all too often, agents at the IRS, Social Security, or the Veterans Administration either insist that we pay more or tell us that we can't get some benefit. This does not necessarily mean that low-level government officials are coldhearted by nature. They may need to fill out many forms and gain approvals from superiors before they can address our claims and questions in a slow-moving process. Whether or not individual government officials are uncaring, it is easy to understand why the bureaucracy often has a negative image in the minds of Americans.

Views about specific government agencies can also be affected by values and beliefs associated with people's political party identification. People who identify themselves as Republicans often believe that the federal government should be smaller and should leave many areas of law and policy under the control of states. By contrast, many people who identify themselves as Democrats may believe that strong national action is needed to address policy issues in ways that benefit all Americans and do not vary by state. Thus public opinion polls show differences in Republicans' and Democrats' expressed views about specific agencies, with Republicans holding markedly more negative views about the EPA, the Department of Health and Human Services, the Department of Justice, the Internal Revenue Service, and the Department of Education.

According to Charles Goodsell, we expect too much from bureaucracies, and we have negative images in part because "we expect bureaucracies not merely to expend maximum possible effort in solving societal problems but to dispose of them entirely, whether solvable or not."[7] Do you agree that government agencies receive blame unfairly for falling short of perfection?

The Advantages of Government Bureaucracy

Officialdom does not exist by accident. Bureaucracies are created and evolve as a means to undertake the purposes and responsibilities of organizations. The German sociologist Max Weber (1864–1920) is known for describing an ideal bureaucracy involving competent, trained personnel with clearly defined job responsibilities under a central authority who keeps detailed records and makes consistent decisions in accordance with established rules. In theory, these are beneficial elements for running an organization efficiently.

If you were in charge of distributing retirement benefits throughout the United States, how would you organize your system of distribution? Would you simply appoint one individual in each state to be the coordinator in charge of the retirees in that state and then send that individual all of the money each month for that state's retirees? This approach appears to eliminate the current centralized bureaucracy of the Social Security Administration, but it also may create many problems. How would you know whether each state coordinator was using the same criteria and rules for determining eligibility for retirement funds? How would you know whether the coordinators were sending out the appropriate amounts of money on time? When agencies are organized in a hierarchical fashion with specialized responsibilities, the federal government can try to diminish the risks from these problems.

One additional advantage, a merit-based system for hiring, has special importance for government bureaucracy. Until a little over a century ago, government employees were hired and fired on the basis of their support for particular political parties and candidates for elective office. This was called the **patronage system,** or **spoils system.** Political parties rewarded their supporters by giving them government jobs. At the same time, supporters of the opposing party were fired as soon as an election placed new leaders in office. "To the victor belongs the spoils," said a prominent Jacksonian Era politician early in the nineteenth century, giving political patronage its alternative name, the *spoils system.* (By "spoils," he was referring to the practice of an army sacking a conquered city and soldiers carrying off whatever they could grab.)

Of course, the spoils system had many problems. There was an abrupt turnover in many government positions after elections in which a different political party gained power. Unqualified people got government jobs despite lacking the knowledge and interest to carry out their tasks properly. Government workers steered benefits and services to fellow partisans and sought to deprive their political opponents of government services. Officials spent too much time doing things that would help keep their party in power and themselves in their jobs. New roads, government contracts, and other benefits went to citizens who supported the elected officials who had hired the government workers. With self-interest unchecked, there were grave risks of corruption, as government workers and political leaders alike traded bribes for favoritism in distributing government services and benefits.

patronage system (spoils system)
A system that rewards the supporters of successful political candidates and parties with government jobs while firing supporters of the opposing party. In earlier eras, government employees throughout the bureaucracy could lose their jobs when a new president was elected from a different political party than his or her own. The same result was true in state and city governments when new governors and mayors were elected. Today new presidents appoint only the top leaders of federal departments and agencies.

civil service system

A government employment system in which employees are hired on the basis of their qualifications and cannot be fired merely for belonging to the wrong political party. It originated with the federal Pendleton Act in 1883 and expanded at other levels of government in the half-century that followed. Today, federal employees in the Internal Revenue Service, National Park Service, U.S. Department of Transportation, and other agencies are hired based on their qualifications and retain their jobs even when new presidents are elected.

Hatch Act

Federal law that limits the participation of federal government employees in political campaigns to protect them from feeling obligated to donate money or work for political candidates.

All these problems came to a head in the early 1880s. During the summer of 1881, a man claiming to be a disappointed office seeker (he was probably insane) shot President James Garfield. Garfield's assassination made him a martyr for the cause of "good government." This event helped push forward previous proposals to reform the employment system within the federal government. Congress and President Chester A. Arthur found themselves under irresistible public pressure to enact legislation establishing a **civil service system** based on merit.

In 1883, Congress passed and President Arthur signed the Pendleton Act, creating the first federal civil service system. Under this act, applicants for specified federal government jobs were supposed to be tested, demonstrate their qualifications, and keep their jobs based on competent performance rather than political affiliation. The new system reduced, but did not entirely eliminate, such problems as unqualified employees and bribery. Over time, more federal jobs were brought under civil service rules, and civil service systems eventually developed as well in state and local governments, especially during the Progressive Era in the first decades of the twentieth century.

The civil service system is still the framework for the federal bureaucracy. Today, the president can appoint the top officials who oversee most federal government agencies. In doing so, the president seeks to steer the bureaucracy in policy directions that reflect the voters' presidential choice in the most recent election. However, except for these high officials and the staff in the Executive Office of the President, the vast majority of other federal workers are civil service employees who remain at their jobs as presidential administrations come and go. Standardization, expertise, and competence would all be endangered—indeed, under today's conditions, they would collapse—if federal agencies experienced the kind of massive turnovers in personnel after each election that were typical of America in the mid-nineteenth century.

Civil service rules protect federal employees from being fired for failing to support a specific political party. Federal employees are further protected by the **Hatch Act** of 1939, a law that limits the participation of federal employees in political campaigns (see Table 8.4). They can vote and attend political rallies, but they cannot

TABLE 8.4   The Hatch Act of 1939

Permitted/Prohibited Political Activities for Federal Employees
Federal employees *may*
• register and vote as they choose.
• assist in voter registration drives.
• express opinions about candidates and issues.
• participate in campaigns where none of the candidates represent a political party.
• contribute money to political organizations or attend political fund-raising functions.
• attend political rallies and meetings.
• join political clubs or parties.
• sign nominating petitions.
• campaign for or against referendum questions, constitutional amendments, and municipal ordinances.
Federal employees *may not*
• be candidates for public office in partisan elections.
• campaign for or against a candidate or slate of candidates in partisan elections.
• make campaign speeches.
• collect contributions or sell tickets to political fund-raising functions.
• distribute campaign material in partisan elections.
• organize or manage political rallies or meetings.
• hold office in political clubs or parties.
• circulate nominating petitions.
• work to register voters for one party only.
• wear political buttons at work.

SOURCE: U.S. Office of Special Counsel, accessed March 3, 2012, http://www.osc.gov/hatchact.htmon.

work on campaigns or endorse candidates. Although this law limits federal workers' political participation, it is intended to prevent them from being pressured by elected officials to donate their money and time to political campaigns. Prior to the implementation of civil service systems, it was very common for government employees to be required to work on political campaigns in order to keep their jobs. The current system spares them from fearing that they will lose promotions, raises, and other benefits for failing to support the party in power.

Despite the often-negative image of bureaucracies, we can summarize the *potential* advantages of bureaucracies. Bear in mind that these potential advantages will remain unfulfilled if the organization, personnel, resources, and supervision within agencies do not ensure that a bureaucracy is actually functioning efficiently.

- **Standardization**. By having a centralized administration and a common set of rules, benefits and services can be provided in a standard fashion that avoids treating similarly situated citizens differently. A retiree in Idaho can receive the same federal benefits and services as a retiree of the same age and employment history in Maine.

- **Expertise and Competence**. When people who work in an agency focus on specific areas of law and policy throughout their careers, they can develop expertise on those issues. This expertise will help them effectively carry out laws and policies and, moreover, permit them to advise Congress and the president on ways to improve law and policy. Presumably, their expertise will make them more competent than people who know little about the subject. Thus, people who work for the EPA are typically hired because of their education and interest in environmental issues, and they develop greater expertise on this subject as they spend years working in this area.

- **Accountability**. Congress can authorize a specific budget for particular programs and then monitor results for the targeted policy area. If $50 million are earmarked to combat air pollution, the existence of an agency dedicated to environmental issues—the EPA—permits those funds to be directed to the targeted issues and not mixed together with funds destined for education, transportation, and defense, all of which are handled by separate agencies in the bureaucracy. After the money is spent, air pollution can be evaluated, and Congress and the president can assess whether the EPA spent the money effectively and whether their intended policies were carried out correctly.

- **Coordination**. Efforts of different agencies can be more effectively coordinated when each has clearly defined responsibilities and a hierarchical structure. Hierarchy enables the leaders in each agency to direct subordinates to work in cooperation with other agencies. For example, if officials in the Department of Education and the Department of Health and Human Services are instructed to cooperate in implementing an antidrug program or an education program aimed at preventing teen pregnancy, the leaders of the respective agencies can work together to delegate shared responsibilities. When individual officials throughout the country act independently on issues, it is much more difficult to coordinate efforts effectively.

In general, these advantages may be helpful in both government and business organizations.

The Problems of Government Bureaucracy

The advantages of a merit system do not mean, however, that government agencies necessarily fulfill their responsibilities efficiently and satisfy the expectations of citizens, the president, and Congress. Many practical problems tarnish the idealistic vision of civil service bureaucracies as effective, efficient organizations. For example, as organizations grow in size, decision-making layers increase between the employee, with whom the average citizen interacts, and the upper-level managers with final authority. Higher-level decision makers may be far removed from the practical policy problems affecting citizens. When decisions must move through a chain of command, there are obvious risks of delay, including the chance that documents will be misplaced or lost so that new forms must be completed to start a decision-making process all over again.

Civil service protections can make it difficult for top officials to motivate government employees and spur them to take actions, especially when those actions require changing an agency's priorities or operating methods. Almost by nature, large organizations are resistant to change. People who have become accustomed to doing their jobs in a specific way may be reluctant to adopt new priorities and directives. Bureaucracies are not typically associated with innovation and bold ideas. They change slowly, and usually in incremental fashion. When the president or Congress wants law and policy to move in a new direction, getting the bureaucracy to reorder its priorities and operate in different ways can be akin to the familiar image of "turning a battleship at sea"—a slow, gradual, laborious process. If executive agencies are slow to implement new laws, they can hinder or even undermine the achievement of a president's policy goals.

For policy change to be effective, laws and programs must be designed by taking account of the resources, characteristics, experience, and organizational structure of the agencies that must implement those laws and programs. Implementation problems can be even more significant when, rather than just providing guidance and supervision for state and local governments, an agency bears responsibility for hiring staff, training personnel, and carrying out new tasks. When agencies are large bureaucracies, it can be exceptionally difficult to organize, implement, and monitor programs effectively.

Let's take an example: the Transportation Security Administration (TSA), which was created in November 2001 in the aftermath of the 9/11 terrorist attacks. The TSA is now part of the Department of Homeland Security. Among other responsibilities, the TSA screens passengers and their baggage for weapons and explosives before they board commercial airliners. An airline passenger's unsuccessful attempt to ignite a bomb as his plane approached the Detroit airport from the Netherlands on Christmas

Transportation Security Administration (TSA) officers provide an essential service in working to protect public safety at airports.

■ *How can we make sure that we have selected the best candidates to become TSA officers and have provided them with necessary training, equipment, and supervision?*

Day in 2009 provided a stark reminder of the need for effective, professional security officials conducting screening and searches at all airports.

In its first few years, the TSA was plagued with problems. Eighteen-thousand screeners were hired and initially put to work without required background checks. Among the 1,200 screeners eventually fired after background checks revealed that they had lied on their applications or had criminal records, several with criminal pasts were permitted to remain on the job for weeks or even months before termination.[8] The federal government paid hundreds of thousands of dollars in claims after screeners were caught stealing from passengers' luggage while searching for weapons and explosives. Morale problems also developed as screeners complained of being required to work overtime without adequate compensation and of being assigned to use baggage-scanning equipment without receiving any training.[9] If the TSA had been given more time for planning, more opportunities to screen and train workers, and more resources to ensure adequate personnel and equipment at each airport, the implementation of the policy might have gone more smoothly. The bureaucracy, however, must work in a constrained environment in which limits on time, resources, and expertise often result in implementation problems.

The challenges of administering the TSA continued in subsequent years as the agency felt pressured to speedily move travelers through security checkpoints in order to avoid causing any flight delays. Moreover, the agency's safety responsibilities remained challenging because the actual tasks at security checkpoints were so routine and repetitive that it was difficult to keep employees attentive and vigilant. In 2015, the Inspector General's Office at the Department of Homeland Security conducted secret tests of TSA effectiveness by sending undercover agents through airport screening while carrying weapons and other illegal items. TSA agents failed to catch 67 of 70 testers for a 95 percent failure rate. As a result of the test failures, the head of TSA was replaced and agents were sent for retraining on security procedures.[10] More problems continued at individual airports in 2016 as a congressional investigation found that TSA officers experienced retaliation from their supervisors if they reported security lapses that would embarrass managers at individual airports.[11] Large bureaucracies that operate at numerous, far-flung locations can be especially difficult to supervise and manage.

Reform of the Bureaucracy

The gigantic size and nationwide responsibilities of modern federal agencies make it extremely difficult for the bureaucracy to live up to the ideals of efficient performance based on management principles in an organizational hierarchy. Some critics argue that alternative approaches to implementation could reduce the problems of government bureaucracy. One suggestion is to try **decentralization**—a reform in which the federal government could give greater independence to regional offices that would be more closely connected to local issues and client populations. Alternatively, states could be given greater authority to handle their own affairs. For example, state inspection agencies could receive federal funds to enforce national air pollution or workplace safety laws. The argument for decentralization rests on a belief that smaller agencies, presumably more closely connected to local problems, can be more efficient and effective. There are risks, however, that decentralization would lead to inconsistent standards and treatment for people in different parts of the country. Officials in one state might vigorously enforce pollution laws, while those in another state might turn a blind eye to such problems because of the economic and political power of polluting industries.

Privatization has also been suggested as a cure for the problems of government bureaucracy. Critics argue that private businesses working under government contracts could deliver services and benefits to citizens with greater efficiency and less

decentralization
Proposed reform for government agencies intended to increase efficiency in administration and create closer contacts with the local public; permits regional and local offices to manage their own performances without close supervision from headquarters.

privatization
The process of turning some responsibilities of government bureaucracy over to private organizations on the assumption that they can administer and deliver services more effectively and inexpensively. During the wars in Iraq and Afghanistan, for example, the government hired private companies to handle food services, transportation of supplies, and even personal protection, such as bodyguards, for American officials in Iraq.

expense than when the bureaucracy handles such matters. All levels of government use private contracts in an effort to save money. Indeed, states have sent convicted offenders to prisons built and operated by private corporations, governments pay private contractors to repair highways and build bridges, and the federal government has hired private contractors to serve as bodyguards for American officials in the war zones of Iraq and Afghanistan.

In theory, businesses and nonprofit agencies are better than the government bureaucracy at finding ways to save money, developing innovations, and responding to feedback from client populations. One way that they save money is through compensation for low-level workers that is less generous than government pay and through flexible personnel policies that allow them to lay off or fire employees whose counterparts in government would have civil service job security protection. Privatization is controversial. In some circumstances, private contractors do not save money and do not deliver services more effectively than government agencies. In addition, it can be difficult to hold private companies accountable for their actions, because they are not necessarily subject to the same oversight laws that govern public agencies. Moreover, there are risks of favoritism and corruption as private companies use campaign contributions, personal contacts with government officials, and lobbying to encourage expenditures of government funds that add to their profits but do not necessarily address the public's needs.

For example, during the Bush administration, critics questioned the basis for lucrative, no-bid contracts awarded to Halliburton Corporation, an oil-services and construction company. The company had been run by Dick Cheney (prior to his becoming the vice president of President Bush), and it made millions of dollars on projects in Iraq despite prior scandals about poor performance and overbilling on government contracts.[12] During the Obama administration, parallel questions were raised about government money provided to alternative energy companies that were ultimately unsuccessful, but reportedly were run by supporters of the administration.[13]

Senior Executive Service (SES)
A program established by Congress In 1978 to enable senior administrators with outstanding management skills to move between jobs in different agencies in order to enhance the performance of the federal bureaucracy.

Periodically, efforts are made to reform the bureaucracy in order to improve its effectiveness. For example, in 1978, Congress established the **Senior Executive Service (SES)**, a program within the federal executive branch that enables senior administrators with outstanding leadership and management skills to be moved between jobs in different agencies in order to enhance the performance of the bureaucracy. The development of the SES was intended to add flexibility in shifting personnel resources within the federal bureaucracy. Then, during President Clinton's administration (1993–2001), Vice President Al Gore led a task force of senior government officials in an effort known as the National Partnership for Reinventing Government. This effort resulted in several laws to better measure the performance of government agencies, increase cooperation between government and business, and otherwise improve the effectiveness of the bureaucracy.

The Lobbying Pathway and Policymaking

8.4   Assess the mechanisms and processes that influence and oversee the federal bureaucracy.

From what you've read so far, you can see the bureaucracy's influence over policy through its responsibilities for implementation of laws enacted by Congress. The effectiveness of agencies' implementation efforts can depend on their resources, information, and expertise. However, the bureaucracy can affect policymaking in other ways.

The bureaucracy also influences the formulation of public policy through the decisions and actions of elites—people with political connections, status, or expertise—and through the day-to-day implementation of laws and regulations by lower-level personnel such as FBI agents, forest rangers, postal workers, water-quality inspectors, and others who have direct contact with the public. If an FBI agent does not follow mandated procedures when investigating a case or arresting a suspect, the laws of Congress and the regulations of the Department of Justice have not been implemented properly. Full and proper implementation of many laws and policies can rest in the hands of relatively low-level officials who make discretionary decisions about how they will treat individuals and businesses when conducting investigations or administering the distribution of government services and benefits.

The Bureaucracy and Legislation

The ideal of the bureaucracy envisions employees with competence and expertise who work in a pyramid-shaped organizational structure with clear lines of authority and supervision. The lines of authority in a bureaucracy's organizational chart are meant to indicate that the downward flow of instructions guides the actions of personnel at each level of the agency. In reality, the decisions and actions of personnel within the bureaucracy are more complicated because of the influence of informal networks and relationships with organizations and actors outside the bureaucracy. In prior decades, political scientists often described the influence of these networks and relationships by focusing on the concept of the **iron triangle**, a concept describing the tight relationship and power over policy issues possessed by three entities sharing joint interests concerning specific policy goals: (1) interest groups concerned with a particular policy issue, (2) the key committee members in Congress and their staff with authority over that issue, and (3) the bureaucracy's leaders and the experts on that particular issue within a given department or subagency. (See Figure 8.3.) Within their sphere of expertise and interest, these iron triangles could, through discussion, communication, and consensus among members, control the writing of laws and the development of policies.

The linkages and power of the iron triangle were enhanced as interest groups provided campaign contributions to legislators on relevant congressional committees and rallied their own members to support or oppose legislative proposals emanating from the iron triangle. The committees in Congress are especially influential in shaping policy. The key committee members could draft legislation, block unwanted bills, and facilitate the passage of desired statutes through the legislative process. The bureaucracy's interested experts could provide needed information, help plan and facilitate implementation, and provide strategic opposition to counterproposals

iron triangle

The tight relationship between employees in government agencies, interest groups, and legislators and their staff members, all of whom share an interest in specific policy issues and work together behind the scenes to shape laws and public policy.

FIGURE 8.3 Iron Triangle

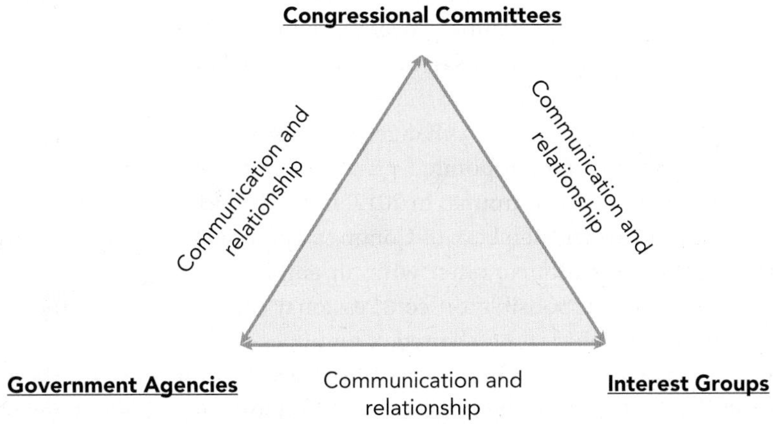

Congressional Committees

Communication and relationship

Communication and relationship

Government Agencies

Communication and relationship

Interest Groups

Gina McCarthy, the administrator of the Environmental Protection Agency, faced tough questioning from a congressional committee in 2016. Angry members of Congress expressed concern about the adequacy of the federal agency's action in response to decisions by state officials in Michigan that contaminated the drinking water in the city of Flint with lead, a toxic metal that is especially harmful to the developing brains of young children.

■ *How does Congress influence the actions of federal agencies?*

generated by those outside of the iron triangle. The concept of the iron triangle helped encourage recognition of the bureaucracy's role in shaping legislation through informal networks.

Contemporary scholars view the iron triangle concept as limited and outdated. The governing system has changed. Growing numbers of interest groups are active in lobbying, and individual members of Congress today have less absolute power over committee processes. With respect to some policy issues, interest groups use strategies that include advertising campaigns to arouse the public and calling the attention of the news media to issues that previously may have been decided largely behind the closed doors of a congressional committee room.

Realizing the inadequacies of the iron triangle framework for all policy issues, scholars now focus on concepts characterized as either **issue networks** or **policy communities**. Guy Peters describes these as "involving large numbers of interested parties, each with substantial expertise in the policy area…. They may contain competing ideas and types of interests to be served through public policy."[14] Both terms describe ongoing relationships and contacts between individuals interested in specific policy issues and areas. These individuals have expertise and remain in contact over time as their particular public policy concerns rise and fall on the nation's policy agenda. At government conferences presenting research on environmental issues, conference attendees who interact with each other are likely to include a variety of individuals representing different perspectives: scholars who study the environment, officials from the EPA, staff members from relevant congressional committees, representatives from interest groups concerned with such issues, and officials from businesses involved in waste disposal, manufacturing processes, and the cleanup of industrial sites.

Some of these individuals may change jobs over the years and move from universities and businesses into appointed positions in government or from congressional committees to interest groups. In 2012, it was reported that more than three-quarters of the 372 former members of Congress employed as lobbyists worked for businesses and interest groups, often with an emphasis on issue areas for which they were previously responsible on congressional committees.[15] A study in 2016 found that former members who chaired committees or had other leadership positions in Congress were most likely to become lobbyists after leaving the national legislature.[16] High officials in the bureaucracy also move in and out of government.

issue networks (policy communities)

Interest groups, scholars, and other experts that communicate about, debate, and interact regarding issues of interest and thus influence public policy when the legislature acts on those issues.

As these actors move between jobs, their interests and expertise keep them in contact with each other through conferences and individual communications as they develop working relationships. When bills are formally proposed, individuals from throughout the network are likely to use their contacts in seeking to amend the bill's wording, lobbying for its passage, or attempting to block its progress through the legislative process. The "revolving door" of employees moving between federal government service and interest groups or lobbying firms raises concerns that an agency may be "captured" or controlled by officials who have long alliances with and commitments to specific interest groups.

For example, Gale Norton, the Secretary of the Interior under President Bush from 2001 to 2006, had previously worked as an attorney for the Mountain States Legal Foundation, an interest group that challenged environmentalist groups in court by arguing against government restrictions on land use and by advocating for the use of federal lands by ranchers, recreational vehicles, and oil exploration companies. When she left her government post, she became a legal advisor for Royal Dutch Shell, an oil company that obtained lucrative federal land leases for obtaining oil from the Interior Department that Norton had been heading.[17] Such "revolving door" job movements between government agencies and the interest groups and businesses with which they deal create risks of the appearance of impropriety or even corruption. Do these individuals improperly use their government authority to steer agency decisions in favor of specific interests in order to obtain a lucrative job or other benefits for themselves? In Gale Norton's case, the U.S. Department of Justice launched a criminal investigation that sought to determine whether she had violated laws against steering government business to favored companies and discussing employment with a company that has dealings with the government within the area of the government official's authority.[18] News reports stated in 2010 that no charges would be filed against her.

The Bureaucracy and Information

Officials appointed by the president to head executive agencies invariably advocate laws—at least in public—that reflect the president's policy agenda. Occasionally, long-time officials within the bureaucracy with experience and expertise may disagree with laws and policies sought by the president and presidential appointees. They may also disagree with new interpretations of existing laws or with presidential efforts to change current policies. These officials may get in touch with their contacts among personnel who work for congressional committees, thereby alerting sympathetic members of Congress to initiate investigations, publicize the president's actions, and oppose efforts to shape law and policy. They may also leak information to the news media in order to bring public attention to issues of concern to them.

An additional role played by officials in the bureaucracy is to provide information for Congress to use in crafting and approving statutes. They provide this information both formally and informally. Formally, some federal agencies, such as the U.S. Census Bureau, regularly send out a steady stream of information to all kinds of congressional committees that are interested in trends in the nation's population as well as in such demographic issues as home ownership, poverty, and education. Other agencies gather, analyze, and provide information about very specific policy issues, usually working only with those congressional committees that are specifically concerned with these issues. Informal communication between the bureaucracy and Congress occurs when legislative staffers or individual members of Congress contact agency officials with questions about policy issues and government programs. These informal contacts can help build relationships within issue networks that lead to cooperative working relationships as members of Congress rely on agency officials for advice when crafting new legislative proposals.

Congressional reliance on officials in the bureaucracy for information can create problems if presidential appointees use their authority to direct subordinates to withhold or distort information as a means of advancing the president's policy agenda. For example, in 2004, several conservative Republicans threatened to oppose President Bush's Medicare bill if it would cost more than $400 billion, but they had been reassured by the White House that it would not. The chief actuary for the Centers for Medicare and Medicaid Services conducted an analysis that indicated the legislation would cost at least $100 billion more, but his superior, the director of the Medicare office, threatened to fire him if he revealed this to members of Congress. Two months after Congress approved the legislation, the White House budget director revealed that the new law would actually cost more than $530 billion.[19]

This risk of distorted information is one reason that Congress also seeks to gather its own information through legislative committees and through the Congressional Budget Office and Government Accountability Office, an investigative agency that reports to Congress. The range of policy issues is so vast, however, that Congress must inevitably rely on officials in the bureaucracy for important information about many public policies. Even though most employees in the federal bureaucracy are civil servants who are not formally affiliated with a political party, they may face pressure from presidential appointees to take actions that violate their own ideals of performing their jobs with neutrality and competence. If they disobey superiors, they may be passed over for promotion, transferred to undesirable positions or offices, or threatened with dismissal based on phony charges of incompetence.

whistleblower

An employee who reports or reveals misconduct by government officials or others.

Some employees within the bureaucracy stand up against actions by executive branch superiors by providing information about misconduct by government officials. Individuals who are willing to provide such information are known as **whistleblowers**, and they often risk workplace retaliation in the form of dismissal, demotions, and other sanctions intended to punish them for their actions and to deter others from revealing politically damaging information. In 2004, for example, an issue emerged in the presidential campaign when a senior civilian contracting official in the U.S. Army Corps of Engineers claimed that Halliburton Corporation, the business previously chaired by Vice President Dick Cheney, had received preferential treatment in the awarding of lucrative contracts for reconstruction projects in Iraq.[20] Because the disclosure triggered investigative actions in Congress, the official's supporters feared that she would suffer retaliation. Her lawyer asserted that she should be shielded by the **Whistleblower Protection Act of 1989**, a federal law intended to prevent officials in the bureaucracy from being punished for their efforts to protect the country from governmental misconduct.

Whistleblower Protection Act of 1989

A federal law intended to prevent employees in the bureaucracy from being punished for reporting or revealing governmental misconduct.

In theory, this statute should protect whistleblowers, but in individual cases, it may be difficult for affected individuals to refute their superiors' claims that they are being punished for poor performance rather than for providing well-intentioned, revealing information. For example, just as her attorney feared, the civilian whistleblower from the Army Corps of Engineers was removed from her position and demoted, with a reduction in salary, after she testified before a congressional committee.[21] Subsequently, however, she filed a lawsuit over her treatment and the government settled the case in 2011 by paying her $970,000.[22] Her case did not prove that whistleblowers will ultimately be protected by the operation of law. The government's willingness to offer a generous settlement may have been the product of the national publicity that her case received. Other potential whistleblowers in government may still be reluctant to come forward after observing her treatment. Thus, questions remain about whether whistleblowers receive sufficient protection to lead them to come forward with information about wrongdoing in government.

Regulations

Depending on their responsibilities, federal agencies may receive rule-making authority from the statutes that Congress enacts. The rule-making process gives officials in the bureaucracy power over the development of public policy. In some cases, the legislation creating an agency will use general language to describe its mission. For example, as the political scientist Robert Katzmann concluded from his study of the FTC, "In the absence of clearly defined statutory objectives, the Federal Trade Commission apparently has wide discretion in determining the goal (or goals) that it should pursue."[23]

General statutory language can become the basis for the bureaucracy's development of its own precise rules—agency-created laws called **regulations**, which govern the topics under a particular agency's jurisdiction. Commentators often describe regulations as filling in the precise details of rules for society based on the broader directives set forth in statutes. In other cases, Congress may enact statutes that specifically delegate to agencies the authority to formulate the precise rules to govern a particular subject.

Statutes written by Congress also specify the procedures that agencies must use in developing regulations. Normally, these procedures include publication of proposed regulations, a period during which the public may comment on the proposals, and a process for hearings about the desirability and potential effects of the proposed regulations. These procedures give interest groups the opportunity to encourage agencies to adopt new proposals, to work for change in proposals that originated with the government or other groups, or to block (if they can) proposed regulations adverse to their interests. For example, as illustrated earlier in this chapter in Pathways of Action, the Environmental Protection Agency (EPA) used its authority under the Clean Air Act by moving forward with proposed regulations to set standards for air pollution.[24] Energy companies and state governments objected to the regulations and also devoted considerable effort to lobbying Congress and filing lawsuits that led the Supreme Court in 2016 to block, at least temporarily, the new rule requiring drastic cutbacks in carbon emissions by power plants.[25] The Timeline feature traces the history of the Clean Air Act and developments affecting the regulation of air pollution.

The rule-making process creates opportunities for shaping regulations. Interested individuals' relationships with officials in the bureaucracy come into play through issue networks. Interest groups that give campaign contributions and endorsements to the president's political party can also lobby overtly. Because some regulations are controversial, agencies are often instructed during election campaigns to slow down the processes by which rules are changed and created so that the political party opposing the president cannot use pending regulations as a campaign issue.[26] Clearly, this rule-making process gives officials in the bureaucracy significant influence over the development of regulations affecting a wide array of policy issues, ranging from air pollution rules to workplace safety regulations to the approval of new drugs and medical treatments.

Although judgments about the desirability of specific regulatory changes always depend on the values of a particular observer, it is generally agreed that presidents have opportunities to exploit the rule-making process to advance their own policy agendas. For example, critics accused the Bush administration of using these tactics to lengthen the hours that long-haul truckers could drive in one shift, despite evidence about the risk of car–truck collisions when drivers are tired; approve logging in federal forests without the usual environmental reviews; dilute rules intended to protect coal miners from black lung disease; and relax air pollution regulations for factories and power plants.[27] The Bush administration and its supporters responded to criticisms by claiming that the government hampers business productivity with too many needless regulations. The Obama administration used the regulatory process to pursue its own goals, including improved gas mileage standards for motor vehicles, government funding for stem-cell research, and federal control over the safety standards for subways and light-rail systems.[28]

regulations
Legal rules created by government agencies based on authority delegated by the legislature. For example, in order to protect public safety, regulations issued by the U.S. Department of Transportation define how many hours each week truck drivers can be on the road and how many hours of rest they must have between driving shifts.

TIMELINE

The Clean Air Act and the Environmental Protection Agency

The Environmental Protection Agency's authority to regulate air pollution emissions from automobiles, energy plants, and factories is one of the most controversial issues of contention between Democrats and Republicans. Although public opinion polls indicate that most Americans support the goal of reducing air pollution, there are significant debates about how much pollution regulation is desirable. Republican politicians, on behalf of their supporters among energy companies and manufacturers, often claim that EPA regulations impose excessively expensive burdens on companies, resulting in plant shutdowns and the loss of jobs. By contrast, Democratic politicians, on behalf of their environmentalist supporters, often favor stricter enforcement of pollution controls because of concerns about public health and the long-term impact of global warming. Thus, the EPA becomes the focus of policy-shaping activities through multiple pathways. Moreover, the agency's orientation changes whenever a different political party wins the presidency.

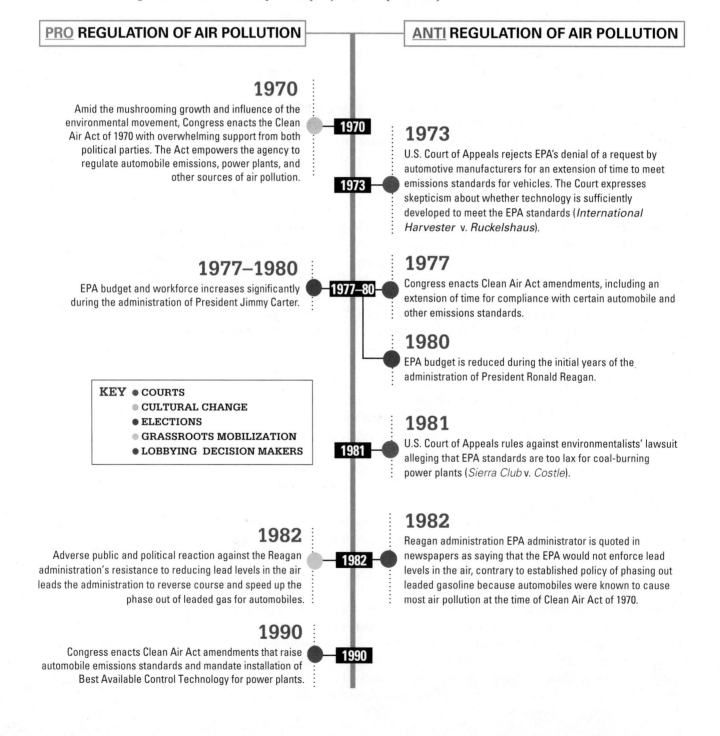

PRO REGULATION OF AIR POLLUTION

ANTI REGULATION OF AIR POLLUTION

1970

Amid the mushrooming growth and influence of the environmental movement, Congress enacts the Clean Air Act of 1970 with overwhelming support from both political parties. The Act empowers the agency to regulate automobile emissions, power plants, and other sources of air pollution.

1973

U.S. Court of Appeals rejects EPA's denial of a request by automotive manufacturers for an extension of time to meet emissions standards for vehicles. The Court expresses skepticism about whether technology is sufficiently developed to meet the EPA standards (*International Harvester* v. *Ruckelshaus*).

1977–1980

EPA budget and workforce increases significantly during the administration of President Jimmy Carter.

1977

Congress enacts Clean Air Act amendments, including an extension of time for compliance with certain automobile and other emissions standards.

1980

EPA budget is reduced during the initial years of the administration of President Ronald Reagan.

KEY
- ● COURTS
- ● CULTURAL CHANGE
- ● ELECTIONS
- ● GRASSROOTS MOBILIZATION
- ● LOBBYING DECISION MAKERS

1981

U.S. Court of Appeals rules against environmentalists' lawsuit alleging that EPA standards are too lax for coal-burning power plants (*Sierra Club* v. *Costle*).

1982

Adverse public and political reaction against the Reagan administration's resistance to reducing lead levels in the air leads the administration to reverse course and speed up the phase out of leaded gas for automobiles.

1982

Reagan administration EPA administrator is quoted in newspapers as saying that the EPA would not enforce lead levels in the air, contrary to established policy of phasing out leaded gasoline because automobiles were known to cause most air pollution at the time of Clean Air Act of 1970.

1990

Congress enacts Clean Air Act amendments that raise automobile emissions standards and mandate installation of Best Available Control Technology for power plants.

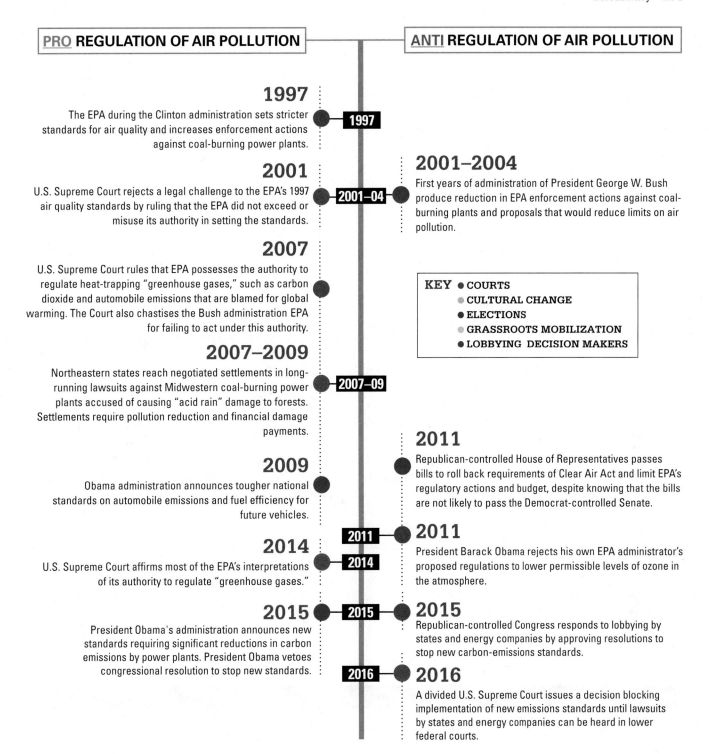

PRO REGULATION OF AIR POLLUTION

1997
The EPA during the Clinton administration sets stricter standards for air quality and increases enforcement actions against coal-burning power plants.

2001
U.S. Supreme Court rejects a legal challenge to the EPA's 1997 air quality standards by ruling that the EPA did not exceed or misuse its authority in setting the standards.

2007
U.S. Supreme Court rules that EPA possesses the authority to regulate heat-trapping "greenhouse gases," such as carbon dioxide and automobile emissions that are blamed for global warming. The Court also chastises the Bush administration EPA for failing to act under this authority.

2007–2009
Northeastern states reach negotiated settlements in long-running lawsuits against Midwestern coal-burning power plants accused of causing "acid rain" damage to forests. Settlements require pollution reduction and financial damage payments.

2009
Obama administration announces tougher national standards on automobile emissions and fuel efficiency for future vehicles.

2014
U.S. Supreme Court affirms most of the EPA's interpretations of its authority to regulate "greenhouse gases."

2015
President Obama's administration announces new standards requiring significant reductions in carbon emissions by power plants. President Obama vetoes congressional resolution to stop new standards.

ANTI REGULATION OF AIR POLLUTION

2001–2004
First years of administration of President George W. Bush produce reduction in EPA enforcement actions against coal-burning plants and proposals that would reduce limits on air pollution.

KEY
● COURTS
◐ CULTURAL CHANGE
● ELECTIONS
◐ GRASSROOTS MOBILIZATION
● LOBBYING DECISION MAKERS

2011
Republican-controlled House of Representatives passes bills to roll back requirements of Clear Air Act and limit EPA's regulatory actions and budget, despite knowing that the bills are not likely to pass the Democrat-controlled Senate.

2011
President Barack Obama rejects his own EPA administrator's proposed regulations to lower permissible levels of ozone in the atmosphere.

2015
Republican-controlled Congress responds to lobbying by states and energy companies by approving resolutions to stop new carbon-emissions standards.

2016
A divided U.S. Supreme Court issues a decision blocking implementation of new emissions standards until lawsuits by states and energy companies can be heard in lower federal courts.

CRITICAL THINKING QUESTIONS

1. How should scientists and environmental experts within the EPA react each time a different political party wins the White House and seeks to steer the EPA in a different direction? What should these "bureaucrats" do if they believe that a particular president is disobeying the mandate of the Clean Air Act?

2. One of the Republican presidential candidates in the 2016 campaign promised to abolish the EPA if elected. Republican critics of environmental regulations claim that the EPA is a "job-killing" agency because of the anti-pollution rules it enforces on energy and manufacturing companies. If the EPA no longer existed, is there an alternative approach to addressing issues of air pollution other than relying on a government agency within the executive branch bureaucracy?

Quasi-Judicial Processes

The bureaucracy affects policy in some agencies through hearings that look similar to the duties of courts in examining evidence and issuing decisions. In the course of making these decisions, officials in the bureaucracy interpret statutes and regulations and thereby shape policy through their application of the law. Depending on the agency and the purpose of the adjudicative procedures, these processes can be formal or informal. There are also differences in the extent to which these processes are adversarial and thereby permit two sides to argue against each other in front of decision makers within the bureaucracy.

Officials in government agencies may use these processes when investigating whether individuals and corporations are obeying laws and regulations. In 2009, for example, the FCC responded to complaints from members of the public by launching an investigation about swearing and an allegedly obscene gesture by award recipients on NBC's broadcast of the Golden Globe awards.[29] Much like judges in a court, the commissioners make their decisions based on an examination of evidence and an interpretation of the law related to broadcast standards. Moreover, their interpretation of the law and their imposition of strong sanctions help shape policy and provide guidance for other broadcasters about permissible program content.

Judicial processes also exist when citizens are denied requested benefits from the government. For example, if people believe that their physical or mental disabilities prevent them from working and that they qualify for disability payments from the Social Security Administration, they must file an application with their local Social Security office and provide medical evidence about their disability. If their local office deems them ineligible, they can appeal to an **administrative law judge (ALJ)** within the Social Security Administration. The ALJ holds a formal hearing, in which the claimant may be represented by an attorney, and medical evidence is presented to document the claimed disability[30] (see Table 8.5). Similar ALJ hearings and quasi-judicial decisions are made in other agencies concerning matters such as immigration and labor union disputes.

As with other judicial-type processes within the bureaucracy, immigration hearings do not receive public attention, and large numbers of cases are processed with relatively little time spent on many of those individual cases. Thus, the risks of error may be greater than in a regular criminal or civil court, in which each side is represented by a lawyer in public proceedings.

administrative law judge (ALJ)
Official who presides over quasi-judicial proceedings within government agencies and renders decisions about disputes governed by statutes, such as appeals from denials of Social Security disability benefits.

TABLE 8.5 Applying for Social Security Disability Benefits

Applicant	Decision makers
• **Step 1.** *Submit application forms.* Records needed to demonstrate that applicant meets the criteria for (1) enough total years worked contributing money to the Social Security system to become eligible for consideration; (2) worked at least half the time in years preceding claimed disability; (3) contact information for doctors. If disability claim is denied, then	After officials in Social Security Administration determine if applicant's work history makes the individual qualified for benefits, medical personnel in state agency receive referral from Social Security Administration to obtain medical records and evaluate applicant's capacity to work.
• **Step 2.** *Request reconsideration.* If disability claim is denied, then	Entire file reviewed by officials in Social Security Administration who did not take part in the original decision.
• **Step 3.** *Appeal decision to quasi-judicial process in Social Security Administration.* If disability claim is denied, then	An administrative law judge (ALJ) within Social Security Administration will conduct a hearing at which the applicant and the applicant's attorney (if represented by counsel) can present evidence and witnesses before ALJ decides whether the original denial of benefits was improper.
• **Step 4.** *Appeal decision to the Appeals Council within the Social Security Administration.* If disability claim is denied, then	Members of the Appeals Council within the Social Security Administration will review records and either deny the claim or refer the case back to the ALJ for further review.
• **Step 5.** *File lawsuit in U.S. District Court.*	U.S. District Court judge considers evidence and determines whether the denial of benefits by the Social Security Administration was improper.

SOURCE: U.S. Social Security Administration, accessed April 11, 2010, http://ssa-custhelp.ssa.gov/cgi-bin/ssa.cfg/php/enduser/std_alp.php?p_page=1&p_cv=1.50&p_pv=&p_prods=&p_cats=50.

Oversight and Accountability

As you've seen in the various ways by which agency officials shape policy, bureaucrats can have significant influence. Yet their actions typically are not noticed by the public or the news media. Without public attention focused on the decisions of agency officials, it is difficult to know what they are doing and to make sure they do not exceed their authority or otherwise make improper decisions. However, oversight mechanisms do exist.

All three branches of government have the power to subject the bureaucracy to oversight and accountability. The president attempts to oversee, guide, and control the bureaucracy through the supervisory authority of political appointees at the top levels of each agency. These appointees are supposed to monitor the work of subordinates and ensure that officials in each agency, as they produce regulations and implement statutes, are working to advance the president's preferred interpretations of laws. The threat of sanctions exists, because even though it may be difficult to dismiss civil service employees for most of their actions, the superiors in each agency can affect promotions, bonuses, and job assignments through the performance evaluations that they conduct annually on each employee.

There is also legislative oversight. This is executed in two simultaneous processes in Congress. The first is to gather information about what the agencies are doing, and the second is to let the agencies know what they need to be doing differently. Oversight by the legislative branch arises when congressional committees summon officials to testify. By pressing these bureaucrats with questions in a public hearing, members of Congress can attempt to discover whether laws are being implemented effectively and justly. If members are unhappy with the performance of officials in specific agencies, they can publicize these problems and thereby cast political blame on the president. This tactic puts pressure on the president and top appointees to ensure that agencies perform properly. Moreover, Congress controls each agency's budget. If agencies disappoint or clash with Congress, they risk losing needed resources. Congressional control over funding therefore creates incentives for cooperation and compliance by officials in the bureaucracy.[31] Judicial oversight comes into play when individuals and interest groups file lawsuits claiming that agencies are not implementing laws properly or are not following proper procedures in creating regulations. The many quasi-judicial processes within the bureaucracy are also subject to oversight through appeals to the federal courts from adverse judgments by ALJs, agency commissions and boards, and other bureaucratic decision makers.

Conclusion

The size of the federal bureaucracy reflects the policy ambitions of the national government. If the government of the United States focused only on national defense, foreign relations, and taxation, as it did in the founding era and for most of the nineteenth century, the federal bureaucracy would be both smaller and narrowly focused on those limited areas. Today, however, Congress writes laws establishing rules and programs covering a host of policy issues, from agriculture to energy to health care. To implement these complex programs, create relevant regulations, and enforce the laws enacted by Congress, the bureaucracy needs sufficient resources and trained personnel.

Despite the negative images the word *bureaucracy* calls to mind, the federal government needs large agencies to gather information, maintain records, educate the public, provide services, and enforce laws. As the national government enters new policy arenas or emphasizes new policy goals, such as homeland security in the aftermath of the terrorist attacks of September 11, 2001, the bureaucracy changes through reorganization and reallocations of money and personnel.

The bureaucracy plays a major role in public policy through a form of the lobbying decision makers pathway. Government agencies influence policy in several ways, none of which are clearly visible to the public or well covered by the media. Personnel in government agencies must implement the laws enacted by Congress and the policy initiatives developed by the president. If officials in the bureaucracy lack resources, knowledge, motivation, or supervision, the impact (or lack thereof) of policies on citizens' lives may differ from the outcomes intended by legislative policymakers and the executive branch.

Congress and the president rely on the bureaucracy for information and expertise about many policy issues. Officials in the bureaucracy may influence legislation through formal testimony to congressional committees as well as through informal contacts in the issue networks with committee staffers and interest groups. Officials in the bureaucracy also create law and policy through rule-making processes for developing, changing, and eliminating regulations. As illustrated by the example of the EPA and air pollution, this regulatory authority can make agencies the focus of significant battles involving lobbying, legislation, and litigation. Modern presidents see the rule-making process as a means to advance their policy agendas without seeking the approval of Congress—and often without announcing to the public the precise implications of the changes that have been made. In light of the bureaucracy's daily involvement in the complete range of policy issues affecting the United States, this component of national government will remain extremely important and influential, despite the fact that the American public does not recognize or understand its actions and impact.

CONFRONTING POLITICS AND POLICY

In 2015, *Forbes* magazine's online edition featured an interview with Alan Collinge, whose experience with escalating fees from his student loan debt led him to form a grassroots action and lobbying organization called StudentLoanJustice.org.[32] In 2008, CNN's Money website had named Collinge as one of its annual "heroes" for his work in seeking to reduce predatory profit-seeking by student loan lenders and to gain for student loan borrowers the same financial protections, such as eligibility for bankruptcy forgiveness, that other borrowers receive.[33] Through the political actions that they organize, such individuals can publicize issues, push for new regulations and legislation, and educate the public as a means to change public policy. In March 2015, President Obama issued a memorandum, titled "The Student Aid Bill of Rights," instructing the Department of Education and other federal agencies to institute new rules and procedures to improve supervision of student loans and provide better communication and complaint procedures for borrowers, among other changes.[34] While these changes in the bureaucracy's efforts to help student loan borrowers cannot be attributable to any one individual, actions of people like Alan Collinge help to contribute to political pressure to make government responsive to student loan borrowers.

ACTION STEPS

1. As a student, do you see problems with student loans that involve insufficiently clear information to borrowers, unnecessary requirements, or excessive fees? If so, list two issues that you believe deserve critical examination.

2. What steps could you take to bring relevant issues of concern to the attention of decision makers in the U.S. Department of Education? List two steps that you could take to seek to have an impact on action by the bureaucracy.

CHAPTER 8

> REVIEW THE CHAPTER

The Federal Bureaucracy

8.1 Trace the development of specific federal departments and agencies. (p. 251)

The bureaucracy in the executive branch of the federal government is composed of departments, independent agencies, independent regulatory commissions, and government corporations that have authority over specific topics across the vast array of policy issues facing the United States. The specific departments were created over the course of history as the country encountered policy issues that required the attention of the federal government. The original departments created at the formation of the Constitution, including Treasury and State, reflected recognition of the flaws in the previous Articles of Confederation. Other departments were created later in history as the nation faced new issues such as urbanization, educational reform, and large numbers of aging veterans from World War II and other wars in need of medical care.

Departments and Independent Agencies

8.2 Analyze the debate over whether the heads of federal agencies should be policy experts or loyal political appointees. (p. 259)

The executive branch is organized into departments. The president appoints a secretary to head each department, as well as the attorney general to lead the Department of Justice. These appointees (plus the heads of a few other designated agencies) constitute the president's cabinet. Political appointees may be politicians or individuals with policy expertise who share the president's policy goals. However, most personnel in the bureaucracy are civil service employees who remain on the job as presidents come and go. Although political appointees are typically committed to the president's agenda, the central role of political appointees at the top of government agencies raises questions

about whether these individuals have enough knowledge about the issue areas for which they bear responsibility.

The Nature of Bureaucracy

8.3 Describe the image people have of the federal bureaucracy, and evaluate the bureaucracy's advantages and disadvantages. (p. 264)

The popular image of the bureaucracy is of large, impersonal organizations that are inefficient and unresponsive. The advantages of a bureaucracy stem from providing organizations with clear lines of authority in which each employee has specific responsibilities and expertise. Ideally, bureaucracies are useful for standardization and consistency in providing government services. However, bureaucracies often fall short of their intended performance goals. As a result, critics have suggested that private businesses should assume responsibility for some of the tasks currently handled by government.

The Lobbying Pathway and Policymaking

8.4 Assess the mechanisms and processes that influence and oversee the federal bureaucracy. (p. 272)

The bureaucracy implements statutes and creates regulations, but its effectiveness is limited by its resources, information, and expertise. Whistleblowers in the bureaucracy provide information about misconduct within agencies. They are supposed to be protected from retaliation because they are helping to enhance accountability by calling attention to agencies' failings. Presidents use the rule-making process to advance policy agendas through regulations and thereby steer the bureaucracy's actions. The rule-making process also provides opportunities for interest groups to influence regulations. Congress uses oversight mechanisms, such as holding hearings that require testimony from agency officials or enacting new legislation to limit actions by government agencies.

> LEARN THE TERMS

bureaucracy, p. 251
departments, p. 256
independent agencies, p. 263
independent regulatory commissions, p. 263
government corporations, p. 263
patronage system (spoils system), p. 267

civil service system, p. 268
Hatch Act, p. 268
decentralization, p. 271
privatization, p. 271
Senior Executive Service (SES), p. 272
iron triangle, p. 273

issue networks (policy communities), p. 274
whistleblowers, p. 276
Whistleblower Protection Act of 1989, p. 276
regulations, p. 277
administrative law judge (ALJ), p. 280

> EXPLORE FURTHER

In the Library

Ashford, Nicholas, and Charles Caldart. *Environmental Law, Policy, and Economics*, Cambridge, MA: MIT Press, 2008.

Foreman, Christopher H., Jr. *Signals from the Hill: Congressional Oversight and the Challenge of Social Regulation.* New Haven, CT: Yale University Press, 1988.

Goodsell, Charles T. *The Case for the Bureaucracy*, 4th ed. Washington, D.C.: CQ Press, 2003.

Gormley, William T., and Steven J. Balla. *Bureaucracy and Democracy: Accountability and Performance,* 2nd ed. Washington, D.C.: CQ Press, 2007.

Kettl, Donald F., and James W. Fesler. *The Politics of the Administrative Process*, 4th ed. Washington, D.C.: CQ Press, 2008.

Meier, Kenneth J., and Laurence J. O'Toole. *Bureaucracy in a Democratic State: A Governance Perspective.* Baltimore, MD: Johns Hopkins University Press, 2006.

Wilson, James Q. *Bureaucracy: What Government Agencies Do and Why They Do It*. New York: Basic Books, 1991.

On the Web

Read about the organization and responsibilities of a federal department, such as the U.S. Department of Transportation at *http://www.dot.gov* or the U.S. Department of Homeland Security at *http://www.dhs.gov.*

Read about the individual appointees in the president's cabinet and find links to the departments of the executive branch at *http://www.whitehouse.gov/government/cabinet.html.*

Independent agencies have their own Web sites, such as the Federal Communications Commission at *http://www.fcc.gov*, the Federal Trade Commission at *http://www.ftc.gov*, and the National Labor Relations Board at *http://www.nlrb.gov.*

Learn about job opportunities and employment policies in the federal civil service at *http://www.usajobs.gov* and at the Web site for the U.S. Office of Personnel Management at *http://www.opm.gov.*

Read a report by the Urban Institute on the privatization of government social services at *http://www.urban.org/publications/407023.html.*

Read published proposed regulations awaiting public comments at *http://www.regulations.gov.*

THE JUDICIARY

Because the Supreme Court is so important for the development of public policy and law, contemporary presidents typically announce nominations of new justices at formal White House press conferences.
■ *What can prevent Republicans and Democrats from reaching agreement about which individuals are best qualified to serve as Supreme Court justices?*

⟶ LEARNING OBJECTIVES

9.1 Explain how American court systems are organized.

9.2 Identify the reasons why American judges are powerful actors in the governing system.

9.3 Outline the selection process for federal judges.

9.4 Explain the theories concerning how Supreme Court justices reach their decisions.

9.5 Characterize the litigation strategies used in the court pathway.

9.6 Evaluate the courts' effectiveness in enforcing judicial decisions.

9.7 Describe the debate over whether it is appropriate for judges to shape public policy in a democracy.

I n February 2016, Supreme Court Justice Antonin Scalia unexpectedly died in his sleep while on a hunting trip in Texas. During his nearly 30 years on the Supreme Court, Justice Scalia became a favorite of political conservatives for his outspoken opposition to policies favored by liberals, such as affirmative action, environmental protection laws, and same-sex marriage. He had provided a key vote in narrow five-member majority decisions on the nine-justice Court. He was also the author of the narrow decision in *District of Columbia* v. *Heller* (2008) declaring that the Second Amendment grants individuals a right to keep handguns in their homes for self-protection.

Because the Republican majority in the U.S. Senate feared that President Barack Obama would nominate a liberal judge to replace Scalia and thereby tip the balance on the Supreme Court in a liberal direction, many senators immediately announced that they would not consider any nominees put forward by the president. They claimed to be following the principle that presidents should not be permitted to appoint new justices during their final year in office. Ideally, they hoped that a Republican candidate would win the presidential election and, after taking office in January 2017, nominate a conservative judge to replace Scalia.

There is nothing in the Constitution about this so-called principle of denying judicial nomination opportunities to a sitting president, so the partisan politics underlying the Republicans' resistance was very clear. Indeed, Democratic senators countered by arguing that when the American people reelected President Obama in November 2012, they were clearly stating who they wanted to choose new federal judges until a new president took office in January 2017. The Republican senators' position, if they adhered to it, guaranteed that there would be only eight justices on the Supreme Court for an entire year after Scalia's death, if not longer. As a result, there was a strong likelihood of 4-to-4 voting ties on important, controversial issues as the Court was evenly-divided between Republican and Democratic appointees in Scalia's absence.

President Obama stated that he had a constitutional duty to nominate someone to fill the vacancy on the Supreme Court. He insisted that the Senate had a constitutional duty to hold hearings and give fair consideration to the nominee prior to voting on whether or not to confirm the individual. Thus, he moved forward with evaluating and interviewing potential Supreme Court nominees. In March 2016, he nominated Judge Merrick Garland, a highly-respected federal court of appeals judge to replace Scalia. Indeed, over the years, a number of Republican senators had praised Garland for being a thoughtful, fair, and moderate judge. Prior to his many years of experience as a federal judge, he had been the lead federal prosecutor in the criminal case that followed the bombing of the Oklahoma City federal building in 1995; an attack that killed 168 people, including many children in a daycare center. In effect, President Obama chose a nominee who should have been acceptable to both Republicans and Democrats in any typical year. However, the fact that Garland, who was less conservative than Scalia, could tip the Court in a more liberal direction meant that Republican leaders in the Senate continued to claim that they would not schedule hearings and would not consider him at all. Yet, the Republican senators also faced the uncertainty about who would be nominated to the Court if the new president in 2017 was the Democratic candidate—someone who might nominate a judge even more liberal than Garland. Eventually, Donald Trump's victory in the November 2016 presidential election rewarded Republican senators for their strategy of opposition and delay. The incoming Republican president had vowed to appoint conservative justices to the Supreme Court, thereby clearing the way for Senate approval of the Republicans' preferred replacement for Scalia.

The political battle over Judge Garland's nomination demonstrated very clearly to the American public that politicians see courts as policy-making institutions that each political party seeks to influence and control. Even though American judges seek to portray courts as neutral institutions that merely interpret and apply the law, judges are drawn from the world of politics and they bring to their decisions values and policy preferences developed through their life experiences and political beliefs. Because federal judges are appointed and can serve in office for life—unlike members of Congress and the President who are selected by voters—a key issue for the American governing system and democracy is the extent to which unelected officials should have influence over important public policies.

HOW MUCH POWER SHOULD JUDGES HAVE?

On June 26, 2015, in the final days of the Supreme Court's term before its summer recess, a courtroom filled with news reporters, lawyers, and spectators heard Justice Scalia announce the Court's decision in a criminal law case, *Johnson* v. *United States*. By an 8-1 vote, the Court invalidated a portion of a statute enacted by Congress. The case concerned a member of a white supremacist group that advocates racial violence. He told an undercover law enforcement officer about weapons and explosives that he manufactured and kept at his home. Because of his prior criminal record, it was a crime for him to possess these weapons. Under the Armed Career Criminal Act (ACCA), he faced a 15-year minimum sentence if he had three prior convictions that were designated as "violent felonies" under federal law. His attorney challenged the government's claim that his prior conviction for unlawful possession of a short-barreled shotgun should be considered a "violent felony." Under the ACCA's words, prior "violent felonies" include "any crime… that…otherwise involves conduct that presents a serious potential risk of physical injury to another." The Supreme Court struck down this language as being too vague to meet constitutional standards and therefore a violation of Johnson's right to due process if the government applied the language to his conviction concerning unlawful possession of the short-barreled shotgun.

On the surface, this decision appears to be a technical matter about legal language and whether it can be applied to specific circumstances. Moreover, the Supreme Court's decisions would ultimately affect the lives of only a relatively small number of Americans who faced charges under that section of the ACCA. Viewed from a broader perspective, however, the Supreme Court's action demonstrated the tremendous power of courts in our governing system. Eight unelected justices on the Supreme Court invalidated a decision made by the American people's 535 elected representatives in Congress. Is it contrary to the principles of democracy to permit appointed judges, who cannot be removed by the voters, to overrule the people's elected representatives? This is an issue of continuous debate. People disagree about whether and when it is proper for unelected judges to invalidate decisions by elected officials.

We are accustomed to viewing courts as third-party dispute resolvers when individuals, interest groups, or businesses have disputes with each other or with government officials. It is important to recognize, however, that lawsuits are also filed in courts by politically motivated actors who desire to use court processes to shape public policy. In recent years, we have seen opponents of various issues, such as President Obama's Affordable Care Act, same-sex marriage, and affirmative action practices in university admissions, file lawsuits to seek rulings by judges that would undo decisions by legislators and other government officials. Indeed, the discussion of bureaucracy in Chapter 8, included the example of states and energy companies using the courts in 2016 in an effort to stop new environmental regulations that would require a reduction in power plants' carbon emissions into the air. Supreme Court decisions about controversial issues may contribute to the public's divided views about whether the Court is doing its job appropriately and well.

⟩ POLL Do you think the Supreme Court is doing a good job?

Court Structure and Processes

9.1 Explain how American court systems are organized.

adversarial system

Legal system used by the United States and other countries in which a judge plays a relatively passive role as attorneys battle to protect each side's interests. In the cases concerning affirmative action in university admissions, for example, the Supreme Court listened to vigorous arguments presented by the government's attorneys as well as opposing arguments from interest group lawyers representing individual applicants opposed to affirmative action.

inquisitorial system

Legal system in most of Europe in which a judge takes an active role in questioning witnesses and seeking to discover the truth.

dual court system

Separate systems of state and federal courts throughout the United States. Each state court system is responsible for interpreting the laws and constitution of that specific state, while the federal courts are responsible for the U.S. Constitution and laws enacted by Congress. For example, the Ohio Supreme Court is the ultimate legal authority over the interpretation of its state's constitution and the statutes enacted by the Ohio legislature.

American courts use an **adversarial system**, in which opposing attorneys represent the interests of their clients. By contrast, many other countries use an **inquisitorial system**, in which judges take an active role in investigating cases and questioning witnesses. The U.S. judicial branch is made up of courts that process disputes, determine whether accused individuals have committed crimes, define individuals' rights, and shape public policy. There are two types of courts—trial and appellate—and both types operate in two parallel court systems—state and federal. Dramatic depictions on television and in movies typically show only one type of proceeding (trials) in one type of court (trial courts). They do not adequately convey the idea that most cases in trial courts are settled through plea bargains or negotiated settlements, rather than through trials. Television portrayals also won't educate you about the U.S. Supreme Court and other appellate courts that consider whether errors occurred when a judge or jury decided a case in a trial court.

Trial Courts

The United States has a **dual court system**. In other words, two court systems, state and federal, exist and operate at the same time in the same geographic areas (see Table 9.1). Sometimes a state court and a federal court are right next door to each other in a downtown district. In small cities and towns, a courthouse may be run by a single judge. In larger cities, a dozen or more judges may hear cases separately in their own courtrooms within a single courthouse. Both court systems handle criminal prosecutions, which involve accusations that one or more individuals broke the law and therefore should be punished. In addition, both systems handle civil lawsuits, in which people or corporations seek compensation from those whom they accuse of violating contracts or causing personal injuries or property damage. Civil lawsuits can also seek orders from judges requiring the government, corporations, or individuals to take specific actions or refrain from behavior that violates the law.

TABLE 9.1 Structure of the American Court System

Federal Court System		State Court System
U.S. Supreme Court		**52 State Supreme Courts***
Original jurisdiction in only limited categories of cases that rarely arise: lawsuits between two states and cases involving foreign ambassadors. Appellate jurisdiction in almost all cases that it decides that arrive from U.S. courts of appeals or state supreme courts.	*Courts of Last Resort*	Appellate jurisdiction for cases concerning state law brought up through their state court systems. There are more than 50 state supreme courts because two states—Texas and Oklahoma—have separate highest courts for civil and criminal cases.
13 U.S. Courts of Appeals		**40 State Courts of Appeals***
No original jurisdiction because no cases are first filed in these courts. These courts handle appeals from cases that were first decided in the U.S. district courts or matters decided by government regulatory commissions.	*Intermediate Appellate Courts*	Appellate jurisdiction over cases from state trial courts. No original jurisdiction. Ten states do not have intermediate appellate courts. Appeals in those states go straight from the trial court to the state supreme court.
94 U.S. District Courts		**State Trial Courts (50 states)**
Original jurisdiction in cases involving federal criminal and civil law; the federal government; lawsuits between citizens of different states for amounts over $75,000; bankruptcy; and admiralty (shipping at sea).	*Trial Courts of General Jurisdiction*	Usually called superior courts, district courts, circuit courts, or courts of common pleas. These courts have original jurisdiction and therefore are the first courts to hear cases concerning state law issues for felonies and other serious matters.
(no limited jurisdiction trial court with life-tenured federal judges)		**Lower-level State Trial Courts**
Federal cases begin in the U.S. district courts.	*Trial Courts of Limited Jurisdiction*	Original jurisdiction for minor criminal and civil cases.

*States use different names for their courts of last resort (e.g., Court of Appeals in New York and Maryland, Supreme Judicial Court in Maine and Massachusetts).

The existence of two court systems within each state reflects American federalism, under which state governments and the federal government both exercise authority over law and public policy. States are free to design their own court systems and to name the different courts within the state. Thus, in some states, trial courts are called "superior courts," while in others, they are known as "district courts," "circuit courts," or "courts of common pleas."

Federal trial courts are called "U.S. district courts." The country is divided into 94 districts. Each state has at least one district and one district court, and larger states have multiple districts. Within each district, there may be multiple judges and courthouses. For example, Wisconsin is divided into the Eastern District of Wisconsin, with courthouses at Milwaukee and Green Bay, and the Western District of Wisconsin, with its courthouse located in Madison. These courts handle cases concerning federal law, such as those based on the U.S. Constitution and statutes (laws) enacted by Congress, as well as certain lawsuits between citizens of different states.

Trial courts use specific rules and processes to reach decisions. Lawyers present arguments to a group of citizen jurors in a jury trial. In such a trial, the judge acts as a "referee," who makes sure proper rules are followed and the jurors understand the rules of law that will guide their decisions in determining the facts and issuing a verdict in favor of one side. When requested by defendants, cases use bench trials, in which a single judge rather than a jury is the decision maker. Trial courts are courts of original jurisdiction, meaning they receive cases first, consider the available evidence, and make the initial decision.

Although the trial is the final possible stage for these lower-level courts, most cases do not get that far. Trial courts actually process most cases through negotiated resolutions, called settlements in civil cases and plea bargains in criminal cases. Settlements and plea bargains can save time and money for lawyers and courts. They may also benefit the individuals involved by providing a mutually agreed upon outcome and, in criminal cases, a less-than-maximum sentence.

Appellate Courts

Appellate courts have appellate jurisdiction, meaning they review specific errors that allegedly occurred in trial court processes or in decisions of appellate courts beneath them in the judicial hierarchy. Most states, as well as the federal court

In 2014, singer Justin Bieber entered a guilty plea to careless driving and resisting arrest charges in Florida. He was required to attend classes on safe driving and anger management. He also donated $50,000 to a youth program. He originally faced more serious drunk driving charges. Bieber's guilty plea avoided the time, expense, and uncertainty of a trial. Yet, his case also demonstrated how vigorous representation by attorneys during plea negotiations can help defendants avoid the most serious possible punishments.

■ *How can we be sure that all defendants, both rich and poor, receive equal treatment, especially because most people cannot make large financial contributions to charities as part of their plea agreements?*

FIGURE 9.1 Geographic Jurisdiction of Federal Courts

The U.S. courts of appeals are divided into regional circuits throughout the country. Each numbered circuit handles appeals from federal cases in a specific set of states.

■ *In which circuit do you live?*

SOURCE: "Map of Federal Court Circuits," Web site of the Administrative Office of the U.S. Courts, accessed April 11, 2010, http://www.uscourts.gov/FederalCourts.aspx.

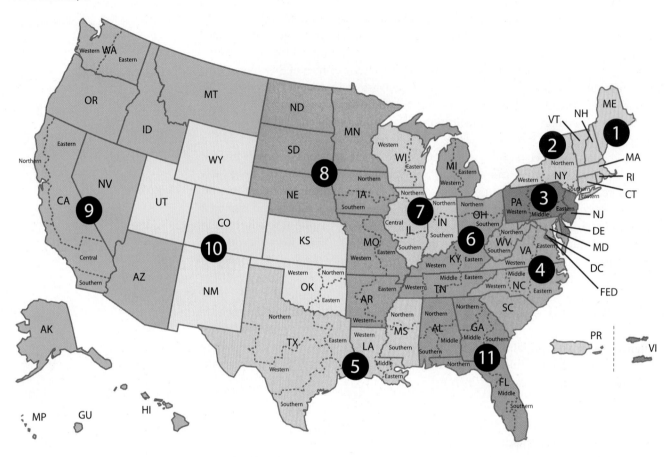

intermediate appellate courts

Courts that examine allegations concerning uncorrected errors that occurred during trials; usually called courts of appeals in state and federal court systems.

courts of last resort

The highest courts in each American court system, typically called supreme courts, that hear selected appeals from the lower courts.

system, have **intermediate appellate courts**. These courts, which are typically called "courts of appeals," hear appeals from judicial decisions and jury verdicts in the trial courts. In the federal system, the U.S. courts of appeals are divided into 11 numbered circuits, and there is also the District of Columbia circuit and a specialized federal circuit for patent and trade cases. The numbered circuits each handle the appeals from districts in specific states (see Figure 9.1). For example, the U.S. Court of Appeals for the Fifth Circuit handles appeals from U.S. district courts in Texas, Louisiana, and Mississippi.[1]

The highest appellate courts in the state and federal systems are **courts of last resort**. In the federal system, the U.S. Supreme Court is the court of last resort. It can also be the court of last resort when issues of federal law, such as questions about civil liberties under the Bill of Rights, arise in cases decided by state supreme courts. State supreme courts are courts of last resort for disputes about the meaning of laws created by a state legislature or about provisions of a state constitution.

There are no juries in appellate courts, and typically three judges hear cases in a state or federal intermediate appellate court. State supreme courts generally have five or seven members, while the U.S. Supreme Court has nine justices. These courts do not make decisions about criminal guilt or issue verdicts in civil cases. Instead, they consider narrow issues concerning alleged errors in the investigation and trial process that were not corrected by the trial judge. Instead of listening to witnesses or examining other evidence, appellate courts consider elaborate written arguments, called **appellate briefs**, submitted by each side's attorneys, as well as oral arguments.

Appellate judges issue detailed written opinions to explain their decisions. The outcome of the case and any announcements of a legal rule are expressed in the **majority opinion**. This opinion represents the views of the majority of judges who heard the case. **Concurring opinions** are written by judges who agree with the outcome favored by the majority but wish to present their own reasons for agreeing with the decision. Appellate decisions are not always unanimous, so judges who disagree with the outcome may write **dissenting opinions** to express their points of disagreement with the views expressed in the majority opinion.[2] Sometimes concurring and dissenting opinions develop ideas that will take hold in later generations and help shape law after new judges are selected for service on appellate courts.

The U.S. Supreme Court

At the top of the American judicial system stands the U.S. Supreme Court. The Court is an unusual appellate court in that it also has original jurisdiction in limited categories of cases defined in Article III of the U.S. Constitution, usually lawsuits between the governments of two states. The U.S. Supreme Court has authority over federal court cases and any decision by a state court (including those of a state supreme court) that concerns the U.S. Constitution or federal law. In particular, the U.S. Supreme Court is regularly called on to decide whether state statutes violate the U.S. Constitution or whether decisions and actions by state and local officials collide with federal constitutional principles. The U.S. Supreme Court's decisions shape law and public policy for the entire country. Policy advocates often seek favorable decisions from the Court when they have been unsuccessful in persuading other branches of government to advance their goals. Table 9.2 gives the names and backgrounds of the current justices of the Court.

Each case goes through several specific stages in the Supreme Court's decision-making process:

- The justices choose 70 to 80 cases to hear from among more than 7,000 petitions submitted annually by people and corporations.

appellate briefs
Written arguments submitted by lawyers in appellate cases.

majority opinion
Appellate court opinion that explains the reasons for the case outcome as determined by a majority of judges.

concurring opinion
Appellate court opinion by a judge who endorses the outcome decided by the majority of judges, but who wants to express different reasons to justify that outcome.

dissenting opinion
Appellate court opinion explaining the views of one or more judges who disagree with the outcome of the case as decided by the majority of judges.

TABLE 9.2 Supreme Court Justices

The rate of support for civil rights and liberties claims is typically used to classify justices as "liberal" (frequent support) or "conservative" (infrequent support).

Name	Sonia Sotomayor	Ruth Bader Ginsburg	Elena Kagan	Stephen G. Breyer	Anthony M. Kennedy	John G. Roberts, Jr.	Samuel A. Alito, Jr.	Clarence Thomas
Support for Civil Rights and Liberties Claims, 2014–2015	73%	69%	69%	69%	54%	42%	27%	19%
Nominated by	Barack Obama	Bill Clinton	Barack Obama	Bill Clinton	Ronald Reagan	George W. Bush	George W. Bush	George H. W. Bush
Date Confirmed	August 6, 2009	August 10, 1993	August 5, 2010	August 3, 1994	February 18, 1988	September 29, 2005	January 31, 2005	October 23, 1991
Confirmation Vote Numbers	68-31	96-3	63-37	87-9	97-0	78-22	58-42	52-48
Previous Experience	Federal Judge, Prosecutor	Federal Judge, Law Professor	Solicitor General of the U.S., Law Professor	Federal Judge, Law Professor	Federal Judge, Law Professor	Federal Judge, Government Lawyer	Federal Judge, Government Lawyer	Federal Judge, Government Administrator

writ of certiorari

A legal action that asks a higher court to call up a case from a lower court; the legal action used to ask the U.S. Supreme Court to accept a case for hearing.

- Nearly all cases are presented to the Court through a petition for a **writ of certiorari**, a traditional legal order that commands a lower court to send a case forward. Cases are selected for hearing through the Court's "rule of four," meaning that four justices must vote to hear a specific case in order for it to be scheduled for oral arguments.

- Attorneys in the chosen cases submit detailed written arguments, called *appellate briefs*, for the justices to study before the case is argued.

- At oral arguments, each side's attorney may speak for only 30 minutes, and the justices often interrupt and ask many questions. The justices also sometimes exchange argumentative comments with each other.

- After oral arguments, the nine justices meet privately in their weekly conference to present their views to each other. When all the justices have stated a position, the chief justice announces the preliminary vote based on the viewpoints expressed. The side that gains the support of five or more justices wins.

- The justices prepare and announce the majority opinion that decides the case as well as additional viewpoints expressed in concurring and dissenting opinions. If the chief justice is in the majority, he designates which justice will write the majority opinion for the Court. If the chief justice is in the minority, then the senior justice in the majority assigns the opinion for the Court. Other justices can decide for themselves whether to write a concurring or dissenting opinion. With the assistance of their law clerks, justices draft preliminary opinions as well as comments on other justices' draft opinions. These draft opinions and comments are circulated to all the justices. They help shape the ultimate reasoning of the final opinions issued in the case and can sometimes persuade wavering justices to change sides.

- When the decision of the Court is publicly announced and the opinions for that case are published, the decision becomes final. The legal rule announced in the decision, however, is not necessarily permanent, because the justices can later change their views. If at least five justices agree that the prior decision was wrongly decided, they can use a new case to overrule the Court's earlier opinion and establish a new rule of law on the subject in question. Presidents often focus on this goal when they select new appointees for the Supreme Court, with the hope that the new justices will vote to overrule decisions with which the president disagrees.

Supreme Court Justice Sonia Sotomayor is sworn in by Chief Justice John Roberts in 2009. Justice Sotomayor's parents were born in Puerto Rico, and she is considered the first Hispanic justice to serve on the nation's highest court.

■ *Is it important that the Supreme Court's composition represents the nation's diversity with respect to race, gender, ethnicity, religion, and other demographic factors? Why or why not?*

The Power of American Judges

9.2 Identify the reasons why American judges are powerful actors in the governing system.

The eighteenth-century authors of the U.S. Constitution did not expect the judicial branch to be as powerful as the executive and legislative branches. Although some of the framers wanted to permit judges to evaluate the constitutionality of statutes, they did not generally believe that the courts would be influential policymaking institutions. In *The Federalist*, No. 78, Alexander Hamilton called the judiciary the "least dangerous" branch of government because it lacked the power of "purse or sword" that the other branches could use to shape policy and spur people to follow their decisions. Congress could use its "power of the purse" to levy taxes or provide government funds in order to encourage or induce people to comply with government policies. The president, as the nation's commander in chief, could use the "sword" of military action to force people to obey laws. But judges produced only words written on paper and thus appeared to lack the power to enforce their decisions.

Hamilton was not wrong to highlight the inherent weakness of the judiciary's structure and authority. He merely failed to foresee how the Supreme Court and other courts would assert their power and gain acceptance as policymaking institutions.

Despite lacking the constitutional power of the "purse" or "sword," the physical imagery of courts, as well as the dress and language associated with judges, helps convey the message that the judicial branch is powerful and different from other branches of government. Many courts operate in majestic buildings with marble columns, purple velvet curtains, fancy woodwork, and other physical embellishments designed to elicit respect for the importance and seriousness of these institutions. Judges wear black robes and sit on benches elevated above other seats in the courtroom, reinforcing their status and conveying a message that other citizens are subordinate to judicial officers. These elements encourage public acceptance of the courts' legitimate power and help to gain citizens' compliance with judicial decisions.

Perhaps even more important than the physical buildings or the judges' dress and language, however, are the structural elements and traditions in the American judicial system that make judges in the United States powerful actors in the country's governing system. These factors include judges' authority over constitutional and statutory interpretation, the power of judicial review, and in the federal court system, judges' protected tenure in office.

Constitutional and Statutory Interpretation

In the United States, although participants in constitutional conventions write constitutions and elected legislators draft laws referred to as **statutes**, these forms of law still require judges to interpret them. Inevitably, the wording of constitutions and statutes contains ambiguities. Whenever there are disputes about the meaning of the words and phrases in constitutions and statutes, those disputes come to courts in the form of lawsuits, and judges are asked to provide interpretations that will settle those disputes. Therefore, judges can provide meaning for law produced by other governmental institutions, as well as for law they develop themselves in judicial decisions. Legal rules created by judges' decisions are typically referred to as case law.

For example, the Eighth Amendment to the U.S. Constitution forbids the government to impose "cruel and unusual punishments." The provision intends to limit the nature of punishments applied to people who violate criminal laws. The words themselves, however, provide no specific guidance about what kinds of punishments are not allowed. Thus judges have been asked to decide which punishments are "cruel and unusual." Are these words violated when prison officials decline to provide

statutes

Laws written by state legislatures and by Congress. For example, the Armed Career Criminal Act was a statute written and enacted by Congress.

medical care to prisoners? How about when a principal paddles a misbehaving student at a public high school? These are the kinds of cases that judges confront.

Statutes provide similar opportunities for judges to shape the law. Statutes for the entire country are produced by Congress. Each state has its own legislature to write laws that apply only within its borders. Judges, when they interpret statutes, are supposed to advance the underlying purposes of the legislature that made the statutes—but those purposes are not always clear. For example, if workers' compensation statutes provide for payments to workers injured "in the course of employment," does that include coverage for a disability resulting from slipping on an icy sidewalk by the employer's business? Inevitably, judges must answer such questions, because legislatures cannot anticipate every possible situation in which issues about a statute's meaning might arise.

As you will see in the later discussion of methods for selecting judges, political battles in the nomination processes for federal judges largely arise from the interpretive authority that American judges possess. Political parties, interest groups, and politicians seek to secure judgeships for people who share their values and who, they hope, will apply those values in judicial decision-making.

Judicial Review

judicial review

The power of American judges to nullify decisions and actions by other branches of government, if the judges decide those actions violate the U.S. Constitution or the relevant state constitution. For example, the Supreme Court invalidated a portion of the Armed Career Criminal Act in 2015 as too vague and thereby violating the due process rights of defendants facing enhanced sentences for prior "violent felonies."

One of the most significant powers of American judges is that of **judicial review**—a process that permits judges to invalidate actions by other governmental actors. Judges can strike down statutes enacted by Congress or invalidate actions by the president (or other executive branch officials) by declaring that those statutes or actions violate the Constitution. As indicated in the examples in Table 9.3, federal judges often use their interpretations of the amendments in the Bill of Rights as the basis for judicial review. A leading constitutional law expert describes judicial review as "certainly the most controversial and at the same time the most fascinating role of the courts of the United States."[3]

Article III of the Constitution defines the authority of the judiciary, yet there is no mention of the judiciary's power of judicial review. The framers of the Constitution were aware of the concept, yet they made no mention of it in the founding document. Did this mean that the idea had been considered and rejected

TABLE 9.3 Judicial Review

Case Name	Date	Vote	Affected Institution	Overview of Case
Arizona Free Enterprise Club's Freedom Club PAC v. *Bennett*	June 27, 2011	5-4	State legislature in Arizona	The U.S. Supreme Court struck down a state law that provided public funds for political candidates to match money privately raised by their opponents. The Court said the law violated the free speech rights of individuals and groups raising and spending private funds in elections.
McDonald v. *City of Chicago*	June 28, 2010	5-4	City Council of Chicago	An ordinance enacted by local officials in Chicago barred the ownership and possession of handguns by anyone other than police officers. The U.S. Supreme Court said its prior decision, striking down such an ordinance in the federal jurisdiction of Washington, D.C., as a violation of the Second Amendment, also applied to laws enacted by states and cities.
National Labor Relations Board v. *Noel Canning*	June 26, 2014	9-0	President	The president cannot make recess appointments to federal posts without Senate confirmation when the Senate is out of session for fewer than 10 days.
Citizens United v. *Federal Election Commission*	January 21, 2010	5-4	Congress	The U.S. Supreme Court invalidated a portion of the Bipartisan Campaign Reform Act of 2002 that sought to prevent corporations from spending funds to support or oppose political candidates. The majority concluded that the statute violated the First Amendment free speech rights of corporations.

by the framers? Apparently not—in *The Federalist*, No. 78, one of the essays written to advocate for the ratification of the Constitution, Hamilton argued in favor of judicial review, asserting not only that legislative acts violating the Constitution must be invalid but also that federal judges must be the ones who decide whether statutes are unconstitutional. According to Hamilton, limitations on congressional actions "can be preserved in practice no other way than through the medium of the courts of justice, whose duty it must be to declare all acts contrary to the manifest tenor of the constitution void." Other Founders, however, worried that judicial review would elevate the power of the judiciary above that of the other governmental branches.

At the beginning of the nineteenth century, the Supreme Court first asserted its authority to review the actions of other governmental branches in the case of *Marbury* v. *Madison* (1803). William Marbury was one of many officials in the administration of Federalist President John Adams who received a last-minute judicial appointment as Adams was leaving office. The appointment of these "midnight judges" was an effort by Adams to place his supporters in positions of judicial influence to counteract the changes in government that would inevitably occur under the administration of the incoming president, Thomas Jefferson. However, in the rush of final activities, the outgoing secretary of state in the Adams administration, John Marshall, never managed to seal and deliver to Marbury his commission as a justice of the peace for the District of Columbia. When Jefferson took office, the incoming secretary of state, James Madison, refused to deliver these commissions to Marbury and several other judicial appointees. Marbury sought his commission by filing a legal action. He followed the requirements of the **Judiciary Act of 1789**, the initial act of Congress that designed the federal court system and established its procedures, by seeking a writ of mandamus from the U.S. Supreme Court. A writ of mandamus is a traditional legal order through which a court directs a government official to take a specific action required by law.

Marbury's legal action presented the Supreme Court with a difficult dilemma. The Court's new chief justice was John Marshall, also a last-minute Adams appointee—and the very man who had failed to seal and deliver Marbury's commission on time in the first place. If Marshall and the other justices decided that Marbury was entitled to his commission, it seemed very likely that President Jefferson and Secretary Madison would simply disobey the Court. If that were to happen, the Court would have had no practical means to force the president to act, undoubtedly tarnishing its legitimacy. Ultimately, the Supreme Court issued a decision that asserted the power of the judiciary without risking any appearance of weakness.

In a unanimous decision written by Chief Justice Marshall, the Court declared that Marbury was indeed entitled to his commission and that the Court possessed the authority to order President Jefferson to have the commission delivered to him. However, the Court declined to issue such an order to the president because—so it declared—the portion of the Judiciary Act of 1789 that directed litigants to file writs of mandamus directly in the Supreme Court was unconstitutional. Therefore, it ruled, Marbury had relied on an unconstitutional statute in seeking a writ of mandamus from the Supreme Court without first proceeding through the lower courts. According to the Court, statutes, such as the Judiciary Act, cannot define the kinds of cases that may be filed directly in the U.S. Supreme Court without being heard first in the lower courts. Article III of the Constitution specifically lists the kinds of cases in which the Supreme Court has original jurisdiction. Other cases must first be filed in lower courts and reach the Supreme Court through the appeals process. Any effort by Congress to expand that list amounts to an improper effort to alter the Constitution by statute rather than by constitutional amendment.

Marbury v. *Madison* (1803)
A case in which the U.S. Supreme Court asserted the power of judicial review, despite the fact that the concept is not explicitly mentioned in the U.S. Constitution. The case represented the first instance in which the Supreme Court declared a statute enacted by Congress, a portion of the Judiciary Act of 1789, to be invalid for violating the Constitution.

Judiciary Act of 1789
Early statute in which Congress provided the initial design of the federal court system.

Chief Justice John Marshall's opinion in *Marbury* v. *Madison* helped to establish the concept of judicial review, an important power for American judges. This power was not specifically granted by the U.S. Constitution.

■ *Do you think judicial review is implied by the Constitution, or did Marshall act improperly in announcing this important judicial power in a Court opinion?*

In general, the Supreme Court has appellate jurisdiction over cases decided in lower courts that are later brought to the highest court through appeals and other posttrial processes. The Constitution specifies that the Supreme Court will make the first or original decision only in cases concerning states and those involving high officials, such as ambassadors. Marbury's action seeking a writ of mandamus did not fit within these narrow categories of cases specified by the Constitution. Ultimately, Marbury did not pursue his case again in the lower courts, and he never received his commission.

The decision in *Marbury* v. *Madison*—one of the most important Supreme Court decisions in American history—asserted the authority and importance of the Supreme Court without actually testing the Court's power in a confrontation with the president. The Court simply asserted the power of judicial review in striking down a portion of the Judiciary Act without providing any elaborate discussion in its opinion that would raise questions about whether such a power even existed under the Constitution.

The Court did not immediately begin to pass judgment on the appropriateness of executive and legislative actions. Instead, it waited more than 50 years before again asserting its power of judicial review. In 1857, in its highly controversial decision in *Dred Scott* v. *Sandford*, the Court invalidated the Missouri Compromise—a series of decisions by Congress in 1820 and 1821 that had put limits on the spread of slavery into western territories. By 1900, the Court came to use the power of judicial review more frequently, and eventually federal courts struck down hundreds of state statutes and more than 100 acts of Congress. Today judicial review is well entrenched in American governing processes and provides a primary source of judicial power.

Federal Judges' Protected Tenure

Article III of the Constitution specifies that federal judges will serve "during good Behaviour." Effectively, that means life-time tenure, since these judges typically are removed through **impeachment** by Congress only if they commit a crime. The tenure granted to federal judges underscores the emphasis that the Constitution places on ensuring the independence of judicial decision makers. If judges are not afraid of losing their jobs by making unpopular decisions, then presumably they will do the right thing (see Figure 9.2). This protection may be especially important when judges make decisions that protect the rights of minorities. For example, many controversial judicial decisions in the mid-twentieth century advancing the equality of African Americans were vigorously criticized because of widespread racial prejudice. At other times, unpopular court decisions have protected the interests of corporations and the wealthy. For example, in 2010, the U.S. Supreme Court outraged critics by ruling that corporations possess rights to freedom of speech that prevent Congress from enacting certain laws that seek to limit how much money corporations can spend in their efforts to influence political campaigns and election outcomes (*Citizens United* v. *Federal Election Commission*, 2010).

Because federal judges are exempted from democracy's traditional accountability mechanism—the need to face periodic elections, which often keeps other public officials from making unpopular decisions—judges are better positioned to make decisions that go against society's dominant values and policy preferences (see again Figure 9.2). This lack of accountability also creates the possibility that judges' decisions will go "too far" in shaping law and policy in ways that are unpopular or detrimental to society, resulting in a backlash against the courts.

A famous example of backlash against the Supreme Court arose in the late 1930s. In 1937, President Franklin D. Roosevelt was frustrated that the life-tenured justices on the Supreme Court were using their power of judicial review to invalidate New Deal legislation that he believed to be necessary to fight the Great Depression. As a result, he proposed restructuring the Supreme Court to permit the president to appoint

impeachment

Process in Congress for removal of the president, federal judges, and other high officials. In 2010, for example, Congress impeached and removed from office Louisiana Federal Judge Thomas Porteous based on corruption and perjury charges.

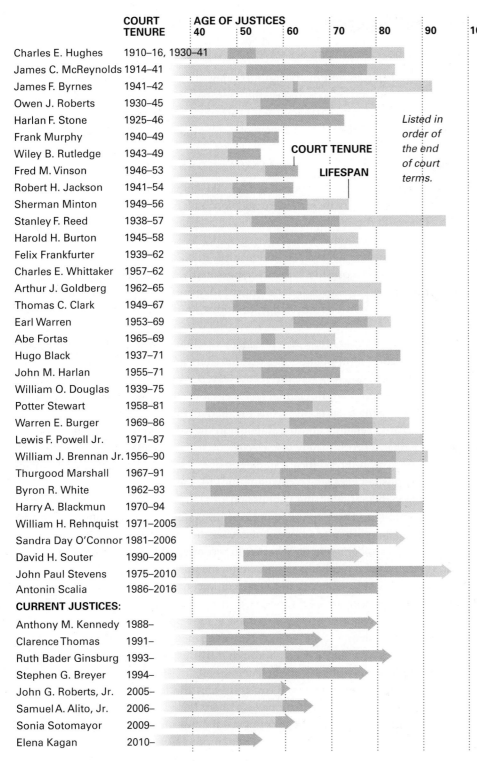

	COURT TENURE	AGE OF JUSTICES

Chart showing justices listed in order of the end of court terms, with bars indicating Court Tenure and Lifespan along an age axis from 40 to 100.

Justice	Court Tenure
Charles E. Hughes	1910–16, 1930–41
James C. McReynolds	1914–41
James F. Byrnes	1941–42
Owen J. Roberts	1930–45
Harlan F. Stone	1925–46
Frank Murphy	1940–49
Wiley B. Rutledge	1943–49
Fred M. Vinson	1946–53
Robert H. Jackson	1941–54
Sherman Minton	1949–56
Stanley F. Reed	1938–57
Harold H. Burton	1945–58
Felix Frankfurter	1939–62
Charles E. Whittaker	1957–62
Arthur J. Goldberg	1962–65
Thomas C. Clark	1949–67
Earl Warren	1953–69
Abe Fortas	1965–69
Hugo Black	1937–71
John M. Harlan	1955–71
William O. Douglas	1939–75
Potter Stewart	1958–81
Warren E. Burger	1969–86
Lewis F. Powell Jr.	1971–87
William J. Brennan Jr.	1956–90
Thurgood Marshall	1967–91
Byron R. White	1962–93
Harry A. Blackmun	1970–94
William H. Rehnquist	1971–2005
Sandra Day O'Connor	1981–2006
David H. Souter	1990–2009
John Paul Stevens	1975–2010
Antonin Scalia	1986–2016

CURRENT JUSTICES:

Justice	Court Tenure
Anthony M. Kennedy	1988–
Clarence Thomas	1991–
Ruth Bader Ginsburg	1993–
Stephen G. Breyer	1994–
John G. Roberts, Jr.	2005–
Samuel A. Alito, Jr.	2006–
Sonia Sotomayor	2009–
Elena Kagan	2010–

Listed in order of the end of court terms.

FIGURE 9.2 U.S. Supreme Court Justices' Length of Service and Age (Justices Leaving the Court Since 1930 and Current Justices as of 2016)

Some justices have served on the Court for several decades and continued to decide cases beyond the age when most people experienced diminished physical capacity and retire from their jobs.

■ *Should we consider limiting the years of service or age of Supreme Court justices? What would be a reason to avoid placing any limitations on Supreme Court justices?*

SOURCE: Web site of the Supreme Court of the United States, 2016, http://www .supremecourt.gov; Carolyn Goldinger, ed., *The Supreme Court at Work*, Washington, D.C.: Congressional Quarterly, 1990.

an additional justice for each serving justice who reached the age of 70. His **"court-packing plan,"** as the press and congressional opponents immediately branded it, would have enabled him to select six new justices immediately and thereby alter the Court's dynamics. Political and public opposition blocked Roosevelt's plan, but his actions demonstrated that decisions by life-tenured judges can stir controversy, especially when those decisions clash with policies preferred by the public and their elected representatives in government. The negative reaction against Roosevelt's attempt to pack the Court also demonstrated how much the American public had come to value the judiciary's independence.

court-packing plan

President Franklin D. Roosevelt's unsuccessful proposal in 1937 to permit the appointment of additional justices to the U.S. Supreme Court. Roosevelt sought to reduce the Court's opposition to his New Deal policies through a plan that would permit the president to appoint a new justice whenever a sitting justice reached 70 years of age.

Judicial Selection

9.3 Outline the selection process for federal judges.

Political parties and interest groups view the judicial selection process as an important means to influence the court pathway. By securing judgeships for individuals who share their political values, these groups can enhance their prospects for success when they subsequently use litigation to shape public policy.

Judicial Selection in the Federal System

The Constitution specifies that federal judges, like ambassadors and cabinet secretaries, must be appointed by the president and confirmed by a majority vote of the U.S. Senate. Thus, both the White House and one chamber of Congress are intimately involved in judicial selection.

Because there are nearly 850 judgeships in the federal district courts and courts of appeals, the president is never personally knowledgeable about all the pending vacancies. For lower federal court judgeships, the president relies heavily on advice from White House aides, senators, and other officials from his own political party.

Traditionally, senators from the president's political party have effectively controlled the selection of appointees for district court judgeships in their own states. Through a practice known as **senatorial courtesy**, senators from the president's party have virtual veto power over potential nominees for their home state's district courts. They are also consulted on nominations for the federal court of appeals that covers their state. Because senators are so influential in the selection of federal district court judges, the judges who ultimately get selected are usually acquainted personally with the senators, active in the political campaigns of the senators and other party members, or accomplished in raising campaign funds for the party.

The process begins with the submission of an appointee's name to the Senate Judiciary Committee. The committee holds hearings on each nomination, including testimony from supporters and opponents. After the Judiciary Committee completes its hearings, its members vote on whether to recommend the nomination to the full Senate. Typically, upon receiving a nomination, the full Senate votes quickly based on the Judiciary Committee's report and vote. But in controversial cases or when asked to confirm appointments to the Supreme Court, the Senate may spend time debating the nomination. A majority of senators must vote for a candidate in order for that person to be sworn in as a federal judge. However, members of the minority political party in the Senate may block a vote through a **filibuster**, keeping discussion going indefinitely unless three-fifths of the Senate's members—60 senators—vote to end it.

Presidents seek to please favored constituencies and to advance their policy preferences in choosing appointees they believe share their values. Interest groups find avenues through which they seek to influence the president's choices as well as the confirmation votes of senators. Judicial selection processes are a primary reason that American courts are political institutions despite their efforts to appear "nonpolitical."

Judicial Selection in the States

Compare the federal judicial selection process with the various processes used to select judges for state court systems. In general, there are four primary methods that states use for judicial selection: partisan elections, nonpartisan elections, and gubernatorial or legislative appointment. Figure 9.3 shows how judges are initially selected in each state, although midterm vacancies in many states are filled by gubernatorial appointment even when elections are the initial selection mechanisms for full terms in office. Each of these methods seeks to emphasize different values, yet they are all closely linked to political processes.

senatorial courtesy

Traditional deference by U.S. senators to the wishes of their colleagues concerning the appointment of individuals to federal judgeships in that state.

filibuster

Process in the United States Senate used to block or delay voting on proposed legislation or on the appointment of a judge or other official by talking continuously. Sixty senators must vote to end a filibuster.

FIGURE 9.3 Primary Methods of Initial Judicial Selection for State Judges

*Some states mix methods, such as having partisan selection of candidates before a nonpartisan election, or having retention elections after processes other than merit selection.

SOURCE: National Center for State Courts Web site, http://www.judicialselection.us/judicial_selection/methods/selection_of_judges.cfm?state.

Both partisan and nonpartisan elections emphasize the importance of popular accountability in a democratic governing system. Yet more than 20 states have eliminated judicial elections to reduce the role of politics and give greater attention to candidates' qualifications when selecting judges. These states have adopted various forms of merit selection systems, usually involving a committee reviewing candidates' qualifications and making recommendations to the governor about which individuals to appoint to judgeships. It is presumed that the committee will focus on the individuals' personal qualities and professional qualifications rather than on political party affiliations. In a few states, governors or legislatures possess the authority to directly appoint individuals of their choice to judgeships.

Judicial Decision-Making

9.4 Explain the theories concerning how Supreme Court justices reach their decisions.

Many people assume that judges make decisions by following established legal rules—and often this is true. However, the political battles over Supreme Court nominations, as well as over judges at other levels of state and federal court systems, reflect the widespread recognition that judges do not merely "follow the law" in making their decisions. In addition, when judges interpret the U.S. Constitution, state constitutions, and statutes, they rely on their own values and judgments. These values and judgments ultimately have a significant effect on public policy affecting many aspects of American life. Therefore, in appointing federal judges, the president seeks to name men and women with a politically compatible outlook. Similarly, the involvement of political parties and interest groups in supporting or opposing judicial candidates reflects their interests in securing judgeships for those individuals they believe will make decisions that advance their policy preferences.[4]

case precedent

A legal rule established by a judicial decision that guides subsequent decisions. The use of case precedent is drawn from the common law system brought from Great Britain to the United States. For example, in order to maintain stability in law, three of the justices in the majority claimed that they followed case precedent in voting to preserve a woman's right of choice concerning abortion in *Planned Parenthood* v. *Casey* (1992) even though they claimed that they did not necessarily agree with the original precedent that established that right in *Roe* v. *Wade* (1973).

Although judges can apply their values in making many kinds of decisions, they do not enjoy complete freedom to decide cases as they wish. Lower-court judges in particular must be concerned that their decisions will be overturned on appeal to higher courts, if they make decisions that conflict with the judgments of justices on courts of last resort. What then guides judges to reach conclusions that are not likely to be overturned? First, they determine the facts of the particular case before them. Next, they make their decision by applying the rules established by higher courts for cases with similar fact situations. When judges apply these established rules, we say that they rely on **case precedent**—the body of prior judicial opinions, especially those from the U.S. Supreme Court and state supreme courts, which establishes the judge-made law developed from interpretations of the U.S. Constitution, state constitutions, and statutes.

Typically, judges will follow the legal principles established by prior cases, no matter what their personal views on the issue. However, if they believe that the precise issue in their case is distinguishable from the issues in prior cases, or if they have new ideas about how such issues should be handled, they can issue an opinion that clashes with established case precedent. Judges make such decisions in the hope that the reasons explained in their opinions will persuade the judges above them to change the prevailing precedent.

For example, when the U.S. Supreme Court decided in 2005 (in *Roper* v. *Simmons*) that the cruel and unusual punishments clause in the Eighth Amendment prohibits the execution of murderers who committed their crimes before the age of 18, it established a new precedent, overturning its previously established precedent permitting execution as punishment for murders committed at the ages of 16 and 17 (*Stanford* v. *Kentucky*, 1989). In reaching its conclusion, the nation's highest court upheld a decision by the Missouri Supreme Court that advocated a new interpretation of the Eighth Amendment (*State ex. rel. Simmons* v. *Roper*, 2003).

The U.S. Supreme Court often seeks to follow and preserve its precedents in order to maintain stability in the law. However, it is not bound by its own precedents, and no higher court can overturn the Supreme Court's interpretations of the U.S. Constitution. Thus, the justices enjoy significant freedom to shape the law by advancing their own theories of constitutional interpretation and by applying their own attitudes and values concerning appropriate policy outcomes from judicial decisions.[5] State supreme courts enjoy similar freedom when interpreting the constitutions and statutes of their own states. Lower-court judges can also apply their own approaches to constitutional and statutory interpretation, especially when facing issues that have not yet been addressed by any court. Their new approaches may be overturned on appeal, but they may also help establish new law if higher courts agree.

Judicial selection battles in the federal courts, especially those related to the nomination of Supreme Court justices, often focus on the nominee's approach to constitutional interpretation. Among the members of the Supreme Court, Justice Clarence Thomas is known for advocating an original intent approach to constitutional interpretation. He and his admirers argue that the Constitution must be interpreted in strict accordance with the original meanings intended by the people who wrote and ratified the document. According to Justice Thomas, constitutional interpretation must follow original intent in order to avoid "judicial activism," in which judges allegedly exceed their proper sphere of authority by injecting their own viewpoints into constitutional interpretation.

The accusation of "judicial activism" is frequently directed by political conservatives against judges whose interpretations of the Bill of Rights lead to broad definitions of rights affecting criminal justice, issues of race and gender, and other policy disputes. That is why the followers of the original intent approach call themselves advocates of "judicial restraint," in which judges defer to the policy judgments of elected officials in the legislative and executive branches of government. In reality, judges with conservative political values can also be "judicial activists" by narrowly interpreting or invalidating statutes concerning environmental regulation, employment discrimination, and other policy areas. Thus, despite their claimed use of "judicial restraint," judges who follow original intent still affect public policy with their decisions. They merely disagree with others about which policies should be influenced by judges.

Critics of original intent argue that there is no way to know exactly what the Constitution's authors intended with respect to each individual word and phrase, or even whether one specific meaning was intended by all of the authors and ratifiers. Moreover, these critics typically argue that the ambiguous nature of many constitutional phrases, such as "cruel and unusual punishments" and "unreasonable searches and seizures," represents one of the document's strengths, because it permits judges to interpret and reinterpret the document in light of the nation's changing social circumstances and technological advances. What would James Madison and the other eighteenth-century Founders of the nation have thought about whether the use of wiretaps and other forms of electronic surveillance violate the Fourth Amendment prohibition on "unreasonable searches"? Critics of original intent argue for a **flexible interpretation** that enables contemporary judges to give meaning to those words in light of current values and policy problems. Nearly all of the Supreme Court justices in the past 50 years have used flexible interpretation, including Ruth Bader Ginsburg and Anthony Kennedy. However, these justices frequently disagree with one another about how much flexibility should apply to various provisions in the Constitution.

As you can see, debates about the proper approach to interpreting the Constitution can be central elements in the political battles over the selection of judges. Presidents try to select judges who they believe share their values and approach to constitutional interpretation, but they cannot accurately predict how a nominee will decide every kind of case, especially because new and unexpected issues emerge each year. Moreover, some Supreme Court justices, as well as judges on lower courts, do change their views over the course of their careers. The views that led the president to select the nominee are not always the views held by nominees

flexible interpretation
An approach to interpreting the U.S. Constitution that permits the meaning of the document to change with evolving values, social conditions, and problems. For example, when the Supreme Court decided that the Eighth Amendment prohibition on "cruel and unusual punishments" forbids the application of the death penalty to offenders with mental development disabilities (*Atkins v. Virginia*, 2002), the majority of justices used a flexible interpretive approach that claimed society's views about punishments for such individuals had changed over time.

Justice Elena Kagan, shown here at her Senate confirmation hearings in 2010, is the former Dean of Harvard Law School and the former Solicitor General of the United States who presented arguments to the Supreme Court on behalf of the U.S. government. Because it was widely believed that Kagan, as an appointee of President Obama, might strengthen the Court's liberal wing, conservative Republican senators opposed her confirmation.

■ *Is it proper for senators to oppose the nomination of a highly-experienced nominee simply because they believe he or she will make decisions with which they will disagree on certain issues?*

at the end of their careers. Justice Harry Blackmun, for example, an appointee of Republican President Richard Nixon, served on the Supreme Court from 1970 to 1994 and became increasingly protective of individuals' rights over the course of his career. Despite the fact that Nixon had envisioned him as a conservative decision maker, he was regarded as one of the Court's most liberal justices at the time of his retirement. On the contemporary Supreme Court, the newest appointees, Justices Sonia Sotomayor and Elena Kagan, have fulfilled the expectations of President Obama and others who supported their nominations by being generally liberal and supportive of constitutional rights.

〉 POLL Do you think the current Supreme Court is conservative, liberal, or moderate? Do you think of *yourself* as conservative, liberal, or moderate?

Political Science and Judicial Decision-Making

Supreme Court justices may claim they apply "judicial restraint" or a "flexible interpretation" of the Constitution in making their decisions, and they may honestly believe that these interpretive approaches guide their decisions. Political scientists, however, question whether the justices' decisions can be explained in this way. Through systematic examination of case decisions and close analysis of justices' opinions, researchers have identified patterns and inconsistencies. These examinations of Supreme Court decisions have led to alternative explanations for the primary factors that shape the justices' decisions.

The idea that justices follow specific theories of constitutional interpretation and carefully consider precedents in making decisions is often labeled the legal model. Critics argue, however, that the justices regularly ignore, mischaracterize, or change precedents when those case decisions seem to impede the desire of the majority of justices to have a case come out a certain way. Justices seem to decide cases on the separation of church and state according to a specific test of whether government actions advance a particular religion. In particular cases, however, they ignore the test if it leads to a result that they do not desire. For example, the justices permitted the Nebraska state senate to hire a minister to lead prayers at the start of each legislative session (*Marsh* v. *Chambers*, 1984). If they had applied the usual test that asked whether or not a government activity has a religious purpose, however, they would presumably have been required to prohibit this entanglement of church and state. Instead, perhaps seeking to avoid public controversy by ruling out legislative prayers, the majority of justices ignored the established legal test in this case and simply declared that legislative prayers are acceptable as a historical tradition.

attitudinal model
An approach to analyzing judicial decision making that looks at individual judges' decision patterns to identify the attitudes and values that guide their decisions.

An alternative theory of judicial decision-making, known as the **attitudinal model**, states that Supreme Court justices' opinions are driven by their attitudes and values. Advocates of this model see the justices' discussion of interpretive theories and precedent as merely a means to obscure the actual basis for decisions and to persuade the public that the decisions are, in fact, based on law. Researchers who endorse the attitudinal model do systematic analyses of judicial decisions to identify patterns that indicate the attitudes and values possessed and advanced by individual justices. Put more simply, the attitudinal theorists argue that some justices decide cases as they do because they are conservative (for example, generally supportive of business interests and expanded power for prosecutors and police) and that others decide cases differently because they are liberal (for example, generally supportive of broad definitions of criminal defendants' rights, environmental regulation, and civil rights).[6]

strategic voting model
An approach to analyzing judicial decision making that identifies strategic decisions made by judges in order to advance their preferred case outcomes.

Other political scientists see judicial decision-making as influenced by a **strategic voting model**.[7] According to this theory, Supreme Court justices vote strategically in order to advance their preferred goals, even if it means voting contrary to their actual attitudes and values in some cases. For example, a chief justice may vote strategically to end up among the majority of justices and thereby retain the authority to decide which justice will write the opinion for the Court. If the chief justice is in the minority after a vote, the senior justice in the majority assigns the opinion. Chief Justice Warren Burger was accused of changing his vote in the controversial abortion decision *Roe* v. *Wade* (1973) when he saw that a majority of his colleagues supported establishing a constitutional right of choice for women. Thus, he was able to assign opinion-writing responsibilities to his long-time friend, Justice Harry Blackmun, whom Burger erroneously believed might write an opinion that established a very weak and limited right of choice.[8]

In recent years, some political scientists have broadened their studies of courts, including judicial decision-making, through what is commonly labeled **new institutionalism**—an approach that emphasizes understanding courts as institutions and seeing the role of courts in the larger political system.[9] The adherents of new institutionalism do not necessarily agree with one another about the causes and implications of judicial action. They do, however, seek to move beyond analyzing judicial decisions solely by looking at the choices of individual Supreme Court justices. Instead, they may focus on the Supreme Court's processes, its reactions to statutes that undercut particular judicial decisions, or its decisions that minimize direct confrontations with other branches of government. Alternatively, the focus could be on judicial inaction, as when the Supreme Court declined to make a decision in a case brought by a U.S. citizen who had been jailed as a suspected terrorist and who had been denied all constitutional rights (*Rumsfeld* v. *Padilla*, 2004). The majority of justices declared that he had originally filed his case in the federal district court of the wrong state. They told him to begin his case again in the lower courts, likely hoping that by the time the case worked its way through the court system again, Congress and the President would have worked out the details of how to process such cases against Americans suspected of terrorist activities.

Political scientists continue to debate which model provides the best explanation for judicial decisions. New models are likely to be developed in the future. For students of American government, these models serve as a reminder that you should not automatically accept government officials' explanations for their decisions and behavior. Systematic examination and close analysis of decisions may reveal influences that the government decision makers themselves do not fully recognize.

new institutionalism

An approach to understanding judicial decision making that emphasizes the importance of courts' structures and processes as well as the courts' role in the governing system.

Action in the Court Pathway

9.5 Characterize the litigation strategies used in the court pathway.

In theory, any individual can make use of the resources of the judicial branch merely by filing a legal action. Such actions may be directed at small issues, such as suing a landlord to recover a security deposit. They may also be directed at significant national issues, including actions aimed at Congress or the president in battles over major public policy issues.

In reality, filing a lawsuit at any level above small-claims courts (where landlord-tenant cases are typically argued) is expensive and requires professional legal assistance. As a result, the courts are not easily accessible to the average American. Typically, this policy-shaping process is used by legal professionals who have technical expertise and financial resources. Nor will courts accept every kind of claim: Claims must be presented in the form of legal cases that embody disputes about rights and obligations under the law. Thus, organized interests and wealthy individuals are often best positioned to make effective use of court processes.

FIGURE 9.4 Policy-Shaping Litigation on the University of Michigan Affirmative Action Cases

Litigation is a long and difficult process. Note how long it took for the cases to travel through the courts, from the denial of admission in 1996 to the Supreme Court's decision in 2003. The final outcome depends on the facts of the case and the persistence, resources, and strategies of the competing sides, as well as the values and interactions of the judges.

■ *Do you have enough knowledge and resources to pursue policy-shaping litigation?*

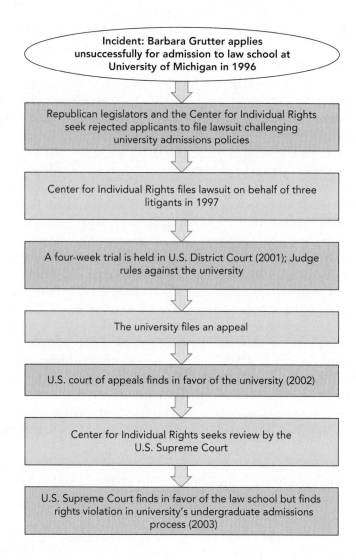

Interest Group Litigation

The court pathway is often attractive to small interest groups because it is possible to succeed with fewer resources than are required for lobbying or mass mobilization. Larger or resource-rich groups also use litigation, but it tends to be just one among several pathways that they use. To be effective in legislatures, for example, groups need lots of money and large numbers of aroused and vocal members. Lobbyists need to spend money by donating to politicians' campaign funds, wining and dining public officials, and mounting public relations campaigns to sway public opinion. By contrast, a small group may be successful using the courts if it has an effective attorney and enough resources to sustain a case through the litigation process. The most important resources for effective litigation are expertise and resources for litigation expenses.[10]

EXPERTISE For effective advocacy in litigation, expertise is essential. This includes thorough knowledge in the areas of law relevant to the case as well as experience in trial preparation or appellate advocacy, depending on which level of the court system is involved in a particular case. Attorneys who have previously dealt with specific issues know the intricate details of relevant prior court decisions and are better able to formulate effective arguments that use those precedents. In addition, attorneys affiliated with large, resource-rich law firms or interest groups have at their disposal teams of attorneys who can handle research and other aspects of investigation and preparation.

LITIGATION RESOURCES   Interest groups and individuals who use the court process must have the resources to handle various expenses in addition to the attorneys' fees, which are generally very high unless the lawyers have volunteered to work pro bono, which translates from the Latin phrase *pro bono publico* as "for the public good," for little or nothing. It means that attorneys and other professionals are waiving their usual fees to work for a cause in which they believe. Some interest groups rely heavily on securing pro bono professional support.

Elements of Strategy

All litigants engage in certain types of strategies—for example, presenting evidence and formulating arguments. Interest groups may benefit from additional opportunities to use specific strategies by choosing which case to pursue or by choosing the court in which a case may be filed.

SELECTION OF CASES   Interest groups seek to find an appropriate **test case** that will serve as the vehicle to persuade judges to change law and policy. Sometimes they can recruit plaintiffs and then provide legal representation and litigation expenses to carry the case through the court system. In challenging laws that restrict choices about abortion, an interest group would rather bring the case on behalf of a teenage rape victim than pursue the case for a married woman who became pregnant after being careless with birth control. The interest group is likely to believe that the rape victim's case will provide more compelling arguments that may generate sympathy from many judges.

Interest groups cannot always choose precisely which cases would best serve their interests. They may pursue any relevant case available at a given moment, because they cannot afford to wait, especially if other cases working their way through the system may lead to adverse judicial decisions.

CHOICE OF JURISDICTION   Another important factor in litigation strategies is the choice of courts in which to pursue a legal action. Because of the country's dual court system, there is often a choice to be made about whether state or federal courts are more likely to produce outcomes favorable to a group's interests. In addition to considering whether state or federal law may be more likely to produce a favorable result, litigators may consider whether a specific federal or state judge would be sympathetic to their values and policy preferences.

FRAMING THE ARGUMENTS   Litigants must make strategic decisions about how to frame the legal issues and arguments that they present in court. In some cases, they must decide which legal issues to raise. Lawyers must assess the judges before whom the case will be presented and make strategic decisions about which arguments will appeal to the particular decision makers who will consider the case.

When an interest group is not itself involved in a case, it may still seek permission to present written arguments as *amicus curiae* (Latin for "a friend of the court"). For example, it is very common for multiple interest groups to submit **amicus briefs**, detailed written arguments that seek to persuade the U.S. Supreme Court to endorse a specific outcome or to adopt reasoning that is favorable to the groups' policy preferences. Amicus briefs can be influential, because justices' opinions sometimes draw from these briefs rather than from the arguments presented by the two parties in the case. Participants in a Supreme Court case typically welcome the submission of amicus briefs on behalf of their side. Indeed, one strategy is to gain the endorsement of as many interest groups as possible to impress the Supreme Court with the broad support that exists for a particular position. Over the course of Supreme Court history, individuals and interest groups have increasingly sought to influence the Court's decisions through amicus briefs. From 1946 through 1955, amicus briefs were filed in only 23 percent of Supreme Court cases, but between 1986 and 1995, they were filed in 85 percent of the cases considered.[11]

test case
A case sponsored or presented by an interest group in the court pathway with the intention of influencing public policy. For example, *Grutter* v. *Bollinger* (2003), the case challenging affirmative action policies at the University of Michigan School of Law, was an unsuccessful test case filed by the Center for Individual Rights.

amicus brief
A written argument submitted to an appellate court by those who are interested in the issue being examined but are not representing either party in the case; often submitted by interest groups' lawyers to advance a specific policy position. For example, when the Supreme Court prepared to hear oral arguments in the health care law case, *National Federation of Independent Business* v. *Sebelius* (2012), the justices received more than two dozen amicus briefs from interest groups and state attorneys general.

TIMELINE

The Battle over Affirmative Action

What remedies are needed to counteract the legacy of discrimination in the United States that hampered employment and education opportunities for women and members of minority groups? The use of "affirmative action" and preferential treatment as a policy tool generated significant disagreement and controversy. Is it a necessary practice to open doors for people hampered by the historic consequences of discrimination? Is it essential for fostering diversity in society's institutions? Or is it an improper form of racial and gender discrimination that violates society's equal protection principles? Note that the affirmative action issue also calls into question the proper role of the judiciary in the governing system, especially when judges strike down affirmative action plans in the awarding of government contracts that were developed by elected officials in other branches of government. For example, if elected members of a city council believe that affirmative action is necessary and, if the voters disagree, those members can be held accountable at the next election. Why should judges determine what public policy will be?

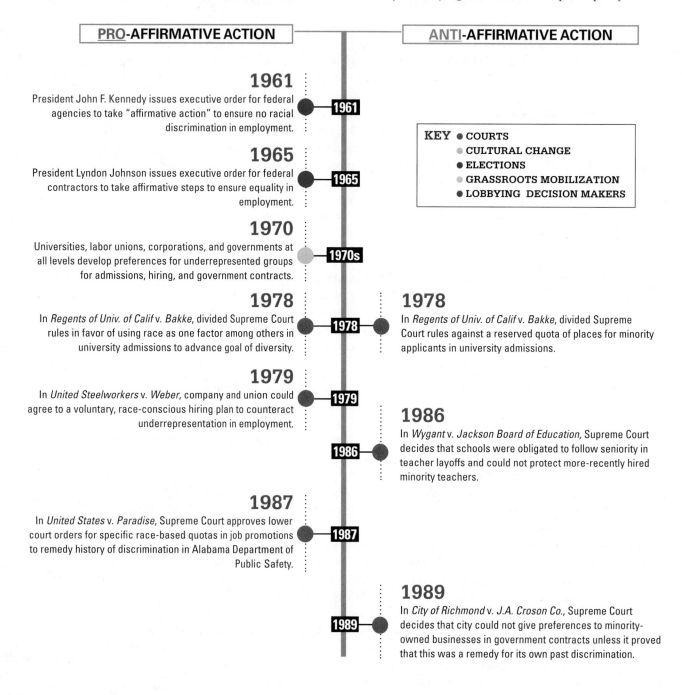

PRO-AFFIRMATIVE ACTION	ANTI-AFFIRMATIVE ACTION

KEY
- ● COURTS
- ◑ CULTURAL CHANGE
- ● ELECTIONS
- ◔ GRASSROOTS MOBILIZATION
- ● LOBBYING DECISION MAKERS

1961 — 1961
President John F. Kennedy issues executive order for federal agencies to take "affirmative action" to ensure no racial discrimination in employment.

1965 — 1965
President Lyndon Johnson issues executive order for federal contractors to take affirmative steps to ensure equality in employment.

1970 — 1970s
Universities, labor unions, corporations, and governments at all levels develop preferences for underrepresented groups for admissions, hiring, and government contracts.

1978 — 1978
In *Regents of Univ. of Calif v. Bakke*, divided Supreme Court rules in favor of using race as one factor among others in university admissions to advance goal of diversity.

1978
In *Regents of Univ. of Calif v. Bakke*, divided Supreme Court rules against a reserved quota of places for minority applicants in university admissions.

1979 — 1979
In *United Steelworkers v. Weber*, company and union could agree to a voluntary, race-conscious hiring plan to counteract underrepresentation in employment.

1986 — 1986
In *Wygant v. Jackson Board of Education,* Supreme Court decides that schools were obligated to follow seniority in teacher layoffs and could not protect more-recently hired minority teachers.

1987 — 1987
In *United States v. Paradise*, Supreme Court approves lower court orders for specific race-based quotas in job promotions to remedy history of discrimination in Alabama Department of Public Safety.

1989 — 1989
In *City of Richmond v. J.A. Croson Co.,* Supreme Court decides that city could not give preferences to minority-owned businesses in government contracts unless it proved that this was a remedy for its own past discrimination.

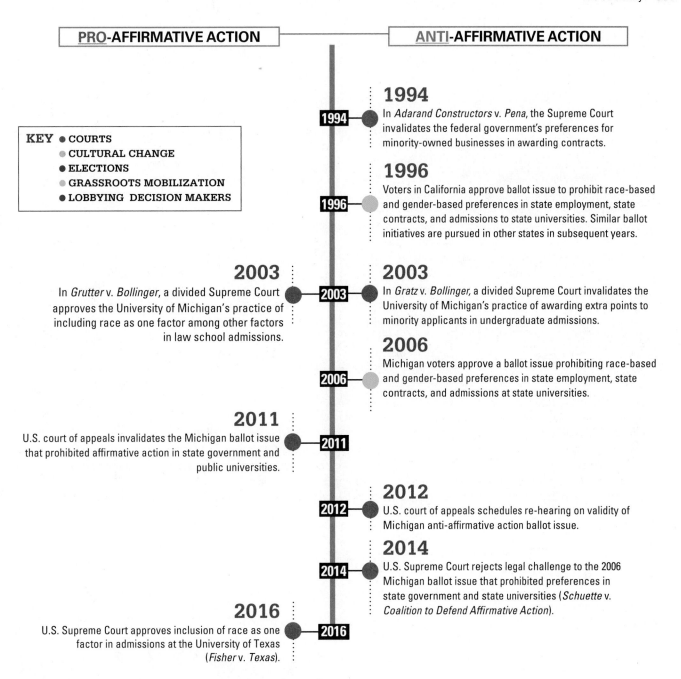

PRO-AFFIRMATIVE ACTION | ANTI-AFFIRMATIVE ACTION

KEY
● COURTS
● CULTURAL CHANGE
● ELECTIONS
● GRASSROOTS MOBILIZATION
● LOBBYING DECISION MAKERS

1994

1994 — In *Adarand Constructors* v. *Pena*, the Supreme Court invalidates the federal government's preferences for minority-owned businesses in awarding contracts.

1996

1996 — Voters in California approve ballot issue to prohibit race-based and gender-based preferences in state employment, state contracts, and admissions to state universities. Similar ballot initiatives are pursued in other states in subsequent years.

2003

In *Grutter* v. *Bollinger,* a divided Supreme Court approves the University of Michigan's practice of including race as one factor among other factors in law school admissions. — 2003

2003

2003 — In *Gratz* v. *Bollinger,* a divided Supreme Court invalidates the University of Michigan's practice of awarding extra points to minority applicants in undergraduate admissions.

2006

2006 — Michigan voters approve a ballot issue prohibiting race-based and gender-based preferences in state employment, state contracts, and admissions at state universities.

2011

U.S. court of appeals invalidates the Michigan ballot issue that prohibited affirmative action in state government and public universities. — 2011

2012

2012 — U.S. court of appeals schedules re-hearing on validity of Michigan anti-affirmative action ballot issue.

2014

2014 — U.S. Supreme Court rejects legal challenge to the 2006 Michigan ballot issue that prohibited preferences in state government and state universities (*Schuette* v. *Coalition to Defend Affirmative Action*).

2016

U.S. Supreme Court approves inclusion of race as one factor in admissions at the University of Texas (*Fisher* v. *Texas*). — 2016

CRITICAL THINKING QUESTIONS

1. Is affirmative action still necessary to create opportunities for those whose opportunities might otherwise be blocked by discrimination? Alternatively, is it necessary or desirable to foster diversity in a university student body or an employer's workforce?

2. Even as its composition has changed over the years, the justices of the Supreme Court have been deeply divided over the permissibility of affirmative action programs. Does the continuing existence of such stark disagreements provide a clue that such controversial policies should actually be worked out through democratic processes that shape policy in the legislative and executive branches of government?

PATHWAYS OF ACTION

CHALLENGING AFFIRMATIVE ACTION

Efforts to undo the country's legacy of discrimination and advance equal opportunity led to the introduction of controversial affirmative action policies that provide assistance to racial minorities, women, and the disabled in education and employment contexts in which they were underrepresented. Americans were deeply-divided on the issue of whether extra assistance or consideration for specific college and job applicants was necessary for remedying past discrimination and desirable for increasing diversity in a student body or workforce. Disappointed white and male applicants to education programs and employment programs filed lawsuits alleging that many affirmative action policies violate laws against discrimination.

The Supreme Court heard several cases concerning such issues and its decisions clarified which specific affirmative action practices are permissible under law. In *Regents of the University of California* v. *Bakke* (1978), a divided Court rejected the use of "quotas" or reserved slots for members of underrepresented groups. However, the majority approved the use of race as one consideration among many as universities sought to create a diverse student body in order to enrich the educational experiences of all students. In the employment context, the Court rejected several policies that gave preferences for government contracts to companies that were owned by women or members of underrepresented groups.

The Center for Individual Rights, an interest group opposed to affirmative action, recruited three unsuccessful applicants to the University of Michigan in order to challenge that university's admissions practices. With the interest group's attorneys carrying these cases forward through the levels of the federal court system, the Supreme Court eventually accepted the cases for hearing. A deeply-divided Court ultimately decided that the university's practice of giving minority applicants a specific number of extra points in the undergraduate admissions process served to improperly discriminate against white applicants (*Gratz* v. *Bollinger,* 2003). However, a slim majority of justices approved the practice of considering race flexibly as one factor among other factors in law school admissions for the purpose of creating a diverse student body (*Grutter* v. *Bollinger,* 2003).

By 2006, Justice Sandra Day O'Connor, the author of *Grutter,* was replaced by Samuel Alito, a more conservative Justice. An organization opposed to affirmative action, the Project on Fair Representation, helped a disappointed applicant to the University of Texas file a case with the hope that there would be a reversal of *Grutter.* However, the Supreme Court merely told lower courts to apply strict scrutiny in looking at universities' admissions (*Fisher* v. *University of Texas,* 2013). A federal appeals court upheld the Texas program in 2014. The Supreme Court heard oral arguments on the issue again in December 2015, but the February 2016 death of Justice Scalia made it likely that the program would survive. Any new majority to change the program depended on his now-missing vote. In June 2016, by a 4-to-3 vote, the Supreme Court upheld the Texas program.

Activists representing both sides of the abortion issue protested outside the Supreme Court in the weeks prior to the Court's 2016 examination of a Texas law restricting abortion clinics.

■ *Could such demonstrations ever influence the justices by informing them of the intensity of people's feelings about an issue? Or do such demonstrations only catch the attention of the news media?*

PUBLIC RELATIONS AND THE POLITICAL ENVIRONMENT   Interest groups have a strong incentive to gain sympathetic coverage from the news media about cases that they pursue through the court pathway. Attorneys often develop relationships with reporters in hopes that sympathetic stories will be written about policy-oriented legal cases. Such stories help educate the public and perhaps shape public opinion about an issue. They may also influence judges, because just like other people, judges read, watch, or listen to the news every day.

Implementation and Impact of Court Decisions

9.6 Evaluate the courts' effectiveness in enforcing judicial decisions.

Court decisions are not automatically implemented or obeyed. Judges have the authority to issue important pronouncements that dictate law and policy, especially with respect to the definition and enforcement of constitutional rights. However, they have limited ability to ensure that their orders are carried out. To see their declarations of law translated into actual public policy, judges must typically rely on public obedience and on enforcement by the executive branch of government.

During the Watergate scandal of the 1970s, in which President Richard Nixon conspired to cover up information about a burglary at Democratic Party offices committed by people working for his reelection campaign, the Supreme Court handed down a decision ordering Nixon to provide a special prosecutor with recordings of secretly taped White House conversations. Years later, Supreme Court Justice Lewis Powell observed that had Nixon refused to comply with the Court's order, "there was no way that we could have enforced it. We had [only] 50 police officers [at the Supreme Court], but Nixon had the [U.S. military at his disposal]."[12] Nixon handed over the tapes, however, and shortly thereafter resigned from office, presumably realizing that public support for his impeachment, already strong, would lead to his conviction by the Senate if he disobeyed a unanimous Court decision that citizens and members of Congress viewed as legitimate.

The weakness of courts has been revealed in a number of cases over the course of American history. In the 1830s, the Cherokee Nation successfully litigated a case against laws that ordered the removal of Cherokees from their lands. The state of Georgia supported removal on behalf of whites who invaded Cherokee lands to search for gold. The U.S. Supreme Court, still led by the aged Chief Justice John Marshall, supported the Cherokees' property rights, but President Andrew Jackson and other officials declined to use their power to enforce the ruling. ("John Marshall has made his decision," Jackson is supposed to have said, "now let him enforce it.") Thus, despite using the court pathway in an appropriate manner to protect their property rights, the Cherokees were eventually forced off their land. A few years later, they were marched at gunpoint all the way to an Oklahoma reservation, with an estimated 4,000 dying along the way. The Cherokees' infamous Trail of Tears forced march and loss of land demonstrated that courts cannot automatically ensure that their decisions are enforced and obeyed. Unlike the situation in the 1970s, in which President Nixon felt strong public pressure to obey the Supreme Court or face impeachment, the Cherokees and the Supreme Court of the 1830s did not benefit from public acceptance and political support.

In modern times, analysts have questioned the effectiveness of courts in advancing school desegregation. Although the Supreme Court earned praise for declaring racial segregation in public schools unconstitutional in *Brown v. Board of Education*, the 1954 decision did not desegregate schools. Racial separation continued in public schools throughout the country for years after the Court's decision. In two highly publicized incidents, military force was necessary to enroll African-American students in all-white institutions. In 1957, President Dwight D. Eisenhower sent troops to force Little Rock Central High School to admit a half-dozen black students, and in 1962, President John F. Kennedy dispatched the U.S. Army to the University of Mississippi so that one African-American student could enroll. In both situations, there had been violent resistance to court orders, but the presidents effectively backed up the judicial decisions with a show of force. In other cities, desegregation was achieved piecemeal, over the course of two decades, as individual lawsuits in separate courthouses enforced the *Brown* mandate.

According to Professor Gerald Rosenberg, the actual desegregation of public schools came only after the president and Congress acted in the 1960s to push policy change, using financial incentives and the threat of enforcement actions to overcome segregation. In Rosenberg's view, courts receive too much credit for policy changes that actually only occur when other actors become involved. Courts receive this credit, in part, because of the symbolism attached to their publicized pronouncements.[13]

Similar arguments can be made about other policy issues. For example, the Supreme Court's decision recognizing a woman's right to make choices about abortion (*Roe* v. *Wade,* 1973) does not ensure that doctors and medical facilities will perform such procedures in all locations or that people have the resources to make use of this right.

Other analysts see the courts differently—as important and effective policymaking institutions. They argue that *Brown* and other judicial decisions about segregation were essential elements of social change. Without these judicial decisions initiating, guiding, and providing legitimacy for change, the changes might not have occurred. For example, until the mid-1960s, southern members of Congress who supported segregation were able to block corrective legislation because the seniority system gave them disproportionate power on congressional committees. In the Senate, they also used the filibuster to prevent consideration of civil rights legislation. Thus, they

The U.S. Supreme Court, shown here in the official 2011 portrait, includes three women for the first time in U.S. history. This small group of unelected officials has significant power to create new law and policy.

■ *Do you think the Supreme Court has used its power appropriately in affecting policy issues? With which Supreme Court decisions do you disagree and why?*

could make sure that proposed bills either died in committee or never came to a vote. In addition, elected officials at all levels of government and in all parts of the country were often too afraid of a backlash from white voters to take strong stands in support of equal protection for African Americans. Analysts point to other court decisions, such as those requiring police officers to inform suspects of their Miranda rights in 1966 and recognizing abortion rights in 1973, to argue that the court pathway has been an important source of policy change.[14] Unelected federal judges were arguably the only actors positioned to push the country into change because they would not lose their jobs as a result of making decisions that were unpopular with some segments of American society.

Judicial Policymaking and Democracy

9.7 Describe the debate over whether it is appropriate for judges to shape public policy in a democracy.

Notwithstanding the framers' expectation that the judiciary would be the weakest branch of government, American judges possess the power to shape public policy. However, this power often stirs up debates about the role of courts in the constitutional governing system. These controversies are most intense when focused on the actions of appointed, life-tenured, federal judges.[15] In a democratic system, how can unelected, long-serving officials be permitted to make important decisions affecting public policy? This is an important question for our government.

The power of the judicial branch poses significant potential risks for American society. What if life-tenured judges make decisions that create bad public policy? What if they make decisions that nullify popular policy choices made by the people's elected representatives or that force those elected representatives to impose taxes needed to implement those decisions? Because of these risks, some critics call judicial policymaking undemocratic. They argue that judges should limit their activities to narrow decisions that address disputes between two parties in litigation and avoid any cases that might lead judges to supersede the preferences of the voters' accountable, elected representatives in the legislative and executive branches. These critics want to avoid the risk that a small number of judicial elites, such as the nine justices on the U.S. Supreme Court, will be able to impose their policy choices on the nation's millions of citizens.

Although judicial policymaking by unelected federal judges does not fit conceptions of democracy based on citizens' direct control over policy through elections, advocates of judicial policymaking see it as appropriate. According to their view, the design of the governing system in the U.S. Constitution rests on a vision of democracy that requires active participation and policy influence by federal judges. Under this conception of democracy, the U.S. Constitution does not permit the majority of citizens to dictate every policy decision. The Constitution facilitates citizen participation and accountability through elections, but the need to protect the rights of individuals under the Bill of Rights demonstrates that the majority should not necessarily control every decision and policy. In 1954, for example, racial segregation was strongly supported by many whites in the North and the South. Should majority rule have dictated that rigid racial segregation continue? In essence, the American conception of constitutional democracy relies on citizen participation and majority rule plus the protection of rights for individuals, including members of unpopular political, religious, racial, and other minority groups.

For example, in the aftermath of the September 11, 2001, terrorist attacks on the World Trade Center and the Pentagon, public opinion polls indicated that a majority of Americans favored requiring Arabs, including those who are U.S. citizens, to undergo special searches and extra security checks before boarding airplanes in the

United States.[16] Imagine that Congress responded by enacting a law that imposed these requirements based on ancestry without regard to its detrimental impact on U.S. citizens of Arab descent. Such a policy, if supported by a majority of citizens, would meet many of the requirements for democratic policymaking. However, it would collide with the Fourteenth Amendment's requirement of "equal protection of the laws" for Americans from all races and ethnic groups.

To ensure that majority interests do not trample the rights of minorities, the Constitution positions federal judges as the decision makers to protect constitutional rights. In this position, because they are appointed, life-tenured officials, federal judges are supposed to have the independence and the insulation from politics necessary to make courageous decisions on behalf of minority group members, no matter how unpopular those minorities may be. In practice, federal judges have not always gone against the wishes of the majority, even when the rights of minority group members were threatened or diminished. Such was the case when the Supreme Court endorsed the detention of innocent Japanese Americans in internment camps during World War II (*Korematsu* v. *United States,* 1944). But in other cases, the Supreme Court and other courts have provided a check against the excesses of majority policy preferences.

There is broad agreement that judges must uphold the U.S. Constitution, state constitutions, and laws enacted by legislatures through the use of their power of interpretation. Disagreements exist, however, about whether judges have acted properly in interpreting the law, especially when judicial decisions shape public policy. Was it improper for the Supreme Court to recognize a constitutional right of privacy that grants women the opportunity to make choices about abortion (*Roe* v. *Wade,* 1973)? Should the U.S. Supreme Court have prevented the Florida courts from ordering recounts of votes during the closely contested presidential election of 2000 (*Bush* v. *Gore,* 2000)? These and other questions will continue to be debated for decades to come for three primary reasons: First, courts are authoritative institutions that shape law and policy in ways that cannot be directly controlled by the public and other institutions of government. Second, court decisions often address controversial issues that reflect Americans' most significant disagreements about social values and public policies. And third, elected officials may choose to avoid taking action on controversial issues, thereby leaving the court pathway as the sole avenue for government action.

Conclusion

The judicial branch serves important functions under the constitutional governing system of the United States. Judges and juries resolve disputes, determine whether criminal defendants are guilty, impose punishment on those convicted of crimes, and provide individuals with a means to challenge actions by government. These functions are carried out in multilevel court systems, made up of trial courts and appellate courts, which exist in each state as well as in a national system under the federal government. Each system is responsible for its own set of laws, though all must be in accord with the U.S. Constitution, "the supreme law of the land."

The judicial branch provides opportunities for individuals and interest groups to seek to shape law and public policy. Through the litigation process in the court pathway, they can frame arguments to persuade judges as to the best approaches for interpreting the law. Judicial opinions shape many significant public policies for society, including those affecting education, abortion, the environment, and criminal justice. These opinions interpreting constitutions and statutes are written by judges who are selected through political processes, including elections in many states and presidential appointment in the federal system. American judges are exceptionally powerful because of their authority to interpret the U.S. Constitution and their ability to block actions by other branches of government through the power of judicial review. The impact of federal judges on major public policy issues raises difficult questions about the proper role of unelected officials in shaping the course of a democracy.

Think back to the Timeline and Pathways of Action features concerning the Supreme Court's decisions on affirmative action in university admissions. In light of what you have learned in this chapter, can you understand why interest groups and state attorneys general pursued a litigation strategy instead of just lobbying Congress on the issue? Do you see why opponents of affirmative action keep returning to the Supreme Court with challenges to universities' admissions policies as they believed—prior to the unexpected death of Justice Scalia in 2016—that the Court's composition leaned in their favor, especially after Justice Alito replaced Justice O'Connor? Ask yourself this question: Is it appropriate for the Supreme Court to decide this issue? Why or why not?

The courts are not easily accessible to citizens, because their use depends on expensive resources, including the patience to sustain extended litigation and the funds to hire expert attorneys and pay for litigation expenses. Because of their resources and expertise, organized interest groups are often better positioned than individual citizens to use the court pathway in pursuing their own policy objectives or in blocking the policy goals of other interest groups. However, the limited ability of judges to implement their own decisions is one factor that leads some observers to debate whether the court pathway provides processes that can consistently and properly develop public policies that are useful and effective.

CONFRONTING POLITICS AND POLICY

In January 2012, protesters from the Occupy Movement staged a demonstration in front of the U.S. Supreme Court on the anniversary of the Court's decision in *Citizens United* v. *Federal Election Committee* (2010). That decision endorsed corporations' political campaign contributions as a form of protected free speech and thereby invalidated limits on corporate campaign spending that had been created by the people's elected representatives in Congress. The decision by the closely-divided Court contributed to massive corporate and organizational spending on political advertising during the 2012 presidential campaign and opened the door to greater levels of spending in subsequent election campaigns. Many critics believe that the *Citizens United* decision improperly gave corporations free speech rights and wrongly equated those speech rights with the act of donating campaign money. The protesters supported a constitutional amendment that would declare that corporations are not the same as people for purposes of possessing rights and would enable Congress to restore the restrictions on campaign spending that the *Citizens United* decision had invalidated. Eleven Occupy protesters were arrested for violating a federal law that prohibits demonstrations on the plaza and steps in front of the Court.

ACTION STEPS

1. Do you believe that the Supreme Court went too far in invalidating campaign finance regulations created by the people's elected representatives in Congress? Give two reasons for your answer.

2. What impact can be produced by public demonstrations and protests in front of the Supreme Court? Would it be a worthwhile expenditure of your time to participate? Give two reasons for your answer.

3. Do you support amending the Constitution in order to undo a Supreme Court decision or is it better to pursue lawsuits that might enable you to persuade the justices to change their minds about a prior decision? Why?

4. Compared with strategies employed involving other branches of government and decision makers, is it easier or more difficult for a citizen to pursue policy goals through litigation that seeks decisions by the judiciary?

⟩ REVIEW THE CHAPTER

Court Structure and Processes

9.1 Explain how American court systems are organized. (p. 288)

The United States has a "dual court system," in which each state, as well as the federal government, operates its own multilevel system with trial and appellate courts. The U.S. Supreme Court carefully selects a limited number of cases each year and then decides important issues of law and policy.

The Power of American Judges

9.2 Identify the reasons why American judges are powerful actors in the governing system. (p. 293)

American judges are powerful because of their authority to interpret constitutions and statutes, their power of judicial review, and in the federal system, their protected tenure in office. They often use their interpretations of rights in the Bill of Rights to invalidate or limit actions by the executive and legislative branches.

Judicial Selection

9.3 Outline the selection process for federal judges. (p. 298)

Federal judges must be appointed by the president and confirmed by the Senate through a political process that involves influence by U.S. senators, predictions about the judges' values and decisions, and activity by political parties and interest groups. States use various methods to select judges, including elections and merit selection.

Judicial Decision-Making

9.4 Explain the theories concerning how Supreme Court justices reach their decisions. (p. 299)

Debates exist about the proper way to interpret the Constitution and statutes, and these debates affect choices about who will be selected to serve as judges. Politicians typically advocate for the selection of judges whom they believe share their preferences concerning public policy. However, scholars recognize that there are several models of judicial decision-making employed by various judges, not all of which simply advance a particular set of policy preferences. While some scholars believe that judges' decisions are guided by personal values, others argue that judges may use case precedents, strategic voting, or concerns about preserving judicial institutions as major influences over decisions.

Action in the Court Pathway

9.5 Characterize the litigation strategies used in the court pathway. (p. 303)

Individuals and interest groups use many strategies in the court pathway. Their likelihood of success is enhanced if they have expertise about the specific legal issues in a case, the resources to initiate and sustain litigation, and the patience to follow the court pathway through each of its stages. Interest groups also select test cases that will best present issues to a court in a favorable manner, and they make additional strategic choices about the court in which they will file a case and the way in which they frame their arguments.

Implementation and Impact of Court Decisions

9.6 Evaluate the courts' effectiveness in enforcing judicial decisions. (p. 309)

Judges cannot always ensure that their decisions are implemented. They must depend on enforcement actions by the executive branch and compliance by the public. As a result, their ability to shape public policy may vary from issue to issue, depending on whether other governmental actors and public opinion support their decisions.

Judicial Policymaking and Democracy

9.7 Describe the debate over whether it is appropriate for judges to shape public policy in a democracy. (p. 311)

Vigorous debates continue to occur about whether it is appropriate for appointed, life-tenured federal judges to create law and public policy in a democracy. Critics of judicial involvement in policymaking argue that democracy is harmed when unelected judges make decisions that should be the sole responsibility of elected officials in the legislative and executive branches. Supporters of judicial action claim that judges cannot avoid shaping policies when fulfilling their responsibility to protect the constitutional rights of individuals and minority group members.

> LEARN THE TERMS

> EXPLORE FURTHER

In the Library

Banks, Christopher, and David O'Brien. *Courts and Judicial Policymaking.* Upper Saddle River, NJ: Pearson, 2008.

Baum, Lawrence. *American Courts: Process and Policy,* 6th ed. Boston: Wadsworth, 2008.

Baum, Lawrence. *Judges and Their Audiences.* Princeton, NJ: Princeton University Press, 2006.

Burns, James MacGregor. *Packing the Court: The Rise of Judicial Power and the Coming Crisis of the Supreme Court.* New York: Penguin Press, 2009.

Canon, Bradley C., and Charles A. Johnson. *Judicial Policies: Implementation and Impact,* 2nd ed. Washington, D.C.: CQ Press, 1999.

Collins, Paul. *Friends of the Supreme Court: Interest Groups and Judicial Decision Making.* New York: Oxford University Press, 2008.

Epstein, Lee, and Jack Knight. *The Choices Justices Make.* Washington, D.C.: CQ Press, 1998.

Epstein, Lee, and Joseph F. Kobylka. *The Supreme Court and Legal Change: Abortion and the Death Penalty.* Chapel Hill, NC: University of North Carolina Press, 1992.

Feeley, Malcolm M., and Edward L. Rubin. *Judicial Policy Making and the Modern State.* New York: Cambridge University Press, 1998.

Goldman, Sheldon. *Picking Federal Judges: Lower Court Selection from Roosevelt Through Reagan.* New Haven, CT: Yale University Press, 1997.

Hume, Robert J. *How Courts Impact Federal Administrative Behavior.* New York: Routledge, 2009.

O'Brien, David. *Storm Center: The Supreme Court in American Politics,* 8th ed. New York, Norton, 2008.

Pacelle, Richard, Brett Curry, and Bryan Marshall. *Decision Making By the Modern Supreme Court.* New York: Cambridge University Press, 2011.

Perry, Barbara. *The Supremes: An Introduction to the U.S. Supreme Court Justices,* 3rd ed. New York: Peter Lang, 2009.

Rosenberg, Gerald N. *The Hollow Hope: Can Courts Bring About Social Change?* 2nd ed. Chicago: University of Chicago Press, 2008.

Sandler, Ross, and David Schoenbrod. *Democracy by Decree: What Happens when Courts Run Government.* New Haven, CT: Yale University Press, 2003.

Yalof, David Alistair. *Pursuit of Justices.* Chicago: University of Chicago Press, 2001.

On the Web

Explore the federal court system at *http://www.uscourts.gov.*

Explore state court systems at *http://www.ncsc.org/.*

Read judicial opinions from the U.S. Supreme Court and other courts at *http://www.law.cornell.edu, http://www.oyez.org,* and *http://supreme.justia.com.*

Examine the contrasting views on judicial decision-making and constitutional interpretation presented on the Web sites of two prominent organizations for lawyers and law students: the Federalist Society for Law and Public Policy Studies *http://www.fed-soc.org* and the American Constitution Society for Law and Policy *http://www.acslaw.org/.*

Discover interest groups that use the court pathway: Washington Legal Foundation *http://www.wlf.org,* Pacific Legal Foundation *http://www.pacificlegal.org,* American Civil Liberties Union *http://www.aclu.org,* and NAACP Legal Defense Fund *http://www.naacpldf.org.*

Learn about upcoming law and policy controversies that will be addressed by the U.S. Supreme Court at the American Bar Association's Web site: *http://www.abanet.org/publiced/preview/briefs/home.html.*

Examine information about lawsuits seeking to persuade judges to tell corrections officials how prisons should be run. Consider whether such litigation and resulting judicial policymaking should be viewed as proper under the U.S. constitutional governing system: *https://www.prisonlegalnews.org.*

POLITICAL SOCIALIZATION AND PUBLIC OPINION

In February 2015 (over a year before this issue erupted on the national stage), the University of California at Irvine designated over twenty public restrooms as "inclusive" for the use of all people. The issue of transgender rights has gotten highly controversial and is unlikely to be quickly resolved.

■ *Do you think that the controversy over bathroom usage is a backlash against the legalization of same-sex marriage or is it an entirely separate issue?*

→ LEARNING OBJECTIVES

10.1 Explain the relationship between public opinion, public policy, and fundamental values.

10.2 Determine how and why public opinion changes and the factors leading to stability in values and beliefs.

10.3 Differentiate between the dominant political ideologies in the United States, and explain how value structures impact public opinion and political action.

10.4 Illustrate how individuals acquire their political values.

10.5 Assess how membership in various social groups impacts political views and behavior.

10.6 Explain how public opinion is measured.

On March 23, 2016, Pat McCrory, the Republican governor of North Carolina, signed into law a bill which requires individuals to use the restroom which corresponds to the biological sex listed on their birth certificate. The law prohibits cities and local governments from expanding "employment" or "public accommodations" protections to groups other than those covered by state law (which covers race, religion, national origin, color, age, biological sex, and handicaps). The law was in reaction to an ordinance passed in Charlotte, the largest city in North Carolina, on February 22, 2016, which expanded the state antidiscrimination laws to include gender identity. The law, among other things, would have allowed transgender people to use restrooms that corresponded to their gender identity. In response to the city ordinance, a special session of the state General Assembly was called where the bill was passed and signed into law by the governor on the same day. Supporters of the bill argue that the state law is designed to protect the privacy of students and defend religious liberty, but others strongly opposed the law as they felt it would have discriminated against already vulnerable adolescents. These debates have proven to be just the beginning of a highly controversial issue. A high-profile boycott by celebrities and businesses quickly emerged following the passage of the North Carolina law. The boycott included business such as PayPal, Deutsche Bank, General Electric, the Dow Chemical Company, Pepsi, Hyatt, Hewlett Packard, Whole Foods, Levis Strauss & Co., and celebrities such as Bryan Adam, Maroon 5, Pearl Jam, Demi Lavato, Nick Jonas, and Bruce Springsteen. The NBA announced in July 2016 that they were moving the 2017 All-Star game from North Carolina in protest against the state law. Frustration over the law was evident in the 2016 gubernatorial election, the closest in the country. At the time of publication, it appears that the sitting governor, Republican Pat McCrory, has lost the race to Democratic challenger, NC Attorney General Roy Cooper. Cooper has pledged to repeal the law.

On May 13, 2016, the Departments of Education and Justice issued rules designed to protect transgender students from bullying. The new guidelines require schools to allow transgender students to use the restroom and locker room that correspond to their gender, not necessarily their sex. The new rules invoke Title IX protection (which prohibits against sex discrimination) and therefore carry the threat of the loss of federal funds for education if the rules are not followed. On May 25, 2016, eleven states sued the federal government over the directive. The lawsuit, lead by Texas, alleges that the federal government did not follow the proper procedures in issuing the directive. The states allege that the federal government bypassed Congress in redefining "sex" to include gender identity. In July 2016, ten more states joined the lawsuit. Pressure is being placed upon the courts to resolve this issue as quickly as possible, although the lawsuits may become moot if the guidelines are rescinded under the administration of President Trump. In an unrelated case, on October 28, 2016, the Supreme Court agreed to hear a case about a Virginia youth who was denied the right to use the bathroom that corresponds to his identified gender (*Gloucester County School Board* v. *GG*). Many anxiously await the ruling, but it may be construed very narrowly and hence fail to adequately address this issue.[1]

When Caitlyn Jenner, formerly known as Bruce Jenner, came out as a transgender woman in April 2015 she was met with strong reactions. She was named one of the 25 Glamour Women of the Year by *Glamour* magazine, was awarded the Arthur Ashe Courage Award at the ESPYS in July 2015, and was selected as Barbara Walters' Most Fascinating Person of 2015. We saw in Chapter 1, public opinion about gay rights has changed dramatically in recent years, but views about gender identity have been slow in changing. Many people were upset at these awards and the backlash against some transgender individuals has been severe. State legislators are reacting to these mixed feelings with a wide variety of legislation from laws prohibiting discrimination based upon gender identity to laws like the one passed in North Carolina. Do you think that public opinion will become more supportive of transgender and transsexual individuals like it has of gays and lesbians?

HOW DO PEOPLE ACQUIRE THEIR POLITICAL VALUES, AND HOW STABLE IS PUBLIC OPINION?

As more and more people come out, we are beginning to see the shame that many carry for being different. National attention has recently been focused upon the issues surrounding bullying of young people because of their actual or perceived sexuality, gender identity, or other issues relating to sexual activity. Concern over the number of suicides by lesbian, gay, transgender, transsexual, and bisexual young people motivated syndicated columnist and author Dan Savage and his partner Terry Miller to create a YouTube video in September 2010 to arouse hope for young people facing harassment. This video inspired others and served as the catalyst for the It Gets Better Project. The Trevor Project, a beneficiary of the It Gets Better Project, is designed to end suicide among LGBT youth. Celebrities, politicians, athletes, and over a half a million everyday people have joined together to end bullying and provide safe zones for youth facing bullying. Why did the public become concerned over bullying, which has existed for a long time?

How do people's opinions change regarding issues such as sexuality? By what processes do people acquire values? Although our culture and political values are relatively stable, change does occur—often gradually, but sometimes with dramatic speed. As you will see with the issues surrounding bullying, when our culture changes, our government responds. In this chapter, you will examine the power of public opinion and culture to bring about change and influence our world.

Public Opinion

10.1 Explain the relationship between public opinion, public policy, and fundamental values.

Our government, Abraham Lincoln reminded us in his Gettysburg Address, is "of the people, by the people, and for the people"—in short, a product and a reflection of the American public. So when you think about public opinion, the concept may at first seem quite straightforward—it is the opinion of the general public. In a society as large and diverse as ours, however, it is no easy job to determine *the* opinion of "the public." It is therefore helpful to think of **public opinion** as a mechanism that quantifies the various opinions held by the population or by subgroups of the population at a particular point in time. A complete picture of the opinions of more than 324 million Americans is difficult to estimate but nevertheless insightful.

Public opinion is grounded in political values, but it can be influenced by a number of sources and life experiences. Despite the fact that we are a highly educated society, this advanced level of education has not directly translated into a more politically informed citizenry. Nearly two-thirds of Americans cannot name a single Supreme Court Justice and over one quarter has no idea which party controls the House or Senate. Those who are politically knowledgeable, however, tend to have more stable political opinions. Many experts and political commentators believe that since most people don't base their opinions on specific knowledge, their opinions are neither rational nor reasonable.[2]

Other scholars have argued that a general sense of political understanding is enough to cast an informed ballot and to form reasonable political opinions.[3] Therefore, even though most citizens cannot name the Chief Justice of the U.S. Supreme Court, they can nevertheless form rational and coherent opinions on issues of public policy and political preferences. It is important to note that research on public opinion most often focuses on the voting population rather than on the general population. This is an important distinction, because the voting population is generally more educated and more politically knowledgeable than the general population.

public opinion

The attitudes of individuals regarding their political leaders and institutions as well as political and social issues. Public opinion tends to be grounded in political values and can influence political behavior.

The Relationship Between Public Opinion and Public Policy

To what extent should public opinion drive public policy? There are many answers to this question, and they reflect assorted takes on the nature of democracy itself. Of central importance is the role of the public in the governing process. How influential should public opinion be? How much attention should our political leaders pay to the public's positions and attitudes? Some authorities believe (though they may not say this openly) that public opinion should have little influence on the behavior and decision making of our leaders. They argue that democracies need to limit the influence of the people, allowing the better-informed and more educated leaders to chart our path. Others argue that political officeholders should give great weight to the views of the people.

Those who believe that democracies need to limit the ability of the public to influence events argue that information must be controlled and narrowly shared. Leaders should do the thinking and the planning, and the masses should step up occasionally to select their leaders in periodic elections and spend the rest of their time as spectators.[4] Many analysts are concerned that public opinion changes too easily and that people are too busy to pay much attention to politics. People are lacking in interest, not in intelligence. Some researchers have found evidence to support the notion that it might be best for leaders to minimize the impact of public opinion and to allow citizens to influence policymakers primarily through elections.[5] This **elitism** was forthrightly expressed in the early days of our republic, but it is not widely acknowledged among political leaders and commentators today.

HISTORICAL VIEWS The Founders, on the whole, thought that too much influence was given to the preferences of the people under the Articles of Confederation. As you've seen, the Articles created a system that was responsive to the broad public but not receptive to the elite. In the new constitutional system they created, the Founders reacted by diminishing the relationship between the government and public opinion. The new system was designed to impose a sort of waiting period on the masses, reflecting the thought that officials should shape public opinion, not respond to it.

For example, *The Federalist*, No. 63, asserts that a "select and stable" Senate would serve as "an anchor against popular fluctuations," which would protect the people from their "temporary errors." In *The Federalist*, No. 49, Madison warns of the "danger of disturbing the public tranquility by interesting too strongly the public passions." Hamilton argues in *The Federalist*, No. 68, for the indirect election of the president by a council of wise men (the Electoral College) who must not react too quickly to the passion of the people, and in *The Federalist*, No. 71, he further warns against following the "sudden breeze of passion" or listening to every "transient impulse" of the public.

The Founders saw the government as our guardian, protecting us from ourselves. They did believe that long-held views—those that lasted over the presidential term and the staggered Senate elections—should affect the course of government. They were more concerned with curbing *transient* ("here today, gone tomorrow") opinions, which they viewed as "common." Today, as we have become more educated and have adopted a political system with near-universal adult suffrage, people have come to expect their government to be open and responsive.

CONTEMPORARY CONSIDERATIONS In direct opposition to this elitist theory— and by far the more commonly held view of contemporary political leaders and political scientists—has been a position based on *pluralism*. Whereas elitists have argued that complex decisions need to be made free from public pressure, pluralists believe that citizens should be informed and should participate in democratic decision making to ensure the health and vitality of the system. They argue that participation by the public gives legitimacy to the political process and governing officials. Pluralists urge

elitism

The theory that a select few—better educated, more informed, and more interested—should have more influence than others in our governmental process. Elites tend to view the world differently than those who are less advantaged.

officials to pay close attention to the desires of the people in charting their actions, because active participation is an essential part of a healthy democracy. This line of reasoning goes back to the ancient Greek philosopher Aristotle, who believed that collective judgments were more likely to be wise and sound than the judgments of a few.

Political scientist Sidney Verba makes a strong case that public opinion, as measured by polls, should be heeded because polls are a more egalitarian form of political expression than other forms of participation, which tend to benefit the more educated and affluent. Since each individual has an equal (but small) chance of being selected to participate in a poll, there is a greater chance that the opinion of the broad public will be accurately determined. Some theorists insist that other forms of political expression are better gauges of public opinion, because they require more effort from people. Verba, however, presents a strong argument that economic differences between the affluent and the less affluent make it difficult for the views of the general population to be heard, because the wealthy are better able to articulate and present their points of view. Hence, to think that the concerns of all demographic groups could be fairly and accurately portrayed without public opinion polls is a bit utopian.[6]

The reality of the situation probably lies somewhere between these two theories. There are times when officials respond to the views of the people—especially when the opinion is fairly popular and when an issue is presented that offers a chance to gain a political advantage. If the voting population is interested in an issue and a dominant viewpoint emerges, elected officials will be under great pressure to pay attention to the opinions and act accordingly. Even unelected officials, including judges, are often influenced by public opinion.

At other times, officials pay less attention to the views of the public, including the views of voters. This is likely to happen when the public has focused relatively little attention on an issue. Officials may also choose not to be responsive when their convictions come into conflict with the views of the people. Elected officials may take unpopular positions that they nevertheless believe in, risking their public support for their beliefs. Knowing when to follow public opinion and when to resist it is one of the marks of a truly great political leader.

One example of public opinion *not* swaying government policy is in the area of gun control. Imposing some form of gun control is popular among a large segment of the citizenry (especially in times following a publicized gun tragedy), but significant federal gun control legislation is rare. Passed in 1993, the Brady Bill, which mandated waiting periods when purchasing handguns, was the first major federal gun control law since 1968—and it was allowed to quietly die in 2004 despite its popularity among a large majority of Americans. The public has shown broad and consistent bipartisan support for requiring expanded background checks to purchase guns as well as preventing the mentally ill from purchasing guns, however no federal gun control legislation was passed.

Consider, however, a different example: drug policy. Following the highly publicized deaths of a few famous athletes, and with increased media coverage of drug abuse and the widespread availability of illicit drugs in the mid-1980s, the public became very concerned with drug abuse, citing it as the nation's most important problem. Congress and the White House struggled to catch up with public concern, each quickly presenting initiatives to address the country's "drug crisis." Significant legislation passed, increasing the role of the federal government in a problem that historically had been viewed as primarily the responsibility of state governments. A major public service campaign was launched to persuade Americans to "just say no" to drugs. A federal "drug czar" was appointed, and a "War on Drugs" was declared.[7] Unlike gun control, this example demonstrates the power of the public in influencing government to respond to a problem. Recently we have seen heightened concern being voiced about opioid abuse and addiction, with pressure being put on the federal government to address what some see as an epidemic.

Why did the government respond to public concerns over drugs but fail to respond to the support for additional gun control provisions? Organized and powerful interest groups vehemently have opposed gun control, whereas no organized interest groups have opposed the War on Drugs. While accurate, this is the simple answer. The complete answer is far more complex. One reason why officials responded to the concern over drugs but not over guns is that people were more worried about the drug crisis than they were about assault weapons. In social science jargon, the drug crisis was simply more "salient" to the population. Moreover, the media reinforced the concern many felt about drug problems, but they did not focus much sustained attention on concerns over the availability of military-style assault weapons. When public officials discuss issues and keep them in the limelight (as they did with drugs), public opinion can often be influenced.

The Relationship Between Public Opinion and Fundamental Values

Shared support for fundamental values tends to temper disagreements and leads to stability in public opinion. Countries that lack agreement on essential values tend to be far more volatile and to have higher levels of unstable public opinion. Most Americans agree on a number of key political values and are proud to live in the United States. Americans believe in majority rule, coupled with the need to protect minority rights. We see fair, free, and competitive elections as essential to our democracy. We feel a strong sense of national loyalty and patriotism, which together provide solid and crucial support for our governmental system. Even though we see problems, we would rather live here than anywhere else. But while we share many common values, we often disagree over their meaning and differ on specific policies related to these values.

PERSONAL LIBERTY One area of broad agreement is support for personal liberty. Our country was founded on the idea of protecting individual liberties and freedoms. As you saw in Chapters 4 and 5, our Constitution and Bill of Rights were written to protect individual freedoms "from" and "to." We are protected

A growing number of Americans are becoming concerned with the power of the government and are increasingly supporting a more Libertarian ideology of limited government. Pictured here is a protest in Florida against red light cameras. Many argue the automated citations run counter to the presumption of innocence and infringe on the rights of citizens.

■ *What do you think? Are red light cameras another example of excessive governmental power or are they a necessary evil to diminish accidents and promote public safety?*

from unreasonable searches, *from* cruel and unjust punishments, and (with the Fourteenth Amendment) *from* discrimination. We are protected against infringement on our freedom *to* practice our religion freely, *to* express our minds, and *to* join with others in forming organizations. Most of us cherish these liberties, but the specific meaning of these freedoms can cause disagreement. Should hate groups have no limits on speech? Can the speech of the wealthy drown out the speech of the poor? When we move from the abstract to specific policies, there is often disagreement.

individualism

An attitude, rooted in classical liberal theory and reinforced by the frontier tradition, that citizens are capable of taking care of themselves with minimal governmental assistance.

INDIVIDUALISM   In addition to freedom, Americans highly value the idea of **individualism**, a belief that goes back to the earliest days of our republic. A reverence for individualism and individual rights is central to our democracy, because the government is expected to protect individuals and design policies that enhance the chances of reaching self-fulfillment. It is also central to our economic system: At the heart of capitalism lies a belief in individualism that in many cases permits individual interests to win out over community interests. (Socialism, by contrast, values community needs over individual wants.) The spirit of individualism also stresses the right of citizens to own property and to control their earnings (hence the conflict over tax policies). Comparing the general sense of individualism in the United States to that in Europe provides a vivid example of how varied opinions can be.

Europeans generally expect their governments to address individual concerns, such as providing health care and alleviating poverty. They believe that such programs are valuable and should be funded. While Americans would like for everyone to have health insurance, for the most part we do not believe it is the government's role to fund universal health insurance programs. The high level of conflict surrounding health care reform in the country since 2009 is evidence of this conflict. The root of this markedly different set of attitudes is the difference of opinion between individual and community responsibility.

equality of opportunity

The belief that all should have equal chances for success in education, employment, and political participation.

equality of outcome

An egalitarian belief that government must work to diminish differences between individuals in society so that everyone is equal in status and value.

EQUALITY   Americans also strongly support the idea of equality, a complex notion involving both political and social aspects. There is near-universal support for political equality: The notion of one person, one vote is deeply embedded in our culture. However when we speak of equality in our society—meaning economic equality, educational attainment, social status, and power, for example—the issue becomes more complex. Most of us believe in the idea of **equality of opportunity** (the belief that everyone should have a chance of success), but many Americans find the idea of **equality of outcome** (using the government to ensure equality) more controversial. Examples of policies that grant equal opportunities for success are public schools and public defenders for people accused of crimes who cannot afford their own lawyers. In contrast, the Equal Pay Act of 1963, which required employers to pay men and women equal wages for equal work, was motivated by a belief in equality of outcome. Today, the idea of equal wages for both sexes is not controversial, but other policies to promote equality are.

Affirmative action is an example of a public policy that tries to achieve equality of opportunity and equality of outcome, depending on how the policy is designed. Affirmative action in college admissions and scholarships provides equality of opportunity, as many well-qualified students might not otherwise have a chance to attend college. Affirmative action in granting governmental contracts to minority-owned construction firms, for example, is motivated by the goal of equality of outcome, ensuring that these firms are treated equally and without bias in business. Current controversies over affirmative action, however, provide a good example of how even though many people agree on the basic notion of equality, disagreement occurs when we put these values into action.

The Stability of Political Beliefs

10.2 Determine how and why public opinion changes and the factors leading to stability in values and beliefs.

Political culture is the set of norms, customs, and beliefs that help citizens understand appropriate ways to act in a political system and provide support for political institutions and practices. It also involves the shared economic and political values about how government should operate. Evidence shows that political culture is relatively stable over time, with party identification being the most stable.[8] Opinions can and do change over a lifetime, but major ways of thinking (partisanship, ideology, and economic and social values) tend to remain stable once a person reaches adulthood. Evidence also exists that adults often adjust their views to adapt to changing political environments and to changing life circumstances.[9]

One source of stability is the broad consensus on the key values we have just discussed. Because our political elites tend to be better educated, they are even more supportive of democratic ideals than are typical individuals. Although we experience conflict, there have been few significant controversies over fundamental issues that have led individuals and groups desiring change to go beyond the established channels to promote their cause. A few exceptions exist: The Civil War is the foremost example of a fundamental conflict, but it ended in the decisive victory of one side, permanently settling the issues of slavery and secession. And a century later, U.S. society faced serious conflicts over the Vietnam War and civil rights. But on the whole, our society has been successful in avoiding violence by using political channels to promote change. Another reason our system is stable is that in the United States, levels of distrust in our institutions of government and our constitutional system (which can be very dangerous and lead to instability) are relatively low. Although trust goes up and down over the years, sufficient levels of trust remain to sustain our system.

political culture

The norms, customs, and beliefs that help citizens understand appropriate ways to act in a political system; also, the shared attitudes about how government should operate.

Shifts in Public Opinion

There have been periods in our history in which large shifts in opinion have occurred; often these shifts have reflected major transformations in American politics. Perhaps the greatest such shift was in the 1760s and 1770s, when overwhelmingly loyal British-American subjects turned into republican rebels against the Crown.

From the 1950s to the 1970s, large increases in support for civil liberties for communists, socialists, and atheists occurred. From the end of World War II through the early 1970s, a national consensus emerged condemning racial segregation. Since the 1960s, opinion has become much more approving of interracial marriage and of equal employment rights for homosexuals. In 1958, only 4 percent of Americans approved of interracial marriages. The number has steadily increased since that time, rising from 20 percent in 1968 to 43 percent in 1983, and reaching 87 percent in 2013.[10] Today, all racial groups in the United States widely accept interracial marriage (though support is greatest among African Americans and Latinos), with young Americans being the most supportive.[11] Support for equal employment opportunities for homosexuals also has risen steadily: 56 percent of Americans supported equal rights in 1977, 71 percent in 1989, and 89 percent in 2008.[12] In 2016, 68 percent of Americans stated that gay or lesbian relations between consenting adults should be legal—up from 56 percent in 2006 and 33 percent in 1986.[13] One of the biggest shifts in public opinion was the 43-percent increase between 1937 and 1978 in the number of people who were willing to vote for a woman candidate for president (increasing from 33 percent in 1937 to 76 percent in 1978).[14]

Most of the significant changes in American public opinion have occurred gradually, over several decades. Rather than sharp changes, we more commonly

FIGURE 10.1 U.S. Public Opinion on Abortion, 1975–2015

As you can see, opinion on this controversial issue has remained fairly stable. In 1975, 54 percent of Americans thought abortion should be legal only under certain circumstances. That number is 50 percent in 2016. Compared to other controversial issues, public opinion on abortion tends to be more stable and consistent over time.

SOURCE: Reprinted By Permission of Gallup, Inc. http://www.gallup.com/poll/1576/abortion.aspx.

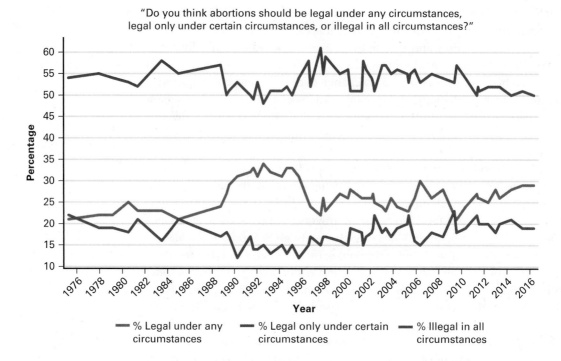

"Do you think abortions should be legal under any circumstances, legal only under certain circumstances, or illegal in all circumstances?"

— % Legal under any circumstances   — % Legal only under certain circumstances   — % Illegal in all circumstances

cohort replacement

Natural phenomenon of generational replacement due to death.

find very slow changes in Americans' beliefs and life circumstances. Attitudes toward abortion, for example, provide a good illustration of the stability of public opinion (see Figure 10.1). Abortion has been a controversial issue since the 1970s, but overall public opinion has remained relatively consistent over the years. Most gradual change can be explained by **cohort replacement**, which simply means that younger people replace older people; and as each generation has experienced a different world, it is logical that each would have different opinions. It is estimated that 50 percent of the electorate is replaced every 20 years.[15] Demographic changes in society also help to explain gradual change, and so does changing technology. For example, computer usage clearly affects the way in which people become informed. The changes in views toward homosexual rights are largely attributed to cohort replacement.

❯ **POLL** Should abortion be legal in all instances, only in certain situations, or should it never be legal?

Sometimes, we do see rather abrupt changes in public opinion, particularly in the area of foreign policy. Political scientists Benjamin Page and Robert Shapiro found that shifts in opinions on foreign policy were three times as rapid as changes in domestic preferences, presumably because the landscape of international politics changed more quickly than that of domestic affairs.[16] Areas that saw abrupt changes were opinions regarding wars (World War II, Korea, Vietnam, the war in Afghanistan), foreign aid, defense spending, and the Middle East.[17] For example, before the attack on Pearl Harbor, public opinion overwhelmingly favored an isolationist foreign policy; those attitudes shifted with dramatic suddenness after December 7, 1941, the day of the attack on Pearl Harbor and the beginning of U.S. involvement in World War II.

The Impact of Popular Culture on Political Opinions and Values

Many people believe that our popular culture can influence our political values and culture, and several historical examples demonstrate ways in which popular culture has had a significant effect. One early example occurred during the abolitionist era; an antislavery movement that began in the North during the early 1800s but did not get onto the mainstream agenda until after the publication of Harriet Beecher Stowe's novel *Uncle Tom's Cabin* in 1851. The novel personalized the horror of slavery and mobilized people who had previously been unaware about the depth of the problem. The book sold more than 300,000 copies in the first year, and within 10 years it had sold more than 2 million copies, becoming the all-time American best-seller. The film *Birth of a Nation* (released in 1916), which glorified the Ku Klux Klan and is arguably one of the most racist movies ever made in the United States, clearly harmed American race relations, especially after it was shown to children in many southern schools as a "history lesson." Finally, Betty Friedan's 1963 book *The Feminine Mystique* invigorated the feminist movement in the 1960s.

Today, politics and entertainment have become increasingly intertwined.[18] Celebrities often make political statements, ranging from open expressions of support for a particular candidate or party to organizing and articulating support for political issues or movements. When discussing the effect of popular culture on political culture, we discover several controversies, most notably focusing on the issue of cause and effect. Does popular culture affect values and beliefs, or do values and beliefs affect popular culture? For example, when Ellen DeGeneres "came out" as a gay woman in 1997 (both personally and as her character, Ellen Morgan, on the then-popular TV show *Ellen*), did she do so because the climate had changed, making it more acceptable to be gay? Or did her coming out lead to changed attitudes toward homosexuality? Was it both? Similar questions can be asked about the circumstances leading Bruce Jenner to publically announce his transition to Caitlyn Jenner. Did the groundbreaking work of others, such as Candis Cayne, Chaz Bono, and Laverne Cox, help make the public more accepting to issues of sexuality and more open to her transition? Similarly, will her actions help the public become more supportive in time or will the backlash felt in some areas grow?

Several theories have been advanced to explain the relationship between popular culture and political culture and public opinion. According to the **catalyst-for-change theory**, popular culture promotes change and shapes the independent attitudes and beliefs of the public. One example of this theory occurred in 1947 when Jackie Robinson became the first black player in Major League Baseball. Watching him display remarkable athletic ability as he played for the Brooklyn Dodgers, and his remarkable control and refusal to respond to the hail of racial slurs from fans that he faced in his first year, caused many people to rethink the common racial stereotypes of the time. In the same way, when Vanessa Williams was crowned the first black Miss America in 1983, many people in society began to think differently about issues of race and beauty.

catalyst-for-change theory
The assertion that public opinion shapes and alters our political culture, thus allowing change.

A second theory sees popular culture as a **barometer of public attitudes**, not as the shaper of those attitudes. According to this theory, Ellen DeGeneres was able to come out because our culture and beliefs had changed, permitting a more tolerant view of homosexuality. Furthermore, this theory explains the popularity of television shows with gay, lesbian, and bisexual characters and actors, such as *Modern Family*, *Empire*, *Girls*, and *Orange is the New Black*—not because they caused us to see homosexuality differently, but because our attitudes had already begun to change.

barometer of public attitudes
The theory that popular culture reflects public opinion.

Still another explanation, **interactive theory**, asserts that popular culture both changes *and* reflects social values and beliefs. In a highly interactive process, popular culture serves as both a catalyst and as a barometer. This last theory seems most logical and dynamic.[19]

interactive theory
The theory that popular culture both shapes and reflects popular opinion.

Consider how public opinion has changed regarding the status of women in our society. Because of a concerted effort to improve the position of women, support for women's equality is higher today than ever in our history. Figure 10.2 shows the changing views about women's leadership skills from 2008 to 2014. In 2008, only 6 percent of respondents thought that women made better political leaders than men (21 percent thought that men made better political leaders than women, while the vast majority—69 percent—thought men and women were equally competent). By 2014, the percentage that thought men and women were equally competent increased to 75 percent with 14 percent thinking men made better leaders (with the increase in the percent that think women are better suited as political leaders, the net difference is now down to 5 percent in favor of men versus 15 percent in 2008).[20] Despite these changes and the fact that women have reached record levels of success in educational attainment and in the workforce, very few have reached the highest levels of political or corporate leadership. Before the rise of the modern Women's Rights Movement in the 1960s, only 46 percent of Americans thought women should be equal with men in business, industry, and government; in 2008, the numbers had risen to 84 percent.[21] Looking at explanations cited by men and women about the dearth of women in the political elite and in top executive positions is telling. The most commonly cited reason is the belief that women are held to higher standards than men, but women are substantially more likely to cite this reason than are men.[22]

> POLL Do you believe men or women generally make better political leaders or are both equally as good?

A number of consequences have emerged from this important cultural change. First, women are seeing growth in opportunities, most notably in education and business. Today, there are more female-headed businesses than ever before. In 2015, 40 percent of students at the nation's top MBA programs were women.[23] Substantially more women are now earning associate's and bachelor's degrees than men, and over half of the doctoral degrees in the United States are awarded to women (though women disproportionately major in the lower-paid and less prestigious fields of education and the humanities). For example, less than 25 percent of doctoral degrees in engineering, computer science, and mathematics are awarded to women while nearly 70 percent of doctorate degrees in education are earned by women.[24]

Although women have made progress in many sectors of society, they are still significantly underrepresented in our government: Women make up nearly 20 percent of Congress, 24.7 percent of statewide elective executive officials, and 24.5 percent of state

Line Judge Sarah Thomas became the first woman to serve as an official for the National Football League in 2015. Prior to this, she was the first woman to officiate a college bowl game in 2009 and was the first woman to officiate in the Big Ten in 2011.

■ *How important do you think it is to see women in roles that used to be exclusively the domain of men?*

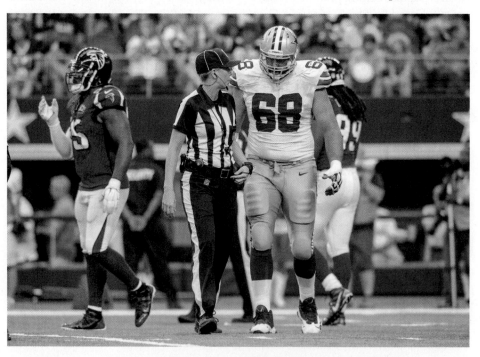

FIGURE 10.2 U.S. Public Opinion on Who Possesses the Most Valued Leadership Traits

One of the most often cited reasons women are not in top executive positions or high political offices is that Americans believe that women are held to higher standards than men. However, when we examine this issue in greater detail, we see that far more women than men think this is the case. Why do you think this pattern emerges? Looking at the changes in the opinion of the public in only six years regarding which sex makes better political leaders is telling. In 2008, 21 percent thought men made better leaders while only 14 percent thought so six years later. The percentage who thought men and women were equally as good increased from 69 percent to 75 percent. Far more think men are better suited to be political leaders, but opinion is changing.

■ *Why do you think the differences between men and women exist? What changes in society do you think are important for the shifting perceptions about women leaders?*

SOURCE: "A Paradox in Public Attitudes. Men or Women: Who's the Better Leader?" Washington, D.C.: Pew Research Center, August 25, 2008, pp. 3; "Women and Leadership: Public Says Women are Equally Qualified, but Barriers Persist," Washington, D.C.: Pew Research Center, January 14, 2015, http://www.pewsocialtrends .org/2015/01/14/women-and-leadership/ accessed on February 16, 2016.

Percent saying men/women generally make better political leaders:

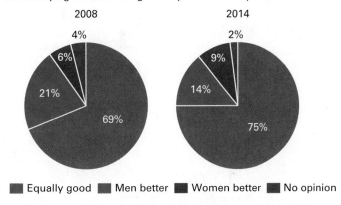

Percent saying each is a major reason more women aren't in top executive business positions or high political offices.

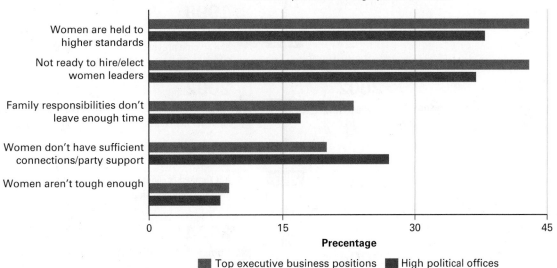

However, if we look at the responses by gender, an interesting pattern emerges:

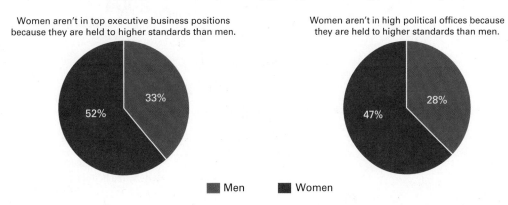

TIMELINE

Bullying in the United States

Bullying has long been accepted in American society. In fact, for generations many thought bullying was a right of passage to be tolerated and even encouraged. This began to change as we saw the devastation that bullying brought to the lives of young people. Bullying began to be seen as a societal problem when it was brought to new levels with the widespread use of social media. While most people see the negative consequences of bullying, controversy exists over what should be done to end bullying. Of central concern is the need to balance free speech and the right for youth to feel safe and protected.

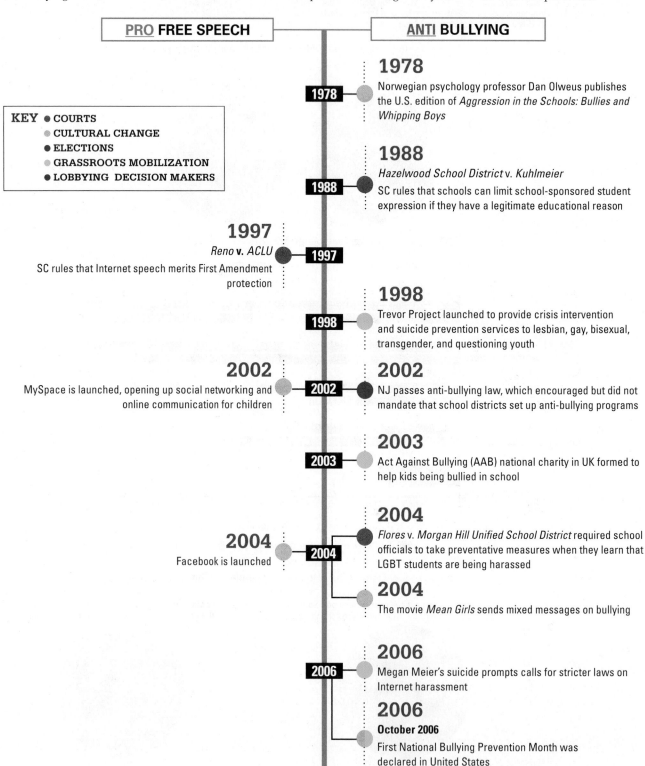

PRO FREE SPEECH   **ANTI BULLYING**

KEY
- COURTS
- CULTURAL CHANGE
- ELECTIONS
- GRASSROOTS MOBILIZATION
- LOBBYING DECISION MAKERS

1978

1978
Norwegian psychology professor Dan Olweus publishes the U.S. edition of *Aggression in the Schools: Bullies and Whipping Boys*

1988

1988
Hazelwood School District v. *Kuhlmeier*
SC rules that schools can limit school-sponsored student expression if they have a legitimate educational reason

1997
Reno **v.** *ACLU*
SC rules that Internet speech merits First Amendment protection

1997

1998

1998
Trevor Project launched to provide crisis intervention and suicide prevention services to lesbian, gay, bisexual, transgender, and questioning youth

2002
MySpace is launched, opening up social networking and online communication for children

2002

2002
NJ passes anti-bullying law, which encouraged but did not mandate that school districts set up anti-bullying programs

2003

2003
Act Against Bullying (AAB) national charity in UK formed to help kids being bullied in school

2004

2004
Flores v. *Morgan Hill Unified School District* required school officials to take preventative measures when they learn that LGBT students are being harassed

2004
Facebook is launched

2004
The movie *Mean Girls* sends mixed messages on bullying

2006

2006
Megan Meier's suicide prompts calls for stricter laws on Internet harassment

2006
October 2006
First National Bullying Prevention Month was declared in United States

KEY
- COURTS
- CULTURAL CHANGE
- ELECTIONS
- GRASSROOTS MOBILIZATION
- LOBBYING DECISION MAKERS

2010

January 14, 2010

Phoebe Prince, 15, hanged herself after being bullied by girls in South Hadley, Massachusetts, for dating an older football player

May 31, 2010

Christian Taylor, 16, committed suicide after months of bullying; his mother said the school did nothing to stop the torment

September 19, 2010

13-year-old Seth Walsh of Tehachapi, CA, committed suicide after years of bullying for being gay

September 21, 2010

Author Dan Savage and his partner post an It Gets Better video clip on YouTube to provide hope for youth being bullied, which launches the It Gets Better Project

September 22, 2010

18-year-old Rutgers freshman Tyler Clementi jumped off the George Washington Bridge after two dorm-mates posted video of him allegedly having sex with another man

2011

January 5, 2011

NJ passed the Anti-Bullying Bill of Rights, the toughest anti-bullying legislation to date (largely in reaction to Tyler Clementi's death)

March 9, 2011

Stopbullying.gov is launched to provide information about resources available to stop bullying

March 10, 2011

White House Conference on Bullying Prevention—President Obama, Michelle Obama, the Department of Education, and the Department of Health and Human Services joined with students, parents, teachers, community activists, and policymakers to discuss effective strategies to stop bullying

2012

Born This Way Foundation created by Lady Gaga, Berkman Center for Internet & Society, Harvard Graduate School of Education, and other organizations

2013

November 2013

Richie Incognito suspended from Miami Dolphins for allegedly harassing fellow offensive lineman, Jonathan Martin. Event triggers conversations around the country about bullying, gender roles, and bystander responsibilities

2015

Karanveer Singh Pannu, a Sikh-American high school student, writes "Bullying of Sikh American Children" to raise awareness of the bullying

2016

February 2016

U.S. Department of Education issues a Press Release "Protecting Our Muslim Youth from Bullying: The Role of the Educator" to fight the heightened targeting of Muslim youth

November 2016

Melania Trump announces that as first lady she will launch an anti-bullying campaign

CRITICAL THINKING QUESTIONS

1. Do you think public information campaigns, like the "It Gets Better" campaign, are changing the way teens view bullying? Imagine a public relations group hired you to develop a campaign against bullying in high schools. What are the strongest arguments you would put forward to end bullying?

2. Should we limit speech, both inside and outside schools, to fight bullying or should we continue to protect this cherished freedom? What is the proper balance between free speech and the right to protect individuals? Should colleges do more to protect students from on-line bullying?

legislators.[25] In 2017, 104 women, the highest in history (though still far below parity and a figure that has grown stagnant), serve in the United States Congress. However, the number of women in corporate leadership positions remains remarkably low. Seven women led Fortune 500 companies in 2005, 15 in 2009, 21 in 2013, and 20 in 2016 (which constitutes 4 percent). Women held only 19.2 percent of board seats on these companies.[26] The Department of Labor examined the "glass ceiling" and found it to be lower than many people thought, often keeping women from top corporate leadership positions.

Political Ideology

10.3 Differentiate between the dominant political ideologies in the United States, and explain how value structures impact public opinion and political action.

political ideology

A consistent set of beliefs that forms a general philosophy regarding the proper goals, purposes, functions, and size of government.

liberal

A person who generally supports governmental action to promote equality, favors governmental intervention in the economy, and supports policies attempting to solve environmental issues.

conservative

A person who believes in limiting government spending, preserving traditional patterns of relationships, and that big government is a threat to personal liberties.

Political ideology is a consistent set of basic beliefs about the proper purpose and scope of government. Americans generally tend to fall into two camps: liberals and conservatives, although at various points in our history, many have been reluctant to identify themselves as either, and some have always identified with other ideologies. In general terms, **liberals** tend to support social and cultural change (especially in connection with issues of equality) and want an activist government that encourages change. **Conservatives**, by contrast, tend to favor traditional views on social, cultural, and economic matters and demand a more limited role for government in most spheres. Although there is some ideological variation within each party, today's Republican Party is, generally speaking, the party of conservatives, whereas most liberals tend to identify with the Democratic Party.

Many Americans believe that liberals prefer more government involvement, while conservatives favor less government involvement. This more-less distinction typically holds true when looking at economic issues and spending on public goods that benefit many people. For instance, liberals favor government spending on environmental protection, education, public transportation, national parks, and social services. In these areas of public policy, conservatives want smaller governmental budgets and fewer governmental programs. However, when it comes to government involvement with respect to social issues, conservatives generally support more governmental intervention in the form of restrictions on abortion, pornography, and LGBT rights while liberals tend to prefer less government intervention in these same areas.

Today, the critical difference between liberals and conservatives concerns not so much the *scope* of governmental activity as the *purpose* of governmental actions. Generally speaking, conservatives approve of using governmental power to promote order, including social order, though there are exceptions to these generalizations. Conservatives typically favor firm police action, swift and severe punishments for criminals, and more laws regulating behavior, such as teen curfews. Such beliefs led many conservatives to support stringent anticommunist domestic and foreign policies in the 1940s and 1950s. Programs to fight domestic terrorism (such as the USA PATRIOT Act, which was initially bipartisan and very popular as an immediate reaction to the attacks of September 11, 2001) now get more conservative than liberal support. Conservatives want to preserve traditional patterns of social relations, including the importance of the domestic role of women in family life and the significance of religion in daily life and school. Conservatives today do not oppose equality, but they tend not to view securing equality as a prime objective of governmental action.

In general, liberals tend to worry more than conservatives do about the civil liberties implications of the USA PATRIOT Act and government surveillance of potential terrorists. Liberals are less likely to approve the use of governmental power to maintain order but are more willing to use governmental power to promote equality. Thus they tend to support laws to ensure that the LGBT community receives equal treatment in employment, housing, and education. They favor policies that encourage businesses to hire and promote women and minorities, and they want to raise the minimum wage and provide greater access to health care for all people.

As you can see in Figure 10.3, political ideology in the United States is relatively stable and consistent over time. Once people develop their ideology, barring major world events, it is unlikely to significantly change throughout their lifetimes. The percentage of those identifying as "conservative" has remained remarkably steady since 1992 (ranging only between 36 and 40 percent) while the percentage identifying as "liberal" has increased from 17 percent in 1992 to 24 percent in 2014. The growth in the number of liberals has come at the expense of the "undecided" or "moderate" category which decreased from 43 percent in 1992 to 34 percent in 2014 (reflecting the manner in which society has become more polarized).

Although not nearly as popular as liberal and conservative ideology, a number of people today identify with populist and libertarian ideology. **Populists** believe that the government can be a positive agent to protect "common people" (which historically included farmers and workers) against the moneyed elite. Populists favor governmental action to promote equality but also support policies to uphold order. **Libertarians** support individual liberty in economic, personal, and social realms over government authority. Libertarians acknowledge that government must have some authority, but they believe that most governmental action must be severely regulated and limited.

〉 POLL How would you classify your political leanings—very conservative, conservative, moderate, liberal, or very liberal?

populist

A person who believes that the government can be a positive agent to protect "common people" against the moneyed elite.

libertarian

A person who supports individual liberty over government authority in economic, personal, and social realms.

Political Socialization

10.4 Illustrate how individuals acquire their political values.

Political socialization is the conscious and unconscious transmission of political culture and values from one generation to another. It is the process by which people learn political information, organize political knowledge, and develop political values. Socialization is not a onetime event; it occurs continuously. The transmission of knowledge as a part of political socialization is a means of teaching one generation the lessons of its predecessors, ideally leading to social stability and better decision-making.

political socialization

The complex process through which people acquire political knowledge and form political values; also the conscious and unconscious transmission of political culture and values from one generation to another.

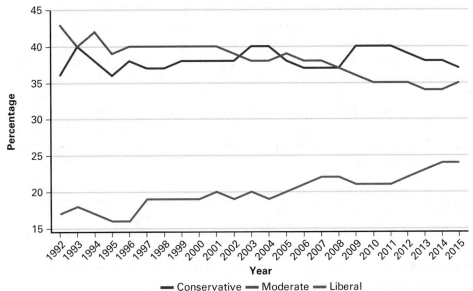

"How would you describe your political views—very conservative, conservative, moderate, liberal or very liberal?"

FIGURE 10.3 Annual Trends in Political Ideology

Political ideology is rather consistent in the United States, unlike other countries which have far more dramatic shifts over time. The United States is becoming a bit more polarized, with fewer people considering themselves moderates today than 20 years ago.

SOURCE: Lydia Saad, "U.S. Liberals at Record 24%, but Still Trail Conservatives." Gallup, January 9, 2015, http://www.gallup.com/poll/180452/liberals-record-trail-conservatives.aspx.

agents of political socialization
Factors that influence how we acquire political facts and knowledge and develop political values.

Research demonstrates that learning during childhood and adolescence affects adult political behavior;[27] we must therefore examine very carefully the process by which people learn about politics. Factors that influence the acquisition of political facts and the formation of values are called **agents of political socialization**. Let's examine six such agents: family, school, peers and community, religion, the media, and events.

❯ **POLL** What are your opinions on the legality of same-sex marriage?

Family

Children learn a wide range of social, moral, religious, economic, and political values from their families, and what they learn can dramatically shape their opinions. When parents are interested in politics, they tend to influence their children to become more politically interested and informed, because children often try to copy the behavior of loved ones.[28] For this reason, families are a very important agent of socialization, serving as an intermediary between children and society.

Observing how parents react to different situations can affect values that are learned and beliefs that are developed. For example, how parents react to the police can set the stage for how children will view authority. Parents' views of poverty can affect the attitudes of their children about welfare and social services. Parents are often most influential in transmitting party identification to their children, especially when both parents are of the same political party. If children do not adopt their parents' political party, they are more likely to define themselves as independents than to align with the opposite party.[29]

Researchers have shown that parents are especially influential in teaching gender roles and racial attitudes. Children who are raised by mothers who work outside the home for wages, for example, tend to have more progressive views of gender. Girls who are encouraged by a parent to be more assertive tend to be more independent and to have more independent careers.[30] Prejudiced parents are more likely to have prejudiced children. Children learn bigotry directly (from parental attitudes and comments) and indirectly (from watching parental interactions with others). Once children are exposed to different factors in adolescence, however, the relationship between parental intolerance and children's bigotry diminishes.[31] Parental influence wanes when children mature and other factors increase in importance.

Recent research concerning the influence of the family on political values has been mixed, finding that the actual levels of influence depend on a number of factors. Families with strong relationships and strong mutual ties tend to be the most likely to transmit values. As the nature of the family changes, we will need to continue examining its influence in shaping the development of children's values. Children today are more likely to be home alone and less likely to spend time with their parents, for example, and the number of families eating together has steadily declined. Moreover, the number of children living in single-parent homes has increased. In 1957, for example, 45 percent of all households were married couples with children; today that number has declined to less than 20 percent. In 2015, 19.76 million children under 18 lived with a single parent (up from 5.83 million in 1970).[32] It's not hard to see that these changes in family structure and interaction may affect the role families will play in influencing children in the future.

School

Schools teach political knowledge, the value of political participation, and the acceptance of democratic principles. Their effectiveness in doing so, however, is debated. Schools seem to be more effective in transmitting basic political knowledge than in creating politically engaged citizens.

Elementary schools introduce children to authority figures outside the family, such as the teacher, the principal, and police officers, while also teaching about the hierarchical nature of power. In doing so, the schools prepare children to accept social order, to follow rules, and to learn the importance of obedience. Children learn that good citizens obey the laws (just as good children obey the rules of the schools and of their parents). School elections for student council and mock presidential elections teach students important democratic principles and procedures, such as the notion of campaigning, voting, and majority rule. Most children emerge from elementary school with a strong sense of nationalism and an idealized notion of American government, thus building a general sense of goodwill for the political system that lays the foundation for future learning.[33] As they mature, children start to see their place in the political community and gain a sense of civic responsibility.

High schools continue building "good citizens" through activities and curriculum. Field trips to the state legislature and classes with explicit political content can result in a greater awareness of the political process and the people involved in it. The school curriculum teaches political facts, while the school atmosphere can affect political values. Students with positive experiences in school, who develop trust in school leaders, faith in the system, and a sense of worthiness are more likely to show higher levels of support for the national political system. Students who feel they are treated fairly by school officials tend to have more trust in officials and feel less alienated from their government.[34] Civics classes in high school are a potentially good mechanism for encouraging student engagement in politics. Researchers have found that the simple existence of such classes is not enough to produce civically engaged students; the dynamic of the class is also important. Civics classes that are taught by people who generally like the subject matter and who themselves are politically engaged are far more successful in positively socializing students. On the whole, however, high school seniors are not very well-informed about politics, are not very interested in politics, and have only moderate levels of support for democratic practices.[35]

Research consistently demonstrates that a college education has a liberalizing effect concerning noneconomic issues. Adults with college experience tend to be more liberal on social issues than adults with less education. Several explanations have been put forward to account for this phenomenon. College tends to make individuals aware of differences between people and allows them to see the complexity of public policy issues. In classes such as the one you are now in, students are exposed to controversies in our society and learn that the issues are far more complicated than previously thought. Moreover, they learn that intelligent people can disagree. Therefore, they tend to be more supportive of changing opinions and less supportive of the status quo. College students often meet a wider range of people than they had contact with in high school, giving them evidence to reject some social stereotypes and prejudices and to accept more diversity. Also, college faculty members are significantly more liberal than their students—and more liberal than most people in society. Notwithstanding individual differences among faculty, those in the liberal arts and the sciences tend to be the most liberal.[36] This disparity leads some conservatives to hypothesize that liberal college faculty indoctrinate students, causing them to become more liberal. Whatever the explanation, people with a college education are generally more liberal on social issues than those who have not been to college.

Schools are important agents of socialization, teaching children not only political facts but also a sense of patriotism and a belief in democratic practices. Children across the country begin their day by pledging allegiance to the American flag and reciting school rules. These practices help create a strong sense of loyalty and nationalism.

■ *Do you think that schools focus too much on allegiance, failing to teach students to critically analyze our government, leaders, and policies? When, if at all, should one learn to question authority?*

Peers and Community

Community and peers are also agents of political socialization. Your community consists of the people, of all ages, with whom you come in contact through work, school, or your neighborhood. Peers are friends, classmates, and coworkers who tend to be around the same age as you and who live in your community. Peer influence tends to be weaker than that of school and family, but our companions do affect us. Differences of opinions and preferences between generations are likely due to peer influence (especially regarding tastes in music, entertainment, clothing, hairstyle, and speech). Peers generally serve to reinforce one another, as people tend to socialize with those like themselves. Research shows that in heterogeneous communities, political participation tends to be higher, with more hotly contested and more competitive elections and more political debate, than in homogeneous environments. People are more likely to participate and pay attention to politics if they believe their vote counts, as is the case when there are a variety of views or disagreements and the election is closely contested.[37]

Politically diverse environments are also more likely to provide interesting stimuli and often result in a greater sense that one can have an effect on government.[38] Minorities living in racially diverse environments tend to have higher political **efficacy** than minorities living in segregated environments. Researchers found that African Americans living in predominantly black communities generally do not experience political socialization in a manner that encourages political participation and civic engagement.[39] Racial segregation tends to develop a sense of isolation and disinterest in the political system. Areas with high voter turnout, with politically engaged adult role models, and with racial diversity appear to be the best environments to raise politically aware and knowledgeable children who have a sense that their voice can count.

Religion

Religions and religious leaders are important instructors, particularly with respect to issues of morality, self-sacrifice, and altruism, and they are important factors in the development of personal identity. Individuals raised in religious households tend to be socialized to contribute to society and to get involved in their communities.[40] Conservative denominations and religions (such as Southern Baptist, traditionalist Catholics, and evangelicals) tend to impart more conservative attitudes (especially regarding abortion and other issues involving personal morality and sexuality) than more liberal churches do.[41] As we saw in Figure 10.4, different religious faiths have different opinions on same sex-marriage (as they do of other social issues). Those raised in religiously diverse communities are more likely to be engaged in politics and have higher levels of political participation.[42] Religion can act as a reinforcing mechanism of community and family values on a wide array of moral and political issues.

The Media

The media are an important agent of political socialization, with varied effects on public opinion. Many authorities believe that the effect of the media on political values and opinions has increased in the past several decades. Today, American children between the ages of 8 and 18 spend more than approximately 53 hours using entertainment media per week (averaging out to nearly 2,800 hours per year).[43] If we add to that the time spent listening to music, reading magazines, and watching movies and music videos, it becomes obvious that entertainment may have a big role in influencing values.

Entertainment media often present behavior at odds with what is approved in the family, schools, and places of worship. Promiscuous sex, drug use, and materialism are common in contemporary programming, with little attention paid to potential consequences. By the time a typical child reaches 18, he or she will have seen 16,000 simulated murders and 200,000 violent acts on television. Shockingly, programming for children often contains more violence than that for adults.[44] What can result is a competition for influence between media, parents, schools, and religion. Many analysts worry that this focus on negativity can adversely affect political efficacy and trust in government.[45]

efficacy
The belief that individuals can influence government. *Internal political efficacy* is the belief that individuals have the knowledge and ability to influence government. *External political efficacy* refers to the belief that governmental officials will respond to individuals.

FIGURE 10.4 Percentage of Americans who Favor Allowing Gays and Lesbians to Marry Legally by Key Demographic Groups

■ *Do the data presented here surprise you? Did you have any idea that opinion on same-sex marriage varied so dramatically by social group? Why do you think this is the case? How do these differences complicate governing?*

SOURCE: "Changing Attitudes on Gay Marriage," (Washington, D.C.: Pew Research Center), July 29, 2015, http://www.pewforum.org/2015/07/29/graphics-slideshow-changing-attitudes-on-gay-marriage/.

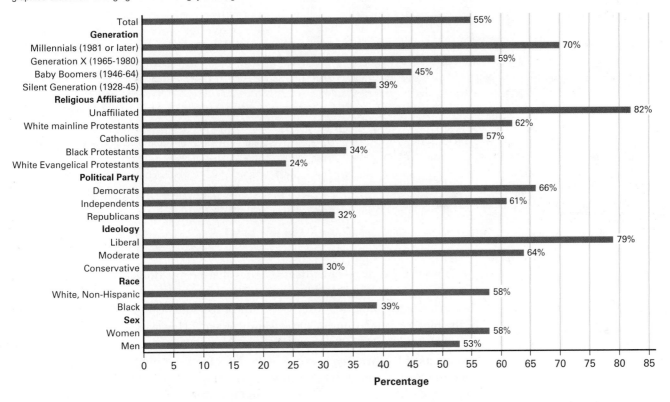

Category	Percentage
Total	55%
Generation	
Millennials (1981 or later)	70%
Generation X (1965-1980)	59%
Baby Boomers (1946-64)	45%
Silent Generation (1928-45)	39%
Religious Affiliation	
Unaffiliated	82%
White mainline Protestants	62%
Catholics	57%
Black Protestants	34%
White Evangelical Protestants	24%
Political Party	
Democrats	66%
Independents	61%
Republicans	32%
Ideology	
Liberal	79%
Moderate	64%
Conservative	30%
Race	
White, Non-Hispanic	58%
Black	39%
Sex	
Women	58%
Men	53%

Nighttime talk-show hosts often joke about politics, governmental officials, and current affairs. Since the departure of long-time favorite, Jon Stewart, John Oliver, host of HBO's *Last Week Tonight with John Oliver*, has grown in popularity. His first show about Donald Trump, from February, 2016, had nearly 26.3 million views in less than four months, becoming the news itself.

■ *Do you think viewers are better informed about politics because of the programs or because they tend to be better educated? Do you consider these shows to be "news programs"? Why or why not?*

PATHWAYS OF ACTION

CELEBRITIES AND GLOBAL ACTIVISM

Celebrities possess the unique ability to focus international attention upon world events. Increasingly, we have seen celebrities use their fame and prominence to raise awareness and money. For example, Global Green USA uses actors, athletes, and musicians (from Serena Williams to Orlando Bloom to Mark Ruffalo) in their "I AM" campaigns to raise awareness of the perils of global warming. The organization Look to the Stars: The World of Celebrity Giving, profiles philanthropic activities. They list Annie Lennox, Elton John, Bono, Bill Clinton, George Clooney, Paul McCartney, Sting, and Ellen DeGeneres as top activists. Matt Damon, for example, is the founder of H₂O Africa (which merged with WaterPartners to create Water.org). He is also one of the founders (along with George Clooney, Brad Pitt, and three others) of Not On Our Watch. He is also active in the ONE Campaign (which works to fight AIDS and poverty in

the developing world), and is an ambassador for ONEXONE (a children's rights organization). Save the Children, an international organization to help children in need around the globe, also has a number of celebrity spokespersons, including Gwyneth Paltrow, Jennifer Garner, America Ferrera, Ben Stiller, Chris Daughtry, Gwen Stefani, Hugh Grant, Keira Knightley, Kelly Clarkson, Sacha Baron Cohen, Randy Jackson, Pink, Julianne Moore, Daniel Radcliffe, Stephen Colbert, and Ben Affleck. Examples of these types of activities abound.

Many celebrities are using their fame to alter the public's perception about our definition of community and social responsibility and to promote a sense of shared global citizenship. While some may diminish celebrity efforts as being superficial and self-serving, their actions speak loudly and focus interest on areas in desperate need of attention.

However, recent research demonstrates that people do learn valid political information from the media, although great variation exists. A 2015 poll by the Pew Research Center found that only one-third of the American public knew that three of the nine Supreme Court justices were women.[46] However, differences existed in knowledge levels depending upon the source of media regularly consumed. Regular consumers of the *New Yorker* and *Atlantic*, NPR (national public radio), and *Hardball* were the best informed, while audiences of religious radio programs, the Weather Channel, CBS News, *Access Hollywood*, and the *National Enquirer* had the lowest levels of political knowledge. In addition to news consumption patterns, other factors like age and educational attainment are related to differences in political knowledge. Generally speaking, younger people are less politically knowledgeable than older people, and the more educated are far more knowledgeable than are the less educated. Politically engaged individuals have much higher levels of political knowledge than those who do not habitually vote or discuss politics.[47]

Social Media

While such an integral part of American society, online news only began to become popular in the late 1990s. When Facebook was created in 2004 and Twitter in 2006, few imagined how fundamentally important they would become for the dissemination of news and sharing of ideas. Traditional news sources (like newspapers and television news programs) have struggled to adapt. Most have transitioned into hybrid delivery systems in which they have both online and traditional stories. Changing technology has profoundly altered the manner in which people consume political news and the manner in which they relate to others and form connections.

Social media has impacted our world in a myriad of ways, many of which are positive but some of which are extremely troubling. Facebook and Twitter have gotten much praise for helping antigovernment protesters unite in Egypt and Tunisia during the Arab Spring demonstrations, which helped bring about massive changes in these Middle Eastern countries in 2011. The ability for the protesters to coordinate activities and plan demonstrations helped sustain the protests and were instrumental in the overthrowing of the totalitarian governments. The Obama presidential campaigns in 2008 and 2012 ushered in a new era of large-scale usage of social media to successfully mobilize voters and enhance virtual connectivity. Black Lives Matter relies heavily upon social media to organize and sustain protests across the country. Academic research is mixed on the extent of the influence of Facebook posts on voting behavior, but some research suggests that close friends and family can influence others to become politically engaged and may influence voting behavior.[48]

As we will see in Chapter 11, people regularly use social media to get news about politics, with young people using Facebook more than any other source as their most popular place to get news about politics and the government. Social media has great potential to expand our world, allowing us to gather information from a huge variety of different sources and augment our exposure to diverse ideas, thoughts, events, and people. However, much of the information on social media is very narrowly cast, allowing many to seek out information which conforms to rather than challenges preconceived world views. Concerns about the objectivity of digital news sources are great. A good deal of the information available online has decidedly partisan bias and is often factually inaccurate or grossly distorted. Professional journalists are taught ethical standards required for good journalism, while many online "journalists" have not been exposed to these ethical requirements and professional training and do not have editorial oversight and accountability. Consequently, being savvy consumers of digital news in this complex marketplace of information is fundamentally important. One highly efficient way to consume news is to follow a few different journalists whom you admire (from a variety of news sources, both domestic and international) on Twitter. Their tweets can keep you informed with balanced news coverage.

Terrorist groups have been very successful in using the Internet and social media to recruit and train followers, coordinate attacks, and raise money. Al-Qaeda, ISIS, Al-Shabab, Boko Haram, the Taliban, and domestic hate groups like the KKK have all been aggressively using social media to advance their political agendas. On October 8, 2015, James Comey, Director of the FBI, stated in testimony before the Senate Committee on Homeland Security and Governmental Affairs that the use of social media by terrorist organizations is one of the greatest threats to national security.[49] On February 5, 2016, Twitter announced that they were suspending 125,000 accounts that have been associated with extremism since mid-2015. They have pledged to take more action to diminish the ability of extremists to use Twitter to support and promote terror, but given the enormous amounts of user-generated content on Twitter, Facebook, YouTube, and other social media platforms, experts are doubtful these efforts will be sufficient.

Events

No event of recent decades has had a more dramatic impact on Americans than the terrorist attacks of September 11, 2001. In response to the attacks, the United States embarked upon two, initially popular though increasingly contentious, wars in Afghanistan and Iraq. In the short term, these events altered public opinion in two ways. First, the public has become more aware of the danger of terrorism. Before the terrorist attacks, many Americans did not believe that our country was vulnerable to terrorist threats. Americans often viewed terrorism as a problem that occurred in other countries (with the clear exception of the Oklahoma City bombing in 1995). Following the 9/11 attacks, the number of Americans who expressed confidence that our government could keep us safe declined significantly. The second observed short-term change was a surge in patriotism and a sense of uniting in battle, especially in the years immediately following the attacks. As time has passed, the urgency of terrorism has diminished, as has the popularity of the wars in Iraq and Afghanistan, but a general sense of fear remains higher than before the attacks.

Research shows that important events can affect the socialization process, because significant events focus national attention. By examining other events in our nation's past that were of great political importance—the attack on Pearl Harbor, the Vietnam War, the assassination of President Kennedy, and the Watergate scandal are all examples—we can see how shocking events can alter politics.

Social Groups and Political Values

10.5 Assess how membership in various social groups impacts political views and behavior.

People with similar backgrounds tend to develop similar political opinions. Dividing Americans along lines of social class, education, religion, race and ethnicity, and gender, these group characteristics also tend to influence public opinion on a variety of domestic and foreign policies.

Before beginning this section, you need to keep in mind several important points. First, we're going to be generalizing about how various factors influence political opinions, but many exceptions exist. Moreover, the effects of specific factors may vary from issue to issue. Rarely do opinions on issues stem from one source—usually, opinions are influenced by many different factors.

We use the term **crosscutting cleavages** to explain how two or more factors work to influence an individual.[50] These cleavages represent splits in the population that separate people into groups and complicate the work of political scientists, for determining which factors are the most important in shaping particular attitudes proves difficult. These cleavages can also moderate opinions and lead to stability over time. Take income as an example. There are many issues on which the poor agree; there are also many issues on which they disagree. As you will see, income has an important effect on opinions, but it is not the only factor. Race, gender, region, and religion (to name a few) also affect individuals.

crosscutting cleavages

Cleavages are divisions in society (such as race, sex, religion) that separate people into groups. A crosscutting cleavage is when two or more cleavages work together to impact political behavior and values.

Economic Bases of Partisanship and Public Opinion

Political socialization does not explain the distribution of party loyalties in the United States. Socialization is helpful in describing *how* rather than *why* an individual acquires party loyalty. An important factor that does determine why an individual becomes a Democrat or a Republican is a person's economic standing and that of his or her parents. One principal generalization that you can make about loyalties to the parties in modern times is that they are often based on socioeconomic status.

Traditionally, Democrats have been regarded as the "party of the people" and Republicans as the "party of the rich." This characterization goes back to the 1800s, but it became more pronounced in the 1930s, when Democratic President Franklin D. Roosevelt launched his New Deal programs in the midst of the Great Depression. Labor legislation, Social Security, and minimum-wage laws all reinforced the Democratic Party's image as the party of the have-nots. Even African Americans, who had aligned with the Republican Party after the Civil War, partly in loyalty to President Abraham Lincoln, abandoned it in the 1930s for the Democratic Party. Ironically, by aligning with the Democrats, African Americans found themselves in the same party with racist white southerners. Beginning in the late 1960s, southern whites who had opposed or remained lukewarm toward racial integration flocked into the Republican ranks.

Generally speaking, social class and party loyalties are not as closely linked in the United States as in other Western democracies, however, distinct differences among white voters based upon social class seemed to have become more pronounced during the 2016 election. Both parties in the United States draw support from upper-, middle-, and lower-status groups. Thus neither party makes overt appeals that reflect sharp class differences. When it comes to purely economic issues, the more affluent tend to be more conservative than the less affluent on fiscal issues such as taxation, *assuming that each group is defining its politics strictly on the basis of self-interest*. But when we add education to the equation, liberal views tend to increase along with rising income. In fact, the higher the level of education a person has received, the more liberal that individual tends to be on social and cultural issues. And because education is highly correlated with income, the relationship is complicated. For example, in 2015 the median weekly earnings by highest level of education showed clear differences:

$1,730 for individuals holding advanced professional degrees;
$1,137 for recipients of bachelor's degrees;
$678 for high school graduates;
$493 for adults with less than a high school diploma.[51]

Education

As we've discussed, education tends to increase citizens' awareness and understanding of political issues, often having a liberalizing effect when it comes to nonfiscal social issues. For example, a college-educated person will be more likely than a less-educated person to choose personal freedom over social order (when they conflict). Thus the more educated groups are more likely to favor gun control and to want limits placed on police authority. Differences based on education in issues of foreign policy also exist. The less-educated tend to favor isolationist policies that would limit the role of the United States on the world scene, whereas the more educated favor greater U.S. engagement in international affairs.[52]

Rather significant differences in many areas of public debate exist based upon educational attainment. Better-educated people tend to be far more likely than the less-educated to support homosexual rights (especially the rights of the LGBT community to adopt children) and far more supportive of abortion rights. Often, however, the more educated (and hence the more affluent) tend to be more fiscally conservative with respect to economic issues like spending on the poor. The least economically secure people (as measured by income and education) tend to be the most supportive of increasing governmental spending on domestic social services, such as Social Security, Medicaid, and other forms of aid to the poor.[53] Whereas college-educated people generally favor governmental spending on social services, many of them are hesitant to support increased social spending, because it will result in higher taxes for them (the more affluent). The less-educated overwhelmingly favor increased government spending on social programs. Based upon early exit polls, significant differences existed between voting patterns in the 2016 presidential election, with the less educated more supportive of Donald Trump than the more educated.

Religion

Religion has always been extremely important in American life. In 2014, Pew Research Center conducted a major study about the religious landscape of the United States (with a similar study conducted in 2007). Their interviews of more than 35,000 Americans from all over the country provide a comprehensive view of the religious views and practices of Americans. They found that over 76 percent of Americans say that they belong to an organized religion (down from 83 percent in 2007), 77 percent say that religion is very or somewhat important to their lives (down from 82 percent in 2007), and 83 percent say that they are absolutely or fairly certain in their belief in God (down from 88 percent in 2007).[54]

Differences in ideology and support of political parties have more effect on voting than do socioeconomic distinctions. When income, education, and occupation are held constant, Catholics and Jews tend to be more liberal and support the Democratic Party, while nonsouthern Protestants tend to be more conservative and support the Republican Party.

In recent decades, these fairly homogeneous alignments have been growing more complicated. Motivated by issues such as abortion and gay rights, "traditional"

Roman Catholics today tend to vote Republican, while other Catholics—especially those strongly committed to the reforms of Vatican Council II in the 1960s—have remained in the Democratic column out of concern over social justice and peace issues. Protestants from the so-called mainline denominations (Episcopalians, most Presbyterians, many Methodists, and some Lutherans, for example) tend to be more split between the political parties.[55] However, white (but not black) evangelicals, who once were mostly either Democrats or nonpolitical, constituted a record 51 percent of the GOP voters in the 2000 presidential election.[56] Based upon early exit polls in 2016, white evangelical Protestants were the most supportive of the Republican Party, with 81 percent voting for Donald Trump, while Mr. Trump won 52 percent of the Catholic vote. In contrast, only 60 percent of all Protestants voted for Mr. Trump. Secretary Clinton won 68 percent of the unaffiliated vote, 71 percent of the Jewish vote, and 58 percent of the minority religious vote.[57]

When we examine the differences among religions on public policy issues, important trends emerge. On almost every nonfiscal issue, Jews consistently take the most liberal policy stances, while Protestants take the most conservative. Catholics typically fall in between.

Figure 10.4 depicts varying degrees of support for same-sex marriage among those who are unaffiliated with a major religion, white mainline Protestants, Catholics, Black Protestants, and white evangelical Protestants. The nonreligious are most supportive while white evangelical Protestants are least supportive. Of the religious groups regularly surveyed (several religious minority groups such as Jews and Muslims are often not sufficiently large enough in national samples to be included for analysis), white mainline Protestants were the most supportive of same-sex marriage in 2015, with Catholics close behind. Figure 10.5 illustrates

FIGURE 10.5　Party Identification by Religious Denomination

In 1988, white evangelical Protestants were evenly divided in their party identification between Democrats and Republicans. However, the division has since increased dramatically. Party loyalties for most other religions have remained more consistent over the same time period.

■ *Why do you think white evangelical Protestants have changed so much more than others? What consequences do you think this will have for both parties?*

SOURCE: "Party Identification Trends, 1992-2014," The Pew Research Center for the People and the Press, April 7, 2015, http://www.people-press.org/2015/04/07/party-identification-trends-1992-2014/#religion.

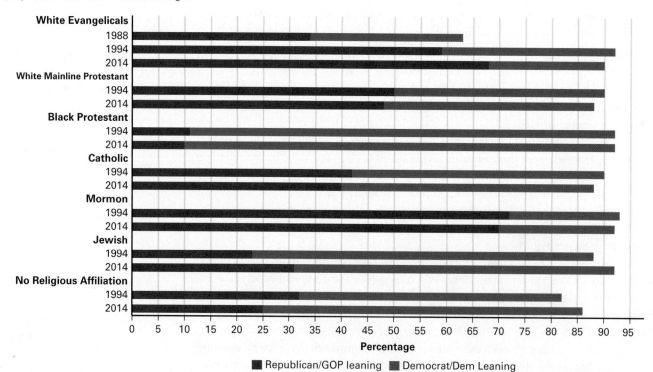

the differences in the distribution of party loyalties based upon religion. White Protestants, especially if they describe themselves as evangelicals, are more likely to be Republicans, while black Protestants (who are mostly evangelicals) are far more likely to be Democrats. The more religious white Catholics (as measured by the regularity of their church attendance) have become more supportive of the Republican Party, whereas the less observant Catholics vote more heavily Democratic (this distinction is less relevant for Hispanic Catholics, as a large percentage are Democrats regardless of religiosity). Jews, on the other hand, have become even more supportive of the Democratic Party than previously, while Mormons are strongly in favor of the Republican Party. Americans who say that they are not members of organized religions are far more likely to be Democrats than Republicans.

Race and Ethnicity

At the beginning of the twentieth century, the major ethnic minorities in America were from Ireland, Germany, Scandinavia, Italy, Poland, and other European countries. They came or descended from those who came to the United States in waves from the 1840s to the early 1900s. These immigrants and their offspring concentrated in urban parts of the Northeast and Midwest. The religious backgrounds of these immigrants differed from the predominant Protestantism of those who had settled colonial America. They were politically energized during the Great Depression, becoming an integral component of the great coalition of Democratic voters that Franklin D. Roosevelt forged in the 1930s. For many years, immigrant groups had political preferences that were consistently different from those of "native" Anglo-Saxons. As these groups have assimilated into society and risen in economic standing, however, these differences have been disappearing.

Since blacks were brought to North America as slaves, they have been at the bottom of the economic, political, and social totem poles. Their disadvantages still exist despite many important social and legal changes in our society.[58] Before the civil rights movement, black participation in American politics was generally quite limited. But in the generation between about 1930 and 1960, racial politics began slowly to change direction. First, during these years, many blacks moved from the South to northern cities, where they encountered very few obstacles to voting. Second, in the 1950s and 1960s, with the rise of black consciousness and the grassroots civil rights movement led by Martin Luther King, Jr., and others, African Americans emerged as a strong, national political force. Civil rights and social policies advanced by the Kennedy and Johnson administrations and the Democratic Congress in the 1960s convinced most blacks that the national Democratic Party was an advocate of racial equality and integration. Since then, black Americans have identified overwhelmingly with the Democratic Party.

Since the 1960s, whites and blacks have evaluated civil rights issues differently. Whites increasingly believe that "a lot" of positive change has occurred with regard to the life circumstances of African Americans, but fewer blacks feel similarly optimistic. Around 60 percent of African Americans say that black poverty is the result of social factors (discrimination, for example), while a plurality of whites (49 percent) attribute black poverty to personal characteristics.[59] Gallup has surveyed Americans about perceptions of race relations regularly since at least 2001. Perceptions remained relatively stable from 2001 through 2013 with around 70 percent of white respondents saying race relations were "very good" or "somewhat good." The percentage of black respondents stating race relations were very or somewhat good averaged around 63 percent. However, the percentage for both groups decreased substantially from 2013 to 2015. In 2015, 45 percent of white respondents stated relations were very or somewhat good, down from 72 percent in 2013. The percentage of African Americans stating that relations were very or somewhat good decreased

FIGURE 10.6 Party Identification by Race

SOURCE: Based on http://www.people-press.org/2015/04/07/party-identification-trends-1992-2014/#religion.

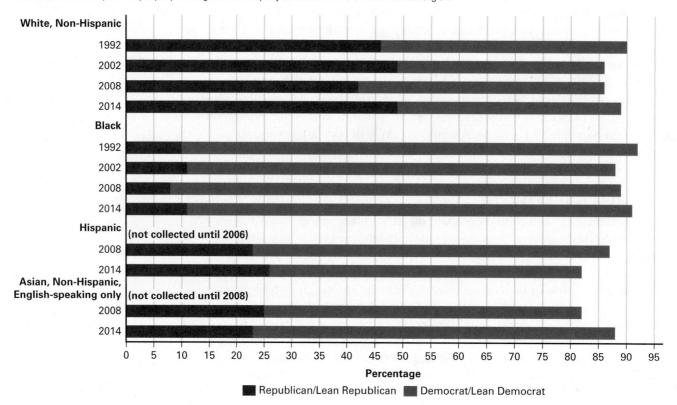

to 51 percent from 66 percent. Perceived relations between whites and Hispanics and Asians have remained relatively stable during this time period.[60] Although Hispanics made up over 17 percent of the general population—in southern states, California, the Southwest, and urban areas in northern states—they represent a sizable and a rapidly growing voting bloc. The Hispanic presence in key border states is very large: 30.2 percent in Arizona, 38.2 percent in Texas, 39 percent in California, and 47 percent in New Mexico. Latinos are the largest racial group in California and New Mexico.[61] Although Hispanics are politically strong in some communities, until the last several election cycles, they lagged behind African Americans in organizing across the nation.

African Americans and members of other minority groups display similar political attitudes for several reasons. First, all racial minorities (excluding second-generation Asians and some Cuban Americans) tend to have low socioeconomic status—a direct result of racism. Substantial differences in earnings continue to exist. Moreover, individuals in all minority groups have been targets of racial prejudice and discrimination. Hence, we should be sensitive to issues of race when evaluating many public policies.

Gender

gender gap

Differences in voting and policy preferences between women and men. After controlling for other factors, women tend to be more liberal and Democratic than men.

A **gender gap** separates American men and women in their patterns of voting behavior, party identification, ways of evaluating presidents, and attitudes toward various public policies. Some political scientists say that the difference in the way men and women vote first emerged in 1920, when newly enfranchised women registered overwhelmingly as Republicans. However, because women did not tend to vote in rates similar to those of men, it was not until the 1980 presidential election that the gender gap attracted much attention.

In that election, when the Republican challenger Ronald Reagan beat the Democratic incumbent Jimmy Carter, he did so with the votes of only 46 percent of the women—but he got the votes of 54 percent of the men. Substantial differences in policy preferences between men and women grew during the 1980s, with women considerably less likely to approve of President Reagan than men were. On many issues, a majority of women embraced the Democratic (or anti-Reagan) position—including a much-publicized movement for declaring a nuclear freeze (a unilateral U.S. cessation in the production and deployment of nuclear weapons), a demand for more spending on social programs, and criticism of the administration's increased defense spending.

According to research from the Center for American Women in Politics at Rutgers University, consistent differences persist between men and women on key issues of public policy. In foreign affairs, women are more likely to oppose U.S. military intervention abroad and are more apt to favor diplomacy in settling foreign disputes. Domestically, women are more likely than men to support programs that protect health care and meet basic human needs, to support restrictions on the possession and use of firearms, and to favor affirmative action and other governmental efforts to achieve racial equality.[62] For example, from 2001 until 2015, women had consistently higher levels of support for same-sex marriage than did men (Figure 10.4). On the whole, women tend to be more liberal on all social issues, from capital punishment to gun ownership to LGBT rights. As a consequence, more women identify with the Democratic Party than the Republican Party (see Figure 10.7). For example, since 1992, around 50 percent of women consistently identify with the Democratic party while on average around 35 percent identify with the Republican Party.[63]

The gender gap, coupled with the fact that more women than men vote, has changed the national agenda and the political landscape. Thus, during the last several presidential and congressional election campaigns, issues of education, health care, prescription drug coverage, and Social Security have dominated the agenda.

FIGURE 10.7 Party Identification by Gender

SOURCE: Based on http://www.people-press.org/2015/04/07/party-identification-trends-1992-2014/#religion.

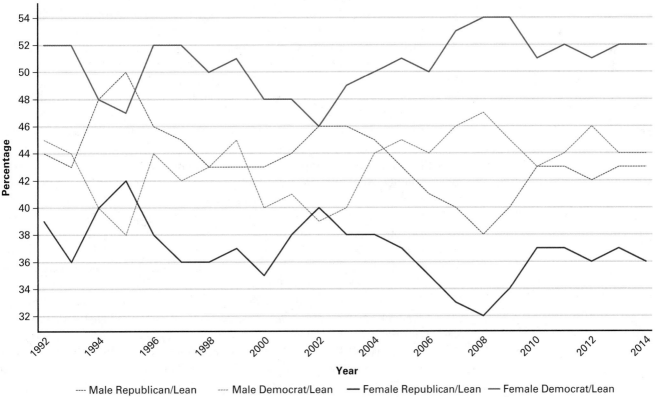

---- Male Republican/Lean Republican   ---- Male Democrat/Lean Democrat   —— Female Republican/Lean Republican   —— Female Democrat/Lean Democrat

Measuring Public Opinion

10.6 Explain how public opinion is measured.

As a wise individual, often said to be Benjamin Disraeli, once tartly observed, "There are three kinds of lies: lies, damned lies, and statistics." Political scientists and professional pollsters measure public opinion in a variety of ways, but polls are the most accurate tool to objectively measure public opinion.

Use of Polls

Polls represent an opportunity to view a snapshot of public opinion, and they allow officials a quick assessment of public policies. People who value citizen participation in a democracy are more likely to see the virtues of polling. Polls allow people to learn the collective preferences of their fellow citizens, but this ability has both positive and negative consequences. On the one hand, polls show people that others in their country may have different opinions, thus enabling individuals to grasp the complexity of many political issues. On the other hand, polls can also silence holders of minority opinions by convincing them that most people don't agree with them on a particular issue.

In examining the influence of polls on the public and on our leaders, Elizabeth Noelle-Neumann developed the theory of a "spiral of silence."[64] When the public learns about the dominant view on something or someone, dissenters come under pressure to remain silent and accept the majority viewpoint. One common way in which this phenomenon manifests itself is the "bandwagon" effect—the tendency for individuals to agree with the candidate or opinion that polls show to be attracting the most support or that receives the most media attention.

Many observers of contemporary politics are wary about using polls in our democracy. They argue that polls can be misleading, giving a false sense of the democratic process.[65] They can also be manipulated to advance a political agenda. Thus overreliance on poll data by our officials can be very dangerous.

The political scientist Benjamin Ginsberg thinks that polls weaken the influence of true public opinion.[66] Polls make it easy—perhaps too easy—for people to express their opinions. Often, polls give the impression that opinions are more strongly held than they really are and can create the impression that people actually have opinions on specific topics when in fact they may not. Other forms of political expression require more time and energy; people with deeply held opinions are therefore more likely to turn to them, giving a truer sense of public opinion. Polls rely on a passive form of expression (respondents do not volunteer to participate; they are solicited), hence you cannot be certain that poll results truly reflect the carefully considered opinion of members of the public who are interested in and care about politics. Polls may simply capture the fleeting thoughts of a group of people who are approached by the pollsters and agree to respond.

Other critics object that polls tend to measure bluntly what is sometimes a very complex entity—the opinions of the people. Reliance on poll data, say these critics, raises many concerns: Suggested opinions, sampling errors, the wording of questions, and the way poll questions are asked can all skew the responses that are obtained. Many critiques of polls emerged following the large number of polls that incorrectly predicted an easy victory for Secretary Clinton. The errors will certainly result in pollsters reconsidering some of their assumptions about the techniques employed in 2016.

One thing is certain though: Public opinion polling is widespread in our society. Each major TV network has paired with a print media organization to conduct polls—CBS News with the *New York Times,* ABC News with the *Washington Post,* and NBC News with the *Wall Street Journal.* And many newsmagazines—*Newsweek, Time,* and *U.S. News and World Report,* for example—routinely commission polls. Every year, several million people are called on to participate in polls. Our government alone conducts over a million survey interviews every year.[67] To avoid being manipulated, individuals should understand how polls are used, constructed, and interpreted.

Modern Polling Techniques

One of the major scientific breakthroughs of the twentieth century was the development of statistical sampling theory, a technique that made possible scientific public opinion polling and survey research. Because opinion poll results are now reported so widely in the media, you must be knowledgeable about polling methods in order to make appropriate use of poll results and avoid being misled or manipulated. Moreover, you must avoid relying on a single poll as a definitive measure of public opinion; often, individual polls provide just a limited "snapshot" view of what the public is thinking.

Researchers almost never question every person in a population; that would be prohibitively expensive and time-consuming. Instead, they take a **sample**—that is, they obtain a portion of the entire population. The goal of sampling is to be able to make generalizations about a group by examining some of its members. Its basic assumption is that individuals can represent the groups out of which they are selected. Because people in similar situations in life are likely to hold similar opinions, studying all of them is not necessary. On the other hand, because every person is somewhat different, talking to enough people from each major group is necessary so that individual uniqueness can be smoothed out and a typical response obtained.

One of the most important elements in a good sample is how *representative* it is of the major social groups that are apt to hold the opinions being researched. Choosing representative samples requires using the correct sampling technique and an appropriate sample size. The sampling technique most widely used today is based on the **probability sample**, a selection procedure in which all potential respondents enter the sample with an equal or known probability of being selected. Good probability techniques should ensure a representative sample if the sample is sufficiently large. Commercial polling agencies, such as Gallup or Harris, normally use national samples of around 1,200 people.

sample

A subset of the population under study; if selected correctly, it represents the population from which it was drawn with reliable and measurable accuracy.

probability sample

Selection procedure in which each member of the target population has a known or an equal chance of being selected. Probability samples are the most commonly employed by professional polling companies.

Survey Research

Once the sample has been drawn, the researcher must turn to the art of developing a good questionnaire that accurately elicits respondents' opinions.

DEVELOPING QUESTIONNAIRES The proper wording and phrasing of the questions are vitally important to producing reliable, objective data. How questions

Pictured here is Nate Silver, a statistician and unabashed numbers geek. Silver is the creator of the popular FiveThirtyEight blog and correctly predicted the winner in all 50 states in the 2012 presidential election as well as in nearly all of the Senate races. He was far less successful in 2016 and was widely criticized, though he was more accurate than others that year.

■ *Do you think we are over dependent upon polling in the United States? What concerns do you have about the uses of polls?*

are worded can dramatically affect the responses people give. Several criteria exist to assist in the development of high-quality questions. First, researchers must use language and vocabulary appropriate for the population under study. For example, different vocabulary would be used in surveying new immigrants to the United States than would be used to poll corporate executives. Questions should also be worded to allow socially acceptable responses, thus minimizing the chance of false replies. If people are not given an acceptable way in which to respond to questions, they may lie.

A good example is voting. People are raised to believe that voting is an important right and responsibility and that a good citizen in our society exercises this right. However, not all people vote. So, when asking about whether a respondent has voted, the researcher will obtain more accurate data if the response options include a socially acceptable reason for nonvoting. If the researcher simply asks, "Did you vote in the last election?" a good percentage of nonvoters might lie to avoid looking bad. However, if respondents are asked, "Did you vote in the last election, or because of work or family responsibilities were you too busy?" nonvoters can say that they were too busy without looking bad. Such sensitivity to social acceptance is an important factor in producing superior questions and research.

Also, to get a person's true opinion, questions must be neutrally worded. Let's say you were interested in a respondent's opinion of underage drinking. A number of ways in which you could phrase your question exist. You could ask, "What is your opinion of irresponsible, underage people who consume alcohol?" You certainly would get an opinion, but would it be an objective one? Probably not, because you characterize the person as irresponsible and are thus leading the respondent to agree with your characterization. A more objectively worded question would be to simply ask, "What is your opinion of underage people consuming alcohol?" Poll results can vary dramatically depending on the manner in which the questions are worded and the alternative responses provided. Reliable polling agencies will provide a copy of the survey if asked.

Once the sample has been drawn and the questionnaire developed, it's time to administer the survey. Questionnaires can be administered in a variety of ways—professionals typically do so in person, by mail, or by telephone. Each technique has advantages and disadvantages. The researcher must choose the method that is most appropriate for the research and also fits the available budget. When conducting political polls, researchers typically try to include only people who are likely to vote.

INTERPRETING PUBLIC OPINION POLLS   Not all polls are released to the general public. Some are conducted to provide politicians with campaign strategies or to determine likely responses to potential stands on an issue. Some groups commission polls but release the results only when they make them appear in a positive light. You must use caution when consuming public opinion data.

Furthermore, understanding how to interpret the information presented in a poll is an important skill to learn. Remember that polls rely on a sample of the target population. Even if all the issues identified earlier are accurately addressed, polls may still be inaccurate. This potential for inaccuracy is an unavoidable cost of using a sample rather than interviewing the entire population (which could never be done even if a pollster had access to unlimited resources). Along with the poll results, the pollster should present two measures of accuracy: the margin of error and the confidence level. We'll provide an example and then explain each.

Say that a hypothetical national poll of likely voters shows that 35 percent of respondents have a favorable opinion of an individual who is considering a run for president. How should you interpret this number? Thirty-five percent of the people who responded to the poll have a favorable view. However, we really aren't interested in the opinion of the poll respondents. We want to use the poll findings to figure out the likely feelings of the general population. To do this, we calculate the **margin of error**—a measurement of the accuracy of the results of a survey—to establish a range in which we think that the actual percentage of favorable ratings will fall. The **confidence level** is the percentage of confidence that we have that the poll truly represents the feelings of everyone in the population.

Going back to the original example, let's say that the margin of error is plus or minus 3 percentage points and that the confidence level is 95 percent. This means that we are 95 percent sure that the actual percentage of people in the country who have favorable opinions of the potential candidate is between 32 and 38 percent.

Although the mathematics of calculating these numbers are complex (and not something that you need to understand), to be an informed consumer, understanding how to interpret and apply both the margin of error and the confidence level is important. In many close elections, the numbers fall within the margin of error. When this happens, the media will say that the election is "too close to call."

Controversies Surrounding Polling

Call-in and Internet surveys, often called *pseudo-polls*, are controversial, because the results are often falsely presented to the public as scientific and reliable. Only individuals watching a particular program on TV, tuning in to a particular radio talk show, or visiting certain Web sites can participate in the poll. In addition, people who call in (especially if there is a cost in time or money) tend to hold more extreme positions than those who do not bother to participate. These surveys may be interesting, but they are statistically unreliable. The most reliable information is obtained when researchers select the respondents, not vice versa.

Contemporary technology has made many people question how representative samples are. Caller ID, call block, and other similar technologies have made reaching many people and selecting a random sample of the population difficult for pollsters. Moreover, refusal rates have been rising, with fewer and fewer of the people reached being willing to cooperate with the pollsters. In some surveys, less than 20 percent of calls result in a completed survey, raising the costs of surveys as well as the level of concern about their accuracy. In the 1960s, two-thirds of contacted people chose to participate. Today, cooperation rates hover around 14 percent for the national surveys that take place over a few days, and overnight surveys often have much lower rates.[68] However, despite these low levels, research indicates that the results are still representative.

Concerns have also arisen over the number of people who no longer use home phones but rely exclusively on cell phones. Research indicates that nearly 29 percent of U.S. homes are wireless-only with no land lines; however, research indicates that except for age, those who are only available by cell phones are similar to those who can be reached via landline phones.[69] This might, however, be a concern if the survey tries to include a large number of college-age individuals, who are more likely to rely exclusively on cell phones and who tend to move a lot.[70] Researchers account for these trends and challenges by weighting the responses to match the demographic composition of the population under study. Research by a number of professional polling organizations indicates that bias associated with issues with response rates are important to note but not insurmountable.[71]

One area of public opinion polling that has recently come under much scrutiny is the media's reporting of polling data during campaigns and elections—and especially the use on election day of exit polls to predict outcomes before the votes are counted. **Exit polls** are taken at selected precincts while voting is in progress, with the pollsters typically asking every 10th voter how he or she has voted and why. In the past, exit polls have been helpful for news organizations as they raced to be the first to predict the winners of elections. But in 1980, having gotten bad news from exit polls in states in the Eastern and Central time zones, President Jimmy Carter conceded defeat to

margin of error

A measurement of the accuracy of the results of a survey to establish a range in which we think that the actual percentage of favorable ratings will fall.

confidence level

The probability that the results found in the sample represent the true opinion of the entire public under study.

exit polls

Surveys of voters leaving polling places; used by news media to gauge how candidates are doing on election day.

Ronald Reagan 3 hours before polls on the West Coast had closed. Democratic officials criticized Carter and the networks, claiming that prematurely publicizing adverse poll data had caused many western Democrats not to vote, affecting many congressional, state, and local elections. As a consequence, the networks agreed not to predict the presidential winner of a state until all polls in that state had closed.

In the 2000 presidential election, the exit polls conducted by the Voter News Service (made up of the four major networks, CNN, and the Associated Press) were flawed by sampling errors. Faulty exit poll results in Florida—as well as forgetting that the state's western panhandle observes Central rather than Eastern time, so that voting was still going on—led CBS to predict the incorrect winner not just once but twice. As a consequence, the networks dropped the Voter News Service and, in 2004, used a new service. Exit polls in the 2004 and 2008 presidential elections were also criticized, especially those conducted in states with close elections. In the future, as we see more and more people choosing early voting, the accuracy of exit polls for predicting winners and providing glimpses into the motivations of voters will be even more precarious. In 2012 Mitt Romney's pollsters believed he was positioned to win the election (they appeared to have underestimated the effectiveness of the Obama campaign's voter mobilization drives). Similarly, most pollsters underestimated the support Donald Trump had across key battleground states and overestimated the enthusiasm Hillary Clinton had, especially among Hispanics, African Americans, and young people.

Poll coverage in elections more generally is also troubling. The media often take the easy road and focus on "horse race" coverage (who's ahead in the polls, who's gaining, and so forth), to the detriment of discussing issues and other matters of substance. In 2004, several weeks before Canada's national election, the Canadian Broadcasting Corporation abruptly quit preelection polling, stating that constantly reporting poll results deflected public attention from issues and emphasized the superficial. Many critics have called for the U.S. networks to follow suit. In May of 2015, Fox News announced that in order for Republican candidates to participate in the first national primary debate, they had to place in the top 10, on average, in the five most recent polls. Many criticized this decision, arguing that candidate standings in polls should not be used to determine participation in such important events.

Given all the concerns about public opinion polling that have been discussed in this chapter, many critics question the wisdom of the incessant reporting of polling to reflect public opinion and desires for social change. Some argue that we must rely on other forms of political expression to voice the views of the public; others believe that pollsters can adapt to these challenges and continue to provide important information about what the public is thinking.

Conclusion

Many people lament a fickle American public that they believe is so quick to change its mind. This may be true of some superficial issues; however, on the whole, levels of public opinion are relatively stable. While opinion does change, it is often slow and incremental, especially when it comes to controversial issues.

Political socialization—the complex process by which people learn political information, organize political knowledge and develop political values—provides a consistent mechanism for transmitting political culture from generation to generation. Important agents for socialization include the family, school, peers, community, religion, the media, and events.

Public opinion polling is an important device to gauge public sentiment and influence change in our society, but predicting when public opinion will be influential may be difficult. Politicians often use poll data to build support for policies and to avoid making unpopular decisions. This creates a reciprocal relationship in which public opinion can influence politicians *and* politicians can use public opinion to influence the people.

Today, public opinion polling operations in the White House have become institutionalized. Each modern administration routinely polls the public.[72] Elites often use poll data to claim legitimacy for their positions. When elites disagree, they try to use poll data to claim the high road, thereby minimizing opposition and garnering additional support for their agenda. Polls become strategic tools by which political leaders seek to sell their views and positions to the public.[73] Politicians often act strategically by "rationally anticipating" shifts in public opinion and examining how these changes can affect future elections. In anticipating these changes, leaders can strategically modify their positions. Thus, public opinion influences politicians directly, through elections, and also indirectly, because they tend to act rationally in anticipating change.[74]

CONFRONTING POLITICS AND POLICY

On Valentine's Day, 2012, Libertarian students at the University of Colorado at Colorado Springs planned events to expose the "dysfunctional lovefest" between corporations and political institutions at their "National Expose Cronyism Day." The student group, Young Americans for Liberty (YAL), joined with 250 groups across the country to draw attention to "crony capitalism" and to show their support for free-market capitalism. The group opposed government bailouts of banks and corporations and believes that governmental officials unduly interfere in the market showing preference to well-funded corporations.[75] YAL is the fastest-growing and most active pro-liberty organization on American college campuses. In 2009, there were only 96 chapters; however, that number grew to more than 600 in 2016.

ACTION STEPS

1. Explore libertarianism by reviewing policy and issue briefs published by the CATO Institute (http://www.cato.org/). Why do you think libertarianism holds a relatively strong ideological attraction for college students?

2. Imagine you were charged with explaining political ideology in the United States to a group of foreign visitors. How would you explain the competing theories? How would you explain the various ideologies of college students today? What examples could you give that demonstrate the link between public opinion and political action? How and when is public opinion influential in guiding government?

⟩ REVIEW THE CHAPTER

Public Opinion

10.1 Explain the relationship between public opinion, public policy, and fundamental values. (p. 318)

Public opinion is a far more complex phenomenon than many people appreciate. Grounded in political values, it tends to be very stable, but it can serve as a mechanism to promote cultural change.

Commentators disagree over the role that public opinion should play in influencing public officials. Some believe public opinion ought to have a limited role in American politics, arguing that people are too easily influenced and manipulated. Other political commentators believe that it is healthy in a democracy for public officials to track public opinion and act in accordance with it.

The Stability of Political Beliefs

10.2 Determine how and why public opinion changes and the factors leading to stability in values and beliefs. (p. 323)

Americans largely agree on a number of fundamental values, including liberty, individualism, democratic institutions, basic principles, and equality. Disagreements occur when the government translates these rather abstract ideas into specific public policies.

Public opinion tends to be stable, though we do see substantial shifts during times of crisis or as a reaction to an important event. As we saw with such issues as gay rights, civil rights, and women's rights, gradual changes in public opinion also occur, as a result of cohort replacement, reflecting and shaping our political and popular culture.

Political Ideology

10.3 Differentiate between the dominant political ideologies in the United States, and explain how value structures impact public opinion and political action. (p. 330)

Political ideology is a consistent set of personal values and beliefs about the proper purpose and scope of government. Once formed, most people's political ideology remains rather stable (barring a critical world or domestic event). The range of political ideologies in the United States is narrower than in other societies; most Americans place themselves fairly close to the center of the political spectrum. Liberals generally believe that government can be a positive actor to advance equality, while conservatives generally support governmental action only to promote order. Political ideology impacts voting behavior, policy preferences, and worldviews.

Political Socialization

10.4 Illustrate how individuals acquire their political values. (p. 331)

People acquire their political knowledge and beliefs through a process called political socialization. Family, schools, community and peers, religious groups, the media, and events all serve as agents of socialization, introducing individuals into the world of politics and influencing individuals' political values, beliefs, opinions, and ideologies.

Social Groups and Political Values

10.5 Assess how membership in various social groups impacts political views and behavior. (p. 338)

People with similar life circumstances and experiences tend to develop similar opinions and values. We see many significant differences between groups based on their income, education, religion, race or ethnicity, and gender. For example, women tend to be more supportive of social programs that benefit the poor and elderly than men. Understanding the socialization process and the way in which demographic factors affect public opinion is important in fully appreciating the diversity of our country.

Measuring Public Opinion

10.6 Explain how public opinion is measured. (p. 344)

Polls are used to measure public opinion on a plethora of issues that are important to Americans; however, poll data can be easily manipulated, and we must be cautious in using poll data to generalize about the population as a whole. Good public opinion polls are useful for gauging public sentiment, but many factors can adversely affect the quality of the data obtained. Such factors include the representativeness of the sample, the wording of the questions posed and the issues explored, and the manner in which questionnaires are administered. Understanding the issues surrounding public opinion polling is an important part of being an informed consumer of political news and information.

＞ LEARN THE TERMS

＞ EXPLORE FURTHER

In the Library

Aldrich, John H., and Kathleen M. McGraw, eds. *Improving Public Opinion Surveys: Interdisciplinary Innovation and the American National Election Studies.* Princeton, NJ: Princeton University Press, 2012.

Asher, Herbert. *Polling and the Public: What Every Citizen Should Know,* 8th ed. Washington, D.C.: CQ Press, 2011.

Clawson, Rosalee, and Zoe Oxley. *Public Opinion: Democratic Ideals, Democratic Practice,* 3rd ed. Washington, D.C.: CQ Press, 2016.

Corrigall-Brown, Catherine. *Patterns of Protest: Trajectories of Participation in Social Movements.* Stanford, CA: Stanford University Press, 2012.

Fiorina, Morris P., Samuel J. Abrams, and Jeremy C. Pope. *Culture War? The Myth of a Polarized America,* 3rd ed. New York: Longman, 2011.

Goidel, Kirby, ed. *Political Polling in the Digital Age: The Challenge of Measuring and Understanding Public Opinion.* Baton Rouge, LA: Louisiana State University Press, 2011.

Jackson, David J. *Entertainment and Politics: The Influence of Pop Culture on Young Adult Political Socialization,* 2nd ed. New York: Lang, 2009.

Kirshner, Ben. *Youth Activism in an Era of Education Inequality.* New York: New York University Press, 2015.

Lay, J. Celeste. *A Midwestern Mosaic: Immigration and Political Socialization in Rural America.* Philadelphia: Temple University Press, 2012.

Leighley, Jan E. and Jonathan Negler. *Who Votes Now? Demographics, Issues, Inequality and Turnout in the United States.* Princeton, NJ: Princeton University Press, 2014.

Lippman, Walter. *Public Opinion.* New York: Harcourt, Brace, 1922.

Nunnally, Shayla C. *Trust in Black America: Race, Discrimination and Politics.* New York: New York University Press, 2012.

Sniderman, Paul M., and Benjamin Highton, eds. *Facing the Challenge of Democracy: Explorations in the Analysis of Public Opinion and Political Participation.* Princeton, NJ: Princeton University Press, 2011.

Zaller, John R. *The Nature and Origins of Mass Opinion.* New York: Cambridge University Press, 1992.

On the Web

For more information on public opinion on current controversies, visit Gallup Organization: *http://www.gallup.com.*

For reports on trends in American public opinion visit PollingReport.com: *http://www.pollingreport.com.*

To explore more about European public opinion visit EUROPA—Public Opinion Analysis of Europe, Eurobarometer Surveys: *http://ec.europa.eu/public_opinion/index_en.htm.*

To learn more about human sexual development visit Kinsey Institute for Research on Sex, Gender, and Reproduction, University of Indiana: *http://www.kinseyinstitute.org/.*

For more information on gay, lesbian, transgender, and transsexual political activism visit National Gay and Lesbian Task Force: *http://thetaskforce.org.*

For more public opinion data visit Polling Report: *http://www.pollingreport.com/.*

To learn more about academic polling visit National Opinion Research Center (NORC), University of Chicago: *http://norc.org.*

For more on public opinion in the United States visit Kaiser Family Foundation: *http://kff.org/polling.*

American National Election Studies is regularly conducted to collect academic data on the voting behavior of Americans. For more information visit *http://www.electionstudies.org.*

For extensive archival survey data visit Roper Center for Public Opinion Research: *http://www.ropercenter.uconn.edu.*

Learn more about an association for public opinion and survey research professionals at American Association for Public Opinion Research (AAPOR): *http://www.aapor.org.*

Pew Research Center for the People and the Press: *http://people-press.org.*

11

THE POLITICS OF THE MEDIA

Through the diligent work of journalists, the truth about the shooting death of 17-year-old Laquan McDonald, who was unarmed, emerged, stimulating wide-spread outrage. Pictured here are protestors on December 24, 2015 calling for the resignation of Chicago Mayor Rahm Emanuel (Democrat).

■ *How important do you think the investigative power of journalists should be? Are there situations where you believe journalists should be censored?*

→ LEARNING OBJECTIVES

11.1 Evaluate the roles played by the media in shaping American politics.

11.2 Outline the development of the American media.

11.3 Illustrate the functions of the media in American politics and society.

11.4 Assess how the media can be influential in American politics.

11.5 Establish how the media have an impact on the cultural values and political opinions of the American public.

11.6 Contrast the rights of a free press to the government's authority to restrict content.

HOW POWERFUL ARE THE MASS MEDIA IN THE UNITED STATES?

On October 20, 2014, Laquan McDonald was shot and killed by Chicago Police Officer Jason Van Dyke. Initially the police reported that the 17-year-old African American teenager lunged at police officers investigating car break-ins. The video of the shooting that occurred less than 30 seconds after Officer Van Dyke arrived at the scene (and six seconds after he exited his vehicle) was only made public after dogged efforts by Chicago journalists. Without the release of the video over fourteen months after the shooting, initial police reports of the incident would have been accepted. The police claimed that McDonald was advancing toward Officer Van Dyke, when in reality he was walking away. McDonald was also repeatedly shot while lying on the ground.

The shooting was initially reported upon by local media with little fanfare and would have been forgotten had it not been for the extraordinary efforts of a few individual journalists and one college professor. On December 8, 2014, Jamie Kalven (a freelance journalist and activist) and Craig Futterman (a University of Chicago Law School professor) issued a statement calling for the release of the police dashcam video of the shooting after being alerted to the horrific nature of the video by a whistleblower. In February 2015, Kalven obtained a copy of the autopsy report where he learned that McDonald was shot 16 times (reports made public prior to this time failed to specify the number of times McDonald was shot). McDonald suffered wounds to the left chest, right chest, left elbow, right elbow, scalp, neck, right upper arm, right hand, right upper leg, left upper back, and right lower back. He also had PCP in his system.

The *Chicago Tribune* filed three separate Freedom of Information Act requests to the police department, the city's legal department, and the Independent Police Review Authority Board. All of the requests were denied. In April, the city approved a $5 million settlement to the McDonald family (before they even filed a lawsuit). Chicago Mayor Rahm Emanuel (Democrat) stated that the police and FBI were withholding the video while they conducted their investigation, and city officials asserted that releasing the video would jeopardize a fair trial. In May 2015, another freelance journalist, Brandon Smith, filed a Freedom of Information Act request with the Chicago Police Department requesting the video. After his request was denied in August, Smith sued the police department to force them to release the video. In November 2015, Illinois Attorney General Lisa Madigan (Democrat) sent a letter to the police stating they could not withhold the video. Later that same month, Cook County Judge Franklin Valderrama ordered the city to release the video by November 25. On November 24, 2015, the graphic and horrific video was released. Mayor Emanuel and Chicago Police Commissioner McCarthy held a press conference at which Smith, the journalist who sued the department to successfully require the release of the video, was not allowed to attend. Hours prior to the release of the video, Officer Van Dyke was arrested on first-degree murder charges. Widespread protests followed the release of the video, the police commissioner was fired, a Justice Department investigation was launched, and a call for the resignation of Mayor Emanuel was made. In August 2016 the police superintendent called for the firing of seven officers for allegedly making false reports in initially supporting Officer Van Dykes's account of the events. Had Smith not so diligently pursued the efforts begun by Kalven and Professor Futterman, the truth about McDonald's death might never have been discovered and the people responsible not held to account.

The media, through their efforts to uncover the facts about events or to cover events of great importance, help us develop a visual image of events—even though we were not present. These impressions attest to the power of the media in shaping the way people think about themselves, their communities, their government, and their world, making the media important actors in shaping and reflecting cultural change. As McDonald's death so powerfully demonstrates, the contemporary media play important roles in investigating events, allowing us to see the world beyond our everyday lives, and providing the opportunity to share experiences and events. This tremendous power, however, comes with great responsibility. One of our aims in this chapter is to look at how important the media are in the cultural change pathway, paying attention not only to the media's potential to impact the political agenda but also to both reflect and shape political culture.

Mass Media

11.1 Evaluate the roles played by the media in shaping American politics.

mass media

The means by which information is transmitted to a large population across a large region. The mass media includes television, radio, magazines, newspapers, and the Internet.

The **mass media** refers to the portion of the media—especially television, radio, newspapers, Internet news sources, and magazines—that is designed to transmit information to a large audience across a large region. The importance of free media in a democratic society cannot be exaggerated. The success of our democracy depends on our being informed and aware about the policy issues facing our nation as well as the action—or inaction—of our government leaders in response to those issues. Your effective involvement as an actor in the country's democratic governing process, whether as a voter, an interest group member, or a political candidate, depends on your knowledge of current events. It is through the media that you see world events beyond those directly observed in your private life. The media show us the "big picture" worlds of politics, entertainment, sports, culture, and economics, as well as the lives of people living in other countries and other cultures.

The media's behavior receives intensive scrutiny, for it is widely asserted that the media are powerful in socializing individuals' attitudes, beliefs, and behaviors. Furthermore, many people believe that the media shape the actions of government officials; some have even called the media the fourth branch of government. However, as you read this chapter, you should question how influential the mass media actually are. Rather than *shaping* our values and beliefs, do the media simply *reflect* them? Or do they do both—shape as well as reflect our cultural values and struggles?

marketplace of ideas

The concept that ideas and theories compete for acceptance among the public, allowing for public debate and heightened awareness.

The media, public opinion, and democracy are linked together in an interactive relationship; each affects the others. All democratic governments must allow for a **marketplace of ideas**, in which differing opinions and values compete for acceptance among the public. The media make possible, on a mass scale, this vitally important public debate over opposing opinions, ideas, and thoughts. The media also serve as a "communications bridge" between the governed and the governing power. This two-way flow of information, from the government to the people and from the people to the government, is fundamental in a representative democracy (and obstructing this two-way information flow is a tactic that dictators use to preserve their power).

Most Americans know that the media are powerful. The media's news coverage can manipulate public opinion, influence policymaking, and affect elections and even the economy, and the entertainment component can also mold our political, social, and economic values. Today, the average American high school senior has spent more time watching TV than attending school.[1] Even what is learned in school is often influenced by the media's portrayal of events. The average American adult spends nearly half of his or her leisure time watching TV, listening to the radio, and reading newspapers or magazines; the single greatest amount of time is spent watching television. Moreover, TV remains the primary source of news and entertainment in the United States, followed closely by the Internet. The Internet is now the second most popular news platform (behind television news); however, an overwhelming number of Americans get their news from multiple sources in a typical day.[2]

The media provide the opportunity for millions to share events and experiences, sometimes—as with urban protestors—with a dramatic power to alter the political climate and world events. We do not observe firsthand most of the things that happen in the world, and therefore we rely on the media to be a mirror to the world and to supply us with almost all of our political knowledge.

Walter Cronkite, the CBS news anchor of the 1960s and 1970s, always ended his broadcast with the words "And that's the way it is." The influence of Cronkite, consistently cited as one of the most trusted people in America, was shown dramatically in 1968. During most of the 1960s, Cronkite had expressed support for the war in Vietnam, but that changed after he visited Southeast Asia in early 1968. Upon returning home, he took the unprecedented step of interjecting a personal opinion at the end of his broadcast on February 27: "For it seems more certain now than ever that the bloody experience of Vietnam is to end in a stalemate." President Johnson, after watching Cronkite's broadcast, is quoted as saying, "That's it. If I've lost Cronkite, I've lost Middle America." A month later, Johnson announced his decision not to seek reelection. Cronkite's words summed up the goal of his news program: his attempt to give Americans a glimpse into the larger world in which they lived. Today, national recognition of top news anchors is low. In 2014, only 27 percent of Americans could recognize a photo of Brian Williams (despite the fact that he was the anchor of *NBC Nightly News*, the single most popular unique source of the news in the United States at the time with an average of 8.5 million viewers per night). In 1985, 47 percent could recognize Dan Rather (the most popular anchor that year).[3]

The media's claim to be a mirror to the world raises many questions. Is this mirror an all-inclusive, unbiased, and neutral representation of world events? Or does the mirror reflect selective pictures, ideas, and opinions? Concerns over the objectivity of the media have caused a good deal of disagreement, which we will discuss throughout this chapter.

Given the impact of the media on public opinion and behavior, many people ask who should control the news. Authoritarian regimes assume that the government knows what's best for its citizens and thus seek to control the flow of information, thereby molding what the public thinks about and believes. Authoritarian governments also believe that news and entertainment programs should not question government or its policies and should instead build support and loyalty. Conversely, democratic societies assume that government officials and candidates for office can and do make mistakes. This assumption is inherent in the American governing structure, with its checks and balances and its division of power. Democracies therefore insist that the public needs a free press to keep government in line. The citizens of a democracy need to challenge the officials' policies and, through public debate and discussion, build consensus and develop better policies. While we may be frustrated at times, especially when we don't agree with the media's portrayal of a news event, a free press is essential for democracy.

From 1962 to 1981, Walter Cronkite (1916–2009) served as anchor of the *CBS Evening News*, becoming one of the most trusted people in the country. His trademark exit line, "And that's the way it is," perfectly characterized his efforts to present fair, accurate, and reliable news to his viewers. He is best remembered for his coverage of the Cuban Missile Crisis, the assassination of President Kennedy, and the Vietnam War.

■ *Do you think we will once again trust and admire journalists as the country did Cronkite? Why or why not?*

The Growth of Mass Media

11.2 Outline the development of the American media.

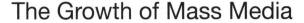

Print media were the first form of mass communication. As technology has developed and changed, so too have the mass media. Today, electronic media are rapidly evolving, with more and more people looking to different sources for information and entertainment.

Print Media

Newspapers were the first mass medium intended to communicate information in a timely fashion to a large audience. The early newspapers were almost always targeted at the elite, and they were created and funded to promote specific political and economic causes. Later newspapers, however, were less expensive and included more sensationalistic coverage designed to appeal to ordinary citizens.

NEWSPAPERS FOR THE ELITE   The first newspaper published in what would become the United States was the *Boston News-Letter,* which began appearing in April 1704. The paper was one page long and was published weekly. By 1725, Boston had three newspapers, and Philadelphia and New York City each had one. At the time of the Revolutionary War five decades later, 50 presses were operating in the 13 colonies.[4] The colonial authorities accepted these early newspapers in part because they generally tried to avoid controversial issues. Many of these early papers relied on government printing jobs as a key source to increase their revenue and could not afford to alienate local officials.

The Revolutionary War changed all this: Newspapers became important tools in building public support for resistance to British policies and, by 1776, for independence. The historian Arthur Schlesinger, Sr. wrote that the war for independence "could hardly have succeeded without an ever alert and dedicated press."[5] By the late 1770s, most presses were actively promoting independence. This activity continued during the war, reporting Patriot successes (often with exaggeration) while downplaying losses.

Newspapers were also used to promote public support for ratifying the Constitution. Compared to the extreme partisanship of the Revolutionary War, their coverage was more balanced, giving opportunities for opponents to discuss their concerns. The best examples of the persuasive use of the press to advance a political agenda are the series of newspaper essays written (anonymously) by Alexander Hamilton, James Madison, and John Jay, later published as *The Federalist Papers.* These essays were powerful and persuasive testimonies in support of the Constitution and helped ensure its ratification in the crucial state of New York. To this day, *The Federalist Papers* remain one of the best expressions of the Founders' original intent.

Following ratification of the Constitution, political leaders of the time thought it very important to promote newspapers, which informed citizens of major issues facing the new government. Sharing information was vital. Americans worried that the new federal government would prove too powerful and too remote for citizens to control. Using the press to report the actions of the new government kept people informed and eased their fears. The spread of political information through the press, declared the House of Representatives, is "among the surest means of preventing the degeneracy of a free government."[6] In view of the difficulties and expenses of publishing newspapers at the time, the federal government provided protection for newspapers by granting them special treatment—for example, by charging a reduced rate of postage for papers mailed to subscribers.

The number and circulation of newspapers in the early nineteenth century grew dramatically. For example, by the early 1830s, there were 12 daily newspapers published in Philadelphia and six in New York City. The number of newspapers published across the country soared, from around 200 in 1800 to around 1,200 in the mid-1830s.[7] These early newspapers were almost always created and funded to promote specific political and economic beliefs. For example, parties and political leaders normally encouraged and helped finance newspapers in important cities. Called **party presses**, these papers were best seen as arms of competing political factions. Most newspapers became unabashedly partisan, reaping rewards when their preferred party won an election and suffering when it lost. These papers were targeted to the elite, were relatively expensive, and did not have many subscribers. Ordinary citizens, however, often heard newspapers being read aloud and argued about in public gathering places, including taverns, inns, and coffeehouses.

NEWSPAPERS FOR THE ORDINARY CITIZEN   The year 1833 saw an important change in the nature of journalism in the United States: the advent of the **penny press**, so called because these daily newspapers cost a penny, versus about six cents for the

party presses
Newspapers popular in the early nineteenth century that were highly partisan and often influenced by political party machines.

penny press
Cheap newspapers containing sensationalized stories sold to members of the working class in the late nineteenth and early twentieth centuries.

established newspapers of the day. These penny papers, the first of which was the *New York Sun,* were marketed to the "common man." (In the sexist thinking of the day, politics, like business, was assumed to be a masculine pursuit, something in which women should not participate.) They offered less political and business coverage but a more diverse range of material—crime and human interest stories, scandals, and sports. These newspapers quickly became very popular, changing the face of journalism by making it a true mass medium. Newspaper publishers covered the costs of publication and made a profit by selling advertising. Unlike earlier newspapers, which had relied on officials or travelers for their political and economic news, the penny presses relied more heavily on reporters who would ferret out stories. These presses were less partisan and were more financially independent of politicians, significantly affecting the way in which politics was covered.[8] This change in the nature of journalism encouraged the press to become freer and more vigorous.

By the mid-nineteenth century, newspapers had become somewhat more objective and fact based. The invention of the telegraph in the 1840s helped this shift. The Associated Press (the world's largest and oldest news agency), created in 1848, inaugurated a new trend in journalism, marked by direct and simple writing designed to appeal to a wide range of readers.

So-called **yellow journalism**, featuring sensationalism, comics, and scandal in a fierce competition to sell papers, became popular at the end of the nineteenth century. (The name came from the yellow-tinted newsprint that some of these papers used.) William Randolph Hearst, one of the earliest practitioners of yellow journalism, forthrightly said, "It is the [*New York*] *Journal*'s policy to engage brains as well as to get news, for the public is even more fond of entertainment than it is of information."[9] As the newspapers' extreme sensation-mongering generated a public backlash, journalists responded by beginning to develop a code of professional ethics. Many newspapers, oriented toward a more "respectable" readership, rejected sensational journalism and still made profits by selling advertising. (The *New York Times* is a prime example.)

In the early twentieth century, the ownership of newspapers became more centralized, the result of competition that forced many papers to close or merge. This trend was well under way by the 1930s, when the Hearst chain (consisting of 26 daily papers in 19 cities) controlled 13 percent of the nation's newspaper circulation. In 1933, six newspaper chains owned 81 daily papers, representing 26 percent of national circulation.[10] This trend has continued, paralleling a drastic shrinkage in the number of newspapers. When the Tribune Media Company merged with the *Los Angeles Times* it owned 13 daily newspapers and 26 TV stations in 21 media markets. Following the merger, the *Tribune* reached nearly 80 percent of U.S. households through one or more media outlets.[11] Currently, the Tribune Media Company is the only multimedia company that owns newspapers and television stations in all three of the largest media markets (New York, Los Angeles, and Chicago). As we'll discuss later in the chapter, many people are concerned with this trend toward concentration of ownership, as well as allegations of the pending "death" of newspapers. Certainly, the environment surrounding the print media is challenging, but their longevity is testimony to their adaptability.

yellow journalism
Sensationalistic stories featured in the daily press around the turn of the twentieth century.

Electronic Media

The twentieth century witnessed an explosion in new means of mass communication, starting with radio and continuing with television and the Internet.

RADIO In 1900, a professor of electrical engineering at the University of Pittsburgh named Reginald Fessenden made the first experimental radio transmission. His successful broadcast made radio communication a reality. During World War I, little was done to exploit this technology commercially, but after the war, there was a rush to set up private radio stations. Presidential election returns were broadcast for the first time in 1920. In 1923, the country had 566 radio stations. At first, radio was primarily an activity for hobbyists who built their own sets. By 1924, however, some 2.5 million Americans owned radio receivers, and the era of mass radio had begun.[12]

When preassembled radios began to be sold in stores, a rapid and dramatic growth of radio audiences occurred. In 1930, for example, radio receivers—14 million of them—were in 45 percent of American households. One decade later, despite the Great Depression, 81 percent of households owned a total of 44 million receivers. By the late 1940s, when television started to become popular, 95 percent of households had radios.[13] Radio had become a source of information and entertainment for practically everyone.

The first radio stations were strictly local, but the formation of radio networks with syndicated programming began in the late 1920s. This trend was encouraged when Congress passed the Radio Act of 1927, which regulated the rapidly growing industry. The Radio Act established the airwaves as a public good, subject to governmental oversight. Under the new federal policy, radio stations were privately owned, with the government regulating the technical aspects and issuing licenses to broadcast on specific frequencies. Freedom-of-speech concerns kept regulation from extending to content.

Not all liberal democracies have privately owned broadcast media. In the United Kingdom, for example, the government owns and controls the British Broadcasting Corporation, known as the BBC. Private stations do exist in Britain and are regulated by an independent regulatory agency, which is responsible to Parliament, but the BBC is the largest broadcasting corporation in the world, sending out programming on television, radio, and the Internet.

Mirroring the trend in American newspaper publishing, radio broadcasting consolidated as the twentieth century wore on. In 1934, one-third of all U.S. radio stations were affiliated with a network, and more than 60 percent were by 1940. Clear Channel Communications currently operates more than 850 radio stations, reaching more than 110 million listeners in over forty countries each week. Today, radio stations that are not affiliated with networks often have weaker signals and face financial problems. Consolidation helps defer costs, but it also concentrates power.

TELEVISION   The arrival of television marked a breakthrough in personalizing communication from officials to the masses, allowing intimate contact in a diverse and large society. Like radio, once television was perfected, it grew at an astounding rate. Television became technically feasible in the late 1930s, but World War II delayed its commercial development. Commercial TV broadcasting began in the late 1940s. In 1950, there were 98 television stations in the United States, with 9 percent of American households having TV sets. Four years later, the number of families owning sets had exploded, from less than 4 million to 28 million. By 1958, some 41 million families had TV sets. Today, more than 1,700 broadcast TV stations are licensed in the United States, 99 percent of households have televisions, and more than 65 percent of all households have three or more sets.[14] When compared with print news and radio, television is unique in two ways—its immediacy (it can show events live) and its visual content, both of which convey a sense of legitimacy to viewers and increase emotional appeal.

Unlike newspapers and radio stations, which first were independently owned and only later consolidated into chains and networks, high costs dictated that almost from the beginning, TV stations were affiliated with networks, thus centralizing ownership. Today, however, the ownership of television broadcasting is becoming more competitive and diverse. In the last 20 or 30 years, network television's audience has changed dramatically. Cable TV, satellite TV, DVRs, Netflix, Hulu, and other streaming media have changed the nature of watching TV, reducing the audience for network programming. Meanwhile, the development of 24/7 news networks, such as CNN, Fox News, and MSNBC, coupled with their popular Web pages, apps, and news alerts have, altered the face of the broadcast media.

Years ago, television watching was a family affair, with most families owning only one television set. In 1975, for example, 57 percent of homes had only one television. Today 99 percent of households own at least one television with 65 percent having three or more.

■ *Should we be concerned over the fact that television watching has become less communal and more isolated? Should families make more of an effort to watch television together?*

THE INTERNET   The Internet has revolutionized the way we communicate. Developed in the early 1980s, it was originally used to network Department of Defense computers, linking the Pentagon with far-flung military bases and defense contractors. Later, it was expanded to include large research universities; e-mail was its first main use. The growth of the Internet is tied directly to the explosive growth of personal computers and the development of graphics programming. (Early e-mail appeared on a blank screen, with no cute graphics or icons, and users had to rely on function keys to send messages manually.) As the technology rapidly developed, the public responded avidly. By the late 1980s, the Internet was coming into widespread public use. Recognizing the Internet's economic potential, companies introduced Web pages and developed marketing techniques for the new medium. Public officials also acted strategically, establishing Web sites through which citizens could contact them electronically. Today, virtually all elected officials and organizations maintain Web pages to provide information and enable citizens to reach them directly.

Many Americans believe that everyone has easy access to the Internet and technology. In fact, while the number of people with access to the Internet has increased greatly, there is still a **technology gap** (also referred to as the **digital divide**) in the United States.[15] According to research conducted by the Pew Center, Internet access has grown dramatically in the last fifteen years. In 2000, only 50 percent of American adults used the Internet; in 2015, that number increased to 84 percent.[16] However, income, education, race, and age all influence a person's access to the Internet. Figure 11.1 gives details on the changing nature of Internet use by key demographics. Today, the differences in use are less pronounced than the patterns evident in 2000, however access to the Internet still varies significantly. Older Americans, for example, are still less likely to use the Internet, but far more seniors are online than 15 years ago. The same pattern is evident for the less educated, those with lower incomes, and racial minority groups. The growth in smartphone ownership has also changed the manner in which people access the Internet. In 2015, 64 percent of Americans had smartphones (up from 35 percent in 2011). For almost 20 percent of smartphone owners, Internet access comes primarily through their phones either because they lack broadband at home or do not have computer access.[17] Ten percent of Americans who own a smartphone do not have access to Internet by any other means. Younger adults and lower-income Americans are especially dependent upon their smartphones for Internet

technology gap (digital divide)
The differences in access to and mastery of information and communication technology between segments of the community (typically for socioeconomic, educational, or geographical reasons).

FIGURE 11.1 Internet use by Selected Characteristics

The Pew Research Center surveyed Americans to examine the availability and usage of the Internet. In this survey, Pew found that access to the Internet is not evenly divided across important demographic groups. People between the ages of 18 and 49 have the highest levels of access, as do those with higher educational attainment. The differences between lower- and higher-income Americans has substantially diminished since 2000. In years past, the differences between major racial groups was larger than it is today, though important differences still exist.

■ *How might the lack of access to the Internet become an issue in the future?*

SOURCE: Andrew Perrin and Maeve Duggan, "Americans' Internet Access: 2000–2015," Pew Research Center, June 26, 2015, http://www.pewinternet .org/2015/06/26/americans-internet-access-2000-2015/.

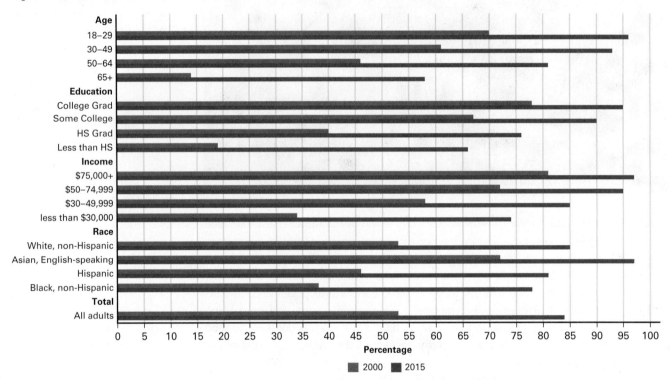

access. Fifteen percent of younger people are smartphone dependent for Internet access. Only 1 percent of people earning more than $75,000 are smartphone dependent while 13 percent of lower-income people rely exclusively upon their phones to access the Internet. Racial minorities are also more reliant upon smartphones for Internet access than are Caucasians.[18]

The benefits made possible by the Internet are likely to be achieved by people who have basic computer skills and thus are already interested in and informed about politics—that is, the educated, the more affluent, and younger people.[19] Although most public libraries provide free Internet access, not all people are able to take advantage of this opportunity (for example, if they have no access to transportation, lack basic computer skills, or are not literate). In July 2015, President Obama announced a new initiative to close the digital divide by bringing high-speed Internet access to poorer communities. President Obama launched a pilot program, ConnectHome, in 27 cities and one tribal nation to connect over 275,000 low-income households to broadband free of charge. The initiative stemmed from a recommendation from the president's Broadband Opportunity Council, created in March 2015. In March 2016, the Federal Communications Commission (FCC) announced a proposal to allow low-income households to use their phone subsidies (Lifeline) for broadband Internet access. Lifeline was initially created to allow low-income households to pay for land-line telephone services. The program was expanded to include cell phones. The new proposal would allow for the program to pay for in-home Internet. In February 2016, Google Fiber announced they were giving away high speed Internet service to thousands of low-income families across the country living in targeted public housing.

FIGURE 11.2 Age Gap for Campaign News Sources

Research shows great variation from generation to generation in news sources. For example, younger people are most likely to get their news online from Facebook, Google News, Yahoo news, as well as a variety of national television news programs. Conversely, Baby Boomers are more likely to get their news from local television news, network and cable news, NPR, and PBS.

SOURCE: Survey conducted March 19 - April 29, 2014. Amy Mitchell, Jeffrey Gottfried, and Katerina Eva Matsa, "Millennials and Political News," Pew Research Center, June 1, 2015, http://www.journalism.org/2015/06/01/facebook-top-source-for-political-news-among-millennials.

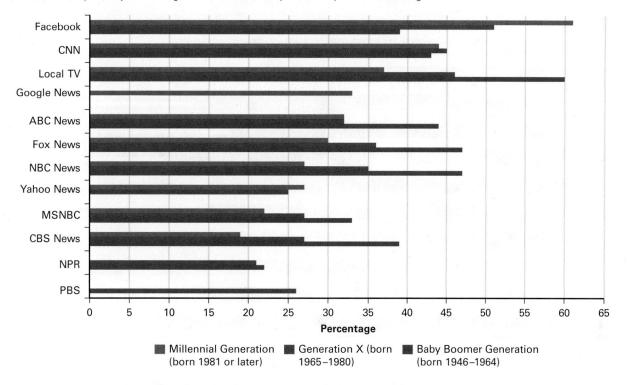

The first area targeted is Kansas City, Missouri. Eventually approximately 1,300 low-income families in Kansas City, Missouri and Kansas, will receive free Internet in their homes. Families in Austin, Texas, already receive free Internet through Google Fiber, however the Kansas City program goes a step further by providing faster connections and downloads.

One needs to use caution when obtaining information from the Web as the very nature of the Internet makes it a potentially dangerous place to get *reliable* information. Anyone with basic computer skills and the interest can create a Web page and a blog—and there is no mechanism to differentiate irrelevant, biased, or intentionally manipulative information from reliable and accurate knowledge. You need to be an informed consumer, aware of the trustworthiness of each online source and careful not to be misled or swayed by imprecise or biased information.

The instantaneous nature of the Internet has dramatically changed news reporting today. For example, Internet users whose service provider offers instantly updated headline news can read the main stories featured in the newspaper many hours before they appear in print. Consequently, the way in which people get their news has changed, with people relying less on local news programs, cable news, nightly network news, newsmagazines, and daily newspapers for information and more on the Internet and news from their service providers. In addition to the issues of race and class with respect to access to the Internet, age also affects the manner in which people consume news. Those under 30 are far more likely to get their news online than from the newspaper or television, whereas people over 50 are more likely to rely on television or the newspaper for their news information (see Figure 11.2).

In addition to changing patterns of news consumption, growth in the use of blogs and social networking sites (such as Facebook and Twitter) as a source of information on campaigns has occurred in the last few years. A remarkable 89 percent of people

FIGURE 11.3 Social Media and the News

A series of national surveys reveal that people are changing their pattern of news consumption from Twitter and Facebook. Adults are increasingly using social media to learn about the news. In two short years, the percentage of people using social media to learn about the news increased significantly.

■ *Do you think this is a positive or a negative trend? Does it matter where people get their news from? Why or why not?*

SOURCE: Social Media and News Survey, March 13–15 & 20–22, 2015, reported in Amy Mitchell and Dana Page, "The Evolving Role of News on Twitter and Facebook," Pew Research Center, July 14, 2015, p. 7, http://www.journalism.org/files/2015/07/Twitter-and-News-Survey-Report-FINAL2.pdf.

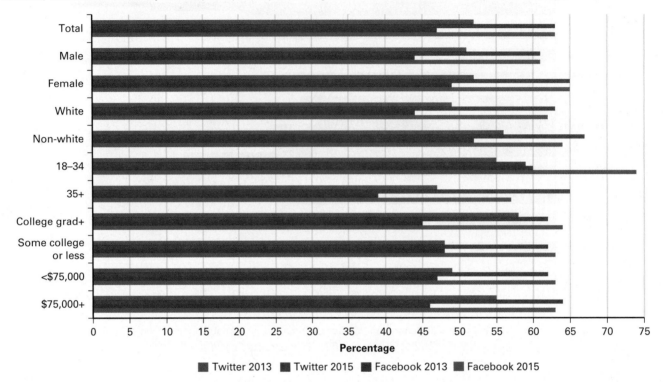

from 18 to 29 use social network sites, with approximately 30 percent of them reporting that they get campaign information from these sites. In total, 71 percent of online adults use Facebook, 22 percent use LinkedIn, 21 percent use Pinterest, 18 percent use Twitter, and 17 percent use Instagram.[20] Historically, fewer people follow the news on Facebook or Twitter, and almost all who regularly follow news on these social networking sites also get their news from other sources.[21] However, in just two years, the percentage of people of all backgrounds using social media to follow the media has grown significantly (Figure 11.3). What is especially interesting about the growth in people using social media to follow the news is that overall usage on each site remained steady during this time period. People are more likely to turn to Twitter to keep track of breaking news than Facebook; more Twitter users (almost 50 percent) follow news organizations compared with only 30 percent of Facebook users.[22] With this said, however, a large percentage of young people report consuming no political news. For example, 31 percent of young people reported that they had not read or viewed news even on digital devices in the previous day. This was the highest percentage of any age group. Another survey in 2012 reported similar results with 29 percent of the 18-to-24 age group saying they had read or viewed no news (on any platform) the previous day.[23]

Digital-First News Media

In the last five years, a number of digital-only news outlets (which rely exclusively on an all-digital platform) have emerged. The results of such ventures have been mixed. There have been a number of notable failures since 2014, but also a few promising starts. First Look Media, launched in January 2014 with $50 million from eBay founder Pierre Omidyar, closed one if its signature news products, The Racket, without ever publishing a single story in October 2014. Gigaom, a tech journalism outlet, closed down abruptly in 2015. Circa, a digital-first news app started in 2012, ran out of capital and suspended operations in 2015. Despite these failed ventures, others have had very good initial success. For example, Vice News, launched in March 2014, claims 1.1 million subscribers and 175 million video views in one year, with an estimated 15 million unique visitors on average per month. Vox.com, a news site lead by Ezra Klein (a former *Washington Post* journalist), had 14 million unique visitors in one month (ranking it 35th in the top 50 news sites). Among the more established digital-only media companies are BuzzFeed and the *Huffington Post* (both of which cover far more than hard news). BuzzFeed is an Internet media company founded in 2006 covering breaking social, entertainment, and political news. As evident in Table 11.1, BuzzFeed is very popular despite having faced controversy after removing posts which were critical of key advertisers. The *Huffington Post* is a politically liberal online news source founded by Arianna Huffington, Kenneth Lerer, Andrew Breitbard, and Jonah Peretti. Founded in 2005, it became the first commercially run digital media entity in the United States to win a Pulitzer Prize in 2012 and is by far the most visited digital-native news entity. More localized coverage is also available in digital-only platforms. For example, the *Texas Tribune*, a non-profit fully online media organization covering Texas politics and designed to promote civic engagement, was created in 2009 by John Thorton (a venture capitalist), and journalists Evan Smith and Ross Ramsey. In early 2016 they had 40 writers and expanded to have a Washington bureau. These digital-native news platforms have further changed the manner in which news is covered and are likely to grow in popularity in the upcoming future.

Technology is rapidly changing politics in other countries as well. In 1988, a pro-democracy uprising in Myanmar was quickly dispelled when the totalitarian government successfully shut the country's borders, expelled foreign journalists and dissidents, and controlled the flow of information. More than 3,000 people were killed in this Asian nation, with little world scrutiny. The government thought it could squash a similar uprising that began in 2007 by once again controlling the media and shielding itself from the world (as it had successfully done a number of times in the past). This time, however, the government did not anticipate the use of technology and how difficult it would be to control. Despite the fact that the country has one of the most repressed and censored media in the world and less than 1 percent of the country has access to the Internet, technology was used to change the nature of the conflict and the world's reaction.

TABLE 11.1 Top Digital-Native News Entities (Unique Visitors in January 2015)

	Total	Desktop	Mobile
HuffingtonPost.com	100,000	44,184	67,095
BuzzFeed.com	77,992	22,749	57,724
BleacherReport.com	44,429	14,645	32,938
BusinessInsider.com	37,309	15,278	24,101
CNET.com	30,482	21,177	11,307
Mashable.com	20,951	9,669	12,029
Slate.com	18,346	7,525	11,533
Vice.com	15,558	4,193	9,375
Gawker.com	14,079	5,724	8,954
Vox.com	13,598	6,070	7,862

SOURCE: comScore Media Metrix, January 2015 U.S. Note: Total digital population is the unduplicated combination of the desktop (web browsing and video) and mobile (websites and apps) traffic figures. For that reason, desktop and mobile figures combined may exceed the total digital population number. Reported in Amy Mitchell and Dana Page, "State of the Media, 2015," Pew Research Center, p. 15, http://www.journalism.org/files/2015/04/FINAL-STATE-OF-THE-NEWS-MEDIA1.pdf.

The embodiment of a revolutionary movement, Wael Ghonim is a reluctant hero. His use of social media facilitated an uprising that changed the face of the Middle East. Pictured at the *Time Magazine* "World's 100 Most Influential People" gala on April 26, 2011, Ghonim became the face of a youth-led revolution in Egypt.

■ *Do you think you could risk your life to advocate for change? What constitutes a modern-day hero?*

Cell phones were used to send text messages, digital photos, and videos, enabling the Buddhist monks to reach a global audience with their desperate calls for democracy. Students throughout the country used text messaging to set up demonstrations and track the location of government soldiers. The government tried to shut down Internet access and cell phone use, but it was rather unsuccessful, especially due to the students' use of satellite telephones. The students' and activists' use of technology made it impossible for the government to isolate itself from global scrutiny.

In analyzing more than 3 million tweets, massive amounts of YouTube videos, and thousands of blog postings, researchers at the University of Washington found that social media played a key role in shaping the political actions and debates surrounding the Arab Spring.[24] Philip Howard, the project lead investigator, stated that "Our evidence suggests that social media carried a cascade of messages about freedom and democracy across North Africa and the Middle East, and helped raise expectations for the success of political uprisings.... Social media became a critical part of the toolkit for greater freedom."[25] Given the success of these pro-democratic movements, we expect future use of Internet, and specifically of social media, to continue to grow. Secretary of State Hillary Clinton began the practice of requiring every diplomat who rotates through the foreign-service institute to get training in social media. Journalist Massimo Calabresi asserts that we now live in a world in which this kind of technology places more power in the hands of the people compared to their rulers.

Functions of the Media

11.3 Illustrate the functions of the media in American politics and society.

The media perform a multitude of functions in the United States, which can be summarized as entertaining, informing, and persuading the public. The media provide people with shared political experiences, which can in turn bring people together and affect public opinion. The media model appropriate behavior and reinforce cultural norms, but they also portray behavior that challenges cultural norms and expectations. And sometimes, they do both at the same time. Because the media are increasingly national in scope, the presentation of some issues in one region to one group will reinforce cultural norms while the same material challenges cultural norms in another region. Consider same-sex marriage. In some regions, these unions are more accepted as normal expressions of love and commitment, while in other regions, the majority of people consider them immoral. When the media portray such unions in the news or in sitcoms, the perspective they use can serve to frame the issue.

Entertainment

Even as entertainment, the media can affect the image of officials and institutions. Consider late-night television, where being the frequent butt of jokes can undermine a leader's public image. The media's negative portrayal of governmental officials, even as entertainment, can have negative effects on public perception and attitudes. Research on media images of public officials from the mid-1950s through the 1990s has demonstrated that the way they were shown was more likely to be negative than positive. The only occupation with worse images was business. Before 1975, our political system itself was twice as likely to be portrayed positively on television than negatively, but by the 1980s, positive portrayals had become uncommon. This shift, the researchers claimed, reflected changes in public opinion in the aftermath of the Vietnam War and the Watergate scandal.[26]

The distinction between entertainment and news has become increasingly blurred as the news divisions of network media come under pressure to be entertaining in hopes of appealing to a broader audience and generating money for the network. A perfect example of this occurred when during the 2008 election campaign *Saturday Night Live*'s Tina Fey began a remarkably successful parody of Republican vice presidential nominee Sarah Palin. Almost immediately upon Senator John McCain's nomination of Governor Palin for the Republican ticket, Fey put on her "power red suit and wig" and began a notable impersonation of the governor that dramatically escalated the ratings of *SNL*. Many critics of Governor Palin quickly seized on Fey's characterizations, using them as evidence that the governor was unsuitable to be the vice president and, if the need arose, president. Fey reprised her portrayal of Governor Palin in January 2016 with a spoof on Palin's endorsement of Donald Trump. *SNL*'s high quality skits—as well as candidate appearances—in the 2016 electoral season have generated a good deal of discussion and attention, further blurring the lines between news and comedy.

Late night makes no attempt to be neutral in presidential elections. For example, John Oliver, host of HBO's *Last Week Tonight*, went on an epic rant against Donald Trump in a 22-minute monologue in February 2016. The monologue had 16 million views in only two days. Politicians often appear on late-night comedy shows, typically trying to personalize themselves. The first presidential candidate to appear on late-night television was John F. Kennedy who appeared on *Tonight Starring Jack Paar* during his 1960 campaign against Richard Nixon. Since this time, it has become increasingly common for candidates to appear on late night. Mitt Romney, while running for president in 2012, was hesitant to appear on late night as he thought he would be facing hostile interviewers. He ultimately appeared on *The Tonight Show*

From its beginnings in 1975, *Saturday Night Live* has made a name for itself by spoofing famous people and politicians. Shown here are two such skits. Chevy Chase is portraying Gerald Ford and Kate McKinnon and Larry David are portraying Hillary Clinton and Bernie Sanders.

■ *How relevant do you think comedy programs are in influencing public opinion of celebrities and politicians?*

with Jay Leno, as he thought Leno would be less hostile toward him. The *Washington Post* tracked late night jokes from September 1, 2015, through January 31, 2016, and found that Republican presidential candidates were the subjects of three times as many jokes as Democratic presidential candidates (1,363 jokes versus 424).[27] However, much of the Republican totals were due to the overwhelmingly large number of jokes targeting Donald Trump (who was the subject of 655 jokes). Hillary Clinton was the second most popular target with over 200 jokes, closely followed by Jeb Bush, Bernie Sanders, and Ben Carson.[28] The clouding of entertainment and news media is not new, but given the popularity of social media sites like YouTube, it may be the first time that such material was so widely accessible and available.

Surveillance, Interpretation, and Socialization

As noted, the distinctive nature of the news media in communicating makes them unique and potentially powerful political actors. In addition to entertaining, the news media have many functions in our society, with great political and social consequences. Harold Lasswell, a prominent political scientist who pioneered studying the effects of the media on American politics, identified three important societal functions of the media: surveillance, interpretation, and socialization.[29]

SURVEILLANCE According to Lasswell, the media have a watchdog role as the "eyes and ears to the world." That is, the media report what's news, thus keeping us informed of significant events not only in our communities but also in the nation and around the globe. Their surveillance function draws attention to problems that need addressing. For example, news coverage on conditions at a local veterans' hospital could demonstrate the need for more oversight and better patient care. The story could then expand, looking at the quality of care in hospitals across the country, perhaps motivating Congress to examine the care our country provides to veterans, enhancing the quality of their lives.

It is important to note, however, that not all surveillance reporting is positive. For example, research has shown that crime is often overreported, making people believe there is more criminal activity in their community than actually exists. Although it can be helpful for the media to probe into scandals and to uncover abuses, emphasizing negativity can also lead to public cynicism. Negative reporting on the economy has drawn much criticism, with some observers asserting that stories that continually report economic downturns can spread fear among investors, causing them to act in ways that actually do worsen the economy.

One aspect of surveillance is **investigative reporting**, in which reporters seek out stories and probe into various aspects of an issue in search of serious problems. Some

investigative reporting
A type of journalism in which reporters thoroughly investigate a subject matter (often involving a scandal) to inform the public, correct an injustice, or expose an abuse.

of the earliest forms of investigative journalism, popular around 1900, were called **muckraking**—an expression that President Theodore Roosevelt coined in describing journalists who, he thought, tried to rake up too much sensational social filth. From the 1870s until World War I, there was a good deal of public interest in reforming government, politics, and business. To generate support for reform, journalists would investigate areas they believed needed to be changed and then present their findings to the public.

One of the most famous examples is Upton Sinclair's examination of the Chicago stockyards. His resulting novel, *The Jungle*, published in 1906, was a scathing exposé of the meatpacking industry. The book created a public outcry for reform during Theodore Roosevelt's administration, leading the federal government to regulate the industry and demand more sanitary conditions to make meat production safer. Muckraking lost public support around 1912, sending investigative journalism into a prolonged lull. The Watergate scandal of the early 1970s not only revived modern investigative journalism but also firmly entrenched it in the contemporary media.

Many Americans welcomed the return of investigative journalism, pointing to the numerous abuses that reporters have uncovered. One excellent example is the *Chicago Tribune*'s investigation into the Illinois death penalty in 1999. The *Tribune* exposed serious flaws in the administration of the death penalty in that state. Its findings ultimately led Governor George Ryan to impose a moratorium on all executions in the state and to appoint a panel to recommend improving the public defender system, which provides lawyers for poor persons accused of committing death-penalty offenses. Some critics, however, believe that investigative journalists often go too far, delving into matters that should be treated confidentially and privately—for example, the behavior of public officials' children. Some areas, these critics say, should be considered off-limits out of respect for individuals' privacy. More recently, the diligent efforts to uncover the truth in the shooting of Laquan McDonald, discussed at the beginning of the chapter, illustrates the power of the media to serve as watchdogs and hold our elected officials and police accountable for their actions.

INTERPRETATION   According to Lasswell, the second societal role of the media is to interpret the news, putting events into context and helping people to understand the complexities of the world. One example occurred upon the death of former president Ronald Reagan in 2004. Retrospective stories in the newspapers and on television put his presidency into context by focusing on his economic and social policies while typically ignoring the more controversial issues of his administration. The media drew historical parallels between Reagan and other presidents and compared his funeral to other presidential funerals. In essence, they put his life and death into context for the nation. The ability to set the context, frame the issue, interpret the facts, and potentially, provide legitimacy for people, issues, or groups gives the media enormous power. In framing how a story is told—in short, by creating heroes and villains—the media tell us, subtly or otherwise, who is "good" and who is "bad" in a way that is difficult to refute thereafter. A more recent example occurred during the Arab Spring. The media characterized the revolutionaries as "reformers" during the very early coverage, thereby painting the uprising in positive terms.

Take the civil rights movement as an example. Interpretive stories in the media about prominent figures and events in the movement have generally been framed to focus on the victims of racism rather than to show that civil rights activists challenged the status quo and broke laws doing so. In 1955, Rosa Parks intentionally and in full awareness broke the law of Montgomery, Alabama, by refusing to give up her seat on a city bus to a white man. Yes, she believed that the law was unjust, but it *was* the law at the time. Media accounts about her at the time of her death in 2005 portrayed her not as a lawbreaker but as a victim and a hero in the struggle for justice. Conversely, the media tended to portray the feminist activists of the late 1960s and early 1970s as

muckraking
Investigating and exposing societal ills such as corruption in politics or abuses in business.

extremist, man-hating, lesbian bra burners when they could have been depicted more sympathetically as women fighting gender oppression and patriarchy.

Interpretive journalism is very much in evidence in reporting on the war in Iraq. When the United States invaded Iraq in 2003, the American media framed the war primarily as a defensive measure, to rid the world of Saddam Hussein's weapons of mass destruction, and secondarily as a war to liberate the oppressed Iraqi people. Framing the invasion in terms of waging the post-9/11 War on Terror, rather than in terms of attacking another nation unprovoked certainly helped generate public support for the initial invasion. However, when neither the alleged stockpiles of weapons of mass destruction nor links between Saddam's Iraq and al-Qaeda were discovered, and as a bitter Iraqi resistance to the American occupation developed along with mounting U.S. military casualties—and as the media repeatedly reported stories of poor planning for the invasion and of post-invasion chaos—the American public's support for the war and for President George W. Bush eroded.

The selection of photos used in reporting news stories involving African American victims of crime and alleged suspects has generated a good deal of controversy. Many people complained that the news coverage of the events in 2005 following Hurricane Katrina and collapse of the levees in New Orleans was racist and relied on racial stereotypes. For example, on August 30, 2005, two news sources—the Associated Press (AP) and Getty Images via Agence France-Presse (AFP)—published two similar pictures with very different captions. In the AP picture, an African American man was described as having "looted" a local grocery store, while in the AFP picture, two Caucasian people were depicted "finding" bread and soda at a local grocery store. Critics contended that the characterizations were based on racial stereotypes and were biased.[30] Others claimed that the captions simply reflected stylistic differences associated with the two news agencies.

More recently the media coverage of the Trayvon Martin/George Zimmerman case generated controversy. The initial pictures used in the media coverage showed photos of both Martin and Zimmerman that were out of date and helped shape the initial public reaction. Martin was shown as a baby-faced, smiling youth in a photo several years old while Zimmerman was initially depicted with an unflattering mug shot taken 7 years prior to the incident. Moreover, the media was widely criticized in their framing of the situation, with some alleging they had a clear agenda to sensationalize the case and others alleging clear instances of bias. *Fox News Magazine* host Geraldo Rivera, a former NBC and ABC employee, asserted that MSNBC made a decision to press for arrest, and ultimate conviction, of George Zimmerman saying the network was "cheerleading for the conviction of George Zimmerman" based upon ideology rather than facts. The *O'Reilly Factor* theorized that left wing extremists are using past crimes against blacks to indict Zimmerman.[31] A Twitter campaign began in 2014 following concern about the photos of Michael Brown (an 18 year old unarmed man killed in Ferguson, Missouri in 2014) used by media organizations covering the story. Some media outlets showed Mr. Brown at his high school graduation in his cap and gown, however most used a photo of him wearing a red jersey and holding up what some thought was a gang sign (his friends state it was a peace sign). The Twitter campaign, #iftheygunnedmedown, drew over 200,000 reposts in which users were asked "If they gunned me down, what photo would you use?" Many supporting the Twitter campaign argued that the selection of photos of black victims often criminalize them by either consciously or unconsciously relying upon stereotypes to help explain why victims of color are partly to blame for their deaths. Such victim-blaming rarely occurs to Caucasians.[32] In 2015, an Iowa newspaper the *Gazette,* posted two stories about local crimes written by the same reporter. Both featured photos of the suspected criminals; one story used yearbook photos of young men in suit jackets and ties; the other used mug shots. By all accounts the crimes were remarkably similar (local burglaries) but the mug shots visually conveyed dramatically different stories. The alleged suspects in the story with mug shots were African Americans, while the alleged suspects in the story with the year book photos were Caucasian.[33] Follow-up stories used mug shots of the white suspects as well (who happened to be wrestlers at the University of Iowa). The newspaper explained the use of the different photos as a timing issue with accessing jail mug shots, but did note that they would be reviewing their policies in the future. As consumers, you need to be conscious of this sort of potential bias and seek numerous sources of news to ensure objectivity.

Many observers of all political stripes are concerned over what they see as bias in news coverage. Some perceive a liberal bias in the news, especially on public radio and television and in such newspapers as the *New York Times;* conservative political commentators such as Glenn Beck and Bill O'Reilly, as well as conservative politicians, make much of this alleged bias. Democrats and liberals counter by asserting that Fox News has a conservative bias, that the mainstream media actually bend over backward to present conservative views, and that a good deal of reporting is, in fact, shaded in a conservative direction. As the 2016 presidential campaign progressed, Donald Trump's claims that the media was biased against him grew very pronounced.

Research on this volatile issue is mixed. In 1995, the Media Studies Center and the Roper Center for Public Opinion surveyed Washington-based reporters and national newspaper editors. They found that 50 percent of reporters identified themselves as Democrats, compared with 34 percent of the national public. Editors were more like the national public than reporters, with 31 percent claiming to be Democrats. Only 4 percent of reporters, however, said that they were Republicans, compared to 28 percent of the public and 14 percent of editors.[34] The research also probed political ideology, finding that reporters are far more likely to call themselves liberal than the general population. Editors were more conservative, dividing along the lines found in the population at large.

In 2004, the Pew Center interviewed national and local reporters and found that 34 percent of national and 23 percent of local reporters considered themselves liberals (compared with 20 percent of the general public). Only 7 percent of national and 12 percent of local reporters self-identified as conservatives (compared with 33 percent of the public); the vast majority of each (54 percent and 61 percent, respectively) claimed they were moderates (compared with 41 percent of the public).[35] These data provide some evidence to bolster assertions that reporters are more likely to be liberals. Other research shows that historically, newspapers have been far more likely to endorse Republican presidential candidates, but the current trend is for papers to remain uncommitted at election time.[36] Research has failed to find empirical evidence that news reporting is biased in favor of either party.[37] So, even though reporters may be more liberal, their professional stance on the whole remains neutral. It is difficult to assess whether their neutrality is the result of the influence of editors and owners (both of whom are more conservative), of their ethical commitments, or of the competitiveness inherent in the modern journalistic environment.

Examining the 2012 presidential election, the Pew Research Center found that Fox News was especially critical of President Obama. In the final stretch of the campaign, nearly half of the coverage of President Obama on Fox News was negative, while only 6 percent was positive. In contrast, CNN had 18 percent positive coverage and 21 percent negative coverage. MSNBC had only 15 percent negative coverage with 39 percent positive. A very different story was found with Mitt Romney. Fox coverage was positive in 28 percent of the stories and negative in only 12 percent. CNN was far more likely to be negative toward Romney than positive (36 percent of the stories were negative with only 11 percent positive). MSNBC was remarkably negative in its portrayal of Romney with 71 percent of stories having a negative tone and 3 percent having a positive tone.[38] The audience each network attracts reflects these trends. Forty-seven percent of those who self-identify as "consistently conservative" get their news from Fox (with 11 percent getting their news from local radio).

The manner in which the actions of individuals are characterized by the media can be significant, influencing the views and opinions of the public. The caption used with the picture of the two Caucasians in the aftermath of Hurricane Katrina (2005) characterized the people as "finding bread and soda," while the caption accompanying the image of the African American stated that the man had "looted" a grocery store.

■ *Do you think these captions indicate that racism is still prevalent in the United States? Why or why not?*

The "consistently liberal" get their news from a more eclectic combination of news sources including CNN (15 percent), NPR (13 percent), MSNBC (12 percent), and the *New York Times* (10 percent).[39]

In addition to concerns about ideological bias, it is important to note that journalists are not demographically representative of the population as most journalists are Caucasian males. Eighty-eight percent of print journalists and editors are white (a percentage which has remained virtually the same since 1994). Only 35 percent of print journalists and editors are female (also virtually unchanged since the late 1990s). Since around 2004, 22 percent of local television news staff have been non-white, with minorities more likely to work in larger media markets than smaller media markets. Dean Baquet became the first executive editor of the *New York Times* in 2014 and Lester Holt became the first solo black anchor in 2015.[40]

However, if we expand the definition of the media to include talk radio, concerns over a liberal bias disappear. Unquestionably, conservative radio personalities and political commentators dominate talk radio, and self-described liberal or left-wing commentators have had difficulty finding a following in this environment. And as for Web sites and blogs, all shades of political opinion seem to have plentiful outlets.

SOCIALIZATION The third societal function of the media that Lasswell identified is to socialize people. The media are an agent of socialization, teaching us political facts and opinions that help form our political belief structures and our political culture. The media also reinforce economic and social values. Simply looking at popular programs provides testimony that the belief in capitalism is alive and well in the United States. Shows such as *The Real Housewives*, which dwell on material acquisitions, reinforce the basic tenets of capitalism—the desire for more drives our economic system.

In winter, young children spend an average of 32 hours a week watching TV. Eighty percent of the programming children watch is intended for adults and generally goes far beyond their life experiences, making the potential for molding their minds greater than that for adults.[41] Therefore, the concern in many areas of society is about programming content and the negative implications of the high levels of violence, sex, and materialism on television. The media can and do promote positive role models for children, celebrating national holidays and heroes, but there is no denying that negative images in the media far outweigh positive illustrations. For adults whose basic ideology and opinions are already formed, the media provide opportunities for reinforcement, especially with so many options available on TV, cable, and the Internet and in the immense variety of print publications. Adults can thus easily find programming to reinforce their ideology and political views; children are more susceptible to what they learn from TV.

Political Use of the Media

11.4 Assess how the media can be influential in American politics.

Political parties, politicians, interest groups, and individuals use the media to manipulate the public and politics. Political elites have always used communication for political purposes. In 350 B.C., the ancient Greek philosopher Aristotle, in his *Rhetoric*, discussed the role of communication in keeping political communities intact. Today's modern mass media simply make the process easier. As you'll see, political leaders often directly appeal to the public (with a televised speech, for example) or indirectly (in advertisements designed to sway public opinion). It is important to realize that communication has always been used for political purposes, although today's technology has made it more sophisticated. In light of their exclusive focus on communication, the mass media in the United States should be considered an important political institution.

How Politicians Make the News

Politicians try very hard to get **earned media coverage**—positive press coverage free of charge. Many of their actions are designed to increase the likelihood that the media will cover them. This is especially significant for officials who are up for reelection. As you will see, people tend to put more credence in what they learn from news programs than in information presented during paid advertisements. Hence earned media coverage is very important for political officials and political candidates. It raises their visibility and exposes them to the public.

Elected officials and other ambitious leaders use various means of getting attention. One popular tactic is to stage **pseudo-events** (a term coined by the historian Daniel J. Boorstin in 1961 to characterize events whose primary purpose is to generate public interest and news coverage).[42] Although the media does not like to cover these staged events, preferring to capture more realistic news, they will often show them for fear of getting scooped by rivals. One of the most famous pseudo-events in recent years occurred on May 1, 2003, when then-President George W. Bush emerged from a Navy jet in full flight gear on the aircraft carrier Abraham Lincoln. He later spoke in front of a huge banner declaring "Mission Accomplished." In a prime-time speech scheduled for that Thursday evening—expected to garner the largest television audience—he declared that the "major combat operations in Iraq have ended" and discussed the defeat of "an ally of Al Qaeda." While President Bush was able to use this staged media event to garner attention, in the long run his words were used against him and his party as the war waged on, often being mentioned even into the 2016 presidential election.

Research into early coverage of the 2016 presidential election clearly demonstrates how successful the two candidates who emerged as front-runners (Donald Trump and Hillary Clinton) have been in generating media coverage. Nate Silver (a statistician and writer who analyzes baseball and elections and is editor-in-chief of FiveThirtyEight blog) analyzed news stories for all presidential candidates in the last six months of the pre-primary years (for example July 2015 through December 2015 for the 2016 presidential nomination) to see how many news stories featured primarily one candidate. Donald

earned media coverage
Airtime provided free of charge to candidates for political office.

pseudo-events
Events that appear spontaneous but are in fact staged and scripted by public relations experts to appeal to the news media or the public.

Trump received 54 percent of the media coverage of the Republican primary (with Jeb Bush coming in second with only 8 percent of the stories). Hillary Clinton received 77 percent of the coverage of the Democratic primary.[43] This huge advantage in free media helps explain why Donald Trump spent much less on paid advertising than most other candidates (through February 2016, the Trump campaign only spent $10 million on television advertising while Jeb Bush spent $82 million, Marco Rubio spent $55 million, Bernie Sanders spent $28.4 million, Hillary Clinton spent $27.9 million, and Ted Cruz spent $22 million).[44] The *New York Times* reported that Trump earned the equivalent of $1.9 billion in freemedia, compared to $313 million by Cruz, $214 million by Bush, and $204 million by Rubio. On the Democratic side, Clinton had a significant advantage over Sanders with $746 million in free media compared to $321 million for Sanders.[45] Trump's remarkable media savvy was a mixed blessing as much of the media coverage was negative.

Politicians try to control the events, but sometimes, they are unsuccessful. President Bush was caught on camera once reading a children's book upside down, provoking much media ridicule. When announcing an elementary school spelling bee, Vice President Dan Quayle once misspelled *potato*. Innumerable jokes about his intelligence dogged him for the rest of his political career. Vice President Joe Biden has made a number of political gaffes. While on the campaign trail in September 2008, during an interview with Katie Couric, Biden remarked "When the stock market crashed, Franklin D. Roosevelt got on the television and didn't just talk about the, you know, the princes of greed. He said, 'Look, here's what happened'"—only experimental TV sets were available in 1929 when the stock market crashed. In March 2010, after introducing President Obama just hours after the health care reform bill passed Congress, he embraced the president and called the bill's passage a "big f***ing deal." In what is likely to go down in history as one of the most significance "gaffes," a video of Donald Trump and Billy Bush discussing women in lewd terms (recorded on a hot mic in 2005) was released by the *Washington Post* on October 7, 2016. Public outrage was intense and a number of women came forward to claim Donald Trump touched them inappropriately (a claim that he vehemently denied). Sometimes damaged by these political gaffes, politicians and their aides spend a great deal of time developing mechanisms to counteract them with positive media attention.

There is often an adversarial relationship between public officials and the media. Officials want to control information about themselves and their policies, including the way such information is framed and presented, while the media reject such "spoon-feeding" and try to retain their independence. Government officials want to be seen in a positive light, whereas the media, perpetually seeking to boost ratings or circulation, always find controversies or conflicts more appealing. At the same time, however, reciprocal relationships bind the media, politicians, and the public together.

Politicians need the media to communicate with their constituents and advance their agendas, the media need politicians to provide news and entertainment, and the public needs both to make informed voting decisions. The media influence the public with programming—but because the media are driven by the profit motive, the public (their source of revenue) influences them. Similarly, the public influences government through elections and by supporting or rejecting policies, and the government influences the public by making and enforcing policies.

How Journalists Report the News

Many people believe that the media's ability to select how and what they report is their greatest source of influence. Called **agenda setting**, it consists of determining which issues will be covered, in what detail, and in what context—and also deciding which stories are not newsworthy and therefore are not going to be covered. Agenda setting figures very prominently in the media's capacity to influence the public and politicians. As a consequence, much concern exists about how and by whom stories are decided to be newsworthy.

agenda setting

The process of featuring specific stories in the media to focus attention on particular issues, thereby setting the political agenda.

In allowing certain stories to get on the public agenda and by sidelining others, the media are said to be acting as **gatekeepers**. Historically, concern stemmed from the fact that no one could check the media's selection of news: The media controlled access by selecting which stories would be covered and from what angle. This has changed recently with more individuals participating in the creation of news. For example, a growing number of Americans contribute to news stories by posting videos online, commenting about news stories, or forwarding news to their friends and acquaintances. However, we should not underestimate the ability of the media to shine the spotlight on issues because of their presumed credibility, access to policy leaders, and resources.[46]

The media set the political agenda, choose how and when political issues get addressed, and decide which stories draw attention to a problem that is important and needs to be fixed. They thus create a political climate that can frame subsequent discussions and shape public opinion. For instance, in June 1998, the media publicized the gruesome death of a black man, James Byrd, Jr., by racist murderers who chained him to the back of a pickup truck and dragged him until he was dead, thus focusing public attention on racial tension and bigotry. In doing so, the media illustrated a problem, discussed its roots, and then demonstrated the need for change, helping set the public agenda. The coverage of the Trayvon Martin, Michael Brown, and Laquan McDonald shootings once again focused the nation's attention on the issue of race and began heated public debates.

The amount of time, space, or prominence such a story receives can dramatically affect whether it will make it onto the political agenda. These decisions, made by senior media managers, are often deliberative and conscious, leading some analysts to worry about potential media bias. Consumers should be skeptical as many stories that are socially, politically, and economically important are still not covered by the media for a variety of reasons.

COVERING THE PRESIDENT   The nature of the interactions and type of relationship with the media differ from president to president. Presidents use the media differently, depending on their personal style. President Clinton averaged 550 public talks each year (many very informal), while President Reagan, dubbed "the Great Communicator," averaged only 320. At the dawn of the television era, President Truman, who is today remembered for his vigorous and colorful ways of expressing himself in public, averaged a mere 88 talks a year.[47] Clinton's ability to communicate and relate to the public earned him a great deal of flexibility, allowing his candidacy and presidency to survive many scandals and even an impeachment trial. The relationship he was able to develop with the people, via the media, increased his popularity, providing some insulation against the serious charges of personal wrongdoing that he eventually faced. President Obama held seven full press conferences in his first year in office (two more than President George W. Bush did in his first year), but he held no full news conferences during the last 5 months of 2009, preferring instead to deliver briefer remarks where he sometimes took questions from the press. President Obama's relatively low number of press conferences the first 7 years of his administration (he averages only 1.7 per month)[48] generated criticism especially in light of his campaign pledge to increase transparency and access in Washington.

There is an interesting dynamic between politicians and the media. Even if the relationship is uneasy, open warfare is rare. On the one hand, the relationship is by definition adversarial, because both sides want to control how information and events are framed. However, as you have seen, both sides need each other, too. Presidents put great effort into creating photo opportunities ("photo ops") and pseudo-events that are visually appealing and releasing to the press information that is favorable to the White House. News media with limited resources will often cooperate, but those with more resources can subject the material to greater scrutiny, often presenting information in a manner contrary to what the White House might prefer.

gatekeepers

A group or individuals who determine which stories will receive attention in the media and from which perspective.

TIMELINE

Women's Rights in the United States

In the last 165 years, women have made great strides in their quest for equality. Once considered the property of their fathers and husbands, women had no control over their own property, children, or bodies. Women had no legal standing to sue or be sued, could not vote, could not enter into contracts, nor be employed in a wide variety of jobs. Even if they were able to work, in many states they did not have the legal right to their own wages. Today women significantly outpace men in educational attainment. Women are more likely to graduate from college than men and more likely to hold a graduate degree than men. Women have made dramatic strides in all fields—including athletics. However, women still lag behind men in pay and economic security.

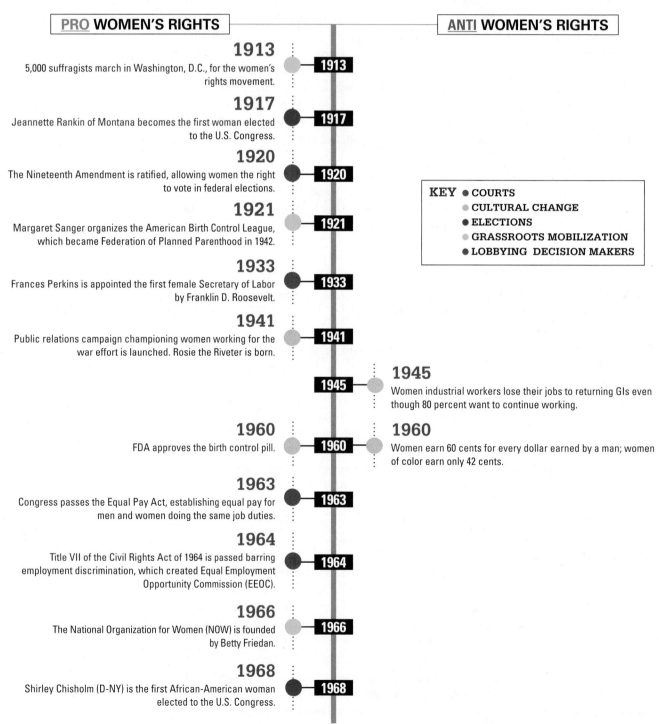

PRO WOMEN'S RIGHTS

ANTI WOMEN'S RIGHTS

1913
5,000 suffragists march in Washington, D.C., for the women's rights movement.
`1913`

1917
Jeannette Rankin of Montana becomes the first woman elected to the U.S. Congress.
`1917`

1920
The Nineteenth Amendment is ratified, allowing women the right to vote in federal elections.
`1920`

1921
Margaret Sanger organizes the American Birth Control League, which became Federation of Planned Parenthood in 1942.
`1921`

KEY
● COURTS
◐ CULTURAL CHANGE
● ELECTIONS
◑ GRASSROOTS MOBILIZATION
● LOBBYING DECISION MAKERS

1933
Frances Perkins is appointed the first female Secretary of Labor by Franklin D. Roosevelt.
`1933`

1941
Public relations campaign championing women working for the war effort is launched. Rosie the Riveter is born.
`1941`

`1945`
1945
Women industrial workers lose their jobs to returning GIs even though 80 percent want to continue working.

1960
FDA approves the birth control pill.
`1960`
1960
Women earn 60 cents for every dollar earned by a man; women of color earn only 42 cents.

1963
Congress passes the Equal Pay Act, establishing equal pay for men and women doing the same job duties.
`1963`

1964
Title VII of the Civil Rights Act of 1964 is passed barring employment discrimination, which created Equal Employment Opportunity Commission (EEOC).
`1964`

1966
The National Organization for Women (NOW) is founded by Betty Friedan.
`1966`

1968
Shirley Chisholm (D-NY) is the first African-American woman elected to the U.S. Congress.
`1968`

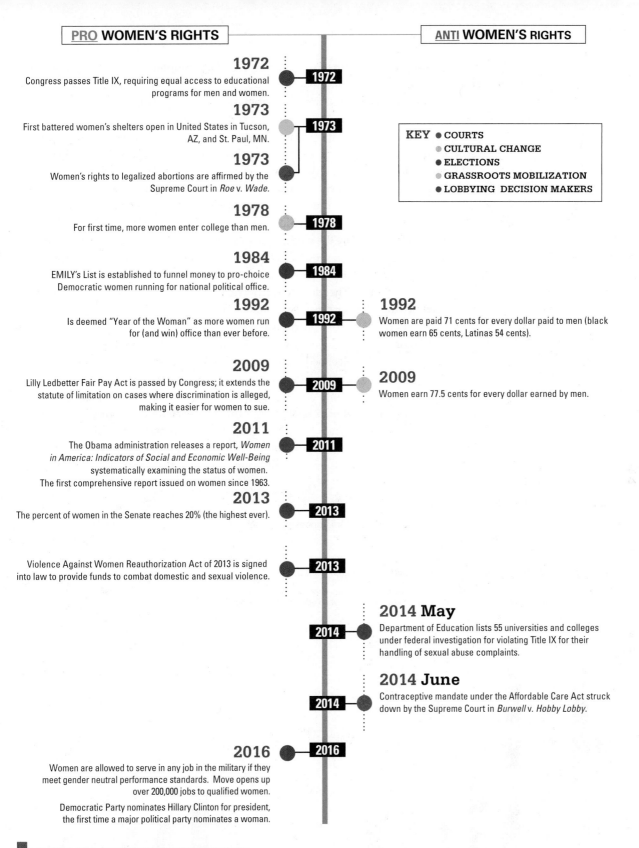

PRO WOMEN'S RIGHTS

ANTI WOMEN'S RIGHTS

KEY
- COURTS
- CULTURAL CHANGE
- ELECTIONS
- GRASSROOTS MOBILIZATION
- LOBBYING DECISION MAKERS

1972
Congress passes Title IX, requiring equal access to educational programs for men and women.

1973
First battered women's shelters open in United States in Tucson, AZ, and St. Paul, MN.

1973
Women's rights to legalized abortions are affirmed by the Supreme Court in *Roe* v. *Wade.*

1978
For first time, more women enter college than men.

1984
EMILY's List is established to funnel money to pro-choice Democratic women running for national political office.

1992
Is deemed "Year of the Woman" as more women run for (and win) office than ever before.

1992
Women are paid 71 cents for every dollar paid to men (black women earn 65 cents, Latinas 54 cents).

2009
Lilly Ledbetter Fair Pay Act is passed by Congress; it extends the statute of limitation on cases where discrimination is alleged, making it easier for women to sue.

2009
Women earn 77.5 cents for every dollar earned by men.

2011
The Obama administration releases a report, *Women in America: Indicators of Social and Economic Well-Being* systematically examining the status of women. The first comprehensive report issued on women since 1963.

2013
The percent of women in the Senate reaches 20% (the highest ever).

2013
Violence Against Women Reauthorization Act of 2013 is signed into law to provide funds to combat domestic and sexual violence.

2014 May
Department of Education lists 55 universities and colleges under federal investigation for violating Title IX for their handling of sexual abuse complaints.

2014 June
Contraceptive mandate under the Affordable Care Act struck down by the Supreme Court in *Burwell* v. *Hobby Lobby.*

2016
Women are allowed to serve in any job in the military if they meet gender neutral performance standards. Move opens up over 200,000 jobs to qualified women.

Democratic Party nominates Hillary Clinton for president, the first time a major political party nominates a woman.

CRITICAL THINKING QUESTIONS

1. Do you think that discrimination is still significant in the United States? Should the government do more to close the pay gap between men and women (currently the median yearly income for women is 80 percent of that for men)?

2. Many consider reproductive freedom for women to be a central component for equal rights, but many women lack the ability to control their reproductive decisions. How important do you think reproductive control is for women to achieve economic and social equality?

SOURCES: http://www.womenatworkmuseum.org/Womens-Rights-timeline.pdf, http://www.annenbergclassroom.org/ Files/Documents/Timelines/WomensRightstimeline.pdf, and http://www.rochester.edu/sba/suffragetimeline.html.

press releases

Written statements that are given to the press to circulate information or an announcement.

news briefing

A public appearance by a governmental official for the purpose of releasing information to the press.

news conference

A media event, often staged, where reporters ask questions of politicians or other celebrities.

The office of the White House press secretary supplies the White House press corps and the Washington-based media with daily information about the administration. The president's press secretary customarily holds a daily press conference. In addition, each administration has an office of communications, which may be structured differently from administration to administration but is always used to oversee long-term public relations and presidential image-making.

Communication from the White House takes three general forms: **press releases**, **news briefings**, and **news conferences**. Press releases and news briefings are the routine ways to release news. Press releases are prepared text in which officials present information to reporters and are worded in hopes that they will be used just as they are, without rewriting. To allow the media to ask direct questions about press releases or current events, the presidential press secretary and other high officials regularly appear for news briefings. News conferences are direct opportunities for the president to speak to the press and the public. Theodore Roosevelt held the first news conference at the White House, but his and all later presidential news conferences until 1961 were conducted in private. In that year, John F. Kennedy was the first president to allow live, televised coverage. In the current age of investigative reporting, the average number of press conferences held each year has declined since President Roosevelt left office; overall, presidents today try to release information in a more cautious, controlled manner (see Figure 11.4).

Doris Graber has identified four major purposes of media coverage of the executive branch.[49] First, the media serve to inform chief executives about current events, highlighting issues that need attention across the nation and the world. Second, the media inform the executive branch about the needs and concerns of the public, by reporting public opinion polls and by publishing letters to the editor and feature stories.

FIGURE 11.4 Presidential Press Conferences

Over the last 70 or so years, the average number of presidential press conferences per month has decreased rather dramatically, from Franklin Roosevelt's high of 6 to Ronald Reagan's low of 0.5.

■ *Why do you think this is the case? Why do you think presidents in the modern era of television are relying on other means to communicate with the country? Do you think this trend isolates the president too much from the press?*

SOURCE: Gerhard Peters, "Presidential News Conferences: Coolidge-Obama," in *The American Presidency Project*, ed. John T. Woolley and Gerhard Peters, Santa Barbara: University of California, accessed on April 5, 2016, http://www.presidency.ucsb.edu/data/newsconferences.php.

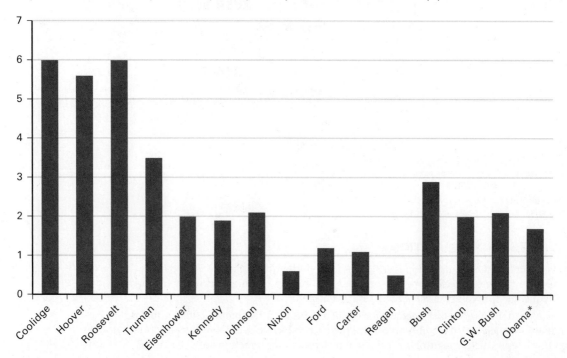

*The Obama statistics are through October 20, 2016.

Third, the media also allow presidents to express their positions and policy proposals directly to the people and other government officials by means of press conferences, televised speeches, and staged events, which always supply the administration in power with ample opportunity to explain its positions and garner support. Finally, the media keep the president in public view, reporting every scrap of available information about the first family's daily life. This reporting is generally framed from a human interest angle, but it also includes evaluations of presidential performance.

All four of these functions allow the public to stay in touch with the actions and life of the president and allow the president to keep in touch with the American

PATHWAYS OF ACTION

THE STRATEGIC USE OF LEAKS

For generations, political actors have utilized leaks to strategically manipulate information. However, new technology allows leaks to be used more purposefully than before. In 2006, The Sunshine Press—an international nonprofit organization funded by such diverse individuals as Chinese dissidents, journalists, mathematicians, and others—launched the Web site WikiLeaks in an effort to expose governmental actions and promote transparency. In the first three years from its debut, the whistleblowing Web site was given a prestigious award from Amnesty International in 2009 for its publication of "Kenya: The Cry of Blood—Extra Judicial Killings and Disappearances." WikiLeaks is famous for leaking a video of U.S. forces killing Iraqi civilians as well as documents about the wars in Afghanistan and Iraq that were previously unavailable to the public. One of its most controversial leaks stemmed from the publication of Guantanamo Bay secret dossiers and the U.S. embassy cables. A U.S. soldier, Chelsea Manning (Manning was diagnosed with gender identity disorder while in the Army and was previously known as Bradley Manning), was sentenced to 35 years in prison for her role in providing unauthorized war logs, cables, and video clips to WikiLeaks. She was convicted for violating the Espionage Act but acquitted of the most serious crime of aiding the enemy. Her supporters consider her a patriot and whistleblower. Following these leaks, the public backlash has grown. Once seen as a renegade Web site, the mainstream media are paying much more attention to WikiLeaks, though its legal status is in flux. To date, perhaps the largest known leak of classified documents has occurred by NSA contractor Edward Snowden. Snowden leaked a variety of documents, including information about numerous surveillance programs. In May 2016 former Attorney General Eric Holder stated that Snowden performed a "public service" by sparking a debate about national surveillance, but stated that he deserved to be punished as he jeopardized American security interests by leaking classified information. He has been granted permission to stay in Russia through 2017 despite being sought by U.S. authorities. More recently, immediately proceeding the 2016 Democratic National Convention, emails were leaked by a suspected Russian hacker showing that the Democratic National Committee (DNC) favored Hillary Clinton during the Democratic primary over her rival, Bernie Sanders. Party rules dictate neutrality. DNC Chair, Debbie Wasserman Schultz, and several others resigned as a result of the scandal. Some of Clinton's paid speeches to big banks were leaked during the general election, which raised questions for many voters about her willingness to regulate the banking industry if elected president.

It seems commonplace today to read a news story or watch a news report in which important information is attributed to an unnamed "high-ranking source" or a "police insider." Why aren't these sources named, and what are the implications of relying on information that is leaked?

There are many reasons why public officials leak information to the press. One is to gauge public reaction, sending up a "trial balloon" to see how a potential policy will be received and reported. For example, when Reagan administration officials considered changing the guidelines for food programs for low-income children to allow ketchup to be considered a vegetable, they leaked this idea to the media. Public outcry was fast and negative, the guidelines remained unchanged, and ketchup was ruled out as a vegetable in federal food programs.[50]

Leaks can also be preemptive. Officials can strategically use leaked information to sway public opinion and pressure other officials. Preemptively leaking material can allow officials to change their minds before making a public vote, as it is often easier to pressure officials before they publicly commit to a position. Unflattering or bad news can also be leaked a little at a time to lessen the damage it might cause. It is common knowledge that the best time to leak bad information is on weekends, when many full-time reporters are off and the public is too busy to watch the news. By Monday morning, the initial impact may have faded or been superseded by other news items.

Leaks are also ways to get information from publicity-shy groups or individuals. People involved with the court system or the police are typically reluctant to release sensitive information. Allowing them a chance to release information without being named could often serve as an important prompt for otherwise silent informants who are hesitant to go on record. It is long-established journalistic practice to grant leakers secrecy so that they are more willing to release information—even if it is illegal to do so.

The public should be skeptical, however, when analyzing material that is not attributed to a source, because it is often released for self-serving reasons. Informants often get to influence how the story is told based on the information they provide, which might not be the full story or the objective truth.[51]

people. Presidents have used this relationship to their advantage, knowing that they can command a great amount of attention and interest in their words and actions. The first media-conscious president was Theodore Roosevelt, who used the White House as a platform to influence public opinion and pursue his political agenda. "I suppose my critics will call that preaching," Theodore Roosevelt said in 1909, "but I have got such a bully pulpit!"

COVERING CONGRESS   For several reasons, the media give far less attention to Congress than to the president. People tend to have more interest in the actions of the president, who is the country's highest-ranking official with a nationwide constituency. No single member of Congress can make that claim or get that recognition. Furthermore, Congress is a much larger institution that requires coalition and consensus building, both of which take time and are not particularly exciting. By contrast, the president is often seen as working alone, so it becomes easier for the press to focus on his actions. Also, as a deliberative body, Congress works slowly, even tediously, and without much drama. Of course, interested people can turn to C-SPAN for gavel-to-gavel congressional coverage—but watching for several hours will reveal just how unexciting such deliberations can be.

The local media often cover the actions and votes of members of Congress, with senators typically getting more attention than representatives, especially in large metropolitan areas that encompass several congressional districts, making it difficult to cover all members of the local congressional delegation in detail. To get mentioned in the local news or local papers, members of Congress often stage pseudo-events and attend local events—even lowly ones like the Watermelon Festival picnic, the Fourth of July parade, or a ribbon-cutting ceremony to celebrate opening a new town library can win visually appealing news coverage.

COVERING THE COURTS   Of the three branches of government, the courts tend to get the least amount of coverage. Why? One reason is that federal judges rarely grant interviews lest their impartiality be questioned. Once appointed, judges normally do not receive much specific personal coverage; rather, attention is focused on their rulings and on the specific cases heard in their courts. The courts, moreover, deliberate and reach their decisions in secret, and very rarely do they allow televised or sound-recorded live coverage of cases as they are being argued.

Another area that receives considerable media attention is controversial confirmation hearings. The Senate must confirm all federal court judges, including Supreme Court justices, after the president has nominated them. Perhaps the most prominent example was the 1991 confirmation hearing for Supreme Court nominee Clarence Thomas. Testifying before the Senate Judiciary Committee, Anita Hill, a University of Oklahoma law professor, accused Thomas of sexual harassment when she was an employee at the U.S. Department of Education, and the Equal Employment Opportunity Commission (EEOC), on which he served in the 1980s. A sharply divided national audience watched the Judiciary Committee's investigation into the charges. The hearings placed the issue of sexual harassment on the national agenda, resulting in many changes in laws, policies, and opinions. They also prompted many women, outraged by the confrontational manner in which Hill was treated by the all-white, all-male Senate Judiciary Committee, to enter politics and seek elected office.[52]

Under most other circumstances, national judges, including Supreme Court justices, rarely generate stories of a personal nature. However, the press does cover their rulings, especially Supreme Court decisions and controversial federal district and appellate court decisions. Reporting on the Supreme Court is difficult, because the Court tends to release several rulings at once, forcing reporters to cover numerous, often technical and difficult opinions. Typically, the press will select one or two main decisions and discuss them in more detail, while a summary box simply mentions the other Supreme Court decisions released that day. Several key decisions (for example,

Roe v. *Wade* [1973] and *Brown* v. *Board of Education* [1954]) attracted enormous press coverage at the time they were released as well as retrospective stories on their anniversaries, follow-up analyses of their consequences, and even later revelations about how the decisions were reached. The media have ignored many important cases, however, and in other instances have presented information that had factual errors, largely because of the complexity of case law.[53]

How Groups Use the Media

Interest groups and outsiders use the media to promote their agendas, employing a variety of techniques. One popular technique is to stage events similar to politicians' pseudo-events. A child advocacy group might stage a rally to support a proposal for greater funding of a health insurance program for children, hoping that the news media will report it. Appearing on the news is very important, especially to groups that do not have large budgets, because positive coverage gives them exposure and often credibility.

A second technique used by groups to get media coverage is to issue press releases and bulletins. The National Organization for Women (NOW), for example, routinely issues press releases on matters of importance to its members. Groups often issue video clips directly to news organizations in hopes that the clips will be aired with no editing to show the group in a positive light. So-called video news releases are designed to make it easy for television stations to use the videos. Groups also provide expert interviews and often have members (who do not necessarily identify themselves as members) write letters to the editor or contribute op-ed articles for local and national newspapers.

Finally, groups with sufficient means will often pay for issue advocacy advertising. One example of this is "Pork—the Other White Meat" commercials prompting consumers to consider including pork in a healthy diet. Because the media are such an important means for groups to raise visibility, win support, and influence both the public and officials, interest groups will continue to be creative in developing attention-grabbing tactics.

The Media and the Public in the Political Arena

11.5 Establish how the media have an impact on the cultural values and political opinions of the American public.

The print media—newspapers, magazines, and other periodicals—tend to cater to an upper-class, better-educated segment of society. Print media are effective in translating facts, while TV is better at conveying emotion and feelings. Thus better-educated people are attracted to the print media, and their readers continue to be better informed about events, reinforcing their advantaged position in society.

The fact that the more affluent have greater access to information than the general society gives them more opportunities to influence politics. For example, announcements of city council meetings or school redistricting plans are usually made in local newspapers. Only individuals who routinely read a local paper will know about proposed changes, public meetings, and scheduled forums. Those who habitually do not read the paper remain uninformed about these events, which may have a significant impact on their lives. A cycle exists: Poorer people pay less attention to the print media, because print stories tend to cater to the interests of the more affluent. And because poor people don't subscribe in large numbers, newspapers continue to ignore the needs of the lower class, perpetuating biases in coverage, access to information, and lack of a diverse audience.

Media in Campaigns

It is a long-standing belief that the media are very powerful actors in elections in the United States; some people go so far as to claim that the media actually determine the outcomes of elections. Although this is certainly an overstatement, the media do have a great deal of power, especially in anointing the "front-running candidates" long before an election. Marking one or two candidates as front-runners usually has a snowball effect: The media and the public pay more attention to them, making it easier for them to get on the news and raise money. The more money they raise, the more prominent their campaign becomes, and the bigger the campaign, the more attention it gets from the media and the public.

Front-runner status develops its own cycle of success—though there is certainly some liability in being declared the front-runner, too. (Front-runners get heightened media scrutiny, for example, which can be fatally damaging if they make gaffes or if skeletons lurk in their closets.) Many people are concerned about the power of the media in determining front-runners, because this tends to prematurely narrow the field of candidates, often very early in the nomination cycle. When the media focus on front-runners in polls and stories, lesser-known candidates often encounter many difficulties, especially with fundraising, and are often forced to withdraw early from the race. Moreover, the media often declare winners based not on the absolute vote total but on how well a candidate does compared to what had been expected.

Bill Clinton, at the time governor of Arkansas, serves as a very good example. Massachusetts Senator Paul Tsongas won the most votes in the 1992 New Hampshire primary, but Clinton, simply because he did better than had been expected, was proclaimed "the winner" by the press. This accolade gave him increased media attention and public support. The "winner" designation sent Clinton's candidacy into high gear, and he went on to win the nomination and the election.

During the last several presidential campaigns, the front-runner status was more difficult to determine for both political parties. In 2008, for the Republicans, former New York City mayor Rudy Giuliani held an early lead in the polls, followed closely by Arizona senator John McCain. Giuliani remained the "front-runner" throughout most of 2007. However, pundits who had all but written off McCain were surprised when Giuliani and McCain were both considered by the media to be front-runners after the second Republican debate in early 2007. The media had an even more difficult time declaring the front-runners for the Democrats. Hillary Clinton, Barack Obama, and John Edwards were all designated with the title at some point during the nomination season. In 2012, at various times, Herman Cain, Newt Gingrich, Rick Perry, and Rick Santorum were all considered front-runners before Mitt Romney finally became the party's nominee. In 2016, Hillary Clinton was the undisputed front-runner for the Democrats, but the Republicans were reluctant to consider Donald Trump a front-runner despite a clear and consistent lead with convention delegates and primary victories.

NEGATIVE COVERAGE   According to a study of the 2012 presidential campaign by the Project of Excellence in Journalism, the Pew Research Center, which analyzed newspaper, broadcast, and cable coverage from late August through October 21, 2012, found that negative coverage of the two main presidential candidates was quite prevalent. Stories and images of President Obama and Governor Romney were overwhelmingly negative. Nineteen percent of stories about President Obama were "favorable" while 30 percent were "unfavorable" (the remaining stories were considered neutral). Thirty-eight percent of Governor Romney's coverage was "unfavorable" while only 15 percent was "favorable." The distribution of favorable and unfavorable coverage was not even in all news sources, as discussed earlier in this chapter. The study also examined social media (Twitter, Facebook, and several million blogs) where coverage was overwhelmingly negative. Statements on Twitter about Governor Romney were negative by a

Presidential debates are often thought to influence presidential elections. They frequently do not, but there are times when especially poor performances can change the momentum of the election. Pictured here is the media center, which is situated nearby the stage where campaign surrogates interact with the media to present their "spin" on the debate. Often it is not objectively how well a candidate does that is important, but how the debate is portrayed against expectations.

■ *Do you think we should consider these events as debates or, since frequently the candidates do not answer the questions posed, would it be better to consider them as joint campaign appearances? Do you think the debates should be more open to minor party candidates?*

4-to-1 margin while 2-to-1 comments about President Obama were negative.[54] Similar analysis of the 2008 general election showed that press treatment of Barack Obama was somewhat more positive than negative, while press coverage of McCain was heavily unfavorable. In the 6 weeks following the summer conventions, unfavorable stories about McCain outweighed favorable ones by a 3-to-1 margin. Obama fared better, with over one-third of stories being clearly positive, and only 29 percent negative (the rest were mixed). As Obama improved in the national polls, his coverage became more positive, while the reverse was true of McCain. Coverage of Alaska Governor Sarah Palin (the Republican vice-presidential candidate) was quite mixed, starting very positively then turning very negative, finally ending with a neutral tone. Interestingly, only about 5 percent of Palin's coverage was on her personal life.[55] The tone of coverage in the 2016 presidential campaign has been remarkably negative. President Obama, clearly frustrated by the tenor of the election, warned about the creation of a "poisonous political climate" and gave an impassioned plea for a more civil political debate as we select his successor.[56] To illustrate two particularly low points, during a Republican primary debate on March 3, 2016, Donald Trump addressed a charge by Marco Rubio that he had "small hands," stating that there was "no problem" with the size of his hands or anything else. At the end of the same month, Ted Cruz and Donald Trump took their fight to a far more personal level when their feud devolved to include attacks on their spouses. Senator Cruz alleged that the Trump campaign was behind infidelity rumors which were published in the *National Enquirer* (a claim which Trump forcefully denied). The Democrats were largely able to remain more civil throughout much of the primary season, but at the later stages of the race for the nomination, the race began to turn more negative as well.

PAID ADVERTISING One key aspect of media usage in campaigns is the need to purchase paid advertising, which is enormously expensive. Paid advertising is essential, however, because research consistently demonstrates that the news media increasingly portray candidates negatively, with fewer and fewer positive stories. Daniel Hallin found that 5 percent of news stories in the 1968 election were positive and 6 percent were negative. By 1988, however, only 1 percent of stories were positive but 16 percent were negative.[57] TV coverage of campaigns has also shrunk, coming to consist chiefly of tiny, frequently repeated visual snippets called **sound bites**. And even the length of the sound bites on network evening news programs shriveled, from

sound bite
A short outtake from a longer film, speech, or interview.

an average of 42.3 seconds in 1968 to 7.2 seconds in 1996.[58] Given these circumstances, candidates desiring to get their message and vision out to the people must pay heavily for advertising.

DEBATES   Televised debates can also be important in affecting the public's perception of candidates. The most infamous example of this impact occurred in the very first televised presidential debate in 1960. John F. Kennedy's strong visual performance allayed the public's fears that he was too young and inexperienced compared to his well-known opponent, Vice President Richard M. Nixon. This debate underscored the importance of television's visual nature. TV viewers saw the physically attractive, tanned, and seemingly relaxed Kennedy verbally sparring with a sweaty, earnest, and less photogenic Nixon, and a majority of television viewers believed that Kennedy won the debate. Those listening to the debate on the radio, however, believed that Nixon had won on the substance of what was said. This stark contrast changed the way in which subsequent candidates have viewed the power of television and underscored the importance of cultivating visual images. Ronald Reagan's masterful performance in the 1980 and 1984 presidential debates showed that despite his advanced years, he was mentally alert and able. (His professional training as an actor helped him, too.) More recently, President Obama's poor performance in the first debate of the 2012 presidential campaign was seized by Governor Mitt Romney to invigorate his stalled campaign, making the November election far more competitive than it was shaping up to be. During the 2016 primary season, the Republican debates were often quite lively, with candidates frequently devolving into personal insults and negative attacks upon each other. The Democratic debates, on the other hand, were far less controversial and offered Bernie Sanders an opportunity to reach a much wider audience of supporters. Donald Trump's widely panned performance in the first presidential debate against Hillary Clinton in 2016 was a pivotal point in the election, serving to invigorate the Democratic base, however, it proved too little to propel Secretary Clinton to victory in this atypical election.

The importance of television in campaigns and elections also has a powerful effect on the pool of eligible candidates and the types of people who are perceived to be "electable." Had TV existed in the 1930s, many believe Franklin D. Roosevelt could not have been elected, because having been crippled by polio, he was confined to a wheelchair. Indeed, Roosevelt worried that his disability would make him seem "weak," and newspaper and newsreel photographers of the day were careful not to show him in his chair or on crutches. Television puts charismatic, telegenic candidates at an advantage; hence candidates for high-profile positions usually hire coaches to teach them how to behave when appearing on television. For example, public opinion polls might show that a candidate is perceived to be "too stuffy." The campaign will then stage outdoor events to make him or her appear more informal, relaxed, and "ordinary." If a candidate is seen as not intellectual enough, events will be staged at a library or university. These coaches work on body language, speech presentations, clothing, and hairstyle. Although this seems superficial, television has made outward appearance crucial. You might wonder if such past presidents as George Washington and Abraham Lincoln could ever be elected today.

Global Issues

CNN reaches nearly every country in the world and can be viewed by 271 million households worldwide. A Russian edition of the *New York Times* is sold in Moscow. MTV is viewed on five continents, in nearly 60 countries with an audience of over 265 million. Such availability of American culture raises concerns for many people, especially in other countries with very different cultures, who fear "McGlobalization." Foreigners worry that our culture and values, many of which they do not share, are "corrupting" citizens in their countries. This concern is especially significant in the Muslim world, where American and Western values are widely perceived as a mortal threat to Islam. Objections to "excessive" American cultural and political influence are heard around the globe, from Canada and France to China. In fact, concerns about American influence led the Chinese government to ban all privately owned satellite dishes. Many historians attribute the fall of communism in the Soviet Union and Eastern Europe in part to exposure to Western thought and values on television. Countries proud of their culture, heritage, and values are greatly troubled by the trend of Americanization made possible by the global media.

Narrowcasting

Another area of concern for many is the trend of cable television and the Internet to appeal to narrower audiences. As television and other mass media have become more specialized, the targeting of specific audiences, known as **narrowcasting**, has become far more common. Some observers worry that specialized programming may cause groups to become more fragmented, as the media no longer cater to a mass audience. Consider the changes in print media and in programming for Spanish speakers in the United States. One study in 2011 found that two-thirds of Hispanic Americans watch Spanish-language programming daily (though second and third generation Hispanics are more likely to watch programming in English and Spanish).[59] A 2015 study found that Spanish-language-dominant homes viewed 78 percent of television in Spanish while multi-language-dominant homes viewed about 50 percent of television in Spanish. English-language-dominant homes (those which speak mostly or only English) watched 97 percent of their television in English.[60] Sixty-two percent of adult Hispanics in the United States speak English or are bilingual.[61] Telemundo and Univision both have nightly news programs, each with a slightly different focus in their stories than the English-language network news programs. Furthermore, because many Hispanic viewers are not watching national English-language news programs, these "mainstream" networks are less likely to offer programming that appeals to Latinos. As a result, the larger English-speaking audience is not sufficiently exposed to issues of concern primarily to Hispanic viewers. An endless cycle can develop that is troubling to many analysts, who worry that specialized programming with a narrow appeal will further fragment groups within American society.

narrowcasting
Creating and broadcasting highly specialized programming that is designed to appeal to a specified subgroup rather than to the general population.

Citizen Journalism

With the advancements in technology and popularity of social networking sites and blogs, more people are actively involved in the creation of news than ever before. Now, more and more often, we are learning about events through the lens of average citizens via cell phone recordings. These videos can be very powerful and have great potential to gain attention and become tools for change. However, informed consumers need to consider the full range of implications of these changes. **Citizen journalism** (also known as *street journalism*) is the idea that nonprofessionals are involved in collecting, reporting, commenting, and disseminating news stories. J. D. Lasica classifies different types of citizen journalism including audience participation at mainstream news outlets (bulletin boards, blogs, videos), independent news and information Web sites (consumer reviews such as trip advisor and YELP), full-fledged participatory news sites (such as South Korea's OhmyNews with the motto "Every Citizen is a Reporter"), collaborative and contributory media sites (such as Slashdot), and broadcasting sites (such as KenRadio).[62]

Bystander and security camera videos have dramatically impacted policing in the United States, leading to protests, state and federal investigations, and heightened debates about race and public policies. Numerous examples of videos, like the one we discussed at the beginning of the chapter, largely depicting white police officers using what is thought to be excessive force have stunned the nation. Such videos are often controversial, as many feel they do not fully show the entire events

citizen journalism
Nonprofessional members of the public who are involved in the collection, reporting, commenting, and dissemination of news stories; also known as street journalism.

Pictured here is U.S. Representative Kevin Brady, R-TX, taking part in the ALS Ice Bucket Challenge. The challenge was designed to raise awareness and money for a devastating disease, ALS.

■ *Do you think that the challenge lost its focus and ultimately was unsuccessful in its goal of raising money for the ALS Association or was it a positive use of social media?*

and can be taken out of context. Supporters of the police, for example, argue that the spectators do not film the entire event and the videos are of only one perspective (typically not the officer's) and can be altered. Even if the material is not intentionally misleading, the lack of context often impacts the ability of the video to capture the "whole story."

Moreover, media outlets, which now compete for news with everyone on the street who owns a cell phone, are increasingly placed in a position to react rather than report. This reactionary cycle can often be riddled with errors and creates a number of concerns. In an attempt to get ahead of a viral video, members of the media can rush to judgment and fail to capture the whole story in their initial reports. We often see this type of reporting during urban crises, protests, and violence. Traditional media sources, such as print newspapers like the *Washington Post* and *New York Times,* have always taken pride in ensuring unbiased and accurate information, verifying sources and accuracy. Stories go through multiple layers of review (typically including an assignment editor, a copyeditor, and at least two section editors). Even with this multi-layered approach, however, errors still occur, especially with so much pressure on media outlets to "break stories." Instant sharing of stories with no verification means a greater likelihood of reporting errors and hoaxes. Consequently, some see citizen journalism as a positive mechanism allowing for more variety of content, promoting diversity, and enhancing participatory democracy, while others view it as something that is dangerous for democracy, since there is nearly no regulation of content or quality—in essence anyone can become a "citizen journalist" with no training or qualifications. The American people's level of trust in the media is significantly lower today than it was 10 or 15 years ago. People are leery of the material they hear on the news and are skeptical of the ability of the media to objectively report the news. As such, they may believe that videos recorded by common citizens are more objective. But are they? As informed consumers, we must be cautious in accepting videos as evidence and proof because they can be filmed—either intentionally or unintentionally—in a biased manner. The broader context is often absent, as the videos are typically recorded after a situation has escalated, thereby failing to document the minutes before the camera was turned on. As consumers, we need to consider the full range of implications of these changes and be thoughtful when consuming "news."

Concentration and Centralization of Ownership

Concern also stems from the trend toward more concentrated media ownership, especially of the print media and in radio broadcasting. As media ownership becomes more centralized, a "nationalization" of the news occurs, which tends to promote a sameness of opinion and experience. Concentration has been under way ever since the rise of broadcast networks and of newspaper chains in the 1930s, but today, it is accelerating.

Competition is generally believed to be healthy, because it makes possible a larger variety of opinions and points of view. There is concern today because much of the news comes from national news services and there is minimal or no competition between papers in major cities—especially between two or more morning or evening papers. Examine your local paper to see how many stories in the first section come from centralized news sources, such as the Associated Press, *New York Times,* or *Washington Post.* You will find that it is not uncommon for the entire first page to be from sources outside your community or state. This trend is evident even in college newspapers, where editorials and stories are often picked up from a news source and do not necessarily reflect the concerns of your particular campus community.

It is widely believed that competition results in the best product, an economic and political belief held by most theorists. Observers of the media enthusiastically approve of **competitive news markets** and regard **news monopolies** as potentially dangerous. Newspaper ownership in recent decades has tended toward monopolies and away from competitive markets.

The changes in broadcasting are less clear. The influence of the networks has diminished thanks to the proliferation of cable and satellite alternatives, although ownership has become more centralized. In 1997, the media critic Ben Bagdikian noted that the number of major media corporations had decreased from more than 50 in the early 1980s to only 10 by the mid-1990s. By 2001, Bagdikian reported, six huge corporations—Time Warner, Disney, Viacom, News Corp., General Electric, and Bertelsmann AG—dominated the mass media.[63] Furthermore, as the media have become deregulated, cross-media ownership is rising, with corporations owning a variety of media outlets, including newspapers, TV and radio stations, newsmagazines, and production companies. In 1995, Capital Cities/ABC owned seven television stations, seven radio networks (with more than 3,000 affiliated stations), 18 radio stations, 75 weekly newspapers, as well as many magazines and trade publications. When it merged with Disney in 1995, this conglomerate grew even larger.[64] In 2012, 90 percent of American media was controlled by six companies (GE [Comcast], NewsCorp, Disney, Viacom, Time Warner, and CBS). These six companies had a total revenue of $275.9 billion and controlled 70 percent of American cable. Comcast, the largest cable operator, home Internet service provider, and the third largest home telephone service provider in the United States, has significant holdings in several cable networks and took control of NBC Universal in 2011 (one of the largest media mergers in recent history).[65] In 2014, five companies (Sinclair, Nexstar, Media General, Gray, and Tribune) owned 32 percent of the nearly 1,400 local television stations nationwide. Sinclair Broadcast Group, the largest local television station owner in the country, purchased 63 stations in 2013 alone. This one company will own, operate, or provide services to 167 stations in 77 media markets reaching nearly 40 percent of the entire population.[66]

Many are concerned with giving so few people such broad access to such a large proportion of the country. However, many others believe the advent of citizen journalism, which has resulted in a massive diversification of media—via millions of Web sites, blogs, forums, wikis, and such—counters the negative impact of this concentration of ownership and allows for healthy debate. In addition, the growing diversity of news consumption (with more people consuming news from multiple sources than in the past) may further lessen concerns about concentration of ownership.

competitive news markets
Locales with two or more news organizations that can check each other's accuracy and neutrality of reporting.

news monopolies
Single news firms that control all the media in a given market.

Governmental Regulations

11.6 Contrast the rights of a free press to the government's authority to restrict content.

All societies have laws regulating the media, most commonly stemming from national security concerns. Laws that define and punish treason and sedition are always necessary to ensure national security; the dilemma is how much regulation is needed before it infringes on personal freedoms. There is a tension between the needs of the government to ensure national security and the desire of a people to be free, as guaranteed by the First Amendment to the Constitution. The 9/11 attacks and President George W. Bush's declaration of the War on Terror, which included enacting the USA PATRIOT Act, threw into high relief these concerns about balancing security and liberty.

Media and Government: A Tense Relationship

The media want to be allowed to report what they think is newsworthy, while the government wants to limit disclosure in order to promote protection. This tension is most evident in wartime. Many people in government want to limit the amount of information shared, seeking to enhance national security. Ideally, from the government's perspective, only information it approves for dissemination would be shared with the public. For example, the government successfully structured the sharing of information during the Gulf War of 1991. Information and images passed through a tightly controlled, centralized governmental "feed," which released video to all the media; hence there was little variety in the information available.

With limited information, however, it is difficult to ensure that the public knows how the war is being fought. Abuses occur during times of war, and many people fear that in the absence of media scrutiny, abuse and cruelty could increase. For instance, does the public have the right to know if a presidential administration or high-ranking military officials approve the use of torture against enemy prisoners? The tension between the public's right to know information to hold officials accountable versus the government's need to conduct war with secrecy to promote victory is very real. The revelations of the abuse of Iraqi prisoners at Abu Ghraib in 2006 as well as U.S. service members burning the Koran in 2012, fanned anti-Americanism throughout the Middle East, putting the lives of American troops in greater danger. However, most citizens agree that the media should have been allowed to share this information to force reforms mandating the humane treatment of prisoners and sensitivity toward the Muslim holy book.

Even nonauthoritarian governments have laws to protect government secrets. For example, in the United States, laws make top-secret documents unavailable for public scrutiny until many years later, after they have been "declassified" (declared no longer secret). Questions of what is and is not "top secret" are often highly controversial. The government has a perspective very different from that of the press, often forcing the courts into the role of arbiter.

Americans of all generations are skeptical about the potential for the media to play a positive impact in our country. In 2010, 40 percent of millennials were positive about the media; by late 2015, those numbers decreased dramatically and became more similar with the views held by other generations. (Figure 11.5). The tension between advancing democratic values, serving as watchdogs, and harming the ability of the government to rule is real and difficult to navigate.

❯ **POLL** Do you think the media has a positive impact on the direction of America these days?

The Right to Privacy

Democratic societies also have laws that protect individuals' privacy and society's morals—for example, bans against obscenity. In terms of the right to privacy, two standards apply—those for public figures and those for private individuals. Courts have traditionally allowed a good deal of latitude in publishing personal information about people in the public eye, including celebrities, athletes, and politicians. Public "personalities" are assumed to have lower expectations for privacy and consequently have less protection. Controversy often stems from the right to privacy of *private* citizens, especially as it pertains to the victims of violent crimes.

A 1975 rape and murder case in Georgia (*Cox Broadcasting Corporation* v. *Cohn*) provides a good example. The victim's family wanted her name withheld from news reports to protect her right to privacy, especially given the vicious sexual assault that preceded her murder. When newspapers nevertheless published her name and gave the specific details of her rape and murder, her family sued, claiming violation of the victim's privacy right. The court disagreed. Because her name was a matter of public record, newspapers were held to be within their rights to publish it. Papers often have policies not to publish the names of rape victims, but these rules are a matter of decency, not of law.

FIGURE 11.5 Public Opinion on Impact of Media on Democracy

SOURCE: Hannah Fingerhut, "Millennials' Views of News Media, Religious Organizations Grow More Negative," The Pew Research Center, January 4, 2016, accessed on March 20, 2016, http://www.pewresearch.org/fact-tank/2016/01/04/millennials-views-of-news-media-religious-organizations-grow-more-negative.

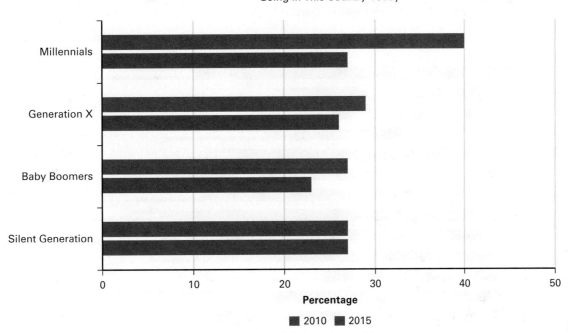

% Who Say News Media Has a Positive Effect on the Way Things Are Going in This Country Today

One area where the right to privacy is protected is when providing a fair trial is in question. The right to privacy of the accused in order to ensure fair treatment in court is enforced, though less strongly today than in the past. Even in cases involving ordinary citizens—and certainly in cases involving celebrities—media coverage of crimes often reaches a saturation level, impelling some observers to question whether any potential jurors can be impartial. To help ensure a fair trial, gag orders can be issued, ordering all participants to refrain from discussing the case. In extreme circumstances, there can be a change of venue (holding the trial in another city), or the judge might even sequester (put into seclusion) jurors to prevent them from consuming news reports and other media coverage of the trial. In the vast majority of criminal trials, however, these extraordinary measures are neither needed nor employed.

Rules Regarding Content and Ownership

The media are prohibited from publishing material that they know to be incorrect. **Libel** laws are designed to protect the reputations of individuals from negative and false reporting. In *New York Times* v. *Sullivan* (1964), the Supreme Court ruled that publishing a falsehood about a public official did not constitute libel unless that official could demonstrate "actual malice"—meaning that the media knew the published information was false or acted recklessly. Three years later, the *Sullivan* ruling was extended to cover celebrities and athletes. These rulings made it far more difficult for a public official or celebrity to sue for libel. It is easier for private citizens to sue for libel, because the standards of proof are lower. Therefore, private individuals are much more successful in bringing lawsuits.

The most controversial issues regarding content are concerns about **prior censorship**—the power of the government to prohibit in advance the publication or broadcast of certain material. Because we believe that a free press is the bedrock of a free society, the American courts are very hesitant to allow prior censorship. Instead, our system of government tends to rely on the threat of punishment after publication in order to keep the press in line. The courts have ruled that prior censorship is

libel

The publication of false and malicious material that defames an individual's reputation.

prior censorship

Forbidding publication of material considered objectionable.

FIGURE 11.6 Public Opinion on Freedom of the Press

Surveys in various countries around the world find wide variation in support for freedom of the press.

■ *What do you think? Is there too much or too little governmental regulation of the media? What factors do you think might change public opinion either way?*

SOURCE: Richard Wike and Katie Simmons, "Global Support for Principle of Free Expression, But Opposition to some Forms of Speech," Pew Research Center, November 18, 2015, accessed on March 20, 2016, http://www.pewglobal.org/2015/11/18/1-support-for-democratic-principles.

It is very important that the media can report the news without state or government censorship in our country.

■ % of Total Who Agree   ■ % of Less Educated Who Agree   ■ % of More Educated Who Agree

allowed only in the most extreme cases. Figure 11.6 provides information about how Americans compare with residents of other countries regarding the importance of a free press. In the United States, 67 percent of people think it is very important to have a free press which is able to function without government censorship. Like in most countries, the more educated are more supportive of this fundamental right than the less educated, though the differences between these two groups are less dramatic than in Germany, France, and South Korea.

> POLL What are your thoughts on the amount of freedom the press has in the United States?

Section 315 of the Communications Act of 1934 (and its many subsequent amendments) provides the central rules regarding censorship of the broadcast media. These rules do not apply to print media or the Internet. The act applied only to the broadcast media, because it was believed at the time that these media, perceived to be quasi monopolies, needed more regulation. When the law was written, the print media seemed to be less monopolistic—and hence more open to ordinary people. Although this is no longer true today, the distinction still applies. Furthermore, as noted earlier, in 1934 the airwaves were considered part of the public domain, to be used for the public good—and therefore in need of government regulation. Consequently, the print media do not have to comply with these regulations, whereas the broadcast media do.

Regulation of the broadcast media falls to the Federal Communications Commission (FCC), an independent regulatory agency created by the Communications Act of 1934 to "serve the public interest, convenience, and necessity." The bipartisan FCC consists of five commissioners. Appointed by the president and confirmed by the Senate, each commissioner serves for 5 years. Many observers want the FCC to be stronger and more independent, but the president and Congress continue to exert a good deal of influence on its decisions.

In addition to privacy and censorship, two other rules exist with respect to television content issues in politics. If a station makes time available to one candidate running for political office, it must make similar time available under similar circumstances to other candidates running for the same office. This is the **equal time rule**. Thus, if the Democratic candidate is allowed to purchase 30 seconds of prime-time television to run an advertisement, the Republican candidate for the same office must also be allowed to purchase 30 seconds of prime time at the same price. The station can refuse to sell time to any candidates from any political party (including minor parties) for particular offices, but if it sells to one, it must sell to the others.

A related and controversial issue regarding access is participation of minor party candidates in presidential debates. In 2004, the Presidential Commission on Presidential Debates ruled that for candidates to participate in the nationally televised presidential debates, they must be constitutionally eligible to hold the office of president, must be on enough state ballots to give them a mathematical chance of securing a majority vote in the Electoral College, and must have the support of 15 percent of the national electorate as measured by public opinion polls. These standards are currently in effect for determining participation eligibility. Given the difficulty of meeting these tests, third-party and independent candidates are generally excluded from the nationally televised debates. The equal time rule does not apply to talk shows and regular newscasts. Thus Seth Meyers can invite one candidate on his show without inviting the others, and just because one candidate's speech is carried on the evening news does not require the network to carry a rival's speech as well.

A similar concept is the **fairness doctrine**, which was in effect from 1949 to 1985. Much broader than the equal time rule, which applies only to political candidates, the fairness doctrine required the broadcast media to allow "reasonable positions" to be presented on controversial issues of public interest. Therefore, we often see or hear news shows that have one person representing one side of an issue and another person speaking for the other side. Although this is not required any longer (partly at the urging of President Ronald Reagan), it is still a common practice.

In addition to regulating the content, the government also regulates the ownership of the media. Until recently, the federal government, attempting to keep the airwaves diverse, limited the number of TV or radio stations that one owner could possess in a single market. The Telecommunications Act of 1996 deregulated many previous ownership restrictions in an attempt to make broadcast media more competitive and responsive to audience concerns and interests, but this deregulation has been controversial. Opponents fear that the law has eliminated the consumer and diversity protections that were present in the Communications Act of 1934. As a result, we are seeing larger and larger mergers, such as Time Warner's acquisition of Turner Broadcasting Company.[67] Even so, one person or entity is still barred from controlling more than 35 percent of network market share and 30 percent of cable market share.[68]

equal time rule

An FCC rule requiring the broadcast media to offer all major candidates competing for a political office equal airtime.

fairness doctrine

Policy that required television and radio broadcasters to provide time for opposing viewpoints on controversial issues so as to ensure fair and balanced reporting: formally abolished in 1987.

The Role of Profits

The standards used for reporting news are controversial. Many critics attack the media's reliance on exploitative and sensational stories in an obsessive search for profits. The quest for profits, it is said, makes the media bloodthirsty hounds, exploiting the misfortune of others. The central question then becomes, "Who should control the media?" Some observers argue that they should police themselves, establishing their own standards of decency and ethics. Others argue that the media simply give us, the public, what we want—if we are displeased with what is being shown, we can use the power of the purse, including boycotts, to influence them.

libertarian view

The idea that the media should be allowed to publish information that they deem newsworthy or of interest to the public without regard to the social consequences of doing so.

social responsibility theory (public advocate model)

The idea that the media should consider the overall needs of society when making decisions about what stories to cover and in what manner: also known as Public Advocate Model.

There are two theories regarding self-imposed control of the media. The **libertarian view** says that the media should show what they think the public wants, with no worry about the consequences. If viewers want violence, give them violence; if they want sex, give them sex. In contrast, the **social responsibility theory** (also called the **public advocate model** of news coverage) states that the media need to balance what viewers want with what is in their best interests. In essence, this theory asserts that the media should promote socially desirable behavior by providing information that advances people's ability to be good citizens, conveying information that allows clear and effective popular decision-making.[69]

The need to make money often leads news people, especially those working in TV, to determine newsworthiness from the perspective of audience appeal rather than political, educational, or social significance. Historically, the networks did not expect to generate profits from news programs, which they believed were a public good, but in recent years, the networks have decided that news programs must not only cover their costs but also generate profits. In 2014, revenue from local newscasts accounted on average for 50 percent of station's overall revenue, up from 40 percent in 2002.[70] Television is dependent on ratings to gauge how much it can charge advertisers. A mere 1 percent increase in the audience can mean millions of dollars in increased advertising revenue. Advertising rates in newspapers are also based on consumption, measured by paid circulation. Changes in programming that reflect profit-driven demands for audience appeal have prompted much criticism.

News journalists increasingly believe that the quest for profits is harming coverage.[71] For example, newspapers have made a variety of changes to increase circulation and profits: They now use more graphics, feature more numerous but shorter stories, provide more news summaries (for example, bulleted lists of how a story relates directly to readers), and put more emphasis on soft news (such as travel, entertainment, weather, and gossip).[72] Similar changes have occurred on TV news shows, the most notable being the increased use of graphics, some of which, like CNN's holograms, add little substantive value to the coverage.

Some commentators on the state of the media believe criticism of these developments is unfair and largely elitist. Critics often assert that the "ideal" citizen *should* want hard news—complex, serious, and socially and politically relevant. But in fact, most people want soft news with light entertainment. Given the reality of their world of daily work, who can blame people for wanting to escape and relax in their leisure time? Hard stories and hard entertainment don't allow for diversion or reprieve. In a democracy, the anti-elitist critics argue, people should be free to choose their own entertainment and sources of information without being criticized for being lowbrow or anti-intellectual. Those who do not accept criticism of the media assert that if we want to make news more factual and intellectual, it nevertheless needs to be presented in a way that is appealing and interesting. This, they say, is the true challenge for reformers.

Conclusion

The media have the potential to dramatically impact the way that most people view world events. Since we usually do not witness most events live and in person, we rely upon the media to show us a picture of the world that would otherwise be impossible. Witnessing the terrorist attacks on September 11, 2001, or the democratic revolutions in the Middle East, or the protests in Ferguson, Missouri, or Chicago, Illinois, on television and online, for example, forever altered the way millions of Americans thought about security, political freedom, race relations, and domestic protests.

The role of traditional media is currently changing as more and more people are getting their news from alternative sources. Americans now are consuming news from more diverse sources than in past generations, with viewer loyalty largely a thing of the past. Moreover, in this digital era, news has become far more immediate and instantaneous.

Growing reliance on social networks and Internet news sources presents great challenges to professional news organizations. Perhaps the greatest changes are in the growth of citizen journalism accompanied by threats to professional ethics and established standards of behavior. The challenges facing traditional media outlets can prove helpful in forcing them to retool their approach and to demonstrate their continued relevancy in this changing environment.

Although many researchers have examined the power of the media and their impact, the results are mixed. People certainly believe that the media are a powerful force in American politics. So do politicians. And because politicians believe the media are powerful, they may alter their behavior based on how that behavior might be portrayed in the media and received by the public. This belief is potentially a strong check on our leaders' actions. However, it is very hard to measure this potential impact of the media. Moreover, attempting to isolate how the media's portrayal of a candidate specifically influences voters is nearly impossible. Was it the image portrayed by the media or the candidate's qualifications or demeanor that registered in the minds of voters? The same quandary applies to the issues: Do people support an education bill because it was favorably reported in the news, or was it favorably reported because people support it? In light of these questions, establishing causal links is very hard. The complex task of decision-making simply has too many alternative variables. Clearly, the power of the media to influence the political agenda is important, because agenda setting affects what people see, think, and talk about. And the media's powers of agenda setting and issue framing also have great potential to influence public opinion.

The media's portrayal of candidates can be highly criticized but their role in holding candidates and officeholders accountable is vital.

■ *On the whole, do you think the mainstream media is biased or do they fulfill their role as governmental watchdog in as neutral manner as possible?*

CONFRONTING POLITICS AND POLICY

On February 16, 2012, Sandra Fluke, a 30-year-old Georgetown University law student, testified at a meeting of the House Democratic Steering and Policy Committee to support mandating health insurance coverage for contraceptives. Rush Limbaugh ignited a firestorm on February 29 when he called her a "slut" and a "prostitute" on his talk-radio show. He continued with similar inflammatory comments for several days until several national sponsors pulled their advertisements from his program and public outcry grew. Women's rights advocates and liberal groups condemned the comments as sexist and called for Clear Channel Communications to cancel his contract. Clear Channel affirmed their support of him. One month following the scandal, the *Washington Post* concluded that advertisers were returning to the show and the outrage had largely passed.[73]

Some made the distinction that Limbaugh is an entertainer rather than a spokesman for conservatives. Does it matter? Moreover, were people too hard on him given the fact his show is designed to inflame and incite passion? Were liberals hypocritical as they did not criticize liberal entertainers for sexist remarks in the past (most notably Bill Maher's comments about Sarah Palin)? Were these comments evidence of a "war on women" or were they more limited to one person's comments on a radio program dependent upon audience share for profits? Similar controversies have occurred in the media coverage of the 2016 presidential election, and are likely to continue in the future, so spending time to analyse your position on this controversy will be helpful.

ACTION STEPS

Select two news stories and examine how they are covered by different sources: newspapers, radio, television network news, cable news, mainstream Internet news sources, and blogs.

1. How does the coverage vary by source?
2. How does the medium affect the way the story is told?
3. Are there differences in content, presentation, or both?
4. Do any sources seem biased? If so, how?

⟩ REVIEW THE CHAPTER

Mass Media

11.1 Evaluate the roles played by the media in shaping American politics. (p. 354)

The media are a powerful force in American politics, with the ability to influence what issues people think about and their response to them. A free and vigorous press is essential for the marketplace of ideas to develop and for democratic debate to thrive.

The need to balance a free press with government regulations raises many delicate issues. In times of war, we generally side with allowing more government regulations, but even then, tension exists. The intimacy and immediacy of television make it exceptionally influential.

The Growth of Mass Media

11.2 Outline the development of the American media. (p. 355)

Newspapers were the first form of mass communication in the United States. When technological improvements allowed newspapers to be produced more cheaply, they became available to the masses, changing the way the news was reported as well as the ways in which governmental officials communicated with the people.

Once introduced, the electronic media quickly spread across the country. Radios were very popular, with ownership growing quickly upon their introduction. The ownership of television sets grew even quicker once technology was developed to allow mass production.

Since the 1980s, the Internet has witnessed remarkable growth. More and more people have access to the Internet, with its usage growing daily. As our world becomes increasingly interdependent, reliance on the mass media for information grows.

Functions of the Media

11.3 Illustrate the functions of the media in American politics and society. (p. 365)

The media perform many important social functions, from monitoring the government to interpreting the news to socializing citizens. These functions all come with the potential for a great degree of power and influence—and responsibility.

Political Use of the Media

11.4 Assess how the media can be influential in American politics. (p. 371)

Since the earliest days of recorded history, individuals have used communication for political purposes. Today, with the advent of technology, mass communication expands the opportunities individuals, leaders, and groups have to advance their political causes. An uneasy relationship between the press and public officials exists. On the one hand, they need each other; on the other, they both want to control the manner in which the news is reported. Officials want to have the news framed supportively, while the media often look for controversy to generate audience interest. Candidates, officials, and groups use many tactics to get positive press coverage, which enhances their legitimacy and visibility and may help garner support.

The Media and the Public in the Political Arena

11.5 Establish how the media have an impact on the cultural values and political opinions of the American public. (p. 379)

The media both shape and reflect our cultural, political, and economic values by serving as a conduit of information and allowing the two-way flow of information. The media conduct public opinion polls, interview people and cover stories, focus attention on issues, and serve as an important link between political leaders and the general public.

Earned media coverage (obtained free of charge) is especially important, because Americans believe it to be more trustworthy and objective than paid advertisements, which are nevertheless important tools to reach an audience. They allow candidates to repeat controlled messages in attempts to sway public opinion.

Governmental Regulations

11.6 Contrast the rights of a free press to the government's authority to restrict content. (p. 385)

The government exercises some regulation of the content and ownership of the media. There are laws dealing with prior restraint, privacy, and those related to accurate and fair reporting. It is complex to balance the competing desires of the press to be free and vigorous and the need for governmental regulation. Generally, we support the most regulation during times of national conflict (typically involving threats to domestic security). However, many argue that the press needs to be most free during times of war to investigate the government to promote accountability and institutional integrity.

> LEARN THE TERMS

> EXPLORE FURTHER

In the Library

Bennett, W. Lance. *News: The Politics of Illusion*. 9th ed. New York: Pearson, 2012.

Boydstun, Amber E. *Making the News: Politics, the Media, and Agenda Setting*. Chicago: University of Chicago Press, 2013.

Croteau, David, William Hoynes, and Stefania Milan. *Media Society: Industries, Images and Audiences*. 5th ed. Thousand Oaks, CA: Sage Publications, 2014.

Dill-Shackleford, Karen E. *How Fantasy Becomes Reality: Information & Entertainment Media in Everyday LIfe*. New York: Oxford University Press, 2016.

Dines, Gail, and Jean M. Humez, eds. *Gender, Race and Class in Media: A Critical Reader*, 4th ed. Thousand Oaks, CA: Sage Publications, 2015.

Entman, Robert. *Scandal and Silence: Responses to Presidential Misconduct*. Cambridge, MA: Polity Press, 2012.

Gonzalez, Juan and Joseph Torres. *News for All the People: The Epic Story of Race and the American Media*. Brooklyn, NY: Verso, 2011.

Graber, Doris A., and Johanna Dunaway. *Mass Media and American Politics*, 9th ed. Washington, D.C.: CQ Press, 2015.

Iyengar, Shanto. *Media Politics: A Citizen's Guide*. 3rd ed. New York: Norton, 2016.

Jones, Jeffrey P. *Entertaining Politics: Satiric Television and Political Engagement*, 2nd ed. Boulder, CO: Rowman & Littlefield, 2010.

Mutz, Diana C. *In-Your-Face Politics: The Consequences of Uncivil Media*. Princeton, NJ: Princeton University Press, 2015.

Potter, James W. *Media Literacy*, 8th ed. Thousand Oaks, CA: Sage Publications, 2016.

On the Web

Presidential campaign commercials from 1952 to 2012 can be found through the Museum of the Moving Image–the Living Room Candidate at *http://www.livingroomcandidate.org/*.

For more information about early radio and related technologies in the United States from 1897 to 1927 visit Early Radio History at *http://earlyradiohistory.us/*.

For collected and preserved historic and contemporary radio and television content, visit Museum of Broadcast Communications at *http://www.museum.tv*.

To compare broadcasting and news from another country visit British Broadcasting Company Web site at *http://www.bbc.co.uk*.

The Freedom Forum at *http://www.freedomforum.org.np* is a nonprofit foundation dedicated to free press and free speech.

Univision at *http://www.univision.com* is a Spanish-language media company serving residents of the United States.

To explore a nonprofit, grassroots citizen's watchdog of the news media, go to Accuracy in Media at *http://www.aim.org*.

Popular cable and news media Web sites are CNN, *http://www.cnn.com*; FOX News, *http://www.foxnews.com*; and the *New York Times*, *http://www.nytimes.com*.

Started as a gossip column and now largely seen as a conservative news reporting Web site is the Drudge Report at *http://www.drudgereport.com*.

OhmyNews is a citizen journalism Web site with the motto "Every Citizen is a Reporter" and is found at *http://english.ohmynews.com/*.

Pew Center for Civic Journalism reports on "experiments" with civic journalism (public journalism) from around the country, found at *http://www.pewcenter.org*.

Slashdot—a technology related "news for nerds" Web site owned by Geeknet, Inc.—is found at *http://slashdot.org/*.

Free Press (*http://www.freepress.net*) is a national nonpartisan, nonprofit organization that works to reform the media through education and advocacy.

INTEREST GROUPS AND CIVIC AND POLITICAL ENGAGEMENT

The face of human trafficking often seems foreign, but it is not. Pictured here is Withelma "T" Lawana Ortiz-Macey, a survivor of abuse and sex trafficking in the foster care system, and Representative Karen Bass, D-CA, at the Foster Youth Shadow Day in May 2016. Ms. Ortiz-Macy is an advocate for youth across the country and has testified before Congress to prevent sex trafficking in the United States.

■ *Did you know that sex trafficking is a domestic problem or did you think it was something that "happened somewhere else"? How do you think we can eliminate sex trafficking and human enslavement today?*

→ LEARNING OBJECTIVES

12.1 Illustrate how beliefs in collective action, self-government, and citizen action laid the foundation for activism and protest in the United States.

12.2 Explain the key factors that facilitate political protest and activism.

12.3 Identify four different types of interest groups, and explain the function of interest groups in a democracy.

12.4 Show how interest groups mobilize their memberships in the face of organizational barriers.

12.5 Describe how interest groups appeal to public officials and the public to gain support for their causes.

12.6 Assess the ways interest groups positively and negatively impact our society.

HOW DO INDIVIDUALS INFLUENCE OUR GOVERNMENT AND OUR SOCIETY THROUGH ORGANIZED ACTION?

So often it seems that individuals, especially young people, cannot make a difference in American politics. However, that simply is not the case. Ordinary young people are literally changing the world every day. Take, for example, a high school senior in Ohio upset over learning she could not vote in her state's presidential primary after preparing all year long in her government class. In early March 2016, Ohio Secretary of State Jon Husted stated he would bar 17-year-olds who will turn 18 before the general elections from voting in the Ohio presidential primary. These teenagers were going to be allowed to vote for some candidates, even for Congress, but not for delegates to nominate presidential candidates. Ohio teens in this category have had the right to participate in presidential primaries in the state since 1981, however Mr. Husted interpreted existing law differently and said they would not be allowed to vote. Katy Spittell, then a 17-year-old, believed this was wrong and unfair so she started an online petition directed toward Mr. Husted and Ohio Governor Kasich. She was able to amass over 1,700 signatures and strategically used social media to pressure Mr. Husted to change his interpretation of the law. Presidential candidate Bernie Sanders joined Ms. Spittell's battle to allow this group of young people to exercise their full voting rights and filed a lawsuit. Ultimately, Ms. Spittell prevailed when an Ohio judge ruled that 17-year-olds must be permitted to vote in this crucial swing state's presidential primary. Ms. Spittell is not alone.

When Ms. Withelma "T" Ortiz Walker was a 24-year-old college student, she testified before Congress about her time as a victim of sex trafficking throughout the western United States. As an activist, this survivor started an online petition on Change.org to encourage the media to stop characterizing child victims and survivors of rape as "child prostitutes" or "child sex workers." In 2016, Ms. Walker worked with the Human Rights Project for Girls to successfully petition the Associated Press to change their style guide in an effort to transform the way we see sex trafficking and the victimization of children. The online petition has proven to be an effective tool for victory in these classic David-versus-Goliath fights.

Activism and Protest in the United States

12.1 Illustrate how beliefs in collective action, self-government, and citizen action laid the foundation for activism and protest in the United States.

Americans claim as our birthright some of the most profound liberties and freedoms. Our Bill of Rights establishes many cherished liberties including freedom of speech, religion, press, and assembly. As a result, we have the unrivaled ability to influence our government and our fellow citizens. We have the freedom to speak our minds and to express our most controversial and complex thoughts—thoughts that might be unpopular or even unreasonable, but still ideas that can be presented in public and compete for acceptance. Furthermore, we have constitutionally guaranteed liberties that allow us to appeal to our government to address our concerns and issues. Using group action has a distinctive appeal to Americans, for whom the tradition is deeply ingrained in the national political culture. In this chapter, we will examine people and groups working to change our society, our laws, and our culture. Grassroots mobilization is an important pathway to influence our society, our government, and our social structures.

Belief in Collective Action

While travelling throughout the United States in 1831 and 1832 and studying our society, Alexis de Tocqueville, a young Frenchman, noted that group activities were essential for the development and maintenance of democracy. Compared to Europeans of his time, he observed, Americans had a much stronger tendency to join together to solve problems, to articulate collective interests, and to form social relationships. He asserted that people living in democratic nations must join together to preserve their independence and freedoms. Collective action is especially important for people who have little influence individually, as like-minded people can come together and act with greater strength. Tocqueville pointed out that the freedom of association allowed "partisans of an opinion" to unite in the electoral arena. In his words,

> The liberty of association has become a necessary guarantee against the tyranny of the majority....There are no countries in which associations are more needed, to prevent the despotism of faction or the arbitrary power of the prince, than those which are democratically constituted....The most natural privilege of man, next to the right of acting for himself, is that of combining his exertions with those of his fellow-creatures, and of acting in common with them. I am therefore led to conclude that the right of association is almost as inalienable as the right of personal liberty.[1]

Tocqueville's journey resulted in the book *Democracy in America*, originally published in 1835. Tocqueville was only 25 years old when he came to America to observe our democracy, yet his account of our society is one of the most perceptive ever published.[2]

The right to associate and to be active in public affairs is one of the most fundamental rights on which participatory democracy depends. To live in a free society, citizens must have the right of association to petition their government to address their grievances and concerns. Such an understanding of the functioning of collective action in democracies goes back to the infancy of our country. The importance of citizen participation is even greater today, because our society has grown far more complex, diverse, and technological, with intimate ties to the global community.

Activism is at the root of our "do something" political culture, and forming groups is essential for political action. Throughout our history, groups have emerged to challenge the status quo—and opposition groups have emerged to fight to preserve the status quo. Our main purpose in the following sections is to illustrate the validity of Tocqueville's observations about the importance of group action in the United States to promote change and to enhance liberty, as well as to provide a context for analyzing contemporary group behavior. These activities are fundamentally important in shaping the very nature and definition of our democracy.

Belief in Self-Government

One central idea underlying our political system is a belief in self-government and citizen action. At the end of the seventeenth century, the English philosopher John Locke argued that people have certain God-given, or natural, rights that are inalienable—meaning that they can neither be taken away by nor surrendered to a government. Locke's social contract theory holds that people set up governments for the very specific purpose of protecting natural rights. All legitimate political authority, said Locke, exists to preserve these natural rights and rests on the consent of the governed. When a ruler acts against the purposes for which government exists, the people have the right to resist and remove the offending ruler. Thomas Jefferson relied on Locke's social contract theory of government when writing the Declaration of Independence; the central premise of this document is that people have a right to revolt when they determine that their government has denied them their legitimate rights.

One consequence of the American Revolution was that faith in collective action, as well as in self-rule, became entrenched in the new United States. Rioting and mass mobilization had proved an effective tool to resist oppressive government. The Revolution also helped establish in the United States the sense of **egalitarianism**—the

egalitarianism
A doctrine of equality that ignores differences in social status, wealth, and privilege.

belief that all people are equal. Our republican form of government, in which power rests in the hands of the people, reinforces this egalitarianism. A faith in the legitimacy of collective action, even violent action, in defense of liberty entered into our political culture.

Influencing Government Through Mobilization and Participation

12.2 Explain the key factors that facilitate political protest and activism.

G rassroots mobilization and interest group activities are essential for a healthy democracy. For democracy to function and to thrive, there must be a collective sense of community: people must feel tied to each other and united with their government, whether or not they agree with its actions. Constitutional guarantees and organized interests facilitate political protest and activism by providing pathways for individuals to influence government.

Constitutional Guarantees

The U.S. Constitution provides substantial guarantees that allow for citizen participation, activism, and mass mobilization. As an example, the Bill of Rights lists liberties that together ensure our right to petition the government. First Amendment freedoms are fundamental in our democracy, because they dramatically determine how we can influence our world, including our fellow citizens and leaders.

In totalitarian systems, lobbying, activism, protest, and other forms of political engagement among citizens are severely limited—indeed, they are usually forbidden and harshly punished. One vivid illustration of this occurred in June 1989, in Beijing, China, when thousands of pro-democracy students gathered in Tiananmen Square to protest political oppression. The world watched in horror as the Chinese government massacred several thousand young pro-democracy protesters on live television. More recently, many Arab Spring protesters in the Middle East were met with violent responses by entrenched governments. These students were demonstrating their desire for rights that all Americans enjoy but that many fail to appreciate.

How do we allow citizens to pursue their self-interest while protecting society's interest as well? Balancing these often competing desires is difficult. One short example illustrates this dilemma. Imagine that a developer wants to build a large factory just outside your neighborhood. You worry about increased traffic, environmental impacts, and decreased property values. What do you do? You could form an association to address your problem, gathering neighbors who share your concerns and petitioning your city council and zoning commission. The neighborhood is rational in its concerns. Factories do alter traffic patterns, affect the local ecosystem, and lower property values. But factories also employ people who might desperately need the work, and they pay taxes that can benefit the entire community. How does the community navigate between the needs of local homeowners and the needs of the larger community? Who should win—homeowners or unemployed people in need of jobs? This difficult question underscores a central dilemma of government.

Organized Interests

Organized interests prompt leaders to "do something"—to address pressing problems in society. Without organized interests, many issues are likely to be overlooked by governments and to develop into real problems. Race rioting in the 1960s, for example, resulted from the frustration of African Americans at being marginalized and disregarded by white society. Years of discrimination and

Using hashtags to gain attention on social media has grown dramatically in popularity. Pictured here is a slogan that stemmed from the #BlackLivesMatter social movement. On December 10, 2015, a memorial was held in New York City to remember the lives of slain NYPD officers Wenjian Liu and Rafael Ramos.

■ *Do you think the #BlackLivesMatter and #BlueLivesMatter slogans are helpful?*

bigotry yielded to frustration and rage—which had no structured outlet. By ignoring the racism that was evident in the United States, Americans created a situation that at last exploded violently.[3] Some feel that history is being repeated with the riots following high-profile police shootings of unarmed African Americans in Ferguson, Missouri, Baltimore, Maryland, Chicago, Illinois, and many other communities.

Pressure from organized interests serves to hold governing officials accountable by forcing them to pay attention to issues that are important to people. Involvement also fosters the acquisition of attributes important to democracy—tolerance, political efficacy (effectiveness), and political trust. Being civically engaged allows people to develop associations and skills that are essential for healthy democratic communities. Moreover, competing groups can counteract the self-serving tendencies of each, balancing perspectives and increasing the likelihood for broader and more diverse representation.

Functions and Types of Interest Groups

12.3 Identify four different types of interest groups, and explain the function of interest groups in a democracy.

Interest groups are organizations outside the government that attempt to influence the government's behavior, decision-making, and allocation of resources. Interest groups perform many valuable functions in our democracy. Often, a tension exists between what is best for the group and its members and what is best for society. This tension can be healthy, however, because it focuses attention on issues that otherwise would not receive much notice and can promote constructive public debate.

interest group
A group of like-minded individuals who band together to influence public policy, public opinion, or governmental officials.

Characteristics of Interest Groups

In our diverse society, people join interest groups to find a place to belong, to articulate their point of view, and to promote their common goals. Three primary characteristics define interest groups. First, they are voluntary associations of joiners. Some interest groups are formal, including trade groups, such as the American Medical

Association (AMA); others are more informal, such as neighborhood groups that form to fight zoning changes. Second, the members of an interest group share common beliefs. Doctors join groups such as the AMA to promote patient care, to safeguard ethics in the practice of medicine, and to ensure their own economic viability. Hunters join organized groups to uphold their gun ownership rights and to ensure access to public land. Third, interest groups focus on influencing government. People join them because they want government policy to reflect their preferences, and consequently, interest groups spend time, energy, and money trying to influence public officials.

As you will see, interest groups use many different tactics in trying to accomplish their goals, but all interest groups exist for the purpose of influencing others—their own members, other like-minded associations, the general public, and elected and appointed officials. **Single-issue interest groups** focus primarily or exclusively on one issue, such as the environment, peace, or abortion. **Multi-issue interest groups**, by contrast, pursue a broader range of issues grouped around a central theme. One example of a multi-issue group is the National Organization for Women (NOW), which works on a number of issues that members believe advance the rights and status of women—educational equality, sexual harassment, reproductive freedom, and pay issues. Similarly, the Christian Coalition strives to promote its values by fighting same-sex marriage, attempting to stop abortion, promoting abstinence-only sex education, and, in general, trying to give religion a greater role in everyday life. Although these two groups often stand on opposite sides of issues, they have in common many characteristics, such as the strength of their members' commitment to the tactics they use in influencing our government and our society.

Functions of Interest Groups

Interest groups enable citizens to peacefully express their concerns to government officials—that is, to exercise their First Amendment right to petition their government. In the United States, interest groups serve the five specific functions shown in

single-issue interest group
A group that is interested primarily in one area of public policy such as the Environmental Defense Fund founded in 1967 to solve critical environmental problems facing the global community.

multi-issue interest group
A group that is interested in pursuing a broad range of public policy issues such as the AARP, which promotes a wide variety of public policies that impact older Americans.

PATHWAYS OF ACTION

LULAC

The League of United Latin American Citizens (LULAC) is one of the oldest and most influential organizations representing Hispanics in the United States. It was founded in 1929 in Corpus Christi, Texas, when three separate Hispanic groups banded together to demand equal rights and opportunities in education, government, law, business, and health care. Today, LULAC, a network of 132,000 community volunteers in the United States and Puerto Rico, organized into over 1000 councils. LULAC provides its members with a number of important services, ranging from conducting citizenship and voter registration drives to pressuring localities into providing more low-income housing. It also strives to help Hispanic youth by providing training programs and educational counseling as well as by offering more than $1 million annually in scholarships. At 14 regional centers, counseling services are provided yearly to more than 18,000 Hispanic students.

Through its activism, LULAC has won a number of important successes that have advanced the civil rights and liberties of Hispanic Americans. In 1945, the California LULAC Council successfully sued to integrate the Orange County school system, which had justified segregation with the claim that Mexican children were "more poorly clothed and mentally inferior to white children."[4] LULAC also provided financial support and attorneys to challenge the practice of excluding Hispanics from juries (*Hernandez* v. *Texas*); in 1954, the U.S. Supreme Court ruled that such exclusion was unconstitutional. In 1966, LULAC marched with and financially supported the largely Spanish-speaking United Farm Workers union in its struggle for minimum wages. LULAC National Education Service Centers, Inc., created in 1973, today serves more than 18,000 Hispanic students a year. The LULAC Institute was established in 1996 to provide model volunteer programs for Hispanic communities, and since 2004, the LULAC Leadership Initiative has been revitalizing Hispanic neighborhoods by creating grassroots programs in 800 Latino communities.

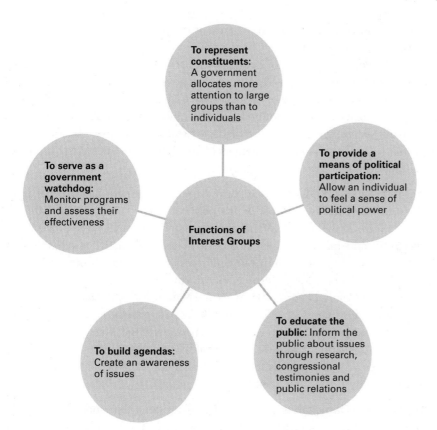

To represent constituents: A government allocates more attention to large groups than to individuals

To provide a means of political participation: Allow an individual to feel a sense of political power

To serve as a government watchdog: Monitor programs and assess their effectiveness

Functions of Interest Groups

To build agendas: Create an awareness of issues

To educate the public: Inform the public about issues through research, congressional testimonies and public relations

FIGURE 12.1 Five Functions of Interest Groups

Many are skeptical about the role interest groups play in the United States, largely because people fail to completely understand the variety of positive functions these groups fulfill.

■ *What would our society be like without interest groups monitoring governmental programs, representing like-minded individuals, promoting political participation, educating the public about complex and controversial issues, and helping raise awareness of issues that would otherwise be ignored?*

Figure 12.1. First, interest groups *represent constituents* before the government. Without the organization and strength of interest groups, individual voices might drown in our complex society.

Second, interest groups provide a *means of political participation*, often coupled with other forms of political activity. Volunteering time, taking part in a group, and contributing money are all important ways in which people can gain a sense of individual and collective power and thus a voice in our society.

A third function of interest groups is to *educate the public*. By sponsoring research, serving as advocates, testifying before congressional committees, conducting public relations campaigns, and engaging in similar activities, members of the public learn about various issues in more detail.

Fourth, interest groups influence policymaking by *building agendas*—that is, simply by bringing an otherwise little-known issue to the forefront. By attempting to educate the public about certain issues or by running public relations campaigns, they focus the attention of both the public and officials on issues that might otherwise be ignored.

Finally, interest groups contribute to the governing process by *serving as government watchdogs*. They monitor government programs, examining their strengths and weaknesses and thereby assessing the effectiveness of programs that are important to their members.

Types of Interest Groups

Interest groups span the political spectrum. To make sense of the variety, it is best to divide interest groups into four categories: economic groups, public interest groups, think tanks and universities, and governmental units. Each type of group exists to advance its goals, which may or may not be in the nation's best interest.

ECONOMIC GROUPS Economic groups include trade associations, labor unions, and professional associations. Trade associations are organized commercial groups, ranging from industrial corporations to agricultural producers. One of the most prominent trade associations is the U.S. Chamber of Commerce.

Labor unions are groups of workers who have joined together to negotiate collectively with employers and to inform the government and the public of their needs. According to the Bureau of Labor Statistics, in 2015 approximately 14.8 million Americans were members of labor unions nationally. **Professional associations** represent people—generally well-paid and highly educated ones—in a specific profession. Two prominent examples are the American Medical Association (AMA) for physicians and the American Bar Association (ABA) for attorneys.

professional association

Organization that represents individuals, largely educated and affluent, in one particular occupational category.

PUBLIC INTEREST GROUPS Over the past 45 years, there has been a dramatic growth in **public interest groups**, which political scientist Jeffrey Berry defines as groups that form in the pursuit of "a collective good, the achievement of which will not selectively and materially benefit the membership or activists of the organization."[5] One of the earliest modern public interest groups was Common Cause, created in 1970 to advocate for governmental reform. The National Association for the Advancement of Colored People (NAACP), the National Rifle Association (NRA), and the environmentalist Sierra Club are all public interest groups, as are the many right-to-life groups that oppose abortion. The AARP (formerly the American Association of Retired Persons) is a public interest group that represents approximately 37.5 million Americans over age 50. It speaks for its members' concerns on such issues as health care, grandparents' rights, and Social Security.

public interest group

Citizen organization that advocates issues of public good, such as protection of the environment.

THINK TANKS **Think tanks** are nonprofit institutions that conduct research and often engage in advocacy on issues of public interest. Think tanks often advocate a strong ideological viewpoint; examples include the conservative American Enterprise Institute and the Heritage Foundation. Universities also use a variety of techniques to petition the government for resources.

think tank

A group of individuals who conduct research in a particular subject or a particular area of public policy.

GOVERNMENTAL UNITS Finally, state- and local-level governmental units form interest groups that petition the federal authorities for help and to otherwise voice their concerns. As we saw in Chapter 3, when Congress cuts its financial support to the states and municipalities while at the same time piling more obligations on them, these government entities have to compete for scarce resources. So, naturally, they form interest groups, too. Two excellent examples of such groups are the National Governors Association (NGA) and the U.S. Conference of Mayors (USCM). The NGA is a bipartisan organization of the nations' governors that helps represent states before the federal government. The USCM is a nonpartisan organization representing cities with populations larger than 30,000. It links national and urban-suburban policy and strengthens federal and city relationships.

The NRA is one of the most powerful lobbies in the United States because they have an active and deeply committed membership.

■ *Do you think the NRA is too powerful, thwarting majority views on gun control?*

The Interest Group Explosion

Between the 1960s and the 1990s, the United States witnessed an explosion in the number and activity level of interest groups. In 1959, 5,843 organizations with a national scope existed. That number almost doubled by 1970, reaching 10,308; a decade later, 14,726 organizations had registered with the federal government. By the mid-1990s, the level of growth had tapered off to slightly over 22,200 national organizations, which is about the number of groups that exist today.[6]

One of the many reasons why interest groups exist in the United States is to unify subgroups of people in our diverse and complex society. As the country grew in size and began to broaden the range of political power exercised by people of different religions, ethnicities, income levels, genders, and racial makeups, differences deepened into

TABLE 12.1   Types of Interest Groups

Type	Examples	Founded	Members	Issue	PAC	Total Expenditures in 2014/2016[†]
Economic	U.S. Chamber of Commerce (http://www.uschamber.com)	1912	3 million businesses	Representation of businesses before the government	Yes	$263,309/$224,918*
	National Association of Realtors (http://www.realtor.org)	1908	1.2 million	Increase the profits of realtors	Yes	$6.2 million/ $6.7 million**
	American Medical Association (http://www.ama-assn.org)	1847	224,503	Physicians' cooperation on important issues	Yes	$2 million/$2.0 million
	American Federation of Teachers (http://www.aft.org)	1916	1.6 million	Improve lives of teachers	Yes	$12 million/ $9.5 million
	AFL-CIO (http://www.aflcio.org/)	1955	12.5 million	Largest federation of Labor unions	Yes	$20.3 million/ $7.3 million
Public interest	AARP (http://www.aarp.org)	1958	37.5 million	Quality of life for older citizens	No	
	Human Rights Campaign (http://www.hrc.org)	1980	1.5 million	Equal rights for gay, lesbian, bisexual, and transgender citizens	Yes	$1.5 million/ $1.3 million
	Sierra Club (http://www.sierraclub.org)	1892	2 million	Environmental protection	Yes	$1 million/$340,115
	National Rifle Association (http://www.nra.org)	1871	5 million	Promote right to bear arms	Yes	$20.8 million/ $18.8 million
	Public Citizen (http://www.citizen.org)	1971	400,000	Representation of consumers	No	
	MoveOn.org (http://www.moveon.org)	1998	7 million	Citizen participation in government	Yes	$10.2 million/ $14.1 million
Think tanks	Brookings Institution (http://www.brookings.edu)	1916	300 resident/ nonresident scholars	Nonprofit research organization	No	
Governmental units	National Governors Association (http://www.nga.org)	1908	50	Bipartisan organization of the nation's governors	No	

[†]2016 Data is based upon reports filed with the FEC and released on October 28, 2016.
*Created a Super PAC that spent $35.5 million in 2014 and $29.8 million in 2016.
**Also has a Super PAC that spent $10.1 million in 2014 and $11.7 million in 2016.
SOURCE: http://www.opensecrets.org.

social divisions or **cleavages**. Many interest groups strive to gather supporters across social cleavages, serving as a unifying factor in a fragmented society. Other interest groups try to exploit cleavages, often using fear to mobilize their supporters.

The nature of our governmental system itself is a second explanation for why interest groups have existed in our society since its earliest days. The American federal system provides many opportunities to influence government at different levels. Groups can appeal to the federal government, to state governments, to county and municipal governments, and to special jurisdictions, such as school districts.

Our federal system helps explain why a larger percentage of Americans are involved in interest groups compared to citizens of other democracies. People who live in more centralized countries, such as the United Kingdom and France, have fewer opportunities to bring pressure on the government. There, a great many issues that would be dealt with locally in the United States are the responsibility of the national legislature. These more unified governments simply do not offer as many points of access as our relatively decentralized system does.

A third explanation of the large growth in interest groups has been put forward by political scientist David Truman. His **disturbance theory** states that groups form whenever individuals perceive other interests as threatening or an event or person disturbs the status quo. Essentially, *social change* causes the growth of interest groups. As society becomes more complex, divisions emerge, which then become the basis for new groups. Not everyone agrees with this theory, however. Others argue that the development of groups depends crucially on the *quality of leadership* of the group.[7] If we

cleavage

Division among people based on at least one social characteristic, such as educational attainment or race.

disturbance theory

The idea that interest groups form when resources become scarce in order to contest the influence of other interest groups.

modify the disturbance theory to include the role of leaders in causing social change, we can offer a hybrid explanation: charismatic individuals come forward to lead the new groups that result from social change.

A fourth explanation for the growth of interest groups in the United States can be attributed to the growth of government. As government takes on new responsibilities, interest groups arise to attempt to influence how the government carries out responsibilities and allocates resources.

A final explanation for the rapid proliferation of interest groups lies in the changing social characteristics of the American population. Today, Americans are more educated and have more disposable income, making it easier for interest groups to target and activate them. In addition, groups have also benefited from new technology, which makes it easier to target potential members and contact interested people.

Interest Group Mobilization

12.4 Show how interest groups mobilize their memberships in the face of organizational barriers.

Before we examine how groups organize, it is important to discuss the barriers that affect organizing—the obstacles that any group must overcome before it can succeed. In this section, we will generalize about the experiences of all groups. It is important to stress, however, that specific subgroups in the American population may face additional barriers and that some barriers may affect certain groups differently than others.

Imagine, for example, that you are troubled by the economic exploitation of Latinos in the construction business in your state and want to organize the workers. However, you learn that the majority of Spanish-speaking construction workers are not citizens or legal immigrants. They would likely be afraid of speaking up or identifying themselves for fear of facing legal repercussions. As another example, imagine that you are a student on a conservative college campus where a number of hate-based crimes have been committed in recent months against homosexual students. You want to form a group composed of homosexual, bisexual, and transgender students and their supporters to pressure the university to protect the students' civil rights. However, students that publicly identify themselves as a member of the group would likely face being ostracized and might even face violence.

In both examples, the pressure would be great to remain silent. Does this mean that neither type of group could be organized? Certainly not, but we must be clear about the barriers that may exist in order to overcome them. Moreover, we must look at barriers that are internalized in individuals and those that reflect the reality of collective action. For example, for you to join a group, you must have confidence in your own abilities to make an important contribution, and you also have to believe that your contribution will make a difference. In smaller, more local organizations, this might be easier to achieve, but in the case of larger groups, it may be more difficult to get a sense that your membership truly matters. As you will see, groups that are successful in recruiting and retaining members are sensitive to each concern and able to overcome these considerations.

Organizational Barriers

The economist Mancur Olson described three key barriers facing people who share concerns and want to create formal problem-resolving organizations.[8] The first barrier is the tendency of individuals to allow others to do work on their behalf. (In essence, why should I spend my time and energy when others will do the work and I will benefit?) This is the **free-rider problem**. Olson notes that free riding is more likely to occur with groups that provide **public goods or collective goods**—things of value

free-rider problem
The fact that public goods can be enjoyed by everyone, including people who do not pay their fair share of the cost for providing those goods.

public goods (collective goods)
Goods—such as clean water, public roads, and community libraries—that are used or consumed by all individuals in society.

NOW (National Organization for Women) used cell phones and the Internet to mobilize a group of supporters from many states in opposition to the closing of a family reproductive health clinic in Charlotte, North Carolina.

■ *Are e-mail or text alerts an effective way to get young people involved with events sponsored by interest groups? What other ways can technology be used to encourage grassroots activism?*

that cannot be given to one group exclusively but instead benefit society as a whole. Clean air is an example. Although one environmentalist group, or more likely a coalition of such groups, gives their time, money, and energy to pass legislation to mandate cleaner automotive emissions, we all benefit from the clean air that legislation provides—even those of us who did not contribute to the group effort. Olson examined the incentives for joining groups from a rational perspective. A person will join a group when the benefits outweigh the costs, but if a person can reap the benefits without incurring any costs, why join? Organized groups must be conscious of the free-rider problem so that they can provide other benefits to members to get them to join.

The second barrier that Olson identified in group formation is cost. This is a chief reason why many people who share common concerns do not organize. For one person to form a viable group that attracts many people and can be influential, money must be spent. It takes money to form and maintain a group, but it also takes a large commitment of time and energy. Some people and groups, of course, are better situated to bear the costs of organizing, most notably the affluent. Less affluent people frequently need to spend their time and energy earning money, including holding second jobs, and they simply cannot volunteer or make large contributions to groups they may support.

The absence of a sense of political efficacy—the belief that one person can make a difference—is the third barrier to interest group formation identified by Olson. Even if you have confidence in your own abilities, you might fall into the pessimistic mind-set of "What can one person do?" Imagine that you are concerned about changing the method of trash collection in your city (going from once to twice a week, for example). "But I'm only one person," you might think. "What can I do by myself?" Such pessimism affects not only people thinking of forming new groups but also those who might join or renew their membership in existing groups. Let's say that you're interested in promoting women's rights. You investigate the National Organization for Women (NOW) and find that it advocates many positions with which you agree. You think about joining but then start to wonder: With 500,000 dues-paying members, what good will my $35 annual dues do? In truth, your dues alone won't do too much for the organization, but you might join once you understand the logic of collective action— that is, when you realize that the dues of 500,000 people come to $17.5 million, a sum that can make a large difference.

Overcoming Organizational Barriers

Any group of people who hope to create and maintain an organization must understand the free-rider problem and other barriers to successful organization and mobilization, so that they can work to overcome them. Groups use many means to make membership attractive so that the benefits of membership outweigh the perceived costs. Organizations must also demonstrate to current and potential members that membership is important and that every member helps advance the collective goal. To overcome these barriers, **selective benefits** may be given to members—benefits that only group members receive, even if the collective good for which they strive remains available to everyone.

SELECTIVE BENEFITS   The first type of selective benefits is **material benefits**—tangible benefits that have value, such as magazines, discounts, and paraphernalia such as T-shirts and plaques. One of the first groups to offer material benefits was the American Farm Bureau. Many people, even nonfarmers, joined the organization in order to receive its insurance discounts. Today, the AARP uses a wider variety of material benefits to encourage membership, including discounts (on pharmacy services, airlines, automobiles, computers, vacations, insurance, restaurants, hotels, and cruises), tax information, magazine subscriptions, legal advice, and credit cards.

In addition to material benefits, which are a major incentive for numerous individuals to join, many groups also offer **solidary benefits**, which are primarily social. Solidary benefits focus on providing activities and a sense of belonging—meetings, dinners, dances, and other such social activities that groups provide to give members a sense of belonging with other like-minded people.

Finally, there are **purposive benefits** of group membership—"the intangible rewards that derive from the sense of satisfaction of having contributed to the attainment of a worthwhile cause."[9] Groups that organize blood drives often try to convey a purposive benefit. The sense of "helping people" and "doing good" are important motivators for many who give blood, encouraging them to endure a modest amount of discomfort and inconvenience.

Many organizations rely on purposive benefits, typically in combination with other benefits, to attract members. For example, because the National Rifle Association (NRA) works for a collective good—advances in protecting gun ownership apply to all citizens—the NRA must fight the free-rider and efficacy problems and recruit dues-paying members to defer its maintenance costs. To encourage people to join, the NRA successfully recruits members by providing a variety of selective benefits, including the following:[10]

- **Material benefits:** Insurance, training, and discounts. The group offers $35,000 life insurance policies to police officers who are members, if they are killed in the line of duty (as well as scholarship to children of officers killed in the line of duty who were active members of the association). It also offers its members gun loss insurance, free accidental death insurance and discounts for eye care, car rentals, hotels, and airfares. The group sponsors training programs for the Olympics and funds research on violent crimes.

- **Solidary benefits:** Safety and training classes (including award-winning Eddy Eagle child safety classes) and shooting competitions (including special tournaments for women and children). Its grassroots group—Friends of the NRA—hosts dinners, national and state conventions, and art contests, and it publishes magazines.

- **Purposive benefits:** The feeling that one is doing something to advance one's view of the Second Amendment of the Constitution and to preserve access to shooting and hunting.

selective benefits
Benefits provided only to members of an organization or group.

material benefits
Benefits that have concrete value or worth.

solidary benefits
Benefits derived from fellowship and camaraderie with other members.

purposive benefits
Intangible rewards people obtain from joining a group they support and working to advance an issue in which they believe.

REQUIRED MEMBERSHIP   Some organizations do not have to encourage membership; they can *demand* it. One prominent example of this is labor unions in many states. In accordance with the National Labor Relations Act of 1935, in some states unions can form agreements with employers that prevent companies from hiring nonunion labor. In other states, "right to work" laws prohibit such contracts, but in nearly 25 states, people can be required, as a condition of employment, to join a union and pay dues. Unions, however, also provide many selective benefits (for example, insurance and employment security) as well as such solidary benefits as dinners, dances, and holiday parties.[11] Although these benefits are more important to recruit members in right-to-work states, they are still used in states that compel membership in order to make the union more attractive and more popular among workers.

Similarly, some corporations use subtle coercion to encourage "voluntary" donations to PACs from executives and their families. Coercion is also prevalent in some professional associations; for example, 33 states and the District of Columbia require attorneys to be members of the state bar association in order to practice law.[12]

The efforts of **patrons**—individuals or organizations that give money to groups—also help form and sustain interest groups. Each year, private organizations such as the Rockefeller and Ford foundations give millions of dollars to citizen groups and think tanks for purposes ranging from conducting research to founding new organizations. Corporations also give hundreds of millions of dollars to interest groups every year. The federal government allocates money to interest groups, generally in the form of a government contract for research or the provision of some other service. For example, the federal government might hire an environmentalist group to help determine how many snowmobiles should be allowed into a national park without harming the ecosystem. Of course, snowmobile companies and the tourist industry may fear that the estimate by the environmentalist group might be too low and may consequently lobby Congress to commission additional research. Few, if any, organizations can rely exclusively on patron support, but support of this sort is very helpful for some.

patrons
Organizations or individuals that contribute money to political leaders or political groups.

The Role of Interest Group Leaders

In addition to using incentives to mobilize support, interest groups use inspirational leadership to build their membership. Charismatic and devoted leaders can entice potential members to join an organization. When people believe in the leaders of an organization, they are more supportive of its goals and more likely to support it financially. Effective leaders "sell" their issues to the public, thus attracting media attention and membership.

CHÁVEZ AND THE UFW   César Chávez provides perhaps the best example of a leader's role in winning success for his organization in what appeared to be hopeless circumstances. Chávez grew up a poor migrant worker farming in states along the U.S.–Mexican border. Because he had to move around with his family to work on farms throughout his childhood, he was able to attend school only sporadically. After serving in the U.S. Navy during World War II, Chávez returned to migratory farm work in Arizona and California. Seeing the desperate circumstances and gross exploitation of farm workers firsthand, Chávez dedicated his life to helping them organize and mobilize to demand fair treatment. In 1962, he organized the National Farm Workers Association, a labor union that later merged with other organizations to form the United Farm Workers of America (UFW).

Chávez's UFW ultimately led a five-year strike by California grape pickers and inspired a national boycott of California grapes. To draw national attention to the grape pickers' plight, Chávez headed a 340-mile march by farm workers across California in

César Chávez was a dynamic leader who organized an unlikely group of activists—migrant farm workers (many of whom were not citizens). Shown here are César Chávez (third from the right) and Coretta Scott King (fourth from the right) leading a march in New York City to build support for a lettuce boycott in 1970. Through marches, protests, and organized boycotts, Chávez was able to improve the working conditions and compensation for thousands of hardworking laborers.

■ *What characteristics do you think are the most important in distinguishing a truly great leader?*

1966 and went on a much-publicized, 25-day hunger strike in 1968. The UFW later led successful campaigns against lettuce growers and other agribusinesses (large, corporate farm industries), demanding fair treatment of farm workers. Chávez and his union gained crucial support from middle-class consumers who boycotted grapes and lettuce harvested by nonunion labor, ultimately forcing the powerful agribusinesses to capitulate.

What is perhaps most remarkable about the success of the groups that Chávez led is their ability to organize the most unlikely people—extremely poor, uneducated immigrants. By the early 1970s, the UFW had grown to 50,000 dues-paying members and had contracts with 300 growers. It succeeded not only in negotiating collective bargaining agreements but also in forcing the enactment of legislation to change migratory pickers' often deplorable working conditions. Activists and scholars alike agree that the success of the UFW owed much to Chávez's energy, appeal, and dedication to social justice. His charisma enabled Chávez to convince farm workers to unite and work with others—for example, California Governor Jerry Brown—to promote their collective interests. As testimony to his commitment to social justice and nonviolent protest, Chávez was posthumously awarded the Presidential Medal of Freedom in 1994.

The UFW is a good example of a group of low-income people uniting to fight large corporations. By overcoming the barriers to organizing, providing membership benefits, and having solid leadership, groups of all kinds can successfully press for change. The challenges are often large, but the rewards can be profound.

Inside and Outside Lobbying

12.5 Describe how interest groups appeal to public officials and the public to gain support for their causes.

The key to understanding influence in our governmental system is to realize that interest groups and individuals use different pathways, often at the same time, to advance their perspectives and petition their government. One pathway may prove a successful vehicle for a group at one point but fail at another time.

Inside Lobbying

inside lobbying

Appealing directly to lawmakers and legislative staff either in meetings, by providing research and information, or by testifying at committee hearings.

Inside lobbying, a tool used in the lobbying decision makers pathway, openly appeals to public officials in the legislature and the executive branch, which includes the bureaucracy. Because inside lobbying is a matter of personal contact with policymakers, it involves some form of direct interaction—often called **gaining access**—between a lobbyist and an agency official, a member of Congress, or a member of the legislator's staff. By having an opportunity to present the group's position directly to lawmakers, staffers, or officials, lobbyists have a greater chance of influencing the decision-making process. To be effective, however, lobbyists must be seen as trustworthy and must develop relationships with individuals who have influence in the relevant policy area.

Another inside lobbying tactic is to testify at congressional committee hearings. Such hearings normally occur when Congress is considering a bill for passage, when committees are investigating a problem or monitoring existing programs, or when a nominee for a high executive or judicial position is testifying before a confirmation vote. Testifying allows an interest group to present its views in public and "on the record," potentially raising its visibility and appealing to political actors.

Organizations spend a great deal of money to lobby the federal government (Table 12.2). Lavish spending, coupled with concerns over corruption, prompted the Lobbying Disclosure Act of 1995. Two components of this legislation regulate direct lobbying. The first component of the law tries to provide "transparency" by requiring lobbyists to register with the federal government and report their activities. Many people believe that having full disclosure will raise public confidence in the system by minimizing the potential for abuse and corruption. The second set of provisions in the law bars certain types of informal lobbying activities that have been used in the past, such as giving expensive gifts, purchasing expensive meals, and paying for trips for members of Congress. Fees (called *honoraria*) for speaking engagements were outlawed in 1992. Even with this legislation, however, many people are concerned with the perception of impropriety and potential for corruption.

gaining access

Winning the opportunity to communicate directly with a legislator or a legislative staff member to present one's position on an issue of public policy.

TABLE 12.2 Spending on Inside Lobbying

In addition to campaign contributions to elected officials and candidates, companies, labor unions, and other organizations spend billions of dollars each year to lobby Congress and federal agencies. Some special interests retain lobbying firms, many of them located along Washington's legendary K Street; others have lobbyists working in-house. A special interest's lobbying activity may go up or down over time, depending on how much attention the federal government is giving the issues. Particularly active clients often retain multiple lobbying firms, each with a team of lobbyists, to press their case for them.

Category	Representative Interest Group	Amount Group Spent On Lobbying In 2015
Corporations	Blue Cross/Blue Shield	$23,383,049
	Boeing Corporation	$21,921,000
Agriculture	American Farm Bureau	$2,792,586
Trade Associations	U.S. Chamber of Commerce	$84,730,000
	National Association of Realtors	$37,788,407
Labor Unions	ALF-CIO (Total combined expenditures)	$5,340,000
	National Education Association	$2,494,515
	Teamsters Union	$1,811,000
Professional Associations	American Medical Assoc.	$21,930,000
Citizen Groups	Gun Owners of America	$1,445,344
	AARP	$8,910,000
Universities	University of Washington	$900,000
	Texas A&M University	$810,000
	Apollo Education Group (owns and operates University of Phoenix)	$1,390,000
Governmental Units	Commonwealth of Puerto Rico	$2,260,000

SOURCE: Center for Responsive Politics, http://www.opensecrets.org/lobbyists.

TIMELINE

Gun Control – A Pendulum Swings

Ratified in 1791, the Second Amendment that states, "A well-regulated Militia, being necessary to the security of a free State, the right of the people to keep and bear Arms, shall not be infringed" still generates controversy today. What should the right to bear arms mean in today's society? Do weapons keep law-abiding citizens safe or make them more vulnerable? What is the best mechanism to balance this precious constitutional right with the need to keep society safe and protected?

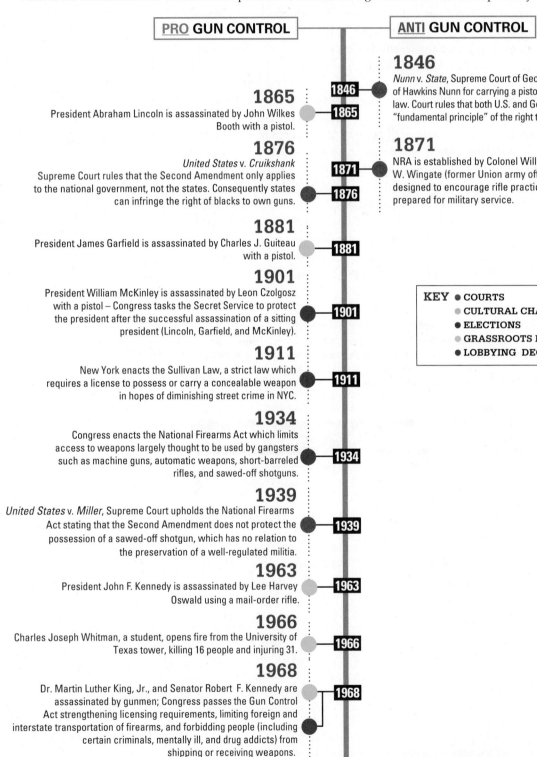

| PRO **GUN CONTROL** | ANTI **GUN CONTROL** |

1846
Nunn v. *State*, Supreme Court of Georgia overrules the conviction of Hawkins Nunn for carrying a pistol in violation of an 1837 state law. Court rules that both U.S. and Georgia constitutions protect the "fundamental principle" of the right to bear arms.

1865
President Abraham Lincoln is assassinated by John Wilkes Booth with a pistol.

1871
NRA is established by Colonel William C. Church and George W. Wingate (former Union army officers) – NRA is initially designed to encourage rifle practice so Americans would be prepared for military service.

1876
United States v. *Cruikshank*
Supreme Court rules that the Second Amendment only applies to the national government, not the states. Consequently states can infringe the right of blacks to own guns.

1881
President James Garfield is assassinated by Charles J. Guiteau with a pistol.

1901
President William McKinley is assassinated by Leon Czolgosz with a pistol – Congress tasks the Secret Service to protect the president after the successful assassination of a sitting president (Lincoln, Garfield, and McKinley).

1911
New York enacts the Sullivan Law, a strict law which requires a license to possess or carry a concealable weapon in hopes of diminishing street crime in NYC.

1934
Congress enacts the National Firearms Act which limits access to weapons largely thought to be used by gangsters such as machine guns, automatic weapons, short-barreled rifles, and sawed-off shotguns.

1939
United States v. *Miller*, Supreme Court upholds the National Firearms Act stating that the Second Amendment does not protect the possession of a sawed-off shotgun, which has no relation to the preservation of a well-regulated militia.

1963
President John F. Kennedy is assassinated by Lee Harvey Oswald using a mail-order rifle.

1966
Charles Joseph Whitman, a student, opens fire from the University of Texas tower, killing 16 people and injuring 31.

1968
Dr. Martin Luther King, Jr., and Senator Robert F. Kennedy are assassinated by gunmen; Congress passes the Gun Control Act strengthening licensing requirements, limiting foreign and interstate transportation of firearms, and forbidding people (including certain criminals, mentally ill, and drug addicts) from shipping or receiving weapons.

KEY
● COURTS
● CULTURAL CHANGE
● ELECTIONS
● GRASSROOTS MOBILIZATION
● LOBBYING DECISION MAKERS

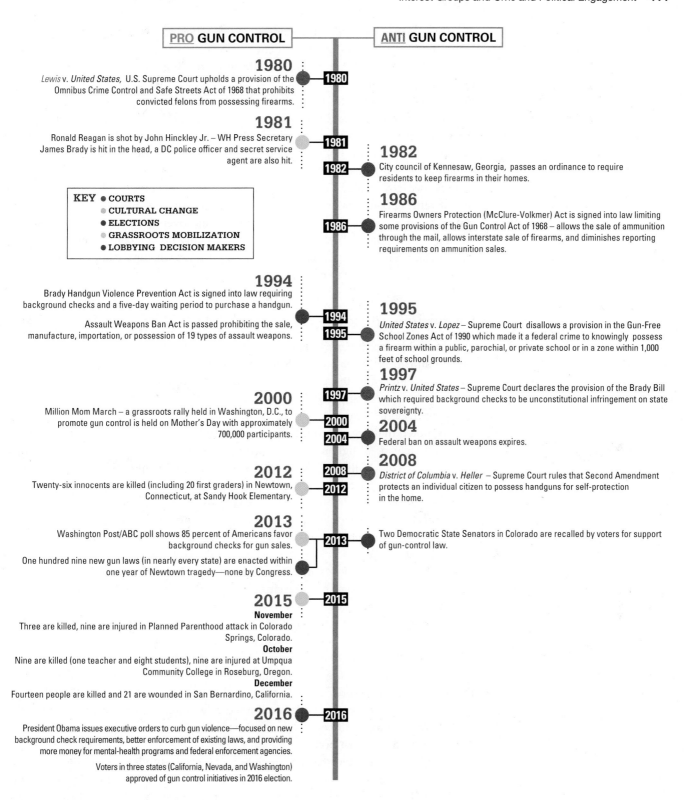

PRO GUN CONTROL   **ANTI GUN CONTROL**

1980
Lewis v. *United States,* U.S. Supreme Court upholds a provision of the Omnibus Crime Control and Safe Streets Act of 1968 that prohibits convicted felons from possessing firearms.

1981
Ronald Reagan is shot by John Hinckley Jr. – WH Press Secretary James Brady is hit in the head, a DC police officer and secret service agent are also hit.

1982
City council of Kennesaw, Georgia, passes an ordinance to require residents to keep firearms in their homes.

1986
Firearms Owners Protection (McClure-Volkmer) Act is signed into law limiting some provisions of the Gun Control Act of 1968 – allows the sale of ammunition through the mail, allows interstate sale of firearms, and diminishes reporting requirements on ammunition sales.

KEY
● COURTS
● CULTURAL CHANGE
● ELECTIONS
● GRASSROOTS MOBILIZATION
● LOBBYING DECISION MAKERS

1994
Brady Handgun Violence Prevention Act is signed into law requiring background checks and a five-day waiting period to purchase a handgun.

Assault Weapons Ban Act is passed prohibiting the sale, manufacture, importation, or possession of 19 types of assault weapons.

1995
United States v. *Lopez* – Supreme Court disallows a provision in the Gun-Free School Zones Act of 1990 which made it a federal crime to knowingly possess a firearm within a public, parochial, or private school or in a zone within 1,000 feet of school grounds.

1997
Printz v. *United States* – Supreme Court declares the provision of the Brady Bill which required background checks to be unconstitutional infringement on state sovereignty.

2000
Million Mom March – a grassroots rally held in Washington, D.C., to promote gun control is held on Mother's Day with approximately 700,000 participants.

2004
Federal ban on assault weapons expires.

2008
District of Columbia v. *Heller* – Supreme Court rules that Second Amendment protects an individual citizen to possess handguns for self-protection in the home.

2012
Twenty-six innocents are killed (including 20 first graders) in Newtown, Connecticut, at Sandy Hook Elementary.

2013
Washington Post/ABC poll shows 85 percent of Americans favor background checks for gun sales.

One hundred nine new gun laws (in nearly every state) are enacted within one year of Newtown tragedy—none by Congress.

Two Democratic State Senators in Colorado are recalled by voters for support of gun-control law.

2015
November
Three are killed, nine are injured in Planned Parenthood attack in Colorado Springs, Colorado.
October
Nine are killed (one teacher and eight students), nine are injured at Umpqua Community College in Roseburg, Oregon.
December
Fourteen people are killed and 21 are wounded in San Bernardino, California.

2016
President Obama issues executive orders to curb gun violence—focused on new background check requirements, better enforcement of existing laws, and providing more money for mental-health programs and federal enforcement agencies.

Voters in three states (California, Nevada, and Washington) approved of gun control initiatives in 2016 election.

CRITICAL THINKING QUESTIONS

1. The National Rifle Association is a powerful lobby, some argue too powerful. Even when public opinion favors heightened gun control, the NRA has been remarkably successful in advancing the agenda of its members. Do you think that interest groups in the United States are "good" or do they wield too much power and influence, thwarting the will of the majority?

2. Should we view the Constitution as a living document, adapting to changing times, or should we be more restricted by the original intent of the founders when interpreting constitutional rights, such as the right to bear arms?

SOURCE: Glenn H. Utter and Robert J. Spitzer, *Encyclopedia of Gun Control & Gun Rights*, 2nd ed., Amenia, NY: Grey House Publishing, Inc., 2011.

This concern proved well founded in 2006 when Jack Abramoff, a top political lobbyist, pled guilty to three felony counts of tax evasion, fraud, and conspiracy to bribe a public official. Abramoff admitted to corrupting governmental officials and defrauding his clients of $25 million. The investigation, which began in 2004, led to the conviction of 12 individuals, including former Representative Bob Ney, former White House official David Safavian, and former interior secretary Steven Griles. Another significant concern regarding lobbying involves what has been characterized by the "revolving door" in which members and/or their staff members leave Congress to become paid lobbyists calling upon their former colleagues and contacts to influence governmental decision-making in their clients' favor. Approximately half of retiring Senators and over 40 percent of retiring members of the House become DC lobbyists (up from 3 percent in 1974) and over 5,400 former congressional staffers have become lobbyists since 1990.[13] Certainly no one begrudges individuals from making a living after careers in Congress, but the wisdom of allowing people to "cash in" is problematic to many.

Outside Lobbying

outside lobbying (grassroots lobbying)

Activities directed at the general public to raise awareness and interest and to pressure officials.

Outside lobbying (or grassroots lobbying), also known as indirect lobbying, is the attempt to influence decision makers indirectly by influencing the public. In appealing directly to the public, interest groups are trying to build public sentiment in order to bring pressure to bear on the officials who will actually make the decisions. David Truman, in his classic analysis of interest groups, *The Governmental Process*, noted that organized interests engage in "programs of propaganda, though rarely so labeled, designed to affect opinions concerning interests" in hopes that concerned citizens will then lobby the government on behalf of whatever the group is trying to accomplish.[14]

There are several advantages in appealing to the public. First, an interest group can indirectly use the people through the elections pathway to directly affect the selection of officials. Citizens can also pressure officials to take action. Moreover, pressure from interest groups can influence which issues the government decides to address as well as the policies it adopts, modifies, or abandons. Appealing directly to the people can also be advantageous, because citizens can take direct actions that can be used to further the group's agenda. By lobbying supporters and the general public, interest groups seek to show public officials that the issue is important to the people.

Examining the activities of more than 90 interest group leaders, political scientist Ken Kollman found that 90 percent of interest groups engage in some kind of outside lobbying.[15] In studying the effect of interest group influence, Matt Grossmann found that interest groups were far more influential than the public in domestic policy areas. He argues that the public plays a limited role in legislative outcomes, especially in areas relating to civil liberties, the environment, and immigration. Rather, interest groups exerted the most power.[16] Figure 12.2 demonstrates that Americans perceive the strong influence interest groups maintain. Interestingly, views about the influence of the National Rifle Association are becoming far more polarized. In 2015, 68 percent of liberals believe that the NRA has too much influence while only 13 percent of conservatives believe the NRA has too much influence. One key element of interest groups influence is their grassroots lobbying efforts. In fact, 75 percent of individuals who contacted members of Congress said they did so at the request of an interest group. Proportionately, more Americans than ever before are communicating with members of Congress, but this surge in communication is not spontaneous. Much of it is the direct result of coordinated efforts by organized interests.[17]

> **POLL** What are your thoughts on the National Rifle Association's influence on gun control legislation in the United States?

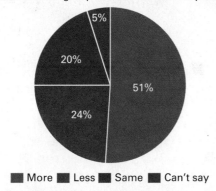

Do you think politicians in Washington these days are more responsive to special-interest groups, or about as responsive to special-interest groups as was the case 20 years ago?

■ More ■ Less ■ Same ■ Can't say

FIGURE 12.2 Americans' Opinions about Influence of Interest Groups in General and the NRA, Specifically

Americans overwhelmingly believe that interest groups exert more influence than voters in national politics.

■ *Do you think that the public has legitimate concerns?*

SOURCES: Survey conducted July 14-20, 2015, by Pew Research Center Hannah Fingerhut, "5 Facts About Guns in the United States," January 5, 2016. http://www.pewresearch.org/fact-tank/2016/01/05/5-facts-about-guns-in-the-united-states/.

Generally speaking, when elected and government officials in Washington make decisions about important issues, how much attention do you feel they actually pay to ... lobbyists and special-interest groups? A great deal, a fair amount, not too much, or none at all?

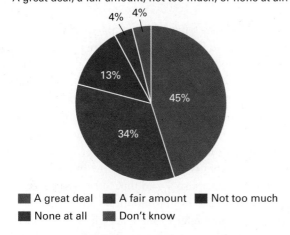

■ A great deal ■ A fair amount ■ Not too much
■ None at all ■ Don't know

Percent who think the NRA has too much influence

■ 2000 ■ 2015

In addition to directly appealing to the public, interest groups also lobby other groups and try to form alliances with them to advance common interests on a particular issue. Coalition building—bringing diverse interests together to advance a cause—is frequently successful. Normally, the coalitions that result are temporary, limited to one specific issue. The more groups cooperate, the easier political action often becomes; conversely, conflict and competition tend to diminish success.

LULAC (League of United Latin American Citizens) conducts voter education campaigns (informing first-time voters of their rights) and voter registration drives in many areas with low voter turnout.

■ *How important is it that interest groups work to inform voters of their rights? Is it possible that new voters could be exploited by interest groups?*

GRASSROOTS MOBILIZATION   Interest groups increasingly rely on grassroots mobilization as a form of outside lobbying to pressure policymakers. A trade association executive interviewed by Kenneth Goldstein gave a good definition of grassroots mobilization: "The identification, recruitment, and mobilization of constituent-based political strength capable of influencing political decisions."[18]

Grassroots work is difficult to measure, and its success is perhaps even more difficult to assess. Most experts, however, believe that grassroots mobilization is becoming far more common. Goldstein found that most Fortune 500 companies have full-time grassroots coordinators with solid plans to present their point of view by stirring up citizen interest, and he also found that the media cover grassroots lobbying with greater frequency today. The depth of support on certain issues is often rather short lived and superficial. Some refer to such artificially stimulated public interest as "Astroturf," because it gives the *appearance* of widespread popularity but has no real depth. Kollman, however, finds evidence that grassroots lobbying is an important tool for getting a group's message to officials.[19]

GRASSROOTS LOBBYING TACTICS   One of the earliest forms of grassroots mobilization was **direct contact**, a process that goes back to the days of the antislavery movement and is still used today because it is so effective. Many Americans believe that indirect lobbying is a new phenomenon. In actuality, indirect lobbying has been going on in our country since its earliest days, although the tools and tactics have evolved with the emergence of new technology. Consider, for example, how westward expansion was sold to the American people. Entities with vested interests in expansion, such as the nineteenth-century railroad companies, stressed in their appeals to the public the ease of obtaining property, the lure of frontier adventure, and the chance of finding wealth by moving west. Westward expansion would have occurred without these marketing campaigns, but capitalizing commercially on the existing public interest accelerated the rate of expansion. Would-be settlers in turn urged the government to aid westward migration. Responding to this pressure, Congress in 1862 passed the Transcontinental Railroad Act and the Homestead Act. By making land grants to the companies that built the western railroads as well as by encouraging western settlement, Congress dramatically increased the value of railroad property. Having committed supporters personally contact fellow citizens is a valuable tool for interest groups. Seeing others who care deeply enough to give of their time and energy can stimulate people to become involved with a cause.

Direct mail is another way for interest groups to contact potential supporters. Modern technology permits mailings to be personalized in ways that allow a group

direct contact
Face-to-face meetings or telephone conversations between individuals.

direct mail
Information mailed to a large number of people to advertise, market concepts, or solicit support.

to frame its message narrowly, so that it appeals to specific types of people. Knowing a good deal about the individuals targeted in its direct-mail campaign helps a well-funded interest group personalize its message and thus make it more efficient. Because modern technology today collects and stores so much personal information, interest groups with substantial financial resources can acquire what they want to know about potential recipients, allowing them to exploit this form of propaganda more effectively.

Many of the events used by interest groups to influence the public and pressure policymakers are designed to provide members with solidary benefits, but they can also raise the organization's image in the community and demonstrate its importance. Labor unions and public interest groups are most likely to engage in this type of behavior, organizing rallies, marches, and mass demonstrations to promote their causes.

Finally, to force the pace of change, interest groups have organized boycotts—the organized refusal of large numbers of people to do business with an opponent as a nonviolent expression of disagreement.

The development in recent decades of more sophisticated means of communication has given interest groups far more options than they once had to motivate supporters, recruit new members, and mobilize the public. To sway public opinion, organized interest groups have aggressively and imaginatively tried to use the media to manipulate what gets reported—and occasionally, they succeed. Pressured by deadlines, some reporters are willing to use in their stories information presented by interest groups. In this era of heightened expectations for investigative reporting, interest groups often try, sometimes covertly, to advance their views by prompting media exposés of controversial issues. Groups also try to have their advocates appear as experts on talk shows. Having someone present the group's position on *The Late Show with Stephen Colbert*, for example, raises the group's visibility and credibility in important ways—because groups must appear credible and trustworthy when using the lobbying decision makers pathway to influence public officials. Staging visually appealing pseudo-events (events that seem to be spontaneous but are actually orchestrated and staged by groups for publicity), such as schoolchildren marching in support of higher teacher pay, is a popular tactic employed because these events are more likely to be shown on the local and even national news.

Many Americans believe an antibusiness bias exists in news coverage. Whether or not such a bias actually exists, citizen groups are often able to invoke sympathy in ways that large corporations cannot. For example, a news story about a local citizen group fighting some huge, impersonal corporation to protect a beautiful stream from pollution is attractive. Such "David-versus-Goliath" stories have a human interest component that is quite appealing to media outlets, which know people like to see the underdog win. To counter this perception of bias, many corporations and industrial groups spend large sums on public relations campaigns to soften their image.

Well-heeled interest groups advertise in major newspapers and magazines as well as on TV and the Internet to increase their visibility and improve their public image. Many of these ads are noncommercial—they are not trying to sell anything or directly attract members but instead are designed to generate favorable public opinion. Because such ads are frequently designed to resemble editorials, they have sometimes been dubbed **advertorials**. For example, drug companies run ads to show that they care about people's health, not just about making money, and oil companies advertise how they are taking pains to protect the environment in efforts to affect public opinion. Advertorials are often intended not only to persuade the public directly but also to influence people who talk to the public, such as journalists and other opinion leaders.

advertorials
Advertisements presented as editorials.

Citizen groups also advertise through the media. Their ads try to inform the public about issues that might concern the group. For example, imagine that a group opposes an issue on the ballot in an upcoming election that would raise the local sales tax to fund a new professional football stadium. What can it do? Certainly, it would want to communicate to the community why it opposes the stadium, because at first, public opinion would probably be rather positive toward the idea (most Americans like professional football and want to attract or keep a local team). So if it hoped to succeed in convincing voters to oppose the increase in sales tax, the anti-stadium group would have to inform citizens about the wider implications of the issue—for example, how a higher sales tax would affect poorer consumers, or how a stadium would radically disrupt traffic patterns.

NEWER TOOLS OF INDIRECT LOBBYING Over the past two decades, the Internet has offered interest groups some of the best possibilities for new tactics. Organized groups can advance their cause in many ways—from Web pages, e-mail campaigns, blogs, viral videos, and social networking sites, which allow people and groups to post information in order to stimulate interest in particular topics, raise public awareness, and influence public opinion. Consumers must use caution when using information posted on these sites, however, because nearly anyone, regardless of level of expertise or knowledge, can set up and maintain a blog. Social networking sites allow groups to appeal to a wide variety of individuals with minimum cost, attracting interest literally from across the globe. The Web has great potential for mobilizing supporters and raising money, but not everyone has access to it or can readily use it. Younger people who are more affluent and better educated access the Web at far greater rates than older, poorer, and less educated people do.

Cliff Landesman of Idealist.org identifies eight purposes for which interest groups use the Web: publicity, public education, communication, volunteer recruitment, research, advocacy, service provision, and fundraising.[20] Certainly, not all groups pursue all eight of these potential uses; many focus on just one or two. For example, many antigovernment groups use bulletin boards to get out their message and communicate with others who share their concerns. Project Vote Smart exists to inform citizens about candidates running for federal office, presenting issue stances in a clear and concise format. One of the early uses of the Web to organize a large-scale march occurred on Mother's Day in 2000. The Million Mom March against gun violence used the Web quite effectively to mobilize supporters. This march of nearly 750,000 individuals started with a Web site created by one woman, Donna Dees-Thomases, whose idea quickly grew into a national movement. Supporters used Web pages to organize the march, create local chapters, provide logistics, attract media coverage, and raise money.[21]

Social media have been very successful in mobilizing grassroots support for a number of causes in the last several years. President Obama was extremely successful in making use of social media during his first campaign, serving to help mobilize youth voters and activists. Following the so-called Facebook election of 2008, Barack Obama has used social media to connect with the public (becoming the first president to have a Twitter account in May 2015). Many politicians have followed his lead. For example, in the 2016 presidential election, Donald Trump regularly posted on Twitter, Hillary Clinton and Jeb Bush "debated" on Twitter, Ted Cruz streamed appearances on Periscope, and the *New York Times* called Bernie Sanders a "king of social media." In August 2016, Donald Trump had 10.8 million followers on Twitter, Hillary Clinton had 8.2 million followers, and Bernie Sanders had 2.4 million followers (note these numbers often are inflated with "fake followers" but the fact that campaigns inflate the numbers indicates how important just this one form of social media has become). Certainly employing social media is an effective tool to enhance awareness but controversies exist. Take for instance the "Kony 2012" campaign organized by the Invisible Children Organization. The Invisible Children organization was created in 2006 to end the use of child soldiers in central Africa. In March 2012 it posted a video on YouTube with a simple (many call simplistic) call to action to help capture Joseph Kony for his crimes against humanity. The video was viewed more than 50 million times in one week sparking a wave of debate and controversy. Most agree that the effort was well intended, but the video has been widely criticized as misleading. Some argue that the people of Uganda are being overshadowed and becoming secondary. Others focus upon the positive results of making youth aware of global crises. The entire event has sparked a debate about the utility and usefulness of social media to tackle complex problems. We will discuss the pros and cons of online engagement later in the chapter. As we saw in the introduction, the use of the online petition has been a powerful tool to push for change and is likely to continue to be used successfully to raise awareness and prompt activism.

CAMPAIGN ACTIVITIES Interest groups play an active role in the elections pathway in local, state, and national election campaigns. Organized groups obviously want to influence elections so that individuals who support their cause will get into office. Groups also want to influence the public during elections in order to sway incumbent policymakers. Groups get involved in elections in many different ways, with their central motivation being to advance their own causes.

Most interest groups take part in electoral politics by rating and endorsing candidates. At every point on the political spectrum, special-interest groups rate the candidates to help influence their supporters and sympathizers. A typical example is the Christian Coalition, which provides voter guides (distributed in sympathetic churches across the nation) that examine candidates' voting records and note what percentage of the time they vote "correctly" on what the group considers key issues. In the same way, the AFL-CIO rates members of Congress on their votes regarding issues important to organized labor, to give supporters a voting cue. So, too, does the U.S. Chamber of Commerce, from the business perspective.

Today, many people worry about the influence that special-interest groups have on elections—and especially about the impact of interest group money on electoral outcomes and the subsequent actions of elected officials. It is important to note, however, that interest groups are simply associations of like-minded people and that many interest groups spend very little money to influence elections. For example, according to the Federal Election Commission (FEC) less than 10 percent of all PACs spent more than $500,000 in 2012. In a democracy, citizens *should* affect elections, even if those citizens are acting collectively. So, while we should certainly scrutinize interest groups' contributions to candidates and political parties, interest group involvement does not necessarily pollute the electoral system. Interest groups can serve as a political cue to their members, other interest groups, voters, and the media. When an interest group donates money to a candidate, it is making a public show of support that can be an important cue for others, either for or against that candidate.

Money has always been important in politics; today's requirement for limited campaign contributions and full disclosure makes the system more transparent and honest. In the days when we did not know how much candidates received in contributions, or from whom they received contributions, we might have naively thought that there was less corruption. However, the opposite was probably true. Despite ready access to contributions, greater scrutiny today likely induces most politicians to be more honest.

On January 21, 2010, in *Citizens United* v. *Federal Election Commission*, a divided Supreme Court overruled two important precedents that had previously limited corporate wealth from unfairly influencing elections.[22] In a 5-4 decision, the Court ruled that the federal government cannot ban political spending by corporations in elections as such bans infringe upon the political speech of corporations. Dissenters argued that corporate money would be sufficiently large to drown out the speech of less funded

FIGURE 12.3   Growth in Independent Expenditures Since 2010

SOURCE: Center for Responsive Politics, https://www.opensecrets.org/outsidespending.

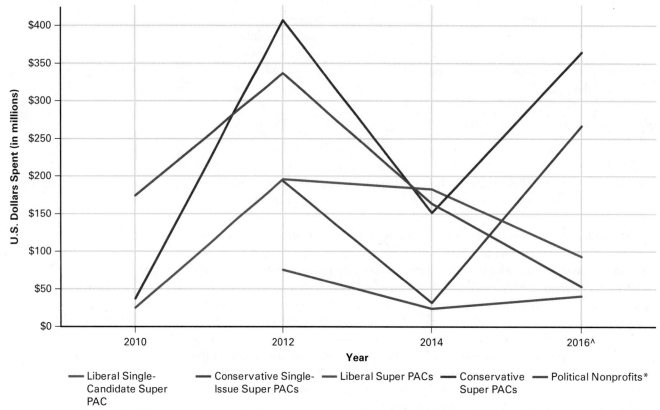

^Final 2016 figures were not disclosed until after publication date.

*Includes: Trade Associations 501 (c)(6), Union 501 (c)(5), Social Welfare Groups 501 (c)(4)

entities (most notably individual citizens) and could serve to corrupt democratic elections. As a consequence of the ruling, a record amount of money has been spent by groups since the decision. For example, independent expenditure-only entities (Super PACs) spent $62.6 million in 2010, $609.4 million in 2012, $345.2 in 2014, and over $1,503 million in 2016. (Figure 12.3). In most elections, Republicans have an advantage as more money is directed to help these candidates. In 2012, nearly 67 percent was spent to benefit conservative candidates. Through October 2016, 64 percent of Super PAC spending benefitted conservative candidates. However, in 2014, Democrats had an advantage, with liberals receiving 51 percent of Super PAC spending. Spending by political non-profits, called "Dark Money" because it is the least transparent and the most difficult to regulate, also increased dramatically. These groups (known by their IRS tax code designations) spent over $335.5 million in the 2012 presidential election.[23]

The Influence of Interest Groups

12.6   Assess the ways interest groups positively and negatively impact our society.

One of the most troubling aspects for many when they consider interest groups is the perception that such groups corrupt politics and politicians. As we have seen, corruption occurs, but more often, it does not. Interest groups do raise and spend a good deal of money, but organizing a diverse society is expensive. Some interests—corporations and professions, for example—are better able to bear these costs than others, such as ordinary citizens. Despite this, as we have seen, citizen groups have thrived and brought about great change.

Interest Group Money

It is difficult to overemphasize the importance of money in mobilization. A significant amount of money is needed just to launch an organization, and continuous funding is needed to maintain it thereafter. Money is needed to recruit members, hire staff, rent offices, pay overhead, and raise additional funds. If the group plans to use many of the tactics discussed in this chapter, substantially more funds will be needed. Advertising and direct mail campaigns are very expensive, and money is also needed to raise more money. Certainly, not many groups can afford the full range of professional services, but for those with sufficient resources, a variety of services can be purchased.

Political scientists have found, not surprisingly, that groups with large resources have many advantages and are more successful.[24] Well-funded groups can afford to hire the best lobbyists and workers, make large campaign contributions, hire specialized professionals, and retain attorneys for legal battles. Moreover, affluent groups can use many lobbying techniques with greater success, for they can sustain such activity over longer periods.

Money is often the key predictor of who wins and who loses in American politics; however, money alone does not always win. For example, in the 2012 presidential election, outside groups and individuals spent over $300 million to oppose President Obama's reelection campaign and the President still won.[25] In the 2016 presidential election, one outside group spent over $81 million to support Governor Jeb Bush in his primary bid, but despite this support, he was unsuccessful. Another group spent over $55 million to support Senator Marco Rubio's unsuccessful presidential bid in 2016.[26] Public support is equally important, which is why interest groups put so much effort into outside lobbying. The women's rights, civil rights, and farm workers movements are perhaps the best examples of less affluent groups exerting great power for change.

Bias in Representation: Who Participates?

At first glance, given the variety of groups, you might think that interest groups represent all Americans equally. They do not. Generally, activists are not typical Americans—most of them are drawn from the elite levels of society. Activists are more politically sophisticated, more knowledgeable, and more involved in their communities. All Americans have the right to form groups, but the fact is that for many reasons, many Americans do not.[27] Educational attainment, family income, and social class are among the largest factors in predicting participation in organized interest groups—and in politics more generally. However, there are exceptions to this general pattern. The least biased form of political participation is voting; not surprisingly, the most skewed form of participation is making campaign contributions: People with more education and more income predominate. Participating in interest groups falls roughly between these two extremes.[28]

Because all American citizens can potentially participate in politics, many observers are not concerned that some Americans choose to remain politically uninvolved. But others are troubled by these patterns of unequal participation and mobilization when they look at the problem from an overall perspective. There is a profound difference among the races, and within races along gender lines, in the level of political participation in the United States. When looking at politics in the aggregate, it is also clear that the immense economic resources of big business give it a disproportionate level of political influence. However, these surplus resources do not automatically equal more power for big business and wealthy individuals. The important distinction to make is whether or not a resource has a tangible political value and can be wielded in the political arena—and at what cost.

Because potential activists *do* have opportunities to organize in American politics, and because one important counterweight to moneyed interests in politics is the power of united and committed citizens, it's important that those with similar interests be mobilized and organized. But we also want to stress how important it is for our democracy that citizens who have traditionally not participated be encouraged to take part in interest group activity. Individuals who participate in group activity, especially those who participate in a diverse range of groups, more often than not tend to develop political tolerance, trust, and a sense of efficacy—qualities that are essential for maintaining a healthy democracy.[29]

Online Activism

Online petitions, like those profiled in the introduction to this chapter, are one of the earliest forms of online activism in the United States. One of the first online petitions was started in 1998. Two computer entrepreneurs, Joan Blades and Wes Boyd, were frustrated at the amount of time Congress was investigating President Bill Clinton's extramarital affair with a White House intern, Monica Lewinsky. They started an online petition to encourage Congress to censure President Clinton and to "move on" and address the pressing problems of the nation. The MoveOn.org petition garnered 100,000 signatures in a week (ultimately getting over 500,000 signatures), and developed into an effective site for regular people to initiate ideas for political change and to organize politically. Since then, a number of other sites have been created to help people organize, perhaps most notable among them is Change.org. The White House has an online petition site (petitions.whitehouse.gov) that guarantees an official response when 100,000 signatures are gathered.

In addition to online petitions, texting has proven to be an effective tool for online organization. Perhaps one of the first effective uses of texting to organize occurred in 1999 at the World Trade Organization protests in Seattle. Activists first used the Internet to organize the protests, then used text messages to coordinate individuals to block traffic and coordinate responses to police actions. In 2006, high school students in Los Angeles used text messages to organize a classroom walk out to protest proposed changes to immigration law. The students also used MySpace (a then-popular social networking site) to get 1,000 students in Fresno to join. Ultimately around 40,000 California students participated in the protests. In 2010, New Jersey Governor Chris Christie announced $820 million in education cuts. Michelle Ryan Lauto (then an 18-year-old college student) created a Facebook event encouraging students to protest and 16,000 students RSVPd "yes" via Facebook and thousands of students across the state joined the walk-out protest. Later that year and into 2011, uprisings sprung up across the Middle East and North Africa (beginning in Tunisia on December 18, 2010). The demonstrations and subsequent revolutions were dubbed the Arab Spring. The uprisings were an example of the remarkable ability for marginalized citizens to organize against repressive governments by using blogs, Twitter, and Facebook. Social media helped break the barrier of fear resulting in youth-led protests spreading hope throughout the Middle East. While lasting democracy has not resulted in many areas, the uprising altered the social contract between the government and the people, laying the seed for the prospect of future democracy.[30]

> POLL Do you believe that retweeting or liking a post on Facebook is a form of activism?

Blogs, an effective tool of citizen journalism, allow nonfiltered commentary and can be an effective tool to promote awareness and activism. Videos uploaded to YouTube can also be effective for groups to reach a broader audience. Microblogging, for example on Twitter, can raise awareness for an event or issue. Hashtags from #BringBackOurGirls, #BlackLivesMatter, #ILookLikeAnEngineer, and #OscarsSoWhite all started conversations about issues of racism and police brutality, the need to diversify Silicon Valley and the tech industry, and the lack of diversity in Hollywood. Most effective change comes from a combination of tools, efficiently using multiple techniques to raise awareness, start conversations, raise money, and organize action.

Despite these many "good" uses of technology to promote action and mobilize for change, a number of concerns have been raised about online "activism." Some wonder if online "activism" actually discourages real action instead giving the impression that activism can occur from one's couch. Simply "liking," retweeting, or sharing a post requires very little commitment and action, but can give the illusion of involvement. Lasting change mandates challenging work and while impassioned online activity can be a start, online "activism" alone is simply insufficient. True change results from the commitment of time, energy, and deeds—not simply clicking from the comfort of your home. Some are concerned that when the novelty of online "activism" wears off and little true change occurs that people will become more disillusioned, more alienated, and less engaged.[31] Most online "activism" is really online awareness—a conversation starter which *can* transition into true activism and involvement, but often does not. One example that demonstrates the powerful way online activity can be both positive and troubling was the ALS ice bucket challenge. The online effort became a cultural phenomenon in 2014 which raised well over $100 million in the United States alone for ALS (a neurodegenerative disease that affects nerve cells in the spinal cord and brain). However, many thought the videos trivialized the disease, which is horrific and tragic, with the "fun" video posts. Moreover, many focused on the "stunt" and did not donate money to the organization and some were concerned over the misuse of water (especially in California given the severe drought in the region). Being sensitive to the limitations and concerns about online activity is important but there is little doubt that digital technology will grow in importance in encouraging political engagement and group activities.

Final Verdict?

Interest groups play a mixed role in our society. On the one hand, they give people opportunities to band together to increase their power and ability to influence fellow citizens and government officials. From an early age, we come to appreciate that there is strength in numbers, thus Americans' solid commitment to collective action. On the other hand, a tension exists. While we believe in collective action as a means for us to influence others, we are often wary of the collective action of groups to which we do not belong or whose views we do not support.

Moreover, it has been asked whether interest groups increase or decrease the influence of individuals: Do interest groups represent ordinary people who would otherwise be powerless? Or do they drown out the voices of ordinary people in favor of special interests?

Participating in groups affects individual citizens in several positive ways. According to some researchers, those who are members of organized interest groups are also more likely to participate in other forms of political activity. Allan Cigler and Mark Joslyn found that people who participated in group activities had higher levels of political tolerance, more trust in elected officials, and a greater sense of political efficacy.[32]

Other research that examined the impact of interest groups on social issues, however, paints a different picture.[33] The growth of interest groups correlates with the growth in distrust in government and fellow citizens, voter cynicism, and lower voting rates. Some hypothesize that when interest groups raise the level of conflict surrounding an issue, they simply alienate the public, thus raising the levels of citizen distrust. However, a different interpretation is also possible—that interest groups form because citizens *do* distrust the government, *are* cynical, and *do* have low participation rates. It could be that people join interest groups in order to organize an otherwise chaotic world.

Conclusion

We have a "how to" element in our government that is focused on bargaining and compromise and is public driven. Organized groups are among the most important actors in motivating the public; yet as a society, we have mixed feelings about interest groups.

On the one hand, we acknowledge the need and show our support for organized action. To help influence change, many of us join organized interests and readily form associations that range from parent organizations in schools and neighborhood improvement groups to larger, nationally oriented organizations. As we saw with the actions of Katy Spittell, and T Walker, the use of online petition drives (and social media campaigns) can help individuals successfully organize for change. Approximately 65 percent of Americans over the age of 18 belong to at least one politically active organization.[34] Even if we don't join organizations, many of us feel that an existing group is representing our interests. For example, many senior citizens are not dues-paying members of the AARP but nevertheless feel that the group represents them.

On the other hand, we also fear organized interests. Polls consistently show that Americans are wary about the influence of "special interests" and believe the "common person" is not adequately represented. In fact, many lobbyists are aware of the perception that others have of them and have even gone so far as to compare their job to that of a glorified pimp! Much of the public believes that interest groups have a great deal of influence with government officials and that their influence has been increasing. Moreover, 83 percent of Americans believe that interest groups have more influence than voters.

Interest groups, as we have emphasized in this chapter, are associations of like-minded people united for a common cause; however, we must be careful not to paint too rosy a picture. Interest groups are primarily concerned with promoting their self-interest. Interest groups are skilled at using public relations to advance their political agenda and fundraise. Even groups that seem to be advancing the best interest of the public may not be. Trade-offs are often inevitable. Consider environmentalist groups. They work to protect the environment so that all of us can benefit, but in the process, they sometimes create difficulties for a community or certain individuals. Forcing a mining company out of business, for example, might be important for the local ecosystem, but it will also throw a large number of people out of work. Therefore, it is debatable whether the behavior of the interest group is in the best interests of the mining community. Such concerns and debates are significant when we examine interest group behavior. To understand fully both the potentially positive and potentially negative impacts of interest group actions, a balanced analysis is essential.

CONFRONTING POLITICS AND POLICY

On October 1, 2011, Molly Katchpole (a 22-year-old from Washington, D.C. living paycheck-to-paycheck) started an online petition to protest a new $5 per month debit card fee proposed by Bank of America. Within four days, 300,000 people had signed the petition on Change.org, making it the largest consumer campaign on the site. Responding to avid online opposition, Bank of America announced that the fee proposal was abandoned. The online petition had an easy victory in a classic David-versus-Goliath fight.

ACTION STEPS

1. Imagine you were upset about a proposed government law. What steps could you take to encourage online protests and build pressure? How can you turn your growing support into a political movement?

2. What sorts of change do you think people can elicit through online activity? List the strategic limitation groups face using online petitions and campaigns to pressure governmental officials.

› REVIEW THE CHAPTER

Activism and Protest in the United States

12.1 Illustrate how beliefs in collective action, self-government, and citizen action laid the foundation for activism and protest in the United States. (p. 396)

From the earliest days of our republic, individuals treasured the notion of collective action. Alexis de Tocqueville characterized our country as a "nation of joiners"—a characterization that is still true today. Early successes with collective action and self-government set the stage for today's commitment. Organized interests provide a safety valve, especially in times of great social, economic, political, and cultural upheaval and change. In their absence, more violent forms of expression might be employed.

Influencing Government Through Mobilization and Participation

12.2 Explain the key factors that facilitate political protest and activism. (p. 398)

Constitutional protections are very important in allowing citizens to petition their government and pursue collective action. The constitutional guarantees of speech, religion, press, and assembly permit them to unite to petition the government about their concerns. These freedoms allow mass movements to develop, often changing both country and culture. Without these protections, we would have great difficulties working with like-minded individuals and influencing our society.

Functions and Types of Interest Groups

12.3 Identify four different types of interest groups, and explain the function of interest groups in a democracy. (p. 399)

Interest groups provide tools for participation, educate the public and governmental officials, and influence policymaking and governmental action. Interest groups consist of economic groups (such as the Chamber of Commerce), public interest groups (including AARP), think tanks (such as the conservative Heritage Foundation and the liberal Brookings Institution), and governmental units (such as the U.S. Conference of Mayors).

Interest Group Mobilization

12.4 Show how interest groups mobilize their memberships in the face of organizational barriers. (p. 404)

The many costs associated with forming and maintaining organized groups include money, time, and overcoming the free-rider and political efficacy problems. To overcome these barriers, interest groups use a variety of tactics, from offering benefits—material, solidary, and purposive—to providing inducements. Leadership is also often a very important factor in group formation, maintenance, and success.

Inside and Outside Lobbying

12.5 Describe how interest groups appeal to public officials and the public to gain support for their causes. (p. 408)

Trying to gain access to present their positions, interest groups lobby directly by contacting officials and their staffs, testifying at congressional hearings, and building long-term relationships with policymakers. Outside lobbying involves trying to influence the government by mobilizing public support. Grassroots mobilization is one highly effective tactic of outside lobbying. Groups rely on traditional tactics such as direct contact and mail but are increasingly using newer techniques such as blogs and social networking sites to reach the general public.

The Influence of Interest Groups

12.6 Assess the ways interest groups positively and negatively impact our society. (p. 418)

Debate exists over the actual influence of interest groups in the United States; however, the consensus among the public is that interest groups are very powerful—perhaps too powerful—relative to the influence of voters and other less organized citizens. The uneven growth pattern, with some groups increasing at much faster rates than others, has led some people to worry about potential bias in the articulation of the needs of some over the desires of individuals and groups with less representation. Despite the negative perceptions associated with interest groups, it is important to remember that they allow for like-minded citizens to join together to participate in politics and to make their voices heard.

⟩ LEARN THE TERMS

⟩ EXPLORE FURTHER

In the Library

Berry, Jeffrey, and Clyde Wilcox. *Interest Group Society*, 6th ed. New York: Routledge, 2016.

Cigler, Allan J., and Burdett A. Loomis, eds. *Interest Group Politics*, 9th ed. Washington, D.C.: CQ Press, 2015.

Drutman, Lee. *The Business of America is Lobbying: How Corporations Became Politicized and Politics Became More Corporate.* New York: Oxford University Press, 2015.

Gilens, Martin. *Affluence & Influence: Economic Inequality and Political Power in America.* New York: Princeton University Press, 2012.

Godwin, Ken, Scott H. Ainsworth and Erik Godwin. *Lobbying and Policymaking.* Washington, D.C.: CQ Press, 2013.

Gray, Virginia, David Lowery and Jennifer K. Benz. *Interest Groups and Health Care Reform across the United States.* Washington, D.C.: Georgetown University Press, 2013.

Grossmann, Matt. *The Not-So-Special Interests: Interest Groups, Public Representation and American Governance.* Stanford, CA: Stanford University Press, 2012.

Homan, Mark S. *Promoting Community Change: Making it Happen in the Real World*, 6th ed. Belmont, CA: Brooks/Cole, 2015.

Leech, Beth L. *Lobbyists at Work.* New York: Springer, 2013.

Mayer, Jane. *Dark Money: The Hidden History of the Billionaires Behind the Rise of the Radical Right.* New York: Doubleday, 2016.

Trigg, Mary K., ed. *Young Women's Activism for Social Change.* Piscataway Township, NJ: Rutgers University Press, 2010.

Wald, Kenneth D. and Allison Calhoun-Brown. *Religion and Politics in the United States*, 7th ed. Lanham, MD: Rowman & Littlefield, 2014.

On the Web

Democracy Matters, a national student organization with a focus on campaign finance reform, is found at *http://www.democracymatters.org*.

Rock the Vote is a nonprofit, nonpartisan organization designed to mobilize and engage young people to vote and become involved in the political process. To register to vote online to find out more information about MTV's efforts to mobilize the youth vote, visit *http://www.rockthevote.org*.

A nonprofit organization that works to strengthen civic knowledge and foster civic values among young people, the Bill of Rights Institute can be located at *http://billofrightsinstitute.org*.

Constitution Society is a nonprofit international organization that provides online resources about constitutional history, law, and government (*http://constitution.org*).

Thousands of interest groups exist in the United States. Here is a brief sample of a variety:
Center for Responsive Politics: *http://www.opensecrets.org*;
Coalition to Stop Gun Violence: *http://www.csgv.org*;
Gun Owners of America: *http://www.gunowners.org*
National Association for the Advancement of Colored People: *http://www.naacp.org*;
National Conference of State Legislatures: *http://www.ncsl.org/*;
U.S. Chamber of Commerce: *http://www.uschamber.com*.

For more information about regional enforcement of environmental law see Commission for Environmental Cooperation (CEC) at *http://cec.org*.

For more information about an environmental group with an international focus visit Greenpeace at *http://www.greenpeace.org/usa/*.

The most active defender of Second Amendment rights is widely recognized to be the National Rifle Association (NRA). For more information visit *http://nra.org*.

Students for a Democratic Society is a student-activist movement with roots going back to the early 1960s: *http://www.studentsforademocraticsociety.org/*.

The Center for Media and Democracy is a nonprofit organization dedicated to investigative reporting: *http://www.prwatch.org*.

For assistance searching blogs see Blog Search at *http://www.blogsearch.google.com*.

For extensive investigative journalism on current controversies visit Center for Public Integrity at *http://www.publicintegrity.org*.

ELECTIONS AND POLITICAL PARTIES IN AMERICA

How we conduct elections in the United States has shifted and changed through the ages. Sometimes the pace of change is slow, while occasionally there are jolts to the system. Without question, the way Donald Trump won the Republican nomination and how he conducted his general election campaign was a shock to the system.

■ *Do you think elections will ever be the same?*

→ LEARNING OBJECTIVES

13.1 Describe the legal challenges that have broadened the democratic character of elections in America.

13.2 Evaluate levels of electoral engagement in America, particularly among young citizens.

13.3 Identify the functions served by political parties in a democracy, and explain how they help organize the governmental process.

13.4 Trace the evolution of political parties in the United States.

13.5 Explain the historic role of minor parties in the U.S. electoral process.

13.6 Outline the process by which party nominees are chosen to run in the general election.

13.7 Explain the process by which we select the president of the United States.

13.8 Assess the critical role that money plays in the election process.

DO ELECTIONS EXPRESS THE HOPES AND CONCERNS OF AVERAGE AMERICANS?

Over the years, political scientists, media pundits, and other students of electoral politics have assembled a set of assumptions, often dubbed rules or axioms, about modern campaigns. There seem to be forces that shape the outcome of an election, and by understanding these dynamics, astute candidates can gain an advantage. For example, Bill Clinton's campaign managers famously posted a reminder of the central theme of their campaign on the wall of the headquarters in 1992: "It's the economy, stupid!" It was a not-so-subtle reminder that a key rule of politics is that voters are concerned, fundamentally, with economic issues. The late Thomas "Tip" O'Neill, who served as Speaker of the House of Representatives in the 1980s, reminded young Democratic colleagues that "all politics is local." As an experienced politician, O'Neill understood that voters pay little attention to a candidate's lofty accomplishments, but instead how he or she will impact their daily lives. Many other rules and truisms have been advanced, some as suggestions and others as cannon.

Did the 2016 presidential election cast many of these truisms to the junk pile? Consider just a few items Many observers had come to believe that the so-called "invisible primary" was critical. This is a stage early in the process when endorsements from prominent officials are stacked up and money begins to flow. Without numerous early endorsements and money, the rule goes, candidates languish. In the fall of 2015, Senator Marco Rubio and former Governor Jeb Bush, both of Florida, completely dominated the invisible primary; they each netted a massive number of endorsements and amassed huge war chests. Rather than getting endorsements, Donald Trump was scorned by most Republican officials and office holders. But neither Rubio nor Bush had any traction once the voting began. Many also believe "big money"—a small number of huge contributors—helps shape the outcome. Yet Bernie Sanders, who certainly gave Hillary Clinton a run for her money (so to speak), raised massive amounts though small contributions. Trump was considerably outspent by his primary opponents and even by the Clinton camp. By historic standards, his expenditures during the nomination phase were measly. There is also the role of media. Most had assumed that a key to winning modern elections is to flood the airways with campaign ads. But Trump bought almost no airtime during the nomination period, relying instead on a dizzying number of appearances on news programs. We used to think that missteps, or gaffs, could damage a candidate's chances. These often come during media appearances. One mistake during the 1976 debate, for instance, seemed to diminish Gerald Ford's reelection prospects. The same sort of thing happened to Michael Dukakis in 1988. Mitt Romney was caught on tape making disparaging comments about "47 percent" of Americans, and some believe it played a role in his defeat. Hillary Clinton made gaffs in the 2016 race, to be sure, but the list of seemingly damaging mistakes made by Donald Trump were staggering—too long to list here. At the top of the list would be the Access Hollywood video where he spoke about his sexual prowess and unwanted advances toward women. The impact of all these missteps and revolutions seemed moot, however, as his polling numbers hardly went down.

This quick list of broken rules and assumptions is just the tip of the iceberg. Many seasoned observers have been left scratching their heads. In so many ways, the 2016 election seemed to change the nature of elections in America.

Why would that be the case? Scholars will wrestle with the implications of this election for decades to come; it was surely one for the record books. Likely, the transformative nature of the election was a product of dramatic social and economic changes. The shrinking of the middle class, stagnant wages, and the withering number of good jobs probably contributed to the uniqueness of the race. Many Trump supporters noted his gaffs and didn't like them, but they were more concerned about new directions. Also, if history is any guide, the way Americans pick leaders has evolved over the two centuries. The election process continues to change. Perhaps elections are the "canary in the coal mine" of our politics—a harbinger of big shifts to come.

Expansion of the Electorate and Other Legal Issues

13.1 Describe the legal challenges that have broadened the democratic character of elections in America.

For elections to be a viable avenue for change, two conditions must be present. First, a citizen must believe that his or her efforts matter. Second, there must be laws affording all citizens the right to participate and there must be a level playing field for candidates. Our system has taken many steps to broaden the right to vote including constitutional amendments and voting and legislative acts to challenge discriminatory practices.

Constitutional Amendments

The first federal constitutional changes that broadened the scope of the electorate were the Fourteenth and Fifteenth Amendments. The first clause of the **Fourteenth Amendment**, ratified in 1868, guaranteed citizenship and the rights of citizenship to all persons born or naturalized in the United States. The second clause gave the states an incentive to grant minority citizens the right to vote, essentially basing representation in both Congress and the Electoral College on the percentage of male citizens over age 21 who could vote.[1,2] In 1870, the **Fifteenth Amendment** was adopted, stating (in its entirety) that "the right of citizens of the United States to vote shall not be denied or abridged by the United States or by any State on account of race, color, or previous condition of servitude."

The **Nineteenth Amendment** enacted in 1920, which gave the vote to women, was the product of a grassroots movement that began in 1848. Frontier life also helped fuel the movement for women's voting rights; on the frontier, women were considered equal partners in the family's fight for survival. The Nineteenth Amendment initiated the most sweeping enlargement of the American electorate in a single act.

The **Twenty-Fourth Amendment** outlawed the poll tax in 1964. A fee imposed on voters, the poll tax had been one of the barriers to African American voting in the South.

The **Twenty-Sixth Amendment**, giving 18-year-old citizens the right to vote, was the most recent change to extend the franchise. By the late 1960s, a growing proportion of Americans were in their late teens and had proved that they could be effective in promoting change. Images of young men going off to die in the Vietnam War but not being able to vote gave the movement its biting edge. The amendment passed with little objection, and the state legislatures ratified it in only three and a half months.[3]

Fourteenth Amendment (1868)
Establishes that each state must guarantee equal protection of the laws to its citizens. In other words, states cannot abridge an individual's civil liberties.

Fifteenth Amendment (1870)
Guarantees the right to vote shall not be denied to anyone on the basis of race.

Nineteenth Amendment (1920)
Granted women the right to vote.

Twenty-Fourth Amendment (1964)
Eliminated the poll tax.

Twenty-Sixth Amendment (1971)
Granted 18-year-old citizens the right to vote.

The struggle for women to have the right to vote was long and difficult.

■ *Do you think young women these days take this struggle, and the entire feminist movement, for granted?*

Voting and Legislative Acts

Article I of the Constitution says, in essence, that as long as Congress remains silent, voting regulations and requirements are left to the states. There were many state-level restrictions on voting in the early days of the Republic. Some states imposed religious qualifications, and most states had property ownership and tax-paying requirements.[4]

CHALLENGING DISCRIMINATORY PRACTICES   Well into the twentieth century, southern states used their power to regulate elections to keep African Americans from the polls. Imposing a variety of restrictions—literacy tests, poll taxes, complicated registration and residency requirements, and the infamous "grandfather clause," which exempted a voter from all these requirements if his (free white) grandfather had voted before 1860—white-ruled southern states managed to disfranchise most blacks.

A favorite exclusionary tool was the white primary. Southern election laws defined political parties as private organizations, with the right to decide their own membership. Thus, while blacks might enjoy the right to vote in the general election, they could not vote in the only election that really counted: the Democratic primary.[5] This practice remained in effect until the Supreme Court ruled in *Smith* v. *Allwright* (1944) that primaries were part of the electoral system, and therefore the exclusion of blacks violated the Fifteenth Amendment.

Voting Rights Act of 1965
Federal statute that effectively attacked literacy tests and other techniques used to prevent African Americans from voting.

CIVIL RIGHTS AND THE VOTING RIGHTS ACT   The Civil Rights Act of 1957 created the U.S. Civil Rights Commission to investigate voting rights violations and to suggest remedies. The most significant change that directly affected elections, however, came with the **Voting Rights Act of 1965**. This law provided that for any congressional district in which fewer than 50 percent of adults went to the polls, a five-year "emergency state" would be triggered. Affected districts could change their election regulations only with the approval of the civil rights division of the Justice Department. In addition, the Justice Department could now send election examiners into the states to register voters and observe elections. Although the act did not end discrimination, it became the most important tool in protecting the right to vote.[6] Election data reflect the act's importance: Overall, in 11 southern states in 1960, a meager 29.7 percent of adult African Americans were registered to vote. By the end of the decade, this figure had more than doubled, to 63.4 percent.[7]

RESIDENCY AND REGISTRATION LAWS   Reforms during the Progressive Era were designed to clean up the all-too-common practice of fraudulent voting in general elections. Party bosses, for example, might pay people to travel around the city voting in numerous polling places. Frequently, dead or nonexistent voters were discovered to have cast ballots. Residency and registration laws were the solution. Residency laws stipulate that a person can vote in a community only if that person has been a resident for a prescribed period. (The length of time varies from state to state, but the Voting Rights Act of 1970 established a maximum of 30 days.) As will be discussed in greater detail below, in some states, a resident can register up to and including Election Day, but in most states, there is a stipulated, pre-Election Day cutoff.

motor voter law
A federal law passed in 1993 requiring states to offer citizens the opportunity to register to vote in many state offices, including motor vehicle offices. The idea was to facilitate voter registration and increase the number of Americans who come to the polls on Election Day.

The idea behind these laws was to reduce corruption, but in recent years they have become controversial, and some people have even suggested that they are the main reason why many Americans do not vote. In their provocatively titled book *Why Americans Still Don't Vote: And Why Politicians Want It That Way*, Frances Fox Piven and Richard Cloward argue these laws have always been about keeping certain types of voters out of the process.[8] Perhaps trying to find a middle ground, Congress in 1993 required states to allow citizens to register to vote at numerous public facilities used by low-income people, such as state motor vehicle, welfare, and employment offices. This so-called **motor voter law** also stipulated that states must permit mail-in registration.

HELP AMERICA VOTE ACT   In the wake of the confusion surrounding the 2000 presidential election, in 2002 Congress passed the Help America Vote Act. This measure was designed to create a more uniform voting system, replacing the haphazard, state-by-state process that had existed for two centuries. The act set federal standards for all voting systems throughout the United States, provided $325 million to update voting systems, required states to create registered voter databases, and called for voter education and poll worker training.

The Controversy Over Voter ID Laws

Several states, including Wisconsin, Texas, Tennessee, South Carolina, Pennsylvania, and Kansas have recently instituted new laws requiring voters to bring state-approved identification cards (such as a driver's license) to voting booths. Indiana already had a similar law on the books. Supporters of these measures argue that IDs are required for many public events, so it simply makes sense that they should be required for voting. These laws will limit corruption and add legitimacy to the process, they argue. Shortly after South Carolina moved to require voter ID cards for all voters, the governor of the state, Republican Nikki Haley, commented, "We continue to improve the levels of South Carolina in terms of integrity, accountability, and transparency. I have heard from people out of state how impressed they are that we took it upon ourselves to say, 'We are going to make sure we maintain the integrity of our voters.'"[9] Those who oppose voter ID measures argue that upward of 10 percent of citizens currently do not have state-recognized ID cards, and that by requiring people to show IDs at the polls will disenfranchise groups of voters. They suggest voter fraud is a tiny issue—certainly less significant than low voter turnout. Moreover, opponents argue that the real intent of the law is not to limit voter fraud, but to keep a particular type of voter from the polls. They point to studies that suggest citizens without state-issued ID cards are disproportionately poor and minority—likely Democratic voters. "A number of state legislatures have taken up these bills and I think that it's a growing concern nationally that the effect is going to be the suppressions of the vote," said Victoria Middleton, executive director for the South Carolina American Civil Liberties Union.[10]

We do know that the legislature and governor in every state that has mandated voter ID laws after the 2010 election were controlled by Republicans. We also know this may not be the last word on the issue. The 1965 Voting Rights Act empowers the Department of Justice to review all election-law changes, especially states with a history of discriminatory voting practices. For example, because a fee is required for obtaining a state-issued photo identification card in Texas, the Department of Justice said in the summer of 2012 that this law, and others like it, may violate the Twenty-Fourth Amendment: the prohibition against poll taxes. Implementation of the new law in Pennsylvania was delayed by the courts because there were worries that many voters would not have enough time to get proper ID before the election.

As the 2016 election approached, the voter ID controversy seemed even more unsettled. The courts had shown some deference to efforts to tighten voter security, but in a series of cases in the summer of 2016 they ruled against laws in North Carolina, North Dakota, and other states. In the North Carolina case, the Supreme Court ruled that certain provisions of the law were deliberate efforts to decrease turnout among African Americans. But in other states, such as Texas and Wisconsin, the laws were simply scaled back. Some states, like Alabama and Georgia, abandoned their ID laws for the 2016 election, but other states, including Kansas, pressing forward. This will likely be a hot-button issue for several years.

TIMELINE

A Brief History of Your Most Basic Right: The Right To Vote

Most scholars agree that the right for all citizens to have a say in selecting leaders—the right to vote—is a critical part of any democracy. The story of "the franchise" in the United States is long and complicated. In the early decades many were kept from the polls because of religious, property, or literacy qualifications. These sorts of limits were eased for white men by the 1840s, but many minority groups faced a much longer struggle. This timeline charts important dates in the story of voting rights in America. It is surely not just a coincidence that as the right to vote expanded, so too did the democratic character of our nation. What is interesting about this is that the framers of our system wanted a limited government, a government by the people, but they were a bit unsure about the electoral process.

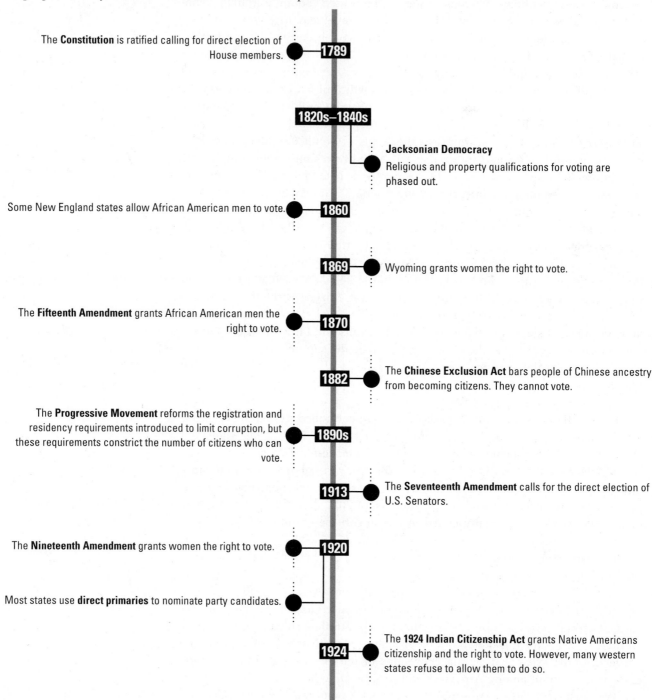

The **Constitution** is ratified calling for direct election of House members. — **1789**

1820s–1840s

Jacksonian Democracy
Religious and property qualifications for voting are phased out.

Some New England states allow African American men to vote. — **1860**

1869 — Wyoming grants women the right to vote.

The **Fifteenth Amendment** grants African American men the right to vote. — **1870**

1882 — The **Chinese Exclusion Act** bars people of Chinese ancestry from becoming citizens. They cannot vote.

The **Progressive Movement** reforms the registration and residency requirements introduced to limit corruption, but these requirements constrict the number of citizens who can vote. — **1890s**

1913 — The **Seventeenth Amendment** calls for the direct election of U.S. Senators.

The **Nineteenth Amendment** grants women the right to vote. — **1920**

Most states use **direct primaries** to nominate party candidates.

1924 — The **1924 Indian Citizenship Act** grants Native Americans citizenship and the right to vote. However, many western states refuse to allow them to do so.

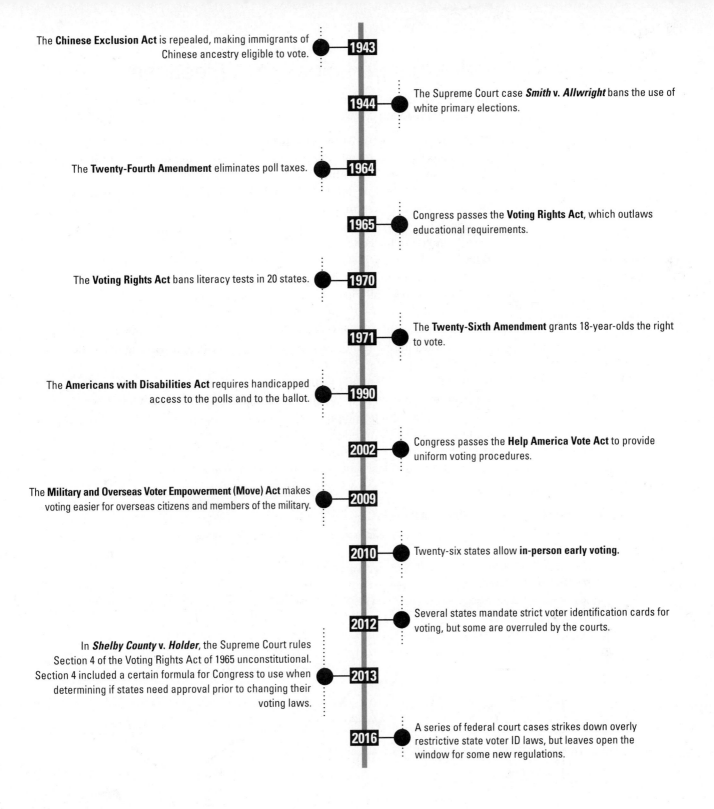

The **Chinese Exclusion Act** is repealed, making immigrants of Chinese ancestry eligible to vote.

1943

1944 The Supreme Court case *Smith* v. *Allwright* bans the use of white primary elections.

The **Twenty-Fourth Amendment** eliminates poll taxes.

1964

1965 Congress passes the **Voting Rights Act**, which outlaws educational requirements.

The **Voting Rights Act** bans literacy tests in 20 states.

1970

1971 The **Twenty-Sixth Amendment** grants 18-year-olds the right to vote.

The **Americans with Disabilities Act** requires handicapped access to the polls and to the ballot.

1990

2002 Congress passes the **Help America Vote Act** to provide uniform voting procedures.

The **Military and Overseas Voter Empowerment (Move) Act** makes voting easier for overseas citizens and members of the military.

2009

2010 Twenty-six states allow **in-person early voting.**

2012 Several states mandate strict voter identification cards for voting, but some are overruled by the courts.

In *Shelby County* v. *Holder*, the Supreme Court rules Section 4 of the Voting Rights Act of 1965 unconstitutional. Section 4 included a certain formula for Congress to use when determining if states need approval prior to changing their voting laws.

2013

2016 A series of federal court cases strikes down overly restrictive state voter ID laws, but leaves open the window for some new regulations.

CRITICAL THINKING QUESTIONS

1. Are there any downsides to defining the democratic character of a nation simply by the right to vote? Can a system that allows all citizens to vote also be oppressive?

2. If voting is a fundamental right, why do so many citizens sit on the side lines each election? Some suggest they do not vote because they are content, but is it not also true that the poor are disproportionately non-voters?

3. Some have suggested that we might try a "voting learner's permit," where 16- and 17-year-olds are given one-half a vote. Do you think this is a good idea? What impact, if any, might the learner's permit program have on adult voter turnout?

Individual Participation in Elections

13.2 Evaluate levels of electoral engagement in America, particularly among young citizens.

There are many ways for citizens to become involved in campaigns and elections. Many citizens are politically active but do not vote, and for some Americans, not voting is either a statement of contentment or a form of political protest. Simply talking about different candidates with friends and family, for example, or reading news stories or watching television programs about election happenings are also types of electoral participation. Any action that is broadly linked to the conduct or outcome of an election can be considered **electoral behavior**.

Another way to think about forms of political participation is to consider the difference between individual and collective participation. Individual participation occurs when a citizen engages in activity aimed at changing public policy without interacting with other citizens. Examples include voting, giving money to a candidate or party, watching political news on television or online, or writing to a candidate or an office holder. Collective participation occurs when a citizen takes action in collaboration with other like-minded citizens. Examples would be attending a rally, discussing politics with friends and family, working at a party or candidate's headquarters, blogging about a political topic, or attending the local meeting of a political party (see Figures 13.1 and 13.2). While individual participation clearly occurs more often, many of the most significant changes in public policy—such as worker rights, civil rights, and environmental legislation—stemmed from collective action.

electoral behavior

Any activity broadly linked to the outcome of a political campaign, such as voting, making phone calls, sending texts, and even talking with friends and neighbors about the upcoming election.

FIGURE 13.1 Forms of Electoral Participation

As this figure suggests, there are many ways individuals can be active in electoral politics.

■ *What was it about the 2008 and 2012 elections that seemed to bring more Americans into the process? The 2016 election was a lively contest, to say the least. Data is still being collected. In the meantime, what is your guess about levels of engagement in the election?*

SOURCE: Based on Graphs 6B "Campaign Participation" and 6D "Political Engagement," American National Election Studies, http://www.electionstudies.org/nesguide/gd-index.htm.

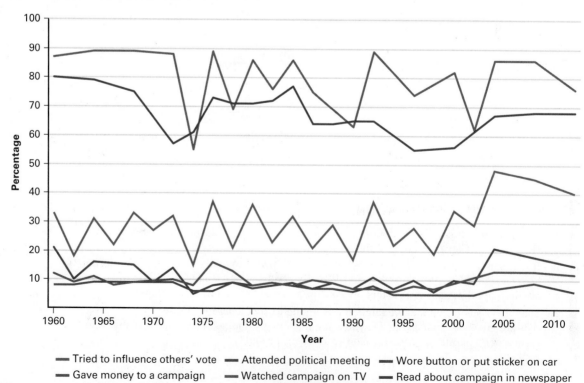

— Tried to influence others' vote — Attended political meeting — Wore button or put sticker on car
— Gave money to a campaign — Watched campaign on TV — Read about campaign in newspaper

FIGURE 13.2 Engagement in Various Forms of Political Participation

■ *The 2016 election was one of the most aggressive races we have seen in generations. What impact do you think all this negativity had on levels of political engagement?*

SOURCE: Based on Aaron Smith, "Civic Engagement in the Digital Age," Pew Research Internet Project, April 25, 2013, http://www.pewinternet.org/2013/04/25/civic-engagement-in-the-digital-age/.

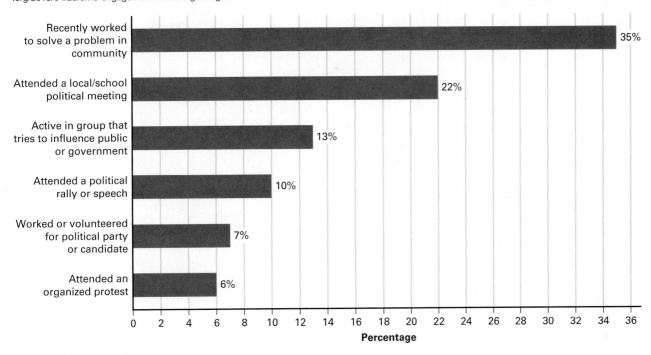

Voter Turnout

In thinking about levels of political participation in any democratic system, we often look at **turnout**—an easily quantifiable number based on the number of citizens who actually vote on Election Day divided by the total number of citizens who are legally qualified to vote in that election. If 1 million residents are allowed to vote but only 600,000 do so, turnout is 0.6, or 60 percent.

To begin, turnout for primary elections is much lower than for general elections. Primaries are used by the parties to select candidates for the general election ballot. Candidates can always run "write in" campaigns, but as you can imagine these efforts rarely succeed. So primary elections are a critically important part of the process. While it depends greatly on the state and the particular contest, turnout in most of these contests is often less than 20 percent—and in many instances in the single digits. Stated a bit differently, candidates who appear on the general election ballot are often picked by less than one-fifth of the electorate.

There was little interest in federal elections during the early days of our republic. Election turnout for presidential elections, measured by the percentage of eligible (male) voters, reached only into the teens until 1800, when it jumped to 31 percent. After what Andrew Jackson called the "corrupt bargain" in the election of 1824, political participation shot up dramatically: In 1828, some 57 percent of eligible voters went to the polls, and by the 1860s, the voting rate had leveled off hovering around 80 percent for the rest of the nineteenth century.

In the early twentieth century, however, Election Day turnouts began to slip. There were a number of likely causes. For one, there was a flood of immigration, causing a population boom in urban areas. Although these new citizens would soon be assimilated into the political process, many of them did not immediately vote. Second, registration laws, residency requirements, and other restrictions during the Progressive Era made it harder for people in the lower socioeconomic class to participate in elections. Finally, the Nineteenth Amendment to the Constitution in 1920 granted women the right to vote, but at first, women were slow to exercise that right.

turnout

The percentage of citizens legally eligible to vote in an election who actually vote in that election. In most recent presidential elections, the turnout is slightly over 50 percent.

FIGURE 13.3 Participation in Presidential Elections

Most Americans believe we are one of the most democratic nations on earth. While that may be true in some respects, our participation in electoral politics is less than stellar. As this figure suggest, turnout since 2008 has continued to decline. In 2016 it was 56 percent.

■ *Why was turnout so modest in 2016 when the race was so dramatic and seemingly so important? Could it be because both candidates were unpopular?*

When Vice President Richard M. Nixon and an upstart senator from Massachusetts by the name of John F. Kennedy squared off in the presidential election in 1960, some 61 percent of the electorate turned out to vote (see Figure 13.3). In the decades since, that figure has dropped more or less steadily. From 1980 until 2000, only about half of eligible voters turned out for presidential elections. Even worse is the participation in midterm congressional elections—the elections between presidential contest years: 2006, 2010, 2014, and so forth.

However, in 2008, roughly 62 percent of eligible voters went to the polls. This figure surpassed all presidential turnout levels since the 1960s. The greatest increases in turnout came from less affluent citizens, young voters, African Americans, and Hispanic Americans. Geographically, the largest increases in turnout were seen in the South and Rocky Mountain states. Dramatic candidates, a lengthy primary campaign, crosscutting issues, and massive get-out-the-vote efforts proved to be a "perfect storm" for voter mobilization in 2008.

Turnout in the 2012 election suggested the previous election may have been an aberration, given that turnout dropped back to roughly 57 percent. Surprisingly, about 12 million fewer voters came to the polls in 2012 than in 2008—even though the nation's population had grown during the four years. It was also the most expensive campaign in our nation's history, and there seems to be a positive relationship between the amount of money spent and voter turnout. Somewhat higher voting rates were seen in so-called swing states, and in those that boasted competitive Senate and gubernatorial races, and controversial ballot initiatives. Voting was depressed in states solidly behind Mitt Romney or Barack Obama, and along the eastern seaboard. Hurricane Sandy had come to shore one week before the election. By all accounts, turnout in the 2012 election was lackluster.

The same can be said about the 2016 election, where the turnout dropped to 56 percent. There was some important variation by state. Donald Trump may have benefited from a slight increase in a few key swing states. For instance, turnout in Florida and Pennsylvania, two big states that proved pivotal to his Electoral College victory, increased by a few percentage points beyond the 2012 levels. But in states like California and Maryland, both solidly Democratic, turnout decreased. A few other non-swing states, like Kansas and Utah, saw dramatic declines as well. It is reasonable to suggest, then, that part of Trump's success came from higher turnout in a few key states. Overall, there was certainly no groundswell of engagement in 2016.

Explaining Modest Turnout

One of the great questions of our day is the cause—or causes—of modest electoral participation. Why was turnout generally higher 50 years ago, even though more Americans attend college, registration barriers have been all but eliminated, and the civil rights movement opened the door to far greater involvement by African Americans and other previously oppressed groups of citizens? With so many positive changes, why would levels of electoral participation be so modest?

There is no clear answer, but theories abound (see Figure 13.4). One possibility is attitudinal change. Increased cynicism, distrust, and alienation are often identified as the root of the problem. Survey data seem to support the claim that negative attitudes about politics have increased over the decades. For instance, in the mid-1950s, about 75 percent of Americans might have been described as trusting their government to "do what is right all or at least most of the time." This number plummeted to just over 20 percent by the early 1990s. About 22 percent of Americans in the 1950s thought "quite a few" politicians were crooked. That number jumped to 50 percent in the mid-1990s and today stands at about 30 percent. Many other indicators suggest that Americans are less confident about government and politics than in previous times.

Closely related to this perspective is what we might call the lifestyle-change theory. According to this hypothesis, life today is simply busier than in the past and offers more distractions. According to the sociologist Robert Putnam, author of the widely

FIGURE 13.4 Why People Don't Vote

One way to read this data is to consider the reasons for not voting, and explore changes that might help. For instance, if "too busy" explains about 27 percent of why people do not vote, should we consider making Election Day a national holiday?

■ *Can you think of other changes that would address some of the reasons for not voting?*

SOURCE: U.S. Election Project.

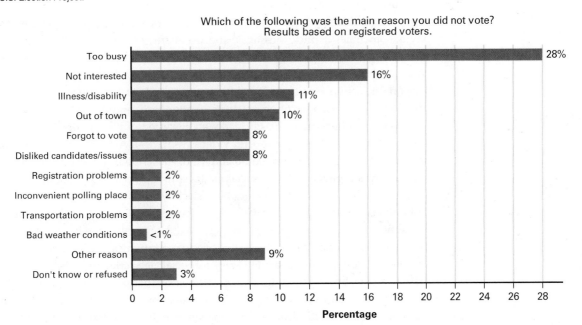

Which of the following was the main reason you did not vote?
Results based on registered voters.

Reason	Percentage
Too busy	28%
Not interested	16%
Illness/disability	11%
Out of town	10%
Forgot to vote	8%
Disliked candidates/issues	8%
Registration problems	2%
Inconvenient polling place	2%
Transportation problems	2%
Bad weather conditions	<1%
Other reason	9%
Don't know or refused	3%

discussed book *Bowling Alone: The Collapse and Revival of American Community*, "I don't have enough time" and "I'm too busy" are the most often heard excuses for social disengagement.[11] We are more distracted by television, new technologies, and social network sites today than in the past, and we have to spend too many hours commuting long distances or putting in extra hours at our jobs to be heavily involved in politics.

However, although changes in attitudes and lifestyles may account for part of the decline, many analysts suggest that the deepest root lies elsewhere. Local-level party organizations—which historically pushed citizens to the polls on Election Day—seem to be withering. A generation ago, many volunteer party workers kept track of which known party members had voted and which had not yet showed up at the polling place. By dinner time on Election Day, those who had delayed voting would get a telephone call or even a visit from one of these workers and be "gently" reminded to vote. Political scientists have tested the relationship between local party vitality and levels of turnout, and the data are convincing: Turnout is much higher in communities that still have strong local parties.[12] But fewer and fewer communities have such organizations.

The nature of campaigns is also cited as a reason for voter alienation. Campaigns, especially for the presidency, have become much longer and more negative, conceivably leading to voter burnout. However, the evidence is not conclusive. Although some studies have found that negative ads do turn voters off, roughly an equal number of other studies have found that turnout actually increases in these negatively charged races.[13] One impressive study suggests that some voters—the less partisan ones—are turned off when the campaign gets nasty but that negative campaigning activates the most partisan voters.[14] Still another line of research suggests that the effects of negative ads depend on the voter's local political culture.[15] A citizen in Provo, Utah, might respond differently to attack ads than, say, a voter in Brooklyn, New York.

Finally, there is the role of the news media. Some social scientists have suggested that the recent turn toward what one scholar has called "attack journalism" or media "feeding frenzies" has repelled voters.[16] In the past, journalists and average citizens alike drew a line between a politician's public and private lives. Probably due to the highly competitive nature of the news business, anything that draws the public's attention seems fair game to the media today.

Armchair Activism?

One of the most popular means for candidates to draw attention and build support is to use social media. Facebook pages and blogs provide information that connects like-minded citizens. Tweets are shared. Instagram, Snapchat, and YouTube posts offer vivid, sometimes explicit messages, and users are encouraged to "like" posts, pages, and pictures, and to retweet messages. They are to pass around Tumblr blogs. As most know, Donald Trump used Twitter extensively during his campaign. Some believe that on-line activism can lead to off-line engagement, such as the wearing of particular clothing or buttons, boycotting products, or attending candidate rallies. While the exact origins of the phenomena are unclear, we all learned of the ALS Ice Bucket Challenge in the summer of 2014 after several videos went viral. As one can imagine, there is a robust and growing literature on the impact of social media on election turnout.

But does engagement with social media spur higher levels of voting? Social media engagement has mockingly been dubbed "slacktivism" and "armchair activism." Media critic and scholar Malcom Gladwell offers a powerful swat at any relationship between social networking sites and broad engagement. Contrary to the hopes of the "evangelists of social media," he argues new modes of communication have not drawn young citizens into the political fray. He writes, "Social networks are effective at increasing participation—by lessening the level of motivation that participation requires."[17] Social media is designed to allow access to information, he argues, but it does not forge connections to other political actors or to the larger political system. "It makes it easier for activists to express themselves, and harder for that expression to have any impact."[18]

Empirical work on this relationship is a bit thin, but one large study suggests little impact. The author of the study writes, "Popular discourse has focused on the use of social media by the Obama campaigns...[and] while these campaigns may have revolutionized aspects of election campaigning online, [there is] little evidence that the social media aspects of the campaigns were successful in changing people's levels of participation."[19] In other words, the early take is that social media does not affect people's likelihood of voting.

Voting and Demographic Characteristics

Another closely related question is why certain groups of Americans participate less than others. Here, too, scholarly findings are inconclusive. One perspective centers on "community connectedness." This theory states that the more connected you are to your community, the more likely you are to vote. Demographic data suggest that poor people, for example, move more often than the affluent do, and they are certainly much less likely to own a home. Every time you change your permanent address, of course, you also need to change your voter registration. Not surprisingly, the level of political participation for these highly mobile people is quite low.

The "costs" of political participation seem to decline as people's level of formal education increases. The Census Bureau reported that 41 percent of registered voters without a high school diploma voted in 2012, as opposed to 75 percent of those with a college degree and 84 percent of those with a graduate degree. Not only does awareness of the mechanics of voting rise with formal education, so do the benefits of voting. People's sense of civic duty seems to build through education. As one pair of political behavior scholars have noted, "Length of education is one of the best predictors of an individual's likelihood of voting."[20]

Young Voters

Finally, there is the issue of age. Age has always been an excellent predictor of who participates in elections. Simply stated, young Americans have always voted at lower rates than older Americans have. This group has less *completed* education, is less affluent, and has much less likelihood of owning a home—all factors that seem related to participation. Younger citizens are also much more mobile, and they often get tripped up by residency requirements and voter registration issues. Yet survey data also suggest that young Americans are eager to contribute to the betterment of society; their rate of volunteering is comparable to the rates of other age groups. But, this willingness to become involved does not always spread to political involvement.

> **POLL** Which of the following best explains why some young Americans don't vote?

1. Too busy
2. Not interested
3. Cynicism and distrust of the system
4. Rules that make it hard to vote, like registration requirements
5. An inability to connect with candidates of either party
6. Other

Many have suggested that the Internet and social media will help young citizens become more connected, and thus bring them into the political process. The Obama "Net-Root" campaign seemed to be a case in point. But the evidence of this from the 2016 election is rather thin.

■ *What is your take: Will these sorts of activities inspire young citizens to get more involved, or is it mere "slactivism?"*

FIGURE 13.5 Self-Reported Voter Turnout in 2012 Presidential Election by Education

Many demographic factors seem to influence the likelihood of voting, particularly levels of education.

■ *Why do you think education is so important in determining who will come to the polls and who will not?*

SOURCE: U.S. Census Bureau, Current Population Survey, November 2012.

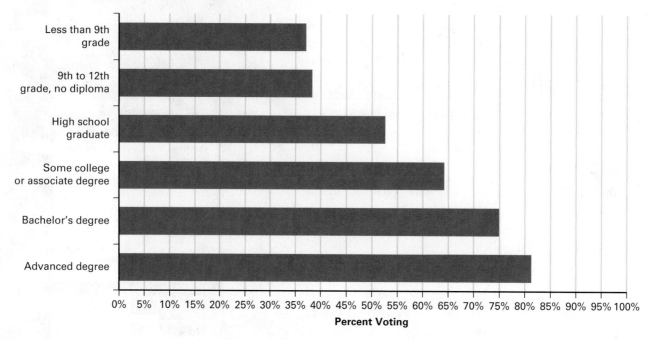

Much to the surprise of scholars, pundits, and older Americans, youth voting made a dramatic turnaround in 2004, and 2008 continued the trend. As you can see in Figure 13.6, voter turnout in 2004 increased among all Americans by about 4 percent, but the increase was greatest among the youngest voters. In 2008, young voters

FIGURE 13.6 Percentage of Turnout By Age Groups, 2004–2016 Elections

This figure clearly shows that older Americans tend to vote more often than do younger Americans.

■ *What impact do you think online engagement will have on levels of youth voting in coming years?*

SOURCE: U.S. Census Bureau, Current Population Survey Select Years, 2012. Figures for 2016 are estimates based on exit polls and other preliminary data compiled by the authors.

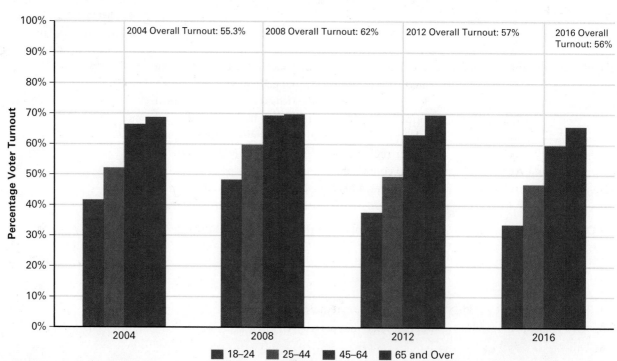

flocked to the polls; about 49 percent of those under 25 came out to vote for either John McCain or Barack Obama.

Why were so many more young voters flocking to the polls? There are a number of possible explanations. For one thing, the earlier decline in youth participation was so startling that many organizations and programs, such as MTV's Rock the Vote and Generation Engage were initiated to bring young people back to the polls. Several new elections pathway organizations also tried bringing voters to the polls, including Americans Coming Together and MoveOn.org. In addition, the intensity of the campaign and the weight of the issues, such as the state of the economy, climate change, the war in Iraq, gay marriage, the future of Social Security, and health care reform caught young voters' attention.

In the aftermath of the 2008 election, those fretting about the long-term stability of our system breathed a sigh of relief. It seemed that young citizens had rediscovered the potential of politics and they were once again making their voices heard. Never shy about proclaiming the impact of their efforts, the folks at Rock the Vote were assertive in their assessment of the long-term implications: "2008 is the year of the young voter. We're not going to take politics as usual anymore, and we won't be ignored. We're taking the country into our hands....Today's youth are a political powerhouse."[21] Surely Democratic operatives were pleased with the change, as their presidential candidate netted some 68 percent of the under-30 vote in 2008. The youth vote was large, progressive, and consequential.

The problem is that the reemergence of young voters may have been a temporary surge, rather than a sea of change. The first indicators of the fleeting resurgence were the 2009 gubernatorial elections in New Jersey and Virginia. In both contests young voters stayed home. Exit polling found that voters under age 30 accounted for just 9 percent of voters in New Jersey (compared with 17 percent in 2008) and 10 percent in Virginia (down from 21 percent in 2008). They also stayed home during the critically important special election to fill the Massachusetts Senate seat vacated by the death of Ted Kennedy in the 2009. All eyes were turned to the Bay State because it represented the "60th seat"—the number of seats that the Democrats needed to overcome GOP filibusters in the Senate. By holding that seat, Barack Obama's agenda of "change," seemingly so important to young voters one year earlier, could continue. Without that seat, the Obama agenda would likely grind to a halt. On Election Day, overall turnout was very high for a special election: a robust 54 percent. Yet generational differences were stark: Turnout for those older than 30 was nearly 60 percent, but for those under 30 it was a scant 15 percent.

By the 2010 midterm election it appeared that the youth engagement bubble had burst. Turnout for those under 30 reached just 22.8 percent, slightly less than in the previous midterm election (2006). Just one in five young Americans came to the polls in 2010, which seems especially thin given the salience of many issues for young voters, particularly the economic crisis, health care reform, and the DREAM Act, for example. Turnout for all voters actually rose in 2010 to 41 percent, signifying that the gap between young and older voters may be *growing*. Finally, coming off of the heels of the "Year of the Youth Vote" (2008), the drop in engagement seems to run against a long line of scholarship that argues that once a citizen votes, repeated acts become habitual.

And yet, youth turnout in the 2012 election moved back to 2008 levels—roughly 49 percent for those voters under 30. This represented about 18 percent of the overall electorate, similar to the percentage four years earlier. Turnout for this group in the 2014 midterms was the lowest ever recorded—21 percent.

Turnout for young Americans in the 2016 election was once again lackluster: 49 percent for those under 30. This was on par with 2012. On the one hand, this figure was a bit lower than many pundits expected. The campaign was intense and, at times, dramatic. For instance, the first debate between Hillary Clinton and Donald Trump set an all-time record for the number of viewers. The campaign was vigorously discussed and debated on social media. But on the other hand, both candidates had low approval ratings, particularly with young voters. Clinton netted some 54 percent from this age group—a figure significantly less than what Obama received four years earlier.

Political Parties in America

13.3 Identify the functions served by political parties in a democracy, and explain how they help organize the governmental process.

One of the great ironies of American politics is that the very forces the framers of our Constitution most feared, political parties, have proved to be the instruments that actually make elections work. One pair of scholars has called them the "institutions Americans love to hate."[22] Nevertheless, by the election of 1800 they had arrived and have been a key aspect of our politics ever since. Most, including some of those early framers, have come to realize that political parties perform important functions in a democracy.

Party Functions

No single definition of political parties satisfies everyone. The principal differences focus on the goals of party activity. One definition, often called the **rational party model**, maintains that parties are organizations that sponsor candidates for political office in hopes of controlling the apparatus of government. A second definition, the **responsible party model**, holds that parties are organizations that run candidates to shape the outcomes of government—that is, to redirect public policy. Rational parties work to win elections in order to control government, whereas responsible parties work hard during elections in order to shape public policy.

With either approach, three factors distinguish political parties from other political organizations such as interest groups, labor unions, trade associations, and political action committees:[23]

1. Political parties run candidates under their own label; interest groups do not.
2. Political parties have a **platform**—a broad range of concerns that they support; interest groups limit their efforts to a narrow range of topics.
3. Political parties are subject to numerous state and local laws. They have some characteristics of private institutions, but in other ways they are similar to public organizations. Scholars have thus dubbed them "quasi-public" institutions. Interest groups, on the other hand, are purely private and free of government regulations.

Just as there is disagreement over the precise definition of *party*, people disagree over what parties contribute to a democratic system. Scholars have suggested that parties do the following:

1. **Organize the election process:** By organizing primary elections, parties enable voters to narrow the pool of office seekers to party **nominees** and establish a platform of issues for their candidates.
2. **Facilitate voter choice:** Given that voters generally do not know everything or even very much about a candidate other than his or her party affiliation, parties help us cast an informed, rational vote. Without party labels, the voter would have to study each candidate's positions in detail.
3. **Recruit candidates:** To win elections, parties try to recruit good, qualified citizens to run for office and to screen out unqualified or corrupt candidates.
4. **Aid candidates:** Parties help candidates put their best foot forward to voters. In the past, party workers would spread the word about their candidates and work on their behalf leading up to Election Day. More recently, parties have begun providing many high-technology campaign services, such as polling, computerized targeting, and radio and television productions. Of course, fundraising has also become a huge part of how parties lend a hand.
5. **Organize a complex government:** The complexity of our government was created by design, part of the checks and balances envisioned by the framers, but in many

rational party model
The goal is to win offices and to control the distribution of government jobs.

responsible party model
The goal is to shape public policy.

platform
The set of issues, principles, and goals that a party supports.

nominees
The individuals selected by a party to run for office under that party's label.

ways, this structure makes united action difficult. Parties counteract this effect by helping bring the many pieces of our system into united action.

6. **Educate citizens and promote involvement:** As each party works to build support for its candidates, the by-product is voter education. Not only do the voters learn more about the candidates because of party activities, they also learn more about government policies and the workings of our system. Also, parties work hard to bring citizens into the electoral process as volunteers, donors, and voters. Many studies have found that communities with strong political parties have higher levels of voting and other modes of political participation.[24]

7. **Ensure accountability:** Because our political system is so complex, it is difficult for voters to know who to give credit to when things go well, or who to blame when they go poorly. If most of the government is controlled by members of the same party, and that party has done a good job, its members tend to be voted back into office. If things get worse, voters are more likely to give the other party a chance. Indeed, this accountability process is at the very heart of self-governance.

Party Elements

One of the most confusing aspects of political parties is precisely what the term *party* implies. Some have suggested parties are similar to business firms seeking to attract consumers (voters) by providing good products (candidates). Others have suggested parties should be understood as networks of aligned groups and individuals. For example, while Rush Limbaugh is not a member of the Republican National Committee, he is supportive of Republican issues and candidates; so in some ways, he could be considered a party leader. In this book, we will instead rely upon the most common approach to describe parties. This approach has carried a great deal of weight in scholarly circles since the 1950s when a prominent political scientist named V. O. Key suggested we might best understand political parties in the United States according to the **tripartite view**, a tripod structure in which political parties have three interrelated elements: party-in-government (PIG), party-in-the-electorate (PIE), and party-as-organization (PO), as illustrated in Figure 13.7.

PARTY-IN-GOVERNMENT Party-in-government refers to the officials who were elected under a party banner. All the Republicans in the House of Representatives, for example, make up one piece of the GOP ("Grand Old Party," which is the nickname for Republicans) party-in-government. They call themselves the Republican Conference, and if they have a majority in the chamber, their leader is the Speaker of the House; if not, he or she is the minority leader (see Chapter 6). Other segments of the Republican party-in-government include the Republicans in the Senate and any president who is a member of the GOP. There are also sub-branches of the national party-in-government, such as governors, state-level elected officials, municipal officials, and so on. Similarly, the Democrats in the House Democrats call themselves the Democratic Caucus, and all the Democrats in the Buffalo City Council consider themselves part of the same team.

tripartite view

Thinking of political parties as consisting of three parts—in-government; in-the-electorate; and as-an-organization.

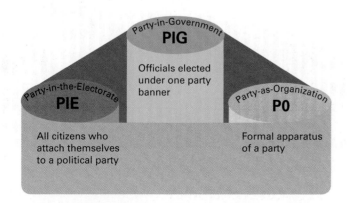

Party-in-Government
PIG
Officials elected under one party banner

Party-in-the-Electorate
PIE
All citizens who attach themselves to a political party

Party-as-Organization
PO
Formal apparatus of a party

FIGURE 13.7 The Three Inter-related Elements of American Political Parties

The three core pieces are represented by party-in-government (PIG), party-in-the-electorate (PIE), and party-as-organization (PO). While few would doubt that each exists, some believe that they should be seen as distinct elements rather than linked together.

■ *When you think of "political party," which element comes to mind?*

There are many ways to measure the extent to which legislators stick with their party, and the most common is called party unity scores. This is the percentage of votes on legislation in which a majority of Republicans oppose a majority of Democrats. It is a measure that can be used to describe the partisan nature of any legislative body, including Congress, state legislatures, county legislatures, and city councils. Regarding Congress, party unity scores have shifted over time, with the average being about 60 percent of votes. A low point was the middle decades of the 20th century when the Democrats controlled Congress, but their Caucus was made up of an awkward mix of Northeastern liberals and Southern conservatives—the latter being dubbed "boll weevils." The two wings of the Democratic Party disagreed passionately on many issues, especially civil rights legislation, leading unit scores to drop into the 30-percent range. By the 1990s, the Republican Party in the South had become significant, making it a more comfortable home for conservative politicians. Today most federal legislators from the South are Republican and party unity scores are much higher. In fact, one of the most significant aspects of contemporary party politics is the record high levels of party unity in Congress, as noted in Figure 13.8. To some, this is evidence that the American electoral politics has become much more polarized in recent decades.

FIGURE 13.8 Party Unity in Congressional Voting

These figures represent the extent to which members of Congress vote with their party on measures that reach the floor.

■ *Why do members of Congress seem more rigid in their partisanship when a growing number of Americans appear to shun hard-core partisanship?*

SOURCE: Based on data from *Congressional Quarterly*, http://media.cq.com/votestudies/ under the Average Unity Scores tab.

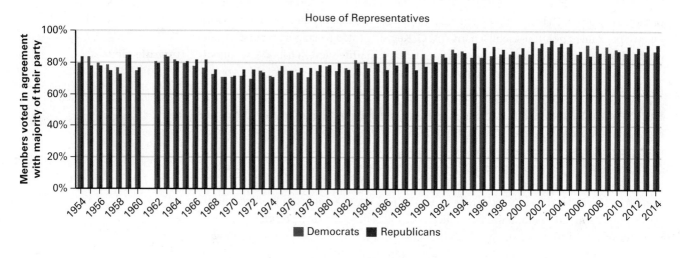

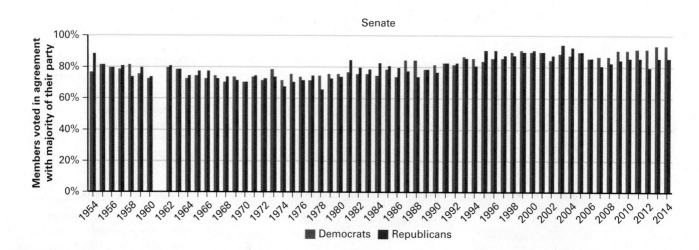

PARTY-IN-THE-ELECTORATE Party-in-the-electorate refers to every citizen who attaches him- or herself to a political party. An average citizen who says "I am a Democrat" or "a Republican" or "a Green" or "a Libertarian" is acknowledging membership in a party-in-the-electorate.[25] Another way of thinking about it is that the party consists of all the voters who consider themselves members of that party.

In many other countries, belonging to a political party can be a big deal. In dictatorships such as China, Cuba, and the former Soviet Union, being a member of the Communist Party—the only legal party—means joining the country's ruling class and gaining valuable career opportunities. It also requires proving political reliability and coming under strict discipline. In democratic countries such as Great Britain, citizens can choose among many parties and can change their affiliation any time they want, but they still have to join up officially, sign a membership card, pay dues, and attend local party meetings. Identifying a British party-in-the-electorate is thus relatively straightforward. Belonging to a party in the United States is very different. In this country, party-in-the-electorate is an ambiguous concept and the source of much scholarly debate.

Some suggest that a person's attitude, or **party identification**, is enough to consider him or her a partisan. Party identification is the belief that a particular party best represents one's interests and outlook toward government and society; it often springs from the childhood socialization process. If a citizen tells a pollster, for example, that he or she thinks of him- or herself as a "strong Republican," the citizen would be considered part of the party-in-the-electorate.

As suggested in Figure 13.9, the percentage of Democratic and Republican identifiers has shifted in the past two decades. In recent years, the number of Democrats seems to be gaining, but so too does the number of nonaligned voters, what we call **independents**. (There are many independents in the United States but no actual Independent Party.)

A number of factors can lead a citizen to choose an allegiance to one party or the other. Social scientists have noted both short- and long-term factors. Short-term factors include an affinity for a particular candidate or concern about a given issue. Many

party identification

A belief that one belongs to a certain party; an emotional connection to a particular party.

independent

A voter who is not registered or affiliated with any political party.

FIGURE 13.9 Trends in Party Identification 1990–2016

Interestingly, this figure shows that Democrats have outnumbered Republicans during much of the last few decades—including 2016. But Donald Trump won the presidency, and Republicans now control both houses of Congress and 33 governorships.

■ *Might there be an important difference between what someone might tell a pollster and how they vote on Election Day?*

SOURCE: "Party Identification," Pew Research Center, http://www.pewresearch.org/data-trend/political-attitudes/party-identification/.

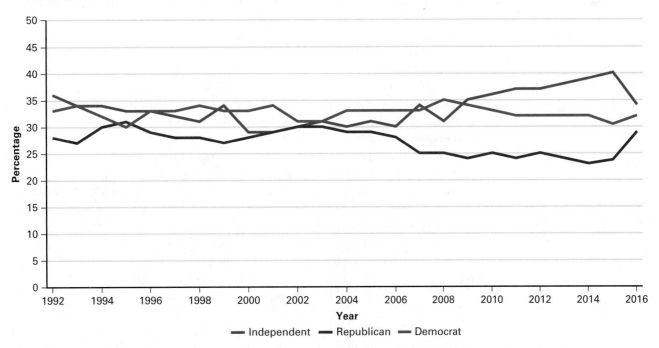

Americans may have moved to the Democratic Party over concerns about the wars in Iraq and Afghanistan, and some have turned to the Republican Party because of concerns over the growing national debt and President Obama's policy initiatives. In all likelihood the 2016 presidential election shifted voter allegiances. That is, Donald Trump did well with white working-class voters—a group that had historically supported Democratic candidates. Hillary Clinton made headway with suburban middle-class voters, especially women, and well-educated voters. In fact, 2016 was the first election since the Depression that a Democrat won a majority of voters with a college degree. Long-term factors, which can be quite powerful, include demographic factors, such as race, level of education, region of the country, and to some extent, even gender.

PARTY-AS-ORGANIZATION   The final piece of the tripod is party-as-organization, which means the formal apparatus of the party, including party headquarters, offices, and leaders. It is the official bureaucracy of the party, and it is found in the form of committees in every state and nearly every community in the nation.

Party organizations exist at each layer of our political system. At the national level are the Democratic National Committee (DNC) and the Republican National Committee (RNC). Each state has both a Republican and a Democratic party, as do most counties and cities across the nation. At the very bottom of the structure, you can still occasionally find ward or precinct organizations. The Chicago Democratic Committee, for example, is made up of a mass of different precinct organizations. Many casual observers of party politics believe that a formal hierarchy connects the layers, with the national parties controlling the state parties and the state organizations dictating orders to the county or municipal committees. This is not the case. An unusual aspect of the American parties is that while there is a good bit of interaction between layers of the system, most of it involving the sharing of resources, few commands find their way down to lower-level committees. For the most part, party organizations at all levels of the system operate as semi-independent units.

The Debate over Party Polarization

As noted previously, party polarization seems to be one of the defining characteristics of American politics in the early part of the twenty-first century. This concept implies that Americans are deeply divided on both ideological and partisan lines. We are increasingly "hard core" Republicans or "hard core" Democrats.

One way to think about sharp divisions is by geography. Figure 13.10 indicates areas of Republican strength in red, blue denotes Democratic strength, and purple an even balance. Clearly, there seems to be distinct partisan regions in the country, but there are also numerous areas that are evenly matched.

Another way of thinking about polarization is the extent to which compromise, middle-of-the-road solutions are supported by party leaders and election officials. One of the authors of this book (Daniel M. Shea) conducted a survey of nearly 500 local party leaders in the summer of 2011. Several of the questions dealt with a willingness to find compromise solutions. Figure 13.11 provides the results of one of these questions. You will note that while 60 percent of local party leaders support the idea of finding compromise solutions, a major partisan difference comes to light. Simply stated, Democratic Party leaders seem much more interested in compromise than do GOP leaders.

Beyond geographic differences and the attitudes of party leaders, the exact dimensions of the recent partisan polarization are a bit unclear. Some scholars, such as Stanford political scientist Morris Fiorina, have suggested the root of the change stems from activists at the ends of the ideological spectrum; hard-core liberals and hard-core conservatives have become especially informed, vocal, and engaged. Most citizens remain moderate, but the wings of the party have become very loud and very active. (Local party leaders would, of course, be part of the "wings.") And because hard-core activists are more likely to vote, particularly in primary elections, the winners tend to be more ideological than their constituent base. Ironically, as middle-of-the-road citizens see their member of Congress and state legislature as firmly committed to

FIGURE 13.10 Partisan Leanings of the Nation, Based on County-Level Election Returns In 2016

Red areas suggest Republican strongholds, while blue areas are Democratic.

■ *Should we be thought of as a blue and red nation, or as a purple nation?*

NOTE: Data available as of November 22, 2016.

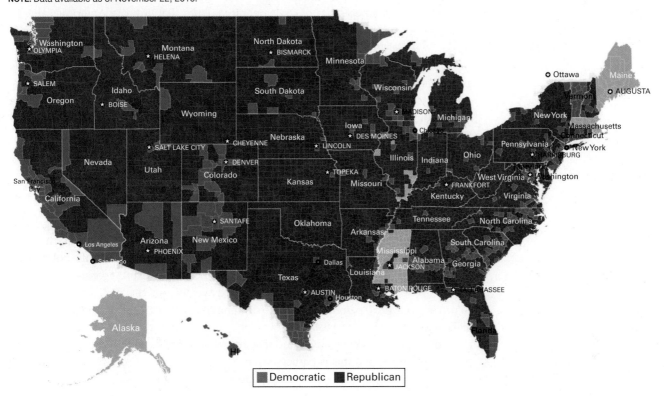

either far-left or far-right policies, they may stay away from the process. They also notice that the tone of politics, given this polarization, has become shrill. It is possible, then, that this type of polarization is actually contributing to lower levels of voting. True ideologues turn out to vote, to be sure, but moderates, who tend to be much less

FIGURE 13.11 Party Leaders and a Willingness to Compromise

This data, compiled by one of the authors of this text in the summer of 2015, suggests GOP leaders are much less anxious to find compromise solutions than are Democratic chairs.

■ *Do you think a willingness to compromise is a function of how well a politician believes he or she might do in the next election? Why compromise if you think you are going to win?*

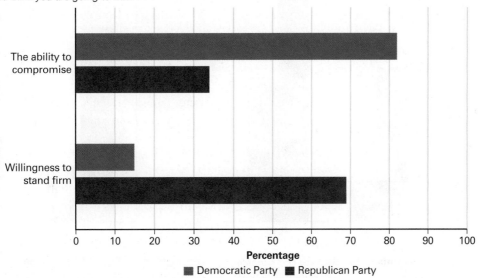

engaged in the process, may be staying home on Election Day. In his book *Disconnect: The Breakdown in Representation in American Politics*, Fiorina writes

> [C]ross-sectional evidence does not rule out the possibility that the long-term decline in voting by independents and ideological moderates is relative to the growing negativity of contemporary politics....[O]rdinary Americans are turned off by the uncivil manner of many members of the political class, their emphasis on issues of limited importance to most people....

Other scholars have suggested the polarization is much more widespread than merely among those at the ideological extremes, and that this change has contributed to higher turnout in recent elections. Consider the writing of Emory University scholar Alan Abramowitz in his book *The Disappearing Center: Engaged Citizens, Polarization and American Democracy*:

> Contrary to the claim that ordinary Americans have been losing interest in government and politics as a result of growing partisan animosity and ideological polarization,...[survey data] shows that Americans today are more interested in politics, better informed about politics, and more politically active than at any time during the past half century.

So which perspective is correct? Has polarization been limited to those at the ideological extremes or has it been more widespread? Several recent studies by the Pew Research Center have added new data to the issue and, for most, settled the debate. In short, the polarization has indeed reached historic highs. The share of Americans who express consistently conservative or consistently liberal opinions has doubled over the past two decades — from about 10 percent to over 20 percent. Two of the defining characteristics of this era relate to a willingness to compromise and feelings toward the other party. With regard to the compromise issue, here again the Pew study found that fewer and fewer seem willing to support compromise solutions, and this is particularly true for conservatives. An even more stunning finding relates to our attitudes toward the opposing party, as noted in Figure 13.12.

FIGURE 13.12   A Rising Tide of Mutual Antipathy

One of the most troubling parts of recent partisan polarization is antipathy for the other side. That is, Democrats don't like or trust Republicans, and vice versa.

■ *How do you think the election of Donald Trump will impact this trend?*

NOTE: Republicans include Republican-leaning independents; Democrats include Democratic-leaning independents.

SOURCE: "Political Polarization in the American Public," Pew Research Center for the People and the Press, June 12, 2014. See: http://www.people-press.org/2014/06/12/political-polarization-in-the-american-public/pp-2014-06-12-polarization-0-06/.

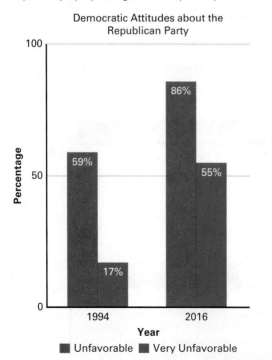

Democratic Attitudes about the Republican Party

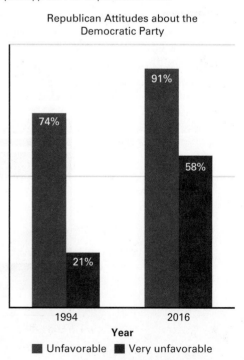

Republican Attitudes about the Democratic Party

A growing number of Americans do not like those of the other party. They would not like to live in a geographic area dominated by that party and would even be upset if their children married someone of that party. Those with strong views, either conservative or liberal, believe that the views of the other side threaten the well-being of the nation. This has always been true for a fraction of the public, but the mushrooming growth of this segment in the last 20 years has stunned even the most seasoned observers. Indeed, antipathy and distrust of the "other" side is a vivid, critically important aspect of contemporary American politics.

Party Eras in American History

13.4 Trace the evolution of political parties in the United States.

Like nearly every other aspect of American government, the nature of the party system has changed over time. From nearly the beginning, political parties have been at the center of the American electoral process, but they must continue to shift and adapt to new conditions.

The Emergence of Parties in America (1790s–1828)

James Madison warned his fellow Americans about the dangers of party-like organizations, which he called "factions," in *The Federalist*, No. 10. A few years later, George Washington, in his famous Farewell Address, suggested much the same: "Let me… warn you in the most solemn manner against the baneful effects of the spirit of party….It is truly [our] worst enemy."

Within a decade after the adoption of the Constitution, however, parties had burst onto the scene. Wishing to fill his cabinet with the best and brightest minds of the day, President Washington selected Thomas Jefferson for secretary of state and Alexander Hamilton for secretary of the treasury. Hamilton and Jefferson passionately disagreed about the future of the nation. Jefferson believed that America's hope lay in small, agriculture-based communities. Hamilton, on the other hand, believed that the future of the nation lay in the development of vibrant cities, and he was convinced that a strong central government was the best mechanism to ensure long-term economic growth.

Partisan animosity got even worse during the presidency of John Adams. Opponents of the administration (led by Jefferson and his "antiparty" friend James Madison) called themselves **Democratic-Republicans**. Supporters of Adams and Hamilton organized the **Federalist Party**, a group that was unrelated to the supporters of the Constitution in 1787–1788, who also called themselves Federalists. One prominent historian described this period as the "great consolidation," when parties finally emerged in America.[26]

The dispute over the legitimacy of political parties was mostly settled with the election of 1800. Even James Madison, who had attacked factions in *The Federalist Papers*, had been an ardent Democratic-Republican (he was elected president as Jefferson's successor in 1808) and in his old age embraced the party system.[27] The Federalists, lacking a large base of support outside New England, gradually faded from the scene.

The Heyday of Parties (1828–1900)

An important event occurred early in our nation's history, what most historians refer to as the **Corrupt Bargain of 1824**. In that year's presidential election, five candidates vied for the office. On Election Day none had received a majority of the Electoral College votes, so the issue was sent to the House of Representatives (as per the Constitution). Most assumed that Andrew Jackson of Tennessee, who had come in first, would win in the House. But that did not happen. There is evidence to suggest

Democratic-Republicans
The first American political party, formed by believers in states' rights and followers of Thomas Jefferson.

Federalist Party
Founded by Alexander Hamilton, its members believed in a strong, centralized government.

Corrupt Bargain of 1824
The alleged secret agreement in the disputed election of 1824 that led the House of Representatives to select John Quincy Adams, who had come in second in the popular vote, as president if he would make Speaker of the House Henry Clay his secretary of state.

a deal was made between Speaker of the House Henry Clay (another candidate that year) and John Quincy Adams of Massachusetts (the son of John Adams, and yet another candidate). If Clay would steer his colleagues in the House to Adams' corner, then Adams, once president, would make Clay secretary of state. This appears to be what happened: Adams became president and Clay secretary of state.

Anger and frustration over the alleged bargain was felt across America, which showed itself in two ways. First, the National Republican Party was torn apart, and by the mid-1830s, another major party, the Whig Party, had arisen. Second, what was left of the National Republicans regrouped as the Democratic Party. The leaders of the Democrats were Andrew Jackson and a New York politician named Martin Van Buren. Jackson, on Van Buren's advice, used local party organizations to rally opposition to Adams. These organizations helped Jackson unseat Adams in 1828, to reelect Jackson in 1832, and to elect Van Buren as his successor in 1836. By that time, Van Buren faced the organized opposition of the Whig Party.

This period was a rebirth of party politics at the community level. Party operatives spread the word that unless average citizens became involved, the nation would be ruled through elite deals like the Corrupt Bargain of 1824.

Party Decline (1900–1970s)

Responding to public outrage over corrupt politics in the post–Civil War era, a number of important changes were gradually made. To strip political machines of their ability to use the patronage jobs by which they controlled government, the merit system (also called the civil service, whereby people earned jobs by doing well on exams) was introduced in 1883 and later expanded. To reduce the ability of bosses to control what happened in polling places, the Australian ballot (or "secret ballot") was instituted;

Pictured here is Boss Tweed, a legendary New York party leader. The Progressive Movement was designed to clean up the corruption of party machines, but some of the reform continues to hinder local party organizations.

■ *Are local party committees still important in the Information Age?*

THE BALLOT

IN COUNTING THERE IS STRENGTH

now voters no longer had to either orally announce their vote or publicly deposit their ballot in the box of one party or the other. And to reduce the chance that bosses would simply handpick nominees who faithfully toed the party line, the direct primary was established. In this system, the rank-and-file would choose the party nominee. These and many other reforms greatly reduced the power of party machines.

The Great Depression dealt another blow to machine politics. The economic crisis of the 1930s tore to shreds the "safety net" that political machines had provided to help out-of-luck citizens get through tough times. To replace these tattered safety nets, President Franklin D. Roosevelt's New Deal established federal Social Security, unemployment insurance, public works projects, and social welfare programs, all of which undermined ordinary people's dependence on political bosses.

By the 1960s, public attitudes about political parties had grown especially sour, and candidates came to realize that parties were no longer necessary or even desirable. Historically, party workers were needed to bring the candidate's message to the voter, but by the 1960s, television and direct mail could reach more voters in a single day than party operatives could contact in weeks. Moreover, new-style campaign consultants burst on the scene in the 1960s. These professionals could be hired, and their allegiance would be solely to the candidate.

What we might call the post-1960 **Candidate-Centered Era** sent repercussions throughout the political system. With candidates pitching themselves as independent, voters saw little reason to hold to any notion of partisanship. As more citizens became independent, voting cues that gave information to citizens about candidates were lost, leading to lower Election Day turnouts. Once in office, elected officials saw little reason to stick to the party caucus, leading to less policy coherence and a less efficient legislative process.

Candidate-Centered Era
After 1960, a period when candidates began to portray themselves as independent from party politics, even though they often ran under a party banner.

Organizational Resurgence (1970s–Present)

By the 1970s, many observers came to believe that parties were fading permanently from the scene. Instead of improving their relations with voters, however, the parties chose to expand their services to candidates. Parties became service-oriented, meaning that they broadened their activities to include a host of high-tech services to candidates. They developed, for example, computerized direct-mail operations, in-house television and radio production studios, and sophisticated polling operations. Simply stated, many party organizations are stronger today because they have adapted to the consultant, service-centered nature of electoral politics.

This change has had significant ramifications. For one thing, sophisticated services require ever-increasing resources. In their efforts to get around campaign finance laws, politicians and their consultants discover new loopholes each year, breeding voter cynicism. At precisely the same time that party organizations are regaining their footing, a growing number of Americans see parties as corrupt. And while the national parties have done well during this period, revitalization has not yet reached the grassroots— that is, local party committees. We now have a party system that is vibrant at the national level, but weak at the local level. Finally, while many candidates appreciate the help they receive, the parties know that they can get more mileage out of targeting only a handful of races. In short, the revitalization of the national party *committees* has been significant, but some believe it has also transformed the nature of the party *system*.

Minor Parties in American Politics

13.5 Explain the historic role of minor parties in the U.S. electoral process.

Unlike most democracies across the globe, the United States boasts a twoparty rather than a multiparty system. Also, a growing number of citizens seem interested in additional choices on Election Day—particularly given the seeming inability of Democrat- and Republican-elected officials to reach compromise solutions. But there seems to be few challenges to the two-party system. Why? The barriers to minor-party success in the United States can be divided into two categories: institutional and attitudinal.

Institutional barriers are the legal impediments created by statutes, by court decisions, or by the Constitution itself. The most significant of these is the single-member district or first-past-the-post system that is used in legislative elections. In many democracies across the globe, a proportional representation system (called "PR") is used. Here, each party receives the number of seats in the legislature roughly proportional to the percentage of votes it gets on election day. Netting 25 percent of the votes, for instance, yields one-fourth of the seats in the legislature. In the American model, legislative districts have only one legislator, who gets into office simply by getting more votes than any other candidate. Imagine that candidates from three parties are competing for a congressional seat. One candidate winds up with 45 percent of the vote, and the others get about 27 percent each. Because the first candidate received more votes than the others—was "the first past the post"—and because only one person can represent the district, that candidate is sent to Washington. The losing parties get nothing for their efforts. Eventually, operatives of the losing parties will consider joining forces if they are not too far apart ideologically. The outcome is a two-party system. This is called Duverger's Law, named after Maurice Duverger, the French scholar who first wrote about this phenomenon in the 1950s.

Another institutional barrier to third parties is the Electoral College, discussed at length next. Because 48 states rely on a winner-take-all system, to have a chance at winning the presidency a candidate has to win states outright; he or she gains nothing by running a strong second. Many states also help sustain the two-party system through **ballot access laws**, schemes created at the turn of the twentieth century to limit the number of candidates on the general election ballot—while at the same time making things easy for the major parties. (After all, members of the two major parties were writing the regulations!)

The second category of barriers to minor-party success is **attitudinal barriers**—perceptions most commonly tied to the wasted-vote syndrome. Because minor-party candidates usually stand little chance of victory, most Americans are reluctant to support such candidates on Election Day, "wasting" (they say) their vote. It is revealing that support for minor-party candidates often peaks several weeks before the election. But as Election Day approaches, voters abandon the minor-party candidate, hoping to add their voice to the contest between the "real" candidates, one of whom everyone knows is going to win. This would also explain why so many Americans tell pollsters that they want more parties in the election process but at the same time minor-party candidates languish on Election Day. A second attitudinal barrier is widespread support for centrist policies. That is, most Americans consider themselves ideologically moderate and in the middle class. This leads them to support middle-of-the-road positions exemplified by the two major parties. Whereas "extremist" parties can do well in other countries, historically they have languished in our system. Given some of the changes discussed in this chapter, perhaps this will change.

ballot access laws

Laws that regulated who's name appears on the general election ballot. In some states it is easier to accomplish than in other states.

attitudinal barriers

Personal beliefs regarding the viability and necessity of minor party candidates. Many will not vote for minor-party candidates because they believe their vote will be wasted.

History of Minor Parties

This is not to suggest that minor parties play no role in our system. It's quite the contrary. Minor parties have sprouted up throughout American political history and have changed the political landscape. They fall into two categories. The first have been the fledgling parties that appeared on the rare occasions when one or both of the major parties were actually collapsing, the second have been the true third parties that periodically challenged the established two-party system and provoked changes in both parties. Table 13.1 identifies many of the significant minor parties throughout American history.

TABLE 13.1   Third Parties in American History

As this table suggests, there have been many minor parties in American history—although their success at the polls has been limited.

■ *Do these organizations play an important role in our political system as most social scientists suggest? What functions would these minor parties afford the system?*

Third Party	Year	Percentage of Popular Vote	Electoral Votes	Fate in Following Years
Anti-Masons	1832	7.8	7	Merges with Whigs by 1836
Free Soil	1848	10.1	0	Fades quickly as Republican Party emerges
Whig-American	1856	21.5	8	Dissolves rapidly; Gone by 1860
Southern Democrat	1860	18.1	72	Dissolves after the election
Peoples' Populist	1892	8.5	22	Endorses Democratic candidate next election
Progressive (T. Roosevelt)	1912	27.5	88	Folds back into Republican Party
Socialist	1912	6	0	Fades quickly
Progressive (R. LaFollette)	1924	16.6	13	Folds back into GOP
States' Rights Democrats	1948	2.4	39	Dissolves after the election
American Independent (G. Wallace)	1968	13.5	46	Wallace runs in 1972, nets 1.5%; Gone
H. Ross Perot	1992	18.9	0	Perot runs in 1996, nets 8%; Gone
Green (R. Nader)	2000	2.7	0	Runs pres. candidates; limited appeal
Libertarian (G. Johnson)	2016	3.5	0	Uncertain

The strongest minor-party presidential candidate in recent years was H. Ross Perot. He netted a huge 18.9 percent of the popular vote—which did not translate into a single Electoral College vote in the 1992 presidential election.

Role of Minor Parties in Our Democracy

Given the challenges that minor parties face in the American system as well as their limited success at the polls throughout our history, you might be tempted to conclude that they are a waste of time—that they play no role in changing the course of government. Nothing could be farther from the truth. Minor parties have played a significant role in shaping public policy by drawing attention to particular issues and by threatening to drain support from the major parties. In fact, it has often been the initial success of minor parties that has led to their downfall: Once a new party dramatizes an issue and shows that there are votes at stake, one (or even both) of the major parties will pick up the issue, and the voters will fall back in line. The major parties are reinvigorated precisely because minor parties nip at the edges of the process. History also shows that minor parties have played a significant role in bringing more citizens into the political process. Voters often begin to feel distrustful of the major parties—or at the very least not represented by them. They slowly withdraw, only to be drawn back into the process by the energy and excitement of minor-party activity.

Parties and The Nomination Process

13.6   Outline the process by which party nominees are chosen to run in the general election.

As you have seen in this chapter, political parties serve many functions. Here, we outline one of the most important: the process of deciding which candidates will appear on the general election ballot under the party's banner—a procedure called *nomination*. For voters, nominations limit their choices on Election Day, but without party nominations we might find dozens or even hundreds of candidates on each ballot.

In the early years, a handful of party leaders did the choosing. At first, few people objected; if the voters did not like the candidates they chose, they could simply vote

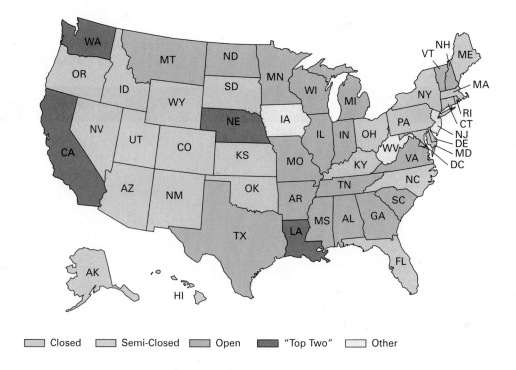

FIGURE 13.13 Primary Systems in the United States

As this figure suggests, the split between open and closed primary states is about even. But this does not mean that they are randomly distributed across the United States.

▪ *Can you see any geographic patterns? If so, what might explain the configuration?*

Closed   Semi-Closed   Open   "Top Two"   Other

direct primary election

The process by which average party members, sometimes called the rank-and-file, are allowed to select party nominees. This process replaced the hand-picked model used by party bosses.

closed primary system

A nomination system where only members of the party are allowed to participate.

open primary system

A nomination system where all are allowed to participate—regardless of their party affiliation.

for someone else. The nomination process changed during the Progressive Era, when laws were passed mandating that the parties get widespread voter input in selecting nominees. We call this process a **direct primary election**. Today, both major parties choose their candidates by letting rank-and-file members (average citizens) vote.

Different Primary Systems

Not every state uses the same primary system (see Figure 13.13). Roughly half the states have what is called a **closed primary system**. In these states, only registered members of the party are allowed to vote in the primary. In some states, the voter must declare his or her party registration in advance of the primary election—often 30 days or so—while in other states, the registration can be done (or changed) on primary day. Either way, the states that rely on this system allow only registered members of the party to vote on prospective nominees. If you are registered as a Democrat or are an independent, you cannot vote in the Republican primary.

Most other states use an **open primary system**. Under it, voters are allowed to participate in the primary election without declaring membership in a party. On primary day, the voter can choose to vote in the Republican primary or the Democratic primary, and no record is kept. (Of course, one cannot vote in both parties' primaries.) Some people have criticized the open primary system because activists in one party can vote for the *weaker* candidates in the other party's primary election. For example, in the 2010 South Carolina Democratic Senate primary, a virtually unheard of candidate, Alvin Greene—who did not campaign, had essentially no resources, and had recently been arrested for showing pornographic pictures to college students—somehow defeated a well-known, well-funded state official. The outcome left many scratching their heads for an explanation; some believe that the open primary system may have allowed Republican supporters to vote for the weakest Democratic candidates. However, most scholars believe this sort of "strategic primary voting" is rare.

There is also a movement in some states to more or less jettison party-based nominations. In 2004, the voters in the state of Washington passed a ballot initiative to create a "top two" nomination process, in which any number of candidates is allowed to run in an initial contest, but only the top two are placed on the general election ballot. These two candidates might be of a different party, or they might not. Louisiana has had a similar system for many years, and Nebraska uses a nonpartisan system, which amounts to a top-two model. And in the spring of 2010, voters in California made a similar switch to a top-two system. Democratic and Republican party leaders in California were stunned, and they quickly filed a federal lawsuit. However, a year later the federal courts ruled that the system adopted by the state was legal.

Presidential Nominations

The framers of the Constitution saw no reason to specify a procedure for nominating presidential candidates. They assumed that the local notables who would gather in each state to cast their Electoral College votes would select the most qualified men. That was how George Washington was unanimously chosen as the first president. When the early party system of Democratic-Republicans and Federalists nevertheless emerged, each party's representatives in Congress named its presidential (and, beginning in 1804, its vice presidential) candidates. The Corrupt Bargain of 1824, however, led to the belief that something less elitist—something that better reflected the will of average voters—should be substituted. The outcome was the **national nominating convention**. The idea was that delegates should be sent from communities across the nation once every 4 years to discuss the strengths and weaknesses of potential candidates and thus produce the best choice. The convention would also be an opportunity to hammer together a party platform as well as rules for conducting party business. The major parties held their first national conventions in 1832 and have done so every 4 years since.

national nominating convention
Events that are held in the summer of presidential election years where party delegates, selected through primaries and caucuses, pick their party's presidential nominee.

One of the sticking points in the convention system was how delegates would be chosen from their communities and what role they might play at the convention. A few states developed mechanisms to allow rank-and-file party members to select delegates, but most simply allowed state and local party bosses to handpick who went to the national convention. Once there, these delegates were obliged to follow the orders of their party leader. This often led to high drama at party conventions. Party bosses used their delegates as negotiating chips, looking to play a key role in nominating the candidate—for what could be better than to be perceived as the party's "kingmaker"?

The strain between party bosses and average party followers came to a head in a fight over the 1968 Democratic presidential nomination. As 1968 began, everyone assumed that President Lyndon B. Johnson would accept his party's renomination. But there arose a groundswell of opposition to Johnson within the Democratic Party over his waging of the Vietnam War. When Johnson failed to win decisively in the March New Hampshire primary, he announced that he was withdrawing from the race.

A sharp division emerged between the party leaders, who backed Vice President Hubert Humphrey, and the "antiwar Democrats," who supported either Minnesota Senator Eugene McCarthy (not to be confused with Senator Joseph McCarthy of Wisconsin, the anticommunist demagogue of the 1950s) and New York Senator Robert F. Kennedy (the late President John F. Kennedy's younger brother and his former attorney general). Kennedy gradually outpaced McCarthy in the primary elections, yet the party bosses continued to back Humphrey, who was staying out of the primaries. Robert Kennedy's assassination in 1968 on the night he won the California primary created a crisis for the antiwar Democrats. Faithful to their bosses, the majority of delegates at the Democratic National Convention in Chicago nominated Humphrey, while thousands of antiwar young people filled the streets in protest outside the convention hall and were beaten and bloodied by police. Humphrey went on to lose the general election to Richard Nixon. The Democratic Party seemed to be in shambles.

After this disastrous election, Democrats implemented a series of changes designed to create a more open, timely, and representative nomination process. Most notably, **binding primaries** were established in most states, where voters picked delegates who

binding primaries
A system where delegates selected through primaries and caucuses are bound to support the candidate that they originally said they would support. That is, they are not allowed to switch their convention vote as they see fit.

Many agree that 1968 was one of the most turbulent years in American history. Here, Robert Kennedy lies dying after being shot on the evening of the California Democratic presidential primary, which he had won. Hubert Humphrey was later given the nomination, even though many "regulars" in the party wanted a true anti–Vietnam War candidate. Four years later, the party had transformed its nomination rules—leading to binding primaries and caucuses.

■ *But have these changes made the system truly more democratic?*

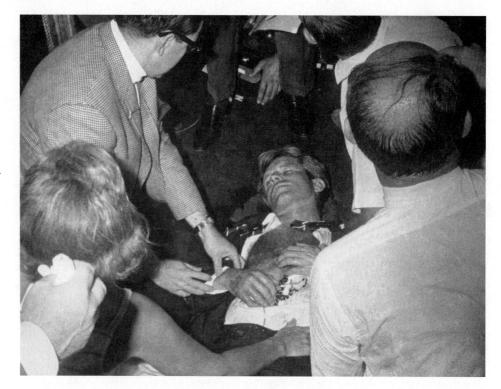

nomination caucus

Essentially, meetings of rank-and-file party members where the qualifications of candidates are discussed and debated, and where a final vote determines the groups' support for each.

pledged their support for a particular presidential candidate. The winners in each state were sent to the convention, where they voted to nominate that candidate. Another way to pick delegates, used in about 15 states, is a **nomination caucus**. Here, rank-and-file party members attend a neighborhood meeting, share ideas and concerns about particular candidates, and cast a ballot for pledged delegates to attend a statewide meeting. There, the same process takes place, and the delegates who win at the state level go to the national party convention. The key difference between primaries and caucuses is that the former is an election and the latter a series of "town hall-like" meetings.

The Republican Party was not bound by the new Democratic Party rules, but as the Democrats moved to what was perceived to be a more open system, the older model lost legitimacy, and the Republicans were obliged to make similar changes.

A Better Process?

The nomination reforms of the early 1970s dramatically transformed the way Americans select presidents. It is hard to overstate the importance of the shift from party boss to voter control. While many have applauded the change, critics point to a number of problems:

- The nomination process may *not* reflect the will of the average party member, let alone the average American, because relatively few people participate in the primaries and caucuses—and the ones who do are much more ideological, more "extremist," than the typical citizen. Turnout in presidential primaries is generally less than 20 percent of eligible voters, and attendance at caucuses rarely gets beyond 10 percent.

- Because candidates win or lose based on how citizens feel about them, the nomination process has become very expensive, time consuming, and negative. Hillary Clinton confronted sustained attacks for more than a year from Vermont Senator Bernie Sanders prior to the 2016 Democratic National Convention, and some of the worst things said about Donald Trump came from other Republican candidates. Candidates who can raise the most money—and raise it the fastest—have historically had an advantage. This money can be used to attack the other candidates, who are all part of the same party. The bitterness of the primaries leaves many Americans distrustful about the electoral process.

- The nomination process puts a premium on winning early primary and caucus contests, which helps raise more money and draw more media hype. Many critics have argued that small and perhaps atypical New Hampshire and Iowa, which hold their events at the very start of the process, exert grossly disproportionate weight in selecting the eventual nominee.

- In an effort to give party leaders and other elected officials (such as governors and members of Congress) a modest say in the nomination process, the Democrats created a special category of delegates in 1984, dubbed superdelegates. This group, which amounts to about 20 percent of the overall number of delegates to the convention, are chosen by the party, not the rank-and-file voters during primaries and caucuses. Superdelegates overwhelmingly backed Hillary Clinton in 2016, leading to deafening calls by Sanders' supporters to get rid of the special category and make the system fairer.

- Finally, following the 2016 nomination process, many began to question the wisdom of a decentralized process. As noted above, the outcome of the reforms of the early 1970s was to allow each state party to create its own process—so long as the outcome is open and fair. This has led to a byzantine mix of rules and dates. Some states, for instance, hold both primaries and caucuses. Others hold primaries, but actually do not select delegates until a state convention is held. In the spring of 2016 Americans learned that in a few states it was possible for a candidate to win the primary, but not receive a majority of that state's delegates.

PATHWAYS OF ACTION

COMING TOGETHER AFTER THE 2016 ELECTION?

Scholars, pundits, public officials, and average Americans seem troubled by the growing ugliness of our politics. The bitter, knock-down, maybe even epic battle between Hillary Clinton and Donald Trump was but the latest installment. And yet, maybe American electoral politics has always been hard hitting. We know that in 1804 Alexander Hamilton died after being shot by Aaron Burr—a low point for political civility in the early days of our political system. We hear of the breakdown of our political process prior to the Civil War and of how Representative Preston S. Brooks of South Carolina used his cane to beat Senator Charles Sumner of Massachusetts into bloody unconsciousness on the floor of the U.S. Senate in 1856. We also know of the infamous floor brawl in the U.S. House of Representatives two years later. More than 50 congressional members joined the melee. Most people have heard about the bruising campaign between Democrat Grover Cleveland and Republican James Blaine and the contentious period of the 1890s. The McCarthy Era was no picnic, and the Vietnam/civil rights/counterculture period of the 1960s was a tough time, to be sure. Perhaps, for better or for worse, uncivil politics are a part of our national tradition.

And yet, there is a growing amount of data to suggest unique forces are at work. Financially successful, highly-charged partisan "news" programs, websites, talk-radio programs, and voter mobilization operations will not disappear after the 2016 election. Reality television shows, ripe with vitriol and rude behavior, are here to stay, and Donald Trump's success may

have exposed the electoral benefits of over-the-top attacks for future candidates.

But do Americans really care about the tone of politics? Do they want to improve the tone of our politics? Shortly before the 2016 election, one of the authors of this text (Shea) conducted a survey of 845 randomly selected voters from across the country. The results are noteworthy. First, a vast majority (upwards of 90 percent) believe a level of respect and civility are important for a healthy democracy. However, a similar number suggest things have gotten particularly bad. For example, 84 percent said that the 2016 election was much more negative than in the past. A full 83 percent said that society had also become less civil.

The good news is that huge majorities expressed a desire to come together after the election. The poll asked, "When the election is over, how important do you think it will be for both sides to cool tempers, shake hands, and come together to confront difficult issues?" A whopping 93 percent of respondents thought it was very or somewhat important. This figure was a even a bit higher for older Americans and for women.

Hyper-partisanship and rough-and-tumble elections are characteristics of our times. But when it comes to the general public, there seems to be genuine interest in cooling things down, confronting some of our nations big issues, and finding compromise solutions. Whether or not elected officials can head down this pathway is difficult to say, but many Americans have their fingers crossed.

Reforming the Process

Is the current process too demanding on the candidates and downright harmful to the electoral process? Many people are beginning to question the utility of the current system and to explore solutions. Indeed, by March 2016—the middle of the nomination process—just one-in-three voters had confidence in their party's system. Does it really make sense, for example, to move from one state to the next, leading to a confusing, frustrating, and drawn-out process? But if the current model does not work, what would?

One alternative would be to drop caucuses and have one national primary day. Just as with the general election, voters from across the nation would pick their party's nominee on the same day. Many suggest that this plan would increase turnout because more people would feel that their vote could make a difference (recall that in the current system the nominee is often determined after a few weeks, leaving some states without a say in the process). But others have argued that the "retail" (meaning intimate, face-to-face) electioneering common in New Hampshire and Iowa would be lost. In its place would be one massive national media campaign.

The so-called Delaware Plan would group four "blocks" of states according to population to determine the order of primaries. The smallest 13 states would go first, then the next 13, then 12 medium states, followed by the largest 12 states. States would remain free to decide between a primary and caucus, and could schedule their event for any time during their appointed period. This plan addresses the problem of front-loading, and supporters argue that it would encourage voter participation and increase grassroots campaign efforts while giving small states—historically not influential—a chance to participate. On the other hand, opponents argue that in this plan money would still play a large role, and instead of a single winner, the plan could produce multiple winners in the many competitions. The main concern is that the four blocks would effectively be four media-centered campaigns. Again, retail campaigning would be lost.

In the wake of the 2008 election, the Republican National Committee took steps that may eventually move the party to a similar system, called the Ohio Plan. Here states will be split into three tiers—early states, small states, and large states—and will vote in that order. The large states would be further broken down into three rotating clusters. This new system was not established for the 2012 or 2016 elections, but there continues to be support for reforms.

Under a rotating primary plan, the nation is split into four regions—Northeast, Midwest, West, and South. Each has about the same number of votes in the Electoral College, based on the most recent census. This plan has the same structure as the Delaware Plan, however, the blocks rotate every presidential election, allowing different regions to be influential each time. The goal is to give all the candidates a fair chance by allowing voters to view them over a longer period of time, and therefore to let a more diverse group choose the frontrunners.

Finally, the regional lottery system uses the blocks created in the rotating primary plan, with the main differences being that the order is determined by a lottery, and leadoff states are not allowed. Scholar Larry Sabato argues, "The key to this plan is the lottery used to determine the order each region will participate in the nominating process. Because candidates are unable to know more than a few months in advance which region will lead off the calendar, homesteading is eliminated and candidates are forced to focus equally on all areas."[28]

The Electoral College

13.7 Explain the process by which we select the president of the United States.

In August of 2004, former vice president Al Gore opened the Democratic National Convention with the following:

> Friends, fellow Democrats, fellow Americans: I'll be candid with you. I had hoped to be back here this week under different circumstances, running for reelection. But you know the old saying: You win some, you lose some. And then there's that little-known third category.

> I didn't come here tonight to talk about the past. After all, I don't want you to think I lie awake at night counting and recounting sheep. I prefer to focus on the future because I know from my own experience that America is a land of opportunity, where every little boy and girl has a chance to grow up and win the popular vote.

The joke, of course, was that while Gore had won the popular vote, he did not win the presidency. And then, to the surprise of many, it happened again in 2016! At writing (Nov. 15, 2016), with a few states conducting recounts, most analysts predict that Donald Trump will net 306 Electoral College votes, to Hillary Clinton's 232. Clinton, however, will end up with roughly one million more popular votes.

The Electoral College

One of the most innovative and controversial aspects of American elections is outlined in the Constitution: use of the **Electoral College** to select the president and vice president. In this process voters in each state choose electors to represent their state at a gathering that chooses the president. Figure 13.14 provides some further details of how the Electoral College works.

It would be hard to overstate the importance of the Electoral College in American politics. Occasionally, it shapes the "winner" of the election but in every election, this awkward procedure shapes the election *process*—from party nominations to the selection of running mates, overall strategy, fundraising activities, candidate events, distributing resources, media coverage, and much else. Depending on which state you live in, citizens will experience presidential campaigns in vastly different ways because of the Electoral College. Many argue that without this institution, elections would be much more democratic. On the other hand, others suggest that given our structure of government, the Electoral College is a necessary, albeit cumbersome, institution.

Electoral College

The procedure for selecting the president and vice president of the United States, defined in Article II of the Constitution, whereby the voters in each state choose electors to attend a gathering where the electors make the final decision.

What Were the Framers Thinking?

The framers believed that only men of the highest caliber and intellect should become president. They worried about politicians with "talents for low intrigue, and the little arts of popularity," as noted by Alexander Hamilton in *The Federalist,* No. 69. So they worried about giving average citizens a direct voice in selecting the president. Instead, they decided that a group of wise citizens should be assembled for the sole purpose of picking the president. But who, exactly, should make up this group? One proposal, which had significant support at the Constitutional Convention, was to let Congress elect the president. Others suggested that this would blur the important separation between the branches. Also, many were concerned that average citizens should have *some* say in the process. The compromise was to allow each state to select its electors by whatever method that state deemed appropriate.

The Electoral College was also a compromise that helped assuage a concern of delegates from small states. There were no political parties at the time, and it was assumed that each state would advance the candidacy of its "favorite son" meaning that each state's most popular politician would run for the presidency. If the selection of

FIGURE 13.14 How to Get to The White House

There are certainly drawbacks to the Electoral College—namely, that candidates who win more popular votes can be denied the presidency. For some, this alone is enough to jettison the scheme. Yet some argue there are problems with a direct election process.

■ *What were some of the reservations that the framers had about direct elections?*

SOURCE: Daniel M. Shea and Bryan Reece, *2008 Election Preview*. Pearson Prentice Hall, 2008, Figure 4.1 (p. 47). Reprinted by permission of Pearson Education, Inc., Glenview, IL.

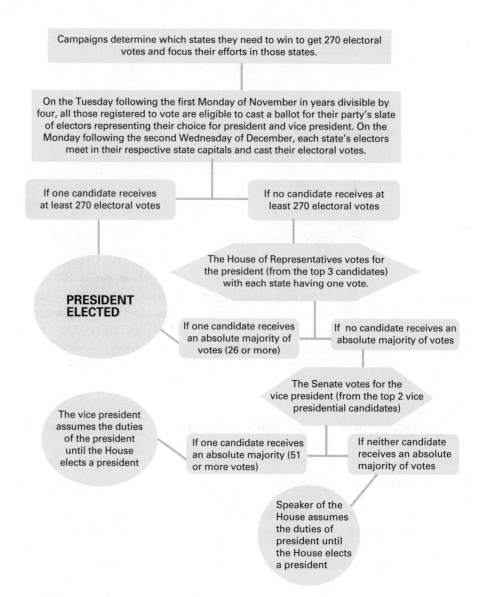

the president was based on popular vote, the largest states (the states with the most voters) would elect their favorite son every time.

So how does the Electoral College solve this problem? The Constitution states that in order to become president, a candidate must receive a majority of Electoral College votes. This does not mean the most votes (a plurality) but rather at least one-half of the overall number of electoral votes cast. When no candidate received at least 50 percent of the votes, the election would be decided in the House of Representatives, where each state, regardless of its size, is given one vote. Because each state would advance a favorite son, and because there were no political parties, most assumed there would be few (if any) elections where a candidate would net a majority of Electoral College votes. As such, it was assumed that in most elections all states, regardless of their population, would have the same role in selecting the president.

When Things Have Gone Wrong

Originally, each elector was given full independence to name any person he saw fit and would cast two votes, naming two different people. The candidate who got the most votes would become president, and the runner-up would become vice president. During the first decades, only a handful of states allowed voters to pick electors; most were chosen by state legislatures. This method worked smoothly during the first two elections, but it began to unravel as soon as Washington announced that he would not accept a third term.

For one thing, political parties—which the framers had neither foreseen emerging nor wanted—burst onto the scene in the 1790s, which led to partisan electors rather than enlightened statesmen doing the choosing. Also, the original design was to have the top vote getter become president and the second-place finisher become vice president, but this proved completely unworkable as soon as competing political parties arose. In the 1796 election, this arrangement meant that John Adams got the presidency and his archrival, the leader of the opposing party, Thomas Jefferson, became vice president. For the next 4 years, each tried to outmaneuver the other.

Finally, the year 1800 brought an electoral rematch between Adams and Jefferson. This time, it seemed that Jefferson had come in first. But, in fact, Jefferson and his running mate, Aaron Burr, were tied: *All* of Jefferson's supporters in the Electoral College had cast their second vote for Burr! The election had to be settled by the House of Representatives. Even though everyone knew that Jefferson was the "top of the ticket," Burr refused to back down, and it took dozens of votes in the House and much wrangling before Jefferson was finally named president and Burr had to settle for the vice presidency. As a result, the **Twelfth Amendment** was adopted, which says that in the Electoral College, the electors must indicate who they are voting for as president and who they are voting for as vice president.

There is yet another controversial part of the process: It is quite possible that the candidate who receives the most popular votes will not receive the most electoral votes. This can happen for two reasons. First, 48 of the 50 states use a winner-takes-all model, also called the **unit rule**, under which the candidate who receives the most popular votes in that state gets all of that state's electoral votes. Second, the original scheme of allowing electors to use their own independent judgment was quickly replaced by partisan considerations. Today, partisan slates of electors compete against one another, meaning that if a Republican candidate wins that state, a Republican slate of electors are sent to the Electoral College. The same is true for Democratic candidates.

These two changes—the unit rule and partisan slates of electors—make it *likely* that the most popular candidate (the highest vote getter) will become the president, but it does not *guarantee* it. In fact, the most popular candidate has been denied the presidency five times in American history:

- In 1824, four candidates were in the running. The second-place finisher was John Quincy Adams, who got 38,000 fewer popular votes than the top vote getter, Andrew Jackson. But no candidate won a majority of the Electoral College. Adams was awarded the presidency when the election was thrown to the House of Representatives, which under the Constitution had to choose among the *three* top Electoral College finishers. The fourth-place finisher, Speaker of the House Henry Clay, threw his support to Adams, who later named Clay as secretary of state. Jackson and his supporters howled that a "corrupt bargain" had deprived him of the White House.

- In 1876, nearly unanimous support from small states gave Republican Rutherford B. Hayes a one-vote margin in the Electoral College, despite the fact that he lost the popular vote to Democrat Samuel J. Tilden by 264,000 votes. The election was decided only when a commission of senators, representatives, and a Supreme Court justice declared Hayes the winner.

- In 1888, Republican candidate Benjamin Harrison lost the popular vote by 95,713 votes to the incumbent Democratic president, Grover Cleveland, but Harrison won by an Electoral College margin of 65 votes. In this instance, some say the Electoral College worked the way it is designed to work by preventing a candidate from winning an election based on support from one region of the country. The South overwhelmingly supported Cleveland, and he won by more than 425,000 votes in six southern states. In the rest of the country, however, he lost by more than 300,000 votes.

- In 2000, Vice President Al Gore had over half a million votes more than George W. Bush (50,992,335 votes to Bush's 50,455,156). But after a recount controversy in

Twelfth Amendment (1804)

Required a separate vote tally in the Electoral College for president and vice president. This change made running on a party ticket much easier.

unit rule

The practice, employed by 48 states, of awarding all of a state's electoral college votes to the candidate who receives the greatest number of popular votes in that state. In these states it is all or nothing!

Florida, and a U.S. Supreme Court ruling in the case of *Bush* v. *Gore* (2000), Bush was awarded the state by 537 popular votes. Thus, Bush became president with 271 electoral votes—the barest possible majority.

- While the exact numbers were not settled at this writing, it seems that in 2016 Donald Trump will receive 306 Electoral College votes, to Hillary Clinton's 232 votes. But Clinton will have received upward of one million more popular votes. This occurred because in several states, like Florida, Ohio, Wisconsin, Michigan, and Pennsylvania, the popular vote outcome was very close—but they all tipped in Trump's favor. Put a bit differently, Trump won by a whisker in several states, leading to a huge electoral vote lead. But there were also several larger states, like California and New York, that gave Clinton an overwhelming majority of the popular vote.

How the Electoral College Shapes Campaign Activities

In addition to having a direct bearing on the outcome of elections, the Electoral College can also impact the way campaigns are conducted. For instance, the unit rule, used in 48 states, puts a premium on winning the right combination of states to net at least 270 (out of 538) electoral votes (see Figure 13.15). Because of the partisan predisposition of voters, the election outcome in many states often is never really a question. For example, Republican candidates regularly win most southern states by large margins—as Mitt Romney did in the 2012 election. The Democrats, on the other hand, can count on West Coast states and most of the New England states. The number of "solidly Democratic" and "solidly Republican" states varies somewhat from year to year, but roughly speaking, there are about 35 to 40. Conversely, only about 10 to 15 states have been "in play" during elections. In 2016, candidates fought it out in just 12 states.

So what, in theory, should be a "national" campaign for the presidency boils down to dramatic, intense efforts in about a dozen states. Campaign operatives struggle to discern which states are solid and which are swing states (states where the outcome of the presidential election is uncertain) and to put together a winning combination. Will Colorado be in play this time? What about the states in the Southwest? Might a Republican from the Northeast put New Hampshire in play? How about a southern Democrat on the ticket—might he or she help create a swing state in that region? These calculations—and many, many others—shape the nature of any presidential campaign and also the outcome of the election.

Moreover, residents living in swing states are bombarded with television ads, pamphlets, mailings, phone calls, rallies, media events, and so forth. In other states, however, the campaigns are relatively nonexistent. Another unfortunate by-product of the unit rule is that voters in solid states feel as if their votes and efforts are irrelevant. Why should a Democrat or Republican in New York or Wyoming, for example, bother to work for a candidate if the outcome of the election in his or her state seems a foregone conclusion? George Edwards, author of *Why the Electoral College Is Bad for America*, has noted, "At base, it violates political equality....It favors some citizens over others depending solely on the state in which they cast their votes for president. So it's an institution that aggregates the popular vote in an inherently unjust manner and allows the candidate who is not preferred by the American public to win the election."[29]

Dump the Electoral College?

Given the outcome of the 2000 election, as well as the other problems, many had expected a popular uprising to abolish the Electoral College. There was, indeed, a modest movement after the election, and it continues to simmer today. But in order to abolish the Electoral College, the Constitution would have to be amended—a complex, difficult process. Surveys suggest that most Americans would like to have

2008

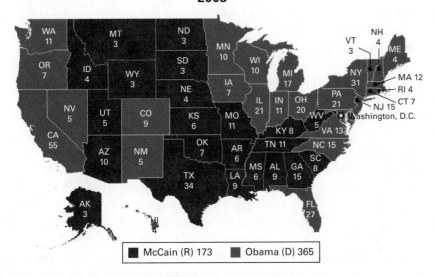

McCain (R) 173   Obama (D) 365

2012

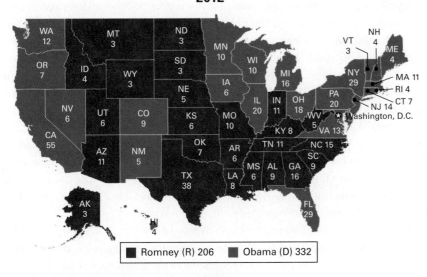

Romney (R) 206   Obama (D) 332

2016

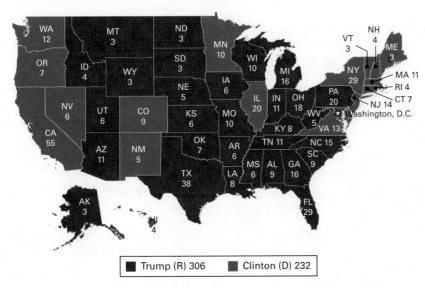

Trump (R) 306   Clinton (D) 232

FIGURE 13.15 Electoral Votes for 2008, 2012, and 2016

■ *Does the Electoral College distort the impact that certain states have on our electoral process? Would that distortion be a valid reason for scrapping the system?*

a direct vote for the presidency; however, the prospects of passing a constitutional amendment seem limited at this time.

Things are happening at the state level, however. In April 2007, for example, Maryland passed a measure that could eventually create a more direct process of choosing the president without amending the Constitution. It passed a law that would award the state's electoral votes to the winner of the national popular vote—so long as other states agree to do the same. The Constitution stipulates that each state can select electors as it sees fit. So if every state agrees to appoint electors who would vote for the winner of the national popular vote, no matter who wins each state, the national popular vote would decide the winner. This would be a way to nullify the Electoral College without amending the Constitution. Nine other states and the District of Columbia have joined this effort, called the National Popular Vote Interstate Compact. But all agree that each will not make this change until the compact boasts states totaling a majority of Electoral College votes.

One of the most significant changes that would result from Maryland's scheme would be the nationalization of presidential campaigns. Candidates would slug it out for votes throughout the nation, not just in particular states. Maryland State Senator Jamie Raskin, sponsor of the measure, said Maryland is largely ignored by presidential candidates during campaigns because they assume it is a solid Democratic state. His hope is that Maryland's plan will start a national discussion and "kick off an insurrection among spectator states—the states that are completely bypassed and side-lined." Also, he argues, "going by the national popular vote will reawaken politics in every part of the country."[30]

Upwards of 40 states have had measures introduced to modify the allocation of Electoral College votes. Not everyone agrees that the system should be dumped, however. Defenders of the Electoral College argue that it adds to the popular support of winners. In other words, somehow we feel that the victor has more legitimacy if the Electoral College vote is won by a landslide, even if that candidate has won the popular vote by only a few percentage points. The Electoral College also forces candidates to strive for wide geographical appeal rather than concentrating all their efforts in a few large states. As noted by columnist George Will, "The system aims not just for majority rule but rule *by certain kinds of majorities.* It encourages candidates to form coalitions of states with various political interests and cultures."[31] Rural states worry that they would fall by the wayside in the pursuit of the largest national vote. Others worry that campaigns would focus almost exclusively on media and that the grassroots efforts, essential to win particular states, would vanish. Figure 13.15 shows the Electoral College vote breakdown in the 2008, 2012, and 2016 elections.

The Role of Money in Elections

13.8 Assess the critical role that money plays in the election process.

In the early days of the Republic, a common practice was to "treat" voters. George Washington, for example, was said to have purchased a quart of rum, wine, beer, and hard cider for every voter in the district when he ran for the Virginia House of Burgesses in 1751 (there were only 391 voters).[32] A common means of spending campaign money during the nineteenth century was to purchase advertisements in newspapers and, more often, to actually purchase a newspaper completely. As technology changed throughout the twentieth century, so did the cost of elections. By the late 1960s, money had become critical for four main reasons:

1. **Decline of Party Organizations.** Given that party organizations were primarily responsible for connecting with voters, candidates needed new ways of reaching out. Many of these new means were extremely costly.
2. **More Voters Up for Grabs.** In 1790, there were fewer than 4 million Americans, almost a quarter of them enslaved. Today, the U.S. population is over 300 million. Reaching such a huge number of voters requires enormous amounts of money.

3. **Television.** In the early 1950s, only a small percentage of homes boasted a television set; by the 1960s, TV was nearly universal. Television changed the way political campaigns were run. And buying advertising time requires huge sums of money.

4. **Campaign Consultants.** Professional campaign consulting burst onto the scene in the 1960s, bringing such sophisticated techniques as direct mail and survey research. These methods proved effective, but they came with a hefty price tag.

In 1952, a presidential election year, *all* campaigns for political office, from president to dogcatcher, added up to approximately $140 million.[33] By 2016, the equivalent figure had swelled to an estimated $10 billion.[34] As noted in Figure 13.16, in the 1960s, it was common for a successful House candidate to spend less than $100,000, but by 2012, the

FIGURE 13.16 Campaign Expenditures

This figure suggests that the cost of elections has grown dramatically, even when inflation is factored in.

■ *What do you think is at the heart of rising elections costs? Does this suggest a serious flaw in the process or a sign of a robust exchange of ideas?*

SOURCE: "The Cost Of Winning An Election, 1986–2014," The Campaign Finance Institute, http://www.cfinst.org/pdf/vital/VitalStats_t1.pdf. The 2016 figures are based on author estimates as of November 15, 2016, using data compiled by the Campaign Finance Institute.

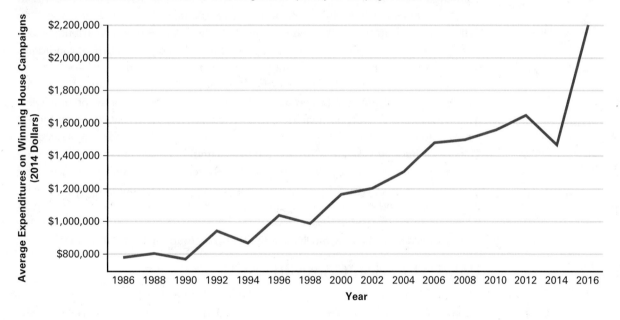

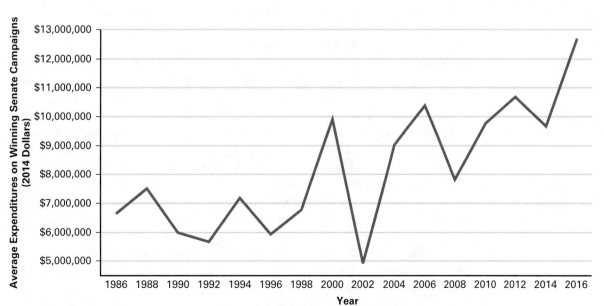

average cost of winning a seat in the House of Representatives topped nearly $2 million. An "expensive" U.S. Senate race in the 1960s was still under half a million dollars; in 2012, the *average* Senate race cost way beyond $12 million. In 2014, several Senate races approached the $30 million mark. Early indications suggest levels in 2016 were significantly higher. Races in Florida, Pennsylvania, and Wisconsin were particularly expensive, but the hands-down most expensive Senate race per voter in 2016 was in New Hampshire, with upward of $40 million being spent in a state with less than one million registered voters. With all that money, you might think races would be more competitive than in the past. In fact, reelection rates for members of the House nearly always stay above 90 percent—sometimes well above 95 percent. It's a bit lower in the Senate, but clearly all incumbents benefit from a dramatic fundraising advantage.

The Rage for Reform

Efforts to control the flow of money in elections date from the Progressive Era, but these measures were largely symbolic. Real reform came in the early 1970s, when members of Congress began to worry about being thrown out of office by a wealthy candidate— perhaps a political novice—who could simply outspend them. The **Federal Election Campaign Act (FECA)** was signed into law by President Richard Nixon in 1971. In brief, the legislation limited how much money candidates could spend, how much an individual or group could give, and how much political parties might contribute. It also established voluntary public financing of presidential elections. Presidential candidates who choose to use this system are limited in the amount they can raise and spend.

Shortly after the amendments took effect, James Buckley, a Conservative Party senator from New York, along with a group of politicians from both ends of the political spectrum, challenged the constitutionality of the law. Buckley argued that spending money was akin to free speech and that limiting it would abridge First Amendment protections. The case of *Buckley* **v.** *Valeo* (1976) was the most significant election-centered court decision in American history. For the most part, the Supreme Court sided with Buckley by striking down provisions of the law that put limits on overall spending, on spending by the candidates, and on spending by independent groups. However, the justices upheld the public funding of presidential elections, so long as it is voluntary, and surprisingly, the Court allowed limits on how much an individual or a group might *give* to a candidate.

Political Action Committees

Another spinoff of FECA and *Buckley* has been the proliferation of political action committees (PACs). Earlier acts of Congress had barred labor unions and corporations from giving money to federal candidates. The idea of PACs was thought up in the 1940s to get around these restrictions. In PACs, none of the monies used to support a candidate came directly from the union or corporation but instead from these groups' independent political units. The contribution limit for PACs was originally five times higher than for individuals, so the number of groups exploded: In 1974, there were roughly 600 PACs, but by 2008, more than 4,600 were giving out contributions.[35]

Political action committees give money to candidates because the interest group that backs them wants a say in public policy. Businesses, for example, want policies that help them make a profit; environmentalists want policies that help protect the natural world; and labor seeks policies that help working men and women. But do these groups, through their PACs, "buy" policies with their contributions? This is a hotly debated issue. The Center for Responsive Politics is a nonpartisan organization that tracks the flow of money in elections. Its Web site (http://www.opensecrets.org) gives detailed information on who gives and who receives campaign money.[36]

Precisely what PACs buy with their contributions is unclear, but the public perceives a problem. Numerous public opinion polls confirm that regardless of what actually happens between contributors and public officials, average Americans regard the money flowing from PACs to candidates as a threat to the democratic process.

Federal Election Campaign Act (FECA)

A law designed to limit the amount of money contributed to campaigns for Congress and the presidency and to broaden donation reporting requirements.

Buckley v. Valeo (1976)

The most significant Supreme Court case on campaign finance in American history. The court ruled that spending money was akin to speech, and therefore protected by the First Amendment.

The Incumbent Fundraising Advantage

Candidates vying for office solicit funds from many sources: individuals (friends, spouses, associates, activists), political parties, PACs, and—believe it or not—other candidates. *Incumbents* are candidates already holding the office and up for reelection, *challengers* are those opposing the incumbents, and *open-seat candidates* are running for seats for which no incumbent is seeking reelection. Political action committees hope that their money will somehow produce support for their policies, which means they hope their money will go to the eventual winner. Accordingly, they prefer to send their funds to incumbents, because those already in office have a head start—the so-called **incumbent advantage**—when it comes to reelection. By sending their money to incumbents, PACs provide an even greater boost to incumbents' chances of reelection.

In some recent elections again, more than 90 percent of incumbent House candidates won even though many Americans are frustrated with "business-as-usual politics." Even in the antiestablishment groundswell that brought Donald Trump to power, some 95 percent of incumbents were sent back to office in 2016. Incumbents have always had an advantage, but critics point to recent changes that have made matters worse. Yale University scholar David Mayhew was one of the first to draw attention to the problem.[37] In his seminal book *Congress: The Electoral Connection*, Mayhew argues that all legislative activity is now geared toward securing reelection. These efforts fall within three categories: *credit claiming*, which is receiving praise for bringing money and federal projects back to the district; *position taking*, or making sure to be on the popular side of issues; and *advertising*, which implies reaching out to constituents in many ways, especially through mailings. Others have pointed to additional sources of incumbent support, such as ongoing media attention, which challengers rarely get.

> **POLL** Would you support a system of government funding of congressional campaigns, so long as candidates could opt in or opt out?

incumbent advantage
The various factors that favor office-holders running for reelection over their challengers. Those already in office have a huge advantage in their efforts to win reelection.

Term Limits

Many reforms have been suggested to reduce the incumbent advantage. One proposal is **term limits**. If we are worried about an unfair advantage given to politicians already in office, why not create more open-seat contests? Limiting legislative terms would guarantee turnover—a stream of new faces, energy, and ideas in the legislature.

term limits
Laws stipulating the maximum number of terms that an elected official may serve in a particular office.

One if the issues that seemed to propel both Trump and Bernie Sanders (D-VT) supporters is the excessive amount of money in elections. But others believe giving money is just another form of political participation—a protected form of free speech.

■ *What is your take: should our government make changes to limit the amount of money in electoral politics or should giving and raising funds remain protected by the 1st Amendment?*

Representatives should know the concerns of average citizens, and what better way of ensuring that than by forcing entrenched legislators to step aside after a fixed period and make way for fresh blood? Opponents of term limits argue that the legislative process is complex, and it takes time to become familiar with the process. Moreover, term limits deny voters a choice—the chance to reelect a legislator who they think may actually be doing a good job.

By the early 1990s, roughly half the states had adopted term limits for state legislators and candidates for federal office. Many legal scholars, however, wondered whether the states had the constitutional power to limit the terms of U.S. House and Senate members. The issue came to a head in the Supreme Court case of *U.S. Term Limits, Inc. v. Thornton* (1995). In a 5-4 decision, the Court majority stated that "allowing individual States to craft their own qualifications for Congress would...erode the structure envisioned by the Framers, a structure that was designed, in the words of the Preamble to our Constitution, to form a 'more perfect Union.'" With that decision, attempts to limit the terms of members of Congress through legislative acts ended; a constitutional amendment remains the only course of action.

Reforming the Reforms: BCRA

While the FECA restrictions limited the amounts individuals and groups could contribute to a candidate, the law put no restrictions on giving money to a political party. By 2000, many Americans had once again come to the conclusion that the campaign finance system was out of whack. One survey found that 75 percent agreed (39 percent "strongly") that "our present system of government is democratic in name only. In fact, special interests run things."[38] Clearly, the reforms of the early 1970s had done little to halt the flow of big money into elections. The public was ripe for change, but reform measures stalled in the legislature. With much effort from Republican Senator John McCain and Democratic Senator Russ Feingold, the **Bipartisan Campaign Reform Act (BCRA)** was passed and signed into law by President George W. Bush in February 2002.

The law was sweeping: It outlawed unlimited contributions to the national political organizations and barred group-sponsored advertisements 30 days before primary elections and 60 days before general elections. Yet the law also raised the contribution limits for individuals, and left open the ability for wealthy individuals to donate **soft money**, virtually unlimited sums of money, to state and local party organizations. The ban on soft money did not apply to political action committees, which were still free to raise unlimited cash.

In 2003, the law was upheld by the Supreme Court in the case *McConnell v. Federal Election Commission*. In a 5-4 decision, the Court affirmed the law's most important elements. It was, according to a *New York Times* account, a "stunning victory for political reform."[39]

The *Citizens United* Bombshell

The most recent chapter in the story of money in American elections was a decision handed down by the Supreme Court in January 2010. The case was ***Citizens United v. Federal Elections Commission***, and it dealt with a provision of the BCRA that outlawed explicit campaigning by nonpartisan groups within 30 days of a general election and 60 days prior to a primary election. Citizens United, a conservative nonprofit corporation, produced a 90-minute documentary called *Hillary: The Movie*, which was highly critical of the New York Senator. They were anxious to distribute it throughout the fall of 2007 and spring of 2008, even though Clinton was running in a series of primaries and caucuses for the Democratic presidential

Bipartisan Campaign Reform Act (BCRA)

Federal law passed in 2002 that outlawed soft-money contributions to party organizations. The bill is also sometimes called McCain–Feingold after the two Senate sponsors.

soft money

Funds contributed through a loophole in federal campaign finance regulations that allowed individuals and groups to give unlimited sums of money to political parties.

Citizens United **v. Federal Elections Commission** (2010)

A Supreme Court case that reversed decades of precedent by declaring unconstitutional laws that ban unions and corporations from using general operating funds on elections.

nomination. Because they were barred from doing so, and because they thought this was a violation of their First Amendment rights, the group took the issue to the federal courts.

The Supreme Court focused its deliberations on the broad issue of the constitutionality of limits on spending by corporations and unions (established a half century before and upheld in several prior cases). In yet another 5–4 decision, the Court ruled that unions and corporations were entitled to spend money from their general treasuries (without the use of PACs) on federal elections, although they could not give money directly to candidates. The decision reverberated across the political system. One commentator, writing for the *National Review Online*, suggested, "The ruling represents a tremendous victory for free speech....The ruling in Citizens United is a straightforward application of basic First Amendment principles."[40] But others feared that the decision would set loose a flood of money and lead to greater corruption. The *New York Times* editorialized, "With a single, disastrous 5-to-4 ruling, the Supreme Court has thrust politics back to the robber-baron era of the 19th century."[41] While accurate figures are somewhat elusive, campaign finance data from the 2010 election suggest a flood of money did, in fact, materialize. Some estimates place the overall spending in the 2010 midterm election at over $3.2 billion, with more than one-half of that coming from outside groups. This is roughly double the amount spent by outside groups in 2008 and in 2006. Republican candidates netted the most from these groups in 2010, but the opposite was true in 2008.[42] Many Americans are troubled by the role played by big money in elections. They believe that it gives some candidates an unfair advantage and spills past the election into the policymaking process. It is one of the many ironies of an open political process: Individuals and interest groups are encouraged to back political candidates vigorously, but in doing so, their efforts distort the playing field. The freedom to participate creates a system with limited participation.

Continuing with the course set in Citizens United, the Supreme Court ruled in April of 2014 that the decades-old cap on the amount an individual can give to federal office candidates in a two-year period was unconstitutional. This case, *McCutcheon* v. *Federal Election Commission*, also yielded a 5-to-4 decision.

Super PACs, Too!

The newest kid on the block is the **Super PAC**. Officially known as "independent expenditure-only committees," Super PACs grew like mushrooms after a summer rain in the wake of recent federal court rulings. These groups are allowed to raise unlimited sums from unlimited sources, including corporations, unions, and other groups— as well as wealthy individuals. With the money they raise, Super PACs can advocate for the defeat or election of federal candidates in various ways—particularly through television ads. Traditional PACs were used, for the most part, by corporations and labor unions. They would collect contributions within prescribed limits ($5,000 or less, in 2008), and spend that money within strict limits (also $5,000). Super PACs, on the other hand, confront few constraints. The one exception is that they are not allowed to coordinate their campaign activities with the candidates they are trying to help. Stated a bit differently, traditional PACs would send checks to candidates, but Super PACs can spend as much as they would like to get a candidate elected so long as they do not coordination their activities with the candidates, hence the term "independent expenditure-only committee." They might run television advertisements, send direct mail, and conduct polls for an individual candidate or a group of candidates, so long as they played no role in process.

An illustration might prove helpful. We might imagine a group of citizens deeply concerned with limiting the sale of hand guns. They learn about Super PACs and

Super PACs

Officially known as "independent expenditure-only committees," these groups are allowed to raise unlimited sums from unlimited sources, including corporations, unions and other groups, as well as wealthy individuals. But, they are not allowed to coordinate their campaign activities and spending with the candidates they are trying to help, hence the term "independent expenditure-only committees."

FIGURE 13.17 The Dramatic Growth of Outside Spending

This figure highlights the dramatic increase in money spent in congressional elections from sources located outside the district—by so-called "outside groups." Twenty years ago, this practice was rare, but today it is common.

■ *Does this practice alter the democratic nature of elections?*

SOURCE: "Outside Spending," OpenSecrets.org: Center for Responsive Politics, https://www.opensecrets.org/outsidespending/. Data for the 2016 election was also compiled from the Center for Responsive Politics, https://www.opensecrets.org/news/2016/10/total-cost-of-2016-election-could-reach-6-6-billion-crp-predicts/.

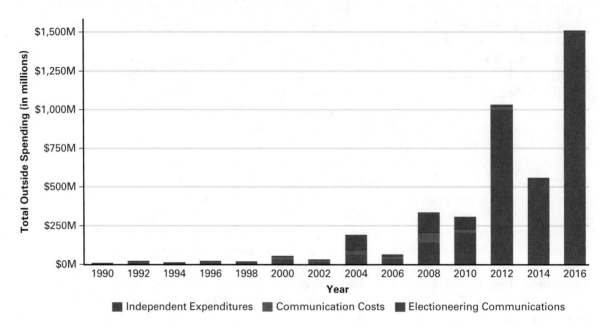

begin collecting funds. They might collect some from small donations, but they might also accept $1 million or more from an individual citizen, and perhaps another $2 million from a corporation. They would have to disclose where this money came from, but they could spend it as they would like so long as they did not coordinate that spending with candidates. They might spread it around between numerous races, or they could dump all of it on a single election.

In the 2010 midterm elections, some 74 of these organizations raised and spent just under $84 million. Leading the way was a unit called American Crossroads, which was created by Karl Rove, a key advisor to President George W. Bush. It supported 10 Republican Senate candidates and 30 Republican House candidates. Another massive conservative Super PAC in the 2010 election was the Club for Growth. Each of these units are "outside groups," given they spend money in districts where they were not located. Figure 13.17 charts the rapid growth of outside group spending.

As is always the case, it takes an election cycle or two for innovative campaign finance approaches to spread throughout the system. That is, by the summer of 2011 it has become clear that Super PACs would be the 800 pound gorillas in the following year's congressional and presidential election. Over 100 of these organizations were created, with many more on the way. Democratic-leaning organizations were being formed at a dizzying pace, and many of the conservative groups that proved effective in 2010 were recharging their war chests. For example, Rove's group collected millions from three billionaires in June of that year: $2 million from Jerry Perenchio, the former Hollywood talent agent and ex-chairman of the Spanish language television network Univision; $1 million from Dallas area hotel magnate Robert Rowling; and $0.5 million from Texas homebuilder Bob Perry.

The 2012 election shattered all campaign finance records. A host of individuals and groups spent lavishly on presidential, Senate, and House candidates. Many individuals spent over $5 million, a larger majority doing so with the hopes of

One of the "truisms" of modern elections is that big money will dominate the system. Pictured here is Vermont Senator Bernie Sanders. While Sanders eventually lost the Democratic nomination to Hillary Clinton, he ran a very strong campaign. Rather than relying on big money contributions, a vast majority of Sanders's funds came from small donations.

■ *Does his campaign suggest concerns about the role of big money are overstated?.*

defeating Barack Obama. For his part, Karl Rove collected and spent upward of $600 million for his Super Pac. To his consternation, and certainly the consternation of his backers, Rove's efforts to win the White House and build a larger Republican majority in Congress were thwarted. Indeed, 2012 proved to be good year for Democrats.

By the 2014 midterm elections, the race for campaign cash had once again reached a fervor pitch. Barack Obama's approval ratings had dipped to the lowest of this administration, and the GOP understood that historically the president's party does poorly in midterm elections. So money flooded into GOP coffers with the hopes of winning the majority in the Senate and expanding their majority in the House. Conversely, many Democratic-leaning organizations raised money furiously with the hopes of staving off a disastrous year.

As expected, the 2016 election saw massive campaign spending. Surprisingly, however, big money did not seem to be a determining factor in the presidential nomination process. Super PACs backing Florida Governor Jeb Bush raised over $100 million before a single primary was held, but Bush never found favor with voters and he got out of the race early. Bernie Sanders raised nearly $250 million in contributions from individuals (including many small donations) and Donald Trump self-financed the nomination stage of this candidacy. By the general election, big money started to pour in on both sides. Candidate spending was hefty, as was SuperPAC and outside expenditures. One of the real surprises was the late surge of party money. Also, the volume of money spent in a handful of House and Senate races was staggering. The Center for Responsive Politics estimates that, when it is all said and done, upward of $6.6 billion will have been spent on the 2016 federal elections.[43]

Conclusion

Americans put a great deal of faith in the election process, and over the past two centuries, many changes have opened the system to more involvement. But at the same time, it seems that only a modest number are willing to get involved. Some of this reluctance might have to do with the mechanics of elections—particularly

In any election there are always unexpected twists and turns. Pictured here is FBI Director James Comey, who announced two weeks before the 2016 election that his agency would be investigating another batch of emails from Hillary Clinton's private server.

■ *Do you think Comey's actions helped shape the outcome of the race or, as they say, was the "cake already baked"?*

the growing volume of money in the system. While it is true that the campaign finance system is also more open, does the flood of money from Super PACs and other sources turn off average citizens? If so, what difference does it make if many Americans do not seem interested in politics and that Americans on the whole turn out to vote less often than citizens in other democracies? Is this really something to worry about?

One way to answer such questions is to take a practical point of view. What policy difference would it make if nonvoters got into the act? Would the government head in a different direction if turnout were higher? Early studies suggested that on the whole, the policy preferences of nonvoters essentially paralleled those of voters. There would be little policy change if we had full election turnout. More recent studies suggest, however, that who votes *does* matter. The low turnout in the 1994 election allowed the Republicans to capture control of both houses of Congress and helped bring George W. Bush to the White House in 2000. Higher turnout among young voters helped bring Barack Obama to office in 2008, but if more young voters had turned out at similar levels in 2016 it is possible the outcome might have been different. Some 54 percent of those under 30 supported Hillary Clinton. Conversely, Donald Trump was brought to power, in large measure, due to higher turnout among a group traditionally less engaged—blue collar whites. In short, public policy is shaped by who comes, and who does not come, to the polls.

Another way to answer such questions is to examine how you define *democracy*. For example, perhaps precise levels of participation are unimportant; so long as enough citizens are involved to make the process competitive, full participation is inconsequential. The people who refrain from involvement in politics are also likely to be the least well informed. Perhaps we do not want these people involved in the process; is an uninformed vote really preferable to none at all? Along similar lines, some people speculate that less informed citizens (the nonvoters) are more prone to radical policy shifts, so their absence at the polls actually adds a degree of stability to public policy. The conservative columnist George Will, in a piece titled "In Defense of Nonvoting," argues that good government—not the right to vote—is the fundamental human right. He suggests that high voting rates in Germany's Weimar Republic (1919–1933) enabled the Nazis to take power in 1933.[44] Declining turnout in America,

Will asserts, is no cause for worry. This perspective is often called the elite democratic model. It insists that so long as fairness and political opportunity are guaranteed, the system is healthy.

The popular democratic model, by contrast, suggests that the character of any political system is not simply the outcome of public policy but also the process by which it is reached. This model puts a premium on electoral involvement. When this occurs, citizens develop an affinity for the system, because they are convinced that they have a stake in whatever policy results from political decisions. Put a bit differently, this theory says that systems of government designed to reflect the will of the people will do so better, and in the long run will be more prosperous and stable, if average citizens join the electoral process. Echoing this sentiment, the political scientist and journalist E. J. Dionne, in his book *Why Americans Hate Politics*, has written that "a nation that hates politics will not long thrive as a democracy."[45] Which of these well-known commentators, Will or Dionne, in your opinion comes closer to the truth?

CONFRONTING POLITICS AND POLICY

Many believe that state policymakers should take steps to enhance the opportunities to vote in any election. The goal of these changes would be to lower the costs of voting (that is, make it easier), and by doing so draw more citizens into the process. Why not allow for early voting, for example, and no-excuse absentee voting. We know that about one-third of the ballots cast in the 2016 election were cast early, and that in about a dozen states over one-half of the ballots are cast in advance of Election Day. Yet how many of these votes would have been cast under the traditional method is unclear. Several studies suggest overall turnout may have actually decreased because of these measures. How could this be the case? It seems that early voting methods may detract from the excitement and energy of Election Day. When there is only one day to vote there is energy, an enthusiasm for fulfilling one's civic duty. As noted by a team of scholars from the University of Wisconsin–Madison, "Early voting dilutes the concentrated activities of Election Day itself that would likely stimulate turnout, an effect not counterbalanced by the increased convenience of voting prior to the election (which, as we have noted, may only provide an alternative outlet for voters who would have voted in any case)."[46, 47]

Several studies have suggested a modest increase in turnout in states with same-day registration: an increase of roughly 5 percentage points. This is when voters can sign-up for voting on Election Day—now possible in 14 states. In most other states, the cut-off is 30 days in advance of the election. Young, more mobile citizens (such as college students) tend to use same-day registration, but it also appears that minority citizens may be more likely to do the same. It also seems that minority residents are more inclined to use early voting techniques, too.

Surprisingly, since 2012 several state legislatures were considering rescinding their early voting laws. As you might guess, this has been, and will continue to be, a controversial topic.

ACTION STEPS

1. Conduct some research on voter registration requirements in your state. What are the rules and regulations and when were they enacted?
2. Conduct some research on the impact of different voter registration laws on voter turnout. Do such laws actually impact the number of citizens who come to the polls?
3. Decide if you believe higher turnout is important. As noted in this chapter, not everyone believes "more is better." Who are the types of citizens that would most likely come to the polls with changes in voter registration laws?
4. Discern the position of state legislators in your area on voter registration laws. You could do this by writing, e-mailing, or calling their office. It might take a few days, but they will likely get back to you.
5. If your legislator has taken a position different from your own, try to schedule a meeting with him or her to discuss the matter. Come in armed with solid information and approach the meeting in a professional, respectful way. You might just be surprised at how effective you might be!

⟩ REVIEW THE CHAPTER

Expansion of the Electorate and Other Legal Issues

13.1 Describe the legal challenges that have broadened the democratic character of elections in America. (p. 426)

On one level, elections take place outside the boundaries of government. As noted in Chapter 1, elections are "processes," not institutions. In fact, some have thought it a bit strange that the framers of our system made little mention of how elections might be conducted. Yet there have been numerous constitutional and legal changes that have redefined the nature and practice of elections in America. Nearly all of these changes, such as the Fifteenth, Nineteenth, and Twenty-Sixth Amendments, and the Voting Rights Act of 1965, have broadened the number of citizens legally entitled to participate in the process.

Individual Participation in Elections

13.2 Evaluate levels of electoral engagement in America, particularly among young citizens. (p. 432)

There are many ways that citizens can become involved in the election process—from voting or attending a rally to sending in a check to a candidate or talking about issues and candidates with friends. For many of us, elections are an important part of our civic lives. To others, electoral participation does not seem to be worth their time and effort. This might be especially true for young citizens. There are signs that this generation has discovered the power and potential of political action, but there are countertrends that suggest they may once again retreat to the side lines.

Political Parties in America

13.3 Identify the functions served by political parties in a democracy, and explain how they help organize the governmental process. (p. 440)

Political parties serve numerous important functions, not the least of which is helping to organize the election process. They also make vote choices easier, recruit candidates, screen candidates, help candidates during elections, overcome constitutional obstruction, educate citizens, and bring citizens into the political process. The three interrelated elements of American political parties are party-in-government, which refers to the elected officials of the same party; party-in-the-electorate, which refers to all citizens who attach themselves to a political party; and, party-as-organization, which refers to the formal apparatus of a party.

Party Eras in American History

13.4 Trace the evolution of political parties in the United States. (p. 447)

Even though parties have been with us from nearly the beginning of our nation, their weight in our system of government has fluctuated. Few speculate that they will regain the prominence they had in the second half of the nineteenth century, but there has been a modest resurgence in recent decades. That is, while local organizations seem to be in trouble, state and national parties are gaining strength, due in large measure to increased financial resources.

Minor Parties in American Politics

13.5 Explain the historic role of minor parties in U.S. electoral process. (p. 449)

Politics in the United States has always centered on the two-party model. Indeed there are a host of institutional factors (such as the Electoral College and the first-past-the-post system) and attitudinal factors (like the wasted-vote syndrome) that appear to keep minor parties at bay. At the same time, minor parties have served important democratic functions—such as raising issues that the major parties are neglecting. Moreover, the number of Americans anxious for more choices on Election Day seems to be on the rise.

Parties and the Nomination Process

13.6 Outline the process by which party nominees are chosen to run in the general election. (p. 451)

One of the core functions of political parties is to run primary elections that determine the candidates for the general election. Open systems allow any registered citizen to vote in the primary, while closed systems permit only party members to cast ballots. In three states there is also a "top-two" system, whereby multicandidate contests lead to two general election candidates, regardless of which party they belong to. The model used to select presidential candidates is evolving and contentious. While some believe the presidential system is broken, exactly what should replace the current system is a topic of fierce debate.

The Electoral College

13.7 Explain the process by which we select the president of the United States. (p. 457)

Many forces shape the conduct of presidential elections, but none is more significant than the Electoral College. This complex, rather odd institution was yet another compromise at the Constitutional Convention, a means to moderate the "passions of the public" and to allow smaller states a greater say in the selection of the president. Today the Electoral College structures how and where campaigns

are conducted and, occasionally, as in the 2000 presidential election, who takes up residence at the White House.

The Role of Money in Elections

13.8 Assess the critical role that money plays in the election process. (p. 462)

Many Americans believe money distorts the election process. A number of laws have been passed to help level the playing field, most recently the Bipartisan Campaign Reform Act. Others argue that giving and collecting money is a form of political action. An important Supreme Court decision in the case of *Citizens United* v. *Federal Election Commission* seemed to buttress this position; the court found limits on corporate and union campaign spending unconstitutional.

〉 LEARN THE TERMS

Fourteenth Amendment (1868),
  p. 427
Fifteenth Amendment (1870), p. 427
Nineteenth Amendment (1920),
  p. 427
Twenty-Fourth Amendment (1964),
  p. 427
Twenty-Sixth Amendment (1971),
  p. 427
Voting Rights Act of 1965, p. 428
motor voter law, p. 429
electoral behavior, p. 432
turnout, p. 433
rational party model, p. 440
responsible party model, p. 440
platform, p. 440

nominees, p. 440
tripartite view, p. 441
party identification, p. 443
independent, p. 443
Democratic-Republicans, p. 447
Federalist Party, p. 447
Corrupt Bargain of 1824, p. 447
Candidate-Centered Era, p. 449
ballot access laws, p. 450
attitudinal barriers, p. 450
direct primary election, p. 452
closed primary system, p. 452
open primary system, p. 452
national nominating convention,
  p. 453
binding primaries, p. 453

nomination caucus, p. 454
Electoral College, p. 457
Twelfth Amendment (1804),
  p. 459
unit rule, p. 459
Federal Election Campaign Act
  (FECA), p. 464
Buckley v. *Valeo* (1976), p. 464
incumbent advantage, p. 465
term limits, p. 465
Bipartisan Campaign Reform Act
  (BCRA), p. 466
soft money, p. 466
Citizens United v. *Federal Elections
  Commission* (2010), p. 466
Super PACs, p. 467

〉 EXPLORE FURTHER

In The Library

Aldrich, John. *Why Parties? The Origin and Transformation of Political Parties in America.* Chicago: University of Chicago Press, 1995.

Bibby, John F., and L. Sandy Maisel. *Two Parties or More? The American Party System,* 2nd ed. Boulder, CO: Westview Press, 2003.

Farrar-Myers, Victoria A., and Diana Dwyre. *Limits and Loopholes: The Quest for Money, Free Speech, and Fair Elections.* Washington, D.C.: Congressional Quarterly, 2007.

Hershey, Marjorie R. *Party Politics in America*, 14th ed. Upper Saddle River, NJ: Pearson Longman, 2010.

Lewis-Beck, Michael, et al. *The American Voter Revisited.* Ann Arbor, MI: University of Michigan Press, 2008.

Maisel, L. Sandy, and Mark D. Brewer. *Parties and Elections in America: The Electoral Process.* Lanham, MD: Rowman and Littlefield, 2009.

Malbin, Michael J., ed., *Life After Reform: When the Bipartisan Campaign Reform Act Meets Politics.* Lanham, MD: Rowman and Littlefield, 2003.

Mayer, William G., and Andrew E. Busch. *The Frontloading Problem in Presidential Nominations.* Washington, D.C.: Brookings Institution Press, 2003.

Patterson, Thomas E. *The Vanishing Voter: Public Involvement in an Age of Uncertainty.* New York: Knopf, 2002.

Piven, Frances Fox, and Richard A. Cloward. *Why Americans Still Don't Vote: And Why Politicians Want It That Way*. Boston: Beacon Press, 2000.

Reichley, A. James. *The Life of the Parties: A History of American Political Parties*. Lanham, MD: Rowman and Littlefield, 2000.

Ryden, David K., ed., *The U. S. Supreme Court and the Electoral Process*. Washington, D.C.: Georgetown University Press, 2000.

Schraufnagel, Scot. *Third Party Blues: The Truth and Consequences of Two-Party Dominance*. New York; Routledge, 2011.

Schumaker, Paul D., and Burdett A. Loomis, eds., *Choosing a President: The Electoral College and Beyond*. Washington, D.C.: Congressional Quarterly, 2002.

Shea, Daniel M. *Let's Vote! The Essentials of the American Electoral Process*. Upper Saddle River, N.J.: Pearson Longman, 2012.

Shea, Daniel M., and John C. Green. *Fountain of Youth: Strategies and Tactics for Mobilizing America's Young Voters*. Lanham, MD: Rowman and Littlefield, 2007.

Theriault, Sean M. *Party Polarization in Congress*. New York: Cambridge University Press, 2008.

White, John K., and Daniel M. Shea. *New Party Politics: From Jefferson and Hamilton to the Information Age*, 2nd ed. Belmont, CA: Wadsworth, 2004.

On the Web

For information on a range of campaign-related issues, see the Federal Election Commission Web site at *http://www.fec.gov*.

For information on levels of political participation in America, see the Center for the Study of the American Electorate Web page at *http://csaelectorate.blogspot.com/*.

For information on youth political engagement, see the Center for Information and Research on Civic Learning and Engagement (CIRCLE) at *http://www.civicyouth.org*.

For a look at the many minor parties in the United States, visit *http://www.dcpoliticalreport.com/PartyLink.htm*.

For more information on the presidential nomination process, visit the PBS NewsHour at *http://www.pbs.org/newshour/extra/lessons_plans/primaries-and-caucuses-how-do-the-parties-choose-a-candidate-lesson-plan/*.

To learn more about the Electoral College, see the U.S. National Archives and Records Administration at *http://www.archives.gov/federal-register/electoral-college/index.html*.

For extensive information on campaign finance, see the Center for Responsive Politics at *http://www.opensecrets.org*.

THE POLICY PROCESS AND ECONOMIC POLICY

The 2013 government shutdown was popularly represented in media with images likes this one. It was the first government shutdown since 1995, over 15 years earlier.

What do you think government shutdowns tell us about the American government's budget policy process? What are the positive and negative aspects of Congress' ability to potentially cause government shutdowns?

→ LEARNING OBJECTIVES

14.1 Identify the major elements of the policymaking process.

14.2 Compare and contrast the three main types of public policies.

14.3 Describe the major ways that the health of the economy is measured.

14.4 Describe the key actors responsible for creating fiscal policy.

14.5 Identify the major sources of U.S. government revenue.

14.6 Identify the major forms of U.S. government expenditures.

14.7 Identify the major instruments of monetary policy.

WHY IS BUDGET POLICY ALSO SOCIAL POLICY?

In October of 2013 the federal government was shutdown for 16 days. Republicans in the GOP-controlled House of Representatives, influenced by Senator Ted Cruz of Texas and outside interest groups like Heritage Action, refused to pass any budget that funded the Patient Protection and Affordable Care Act (also known as simply the Affordable Care Act or Obamacare). The Affordable Care Act was one of Democratic President Barack Obama's most important policy accomplishments, and something he strongly supported.

While Obamacare was strongly supported by President Obama and Congressional Democrats, Congressional Republicans strongly opposed it. Republicans in the House of Representatives and Senate had campaigned against it in 2010 and 2012 (they would also do so in 2014). Opinion polls showed a similar divide among Americans in the public, with Republicans disliking the Act and Democrats in favor of it.

In Congress, Democrats generally believed that Obamacare was constitutional, helped provide health insurance to poor Americans who previously could not afford it, and lowered overall health care costs. Republicans in Congress often asserted that it was unconstitutional, increased the cost of health care, and caused people to lose health care that they already had and liked. Additionally, Republicans pointed out that many of the formerly uninsured who received health insurance through the Affordable Care Act got it through Medicaid, which some studies show produces no better health outcomes than having no insurance at all. Democrats countered that if Medicaid was such a bad program, public opinion would not be so strongly in favor of it!

Complicating the debate over Obamacare was that it was, like many pieces of legislation, not everyone's desired policy. Many Congressional Democrats, even though they liked the Affordable Care Act, would have preferred legislation creating a government-run health care system similar to that found in Canada. This kind of proposal is often known as a "public option" or "single payer." Most Congressional Republicans, on the other hand, would have preferred health care legislation that allowed Americans to deduct health insurance costs from their taxes and gave those on Medicaid a health credit they could use toward the private insurance plan of their choice.

All of these health care proposals, including the implemented Affordable Care Act, cost taxpayer money. Therefore, the decision of whether to pass them or fund them or not fundamentally affects the lives of millions of Americans. Budget policy is social policy.

The 2013 government shutdown eventually ended. Due to fears about how the public would perceive their party's role in the shutdown, enough Congressional Republicans eventually decided to pass a budget that included funding for Obamacare, even though many of their co-partisans opposed it. Though this particular shutdown ended relatively quickly, its political effects endured. The role of shutdowns and potential shutdowns in budget negotiations continues to highlight the importance of Congress' budgetary power.

Furthermore, Obamacare and the 2013 shutdown played an important role in the 2016 presidential primaries and election. Several Republican candidates were in Congress during the shutdown and favored eliminating Obamacare. In contrast, the Democratic candidates for president wanted to maintain and build on Obamacare with new legislation. With the victory of Donald Trump and the Republicans maintaining control of the House and Senate in the 2016 elections, the future of Obamacare is uncertain. Repealing Obamacare was a high priority for Republican voters, but President-elect Trump had not yet made clear whether he supported a partial or full repeal of the Affordable Care Act.

The Obamacare and Medicaid debates, and 2013 government shutdown, provide a clear example of how public policies are the product of complex interactions among political actors that determine what government does or does not do. Health care also demonstrates the confluence between economic and social concerns and the multi-faceted interactions among political actors that define policymaking in a democracy.

Making Public Policy

14.1   Identify the major elements of the policymaking process.

The battles over health care described in this chapter's introduction provide a glimpse into just a small portion of the broader policymaking process in the United States. Making public policy involves numerous components in a series of interconnected steps. Each step affects all the others and in turn influences the ultimate form and shape of the policies that are produced or not produced by the government. Debates on the very existence of a problem often create a highly charged political atmosphere even before any discussion of potential solutions ever takes place. Take Medicare for example. Republicans like Paul Ryan have argued that the underlying economics of the Medicare system make it unsustainable as the population of senior citizens grows. Conversely, Congressional Democrats contend that the fundamentals of the system are sound and with some modest changes the system can be made solvent for the long term. In this section we examine how steps in the policy process such as problem identification shape public policies and how those policies in turn affect the daily lives of Americans.

Think about public policy as what comes after the equal sign in a mathematical equation. The structure of government plus the political process form the elements on the left side of the equation. The sum of these interactions equals the policies that affect each citizen. Any change caused by the effects of the policies (the right side of the equation) influences the structure of the government and the political process (the left side of the equation), and vice versa (see Figure 14.1).

Public policy is more than just a law, the action of an agency, or a court decision. For a complete understanding of public policy, you must know why these tangible outputs of government exist in the first place and anticipate how they may change in the future.

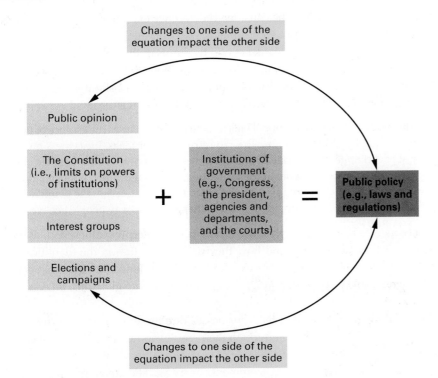

FIGURE 14.1   Public Policy Equation

The form and shape of public policies can be compared to the output of a mathematical equation. Just as the various components on the left side determine the ultimate result on the right side of the equation, so do the various political pressures and institutional characteristics produce the makeup of public policies.

■ *How do public policies alter the political pressures (e.g., interest groups, elections, public opinion) that played a major role in their creation?*

Politicians, members of the media, and average citizens often draw a distinction between politics and policy. This difference rests on the notion that politics is like a game, or even a war, in which strategies are used to gain advantages over opponents and win battles. (The very word *campaign* is borrowed from the vocabulary of warfare.) Policy is the output of politics and, to some people, not political in itself. You may have heard commentators praising presidential debates as a time for "setting politics aside," forcing the candidates to deal with *policy* issues. But this common notion of an either-or relationship is an artificial way of thinking about these two concepts.

As defined, public policy is what you get after the equal sign in the equation of politics plus government. Elections, social movements, interest group activity, and the actions of political institutions such as Congress or the federal courts all go into the equation *before* this equal sign. Using this metaphor, public policy is inherently political. It reflects the exercise of power in our system of government, our economic system, and our society in general.

Social scientists and other policy specialists often think about public policy as a collection of phases in a process, as though the intricacies of the process were somehow disconnected from the political world. There is a well-worn approach to the study of the process of policy formation, usually called the policy process model, which begins with the identification of a problem and concludes with the analysis of the effectiveness of the solutions applied to that problem.[1] This model forms the core of this chapter, but we will also help you see the pathways that connect politics with public policy and the effect of these variables on the public as well as other segments of our society and political world.

As you read this chapter, keep in mind that theories about policy and the process of public policymaking are not just abstract stabs at ideas motivated by academic curiosity. Rather, the need to theorize comes from the desire to make sense of what seems, at first, like a tangled mass of motivations, actors, and actions.

The Steps of Policymaking

In this section we begin to examine the key aspects of the policy process model. The model describes policymaking in five or six distinct steps that include functions such as problem identification, policy formulation, and policy evaluation. While the policy process model is very useful in describing key features of policymaking, it does have limitations that we feel should be considered before we explore its elements. Taking a different approach to the study of policymaking is Deborah Stone, one of several political scientists trying to get us to think beyond the limits of the policy process model. In Stone's view, the policy process model lacks connections to the ways that real people and their governments make decisions about policy. She uses slightly different terms to describe a major shortcoming of this model, but her point is clear:

> The production [process] model fails to capture what I see as the essence of policymaking in political communities: the struggle over ideas. Ideas are a medium of exchange and a mode of influence even more powerful than money and votes and guns...Ideas are at the center of all political conflict. Policymaking, in turn, is a constant struggle over the criteria for classification, the boundaries of categories, and the definition of ideals that guide the way people behave.[2]

For Stone, the heart of policymaking is how people interpret values, such as equity, efficiency, security, and liberty, and how they use these values in the identification of problems and possible solutions. For example, most people would agree that equality is a highly desirable goal for our society. Should we therefore guarantee an equal level of health care for all citizens? Or should the government simply offer the *opportunity* for health care through policies that help businesses hire more workers, who might then receive some health care coverage through their employers? Our answers to such questions reflect our preferences about the role of government in our lives. They also reflect the influence exerted on us by the government, the media, and other organized interests.

Take for example the issue of health care. In 2010 the United States Congress passed and President Obama signed into law the Affordable Care Act, which transformed the way that health care would be paid for in the United States. This law was the culmination of a year-long battle in Congress that was incredibly heated and partisan in nature. While the Affordable Health Care Act was passed during the administration of Barack Obama, he was not the first president to attempt major reform of the American health care system. In the early 1990s, debate about health care coverage for the roughly 40 million Americans who lacked insurance (today's numbers are even higher; see Figure 14.2) took center stage. President Clinton presented a plan to provide health care coverage that mobilized both supporting and opposing forces much like the divisions formed during the 2010 debates. Some critics charged that the bill was done in by an oppressive and misleading lobbying campaign, led by the nation's health care and health insurance industries. The lobbying campaign featured TV ads voicing opposition to an overly complex policy that would ultimately hurt the average health care consumer and urging people to contact their government representatives. The ads worked, and public support for Clinton's plan slipped drastically. Opinion polls taken at the time still showed strong support for the basic idea of insuring those who lacked coverage, but the Clinton plan was dead in the water.[3] In 2009, Obama sought to avoid a repeat of this result by encouraging compromise, but he nevertheless encountered many of the same difficulties Clinton faced 15 years earlier.[4]

Using the policy process model, we might say that President Clinton put health care onto the nation's agenda, but it then failed to move successfully through the other phases of the process. This is a fairly accurate statement, but it tells us very little about the pathways of politics or what actually happened along the way. This is where ideas about how people view what is good and desirable in government and politics become important.

Much of what we know about public policy and how it is made can be related to the policy process model, which we mentioned earlier in the chapter. Like all models, it is a generalization—a simplified representation of reality. It must exclude some complexities in order to make a very intricate process easier to understand.

FIGURE 14.2 Uninsured Americans Under Age 65

■ *How would you resolve this dilemma? Does the percentage of uninsured Americans surprise you? Why is the highest percentage indicated for the 26–34 age group?*

SOURCE: U.S. Census Bureau, 2015 Current Population Survey Report.

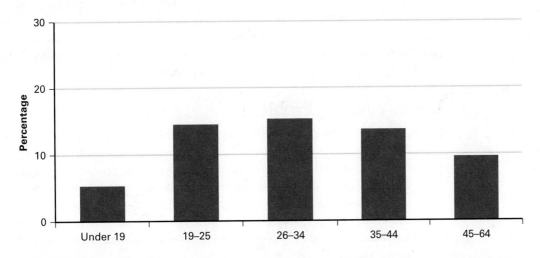

FIGURE 14.3 The Policymaking Process

The policy process model presents a picture of policymaking that begins with the identification of a problem and eventually moves to reexamination of the solution or solutions to that problem. Real-world policymaking is not always so orderly. It may begin at some point other than the identification of a problem.

Problem Identification—Publicize a problem and demand government action.
Participants: Media • Interest Groups • Citizen Initiatives • Public Opinion

Agenda Setting—Decide what issues will be resolved and what matters government will address.
Participants: Elites • President • Congress

Policy Formulation—Develop policy proposals to resolve issues and ameliorate problems.
Participants: Think Tanks • Presidents and Executive Office • Congressional Committees • Interest Groups

Policy Legitimation—Select a proposal, generate political support for it, enact it into law, and rule on its Constitutionality.
Participants: Interest Groups • President • Congress • Courts

Policy Implementation—Organize departments and agencies, provide payments or services, and levy taxes.
Participants: President and White House • Executive Departments and Agencies

Policy Evaluation—Report outputs of government programs, evaluate policy impact on target and nontarget groups, and propose changes and "reforms."
Participants: Executive Departments and Agencies • Congressional Oversight Committees • Mass Media • Think Tanks • Interest Groups

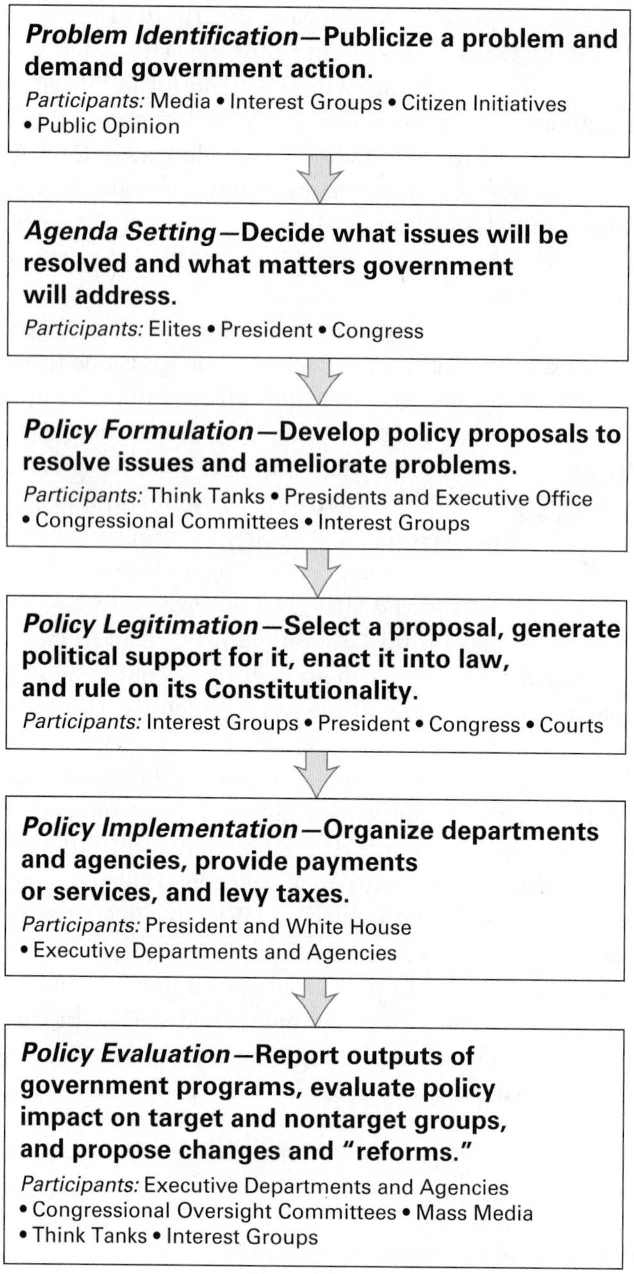

Although scholars in the field of public policy disagree over some details, the major parts of the policy process model are generally thought to consist of the six steps shown in Figure 14.3: (1) identifying the problem, (2) setting an agenda, (3) formulating policy, (4) legitimizing policy, (5) implementing policy, and (6) evaluating policy (some versions of the model omit policy evaluation, viewing it as an administrative or academic pursuit and therefore disconnected from politics).

Identifying the Problem

Just how do we know that a problem exists? Perhaps no issue more clearly demonstrates the complexity and importance of problem identification in the formation of policy than global warming, one aspect of climate change. Since the 1980s scientists have warned that the burning of fossil fuels was leading to conditions that trap heat in the atmosphere and thus raise global temperatures. For many years, the scientists' warnings about global warming were based on measurements of increasing carbon dioxide in the atmosphere and computer models that indicated increasing

In the policy debates surrounding climate change and global warming in particular, the condition of Arctic species such as the polar bear have taken on symbolic importance. While many Americans believe that climate change is occurring, there is still considerable debate about how much of a problem climate change poses and what kinds of policies should be adopted to address increasing global temperatures.

■ *Why has it proved difficult for policymakers to clearly identify the problems associated with global warming?*

atmospheric carbon dioxide would lead to higher global temperatures over the next century. Among the projected effects of global warming were melting glaciers and polar ice, higher sea levels, more intense hurricanes, and prolonged droughts.[5] While the projections of scientists caught the attention of government officials both in the United States and abroad, difficulties in establishing the magnitude and timing of climate change have plagued efforts to create policies that address global warming.

Proponents of government efforts to address global warming have contended that the increased levels of carbon dioxide in the atmosphere and the projections from climatologists regarding major global impacts from higher temperatures on the planet are enough information to spur the government to act on the problem. Supporters of immediate action to address global warming also note existing evidence of climate change—including retreating glaciers, species migration, and some of the hottest years on record—as clear signs that the problem has already been observed and that actions to confront global warming are therefore needed immediately.[6] To these individuals there is no question that the problem exists.

Opponents of government actions to address global warming have consistently held that there is not enough evidence available to firmly establish that humans are altering the planet's climate, and they maintain that any recent warming is the product of natural cycles. The critics of global warming theory contend that climate change is simply a theory and that costly policies aimed at reducing carbon emissions are unnecessary until the problem can be more firmly established. These critics also point to hacked e-mails from climate scientists as evidence that climatologists have manipulated data to show greater signs of warming than have actually occurred.[7]

Without a doubt, some problems simply cry out for action. Terrorism on American soil crystallized in an unforgettable display of violence and brutality on September 11, 2001. Such events, including many of far lower magnitude, are known as **focusing events**—moments that bring a problem to the attention of both the public and policymakers. At least at first, there is no debate about the existence of a problem, and the event serves as a **trigger mechanism**, a means of propelling an established problem on to the next stage of the policy process, setting an agenda.[8]

focusing events
Moments that capture attention and highlight the existence of a problem.

trigger mechanism
The means, often tied to focusing events, to push a recognized problem further along in the policy cycle.

Driving while distracted has become one of the leading causes of automobile accidents in the United States, and the issue has been identified by many government officials as a significant safety problem facing all of us.

■ *Why has this issue been quickly placed on policy agendas in both Washington, D.C., and state capitals, while other issues struggle to gain the attention of government officials?*

issue-attention cycle

The pattern of problems quickly gathering attention but then failing to remain in the spotlight.

Setting an Agenda

At some point in your life, you have probably attended at least one meeting of a school club, a town planning board, or some other formal gathering. To make good use of time and provide structure, well-organized meetings are always planned around an *agenda,* a list of issues and ideas up for discussion or actions to be undertaken. Of course, this is probably old news to you, but what you may not have thought about is the power available to the individuals who set the agenda. Many groups and organizations use rules that exclude or severely limit any action on—or even discussion of—items not listed on the agenda. The ability to exclude an item from the agenda, for whatever reason, is a powerful way to control what government does.[9]

Like problem identification, agenda setting in the absence of a major crisis is largely determined by the organization and resources of individuals and coordinated interests. People and groups who can best articulate their position or who have what it takes to gain access to policymakers (such as money for reelection campaigns, the support of group members, or well-connected lobbyists) will usually succeed in getting their problem on the agenda.

Once a problem is on the agenda, how do you keep it there? There is no guarantee that policymakers will consistently treat an issue as a high priority, year in and year out. Anthony Downs has created a valuable way of thinking about the nature of agenda items that he calls the **issue-attention cycle**.[10] Downs argues that some issues are more likely to remain on the formal agenda, just as others are doomed to fade away. Even issues that affect small slices of the population that lack political, economic, or social clout, or that are difficult to address may first grab lots of attention, but they usually fall off the agenda because of the cost and inconvenience associated with solving them or the inability of the affected parties to keep the decision makers' attention.

For example, during the early 1990s contaminated drinking water in Milwaukee, Wisconsin, caused by a faulty treatment plant, led to hundreds of thousands of individuals becoming ill and over 100 people dying from the waterborne diseases that they ingested. The high number of deaths from the water contamination focused national attention on the need for improved treatment facilities, and Congress passed legislation to prevent the type of tragedy that occurred in Milwaukee from happening again. But as time passed, the major costs associated with fully ensuring safe drinking water in the United States and the absence of additional dramatic events, pushed drinking water concerns lower on the government's agenda. Even a major 2009 report that found the water provided to more than 49 million people was contaminated with illegal concentrations of chemicals and dangerous bacteria failed to make Congress give this issue greater attention.[11] In 2016, drinking water safety briefly became a major policy issue again. Due in part to bureaucratic failure and a lack of attention from important policymakers, many residents of Flint, Michigan, consumed drinking water contaminated with toxic levels of lead. Both Michigan Governor Rick Snyder and President Obama were involved in fixing the problem, but after a brief period of public attention, drinking water concerns again fell off the national policy agenda.

Formulating and Legitimizing Policy

Many actors both inside and outside of government can affect the agenda-setting process. Once a problem makes it onto the agenda, however, the political pathways haven't reached their end. In fact, the next phase of the policymaking process, formulation, is as politically driven as agenda setting—if not more so.

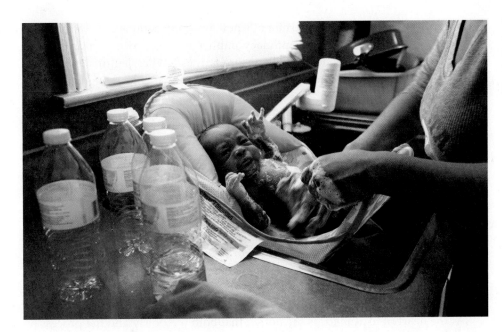

To avoid exposing her baby to tap water contaminated with toxic levels of lead, a woman in Flint, Michigan, uses bottled water to bathe her child.

■ *Why is water policy something that we rarely think about?*

FORMULATING POLICY   Formulating policy means crafting solutions to identified problems. Of course, how you define the problem will frame the acceptable solutions. Was the terrorist attack on 9/11 a crime against U.S. citizens and property, or was it an act of war? If your answer, like that of the Bush administration, is "war," then solely legal actions (such as capturing those who planned and funded the attacks, trying them in court, and possibly, sentencing them to death) won't do. If your answer is "crime," the solution is simply to track down the "bad guys" and bring them to justice.

Solutions can come in many forms. Clearly, the laws passed by legislatures, like those passed by Congress, are attempts to solve problems. The legislative process itself, including the introduction of bills, hearings, and floor debates, are all parts of formulating public policy: At each of these stages, the solution can change and evolve. When presidents issue executive orders directing the federal government to do—or to stop doing—various things, they are also engaged in problem solving. For example, after Barack Obama was sworn in as president in 2009, one of his first executive orders repealed a Bush administration ban on federal funding of research that uses embryonic stem cells. The decisions made by courts, especially the U.S. Supreme Court, are policies because other branches of government and the nation's citizens are bound by these decisions as though they were laws passed by Congress.

In today's federal government, each access point—Congress, the president, the Supreme Court, and the federal bureaucracy—is connected to us by one or more of the pathways of political action. Not all pathways offer an equally open journey to one of these centers of policy formulation. Of the four access points, Congress is the most accessible. Elections can change congressional membership. Lobbying, along with interest group and social movement activism, can influence the nature of solutions. Congress—in particular the House of Representatives, "the people's house"—was designed by the framers to be the most open of the policymaking institutions of the federal government. However, the fact that dislodging incumbents from their seats is difficult has, in many critics' eyes, made the House more immune to pressure from dissatisfied constituents. Although most of the opportunities for policymaking (and the greatest opportunity for citizen influence) still lie with Congress, the presidency and the federal courts have grown in power in ways far beyond what our country's founders imagined.

LEGITIMIZING POLICY   A government's policymaking actions can confer legitimacy on the policies it makes. Legitimacy implies fairness; formal rules and the ability to see the process in action help ensure fairness. When legitimacy is established, people are willing to accept policies—even if they dislike them. Legitimacy is different from coercion, which is the threat or actual use of force or punishment to secure compliance with a policy. The most vivid example of such coercion in American history was the action of President Lincoln and Congress in raising armies to crush the South's attempted secession. The seceding states in the South had viewed Lincoln's election, by northern votes alone, as illegitimate. Massive coercion is necessary to obtain compliance with policies that are widely seen as illegitimate, but policies that are viewed by the public as being fair generally require very little, if any, such action. The fair and open nature of the policymaking process helps ensure that solutions are not favoring one part of society as a pay-off or a special favor. If Congress did all its work behind closed doors or the process by which the Supreme Court renders decisions were to change from case to case, we might justifiably wonder about the legitimacy of the decisions made by these institutions.

At the heart of legitimacy is the notion that both the policy and the process by which the policy was made conformed to the rules of the system. Of course no rule is more important in American politics than the Constitution of the United States. When a policy is passed by Congress and signed by the president it may temporarily take on the signs of legitimacy, but its ultimate acceptance as the legitimate law of the land may have to wait for the courts to weigh in. As was discussed in length back in Chapter 9, the judicial system has an important say in determining if a law conforms to the rules for governing established by the Constitution. The Affordable Care Act of 2010 provides a clear and important example of the Court's role in legitimizing a public policy in the United States. Shortly after the health care law was passed in 2010, its constitutional legitimacy was challenged in the federal courts on the grounds that the law's provision requiring Americans to purchase health insurance was in violation of the Constitution's provisions. While the Affordable Care Act law was in operation for over a year before the court heard the first case on it in 2012, it did not receive full legitimacy in the eyes of the courts or many Americans until the court weighed in with decisions on its constitutionality in 2012 and 2015.

Implementing Policy

Once policies have been created, someone actually has to do something with them. As its name implies, the executive branch of government is charged with executing or implementing the policies made by a legislature, the courts, or the executive branch itself. The framers divided up the functions of government in order to lessen the chance that it might take away the people's liberty. The result is that policy implementation is largely done by the executive branch. The other two branches, however, also influence how the policies they make are carried out. Add to this the openness of the government to citizen activity, and a picture emerges of implementation as a highly political process.

This may seem like simple common sense, but for a long time, political scientists and other scholars of public policy did not see the links between politics and implementation. In fact, one branch of political science focuses on *public administration* as distinct from *public policy*. This view of a policy–administration divide may have been based on a desire to separate the executors of policy from outside pressure, so that good policy would not be subverted by biased implementation. This sounds like a reasonable goal, and if we take this idea to a more everyday level, its worth becomes even more apparent.

Many of us, driving above the speed limit, have passed a police officer and yet received no ticket. We clearly broke the law—a policy setting a maximum speed limit. What explains the lack of a ticket in this case is the **discretion** given to the individuals who implement policy. Perhaps going a few miles over the speed limit is acceptable for that stretch of road at that time of the day with that level of traffic and that weather. A change in one of these circumstances might mean getting a ticket. Formulating a law for each stretch of highway, while factoring in things such as road conditions and weather, would be nearly impossible, so legislatures often write laws with the presumption that the executive branch will use reasonable discretion in applying them. The key word in this presumption is *reasonable*. What if a police officer pulled over all drivers sporting a Republican bumper sticker who exceeded the speed limit by *any* amount? Or what if this officer gave speeding tickets only to African Americans? These are dramatic examples of prejudice (which, unfortunately, sometimes occur), but there are other, more subtle ways in which discretion is used that are out of step with the intent of policy and demonstrate the political aspect of implementation. Knowing this, legislators must be especially attuned to the implementation process.

discretion
The power to apply policy in ways that fit particular circumstances.

Since all democratic legislatures, including the U.S. Congress, are bodies in which majorities are needed to pass laws, legislation is often written in ways designed to attract wide support among the diverse membership. One way to do this is to write a vaguely worded policy that allows legislators to read their own interests and the interests of their constituents into the proposal.

Because of the need for vaguely worded policy, and the need to rely on the executive branch for expert formulation of the details and implementation, legislators cannot simply walk away from a policy once it is in the implementation phase. Legislatures typically review policy implementation through oversight. Legislative oversight takes two forms, reauthorization and investigation.

Evaluating Policy

Perhaps the most overlooked and undervalued step in the policymaking process is evaluation. In its most basic form evaluations ask the simple question, did the policy work? While simple in concept, evaluation is anything but simple in practice. For example the simple exercise of determining the criteria of evaluation may be quite difficult and contentious. In the area of defense policy determining the effectiveness of budget allocations is quite problematic. On one hand an evaluation may indicate that the billions of dollars spent on a weapons technology contributed to the nation's safety from foreign attack. However, the evaluation may question if the same outcome (i.e., no foreign attack) may have been achieved at a much smaller price tag or with no money spent at all. Unlike the world of business where ultimate success can be determined by bottom line measures such as profits and losses, evaluation of policy effectiveness is more complex and often less conclusive.

The issue of health care reform is illustrative of the complexities of policy evaluations and the importance of criteria selection. If, after a few years, experts judge that the Affordable Care Act has reduced overall health care costs and increased coverage, one might reasonably call the policy a success. However, if neither of those two things happen, or one of those two but not both happens, the overall effectiveness of the policy could reasonably be called into question. Evaluating the overall effectiveness of a policy can sometimes be as difficult as the actual formulation of the policy itself.

TIMELINE

Environmental Movement

As scientific evidence shows increased global warming, a reduction in rain forests, and higher levels of pollution, the international community struggles to cope. Governments today must strike a delicate balance between economic growth and development and environmental protections. If there is too much regulation of business to protect the environment, businesses may relocate to other countries or regions, harming the U.S. economy. If there is too little regulation, the environment suffers because businesses don't want to risk the higher costs that go along with environmentally friendly practices. How far should the government go to protect our environment?

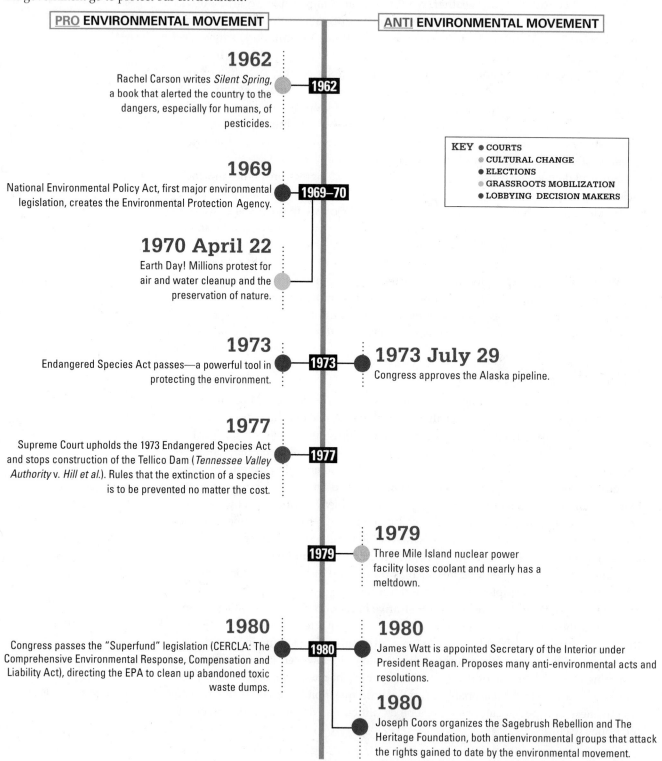

PRO ENVIRONMENTAL MOVEMENT

ANTI ENVIRONMENTAL MOVEMENT

1962 | 1962
Rachel Carson writes *Silent Spring*, a book that alerted the country to the dangers, especially for humans, of pesticides.

KEY
● COURTS
● CULTURAL CHANGE
● ELECTIONS
● GRASSROOTS MOBILIZATION
● LOBBYING DECISION MAKERS

1969 | 1969–70
National Environmental Policy Act, first major environmental legislation, creates the Environmental Protection Agency.

1970 April 22
Earth Day! Millions protest for air and water cleanup and the preservation of nature.

1973 | 1973
Endangered Species Act passes—a powerful tool in protecting the environment.

1973 July 29
Congress approves the Alaska pipeline.

1977 | 1977
Supreme Court upholds the 1973 Endangered Species Act and stops construction of the Tellico Dam (*Tennessee Valley Authority* v. *Hill et al.*). Rules that the extinction of a species is to be prevented no matter the cost.

1979 | **1979**
Three Mile Island nuclear power facility loses coolant and nearly has a meltdown.

1980 | 1980
Congress passes the "Superfund" legislation (CERCLA: The Comprehensive Environmental Response, Compensation and Liability Act), directing the EPA to clean up abandoned toxic waste dumps.

1980
James Watt is appointed Secretary of the Interior under President Reagan. Proposes many anti-environmental acts and resolutions.

1980
Joseph Coors organizes the Sagebrush Rebellion and The Heritage Foundation, both antienvironmental groups that attack the rights gained to date by the environmental movement.

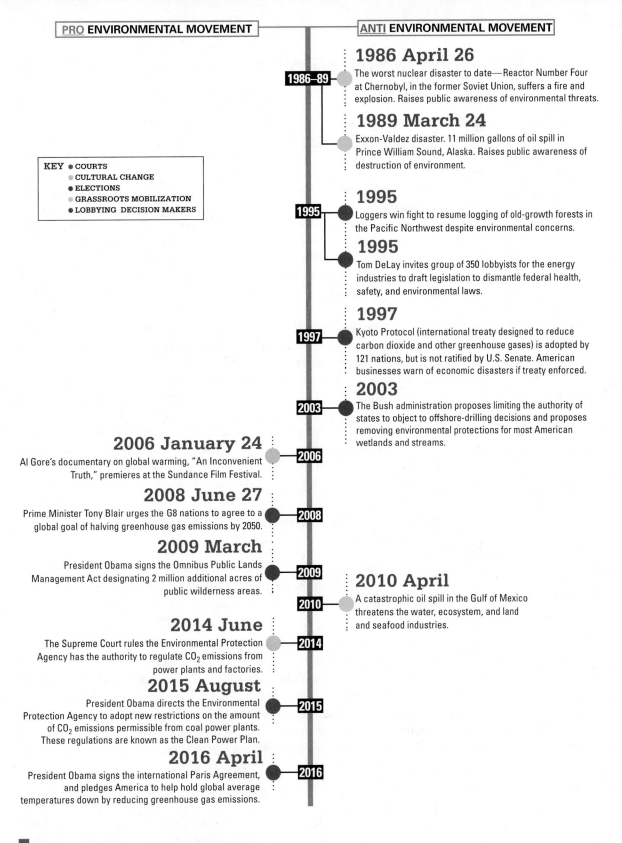

PRO ENVIRONMENTAL MOVEMENT

ANTI ENVIRONMENTAL MOVEMENT

KEY
- ● COURTS
- ● CULTURAL CHANGE
- ● ELECTIONS
- ● GRASSROOTS MOBILIZATION
- ● LOBBYING DECISION MAKERS

1986 April 26
The worst nuclear disaster to date—Reactor Number Four at Chernobyl, in the former Soviet Union, suffers a fire and explosion. Raises public awareness of environmental threats.

1989 March 24
Exxon-Valdez disaster. 11 million gallons of oil spill in Prince William Sound, Alaska. Raises public awareness of destruction of environment.

1995
Loggers win fight to resume logging of old-growth forests in the Pacific Northwest despite environmental concerns.

1995
Tom DeLay invites group of 350 lobbyists for the energy industries to draft legislation to dismantle federal health, safety, and environmental laws.

1997
Kyoto Protocol (international treaty designed to reduce carbon dioxide and other greenhouse gases) is adopted by 121 nations, but is not ratified by U.S. Senate. American businesses warn of economic disasters if treaty enforced.

2003
The Bush administration proposes limiting the authority of states to object to offshore-drilling decisions and proposes removing environmental protections for most American wetlands and streams.

2006 January 24
Al Gore's documentary on global warming, "An Inconvenient Truth," premieres at the Sundance Film Festival.

2008 June 27
Prime Minister Tony Blair urges the G8 nations to agree to a global goal of halving greenhouse gas emissions by 2050.

2009 March
President Obama signs the Omnibus Public Lands Management Act designating 2 million additional acres of public wilderness areas.

2010 April
A catastrophic oil spill in the Gulf of Mexico threatens the water, ecosystem, and land and seafood industries.

2014 June
The Supreme Court rules the Environmental Protection Agency has the authority to regulate CO_2 emissions from power plants and factories.

2015 August
President Obama directs the Environmental Protection Agency to adopt new restrictions on the amount of CO_2 emissions permissible from coal power plants. These regulations are known as the Clean Power Plan.

2016 April
President Obama signs the international Paris Agreement, and pledges America to help hold global average temperatures down by reducing greenhouse gas emissions.

CRITICAL THINKING QUESTIONS

1. Since most regulations to promote clean air and water cost businesses extra money, some believe that they can unduly harm our economy as businesses have less operating funds to expand and invest. Do you think that these concerns are reasonable? Or do you think that environmental protection is worth the costs?

2. Should public opinion influence our environmental policy or should we rely upon the recommendations of the scientific community? How large of a role do you think business leaders ought to play? How should we as a society balance these competing needs?

Types of Public Policy

14.2 Compare and contrast the three main types of public policies.

Public policies can do many things. Policies can provide us with resources to protect our health and safety. They can determine what we learn in public schools and how clean the drinking water is that we draw from the faucets in our homes. Public policies can establish how fuel-efficient the cars we drive must be and how much money is taken from our pay checks each week to pay for government services. While public policies have varied impacts on the lives of the individuals that they were designed to affect, almost all policies possess some economic ramifications for the government that creates them or the citizens that the policies apply to. Even laws that don't appear to involve monetary resources usually have some financial ramifications. Take for example voter identification laws. Between 2011 and 2016, many states passed laws that required individuals to show identification when they go to vote. On the surface such a law appears devoid of financial implications but digging a little deeper it is clear the law has numerous impacts that involve money. For example, the process of administering the laws will cost millions in training of voting station personnel to understand the procedures for verification of identification and for those without identification there will be costs involved in getting IDs to allow them to vote. You may even attend a college that has had to provide new identification cards for all of their students just to conform with the rules established by a voter identification law. But while almost all public policies have some economic ramifications, there are key differences that can affect the process and outcomes that we observe. In the next section we examine the major types of public policies and the role that money plays in each of those categories.

Categorizing Policies by Basic Functions of Government

policy categories

A way of classifying policies by their intended goal and means of carrying out that goal.

A key approach to studying public policy involves creating **policy categories** that classify what policies do and how they do it. To do this, political scientists have identified three basic functions of government: **distribution**, **regulation**, and **redistribution**.[12]

distribution

Government providing things of value to specific groups.

DISTRIBUTION   A government *distributes* a society's resources, such as wealth, services, or other things of value, when it gives benefits to specific groups in that society. When undertaken by a legislature, such distribution is often given the negative label "pork barrel" spending because it seems designed to bring credit to the legislator who proposed it. Public policies dealing with economic development often fall into the distributive category. For example, when a city offers to help with the cost of construction of a stadium or arena for a professional sports franchise the city is distributing the public's resources largely for the benefit of a private business (i.e., the sports franchise) and its patrons (i.e., its fans).

regulations

Legal rules created by government agencies based on authority delegated by the legislature.

redistribution

Government providing a broad segment of the society with something of value.

REGULATION   *Regulation* takes place when a government uses legislative, military, or judicial power to stop an action by a person, organization, or group or when it mandates other behaviors or actions. For example, because of the actions of environmental organizations and engaged citizens, today's energy producers must meet federal regulations designed to limit air pollution. If an electric plant does not meet these requirements, its owners can be fined or punished in other ways. While regulatory policies may not seem like they involve financial resources, in most cases regulations require either government expenditures to enforce the regulations or compliance costs for those being regulated. Take for example the drinking age. To ensure that individuals under the age of 21 do not consume or purchase alcohol, governments must allocate resources (i.e., money and personnel) to monitoring establishments that sell and serve alcoholic beverages and to the prosecution of those who violate these rules.

REDISTRIBUTION   *Redistribution* resembles distribution in many ways, but instead of a specific group benefiting from the actions of government, a much larger segment of society receives goods or services. Of course, redistributive policies mean that resources are taken from one part of society and given to another. An example of a redistributive policy is taxing workers to fund social welfare programs for the poor. Because redistributive policies usually pit one social class against another, they are generally the most difficult policies to enact and implement. Sometimes, as is the case with Social Security benefits, the redistribution occurs across generations, with one generation paying in to the system while another is drawing out an unequal amount.

Because all government policies can be placed in one of these three categories, this approach allows us to see the way governments operate and, with a bit more thought, how each of the pathways of political action can influence each of these government functions.

Categorizing Policies by Tangible or Symbolic Benefits

Categorizing policies by the nature of their benefits is also useful. Policies themselves can produce either tangible benefits for the public or merely symbolic benefits.[13]

TANGIBLE BENEFIT   A tangible benefit such as federal assistance for victims of hurricanes and other natural disasters, is something that the recipients will experience in a material way—for instance, receiving truckloads of clean drinking water and dry ice to preserve food. Health care insurance from the federal government is a major source of tangible benefits for citizens of the United States who are enrolled in programs such as Medicare. Take for example the prescription drug plan (Medicare Part D). Under this plan recipients are entitled to receive prescriptions that are largely financed through government payments. Of course money itself is one of the most important tangible benefits. If you receive a grant in aid to help finance your tuition expenses you have received a tangible benefit from your government.

SYMBOLIC BENEFIT   A symbolic benefit does not offer concrete, material results; it provides a theoretical solution to a problem. For example, the independent commission that investigated the intelligence failures leading up to 9/11 could not directly change the U.S. government's antiterrorism policy, nor could it restore life to the almost 3,000 people who perished in those attacks. The commission also could not ensure adoption of all of its suggestions. Still, the actions of the commission communicated to the public that the government was working to solve this very difficult problem. The benefit—the feeling of security we may get from knowing that intelligent and dedicated people are trying to make us safer—may not help put food on the table, but it is still a benefit.

Economic Policy

As we have attempted to demonstrate from the start of this chapter public policies and economics are deeply intertwined. Almost every type of policy that we have discussed so far has some type of financial implication for either the government that creates the policies or the citizens that are affected by the policies themselves. However, there are certain types of policies that are more explicitly tied to the use of government's financial resources and its ability to shape the broader health of the economy. Traditionally, scholars examine economic policy through the two broad approaches that government uses to affect the economy: (1) fiscal policy and (2) monetary policy. In the next sections we examine the details of these two key areas of policy and discuss some of the impacts on social policies, such as Medicare, that come about through fiscal and monetary tools. But before we get to the tools on how to manage the economy, it's valuable to first examine some core measures of economic performance and the institutions of government that attempt to manage economic performance.

Measuring Economic Performance

14.3 Describe the major ways that the health of the economy is measured.

When economists gauge the economy's performance, they usually focus on five figures: (1) inflation, (2) unemployment, (3) gross domestic product, (4) the balance of trade, and (5) the budget deficit (or surplus). These measures matter to politicians as well. A healthy economy helps incumbents stay in office. Let's examine each of these figures in turn.

Inflation

inflation

An increase in prices over time.

Inflation measures the rate at which prices increase. The classic definition of inflation is "too many dollars chasing too few goods." We all know that inflation is bad and that high inflation rates can undermine and distort all other aspects of the economy. When inflation is out of control, it can wipe out middle class savings, devalue the dollar, and cause immense social and political unrest. When we look at monetary policy later in this chapter, we will see that inflation has been the major area of concern for the Fed since the mid-1970s. At that time, inflation ran at more than 10 percent annually, topping out at 13.5 percent in 1980. Since that period, it has dropped back toward its historic norm of between 2 and 3 percent per year. The inflation rate is measured by the **Consumer Price Index (CPI)**, a figure computed by the Department of Labor. Calculated at regular intervals, the CPI is based on the changing costs of a specified "market basket" of goods and services.

Consumer Price Index (CPI)

Figure representing the cost of a specific set of goods and services tracked at regular intervals by the Department of Labor.

The government must also guard against **deflation**—dropping prices. Although deflation might sound good, falling prices discourage spending. If prices are going down, consumers refuse to spend today in hopes of paying less tomorrow. Consumers who sit on their wallets are not engaging in the kind of economic activity that creates jobs and a vibrant economy.

deflation

A decrease in prices over time.

Unemployment

unemployment rate

The percentage of Americans who are currently not working but are seeking jobs.

The **unemployment rate** measures the percentage of Americans who are out of work. It is not a perfect measure because it accounts only for people who identify themselves as actively seeking work, and sampling techniques are used in calculating it. Those who have given up looking for jobs are not counted, either as employed or unemployed—they are regarded as simply outside the workforce. The several million "undocumented" workers and the people involved in the illegal or "underground" economy are also left out. Unemployment therefore is often understated in particular geographic areas or during periods of great poverty. A "good" unemployment rate is around 5 percent. (One hundred percent employment would be impossible; a certain number of people are always between jobs or just entering the workforce.) In the 1980s, many economists considered 5 percent to be full employment, only to have unemployment drop below that figure in the late 1990s and again in 2005 and 2006. However, during the deep recession in 2008 and 2009, the unemployment level reached 10 percent before slowly declining to 8 percent in the spring of 2012. By November 2016, the national unemployment rate had dropped to 4.9 percent. More detailed employment statistics are noted in Figure 14.4.

Sometimes a slight uptick in unemployment can be a sign of a vibrant economy—people are more willing to leave a job they don't like when they are confident they can find better work elsewhere, and those who hadn't previously sought work become active job seekers. Employment rates that are too low, on the other hand, can make Wall Street wary of wage-driven inflation; when employers have trouble finding people to fill all available jobs, they have to pay their workers more. That's why the stock market often drops in response to "good" employment news.

FIGURE 14.4   Unemployment Rate

This figure charts unemployment levels over the last two decades. What this figure does not show, however, is the level of "underemployment"—the percentage of Americans who are working less than they would prefer, likely due to cutbacks. Most economists put this figure in November of 2016 at 10–13 percent.

■ *How would a Keynesian economist and a monetarist differ in their approaches to dealing with the problem of high unemployment?*

SOURCE: Bureau of Labor Statistics.

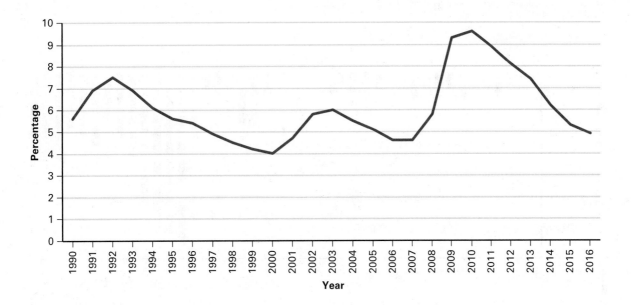

Gross Domestic Product

Gross domestic product (GDP)—the value of all the goods and services produced in a nation—measures the size of the American economy. Generally, economic growth is good, but overly rapid economic growth can be harmful because it can feed inflation. This is where the Fed will step in to try to curb runaway growth before inflation can gain a foothold. A good growth target for GDP for the U.S. economy is between 3 and 4 percent. Rapidly developing countries such as China and India have experienced much higher growth rates. The growth rate commonly reported in the media is the "real GDP" rate—GDP adjusted to account for the effects of the CPI, so that actual economic growth does not falsely include the rate of inflation.

gross domestic product (GDP)
The value of all goods and services produced in a nation.

Balance of Trade

The **balance of trade** measures the difference between imports and exports. A positive balance means that a nation has a trade surplus—it exports more goods than it imports. A negative balance of trade means a trade deficit—the country imports more goods than it exports. The United States has been running a significant trade deficit for years. The same American consumers who express their concerns about the outsourcing of American jobs also love to buy cheap imported goods. The U.S. trade deficit in goods was $531.5 billion in 2015, which represented the largest deficit since 2012. This increase is due in part to weaker economies in other countries reducing demand for American exports.[14]

balance of trade
The net difference between a nation's imports and its exports.

The Budget Deficit

A major concern for the U.S. economy has been the budget deficit and the rising national debt. The **budget deficit** is the amount by which, in a given year, government spending exceeds government revenue. (The rare circumstance when revenue

budget deficit
The amount by which a government's expenditures exceed its revenues.

FIGURE 14.5 Federal Deficits and Surpluses

The federal government has operated with budget deficits for most of the past 20 years. The few years of budget surpluses were caused by a thriving economy in the late 1990s. The return to budget deficits came after 9/11, when the federal government cut taxes and then soon initiated expensive military actions in Afghanistan and Iraq and also experienced rising costs in entitlement programs. Deficits grew even more during the Great Recession in 2009 and 2010, and continued to be a problem every year after.

■ *Does the size of the budget deficits worry you? How would you resolve this problem?*

NOTE: Values for Fiscal Years 2016–2021 are based on OMB estimates.

SOURCE: U.S. Office of Management and Budget, "Historical Tables," Budget of The United States Government, Historical Tables, annual. Accessed at https://www.whitehouse.gov/omb/budget/Historicals.

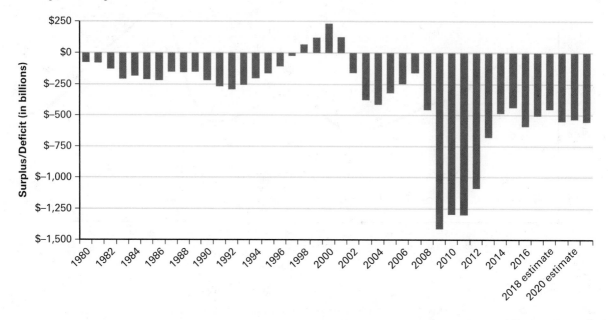

budget surplus

The amount by which a government's revenues exceed its expenditures.

national debt

The nation's cumulative deficits.

outstrips expenditures is called a **budget surplus**; see Figure 14.5.) The net sum of the budget deficit minus the surplus is the **national debt**, or the amount that the government owes. With the exception of the four years between 1998 and 2001, the United States has run a budget deficit every year since 1970. That has added up to a national debt of about $19 trillion by early 2016.[15] When the nation went into an economic crisis in the fall of 2008, the Congress and President Bush put together a $700 billion bailout program to shore up U.S. financial institutions. The spending for the bailout package also moved Congress and President Bush to increase the amount the nation can legally borrow to cover U.S. debts from $10.4 billion to $11.3 billion, with President Obama and Congress again raising the debt ceiling to over $15 billion in 2012. The national debt must be financed through money that is borrowed—with interest—both at home and abroad, which makes balancing the budget that much harder with each passing year.

With the Republican takeover of the House of Representatives in the wake of the 2010 midterm elections, and takeover of the Senate after the 2014 midterm elections, the politics of deficit financing took an interesting turn. The Republican Party campaigned on a pledge to reduce government spending and to shrink the federal deficit if returned to control in Congress. Meanwhile, President Obama continued to argue for substantial government spending to help stimulate the federal economy to grow out of a stagnated period. With President-elect Trump set to take office in January 2017 along with a Republican-controlled Congress, reducing the budget deficit will be an important issue. However, there may be some disagreement between Republican President Trump and the Congressional GOP. Republicans in Congress may want to decrease spending by reforming entitlements, but President-elect Trump seems less in favor of this kind of policy change. The only certainty appears to be a dire fiscal picture in the near future.[16] According to Congressional Budget Office estimates, the budget deficit will approach $600 billion in 2016 and rise to $739 billion by 2020.[17]

The Key Players in the Development of Economic Policy

14.4   Describe the key actors responsible for creating fiscal policy.

The game of politics is all about deciding who gets what, and part of that involves deciding who pays for what. That is what **fiscal policy**—the politics of taxing and spending—is all about. With the federal budget now at $3.7 trillion, there is a lot of money up for grabs. As you learned in the preceding section, the federal government is currently spending more money than it is collecting in taxes, creating a budget deficit. Collectively, our deficits added up to a national debt of about $19 trillion in February 2016. The stage is set for the national debt to become much larger.

Technically, the United States has two budgets. The first is "on budget" and includes general revenue from income tax and corporate taxes, paying for things such as defense, NASA, and poverty prevention programs. The second is "off budget" and includes money from the Social Security and Medicare payroll taxes and trust funds. In reality, this separation is a legalistic fiction. For our purposes, we are going to view the budget as a unified, integrated whole, except when we specifically discuss on-budget and off-budget aspects.

fiscal policy
Taxation and spending decisions made by the government.

Major Actors

Budgets are created through interactions between Congress and the president, but there are several other major actors in the realm of fiscal policy, the most significant of which is the **Congressional Budget Office (CBO)**. A research arm of Congress, the CBO was created by the Budget and Impoundment Act of 1974. The act had numerous purposes, but one of the key aspects was to give Congress a stronger position in dealing with the president on budgetary matters, thus fundamentally changing how the budget of the United States is crafted. Before this Act, the White House **Office of Management and Budget (OMB)** had the primary responsibility for drawing up the budget. The president would present the basic document, and Congress would make adjustments. Since 1975, the CBO has created long-term budget outlooks, analyses of the president's proposed budget, and fiscal impact statements for every bill that comes out of a congressional committee. As a result, Congress has become a more prominent player in creating the budget. The OMB still draws up a budget, and although that budget sometimes has some influence, it is often "dead on arrival" when it gets to Congress.

The OMB provides the president with information and guidance. The power of the veto gives the president an important role in determining the final budget, which is always a compromise. Of course, the OMB carries a little more weight when the presidency and Congress are both controlled by the same party. Since 1946, the president has also had the "help" of the **Council of Economic Advisers (CEA)**. The CEA was created by Congress back when the initial budget document was primarily the chief executive's responsibility in order to help the White House make budget decisions. The CEA's three members are usually leading academic economists and are appointed by the president. Some presidents, notably John F. Kennedy, have relied heavily on the CEA; others, such as Ronald Reagan, have all but ignored it. In 1993, the National Economic Council (NEC) was established to advise the president on economic policy.

Congressional Budget Office (CBO)
The research arm of Congress, a major player in budget creation.

Office of Management and Budget (OMB)
A cabinet-level office that monitors federal agencies and provides the president with expert advice on policy-related topics.

Council of Economic Advisers (CEA)
A group of economists within the Executive Office of the President, appointed by the president to provide advice on economic policy.

Key Congressional Players

As discussed earlier, committees do the real work of Congress. Although the Constitution requires that all revenue bills originate in the House, the 435 House members sitting together could never write a budget. Instead, appropriations and tax bills are products of committees in the Senate and the House. Each chamber has an appropriations committee, which has primary responsibility for deciding where federal money should be spent. The House Ways and Means Committee is responsible for tax bills. The Senate Finance Committee serves as its counterpart. The House and Senate also each have budget committees that review the fiscal process.

Revenue

14.5 Identify the major sources of U.S. government revenue.

In 2015, the U.S. government collected about $3.3 trillion in revenue. The largest portion of that total came from taxes on individual income, at $1.54 trillion. Taxes to fund the Social Security program, referred to as *Social Security (Insurance) taxes* or **payroll taxes**, produced another $1.065 trillion. Revenue from corporate taxes yielded $344 billion. Customs duties and miscellaneous taxes accounted for $86 billion. Excise revenues totaled $98 billion, and estate and gift revenues accounted for $19 billion.[18] The tax burden for the majority of Americans comes in the form of income tax and Social Security.

Income tax is levied on wages, rent, interest, and profit, while payroll tax is levied on wage earnings. Income tax is a **progressive tax**—the more money you make, the higher the percentage you pay in taxes, up to a top rate of 39.6 percent. The Social Security tax, on the other hand, is a **regressive tax**. If you make enough money, your Social Security tax burden drops. At first glance, payroll taxes seem flat—everyone pays the same rate. However, this tax is collected only on the first $118,500 of income; earnings (from salaries and self-employment) above that level are not subject to the Social Security tax. So, the tax burden for higher-income earners is felt more heavily through income taxes, while those with lower incomes are hit harder by payroll taxes.

Income Taxes

Taxes on income made up just over 8.1 percent of GDP in 2014. Currently, there are seven different income taxation levels in the United States (see Table 14.1). For comparison, we show the rates for a single person and for a married couple filing jointly. As you earn

payroll taxes
A tax on earnings that funds Social Security and Medicare.

progressive tax
A tax structured such that higher-income individuals pay a larger percentage of their income in taxes.

regressive tax
A tax structured such that higher-income individuals pay a lower percentage of their income in taxes.

FIGURE 14.6 The Federal Revenue Budget

Federal government revenue comes primarily from individual income tax and payroll taxes for Social Security and Medicare.

■ *How can an increase in the unemployment rate affect tax revenues?*

SOURCE: "Budget and Economic Data: Detailed Revenue Projections," Congressional Budget Office, https://www.cbo.gov/about/products/budget_economic_data#7.

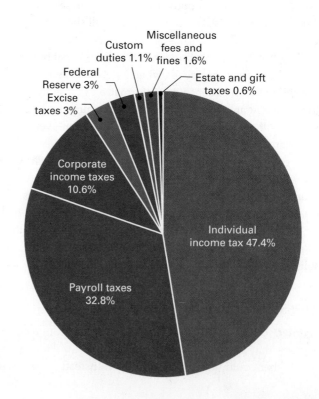

TABLE 14.1   Tax Brackets, 2016

Schedule X: Single Taxpayer			Schedule Y-1: Married Taxpayers Filing Jointly or Qualifying Widow or Widower		
If Taxable Income Is Over	But Not Over	The Tax Is	If Taxable Income Is Over	But Not Over	The Tax Is
$0	$9,275	10% of the amount over $0	$0	$18,550	10% of the amount over $0
$9,275	$37,650	$927.50 plus 15% of the amount over $9,275	$18,550	$75,300	$1,855 plus 15% of the amount over $18,550
$37,650	$91,150	$5,183.75 plus 25% of the amount over $37,650	$75,300	$151,900	$10,367.50 plus 25% of the amount over $75,300
$91,150	$190,150	$18,558.75 plus 28% of the amount over $91,150	$151,900	$231,450	$29,517.50 plus 28% of the amount over $151,900
$109,150	$413,350	$46,278.75 plus 33% of the amount over $190,150	$231,450	$413,350	$51,791.50 plus 33% of the amount over $231,450
$413,350	$415,050	$119,934.75 plus 35% of the amount over $413,350	$413,350	$466,950	$111,818.50 plus 35% of the amount over $413,350
$415,050	no limit	$120,529.75 plus 39.6% of the amount over $415,050	$466,950	no limit	$130,578.50 plus 39.6% of the amount over $466,950

SOURCE: Internal Revenue Service.

more money in a given year, you move into a higher **marginal tax bracket**—*marginal* meaning the tax rate you pay on the last dollar you earn that year. Everyone pays 10 percent on the first dollar of taxable income, but not all dollars are taxed: In addition to the taxpayer's personal deduction, there is a deduction for each dependent (such as a child under 18), and the taxpayer either gets a standard deduction or itemizes deductions and subtracts them from gross earnings. In 2014, a family of four paid no taxes, as long as the family's gross income was under $37,923 annually.[19] The tax brackets in Table 14.1 cover net income after all these deductions—known as *taxable income*. The tax codes are so complicated and deductions are so difficult to understand that it is almost impossible for many taxpayers to calculate their own taxes. Each year, more and more Americans use tax software programs or hire outside experts or accountants to prepare their tax returns.

marginal tax bracket

The tax rate you pay on the last dollar that you earn in a given year.

Payroll Taxes

Social Security taxes make up 5.9 percent of GDP. They take the form of a payroll tax, a tax split so that employees pay half and their employers pay the other half. Each pays 6.2 percent into the Social Security Trust Fund and 1.45 percent into the Medicare trust fund. In effect, this tax split obscures the full impact of its burden—half is hidden in your employee benefits. If you are self-employed, however, you carry the full burden: 15.3 percent of the first $118,500 of the net income from your business or profession.

The Tax Burden

So, who pays what? Analysis of household income and tax burden by the CBO shows that the top 10 percent of earners pay about 50 percent of taxes. The bottom 20 percent pay only about 1 percent. Those numbers are a little skewed, however, as they include only the employee's portion of the payroll tax. The top 1 percent of earners pays 24 percent of federal taxes. The bottom line is this: Most American workers pay more per year in payroll taxes than they do in income taxes.

Critics argue that the CBO analysis is flawed because it measures income, not wealth. Capital gains, such as the increase in the value of stock someone owns, are taxed at a lower rate than earned income. Profits from stock and real estate transactions are taxed only when they are sold, so capital gains can accumulate for years without generating any government revenue. As a result, the wealthy—especially the nonworking wealthy—escape taxation on the vast majority of their assets. Critics contend that the poor have little opportunity to accumulate wealth.

Corporate Taxes

Taxes on corporations generate about 11 percent of the federal government's revenue. The United States has one of the highest effective corporate tax rates in the industrialized world, with a top tax rate of 35 percent. Taking into account state corporate taxes as well, the average U.S. corporation has an effective marginal tax rate of almost 40 percent on its net income. At the same time, corporate tax collection amounts to only about 2 percent of GDP, well below the international average of about 3.4 percent. The disparity between the tax rate and the taxes actually collected is explained by the numerous deductions and credits that federal and state laws provide.

The U.S. corporate tax system also has numerous write-offs, often targeted to specific industries that result from successful lobbying, which are intended to elicit certain corporate behavior. Tax reforms implemented in 2003, for example, allowed many businesses to write off their expenses faster. One provision, called the SUV loophole, allowed businesses to deduct luxury sport utility vehicles from their income provided that the vehicles were used for business purposes. Many critics of business tax policy brand such incentives "corporate welfare." As the country struggled to come out of recession, the Obama administration offered various forms of tax breaks for business entities, including small businesses. In 2010, President Obama announced that small businesses would receive a $5,000 tax credit for each job created during the year. The maximum amount of tax credits received per firm was set at $500,000.[20]

Corporate income tax revenues depend, of course, on whether companies make a profit. During a recession, corporate profits can plummet or even vanish completely. The consensus among most business experts is that worldwide, corporate tax revenues are in a period of decline. This trend began at the end of the Cold War and the breakup of the Soviet Union in the early 1990s. As nations try to remain competitive, this downward trend is likely to continue, keeping pressure on the United States to lower its corporate tax rates.

Other Taxes

Other taxes include excise taxes, customs duties, inheritance taxes, and miscellaneous receipts. Excise taxes levied on fuel, alcohol, and tobacco are paid by the producer and are folded into the price of the product. Customs duties are taxes on foreign-made goods imported into the United States and, like excise taxes, are part of the consumer's final price. Inheritance taxes are on the asset value of a person's estate. Miscellaneous receipts include income earned by the Federal Reserve in its day-to-day operations.

Critics of our tax system maintain that the "sin taxes" on alcohol and tobacco add to the regressivity of the overall system. Because today the poor are more likely to smoke than the wealthy, and because their income is smaller, tobacco taxes eat up a larger percentage of a poor person's income than a richer person's income.

Despite increased imports, customs duty income has remained relatively stable, due in large part to our expansion of free-trade zones and worldwide limits on tariffs.

Tax Analysis

Finding the optimum tax rate is a difficult job for the government to perform. At first glance, you might think that generating more revenue is a simple matter of raising tax rates, but as you will see, it is not that simple.

In the mid-1970s, Arthur Laffer, a professor at the University of Southern California, was conversing with a *Wall Street Journal* columnist, when he sketched out an interesting theory on a cocktail napkin. Laffer reasoned that

The floor of the New York Stock Exchange in New York City, where stock transactions affect the ownership and value of corporations. The decisions of corporate leaders to expand their businesses or, alternatively, lay off employees also affect government tax revenues.

■ *If you were the president or a member of Congress, how would you react if a major corporation announced that it was going to lay off 20,000 workers?*

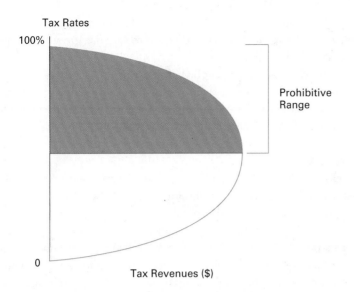

Tax Rates

100%

Prohibitive Range

0

Tax Revenues ($)

FIGURE 14.7 The Laffer Curve

The Laffer curve represents an economist's theory about how to design tax rates in a manner that will help the government and the economy. It argues that setting tax rates too high will actually reduce the amount of revenue collected by government.

■ *Are there any specific assumptions that underlie this theory? Should the theory be proven before it is adopted by government officials?*

if the tax rate is zero, government revenue is zero. That's pretty obvious—zero times anything is zero. Laffer maintained, however, that government revenue will also be zero if the tax rate is 100 percent. Why? Because if the government takes all their earnings, no one will go to work! Zero times everything is still zero. Laffer sketched out a graph, now known as the **Laffer curve**, to demonstrate that there exists some rate of taxation above which government revenue drops (see Figure 14.7). A sufficiently high tax rate, Laffer concluded, discourages productivity.

Laffer was one of the chief proponents of supply-side economics, the theory that cutting taxes would grow the economy, thereby ultimately increasing government revenues. The supply-siders were the major theoretical force behind President Reagan's tax cut policies of the early 1980s. Although opponents argue that the tax cuts were a failure because the deficit exploded during the Reagan years, revenues did increase dramatically. From 1980 to 1990, government revenues almost doubled, from $517 billion to over $1 trillion. Spending, however, skyrocketed from $591 billion to $1.25 trillion. A yearly deficit that had been about $70 billion at the beginning of the decade had ballooned to over $220 billion by the end. Congress and the president spent all the new revenue—plus an additional $1.7 trillion that had to be raised by borrowing.

The bottom line on tax revenue seems to be this:

1. Over a period of several years, revenues increase.
2. If the government raises marginal tax rates, revenue goes up. (Overall economic growth might slow a bit, but tax revenue rises.)
3. If the government cuts marginal tax rates, revenue goes up. (It might dip at first during a transitional period, but that decline won't last for long as the overall economy grows; a smaller percentage of a larger pie can still lead to a larger piece of pie.)

An important question that arises when we analyze the tax system is equity. Is it fair? No one likes paying taxes, but the government needs a source of revenue to fund even the most minimal services. Should the wealthy be taxed at a higher rate—a more progressive rate—in order to provide more services for the poor? Critics argue that the current economic system is unfair. They say that the disparity between rich and poor is too wide. Despite significant gains in real GDP (GDP after factoring out inflation), most real-wage increases have gone to the wealthiest Americans. Would a more progressive tax system help reverse that trend? Or would it discourage the wealthy from putting forth the extra effort and productive investments that lead to gains in productivity? A related question follows: Does fairness matter as much as efficiency?

Laffer curve

An economic model that maintains that a higher rate of taxation can result in lower government revenues.

Should the government try to foster an economic system that generates revenue while boosting the overall economy, or is it preferable to sacrifice growth for equity? Many Americans disagree about the answers.

The U.S. tax code is long, complicated, and not particularly efficient. Its evolution over the years has turned it into a mishmash of special-interest tax breaks and exemptions. Many of those exemptions—such as the home mortgage interest exemption—benefit such a wide range of taxpayers, that any attempt to revise the code stirs up wide-ranging opposition. Nonetheless, numerous reforms have been offered in recent years.

Major reform initiatives fall under one of two basic concepts: a flat tax or a national sales tax. The most common variant of the flat tax is one offered by former U.S. Congressman Dick Armey, a Republican from Texas (and a former economics professor). Under his proposal, married couples would receive a $26,000 standard exemption plus a personal exemption of just over $5,000 for each family member. There would be no other deductions. All income over the exempted amount would be taxed at 17 percent. Net business income would be likewise taxed at 17 percent. This flat tax would generate a little less revenue than the present system, and the large standard deduction would make this tax modestly progressive. Many lower-income families would pay no income tax at all, and most taxpayers would not need to hire accountants to do their taxes.

Under a proposed national sales tax, the federal government would collect a surcharge of about 23 percent on purchases of all goods and services. Because such a sales tax would, by its nature, be regressive (low-income people typically have to spend everything they earn; higher-income people can save part of their income), each household would receive a rebate check at the beginning of each month, equal to 23 percent of poverty-level income based on family size. Although the tax rate might seem high, the sales tax would replace both income and payroll taxes. Many economists believe that under this plan, retail prices for many goods would drop: They argue that a significant portion of the cost of goods comes from embedded taxes. One aim of the national sales tax would be to bring illegal business activities under the tax umbrella. No one is suggesting that drug dealers would collect and pay taxes on their sales, but when they spend their profits, they would make a greater contribution to the legitimate economy.

In 2012 tax reform centered on the so called "Buffet Rule" that was designed to make the wealthiest Americans pay a higher tax rate than in the past. Named for billionaire investor Warren Buffett, the Buffet Rule was proposed by President Obama and called for a law where no household making more than a $1 million should pay a smaller share of their income in taxes than middle-class families pay. This outcome would be accomplished by limiting the degree to which the very wealthy can take advantage of loopholes and tax rates that allow them to pay less of their income in taxes than middle-class families.[21]

In the 2016 presidential election, tax reform ideas varied greatly between Democrats and Republicans. During the Democratic presidential primary, former Secretary of State Hillary Clinton and Senator Bernie Sanders put forth tax reform plans focused on enacting the Buffet Rule, raising the top marginal income tax rates, and increasing various other tax rates that primarily directly affect upper-income households, including the capital gains tax. Flat tax proposals were common in the Republican presidential primary, and featured in the tax plans of Senators Ted Cruz and Rand Paul. Senator Marco Rubio's plan eliminated the capital gains tax entirely. Eventual Republican nominee Donald Trump initially proposed large reductions in the top income tax rates.

› **POLL** How would you reform American tax policy? What are your goals in doing so? What intended and unintended effects do you believe your proposed reform will have?

Expenditures

14.6 Identify the major forms of U.S. government expenditures.

In President Obama's proposed 2017 budget, the U.S. government's largest expenditure was for Social Security, with an estimated outlay of $976 billion. The budget also proposed spending a little over $600 billion apiece for national defense and Medicare, while spending $568 billion on other health care programs. Income security, which you will learn about shortly, accounted for $550 billion. Interest on the national debt ate up $303 billion. All other major spending programs, including education, science, transportation, and veterans' benefits, accounted for less than $200 billion each.[22]

According to Congressional Budget Office, the budget deficit for 2016 was expected to be around $534 billion or 3 percent of GDP.[23] Government expenditures continually expand, in part because levels of "current services" have become the baseline for most government programs. This means that the starting point for next year's budget is this year's budget, plus increases needed because of increased population and inflation. When politicians talk about balancing "the budget," they are generally referring to the current services budget. So, even if spending increases from one year to the next, government officials can claim that they have cut the budget, as long as the rate of increase is below the current services projection.

> POLL How do you feel about what you and your family pay in taxes, considering the benefits you enjoy from the national government?

Social Security

The U.S. government's Social Security program was established in 1935 during the Great Depression. At that time, more than half of the elderly lived in poverty, and the program's goal was to provide a minimal pension for older Americans. In many ways, Social Security was a conservative response to the far more radical demands during the 1930s for guaranteed levels of income and more substantive aid to the poor. The initial payroll tax rate was 1 percent, paid by both employee and employer, and it was levied on only the first $3,000 of annual income. At first, monthly benefits were not indexed to inflation—what you received was what you expected to receive for life. Not until the 1950s did Congress authorize a cost-of-living adjustment (COLA), and not until 1975 did these COLA increases become annual and automatic. Originally, Social Security covered only employees of industrial and commercial firms, excluding farm workers and domestic servants. Since then, it has been expanded to include not only those workers but also retirement-age surviving spouses, dependents, and disabled working-age people.

Technically, Social Security is an independent, off-budget program. It was originally intended to be self-financing. As long as there were several workers for each retiree, that concept worked fairly well. In the 1970s, however, Social Security started running a slight deficit. It was evident that the problem would worsen over time. Americans were getting older. There were fewer workers per retiree, and retirees were living longer. Anyone examining the demographics could see more substantial problems on the horizon. When baby boomers started to retire and the smaller Generation X took its place in the workforce, an even greater burden fell on the remaining workers.

In 1983, a special commission headed by the economist Alan Greenspan generated a number of reform measures that were enacted by Congress. The central purpose of the reforms was to create a surplus, known as the **Social Security Trust Fund**, which would save money over the years to help bridge the gap created as the boomers retired. It did this primarily in two ways. First, the retirement age was raised: Over

Social Security Trust Fund

A fund to pay future Social Security benefits, supposedly being built through today's payroll tax.

several years, the age for drawing full retirement benefits increased from 65 to 67. Second, the reform significantly increased payroll taxes—again, over a period of years—to the relatively high rate that now prevails. The reforms also raised the tax rate on the self-employed, so that they pay the combined rate paid by employers and employees. As a result, Social Security immediately began running a surplus, surpassing $50 billion a year by 1989 and $100 billion by 1999. In 2005, the surplus was $173 billion. However, as ever more Baby Boomers have retired in recent years, Social Security payments have started to outstrip payroll taxes. In 2014, Social Security ran a deficit of $74 billion.[24] Yearly deficits are expected to grow even larger in the future.

By the time we get to 2018, when Social Security is expected to start paying out more than it is bringing in, the fund will be worth more than $4 trillion. The problem is that the trust fund money is not sitting in a vault somewhere. It has already been spent. One reason the nation has been able to run such large deficits over the past couple of decades is that the Treasury has borrowed money from the Social Security Trust Fund, depositing an electronic IOU in its place. Although, as we have said, Social Security is supposed to be off-budget, deficit figures subtract the Social Security surplus. In fact, a closer look at the alleged surpluses from 1998 through 2001 shows mainly smoke and mirrors. On-budget surpluses occurred in only two of those years, and in one of those years, the surplus was less than $1 billion. The reported cumulative surplus of $559 billion amounted to an on-budget surplus of only $23 billion!

If the $4 trillion has already been spent, does that mean it is gone? Not really. The government owes itself electronic IOUs, which have also accrued interest payments. Does this mean that the federal government will default on its Social Security obligations—that when *you* retire, there will be no Social Security for you? Despite the claims of some conservative pundits, no. The strength of the American dollar, and the confidence that it engenders, depends on the United States meeting its financial obligations. The United States, thus far, has never defaulted on its debt—even to itself—and it would be financial suicide if it were to start now. The long-term consequences of rising Social Security obligations and decreasing surpluses, however, will have significant implications for future U.S. budgets.

Defense

The nation's largest on-budget appropriations are for defense. Roughly $573 billion was authorized for defense spending in 2016. Since the dawn of history, war and defense have been expensive propositions. Many factors lead to the high costs of maintaining the armed forces. Of course, military personnel need to be paid. Salary and retirement benefits comprise a large portion of the U.S. military budget. In addition, the armed services provide housing and medical care for soldiers and their families, and the military employs a large number of civilian personnel. Throw in administrative costs, base construction and upkeep, training, and logistics, and more than half of the military budget goes for operations and support.

The second large area of defense spending includes the development, testing, and procurement of weapons systems. Weapons development and procurement are always controversial, especially in a world in which the United States is clearly the dominant superpower. The air force, for example, has to decide whether to proceed with the purchase of additional, sophisticated F-22 fighters or if it would be better served by ordering more of the cheaper but newer Joint Strike Fighters. The marines have to decide whether their long-term interests are best served by buying more conventional heavy-lift helicopters or by transitioning to the more expensive but faster tilt-rotor aircraft. The army has to decide whether it needs more reconnaissance helicopters or if it should transition to unmanned drones. The navy has to decide whether to keep all 11 of its massive, nuclear-powered aircraft carriers or build smaller, nonnuclear carriers to allow it to spread its presence over a greater area.

All of these decisions must be made within the context of what is best for national security and for military personnel and within the scope of the overall budget. It also requires military leaders and members of Congress to make certain assumptions about future threat levels that are difficult to predict and that may well change over time. Will China emerge as a major threat? If so, will the Chinese match us technologically or try to offset our power with a larger but less sophisticated military? Will we remain the sole global superpower? How can we fashion rapid-response units that can take the field in several global hotspots at one time? What should be our worst-case scenario for planning troop and asset deployment? Uncertainty makes each of these decisions difficult and potentially costly in terms of both dollars and security. These decisions are also influenced by the lobbying decision makers pathway because companies that supply planes, ships, and other equipment will pressure their congressmen as well as Department of Defense officials to buy their products.

Many Americans believe that the war on terror and the expenses related to Afghanistan and Iraq have led to increased defense spending, as a percentage of the budget or GDP. However, despite the fact that defense spending, in dollars, is at record levels, it is much lower as a percentage of both GDP and the overall budget than it was during the latter stages of the Cold War—and far below the levels during World War II. In 1944, at the height of World War II, military spending accounted for more than 80 percent of the federal budget and 38 percent of GDP. Cold War defense spending peaked in the late 1980s at 27 percent of the federal budget and 6 percent of GDP. Today, defense absorbs about 16 percent of the budget and about 3.5 percent of GDP.[25]

› POLL How much should our government spend on defense? Is there a fundamental tradeoff between defense spending and economic spending, or does one help the other? Why?

Nevertheless, these percentages could increase depending on developments in Iraq, Afghanistan, and the defense against ISIS and global terrorism. More importantly, the figures cited above do not take into account the fact that, under the Bush administration, war spending was requested through off-budget measures like emergency supplemental bills. These supplemental bills were not included in the White House deficit projections.

An American serviceman takes a photograph of a fellow soldier in front of a drone.

■ *What is the best way to use drones in American foreign policy?*

Barack Obama campaigned on a promise to reduce military spending and introduce more transparency in war spending. President Obama's budgets, however, initially exceeded President Bush's combined defense and supplemental budgets, which in 2008 totaled $623.1 billion.[26] President Obama's 2011 defense budget proposal, sent to Congress in February 2010, totaled $708 billion. This figure included $159 billion to support overseas contingency operations, primarily in Afghanistan and Iraq. However, by the end of his second term, with U.S. presence in Iraq and Afghanistan greatly diminished, President Obama did reduce defense spending below what it was at the end of the Bush administration.

In November of 2016, President-elect Trump seemed committed to getting Congress to increase defense spending. Estimates suggests this increase could be up to $80 billion annually.

Income Security

income security

The notion that the government should establish programs that provide a safety net for society's poorest members.

The idea behind **income security** is that the government should provide a safety net for the most vulnerable members of society. The largest components of the income security program are the earned-income credit, the child tax credit, supplemental security income, unemployment compensation, and food stamps. Together, these programs comprise almost three-fourths of total federal income security spending. Unemployment payments tend to rise and fall, depending on the state of the economy; they fell as the economy recovered from its post–9/11 slump and then rose as the economy struggled in 2009. The food stamp program is administered by the Department of Agriculture. In 2016, over 45 million Americans received food stamps. This figure represented a 60 percent increase since 2008.[27] Smaller income security programs include Temporary Assistance to Needy Families (TANF); the Women, Infants, and Children (WIC) program; and federal child support enforcement measures. Even smaller amounts go to foster care and adoption assistance. The number of families receiving TANF has been cut in half in the past decade as a result of the Welfare Reform Act of 1996. The cash portion of income assistance, TANF is often referred to generically as "welfare."

Government Medical Care

Health care reform was an important issue in the 2008, 2012, and 2016 presidential elections because of growing costs to both citizens and the federal government. As noted in Figure 14.8, without significant change, the percentage of health care–related spending by the federal government (for example, for Medicare and Medicaid) is projected to grow dramatically.

Medicare and Medicaid are two separate, often-confused programs with common origins. Both were established in the mid-1960s as part of President Lyndon Johnson's Great Society. Since then, exploding medical costs have been one of the largest contributors to increased government spending. Over the past 40 years, health care costs have outstripped the general rate of inflation. Part of this is due to improvements in treatment procedures, most of which are very expensive. Improvements in the quality of health care lead to longer life expectancy, which means that the average senior citizen spends more years receiving Medicare coverage and that coverage costs far more than it did in the past.

Medicare

Health care coverage for senior citizens.

Medicare provides health insurance coverage for retired people (beginning at age 65) as well as for disabled younger people. In 1974, Medicare spending accounted for 0.7 percent of GDP; today, it is over 3 percent. By 2050, if no reforms are enacted, Medicare spending alone will account for between 8 and 9 percent of the *total* U.S. economy.

Medicare is for the general over-65 population and the disabled; the economically disadvantaged receive health services through **Medicaid**. Under this joint

FIGURE 14.8   Federal Entitlement Spending and National Debt Interest Payments Over Time

Social Security, Medicare, Medicaid, and interest on the national debt are projected to consume virtually all federal revenue within the next 25 years.

■ *How will tax policy be impacted by the increasing share of entitlement expenditures as a percentage of GDP?*

SOURCE: Congressional Budget Office and Office of Management and Budget, The 2015 Long-Trem Budget outlook, "Summary Data for the extended Alternatives Fiscal Scenario," www.cbo.gov/publication/50250.

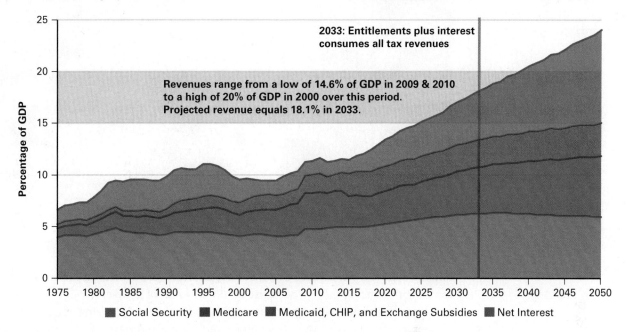

program between the federal government and the states, the federal government provides an average of 57 percent of Medicaid's financing. Because some states provide more services than others, matching percentages vary. Most of the 71 million Medicaid enrollees are children and pregnant women, but the overwhelming amount of Medicaid funding goes to the elderly and disabled. Much of that money is spent on nursing homes, home health care, and social services for retired people who have exhausted their life savings.

Five years after it was established in 1965, Medicaid spending comprised 0.3 percent of GDP; today, it accounts for 1.7 percent. If increases continue at current levels, total spending could hit 5 percent of GDP by 2050. These figures help explain the prominent and controversial role that Medicaid plays in the contemporary budget battles that we discussed in the opening of the chapter.

Medicaid
Health care coverage for the poor.

Interest and Other Spending

As government debt rises, interest payments also rise. Almost 7 percent of the total budget goes to pay interest on the debt. In the 2015 fiscal year, interest payments on debt amounted to about $223 billion, which constitutes a significant portion of the budget deficit of $439 billion that occurred in that year.

That's only part of the story, however. Notes held by the Social Security and Medicare trust funds also receive interest payments. Using smoke-and-mirrors accounting again, the federal government considers this interest to be income, offsetting total interest payments. Since the trust fund interest technically accrues, a truer mark of interest costs is much higher. That's because the debt held by government trust funds is about two-thirds the size of the trust fund held by the public.

The size of the debt is only one factor when it comes to interest payments. Because interest rates are set by the open market, an issue we'll discuss when we cover monetary policy later in the chapter, the cost of financing the debt can rise or

With the life expectancy of Americans increasing, more and more people are receiving Medicare benefits. The program is costly and will continue to require greater spending to cover advances in medical treatment and the expanding pool of recipients.

■ *What fiscal policy measures can help cover these rising costs for Medicare?*

fall independently of the size of the debt. If interest rates were to rise from 4 to 5 percent, debt-financing costs would rise by 25 percent. Of course, the government has its debt instruments spread over several years, with varying lengths of maturity, so a temporary rate change would have little overall impact. An extended period of rising rates, however, could force the government to issue more of its notes at a higher cost, thereby driving up the long-term cost of borrowing.

In an effort to trim deficits in his 2016 budget proposal, President Obama pushed Congress to enact about $3 trillion in new taxes and fees over the next 10 years. The requested increases in spending in his proposal, however, more than offset this estimated increase in government revenue over the next 10 years. Under the President's proposal, the accumulated debt held by the public would increase by over $7 trillion by 2026.[28]

Spending for all other programs falls significantly below those that we have discussed in detail. For example, the president's 2016 budget requested $64.9 billion for the Department of Education. NASA's share is $19 billion. The Department of Energy, according to the president's proposal, will receive about $32.5 billion. The Department of Transportation will get approximately $98.1 billion. The Department of Agriculture budget is slated at $24.6 billion. The Environmental Protection Agency (EPA) will receive $8.3 billion. With a proposed $29 billion budget, the Department of Justice will run the federal prisons, the Federal Bureau of Investigation (FBI), the Drug Enforcement Agency (DEA), and the Bureau of Alcohol, Tobacco, Firearms, and Explosives (ATF), as well as the U.S. Attorney's Office.[29]

One of the difficulties of creating the budget at the federal level is caused by the pervasiveness of **entitlements**—mandatory spending required by law that is not subject to the budgetary process. Entitlements account for three out of every five dollars that the federal government spends. Almost all of the spending on Social Security and Medicare is mandatory, as are large percentages of spending on income security and Medicaid. Federal law requires that all who meet certain specifications are entitled to certain benefits. Since discretionary spending (spending that is not mandatory; Congress determines how much funding it will supply each year) accounts for less than half the total budget, congressional hands are somewhat tied as legislators attempt to constrain spending. Of course, since Congress wrote the laws enacting the entitlements in the first place, it can rework legislation to alleviate this complication.

entitlements

Government expenditures required by law.

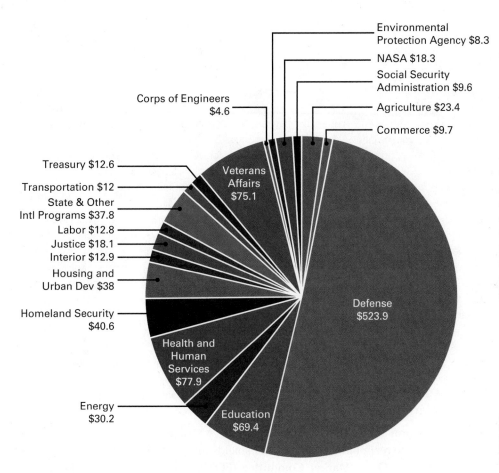

Corps of Engineers $4.6

Environmental Protection Agency $8.3

NASA $18.3

Social Security Administration $9.6

Agriculture $23.4

Commerce $9.7

Treasury $12.6

Transportation $12

State & Other Intl Programs $37.8

Labor $12.8

Justice $18.1

Interior $12.9

Housing and Urban Dev $38

Homeland Security $40.6

Health and Human Services $77.9

Energy $30.2

Education $69.4

Veterans Affairs $75.1

Defense $523.9

FIGURE 14.9 President Obama's 2017 Proposed Budget (In Billions)

In February 2016, President Obama proposed the federal budget. Budgets are an expression of an administration's priorities and of the contemporary needs of the nation at large. It is important to note that this figure does not include mandatory federal expenditures for items such as interest on the national debt and entitlement expenditures for items such as Social Security benefits. These items make up an increasingly large portion of overall federal spending and contribute significantly to federal deficits and the national debt.

■ *Do you think the allocation of resources to secure the nation's defense compromises our needs in health and education sectors? How do the budget data show us that policy priorities are set by domestic as well as international considerations? Explain your answer.*

SOURCE: "Department Fact Sheets," Office of Management and Budget, Department Fact Sheets. Accessed at https://www.whitehouse.gov/omb/budget/agency-fact-sheets.

As you might suspect, however, that would tend to anger the people benefiting from the current system. All of these spending discussions lead back to one central point: It is still *your* money. The only way you can influence how it is spent is to let federal officials know what you think about their priorities.

Monetary Policy

14.7 Identify the major instruments of monetary policy.

In the simplest terms, **monetary policy** involves the management of the supply of money in circulation within the United States. It is essential to strike a balance. Too much money coursing through the economy will be inflationary—remember the definition of inflation as "too much money chasing too few goods." Too little money will stifle economic growth. Keeping the balance right by managing monetary policy is the job of the Federal Reserve Board of Governors and its Federal Open Market Committee.

The Federal Reserve Board

Created in 1913 by an act of Congress, the **Federal Reserve System (the Fed)** is our nation's independent central bank. (In most other Western nations, the central bank is controlled by the national government.) Although it is accountable to Congress, the Fed is free from political pressure because of the way it is structured. The seven members of its Board of Governors are appointed by the president of the United States, but they hold staggered, 14-year terms. That makes it difficult for any president or for Congress to exert too much influence over its policies. Moreover, there are 12 regional Federal Reserve banks within the system, each of which selects its own president,

monetary policy

Money supply management conducted by the Federal Reserve.

Federal Reserve System (the Fed)

The independent central bank of the United States.

PATHWAYS OF ACTION

AARP

Founded in 1958 as the American Association of Retired Persons, AARP ranks as one of the nation's most powerful interest groups. Claiming more than 35 million members, AARP has an additional advantage: Its members vote. Americans older than 50—the minimum age to join AARP—are the demographic group most likely to vote. Add in the fact that interest group members are more likely to vote than average citizens, and the organization's power becomes even more formidable.

Advocating for Social Security and Medicare, AARP played a key role in pushing through prescription drug coverage for seniors. However, the organization believes both that more needs to be done to make medical care more affordable and that patients should be able to purchase prescription medicine from other countries (for example, Canada) if that option is less expensive. Although AARP supports maintaining current Social Security benefits for the already retired, it recognizes that the system faces long-term problems. AARP's leaders believe that the sooner incremental changes are made, the better. Although they opposed President George W. Bush's proposal to put a portion of the payroll tax into private accounts—they were instrumental in defeating this idea before it ever got out of the starting gate—they do advocate the creation of separate private accounts as a supplement to Social Security. AARP also works at both the state and national levels for laws that protect senior citizens from predatory lending practices and financial scams.

AARP is nonpartisan. It does not endorse particular candidates. Because more than half of all seniors belong to AARP—many of them attracted by the peripheral benefits that this group offers, such as discounts on a wide range of products and services, tax information, magazine subscriptions, legal advice, and credit cards—membership crosses demographic and political lines. As a result, its members do not vote as a bloc, which reduces its political power to some degree. In fact, in 2009, when AARP deviated from its nonpartisan position to endorse President Obama's health care reform plan, thousands of AARP members cancelled their memberships in protest.[30] However, in general, politicians throughout the country realize the danger in taking positions contrary to policies supported by this powerful organization.

Federal Open Market Committee (FOMC)

The policymaking arm of the Federal Reserve Board of Governors.

reserve ratios

Minimum percentage of deposits that a financial institution must keep on hand.

federal funds rate

The interest rate that banks charge each other for overnight loans.

open-market operations

The buying and selling of securities by the Federal Reserve Board to manipulate the money supply.

subject to approval by the Board of Governors. Although the presidents' terms are 5 years, most are reappointed. This further shields the Fed from political pressure.

The **Federal Open Market Committee (FOMC)**, the Fed's policymaking arm, consists of the seven governors, the president of the New York Federal Reserve Board (who has a permanent seat), and four of the remaining 11 regional presidents, who serve on a rotating basis. The other seven presidents offer input.

Maximizing GDP and employment while minimizing inflation, which has been compared to walking a tightrope while carrying a chainsaw, has been a formal part of the Fed's job description since 1977. When GDP is high and employment is full, the risk of inflation is always present. A tight job market can drive up wages (which sounds good), but that can drive up prices (which is bad). Over the long term, inflation will undercut employment. A stagnant or declining GDP, mounting unemployment, or rapid inflation, whether they occur simultaneously or separately, will all trigger domestic and international demands that the Fed "do something."

The FOMC has five main tools to manipulate monetary policy. The first is **reserve ratios**—the amount of cash that the Fed requires member banks to keep on hand in order to insure against a run on deposits. (Such runs last occurred, on a major scale, during the Great Depression.) By raising the reserve ratio—in effect, lowering the amount of money that banks can loan out—the Fed can reduce the money supply. This is not a particularly effective Fed instrument, however, because most banks keep more cash than they are required to.

The second tool is the **federal funds rate**—a market-driven interest rate that banks charge one another for short-term (often overnight) loans. Rates drop when there is excess money in the system; they rise when available loan money is restricted. In fact, interest rates are essentially the "price" of money. Like any other commodity, its price goes up when there is more demand than supply, and its price drops when there is more supply than demand. Because the funds rate is market-driven—member banks negotiate interest rates, with each participant looking for the best deal possible—the Fed has no direct control over this rate. It does, however, greatly influence this rate through the third tool, its **open-market operations**, by which it manipulates the total amount of money available in the market.

Most open-market operations today are carried out electronically, but consider the following simple example. Picture a huge safe with a divider down the middle. On the left side are piles of money. On the right side are piles of treasury bills (T-bills) and savings bonds—the federal government's IOUs. This hypothetical safe belongs to the Fed. Now, suppose that the Fed wants the federal funds rate to rise. Because the Fed cannot set this rate directly, it needs to make money scarcer so that interest rates rise. It takes some of its T-bills and savings bonds from the right side of the safe and sells them on the open market. It takes the cash that it receives from these sales and puts it in the left side of the safe, thus removing those funds from the circulating money supply. With less money available, the federal funds rate will rise. Higher interest rates will put the brakes on the economic engine. Because the member banks immediately pass higher rates on to their customers, businesses and consumers are less likely to borrow, which slows business expansion and spending. If, by contrast, the Fed wants the federal funds rate to fall, it takes money from the left side of the safe and puts it into circulation to buy securities from the open market, thus increasing the supply (and lowering the price) of money.

The fourth way that the Fed can intervene is though the **discount rate**—the interest rate that the Fed charges its member banks for loans. The discount rate is generally about 0.1 percent above the federal funds rate. Although the discount rate does not directly set the **prime rate**—the rate that banks charge their best customers—there is significant correlation between the two.

Finally, the Fed, using the fifth tool, can buy and sell foreign currencies in an effort to stabilize world financial markets and currency exchange rates. Although this instrument is generally not used to affect the U.S. money supply, it is sometimes used to adjust the value of the dollar relative to other currencies.

The most significant of these tools are open-market operations and the discount rate. True monetarists favor creating a target money supply and manipulating policy to achieve that goal. Other economists, with less strictly monetarist views, choose different targets to keep inflation under control.

The Fed in Action

When Paul Volcker was appointed chairman of the Board of Governors in 1979, the economy was teetering on the edge of disaster. Skyrocketing energy prices, declining productivity, huge budget deficits, and a malignant condition that the media dubbed **stagflation** (the combination of a stagnant GDP, rising unemployment, and rapid inflation) had thrown the U.S. economy into its worst shape since the Great Depression. Volcker had to make a hard decision. If the Fed cut the money supply, interest rates would rise. That made sense. Less of a commodity drives up the price. But if the money supply went up, interest rates would rise as well. That seemed to violate the rule of supply and demand, but there was another culprit here: inflationary expectations. Inflation erodes the value of money. One dollar today will purchase more than one dollar will buy five years from now, because prices will have increased. Banks and other lending institutions figured out where they thought inflation was headed and only lent at rates high enough to compensate for the devaluing effects of the expected inflation. That particular set of circumstances also violated the **Phillips curve**—an economic model that assumes an inverse relationship between unemployment and inflation.

By tightening the money supply, Volcker's Fed could hold down inflation, but according to the Phillips curve, this would drive up unemployment. Advocates of the Phillips curve argued that a certain level of inflation was acceptable as long as employment was maximized, but surprisingly, both inflation and unemployment shot up in the 1970s. For some economists, the validity of Keynesian macroeconomics—the pillar of post–World War II economic policy—was in doubt. Heading into the 1976

discount rate
The rate the Fed charges member banks for short-term loans.

prime rate
The interest rate that a bank charges its best customers.

stagflation
The combination of stagnant GDP, rising unemployment, and rapid inflation.

Phillips curve
An economic model that assumes an inverse relationship between unemployment and inflation.

presidential elections, Democrats coined the term "misery index" to denote the sum of the unemployment and inflation rates. This phrase would come back to haunt them in 1980.

From Volcker's perspective, the economy's problem was "loose money." The "accommodating" policy that the Fed pursued during the 1970s, along with generous federal spending on domestic and Cold War defense programs, had produced inflationary expectations. As banks forced interest rates up, unemployment rose. Volcker understood that the first order of business was to kill those inflationary expectations—"to wring inflation out of the economy," as it was said at the time. He put a stranglehold on the money supply.

Volcker knew that his prescription would be painful. Tight money drove up interest rates and unemployment, but it killed inflation. After inflation had been brought under control, in the early 1980s, Volcker allowed the money supply to expand, but not fast enough to reignite inflationary expectations. More money in circulation lowered its price, meaning that interest rates fell. With lower interest rates, unemployment rates began to ease. In 1983, President Ronald Reagan appointed Volcker to a second 4-year term as chairman, during which he continued to maintain a relatively tight money supply.

During Volcker's reign, the Fed focused on fighting inflation by controlling the actual amount of money in circulation. The problem with this approach is that money is hard to define—and even harder to measure. The narrowest definition of money is cash in circulation. A broader definition includes checking and savings accounts, and certificates of deposit, but even this broader definition is perhaps inadequate in a society where credit is relatively easy to obtain and people can spend money they do not actually have. That is one reason why Volcker's successor, Alan Greenspan (appointed in 1987), focused more on inflationary risk and interest rates—particularly the discount rate—and less on targeting a certain supply of money. Greenspan's successor, Ben Bernanke (appointed in 2006 and reappointed in 2010), struggled to hit a specific inflation target. His successor, Janet Yellen, appointed by Barack Obama in 2014, also pledged to keep inflation at an acceptable level.

One of the problems the Fed faces in enacting monetary policy is the significant lag time between Fed action and economic results. Efforts to slow the economy and control inflation—such as raising the discount rate—will not affect inflation and unemployment until months later, so the Fed has to be right twice: First, it needs to know where the economy is headed; second, after making the correct initial determination, it needs to conjure up the correct response to the circumstances that it believes are emerging. To make things even more difficult, it has to be right every time, or its actions can make things worse. (Many economists and economic historians blame the length and severity of the Great Depression, to a significant degree, on the Fed's bad policy choices.) Both the Fed and the Department of the Treasury are in a similar bind as they attempt to deal with the fallout of the financial crisis that froze credit markets and sent stocks on a wild up-and-down ride in the fall of 2008; any actions they take may not yield immediate results or may produce unintended consequences. In an effort to stem the financial crisis, the nation's central bank purchased mortgages, long-term Treasury bills, and the debt of mortgage financial giants Freddie Mac and Fannie Mae. Bernanke acknowledged that the Fed will, at some point, have to tighten its monetary policy by raising interest rates. Given the precarious nature of the economy, it is not clear when it will pursue policies that will tighten financial conditions.[31]

Janet Yellen, appointed to head the Federal Reserve by Barack Obama in 2014, is the first woman appointed to this important post.

■ *In what ways can the treasury secretary and chairman of the Federal Reserve work together to improve economic conditions in the United States?*

Monetary Policies Versus Fiscal Policies

Monetary and fiscal policies do not always work together. Fiscal actions, taken by politicians, tend to inflate the economy. Elected officials are continually trying to serve their constituents and get through the next election cycle; their goal is to keep the economy going until their jobs are secured. The monetary policies of the Fed, by contrast, are focused on long-term economic interests. Former Fed Chairman Greenspan often voiced concerns about rising budget deficits, and Congress, for its part, has often criticized the Fed for keeping too tight a rein on the money supply.

Many Americans believe that the Federal Reserve Bank is free from political pressure. Given that its mandate is to supervise monetary policy with a view to long-term economic stability, the Fed's actions should not take into account election cycles. Yet, it is obvious that fiscal deficits, which may be the result of political choice, are in part accommodated by looser monetary policy. Secretaries of Treasury have regularly consulted with the chair of the Fed in matters relating to macroeconomic management. Congress also schedules regular hearings for the chair, not only to hear about the state of the economy, but also to put political pressure on it to act in certain ways. Some members of Congress have occasionally gone so far as to threaten the Fed's independence.

As Ben Bernanke came up for confirmation for a second term in early 2010, Congress grilled him about monetary policy maneuvers. Senate Banking Committee Chair Chris Dodd faulted the Fed for lax regulations that contributed to the financial crisis, while Senate Majority Leader Harry Reid wanted to know Bernanke's position on whether the government should pressure banks to ease terms on mortgage loans.[32] In an op-ed published in the *Washington Post*, Bernanke warned that congressional measures to curb the Fed's bank regulatory power or any attempts to audit its monetary policy deliberations would undermine the bank's autonomy and ability to promote financial stability.[33] Clearly, the Fed's autonomy from political interference is not absolute.

When push comes to shove, though, the Fed has more weapons in its arsenal than Congress. By tightening the money supply sufficiently, it can significantly reduce the inflationary aspects of tax cuts or increased government spending. A concerted effort by the Fed could even put pressure on Congress to bring the debt problem under control. By tightening the money supply and driving up interest rates, the Fed could make deficit financing so expensive that it becomes a big issue sooner rather than later. During recessions, as we have seen recently, both Congress and the Fed have allowed for expansionary fiscal and monetary policies.

Conclusion

Now that you have learned more about public policy and the particular role that economics and fiscal concerns play in this area of American government, let's go back to our original discussion of health care reform. It is almost impossible to talk about the social policies of providing health care to the nation's citizens without a thorough understanding of the economics and financial considerations that are involved in such an endeavor. When Congressional Democrats and Republicans were unable to pass a budget for a few weeks in the fall of 2013, their disagreement was as much about reconstructing fiscal policy in the United States as it was about addressing the health care needs of millions of Americans. Fiscal policy and social policy are inextricably linked.

Comprehensive policy change, like that being considered for Medicaid and health care generally, is unusual in the United States for a number of reasons. Our fragmented branches of government, the existence of political parties, the power of interest groups and social movements that are often in competition with one another— these are a few of the main factors that fulfill what James Madison sought in his plan for the Constitution. No single interest or faction, even one comprising a majority of the population, can easily take control of such a system and use it to its own advantage. No one disputes the influence of so-called special interests, but congressional policymaking is often a reflection of an increasing diversity of interests in our nation of over 300 million people.

For many if not most policy issues, there is no one public good but rather a wide range of solutions for the many different people in a single congressional district or state. Even when there is widespread concern about a major aspect of society, as with health care, agreement on the best solution may be difficult to achieve. Of course agreement on public policy is even more challenging given the economic realities of government. The underpinnings of our democracy both shape and are shaped by the making and implementation of economic policy. Who gets what, when, and how are questions we have asked before in this book because they speak to the essential characteristic of our democracy. The choices made by policymakers about financial and monetary matters clearly reflect the value choices that form the answers to these questions.

Even among each party's politicians, there is sometimes considerable disagreement over healthcare policy. Many Congressional Republicans, like Paul Ryan, want to repeal Obamacare entirely and then replace it with other reforms. In contrast, President-elect Trump may favor only a partial repeal of the Affordable Care Act. Within the Democratic Party, politicians are split between wanting to fix the less effective aspects of Obamacare while supporting the Act overall and replacing it with a more government-centered healthcare system.

CONFRONTING POLITICS AND POLICY

No one has to tell you about the high cost of higher education in the United States—you see it every time a tuition bill appears in your mail. Your experiences confirm the hard numbers that show the cost of college increasing at rates much higher than the overall rate of inflation. During the 2015 and 2016 academic year, the price for studying and living on campus at the average public university for in-state students was $24,061. That is a 12.1% increase since 2012. The cost of living and studying at one of the nation's private colleges was $47,831 in annual expenses in 2015–2016.[34] That is a 13.2% increase since 2012. For comparison, the overall increase in inflation between 2011 and 2016 was only about 7%. While there are many factors that contribute to inflation, the role of government policies in these rising price tags is significant. With state budgets facing large deficits, policymakers have made major cuts to public higher education budgets in recent years. According to the American Academy of Arts & Sciences, between 2008 and 2013, states reduced spending on the median public institution by about 20%.[35]

And at the national level, former House Budget Committee Chairman (now Speaker of the House) Paul Ryan released a budget proposal that included a number of reductions to the size and availability of federal grants for higher education.[36] With public financial support for higher education waning and tuition skyrocketing many are now questioning the accessibility of a college degree for America's young people. What must happen for the government to invest more financial resources in higher education, and what role can students themselves have in making those policy changes occur?

ACTION STEPS

1. Imagine that you have been appointed by your college to travel to your state capital to lobby the governor and state legislators to increase the level of appropriations for colleges and financial aid for students. What kind of strategies would you use to get the attention of the policymakers in your state? Once you have their attention, what types of arguments can you make why higher education is a good investment of public financial resources? Finally, how can you convince them that higher education is more important than other areas of public policy such as transportation, criminal justice, and health care?

2. Why do you think policymakers at both the national and state levels have targeted higher education for spending cuts? Would members of the public be willing to pay higher taxes if they were assured that the money would be used to decrease the cost of higher education? Does government have a responsibility to assist students with paying the costs of their higher education?

> REVIEW THE CHAPTER

Making Public Policy

14.1 Identify the major elements of the policymaking process. (p. 477)

The types of public policies formed within a democracy, and specifically the form used in the United States, is greatly influenced by the process that is used to develop policy. From getting attention of government officials to recognize the need for a policy to the eventual implementation of the policy itself, key characteristics of the process can shape the types of policies that are produced by government. Thus if we are to think of public policies as the output on the right side of the equation we need to understand everything on the left side of the equation that can be categorized as elements of the policymaking process.

Types of Public Policy

14.2 Compare and contrast the three main types of public policies. (p. 488)

Public policies can be categorized by issue area (such as the environment, education, and agriculture) or by the functions of government necessary to carry out the policy. The three basic types of policy based on the functions of government are distribution, regulation, and redistribution. It is also possible to categorize policy outputs as either tangible or symbolic.

Measuring Economic Performance

14.3 Describe the major ways that the health of the economy is measured. (p. 490)

The relationship between government and the economy is multifaceted. The United States government utilizes many policy tools to effect changes upon the condition of the nation's economy. Those conditions are measured through a number of variables related to economic performance and the financial standing of the government itself. Among the most important measures of the health of the U.S. economy are inflation, employment, gross domestic product, the budget deficit or surplus, and the balance of trade.

The Key Players in the Development of Economic Policy

14.4 Describe the key actors responsible for creating fiscal policy. (p. 493)

Fiscal policy encompasses the taxing and spending decisions made by the government. The Congressional Budget Office is an important source of budgetary analysis and planning. Congress and its relevant committees shape the budget. The congressional committees make changes to the president's budgetary proposal crafted by the Office of Management and Budget.

Revenue

14.5 Identify the major sources of U.S. government revenue. (p. 494)

The largest source of revenue for the U.S. government is the income tax, the payroll tax is second, and corporate taxes are third. Taxation decisions affect both economic performance and the perception of equity. Under a progressive taxation system, higher-income people pay a larger percentage of their income in taxes. Under a regressive system, lower-income people pay a higher percentage of their income in taxes.

Expenditures

14.6 Identify the major forms of U.S. government expenditures. (p. 499)

The largest areas of expenditure for the United States are Social Security and defense, with income security being the third largest. Because of debt and long-term commitments for Social Security, medical care, and defense expenditures, the United States faces significant budgetary challenges in the future.

Monetary Policy

14.7 Identify the major instruments of monetary policy. (p. 505)

Monetary policy involves managing the nation's money supply in order to stabilize inflation, interest rates, and employment. The Federal Reserve Board's Federal Open Market Committee (FOMC) has primary responsibility for setting monetary policy. The primary instruments of the FOMC are the discount rate and open-market operations. The Fed uses the FOMC to regulate money supply through the buying and selling of Treasury bills. It also uses the discount rate—a rate it charges commercial banks for borrowing its funds—to control the money supply. Selling Treasury bills and raising the discount rate reduces the money supply in the economy; buying Treasury bills and lowering the discount rate has the opposite effect.

⟩ LEARN THE TERMS

focusing events, p. 481
trigger mechanism, p. 481
issue-attention cycle, p. 482
discretion, p. 485
policy categories, p. 488
distribution, p. 488
regulation, p. 488
redistribution, p. 488
inflation, p. 490
Consumer Price Index (CPI), p. 490
deflation, p. 490
unemployment rate, p. 490
gross domestic product (GDP),
 p. 491
balance of trade, p. 491
budget deficit, p. 491

budget surplus, p. 492
national debt, p. 492
fiscal policy, p. 493
Congressional Budget Office (CBO),
 p. 493
Office of Management and Budget
 (OMB), p. 493
Council of Economic Advisers
 (CEA), p. 493
payroll tax, p. 494
progressive tax, p. 494
regressive tax, p. 494
marginal tax bracket, p. 495
Laffer curve, p. 497
Social Security Trust Fund, p. 499
income security, p. 502

Medicare, p. 502
Medicaid, p. 503
entitlements, p. 504
monetary policy, p. 505
Federal Reserve System (the Fed),
 p. 505
Federal Open Market Committee
 (FOMC), p. 506
reserve ratios, p. 506
federal funds rate, p. 506
open-market operations, p. 506
discount rate, p. 507
prime rate, p. 507
stagflation, p. 507
Phillips curve, p. 507

⟩ EXPLORE FURTHER

In the Library

Béland, Daniel, and Alex Waddan. *The Politics of Policy Change*, Washington, D.C.: Georgetown University Press, 2012.

Derthick, Martha A. *Up in Smoke*. Washington, D.C.: CQ Press, 2002.

Friedman, Thomas L. *The Lexus and the Olive Tree: Understanding Globalization*. New York: Farrar, Straus and Giroux, 2000.

Greenspan, Alan. *The Age of Turbulence: Adventures in a New World*. New York: Penguin Books, 2007.

Greider, William. *Secrets of the Temple: How the Federal Reserve Runs the Country*. New York: Touchstone, 1987.

Hudson, William. *The Libertarian Illusion: Ideology, Public Policy and the Assault on the Common Good*. Washington, D.C.: CQ Press, 2007.

Kahn, Alfred E. *Lessons from Deregulation: Telecommunications and Airlines After the Crunch*. Washington, D.C.: Brookings Institution Press, 2004.

Kingdon, John W. *Agendas, Alternatives, and Public Policies*. New York: Harper and Row, 1984.

Lindblom, Charles E., and Edward J. Woodhouse. *The Policy-Making Process*, 3rd ed. Englewood Cliffs, NJ: PrenticeHall, 1993.

Menard, Claude, and Michel Ghertman, eds. *Regulation, Deregulation and Reregulation: Institutional Perspectives*. Northampton, MA: Edward Elgar Press, 2009.

Schick, Allen. *The Federal Budget: Politics, Policy, Process*, 3rd ed. Washington, D.C.: Brookings Institution, 2007.

Skidelsky, Robert. *Keynes: The Return of the Master*. New York: Penguin Books, 2009.

Spitzer, Robert J. *The Politics of Gun Control*. Washington, D.C.: CQ Press, 2004.

Stiglitz, Joseph. *Globalization and Its Discontents*. New York: W.W. Norton, 2003.

Stone, Deborah. *Policy Paradox: The Art of Political Decision Making*. New York: Norton, 1997.

Theodoulou, Stella Z., and Chris Kofinis. *The Art of the Game: Understanding American Public Policy Making*. Belmont, CA: Wadsworth, 2004.

Wessel, David. *Red Ink: Inside the High Stakes Politics of the Federal Budget*. New York: Crown Business, 2012.

Woodward, Bob. *Maestro: Greenspan's Fed and the American Boom*. New York: Simon and Schuster, 2000.

Zietlow, Rebecca. *Enforcing Equality: Congress, the Constitution, and the Protection of Individual Rights*. New York: NYU Press, 2006.

On the Web

Learn about the roles of the departments and agencies of the federal government in formulating distributive, regulatory, and redistributive public policies: *http://www.firstgov.gov/Agencies/Federal/Executive.shtml*.

The House of Representatives is a policymaker with oversight functions. Find out what it is doing in both these areas: *http://www.house.gov*.

The Senate is also a policymaker with oversight functions: *http://www.senate.gov*.

Presidents are powerful policy players. To see what issues the president supports, go to *http://www.whitehouse.gov*.

Learn about the federal courts and their roles as policymakers: *http://www.firstgov.gov/Agencies/Federal/Judicial.shtml*.

Everyday Democracy offers ideas and tools for citizen involvement in public policy: *http://www.everyday-democracy.org/*.

The Occupational Health and Safety Administration (OHSA) is an agency of the U.S. Department of Labor. It is responsible for issuing and enforcing standards for workplace safety and health. For more information on the agency, please visit *http://www.osha.gov*.

The Environmental Protection Agency (EPA) is a federal agency charged with issuing and ensuring environmental standards. For more on EPA activities, please visit *http://www.epa.gov*.

The Food and Drug Administration (FDA) is an agency of the U.S. Department of Health and Human Services. It is responsible for promoting and protecting public health. It regulates and supervises standards in food and pharmaceutical industries, among others. For more information on the agency, please visit *http://www.fda.gov*.

Information on the Federal Reserve can be found at *http://www.federalreserve.gov/*.

See Progressive Policy Institute's link to fiscal and economic policy issues at *http://www.progressivepolicy.org/issues/*.

The Office of Management and Budget (OMB) is a cabinet-level office that prepares the president's budget. For information about the budget, please visit *http://www.whitehouse.gov/omb*.

The Congressional Budget Office (CBO) is the primary congressional agency that reviews the congressional budget. For a congressional analysis of the president's budget, please visit *http://www.cbo.gov*.

The United States General Accountability Office (GAO) is the "investigative arm of Congress" and is charged to help improve the performance and accountability of the U.S. federal-government in order to benefit the American people. For more information on GAO activities, please visit *http://www.gao.gov*.

The National Center for Policy Analysis (NCPA) is a nonpartisan think tank that researches and evaluates public policy areas such as health care, taxes, Social Security, welfare, criminal justice, and education and environmental regulation. For more information about NCPA activities, please visit *http://www.ncpa.org*.

Read about the Concord Coalition, a nonpartisan group lobbying for sound fiscal policy at *http://www.concord-coalition.org*.

FOREIGN AND NATIONAL SECURITY POLICY

Russian President Putin and Syrian Bashar al-Assad meet. Russian military intervention in Syria to support Assad was one of the most important international developments of 2015.

■ *What, if anything, should America do to counter Russia military expansionism in Eastern Europe and the Middle East?*

→ LEARNING OBJECTIVES

15.1 Compare and contrast four different approaches to American foreign policy.

15.2 Establish three links between American foreign and domestic policy.

15.3 Assess pathways for citizen participation in foreign policymaking.

15.4 Analyze how political institutions compete for influence in making foreign policy.

15.5 Outline the major foreign policy issues confronting the United States today.

During President Obama's second term, the United States faced an array of difficult foreign policy questions. Since the 2014 Congressional elections, the number of "hot spots" across the globe has grown. These issues ranged from Iran and North Korea's nuclear programs, the economic crisis in the Euro zone, the volatile political situation in Afghanistan and Iraq, and the region-destabilizing Syrian Civil War. Perhaps the greatest challenges, however, came from three states that sought to revise to international status quo. Russia, China, and **ISIS** (the Islamic State in Iraq and Syria, which will be discussed in more detail later in this chapter) all sought to assert more control over their own sphere of influence and weaken American global hegemony in various ways.

Under President Vladimir Putin's leadership, Russia has aggressively expanded its territory and influence and challenged American and European Union leadership in Eastern Europe and the Middle East. Putin has expanded the reach of Russia's armed forces with exercises across the world and near American territory, established new Russian military bases in Syria through an alliance with Syrian President Bashar al-Assad, and restored Russian influence over former Soviet Bloc states like Kazakhstan.

Effective Russian territory now includes South Ossetia, Crimea, and parts of Eastern Ukraine. The challenge to international stability from Putin is all the more remarkable because for many it was unexpected. In President Obama's first term, America attempted a widely published "Russian reset" of cooperation with Russia that many people thought would lead to better relations in the future. In fact, during the 2012 presidential election, Democrats and Republicans did not even agree over whether Russia was a political threat.

China has also sought to assert more international power, in ways that disrupt the international order or challenge American leadership. The Chinese government has been building manmade islands in the South China Sea, presumably to use as naval or air bases, in neutral territory or areas claimed by American allies like Japan. In addition, the Chinese government is widely suspected of using cyber warfare to weaken American electronic security systems.

Since 2014, a new state that exerts effective control over large areas of Iraq and Syria has aggressively invaded the Middle East. ISIS is currently attempting to conquer Iraq, challenging the American-backed government there, and is active in Libya and Afghanistan as well. ISIS also recruits and sponsors terrorists all over the world.

In the Syrian Civil War, ISIS is fighting against both other rebel groups and President Assad. The American military is currently conducting airstrikes and advising and assisting other rebel groups against ISIS. However, the United States also opposes the current Syrian government of President Assad and has insisted that he step down. Assad's leadership is supported by Russia and the Russian military. The Syrian Civil War has destabilized the entire surrounding region and has caused a refugee crisis in Europe. By 2016, the estimated death toll in the civil war was close to 500,000 people. Both the Assad government and ISIS have committed gross human rights violations.

The foreign policy challenges of Russia, China, and ISIS must all be dealt with by the Trump administration in 2017. President-elect Trump has signaled that he may work to find more common ground with Russia in American foreign policy, especially in cooperating to destroy ISIS. The Trump administration is expected to aggressively confront China on trade, which could include high tariffs on goods imported from China. Nevertheless, at least one major foreign policy problem that the United States faced during President Obama's second term may be solved: the issue of Iran's nuclear weapons program. Under the Joint Comprehensive Plan of Action (or JCPOA, discussed later in this chapter), Iran no longer appears to be developing the fissile material for a nuclear bomb.

ISIS

The Islamic State in Iraq and Syria. ISIS controls a wide swath of territory in Syria and Iraq, and is challenging both the Russian-backed Syrian government of Bashar al-Assad and the U.S.-backed Iraqi government.

Expectations regarding American leadership's support of pro-democracy voices are tempered by the realization that our policies are not always consistent with the aspirations of those that want to dismantle authoritarian regimes. In March 2012, for example, the U.S. Congress approved a $1.3 billion military aid package to Egypt despite that country's military not relinquishing power to a democratically elected government. U.S. human rights and civil society groups have also drawn attention to the problem of fragile and failed states. Beyond the humanitarian crisis brought about by these states' inability to deliver basic public goods to their populations, analysts are concerned about the security and strategic ramifications of weak governance in distant parts of the globe.

There is an added complication. As noted in Chapter 7, political scientist Aaron Wildavsky introduced the "two presidency" thesis (sometimes called the dual presidency model) in 1966. Wildavsky argued that presidents are often frustrated when it comes to domestic affairs, given the numerous actors and Congress's ability to check presidential initiatives. Instead, presidents are significantly better equipped to lead in foreign policy and defense matters. Not surprisingly, they will often turn to foreign policy later on in their tenure. This pattern may be true of Barack Obama, who in his second term concluded both a high-profile international Paris Agreement on climate change and the aforementioned JCPOA.

Competing Principles for American Foreign Policy

15.1 Compare and contrast four different approaches to American foreign policy.

Today, there are two major approaches to U.S. interaction with the rest of the world. Both perspectives view the United States as a leading power in world politics. They differ, however, on what the United States should try to accomplish from this position of strength. A group we'll call the "transformers" believes that the United States should try to transform the international system in a way that will not just protect American goals and values but allow them to prosper and become universally accepted. According to the second group, the "maintainers," the United States should consolidate its gains as the victor in the Cold War and not try to impose itself or its values on others. Within each perspective, we can identify two major competing camps, for a total of four different stances on American foreign policy (see Table 15.1). After describing the beliefs of these four groups, we will bring them into sharper focus by examining the position of each on the wars in Iraq and Afghanistan.

TABLE 15.1   Four Perspectives on Foreign Policy

Transformers: perspectives and beliefs	Maintainers: perspectives and beliefs
Neoconservatives	**Conservatives**
• The United States must enforce the rules on other countries (although not necessarily abide by them), because it is the sole unchallenged superpower. • Military power is the most important factor in foreign policy. • The United States must be able to act unilaterally, as its leaders see fit, in dealing with foreign policy problems; international organizations may come between the United States and its best interests. • Spreading democracy to other nations is in the best interests of the United States.	• The United States must be prepared to use military force. • Global interests may be different from U.S. interests. • Power is an important asset; it must be maintained and used carefully. • Power is more effective if it is viewed as legitimate.
Neoliberals	**Isolationists**
• Spreading democracy is in the American national interest. • Nonmilitary means are preferred over military action. • Support from international organizations and agreements can be important to future endeavors.	• Military power should be used as a shield to protect U.S. interests. • The United States is minimally accountable to its allies and the international community. • Foreign policy should consist mostly of cultural, commercial, and diplomatic interactions.

Transformers

Both the neoconservative and neoliberal transformers are optimists. They view the United States as being in an unchallenged position to bring about fundamental changes in other states that will protect American goals and values and allow them to prosper and become universally accepted.

NEOCONSERVATIVES   The **neoconservatives** are a group that occupied prominent foreign policy positions in both Bush administrations.[1] Four common themes tend to unite neoconservatives in their views on American foreign policy. First, because the United States is the sole remaining superpower, it plays a fundamentally different role in world politics than other countries do. This means that the United States is in a position to force others to follow rules of proper behavior, but it does not have to abide by those rules itself. Second, the ever-present military power of the United States is the central instrument of American foreign policy, and the United States should not be apologetic or timid about using it. Third, neoconservatives believe that unilateralism is the proper approach for dealing with foreign policy problems. Instead of helping the United States achieve its goals, alliances such as the **North Atlantic Treaty Organization (NATO)** and international institutions such as the United Nations more often than not place roadblocks in its way. Rather than be hamstrung by these bodies, neoconservatives insist that America must always be free to act in response to the wishes of American leaders. Fourth, neoconservatives believe that it is in the American national interest to spread democracy around the world. They would be at odds with President Obama's reduction in the American presence and number of troops in Iraq and Afghanistan since 2009.

NEOLIBERALS   While neoconservative transformers think about world politics in terms of conflict and struggle, with few opportunities for cooperation, **neoliberals** see in much of the world the potential for shared identity and cooperation.[2] Neoliberals do not presume that nations automatically share interests or that cooperation can be easily generated. They do, however, value international institutions and regimes as a way to manage and coordinate expectations among nations and other international actors. Neoliberals fear that neoconservative principles will provoke a global backlash that will increase American insecurity and lead to a world less supportive of American values. Democratic presidential candidate and former Secretary of State Hillary Clinton demonstrates many of the characteristics of a neoliberal.

Neoliberal transformers share three common objectives. Similar to neoconservatives, neoliberals seek to spread democracy to further American national interests. However, whereas neoconservatives stress the ability of the United States to come into a society and build democracy, neoliberals maintain that democracy is best built from within, by local political forces. Second, neoliberals tend to stress nonmilitary means for achieving foreign policy ends. They favor foreign aid and economic assistance programs, especially when the aid is made dependent on conditions such as respect for human rights. Neoliberals do not reject the use of military force outright, however. Third, in contrast to the neoconservative embrace of unilateralism, neoliberals stress the importance of international institutions and agreements as ways of accomplishing foreign policy objectives.

Maintainers

Whereas both the neoconservative and neoliberal transformers are optimists, the conservative and isolationist maintainers are pessimists. Maintainers see the international system as a threat to American interests.

CONSERVATIVES   Conservatives believe that an effective American foreign policy must be built around four themes. First is the realization that to protect its

neoconservatives
People who believe that the United States has a special role to play in world politics; they advocate the unilateral use of force and the pursuit of a value-based foreign policy.

North Atlantic Treaty Organization (NATO)
A military alliance set up by the United States and its Western European allies initially for the purpose of containing the expansion of the former Soviet Union.

neoliberals
People who believe that cooperation is possible through the creation and management of international institutions, organizations, and regimes.

interests, the United States must be prepared to act militarily. Diplomacy and economic aid are no substitutes for military power. Second, American national interests are limited and not identical to global interests. When the two are in conflict, national interests must always take precedence. Global crusades, whether to build democracy or defeat terrorism, are dangerous, because they divert the United States from real and more immediate dangers. Third, power—especially military power, as the key measure that countries use to compare one another—must be refreshed constantly and used carefully. It is better to take action through alliances and coalitions than it is to act alone so that the costs and risks of military action can be shared. Fourth, the exercise of American power is most effective when others view it as legitimate.[3]

ISOLATIONISTS Isolationist maintainers have little doubt about the importance of military power and the need to defend American national interests. Where they part company from the conservative maintainers is in the number and range of events abroad that call for military action by America. For isolationists, the major threats to U.S. security come from an overactive foreign policy and responses that threaten to undermine core American values.[4] Three themes guide isolationist foreign policy thinking. First, American foreign policy must concentrate on protecting American lives and property, the territory of the United States, and the integrity of the American political system. To do so, American military power must become less a lance to strike out at others and more a shield to defend our homeland. Second, American responsibility to allies and the international community is minimal. Other countries must learn to become responsible for their own defense. Third, the proper way for the United States to be active in the world is through cultural, commercial, and diplomatic interactions. Foreign aid should be reduced and American troops brought home.

Conflicting Evaluations of the Wars in Iraq and Afghanistan

On March 19, 2003, following much public debate in the United States, political maneuvering at the United Nations, and the presentation of a 48-hour ultimatum to Iraq's dictator, Saddam Hussein, the Iraq War began. President George W. Bush had branded Iraq part of an "axis of evil," along with North Korea and Iran, in his 2002 State of the Union address. The Bush administration argued that Iraq's possession of **weapons of mass destruction** required preemptive military action on the part of the United States. (That claim was later recognized as incorrect.) The military operation was a spectacular success. On April 9, Baghdad fell, and on May 1, President Bush declared an end to major combat operations. By December 2003, Saddam Hussein was captured.

The early success in Iraq followed similar successes in Afghanistan. In the aftermath of the 2001 terrorist attacks in the United States, a coalition of nations used military force to bring down the Taliban-led government in Afghanistan and replaced it with a democratically elected government led by Hamid Karzai. The early military actions in Afghanistan included relatively few casualties among coalition forces, and there was a general sense that the situation in that nation was under control. However the early appraisals of success in Iraq and Afghanistan would prove to be premature and overly optimistic.

In Iraq violent opposition continued throughout the region, however, and the American occupation of Iraq proved far more difficult than expected. In July 2003, deaths among U.S. combat forces in Iraq reached the level of the 1991 Persian Gulf War. By April 2012, there had been about 4,500 deaths of U.S. combat forces in Iraq. The Iraqi body count had surpassed 100,000.[5]

weapons of mass destruction
Weapons capable of inflicting widespread devastation on civilian populations.

Political and economic setbacks, unforeseen by the war's planners, were numerous. Iraq's oil production was slow to recover, and U.S. funds aimed at economic recovery had to be diverted to improve security. Amid seemingly endless sectarian and ethnic strife, Iraqi political leaders repeatedly failed to meet reestablished deadlines to lay the foundation for a new democratic political order. By December 2011, U.S. troops were pulled out of Iraq. Serious questions, however, remain about Iraq's transition toward democracy, as the post-Saddam rulers continue to deal with sectarian violence and intra-elite political squabbles amidst challenges posed by economic turmoil and weak governance. Within days of U.S. troop withdrawal, Sunni prime minister Nouri-al-Maliki's government issued an arrest warrant against Shia vice president Tareq al-Hashemi, leading the influential Al-Iraqiya list to boycott parliament and leave cabinet positions. Although members of the bloc returned to parliament in January 2012, the fragility of Iraq's governing coalition remains a cause for concern. In addition to the existential threat of ISIS, the current Iraqi government faces a political threat from its people, who widely view it as corrupt and incompetent, and the economic threat of relatively low oil prices. In April of 2016, hundreds of protesters invaded the Iraqi Parliament to demand change.[6]

The early successes in Afghanistan were replaced with deteriorating security conditions and a resurgence of the Taliban in many regions of the nation. After becoming president in 2009, Barack Obama decided to increase American troop levels to combat the resurgent Taliban, in a manner similar to the strategy used earlier in Iraq. The Afghanistan troop surge had some success, and Americans received a morale boost when Navy SEALS killed Osama Bin Laden in May of 2011. The U.S. and Afghanistan signed a Strategic Partnership Agreement one year later. President Obama began to decrease American military presence in Afghanistan in 2012, and the reduction of forces continued until December of 2014, when official American and NATO combat operations ceased.

The U.S. did not leave Afghanistan entirely, however. About 10,000 American military personal have remained since 2014. While most of the continuing fight against the Taliban and new battle against ISIS in Afghanistan is conducted by

In late 2011 the last American combat troops leave Iraq after nearly 9 years of service in that country. During those 9 years over 4,400 Americans died in Iraq, with almost 32,000 injured while stationed in that war-torn nation. During the years that American troops served in Iraq, public opinion in the United States regarding the war increasingly favored bringing the troops home and ending the war.

■ *What role should public opinion play in the decisions that the president and Congress make regarding use of military personnel in foreign countries?*

Afghan troops, the remaining U.S. soldiers assist in support, protection, and counterterrorism operations. Analysts are uncertain about what the Trump administration plans to do in Afghanistan, other than continue the American commitment to destroy ISIS there.

We'll now evaluate the Iraq and Afghanistan conflicts from the four foreign policy perspectives we have introduced. We will consider the judgments of each camp in turn, beginning with the neoconservatives, who dominated the Bush administration's decision-making.

NEOCONSERVATIVE EVALUATION Neoconservatives view the wars in Iraq and Afghanistan as essential to the future security of the United States. The Taliban harbored terrorists in Afghanistan and therefore posed a direct threat to Americans. Removing Saddam Hussein from power was necessary, even if he did not have weapons of mass destruction, because his was a dangerous and aggressive government that once had these weapons and, if permitted, would obtain them again. Removing him from power was also necessary in order to build democracy in Iraq and set the stage for the democratization of the Middle East. In the neoconservative view, the United States cannot leave Iraq until democracy and economic recovery are assured, just as they were in post–World War II West Germany and Japan.

NEOLIBERAL EVALUATION Neoliberals shed no tears over the downfall of the Taliban and Saddam Hussein, recognizing that both had abysmal records of human rights abuses, and in the case of Hussein a history of foreign incursions. Before the war, however, neoliberals had asserted that nonmilitary means, such as economic sanctions and UN-led weapons inspection were preferable lines of action for controlling or removing these regimes. They had also cautioned that occupying and reconstructing these nations would be difficult and that democracy could not be imposed from outside. Neoliberals also maintain that if the reconstruction in these nations is to succeed, the United Nations must play a larger role.

CONSERVATIVE EVALUATION Conservatives made some key distinctions between the wars in Iraq and Afghanistan. First, conservatives favored the broader and more engaged international alliance employed in Afghanistan to the more U.S.-centered approach used in Iraq. They believed that such cooperation would reduce the political and economic costs to the United States, both in the actual fighting of the war and during the subsequent occupation. Second, conservatives saw the Iraq War as having distracted the United States from pursuing the true enemy: Osama bin Laden and his terrorists. In their view, the Iraq War gave anti-American terrorism new life, as Iraq became a magnet for international terrorist groups. Related to this is the conservatives' concern that by acting unilaterally, the United States disrupted the balance of global politics, in the end leaving America less secure. It may be argued that President Obama was partial to this view on the Iraq war.

ISOLATIONIST EVALUATION Finally, the isolationists generally supported the war in Afghanistan because it was a direct response to the 9/11 terrorist attacks. They saw little value added in the Iraq War, and they regard attempts at building democracy in Iraq and the Middle East as a "fool's errand." Isolationists would prefer to focus on more rigorous efforts to promote homeland security.

Echoes from the Past

Americans have almost always disagreed about the proper ways to interact with the rest of the world. These diverging attitudes have long been shaped by specific historical circumstances, America's strategic interests, and the different foreign policy preferences of American leaders. During the American Revolution, Congress sent diplomats to Europe pleading for crucial military and financial help to defeat the British. Upon leaving office in 1796, President George Washington recommended a foreign policy of isolation and noninvolvement. Succeeding presidents generally kept engagement with other countries close to home in the Western Hemisphere.

Only on the eve of the twentieth century, with the Spanish-American War (1898), did the United States become a major player on the world stage. By defeating Spain, the United States acquired an overseas territory, the Philippines. Under the first twentieth-century presidents—Theodore Roosevelt, William Howard Taft, and Woodrow Wilson—the United States carved out a sphere of influence in Mexico, Central America, and the Caribbean. In 1917, Wilson took the United States into World War I, and American forces contributed significantly to defeating Germany in 1918. Wilson took an active role in negotiating the peace treaty (the Treaty of Versailles) and in creating the League of Nations. But the Senate rejected joining the League of Nations, and American foreign policy in the 1920s was largely confined to bolstering U.S. influence in Latin America. During the 1930s, the United States gave little support to the democratic nations of Britain and France after Adolf Hitler came to power in Germany.

Japan's attack on Pearl Harbor on December 7, 1941, changed forever how Americans saw the outside world. The "Fortress America" strategy of relying on the protection of the oceans no longer seemed realistic. The nation mobilized its military might and achieved victory in Europe and Asia. With World War II over and the onset of the Cold War, the United States had no choice but to play a major and sustained role in world affairs. The United States helped create the United Nations; international economic organizations, such as the World Bank and the International Monetary Fund; and alliances, such as NATO. The struggle against the Soviet Union and communism became global, especially after communist revolutionaries triumphed in China in 1949. The image of dominoes, standing precariously on edge and tumbling one after the other, was frequently invoked to represent this conflict. No country, in this metaphor, could be allowed to fall to communism, because that would set off a chain reaction in which one country after another would "go communist." The end of the Cold War did not bring the peace dividend many had hoped for.

The events of September 11, 2001, thrust America into a global "war on terror." Under President Bush's leadership, a multilateral coalition (a coalition made up of several nations) was formed to invade Afghanistan and remove the Taliban from power. NATO presence and European support remain in Afghanistan today, as the country struggles to find stability. With Iraq, however, President Bush and his neoconservative foreign policymakers found it hard to form a broad multilateral coalition. Eventually, the United States and Great Britain led a "coalition of the willing" that bypassed the UN, to invade Iraq and enforce regime change. Powerful countries like France, Germany, and Russia opposed the invasion of Iraq. The legitimacy of the invasion was called into question from the beginning, and the continued sectarian violence and lack of real stability further alienated the broader global community.

As previously mentioned, President Obama's decision to withdraw troops from Iraq was followed by the announcement of a timeline to withdraw troops from Afghanistan by 2014. After his December 2009 decision to send 30,000 more troops to Afghanistan, the total number of U.S. troops there increased to 100,000. In Afghanistan, U.S. troops work within the NATO command structure, rather than acting unilaterally. This fit with President Obama's neoliberal philosophy when it came to international relations. The United States worked through NATO in supporting anti-Gaddafi forces in the ouster of the Libyan leader. In his second term, with the support of several NATO allies (known as the Global Coalition to Counter the Islamic State of Iraq and the Levant), Barack Obama directed the U.S. military to conduct air strikes in Syria and deploy American soldiers to advise and assist Syrian rebels against ISIS in Operation Inherent Resolve.

Links Between Foreign and Domestic Policy

15.2 Establish three links between American foreign and domestic policy.

We commonly talk of American foreign policy and domestic policy as two separate realms, but the boundary separating domestic and foreign policy is not, and never has been, watertight. In this section, we will examine three different links between American foreign and domestic policy. First, American foreign policy is often based on ideas and values that guide domestic policy. Second, the U.S. political decision-making process is influenced by the presence and activity of a number of international factors, including lobbyists. Finally, and perhaps most important, U.S. foreign policy can affect the distribution of costs and benefits among different groups in the United States.

Domestic Policy Values Guide American Foreign Policy

Let's first consider the impact of domestic policy values on American foreign policy by looking at how the United States approaches human rights and environmental issues at the global level.[7] Three guiding principles lie at the heart of our country's human rights foreign policy. First, American policy, both domestic and foreign, emphasizes individual legal rights and civil liberties; it pays less attention to economic and social rights. Second, Washington usually regards hostile, overly strong governments as the primary threat to human rights; rarely does American policy see a need to strengthen foreign governments in order to promote human rights. Third, American foreign policy generally rejects violence as a means for promoting human rights. Attempts to advance workers' rights or civil rights through violence have never been received favorably in the United States; instead, we generally look to legal and electoral means of promoting rights. Because this historical experience is not shared by many other countries, American calls for rejecting violence as a means of change are often met with skepticism.

The influence of American domestic policy values on its foreign policy is also evident in U.S. environmental policy. By and large, international environmental proposals put forward by the United States have not imposed new costs on Americans; they have instead sought to persuade other countries to adopt American standards. For example, the United States was one of the strongest advocates of a 10-year ban on commercial whaling, an area in which the United States has few economic interests but many citizens who worry about the fate of the world's whale population. But the United States has also vigorously opposed efforts to establish an international register of toxic chemicals, and it has refused to ratify the 1997 **Kyoto Protocol** on reducing greenhouse gases—in both cases citing the costs to American firms and the threat to American living standards. Todd Stern, President Obama's chief climate change negotiator, stated in September 2011 that the United States felt that the Kyoto protocol would not be supported by major economies other than those in the E.U. once the protocol's provisions expired in 2012.[8]

In President Obama's first and second terms, the administration promised greater U.S. leadership on international environmental accords. When both America and China signed the international **Paris Agreement** in April 2016 and pledged to help hold global average temperatures down by reducing greenhouse gas emissions, many observers viewed it as a fulfilling of those promises.

International Factors Influence U.S. Political Activity

Foreign lobbying has become big business in Washington. Between 1998 and 2004, companies with headquarters in 78 foreign nations spent more than $620 million lobbying the U.S. government. These companies employed 550 lobbying firms and a total

Kyoto Protocol

An international agreement to address the problem of global warming. The United States was involved in its negotiation but has refused to ratify the agreement, citing excessive economic costs.

Paris Agreement

An international agreement signed by representatives of over 150 countries, and with the support of American President Barack Obama and Chinese President Xi Jinping. The signatories agreed to take efforts to reduce global warming by decreasing emissions of greenhouse gases like carbon dioxide.

President Obama and Chinese President Xi Jinping shake hands, symbolizing their shared interests in promoting the Paris Agreement.

■ *What are the challenges to pursuing international climate change agreements? How might these challenges affect American policy on climate change?*

of 3,800 lobbyists—more than 100 of them former members of Congress. Between July 2007 and December 2008, about 340 foreign interests representing governments, separatist groups, and for-profit corporations, spent about $87 million on lobbying efforts in the United States.[9] These lobbying groups are registered with the Department of Justice.

In 1990, with his capital city under attack by rebel forces, Liberian President Samuel Doe paid a Washington lobbyist $800,000 to improve his image and increase lukewarm U.S. support. (It didn't help—Doe was later overthrown and executed by the rebels.) In 2008, Liberia spent about $560,000 on U.S. lobbying efforts.[10] In 1990, former South African political prisoner Nelson Mandela traveled to Washington, in part to lobby Congress to keep economic sanctions in place against the white-supremacist government that ruled his country. And in 2003, Bob Livingstone, a former Republican representative from Louisiana and one-time chair of the House Appropriations Committee, helped Turkey defeat an attempt by the Republican-controlled Congress to take away $1 billion worth of foreign aid because of its failure to help the United States in the Iraq War. Countries like Pakistan, Indonesia, and Djibouti, despite their dubious human rights record, have received billions of dollars of additional military aid because of lobbying efforts in the post-9/11 period. Many of the funds have been disbursed without adequate congressional oversight.[11] Many foreign governments are deeply concerned about American foreign aid legislation and arms sales. To secure their objectives in these areas, they pursue a two-step lobbying campaign. First, they try to gain leverage by lobbying the executive branch, usually the White House, the State Department, and the Defense Department. Second, as already noted, they also lobby Congress.

The primary concern of foreign firms that operate in the United States is the ability of their affiliates to conduct business profitably and without hindrance. Between 1998 and 2004, for example, 22 foreign companies operating in the United States actively lobbied the Environmental Protection Agency over issues connected with the agency's Superfund cleanup policies. At the state and local levels, taxation, zoning, and education, as well as labor laws and policies, are all of considerable concern to foreign firms. In one well-known case, Sony threatened to stop planned construction of new plants in California and Florida unless those states repealed portions of their tax codes that would have taxed Sony on its worldwide sales rather than on its sales of items produced in that particular state. After both states changed their tax laws, Sony went ahead and built the new plants. In 2005, Toyota was planning the location of a new automotive plant, in either the United States or Canada. Although several U.S. states offered more lucrative tax packages, both the national government and several provincial governments in Canada offered money for worker training; in addition, the Canadian system of universal health care would allow Toyota to save on the cost of health care benefits. Canada ended up getting the plant.

The scale of foreign political activity in the United States has repeatedly raised two concerns. The first is that the more our representatives listen to foreign lobbyists, the less they will hear from the American public. The second is that foreign interests and American interests are not always compatible. By listening to and responding to foreign voices, policymakers may ignore or, worse, harm American national interests. This concern is reinforced by periodic revelations of foreign attempts at bribery and espionage, such as the foreign hacks of Office of Personnel Management data in 2015, which were strongly suspected of being backed by the Chinese government.

As an additional example, in 2002, it was revealed that Taiwan kept a secret $100 million fund to buy influence in this country. In 2005, two former employees of a pro-Israeli lobbying firm were indicted for disclosing U.S. defense information. The American Israel Public Affairs Committee (AIPAC) is an influential group that lobbies the United States government on behalf of Israel. Yet, it is not a foreign lobby, since it does not receive funds from Israel and hence does not need to register as an Israeli lobby. It has over 100,000 members who are mostly American Jews.[12] In 2007, two influential scholars—John Mearsheimer and Stephen Walt—published their controversial book *The Israel Lobby and U.S. Foreign Policy*. The authors argue that U.S foreign policy is held hostage to narrowly defined Israeli interests, often represented by the AIPAC. As expected, the book received scathing criticism from pro-Israel groups in the American political process. Not all foreign lobbies are acting on behalf of sovereign countries. On March 19–20, 2012, the International Campaign for a Free Tibet, along with a number of pro-Tibet groups, visited the U.S. Congress during the fourth annual Tibet Lobby Day, urging the U.S. government to put pressure on China to recognize Tibet's right to self-determination.[13] Former Pennsylvania Governor Ed Rendell was investigated by the Treasury for accepting funds to speak on behalf of the Iranian exile group Mujahideen-e Khalq, which is on the U.S. government's list of foreign terrorist organizations.[14]

globalization

The expansion of economic interactions between countries.

The ever-increasing pace of **globalization**—the expansion of economic interactions between countries—has added a third concern. Foreign governments and firms might not stop at seeking to influence American political decisions; they might also seek to influence American economic decisions in ways that harm the United States. In 2005, it was announced that CNOOC Ltd., a Chinese government–controlled oil company, was attempting to buy Unocal Corporation, the third-largest U.S. oil company. When the news broke, many American lawmakers raised economic and security issues and threatened to block the takeover. In their view, China was a major competitor with the United States for global influence and power. Faced with this opposition, CNOOC withdrew its $18.4 billion offer—clearing the way for Chevron, the second-largest American oil company, to acquire Unocal, even though its offer was $700 million less.

> POLL Some Americans see China as a threat to America. Others see it as one of our most important trading/economic partners. Which do you think it is? What evidence would you use to argue one way or the other?

In another example of the risks of globalization, a disastrous oil spill in the Gulf of Mexico in 2010 threw British Petroleum (BP), the foreign corporation responsible, under American public scrutiny and led to presidential and congressional criticism. Aside from questions about lack of adequate regulation in off-shore drilling, BP was targeted by politicians and the media for its poor risk-management and damage control strategies. This oil spill raised concerns that private foreign investment and investments by foreign countries in the U.S. economy undermine the sovereignty of the United States.

British demonstrators rally in favor of leaving the European Union (a decision known as Brexit) and in favor of remaining in the European Union. In June of 2016, the United Kingdom held a referendum on Brexit. The pro-Brexit side won with 52% of the vote.

■ *What is the nature of America's relationship with the United Kingdom? How is that different than our relationship with the European Union?*

As countries like China, Russia, and Middle Eastern petro-states create their sovereign wealth funds—country-owned funds that invest globally—questions of sovereignty and influence come to the forefront. Policymakers are concerned about the increased leverage of foreign countries in our domestic political process, as these states ramp up their investments in our economy. At the same time, we need to appreciate that U.S. firms are also investing globally, and many originating U.S. firms are now owned by international bodies of shareholders. As the volume of international trade and investments increases with globalization, Americans need to assess the international and domestic gains and losses from such activities.

International and Domestic Gains and Losses

As we consider the costs and benefits from international trade and investments, we must realize that citizens and governments of other countries are also engaged in their own respective cost-benefit assessments. For example, many developing countries will not enter into international trade agreements until the United States ends the practice of providing subsidies to its farmers. Developing countries believe such subsidies give U.S. farmers unfair advantages in international markets. But prospects for ending these subsidies—which today go mainly to agribusinesses and the wealthiest farmers—are small because of the power of agricultural lobbies in the U.S. Congress. The current farm bill subsidizes agriculture to the tune of $20 billion.[15] Talks sponsored by the World Trade Organization on trade liberalization have met with many obstacles due to the persistence of European Union and U.S. agricultural subsidies. Developing countries point to "hypocrisy" when the United States insists that they open their markets via deregulation, privatization, and trade liberalization.

Just as globalization of trade and investment has complex economic ramifications for Americans, foreign policy operations can also have economic spillover effects. The fact that we spend vast resources pursuing foreign policy objectives in Iraq and Afghanistan forces us to make sacrifices on the domestic front. As the cost of conducting an interventionist foreign policy increases, requiring that domestic programs be canceled, cut back, or delayed because of economic pressures, support for foreign policy decreases.[16]

The Democratic Party used to be the low-taxes party, going back to its days as an agrarian party based in the South and West. The GOP had always been more protectionist (meaning it believes in protecting domestic producers and workers from foreign competition) because protectionism appealed to manufacturers and (often) workers who feared "cheap foreign competition." Protectionism was widely—and rightly—blamed for intensifying the Great Depression, however, so in the post-World War II world, U.S. foreign policy favored trade liberalization and the expansion of American exports. Today, the Democrats are becoming increasingly protectionist to appeal to workers threatened with job loss and to environmentalists worried about the environmental impact of industrializing the developing world. And the Republicans have become the party of free trade, because they represent the interests of export-oriented American businesses and emphasize the benefits of international trade to American consumers. Economic downturns heighten concerns about protecting American jobs across the political spectrum. Right-wing and left-wing populists rally against outsourcing and "unfair" foreign economic competition. In 2016, both Democratic presidential candidate Hillary Clinton and Republican presidential candidate Donald Trump campaigned against international trade agreements which hurt American blue-collar workers.

Americans also weigh the cost of foreign policy by counting the number of battlefield deaths. This grim equation first contributed to the erosion of the American public's support of the Vietnam War—which ultimately cost the lives of more than 55,000 U.S. troops—in the late 1960s and early 1970s. The conventional wisdom is that the greater the number of American deaths in a foreign war, the less support Americans give to the president who is waging that war. To some extent, this happened to President George W. Bush. In 2006, as casualties mounted and Iraq showed little sign of ending its insurgency and establishing a viable government, Bush's standing in public opinion polls (overall job rating, handling of the war, and honesty) plummeted to record lows. A decline in presidential popularity does not appear to be automatic, however. Even as battlefield deaths mount, solidarity among political elites and a widely accepted military mission may keep a president's standing in the opinion polls high.[17] The U.S. experience in Vietnam, however, suggests that such public support cannot be maintained indefinitely in the absence of visible military success. While President Bush was able to win reelection in 2004, the increasing unpopularity of the Iraq War (coupled with other issues) is partly to blame for the Republican Party's loss of both houses of Congress in 2006 and the White House in 2008.

Public concerns about the benefits and costs of American foreign policy today run high in two areas: international trade policy and protection of civil liberties. In 2015, the Obama administration battled in the House of Representatives for passage of Trade Promotion Authority (TPA). TPA gave the president the power to submit certain kinds of international trade agreements to Congress under special rules that prevent amendments to the agreement and force an immediate yes-or-no vote on the agreement. TPA passed the House by a vote of 218-208 and gave President Obama TPA. Supporters argue that TPA is vital to the overall economic health of the U.S. economy in an era of globalization, because it makes it easier for the president to negotiate trade agreements with foreign countries and provide consumers with more choices at competitive prices. Some opponents argue that making it easier for trade agreements to pass Congress will lead to the loss of American jobs as firms move overseas to produce goods and then sell them in the American market. Other opponents argue that TPA gives too much power to the president.

The second area of public concern is how to safeguard civil liberties while fighting the war against terrorism. Particularly worrisome to some are provisions of the USA PATRIOT Act. The PATRIOT Act was passed after 9/11 and renewed in 2006 and 2011. It was renewed again, in part, in 2015 after briefly expiring. The provisions of the Act can give law enforcement officials access to an individual's private information without his or her knowledge. New federal laws also curtail the rights of foreigners who are detained on suspicion of being or aiding terrorists. Suspects can be detained for indefinite periods without being charged with a crime or having access to legal representation. Revelations that the Bush and Obama administrations, on their own authority, approved and conducted electronic eavesdropping inside the United States were equally controversial. However, while Congress did reauthorize much of the PATRIOT Act in the USA FREEDOM Act in 2015, it ended the NSA's (National Security Agency's) bulk collection of Americans' phone data.[18]

The Domestic Context of American Foreign Policymaking

15.3 Assess pathways for citizen participation in foreign policymaking.

Perhaps more than any other aspect of policy in the United States, the making and carrying out of foreign policy seems distant and remote to most Americans. It can be argued that Americans' reluctance to find pathways for expression of their views on American foreign policy, whether supportive or critical, is a major weakness. After all, successful foreign policy must combine a well-crafted response to international challenges and opportunities with public support. Others argue that the public should leave foreign policy to the experts. The question then becomes, who are the experts? The president and his advisers? Professional military and diplomatic officials? Congress? The seemingly knowledgeable journalists and academics who voice their support for or criticism of American foreign policy?

To answer these questions, we will examine public opinion, elections, interest group activity, and political protest in search of pathways for citizen participation in the making of American foreign policy. We will then turn to the national-level political institutions that deal with foreign policy.[19]

Keep in mind that some individuals are better positioned than others to influence public policy. They come from varied backgrounds, but what sets them apart is the knowledge they possess and, even more important, the access they have to policymakers. Some are former government officials now at a think tank or university. Others are major contributors to a political party or leaders in organizations on whose support political parties depend to win elections. Still others are opinion leaders who provide commentaries in the news.

Public Opinion

Public opinion provides a first pathway for most citizens to express their views about American foreign policy. Although they may claim not to be influenced by opinion polls in their decision-making, every president since Richard Nixon has employed pollsters to find out what the public thinks.

The influence of public opinion on American foreign policy can be seen in two ways. First, public opinion can serve as a source of public policy innovation, as when it pressured the Bush administration to create the Department of Homeland Security and the position of director of national intelligence after the 9/11 terrorist attacks. Alternatively, public opinion can restrain innovation or serve as a policymaking resource to preserve the status quo.

One of the major obstacles President Franklin D. Roosevelt faced in the 1930s, despite being well aware of the growing danger of Nazi Germany, was the American public's strongly isolationist mood. In fact, FDR's efforts to aid Great Britain and the Soviet Union in their resistance to German aggression in the years leading up to World War II were severely constrained by domestic isolationism; only the attack on Pearl Harbor removed this obstacle. American policymakers in the 1970s and 1980s worried about the so-called **Vietnam syndrome**, the belief that the public was no longer willing to support a prolonged military presence abroad that caused appreciable losses of American soldier's lives if it looked like it might become an unwinnable "quagmire."

Vietnam syndrome

The belief, attributed to the American experience in Vietnam, that the public will not support the use of military force if it results in significant American casualties.

Concern about the Vietnam syndrome compelled President Reagan to withdraw American forces from Lebanon in 1983 and President Clinton to beat a hasty retreat from Somalia 10 years later—in both cases, these actions were taken after it became apparent that American military casualties were rising.

Policymakers tend to regard public opinion as a resource to be mobilized in international conflicts. They want to show foreign leaders that the American public is united behind the president. This happens almost reflexively when crises erupt that are perceived as threatening American security or when American troops are sent into combat. This **"rally 'round the flag" effect** was very noticeable at the start of the Iraq War. President George W. Bush's rating in the polls jumped 13 points the moment the war began. He had experienced an even bigger leap—39 percentage points—right after the 9/11 attacks.

What conditions are necessary for policymakers to hear the public's voice? Research seems to confirm that at least 50 percent of the American public must be in agreement on a foreign policy issue before their opinion has any influence.[20] Public opinion is likely to be heard most clearly in the agenda-building and ratification stages of foreign policy decision-making. Between those two stages, the institutional forces in the executive branch and Congress are the focus of attention.

Elections

The winning candidate in modern presidential elections claims that the results provide a mandate for that candidate's program, and foreign policy is no exception. Do elections really serve as a pathway for influencing foreign policy decisions? The evidence is mixed at best. Both major-party candidates tend to be on the same side of the issue. In 1980, both incumbent President Jimmy Carter and challenger Ronald Reagan favored increasing U.S. military capabilities. In 2008, both presidential contenders Barack Obama and John McCain stood firm in their commitments to defeat terrorism, but they diverged when it came to the U.S. presence in Iraq. Obama committed to withdrawing from Iraq within a defined timeline, while McCain promised to remain in Iraq until the mission was completed. Often, presidential elections turn out to be less a debate over foreign policy and more a contest about whom the public trusts to achieve those goals. In the 2012 election between President Obama and Mitt Romney, foreign policy largely took a back seat to domestic economic concerns, but the two disagreed about the extent to which Vladimir Putin's Russia was a foreign policy threat. Trade and America's global commitments were major issues in the 2016 presidential election between Donald Trump and Hillary Clinton. Trump favored more tariffs and less free trade with countries like China and Mexico and less American commitment to international organizations like NATO. Clinton supported continuing strong American involvement in international organizations and less restrictions on trade than Trump. Both candidates were more opposed to free trade than Romney and Obama in the 2012 campaign.

Part of the problem is that the American public tends not to be well informed about foreign policy issues. In 1964, at the height of the Cold War, only 38 percent of Americans knew that the Soviet Union was not a member of NATO. In 1979, only 23 percent knew which two countries were participating in the **Strategic Arms Limitation Talks (SALT)** (it was the United States and the Soviet Union, who were negotiating limits on the size of their respective nuclear forces). In 1993, 43 percent of Americans could not identify the continent on which Somalia was located, where American peacekeeping forces were facing significant local opposition. And in 2003, an amazing 68 percent of Americans believed—incorrectly—that Iraq had played a major role in the 9/11 terrorist attacks. Some members of Congress believe that the low level of their constituents' information makes incumbents dangerously vulnerable. Challengers can win—and have won—elections by taking foreign policy and national defense votes out of context and misrepresenting them in a negative light.

There is one way in which presidential elections clearly have influenced American foreign policy. Foreign governments rarely try to do serious business

"rally 'round the flag" effect

The expectation that Americans will unite behind the nation's leaders in times of crisis.

Strategic Arms Limitation Talks (SALT)

Negotiations between the United States and Soviet Union during the Cold War that produced two major agreements on limiting the size of each country's nuclear forces.

FIGURE 15.1 How Americans' Knowledge Of Where Ukraine Is Affects Their View On Whether To Intervene There

American public opinion on foreign policy is sometimes uninformed, and this can affect what the public demands from the federal government. Many Americans do not know where Ukraine is located. This lack of knowledge is alarming, because Russian intervention in Ukraine has become an important concern of American foreign policy. Ukraine is located southwest of Russia and southeast of Poland, as the map below shows.

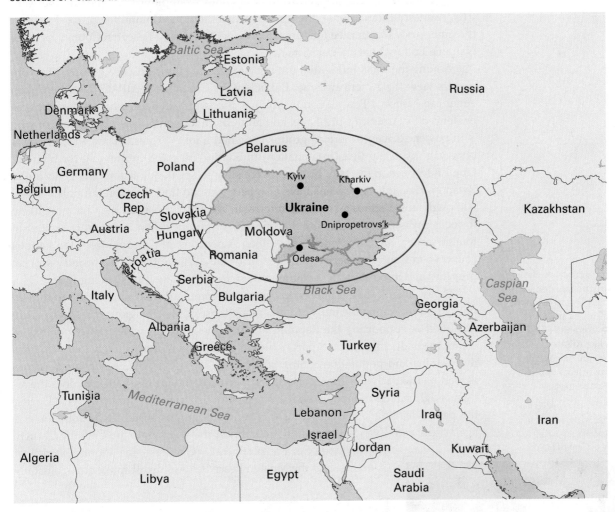

with the United States during presidential elections. Foreign policy measures initiated at that time have always run the risk of failure. During the Cold War, every political candidate dreaded being attacked as "soft on communism"; fear of that accusation was one factor that pulled Lyndon Johnson into the Vietnam War and kept him from cutting his losses. In anticipation of an upcoming election, a president often tries to tie up the loose ends of major foreign policy initiatives—such as trade agreements, treaties, and military activity—in order to keep them from becoming electoral issues.[21]

Similarly, in a post–9/11 era American presidents and their challengers in elections have had to demonstrate that they will be vigilant in protecting the nation from terrorist threats. This is particularly true for Democrats like John Kerry and Barack Obama, who were targeted in their campaigns for being too concerned about the legal rights of those accused of terrorist acts and therefore not as steadfast as they should be in protecting the safety of American citizens. In March 2011, President Obama reversed his 2-year-old order to re-allow military trials of detainees to resume at Guantanamo Bay. Critics stated that, in essence, he failed to fulfill his promise to close the camp.[22] Obama did ask Congress to close Guantanamo in 2016. However, President-elect Donald Trump pledged to keep Guantanamo Bay open. He also promised to reinstate many enhanced interrogation techniques used by the Bush administration to fight against terrorism.

Interest Groups

The third avenue down which the public can travel to express its outlook on foreign policy issues is interest group activity. A wide variety of groups use this pathway to influence American foreign policy. A representative list of interest groups active in trying to influence U.S. policy toward China, for example, would include the AFL-CIO, Amnesty International, the Christian Coalition, the Committee of 100 for Tibet, the Emergency Committee for American Trade, the Family Research Council, and the National Endowment for Democracy.

Among the most influential interest groups are ethnic-identity groups. Most observers view the American Israel Public Affairs Committee (AIPAC) and the Cuban American National Foundation (CANF) as the two most successful such groups, as evidenced by America's pro-Israel and anti-Castro foreign policies, regardless of who is in power. African American groups have had a mixed record. They were active in opposing apartheid (legal segregation) in South Africa and in pressing for humanitarian intervention in Haiti, but they were slow to speak out against the genocide in Rwanda. Hispanic Americans have also been slow to find their foreign policy voice. Although most Latinos take a deep interest in immigration issues, they are more likely to focus on issues related to their countries of origin. When it comes to American foreign policy, Mexican Americans, Cuban Americans, and people from the various countries in Central America and the Caribbean all have their own country-specific priorities and interests, and sometimes, these lead to antagonisms among them.

Today, religion-based interest groups are becoming increasingly active on foreign policy issues. Among the most prominent are those on the "religious right." Primarily identified as supporting the Republican Party, these groups were firm opponents of communism during the latter part of the Cold War. Today, they actively lobby on family planning and population control policies and in support of Christians persecuted abroad, particularly in China, Russia, and Sudan. By no means, however, does the religious right have a monopoly on religiously motivated interest group activity. During the period leading up to the Iraq War, religious groups were active both for and against the war. Evangelicals tended to support the war, while the Catholic Church, the Religious Society of Friends (Quakers), the World Council of Churches, and the Muslim Peace Fellowship all spoke out against it.

During his campaign to win the 2016 Republican Party nomination for president, Donald Trump delivered a speech to the American Israel Political Action Committee (AIPAC). Organizations like AIPAC use lobbying to exert pressure on government officials to adopt foreign policies favorable to their interests.

■ *Do powerful interest groups such as AIPAC limit the ability of government officials to adopt policies that serve the best interest of the United States?*

Political Protest

Globalization has aroused much debate among Americans, particularly on college campuses. Images in the media of protesters clashing with police in Seattle in December 1999 at a meeting of the World Trade Organization (WTO) brought back for many vivid memories of political protests against the war in Vietnam—a prominent feature on the American political landscape in the late 1960s and early 1970s. Globalization as a political issue has succeeded in mobilizing protesters largely because it taps into two important contemporary issues: quality of life as well as civil rights and liberties.

Images of demonstrators in the streets are an important reminder that the public voice is expressed through both officially sanctioned and unofficial pathways. Not unexpectedly, administrations tend to dismiss protest activity as unimportant, but political protests on the scale of the peace movement and the anti-globalization movement can alter the political agenda, forcing policymakers to confront issues they otherwise would ignore. Protests can also bring new voices into the political process and reenergize long-established political forces, such as labor unions.

PATHWAYS OF ACTION

BONO AND ONE

In the post-9/11 age, national security concerns have been more intricately linked with questions of global poverty and inequity. Increased attention is being paid to the gulf between the "haves" and "have-nots" both within and across countries. Economic stagnation, conflict, extreme poverty, high debt burden, and corruption are all interrelated phenomena, and can pose national and international security threats. Nowhere are these problems more obvious than in sub-Saharan Africa. As the world's richest states contemplate ways of aiding Africa, nongovernmental initiatives have mobilized grass-root organizations and activists in an effort to help stabilize the continent.

One such organization is exemplified by "ONE," co-founded by rock icon Bono—lead singer of the Irish rock band U2. ONE's origins date back to 2002, when Bono, along with fellow musician Bob Geldof (of Live Aid fame), Bobby Shriver, and Jamie Drummond joined forces with Bill and Melinda Gates to form DATA (Debt, AIDS, Trade, Africa), which attempted to induce African states into promoting democracy, accountability, and transparency in return for debt forgiveness, Western help in the fight against AIDS, and the promise of more open and "fair" Western economies as export markets. In 2004, DATA, along with 10 other leading antipoverty organizations joined forces to create ONE—a nonpartisan campaign aimed at mobilizing Americans in the fight against extreme poverty and preventable global disease. It is no surprise that a lot of the organization's activity is focused on Africa.

The organization's campaign to raise awareness and funds and to bring policy shifts was matched by its drive to secure membership. Within a year of its formation, over 2 million grassroots activists joined its ranks. These activists contact members of Congress about pressing global development needs and mobilize new and old constituencies across communities and campuses in the United States.

ONE's activities against poverty and human misery are directly linked to security issues. As the organization points out in its Web page, there are 50 percent more infant deaths in sub-Saharan African countries that are embroiled in conflict, in comparison to those that are not. The conflict ridden countries account for 15 percent more undernourished people, and 20 percent more adult illiteracy than countries at peace. The same source cites that sub-Saharan Africa loses about $148 billion a year to corruption. This amounts to about a quarter of the region's GDP. The average cost of armed conflict in 23 sub-Saharan countries between 1990 and 2005 was about $18 billion a year or 15 percent of these states' GDP. These lost funds and resources not only impoverish the people, but also sustain these conflicts and push the states toward failure.

About 11,700 people die each day from HIV/AIDS, tuberculosis, and malaria. Almost two-thirds of these people are living in sub-Saharan Africa. At least 2.8 billion people around the world do not have adequate access to clean water, while 4,100 children die each day of diarrhea, which is spread through poor sanitation and hygiene. These dismal statistics threaten not only national and regional stability, but also global stability. ONE activists are engaged in work that links humanitarian, development, sustainability, and security issues related to our existence. ONE's policy activism has been instrumental in the area of debt forgiveness. Ninety-three billion dollars of debt has been cancelled for sub-Saharan countries since 1996. To find out more about ONE and its campaigns, visit http://www.one.org/us/.

U2's lead singer Bono has been a major force in the formation of ONE, an organization that has worked to have the debt of developing nations either reduced or forgiven as a means of helping nations to grow out of poverty.

■ *Why would the presence of a celebrity increase the likelihood that a government would pay attention to the requests of an organization?*

SOURCE: "Bono, Gates Unveil "DATA" Agenda for Africa," http://archives.cnn.com/2002/TECH/industry/02/02/gates.bono.africa/.

Political Institutions and Foreign Policymaking

15.4 Analyze how political institutions compete for influence in making foreign policy.

As in other policy areas, the Constitution allocates political power among the president, Congress, and the courts in the formation of foreign policy. Three constitutionally defined powers are controversial. The first is treaty-making power. The Constitution states that the president, by and with the consent of the Senate, has the power to make treaties. Confirmation by two-thirds of the Senate is required for ratification of a treaty. Presidents can get around this requirement by signing an executive agreement with another country, which does not require any congressional action.

The second constitutionally defined power is appointment. Presidents nominate ambassadors and other key foreign policy officials to their posts, who must then be confirmed by the Senate. Once again, a president may get around Congress by using personal representatives to conduct negotiations or by making recess appointments—nominations that are automatically approved because Congress is not in session. (Recess appointees do not hold office with the same permanent tenure as confirmed appointees, however, so this is used as a stopgap measure.)

Finally, there are the war powers. The Constitution gives to Congress the power to declare war and the power to raise and maintain military forces. The president is constitutionally designated as commander in chief. A major issue here is that since World War II, no American war has been formally declared by Congress.

The Executive Branch

In today's public eye, the president makes American foreign policy. It is the president who announces decisions on war and peace; meets foreign leaders at the White House, at international summit conferences, or in foreign capitals; and signs treaties and international agreements. Presidents do not make foreign policy decisions in isolation,

In 2011 President Barack Obama along with Secretary of State Hillary Clinton and other foreign policy advisors watch as a Navy SEAL team carry out the mission in Pakistan that would lead to the death of Osama bin Laden. While successful in killing the master mind of the 9/11 terrorist attacks, the decision to send U.S. troops into Pakistan jeopardized relations with one of the key nations in one of the most turbulent regions of the world.

■ *Under what conditions should the United States send its troops into foreign nations without the consent of those nations?*

however. We have already noted that through public opinion polling, they are kept well aware of the domestic political consequences of their foreign policy decisions.

CHIEF OF STAFF The White House chief of staff plays an increasing role in foreign policy matters.[23] Rahm Emmanuel, Barack Obama's former chief of staff, was a key player on foreign policy issues during the first years of the Obama administration, which included a strong role in shaping the White House's opposition to Israeli settlement expansion. Howard Baker, Jr., formerly an influential Republican senator, served as chief of staff in the last years of President Ronald Reagan's administration. During that time, he played an important part in controlling the backlash from Reagan's possible involvement in the Iran-Contra affair, and influenced Reagan to hold frequent summit conferences with Soviet leader Mikhail Gorbachev with the goal of ending the Cold War.

THE VICE PRESIDENCY A relatively new foreign policy voice from within the White House comes from the vice president.[24] Dick Cheney, George W. Bush's vice president, once served as chief of staff to President Gerald Ford and as secretary of defense to President George H. W. Bush. Within George W. Bush's administration, Cheney was a powerful advocate of the Iraq War, and some observers considered him the architect of the president's foreign policy, at least during Bush's first term. Although Cheney's role in foreign policy far exceeded that of many vice presidents, Dan Quayle, the vice president under George H. W. Bush, had been active in designing Latin American policy, and Al Gore, Bill Clinton's vice president, established himself as an expert on Russia.

When Joe Biden joined Barack Obama's presidential campaign, he immediately added foreign policy expertise. Biden, the former chair of the Senate Foreign Relations Committee, was known and respected around the world. Once in office, Biden quickly distinguished himself as influential in articulating and shaping the administration's foreign policy (especially in Afghanistan). Despite their recent prominence in foreign policy matters, vice presidents have only as much influence and authority as presidents accord them.

NATIONAL SECURITY COUNCIL A modern president's most important source of advice about foreign policy problems inside the White House is the National Security Council (NSC).[25] The NSC was created in 1947, at the beginning of the Cold War. At the same time, the Central Intelligence Agency (CIA) was established, and the old war and navy departments were consolidated to form the Department of Defense. These changes represented a wide-ranging reorganization of the foreign affairs bureaucracy under the 1947 National Security Act. The term *foreign affairs bureaucracy* is used to describe those bureaucratic units most deeply involved in shaping foreign policy, which commonly include the State Department, the Defense Department, and the CIA. One of the major lessons learned from the attack on Pearl Harbor and World War II was that to protect the United States, much greater coordination and communication were needed among the foreign affairs and domestic bureaucracies.

The NSC has evolved over time. Since its inception, the NSC has grown from a small presidential staff of 10 people to a bureaucratic body that at times has employed more than 200, including 100 professional national security analysts. Finding the NSC too large and unmanageable in times of crisis, presidents have routinely relied for advice on smaller groups, such as Lyndon Johnson's "Tuesday Lunch Group" during the Vietnam War and Jimmy Carter's "Friday Breakfast Group" during the Soviet Union's 1979 invasion of Afghanistan and the Iranian hostage crisis. Similarly, George W. Bush established the "War Cabinet" to help with the planning and conduct of the Afghanistan and Iraq wars.

The NSC staff is charged with making policy recommendations and overseeing the implementation of foreign policy decisions. The president sets up the organizational structure for the NSC. Barack Obama significantly expanded the NSC structure to add the attorney general, the secretaries of the treasury and of homeland security, the U.S. ambassador to the United Nations, and the chief of staff to the council. President Obama also sought to increase coordination between national security agencies through the creation of Interagency Policy Committees (IPCs). These committees are tasked with managing development and implementation of national security policies when multiple agencies (such as the CIA and Homeland Security) are involved.

Presidents have turned to the NSC staff for advice out of frustration with the advice they have received from the State Department, the Defense Department, and the CIA. Too often, presidents have felt that these foreign policy bureaucracies have not been sensitive enough to presidential perspectives in making foreign policy. The big issue is time frame. Foreign policy professionals are sensitive to how foreign governments will respond over the long term. Presidents, on the other hand, think in terms of 4-year electoral cycles and are of course vitally concerned with how members of the American public will judge their immediate response to events.

NATIONAL SECURITY ADVISER　The national security adviser was initially intended to be a kind of neutral referee, managing the NSC and reporting to the president. This changed during the Kennedy and Johnson administrations, when national security advisers began openly to advocate policy solutions and paid less attention to their managerial role. Henry Kissinger (under Nixon), Zbigniew Brzezinski (under Carter), Colin Powell (under Reagan), and Condoleezza Rice (under George W. Bush) are among the most visible and most powerful recent national security advisers. President Obama's national security adviser, Susan Rice, played a central role in formulating American foreign policy, but that role was frequently challenged by other high officials, most notably the secretary of state and the secretary of defense.

STATE DEPARTMENT　According to historical tradition, the president looks first to the State Department in making foreign policy. The State Department is the formal channel of information between the United States and foreign governments and serves as a resource for senior policymakers. Each year, the State Department represents the United States at meetings of more than 50 major international organizations and at more than 800 international conferences. From day to day, the State Department also plays a central role in managing American foreign policy through U.S. embassies abroad, where the ambassador serves as chief of mission and heads the "country team," which is made up of all U.S. personnel assigned to an embassy. CIA officials (who often operate covertly) are left out of the official accounting. Complicating the difficulty of asserting control over such a diverse set of government agencies is the fact that ambassadors frequently are not career foreign service officers. Many—especially in glamorous European capital cities—are political appointees who were made ambassadors as a reward for campaign contributions or as consolation after an election loss or retirement. For example the highly prestigious post of ambassador to the United Kingdom was given to Louis Sussman, a lawyer and banker who raised over $200,000 for the Obama campaign in 2008. He replaced Robert Tuttle, a car dealer and art collector who made large contributions to the campaigns of George W. Bush. The examples of Sussman and Tuttle demonstrate that expertise in foreign relations is by no means a requirement to serve in high ranking positions in the diplomatic core.

DEPARTMENT OF DEFENSE　For most of its history, the military security of the United States was provided by forces under the direction of the War Department and the Department of the Navy. These two departments coordinated the activity of the armed forces under the sole direction of the president. This changed dramatically with the passage of the National Security Act in 1947, which established the offices of the secretary of defense and chairman of the joint chiefs of staff and created the National Military Establishment. In 1949, the National Military Establishment was renamed the Department of Defense.

Secretaries of defense have generally adopted one of two approaches. Generalists will defer to military know-how and see themselves as the military's representatives in policy deliberations with the president and other foreign affairs bureaucracies. Secretaries who see themselves as experts in defense matters seek to shape and control the Defense Department in accordance with their views. Donald Rumsfeld, George W. Bush's former secretary of defense, quickly established himself as a controversial military authority whose ideas about how to fight the war on terror, drive Saddam Hussein from power, and occupy Iraq after the war often clashed with those of the professional military officers. These disagreements became public in 2006, when six retired generals, some with combat commands in Iraq, voiced their opposition to Rumsfeld and called for his resignation. He stepped down in December of that year. Robert M. Gates, director of the CIA in the administration of George H. W. Bush from 1991 until the start of 1993, was President George W. Bush's choice to succeed Rumsfeld in 2006. As a past head of the Central Intelligence Agency, Gates brought a unique background to the job—one that was hailed by some observers and objected to by others. Despite some criticisms at his appointment, Gates was kept on as Secretary of Defense under President Obama, indicating that his more consensual and less controversial approach to managing the Department of Defense had won him bipartisan support. At the same time, he could not avoid controversy when it came to the question of defense funding. In May 2011, on behalf of the Obama Administration, he proposed a $78 billion cut in U.S. defense programs over the next 5 years. It was reported that although both he and the chairman of joint chief of staffs, Admiral Mike Mullen, recommended to the White House that a 2–3 percent increase in defense budget was required, President Obama was responsive to a 1 percent increase in defense budget in 2011.[26] Gates emphasized that the defense cuts must be prioritized and be strategic. In May 2011, while delivering his last major policy speech during his tenure as Secretary of Defense, he stated "The overarching goal will be to preserve a U.S. military capable of meeting crucial national security priorities even if fiscal pressure requires reductions in that force's size."[27]

A major point of debate among civilian and military officials in the Pentagon is the future size and shape of the military. How much emphasis should be given to information technologies in planning for and fighting future wars? For what type of conflicts should the military be trained? The type of military operation that defeated the Iraqi army in 2003 is very different from counterinsurgency operations against terrorists or humanitarian interventions to halt genocide. One consequence of an increased emphasis on technology is a reduction in the size of the military, both at home and abroad. This means reliance on National Guard units for combat missions and the closure of many military bases—both of which can be very disruptive to and unpopular with local communities in the United States.

Another longstanding issue involves the conditions under which American military forces should be sent into combat. There are two poles in this debate: the Powell Doctrine and the McNamara Doctrine. The **Powell Doctrine**, named for Colin Powell, calls for the decisive use of American military only when there is clear public support for the use of force and an exit strategy is in place. According to the **McNamara Doctrine**, named for Robert McNamara, the secretary of defense during much of the Vietnam War, limited and graduated use of military force is permissible when there is a recognized problem demanding a military response, with or without public support. The professional military tends to favor the Powell Doctrine, and Defense Department civilians are more likely to advocate a position in line with the McNamara Doctrine.

Regardless of the prevailing view concerning the use of military force, the military does not have the final say. Under the Constitution, the president is commander in chief, and in the United States, the military has traditionally deferred to civilian authority.

Powell Doctrine

A view that cautions against the use of military force, especially where public support is limited, but states that once the decision to use force has been made, military power should be applied quickly and decisively.

McNamara Doctrine

A view that military power can be applied to situations in controlled and limited amounts that rise over time and that public support should not be a major factor governing its use.

covert action

Efforts to secretly influence affairs in another state, which may include propaganda, disinformation campaigns, bribery, fomenting political and economic unrest, and, in the extreme, assassination.

intelligence

Gathering and analyzing information and communications, often secret, about potential enemies and other national security matters.

CENTRAL INTELLIGENCE AGENCY We often associate the Central Intelligence Agency with **covert action**, but one of the agency's primary functions is the gathering of **intelligence**—information that has been *evaluated* and is not simply news snippets or rumors. Ideally, intelligence should provide policymakers with enough warning and insight to allow them to act in the face of a challenge to American security interests. This is not easy, because surprise is a constant element of global politics.[28]

The CIA's ability to undermine surprise, or at least reduce its negative consequences, is determined largely by two factors. The first is the relationship between the CIA and the president. The second is the relationship between the CIA and the other intelligence agencies.

There are several points of friction in the relationship between the CIA and the president. First, the logic of intelligence clashes with the logic of policymaking. Good intelligence limits policy options by clarifying the assumptions behind and consequences of various policy options, but good policymaking often requires keeping as many options open for as long as possible. Second, how close should intelligence be to policy? The traditional answer is that intelligence and policy must be kept separate so that the intelligence is not infected by policy considerations and can provide neutral information. Intelligence that is kept separate from policy is likely to be useless, however, because intelligence cannot inform policymaking if it is not aware of policy. Third, there is often a difference between the type of information the president wants to receive and the type of information the CIA is inclined to collect. Policymakers are most eager to obtain information that will help them convince Congress and the American public about the merits of their favored policy. They are frustrated by intelligence that is impossible to use because it is tentative, secretive, or not easily understood. Finally, the CIA is not the president's only source of intelligence. It is in competition for the president's attention with interest groups, lobbyists, the media, and well-placed individuals. Presidential candidate Barack Obama had stated that he would undertake "a top to bottom review of the threats we face and our abilities to confront them." This would involve a sweeping overhaul of his predecessor's War on Terror, which, according to Obama, was compromising American values. It has, however, been claimed that rhetoric aside, President Obama "believed in a vigorous, aggressive continuing counterterrorism effort." According to CIA's Acting General Counsel during the Bush Administration John Rizzo, "With a notable exception of the enhanced interrogation program, the incoming Obama administration changed virtually nothing with respect to existing CIA programs and operations."[29] This may suggest that institutional reform and change in a complex policy environment is extremely difficult, even for a president who ran on a campaign promising extensive reforms.

The CIA has a unique relationship with other members of what is known as the "intelligence community." Besides the CIA, the most prominent members of that community are the intelligence units of each branch of the military, the State Department, the Federal Bureau of Investigation (FBI), the National Security Agency (in charge of protecting America's secret communication codes as well as breaking the codes of others), the Defense Intelligence Agency (whose director is the primary adviser to the secretary of defense on military intelligence matters), and the National Reconnaissance Office (charged with developing American information-gathering technology).

Turf wars between these organizations are not uncommon as each seeks to protect its mission from being encroached on by others. Today, one of the most serious disputes is between the CIA, the State Department, and the Pentagon over covert (secret) action. Covert action has traditionally been carried out by the CIA. Since 9/11, however, the military has played an increasing role, and it does not need the approval of the ambassador to a country to carry out such operations.

The various members of the intelligence community often have different approaches to foreign policy problems. Consider the issue of spies. The FBI takes a law enforcement perspective, indicating that people suspected of engaging in espionage for foreign governments should be arrested and prosecuted for breaking the law. The CIA prefers to let spies continue to operate so that it can watch them, discover their contacts, and feed them misinformation. Nor does the CIA want its own operations revealed in a public trial.

Until 2006, when the position of director of national intelligence (DNI) was created, the head of the CIA and the head of the rest of the intelligence community were one and the same, an individual who held the title of director of central intelligence (DCI). Today, these positions are held by two different officials. During the time that the CIA and the intelligence community were both led by the DCI, the DCI had budget authority only over the CIA, so an estimated 80 to 90 percent of the intelligence community's budget was beyond the DCI's control, falling instead under the control of the Pentagon. In the federal government, budget control gives powerful bureaucratic leverage. One of the many unresolved problems facing the director of national intelligence today is that the position lacks effective budget control over all members of the intelligence community.

Concerns about the ability of the CIA to coordinate and share its intelligence information with other agencies continue years after the attacks of 9/11. In December 2009, an attempt to blow up a jet bound for Detroit, Michigan, demonstrated that CIA procedures had problems that had not been resolved through post-9/11 reforms. In particular, the agency had collected information about the attempted bomber, Umar Farouk Abdulmutallab, but had not shared it with the Transportation Safety Administration (TSA), which is responsible for maintaining the federal government's no-fly list. This incident prompted a change in CIA policies, which requires that the agency formally disseminate information on suspected extremists and terrorists within 48 hours and expand name traces on possible extremists and terrorists.[30]

DEPARTMENT OF HOMELAND SECURITY   The Department of Homeland Security (DHS) is the newest part of the intelligence community. More than any other government unit, the DHS occupies a gray area between the domestic and foreign policy bureaucracies.[31] The DHS came into existence in November 2002 in response to the terrorist attacks of 9/11. Its creation was the largest bureaucratic transformation in American history, affecting 170,000 employees and combining 22 different agencies from eight different departments. The DHS swallowed up the Federal Emergency Management Agency (FEMA), the Coast Guard, the Secret Service, the Customs Service, the Immigration and Naturalization Service (INS), and the recently created Transportation Security Administration. Formation of the DHS did not affect the FBI and the CIA directly, but the new DHS does have an intelligence and threat analysis unit that makes it a challenger to these traditional intelligence-gathering agencies in the policymaking process.

The newness of the DHS makes it difficult to judge the role it will play in foreign policy decision-making. Its first major venture into policymaking, devising a color-coded nationwide terrorist threat alert system, was not well received. Tom Ridge, its first secretary, left office amid criticism for failing to navigate the shoals of bureaucratic warfare. His successor, Michael Chertoff, quickly proposed a wide range of organizational reforms intended to improve the glaring inadequacies of its organizational performance, which became apparent in the government's response to Hurricane Katrina in September 2005. These proposed reforms included faster funding for first responders, tighter security in American ports, and improved cooperation with intelligence agencies.

Under the Obama administration, the DHS took greater interest in the threats from "domestic terrorists." Domestic terrorists can come in the form of American-born individuals who go abroad to receive training on the use of terrorist techniques or in the form of Americans who plot and train for terrorist strikes within the borders of the nation. In April 2009, the DHS issued a report that warned of the rise of Christian militias, right-wing extremists, and domestic terrorists. These warnings proved to be well founded with the 2010 arrest of nine heavily armed Christian militia members that were plotting to kill law enforcement officers and then attack the funeral procession as part of their fight against the government.[32] Former secretary of DHS Janet Napolitano focused the organization's efforts on securing the nation's southwest border by deploying additional personnel and advanced technology, while increasing collaboration with the Mexican government to combat the actions of violent drug cartels and the problem of illegal immigration.[33]

Congress

If you go by newspaper and television accounts, it would seem that the president and Congress are always in conflict over the conduct of American foreign policy. This is not the case. Viewed over time, presidential-congressional relations in foreign policy have alternated between long stretches of presidential dominance and moments when Congress emerged as an important force, fully capable of frustrating presidential initiatives. These swings depend on two factors: the level of congressional *activity* and the level of congressional *assertiveness*.[34] In turn, these two factors are influenced by many other considerations, including the party in control of the White House and of the Congress; the size of the majority one party has in the House, the Senate, or in both houses of Congress; the timing of presidential and congressional elections; the popularity of the president and the Congress with the American public; the impact of interest groups and movements on political actors; the goals and skills of the president and the leadership of the Congress; and a host of other political forces.

containment

A Cold War strategy that sought to control and encircle the Soviet Union rather than defeat it militarily.

SUPPORTIVE CONGRESS A supportive Congress is actively engaged in foreign policy issues but does not try to assert control over them. From the onset of the Cold War around 1947 until the late 1950s, Congress was largely supportive. Relations between the president and Congress were positive. These were the years of "bipartisan" foreign policy, when "politics stopped at the water's edge," meaning that differences between Republicans and Democrats hardly surfaced in foreign policy decision-making. A broad consensus existed that the Soviet Union and communism were the enemy and that **containment**—a Cold War strategy that sought to control and encircle the Soviet Union rather than defeat it militarily—was the proper strategy for meeting the threat. Congress saw its role as supporting the president and providing him with the means to carry out his foreign policy. Exceptions to this rule involved a good dose of domestic politics. One such case was the McCarthy hearings, primarily conducted by Republicans, into charges that communists had infiltrated the State Department (controlled by Democrats) and the Defense Department and were responsible for such key foreign policy setbacks as the triumph of communism in China, described at the time as the "loss of China."

STRATEGIC CONGRESS From roughly 1958 through 1968, a "strategic" Congress emerged, mostly encountering presidents from the same Democratic Party that also controlled Congress. This meant that Congress was not particularly active but was willing to be assertive on selected issues. Resolutions of support for presidential foreign policy initiatives were still the rule. Notable examples occurred in 1961, after the failed Bay of Pigs invasion of Cuba to remove Fidel Castro from power; during the 1962 Cuban Missile Crisis, when the world reached the brink of a Soviet–American nuclear confrontation; and in 1964, when Congress passed almost unanimously and with little debate the Gulf of Tonkin Resolution, which gave President Lyndon Johnson a virtual free hand to confront North Vietnam militarily. Key members of Congress, however, such as Senator J. William Fulbright, who chaired the Senate Foreign Relations Committee, clashed with President Johnson as the Vietnam War escalated with little evidence of success. The second issue on which Congress was active during this period was military strength. The biggest military issue of the time was the "missile gap"—the idea that the Soviet Union was ahead of the United States in missile production, and that the president had not done enough to protect American national security. In the 1960 presidential campaign, which pitted Democratic candidate John F. Kennedy against Republican Richard Nixon, the Democrats used the "missile gap" very effectively. Once in office, however, Kennedy discovered that no such gap existed.

COMPETITIVE CONGRESS   From 1969 into the mid-1980s, a time that featured divided government and a Congress that was reacting to the excessive use of presidential power by Lyndon Johnson and Richard Nixon, Congress was *competitive*—both active and assertive. During that time, Congress challenged presidents on both the content and the conduct of American foreign policy. For example, in 1974, the Jackson-Vanik Amendment, which made improved economic relations with the Soviet Union contingent on allowing persecuted Jews to emigrate more freely, openly challenged President Richard Nixon's policies toward the Soviet Union. Since better economic relations were a key aspect of Nixon's foreign policy of **détente**, which was designed to improve relations with the Soviets and lessen international tensions, this amendment became a major problem in Nixon's negotiations with the Kremlin. At the end of the 1970s, President Jimmy Carter faced a congressional challenge over the Panama Canal Treaty, which restored the canal to Panamanian control, removing a key irritant from U.S.-Latin American relations.

détente
Reduction of tension or strained relations between previously hostile nations.

Carter managed to get the treaty approved by the Senate, but only after making concessions to senators who had raised strong objections. In the 1980s, congressional-presidential struggles focused largely on President Reagan's policy of staunch support for the Contra rebels in Nicaragua despite congressional prohibitions on funding rebel activity. A complex arms sales program to Iran was engineered behind the scenes to help accomplish the fall of the Sandinista government in Nicaragua as well as the release of Americans held captive in Lebanon; when revealed, it became known as the Iran-Contra affair.

WAR POWERS RESOLUTION   The most important challenge to the president's ability to conduct foreign policy has been the War Powers Resolution, which Congress passed over President Nixon's veto in 1973. This law sought to limit the president's ability to use military force by requiring that Congress receive formal notification of troop deployment abroad into combat situations and issue its approval. If congressional approval is not granted, the forces must be withdrawn within 60 days. Although all presidents since 1973 have objected to this law on the grounds that it is unconstitutional, they have all observed it when committing American forces abroad. President George H. W. Bush was careful to obtain a supportive congressional vote before launching the Gulf War in 1991, and Bill Clinton did likewise before he committed American forces to the brief war that NATO waged against Serbia over Kosovo in 1999. So far, Congress has never exercised its power to withdraw military forces.

REEMERGENCE OF THE STRATEGIC CONGRESS   A strategic Congress slowly began to reemerge in the mid-1980s, a pattern that was the norm until September 11, 2001. During this period, Congress pulled back from broad-based challenges to the president's conduct of foreign policy and concentrated on a smaller set of highly visible issues. Foremost among these was the annual vote granting China "most favored nation" status; the Comprehensive Nuclear Test Ban Treaty (rejected in 1999); and the North American Free Trade Agreement (passed in 1993).

DISENGAGED CONGRESS   The 9/11 terrorist attacks brought back a disengaged Congress. In the immediate aftermath of 9/11, Congress ceded much of its authority and initiative in making crucial foreign policy decisions to the president, including mobilization of resources for the War on Terror. Public opinion poll numbers rose into the 90-percent range for the president, and Congress also benefited from renewed support from the public during this time of national crisis. With both houses of Congress in the hands of the Republican Party and the party's leader in the White House, there was little incentive for either the House or the Senate to challenge President Bush. However, after the 2006 elections returned the Democrats to power in the Congress, the president and his executive branch were treated to a strong dose of congressional oversight as committees reasserted their role of watchdog over the actions of the administration. Members of both parties voiced concern over the Bush administration's postwar policies in Iraq, the use of torture on suspected terrorists in American custody, and the claim of inherent presidential authority to order electronic wiretaps on Americans in order to prosecute the War on Terror. The centerpiece of President Bush's post-9/11 national security legislation, the USA PATRIOT Act, was renewed in 2006 after strongly debated changes were made, and then again in part in 2011 and 2015 under the Obama administration.

When Barack Obama took office in 2009 with Democrats controlling both the Senate and House, it was reasonable to expect that his foreign policy initiatives would gain strong backing from Democratic members of Congress. But on the most significant foreign policy decision of Obama's first year in the White House, increasing troop levels by 30,000 in Afghanistan, the president received his greatest opposition from members of his own party and solid support from Republican lawmakers. This situation demonstrates how members of Congress and presidents view foreign policy in strikingly different ways.

LEGISLATION, FUNDING, AND OVERSIGHT   Congress most frequently uses three tools to influence foreign policy: legislation, funding, and oversight. Congress often seeks to assert its influence by attaching amendments to foreign policy legislation that place conditions on the president's actions. It may also target foreign aid and military assistance money for certain countries, as it has done repeatedly for Israel and Egypt. It may make foreign aid conditional on annual reports that give passing grades on such matters as human rights, antidrug and antiterrorism efforts, and nuclear weapons control. Presidents can ignore these limitations, however, by certifying that assistance is in the "national interests" of the United States. Presidents have used this power to continue foreign aid to Mexico and Panama despite those countries' poor records in the War on Drugs and to Pakistan after 9/11 in spite of its questionable record in opposing terrorism and enforcing nuclear nonproliferation.

Congressional budgetary powers are equally blunt and hard to use with finesse, in part because of the committee structure within Congress. In 2003, the Bush administration asked Congress for funds to help rebuild Iraq, yet delays resulting from the insurgency and bureaucratic battles prevented much of this money from being spent. Perhaps the biggest obstacle to using its budgetary powers to control American foreign policy is that whereas programs require funding, presidential policy announcements do not. Congress often finds itself reluctant to undercut a president once the White House has publicly committed the United States to a course of action with important international implications. In the case of Iraq, the notion of simply defunding the ongoing troop deployment in Iraq was derided by Republican opponents as "selling out the troops"—something the Democratic leaders in Congress could hardly see as an appealing perception about their party.

Several factors limit the impact of congressional oversight. One is the small political payoff for a great investment of time. Constituent work and shaping of domestic legislation are much more valuable for reelection purposes. A second limiting factor is organization: More than 80 committees have some kind of jurisdiction over the sprawling Department of Homeland Security. Third, most congressional oversight of foreign policy tends to be after the fact. For example, the 9/11 hearings were highly visible undertakings, fraught with emotion and geared toward establishing blame. Routine oversight of foreign policy programs involves far less effort and minimal media attention.

Presidents and critics of Congress tend to see the legislature as an obstacle course that must be run in order to formulate and carry out a coherent foreign policy. Defenders see congressional input as vital to keeping the government in touch with the national mood and ensuring long-term public support for American foreign policy.

The Supreme Court

The Supreme Court seldom voices an opinion regarding American foreign policy. Over the course of its history, however, the Court has produced three types of rulings dealing with foreign policy. First, when there is a conflict between state laws and treaties on a subject involving American foreign policy, the Court has ruled consistently that treaties take precedence over state laws. Second, the Court has consistently supported the president in conflicts with Congress. For example, it has ruled that executive agreements, which do not require congressional approval, have the same validity as treaties, which do require such approval. Finally, the Supreme Court has been reluctant to grant the government broad powers that may restrict American civil liberties and constitutionally guaranteed freedoms. With its more recent decisions in cases dealing with the treatment of accused terrorists and surveillance conducted without the use of a warrant in the United States, the Court has shown a willingness to moderately curtail the powers of the executive branch.

Foreign Policy and National Security Issues

15.5 Outline the major foreign policy issues confronting the United States today.

T he United States faces many current foreign policy problems and challenges. We will examine three categories of foreign policy problems: military security, economic, and human welfare. Although we will discuss them separately, in many cases these problems are intimately connected.

For instance, because there is no cure, it is tempting to treat acquired immunodeficiency syndrome (AIDS) as a health problem, which would put it in the human welfare category. Consider, however, that according to the World Bank, the spread of the human immunodeficiency virus (HIV) and AIDS is in part responsible for the decreased economic growth rate in sub-Saharan African countries. In Africa, the HIV/AIDS pandemic also raises complex military security issues: The presence of large numbers of infected people can be seen as a threat that needs to be contained by neighboring countries, and the presence of a large number of infected individuals within a country's armed forces can drastically reduce its ability to carry out military missions or defend itself from foreign invasion. Furthermore, the lack of ability to resolve this public health issue, along with a myriad of economic and social crises, can push a sub-Saharan state to the brink of failure. Failed states pose a threat to regional and global security.

Military Security Issues

Combating terrorism and stopping the proliferation of weapons of mass destruction (nuclear, chemical, and biological weapons, as well as ballistic missile delivery systems) top everyone's list of pressing military security issues. Responding to them is a challenge not only because of the elevated level of danger but also because the nature of the problem changes constantly.

TERRORISM In the early 1990s, the intelligence community's dominant view was that Middle Eastern terrorists were controlled, or at least heavily influenced, by hostile regional powers such as Iran, Syria, and Libya. When President Clinton signed an executive order imposing sanctions on 12 Middle Eastern terrorist groups in 1995, al Qaeda was not even on the list. The United States was aware of Osama bin Laden but regarded him as a financier of international terrorism, not as a terrorist himself. Our understanding of terrorism changed slowly during the 1990s, and portions of the intelligence community began to speak of a new breed of radical Islamic terrorism that operated independently of government control. Gradually, bin Laden's activities came under closer watch, and in 1996, the CIA Counterterrorist Center set up a special office to deal with him alone. Still, few experts in either the Clinton or the George W. Bush administrations placed this new terrorist threat above all others, despite strong evidence of al Qaeda's complicity in the 1998 bombings of American embassies in Kenya and Tanzania and the attack on the *U.S.S. Cole* in Aden in 2000.

After 9/11, the United States moved quickly to destroy al Qaeda's sanctuary in Afghanistan, and to a large extent, it succeeded. However, even with the defeat of much of al Qaeda since 2001 and killing of Osama bin Laden in 2011, terrorist attacks on American and European soil have continued over the past 15 years. Events like the March 2004 train bombing in Madrid, July 2005 attacks on the London mass transit system, December 2009 attempted bombing of a Northwest Airlines flight, May 2015 shooting in Garland, Texas, and November 2015 suicide bombings in Paris underscore the threat that the United States and other Western democracies face from terrorism.

This threat is even more serious because of the variety of forms and organizational structures that contemporary terrorist groups use. Many terrorist groups on the State Department's list of Foreign Terrorist Organizations are now geographically dispersed, with individual agents who are mostly autonomous and self-sufficient. Instead of being highly centralized and directed by a single leader, such as bin Laden, or a single source, such as al Qaeda, these groups now operate as a coalition of independent **jihadist** (Islamic holy war) agents, linked by an anti-Western ideology and the Internet. The number of jihadist-related Web sites has grown from dozens in 2001 to thousands today; these sites provide training information and even manuals on how to build and deploy biological and chemical weapons to terrorists around the globe. These kinds of terrorist organizations are non-state political actors, and their autonomy and intercontinental dispersion makes it difficult for the American government to destroy them quickly.

Before the rise of ISIS (the Islamic State of Syria and the Levant; it's also known as ISIL and Daesh), most of the terrorist threats to the United States and European democracies consisted of non-state actors. These terrorist groups didn't have sovereign control of sizeable geographic territory or formal government exercising that control. Many of them, including bin Laden's al Qaeda, did not desire to create a country themselves. ISIS changed all of that.

ISIS originally developed as a splinter group from al Qaeda in Iraq during the Bush administration. The Syrian Civil War (2011–) and continued instability in Iraq during President Obama's second term created a power vacuum across a large geographic area in the Middle East. After a variety of leadership and name changes, the group, now led by Abu Bakr al-Baghdadi, formally broke off from al Qaeda and seized a wide swath of territory in Syria and Iraq. After consolidating its gains, ISIS has formed governments in this territory and ruled according to its perverse interpretation of Islamic law. The justice and administration of ISIS in its state includes rampant rape, slavery, and genocide.

While much of ISIS is located within a particular geographic area in Syria and Iraq, the chaotic nature of the Syrian Civil War and unrest in Iraq make ISIS difficult to destroy. There are a variety of armed, violent non-state actors in both areas, some of which compete with ISIS. Additionally, there are multiple state actors involved in

jihadists
Participants in a crusade or holy war, especially in defense of Islam.

the Syrian Civil War, including the Syrian government of Bashar al-Assad and Russia. While they both oppose ISIS, they also complicate Western action against ISIS.

Additionally, ISIS is active in Afghanistan and Libya. It draws potential terrorist migrants to its territory in Syria and Iraq from around the world. ISIS recruits effectively online on social media and uses the Internet to appeal to sympathizers in other countries. Defeating ISIS represents a serious challenge for American leaders.

WEAPONS OF MASS DESTRUCTION   A fundamental reality of the nuclear age is that the knowledge needed to build nuclear, chemical, and biological weapons is readily available. Of even greater concern is that security at many facilities in the former Soviet Union where weapons of mass destruction were once built or stored still leaves much to be desired. Until recently, the U.S. position was that the spread of weapons of mass destruction needed to be stopped because they were dangerous weapons in their own right. The Bush administration's position was that it is not so much the proliferation of such weapons as the identity of the recipients. American policymakers therefore do not view Israeli or Indian nuclear weapons in the same light as Iranian and North Korean nuclear weapons projects. The ultimate nightmare scenario involves theft and use of one of these weapons of mass destruction by a terrorist group.

President Obama was forceful on issues of nuclear proliferation. In his Nobel Peace Prize acceptance speech, he spoke of the need for nuclear disarmament and the peaceful use of nuclear energy. In March 2010, he agreed to a nuclear arms reduction treaty with Russian President Dmitry Medvedev, limiting each side to 1,550 warheads. The treaty reduces the nuclear warhead limit by 30 percent.[35] In July 2015, the Obama administration, United Nations Security Council, Germany, the European Union, and Iranian government signed the Joint Comprehensive Plan of Action (JCPOA) agreement. JCPOA lifted various economic sanctions against Iran in exchange for Iran allowing more international inspections of its nuclear facilities, reducing operations at its nuclear facilities, and agreeing to refrain from using its nuclear reactors to produce fissile material for nuclear weapons.[36]

PREEMPTION AND DETERRENCE   In its *2002 National Security Strategy for the United States*, the Bush administration advanced a new strategic doctrine of **preemption**—a

ISIS poses both a terrorist threat to America and other Western democracies, and an existential threat to surrounding Middle Eastern countries like Syria and Iraq. Defeating ISIS will require the formulation of a new American grand strategy in the Middle East.

■ *What measures can the United States take to combat ISIS? What are the risks of the various measures that can be used?*

preemption
A military strategy based on striking first in self-defense.

TIMELINE

The Use of U.S. Military Forces in the War On Terror

After the terrorist attacks of September 11, 2001, it was clear to the world that the United States would take some type of forceful action to retaliate for the loss of over 3,000 lives. The size and brutality of the acts of terrorism in New York, at the Pentagon, and in a field in rural Pennsylvania made some type of action inevitable. What was unclear was how and where the armed forces of the United States should be used. Ultimately, the decisions made by the nation's leaders resulted in millions of American soldiers serving in combat situations in Iraq and Afghanistan, with thousands losing their lives and many more suffering both physical and mental harm from their service. Were the decisions to send U.S. troops to Iraq and Afghanistan in the wake of the 9/11 attacks appropriate responses to the loss of American lives? Under what conditions should troops be committed to combat situations on foreign soil?

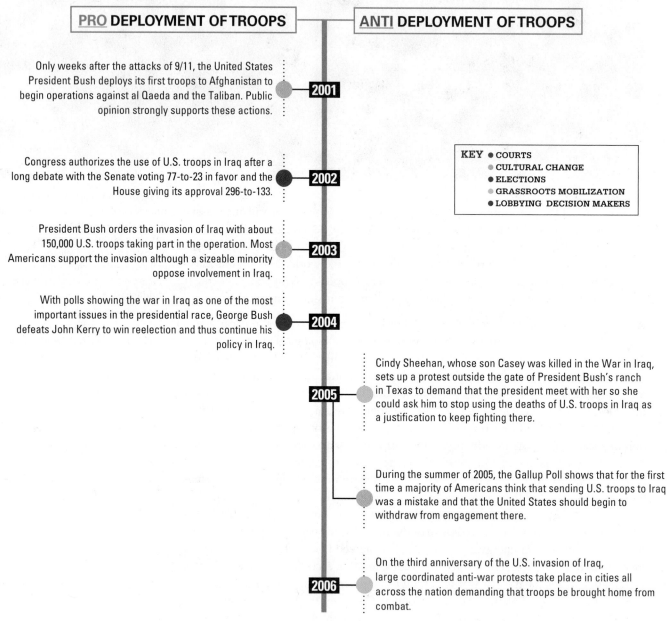

PRO DEPLOYMENT OF TROOPS

ANTI DEPLOYMENT OF TROOPS

2001 — Only weeks after the attacks of 9/11, the United States President Bush deploys its first troops to Afghanistan to begin operations against al Qaeda and the Taliban. Public opinion strongly supports these actions.

2002 — Congress authorizes the use of U.S. troops in Iraq after a long debate with the Senate voting 77-to-23 in favor and the House giving its approval 296-to-133.

KEY
- COURTS
- CULTURAL CHANGE
- ELECTIONS
- GRASSROOTS MOBILIZATION
- LOBBYING DECISION MAKERS

2003 — President Bush orders the invasion of Iraq with about 150,000 U.S. troops taking part in the operation. Most Americans support the invasion although a sizeable minority oppose involvement in Iraq.

2004 — With polls showing the war in Iraq as one of the most important issues in the presidential race, George Bush defeats John Kerry to win reelection and thus continue his policy in Iraq.

2005 — Cindy Sheehan, whose son Casey was killed in the War in Iraq, sets up a protest outside the gate of President Bush's ranch in Texas to demand that the president meet with her so she could ask him to stop using the deaths of U.S. troops in Iraq as a justification to keep fighting there.

During the summer of 2005, the Gallup Poll shows that for the first time a majority of Americans think that sending U.S. troops to Iraq was a mistake and that the United States should begin to withdraw from engagement there.

2006 — On the third anniversary of the U.S. invasion of Iraq, large coordinated anti-war protests take place in cities all across the nation demanding that troops be brought home from combat.

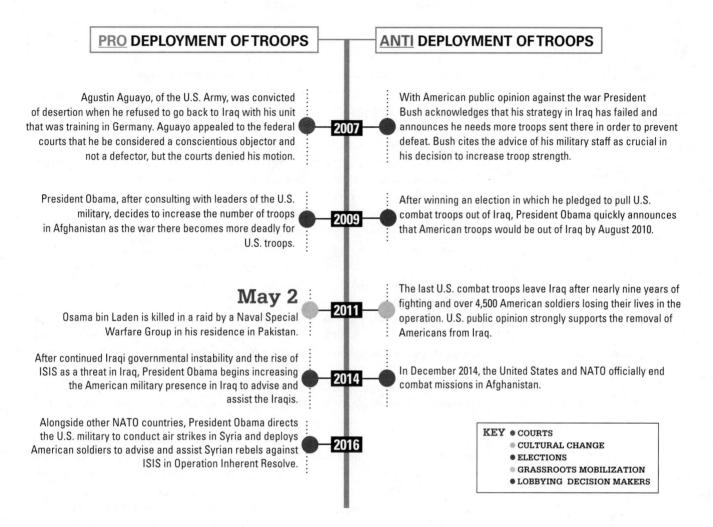

PRO DEPLOYMENT OF TROOPS

ANTI DEPLOYMENT OF TROOPS

2007

Agustin Aguayo, of the U.S. Army, was convicted of desertion when he refused to go back to Iraq with his unit that was training in Germany. Aguayo appealed to the federal courts that he be considered a conscientious objector and not a defector, but the courts denied his motion.

With American public opinion against the war President Bush acknowledges that his strategy in Iraq has failed and announces he needs more troops sent there in order to prevent defeat. Bush cites the advice of his military staff as crucial in his decision to increase troop strength.

2009

President Obama, after consulting with leaders of the U.S. military, decides to increase the number of troops in Afghanistan as the war there becomes more deadly for U.S. troops.

After winning an election in which he pledged to pull U.S. combat troops out of Iraq, President Obama quickly announces that American troops would be out of Iraq by August 2010.

2011

May 2
Osama bin Laden is killed in a raid by a Naval Special Warfare Group in his residence in Pakistan.

The last U.S. combat troops leave Iraq after nearly nine years of fighting and over 4,500 American soldiers losing their lives in the operation. U.S. public opinion strongly supports the removal of Americans from Iraq.

2014

After continued Iraqi governmental instability and the rise of ISIS as a threat in Iraq, President Obama begins increasing the American military presence in Iraq to advise and assist the Iraqis.

In December 2014, the United States and NATO officially end combat missions in Afghanistan.

2016

Alongside other NATO countries, President Obama directs the U.S. military to conduct air strikes in Syria and deploys American soldiers to advise and assist Syrian rebels against ISIS in Operation Inherent Resolve.

KEY
● COURTS
● CULTURAL CHANGE
● ELECTIONS
● GRASSROOTS MOBILIZATION
● LOBBYING DECISION MAKERS

CRITICAL THINKING QUESTIONS

1. Public opinion on the use of American troops shifted dramatically over the course of the wars in Iraq and Afghanistan. Should public views on the use of the nation's armed forces play a major role in shaping the decisions of the nation's leaders or do such opinions actually cause leaders to make decisions that reflect emotion rather than strong evidence?

2. What are the conditions that must be present if the United States is to commit the members of its armed forces to combat in a foreign nation? Should there be a clear "exit strategy" established anytime the nation sends U.S. troops to fight in a foreign land?

deterrence

A military strategy associated with the Cold War that sought to prevent an unwanted military action from taking place by raising the prospect of large-scale retaliation.

means of dealing with terrorism and the proliferation of weapons of mass destruction by striking first in self-defense. The Iraq War is an example of preemption in action. The Bush administration argued that preemption is necessary because the strategies that were used successfully during the Cold War, do not work against these shadowy and often stateless enemies. **Deterrence** threatens a state-based enemy with swift and overwhelming retaliation for actions such as nuclear attacks or acts of aggression.

Preemption is controversial for several reasons. First, containment and deterrence may be effective against some enemies. If this is true, then preemption might be a policy of last resort rather than the first choice. Second, preemption cannot be carried out very often. The human and economic costs of invading Iraq have shown that it would be difficult to respond effectively to threatening activity by North Korea or Iran. Also, if the United States justifies preemption, other countries might adopt the same policy. This would be especially troubling in the event of an escalation in the conflicts that now simmer between India and Pakistan, China and Taiwan, and Israel and its Arab neighbors. A third concern is morality. Going first in self-defense is an age-old principle of world politics, but the price for being wrong is also very high, including being seen as the aggressor and becoming the object of global condemnation and a potential target for retaliation.

Another element of the Bush administration's strategy for countering terrorist threats was to build a national ballistic missile defense system. It would function as a shield protecting the United States from weapons of mass destruction delivered by intercontinental ballistic missiles.[37] The idea for such a system, which goes back to the 1950s, was actively pursued in the 1980s by the Reagan administration. One of the major roadblocks, then as now, is the technological challenge of building and operating such a system. The system would have to work flawlessly the first time and every time—yet simulating all threat conditions would be almost impossible.

The expense of the system was also a concern because of the fact that terrorists could strike devastatingly at the United States without using ballistic missiles. Only against a "rogue state," such as Iran or North Korea might a missile shield offer any potential protection. Russia objected vehemently to the Bush administration's plan to install a tracking radar in Poland and 20 interceptors in the Czech Republic, primarily to ward off a possible Iranian threat, when Iran did not as of yet possess medium range missiles. The Obama administration's decision to cancel the Bush plan was hailed by Russia. However, tensions rose again as the Obama administration, in 2010, announced plans to install medium rage interceptors in Romania. Russia felt that it would threaten its long-range nuclear missile force.[38] These interceptor missiles were installed and became operational in 2016.[39]

Economic and Foreign Trade Issues

The most fundamental economic issue in American foreign policy is how to respond to the growing pace of globalization. Goods, people, ideas, and money now move across national borders more frequently and with greater speed than ever before. Consider that from about 1996 to 2004, Europeans invested more capital in the state of Texas than Americans invested in the entire nation of Japan, and that large American technology firms, such as Microsoft, earn about half of their total revenues from their European operations. Although there are tremendous economic benefits from this heightened economic activity (including many relatively cheap imported consumer goods), there are also significant costs. Jobs are lost to foreign countries, and national policies in areas such as workers' rights and environmental regulation must give way to international standards.

For example, the Byrd Amendment was enacted by Congress in 2000 to provide the aging American steel industry with $710 million worth of financial aid to offset losses suffered as a result of steel imports from Europe, Canada, South Korea, and Japan. The World Trade Organization (WTO)—the international organization that oversees international trade—ruled in 2003 that the Byrd Amendment constitutes an unfair trading practice and must end. The WTO ruling also gave other countries the right to impose penalties on U.S. exports until the United States complies with the ruling, which as of 2016, it had not done. President Obama initially planned to include a "Buy American" clause in his stimulus package, whereby most of the government's infrastructure and public works spending would go to American suppliers. While popular with the Democrats and unions, many worried that such a clause violated WTO regulations that limit discrimination in government spending, which could bring retaliation from the E.U. and sanctions from the WTO.[40] In February 2009, President Obama backed down from the "Buy American" clause in the face of strong international opposition, stating that he did not want to start a trade war.[41] In the face of opposition from trading partners, the "Buy American" clause was not included in the stimulus package. During the 2012 presidential election campaign, President Obama ran on the promise of a "renaissance" in American manufacturing. He credited his policies for the revival of the U.S. automobile industry and pledged to create a $1 billion network of advanced manufacturing institutes across the nation.[42] He also urged businesses to "insource" jobs back to the United States. During the 2016 presidential election campaign, President-elect Donald Trump proposed changing some aspects of America's longstanding commitment to free trade. In particular, Trump favored renegotiating NAFTA (the North American Free Trade Agreement) with Mexico and Canada and refused to sign TPP (the Trans-Pacific Partnership). Democratic candidate Hillary Clinton also opposed TPP.

> POLL What do you think foreign trade means for America? Do you see foreign trade more as an opportunity for economic growth through increased U.S. exports or a threat to the economy from foreign imports?

GLOBAL ECONOMIC POWERS How should the United States respond to the growing economic power of other nations? As of 2016, China remains the world's largest recipient of foreign direct investment. It is one of the world's third-largest traders, and it is the largest trading partner for Japan, the second-largest for Europe, Russia, and the United States. China also holds the world's largest currency reserves. Because many technologies being traded globally today can be used for both commercial and military applications, the stronger China grows economically, the more powerful it is likely to become militarily. As it grows economically and militarily, the political influence of this communist country will increase in Asia and around the world. Recently, China has expanded its presence along major trade routes in the South China Sea by building artificial islands. These islands could be used to station military forces in areas claimed by neighboring countries. In addition, China's industrial growth is placing an immense strain on the global environment, with grave implications for climate change and fossil fuel depletion. Yet globalization makes it expensive, if not impossible, to isolate China and curb its growth without causing serious harm to the American economy and to the competitive position of U.S. firms abroad. The United States is politically reliant on China in matters related to Iran and North Korea. China's increasing presence and influence in Africa is elevating its geopolitical influence globally. At the same time, the United States and China lock heads over China's currency manipulation in ways that exacerbate the U.S. trade deficit and Chinese surplus. A devalued Chinese currency makes Chinese exports to the United States appear cheaper, while making U.S. exports to China more expensive.

Human Welfare Issues

Human welfare issues focus on improving the lives of people around the world. For some Americans, addressing such challenges is an act of unselfishness and a statement about the shared humanity of people around the world. Those who take a more pragmatic approach believe that human rights abuses are a prime contributor to

FIGURE 15.2 Foreign Aid Spending, 2015

Though the United States contributes the most foreign aid by far in terms of dollars, it is near the bottom of the pack of developed nations in terms of the portion of GNI spent in aid. The United Nations agreed on a target goal of 0.7 percent of GNI. Most nations fall short of this goal. America spent only of 0.17 percent of GNI on foreign aid in 2015.

■ *Do you think the United States has a moral obligation to be more generous, or is our substantially larger contribution sufficient?*

SOURCE: "Official Development Assistance (ODA)," Organization for Economic Co-operation and Development (OECD) (2015), https://data.oecd.org/oda/net-oda.htm.

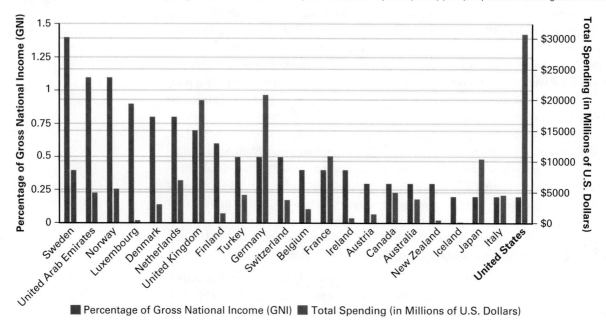

■ Percentage of Gross National Income (GNI)   ■ Total Spending (in Millions of U.S. Dollars)

the domestic and international tensions that threaten U.S. interests. Americans have mobilized on behalf of victims of human rights abuses across the world. STAND is a Student Anti-Genocide Coalition that unites student groups across American college campuses and around the world to put an end to genocide in Darfur and other parts of the world. STAND is the student-led division of the organization Genocide Intervention and it seeks to "empower individuals and communities with the tools to prevent and stop genocide."[43]

The group Invisible Children is an American-based organization that has been working to raise awareness about the abuses committed by the Lord's Resistance Army (LRA) in Central Africa. They have sought to bring LRA's leader Joseph Kony to justice. Kony has been accused of abducting children who are forced to commit horrific crimes against their own communities and forced to serve as child soldiers in the LRA. The International Criminal Court at The Hague, in the Netherlands, has charged Kony with crimes against humanity and war crimes. As of 2016, he is still at-large.

Genocide

The deliberate and systematic extinction of an ethnic or cultural group.

GENOCIDE   Defined by the United Nations as "the intent to destroy, in whole or in part, a national ethnic, racial, or religious group," **genocide** is the most extreme category of human rights violation. The number of victims of genocide in the twentieth century is staggering. Six million Jews, as well as millions more Gypsies (Roma) and various other European minorities, perished in the most notorious instance of modern genocide, the Nazi Holocaust. More than a million Armenians in the Ottoman Empire were killed in genocidal attacks, and in the wars in Southeast Asia in 1975, well over a million Cambodians were massacred by communist guerrillas in the Cambodian "killing fields." Large-scale genocide also occurred in the 1990s in the central African country of Rwanda as well as in Bosnia and other parts of the former Yugoslavia in Eastern Europe. Between 1992 and 1995, about 200,000 predominantly Muslim Bosnians were killed by Serbs and Croats. An estimated 800,000 Rwandans were slaughtered in just a few months in 1994.

Most recently, genocide has raged in Sudan, a vast country in northeastern Africa with mixed Arab and black populations. From early July 2003 through 2004, an estimated 50,000 people were killed in Sudan, and another 2 million, desperately short of medicine and food, were driven into the desert region called Darfur.[44] By 2010, it was estimated that up to 300,000 people had died and 2.5 million more had been displaced.[45] In 2016, African Union/United Nations Hybrid Operations had almost 21,000 uniformed personnel (troops and police) deployed in Darfur under UN Security Council Resolution 1881.[46] This is the second-largest current deployment of UN troops.

In spite of these horrific numbers, no clear-cut policy toward genocide has been enunciated in the United States, the United Nations, or anywhere else in the world. The genocide in Rwanda and the former Yugoslavia brought only tepid reactions from the Western powers. Both the U.S. House of Representatives and UK Parliament have spoken out about ISIS committing genocide against Christians and Yazidis (a Kurdish religious group) in the territory it controls in Syria and Iraq, but two dilemmas face any attempt to formulate policies against genocide. The first is that the pace of killing sometimes is much faster than the ability of countries to respond. In Rwanda, at least half of the 500,000 Tutsi victims were killed by their Hutu neighbors in three weeks. In 1995, Bosnian Serbs murdered 7,000 Muslims in one day in the town of Srebenica. Second, there is what is known as the "moral hazard": Knowing that the United States and others will respond to genocide may actually encourage some to provoke violence against their people in hopes of involving outside forces.

LAND MINES   One of the greatest tragedies of modern warfare is that the killing and maiming of people often continues after the fighting ends. The culprit? Land mines. It is estimated that about 120 million land mines are still concealed in more than 80 countries today. Annually, they kill or seriously injure 26,000 people—an average of one person every 26 minutes. Each year, some 100,000 land mines are deactivated, but another 2 million are placed in the ground. The United States has played an ambiguous role in the land mine issue. It was a leader in the initial global effort to do away with them and actively funds and supports demining efforts around the world. On the other hand, the United States has refused to sign the 1997 Ottawa Treaty banning the use of land mines in war, maintaining that continued research and development efforts are necessary to preserve military capabilities in potential combat zones such as the Korean peninsula. In place of the Ottawa Treaty, the United States proposes a worldwide ban on land mines that do not deactivate themselves after a given period of time. The Obama administration continues to "review its policy on land mines" while refusing to sign a comprehensive treaty to ban them.[47] The issue of landmines is hard to ignore. There have been reports that as recently as March 2012, the Syrian army placed landmines alongside Syria's borders with Turkey and Lebanon, in order to deter citizens from fleeing to neighboring countries to escape from the regime's tyranny and violence.[48] ISIS has used landmines as a terror weapon against opposing militaries and civilians retaking areas it once controlled.

HUMAN TRAFFICKING   It is important to keep in mind that human welfare issues are not solely a result of civil wars or international conflicts. Consider the plight of women and children who are transported across borders as sex slaves. The global trafficking of people is now a $12 billion-a-year industry, involving 500,000 to 2,000,000 individuals.[49] Human trafficking is now the third-largest illegal business on earth, following drug and weapons trafficking. The United States is not immune from this problem. It is estimated that 14,500 to 17,500 people are transported into the United States each year for the sex trade or other forms of economic exploitation, and as many as a million people may have been illegally smuggled into the United States since 2000.[50] Since the passage of the little-noticed Trafficking Victims Protection Act by Congress in 2000, the United States is required to cut off most nonhumanitarian foreign aid to countries not making an effort to eliminate this problem. While global enforcement efforts have increased in the last decade, the Department of Justice convicted only 184 people of human trafficking in 2014.[51]

CLIMATE CHANGE   It is increasingly obvious that environmental issues are a major national security issue for the United States. The relationship between environmental degradation and emerging security risks has become more apparent as the scale and intensity of environmental problems have evolved. In particular, the issue of climate change has been identified as one of the most important threats to long-term international stability. Climate change has been linked to increasing sea levels, more intense storms, and prolonged droughts. These factors have devastating impacts on living conditions throughout the planet and most notably in developing nations.

Under stress from global warming-induced environmental damage, developing countries are more prone to political, economic, and social unrest that can in turn create greater instability at the international level. The U.S. Defense Department has listed climate change among the security threats identified in the 2014 Quadrennial Defense Review, the report that updates Pentagon priorities every 4 years. And in 2009, the CIA created a new Center on Climate Change and National Security, demonstrating that the federal government's defense and intelligence organizations acknowledge the threats that climate change poses to the nation.[52]

OTHER ISSUES   This short account hardly does justice to the full range of human welfare issues that the United States must face. If you, like many people, are concerned about gasoline prices, perhaps you consider the price of oil and America's dependence on foreign oil the most important foreign policy issue. Or your primary focus may be the issue of religious freedom; many nations around the world

Retreating glaciers are one of the most visible signs of the planet's warming climate. Melting glaciers and polar ice threaten to increase sea levels that will inundate low-lying areas throughout the planet.

■ *Why has it been difficult to get global cooperation on policies that would reduce the emission of greenhouse gases and what role has the United States played in the failure of the international community to address this growing problem?*

do not permit individuals to practice their religious beliefs freely or to convert from one religion to another. Other important issues include child labor, the status of women, poverty, and access to health care. Almost 3 billion people—nearly half the world's population—live on less than $2 a day. There are 400 million children in the world who have no access to safe water, and 270 million have no access to health services.

Conclusion

As discussed at the beginning of this chapter, the decision of President Barack Obama to use airstrikes against ISIS in Syria in Operation Inherent Resolve, but also oppose President Assad, provides an excellent example of the complexities of U.S. foreign policy. As a world superpower, the United States maintains a combination of economic and military power that is unmatched. With this unique position every one of its foreign policy decisions sends ripples throughout the world and often determines the life and death of both Americans and non-Americans in every corner of the globe. What President-elect Donald Trump decides to do in foreign policy in 2017 will no doubt be different than what a President Hillary Clinton would have done. This is particularly true in American foreign policy toward Mexico, China, Russia, and Syria. Citizens of those countries are paying close attention to the new Trump administration. As you've learned, however, American foreign policy is complex. Even expert analysts cannot predict precisely how American foreign policy will be different at the end of 2017.

In this chapter, we have looked at the broad outlines of that debate as they are framed by neoconservatives, neoliberals, conservatives, and isolationists. These competing ideas draw on and bring together long-established ways of thinking about American foreign policy, dating back to the founding of the United States.

The making of American foreign policy is the product of the interaction between people and institutions. The American public expresses its voice through public opinion, elections, interest group activity, and political protest. Policymakers often have difficulty understanding what they hear from the public. They also have a desire to use the American public to help achieve their goals, which often reduces their willingness to listen. Presidents face a similar dilemma in reaching out for advice, whether to their White House staff or to the foreign policy bureaucracy. They want and need information but often hear unwelcome news. Competition among offices in the White House and within the foreign affairs bureaucracy provides the president with many choices of information sources and sets the stage for controversy. This controversy is often played out in public, especially when it involves conflict between the president and Congress.

One must also consider an economic climate that raises questions about the domestic costs and economic burden of projecting and promoting U.S. foreign policy objectives globally. Even limited U.S. operations in Syria, Iraq, and Afghanistan require a considerable amount of resources that U.S. taxpayers and the government need to provide. Many would argue that these resources are desperately needed at home. It may be argued that investments in U.S. infrastructure, research and development, education, and health care systems are needed to enhance our economic competitiveness and to protect manufacturing jobs. National-security and foreign-policy concerns compete with pocketbook concerns, and this competition is amplified during election season.

Both Democratic candidate Hillary Clinton and Republican candidate Donald Trump balanced these considerations in their messages to voters in the 2016 presidential election. As a global superpower, our international leadership role in an increasingly uncertain global environment is critical. At the same time, isolationists will challenge the costs of global engagement, especially during times of domestic economic hardship.

Finally, it is important to remember that terrorism is not the only foreign policy issue facing the United States today. A wide range of military security, economic, and human welfare issues are on the national agenda. Failure to address them adequately today may hold dire consequences for the future.

CONFRONTING POLITICS AND POLICY

As teenagers, Americans struggle to balance their schedule between academics, extracurricular, and leisure activities. In many parts of the world, such luxuries are not accorded to the youth, who are mired in poverty and conflict. It is estimated that many tens of thousands of child soldiers are being forced into combat in countries as diverse as Afghanistan, Central African Republic, the Philippines, and Uganda. Children under 18 have been involved in government and non-state armed groups. They are placed in precarious conditions against their will. It is a global challenge to release, disarm, demobilize, and reintegrate these child soldiers into their native societies. The United Nations is striving for a universal ratification of the Optional Protocol to the Convention on the Rights of the Child on the involvement of children in armed conflict.[53] Many feel that countries like the United States should be more forceful in ensuring that this measure is universally ratified. This could mean that the United States' foreign aid policy would have to be modified, in relation to countries accused of involving child soldiers.

ACTION STEPS

1. Imagine that the NGO Child Soldiers International hired you to manage its operations in the United States. As part of your responsibilities, you are required to launch a new public relations campaign to mobilize public opinion in favor of a more assertive U.S. foreign policy to deal with the scourge of child labor. What kind of message would you need to transmit to achieve your goal? How would you work with American civil society groups? How would you mobilize constituents to put pressure on their Congressmen and women and on the president of the United States? What role would the media play in your campaign?

2. Why do you think most Americans are not concerned about the issue of child soldiers? Could you explain to your friends that there is a moral as well as strategic reason to take this issue seriously?

⟩ REVIEW THE CHAPTER

Competing Principles for American Foreign Policy

15.1 Compare and contrast four different approaches to American foreign policy. (p. 516)

Four different schools of thought have existed throughout American history and continue to influence today's thinking on foreign policy. Two groups of "transformers" (neoliberals and neoconservatives) and two groups of "maintainers" (conservatives and isolationists) differ in their view of the proper content and conduct of American foreign policy. Neoliberals look to international organizations and agreements as ways for the United States to engage in foreign policy, while neoconservatives are more supportive of unilateral actions by the United States, if those actions help to preserve the nation's interests and standing in the world. Conservatives believe that the United States should not have to bear the burden for foreign policies that provide benefits to countries other than the United States, and isolationists seek to minimize U.S. entanglements with matters in other parts of the world.

Links Between Foreign and Domestic Policy

15.2 Establish three links between American foreign and domestic policy. (p. 522)

Three types of linkages exist between American foreign policy and domestic policy. First, American foreign policy is often influenced by some of the same values that guide domestic policy. Second, the U.S. political decision-making process is influenced by the efforts of lobbyists that represent foreign nations, groups, and businesses. Finally, U.S. foreign policy affects the distribution of costs and benefits among individuals and groups in the United States.

For more information on globalization, see the United Nations Environmental Program Web page at http://www.unep.org/.

The Domestic Context of American Foreign Policymaking

15.3 Assess pathways for citizen participation in foreign policymaking. (p. 527)

Public opinion, elections, interest group activity, and political protest are four different means by which the public can use pathways to influence foreign policy decisions. Many of the same factors that affect the making of domestic policy also play a role in shaping American foreign policy, but additional factors include lobbyists for foreign nations and other groups that exert influence on the adoption of U.S. policy toward other countries.

Political Institutions and Foreign Policymaking

15.4 Analyze how political institutions compete for influence in making foreign policy. (p. 532)

The president does not make foreign policy decisions alone but relies heavily on advisers and staff within the White House. The relationship between the president and Congress is dynamic and varies from strategic to competitive. Regardless of how they interact, Congress has a fixed number of tools at its disposal to influence foreign policy. The Supreme Court intervenes only rarely in foreign policy matters, but occasionally it reviews a case important to national security and foreign policy issues.

Foreign Policy and National Security Issues

15.5 Outline the major foreign policy issues confronting the United States today. (p. 541)

A complex set of military security, economic, and human welfare issues confronts the United States today. While terrorist threats capture much of the public's attention, other issues such as trade, human trafficking, and environmental degradation increasingly affect the security of the nation.

〉 LEARN THE TERMS

ISIS, p. 515
neoconservatives, p. 517
North Atlantic Treaty Organization
(NATO), p. 517
neoliberals, p. 517
weapons of mass destruction, p. 518
Kyoto Protocol, p. 522
Paris Agreement, p. 522

globalization, p. 524
Vietnam syndrome, p. 527
"rally 'round the flag" effect,
  p. 528
Strategic Arms Limitation Talks
(SALT), p. 528
Powell Doctrine, p. 535
McNamara Doctrine, p. 535

covert action, p. 536
intelligence, p. 536
containment, p. 538
détente, p. 539
jihadists, p. 542
preemption, p. 543
deterrence, p. 546
genocide, p. 548

〉 EXPLORE FURTHER

In the Library

Bacevich, Andrew. *The Limits of Power: The End of American Exceptionalism.* New York: Metropolitan/Holt, 2009.

Bales, Kevin, and Ron Soodalter. *The Slave Next Door: Human Trafficking and Slavery in America Today.* Berkeley, CA: University of California Press, 2009.

Ikenberry, G. John. *American Foreign Policy: Theoretical Essays,* 5th ed. Upper Saddle River, NJ: Prentice Hall, 2005.

Kohut, Andrew, and Bruce Stokes. *America Against the World.* New York: Times Books, 2006.

Mearsheimer, John J., and Stephen M. Walt. *The Israel Lobby and U.S. Foreign Policy.* New York: Farrar, Straus and Giroux, 2007.

Sobel, Richard. *The Impact of Public Opinion on U.S. Foreign Policy Since Vietnam.* New York: Oxford University Press, 2001.

Woodward, Bob. *Plan of Attack.* New York: Simon and Schuster, 2004.

Zakaria, Fareed. *The Post American World.* New York: Norton, 2008.

On the Web

Information regarding the work of the U.S. State Department including the activities of the Secretary of State are found at *http://www.state.gov/.*

Learn more about Woodrow Wilson and the League of Nations at *http://www.indiana.edu/~league/.*

For more information on globalization, see the United Nations Environmental Program Web page at *http://www.unep.org/.*

World Public Opinion.org, offers comprehensive information on public opinion around the world on international issues at *http://www.worldpublicopinion.org.*

The Central Intelligence Agency provides information on the global infectious disease threat and its implications for the United States at *http://www.fas.org/irp/threat/nie99-17d.htm.*

Foreign Service dispatches and periodic reports on U.S. foreign policy can be found at *http://www.unc.edu/depts/diplomat.*

Information on the national security strategy of the United States is available at *http://www.whitehouse.gov/nsc/nss.html.*

Information on the International Campaign to Ban Landmines can be found at *http://www.icbl.org/.*

Examine the 9-11 Commission's report online at *http://www.9-11commission.gov/.*

By the early 1770s, relations between Great Britain and 13 colonies in North America had become strained. Actual hostilities broke out in 1775 at Lexington and Concord, marking the beginning of the Revolutionary War. But the "patriot cause" was not universally accepted throughout the colonies. A second Continental Congress was called, and on May 10, 1775, representatives appointed by state legislatures from all of the colonies except Georgia convened in Philadelphia. A committee consisting of John Adams, Benjamin Franklin, Robert R. Livingston, Roger Sherman, and a slim, quiet delegate from Virginia named Thomas Jefferson (the "Committee of Five") was formed to draft a statement that would justify a war for independence. Adams suggested that Jefferson take the first stab at writing a draft document. With a few minor edits from Adams and Franklin, Jefferson presented his "Declaration" to the Continental Congress on June 28, 1776. Many agree that it is one of the most eloquent political statements ever written.

The Preamble of the Declaration is influenced by Enlightenment philosophy, a seventeenth-century European intellectual movement that held that all questions of math, science, and government could be solved through clear logic and careful experimentation. As such, it rejected superstition and religious "truths."

These words also clearly reflect the writings of English philosopher John Locke (1632–1704), particularly his *Second Treatise on Government*. Jefferson also seemed to be "borrowing" from the Virginia Declaration of Rights, which had been adopted about a month earlier.

Jefferson presents a notion of natural rights. That is, individuals possess certain privileges—certain guarantees by virtue of being human. These rights are *not* granted by government, but instead by God, or what Jefferson calls the "Creator." They cannot be given, nor can they be taken away.

Here Jefferson introduces the social contract theory, drawn in large measure from the writings of John Locke. Humans have the option of living alone in what he called "the state of nature." According to this theory, humans originally lived without government or laws, enjoying complete personal freedom. Yet the state of nature meant "a war of all against all," in which—in the words of another philosopher, Thomas Hobbes—life was "solitary, poor, nasty, brutish, and short." To end this perpetual conflict and insecurity, people created governments, thereby giving up some of their freedoms in order to protect their lives and their property.

Jefferson also agreed with Locke that governments, having been created by the people to protect their rights, are limited; they get their powers from the will of the people and no one else. (In arguing this, Locke was attacking the traditional claim that kings ruled by the will of God.)

When a government fails to respect the will of the people—that is, when it appears no longer to be limited—it becomes the right, indeed the obligation, of citizens to change the government. This passage is Jefferson's call for revolution.

Appendix 1

The Declaration of Independence of the Thirteen Colonies

In Congress, July 4, 1776

The Unanimous Declaration of the Thirteen United States of America

When in the Course of human events, it becomes necessary for one people to dissolve the political bands which have connected them with another, and to assume among the powers of the earth, the separate and equal station to which the Laws of Nature and of Nature's God entitle them, a decent respect to the opinions of mankind requires that they should declare the causes which impel them to the separation.

We hold these truths to be self-evident, that all men are created equal, that they are endowed by their Creator with certain unalienable Rights, that among these are Life, Liberty and the pursuit of Happiness. That to secure these rights, Governments are instituted among Men, deriving their just powers from the consent of the governed, that whenever any Form of Government becomes destructive of these ends, it is the Right of the People to alter or to abolish it, and to institute new Government, laying its foundation on such principles and organizing its powers in such form, as to them shall seem most likely to effect their Safety and Happiness.

> Here Jefferson seems to provide a caution: Governments should be responsive to the will of the people, but just because the public is upset with government does not imply the need for revolution. Yes, governments can be changed, but not for "light and transient causes."
>
> This next section is called the List of Grievances, which is essentially a laundry list of all the bad things that the British Government has done to the colonies. The idea here was to create such a long and powerful list that few would disagree with the need for a change.

> In all these passages, "He" refers to King George III.

> Precisely what defined a "government by the people" was still a bit vague at this time, but many suspected that representative assemblies were a necessary ingredient. So when the King dissolved these legislatures it seemed that he was striking a direct blow against self-rule.

Prudence, indeed, will dictate that Governments long established should not be changed for light and transient causes; and accordingly all experience hath shewn, that mankind are more disposed to suffer, while evils are sufferable, than to right themselves by abolishing the forms to which they are accustomed. But when a long train of abuses and usurpations, pursuing invariably the same Object evinces a design to reduce them under absolute Despotism, it is their right, it is their duty, to throw off such Government, and to provide new Guards for their future security. —Such has been the patient sufferance of these Colonies; and such is now the necessity which constrains them to alter their former Systems of Government. The history of the present King of Great Britain [George III] is a history of repeated injuries and usurpations, all having in direct object the establishment of an absolute Tyranny over these States. To prove this, let Facts be submitted to a candid world.

He has refused his Assent to Laws, the most wholesome and necessary for the public good.
He has forbidden his Governors to pass Laws of immediate and pressing importance, unless suspended in their operation till his Assent should be obtained; and when so suspended, he has utterly neglected to attend to them.

He has refused to pass other Laws for the accommodation of large districts of people, unless those people would relinquish the right of Representation in the Legislature, a right inestimable to them and formidable to tyrants only.

He has called together legislative bodies at places unusual, uncomfortable, and distant from the depository of their public Records, for the sole purpose of fatiguing them into compliance with his measures.

He has dissolved Representative Houses repeatedly, for opposing with manly firmness his invasions on the rights of the people.

He has refused for a long time, after such dissolutions, to cause others to be elected; whereby the Legislative powers, incapable of Annihilation, have returned to the People at large for their exercise; the State remaining in the mean time exposed to all the dangers of invasion from without, and convulsions within.

He has endeavoured to prevent the population of these States; for that purpose obstructing the Laws for Naturalization of Foreigners; refusing to pass others to encourage their migrations hither, and raising the conditions of new Appropriations of Lands.

He has obstructed the Administration of Justice, by refusing his Assent to Laws for establishing Judiciary powers.

An independent judiciary was also an element deemed essential for democratic governance, and the King's control of the courts seems a clear illustration of tyranny.

He has made Judges dependent on his Will alone, for the tenure of their offices, and the amount and payment of their salaries.

He has erected a multitude of New Offices, and sent hither swarms of Officers to harass our people, and eat out their substance.

He has kept among us, in times of peace, Standing Armies without the consent of our legislatures.

While most countries keep "standing armies" these days, in the eighteenth-century armies were assembled only when war was at hand. Many colonists saw the King's army as an instrument of aggression and control.

He has affected to render the Military independent of and superior to the Civil power.

He has combined with others to subject us to a jurisdiction foreign to our constitution and unacknowledged by our laws; giving his Assent to their Acts of pretended Legislation:

For Quartering large bodies of armed troops among us:

What is interesting about the list of grievances is that many of the items refer to more theoretical matters pertaining to just governance and the rights of citizens. But other items point to pragmatic issues, such as improperly taking money from colonists. Make no mistake, the Revolution was about creating a democratic system of government, a government responsive to "the people," but it was also about creating a system where average citizens could prosper financially.

For protecting them, by a mock Trial, from punishment for any Murders which they should commit on the Inhabitants of these States:

For cutting off our Trade with all parts of the world:

For imposing Taxes on us without our Consent:

For depriving us, in many cases, of the benefits of Trial by Jury:

Many colonists were anxious to pursue independence because they believed in self-rule, but many others were mostly interested in commercial issues (economic gain). So the "open trade" issue was critical for building broad public support for independence.

For transporting us beyond Seas to be tried for pretended offences:

For abolishing the free System of English Laws in a neighbouring Province, establishing therein an Arbitrary government, and enlarging its Boundaries so as to render it at once an example and fit instrument for introducing the same absolute rule into these Colonies:

For taking away our Charters, abolishing our most valuable Laws, and altering fundamentally the Forms of our Governments:

Again, many saw colonial assemblies as the foundation of a free society, so the King's suspension of their laws suggested tyrannical rule.

With the French and Indian War only a few years distant, many of the colonists continued to have grave fears about hostilities with Native Americans. So to suggest that the King was inflaming conflict was no small matter.

This was perceived as especially harsh language. To call the King "a Tyrant" was considered an act of treason.

Was the Declaration of Independence effective in rallying support behind the revolutionary cause? We do know that many New Yorkers were so inspired upon hearing these words that they toppled a statue of King George and had it melted down to make 42,000 bullets for war. Still, many balked at joining the Revolution and even enlisted in the British Army. We also know that public support for the Continental Army, headed by George Washington, lagged considerably throughout the Revolution.

For suspending our own Legislatures, and declaring themselves invested with power to legislate for us in all cases whatsoever.

He has abdicated Government here, by declaring us out of his Protection and waging War against us.

He has plundered our seas, ravaged our Coasts, burnt our towns, and destroyed the lives of our people.

He is at this time transporting large Armies of foreign Mercenaries to compleat the works of death, desolation and tyranny, already begun with circumstances of Cruelty and perfidy scarcely paralleled in the most barbarous ages, and totally unworthy the Head of a civilized nation.

He has constrained our fellow Citizens taken Captive on the high Seas to bear Arms against their Country, to become the executioners of their friends and Brethren, or to fall themselves by their Hands.

He has excited domestic insurrections amongst us, and has endeavoured to bring on the inhabitants of our frontiers, the merciless Indian Savages, whose known rule of warfare, is an undistinguished destruction of all ages, sexes and conditions.

In every stage of these Oppressions We have Petitioned for Redress in the most humble terms: Our repeated Petitions have been answered only by repeated injury. A Prince whose character is thus marked by every act which may define a Tyrant, is unfit to be the ruler of a free people.

Nor have We been wanting in attentions to our British brethren. We have warned them from time to time of attempts by their legislature to extend an unwarrantable jurisdiction over us. We have reminded them of the circumstances of our emigration and settlement here. We have appealed to their native justice and magnanimity, and we have conjured them by the ties of our common kindred to disavow these usurpations, which would inevitably interrupt our connections and correspondence. They too have been deaf to the voice of justice and of consanguinity. We must, therefore, acquiesce in the necessity, which denounces our Separation, and hold them, as we hold the rest of mankind, Enemies in War, in Peace Friends.

We, therefore, the Representatives of the united States of America, in General Congress, Assembled, appealing to the Supreme Judge of the world for the rectitude of our intentions, do, in the Name, and by the Authority of the good People of these Colonies, solemnly publish and declare, That these United Colonies are, and of Right ought to be Free and Independent States; that they are Absolved from all Allegiance to the British Crown, and that all political connection between them and the State of Great Britain, is and ought to be totally dissolved; and that as Free and Independent States, they have full Power to levy War, conclude Peace, contract Alliances, establish Commerce, and to do all other Acts and Things which Independent States may of right do. And for the support of this Declaration, with a firm reliance on the protection of divine Providence, we mutually pledge to each other our Lives, our Fortunes and our sacred Honor.

The signers of the Declaration represented the new states as follows:

NEW HAMPSHIRE
Josiah Bartlett, William Whipple, Matthew Thornton

MASSACHUSETTS
John Hancock, Samuel Adams, John Adams, Robert Treat Paine, Elbridge Gerry

RHODE ISLAND
Stephen Hopkins, William Ellery

CONNECTICUT
Roger Sherman, Samuel Huntington, William Williams, Oliver Wolcott

All the signers assumed that they were, in effect, signing their own death warrant if indeed the Revolution were to fail. The above paragraph, about absolving allegiances to the British Crown and creating independent states, would surely be interpreted as treason in England. Signing the Declaration was an act of true courage.

On July 19, 1776, Congress ordered a copy be handwritten for the delegates to sign, which most did on August 2, 1776. Two delegates never signed at all. As new delegates joined the Congress, they were also allowed to sign. A total of 56 delegates eventually signed.

The first and most famous signature on the embossed copy was that of John Hancock, President of the Continental Congress.

NEW YORK
William Floyd, Philip Livingston, Francis Lewis, Lewis Morris

NEW JERSEY
Richard Stockton, John Witherspoon, Francis Hopkinson, John Hart, Abraham Clark

PENNSYLVANIA
Robert Morris, Benjamin Rush, Benjamin Franklin, John Morton, George Clymer, James Smith, George Taylor, James Wilson, George Ross

Franklin was the oldest signer, at 70.

DELAWARE
Caesar Rodney, George Read, Thomas McKean

MARYLAND
Samuel Chase, William Paca, Thomas Stone, Charles Carroll of Carrollton

VIRGINIA
George Wythe, Richard Henry Lee, Thomas Jefferson, Benjamin Harrison, Thomas Nelson, Jr., Francis Lightfoot Lee, Carter Braxton

Two future presidents signed the Declaration — Thomas Jefferson and John Adams.

NORTH CAROLINA
William Hooper, Joseph Hewes, John Penn

SOUTH CAROLINA
Edward Rutledge, Thomas Heyward, Jr., Thomas Lynch, Jr., Arthur Middleton

Edward Rutledge, at age 26, was the youngest signer of the Declaration.

GEORGIA
Button Gwinnett, Lyman Hall, George Walton

After its adoption by the Congress, a handwritten draft was then sent a few blocks away to the printing shop of John Dunlap. Through the night between 150 and 200 copies were made, now known as "Dunlap broadsides." One was sent to George Washington on July 6, who had it read to his troops in New York on July 9. The 25 Dunlap broadsides still known to exist are the oldest surviving copies of the document. The original handwritten copy has not survived.

The signed copy of the Declaration of Independence is on display at the National Archives.

"We, the people." Three simple words are of profound importance and contentious origin. Every government in the world at the time of the Constitutional Convention was some type of monarchy, wherein sovereign power was bestowed from the top. The Founders of our new country rejected monarchy as a form of government and proposed instead a republic, which would draw its sovereignty from the people.

It is this very sense of empowerment that allows the "people" to influence our government and shape the world in which we live. We are among the freest people in the world largely because of this document. We are presented with multiple pathways to influence our government and better our lives.

Article I. The very first article in the Constitution established the legislative branch of the new national government. Why did the framers start with the legislative power instead of the executive branch? The framers truly believed it was the most important component of the new government.

It was also something that calmed the anxieties of average citizens. That is, they had experience with "legislative-centered governance" under the Articles and even during the colonial period. It was not perfect, but the legislative process seemed to work.

Section 1. Section 1 established a bicameral (two-chamber) legislature, or an upper (Senate) and lower (House of Representatives) organization of the legislative branch.

A bicameral legislature offers more opportunities to influence the policy process, as you can appeal to both your Senators and your representatives through the lobbying decision makers pathway, or indirectly through the elections pathway, the grassroots mobilization pathway, or the cultural change pathway. If you do not like a law passed by Congress, you can appeal to the courts to invalidate it or to change its meaning.

Section 2 Clause 1. This section sets the term of office for House members (2 years) and indicates that those voting for Congress will have the same qualifications as those voting for the state legislatures. Originally, states limited voters to white property owners. Some states even had religious disqualifications, for instance, if citizens were Catholic or Jewish.

There was a great deal of discussion about how long a legislator should sit in office before appealing to constituents for reelection. Short terms of office, such as the two years used in the House of Representatives, help force members to pay attention to the needs of their constituents.

Clause 2. This section sets forth the basic qualifications of a -representative: at least 25 years of age, a U.S. citizen for at least seven years, and a resident of the state in which the district is located. Note that the Constitution does not require a person to be a resident of the district he or she represents.

Clause 2 does not specify how many terms a representative can serve in Congress, but some critics support limiting the number of terms members can serve in order to make Congress more in touch with the citizenry—and to overcome some of the advantages incumbents have created to help win elections. Currently the average length of service in the House is nine years (4.6 terms).

Appendix 2

The Constitution of the United States

The Preamble

We, the People of the United States, in Order to form a more perfect Union, establish Justice, insure domestic Tranquility, provide for the common defence, promote the general Welfare, and secure the Blessings of Liberty to ourselves and our Posterity, do ordain and establish this Constitution for the United States of America.

Article I
The Legislative Article
Legislative Power

SECTION 1. All legislative Powers herein granted shall be vested in a Congress of the United States, which shall consist of a Senate and House of Representatives.

House of Representatives: Composition; Qualifications; Apportionment; Impeachment Power

SECTION 2 CLAUSE 1. The House of Representatives shall be composed of Members chosen every second Year by the People of the several States, and the Electors in each State shall have the Qualifications requisite for Electors of the most numerous Branch of the State Legislature.

CLAUSE 2. No Person shall be a Representative who shall not have attained to the Age of twenty five Years, and been seven Years a Citizen of the United States, and who shall not, when elected, be an Inhabitant of that State in which he shall be chosen.

CLAUSE 3. Representatives and direct Taxes[1] shall be apportioned among the several States which may be included within this Union,

Clause 3. This clause contains the Three-Fifths Compromise, in which Native Americans and African Americans were only counted as three-fifths of a person for congressional representation purposes. This clause also addresses the question of congressional reapportionment every 10 years, which requires a census. Since the 1911 Reapportionment Act, the size of the House of Representatives has been set at 435. This is the designated size that is reapportioned every 10 years. Based on changes of population, some states gain and some states lose representatives.

While the Constitution never directly addresses the issue of slavery, this clause and others clearly condone its existence. It ultimately took the Civil War (1861–1865) to resolve the issue of slavery.

Clause 4. This clause provides a procedure for replacing a U.S. representative in the case of death, resignation, or expulsion from the House. Essentially, the governor of the representative's state will determine the selection of a successor. Generally, if less than half a term is left, the governor will appoint a successor. If more than half a term is remaining, most states require a special election to fill the vacancy.

Clause 5. Only one officer of the House is specified, the Speaker. The House decides all other officers. This clause also gives the House authority for impeachments—the determination of formal charges—against officials of the executive and judicial branches.

Interestingly, this clause does not stipulate that the Speaker be a member of Congress. The House might choose an outsider to run their chamber, but this has never happened—and will likely not happen in the future.

Section 3 Clause 1. This clause treats each state equally—all have two senators. Originally, state legislators chose senators, but since passage and ratification of the Seventeenth Amendment, they are now elected by popular vote. This clause also establishes the term of a senator—six years, three times that of a House member.

This clause is very important when thinking about pathways of change. For one, it creates a mechanism by which the minority, through their senators, can thwart the will of the majority. Each state has the same number of senators. A majority of senators, representing states with small populations, have the ability to control the process—or at least stall things. In our system "majority will" does not always prevail.

Also, six-year terms give senators the chance to worry only periodically about an approaching reelection. Unlike members of the House, who come up for reelection so frequently that their actions may be constantly guided by a concern for pleasing the voters, this extended term in office offers senators some leeway to do what they think is best for their state and the nation, rather than what might be seen as popular.

Clause 2. To prevent a wholesale replacement of senators every six years, this clause provides that one-third of the Senate will be elected every two years. In other words, in order to remove at least one-half of the Senators from office, two elections are needed.

Senate vacancies are filled in the same way as the House—either appointment by the governor or by special election. Currently the average length of service in the Senate is 11.3 years (slightly less than two terms).

Clause 3. This clause sets forth the qualifications for U.S. senator: at least 30 years old, a U.S. citizen for at least nine years, and a citizen of a state. The equivalent age of 30 today would be 54 years old. The average age of a U.S. senator at present is 59.5 years.

according to their respective Numbers, which shall be determined by adding to the whole Number of free Persons, including those bound to Service for a Term of Years, and excluding Indians not taxed, three fifths of all other Persons.[2] The actual Enumeration shall be made within three Years after the first Meeting of the Congress of the United States, and within every subsequent Term of ten Years, in such Manner as they shall by Law direct. The Number of Representatives shall not exceed one for every thirty Thousand, but each State shall have at Least one Representative; and until such enumeration shall be made, the State of New Hampshire shall be entitled to chuse three, Massachusetts eight, Rhode-Island and Providence Plantations one, Connecticut five, New-York six, New Jersey four, Pennsylvania eight, Delaware one, Maryland six, Virginia ten, North Carolina five, South Carolina five, and Georgia three.

CLAUSE 4. When vacancies happen in the Representation from any State, the Executive Authority thereof shall issue Writs of Election to fill such Vacancies.

CLAUSE 5. The House of Representatives shall chuse their Speaker and other Officers; and shall have the sole Power of Impeachment.

Senate Composition: Qualifications, Impeachment Trials

SECTION 3 CLAUSE 1. The Senate of the United States shall be composed of two Senators from each State, chosen by the Legislature thereof,[3] for six Years; and each Senator shall have one Vote.

CLAUSE 2. Immediately after they shall be assembled in Consequence of the first Election, they shall be divided as equally as may be into three Classes. The Seats of the Senators of the first Class shall be vacated at the Expiration of the second Year, of the second Class at the Expiration of the fourth Year, and of the third Class at the Expiration of the sixth Year, so that one third may be chosen every second Year; and if Vacancies happen by Resignation, or otherwise, during the Recess of the Legislature of any State, the Executive thereof may make temporary Appointments until the next Meeting of the Legislature, which shall then fill such Vacancies.[4]

CLAUSE 3. No Person shall be a Senator who shall not have attained to the Age of thirty Years, and been nine Years a Citizen of the United States, and who shall not, when elected, be an Inhabitant of that State for which he shall be chosen.

CLAUSE 4. The Vice President of the United States shall be President of the Senate, but shall have no Vote, unless they be equally divided.

CLAUSE 5. The Senate shall chuse their other Officers, and also a President pro tempore, in the Absence of the Vice President, or when he shall exercise the Office of President of the United States.

CLAUSE 6. The Senate shall have the sole Power to try all Impeachments. When sitting for that Purpose, they shall be on Oath or Affirmation. When the President of the United States is tried, the Chief Justice shall preside: And no Person shall be convicted without the Concurrence of two thirds of the Members present.

CLAUSE 7. Judgment in Cases of Impeachment shall not extend further than to removal from Office, and disqualification to hold and enjoy any Office of honor, Trust or Profit under the United States: but the Party convicted shall nevertheless be liable and subject to Indictment, Trial, Judgment and Punishment, according to Law.

Congressional Elections: Times, Places, Manner

SECTION 4 CLAUSE 1. The Times, Places and Manner of holding Elections for Senators and Representatives, shall be prescribed in each State by the Legislature thereof; but the Congress may at any time by Law make or alter such Regulations, except as to the Places of chusing Senators.

CLAUSE 2. The Congress shall assemble at least once in every Year, and such Meeting shall be on the first Monday in December, unless they shall by Law appoint a different Day.[5]

Powers and Duties of the Houses

SECTION 5 CLAUSE 1. Each House shall be the Judge of the Elections, Returns and Qualifications of its own Members, and a Majority of each shall constitute a Quorum to do Business; but a smaller Number may adjourn from day to day, and may be authorized to compel the Attendance of absent Members, in such Manner, and under the Penalties as each House may provide.

Clause 4.   The only constitutional duty of the vice president is specified in this clause—president of the Senate. This official only has a vote if there is a tie vote in the Senate; then the vice president's vote breaks the tie.
    The split between Democrats and Republicans in Congress has been tiny in recent years. Not surprisingly, the Vice President has been called upon to cast several deciding votes.

Clause 5.   One official office in the U.S. Senate is specified—temporary president, who fills in during the vice president's absence (which is normally the case). All other Senate officers are designated and selected by the Senate.

Clause 6, 7.   The Senate acts as a trial court for impeached federal officials. If the accused is the president, the Chief Justice of the U.S. Supreme Court presides. Otherwise, the vice president normally presides. Conviction of the charges requires a two-thirds majority vote of those senators present at the time of the vote. Conviction results in the federal official's removal from office and disqualification to hold any other federal appointed office.

Section 4 Clause 1.   Through the years this clause has proven to be a critical aspect of the elections pathway. By allowing states to regulate elections procedures (that is, until Congress acts), the types of citizens able to participate in the process have been limited. First, religious and property qualifications were common, and many southern states used this provision to discriminate against black voters until the 1960s. Many states barred women from voting in elections until the ratification of the Nineteenth Amendment, and still others kept 18-year-olds out until the Twenty-Fifth Amendment.
    Lingering issues include residency and registration requirements. In some states citizens can register to vote on Election Day, but in many others they have to take this step 30 days in advance. Indeed, many argue that residency and registration requirements unnecessarily inhibit voting, especially for young people who tend to be more mobile. Others argue that such laws help to reduce voter fraud.

Clause 2.   The states determine the place and manner of electing representatives and senators, but Congress has the right to make or change these laws or regulations, except for the election sites. Congress is required to meet annually, and now, by law, annual meetings begin in January.

Section 5 Clause 1.   This clause enables each legislative branch to essentially make its own rules. Normally, to take a vote, a quorum is necessary. But if no votes are scheduled, fewer than a quorum can convene a session.

Clause 2. Essentially, each branch promulgates its own rules and punishes its own members. Knowing exactly how each chamber of the legislature conducts its proceedings is essential for political activists. The lobbying decision makers pathway can be a potent means of shifting public policy, but only when internal rules are well understood. Perhaps this is one of the reasons why former members of Congress make such good lobbyists.

Clause 3. An official record called the Congressional Record, House Journal, etc., is kept for all sessions. It is a daily account of House and Senate floor debates, votes, and members' remarks. However, a record is not printed if a proceeding is closed to the public for security reasons. Many votes are by voice vote, and if at least one-fifth of the members request, a recorded vote of Yeas and Nays will be conducted and documented. This procedure permits analysis of congressional role-call votes.

Clause 4. This clause prevents one house from adjourning for a long period of time or to some other location without the consent of the other house.

Section 6 Clause 1. This section refers to a salary paid to senators and members of the House from the U.S. Treasury. This clearly states that federal legislators work for the entire nation, and not for their respective states.

In 2014, the salary for members of Congress was $174,000; some leadership positions, like Speaker of the House, receive a higher salary. The Speaker receives a salary of $223,500. Members of Congress receive many other benefits: free health care, fully funded retirement system, free round trips to their home state or district, etc. This section also provides immunity from arrest or prosecution for congressional actions on the floor or in travel to and from the Congress. For example, few members of Congress have ever been charged with drunk driving.

Clause 2. This section prevents the United States from adopting a parliamentary democracy, since congressional members cannot hold executive offices and members of the executive branch cannot be members of Congress.

Section 7 Clause 1. This clause specifies one of the few powers specific to the U.S. House—revenue bills. Since the House was intended to be more closely tied to the people (since members are elected more frequently and they represent fewer people than the Senate), the Founders wanted to grant them the power of the purse.

Given that much of politics centers on the allocation of scarce resources (the distribution of money), this provision is a key piece of information for would-be political activists.

CLAUSE 2. Each House may determine the Rules of its Proceedings, punish its Members for disorderly Behaviour, and, with the Concurrence of two thirds, expel a Member.

CLAUSE 3. Each House shall keep a Journal of its Proceedings, and from time to time publish the same, excepting such Parts as may in their Judgment require Secrecy; and the Yeas and Nays of the Members of either House on any question shall, at the Desire of one fifth of those Present, be entered on the Journal.

CLAUSE 4. Neither House, during the Session of Congress, shall, without the Consent of the other, adjourn for more than three days, nor to any other Place than that in which the two Houses shall be sitting.

Rights of Members

SECTION 6 CLAUSE 1. The Senators and Representatives shall receive a Compensation for their Services, to be ascertained by Law, and paid out of the Treasury of the United States. They shall in all Cases, except Treason, Felony and Breach of the Peace, be privileged from Arrest during their Attendance at the Session of their respective Houses, and in going to and returning from the same; and for any Speech or Debate in either House, they shall not be questioned in any other Place.

CLAUSE 2. No Senator or Representative shall, during the Time for which he was elected, be appointed to any civil Office under the Authority of the United States, which shall have been created, or the Emoluments whereof shall have been encreased during such time; and no Person holding any Office under the United States, shall be a Member of either House during his Continuance in Office.

Legislative Powers: Bills and Resolutions

Section 7 Clause 1. All Bills for raising Revenue shall originate in the House of Representatives; but the Senate may propose or concur with Amendments as on other Bills.

CLAUSE 2. Every Bill which shall have passed the House of Representatives and the Senate, shall, before it becomes a Law, be presented to the President of the United States; If he approve he shall sign it, but if not he shall return it, with his Objections to that House in which it shall have originated, who shall enter the Objections at large on their Journal, and proceed to reconsider it. If after such Reconsideration two thirds of that House shall agree to pass the Bill, it shall be sent, together with the Objections, to the other House, by which it shall likewise be reconsidered, and if approved by two thirds of that House, it shall become a Law. But in all such Cases the Votes of both Houses shall be determined by yeas and Nays, and the Names of the Persons voting for and against the Bill shall be entered on the Journal of each House respectively. If any Bill shall not be returned by the President within ten Days (Sundays excepted) after it shall have been presented to him, the Same shall be a Law, in like Manner as if he had signed it, unless the Congress by their Adjournment prevent its Return, in which Case it shall not be a Law.

CLAUSE 3 Every Order, Resolution, or Vote to which the Concurrence of the Senate and House of Representatives may be necessary (except on a question of Adjournment) shall be presented to the President of the United States; and before the Same shall take Effect, shall be approved by him, or being disapproved by him, shall be repassed by two thirds of the Senate and House of Representatives, according to the Rules and Limitations prescribed in the Case of a Bill.

Powers of Congress

Section 8 Clause 1. The Congress shall have Power To lay and collect Taxes, Duties, Imposts and Excises, to pay the Debts and provide for the common Defence and general Welfare of the United States; but all Duties, Imposts and Excises shall be uniform throughout the United States.

CLAUSE 2. To borrow Money on the credit of the United States;

CLAUSE 3. To regulate Commerce with foreign Nations, and among the several States, and with the Indian Tribes;

CLAUSE 4. To establish an uniform Rule of Naturalization; and uniform Laws on the subject of Bankruptcies throughout the United States;

Clause 2. The heart of the checks and balances system is contained in this clause. Both the House and Senate must pass an identical bill and present it to the president. If the president fails to act on the bill within 10 days (not including Sundays), the bill will automatically become law if Congress is in session. If the president signs the bill, it becomes law. If the president vetoes the bill and sends it back to Congress, this body may override the veto by a two-thirds vote in each branch. This vote must be a recorded vote.

The systems of checks and balances, as well as a division of power at the federal level, allow many ways to pursue change by a variety of pathways.

Clause 3. This clause covers every other type of legislative action other than a bill. Essentially, the same procedures apply in most cases. There are a few exceptions. For example, a joint resolution proposing a new congressional amendment is not subject to presidential veto.

Section 8 Clause 1, 2. This power allows the federal government to deficit-spend (which most states are not allowed to do). Thus, when times of economic difficulty arise, individuals and groups can petition government for financial aid and relief with job shortages.

Clause 3. This is one of the most sweeping powers granted Congress, because so much can be linked to interstate "commerce." Since the early twentieth century, the U.S. Supreme Court has defined interstate commerce broadly and thereby enabled Congress to use this power to pass antidiscrimination laws, criminal justice laws, and other statutes.

Clause 4. This provision helps us understand why Congress, rather than state legislatures, has been at the center of the recent immigration reform debate.

Clause 5, 6, 7. Congressional power over coining money, counterfeiting, and post offices provides the justification for the creation of many criminal laws that are handled by federal law enforcement agencies such as the Federal Bureau of Investigation (FBI) and Secret Service. Because these matters are specified as under federal authority in the Constitution, it is a federal crime—rather than a state crime—to counterfeit money and engage in mail fraud. Most other kinds of crimes, such as murders, robberies, and burglaries victimizing ordinary citizens, are governed by state law.

Clause 9. Congress is responsible for the design of and procedures used in the federal court system. The U.S. Supreme Court is the only court created by the Constitution (see Article III). The lower federal courts are created by—and can be changed by—laws enacted by Congress. When there are changes in the design of the federal court system, such as the creation of a new court, these matters are under the power of Congress rather than under the control of the Supreme Court.

Clause 10, 11. Although Congress possesses the exclusive authority to declare war, presidents use their powers as commander-in-chief (see Article II) to initiate military actions even when there is no formal congressional declaration of war. There have been periodic disputes about whether presidents have exceeded their authority and ignored the Constitution's explicit grant of war-declaring power to Congress.

Clause 11, 12, 13. These three clauses, clauses 11, 12, and 13, ensure that Congress is involved in foreign policy decisions; thus citizens and groups can appeal to Congress if they do not like the president's foreign policy decisions or actions. Giving Congress the power to make appropriations to fund the military is potentially a significant power they have in rivaling the president for influence.

Clause 14, 15, 16. These clauses establish what are known as the "expressed" or "specified" powers of Congress.

Clause 17. This clause establishes the seat of the federal government, which was first located in New York. It eventually was moved to Washington, D.C., when both Maryland and Virginia ceded land to the new national government, which then established the District of Columbia.

CLAUSE 5. To coin Money, regulate the Value thereof, and of foreign Coin, and fix the Standard of Weights and Measures;

CLAUSE 6. To provide for the Punishment of counterfeiting the Securities and current Coin of the United States;

CLAUSE 7. To establish Post Offices and post Roads;

CLAUSE 8. To promote the Progress of Science and useful Arts, by securing for limited Times to Authors and Inventors the exclusive Right to their respective Writings and Discoveries;

CLAUSE 9. To constitute Tribunals inferior to the supreme Court;

CLAUSE 10. To define and punish Piracies and Felonies committed on the high Seas, and Offences against the Law of Nations;

CLAUSE 11. To declare War, grant Letters of Marque and Reprisal, and make Rules concerning Captures on Land and Water;

CLAUSE 12. To raise and support Armies, but no Appropriation of Money to that Use shall be for a longer Term than two Years;

CLAUSE 13. To provide and maintain a Navy;

CLAUSE 14. To make Rules for the Government and Regulation of the land and naval Forces;

CLAUSE 15. To provide for calling forth the Militia to execute the Laws of the Union, suppress Insurrections and repel Invasions;

CLAUSE 16. To provide for organizing, arming, and disciplining, the Militia, and for governing such Part of them as may be employed in the Service of the United States, reserving to the States respectively, the Appointment of the Officers, and the Authority of training the Militia according to the discipline prescribed by Congress;

CLAUSE 17. To exercise exclusive Legislation in all Cases whatsoever, over such District (not exceeding ten Miles square) as may, by Cession of particular States, and the Acceptance of Congress, become the Seat of the Government of the United States, and to exercise like Authority over all Places purchased by the Consent of the Legislature of the State in which the Same shall be, for the Erection of Forts, Magazines, Arsenals, dock-Yards, and other needful Buildings;

CLAUSE 18. To make all Laws which shall be necessary and proper for carrying into Execution the foregoing Powers, and all other Powers vested by this Constitution in the Government of the United States, or in any Department or Officer thereof.

Powers Denied to Congress

SECTION 9 CLAUSE 1 The Migration or Importation of such Persons as any of the States now existing shall think proper to admit, shall not be prohibited by the Congress prior to the Year one thousand eight hundred and eight, but a Tax or duty may be imposed on such Importation, not exceeding ten dollars for each Person.

CLAUSE 2. The Privilege of the Writ of Habeas Corpus shall not be suspended, unless when in Cases of Rebellion or Invasion the public Safety may require it.

CLAUSE 3. No Bill of Attainder or ex post facto Law shall be passed.

CLAUSE 4. No Capitation, or other direct, Tax shall be laid, unless in Proportion to the Census or Enumeration herein before directed to be taken.[6]

CLAUSE 5. No Tax or Duty shall be laid on Articles exported from any State.

CLAUSE 6. No Preference shall be given by any Regulation of Commerce or Revenue to the Ports of one State over those of another; nor shall Vessels bound to, or from, one State, be obliged to enter, clear, or pay Duties in another.

CLAUSE 7. No Money shall be drawn from the Treasury, but in Consequence of Appropriations made by Law; and a regular Statement and Account of the Receipts and Expenditures of all public Money shall be published from time to time.

Clause 18. This clause, known as the "Elastic Clause," provides the basis for the doctrine of "implied" congressional powers, which was first introduced in the U.S. Supreme Court case of *McCulloch* v. *Maryland* (1819). It greatly expanded the power of Congress to pass legislation and make regulations.
  The "Necessary and Proper" Clause increases the powers of Congress, granting the legislature a great deal more authority and influence in our system of government. It has proven essential in creating a strong national government and in placing Congress at the center of the policy process.

Section 9 Clause 1. This clause was part of the Three-Fifths Compromise. Essentially, the new Congress was prohibited from stopping the importation of slaves until 1808, but it could impose a head tax not to exceed $10 for each slave.
  Condoning slavery, from today's perspective, clearly clashed with the Declaration of Independence's assertion that all men are created equal. It is hard to understand the hypocrisy of a free society with slaves. Without this provision, however, southern delegates would have left the Constitutional Convention, and southern states would not have voted to ratify the new Constitution.

Clause 2. Habeas Corpus is a judicial order forcing law enforcement authorities to produce a prisoner they are holding, and to justify the prisoner's continued confinement. Congress cannot suspend the writ of habeas corpus except in cases of rebellion or invasion. The writ of habeas corpus permits a judge to inquire about the legality of detention or deprivation of liberty of any citizen. This is one of the few legal protections for individuals enshrined in the Constitution before the Bill of Rights.

Clause 3. This provision prohibits Congress from passing either bills of attainder (an act of legislature declaring a person or group of persons guilty of some crime, and punishing them, without benefit of a trial) or ex post facto laws (retroactive crimes after passage of legislation). Similar restrictions were put in many state constitutions. These protections were among the few specifically provided for individuals in the body of the Constitution before the creation of amendments.

Clause 4. This clause was interpreted to prevent Congress from passing an income tax. When the Supreme Court struck down congressional efforts to impose an income tax, passage of the Sixteenth Amendment in 1913 counteracted the Supreme Court decision and gave Congress this power.

Clause 5. This section establishes free trade within the United States That is, one state cannot tax the importation of domestic goods, and the federal government cannot tax state exports.

Clause 6. This clause also applies to free trade within the United States The national government cannot show any preference to any state or maritime movements among the states.

Clause 7. This clause prevents any expenditure unless it has been provided for in an appropriations bill enacted by Congress. At the beginning of most fiscal years, Congress has not completed the budget. Technically, the government cannot then spend any money, and would have to shut down. So Congress usually passes a Continuing Resolution Authority providing temporary authority to continue to spend money until the final budget is approved and signed into law.

Clause 8. Feudalism would not be established in the new country. We would have no nobles. No federal official can accept a title of nobility (even honorary) without permission of Congress.

This section sets out the prohibitions on state actions.

Section 10 Clause 1. This clause is a laundry list of denied powers. These restrictions cannot be waived by Congress. States cannot engage in foreign relations or acts of war. Letters of marque and reprisal were used to provide legal cover for privateers. The federal government's currency monopoly is established. The sanctity of contracts is specified, and similar state prohibitions are specified for bills of attainder, ex post facto, etc.

Clause 2. This section establishes the monopoly control of the national government in matters of both national and international trade. The only concession to states is health and safety inspections.

Clause 3. This final section of the Legislative article establishes the war monopoly power of the national government. The only exception to state action is actual invasion or threat of imminent danger.

Article II. This article establishes an entirely new concept in government—an elected executive power. This was a touchy topic in 1787. On one hand, there was great worry about executive power—it was seen as the root of tyranny. On the other hand, many believed that a powerful executive was necessary for long-term stability for the new nation. The right balance was a system with a strong executive, where the executive's power could be limited.

Section 1 Clause 1. This clause establishes the executive power in the office of the president of the United States of America. It also establishes a second office—vice president. A four-year term was established, but not a limit on the number of terms. A limit was later established by the Twenty-Second Amendment.

Clause 2. This paragraph establishes the Electoral College to choose the president and vice president. Each state can determine how electors will be allotted to different candidates. For instance, today 48 states give the candidate who receives the most votes from citizens all of its electoral votes. This "winner-take-all" system puts an important twist on presidential election strategy. The trick for the candidates is to amass 270 electoral votes from different combinations of states.

    Another implication of this system of choosing an executive is that it is possible for one candidate to receive more votes from citizens than other candidates, but still not become president. This has occurred four times in American history, most recently in 2000, when Al Gore received roughly 500,000 votes more than George W. Bush but fewer Electoral College votes.

CLAUSE 8. No Title of Nobility shall be granted by the United States: And no Person holding any Office of Profit or Trust under them, shall, without the Consent of Congress, accept of any present, Emolument, Office, or Title, of any kind whatever, from any King, Prince, or foreign State.

Powers Denied to the States

SECTION 10 CLAUSE 1. No State shall enter into any Treaty, Alliance, or Confederation; grant Letters of Marque and Reprisal; coin Money; emit Bills of Credit; make any Thing but gold and silver; Coin a Tender in Payment of Debts; pass any Bill of Attainder, ex post facto Law, or Law impairing the Obligation of Contracts, or grant any Title of Nobility.

CLAUSE 2. No State shall, without the Consent of the Congress, lay any Imposts or Duties on Imports or Exports, except what may be absolutely necessary for executing its inspection Laws: and the net Produce of all Duties and Imposts, laid by any State on Imports or Exports, shall be for the Use of the Treasury of the United States; and all such Laws shall be subject to the Revision and Controul of the Congress.

CLAUSE 3. No State shall, without the Consent of Congress, lay any Duty of Tonnage, keep Troops, or Ships of War in time of Peace, enter into any Agreement or Compact with another State, or with a foreign Power, or engage in War, unless actually invaded, or in such imminent Danger as will not admit of delay.

Article II
The Executive Article
Nature and Scope of Presidential Power

Section 1 Clause 1. The executive Power shall be vested in a President of the United States of America. He shall hold his Office during the Term of four Years, and, together with the Vice President, chosen for the same Term, be elected as follows:

CLAUSE 2. Each State shall appoint, in such Manner as the Legislature thereof may direct, a Number of Electors, equal to the whole Number of Senators and Representatives to which the State may be entitled in the Congress: but no Senator or Representative, or Person holding an Office of Trust or Profit under the United States, shall be appointed an Elector.

CLAUSE 3. The Electors shall meet in their respective States, and vote by Ballot for two Persons, of whom one at least shall not be an Inhabitant of the same State with themselves. And they shall make a List of all the Persons voted for, and of the Number of Votes for each; which List they shall sign and certify, and transmit sealed to the Seat of the Government of the United States, directed to the President of the Senate. The President of the Senate shall, in the Presence of the Senate and House of Representatives, open all the Certificates, and the Votes shall then be counted. The Person having the greatest Number of Votes shall be the President, if such Number be a Majority of the whole Number of Electors appointed; and if there be more than one who have such Majority and have an equal Number of Votes, then the House of Representatives shall immediately chuse by Ballot one of them for President; and if no Person have a Majority, then from the five highest on the List the said House shall in like Manner chuse the President. But in chusing the President, the Votes shall be taken by States, the Representation from each State having one Vote; A quorum for this Purpose shall consist of a Member or Members from two thirds of the States, and a Majority of all the States shall be necessary to a Choice. In every Case, after the Choice of the President, the Person having the greatest Number of Votes of the Electors shall be the Vice President. But if there should remain two or more who have equal Votes, the Senate shall chuse from them by Ballot the Vice President.[7]

CLAUSE 4. The Congress may determine the Time of chusing the Electors, and the Day on which they shall give their Votes; which Day shall be the same throughout the United States.

CLAUSE 5. No Person except a natural born Citizen, or a Citizen of the United States, at the time of the Adoption of this Constitution, shall be eligible to the Office of President; neither shall any Person be eligible to that Office who shall not have attained to the Age of thirty five Years, and been fourteen Years a Resident within the United States.

CLAUSE 6. In Case of the Removal of the President from Office, or of his Death, Resignation, or Inability to discharge the Powers and Duties of the said Office, the Same shall devolve on the Vice President, and the Congress may by Law provide for the Case of Removal,

Clause 3. This paragraph has been superseded by the Twelfth Amendment. The original language provided for a House election in the case of no majority vote or a tie vote among the top five candidates. Now the number of candidates is three. The Senate is to select the vice president if a candidate does not have an electoral majority or in the case of a tie vote. The Senate considers only the top two candidates. The amendment also clarifies that the qualifications of the vice president are the same as those for president.

Clause 4. Congress is given the power to establish a uniform day and time for the state selection of electors.

Clause 5. The qualifications for the offices of president and vice president are specified here—at least 35 years old, 14 years resident in the United States, and a natural-born citizen. The Fourteenth Amendment clarified who is a citizen of the United States, a person born or naturalized in the United States and subject to its jurisdiction. But the term "natural-born citizen" is unclear and has never been further defined by the judicial branch. Does it mean born in the United States or born of U.S. citizens in the United States or somewhere else in the world? Unfortunately, there is no definitive answer.

Clause 6. This clause concerns presidential succession and has been modified by the Twenty-Fifth Amendment. Upon the death, resignation, or impeachment conviction of the president, the vice president becomes president. The new president nominates a new vice president, who assumes the office if approved by a majority vote in both congressional branches. The president is also now able to notify the Congress of his or her inability to perform the duties of office.

Clause 7. This section covers the compensation of the president, which cannot be increased or decreased during his or her office. The current salary is $400,000 per year. The prohibition against decreasing the president's salary was considered an important part of the separation of powers. If Congress were at odds with the president and also able to decrease his pay, then it could drive him from office or punish him by reducing his salary.

Clause 8. This final clause in Section 1 is the oath of office administered to the new president. Interestingly, the phrase "so help me God," is not part of this oath, but has become customary in recent years.

Section 2 Clause 1. This clause establishes the president as commander-in-chief of the U.S. armed forces. George Washington was the only U.S. president to actually lead U.S. armed forces, during the Whiskey Rebellion.

The second provision is the basis for cabinet meetings that are used to hear the opinions of executive department heads. The last provision grants an absolute pardon or reprieve power for the president.

Since the president is commander-in-chief, citizens and groups concerned with U.S. foreign policy (especially armed military conflicts) can hold the president accountable for policy decisions. Litigation, protests, marches, and electoral battles have all been used by citizens dissatisfied with presidential foreign policy decisions.

Clause 2. This clause covers two important presidential powers: treaty making and appointments. The president (through the State Department) can negotiate treaties with other nations, but these do not become official until ratified by a two-thirds vote of the U.S. Senate.

The president is empowered to appoint judges, ambassadors, and other U.S. officials (cabinet officers, military officers, agency heads, etc.) subject to Senate approval.

These powers are important to ensure the division of power between the three branches of our national government as well as the system of checks and balances. Sharing these powers allows for input by the people and organized groups. The Senate approves most treaties and most presidential appointments, especially if it is controlled by members of the same party as the president. But this is not always true; many treaties and appointments have been rejected, often because the Senate was responding to strong public opinion.

Clause 3. This allows recess appointments of the officials listed in Clause 2 above. These commissions automatically expire unless approved by the Senate by the end of the next session. Presidents have used this provision to fill jobs when the nomination process is stalled.

Death, Resignation or Inability, both of the President and Vice President, declaring what Officer shall then act as President, and such Officer shall act accordingly, until the Disability be removed, or a President shall be elected.[8]

CLAUSE 7. The President shall, at stated Times, receive for his Services, a Compensation, which shall neither be encreased nor diminished during the Period for which he shall have been elected, and he shall not receive within that Period any other Emolument from the United States, or any of them.

CLAUSE 8. Before he enter on the Execution of his Office, he shall take the following Oath or Affirmation:—"I do solemnly swear (or affirm) that I will faithfully execute the Office of President of the United States, and will to the best of my Ability, preserve, protect and defend the Constitution of the United States."

Powers and Duties of the President

Section 2 Clause 1. The President shall be Commander in Chief of the Army and Navy of the United States, and of the Militia of the several States, when called into the actual Service of the United States; he may require the Opinion, in writing, of the principal Officer in each of the executive Departments, upon any Subject relating to the Duties of their respective Offices, and he shall have Power to grant Reprieves and Pardons for Offences against the United States, except in Cases of Impeachment.

CLAUSE 2. He shall have Power, by and with the Advice and Consent of the Senate, to make Treaties, provided two thirds of the Senators present concur; and he shall nominate, and by and with the Advice and Consent of the Senate, shall appoint Ambassadors, other public Ministers and Consuls, Judges of the supreme Court, and all other Officers of the United States, whose Appointments are not herein otherwise provided for, and which shall be established by Law: but the Congress may by Law vest the Appointment of such inferior Officers, as they think proper, in the President alone, in the Courts of Law, or in the Heads of Departments.

CLAUSE 3. The President shall have Power to fill up all Vacancies that may happen during the Recess of the Senate, by granting Commissions which shall expire at the End of their next Session.

SECTION 3. He shall from time to time give to the Congress Information of the State of the Union, and recommend to their Consideration such Measures as he shall judge necessary and expedient; he may, on extraordinary Occasions, convene both Houses, or either of them, and in Case of Disagreement between them, with Respect to the Time of Adjournment, he may adjourn them to such Time as he shall think proper; he shall receive Ambassadors and other public Ministers; he shall take Care that the Laws be faithfully executed, and shall Commission all the Officers of the United States.

SECTION 4. The President, Vice President and all civil Officers of the United States, shall be removed from Office on Impeachment for, and Conviction of, Treason, Bribery, or other high Crimes and Misdemeanors.

Article III
The Judicial Article
Judicial Power, Courts, Judges

SECTION 1. The judicial Power of the United States, shall be vested in one supreme Court, and in such inferior Courts as the Congress may from time to time ordain and establish. The Judges, both of the supreme and inferior Courts, shall hold their Offices during good Behaviour, and shall, at stated Times, receive for their Services, a Compensation, which shall not be diminished during their Continuance in Office.

Jurisdiction

Section 2 Clause 1. The judicial Power shall extend to all Cases, in Law and Equity, arising under this Constitution, the Laws of the United States, and Treaties made, or which shall be made, under their Authority;—to all Cases affecting Ambassadors, other public Ministers and Consuls;—to all Cases of admiralty and maritime Jurisdiction;—to Controversies to which the United States shall be a Party;—to Controversies between two or more States—between a State and Citizens of another State;[9]—between Citizens of different States;—between Citizens of the same State claiming Lands under Grants of different States, and between a State, or the Citizens thereof, and foreign States, Citizens, or Subjects.

Section 3. This section provides for the annual State of the Union address to a joint session of Congress. Presidents have learned that the ability to reach out to the public can be a source of tremendous power. The State of the Union Address is thus an important opportunity to speak directly to the American public, build support for initiatives, and shape the policy agenda. The president is also authorized to call special meetings of either the House or Senate. If there is disagreement between the House and Senate regarding adjournment, the president may adjourn them. This would be extremely rare. The next-to-last provision, to faithfully execute laws, provides the basis for the whole administrative apparatus of the executive branch.

Section 4. This section provides the constitutional authority for the impeachment and trial of the president, vice president, and all civil officers of the United States for treason, bribery, or other high crimes and misdemeanors (the exact meaning of this phrase is unclear and is often more political than judicial). Impeachment proceedings have been undertaken against two presidents in American history: Andrew Johnson, in 1868, and Bill Clinton in 1998. In both cases the Senate failed to convict the president, and both were allowed to stay in office. Richard Nixon would have also confronted impeachment proceedings in 1974 for his involvement in the Watergate scandal, but he resigned from office and avoided the process.

Article III Section 1. This section establishes the judicial branch in very general terms. It only provides for the Supreme Court; Congress must create the court system. It first did so in the Judiciary Act of 1789, when it established 13 district courts (one for each state) and three appellate courts. All federal judges hold their offices for life and can only be removed for breaches of good behavior—a very ambiguous term. Federal judges have been removed for drunkenness, accepting bribes, and other misdemeanors. To date, no justice of the U.S. Supreme Court has ever been removed.

The tenure of judges in office, which can be for life, is meant to give judges the ability to make decisions according to their best judgments without facing the prospect of removal from office for issuing an unpopular judgment. While this protected tenure is an undemocratic aspect of the Constitution in the sense that it removes federal judges from direct electoral accountability, it has been an important aspect of the judiciary's ability to enforce civil rights and liberties on behalf of minority groups and unpopular individuals.

This protected tenure is one aspect of government that makes the court pathway especially attractive to individuals, small groups, and others who lack political power. For example, federal judges acted against racial discrimination in the 1950s at a time when most white Americans accepted the existence of such discrimination when applied to African Americans. The salary of federal judges is set by congressional act but can never be reduced.

Section 2 Clause 1, 2, 3. This section establishes the original and appellate jurisdiction of the U.S. Supreme Court. Original jurisdiction cases are essentially limited to disputes between states. The Eleventh Amendment limited the ability of individuals to sue states. Even in these cases involving states, the Supreme Court now typically appoints a special judge to hear the evidence and make a recommendation to the justices rather than hold an actual trial at the Supreme Court. Since 1925, the Supreme Court no longer hears every case on appeal but can select which cases it will accept, which is now only about 75–85 cases per year. Although this provision mentions trial by jury in all cases, the Supreme Court's interpretations of the jury trial right, also contained in the Sixth Amendment, limits the right to criminal cases involving serious crimes with punishments of six months or more of imprisonment.

CLAUSE 2. In all Cases affecting Ambassadors, other public Ministers and Consuls, and those in which a State shall be Party, the supreme Court shall have original Jurisdiction. In all the other Cases before mentioned, the supreme Court shall have appellate Jurisdiction, both as to Law and Fact, with such Exceptions, and under such Regulations as Congress shall make.

CLAUSE 3. The Trial of all Crimes, except in Cases of Impeachment, shall be by Jury; and such Trial shall be held in the State where the said Crimes shall have been committed; but when not committed within any State, the Trial shall be at such Place or Places as the Congress may by Law have directed.

Treason

Section 3 Clause 1. Treason against the United States, shall consist only in levying War against them, or in adhering to their Enemies, giving them Aid and Comfort. No Person shall be convicted of Treason unless on the Testimony of two Witnesses to the same overt Act, or on Confession in open Court.

CLAUSE 2. The Congress shall have Power to declare the Punishment of Treason, but no Attainder of Treason shall work Corruption of Blood, or Forfeiture except during the Life of the Person attainted.

Article IV
Interstate Relations
Full Faith and Credit Clause

Section 1. Full Faith and Credit shall be given in each State to the public Acts, Records, and judicial Proceedings of every other State. And the Congress may by general Laws prescribe the Manner in which such Acts, Records and Proceedings shall be proved, and the Effect thereof.

Privileges and Immunities; Interstate Extradition

Section 2 Clause 1. The Citizens of each State shall be entitled to all Privileges and Immunities of Citizens in the several States.

CLAUSE 2. A person charged in any State with Treason, Felony or other Crime, who shall flee from Justice, and be found in another State, shall on Demand of the executive Authority of the State from which he fled, be delivered up, to be removed to the State having Jurisdiction of the Crime.

Section 3 Clause 1, 2. Treason is the only crime defined in the U.S. Constitution. Congress established the penalty of death for treason convictions. Note that two witnesses are required to convict anyone of treason.

Article IV Section 1. This section provides that the official acts and records (for example, marriages and divorces) of one state will be recognized and given credence by other states. It is one of several clauses that were designed to create a strong national government. Concerns about this clause have taken on new importance in recent years, as the gay marriage issue has heated up in most state legislatures.

Section 2 Clause 1. This clause requires states to treat citizens of other states equally. For example, when driving in another state, a driver's license is recognized.

Clause 2. A criminal fleeing to another state, if captured, can be returned to the state where the crime was committed. But this is not an absolute (extradition). A state's governor can refuse, for good reason, to extradite someone to another state.

CLAUSE 3. No person held to Service or Labour in one State, under the Laws thereof, escaping into another, shall, in Consequence of any Law or Regulation therein, be discharged from such Service or Labour, but shall be delivered up on Claim of the Party to whom such Service or Labour may be due.[10]

> **Clause 3.** This clause was included to cover runaway slaves. It has been made inoperable by the Thirteenth Amendment, which abolished slavery.

Admission of States

Section 3 Clause 1. New States may be admitted by the Congress into this Union; but no new State shall be formed or erected within the Jurisdiction of any other State; nor any State be formed by the Junction of two or more States, or Parts of States, without the Consent of the Legislatures of the States concerned as well as of the Congress.

CLAUSE 2. The Congress shall have Power to dispose of and make all needful Rules and Regulations respecting the Territory or other Property belonging to the United States; and nothing in this Constitution shall be so construed as to Prejudice any Claims of the United States, or of any particular State.

> **Section 3 Clause 1, 2.** This section concerns the admission of new states to the Union. In theory, no state can be created from part of another state without permission of the state legislature. But West Virginia was formed from Virginia during the Civil War without the permission of Virginia, which was part of the Confederacy. With 50 states now part of the Union, this section has not been used for many decades. The only foreseeable future use may be in the case of Puerto Rico or perhaps Washington, D.C.

Republican Form of Government

SECTION 4. The United States shall guarantee to every State in this Union a Republican Form of Government, and shall protect each of them against Invasion; and on Application of the Legislature, or of the Executive (when the Legislature cannot be convened) against domestic Violence.

> **Section 4.** This section commits the federal government to guarantee a republican form of government to each state and to protect the states against foreign invasion or domestic insurrection.
>
> By mandating a republican form of government, the Constitution guarantees that power rests in the hands of the citizens and is exercised by their elected representatives. As such, citizens are able to appeal directly to their governing officials through several pathways, such as through the courts, via elections, or by lobbying.

Article V
The Amending Power

The Congress, whenever two thirds of both Houses shall deem it necessary, shall propose Amendments to this Constitution, or, on the Application of the Legislatures of two thirds of the several States, shall call a Convention for proposing Amendments, which, in either Case, shall be valid to all Intents and Purposes, as Part of this Constitution, when ratified by the Legislatures of three fourths of the several States, or by Conventions in three fourths thereof, as the one or the other Mode of Ratification may be proposed by the Congress; Provided that no Amendment which may be made prior to the Year One thousand eight hundred and eight shall in any Manner affect the first and fourth Clauses in the Ninth Section of the first Article; and that no State, without its Consent, shall be deprived of its equal Suffrage in the Senate.

> **Article V.** Amendments to the U.S. Constitution can be originated by a two-thirds vote in both the U.S. House and Senate or by two-thirds of the state legislatures asking for a convention to propose amendments. Proposed amendments, by either route, must be approved by three-fourths of state legislatures or by three-fourths of conventions convened in the states for purposes of ratification. Only one amendment has been ratified by the convention method—the Twenty-First Amendment, to repeal the Eighteenth Amendment establishing Prohibition.
>
> Thousands of amendments have been proposed; few have been passed by two-thirds vote in each branch of Congress. The Equal Rights Amendment was one such case, but it was not ratified by three-fourths of state legislatures. There have only been 27 successful amendments to the U.S. Constitution.
>
> Since both the federal and state levels of government are involved in amending the Constitution, interested parties have several strategies to pursue to increase the likelihood that a proposed amendment is successful or is defeated.

Clause 1. This clause made the new national government responsible for all debts incurred during the Revolutionary War. This was very important to banking and commercial interests.

Clause 2. This is the National Supremacy Clause, which provides the basis for the supremacy of the national government. This seems to be a rather straightforward issue these days, but until the conclusion of the Civil War, "national supremacy" was not a settled concept.

Clause 3. This clause requires essentially all federal and state officials to swear or affirm their allegiance to and support of the U.S. Constitution. Note that a religious test was prohibited for federal office. However, some states used religious tests for voting and office qualification until the 1830s.

Article VII. In the end, all 13 states ratified the Constitution. But it was a close call in several states.

Realizing the unanimous ratification of the new Constitution by the 13 states might never have occurred, the framers wisely specified that only nine states would be needed for ratification. Even this proved to be a test of wills between Federalists and Anti-Federalists, leading to publication of the great political work *The Federalist Papers*.

The first ten amendments were ratified on December 15, 1791, and form what is known as the "Bill of Rights."

The Bill of Rights applied at first only to the federal government and not to state or local governments. Beginning in 1925 in the case of *Gitlow* v. *New York*, the U.S. Supreme Court began to selectively incorporate the Bill of Rights, making its provisions applicable to state and local governments, with some exceptions, which will be discussed at the appropriate amendment.

Until the Supreme Court incorporated the Bill of Rights to include protections from state governments, citizens had to look to state constitutions for protections of civil liberties.

Amendment 1. This amendment protects five fundamental freedoms: religion, speech, press, assembly, and petition. The press is the only business that is specifically protected by the U.S. Constitution. Freedom of religion and speech are two of the most contentious issues and generate a multitude of Supreme Court cases.

These freedoms are crucial for nearly every pathway of change; without each fundamental right, individuals and groups could not pursue change without fear of reprisal. This amendment is perhaps the most crucial to guarantee a free society.

Article VI
The Supremacy Act

CLAUSE 1. All Debts contracted and Engagements entered into, before the Adoption of this Constitution, shall be as valid against the United States under this Constitution, as under the Confederation.

CLAUSE 2. This Constitution, and the Laws of the United States which shall be made in Pursuance thereof; and all Treaties made, or which shall be made, under the Authority of the United States, shall be the supreme Law of the Land; and the Judges in every State shall be bound thereby, any Thing in the Constitution or Laws of any State to the Contrary notwithstanding.

CLAUSE 3. The Senators and Representatives before mentioned, and the Members of the several State Legislatures, and all executive and judicial Officers, both of the United States and of the several States, shall be bound by Oath or Affirmation, to support this Constitution; but no religious Test shall ever be required as a Qualification to any Office or public Trust under the United States.

Article VII

Ratification

The Ratification of the Conventions of nine States, shall be sufficient for the Establishment of this Constitution between the States so ratifying the Same.

Done in Convention by the Unanimous Consent of the States present the Seventeenth Day of September in the Year of our Lord one thousand seven hundred and Eighty seven and of the Independence of the United States of America the Twelfth. In Witness whereof We have hereunto subscribed our Names.

Amendments
The Bill of Rights

AMENDMENT 1

RELIGION, SPEECH, ASSEMBLY, AND PETITION

Congress shall make no law respecting an establishment of religion, or prohibiting the free exercise thereof; or abridging the freedom of speech, or of the press; or the right of the people peaceably to assemble, and to petition the Government for a redress of grievances.

AMENDMENT 2

MILITIA AND THE RIGHT TO BEAR ARMS

A well-regulated Militia, being necessary to the security of a free State, the right of the people to keep and bear Arms, shall not be infringed.

AMENDMENT 3

QUARTERING OF SOLDIERS

No Soldier shall, in time of peace be quartered in any house, without the consent of the Owner, nor in time of war, but in manner to be prescribed by law.

AMENDMENT 4

SEARCHES AND SEIZURES

The right of the people to be secure in their persons, houses, papers, and effects, against unreasonable searches and seizures, shall not be violated, and no Warrants shall issue, but upon probable cause, supported by Oath or affirmation, and particularly describing the place to be searched, and the persons or things to be seized.

AMENDMENT 5

GRAND JURIES, SELF-INCRIMINATION, DOUBLE JEOPARDY, DUE PROCESS, AND EMINENT DOMAIN

No person shall be held to answer for a capital, or otherwise infamous crime, unless on a presentment or indictment of a Grand jury, except in cases arising in the land or naval forces, or in the Militia, when in actual service in time of War or public danger; nor shall any person be subject for the same offence to be twice put in jeopardy of life or limb; nor shall be compelled in any criminal case to be a witness against himself, nor be deprived of life, liberty, or property, without due process of law; nor shall private property be taken for public use, without just compensation.

Amendment 2.   Those who favor gun ownership, either for protection, hunting, or sport, cite this amendment. This is the amendment most recently incorporated for application to state and local governments. The Supreme Court applied this amendment to state and local governments with its decision in *McDonald* v. *City of Chicago* (2010).

There is controversy as to the meaning of this amendment. Some believe that it specifically refers to citizen militias, which were common at the time of the Constitution but now have been replaced by permanent armed forces (state national guard units), thereby allowing the federal government to regulate gun ownership. Others believe that the amendment refers to individuals directly, therefore guaranteeing private citizens the right to own guns.

Amendment 3.   It was the practice of the British government to insist that colonists provide room or board to British troops. This amendment was designed to prohibit this practice. Today, military and naval bases provide the necessary quarters and this issue does not arise. This amendment has not been incorporated and applies only against the federal government.

Amendment 4.   This extremely important amendment is designed to prevent the abuse of police powers. Essentially, unreasonable searches or seizures of homes, persons, or property cannot be undertaken without probable cause or a warrant that specifically describes the place to be searched, the person involved, and the suspicious things to be seized.

People who believe that these rights have been violated have successfully used the court-centered pathway for protection, either by seeking to have improperly obtained evidence excluded from use in court or by seeking money damages from police officials to compensate for the invasion of a home or an improper search of an individual's body.

Many people feel that the rights of the accused are often given more precedence than the rights of victims. The Constitution does not contain rights for victims, but a constitutional amendment has been proposed to protect victims' rights. This does not mean that victims are unprotected by the law. States and the federal government have statutes that provide protections and services for crime victims.

Amendment 5.   Only a grand jury can indict a person for a federal crime. (This provision does not apply to state and local governments because it has not been incorporated by the Supreme Court.) This amendment also covers double jeopardy, or being tried twice for the same crime in the same jurisdiction. This amendment also covers the prohibition of compelled self-incrimination. The deprivation of life, liberty, or property is prohibited unless due process of law is applied. This provision applies to the federal government, and there is a parallel provision that applies to state and local governments in the Fourteenth Amendment. Finally, private property may not be taken under the doctrine of "eminent domain" unless the government provides just compensation.

Amendment 6.   This amendment requires public trials by jury for criminal prosecutions. However, the Supreme Court only applies the right to trial by jury to serious offenses, not petty offenses. Anyone accused of a crime is guaranteed the rights to be informed of the charges; to confront witnesses; to subpoena witnesses for their defense; and to have a lawyer for their defense. The government must provide a lawyer for a defendant unable to afford one for any case in which the defendant faces the possibility of a jail or prison sentence.

There are serious questions about the adequacy of attorney performance and resources for criminal defense. In some jurisdictions, there are not enough defense attorneys for poor defendants, so that the attorneys spend little time on each case. In addition, the Supreme Court does not have strict standards for attorney performance, so some defendants have been represented by attorneys who know very little about criminal law.

Amendment 7.   The right to trial by jury in civil cases will never be incorporated by the Supreme Court for application against state and local governments, because it would impose a huge financial burden (jury trials are very expensive).

Amendment 8.   The Supreme Court has not clearly defined the limits imposed by prohibition of excessive bail or excessive fines. Thus these rights rarely arise in legal cases, and bail amounts in excess of $1 million will periodically be imposed for serious crimes or wealthy defendants. The prohibition on cruel and unusual punishments focuses on criminal punishments, not other contexts (such as the punishment of children in public schools or civil fines against businesses). Cruel and unusual punishments are defined according to current societal values and thus the definition of what is "cruel and unusual" can change over time. This provision bars punishments that are either excessive or torturous.

Capital punishment is covered by this amendment, as well as the treatment of prisoners inside prisons. Court cases challenging the constitutionality of capital punishment cite this amendment's language prohibiting cruel and unusual punishment. For a period of four years (1973–1976), the Supreme Court banned capital punishment as it was then being applied by the states. When states modified their statutes to provide a two-part judicial process of guilt determination and punishment, the Supreme Court allowed the reinstitution of capital punishment by the states.

Amendment 9.   This amendment implies that there may be other rights of the people not specified by the previous amendments, but the wording gives no guidance about what those rights might be. Instead, when the Supreme Court has identified rights not specifically mentioned in the Bill of Rights, it has tended to claim that these rights, such as privacy and the right to travel between states, are connected to the right to "due process" found in the Fifth and Fourteenth Amendments.

Amendment 10.   The Tenth Amendment was seen as the reservoir of reserved powers for state governments. But the doctrine of implied national government powers, which was established by the U.S. Supreme Court in *McCulloch* v. *Maryland* (1819), undercut the words and apparent intent of this amendment. With the exception of a few decisions, the Supreme Court has generally deferred to assertions of federal power since the 1930s.

AMENDMENT 6

CRIMINAL COURT PROCEDURES

In all criminal prosecutions, the accused shall enjoy the right to a speedy and public trial, by an impartial jury of the State and district wherein the crime shall have been committed, which district shall have been previously ascertained by law, and to be informed of the nature and cause of the accusation; to be confronted with the witnesses against him; to have compulsory process for obtaining witnesses in his favor, and to have the Assistance of Counsel for his defence.

AMENDMENT 7

TRIAL BY JURY IN COMMON LAW CASES

In Suits at common law, where the value in controversy shall exceed twenty dollars, the right of trial by jury shall be preserved, and no fact tried by a jury shall be otherwise reexamined in any Court of the United States, than according to the rules of the common law.

AMENDMENT 8

BAIL, CRUEL AND UNUSUAL PUNISHMENT

Excessive bail shall not be required, nor excessive fines imposed, nor cruel and unusual punishments inflicted.

AMENDMENT 9

RIGHTS RETAINED BY THE PEOPLE

The enumeration in the Constitution, of certain rights, shall not be construed to deny or disparage others retained by the people.

AMENDMENT 10

RESERVED POWERS OF THE STATES

The powers not delegated to the United States by the Constitution, nor prohibited by it to the States, are reserved to the States respectively, or to the people.

AMENDMENT 11

SUITS AGAINST THE STATES

[Ratified February 7, 1795]

The Judicial power of the United States shall not be construed to extend to any suit in law or equity, commenced or prosecuted against one of the United States by Citizens of another State, or by Citizens or Subjects of any Foreign State.

AMENDMENT 12

ELECTION OF THE PRESIDENT

[Ratified June 15, 1804]

The Electors shall meet in their respective states, and vote by ballot for President and Vice-President, one of whom, at least, shall not be an inhabitant of the same state with themselves; they shall name in their ballots the person voted for as President, and in distinct ballots the person voted for as Vice-President, and they shall make distinct lists of all persons voted for as President, and of all persons voted for as Vice-President, and of the number of votes for each, which lists they shall sign and certify, and transmit sealed to the seat of the government of the United States, directed to the President of the Senate;—The President of the Senate shall, in the presence of the Senate and House of Representatives, open all the certificates and the votes shall then be counted;—The person having the greatest number of votes for President, shall be the President, if such number be a majority of the whole number of Electors appointed; and if no person have such majority, then from the persons having the highest numbers not exceeding three on the list of those voted for as President, the House of Representatives shall choose immediately, by ballot, the President. But in choosing the President, the votes shall be taken by states, the representation from each state having one vote; a quorum for this purpose shall consist of a member or members from two-thirds of the states, and a majority of all the states shall be necessary to a choice. And if the House of Representatives shall not choose a President whenever the right of choice shall devolve upon them, before the fourth day of March next following, then the Vice-President shall act as President, as in the case of the death or other constitutional disability of the President.[11] The person having the greatest number of votes as Vice-President, shall be the Vice-President, if such a number be a majority of the whole numbers of Electors

Amendment 11.   Article III of the U.S. Constitution originally allowed federal jurisdiction in cases of one state citizen against another state citizen or state. This amendment removes federal jurisdiction in this area. In essence, states may not be sued in federal court by citizens of another state or country.

Amendment 12.   This was a necessary amendment to correct a flaw in the Constitution covering operations of the Electoral College. In the election of 1800, Thomas Jefferson and Aaron Burr, both of the same Democratic Republican party, received the same number of electoral votes, 73, for president. Article II of the original Constitution specified that each elector would cast two ballots. It did not specify for whom. This amendment clarifies that the electoral vote must be specific for president and vice president. The original Constitution provided that if no candidate received a majority of electoral votes, the House would decide from the candidates with the top five vote totals. This amendment reduces the candidate field to the top three vote totals. If the House delays in this selection past the fourth day of March, the elected vice president will act as president until the House selects the president. The original Constitution provided that the candidate with the second highest number of electoral votes would become vice president.

This amendment, which requires a separate vote tally for vice president, provides for selection by the U.S. Senate if no vice presidential candidate receives an electoral vote majority.

appointed, and if no person have a majority, then from the two highest numbers on the list, the Senate shall choose the Vice-President; a quorum for the purpose shall consist of two-thirds of the whole number of Senators, and a majority of the whole number shall be necessary to a choice. But no person constitutionally ineligible to the office of President shall be eligible to that of Vice-President of the United States.

AMENDMENT 13

PROHIBITION OF SLAVERY

[Ratified December 6, 1865]

SECTION 1. Neither slavery nor involuntary servitude, except as a punishment for crime whereof the party shall have been duly convicted, shall exist within the United States, or any place subject to their jurisdiction.

SECTION 2. Congress shall have power to enforce this article by appropriate legislation.

AMENDMENT 14

CITIZENSHIP, DUE PROCESS, AND EQUAL PROTECTION OF THE LAWS

[Ratified July 9, 1868]

SECTION 1. All persons born or naturalized in the United States, and subject to the jurisdiction thereof, are citizens of the United States and of the State wherein they reside. No State shall make or enforce any law which shall abridge the privileges or immunities of citizens of the United States; nor shall any State deprive any person of life, liberty, or property, without due process of law; nor deny to any person within its jurisdiction the equal protection of the laws.

SECTION 2. Representatives shall be apportioned among the several States according to their respective numbers, counting the whole number of persons in each State, excluding Indians not taxed. But when the right to vote at any election for the choice of electors for President and Vice President of the United States, Representatives in Congress, the Executive and Judicial officers of a State, or the members of the Legislature thereof, is denied to any of the male inhabitants of such State, being twenty-one years of age, and citizens of the United States, or in any way abridged, except for participation in rebellion, or other crime, the basis of representation therein shall be reduced in the proportion which the number of such male citizens shall bear to the whole number of male citizens twenty-one years of age in such State.[12]

Amendment 13. This is the first of the three Civil War amendments. Slavery is prohibited under all circumstances. Involuntary servitude is also prohibited unless it is a punishment for a convicted crime.

Amendment 14 Section 1. This section defines the meaning of U.S. citizenship and protection of these citizenship rights. It also establishes the Equal Protection Clause, meaning that each state must guarantee fundamental rights and liberties to all of its citizens. It extended the provisions of the Fifth Amendment of due process and protection of life, liberty, and property and made these applicable to the states. The Due Process Clause has been especially important for the expansion of civil rights and liberties as the Supreme Court interpreted it in a flexible manner to recognize new rights (e.g., privacy, right of choice for abortion, etc.) and to apply the Bill of Rights against the states.

Section 2. This section changed the Three-Fifths Clause of the original Constitution. At the time of ratification of this amendment, all male citizens, 21 or older, were used to calculate representation in the House of Representatives. If a state denied the right to vote to any male 21 or older, the number of denied citizens would be deducted from the overall state total to determine representation.

This is the first time that gender was entered into the Constitution. It was not until 50 years later (in 1920 with the Nineteenth Amendment) that women were granted the right to vote.

SECTION 3. No person shall be a Senator or Representative in Congress, or elector of President and Vice President, or hold any office, civil or military, under the United States, or under any State, who, having previously taken an oath, as a member of Congress, or as an officer of the United States, or as a member of any State legislature, or as an executive or judicial officer of any State, to support the Constitution of the United States, shall have engaged in insurrection or rebellion against the same, or given aid or comfort to the enemies thereof. But Congress may by a vote of two-thirds of each House, remove such disability.

SECTION 4. The validity of the public debt of the United States, authorized by law, including debts incurred for payment of pensions and bounties for services in suppressing insurrection or rebellion, shall not be questioned. But neither the United States nor any State shall assume or pay any debt or obligation incurred in aid of insurrection or rebellion against the United States, or any claim for the loss or emancipation of any slave; but all such debts, obligations and claims shall be held illegal and void.

SECTION 5. The Congress shall have power to enforce, by appropriate legislation, the provisions of this article.

AMENDMENT 15

THE RIGHT TO VOTE

[Ratified February 3, 1870]

SECTION 1 The right of citizens of the United States to vote shall not be denied or abridged by the United States or by any State on account of race, color, or previous condition of servitude.

SECTION 2. The Congress shall have power to enforce this article by appropriate legislation.

AMENDMENT 16

INCOME TAXES

[Ratified February 3, 1913]

The Congress shall have power to lay and collect taxes on incomes, from whatever source derived, without apportionment among the several States, and without regard to any census or enumeration.

Section 3.   This section disqualifies from federal office or elector for president or vice president anyone who rebelled or participated in an insurrection (that is, the Confederate Army after the Civil War) against the Constitution. This was specifically directed against citizens of southern states. Congress by a two-thirds vote could override this provision.

Section 4, 5.   Section 4 covers the Civil War debts; Section 5 grants to Congress the very specific authority to create legislation that will implement and enforce the provisions of the Fourteenth Amendment.

Unlike the Bill of Rights, which is intended to protect individuals by limiting the power of the federal government, including Congress, Section 5 intends to empower Congress to create laws that will protect individuals from actions by states that violate their rights.

Although the Thirteenth and Fourteenth Amendments were designed to end slavery, and provide citizenship, due process, and equal protection rights for freed slaves and their offspring, they were interpreted very narrowly until the 1960s. Civil rights activists had to use the court-centered, cultural change, and grassroots mobilization pathways to force legal, political, and social change to allow all individuals, regardless of color or race, to enjoy full civil rights.

Amendment 15 Section 1, 2.   This final Civil War amendment states that voting rights could not be denied by any states on account of race, color, or previous servitude. It did not mention gender. Accordingly, only male citizens 21 or over were guaranteed the right to vote by this amendment. Some states sought to defeat the intent of the amendment by adopting additional restrictions to voting rights (such as poll taxes, whites-only primaries, and literacy tests) in order to block the participation of African American voters. These restrictions were eliminated in the 1960s as civil rights activists effectively used several pathways for change: court-centered, lobbying decision makers, and grassroots mobilization.

Amendment 16.   Article I, Section 9 of the original Constitution prohibited Congress from enacting a direct tax unless in proportion to a census. Congress in 1894 passed an income tax law, levying a 2 percent tax on incomes over $4,000. In 1895, the U.S. Supreme Court in a split decision (5–4) found that the income tax was a direct tax not apportioned among the states and was thus unconstitutional. Thus, Congress proposed an amendment allowing it to enact an income tax. Once this amendment was ratified, the flow of tax money to Washington increased tremendously.

Amendment 17. Before this amendment, U.S. senators were selected by state legislatures. Now U.S. senators would be selected by popular vote in each state. Further, the governor of each state may fill vacancies, subject to state laws.

Amendment 18. This amendment was largely the work of the Women's Christian Temperance Union and essentially banned the manufacture, sale, or transportation of alcoholic beverages. Unintended consequences of this attempt to legislate morality were the brewing of "bathtub gin" and moonshine liquor and the involvement of organized crime in importing liquor from Canada. The Twenty-First Amendment repealed this provision. This is also the first amendment where Congress fixed a period for ratification—seven years.

Amendment 19. Women achieved voting parity with men. It took enormous efforts by a large number of women and men to win this right, spanning over 70 years (from the call for the right to vote at the first women's rights convention in Seneca Falls, New York, in 1848). Suffragists protested, sued, marched, lobbied, and were imprisoned in their battle to win equal voting rights for men and women.

AMENDMENT 17

DIRECT ELECTION OF SENATORS

[Ratified April 8, 1913]

The Senate of the United States shall be composed of two Senators from each State, elected by the people thereof, for six years; and each Senator shall have one vote. The electors in each State shall have the qualifications requisite for electors of the most numerous branch of the State legislatures.

When vacancies happen in the representation of any State in the Senate, the executive authority of such State shall issue writs of election to fill such vacancies: Provided, That the legislature of any State may empower the executive thereof to make temporary appointments until the people fill the vacancies by election as the legislature may direct.

This amendment shall not be so construed as to affect the election or term of any Senator chosen before it becomes valid as part of the Constitution.

AMENDMENT 18

PROHIBITION

[Ratified January 16, 1919. Repealed December 5, 1933 by Amendment 21]

SECTION 1. After one year from the ratification of this article the manufacture, sale, or transportation of intoxicating liquors within, the importation thereof into, or the exportation thereof from the United States and all territory subject to the jurisdiction thereof for beverage purposes is hereby prohibited.

SECTION 2. The Congress and the several States shall have concurrent power to enforce this article by appropriate legislation.

SECTION 3. This article shall be inoperative unless it shall have been ratified as an amendment to the Constitution by the legislatures of the several States, as provided in the Constitution, within seven years from the date of the submission hereof to the States by the Congress.[13]

AMENDMENT 19

FOR WOMEN'S SUFFRAGE

[Ratified August 18, 1920]

The right of the citizens of the United States to vote shall not be denied or abridged by the United States or by any State on account of sex.

Congress shall have power to enforce this article.

AMENDMENT 20

THE LAME DUCK AMENDMENT

[Ratified January 23, 1933]

SECTION 1.   The terms of the President and Vice President shall end at noon on the 20th day of January, and the terms of the Senators and Representatives at noon on the 3d day of January, of the years in which such terms would have ended if this article had not been ratified; and the terms of their successors shall then begin.

SECTION 2.   The Congress shall assemble at least once in every year, and such meeting shall begin at noon on the 3d day of January, unless they shall by law appoint a different day.

SECTION 3.   If, at the time fixed for the beginning of the term of the President, the President elect shall have died, the Vice President elect shall become President. If a President shall not have been chosen before the time fixed for the beginning of his term, or if the President elect shall have failed to qualify, then the Vice President elect shall act as President until a President shall have qualified; and the Congress may by law provide for the case wherein neither a President elect nor a Vice President elect shall have qualified, declaring who shall then act as President, or the manner in which one who is to act shall be selected, and such person shall act accordingly until a President or Vice President shall have qualified.

SECTION 4.   The Congress may by law provide for the case of the death of any of the persons from whom the House of Representatives may choose a President whenever the right of choice shall have devolved upon them, and for the case of the death of any of the persons from whom the Senate may choose a Vice President whenever the right of choice shall have devolved upon them.

SECTION 5.   Sections 1 and 2 shall take effect on the 15th day of October following the ratification of this article.

SECTION 6.   This article shall be inoperative unless it shall have been ratified as an amendment to the Constitution by the legislatures of three-fourths of the several States within seven years from the date of its submission.

Amendment 20.   Called the Lame Duck amendment, this amendment fixes the dates for the end of presidential and legislative terms. A new president is elected in November, but the current president remains in office until January 20 of the following year, thus the term "lame duck." Legislative terms begin earlier, on January 3.

Amendment 21. This unusual amendment nullified the Eighteenth Amendment. The amendment called for the end of Prohibition unless prohibited by state laws.

This is the only instance of one amendment nullifying another. Here, governmental actions reflected the will of the majority. Initially, there was concern that the production and consumption of alcohol was detrimental to society, but as time passed, public opinion shifted. The public became less concerned about consumption and more worried about the illegal manufacture of alcohol and the subsequent growth of illegal markets and urban violence.

Amendment 22. This amendment could be called the Franklin D. Roosevelt amendment. It was FDR who broke the previously unwritten rule, established by George Washington, of serving no more than two terms as president. Democrat Roosevelt won election to an unprecedented four terms as president (although he died before completing his fourth term). When the Republicans took control of the Congress in 1948, they pushed through the Twenty-Second Amendment, limiting the U.S. president to a lifetime of two full four-year terms of office.

Amendment 23. This amendment gave electoral votes to the residents of Washington, D.C., which is not a state and thus not included in the original scheme of state electoral votes. Currently, Washington, D.C., has 3 electoral votes, bringing the total of presidential electoral votes to 538. Residents of Washington, D.C., do not, however, have voting representation in Congress. Puerto Ricans are citizens of the United States but have no electoral votes. Both Washington, D.C., and Puerto Rico are represented in Congress by nonvoting delegates.

AMENDMENT 21

REPEAL OF PROHIBITION

[Ratified December 5, 1933]

SECTION 1. The eighteenth article of amendment to the Constitution of the United States is hereby repealed.

SECTION 2. The transportation or importation into any State, Territory, or possession of the United States for delivery or use therein of intoxicating liquors, in violation of the laws thereof, is hereby prohibited.

SECTION 3. This article shall be inoperative unless it shall have been ratified as an amendment to the Constitution by conventions in the several States, as provided in the Constitution, within seven years from the date of the submission hereof to the States by the Congress.

AMENDMENT 22

NUMBER OF PRESIDENTIAL TERMS

[Ratified February 27, 1951]

SECTION 1. No person shall be elected to the office of the President more than twice, and no person who has held the office of President, or acted as President, for more than two years of a term to which some other person was elected President shall be elected to the office of the President more than once. But this article shall not apply to any person holding the office of President when this article was proposed by the Congress, and shall not prevent any person who may be holding the office of President, or acting as President, during the term within which this article becomes operative from holding the office of President or acting as President during the remainder of such term.

SECTION 2. This article shall be inoperative unless it shall have been ratified as an amendment to the Constitution by the legislatures of three-fourths of the several states within seven years from the date of its submission to the states by the Congress.

AMENDMENT 23

PRESIDENTIAL ELECTORS FOR THE DISTRICT OF COLUMBIA

[Ratified March 29, 1961]

SECTION 1. The District constituting the seat of government of the United States shall appoint in such manner as the Congress may direct:

A number of electors of President and Vice President equal to the whole number of Senators and Representatives in Congress to which the

District would be entitled if it were a state, but in no event more than the least populous state; they shall be in addition to those appointed by the states, but they shall be considered, for the purposes of the election of President and Vice President, to be electors appointed by a state; and they shall meet in the District and perform such duties as provided by the twelfth article of amendment.

SECTION 2. The Congress shall have power to enforce this article by appropriate legislation.

AMENDMENT 24

THE ANTI-POLL TAX AMENDMENT

[Ratified January 23, 1964]

SECTION 1. The right of citizens of the United States to vote in any primary or other election for President or Vice President, for electors for President or Vice President, or for Senator or Representative in Congress, shall not be denied or abridged by the United States or any state by reason of failure to pay any poll tax or other tax.

SECTION 2 The Congress shall have power to enforce this article by appropriate legislation.

AMENDMENT 25

PRESIDENTIAL DISABILITY, VICE PRESIDENTIAL VACANCIES

[Ratified February 10, 1967]

SECTION 1. In case of the removal of the President from office or of his death or resignation, the Vice President shall become President.

SECTION 2. Whenever there is a vacancy in the office of the Vice President, the President shall nominate a Vice President who shall take the office upon confirmation by a majority vote of both Houses of Congress.

SECTION 3. Whenever the President transmits to the President pro tempore of the Senate and the Speaker of the House of Representatives his written declaration that he is unable to discharge the powers and duties of his office, and until he transmits to them a written declaration to the contrary, such powers and duties shall be discharged by the Vice President as Acting President.

SECTION 4. Whenever the Vice President and a majority of either the principal officers of the executive departments, or of such other body as Congress may by law provide, transmit to the President pro tempore of the Senate and the Speaker of the House of Representatives their

Amendment 24. The poll tax was a procedure used mostly in southern states to discourage poor white and black voters from registering to vote. Essentially, one would have to pay a tax to register to vote. The tax was around $34 per year (sometimes retroactive), which amounted to a great deal of money to the poor, serving to disenfranchise a great proportion of the poor. As part of the fight for universal voting rights for all, the poll tax was abolished. Literacy tests, another device to disqualify voters, were abolished by the Voting Rights Act of 1965.

By banning this tax (coupled with other civil rights reforms), the United States delivered what the civil rights amendments promised—full voting rights for all citizens regardless of race.

Amendment 25. President Woodrow Wilson's final year in office was marked by serious illness. It is rumored that his wife acted as president. There was no constitutional provision to cover an incapacitating illness of a president. This amendment provides a procedure for this eventuality. The president can inform congressional leaders of his or her incapacitation, and the vice president then takes over. When the president recovers, he or she can inform congressional leaders and resume office.

The amendment also recognizes that the president may not be able or wish to indicate this lack of capacity. In this case, the vice president and a majority of cabinet members can inform congressional leaders, and the vice president takes over. When the president informs congressional leadership that he or she is back in form, he or she resumes the presidency unless the vice president and a majority of the cabinet members disagree. Then Congress must decide who is to be president. The likelihood that this procedure will ever be used is relatively small.

The most immediate importance of this amendment concerns the office of vice president. The original Constitution did not address the issue of a vacancy in this office. This amendment was ratified in 1967, only a few years before it was needed. In 1973, the sitting vice president, Spiro Agnew, resigned his office. Under the provisions of this amendment, President Nixon nominated Gerald Ford as vice president. As a former member of the House, Ford was quickly approved by the Congress. But a year later, President Nixon also resigned. Now Vice President Ford became President Ford, and he in turn appointed Nelson Rockefeller as the new vice president. For the first time in our history, neither the president nor the vice president were selected by the Electoral College after a national election.

written declaration that the President is unable to discharge the powers and duties of his office, the Vice President shall immediately assume the powers and duties of the office as Acting President.

Thereafter, when the President transmits to the President pro tempore of the Senate and the Speaker of the House of Representatives his written declaration that no inability exists, he shall resume the powers and duties of his office unless the Vice President and a majority of either the principal officers of the executive department, or of such other body as Congress may by law provide, transmit within four days to the President pro tempore of the Senate and the Speaker of the House of Representatives their written declaration that the President is unable to discharge the powers and duties of his office. Thereupon Congress shall decide the issue, assembling within forty-eight hours for that purpose if not in session. If the Congress, within twenty-one days after receipt of the latter written declaration, or, if Congress is not in session, within twenty-one days after Congress is required to assemble, determines by two-thirds vote of both Houses that the President is unable to discharge the powers and duties of his office, the Vice President shall continue to discharge the same as Acting President; otherwise, the President shall resume the powers and duties of his office.

AMENDMENT 26

EIGHTEEN-YEAR-OLD VOTE

[Ratified July 1, 1971]

SECTION 1 The right of citizens of the United States, who are 18 years of age or older, to vote, shall not be denied or abridged by the United States or by any state on account of age.

SECTION 2 The Congress shall have power to enforce this article by appropriate legislation.

AMENDMENT 27

CONGRESSIONAL SALARIES

[Ratified May 7, 1992]

No law varying the compensation for the services of the Senators and Representatives shall take effect until an election of Representatives shall have intervened.

Amendment 26 Section 1, 2.   During the Vietnam War, 18-year-olds were being drafted and sent out to possibly die in the service of their country. Yet they did not even have the right to vote. This incongruity led to the Twenty-Sixth Amendment, which lowered the legal voting age from 21 to 18.

Before the passage of this amendment, young people, being denied the ability to express themselves peacefully with the vote, often felt frustrated with their inability to express their concerns and influence public policy. With the passage of this amendment, those citizens over the age of 18 could pursue the election-centered pathway (and others) to instigate change.

Amendment 27.   This is a "sleeper" amendment that was part of 12 amendments originally submitted by the first Congress to the states for ratification. The states only ratified 10 of the 12, which collectively became known as the Bill of Rights. But since Congress did not set a time limit for ratification, the other two amendments remained on the table. Much to the shock of the body politic, in 1992, three-fourths of the states ratified original amendment 12 of 12. This reflected the disgust of seeing Congress continuing to increase its salary and benefits. The amendment delays any increase of compensation for at least one election cycle.

---

1 Modified by the 16th Amendment
2 Replaced by Section 2, 14th Amendment
3 Repealed by the 17th Amendment
4 Modified by the 17th Amendment
5 Changed by the 20th Amendment

6 Modified by the 16th Amendment
7 Changed by the 12th and 20th Amendments
8 Modified by the 25th Amendment
9 Modified by the 11th Amendment
10 Repealed by the 13th Amendment

11 Changed by the 20th Amendment
12 Changed by the 26th Amendment
13 Repealed by the 21st Amendment

The Federalist, No. 10, James Madison

To the People of the State of New York: Among the numerous advantages promised by a well-constructed union, none deserves to be more accurately developed than its tendency to break and control the violence of faction. The friend of popular governments, never finds himself so much alarmed for their character and fate, as when he contemplates their propensity of this dangerous vice. He will not fail, therefore, to set a due value on any plan which, without violating the principles to which he is attached, provides a proper cure for it. The instability, injustice, and confusion introduced into the public councils, have, in truth, been the mortal diseases under which popular governments have every where perished; as they continue to be the favorite and fruitful topics from which the adversaries to liberty derive their most specious declamations. The valuable improvements made by the American constitutions on the popular models, both ancient and modern, cannot certainly be too much admired; but it would be an unwarrantable partiality, to contend that they have as effectually obviated the danger on this side, as was wished and expected. Complaints are everywhere heard from our most considerate and virtuous citizens, equally the friends of public and private faith, and of public and personal liberty, that our governments are too unstable; that the public good is disregarded in the conflicts of rival parties; and that measures are too often decided, not according to the rules of justice, and the rights of the minor party, but by the superior force of an interested and overbearing majority. However anxiously we may wish that these complaints had no foundation, the evidence of known facts will not permit us to deny that they are in some degree true. It will be found, indeed, on a candid review of our situation, that some of the distresses under which we labor have been erroneously charged on the operations of our governments; but it will be found, at the same time, that other causes will not alone account for many of our heaviest misfortunes; and, particularly, for that prevailing and increasing distrust of public engagements, and alarm for private rights, which are echoed from one end of the continent to the other. These must be chiefly, if not wholly, effects of the unsteadiness and injustice, with which a factious spirit has tainted our public administrations.

By a faction, I understand a number of citizens, whether amounting to a majority of the whole, who are united and actuated by some common impulse of passion, or of interest, adverse to the rights of other citizens, or to the permanent and aggregate interests of the community.

There are two methods of curing the mischiefs of faction: the one, by removing its causes; the other, by controlling its effects.

There are again two methods of removing the causes of faction: the one, by destroying the liberty which is essential to its existence; the other, by giving to every citizen the same opinions, the same passions, and the same interests.

It could never be more truly said, than of the first remedy, that it was worse than the disease. Liberty is to faction what air is to fire, an aliment without which it instantly expires. But it could not be a less folly to abolish liberty, which is essential to political life, because it nourishes faction, than it would be to wish the annihilation of air, which is essential to animal life, because it imparts to fire its destructive agency.

The second expedient is as impracticable, as the first would be unwise. As long as the reason of man continues fallible, and he is at liberty to exercise it, different opinions will be formed. As long as the connection subsists between his reason and his self-love, his opinions and his passions will have a reciprocal influence on each other; and the former will be objects to which the latter will attach themselves. The diversity in the faculties of men, from which the rights of property originate, is not less an insuperable obstacle to an uniformity of interests. The protection of these faculties is the first object of government. From the protection of different and unequal faculties of acquiring property, the possession of different degrees and kinds of property immediately results; and from the influence of these on the sentiments and views of the respective proprietors, ensues a division of the society into different interests and parties.

The latent causes of faction are thus sown in the nature of man; and we see them everywhere brought into different degrees of activity, according to the different circumstances of civil society. A zeal for different opinions concerning religion, concerning government, and many other points, as well of speculation as of practice; an attachment to different leaders ambitiously contending for preeminence and power; or to persons of other descriptions whose fortunes have been interesting to the human passions, have, in turn, divided mankind into parties, inflamed them with mutual animosity, and rendered them much more disposed to vex and oppress each other, than to cooperate for their common good. So strong is this propensity of mankind, to fall into mutual animosities, that where no substantial occasion presents itself, the most frivolous and fanciful distinctions have been sufficient to kindle their unfriendly passions and excite their most violent conflicts. But the most common and durable source of factions, has been the various and unequal distribution of property. Those who hold, and those who are without property, have ever formed distinct interests in society. Those who are creditors, and those who are debtors, fall under a like discrimination. A landed interest, a manufacturing interest, a mercantile interest, a moneyed interest, with many lesser interests, grow up of necessity in civilized nations, and divide them into different classes, actuated by different sentiments and views. The regulation of these various and interfering interests forms the principal task of modern legislation, and involves the spirit of the party and faction in the necessary and ordinary operations of the government.

No man is allowed to be a judge in his own cause; because his interest will certainly bias his judgment, and, not improbably, corrupt his integrity. With equal, nay, with greater reason, a body of men are unfit to be both judges and parties at the same time; yet what are many of the most important acts of legislation, but so many judicial determinations, not indeed concerning the right of single persons, but concerning the rights of large bodies of citizens? And what are the different classes of legislators, but advocates and parties to the causes which they determine? Is a law proposed concerning private debts? It is a question to which the creditors are parties on one side, and the debtors on the other. Justice ought to hold the balance between them. Yet the parties are, and must be, themselves the judges; and the most numerous party, or, in other words, the most powerful faction, must be expected to prevail. Shall domestic manufacturers be encouraged, and in what degree, by restrictions on foreign manufacturers? Are questions which would be differently decided by the landed and the manufacturing classes; and probably by neither with a sole regard to justice and the public good. The apportionment of taxes, on the various descriptions of property, is an act which seems to require the most exact impartiality; yet there is, perhaps, no legislative act, in which greater opportunity and temptation are given to a predominant party to trample on the rules of justice. Every shilling, with which they overburden the inferior number, is a shilling saved to their own pockets.

It is in vain to say, that enlightened statesmen will be able to adjust these clashing interests, and render them all subservient to the public good. Enlightened statesmen will not always be at the helm, nor, in many cases, can such an adjustment be made at all, without taking into view indirect and remote considerations, which will rarely prevail over the immediate interest which one party may find in disregarding the rights of another, or the good of the whole.

The inference to which we are brought is, that the causes of faction cannot be removed; and that relief is only to be sought in the means of controlling its effects.

If a faction consists of less than a majority, relief is supplied by the republican principle, which enables the majority to defeat its sinister views, by regular vote. It may clog the administration, it may convulse the society; but it will be unable to execute and mask its violence under the forms of the Constitution. When a majority is included in a faction, the form of popular government, on the other hand, enables it to sacrifice to its ruling passion or interest, both the public good and the rights of other citizens. To secure the public good, and private rights, against the danger of such a faction, and at the same time to preserve the spirit and the form of popular government, is then the great object to which our inquiries are directed. Let me add, that it is the great desideratum, by which alone this form of government can be rescued from the opprobrium under which it has so long laboured, and be recommended to the esteem and adoption of mankind.

By what means is this object attainable? Evidently by one of two only. Either the existence of the same passion or interest in a majority, at the same time, must be prevented; or the majority, having such coexistent passion or interest, must be rendered, by their number and local situation, unable to concert and carry into effect schemes of oppression. If the impulse and the opportunity be suffered to coincide, we well know that neither moral nor religious motives can be relied on as an adequate control. They are not found to be such on the injustice and violence of individuals, and lose their efficacy in proportion to the number combined together; that is, in proportion as their efficacy becomes needful.

From this view of the subject, it may be concluded, that a pure democracy, by which I mean a society consisting of a small number of citizens, who assemble and administer the government in person, can admit of no cure for the mischiefs of faction. A common passion or interest will, in almost every case, be felt by a majority of the whole; a communication and concert, results from the form of government itself; and there is nothing to check the inducements to sacrifice the weaker party, or an obnoxious individual. Hence, it is, that such democracies have ever been spectacles of turbulence and contention; have ever been found incompatible with personal security, or the rights of property; and have in general been as short in their lives, as they have been violent in their deaths. Theoretic politicians, who have patronized this species of government, have erroneously supposed, that by reducing mankind to a perfect equality in their political rights, they would, at the same time be perfectly equalized and assimilated in their possessions, their opinions, and their passions.

A republic, by which I mean a government in which the scheme of representation takes place, opens a different prospect, and promises the cure for which we are seeking. Let us examine the points in which it varies from pure democracy, and we shall comprehend both the nature of the cure and the efficacy which it must derive from the union.

The two great points of difference, between a democracy and a republic, are, first, the delegation of the government, in the latter, to a small number of citizens, elected by the rest; secondly, the greater number of citizens, and greater sphere of country, over which the latter may be extended.

The effect of the first difference is, on the one hand, to refine and enlarge the public views, by passing them through the medium of a chosen body of citizens, whose wisdom may best discern the true interest of their country, and whose patriotism and love of justice, will be least likely to sacrifice it to temporary or partial considerations. Under such a regulation, it may well happen, that the public voice, pronounced by the representatives of the people, will be more consonant to the public good, than if pronounced by the people themselves, convened for the purpose. On the other hand the effect may be inverted. Men of factious tempers, of local prejudices, or of sinister designs, may by intrigue, by corruption, or by other means, first obtain the suffrages, and then betray the interest of the people. The question resulting is, whether small or extensive republics are most favourable to the election of proper guardians of the public weal; and it is clearly decided in favour of the latter by two obvious considerations.

In the first place, it is to be remarked that, however small the republic may be, the representatives must be raised to a certain number, in order to guard against the cabals of a few; and that however large it may be, they must be limited to a certain number, in order to guard against the confusion of a multitude. Hence, the number of representatives in the two cases not being in proportion to that of the constituents, and being proportionally greatest in the small republic, it follows, that if the proportion of fit characters be not less in the large than in the small republic, the former will present a greater option, and consequently a greater probability of a fit choice.

In the next place, as each representative will be chosen by a greater number of citizens in the large than in the small republic, it will be more difficult for unworthy candidates to practice with success the vicious arts, by which elections are too often carried; and the suffrages of the people being more free, will be more likely to centre in men who possess the most attractive merit, and the most diffusive and established characters.

It must be confessed, that in this, as in most other cases, there is a mean, on both sides of which inconveniences will be found to lie. By enlarging too much the number of electors, you render the representatives too little acquainted with all their local circumstances and lesser interests; as by reducing it too much, you render him unduly attached to these, and too little fit to comprehend and pursue great and national objects. The federal constitution forms a happy combination in this respect; the great and aggregate interests being referred to the national, the local and particular to the state legislatures.

The other point of difference is, the greater number of citizens, and extent of territory, which may be brought within the compass of republican, than of democratic government; and it is this circumstance principally which renders factious combinations less to be dreaded in the former, than in the latter. The smaller the society, the fewer probably will be the distinct parties and interests composing it; the fewer the distinct parties and interests, the more frequently will a majority be found of the same party; and the smaller the number of individuals composing a majority, and the smaller the compass within which they are placed, the more easily will they concert and execute their plans of oppression. Extend the sphere, and you take in a greater variety of parties and interests; you make it less probable that a majority of the whole will have a common motive to invade the rights of other citizens; or if such a common motive exists, it will be more difficult for all who feel it to discover their own strength, and to act in unison with each other. Besides other impediments, it may be remarked, that where there is a consciousness of unjust or dishonourable purposes, communication is always checked by distrust, in proportion to the number whose concurrence is necessary.

Hence, it clearly appears, that the same advantage, which a republic has over a democracy, in controlling the effects of faction, is enjoyed by a large over a small republic—is enjoyed by the union over the states composing it. Does this advantage consist in the substitution of representatives, whose enlightened views and virtuous sentiments render them superior to local prejudices, and to schemes of injustice? It will not be denied that the representation of the union will be most likely to possess these requisite endowments. Does it consist in the greater security afforded by a greater variety of parties, against the event of any one party being able to outnumber and oppress the rest? In an equal degree does the increased variety of parties, comprised within the union, increase the security? Does it, in fine, consist in the greater obstacles opposed to the concert and accomplishment of the secret wishes of an unjust and interested majority? Here, again, the extent of the union gives it the most palpable advantage.

The influence of factious leaders may kindle a flame within their particular states, but will be unable to spread a general conflagration through the other states; a religious sect may degenerate into a political faction in a part of the confederacy; but the variety of sects dispersed over the entire face of it, must secure the national councils against any danger from that source: a rage for paper money, for an abolition of debts, for an equal division of property, or for any other improper or wicked project, will be less apt to pervade the whole body of the union than a particular member of it; in the same proportion as such a malady is more likely to taint a particular county or district, than an entire state.

In the extent and proper structure of the union, therefore, we behold a republican remedy for the diseases most incident to republican government. And according to the degree of pleasure and pride we feel in being republicans, ought to be our zeal in cherishing the spirit, and supporting the character of federalists.

The Federalist, No. 51, James Madison

To what expedient, then, shall we finally resort, for maintaining in practice the necessary partition of power among the several departments as laid down in the Constitution? The only answer that can be given is that as all these exterior provisions are found to be inadequate the defect must be supplied, by so contriving the interior structure of the government as that its several constituent parts may, by their mutual relations, be the means of keeping each other in their proper places. Without presuming to undertake a full development of this important idea I will hazard a few general observations which may perhaps place it in a clearer light, and enable us to form a more correct judgment of the principles and structure of the government planned by the convention.

In order to lay a due foundation for that separate and distinct exercise of the different powers of government, which to a certain extent is admitted on all hands to be essential to the preservation of liberty, it is evident that each department should have a will of its own; and consequently should be so constituted that the members of each should have as little agency as possible in the appointment of the members of the others. Were this principle rigorously adhered to, it would require that all the appointments for the supreme executive, legislative, and judiciary magistracies should be drawn from the same fountain of authority, the people, through channels having no communication whatever with one another. Perhaps such a plan of constructing the several departments would be less difficult in practice than it may in contemplation appear. Some difficulties, however, and some additional expense would attend the execution of it. Some deviations, therefore, from the principle must be admitted. In the constitution of the judiciary department in particular, it might be inexpedient to insist rigorously on the principle: first, because peculiar qualifications being essential in the members, the primary consideration ought to be to select that mode of choice which best secures these qualifications; second, because the permanent tenure by which the appointments are held in that department must soon destroy all sense of dependence on the authority conferring them.

It is equally evident that the members of each department should be as little dependent as possible on those of the others for the emoluments annexed to their offices. Were the executive magistrate, or the judges, not independent of the legislature in this particular, their independence in every other would be merely nominal.

But the great security against a gradual concentration of the several powers in the same department consists in giving to those who administer each department the necessary constitutional means and personal motives to resist encroachments of the others. The provision for defense must in this, as in all other cases, be made commensurate to the danger of attack. Ambition must be made to counteract ambition. The interest of the man must be connected with the constitutional rights of the place. It may be a reflection on human nature that such devices should be necessary to control the abuses of government. But what is government itself but the greatest of all reflections on human nature? If men were angels, no government would be necessary. If angels were to govern men, neither external nor internal controls on government would be necessary. In framing a government which is to be administered by men over men, the great difficulty lies in this: you must first enable the government to control the governed; and in the next place oblige it to control itself. A dependence on the people is, no doubt, the primary control on the government; but experience has taught mankind the necessity of auxiliary precautions.

This policy of supplying, by opposite and rival interests, the defect of better motives, might be traced through the whole system of human affairs, private as well as public. We see it particularly displayed in all the subordinate distributions of power, where the constant aim is to divide and arrange the several offices in such a manner as that each may be a check on the other—that the private interest of every individual may be a sentinel over the public rights. These inventions of prudence cannot be less requisite in the distribution of the supreme powers of the State.

But it is not possible to give to each department an equal power of self-defense. In republican government, the legislative authority necessarily predominates. The remedy for this inconveniency is to divide the legislature into different branches; and to render them, by modes of election and different principles of action, as little connected with each other as the nature of their common functions and their common dependence on the society will admit. It may even be necessary to guard against dangerous encroachments by still further precautions. As the weight of the legislative authority requires that it should be thus divided, the weakness of the executive may require, on the other hand, that it should be fortified. An absolute negative on the legislature appears, at first view, to be the natural defense with which the executive magistrate should be armed. But perhaps it would be neither altogether safe nor alone sufficient. On ordinary occasions it might not be exerted with the requisite firmness, and on extraordinary occasions it might be perfidiously abused. May not this defect of an absolute negative be supplied by some qualified connection between this weaker department and the weaker branch of the stronger department, by which the latter may be led to support the constitutional rights of the former, without being too much detached from the rights of its own department?

If the principles on which these observations are founded be just, as I persuade myself they are, and they be applied as a criterion to the several State constitutions, and to the federal Constitution, it will be found that if the latter does not perfectly correspond with them, the former are infinitely less able to bear such a test.

There are, moreover, two considerations particularly applicable to the federal system of America, which place that system in a very interesting point of view.

First. In a single republic, all the power surrendered by the people is submitted to the administration of a single government; and the usurpations are guarded against by a division of the government into distinct and separate departments. In the compound republic of America, the power surrendered by the people is first divided between two distinct governments, and then the portion allotted to each subdivided among distinct and separate departments. Hence a double security arises to the rights of the people. The different governments will control each other, at the same time that each will be controlled by itself.

Second. It is of great importance in a republic not only to guard the society against the oppression of its rulers, but to guard one part of the society against the injustice of the other part. Different interests necessarily exist in different classes of citizens. If a majority be united by a common interest, the rights of the minority will be insecure. There are but two methods of providing against this evil: the one by creating a will in the community independent of the majority—that is, of the society itself; the other, by comprehending in the society so many separate descriptions of citizens as will render an unjust combination of a majority of the whole very improbable, if not impracticable. The first method prevails in all governments possessing an hereditary or self-appointed authority. This, at best, is but a precarious security; because a power independent of the society may as well espouse the unjust views of the major as the rightful interests of the minor party, and may possibly be turned against both parties. The second method will be exemplified in the federal republic of the United States. Whilst all authority in it will be derived from and dependent on the society, the society itself will be broken into so many parts, interests and classes of citizens, that the rights of individuals, or of the minority, will be in little danger from interested combinations of the majority. In a free government the

security for civil rights must be the same as that for religious rights. It consists in the one case in the multiplicity of interests, and in the other in the multiplicity of sects. The degree of security in both cases will depend on the number of interests and sects; and this may be presumed to depend on the extent of country and number of people comprehended under the same government. This view of the subject must particularly recommend a proper federal system to all the sincere and considerate friends of republican government, since it shows that in exact proportion as the territory of the Union may be formed into more circumscribed Confederacies, or States, oppressive combinations of a majority will be facilitated; the best security, under the republican forms, for the rights of every class of citizen, will be diminished; and consequently the stability and independence of some member of the government, the only other security, must be proportionally increased. Justice is the end of government. It is the end of civil society. It ever has been and ever will be pursued until it be obtained, or until liberty be lost in the pursuit. In a society under the forms of which the stronger faction can readily unite and oppress the weaker, anarchy may as truly be said to reign as in a state of nature, where the weaker individual is not secured against the violence of the stronger; and as, in the latter state, even the stronger individuals are prompted, by the uncertainty of their condition, to submit to a government which may protect the weak as well as themselves; so, in the former state, will the more powerful factions or parties be gradually induced, by a like motive, to wish for a government which will protect all parties, the weaker as well as the more powerful. It can be little doubted that if the State of Rhode Island was separated from the Confederacy and left to itself, the insecurity of rights under the popular form of government within such narrow limits would be displayed by such reiterated oppressions of factious majorities that some power altogether independent of the people would soon be called for by the voice of the very factions whose misrule had proved the necessity to it. In the extended republic of the United States, and among the great variety of interests, parties, and sects which it embraces, a coalition of a majority of the whole society could seldom take place on any other principles than those of justice and the general good; whilst there being thus less danger to a minor from the will of a major party, there must be less pretext, also, to provide for the security of the former, by introducing into the government a will not dependent on the latter, or, in other words, a will independent of the society itself. It is no less certain that it is important, notwithstanding the contrary opinions which have been entertained that the larger the society, provided it lie within a practicable sphere, the more duly capable it will be of self-government. And happily for the republican cause, the practicable sphere may be carried to a very great extent by a judicious modification and mixture of the federal principle.

Anti-Federalist, Brutus, October 18, 1787

To the Citizens of the State of New York: When the public is called to investigate and decide upon a question in which not only the present members of the community are deeply interested, but upon which the happiness and misery of generations yet unborn is in great measure suspended, the benevolent mind cannot help feeling itself peculiarly interested in the result.

In this situation, I trust the feeble efforts of an individual, to lead the minds of the people to a wise and prudent determination, cannot fail of being acceptable to the candid and dispassionate part of the community. Encouraged by this consideration, I have been induced to offer my thoughts upon the present important crisis of our public affairs.

Perhaps this country never saw so critical a period in their political concerns. We have felt the feebleness of the ties by which these United-States are held together, and the want of sufficient energy in our present confederation, to manage, in some instances, our general concerns. Various expedients have been proposed to remedy these evils, but none have succeeded. At length a Convention of the states has been assembled, they have formed a constitution which will now, probably, be submitted to the people to ratify or reject, who are the fountain of all power, to whom alone it of right belongs to make or unmake constitutions, or forms of government, at their pleasure. The most important question that was ever proposed to your decision, or to the decision of any people under heaven, is before you, and you are to decide upon it by men of your own election, chosen specially for this purpose. If the constitution, offered to your acceptance, be a wise one, calculated to preserve the invaluable blessings of liberty, to secure the inestimable rights of mankind, and promote human happiness, then, if you accept it, you will lay a lasting foundation of happiness for millions yet unborn; generations to come will rise up and call you blessed. You may rejoice in the prospects of this vast extended continent becoming filled with freemen, who will assert the dignity of human nature. You may solace yourselves with the idea, that society, in this favoured land, will fast advance to the highest point of perfection; the human mind will expand in knowledge and virtue,

and the golden age be, in some measure, realised. But if, on the other hand, this form of government contains principles that will lead to the subversion of liberty—if it tends to establish a despotism, or, what is worse, a tyrannic aristocracy; then, if you adopt it, this only remaining assylum for liberty will be shut up, and posterity will execrate your memory.

Momentous then is the question you have to determine, and you are called upon by every motive which should influence a noble and virtuous mind, to examine it well, and to make up a wise judgment. It is insisted, indeed, that this constitution must be received, be it ever so imperfect. If it has its defects, it is said, they can be best amended when they are experienced. But remember, when the people once part with power, they can seldom or never resume it again but by force. Many instances can be produced in which the people have voluntarily increased the powers of their rulers; but few, if any, in which rulers have willingly abridged their authority. This is a sufficient reason to induce you to be careful, in the first instance, how you deposit the powers of government.

With these few introductory remarks, I shall proceed to a consideration of this constitution:

The first question that presents itself on the subject is, whether a confederated government be the best for the United States or not? Or in other words, whether the thirteen United States should be reduced to one great republic, governed by one legislature, and under the direction of one executive and judicial; or whether they should continue thirteen confederated republics, under the direction and controul of a supreme federal head for certain defined national purposes only?

This enquiry is important, because, although the government reported by the convention does not go to a perfect and entire consolidation, yet it approaches so near to it, that it must, if executed, certainly and infallibly terminate in it.

This government is to possess absolute and uncontroulable power, legislative, executive and judicial, with respect to every object to which it extends, for by the last clause of section 8th, article 1st, it is declared "that the Congress shall have power to make all laws which shall be necessary and proper for carrying into execution the foregoing powers, and all other powers vested by this constitution, in the government of the United States; or in any department or office thereof." And by the 6th article, it is declared "that this constitution, and the laws of the United States, which shall be made in pursuance thereof, and the treaties made, or which shall be made, under the authority of the United States, shall be the supreme law of the land; and the judges in every state shall be bound thereby, any thing in the constitution, or law of any state to the contrary notwithstanding." It appears from these articles that there is no need of any intervention of the state governments, between the Congress and the people, to execute any one power vested in the general government, and that the constitution and laws of every state are nullified and declared void, so far as they are or shall be inconsistent with this constitution, or the laws made in pursuance of it, or with treaties made under the authority of the United States.—The government then, so far as it extends, is a complete one, and not a confederation. It is as much one complete government as that of New-York or Massachusetts, has as absolute and perfect powers to make and execute all laws, to appoint officers, institute courts, declare offences, and annex penalties, with respect to every object to which it extends, as any other in the world. So far therefore as its powers reach, all ideas of confederation are given up and lost. It is true this government is limited to certain objects, or to speak more properly, some small degree of power is still left to the states, but a little attention to the powers vested in the general government, will convince every candid man, that if it is capable of being executed, all that is reserved for the individual states must very soon be annihilated, except so far as they are barely necessary to the organization of the general government. The powers of the general legislature extend to every case that is of the least importance—there is nothing valuable to human nature, nothing dear to freemen, but what is within its power. It has authority to make laws which will affect the lives, the liberty, and property of every man in the United States; nor can the constitution or laws of any state, in any way prevent or impede the full and complete execution of every power given. The legislative power is competent to lay taxes, duties, imposts, and excises;—there is no limitation to this power, unless it be said that the clause which directs the use to which those taxes, and duties shall be applied, may be said to be a limitation: but this is no restriction of the power at all, for by this clause they are to be applied to pay the debts and provide for the common defence and general welfare of the United States; but the legislature have authority to contract debts at their discretion; they are the sole judges of what is necessary to provide for the common defence, and they only are to determine what is for the general welfare; this power therefore is neither more nor less, than a power to lay and collect taxes, imposts, and excises, at their pleasure; not only [is] the power to lay taxes unlimited,

as to the amount they may require, but it is perfect and absolute to raise them in any mode they please. No state legislature, or any power in the state governments, have any more to do in carrying this into effect, than the authority of one state has to do with that of another. In the business therefore of laying and collecting taxes, the idea of confederation is totally lost, and that of one entire republic is embraced. It is proper here to remark, that the authority to lay and collect taxes is the most important of any power that can be granted; it connects with it almost all other powers, or at least will in process of time draw all other after it; it is the great mean of protection, security, and defence, in a good government, and the great engine of oppression and tyranny in a bad one. This cannot fail of being the case, if we consider the contracted limits which are set by this constitution, to the late [state?] governments, on this article of raising money. No state can emit paper money—lay any duties, or imposts, on imports, or exports, but by consent of the Congress; and then the net produce shall be for the benefit of the United States: the only mean therefore left, for any state to support its government and discharge its debts, is by direct taxation; and the United States have also power to lay and collect taxes, in any way they please. Every one who has thought on the subject, must be convinced that but small sums of money can be collected in any country, by direct taxe[s], when the foederal government begins to exercise the right of taxation in all its parts, the legislatures of the several states will find it impossible to raise monies to support their governments. Without money they cannot be supported, and they must dwindle away, and, as before observed, their powers absorbed in that of the general government.

It might be here shewn, that the power in the federal legislative, to raise and support armies at pleasure, as well in peace as in war, and their controul over the militia, tend, not only to a consolidation of the government, but the destruction of liberty.—I shall not, however, dwell upon these, as a few observations upon the judicial power of this government, in addition to the preceding, will fully evince the truth of the position.

The judicial power of the United States is to be vested in a supreme court, and in such inferior courts as Congress may from time to time ordain and establish. The powers of these courts are very extensive; their jurisdiction comprehends all civil causes, except such as arise between citizens of the same state; and it extends to all cases in law and equity arising under the constitution. One inferior court must be established, I presume, in each state, at least, with the necessary executive officers appendant thereto. It is easy to see, that in the common course of things, these courts will eclipse the dignity, and take away from the respectability, of the state courts. These courts will be, in themselves, totally independent of the states, deriving their authority from the United States, and receiving from them fixed salaries; and in the course of human events it is to be expected, that they will swallow up all the powers of the courts in the respective states.

How far the clause in the 8th section of the 1st article may operate to do away all idea of confederated states, and to effect an entire consolidation of the whole into one general government, it is impossible to say. The powers given by this article are very general and comprehensive, and it may receive a construction to justify the passing almost any law. A power to make all laws, which shall be *necessary and proper*, for carrying into execution, all powers vested by the constitution in the government of the United States, or any department or officer thereof, is a power very comprehensive and definite [indefinite?], and may, for ought I know, be exercised in a such manner as entirely to abolish the state legislatures. Suppose the legislature of a state should pass a law to raise money to support their government and pay the state debt, may the Congress repeal this law, because it may prevent the collection of a tax which they may think proper and necessary to lay, to provide for the general welfare of the United States? For all laws made, in pursuance of this constitution, are the supreme lay of the land, and the judges in every state shall be bound thereby, any thing in the constitution or laws of the different states to the contrary notwithstanding.—By such a law, the government of a particular state might be overturned at one stroke, and thereby be deprived of every means of its support.

It is not meant, by stating this case, to insinuate that the constitution would warrant a law of this kind; or unnecessarily to alarm the fears of the people, by suggesting, that the federal legislature would be more likely to pass the limits assigned them by the constitution, than that of an individual state, further than they are less responsible to the people. But what is meant is, that the legislature of the United States are vested with the great and uncontroulable powers, of laying and collecting taxes, duties, imposts, and excises; of regulating trade, raising and supporting armies, organizing, arming, and disciplining the militia, instituting courts, and other general powers. And are by this clause invested with the power of making all laws, *proper and necessary*, for carrying all these into execution; and they may so exercise this power as entirely to annihilate all the state governments, and reduce this country to one single government. And if they may do it, it is pretty certain they will; for it will be found that the power retained by individual states, small as it is, will be a clog upon the wheels of the government of the United States; the latter therefore will be naturally inclined to remove it out of the way. Besides, it is a truth confirmed by the unerring experience of ages, that every man, and every body of men, invested with power, are ever disposed to increase it, and to acquire a superiority over every thing that stands in their way.

This disposition, which is implanted in human nature, will operate in the federal legislature to lessen and ultimately to subvert the state authority, and having such advantages, will most certainly succeed, if the federal government succeeds at all. It must be very evident then, that what this constitution wants of being a complete consolidation of the several parts of the union into one complete government, possessed of perfect legislative, judicial, and executive powers, to all intents and purposes, it will necessarily acquire in its exercise and operation.

Let us now proceed to enquire, as I at first proposed, whether it be best the thirteen United States should be reduced to one great republic, or not? It is here taken for granted, that all agree in this, that whatever government we adopt, it ought to be a free one; that it should be so framed as to secure the liberty of the citizens of America, and such an one as to admit of a full, fair, and equal representation of the people. The question then will be, whether a government thus constituted, and founded on such principles, is practicable, and can be exercised over the whole United States, reduced into one state?

If respect is to be paid to the opinion of the greatest and wisest men who have ever thought or wrote on the science of government, we shall be constrained to conclude, that a free republic cannot succeed over a country of such immense extent, containing such a number of inhabitants, and these encreasing in such rapid progression as that of the whole United States. Among the many illustrious authorities which might be produced to this point, I shall content myself with quoting only two. The one is the baron de Montesquieu, spirit of laws, chap. xvi. vol. I [book VIII]. "It is natural to a republic to have only a small territory, otherwise it cannot long subsist. In a large republic there are men of large fortunes, and consequently of less moderation; there are trusts too great to be placed in any single subject; he has interest of his own; he soon begins to think that he may be happy, great and glorious, by oppressing his fellow citizens; and that he may raise himself to grandeur on the ruins of his country. In a large republic, the public good is sacrificed to a thousand views; it is subordinate to exceptions, and depends on accidents. In a small one, the interest of the public is easier perceived, better understood, and more within the reach of every citizen; abuses are of less extent, and of course are less protected." Of the same opinion is the marquis Beccarari.

History furnishes no example of a free republic, any thing like the extent of the United States. The Grecian republics were of small extent; so also was that of the Romans. Both of these, it is true, in process of time, extended their conquests over large territories of country; and the consequence was, that their governments were changed from that of free governments to those of the most tyrannical that ever existed in the world.

Not only the opinion of the greatest men, and the experience of mankind, are against the idea of an extensive republic, but a variety of reasons may be drawn from the reason and nature of things, against it. In every government, the will of the sovereign is the law. In despotic governments, the supreme authority being lodged in one, his will is law, and can be as easily expressed to a large extensive territory as to a small one. In a pure democracy the people are the sovereign, and their will is declared by themselves; for this purpose they must all come together to deliberate, and decide. This kind of government cannot be exercised, therefore, over a country of any considerable extent; it must be confined to a single city, or at least limited to such bounds as that the people can conveniently assemble, be able to debate, understand the subject submitted to them, and declare their opinion concerning it.

In a free republic, although all laws are derived from the consent of the people, yet the people do not declare their consent by themselves in person, but by representatives, chosen by them, who are supposed to know the minds of their constituents, and to be possessed of integrity to declare this mind.

In every free government, the people must give their assent to the laws by which they are governed. This is the true criterion between a free government and an arbitrary one. The former are ruled by the will of the whole, expressed in any manner they may agree upon; the latter by the will of one, or a few. If the people are to give their assent to the laws, by persons chosen and appointed by them, the manner of the choice and the number chosen, must be such, as to possess, be disposed, and consequently qualified to declare the sentiments of the people; for if they do not know, or are not disposed to speak the sentiments of the people, the people do not govern, but the sovereignty is in a few. Now, in a large extended country, it is impossible to have a representation, possessing the sentiments, and of integrity, to declare the minds of the people, without having it so numerous and unwieldly, as to be subject in great measure to the inconveniency of a democratic government.

The territory of the United States is of vast extent; it now contains near three millions of souls, and is capable of containing much more than ten times that number. Is it practicable for a country, so large and so numerous as they will soon become, to elect a representation, that will speak their sentiments, without their becoming so numerous as to be incapable of transacting public business? It certainly is not.

In a republic, the manners, sentiments, and interests of the people should be similar. If this be not the case, there will be a constant clashing of opinions; and the representatives of one part will be continually striving against those of the other. This will retard the operations of government, and prevent such conclusions as will promote the public good. If we apply this remark to the condition of the United States, we shall be convinced that it forbids that we should be one government. The United States includes a variety of climates. The productions of the different parts of the union are very variant, and their interests, of consequence, diverse. Their manners and habits differ as much as their climates and productions; and their sentiments are by no means coincident. The laws and customs of the several states are, in many respects, very diverse, and in some opposite; each would be in favor of its own interests and customs, and, of consequence, a legislature, formed of representatives from the respective parts, would not only be too numerous to act with any care or decision, but would be composed of such heterogenous and discordant principles, as would constantly be contending with each other.

The laws cannot be executed in a republic, of an extent equal to that of the United States, with promptitude.

The magistrates in every government must be supported in the execution of the laws, either by an armed force, maintained at the public expence for that purpose; or by the people turning out to aid the magistrate upon his command, in case of resistance.

In despotic governments, as well as in all the monarchies of Europe, standing armies are kept up to execute the commands of the prince or the magistrate, and are employed for this purpose when occasion requires: But they have always proved the destruction of liberty, and [are] abhorrent to the spirit of a free republic. In England, where they depend upon the parliament for their annual support, they have always been complained of as oppressive and unconstitutional, and are seldom employed in executing of the laws; never except on extraordinary occasions, and then under the direction of a civil magistrate.

A free republic will never keep a standing army to execute its laws. It must depend upon the support of its citizens. But when a government is to receive its support from the aid of the citizens, it must be so constructed as to have the confidence, respect, and affection of the people." Men who, upon the call of the magistrate, offer themselves to execute the laws, are influenced to do it either by affection to the government, or from fear; where a standing army is at hand to punish offenders, every man is actuated by the latter principle, and therefore, when the magistrate calls, will obey: but, where this is not the case, the government must rest for its support upon the confidence and respect which the people have for their government and laws. The body of the people being attached, the government will always be sufficient to support and execute its laws, and to operate upon the fears of any faction which may be opposed to it, not only to prevent an opposition to the execution of the laws themselves, but also to compel the most of them to aid the magistrate; but the people will not be likely to have such confidence in their rulers, in a republic so extensive as the United States, as necessary for these purposes. The confidence which the people have in their rulers, in a free republic, arises from their knowing them, from their being responsible to them for their conduct, and from the power they have of displacing them when they misbehave: but in a republic of the extent of this continent, the people in general would be acquainted with very few of their rulers: the people at large would know little of their proceedings, and it would be extremely difficult to change them. The people in Georgia and New-Hampshire would not know one another's mind, and therefore could not act in concert to enable them to effect a general change of representatives. The different parts of so extensive a country could not possibly be made acquainted with the conduct of their representatives, nor be informed of the reasons upon which measures were founded. The consequence will be, they will have no confidence in their legislature, suspect them of ambitious views, be jealous of every measure they adopt, and will not support the laws they pass. Hence the government will be nerveless and inefficient, and no way will be left to render it otherwise, but by establishing an armed force to execute the laws at the point of the bayonet—a government of all others the most to be dreaded.

In a republic of such vast extent as the United-States, the legislature cannot attend to the various concerns and wants of its different parts. It cannot be sufficiently numerous to be acquainted with the local condition and wants of the different districts, and if it could, it is impossible it should have sufficient time to attend to and provide for all the variety of cases of this nature, that would be continually arising.

In so extensive a republic, the great officers of government would soon become above the controul of the people, and abuse their power to the purpose of aggrandizing themselves, and oppressing them. The trust committed to the executive offices, in a country of the extent of the United-States, must be various and of magnitude. The command of all the troops and navy of the republic, the appointment of officers, the power of pardoning offences, the collecting of all the public revenues, and the power of expending them, with a number of other powers, must be lodged and exercised in every state, in the hands of a few. When these are attended with great honor and emolument, as they always will be in large states, so as greatly to interest men to pursue them, and to be proper objects for ambitious and designing men, such men will be ever restless in their pursuit after them. They will use the power, when they have acquired it, to the purposes of gratifying their own interest and ambition, and it is scarcely possible, in a very large republic, to call them to account for their misconduct, or to prevent their abuse of power.

These are some of the reasons by which it appears, that a free republic cannot long subsist over a country of the great extent of these states. If then this new constitution is calculated to consolidate the thirteen states into one, as it evidently is, it ought not to be adopted.

Though I am of opinion, that it is a sufficient objection to this government, to reject it, that it creates the whole union into one government, under the form of a republic, yet if this objection was obviated, there are exceptions to it, which are so material and fundamental, that they ought to determine every man, who is a friend to the liberty and happiness of mankind, not to adopt it. I beg the candid and dispassionate attention of my countrymen while I state these objections—they are such as have obtruded themselves upon my mind upon a careful attention to the matter, and such as I sincerely believe are well founded. There are many objections, of small moment, of which I shall take no notice—perfection is not to be expected in any thing that is the production of man—and if I did not in my conscience believe that this scheme was defective in the fundamental principles—in the foundation upon which a free and equal government must rest—I would hold my peace.

Appendix 6

The Gettysburg Address, Abraham Lincoln

Gettysburg, Pennsylvania
November 19, 1863

Four score and seven years ago our fathers brought forth on this continent, a new nation, conceived in Liberty, and dedicated to the proposition that all men are created equal.

Now we are engaged in a great civil war, testing whether that nation, or any nation so conceived and so dedicated, can long endure. We are met on a great battlefield of that war. We have come to dedicate a portion of that field, as a final resting place for those who here gave their lives that that nation might live. It is altogether fitting and proper that we should do this.

But, in a larger sense, we can not dedicate—we can not consecrate—we can not hallow—this ground. The brave men, living and dead, who struggled here, have consecrated it, far above our poor power to add or detract. The world will little note, nor long remember what we say here, but it can never forget what they did here. It is for us the living, rather, to be dedicated here to the unfinished work which they who fought here have thus far so nobly advanced. It is rather for us to be here dedicated to the great task remaining before us—that from these honored dead we take increased devotion to that cause for which they gave the last full measure of devotion—that we here highly resolve that these dead shall not have died in vain—that this nation, under God, shall have a new birth of freedom—and that government of the people, by the people, for the people, shall not perish from the earth.

Source: *Collected Works of Abraham Lincoln*, edited by Roy P. Basler. The text above is from the so-called "Bliss Copy," one of several versions which Lincoln wrote, and believed to be the final version. For additional versions, you may search *The Collected Works of Abraham Lincoln* through the courtesy of the Abraham Lincoln Association.

Related Links

Battlefield Map (Library of Congress): https://www.loc.gov/item/99439128/
Civil War Institute (Gettysburg College): http://www.gettysburg.edu/cwi/
Gettysburg Address Exhibit (Library of Congress): https://www.loc.gov/exhibits/gettysburg-address/

Gettysburg Address Eyewitness (National Public Radio): http://www.npr.org/programs/lnfsound/stories/990215.stories.html
Gettysburg Address News Article (New York Times): http://www.nytimes.com/learning/general/onthisday/big/1119.html
Gettysburg Address Teacher Resource (C-SPAN): http://www.c-span.org/video/?313031-1/historians-writers-remember-battle-gettysburg
Gettysburg Civil War Photographs (Library of Congress): http://www.loc.gov/teachers/classroommaterials/connections/civil-war-photographs/
Gettysburg Discussion Group (Bob & Dennis Lawrence): http://www.gdg.org/
Gettysburg Events (NPS): https://www.nps.gov/gett/planyourvisit/calendar.htm
Gettysburg National Military Park (NPS): https://www.nps.gov/gett/index.htm
Letter of Invitation to Lincoln (Library of Congress): https://www.loc.gov/exhibits/treasures/trt031.html
Lincoln at Gettysburg: http://www.smithsonianmag.com/history/Interactive_Seeking_Abraham_Lincoln_at_the_Gettysburg_Address-180947919/?no-ist
Lincoln at Gettysburg Photo Tour: http://www.abrahamlincolnonline.org/lincoln/tours/gettytour.htm
Lincoln Fellowship of Pennsylvania: http://www.lincolnfellowship.org/
Lincoln's Invitation to Stay Overnight (Library of Congress): https://www.loc.gov/exhibits/treasures/trt030.html
Lincoln's Letter from Edward Everett (Library of Congress): https://www.loc.gov/exhibits/treasures/trt032.html
Reading of the Gettysburg Address (NPR): http://www.npr.org/templates/story/story.php?storyId=1512410
Recollections of Lincoln at Gettysburg (Bob Cooke): http://www.abrahamlincolnonline.org/lincoln/news/recollect.htm
Response to a Serenade: http://www.abrahamlincolnonline.org/lincoln/speeches/serenade.htm
Seminary Ridge Historic Preservation Foundation: http://seminaryridgemuseum.weebly.com/
The Gettysburg Powerpoint Presentation (Peter Norvig): http://norvig.com/Gettysburg/
Wills House: https://www.nps.gov/gett/planyourvisit/david-wills-house.htm

Related Books

Graham, Kent. *November: Lincoln's Elegy at Gettysburg.* Bloomington, IN: Indiana University Press, 2001.

Hoch, Bradley R. and Boritt, Gabor S. *The Lincoln Trail in Pennsylvania.* University Park, PA: Pennsylvania State University Press, 2001.

Kunhardt, Philip B., Jr. *A New Birth of Freedom—Lincoln at Gettysburg.* Boston: Little, Brown, 1983.

Wills, Garry. *Lincoln at Gettysburg: The Words That Remade America.* New York: Touchstone Books, 1993.

Appendix 7

Presidents and Congresses, 1789–2017

Term	President and Vice President	Party of President	Congress	Majority Party House	Majority Party Senate
1789–97	**George Washington**	None	1st	N/A	N/A
	John Adams		2d	N/A	N/A
			3d	N/A	N/A
			4th	N/A	N/A
1797–1801	**John Adams**	Fed	5th	N/A	N/A
	Thomas Jefferson		6th	Fed	Fed
1801–09	**Thomas Jefferson**	Dem Rep	7th	Dem Rep	Dem Rep
	Aaron Burr (1801–05)		8th	Dem Rep	Dem Rep
	George Clinton (1805–09)		9th	Dem Rep	Dem Rep
			10th	Dem Rep	Dem Rep
1809–17	**James Madison**	Dem Rep	11th	Dem Rep	Dem Rep
	George Clinton (1809–12)[1]		12th	Dem Rep	Dem Rep
	Elbridge Gerry (1813–14)[1]		13th	Dem Rep	Dem Rep
			14th	Dem Rep	Dem Rep
1817–25	**James Monroe**	Dem Rep	15th	Dem Rep	Dem Rep
	Daniel D. Tompkins		16th	Dem Rep	Dem Rep
			17th	Dem Rep	Dem Rep
			18th	Dem Rep	Dem Rep
1825–29	**John Quincy Adams**	Nat'l Rep	19th	Nat'l Rep	Nat'l Rep
	John C. Calhoun		20th	Dem	Dem
1829–37	**Andrew Jackson**	Dem	21st	Dem	Dem
	John C. Calhoun (1829–32)[2]		22d	Dem	Dem
	Martin Van Buren (1833–37)		23d	Dem	Dem
			24th	Dem	Dem
1837–41	**Martin Van Buren**	Dem	25th	Dem	Dem
	Richard M. Johnson		26th	Dem	Dem
1841	**William H. Harrison**[1]	Whig	27th	Whig	Whig
	John Tyler (1841)				
1841–45	**John Tyler**	Whig	28th	Dem	Whig
	(VP vacant)				
1845–49	**James K. Polk**	Dem	29th	Dem	Dem
	George M. Dallas		30th	Whig	Dem
1849–50	**Zachary Taylor**[1]	Whig	31st	Dem	Dem
	Millard Fillmore				
1850–53	**Millard Fillmore**	Whig	32d	Dem	Dem
	(VP vacant)				
1853–57	**Franklin Pierce**	Dem	33d	Dem	Dem
	William R. D. King (1853)[1]		34th	Rep	Dem
1857–61	**James Buchanan**	Dem	35th	Dem	Dem
	John C. Breckinridge		36th	Rep	Dem

[1] Died in office.
[2] Resigned from the vice presidency.

Term	President and Vice President	Party of President	Congress	Majority Party House	Majority Party Senate
1861–65	**Abraham Lincoln**[1]	Rep	37th	Rep	Rep
	Hannibal Hamlin (1861–65)		38th	Rep	Rep
	Andrew Johnson (1865)				
1865–69	**Andrew Johnson**	Rep	39th	Union	Union
	(VP vacant)		40th	Rep	Rep
1869–77	**Ulysses S. Grant**	Rep	41st	Rep	Rep
	Schuyler Colfax (1869–73)		42d	Rep	Rep
	Henry Wilson (1873–75)[1]		43d	Rep	Rep
			44th	Dem	Rep
1877–81	**Rutherford B. Hayes**	Rep	45th	Dem	Rep
	William A. Wheeler		46th	Dem	Dem
1881	**James A. Garfield**[1]	Rep	47th	Rep	Rep
	Chester A. Arthur				
1881–85	**Chester A. Arthur**	Rep	48th	Dem	Rep
	(VP vacant)				
1885–89	**Grover Cleveland**	Dem	49th	Dem	Rep
	Thomas A. Hendricks (1885)[1]		50th	Dem	Rep
1889–93	**Benjamin Harrison**	Rep	51st	Rep	Rep
	Levi P. Morton		52d	Dem	Rep
1893–97	**Grover Cleveland**	Dem	53d	Dem	Dem
	Adlai E. Stevenson		54th	Rep	Rep
1897–1901	**William McKinley**[1]	Rep	55th	Rep	Rep
	Garret A. Hobart (1897–99)[1]		56th	Rep	Rep
	Theodore Roosevelt (1901)				
1901–09	**Theodore Roosevelt**	Rep	57th	Rep	Rep
	(VP vacant, 1901–05)		58th	Rep	Rep
	Charles W. Fairbanks (1905–09)		59th	Rep	Rep
			60th	Rep	Rep
1909–13	**William Howard Taft**	Rep	61st	Rep	Rep
	James S. Sherman (1909–12)[1]		62d	Dem	Rep
1913–21	**Woodrow Wilson**	Dem	63d	Dem	Dem
	Thomas R. Marshall		64th	Dem	Dem
			65th	Dem	Dem
			66th	Rep	Rep
1921–23	**Warren G. Harding**[1]	Rep	67th	Rep	Rep
	Calvin Coolidge				
1923–29	**Calvin Coolidge**	Rep	68th	Rep	Rep
	(VP vacant, 1923–25)		69th	Rep	Rep
	Charles G. Dawes (1925–29)		70th	Rep	Rep
1929–33	**Herbert Hoover**	Rep	71st	Rep	Rep
	Charles Curtis		72d	Dem	Rep
1933–45	**Franklin D. Roosevelt**[1]	Dem	73d	Dem	Dem
	John N. Garner (1933–41)		74th	Dem	Dem
	Henry A. Wallace (1941–45)		75th	Dem	Dem
	Harry S Truman (1945)		76th	Dem	Dem
			77th	Dem	Dem
			78th	Dem	Dem

[1] Died in office.

Term	President and Vice President	Party of President	Congress	Majority Party	
				House	Senate
1945–53	**Harry S Truman**	Dem	79th	Dem	Dem
	(VP vacant, 1945–49)		80th	Rep	Rep
	Alben W. Barkley (1949–53)		81st	Dem	Dem
			82d	Dem	Dem
1953–61	**Dwight D. Eisenhower**	Rep	83d	Rep	Rep
	Richard M. Nixon		84th	Dem	Dem
			85th	Dem	Dem
			86th	Dem	Dem
1961–63	**John F. Kennedy**[1]	Dem	87th	Dem	Dem
	Lyndon B. Johnson (1961–63)				
1963–69	**Lyndon B. Johnson**	Dem	88th	Dem	Dem
	(VP vacant, 1963–65)		89th	Dem	Dem
	Hubert H. Humphrey (1965–69)		90th	Dem	Dem
1969–74	**Richard M. Nixon**[3]	Rep	91st	Dem	Dem
	Spiro T. Agnew (1969–73)[2]		92d	Dem	Dem
	Gerald R. Ford (1973–74)[4]				
1974–77	**Gerald R. Ford**	Rep	93d	Dem	Dem
	Nelson A. Rockefeller[4]		94th	Dem	Dem
1977–81	**Jimmy Carter**	Dem	95th	Dem	Dem
	Walter Mondale		96th	Dem	Dem
1981–89	**Ronald Reagan**	Rep	97th	Dem	Rep
	George Bush		98th	Dem	Rep
			99th	Dem	Rep
			100th	Dem	Dem
1989–93	**George Bush**	Rep	101st	Dem	Dem
	J. Danforth Quayle		102d	Dem	Dem
1993–2001	**William J. Clinton**	Dem	103d	Dem	Dem
	Albert Gore, Jr.		104th	Rep	Rep
			105th	Rep	Rep
			106th	Rep	Rep
2001–2009	**George W. Bush**	Michael R. Pence	107th	Rep	Dem
	Richard Cheney		108th	Rep	Rep
			109th	Rep	Rep
			110th	Dem	Dem
			113th	Rep	Dem
			114th	t/c	t/c
2009–2017	**Barack H. Obama**	Dem	111th	Dem	Dem
	Joseph R. Biden, Jr.		112th	Rep	Dem
			113th	Rep	Dem
			114th	Rep	Rep
2017–	**Donald J. Trump**	Rep	115th	Rep	Rep
	Michael R. Pence				

[1] Died in office.
[2] Resigned from the vice presidency.
[3] Resigned from the presidency.
[4] Appointed vice president.

SUPREME COURT JUSTICES

Name[1]	Years on Court	Appointing President	Name[1]	Years on Court	Appointing President
JOHN JAY	1789–1795	Washington	Ward Hunt	1873–1882	Grant
James Wilson	1789–1798	Washington	MORRISON R. WAITE	1874–1888	Grant
John Rutledge	1790–1791	Washington	John M. Harlan	1877–1911	Hayes
William Cushing	1790–1810	Washington	William B. Woods	1881–1887	Hayes
John Blair	1790–1796	Washington	Stanley Matthews	1881–1889	Garfield
James Iredell	1790–1799	Washington	Horace Gray	1882–1902	Arthur
Thomas Johnson	1792–1793	Washington	Samuel Blatchford	1882–1893	Arthur
William Paterson	1793–1806	Washington	Lucious Q. C. Lamar	1888–1893	Cleveland
JOHN RUTLEDGE[2]	1795	Washington	MELVILLE W. FULLER	1888–1910	Cleveland
Samuel Chase	1796–1811	Washington	David J. Brewer	1890–1910	B. Harrison
OLIVER ELLSWORTH	1796–1800	Washington	Henry B. Brown	1891–1906	B. Harrison
Bushrod Washington	1799–1829	J. Adams	George Shiras, Jr.	1892–1903	B. Harrison
Alfred Moore	1800–1804	J. Adams	Howel E. Jackson	1893–1895	B. Harrison
JOHN MARSHALL	1801–1835	J. Adams	Edward D. White	1894–1910	Cleveland
William Johnson	1804–1834	Jefferson	Rufus W. Peckman	1896–1909	Cleveland
Brockholst Livingston	1807–1823	Jefferson	Joseph McKenna	1898–1925	McKinley
Thomas Todd	1807–1826	Jefferson	Oliver W. Holmes	1902–1932	T. Roosevelt
Gabriel Duvall	1811–1835	Madison	William R. Day	1903–1922	T. Roosevelt
Joseph Story	1812–1845	Madison	William H. Moody	1906–1910	T. Roosevelt
Smith Thompson	1823–1843	Monroe	Horace H. Lurton	1910–1914	Taft
Robert Trimble	1826–1828	J. Q. Adams	Charles E. Hughes	1910–1916	Taft
John McLean	1830–1861	Jackson	EDWARD D. WHITE	1910–1921	Taft
Henry Baldwin	1830–1844	Jackson	Willis Van Devanter	1911–1937	Taft
James M. Wayne	1835–1867	Jackson	Joseph R. Lamar	1911–1916	Taft
ROGER B. TANEY	1836–1864	Jackson	Mahlon Pitney	1912–1922	Taft
Philip P. Barbour	1836–1841	Jackson	James C. McReynolds	1914–1941	Wilson
John Cartron	1837–1865	Van Buren	Louis D. Brandeis	1916–1939	Wilson
John McKinley	1838–1852	Van Buren	John H. Clarke	1916–1922	Wilson
Peter V. Daniel	1842–1860	Van Buren	WILLIAM H. TAFT	1921–1930	Harding
Samuel Nelson	1845–1872	Tyler	George Sutherland	1922–1938	Harding
Levi Woodbury	1845–1851	Polk	Pierce Butler	1923–1939	Harding
Robert C. Grier	1846–1870	Polk	Edward T. Sanford	1923–1930	Harding
Benjamin R. Curtis	1851–1857	Fillmore	Harlan F. Stone	1925–1941	Coolidge
John A. Campbell	1853–1861	Pierce	CHARLES E. HUGHES	1930–1941	Hoover
Nathan Clifford	1858–1881	Buchanan	Owen J. Roberts	1930–1945	Hoover
Noah H. Swayne	1862–1881	Lincoln	Benjamin N. Cardozo	1932–1938	Hoover
Samuel F. Miller	1862–1890	Lincoln	Hugo L. Black	1937–1971	F. Roosevelt
David Davis	1862–1877	Lincoln	Stanley F. Reed	1938–1957	F. Roosevelt
Stephen J. Field	1863–1897	Lincoln	Felix Frankfurter	1939–1962	F. Roosevelt
SALMON P. CHASE	1864–1873	Lincoln	William O. Douglas	1939–1975	F. Roosevelt
William Strong	1870–1880	Grant	Frank Murphy	1940–1949	F. Roosevelt
Joseph P. Bradley	1870–1892	Grant	HARLAN F. STONE	1941–1946	F. Roosevelt

[1]Capital letters designate Chief Justices
[2]Never confirmed by the Senate as Chief Justice

Name[1]	Years on Court	Appointing President
James F. Brynes	1941–1942	F. Roosevelt
Robert H. Jackson	1941–1954	F. Roosevelt
Wiley B. Rutledge	1943–1949	F. Roosevelt
Harold H. Burton	1945–1958	Truman
FREDERICK M. VINSON	1946–1953	Truman
Tom C. Clark	1949–1967	Truman
Sherman Minton	1949–1956	Truman
EARL WARREN	1953–1969	Eisenhower
John Marshall Harlan	1955–1971	Eisenhower
William J. Brennan, Jr.	1956–1990	Eisenhower
Charles E. Whittaker	1957–1962	Eisenhower
Potter Stewart	1958–1981	Eisenhower
Byron R. White	1962–1993	Kennedy
Arthur J. Goldberg	1962–1965	Kennedy
Abe Fortas	1965–1970	L. Johnson
Thurgood Marshall	1967–1991	L. Johnson
WARREN E. BURGER	1969–1986	Nixon
Harry A. Blackmun	1970–1994	Nixon
Lewis F. Powell, Jr.	1971–1987	Nixon
William H. Rehnquist	1971–1986	Nixon
John Paul Stevens	1975–2010	Ford
Sandra Day O'Connor	1981–2006	Reagan
WILLIAM H. REHNQUIST	1986–2005	Reagan
Antonin Scalia	1986–2016	Reagan
Anthony Kennedy	1988–	Reagan
David Souter	1990–2009	G. H. W. Bush
Clarence Thomas	1991–	G. H. W. Bush
Ruth Bader Ginsburg	1993–	Clinton
Stephen Breyer	1994–	Clinton
JOHN G. ROBERTS, JR.	2005–	G. W. Bush
Samuel A. Alito, Jr.	2006	G. W. Bush
Sonia Sotomayor	2009–	Obama
Elena Kagan	2010–	Obama

[1]Capital letters designate Chief Justices
[2]Never confirmed by the Senate as Chief Justice

Glossary

accommodationist   An interpretive approach to the Establishment Clause of the First Amendment that would permit government financial support for certain religious programs, or would permit government sponsorship of religious practices, such as prayer in public schools.

administrative law judge (ALJ)   Official who presides over quasi-judicial proceedings within government agencies and renders decisions about disputes governed by statutes, such as appeals from denials of Social Security disability benefits.

adversarial system   Legal system used by the United States and other countries in which a judge plays a relatively passive role as attorneys battle to protect each side's interests. In the cases concerning affirmative action in university admissions, for example, the Supreme Court listened to vigorous arguments presented by the government's attorneys as well as opposing arguments from interest group lawyers representing individual applicants opposed to affirmative action.

advertorials   Advertisements presented as editorials.

affirmative action   Measures taken in hiring, recruitment, employment, and education to remedy past and present discrimination against members of specific groups. For example, affirmative action efforts can range from advertising employment and educational opportunities in publications with primarily minority or female readers to giving extra credit in university admissions processes to underrepresented groups, including racial minorities, poor people, women, and the disabled.

agenda setting   The process of featuring specific stories in the media to focus attention on particular issues, thereby setting the political agenda.

agents of political socialization   Factors that influence how we acquire political facts and knowledge and develop political values.

amicus brief   A written argument submitted to an appellate court by those who are interested in the issue being examined but are not representing either party in the case; often submitted by interest groups' lawyers to advance a specific policy position. For example, when the Supreme Court prepared to hear oral arguments in the health care law case, *National Federation of Independent Business* v. *Sebelius* (2012), the justices received more than two dozen amicus briefs from interest groups and state attorneys general.

Anti-Federalists   Opponents of ratification of the U.S. Constitution in 1787 and 1788. This group worried that the new system would give the national government too much power, at the expense of state rights and individual liberties. (Note that those opposed to the Federalist Party in the late 1790s were not Anti-Federalists but rather Democratic-Republicans.)

appellate briefs   Written arguments submitted by lawyers in appellate cases.

at-large districts   Districts encompassing an entire state, or large parts of a state, in which House members are elected to represent the entire area. Small states, like Wyoming and Vermont, have at-large legislators because they have just one legislative district (the entire state).

attitudinal barriers   Personal beliefs regarding the viability and necessity of minor party candidates. Many will not vote for minor-party candidates because they believe their vote will be wasted.

attitudinal model   An approach to analyzing judicial decision making that looks at individual judges' decision patterns to identify the attitudes and values that guide their decisions.

authoritarian regime   A system in which leaders have no formal or legal restraints, but are constrained by informal structures like religious groups or military leaders.

authority   The recognized right of an individual, group, or institution to make binding decisions for society. While some might disagree with certain Supreme Court decisions, for instance, most recognize the Court's authority in our system of government.

Baker v. *Carr* **(1961)**   Supreme Court case that set the standard that House districts must contain equal numbers of constituents, thus establishing the principle of "one person, one vote."

balance of trade   The net difference between a nation's imports and its exports.

ballot access laws   Laws that regulated who's name appears on the general election ballot. In some states it is easier to accomplish than in other states.

barometer of public attitudes   The theory that popular culture reflects public opinion.

bench trials   Trials in which a judge presides without a jury. The judge makes determinations of fact and law.

bicameral legislature   A legislature composed of two houses. Not only is Congress bicameral, consisting of the House and the Senate, but 49 of the 50 states also have a two-house legislature. Since 1934, Nebraska has had a unicameral (one house) legislature.

Bill of Rights   The first 10 amendments to the U.S. Constitution, ratified in 1791, protecting civil liberties. Freedom of speech, for instance, is one of our core civil liberties, protected in the First Amendment.

bill sponsor   The member of Congress who introduces a bill.

binding primaries   A system where delegates selected through primaries and caucuses are bound to support the candidate that they originally said they would support. That is, they are not allowed to switch their convention vote as they see fit.

Bipartisan Campaign Reform Act (BCRA) Federal law passed in 2002 that outlawed soft-money contributions to party organizations. The bill is also sometimes called McCain–Feingold after the two Senate sponsors.

block grants Funds given to states that allow substantial discretion to spend the money with minimal federal restrictions. State and local governments tend to prefer block grants to other forms of grants-in-aid, as there is more flexibility in how the money is spent.

***Brown v. Board of Education of Topeka* (1954)** A U.S. Supreme Court decision that overturned *Plessy* v. *Ferguson* (1896) and declared that government-mandated racial segregation in schools and other facilities and programs violates the Equal Protection Clause of the Fourteenth Amendment.

***Buckley v. Valeo* (1976)** The most significant Supreme Court case on campaign finance in American history. The court ruled that spending money was akin to speech, and therefore protected by the First Amendment.

budget deficit The amount by which a government's expenditures exceed its revenues.

budget surplus The amount by which a government's revenues exceed its expenditures.

bureaucracy An organization with a hierarchical structure and specific responsibilities intended to enhance efficiency and effectiveness. In government, it refers to departments and agencies in the executive branch. For example, the Internal Revenue Service (IRS) is an agency in the federal bureaucracy that carries out national tax laws through collection of income taxes and investigation of individuals and businesses that fail to pay the taxes required by the laws created by Congress.

cabinet A group of presidential advisers, primarily the secretaries of federal departments. The size of the cabinet has varied through the years, but lately it has been composed of roughly 20 members.

Candidate-Centered Era After 1960, a period when candidates began to portray themselves as independent from party politics, even though they often ran under a party banner.

capital punishment A criminal punishment, otherwise known as the *death penalty*, in which a person is subject to execution after conviction. Reserved for the most serious offenses of murder and treason.

capitalism An economic system where business and industry are privately owned and there is little governmental interference.

case precedent A legal rule established by a judicial decision that guides subsequent decisions. The use of case precedent is drawn from the common law system brought from Great Britain to the United States. For example, in order to maintain stability in law, three of the justices in the majority claimed that they followed case precedent in voting to preserve a woman's right of choice concerning abortion in *Planned Parenthood* v. *Casey* (1992) even though they claimed that they did not necessarily agree with the original precedent that established that right in *Roe* v. *Wade* (1973).

catalyst-for-change theory The assertion that public opinion shapes and alters our political culture, thus allowing change.

categorical grants Grants of money from the federal government to state or local governments for very specific purposes. These grants often require that funds be matched by the receiving entity.

checks and balances A system in our government where each branch (legislative, executive, judicial) has the power to limit the actions of others. For example, even though President Obama announced a decision to send 30,000 additional troops to Afghanistan in December 2009, it did not automatically mean that Congress would appropriate the funds necessary to carry out the plan.

citizen journalism Nonprofessional members of the public who are involved in the collection, reporting, commenting, and dissemination of news stories; also known as street journalism.

***Citizens United v. Federal Elections Commission* (2010)** A Supreme Court case that reversed decades of precedent by declaring unconstitutional laws that ban unions and corporations from using general operating funds on elections.

civil liberties Individual freedoms and legal protections guaranteed by the Bill of Rights that cannot be denied or hindered by government. For example, the First Amendment right to freedom of speech was protected for Westboro Baptist Church's members despite the fact that many Americans find the presentation of their messages near military funerals to be very offensive.

civil rights Public policies and legal protections concerning equal status and treatment in American society to advance the goals of equal opportunity, fair and open political participation, and equal treatment under the law without regard to race, gender, disability status, and other demographic characteristics.

Civil Rights Act of 1964 A federal statute that prohibited racial discrimination in public accommodations (hotels, restaurants, theaters), employment, and programs receiving federal funding.

civil service system A government employment system in which employees are hired on the basis of their qualifications and cannot be fired merely for belonging to the wrong political party; it originated with the federal Pendleton Act in 1883 and expanded at other levels of government in the half-century that followed. Today, federal employees in the Internal Revenue Service, National Park Service, U.S. Department of Transportation, and other agencies are hired based on their qualifications and retain their jobs even when new presidents are elected.

clear and present danger test A test for permissible speech articulated by Justice Oliver Wendell Holmes in *Schenck* v. *United States* (1919) that allows government regulation of some expressions, such as prohibiting people from creating danger by falsely shouting "fire" in crowded theater, words that are likely to cause people to be needlessly injured when they rush to flee the building.

cleavage Division among people based on at least one social characteristic, such as educational attainment or race.

closed primary system A nomination system where only members of the party are allowed to participate.

cloture A rule declaring the end of a debate in the Senate. In most instances it takes 60 votes for cloture, meaning that even a minority of senators can hold up legislation.

cohort replacement Natural phenomenon of generational replacement due to death.

compelled self-incrimination Being forced through physical abuse or other coercion to provide testimony against oneself in a criminal case, a practice that is prohibited by the Fifth Amendment.

competitive news markets Locales with two or more news organizations that can check each other's accuracy and neutrality of reporting.

compulsory process A right contained in the Sixth Amendment to enable criminal defendants to use court orders to require witnesses to appear and to require the production of documents and other evidence.

concurring opinion Appellate court opinion by judge who endorses the outcome decided by the majority of judges, but wants to express different reasons to justify that outcome.

conference committee A committee of members of the House and Senate that irons out differences in similar measures that have passed both houses to create a single bill. The goal of the committee is to find common ground and emerge with a single bill. This process has become more difficult in recent years.

confidence level The probability that the results found in the sample represent the true opinion of the entire public under study.

confrontation A right contained in the Sixth Amendment for criminal defendants to see their accusers in court and hear at first hand the accusations and evidence being presented against them.

Congressional Budget Office (CBO) The research arm of Congress, a major player in budget creation.

conscience model of representation The philosophy that legislators should follow the will of the people until they truly believe it is in the best interests of the nation to act differently.

conservative A person who believes in limiting government spending, preserving traditional patterns of relationships, and that big government is a threat to personal liberties.

Constitutional Convention A meeting in Philadelphia in 1787 at which delegates from the colonies drew up a new system of government. The finished product was the Constitution of the United States.

constitutional government A system where there are both formal and informal constraints on the exercise of power.

constitutional monarchy A system of government in which a royal family, and often a king or queen, serves as a symbolic figurehead. Real government authority rests with another body, usually a parliament.

Consumer Price Index (CPI) Figure representing the cost of a specific set of goods and services tracked at regular intervals by the Department of Labor.

containment A Cold War strategy that sought to control and encircle the Soviet Union rather than defeat it militarily.

cooperative federalism A system in which the powers of the federal and state government are intertwined and shared. Each level of government shares overlapping power, authority, and responsibility.

Corrupt Bargain of 1824 The alleged secret agreement in the disputed election of 1824 that led the House of Representatives to select John Quincy Adams, who had come in second in the popular vote, as president if he would make Speaker of the House Henry Clay his secretary of state.

Council of Economic Advisers (CEA) A group of economists within the Executive Office of the President, appointed by the president to provide advice on economic policy.

court-packing plan President Franklin D. Roosevelt's unsuccessful proposal in 1937 to permit the appointment of additional justices to the U.S. Supreme Court to enhance the support for New Deal initiatives.

court-packing plan President Franklin D. Roosevelt's unsuccessful proposal in 1937 to permit the appointment of additional justices to the U.S. Supreme Court. Roosevelt sought to reduce the Court's opposition to his New Deal policies through a plan that would permit the president to appoint a new justice whenever a sitting justice reached 70 years of age.

courts of last resort The highest courts in each American court system, typically called supreme courts, that hear selected appeals from the lower courts.

covert action Efforts to secretly influence affairs in another state, which may include propaganda, disinformation campaigns, bribery, fomenting political and economic unrest, and, in the extreme, assassination.

creative federalism A system in which the role of the federal government is expanded by providing financial incentives for states to follow congressional initiatives. Creative federalism establishes programs that are funded and regulated by Congress centralizing congressional authority over the states to provide social services. Many oppose this system because they believe that it usurps the authority of states and makes the national government too powerful.

crosscutting cleavages Cleavages are divisions in society (such as race, sex, religion) that separate people into groups. A crosscutting cleavage is when two or more cleavages work together to impact political behavior and values.

decentralization Proposed reform for government agencies intended to increase efficiency in administration and create closer contacts with the local public; permits regional and local offices to manage their own performances without close supervision from headquarters.

de facto segregation Racial segregation in housing and schools that was presumed to occur through people's voluntary choices about where they wanted to live but was actually facilitated by the discriminatory actions of landlords, real estate agents, and banks.

deflation A decrease in prices over time.

de jure segregation Racial segregation mandated by laws and policies created by government officials.

delegate model of representation The philosophy that legislators should adhere to the will of their constituents. If most constituents want a particular measure, a legislator with this view would feel compelled to support it, regardless of his or her personal feelings.

democracy   A political system in which all citizens have a chance to play a role in shaping government action and are afforded basic rights and liberties.

Democratic-Republicans   The first American political party, formed by believers in states' rights and followers of Thomas Jefferson.

department   Any of the 15 major government agencies responsible for specific policy areas whose heads are usually called secretaries and serve in the president's cabinet. For example, the U.S. Department of State, led during the Obama administration by Secretary John Kerry, the former U.S. senator from Massachusetts, is responsible for managing relationships with foreign governments and issuing passports to U.S. citizens.

détente   Reduction of tension or strained relations between previously hostile nations.

deterrence   A military strategy associated with the Cold War that sought to prevent an unwanted military action from taking place by raising the prospect of large-scale retaliation.

devolution   The transfer of jurisdiction and fiscal responsibility for particular programs from the federal government to state or local governments. State governments generally like certain components of devolution, most notably responsibility over decision making that impacts their residents; however, the fiscal responsibility that often comes with devolution is often difficult for states and localities to bear.

dictator   A ruler who holds absolute governmental authority and usually arrives at the post through a violent uprising.

Dillon's rule   Iowa state court decision in 1868 that narrowly defined the power of local governments and established the supremacy of state governments when conflict exists with localities. Subsequently upheld by the Supreme Court.

direct contact   Face-to-face meetings or telephone conversations between individuals.

direct mail   Information mailed to a large number of people to advertise, market concepts, or solicit support.

direct primary election   The process by which average party members, sometimes called the rank-and-file, are allowed to select party nominees. This process replaced the hand-picked model used by party bosses.

discount rate   The rate the Fed charges member banks for short-term loans.

discretion   The power to apply policy in ways that fit particular circumstances.

dissenting opinion   Appellate court opinion explaining the views of one or more judges who disagree with the outcome of the case as decided by the majority of judges.

distribution   Government providing things of value to specific groups.

disturbance theory   The idea that interest groups form when resources become scarce in order to contest the influence of other interest groups.

doctrine of nullification   Theory that state governments had a right to rule any federal law unconstitutional and therefore null and void. The doctrine was ruled unconstitutional but contributed to the secession of southern states from the Union and ultimately the Civil War.

doctrine of secession   The theory that state governments had a right to declare their independence and create their own form of government. Eleven southern states seceded from the Union in 1860–1861, created their own government (the Confederate States of America), and thereby precipitated the Civil War. The Civil War demonstrated that the doctrine was invalid, but the idea that state governments ought to be very powerful and act in their own self-interest has resurfaced from time to time.

double jeopardy   Being tried twice for the same crime, a practice prohibited by the Fifth Amendment.

dual court system   Separate systems of state and federal courts throughout the United States. Each state court system is responsible for interpreting the laws and constitution of that specific state, while the federal courts are responsible for the U.S. Constitution and laws enacted by Congress. For example, the Ohio Supreme Court is the ultimate legal authority over the interpretation of its state's constitution and the statutes enacted by the Ohio legislature.

dual federalism   A theory stating that the powers of the federal and state governments are strictly separate, with interaction often marked by tension rather than cooperation. Under a system of dual federalism, governments have separate spheres of responsibilities and influence and do not cooperate among themselves.

Due Process Clause   A statement of rights in the Fifth Amendment (aimed at the federal government) and the Fourteenth Amendment (aimed at state and local governments) that protects against arbitrary deprivations of life, liberty, or property. The Fourteenth Amendment phrase is also interpreted by the Supreme Court to expand a variety of rights, such as identifying a right to privacy in the concept of personal "liberty" that the clause protects against arbitrary government interference.

earmarks/pork-barrel legislation   Legislation that benefits one state or district; also called *particularized legislation*. For example, a legislator might work diligently to get federal monies for the construction of a new stretch of an interstate highway.

earned media coverage   Airtime provided free of charge to candidates for political office.

efficacy   The belief that individuals can influence government. *Internal political efficacy* is the belief that individuals have the knowledge and ability to influence government. *External political efficacy* refers to the belief that governmental officials will respond to individuals.

egalitarianism   A doctrine of equality that ignores differences in social status, wealth, and privilege.

Elastic Clause/Necessary and Proper Clause   Constitution grants Congress the power to pass all laws "necessary and proper" for carrying out the list of expressed powers. This allows Congress to move on a broad host of matters so long as they can be linked to one of the enumerated (specifically stated) powers. It greatly enhances the power of the national government.

electoral behavior   Any activity broadly linked to the outcome of a political campaign, such as voting, making phone calls, sending texts, and even talking with friends and neighbors about the upcoming election.

Electoral College   The procedure for selecting the president and vice president of the United States, defined in Article II of the Constitution, whereby the voters in each state choose electors to attend a gathering where the electors make the final decision.

elitism   The theory that a select few—better educated, more informed, and more interested—should have more influence than others in our governmental process. Elites tend to view the world differently than those who are less advantaged.

entitlements   Government expenditures required by law.

equality of condition   A conception of equality that exists in some countries that value equal economic status as well as equal access to housing, health care, education, and government services. For example, governing systems that emphasize equality of condition provide health care, generous unemployment benefits, and government-financed opportunities to attend universities. This is also referred to by some as equality of outcome.

equality of opportunity   A conception of equality that seeks to provide all citizens with opportunities for participation in the economic system and public life but accepts unequal results in income, political power, and property ownership.

equality of outcome   An egalitarian belief that government must work to diminish differences between individuals in society so that everyone is equal in status and value.

equal time rule   An FCC rule requiring the broadcast media to offer all major candidates competing for a political office equal airtime.

Establishment Clause   A clause in the First Amendment guaranteeing freedom from religion by providing a basis for Supreme Court decisions limiting government support for and endorsement of particular religions.

exclusionary rule   A general principle stating that evidence obtained illegally cannot be used against a defendant in a criminal prosecution. The Supreme Court has allowed certain exceptions to the rule in particular circumstances, such as when evidence obtained through an improper search would have eventually been discovered by the police later through actions permitted by law.

executive agreements   Binding commitments between the United States and other countries agreed to by the president but, unlike treaties, not requiring approval by the Senate.

Executive Office of the President (EOP)   A group of presidential staff agencies created in 1939 that provides the president with help and advice. Many suggest the growing powers of the presidency spring in large measure from the expansion of the EOP.

executive order   A regulation made by the president that has the effect of law. In the summer of 2012, for example, President Obama issued an executive order limiting the deportation of some illegal immigrant children brought to the United States by their parents.

exit polls   Surveys of voters leaving polling places; used by news media to gauge how candidates are doing on election day.

expressed powers   The powers explicitly granted to the national government in the U.S. Constitution. For instance, Article I, Section 8 grants Congress the power to regulate commerce, and Article II, Section 2 stipulates that presidents will be commander in chief of the Army and Navy.

fairness doctrine   Policy that required television and radio broadcasters to provide time for opposing viewpoints on controversial issues so as to ensure fair and balanced reporting: formally abolished in 1987.

Federal Election Campaign Act (FECA)   A law designed to limit the amount of money contributed to campaigns for Congress and the presidency and to broaden donation reporting requirements.

federal funds rate   The interest rate that banks charge each other for overnight loans.

Federal Open Market Committee (FOMC)   The policymaking arm of the Federal Reserve Board of Governors.

Federal Reserve System (the Fed)   The independent central bank of the United States.

federal system   A system of government in which power and authority are divided between a central government and regional subunits.

Federalist Party   Founded by Alexander Hamilton, its members believed in a strong, centralized government.

Federalists   Supporters of the ratification of the U.S. Constitution. James Madison was one of the leading Federalists during this time. By the late 1790s, it was the name given to one of the first political parties, headed by Alexander Hamilton and John Adams. Many of the early Federalists, such as Madison, later joined the Democratic-Republican Party, in opposition to the Federalist Party.

Fifteenth Amendment (1870)   Guarantees the right to vote shall not be denied to anyone on the basis of race.

filibuster   A process in the U.S. Senate used to block or delay voting on proposed legislation or on an appointment of a judge or other official by talking continuously. Sixty senators must vote to end a filibuster. With a hyper-partisan legislature, the requirement to get 60 votes to move things along has created a very slow process. Some would suggest this rule worsens legislative gridlock.

fiscal policy   Taxation and spending decisions made by the government.

flexible interpretation   An approach to interpreting the U.S. Constitution that permits the meaning of the document to change with evolving values, social conditions, and problems. For example, when the Supreme Court decided that the Eighth Amendment prohibition on "cruel and unusual punishments" forbids the application of the death penalty to offenders with mental development disabilities (*Atkins* v. *Virginia*, 2002), the majority of justices used a flexible interpretive approach that claimed society's views about punishments for such individuals had changed over time.

focusing events   Moments that capture attention and highlight the existence of a problem.

formula grants   Specific type of categorical grant in which money is allocated and distributed based upon a prescribed formula.

Fourteenth Amendment (1868)   Establishes that each state must guarantee equal protection of the laws to its citizens. In other words, states cannot abridge an individual's civil liberties.

Free Exercise Clause   A clause in the First Amendment guaranteeing freedom to practice one's religion without government interference as long as those practices do not harm other individuals or society.

free-rider problem   The fact that public goods can be enjoyed by everyone, including people who do not pay their fair share of the cost for providing those goods.

French and Indian War   Also called the Seven Year's War, this was a series of military battles between Britain and France in North America between 1754 and 1763. The French received support from a number of Indian tribes. Britain won the war, but it proved quite costly—leading to novel ways of raising money from the colonists.

gaining access   Winning the opportunity to communicate directly with a legislator or a legislative staff member to present one's position on an issue of public policy.

gatekeepers   A group or individuals who determine which stories will receive attention in the media and from which perspective.

gender gap   Differences in voting and policy preferences between women and men. After controlling for other factors, women tend to be more liberal and Democratic than men.

genocide   The deliberate and systematic extinction of an ethnic or cultural group.

gerrymandering   Drawing legislative district boundaries in such a way as to gain political advantage. With the rise of partisanship in most state legislatures, many assume that party-based gerrymandering will be more common in the years to come.

globalization   The expansion of economic interactions between countries.

going public   Appealing directly to the people to garner support for presidential initiatives. For instance, presidents will often hold a press conference or an address in the White House Rose Garden when they are looking to build public support for a proposal that is languishing in Congress.

government corporations   Agencies with independent boards and the means to generate revenue through sales of products and services, fees, or insurance premiums that are intended to run like private corporations.

grants-in-aid   Funds given from one governmental unit to another governmental unit for specific purposes. Such grants cover a wide array of programs, helping to equalize services among states and allow the federal government to influence policymaking at state and local levels.

Great Compromise/Connecticut Compromise   An agreement at the Constitutional Convention that the new national government would have a House of Representatives—in which the number of members would be based on each state's population—and a Senate—in which each state would have the same number of representatives.

Great Squeeze   A period prior to the American Revolution when the British Parliament sought to recoup some of the costs associated with the French and Indian War by levying new taxes and fees on colonists. Two examples of these measures would be the Sugar Act and the Stamp Act.

gross domestic product (GDP)   The value of all goods and services produced in a nation.

Hatch Act   Federal law that limits the participation of federal government employees in political campaigns to protect them from feeling obligated to donate money or work for political candidates.

hearings   Committee sessions for taking testimony from witnesses and for collecting information on legislation under consideration or for the development of new legislation.

home rule   The right of a city with a population of more than 5,000 to adopt any form of government residents choose, provided that it does not conflict with the state constitution or statutes.

impeachment   Process in Congress for removal of the president, federal judges, and other high officials. In 2010, for example, Congress impeached and removed from office Louisiana Federal Judge Thomas Porteous based on corruption and perjury charges.

income security   The notion that the government should establish programs that provide a safety net for society's poorest members.

incorporation   The process used by the Supreme Court to protect individuals from actions by state and local governments by interpreting the Due Process Clause of the Fourteenth Amendment as containing selected provisions of the Bill of Rights. For example, in *Klopfer* v. *North Carolina* (1967), the U.S. Supreme Court held that the Sixth Amendment right to a speedy trial is fundamental to the criminal justice process and therefore applies to state criminal trials through the Fourteenth Amendment's Due Process Clause.

incumbent advantage   The various factors that favor office-holders running for reelection over their challengers. Those already in office have a huge advantage in their efforts to win reelection.

independent   A voter who is not registered or affiliated with any political party.

independent agencies   Federal agencies with narrow responsibilities for a specific policy issue, such as the environment, not covered by one of the fifteen federal departments.

independent regulatory commissions   Organizational entities in the federal government that are not under the control of the president or a department.

individualism   An attitude, rooted in classical liberal theory and reinforced by the frontier tradition, that citizens are capable of taking care of themselves with minimal governmental assistance.

inflation   An increase in prices over time.

inner cabinet   The advisers considered most important to the president—usually the secretaries of the departments of state, defense, treasury, and justice.

inquisitorial system   Legal system in most of Europe in which a judge takes an active role in questioning witnesses and seeking to discover the truth.

inside lobbying   Appealing directly to lawmakers and legislative staff either in meetings, by providing research and information, or by testifying at committee hearings.

institutional presidency   The concept of the presidency as a working collectivity—a massive network of staff, analysts, and advisers with the president as its head.

intelligence   Gathering and analyzing information and communications, often secret, about potential enemies and other national security matters.

interactive theory   The theory that popular culture both shapes and reflects popular opinion.

interest group   A group of like-minded individuals who band together to influence public policy, public opinion, or governmental officials.

intermediate appellate courts   Courts that examine allegations concerning uncorrected errors that occurred during trials; usually called courts of appeals in state and federal court systems.

investigative reporting   A type of journalism in which reporters thoroughly investigate a subject matter (often involving a scandal) to inform the public, correct an injustice, or expose an abuse.

Iran-Contra affair   The Reagan administration's unauthorized diversion of funds from the sale of arms to Iran to support the Contras, rebels fighting to overthrow the leftist government of Nicaragua.

iron triangle   The tight relationship between employees in government agencies, interest groups, and legislators and their staff members, all of whom share an interest in specific policy issues and work together behind the scenes to shape laws and public policy.

issue networks (policy communities)   Interest groups, scholars, and other experts that communicate about, debate, and interact regarding issues of interest and thus influence public policy when the legislature acts on those issues.

issue-attention cycle   The pattern of problems quickly gathering attention but then failing to remain in the spotlight.

jihadists   Participants in a crusade or holy war, especially in defense of Islam.

Jim Crow laws   Laws enacted by southern state legislatures after the Civil War that mandated rigid racial segregation. For example, such laws not only required separate bank teller windows and elevators but also separate Bibles for swearing in African American witnesses in court.

judicial review   The power of American judges to nullify decisions and actions by other branches of government, if the judges decide those actions violate the U.S. Constitution or the relevant state constitution. For example, the Supreme Court invalidated a portion of the Armed Career Criminal Act in 2015 as too vague and thereby violating the due process rights of defendants facing enhanced sentences for prior "violent felonies."

Judiciary Act of 1789   Early statute in which Congress provided the initial design of the federal court system.

Kyoto Protocol   An international agreement to address the problem of global warming. The United States was involved in its negotiation but has refused to ratify the agreement, citing excessive economic costs.

Laffer curve   An economic model that maintains that a higher rate of taxation can result in lower government revenues.

Lemon **test**   A three-part test for Establishment Clause violations announced by the U.S. Supreme Court in *Lemon* v.

Kurtzman (1971) that examines whether government policies support religious programs or cause excessive entanglement between government and religion.

libel   The publication of false and malicious material that defames an individual's reputation.

liberal   A person who generally supports governmental action to promote equality, favors governmental intervention in the economy, and supports policies attempting to solve environmental issues.

libertarian   A person who supports individual liberty over government authority in economic, personal, and social realms.

libertarian view   The idea that the media should be allowed to publish information that they deem newsworthy or of interest to the public without regard to the social consequences of doing so.

majority leader   The head of the majority party in the Senate; the second-highest-ranking member of the majority party in the House.

majority opinion   Appellate court opinion that explains the reasons for the case outcome as determined by a majority of judges.

Marbury **v.** *Madison* **(1803)**   A case in which the U.S. Supreme Court asserted the power of judicial review, despite the fact that the concept is not explicitly mentioned in the U.S. Constitution. The case represented the first instance in which the Supreme Court declared a statute enacted by Congress, a portion of the Judiciary Act of 1789, to be invalid for violating the Constitution.

margin of error   A measurement of the accuracy of the results of a survey to establish a range in which we think that the actual percentage of favorable ratings will fall.

marginal tax bracket   The tax rate you pay on the last dollar that you earn in a given year.

marketplace of ideas   The concept that ideas and theories compete for acceptance among the public, allowing for public debate and heightened awareness.

mass media   The means by which information is transmitted to a large population across a large region. The mass media includes television, radio, magazines, newspapers, and the Internet.

material benefits   Benefits that have concrete value or worth.

Mayflower Compact   A document setting-up a set of laws for the Pilgrims who landed at Plymouth, Massachusetts, in 1620. It was truly significant because they did not simply pick a leader to make decisions, but instead established rules that all would follow.

McCulloch **v.** *Maryland* **(1819)**   U.S. Supreme Court decision that defined the respective powers of the state and federal governments. The opinion established that the Constitution grants to Congress implied powers for implementing the Constitution's express powers in order to create a functional national government, and that state action may not impede valid constitutional exercises of power by the Federal government.

McNamara Doctrine   A view that military power can be applied to situations in controlled and limited amounts that rise over time and that public support should not be a major factor governing its use.

Medicaid   Health care coverage for the poor.

Medicare   Health care coverage for senior citizens.

minority leader   The leading spokesperson and legislative strategist for the minority party in the House or the Senate.

Miranda v. Arizona **(1966)**   A U.S. Supreme Court decision that requires police officers, before questioning a suspect in custody, to inform that suspect about the right to remain silent and to have a lawyer present during custodial questioning. These warnings are intended to protect people from feeling pressured to incriminate themselves without being aware of their rights.

modern presidency   A political system in which the president is the central figure and participates actively in both foreign and domestic policy.

monarchy   A system of government in which the ruler is established through heredity. This person (sometimes an entire family) holds absolute governmental power.

monetary policy   Money supply management conducted by the Federal Reserve.

monopolies   Exclusive control by companies over most or all of a particular industry.

motor voter law   A federal law passed in 1993 requiring states to offer citizens the opportunity to register to vote in many state offices, including motor vehicle offices. The idea was to facilitate voter registration and increase the number of Americans who come to the polls on Election Day.

muckraking   Investigating and exposing societal ills such as corruption in politics or abuses in business.

multi-issue interest group   A group that is interested in pursuing a broad range of public policy issues such as the AARP, which promotes a wide variety of public policies that impact older Americans.

narrowcasting   Creating and broadcasting highly specialized programming that is designed to appeal to a specified subgroup rather than to the general population.

National Association for the Advancement of Colored People (NAACP)   Civil rights advocacy group founded by African Americans and their white supporters in 1909 that used the court pathway to fight racial discrimination in the 1930s through the 1950s and later emphasized elections and lobbying pathways.

national debt   The nation's cumulative deficits.

national nominating convention   Events that are held in the summer of presidential election years where party delegates, selected through primaries and caucuses, pick their party's presidential nominee.

natural rights   Basic rights that no government can deny. For example, the right to a fair, impartial trial would be considered a natural right, as would the right to speak out against government corruption.

Necessary and Proper Clause   A statement in Article I, Section 8, of the U.S. Constitution that grants Congress the power to pass all laws "necessary and proper" for carrying out the list of expressed powers providing basis for implied Congressional power. Also known as the Elastic Clause as it stretches Congressional power and authority.

neoconservatives   People who believe that the United States has a special role to play in world politics; they advocate the unilateral use of force and the pursuit of a value-based foreign policy.

neoliberals   People who believe that cooperation is possible through the creation and management of international institutions, organizations, and regimes.

New Deal   A set of policies and programs advanced by Franklin D. Roosevelt in the 1930s with the aim of pulling the nation out of the Depression.

New Deal   Programs designed by President Franklin D. Roosevelt to bring economic recovery from the Great Depression by expanding the role of the federal government in providing employment opportunities and social services, advanced social reforms to serve the needs of the people, greatly expanding the budget and activity of the federal government. Its ultimate success helped redefine the very nature of federalism and how Americans viewed their national government.

new institutionalism   An approach to understanding judicial decision making that emphasizes the importance of courts' structures and processes as well as the courts' role in the governing system.

New Jersey Plan   A scheme for government advanced at the Constitutional Convention that was supported by delegates from smaller states. It called for equal representation of states in a unicameral legislature. Under this approach, each state would have the same say in the national legislature, and the executive branch would have modest powers.

news briefing   A public appearance by a governmental official for the purpose of releasing information to the press.

news conference   A media event, often staged, where reporters ask questions of politicians or other celebrities.

news monopolies   Single news firms that control all the media in a given market.

Nineteenth Amendment (1920)   Granted women the right to vote.

nomination caucus   Essentially, meetings of rank-and-file party members where the qualifications of candidates are discussed and debated, and where a final vote determines the groups' support for each.

nominees   The individuals selected by a party to run for office under that party's label.

North Atlantic Treaty Organization (NATO)   A military alliance set up by the United States and its Western European allies initially for the purpose of containing the expansion of the former Soviet Union.

Obergefell v. Hodges **(2015)**   The U.S. Supreme Court's momentous decision that declared same-sex marriage is a protected right under the Fourteenth Amendment's Due Process and Equal Protection Clauses.

Office of Management and Budget (OMB)   A cabinet-level office that monitors federal agencies and provides the president with expert advice on fiscal policy-related topics.

oligarchy A system of government in which a small group of elites, sometimes the very wealthy or an assembly of religious leaders, control most of the governing decisions.

open-market operations The buying and selling of securities by the Federal Reserve Board to manipulate the money supply.

open primary system A nomination system where all are allowed to participate—regardless of their party affiliation.

outside lobbying (grassroots lobbying) Activities directed at the general public to raise awareness and interest and to pressure officials.

oversight The responsibility of Congress to keep an eye on agencies in the federal bureaucracy to ensure that their behavior conforms to its wishes. Perhaps not surprisingly, many see this function as taking a more partisan flavor in recent years—particularly when one party controls Congress and the other the White House.

Paris Agreement An international agreement signed by representatives of over 150 countries, and with the support of American President Barack Obama and Chinese President Xi Jinping. The signatories agreed to take efforts to reduce global warming by decreasing emissions of greenhouse gases like carbon dioxide.

party identification A belief that one belongs to a certain party; an emotional connection to a particular party.

party presses Newspapers popular in the early nineteenth century that were highly partisan and often influenced by political party machines.

party unity scores Various measures of how often legislators of the same party stick together. When these measures are high, the level of bipartisanship is low. In recent years, party unity scores have been at record high levels.

pathways of action The activities of citizens in American politics that affect the creation, alteration, and preservation of laws and policies. For instance, average citizens can change the course of public policy by bringing new officials into government through elections and by lobbying existing legislators.

patronage system (spoils system) A system that rewards the supporters of successful political candidates and parties with government jobs while firing supporters of the opposing party. In earlier eras, government employees throughout the bureaucracy could lose their jobs when a new president was elected from a different political party than his or her own. The same result was true in state and city governments when new governors and mayors were elected. Today new presidents appoint only the top leaders of federal departments and agencies.

patrons Organizations or individuals that contribute money to political leaders or political groups.

payroll taxes A tax on earnings that funds Social Security and Medicare.

penny press Cheap newspapers containing sensationalized stories sold to members of the working class in the late nineteenth and early twentieth centuries.

personal presidency The notion that there are greater and greater expectations placed on presidents, due in large measure to the way they run for office. At the same time, presidents are often unable to deliver on the promises they made during campaigns.

Phillips curve An economic model that assumes an inverse relationship between unemployment and inflation.

Pilgrims Puritans who sailed from Europe in the early 1600s to North America with the aim of settling the land and starting a new life. More generally, this term can mean a person who journeys to a holy land.

platform The set of issues, principles, and goals that a party supports.

plea bargaining Negotiation process in which prosecutors seek a quick, certain conviction without a trial by agreeing to reduce charges or recommend a less-than-maximum sentence in exchange for the defendant's voluntary plea of guilty.

***Plessy* v. *Ferguson* (1896)** A U.S. Supreme Court decision that endorsed the legality of racial segregation laws by permitting "separate but equal" services and facilities for African Americans, even though the services and facilities were actually inferior, such as markedly inferior schools for African American children.

pluralism A system of government in which there are multiple groups vying for power.

pocket veto The president's killing of a bill that has been passed by both houses of Congress, simply by not signing it within 10 days of the bill's passage.

police powers The powers reserved to state governments related to the health, safety, and well-being of citizens. For example, many consider the job of educating children to be the concern of local governments—a police power.

policy categories A way of classifying policies by their intended goal and means of carrying out that goal.

political culture The norms, customs, and beliefs that help citizens understand appropriate ways to act in a political system; also, the shared attitudes about how government should operate.

political equality Fundamental value underlying the governing system of the United States that emphasizes all citizens' opportunities to vote, run for office, own property, and enjoy civil liberties protections under the Constitution.

political ideology A consistent set of beliefs that forms a general philosophy regarding the proper goals, purposes, functions, and size of government.

political socialization The complex process through which people acquire political knowledge and form political values; also the conscious and unconscious transmission of political culture and values from one generation to another.

politico model of representation Legislators follow their own judgment until the public becomes vocal about a particular matter, at which point they should follow the dictates of constituents.

politics The process by which the actions of government are determined. For example, by appealing to members of the city council to change the new housing ordinance, several students decided to roll up their sleeves and become engaged in local politics.

populist A person who believes that the government can be a positive agent to protect "common people" against the moneyed elite.

Powell Doctrine   A view that cautions against the use of military force, especially where public support is limited, but states that once the decision to use force has been made, military power should be applied quickly and decisively.

power   The ability to exercise control over others and get them to comply. For instance, the National Rifle Association wields power because many legislators fear upsetting their large, active membership.

preemption   A military strategy based on striking first in self-defense.

prerogative power   Extraordinary powers that the president may use under certain conditions, such as during times of war.

press releases   Written statements that are given to the press to circulate information or an announcement.

press shield law   A statute enacted by a legislature establishing a reporter's privilege to protect the confidentiality of sources.

prime rate   The interest rate that a bank charges its best customers.

prior censorship   Forbidding publication of material considered objectionable.

prior restraint   Effort by government to prohibit or prevent the publication of information or viewpoints. Since its decision in *Near* v. *Minnesota* (1931), the U.S. Supreme Court has generally forbidden prior restraint as a violation of the First Amendment protection for freedom of the press.

privatization   The process of turning some responsibilities of government bureaucracy over to private organizations on the assumption that they can administer and deliver services more effectively and inexpensively. During the wars in Iraq and Afghanistan, for example, the government hired private companies to handle food services, transportation of supplies, and even personal protection, such as bodyguards, for American officials in Iraq.

probability sample   Selection procedure in which each member of the target population has a known or an equal chance of being selected. Probability samples are the most commonly employed by professional polling companies.

professional association   Organization that represents individuals, largely educated and affluent, in one particular occupational category.

progressive tax   A tax structured such that higher-income individuals pay a larger percentage of their income in taxes.

project grants   A type of categorical grant in which a competitive application process is required for a specific project (often scientific or technical research or social services).

pseudo-events   Events that appear spontaneous but are in fact staged and scripted by public relations experts to appeal to the news media or the public.

public goods (collective goods)   Goods—such as clean water, public roads, and community libraries—that are used or consumed by all individuals in society.

public interest group   Citizen organization that advocate issues of public good, such as protection of the environment.

public opinion   The attitudes of individuals regarding their political leaders and institutions as well as political and social issues. Public opinion tends to be grounded in political values and can influence political behavior.

public policy   What government decides to do or not do; government laws, rules, or expenditures. For instance, it is state public policy that you must be 21 years old to purchase alcohol.

purposive benefits   Intangible rewards people obtain from joining a group they support and working to advance an issue in which they believe.

"rally 'round the flag" effect   The expectation that Americans will unite behind the nation's leaders in times of crisis.

rational party model   The goal is to win offices and to control the distribution of government jobs.

reapportionment   The process by which seats in the House of Representatives are reassigned among the states to reflect population changes following the Census (every 10 years). In recent decades Sun Belt states have netted more seats, and Rust Belt states have lost seats.

reasonable time, place, and manner restrictions   Permissible government regulations on freedom of speech that seek to prevent disruptions or threats to public safety in the manner in which expressions are presented, such as blocking a street to stage a protest march. Such regulations cannot be used to control the content of political speech.

reciprocity/logrolling   Supporting a legislator's bill in exchange for support of one's own bill.

redistribution   Government providing a broad segment of the society with something of value.

redistricting   The process of redrawing legislative district boundaries within a state to reflect population changes. The shifting of district boundaries can have massive political implications. At times, two sitting legislators are placed in the same district, for example. They are forced to run against each other.

regressive tax   A tax structured such that higher-income individuals pay a lower percentage of their income in taxes.

regulations   Legal rules created by government agencies based on authority delegated by the legislature. For example, in order to protect public safety, regulations issued by the U.S. Department of Transportation define how many hours each week truck drivers can be on the road and how many hours of rest they must have between driving shifts.

reporter's privilege   The asserted right of news reporters to promise confidentiality to their sources and to keep information obtained from sources, including evidence of criminal activity, secret. The U.S. Supreme Court has held that reporter's privilege is not a component of the First Amendment's protection for freedom of the press.

representative democracy   A system in which citizens select, through an open and fair process, a smaller group to carry out the business of government on their behalf.

republic   A system of government in which members of the general public select agents to represent them in political decision-making. For example, most campus student governments can be considered republics because elections are held to choose student representatives.

reserve ratios   Minimum percentage of deposits that a financial institution must keep on hand.

responsible party model   The goal is to shape public policy.

right to privacy   A constitutional right created and expanded in U.S. Supreme Court decisions concerning access to contraceptives, abortion, private sexual behavior, and other matters, even though the word *privacy* does not appear in the Constitution. A majority of Supreme Court justices since the 1960s have identified privacy protections as among the rights within the concept of protected liberty in the Due Process Clause of the Fourteenth Amendment.

Roe v. Wade **(1973)**   Controversial U.S. Supreme Court decision that declared women have a constitutional right to choose to terminate a pregnancy in the first six months following conception.

rotation   The staggering of senatorial terms such that one-third of the Senate comes up for election every 2 years. Even if voters are ripping mad throughout the nation, only one-third of the Senate can be removed in a particular election.

sample   A subset of the population under study; if selected correctly, it represents the population from which it was drawn with reliable and measurable accuracy.

selective benefits   Benefits provided only to members of an organization or group.

senatorial courtesy   Traditional deference by U.S. senators to the wishes of their colleagues concerning the appointment of individuals to federal judgeships in that state.

Senior Executive Service (SES)   A program established by Congress in 1978 to enable senior administrators with outstanding management skills to move between jobs in different agencies in order to enhance the performance of the federal bureaucracy.

seniority   Length of time served in a chamber of the legislature. Members with greater seniority have traditionally been granted greater power.

separationist   An interpretive approach to the Establishment Clause of the First Amendment, which requires a "wall of separation" between church and state, including prohibitions on using government money for religious programs.

Seventeenth Amendment   Change to the U.S. Constitution, ratified in 1913, which provides for the direct election of senators. Without this change, we would not vote for our senators, but instead they would be chosen by the state legislature.

sharing of powers   The U.S. Constitution's granting of specific powers to each branch of government while making each branch also partly dependent on the others for carrying out its duties. For example, the Supreme Court ruled that "separate but equal" educational systems were unconstitutional in 1954, but the task of actually desegregating schools was left to President Eisenhower.

Shays's Rebellion   An armed uprising in western Massachusetts in 1786 and 1787 by small farmers angered over high debt and tax burdens. This event helped bring about the Constitutional Convention, as many worried that similar events would happen unless there were changes.

signing statement   A written proclamation issued by the president regarding how the executive branch intends to interpret a new law. Occasionally these statements seem to contradict what Congress had in mind, making them quite controversial.

single-issue interest group   A group that is interested primarily in one area of public policy such as the Environmental Defense Fund founded in 1967 to solve critical environmental problems facing the global community.

social contract theory   A political theory that holds individuals give up certain rights in return for securing certain freedoms. If the government breaks the social contract, grounds for revolution exist. This notion was at the core of the Declaration of Independence.

social responsibility theory (public advocate model)   The idea that the media should consider the overall needs of society when making decisions about what stories to cover and in what manner: also known as public advocate model.

Social Security Trust Fund   A fund to pay future Social Security benefits, supposedly being built through today's payroll tax.

Social Security   A federal program started in 1935 that taxes wages and salaries to pay for retirement benefits, disability insurance, and hospital insurance.

socialism   An economic system in which the government owns and controls most factories and much or all of the nation's land.

soft money   Funds contributed through a loophole in federal campaign finance regulations that allowed individuals and groups to give unlimited sums of money to political parties.

solidary benefits   Benefits derived from fellowship and camaraderie with other members.

sound bite   A short outtake from a longer film, speech, or interview.

sovereignty   The exclusive right of an independent state to reign supreme and base absolute power over a geographic region and its people.

Speaker   The presiding officer of the House of Representatives, who is also the leader of the majority party in the House.

special governments   Local governmental units established for very specific purposes, such as the regulation of water and school districts, airports, and transportation services. Decisions made by special governments tend to have a very large impact on the daily lives of individuals but typically garner less media attention.

specialization   A norm suggesting that members of both chambers have extensive knowledge in a particular policy area. One member might specialize in military matters, while another might focus on agricultural issues. This norm serves the needs of the full chamber.

stagflation   The combination of stagnant GDP, rising unemployment, and rapid inflation.

statutes   Laws written by state legislatures and by Congress. For example, the Armed Career Criminal Act was a statute written and enacted by Congress.

stewardship model   A theory of robust, broad presidential powers; the idea that the president is only limited by explicit restrictions in the Constitution. This model, now completely accepted, set the stage for a broad expansion of presidential powers.

Strategic Arms Limitation Talks (SALT) Negotiations between the United States and Soviet Union during the Cold War that produced two major agreements on limiting the size of each country's nuclear forces.

strategic voting model An approach to analyzing judicial decision making that identifies strategic decisions made by judges in order to advance their preferred case outcomes.

strict scrutiny An exacting test for violations of fundamental rights by requiring the government to demonstrate a compelling interest when policies and practices clash with certain constitutional rights. The government may persuade judges, for example, that national security interests or health and safety interests outweigh the exercise of free speech or religion in specific situations.

subcommittees Specialized groups within standing committees. For example, a subcommittee of the House Education and Labor Committee is Early Childhood, Elementary, and Secondary Education.

Super PACs Officially known as "independent expenditure-only committees," these groups are allowed to raise unlimited sums from unlimited sources, including corporations, unions and other groups, as well as wealthy individuals. But, they are not allowed to coordinate their campaign activities and spending with the candidates they are trying to help, hence the term "independent expenditure-only committees."

symbolic speech The expression of an idea or viewpoint through an action, such as wearing an armband or burning an object. Symbolic speech can enjoy First Amendment protections.

technology gap (digital divide) The differences in access to and mastery of information and communication technology between segments of the community (typically for socioeconomic, educational, or geographical reasons).

term limits Laws stipulating the maximum number of terms that an elected official may serve in a particular office.

test case A case sponsored or presented by an interest group in the court pathway with the intention of influencing public policy. For example, *Grutter* v. *Bollinger* (2003), the case challenging affirmative action policies at the University of Michigan School of Law, was an unsuccessful test case filed by the Center for Individual Rights.

The Federalist Papers A series of 85 essays in support of ratification of the U.S. Constitution that were written by James Madison, Alexander Hamilton, and John Jay and published under the byline Publius in New York City newspapers between October 27, 1787, and May 28, 1788. We often turn to these essays to better understand the intent of the framers.

think tank A group of individuals who conduct research in a particular subject or a particular area of public policy.

totalitarian regime A system of government in which the ruling elite holds all power and controls all aspects of society. Nazi Germany was a totalitarian government in the 1930s and early 1940s.

totalitarian regime A system of government in which there are no limits on the power and authority of the rulers.

treaty A formal agreement between governments. For example, in the 1970s the United States joined many other nations in agreeing to limit the testing and development of nuclear weapons.

trial by jury A right contained in the Sixth Amendment to have criminal guilt decided by a body of citizens drawn from the community.

trigger mechanism The means, often tied to focusing events, to push a recognized problem further along in the policy cycle.

tripartite view Thinking of political parties as consisting of three parts—in-government; in-the-electorate; and as-an-organization.

trustee model of representation The philosophy that legislators should consider the will of the people but act in ways they believe best for the long-term interests of the nation, at which time, the precise "will of the people" is set aside.

turnout The percentage of citizens legally eligible to vote in an election who actually vote in that election. In most recent presidential elections, the turnout is slightly over 50 percent.

Twelfth Amendment (1804) Required a separate vote tally in the Electoral College for president and vice president. This change made running on a party ticket much easier.

Twenty-Fourth Amendment (1964) Eliminated the poll tax.

Twenty-Sixth Amendment (1971) Granted 18-year-old citizens the right to vote.

unemployment rate The percentage of Americans who are currently not working but are seeking jobs.

unit rule The practice, employed by 48 states, of awarding all of a state's electoral college votes to the candidate who receives the greatest number of popular votes in that state. In these states it is all or nothing!

unitary system A system of government in which political power and authority are located in one central government that runs the country and that may or may not share power with regional subunits.

universal suffrage The right to vote for all adult citizens.

veto The disapproval of a bill or resolution by the president. A veto can be overturned by two-thirds vote in both houses of Congress.

Vietnam syndrome The belief, attributed to the American experience in Vietnam, that the public will not support the use of military force if it results in significant American casualties.

Virginia Plan A plan made by delegates to the Constitutional Convention from several of the larger states calling for a strong national government with a bicameral legislature, a national executive, a national judiciary, and legislative representation based on population. Much of this plan found its way into the Constitution, shaping the system we live under today.

voting cues Summaries encapsulating the informed judgment of others in the legislature; members of Congress rely on these to streamline the decision-making process.

Voting Rights Act of 1965   A federal statute that effectively attacked literacy tests and other techniques used to prevent African Americans from voting.

War Powers Resolution   A measure passed by Congress in 1973 designed to limit presidential deployment of troops unless Congress grants approval for a longer period. Every president since the passage of this measure has argued that it is unconstitutional, and has not agreed to abide by its provisions.

warrant   A judicial order authorizing a search or an arrest. Under the Fourth Amendment, police and prosecutors must present sufficient evidence to constitute "probable cause" in order to obtain a warrant from a judge.

weapons of mass destruction   Weapons capable of inflicting widespread devastation on civilian populations.

Whig model   A theory of restrained presidential powers; the idea that presidents should use only the powers explicitly granted in the Constitution. Under this approach Congress, not the president, would lead the policy process.

whips   Assistants to House and Senate leaders, responsible for drumming up support for legislation and for keeping count of how members plan to vote on different pieces of legislation. Given the rise of partisanship in Congress, the job of the whips has become much more intense.

whistleblower   An employee who reports or reveals misconduct by government officials or others.

Whistleblower Protection Act of 1989   A federal law intended to prevent employees in the bureaucracy from being punished for reporting or revealing governmental misconduct.

writ of certiorari   A legal action that asks a higher court to call up a case from a lower court; the legal action used to ask the U.S. Supreme Court to accept a case for hearing.

yellow journalism   Sensationalistic stories featured in the daily press around the turn of the twentieth century.

Endnotes

CHAPTER 1

1. Employment of homosexuals and other sex perverts in government; interim report submitted to the Committee on Expenditures in the Executive Departments by its Subcommittee on Investigations pursuant to S. Res. 280, 81st Congress, a resolution authorizing the Committee on Expenditures in the Executive Departments to carry out certain duties. 1950. Accessed at: http://www.worldcat .org/title/employment-of-homosexuals-and-other-sex-perverts-in-government-interim-report-sub-mitted-to-the-committee-on-expenditures-in-the-executive-departments-by-its-subcommittee-on-investigations-pursuant-to-s-res-280-81st-congress-a-resolution-authorizing-the-commit-tee-on-expenditures-in-the-executive-departments-to-carry-out-certain-duties/oclc/11575400.
2. Human Rights Watch, "Egypt: Year of Abuses Under al-Sisi," June 8, 2015, https://www.hrw.org/news/2015/06/08/egypt-year-abuses-under-al-sisi.
3. Mothers Against Drunk Driving, "MADD Statistics," http://www.madd.org/statistics/.
4. Virginia Gray and David Lowery, "Where Do Policy Ideas Come From? A Study of Minnesota Legislators and Staffers," *Journal of Public Administration Research and Theory* 10 (2000): 573–595.
5. George F. Cole and Christopher E. Smith, *The American System of Criminal Justice*, 12th ed. (Belmont, CA: Wadsworth, 2008).
6. Greg Lukianoff and Jonathan Haidt, "The Coddling of the American Mind," *Atlantic* (September 2015).
7. Quoted in John K. White and Daniel M. Shea, *New Party Politics: From Jefferson and Hamilton to the Information Age*, 2nd ed. (Belmont, CA: Wadsworth, 2004), 13.
8. Thomas Dye, *Politics in America*, 8th ed. (New York: Pearson Education, 2009), 25.
9. For an interesting discussion of the link between political culture and system stability, see Oliver H. Woshinsky, *Culture and Politics* (Upper Saddle River, NJ: Prentice Hall, 1995).
10. Ibid., 117–118.
11. Gunnar Myrdal, *An American Dilemma: The Negro Problem and Modern Democracy* (New York: Harper, 1944), 27.
12. Ibid.
13. Arthur M. Schlesinger Jr., *The Disuniting of America: Reflections on a Multicultural Society* (New York: Norton, 1992), 27.
14. Albert Su, "Ron Paul Support Grows on College Campuses," CBSNews.Com, February 11, 2009.

CHAPTER 2

1. Ernesto Dal Bo, Pedro Dal Bo, and Jason Snyder, "Political Dynasties,"Social Science Research Network, accessed May 26, 2006, http://ssrn.com/abstract=909251 or http://dx.doi.org/10.2139/ssrn.909251.
2. Max Weber, "Politics as a Vocation" (1918), in *From Max Weber: Essays in Sociology*, ed. H. H. Gerth and C. Wright Mills (New York: Oxford University Press, 1946), 128.
3. Theodore J. Lowi and Benjamin Ginsberg, *American Government: Freedom and Power*, 2nd ed. (New York: Norton, 1992), 10.
4. Ibid.
5. David McCullough, *John Adams* (New York: Simon and Schuster, 2001), 60.
6. Ibid.
7. Barbara Ehrenreich, "Their George and Ours," *New York Times*, July 4, 2004, sec. 4, 9.
8. "Thomas Paine: Life in America," Encyclopaedia Britannica Online, 2004, http://search.eb.com.
9. "Articles of Confederation," Encyclopaedia Britannica Online, 2004, http://search.eb.com.
10. Bruce Miroff, Raymond Seidelman, and Todd Swanstrom, *The Democratic Debate: An Introduction to American Politics*, 4th ed. (Boston: Houghton Mifflin, 2007), 26.
11. Joseph J. Ellis, *Founding Brothers: The Revolutionary Generation* (New York: Vintage Books, 2002), 94.
12. Ibid., 91.
13. Alexander Hamilton, James Madison, and John Jay, *The Federalist*, No. 57.
14. "Essays of Brutus, No. 1," in *The Complete Anti-Federalist*, ed. Herbert Storing (Chicago: University of Chicago Press, 1981).

CHAPTER 3

1. For more information about childhood obesity see the Center for Disease Control's (CDC) Web page, http://www.cdc.gov/healthyschools/obesity/facts.htm.
2. For more information on unfunded mandates and the challenges of federalism, see the Council of State Governments' Web page, http://www.csg.org.
3. M. Judd Harmon, *Political Thought: From Plato to the Present* (New York: McGraw-Hill, 1964), 289.
4. National Conference of State Legislatures, accessed on November 26, 2011, http://www.ncsl.org/Default.aspx?TabID=746&tabs=1116,112,764#1116.
5. The Council of State Governments, accessed on November 26, 2011, http://www.csg.org/knowledgecenter/docs/TIA_FF_StateCompensation_final.pdf.
6. Legislator demographic information is from the National Conference of State Legislatures, accessed on February 9, 2016, http://www.ncsl.org/research/about-state-legislatures/who-we-elect.aspx. It should be noted that not all legislators supply the organization with pertinent demographic data so the information provided here is from self-reporting (though participation is relatively high for their national organization).
7. Council of State Governments, Knowledge Center, accessed on February 9, 2016, http://knowledgecenter.csg.org/kc/content/governors-salaries-2015.

8. "State Court Budgets and Judicial Salaries," Ballotpedia, accessed on February 8, https://ballotpedia.org/State_court_budgets_and_judicial_salaries#tab=Salaries, 2016.

9. Jesse J. Richardson Jr., Meghan Zimmerman Gough, and Robert Puentes, "Is Home Rule the Answer?" The Brookings Institution, January 2003, accessed on December 2, 2009, http://www.brookings.edu/reports/2003/01metropolitanpolicy_richardson.aspx.

10. Federal law requires the U.S. Census Bureau to conduct a Census of Governments of all state and local government organizations units every five years. The last Census of Governments was conducted in October 2012. Accessed on July 28, 2014, https://www.census.gov/govs/cog2012/.

11. See Howard Gillman, *The Constitution Besieged: The Rise and Demise of Lochner Era Police Powers Jurisprudence* (Durham, NC: Duke University Press, 1993).

12. Morton Grozdins, *The American System,* ed. Daniel J. Elazar (Chicago: Rand McNally, 1966).

13. U.S. Government Accountability Office, "Grants to State and Local Governments, September 25, 2012," accessed on February 9, 2016, http://www.gao.gov/products/GAO-12-1016; U.S. Government Accountability Office, "Management of Federal Grants to State and Local Governments," accessed on February 9, 2016, http://www.gao.gov/key_issues/management_of_federal_grants_to_state_local/issue_summary.

14. Cheryl H. Lee, Tereese Dyson, Matthew Park, Calvin Handy and Marquita Buchanan Reynolds, "Economy-Wide Statistics Briefs: Public Sector, State Government Finances Summary: 2013," February 2015, accessed on February 9, 2016, http://www2.census.gov/govs/state/g13-asfin.pdf); "Federal Spending in the States – 2004 to 2013" The Pew Charitable Trusts, December 2, 2014, accessed on February 9, 2016, http://www.pewtrusts.org/en/research-and-analysis/issue-briefs/2014/12/federal-spending-in-the-states.

15. According to the National Conference of State Legislatures, accessed on February 10, 2016, http://www.ncsl.org/research/immigration/state-laws-related-to-immigration-and-immigrants.aspx.

16. Max Fisher, "Map: How the World's Countries Compare on Income Inequality (the U.S. Ranks Below Nigeria)," *Washington Post*, September 27, 2013, accessed on July 26, 2014, http://www.washingtonpost.com/blogs/worldviews/wp/2013/09/27/map-how-the-worlds-countries-compare-on-income-inequality-the-u-s-ranks-below-nigeria/; Alanna Petroff, "U.S. and Israel Have Worst Inequality in the Developed World," *CNN Money,* May 21, 2015, accessed on February 14, 2016, http://money.cnn.com/2015/05/21/news/economy/worst-inequality-countries-oecd/.

17. Cheryl H. Lee, Tereese Dyson, Matthew Park, Calvin Handy and Marquita Buchanan Reynolds, "State Government Finances Summary: 2013: Economy-Wide Statistics Briefs, Public Sector," United States Census, U.S. Department of Commerce, released February 2015, accessed on February 13, 2016, http://www2.census.gov/govs/state/g13-asfin.pdf.

18. The Pew Center on the States, accessed on November 26, 2011, http://www.pewtrusts.org/en/multimedia/data-visualizations/2014/fiscal-50#ind0.

19. Marshall Clement, Matthew Schwarzfeld, and Michael Thompson, "The National Summit on Justice Reinvestment and Public Safety," Justice Center: The Council of State Governments, January 2011, accessed on November 26, 2011, http://www.pewcenteronthestates.org/initiatives_detail.aspx?initiativeID=59068.

20. "The Price of Incarceration: What Incarceration Costs Taxpayers," Center on Sentencing and Corrections: VERA Institute of Justice, updated July 2012, accessed on July 29, 2014, http://www.vera.org/sites/default/files/resources/downloads/price-of-prisons-updated-version-021914.pdf.

21. Roy Walmsley, "World Prison Population List, 10th ed.," International Centre for Prison Studies (ICPS) (University of Essex) accessed on February 13, 2016, http://www.apcca.org/uploads/10th_Edition_2013.pdf.

22. Richard Marosi, "Latest Drug Tunnel, Pot Seizures May Reflect Rise of Sinaloa Cartel," *Los Angeles Times.* December 1, 2011, accessed on December 1, 2011, http://www.latimes.com/news/local/la-me-border-tunnel-20111201,0,5158944.story.

CHAPTER 4

1. Jess Aloe, "Proposed Law Could Allow Warrantless Phone Searches," *Burlington Free Press*, January 17, 2016, http://www.burlingtonfreepress.com.

2. Henry J. Abraham, *Freedom and the Court: Civil Rights and Liberties in the United States,* 5th ed. (New York: Oxford University Press, 1988), 41.

3. Ibid., 206.

4. *Engel* v. *Vitale,* 370 U.S. 421, 431 (1962).

5. Linda Greenhouse, "Documents Reveal the Evolution of a Justice," *New York Times*, March 4, 2004, A16.

6. "'Irvine 11' Students Plan to Appeal Convictions," *Los Angeles Times*, September 23, 2011, http://latimesblogs.latimes.com.

7. Julie Tate, "Bradley Manning Sentenced to 35 Years in WikiLeaks Case," *Washington Post*, August 21, 2013, http://www.washingtonpost.com.

8. Joshua Lipton, "Vanessa Leggett: Why She Wouldn't Give Up Her Notes," *Columbia Journalism Review* (March–April 2002) accessed on August 23, 2008, http://www.cjr.org/issues/2002/2/qa-leggett.asp.

9. Craig Uchida and Timothy Bynum, "Search Warrants, Motions to Suppress, and 'Lost Cases': The Effects of the Exclusionary Rule in Seven Jurisdictions," *Journal of Criminal Law and Criminology* 81 (1991): 1034–1066.

10. Brad Heath, "U.S. Secretly Tracked Billions of Phone Calls for Decades," *USA Today*, April 8, 2015, http://www.usatoday.com; Kim Zetter, "Yes, the Government's Stingray Spy Technology Can Record Your Calls," *Slate*, October 29, 2015, http://www.slate.com.

11. George F. Cole and Christopher E. Smith, *Criminal Justice in America,* 4th ed. (Belmont, CA: Wadsworth, 2004), 10.

12. See Lee Epstein and Joseph Kobylka, *The Supreme Court and Legal Change* (Chapel Hill: University of North Carolina Press, 1992).

13. Mark Costanza, *Just Revenge: Costs and Consequences of the Death Penalty* (New York: St. Martin's Press, 1997), 95–111.

14. Death Penalty Information Center, February 2016, http://www.deathpenaltyinfo.org.

15. Adam Liptak, "Supreme Court to Hear Texas Abortion Law Case," *New York Times*, November 13, 2015, http://www.nytimes.com.

16. Christopher E. Smith, *Courts and the Poor* (Chicago: Nelson-Hall, 1991), 118.

CHAPTER 5

1. "'Enough Is Enough': Tens of Thousands March to Protest Police Violence," CBS News, December 13, 2014, available at http://www.cbsnews.com/news/eric-garner-ferguson-missouri-protesters-converge-on-washington/; Greg Botelho, Holly Yan, and Dana Ford, "Baltimore Protests: Crowds, Police Stand Off After Curfew," CNN News, April 29, 2015, available at http://www.cnn.com/2015/04/28/us/baltimore-riots/.

2. See, for example, Charles R. Epp, Steven Maynard-Moody, and Donald Haider-Markel, *Pulled Over: How Police Stops Define Race and Citizenship*, Chicago, IL: University of Chicago Press, 2014; James McKinley, "Study Finds Racial Disparity in Criminal Prosecutions," *New York Times*, July 4, 2014, available at http://www.nytimes.com/2014/07/09/nyregion/09race.html; New York Civil Liberties Union, "Stop-and-Frisk Data," 2015, available at http://www.nyclu.org/content/stop-and-frisk-data; Sharon LaFraniere and Andrew Lehren, "The Disproportionate Risks of Driving While Black," *New York Times*, October 24, 2015, available at http://www.nytimes.com/2015/10/25/us/racial-disparity-traffic-stops-driving-black.html.

3. Julia Craven, "Black Lives Matter Co-Founder Reflects on the Origins of the Movement," *Huffington Post*, September 30, 2015, available at http://www.huffingtonpost.com/entry/black-lives-matter-opal-tometi_us_560c1c59e4b0768127003227; Janell Ross, "How Black Lives Matter Moved from a Hashtag to a Real Political Force," *Washington Post*, August 19, 2015, available at https://www.washingtonpost.com/news/the-fix/wp/2015/08/19/how-black-lives-matter-moved-from-a-hashtag-to-a-real-political-force/.

4. Mark Berman and Wesley Lowry, "The 12 Key Highlights from the DOJ's Scathing Ferguson Report," *Washington Post*, March 4, 2015, available at https://www.washingtonpost.com/news/post-nation/wp/2015/03/04/the-12-key-highlights-from-the-dojs-scathing-ferguson-report/; Civil Rights Division, U.S. Department of Justice, *Investigation of the Ferguson Police Department*, March 4, 2015, available at http://www.justice.gov/sites/default/files/opa/press-releases/attachments/2015/03/04/ferguson_police_department_report.pdf.

5. Lisa Seville and Hannah Rappleye, "Probation Firm Extorted Money from Poor in Alabama, Suit Charges," NBC News, March 13, 2015, available at http://www.nbcnews.com/news/us-news/probation-firm-extorted-money-poor-alabama-suit-charges-n323036; Jessica Pishko, "Locked Up for Being Poor," *Atlantic*, February 25, 2015, available at http://www.theatlantic.com/national/archive/2015/02/locked-up-for-being-poor/386069/.

6. Rodney Balko, "The Black Lives Matter Policy Agenda Is Practical, Thoughtful—and Urgent," *Washington Post*, August 25, 2015, available at https://www.washingtonpost.com/news/the-watch/wp/2015/08/25/the-black-lives-matter-policy-agenda-is-practical-thoughtful-and-urgent/.

7. John Eligon, "Emboldened by Protests, Black Lives Matter Activists Move from Street to Ballot," *New York Times*, February 6, 2016, available at http://www.nytimes.com/2016/02/07/us/emboldened-by-protests-black-lives-matter-activists-move-from-street-to-ballot.html.

8. For example, see Peter Kolchin, *American Slavery, 1619–1877*, New York, NY: Hill and Wang, 1993; Walter Johnson,

Soul by Soul: Life Inside the Antebellum Slave Market, Cambridge, MA: Harvard University Press, 1999; Ira Berlin, Marc Favreau, and Steven F. Miller, eds., *Remembering Slavery*, New York, NY: New Press, 1998; John Hope Franklin and Loren Schweninger, *Runaway Slaves: Rebels on the Plantation*, New York, NY: Oxford University Press, 1999.

9. For example, see Andrew Hacker, *Two Nations: Black and White, Separate, Hostile, Unequal*, New York, NY: Scribner, 1992; Tom Wicker, *Tragic Failure: Racial Integration in America*, New York, NY: Morrow, 1996.

10. Eric Foner, *The Story of American Freedom*, New York, NY: Norton, 1998, p. 104.

11. David E. Kyvig, *Explicit and Authentic Acts: Amending the U.S. Constitution, 1776–1995*, Lawrence, KS: University Press of Kansas, 1996, p. 182.

12. William Gillette, *Retreat from Reconstruction, 1869–1879*, Baton Rouge, LA: Louisiana State University Press, 1979, pp. 335–347.

13. Ronald Takaki, *A Different Mirror: A History of Multicultural America*, Boston, MA: Little, Brown, 1993, pp. 191–221.

14. Ibid., p. 138.

15. See Richard Kluger, *Simple Justice*, New York, NY: Random House, 1975, pp. 657–747.

16. *Grutter v. Bollinger*, 539 U.S. 306, 325 (2003).

17. *Hutchinson v. Cuyahoga County Board of Commissioners*, Case No. 1:08-CV-2966, U.S. District Court for the Northern District of Ohio, April 25, 2011.

18. "Court Upholds Damage Cap in Cincinnati Teen's Stage Collapse Lawsuit," WLWT-TV News, July 1, 2015, available at http://www.wlwt.com/news/court-upholds-5-million-cap-in-indiana-stage-collapse-case/33912676.

19. "An Interview with Congressman Charles Diggs," in Juan Williams, *Eyes on the Prize: America's Civil Rights Years*, New York, NY: Viking, 1987, p. 49.

20. Ibid., p. 52.

21. See Gunnar Myrdal, *An American Dilemma: The Negro Problem and Modern Democracy*, New York, NY: Harper, 1944.

22. Taylor Branch, *Parting the Waters: America in the King Years, 1954–1963*, New York, NY: Simon and Schuster, 1988, pp. 128–205.

23. Williams, *Eyes on the Prize*, pp. 208–217.

24. Ibid., pp. 184–195.

25. Branch, *Parting the Waters*, p. 891.

26. Williams, *Eyes on the Prize*, pp. 197–200.

27. Ibid., pp. 276–277.

28. Gerald Gunther, *Constitutional Law*, 11th ed., Mineola, NY: Foundation Press, 1985, p. 932.

29. Eleanor Flexner, *Century of Struggle: The Women's Rights Movement in the United States*, rev. ed., Cambridge, MA: Harvard University Press, 1975, pp. 154–158.

30. Ibid., pp. 167–171, 295.

31. Ibid., p. 228.

32. Ibid., p. 300.

33. Oscar J. Martinez, "A History of Chicanos/Mexicanos along the U.S.–Mexico Border," in *Handbook of Hispanic Cultures in the United States: History*, Alfredo Jimenez, ed., Houston, TX: Arte Publico Press, 1994, pp. 261–280.

34. Pedro Caban, Jose Carrasco, Barbara Cruz, and Juan Garcia, *The Latino Experience in U.S. History*, Paramus, NJ: Globe Fearon, 1994, pp. 208–220.

35. Ibid., pp. 282–287.

36. "CFBB and Department of Justice Take Action Against Provident Funding Associates for Discriminatory

Mortgage Pricing," Press Release, U.S. Consumer Federal Protection Bureau, May 28, 2015, available at http://www.consumerfinance.gov/newsroom/cfpb-and-department-of-justice-take-action-against-provident-funding-associates-for-discriminatory-mortgage-pricing/.

37. "Alabama's Second Thoughts," *New York Times*, December 17, 2011, available at http://www.nytimes.com/2011/12/18/opinion/sunday/alabamas-second-thoughts.html?_r%3D0.

38. For example, see Matthew R. Durose, Erica L. Schmitt, and Patrick Langan, *Contacts Between Police and the Public: Findings from the 2002 National Survey,* Washington, D.C.: U.S. Bureau of Justice Statistics, 2005; Robin Shepard Engel and Jennifer M. Calnon, "Examining the Influence of Drivers' Characteristics during Traffic Stops with Police: Results from a National Survey," *Justice Quarterly 21,* 2004: pp. 49–90.

39. Tierney Sneed, "Obama's Policing Task Force Releases Report," *U.S. News and World Report*, March 2, 2015, available at http://www.usnews.com/news/articles/2015/03/02/obamas-policing-task-force-releases-report; Al Baker, "Police Leaders Unveil Principles Intended to Shift Policing Practices Nationwide," *New York Times,* January 29, 2016, available at http://www.nytimes.com/2016/01/30/nyregion/police-leaders-unveil-principles-intended-to-shift-policing-practices-nationwide.html?_r%3D0.

40. "How Long Would They Lock Up Your Killer?" *Legal Affairs,* July–August 2004, p. 25.

41. Todd Leopold, "Boy Scouts Change Policy on Gay Leaders," CNN.com, July 28, 2015, available at http://www.cnn.com/2015/07/27/us/boy-scouts-gay-leaders-feat/.

42. Teni Adedeji, "The Merits of Civil Protest at UCSB," *The Bottom Line,* February 7, 2016, available at https://thebottomline.as.ucsb.edu/2016/02/the-merits-of-civil-protest-at-ucsb.

CHAPTER 6

1. Thomas Friedman, "Where Did 'We' Go?" *New York Times*, September 30, 2009, http://www.nytimes.com/2009/09/30/opinion/30friedman.html.

2. Kelly D. Patterson and Daniel M. Shea, eds., *Contemplating the People's Branch* (Upper Saddle River, NJ: Prentice Hall, 2000), 6.

3. Gary W. Cox and Jonathan N. Katz, *Elbridge Gerry's Salamander* (Cambridge, England: Cambridge University Press, 2002), 3.

4. As cited in Robert Barnes, "Supreme Court Appears Conflicted On Dismissal of Gerrymandering Case," *Washington Post,* November 4, 2015,

5. Adam Clymer, "Why Iowa Has So Many Hot Seats," *New York Times,* October 27, 2002, A22.

6. L. Sandy Maisel, *Parties and Elections in America: The Electoral Process,* 3rd ed. (Lanham, MD: Rowman and Littlefield, 1999), 207.

7. Cox and Katz, *Elbridge Gerry's Salamander,* 12–13.

8. Ibid., 25–28.

9. Chris Cillizza, "Reapportionment Winners and Losers," *Washington Post,* December 21, 2010, http://voices.washingtonpost.com/thefix/redistricting/reapportionment-winners-and-lo.html.

10. Roger H. Davidson, Walter J. Oleszek, and Frances E. Lee. *Congress and Its Members,* 12th ed. (Washington, D.C.: CQ Press, 2009), 199.

11. Ibid., 205.

12. Robert Pear, "Passions Flare as House Debates Birth Control Rule," *New York Times*, February 16, 2012.

13. David J. Vogler, *The Politics of Congress* (Madison, WI: Brown and Benchmark, 1993), 76.

14. Michael J. Malbin, *Unelected Representatives: Congressional Staff and the Future of Representative Government* (New York: Basic Books, 1979).

15. Charles Peters, *How Washington Really Works* (Reading, MA: Addison-Wesley, 1992), 133; Fred Harris, *In Defense of Congress* (New York: St. Martin's Press, 1995), 40–41.

16. Patterson and Shea, *Contemplating the People's Branch,* 133–134.

17. Adam Nagourney, "Democrats Reel As Senator Says No to Third Term," *New York Times*, February 15, 2010, A1.

18. Josh Tyrangiel, "A Congressional Exit Interview," *Bloomberg Businessweek,* July 21, 2012, http://www.businessweek.com/printer/articles/31850-a-congressional-exit-interview.

19. Jackie Calmes, "Party Gridlock in Washington Feeds Fears of Debt Crisis," *New York Times,* February 17, 2010, A1.

20. Ibid., 136.

21. Alexander Burns, "VP: Constitution on Its Head," POLITICO, January 18, 2010, http://www.politico.com/politico44/perm/0110/biden_slams_filibuster_fe40df44-9045-4c26-a715-51c427035eae.html.

22. Donald R. Matthews, *U.S. Senators and Their World* (New York: Vintage Books, 1960).

23. Ibid., 97.

24. Ibid., 99.

25. Barbara Sinclair, *Unorthodox Lawmaking: New Legislative Processes in the U.S. Congress,* 3rd ed. (Washington, D.C.: Congressional Quarterly, 2007).

26. Davidson and Oleszek, *Congress and Its Members,* 12th ed., 234.

27. Paul Singer, "Members Offered Many Bills But Passed Few," *CQ Politics OnLine,* December 1, 2008, http://www.rollcall.com/issues/54_61/news/30466-1.html.

28. Center for American Women and Politics, accessed November 11, 2016, http://www.cawp.rutgers.edu/current-numbers.

29. Congressional Black Caucus, accessed February 2004, http://www.congressionalblackcaucus.net.

30. Ibid.

31. Stephen J. Wayne, *Is This Any Way to Run a Democratic Election?* 2nd ed. (Boston: Houghton Mifflin, 2003), 54.

32. Center for Responsive Politics, "Personal Finances of Members of Congress," accessed May 31, 2016, http://www.opensecrets.org/pfds/.

33. U.S. Census Bureau, "Income," accessed February 2004, http://www.census.gov/hhes/www/income.html.

34. Roger H. Davidson and Walter Oleszek, *Congress and Its Members,* 7th ed. (Washington, D.C.: CQ Press, 2000), 128–129.

35. Roger H. Davidson and Walter Oleszek, *Congress and Its Members,* 10th ed. (Washington, D.C.: CQ Press, 2006), 479.

36. Harris, *In Defense of Congress,* 59.

37. Gallup Polling, "Congress and the Public." accessed May 31, 2016, http://www.gallup.com/poll/1600/congress-public.aspx.

38. Morris Fiorina, *Disconnect: The Breakdown of Representation in American Politics* (Norman, OK: University of Oklahoma Press, 2009), 143.

CHAPTER 7

1. Theodore J. Lowi and Benjamin Ginsberg, *American Government: Freedom and Power* (New York: Norton, 1990), 241.
2. John Locke, *The Second Treatise on Government*, cited in ibid., 241.
3. Sidney M. Milkis and Michael Nelson, *The American Presidency: Origins and Development, 1776–1998* (Washington, D.C.: CQ Press, 1999), 26.
4. Milkis and Nelson, *American Presidency, 1776–1998*, 28.
5. David Mervin, *The President of the United States* (New York: Harvester Press, 1993), 22.
6. Michael Nelson, ed., *The Evolving Presidency*, 2nd ed. (Washington, DC: CQ Press, 2004), 10.
7. Robert Dallek, *Hail to the Chief: The Making and Unmaking of American Presidents* (New York: Hyperion, 1996), 14.
8. Theodore Roosevelt, "The Stewardship Doctrine," in *Classics of the American Presidency*, ed. Harry Bailey (Oak Park, IL: Moore, 1980), 35–36.
9. Dallek, *Hail to the Chief*, 18.
10. Michael A. Genovese, *The Power of the American Presidency, 1789–2000* (New York: Oxford University Press, 2001), 132.
11. Ibid, 143.
12. Sidney M. Milkis and Michael Nelson, *The American Presidency: Origins and Development, 1776–2002* (Washington, D.C.: CQ Press, 2003), 424.
13. Ibid.
14. Ibid., 428.
15. Nathan Miller, *FDR: An Intimate History* (Lanham, MD: Madison Books, 1983), 276.
16. Edward S. Greenberg and Benjamin I. Page, *The Struggle for Democracy*, 5th ed. (New York: Longman, 2002), 361.
17. Milkis and Nelson, *American Presidency, 1776–2002*, 438.
18. Ibid., 440.
19. Richard Neustadt, *Presidential Power* (New York: Wiley, 1960), 193.
20. Stephen Skowronek, *The Politics Presidents Make: From John Adams to George Bush* (Cambridge, MA: Harvard University Press, 2008).
21. Gary King and Lyn Ragsdale, *The Elusive Executive: Discovering Statistical Patterns in the Presidency* (Washington, D.C.: CQ Press, 1988), 35.
22. The Supreme Court case was *United States* v. *Curtis Wright Corp.*, 299 U.S. 304 (1936).
23. Louis Fisher, "Invitation to Struggle: The President, Congress, and National Security," in *Understanding the Presidency*, eds. James P. Pfiffner and Roger Davidson (New York: Longman, 1996), 269.
24. Abraham Lincoln, "A Special Session Message, July 4, 1861," cited in Genovese, *Power of the American Presidency*, 81.
25. Aaron Wildavsky, "The Two Presidencies," *Trans-Action* 4 (1966): 7–14.
26. Theodore J. Lowi, *The Personal President: Power Invested, Promise Unfulfilled* (Ithaca, NY: Cornell University Press, 1985), xii.
27. Dallek, *Hail to the Chief*, xx.
28. Sean Wilentz, "The Worst President Ever?" *Rolling Stone*, April 21, 2006.
29. These points are made by political scientist Fred I. Greenstein, "A Change and Continuity in Modern Presidency," in *The New American Political System*, ed. Anthony King (Washington, D.C.: American Enterprise Institute, 1978), 45–46.

CHAPTER 8

1. Emily Wax-Thibodeaux, "One Year After VA Scandal, the Number of Veterans Waiting for Care Is Up 50 Percent," *Washington Post*, June 23, 2015, https://www.washingtonpost.com/news/federal-eye/wp/2015/06/23/one-year-after-va-scandal-the-number-of-veterans-waiting-for-care-is-up-50-percent/.
2. U.S. Environmental Protection Agency, *The Benefits and Costs of the Clean Air Act from 1990 to 2020* (Washington, D.C.: U.S. Environmental Protection Agency, 2011).
3. Timothy Cama, "Obama Vetoes GOP Push to Kill Climate Rules," *The Hill*, December 19, 2015, http://thehill.com/policy/energy-environment/263805-obama-vetoes-gop-attempts-to-kill-climate-rules.
4. David G. Savage, "Supreme Court Deals Blow to Obama by Putting His Climate Change Rules on Hold," *Los Angeles Times*, February 9, 2016, http://www.latimes.com/nation/la-na-court-obama-climate-change-20160209-story.html.
5. Eric Lipton and Scott Shane, "Leader of Federal Effort Feels the Heat," *New York Times*, September 3, 2005, accessed July 21, 2008, http://www.nytimes.com/2005/09/03/national/nationalspecial/03fema.html?_r=1&oref=slogin; See also Daren Fonda and Rita Healy, "How Reliable Is Brown's Resume?" *Time*, September 8, 2005, accessed July 21, 2008, http://www.time.com/time/nation/article/0,8599,1103003,00.html.
6. Pew Research Center for the People and the Press, "Performance and Purpose: Constituents Rate Government Agencies," accessed July 21, 2008, http://people-press.org/report/41/.
7. Charles T. Goodsell, *The Case for Bureaucracy* (Chatham, NJ: Chatham House, 1983), 15.
8. "TSA Takes Heat for Background Check Miscues," *Government Security*, February 11, 2004, accessed July 21, 2008, http://govtsecurity.securitysolutions.com/ar/security_tsa_takes_heat_index.htm.
9. Jeff Johnson, "TSA Screeners Claim They're 'Being Used for Cannon Fodder,'" CNSNews.com, accessed March 20, 2008, http://www.cnsnews.com/ViewPrint.asp?Page=%5CPolitics%5Carchive%5C200303%5CPOL20030304b.html.
10. Ron Nixon, "After Lapses, T.S.A. Will Target Screening in Overhaul," *New York Times*, July 28, 2015, http://www.nytimes.com/2015/07/29/us/politics/transportation-security-administration-targets-screening-in-overhaul.html.
11. Ron Nixon, "T.S.A. Lapses, Retaliation and Bonuses Are Investigated by House Panel," *New York Times*, February 23, 2016, http://www.nytimes.com/2016/02/24/us/politics/tsa-lapses-retaliation-and-bonuses-are-investigated-by-house-panel.html.
12. Maud S. Beelman, "Halliburton Lobby Costs See Big Drop," *Boston Globe*, March 27, 2004, accessed March 3, 2012, http://www.boston.com/news/nation/articles/2004/03/27/halliburton_lobby_costs_see_big_drop/?page=full.
13. Matthew L. Wald and Charlie Savage, "Furor Over Loans to Failed Solar Firm," *New York Times*, September 14, 2011, accessed on March 3, 2012, http://www.nytimes.com/.
14. B. Guy Peters, *American Public Policy: Promise and Performance*, 5th ed. (Chatham, NJ: Chatham House, 1999), 33.
15. "Revolving Door," Center for Responsive Politics Web site, accessed March 3, 2012, http://www.opensecrets.org/revolving/top.php?display=Z.

16. Jeffrey Lazurus, "Which Members of Congress Become Lobbyists? The Ones with the Most Power: Here's the Data," *Washington Post*, January 15, 2016, https://www.washingtonpost.com/news/monkey-cage/wp/2016/01/15/which-members-of-congress-become-lobbyists-the-ones-with-the-most-power-heres-the-data/.

17. Jim Tankersley and Josh Meyer, "Former Interior Secretary Gale Norton Is Focus of Corruption Probe," *Los Angeles Times*, September 17, 2009, accessed April 11, 2010, http://articles.latimes.com/2009/sep/17/nation/na-norton17.

18. Ibid.

19. Tony Pugh, "Medicare Cost Estimates Concealed, Expert Says," *San Diego Union-Tribune*, accessed July 21, 2008, http://www.cnsnews.com/ViewPrint.asp?Page=%5CPolitics%5Carchive%5C200303%5CPOL20030304b.html.

20. "General: Army Leaned on Whistleblower," CBSNews.com, accessed July 21, 2008, http://www.cbsnews.com/stories/2004/10/28/national/main652183.shtml.

21. Neely Tucker, "A Web of Truth," *Washington Post*, October 19, 2005, C1.

22. Joe Davidson, "Whistleblower 'Bunny' Greenhouse Wins Settlement Near $1 Million," *Washington Post*, July 26, 2011, https://www.washingtonpost.com.

23. Robert A. Katzmann, *Regulatory Bureaucracy* (Cambridge, MA: MIT Press, 1980), 180.

24. Timothy Cama, "Obama Vetoes GOP Push to Kill Climate Rules," *The Hill*, December 19, 2015, http://thehill.com/policy/energy-environment/263805-obama-vetoes-gop-attempts-to-kill-climate-rules.

25. David G. Savage, "Supreme Court Deals Blow to Obama by Putting His Climate Change Rules on Hold," *Los Angeles Times*, February 9, 2016, http://www.latimes.com/nation/la-na-court-obama-climate-change-20160209-story.html.

26. Nicholas Ashford and Charles Caldart, *Environmental Law, Policy, and Economics* (Cambridge, MA: MIT Press, 2008), 522–523.

27. Joel Brinkley, "Out of Spotlight, Bush Overhauls U.S. Regulations," *New York Times*, August 14, 2004, accessed July 21, 2008, http://www.nytimes.com/2004/08/14/politics/14bush.html?ex=1250136000&en=1bf32d7574b25b2b&ei=5090.

28. Joe Stephens and Lena H. Sun, "Federal Oversight of Subways Proposed," *Washington Post*, November 15, 2009, accessed April 11, 2010, http://www.washingtonpost.com/wpdyn/content/article/2009/11/14/AR2009111402459.html.

29. Catherine Elsworth, "Golden Globes Investigated for Breaching Indecency Rules," *London Telegraph*, January 15, 2009, accessed April 11, 2010, http://www.telegraph.co.uk/news/worldnews/northamerica/usa/4249694/Golden-Globes-investigated-for-breaching-indecency-rules.html.

30. See Donna Price Cofer, *Judges, Bureaucrats, and the Question of Independence* (Westport, CT: Greenwood Press, 1985).

31. Steve Kanigher, "UNLV Law Students Force Key Change in Deportation Cases," *Las Vegas Sun*, May 30, 2011, http://www.mariowire.com/2011/05/30/unlv-law-sudents-change-deportation-cases/.

32. Peter J. Reilly, "Interview with Student Loan Activist Alan Collinge on Bankruptcy Protection," *Forbes*, October 28, 2015, http://www.forbes.com/sites/peterjreilly/2015/10/28/interview-with-student-loan-activist-alan-collinge-on-bankruptcy-protection/#678fc6116438.

33. "Hero: Alan Collinge," CNN.com, updated December 12, 2008, http://money.cnn.com/galleries/2008/news/0812/gallery.heroes_zeros_2008/5.html.

34. "Presidential Memorandum—Student Aid Bill of Rights," The White House Web site, March 10, 2015, https://www.whitehouse.gov/the-press-office/2015/03/10/presidential-memorandum-student-aid-bill-rights.

CHAPTER 9

1. Christopher E. Smith, *Courts, Politics, and the Judicial Process*, 2nd ed. (Chicago: Nelson-Hall, 1997), 37.

2. Stephen L. Wasby, *The Supreme Court in the Federal Judicial System*, 4th ed. (Chicago: Nelson-Hall, 1993), 56–57, 238–244.

3. Henry J. Abraham, *The Judicial Process*, 6th ed. (New York: Oxford University Press, 1993), 96–97.

4. Christopher E. Smith, "Polarization and Change in the Federal Courts: *En Banc* Decisions in the U.S. Courts of Appeals," *Judicature* 74 (1990): 133–137.

5. Lawrence Baum, *Judges and Their Audiences* (Princeton, NJ: Princeton University Press, 2006), 19–24.

6. Jeffrey A. Segal and Harold J. Spaeth, *The Supreme Court and the Attitudinal Model* (New York: Cambridge University Press, 1993), 64–73.

7. Thomas H. Hammond, Chris W. Bonneau, and Reginald S. Sheehan, *Strategic Behavior and Policy Choice on the U.S. Supreme Court* (Palo Alto, CA: Stanford University Press, 2005).

8. David M. O'Brien, *Storm Center: The Supreme Court in American Politics*, 8th ed. (New York: Norton, 2008).

9. Herbert Kritzer, "Martin Shapiro: Anticipating the New Institutionalism," in *The Pioneers of Judicial Behavior*, ed. Nancy Maveety (Ann Arbor, MI: University of Michigan Press, 2003), 387.

10. Wasby, *The Supreme Court*, 155.

11. Joseph D. Kearney and Thomas W. Merrill, "The Influence of Amicus Curiae Briefs on the Supreme Court," *University of Pennsylvania Law Review* 148 (2000): 753. See also Paul M. Collins Jr., "Lobbyists Before the U.S. Supreme Court," *Political Research Quarterly* 60 (2007): 55–70.

12. Jeff Yates, *Popular Justice: Presidential Prestige and Executive Success in the Supreme Court* (Albany, NY: State University of New York Press, 2002), 2.

13. Gerald Rosenberg, *The Hollow Hope: Can Courts Bring About Social Change?* (Chicago: University of Chicago Press, 1991).

14. Bradley C. Canon, "The Supreme Court and Policy Reform: The Hollow Hope Revisited," in *Leveraging the Law: Using the Courts to Achieve Social Change*, ed. David A. Schultz (New York: Lang, 1998), 215–249.

15. See Richard E. Morgan, *Disabling America: The "Rights Industry" in Our Time* (New York: Basic Books, 1984); Jeremy Rabkin, *Judicial Compulsions: How Public Law Distorts Public Policy* (New York: Basic Books, 1989).

16. Gallup Poll, "Civil Liberties," national opinion poll conducted September 14–15, 2001, http://www.galluppoll.com.

CHAPTER 10

1. Madlin Mekelburg and John Reynolds, "The Brief: Paxton Shopped Districts for Transgender Policy Lawsuit," May 27, 2016, *Texas Tribune,* accessed on May 27, 2016, https://www.texastribune.org/2016/05/27/brief-may-27-2016/

2. For instance, see the seminal work by Angus Campbell, Philip Converse, Warren Miller, and Donald Stokes, *The American Voter* (Chicago: University of Chicago Press, 1960).

3. For instance, see V. O. Key, Jr., *The Responsible Electorate* (Cambridge, MA: Belknap Press, 1966); see also Warren E. Miller and J. Merrill Shanks, *The New American Voter* (Cambridge, MA: Harvard University Press, 1996).

4. Walter Lippmann, *Public Opinion* (New York: Harcourt, Brace, 1922).

5. Robert Weissberg, *Polling, Policy, and Public Opinion: The Case Against Heeding the "Voice of the People"* (New York: Palgrave-Macmillan, 2002).

6. Sidney Verba, *Participation in America: Political Democracy and Social Equality* (Chicago: University of Chicago Press, 1972).

7. Herbert Asher, *Polling and the Public: What Every Citizen Should Know,* 6th ed. (Washington, D.C.: CQ Press, 2004), 195.

8. Starting with the seminal research of Philip E. Converse, "The Nature of Belief Systems in Mass Publics," in *Ideology and Discontent,* ed. David E. Apter (New York: Free Press, 1964), 206–261.

9. Robert S. Erikson and Kent L. Tedin, *American Public Opinion,* 5th ed. (Boston: Allyn and Bacon, 1995), 144.

10. Frank Newport, "In U.S., 87% Approve of Black-White Marriage, vs. 4% in 1958," Gallup Poll, accessed on March 3, 2016, http://www.gallup.com/poll/163697/approve-marriage-blacks-whites.aspx.

11. Ibid.

12. Lydia Saad, "Tolerance for Gay Rights at High-Water Mark," Gallup Poll, accessed on May 29, 2007, http://www.gallup.com/poll/27694/Tolerance-Gay-Rights-HighWater-Mark.aspx; "Indepth Issues – Gay and Lesbian Rights," Gallup Polls, accessed on March 4, 2016, http://www.gallup.com/poll/1651/gay-lesbian-rights.aspx.

13. "In depth Issues – Gay and Lesbian Rights," Gallup Polls, accessed on March 4, 2016, http://www.gallup.com/poll/1651/gay-lesbian-rights.aspx.

14. Jeffrey M. Jones and David W. Moore, "Generational Differences in Support for a Woman President," June 17, 2003, accessed on May 27, 2016, http://www.gallup.com/poll/8656/generational-differences-support-woman-president.aspx.

15. Paul Abramson, *Political Attitudes in America* (San Francisco: Freeman, 1983).

16. Benjamin I. Page and Robert Y. Shapiro, *The Rational Public* (Chicago: University of Chicago Press, 1992), 178.

17. Ibid., 179.

18. See David J. Jackson, *Entertainment and Politics: The Influence of Pop Culture on Young Adult Political Socialization* (New York: Lang, 2002), ch. 1.

19. See Daniel Shea, "Introduction: Popular Culture—The Trojan Horse of American Politics?" in *Mass Politics: The Politics of Popular Culture,* ed. Daniel Shea (New York: St. Martin's/Worth, 1999).

20. "A Paradox in Public Attitudes. Men or Women: Who's the Better Leader? A paradox in Public Attitudes," Paul Taylor, Project Director, accessed on January 2, 2010, http://pewsocialtrends.org/pubs/708/gender-leadership; "Women and Leadership: Public Says Women are Equally Qualified, but Barriers Persist," Pew Research Center, January 14, 2015, accessed on February 16, 2016, http://www.pewsocialtrends.org/2015/01/14/women-and-leadership/.

21. "The ANES Guide to Public Opinion and Electoral Behavior," *American National Election Studies,* Table 4C.1, accessed on January 21, 2012, http://electionstudies.org/nesguide/toptable/tab4c_1.htm.

22. "Women and Leadership: Public Says Women are Equally Qualified, but Barriers Persist." Pew Research Center, January 14, 2015, accessed on February 16, 2016, http://www.pewsocialtrends.org/2015/01/14/women-and-leadership/.

23. Gwen Moran, "Women Now Make Up 40 Percent of Students at Top MBA Programs," *Fortune,* November 9, 2015, accessed on March 4, 2016, http://fortune.com/2015/11/09/women-mba-40-percent/.

24. Jeff Allum, "Graduate Enrollment and Degrees: 2003 to 2013", Council of Graduate Schools, September 2014, accessed on March 4, 2016, http://cgsnet.org/ckfinder/userfiles/files/GED_report_2013.pdf.

25. "Current Numbers of Women Officeholders," Center for American Women in Politics, accessed on March 4, 2016, http://www.cawp.rutgers.edu/current-numbers.

26. "Women CEOs of the S&P," Catalyst, accessed on March 4, 2016, http://www.catalyst.org/knowledge/women-ceos-sp-500.

27. Jackson, *Entertainment and Politics,* 9.

28. M. Kent Jennings and Richard G. Niemi, *Generations and Politics: A Panel Study of Young Adults and Their Parents* (Princeton, NJ: Princeton University Press, 1981).

29. Stuart Oskamp, *Attitudes and Opinions,* 2nd ed. (Englewood Cliffs, NJ: Prentice Hall, 1991), 160.

30. Ibid., ch. 15.

31. David Easton, *A Systems Analysis of Political Life* (New York: Wiley, 1965).

32. U.S. Census Bureau, *America's Families and Living Arrangements, 2015* (Washington, D.C.: Government Printing Office, September 2015).

33. James G. Gimpel, J. Celeste Lay, and Jason E. Schuknecht, *Cultivating Democracy: Civic Environments and Political Socialization in America* (Washington, D.C.: Brookings Institution Press, 2003), 147.

34. Lee Anderson, *The Civics Report Card* (Princeton, NJ: Educational Testing Service, 1990).

35. U.S. Census Bureau, *Educational Attainment in the United States, 2003* (Washington, D.C.: Government Printing Office, 2003).

36. Ernest Boyer and Mary Jean Whitelaw, *The Condition of the Professorate* (New York: Harper and Row, 1989).

37. Gimpel, Lay, and Schuknecht, *Cultivating Democracy,* 63.

38. Ibid.

39. Ibid., 92.

40. See, for instance, Penny Edgell Becker and Pawan H. Dhingra, "Religious Involvement and Volunteering: Implications for Civil Society," *Sociology of Religion* 62 (2001): 315–335; Corwin Smidt, "Religion and Civic Engagement: A Comparative Analysis," *Annals of the American Academy of Political and Social Sciences* 565 (1999): 176–192.

41. Gimpel, Lay, and Schuknecht, *Cultivating Democracy,* 142.

42. Ibid., 143.

43. Kaiser Family Foundation, "Daily Media Use Among Children and Teens up Dramatically from Five Years Ago," accessed on February 20, 2010, http://www.kff .org/entmedia/entmedia012010nr.cfm.

44. Statistic Brain, "Television Watching Statistics," accessed on August 5, 2014, http://www.statisticbrain.com/ television-watching-statistics/; University of Michigan, "Your Child: Development & Behavior Resources," accessed on March 7, 2016, http://www.med.umich .edu/yourchild/topics/tv.htm.

45. See, for instance, Gimpel, Lay, and Schuknecht, *Cultivating Democracy,* 35.

46. "What the Public Knows – In Pictures, Words, Maps and Graphs," April 28, 2015, accessed on March 7, 2016, http://www.people-press.org/2015/04/28/what-the-public-knows-in-pictures-words-maps-and-graphs/2/.

47. Ibid.

48. Robert M. Bond, James H. Fowler, et al., "A 61-Million-Person Experiment in Social Influence and Political Mobilization," *Nature,* September 2012, vol 489, issue 7415, 295-298

49. https://www.fbi.gov/news/testimony/threats-to-the-homeland.

50. Paul Lazarfeld, Bernard Berelson, and Hazel Gaudet, *The People's Choice* (New York: Columbia University Press, 1944).

51. Bureau of Labor Statistics, "Earnings and unemployment rates by educational attainment," February 12, 2016, accessed on March 7, 2016, http://www.bls.gov/emp/ ep_chart_001.htm.

52. Robert S. Erikson and Kent L. Tedin, *American Public Opinion,* 183.

53. William H. Flanigan and Nancy H. Zingale, *Political Behavior of the American Electorate,* 11th ed. (Washington, D.C.: CQ Press, 2006), 132.

54. Pew Research, "Religion & Public Life," November 7, 2012, accessed on August 5, 2014, http://www.pewforum .org/files/2013/05/report-religious-landscape-study-full .pdf; Pew Research, "Religion & Public Life," May 12, 2015, accessed on March 7, 2016, http://www.pewforum .org/religious-landscape-study/.

55. Flanigan and Zingale, *Political Behavior,* 106.

56. James L. Guth et al., "A Distant Thunder? Religious Mobilization in the 2000 Elections," in *Interest Group Politics,* 6th ed., ed. Allen J. Cigler and Burdett A. Loomis (Washington, D.C.: CQ Press, 2002), 161–184.

57. Exit polls, http://edition.cnn.com/election/results/ exit-polls/national/president, accessed on November 11, 2016.

58. Oskamp, *Attitudes and Opinions,* 390.

59. Ibid., 391.

60. "In Depth Issues – Race Relations," Gallup Polls, accessed on March 7, 2016, http://www.gallup.com/poll/1687/ race-relations.aspx.

61. Latinos will surpass whites as the largest racial/ ethnic group in California according to the "Governor's Budget Summary, 2014-15," State of California, http:// www.ebudget.ca.gov/2014-15/pdf/BudgetSummary/ FullBudgetSummary.pdf.

62. Center for American Women and Politics, *The Gender Gap: Attitudes on Public Policy Issues* (New Brunswick, NJ: Eagleton Institute of Politics, Rutgers University, 1997); Susan J. Carroll and Richard F. Fox, eds., *Gender and Elections* (New York: Cambridge University Press, 2006).

63. "Party Identification Trends – 1992–2014," Pew Research Center, accessed on March 7, 2015, http://www.people-press.org/2015/04/07/party-identification-trends-1992-2014/#gender.

64. Reported in Justin Lewis, *Constructing Public Opinion: How Political Elites Do What They Like and Why We Seem to Go Along with It* (New York: Columbia University Press, 2001), 34.

65. Asher, *Polling and the Public,* 23.

66. Benjamin Ginsberg, *The Captive Public: How Mass Opinion Promotes State Power* (New York: Basic Books, 1986).

67. Lewis, *Constructing Public Opinion,* 41.

68. Floyd J. Fowler, Jr., *Survey Research Methods,* 4th ed. (Thousand Oaks, CA: SAGE Publications, 2009), ch. 4; Pew Research Center for the People & the Press, "Assessing the Representativeness of Public Opinion Surveys," May 15, 2013, accessed on August 5, 2014, http://www.people-press.org/2012/05/15/assessing-the-representativeness-of-public-opinion-surveys/.

69. Scott Keeter, "Research Roundup: Latest Findings on Cell Phones and Polling," Pew Research Center, May 22, 2009, accessed on January 2, 2010, http://pewresearch.org/ pubs/848/cell-only-methodology; Stephen J. Blumberg et al., "Wireless Substitution: State-level Estimates From the National Health Interview Survey, January 2007-June 2010," *National Health Statistics Reports,* no 39. (Hyattsville, MD: National Center for Health Statistics. 2011); Jeffrey Sparshott, "More People Say Goodbye to Their Landlines," September 5, 2013, *Wall Street Journal* online, accessed on August 5, 2014, http://online.wsj.com/news/ articles/SB10001424127887323893004579057402031104502.

70. Ibid.

71. See for instance, Drew Desliver and Scott Keeter, "The Challenges of Polling When Fewer People are Available to be Polled," July 21, 2015, accessed on March 7, 2016, http://www.pewresearch.org/fact-tank/2015/07/21/the-challenges-of-polling-when-fewer-people-are-available-to-be-polled/.

72. Ibid., C25.

73. For instance, see Lewis, *Constructing Public Opinion,* 37.

74. James A. Stimson, *Public Opinion in America,* 2nd ed. (Boulder, CO: Westview Press, 1999), 122.

75. Bob Berwyn, "Libertarian students use Valentine's Day to expose unhealthy lovefest between big business and political institutions," February 14, 2012, accessed on May 27, 2016, http://summitcountyvoice.com/2012/02/14/libertarian-students-use-valentines-day-to-expose-unhealthy-lovefest-between-big-business-and-political-institutions/.

CHAPTER 11

1. "Daily Media Use Among Children and Teens up Dramatically from Five Years Ago," Kaiser Family Foundation, January 20, 2010, accessed on May 17, 2012, http://www .kff.org/entmedia/entmedia012010nr.cfm.

2. Andrea Caumont, "12 Trends Shaping Digital News," The Pew Research Center for the People and the Press, October 16, 2013. http://www.pewresearch.org/fact-tank/2013/10/16/12-trends-shaping-digital-news/.

3. Michael Barthel, "America's News Anchors Are Less Recognizable Now, but Network News is Still Alive," Pew Research Center, February 12, 2015, http://www.pewresearch.org/fact-tank/2015/02/12/americas-news-anchors-are-less-recognizable-now-but-network-news-is-still-alive/.

4. Alfred McClung Lee, *The Daily Newspaper in America* (New York: Macmillian, 1937), 21.

5. Quoted in Philip Davidson, *Propaganda and the American Revolution, 1763–1783* (Chapel Hill, NC: University of North Carolina Press, 1941), 285.

6. *Messages and Papers of the Presidents 1789–1908,* vol. 1 (Washington, D.C.: Bureau of National Literature and Art, 1909), 132.

7. Lee, *Daily Newspaper in America,* 716–717.

8. See Jan E. Leighley, *Mass Media and Politics: A Social Science Perspective* (Boston: Houghton Mifflin, 2004), ch. 1.

9. Quoted in W.W. Swanberg, *Citizen Hurst* (New York: Scribner, 1961), 90.

10. Lee, *Daily Newspaper in America,* 215–216.

11. Doris A. Graber, *Mass Media and American Politics,* 8th ed. (Washington, D.C.: CQ Press, 2006), 38.

12. Edwin Emery and Michael Emery, *The Press and America* (Englewood Cliffs, NJ: Prentice Hall, 1984), 372–379.

13. Frank Luther Mott, *American Journalism, A History: 1690–1960* (New York: Macmillian, 1962), 679.

14. "Television Watching Statistics," Statistic Brain, http://www.statisticbrain.com/television-watching-statistics/.

15. See, for instance, Christopher P. Latimer, "The Digital Divide: Understanding and Addressing," accessed on May 15, 2008, http://www.nysfirm.org/documents/html/whitepapers/nysfirm_digital_divide.htm.

16. Andrew Perrin and Maeve Duggan, "Americans' Internet Access: 2000-2015," June 26, 2015, Pew Research Center: Internet, Science and Tech, accessed on March 29, 2016, http://www.pewinternet.org/2015/06/26/americans-internet-access-2000-2015/.

17. Aaron Smith and Dana Page, "U.S. Smartphone Use in 2015," Pew Research Center, April 1, 2015. accessed on March 29, 2016, http://www.pewinternet.org/files/2015/03/PI_Smartphones_0401151.pdf.

18. Ibid.

19. See, for instance, Kathy Koch, "The Digital Divide," in *The CQ Researcher Online* 10.3 (2000), published January 28, 2000, document ID: cqresrre2000012800; Aaron Smith, Kay Lehman Schlozman, Sidney Verba, and Henry Brady, "The Internet and Civic Engagement," Pew Internet and American Life Project, September 1, 2009, accessed on April 5, 2010, http://www.pewinternet.org/Reports/2009/15?The-Internet-and-Civic-Engagement.aspx.

20. Maeve Duggan and Aaron Smith, "Social Media Update 2013," accessed on August 7, 2014, http://www.pewinternet.org/2013/12/30/social-media-update-2013/.

21. Amy Mitchell and Tom Rosenstiel, "The State of the News Media 2012: An Annual Report of American Journalism," Pew Research Center's Project for Excellence in Journalism, accessed on May 12, 2012, http://stateofthemedia.org/2012/overview-4/major-trends/.

22. Amy Mitchell and Dana Page, "The Evolving Role of News on Twitter and Facebook," p. 7, Pew Research Center, July 14, 2015, http://www.journalism.org/files/2015/07/Twitter-and-News-Survey-Report-FINAL2.pdf.

23. Pew Research Center for the People and the Press, "In Changing News Landscape, Even Television Is Vulnerable," September 27, 2012.

24. Reported in Catherine O'Donnell, "New study quantifies use of social media in Arab Spring," UW News and Information, September 12, 2011, accessed on May 16, 2012, http://www.washington.edu/news/articles/new-study-quantifies-use-of-social-media-in-arab-spring.

25. Ibid.

26. S. Robert Lichter, Linda S. Lichter, and Daniel Amundson, "Government Goes Down the Tube: Images of Government in TV Entertainment, 1955–1998," *The International Journal of Press/Politics* 5 (2000): 96–103.

27. S. Robert Lichter, Stephen J. Farnsworth, and Deanne Canieso, "Late Night Tells 3 Times as Many Jokes About 2016 Republicans as Democrats," March 8, 2016, https://www.washingtonpost.com/news/the-fix/wp/2016/03/08/late-night-tells-3-times-as-many-jokes-about-2016-republicans-as-democrats/.

28. Ibid.

29. Harold D. Lasswell, "The Structure and Function of Communication in Society," in *Mass Communications,* ed. Wilbur Schramm (Urbana, IL: University of Illinois Press, 1969), 103.

30. For a good analysis of the issue of race and media coverage, see Robert M. Entman and Andrew Rojecki, *The Black Image in the White Mind: Media and Race in America* (Chicago: University of Chicago Press, 2001).

31. Reported in Jerry L. Yeric, *Mass Media and the Politics of Change* (Itasca, IL: Peacock Publishers, 2001), ch. 6.

32. Renee Lewis, "Ferguson Reports Raise Questions on Media Criminalization of Blacks," *Aljazeera America,* August 14, 2014, http://america.aljazeera.com/articles/2014/8/14/ferguson-media-iftheygunnedmedown.html.

33. Adam Carros and Zack Kucharski, "Gazette, KCRG-TV9 Photos Explained," *The Gazette,* April 3, 2015, accessed on April 5, 2016, http://www.thegazette.com/subject/opinion/guest-columnists/gazette-kcrg-tv9-photos-explained-20150403.

34. "Bottom-Line Pressure Now Hurting Coverage, Say Journalists," Pew Research Center for the People and the Press, accessed on May 23, 2004, http://people-press.org/reports/display.php3?PageID=825.

35. "Journalist Survey," Pew Research Center: Journalism & Media Staff, March 13, 2004, accessed on October 14, 2016, http://www.journalism.org/2004/03/13/journalist-survey/.

36. See Yeric, *Mass Media and the Politics of Change;* and Graber, *Mass Media and American Politics.*

37. Graber, *Mass Media and American Politics,* 198.

38. Jesse Holcomb, "5 Facts about Fox News," Pew Research Center, January 14, 2014, accessed on April 5, 2016, http://www.pewresearch.org/fact-tank/2014/01/14/five-facts-about-fox-news/.

39. Amy Mitchell, Jeffrey Gottfried, Jocelyn Kiley and Katerina Eva Matsa, "Political Polarization & Media Habits," Pew Research Center, October 21, 2014, accessed on April 1, 2016, http://www.journalism.org/2014/10/21/political-polarization-media-habits/.

40. Monica Anderson, "As the NY Times' first black executive editor, Dean Baquet is in a distinct minority," Pew Research Center, May 28, 2014, http://www.pewresearch

.org/fact-tank/2014/05/28/as-the-new-york-times-first-black-executive-editor-dean-baquet-is-in-a-distinct-minority/; see also, ASNE Newsroom Census, http://asne.org/content.asp?admin=Y&contentid=121.

41. University of Michigan, Health System. Your Child: Development & Behavior Resources, accessed on October 14, 2016, http://www.med.umich.edu/yourchild/topics/tv.htm.

42. Daniel J. Boorstin, The Image: A Guide to Pseudo-Events in America (New York: Vintage, 1961).

43. Nate Silver, "Trump Boom or Trump Bubble?" FiveThirtyEight, December 15, 2015, accesssed on April 3, 2016, http://fivethirtyeight.com/features/trump-boom-or-trump-bubble/.

44. Nicholas Confessore and Karen Yourish, "Measuring Donald Trump's Mammoth Advantage in Free Media," *New York Times*, March 15, 2016, accessed on April 1, 2016, http://www.nytimes.com/2016/03/16/upshot/measuring-donald-trumps-mammoth-advantage-in-free-media.html.

45. Ibid.

46. Ibid., 271.

47. "Presidential News Conferences: Coolidge-Obama," The American Presidency Project at UC Santa Barbara, as of April 20, 2012, accessed on May 9, 2012, http://www.presidency.ucsb.edu/data/newsconferences.php.

48. Graber, *Mass Media and American Politics*, 185; Gerhard Peters, "Presidential News Conferences: Coolidge-Obama," in *The American Presidency Project*, ed. John T. Woolley and Gerhard Peters (Santa Barbara, CA: University of California), accessed on April 5, 2016, http://www.presidency.ucsb.edu/data/newsconferences.php. The Obama statistics are through February 2016.

49. Graber, Mass Media and American Politics, chapter 7.

50. See, for instance, Bennett, *News: The Politics of Illusion*.

51. Ibid.

52. For a good discussion of the impact the Thomas hearings had in mobilizing women voters and candidates, see Linda Witt, Karen M. Paget, and Glenna Matthews, Running as a Woman: Gender and Power in American Politics (New York: Free Press, 1994).

53. See for Instance, Graber, Mass Media and American Politics, 311; see also Vincent James Strickler and Richard Davis, "The Supreme Court and the Press," in Media, Power and Politics, e. Mark J. Roxell (Landham, MD: Rowman and Littlefield, 2003).

54. "Winning the Media Campaign: How the Press Reported the 2008 General Election," The Pew Research Center's Project for Excellence in Journalism, October 22, 2008, accessed on April 30, 2012, http://www.journalism.org/analysis_report/winning_media_campaign.

55. Ibid.

56. David Nakamura and Greg Jaffe, "Frustrated by 2016 Tone, Obama Warns of 'Poisonous Political Climate'," *Washington Post*, February 10, 2016. accessed on March 30, 2016, https://www.washingtonpost.com/news/post-politics/wp/2016/02/10/frustrated-by-2016-tone-obama-returns-to-political-roots-to-rekindle-hope-of-2008/.

57. S. Robert Lichter and Richard E. Noyes, "There They Go Again: Media Coverage of Campaign '96," in *Political Parties, Campaigns, and Elections*, ed. Robert E. DeClerico (Upper Saddle River, NJ: Prentice Hall, 2000), 98.

58. Daniel C. Hallin, "Sound Bit News: Television Coverage of Elections, 1968–1988," *Journalism of Communication* 42 (1992): 15.

59. Ana Vecina Suarez, Hispanic Media USA: A Narrative Guide to Print and Electronic Media in the United States (Washington, D.C.: Media Institute, 1987).

60. Claudia Pardo and Charles Dreas, "Three Things You Thought You Knew About U.S. Hispanic's Engagement With Media… And Why You May Have Been Wrong," Nielsen Company, 2011, accessed on April 5, 2016, http://www.nielsen.com/content/dam/corporate/us/en/newswire/uploads/2011/04/Nielsen-Hispanic-Media-US.pdf.

61. Katernia Eva Matsa, "Hispanic Media: Fact Sheet," Pew Research Center, April 29, 2015, accessed on April 5, 2016, http://www.journalism.org/2015/04/29/hispanic-media-fact-sheet/.

62. J.D. Lasica, "What is Participatory Journalism?" Online Journalism Review, August 7, 2003, assessed on October 14, 2016, http://www.ojr.org/ojr/workplace/1060217106.php.

63. Ben H. Bagdikian, The Media Monopoly, 5th ed. (Boston: Beacon Press), p. x.

64. "Who Owns the News Media," The State of the News Media, 2011, Pew Research Center's Project for Excellence in Journalism, accessed on May 16, 2012, http://stateofthemedia.org/media-ownership/.

65. For a good discussion of deregulation, see Leighley, *Mass Media and Politics*, ch. 2.

66. Katerina Eva Matsa, "The Acquisition Binge in Local TV," Pew Research Center, May 12, 2014, accessed on April 7, 2016, http://www.pewresearch.org/fact-tank/2014/05/12/the-acquisition-binge-in-local-tv/.

67. For a good discussion of deregulation, see Leighley, *Mass Media and Politics*, chapter 2.

68. Graber, *Mass Media and American Politics*, p. 49.

69. Ibid., 19-21.

70. Katerina Eva Matsa, "5 Facts About the State of Local TV Newsrooms," Pew Research Center, July 23, 2014, accessed on April 8, 2016, http://www.pewresearch.org/fact-tank/2014/07/23/5-facts-about-the-state-of-local-tv-newsrooms/.

71. "Bottom-Line Pressures Now Hurting Coverage, Say Journalists," The Pew for the People and the Press, May 23, 2004, accessed on May 17, 2012, http://people-press.org/report/214/.

72. Leighley, *Mass Media and Politics*, 80.

73. Farhi, Paul, "Limbaugh Sees Heat Over Comments Turn Down to a Simmer," *Washington Post*, March 28, 2012, accessed on April 30, 2012, http://www.washingtonpost.com/lifestyle/style/limbaugh-sees-heat-over-comments-turn-down-to-a-simmer/2012/03/28/gIQAspEKhS_print.html.

CHAPTER 12

1. Alexis de Tocqueville, *Democracy in America*, vol. 1, ed. Richard Heffner (New York: New American Library, 1956; originally published 1835), 220.

2. His actual charge was to examine our penal system, but his true interest was to examine our democracy so that he could take lessons back to France.

3. For a good discussion of the importance of organized groups in democratic theory, see Jane Mansbridge, "A Deliberative Theory of Interest Representation," in

The Politics of Interests: Interest Groups Transformed, ed. Mark P. Petracca (Boulder, CO: Westview Press, 1992).

4. League of United Latin American Citizens, accessed on June 1, 2008, http://www.lulac.org.

5. Jeffrey M. Berry, *Lobbying for the People: The Political Behavior of Public Interest Groups* (Princeton, NJ: Princeton University Press, 1977), 7.

6. Frank R. Baumgartner and Beth L. Leech, *Basic Interests: The Importance of Groups in Politics and in Political Science* (Princeton, NJ: Princeton University Press, 1998), 103.

7. Robert Salisbury, "An Exchange Theory of Interest Groups," *Midwest Journal of Political Science* 13 (February 1969): 1–32.

8. Mancur Olson, *The Logic of Collective Action* (Cambridge, MA: Harvard University Press, 1971).

9. James Q. Wilson, *Political Organizations* (New York: Basic Books, 1974), 34.

10. Adapted from National Rifle Association, http://www.nra.org.

11. Anthony Nownes, *Pressure and Power: Organized Interests in American Politics* (Boston: Houghton Mifflin, 2001), 50.

12. Ibid., 51.

13. T.W. Farnam, "Study Shows Revolving Door of Employment Between Congress, Lobbying Firms," *Washington Post*, September 12, 2011, accessed on March 10, 2012, http://www.washingtonpost.com/politics/study-shows-revolving-door-of-employment-between-congress-lobbying-firms/2011/09/12/gIQAxPYROK_story.html; Mark Leibovich, *This Town: Two Parties and a Funeral — Plus Plenty of Valet Parking! — in America's Gilded Capital* (New York: NY: Blue Rider Press, 2013), 330; see also, Janine Wedel, *Unaccountable: How Anti-Corruption Watchdogs and Lobbyists Sabotaged America's Finance, Freedom and Security* (New York: Pegasus Books, 2014).

14. David B. Truman, *The Governmental Process: Political Interests and Public Opinion,* 2nd ed. (New York: Knopf, 1971).

15. Ken Kollman, *Outside Lobbying: Public Opinion and Interest Group Strategies* (Princeton, NJ: Princeton University Press, 1998), 58.

16. Matt Grossmann, *Artists of the Possible: Governing Networks and American Policy Change Since 1945* (New York: NY, Oxford University Press, 2014).

17. Kenneth M. Goldstein, *Interest Groups, Lobbying, and Participation in America* (Cambridge, England: Cambridge University Press, 1999), 111, 125; see also Nownes, *Pressure and Power.*

18. Goldstein, *Interests Groups,* p. 3.

19. Kollman, *Outside Lobbying.*

20. Cliff Landesman, "Nonprofits and the World Wide Web," Idealist.org, accessed on March 22, 2010, http://www.idealist.org/if/i/en/av/FAQText/319-38.

21. Christopher J. Bosso and Michael Thomas Collins, "Just Another Tool? How Environmental Groups Use the Internet," in Allan Cigler and Burdett Loomis, *Interest Group Politics,* 6th ed. (Washington: CQ Press, 2002), 101.

22. The Supreme Court overturned the precedents established in 1990, *Austin* v. *Michigan Chamber of Commerce,* and in 2003, *McConnell* v. *Federal Election Commission.*

23. "Super PACs," Center for Responsive Politics, accessed on October 15, 2016, https://www.opensecrets.org/outsidespending/summ.php?cycle=2012&chrt=V&disp=O&type=S; "Political Nonprofits (Dark Monday)," Center for Responsive Politics, accessed on October 15, 2016, https://www.opensecrets.org/outsidespending/nonprof_summ.php.

24. Darrell W. West and Burdett A. Loomis, *The Sound of Money* (New York: Norton, 1998).

25. 2012. Outside Spending, by Race, accessed on July 31, 2014, https://www.opensecrets.org/outsidespending/summ.php?cycle=2012&disp=R&pty=A&type=G.

26. "Super PACs," Center for the Responsive Politics, accessed on May 1, 2016, https://www.opensecrets.org/pacs/superpacs.php?cycle=2016.

27. Truman, *Governmental Process.*

28. Sidney Verba, Kay Lehman Schlozman, and Henry E. Brady, *Voice of Equality: Civic Volunteerism in American Politics* (Cambridge, MA: Harvard University Press, 1995), 150–154.

29. Allan J. Cigler and Mark Joslyn, "Group Involvement and Social Capital Development," in *Interest Group Politics,* 6th ed., ed. Allan J. Cigler and Burdett A. Loomis (Washington, D.C.: CQ Press, 2002), ch. 2.

30. For a good timeline of the international use of online activism see http://mashable.com/2011/08/15/online-activism/#gallery/history-of-internet-activism/50bde23f97b2f87f130001fb; for more information about online activism see the University of Washington's Digital Activism Research Project, http://digital-activism.org/ and "Digital and Online Activism, Reset: Smart Approaches to Sustainability," https://en.reset.org/knowledge/digital-and-online-activism.

31. See for example, Micah White, "Clicktivism is Ruining Leftist Activism," *Guardian,* August 12, 2010, accessed on April 30, 2016, http://www.theguardian.com/commentisfree/2010/aug/12/clicktivism-ruining-leftist-activism.

32. Allan Cigler and Mark R. Joslyn, "The Extensiveness of Group Membership and Social Capital: The Impact on Political Tolerance Attitudes," *Political Research Quarterly,* 55 (2002), p. 7–25.

33. For instance, see Matthew J. Burbank, Ronald J. Hrebenar, and Robert C. Benedict, *Parties, Interest Groups, and Political Campaigns* (Boulder, CO: Paradigm Publishers, 2008).

34. Verba, Schlozman, and Brady, *Voice of Equality,* 81–82.

CHAPTER 13

1. Nicholas Confessor and Jess Bidgood, "Little to Show for Cash Flood by Big Donors," *New York Times,* November 7, 2012.

2. Alan P. Grimes, *Democracy and the Amendments to the Constitution* (Lexington, MA: Lexington Books, 1978), 44–45.

3. Ibid., 131, 142–147.

4. Alexsander Keyssar, *The Right to Vote: The Contested History of Democracy in the United States* (New York: Basic Books, 2000).

5. Ibid., 111.

6. Ibid., 264–265.

7. L. Sandy Maisel, *Parties and Elections in America: The Electoral Process,* 3rd ed. (Lanham, MD: Rowman and Littlefield, 1999), 97.

8. Frances Fox Piven and Richard A. Cloward, *Why Americans Still Don't Vote: And Why Politicians Want It That Way* (Boston, Beacon Press, 2000).

9. Yvonne Wenger, "Debate Rages Over South Carolina's Voter ID Law," Postandcourier.com, May 19, 2011,

http://www.postandcourier.com/news/2011/may/19/debate-rages-over-south-carolinas-voter-id-law/.

10. Kevin Dolak, "State Voter ID Laws Draw National Scrutiny," ABCNEWS.Com, September 8, 2011.

11. These data, and much else, can be found in the American National Election Study Guide to Public Opinion and Electoral Behavior, http://www.electionstudies.org/.

12. Robert Putnam, *Bowling Alone: The Collapse and Revival of American Community* (New York: Simon and Schuster, 2000), 189.

13. John P. Frendreis, James L. Gibson, and Laura L. Vertz, "Electoral Relevance of Local Party Organizations," *American Political Science Review* 84 (1990): 225–235; Stephen Brooks, Rick Farmer, and Kyriakos Pagonis, "The Effects of Grassroots Campaigning on Political Participation" (paper presented at the annual meeting of the Southern Political Science Association, Atlanta, GA, November 8–10, 2001).

14. For details of these studies, see Richard Lau, Lee Sigelman, Caroline Heldman, and Paul Babbit, "The Effects of Negative Political Advertising: A Meta-Analytic Assessment," *American Political Science Review* 93 (1999): 851–875.

15. Stephen Ansolabehere and Shanto Lyengar, *Going Negative: How Political Advertisements Shrink and Polarize the Electorate* (New York: Free Press, 1995).

16. Kelly D. Patterson and Daniel M. Shea, "Local Political Context and Negative Campaigns: A Test of Negative Effects Across State Party Systems," *Journal of Political Marketing* 3 (2004): 1–20.

17. Malcolm Gladwell, "Small Change: Why the Revolution Will Not Be Tweeted," *New Yorker* (October 4, 2010).

18. Ibid.

19. Shelley Boulianne, "Does Internet Use Affect Engagement? A Meta-Analysis of Research." *Political Communications*, vol. 26, issue 2 (2014).

20. Larry J. Sabato, *Feeding Frenzy: How Attack Journalism Has Transformed American Politics* (New York: Free Press, 1993).

21. William H. Flanigan and Nancy H. Zingal, *Political Behavior and the American Electorate*, (Washington, D.C.: CQ Press, 1998), 40.

22. Rock the Vote, 2008, "Who Are Young Voters?" Rock the Vote Web site, http://www.rockthevote.org/about/about-young-voters/who-are-young-voters/.

23. Colin Campbell and Bert A. Rockman, "Introduction," in *The Clinton Presidency: First Appraisals*, ed. Colin Campbell and Bert A. Rockman (Chatham, NJ: Chatham House, 1996), 14.

24. John K. White and Daniel M. Shea, *New Party Politics: From Jefferson and Hamilton to the Information Age* (New York: Bedford St. Martin's, 2004), 19.

25. See, for example, John P. Frendreis, James L. Gibson, and Laura L. Vertz, "Electoral Relevance of Local Party Organizations," *American Political Science Review* 84 (1990): 225–235.

26. White and Shea, *New Party Politics,* 20.

27. William Nisbet Chambers, *Political Parties in a New Nation: The American Experience, 1776–1809* (New York: Oxford University Press, 1963).

28. E. E. Schattschneider, *Party Government* (New York: Rinehart, 1942), 1.

29. "The Report of the National Symposium on Presidential Selection," The Center for Governmental Studies at the University of Virginia (2001), http://www.centerforpolitics.org/downloads/rnsps.pdf.

30. As stated on National Public Radio, *Morning Edition,* October 19, 2004, http://www.npr.org/templates/story/story.php?storyId=4115994.

31. Associate Press, "Maryland Sidesteps Electoral College," MSNBC, April 11, 2007, accessed on September 19, 2007, http://www.msnbc.msn.com/id/18053715/.

32. George Will, "From Schwarzenegger, a Veto for Voters' Good," *Washington Post,* October 12, 2006, A27.

33. John K. White and Daniel M. Shea, *New Party Politics: From Jefferson and Hamilton to the Information Age* (New York: Bedford St. Martin's, 2000), 210.

34. Alan Hunt, "How Record Spending will Affect the 2016 Election," *BloombergView* April 26, 2016, https://www.bloomberg.com/view/articles/2015-04-26/how-record-spending-will-affect-2016-election.

35. Howard L. Reiter, *Parties and Elections in Corporate America* (New York: St. Martin's Press, 1987), 171.

36. White and Shea, *New Party Politics,* 220.

37. "Tracking the Payback," Center for Responsive Politics, http://www.opensecrets.org/payback/index.asp, April 23, 2003.

38. David Mayhew, *Congress: The Electoral Connection* (New Haven, CT: Yale University Press, 1974).

39. Roper Center for Public Opinion Research, 1994, cited in Center for Responsive Politics, *The Myths About Money in Politics* (Washington, D.C.: Center for Responsive Politics, 1995), 19.

40. "A Campaign Finance Triumph" [editorial], *New York Times,* December 11, 2003, 42A.

41. Paul Sherman, "Citizens United Decision Means More Free Speech," *National Review* Online, January 21, 2010, http://bench.nationalreview.com/post/?q=MGVlYzczZjZlMTM1YWVlYjJhMzA3NzJjMTVhYmUwZDg=.

42. "The Court's Blow to Democracy" [editorial], *New York Times,* January 21, 2010A30.

43. Center for Responsive Politics, "Total Cost of 2016 Election Could Reach $6.6 Billion," October 25, 2016, https://www.opensecrets.org/news/2016/10/total-cost-of-2016-election-could-reach-6-6-billion-crp-predicts/.

44. Kenneth Vogel, "Campaign Finance Reform: R.I.P?" Politico.com, October 13, 2010, http://www.politico.com/news/stories/1010/43515.html.

45. The Pew Research Center funds the Pew Internet & American Life Project. The Project "produces reports that explore the impact of the Internet on families, communities, work and home, daily life, education, health care, and civic and political life." Reports can be found at http://www.pewinternet.org.

46. Technorati (http://www.technorati.com) is a search engine similar to Google; however, it is exclusively devoted to blogs. They produce a regular industry report (State of the Blogosphere) based on their total indexed blogs.

47. Burden, Barry C., David T. Canon, Kenneth R. Mayer, Donald P. Moynihan "The Effects and Costs of Early Voting, Election Day Registration, and Same Day Registration in the 2008 Elections," (paper presented to the Pew Charitable Trusts, December 21, 2009), http://www.pewcenteronthestates.org/uploadedFiles/wwwpewcenteronthestatesorg/Initiatives/MVW/UWisconsin.pdf.

CHAPTER 14

1. For a well-known example, see Charles E. Lindblom and Edward J. Woodhouse, *The Policy-Making Process,* 3rd ed. (Englewood Cliffs, NJ: Prentice Hall, 1993).

2. Deborah Stone, *Policy Paradox: The Art of Political Decision Making* (New York: Norton, 1997), 11.

3. Theda Skocpol, *Boomerang: Health Care Reform and the Turn Against Government* (New York: Norton, 1997).

4. Matt Spetalnick, "Obama Launches New Push for Healthcare Overhaul," *Washington Post*, January 9, 2010, A1.

5. National Aeronautic and Space Administration, *World Book at NASA*, accessed on January 20, 2010, http://www.nasa.gov/worldbook/global_warming_worldbook.html.

6. Intergovernmental Panel on Climate Change, *Climate Change 2007 Synthesis Report* (Geneva: IPCC, 2007).

7. Keith Johnson, "Climate Emails Stoke Debate," *Wall Street Journal*, November 23, 2009, A3.

8. Roger W. Cobb and Charles D. Elder, *Participation in American Politics: The Dynamics of Agenda Building* (Baltimore: Johns Hopkins University Press, 1983), 82–93.

9. For a fascinating discussion of how power is exercised by controlling the agenda, see Peter Bachrach and Morton S. Baratz, "Two Faces of Power," *American Political Science Review* 56 (1962): 947–952.

10. Anthony Downs, "Up and Down with Ecology: The 'Issue-Attention Cycle,'" *Public Interest* (Summer 1972): 38–50.

11. Charles Duhigg, "Millions in U.S. Drink Dirty Water, Records Show," *New York Times*, December 7, 2009, A1.

12. Theodore J. Lowi, "American Business, Public Policy Case Studies, and Political Theory," *World Politics* 16 (1965): 677–715.

13. Murray Edelman, *The Symbolic Uses of Politics* (Urbana, IL: University of Illinois Press, 1967), ch. 2.

14. "US Trade Deficit Grows in 2015 as Exports Weaken," L'Agence France-Presse (AFP), February 5, 2016, https://www.yahoo.com/news/us-trade-deficit-grows-2015-exports-weaken-135439974.html?ref=gs.

15. Stephen Dinan, "Federal Debt Hits $19 Trillion; New Record Set," *Washington Times*, February 1, 2016, http://www.washingtontimes.com/news/2016/feb/1/federal-debt-hits-19-trillion-new-record-set/.

16. "U.S. Fiscal Year Budget Deficit Narrows to $439 Billion," Reuters, October 15, 2015, http://www.reuters.com/article/us-usa-budget-idUSKCN0S92K920151015.

17. "The Budget and Economic Outlook: 2015 to 2025," Congressional Budget Office, January 26, 2015, https://www.cbo.gov/publication/49892.

18. "Table 2.1 – Receipts By Source: 1934-2021," https://www.whitehouse.gov/omb/budget/Historicals.

19. "Historical Federal Income Tax Rates for a Family of Four," Tax Policy Center, July 1, 2015, http://www.taxpolicycenter.org/statistics/historical-federal-income-tax-rates-family-four.

20. Alice Gomstyn, "Obama Announces $33B Hiring Tax Credit," ABC News Business Unit, January 29, 2010, http://abcnews.go.com/Business/Obama/obama-tax-credit-33-billion-hiring-jobs/story?id=9697334.

21. "White House Report – The Buffett Rule: A Basic Principle of Tax Fairness", http://www.whitehouse.gov/economy/buffett-rule.

22. "What Obama Wants the Government to Spend Money on in His Final Presidential Budget," *Washington Post*, February 8, 2016, https://www.washingtonpost.com/graphics/politics/presidential-budget-2017/.

23. Robert Schroeder, "CBO Cuts 2016 Budget Deficit Estimate by $10 Billion," MarketWatch, March 24, 1016, http://www.marketwatch.com/story/cbo-cuts-2016-budget-deficit-estimate-by-10-billion-2016-03-24-14103428.

24. Drew Desilver, "5 Facts About Social Security," Pew Research Center, August 18, 2015, http://www.pewresearch.org/fact-tank/2015/08/18/5-facts-about-social-security/.

25. "Policy Basics: Where Do Our Federal Tax Dollars Go?" http://www.cbpp.org/research/federal-budget/policy-basics-where-do-our-federal-tax-dollars-go.

26. "Department of Defense," Office of Management and Budget, http://www.whitehouse.gov/omb/rewrite/budget/fy2008/defense.html.

27. Glenn Kessler, "Barack Obama, The Food Stamp President," *Washington Post*, December 8, 2011, http://www.washingtonpost.com/blogs/fact-checker/post/barack-obama-the-food-stamp-president/2011/12/07/gIQAzTdQdO_blog.html.

28. Jackie Calmes, "Obama's Last Budget, and Last Budget Battle With Congress," *New York Times*, February 9, 2016, http://www.nytimes.com/2016/02/10/us/politics/obama-budget-cybersecurity-congress.html?_r=0.

29. "Department Fact Sheets:The Federal Budget 2016," Office of Management and Budget, https://www.whitehouse.gov/omb/budget_factsheets_departments/.

30. "Thousands Quit AARP over Health Reform." CBSNews, August 17, 2009, http://www.cbsnews.com/stories/2009/08/17/eveningnews/main5247916.shtml.

31. Jennifer Liberto, "Bernanke Lays Out Plan for Tighter Money," *CNN Money*, http://money.cnn.com/2010/02/10/news/economy/fed_unwinding/.

32. Scott Lanman and Alison Vekshin. "Bernanke Meets Reid as Senate Prepares for Confirmation Vote," Businessweek, January 21, 2010, http://www.businessweek.com/new/2010-01-21/bernanke-meets-reid-as-Senate-prepares-for-confirmation-vote.html.

33. "Bernanke: Don't Tamper with the Fed," *CNN Money*, November 28, 2009, http://money.cnn.com/2009/11/28/news/economy/bernanke_oped/index.htm?postversion=2009112810.

34. "Average Estimated Undergraduate Budgets," http://trends.collegeboard.org/college-pricing/figures-tables/average-estimated-undergraduate-budgets-2015-16.

35. "Public Research Universities: Changes In State Funding," https://www.amacad.org/multimedia/pdfs/publications/researchpapersmonographs/PublicResearchUniv_Changes-InStateFunding.pdf.

36. Libby A. Nelson, "Tough Budget for Loans and Pell," *Inside Higher Ed*, March 21, 2012, http://www.insidehighered.com/news/2012/03/21/higher-education-proposals-2013-republican-budget.

CHAPTER 15

1. Charles Krauthammer, "The Unipolar Moment Revisited," *National Interest* (Winter 2002–2003): 5–18; Max Boot, *The Savage Wars of Peace* (New York: Basic Books, 2002).

2. G. John Ikenberry, *After Victory: Institutions, Strategic Restraint, and the Rebuilding of Order After Major Wars* (Princeton, NJ: Princeton University Press, 2001).

3. Robert Tucker and David Hendrickson, "The Sources of American Legitimacy," *Foreign Affairs* 83 (2004): 18–32;

Henry Nau, "No Enemies on the Right," *National Interest* (Winter 2004–2005): 19–28.

4. Gary Dempsey, with Roger Fontaine, *Fool's Errands: America's Recent Encounters with Nation Building* (Washington, D.C.: Cato Press, 2001).

5. Iraqi Body Count, http://www.iraqbodycount.org/.

6. Susannah George, "Iraqi Protestors Pour into Green Zone, Storm Parliament," ABCNews, April 30, 2016, http://bigstory.ap.org/article/3e2c0f86273b405a885a0b19a2cfd8e3/anti-government-protesters-breach-baghdads-green-zone.

7. Glenn Hastedt, ed., *One World, Many Voices* (Englewood Cliffs, NJ: Prentice Hall, 1995), 240–250, 288–300.

8. "Obama's Envoy for Climate Change Casts Doubt on Kyoto Protocol," *Guardian*, http://www.guardian.co.uk/environment/2011/sep/19/us-envoy-climate-change-emissions.

9. "Foreign Interests Spend $87 Million Lobbying in U.S," All Business, http://www.allbusiness.com/government/government-bodies-offices-us-federal-government/13708212-1.html.

10. "U.S. Foreign Lobbying, Terrorism Influencing Post 9/11 U.S. Military Aid and Human Rights," The Center for Public Integrity, http://projects.publicintegrity.org/NewsRelease.aspx?id=101.

11. Ibid.

12. "American Israel Public Affairs Committee (AIPAC)," *New York Times*, http://topics.nytimes.com/top/reference/timestopics/organizations/a/american_israel_public_affairs_committee_aipac/index.html.

13. "Tibet Lobby Day Setting Records in U.S. Capitol," International Campaign for Tibet, http://www.savetibet.org/media-center/ict-press-releases/tibet-lobby-day-setting-records-us-capitol.

14. Christina Wilkie, "Ed Rendell, Investigated In Mujahideen-e Khalq Speaker Fees, Backs 'Terrorist' Group." *Huffington Post*, March 12, 2012, http://www.huffingtonpost.com/2012/03/12/ed-rendell-investigated-mujahideen-e-khalq_n_1340566.html.

15. Dan Charles, "Farm Subsidies Persist and Grow, Despite Talk of Reform," NPR, February 1, 2016, http://www.npr.org/sections/thesalt/2016/02/01/465132866/farm-subsidies-persist-and-grow-despite-talk-of-reform.

16. Peter Trubowitz, *Defining the National Interest* (Chicago: University of Chicago Press, 1998).

17. Miroslav Nincic, "Domestic Costs, the U.S. Public and the Isolationist Calculus," *International Studies Quarterly* 41 (1997): 593–610; Bruce Jentleson, "The Pretty Prudent Public: Post-Vietnam American Opinion on the Use of Force," *International Studies Quarterly* 36 (1990): 49–74.

18. Jim Abrams, "Patriot Act Extension Signed by Obama." *Huffington Post*, May 27, 2011, http://www.huffingtonpost.com/2011/05/27/patriot-act-extension-signed-obama-autopen_n_867851.html.

19. For a more extensive discussion, see Glenn Hastedt, *American Foreign Policy: Past, Present, Future*, 6th ed. (Upper Saddle River, NJ: Prentice Hall, 2006).

20. Thomas Graham, "Public Opinion and U.S. Foreign Policy," in *The New Politics of American Foreign Policy*, ed. David Deese (New York: St. Martin's Press, 1994), 190–215.

21. William Quandt, "The Electoral Cycle and the Conduct of American Foreign Policy," *Political Science Quarterly* 101 (1986): 825–837.

22. Scott Shane and Mark Landler, "Obama Clears way for Guantanamo Trials," *New York Times*, March 7, 2011, http://www.nytimes.com/2011/03/08/world/americas/08guantanamo.html.

23. David Cohen, Chris Dolan, and Jerel Rosati, "A Place at the Table," *Congress and the Presidency* 29 (2002): 119–149.

24. Paul Kengor, "The Vice President, the Secretary of State, and Foreign Policy," *Political Science Quarterly* 115 (2000): 175–190.

25. Amy Zegart, *Flawed by Design: The Evolution of the CIA, JCS, and NSC* (Stanford, CA: Stanford University Press, 2000).

26. Tom Mahnken. "Gates Defense Cuts: A Glass Half-Full, but Also Half-Empty" *Foreign Policy*, January 7, 2011, http://shadow.foreignpolicy.com/posts/2011/01/07/gates_s_defense_cuts_a_glass_half_full_but_also_half_empty.

27. Fred Baker III, "Gates: Defense Cuts Must Be Prioritized, Strategic," U.S Department of Defense, http://www.defense.gov/news/newsarticle.aspx?id=64059.

28. Loch Johnson and James Wirtz, eds., *Strategic Intelligence: Windows into a Secret World* (Los Angeles: Roxbury, 2004).

29. Sarah Moughty, "Top CIA Official: Obama Changed Virtually None of Bush's Controversial Programs," *Frontline: Top Secret America*, September 1, 2011, http://www.pbs.org/wgbh/pages/frontline/iraq-war-on-terror/topsecretamerica/top-cia-official-obama-changed-virtually-none-of-bushs-controversial-programs/.

30. Michael Scherer, "The CIA Announces Further Changes to Respond to Intel Failure," *Time*, January 7, 2010, http://swampland.blogs.time.com/2010/01/07/the-cia-announces-further-changes-to-respond-to-intel-failure/.

31. Glenn Hastedt, "The Department of Homeland Security: Politics of Creation," in *Contemporary Cases in American Foreign Policy*, ed. Ralph Carter (Washington, D.C.: CQ Press, 2004).

32. Nick Bunkley, "Militia Charged with Plotting to Murder Officers," *New York Times*, March 29, 2010, http://www.nytimes.com/2010/03/30/us/30militia.html.

33. "Secretary Janet Napolitano," Department of Homeland Security, http://www.dhs.gov/xabout/structure/gc_1232568253959.shtm.

34. James Scott and Ralph Carter, "Acting on the Hill," *Congress and the Presidency* 29 (2002): 151–169.

35. "U.S. and Russia Announce Deal to Cut Nuclear Weapons," British Broadcasting Company, accessed on March 26, 2010, http://news.bbc.co.uk/2/hi/europe/8589385.stm.

36. "The Historic Deal that Will Prevent Iran from Acquiring a Nuclear Weapon: How the U.S. and the International Community Will Block All of Iran's Pathways to a Nuclear Weapon," The White House, President Barack Obama, https://www.whitehouse.gov/issues/foreign-policy/iran-deal.

37. Ashton Carter, "How to Counter WMD," *Foreign Affairs* (September 2004): 72–85.

38. "US-Russia Treaty Stalls over Obama Missile Defense Plan," *McClatchy Newspapers*, March 1, 2010, http://www.mcclatchydc.com/2010/03/01/89641/us-russia-treaty-stalls-over-obama.html.

39. Steven Beardsley, "European Missile Shield Marks Milestone as New Threats Emerge," *Stars and Stripes*, May 10, 2016, http://www.stripes.com/news/european-missile-shield-marks-milestone-as-new-threats-emerge-1.408902.

40. Neil King, Jr. and John W. Miller, "Obama Risks Flap on 'Buy American'," *Wall Street Journal*, February 4, 2009, http://online.wsj.com/article/SB123370411879745425.html.

41. "Obama backs down on 'Buy American' clause," EurActiv, http://www.euractiv.com/en/trade/obama-backs-buy-american-clause/article-179157.

42. Kathleen Hennessey. "Obama Hails Jobs Report, Pitches Manufacturing Initiative," *Los Angeles Times*, March 9, 2012, http://articles.latimes.com/2012/mar/09/nation/la-na-obama-richmond-20120310.

43. "Mission," STAND, http://www.standnow.org/about/mission.

44. Scott Straus, "Darfur and the Genocide Debate," *Foreign Affairs* (January–February 2005): 123–133.

45. "UNAMID—Background," African Union - United Nations Mission in Darfur, http://unamid.unmissions.org/Default.aspx?tabid=890.

46. "UNAMID—Facts and Figures," African Union - United Nations Mission in Darfur, http://www.un.org/en/peacekeeping/missions/unamid/facts.shtml.

47. REUTERS, "Review of Land Mine Treaty to 'Take Some Time,' State Dept. Says," *New York Times*, November 25, 2009, http://www.nytimes.com/2009/11/26/world/americas/26mines.html.

48. Bassem Mroue, "Syria Uses Land Mines at Borders," *Washington Times*, March 13, 2012, http://www.washingtontimes.com/news/2012/mar/13/syria-uses-land-mines-at-borders/?page=all.

49. "Trafficking and HIV/Aids Project Fact Sheet," United Nations Educational Scientific and Cultural Organization, http://www.unescobkk.org/culture/our-projects/cultural-diversity/trafficking-and-hivaids-project/projects/trafficking-statistics-project/data-comparison-sheet/.

50. "United States of America Fact Sheet," HumanTrafficking.org, http://www.humantrafficking.org/countries/united_states_of_america.

51. Office to Monitor and Combat Trafficking in Persons, "2015 Trafficking in Persons Report," U.S. Department of State, http://www.state.gov/j/tip/rls/tiprpt/countries/2015/243559.htm.

52. John M. Broder, "Climate Change as Threat to U.S. Security," *New York Times*, August 8, 2009, http://www.nytimes.com/2009/08/09/science/earth/09climate.html.

53. The full text of the Optional Protocol is available at http://www2.ohchr.org/english/law/pdf/crc-conflict.pdf.

Credits

Index

Note: Page numbers followed by "t" refer to material in a table; "m" refers to a map; "f" refers to a figure; "p" refers to a picture or its caption.